ANNUAL REVIEW OF
PSYCHOLOGY

EDITORIAL COMMITTEE (1993)

ANNUAL REVIEW OF PSYCHOLOGY

VOLUME 44, 1993

LYMAN W. PORTER, *Editor*
University of California, Irvine

MARK R. ROSENZWEIG, *Editor*
University of California, Berkeley

ANNUAL REVIEWS INC.   4139 EL CAMINO WAY   P.O. BOX 10139   PALO ALTO, CALIFORNIA   94303-0897

ANNUAL REVIEWS INC.
Palo Alto, California, USA

International Standard Serial Number: 0066-4308
International Standard Book Number: 8243-0244-3
Library of Congress Catalog Card Number: 50-13143

Annual Review and publication titles are registered trademarks of Annual Reviews Inc.

The paper used in this publication meets the minimum requirements of American National Standards for Information Sciences—Permanence of Paper for Printed Library
Materials, ANZI Z39.48-1984

Annual Reviews Inc. and the Editors of its publications assume no responsibility for
the statements expressed by the contributors to this *Review.*

Typesetting by Ruth McCue-Saavedra, Loralee B. Burke, and the Annual Reviews
Inc. Editorial Staff

PRINTED AND BOUND IN THE UNITED STATES OF AMERICA

PREFACE

This year's volume of the *Annual Review of Psychology* features a chapter on psychology in a country undergoing many changes and becoming increasingly active on the world stage—China. The chapter is authored by Zhong-Ming Wang of the Department of Psychology, Hangzhou University, in the People's Republic of China, and is dedicated to a distinguished pioneer in Chinese psychology, Professor Li Chen.

In keeping with the increasing global scope of psychology, another chapter in this year's volume written by non-American psychologists is "A Holistic View of Personality: A Model Revisited," by David Magnusson and Bertil Törestad of the Department of Psychology, Stockholm University.

Continuing our series of prefatory chapters by distinguished senior psychologists, this year Richard Lazarus, of the University of California, Berkeley, contributes "From Psychological Stress to the Emotions: A History of Changing Outlooks." This volume's "special topic" chapter (a chapter not directly related to our master plan's set of regularly recurring topics) is by Paul Karoly, of Arizona State University: "Mechanisms of Self-Regulation: A Systems View."

The coeditors take this opportunity to thank Auke Tellegen for his splendid service to the Editorial Committee, completing a six-year term that included— at his follow Committee members' request—an additional year beyond the normal five. Again this year, the Committee has asked a member, John Darley, to stay on for an additional year to help regularize the terms of those joining and departing the *Review*; and we gratefully welcome two new members to the Committee: Terrence Wilson and Mavis Hetherington.

LYMAN W. PORTER
MARK R. ROSENZWEIG
COEDITORS

ANNUAL REVIEWS INC. is a nonprofit scientific publisher established to promote the advancement of the sciences. Beginning in 1932 with the Annual Review of Biochemistry, the Company has pursued as its principal function the publication of high quality, reasonably priced Annual Review volumes. The volumes are organized by Editors and Editorial Committees who invite qualified authors to contribute critical articles reviewing significant developments within each major discipline. The Editor-in-Chief invites those interested in serving as future Editorial Committee members to communicate directly with him. Annual Reviews Inc. is administered by a Board of Directors, whose members serve without compensation.

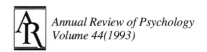

Annual Review of Psychology
Volume 44(1993)

CONTENTS

FROM PSYCHOLOGICAL STRESS TO THE EMOTIONS:
A HISTORY OF CHANGING OUTLOOKS, *R. S. Lazarus*   1–21

MECHANISMS OF SELF-REGULATION: A SYSTEMS VIEW,
Paul Karoly   23–51

PSYCHONEUROIMMUNOLOGY: CONDITIONING AND STRESS,
Robert Ader and Nicholas Cohen   53–85

PSYCHOLOGY IN CHINA: A REVIEW DEDICATED TO LI CHEN,
Zhong-Ming Wang   87–116

ATTITUDES AND ATTITUDE CHANGE, *James M. Olson
and Mark P. Zanna*   117–54

SOCIAL COGNITION AND SOCIAL PERCEPTION, *Susan T. Fiske*   155–94

ORGANIZATIONAL BEHAVIOR: LINKING INDIVIDUALS
AND GROUPS TO ORGANIZATIONAL CONTEXTS,
Richard T. Mowday and Robert I. Sutton   195–229

ENGINEERING PSYCHOLOGY IN A CHANGING WORLD,
William C. Howell   231–63

THINKING, *Keith J. Holyoak and Barbara A. Spellman*   265–315

MAMMALIAN BRAIN SUBSTRATES OF AVERSIVE CLASSICAL
CONDITIONING, *David G. Lavond, Jeansok J. Kim,
and Richard F. Thompson*   317–42

INDIVIDUALITY AND DIVERSITY: THEORY AND RESEARCH
IN COUNSELING PSYCHOLOGY, *Nancy E. Betz
and Louise F. Fitzgerald*   343–81

INFORMATION PROCESSING MODELS: MICROSCOPES
OF THE MIND, *Dominic W. Massaro and Nelson Cowan*   383–425

A HOLISTIC VIEW OF PERSONALITY: A MODEL REVISITED,
David Magnusson and Bertil Törestad   427–51

THE STRUCTURE AND ORGANIZATION OF MEMORY, *Larry R. Squire,
B. Knowlton, and G. Musen*   453–95

CULTURAL PSYCHOLOGY: WHO NEEDS IT?, *Richard A. Shweder
and Maria A. Sullivan*   497–523

SOCIAL AND COMMUNITY INTERVENTIONS, *Murray Levine,*
    Paul A. Toro, and David V. Perkins   525–58
SOCIAL-COGNITIVE MECHANISMS IN THE DEVELOPMENT
    OF CONDUCT DISORDER AND DEPRESSION, *Kenneth A. Dodge*   559–84
SOCIAL FOUNDATIONS OF COGNITION, *John M. Levine,*
    Lauren B. Resnick, and E. Tory Higgins   585–612
CHILD CARE RESEARCH: ISSUES, PERSPECTIVES, AND RESULTS,
    Sandra Scarr and Marlene Eisenberg   613–44
PROGRAM EVALUATION, *Lee Sechrest and A. J. Figueredo*   645–74
ANIMAL BEHAVIOR: A CONTINUING SYNTHESIS,
    William Timberlake   675–708

INDEXES

Author Index   709
Subject Index   739
Cumulative Index of Contributing Authors, Volumes 35–44   757
Cumulative Index of Chapter Titles, Volumes 35–44   760

SOME RELATED ARTICLES IN OTHER *ANNUAL REVIEWS*

From the *Annual Review of Neuroscience,* Volume 15 (1992)

Development of Local Circuits in Mammalian Visual Cortex,
    Lawrence C. Katz and Edward M. Callaway
Adrenergic Receptors as Models for G Protein–Coupled Receptors,
    Brian Kobilka
*Moving in Three-Dimensional Space: Frames of Reference, Vectors,
    and Coordinate Systems,* J. F. Soechting and M. Flanders
Neural Mechanisms of Tactual Form and Texture Perception,
    K. O. Johnson and S. S. Hsiao
*The Neostriatal Mosaic: Multiple Levels of Compartmental Organization
    in the Basal Ganglia,* Charles R. Gerfen
The Role of the Amygdala in Fear and Anxiety, Michael Davis
The Organization and Reorganization of Human Speech Perception,
    Janet F. Werker and Richard C. Tees

From the *Annual Review of Public Health,* Volume 13 (1992)

*Biological Interactions and Potential Health Effects of
    Extremely-Low-Frequency Magnetic Fields from Power Lines
    and Other Common Sources,* T. S. Tenforde
Worksite Drug Testing, Diana Chapman Walsh, Lynn Elinson,
    and Lawrence Gostin
Depression: Current Understanding and Changing Trends, Myrna M. Weissman
    and Gerald L. Klerman
Acute Confusional States in Older Adults and the Role of Polypharmacy,
    Ronald B. Stewart and William E. Hale
Cognitive Impairment: Dementia and Alzheimer's Disease, Eric B. Larson,
    Walter A. Kukull, and Robert L. Katzman

From the *Annual Review of Medicine,* Volume 43 (1992)

Suicide: Risk Factors and Prevention in Medical Practice, Randall D. Buzan
    and Michael P. Weissberg

From the *Annual Review of Anthropology,* Volume 20 (1991)

Human Behavioral Ecology, Lee Cronk
Prototypes Revisited, Robert E. Maclaury

From the *Annual Review of Anthropology,* Volume 21 (1992)

Language and World View, Jane Hill and Bruce Mannheim
Shamanisms Today, Jane Monig Atkinson

Annu. Rev. Psychol. 1993. 44:1–21

FROM PSYCHOLOGICAL STRESS TO THE EMOTIONS: A History of Changing Outlooks

R. S. Lazarus

Department of Psychology, University of California, Berkeley, California 94720

KEYWORDS: psychological stress, emotion, relational meaning, core relational themes, appraisal, coping

CONTENTS

EARLY APPROACHES TO STRESS.. 2
THE COGNITIVE MEDIATIONAL APPROACH: APPRAISAL 5
COPING WITH STRESS 8
REGARDING STRESS AS A SUBSET OF THE EMOTIONS 10
A COGNITIVE-MOTIVATIONAL-RELATIONAL THEORY OF EMOTION 12
    Relational Meaning: Core Relational Themes.. 13
    The Separate Appraisal Components.. 14
    Coping and Emotion... 16
FINAL THOUGHTS 17

Research scholars are products of their times but their work also changes the way scientific issues are studied after them. This reciprocal influence between the outlook of a period and the research people do has been particularly evident in the study of psychological stress and the emotions during the period of my academic life from post-World War II to the present. In pursuing issues about stress and the emotions that have been of particular interest to me, historical shifts of great moment are revealed, which I intend to highlight in this essay.

1

0066-4308/93/0201-0001$02.00

EARLY APPROACHES TO STRESS

The term stress, meaning hardship or adversity, can be found—though without a programmatic focus—at least as early as the 14th century (Lumsden 1981). It first seems to have achieved technical importance, however, in the 17th century in the work of the prominent physicist-biologist, Robert Hooke (see Hinkle 1973). Hooke was concerned with how man-made structures, such as bridges, must be designed to carry heavy loads and resist buffeting by winds, earthquakes, and other natural forces that could destroy them. *Load* referred to a weight on a structure, *stress* was the area over which the load impinged, and *strain* was the deformation of the structure created by the interplay of both load and stress.

Although these usages have changed somewhat in the transition from physics to other disciplines, Hooke's analysis greatly influenced early 20th century models of stress in physiology, psychology, and sociology. The theme that survives in modern times is the idea of stress as an external load or demand on a biological, social, or psychological system.

During World War II there was considerable interest in emotional breakdown in response to the "stresses" of combat (e.g. Grinker & Spiegel 1945). The emphasis on the psychodynamics of breakdown—referred to as "battle fatigue" or "war neurosis"—is itself historically noteworthy, because in World War I the perspective had been neurological rather than psychological; the World War I term for breakdown was "shell shock," which expressed a vague but erroneous notion that the dysfunction resulted from brain damage created by the sound of exploding shells.

After World War II it became evident that many conditions of ordinary life—for example, marriage, growing up, facing school exams, and being ill—could produce effects comparable to those of combat. This led to a growing interest in stress as a cause of human distress and dysfunction. The dominant model—parallel with Hooke's analysis—was basically that of input (load or demand on systems) and output (strain, deformation, breakdown). The main epistemology of the American academic psychology of those days, namely, behaviorism and positivism, made this type of model appear scientific and straightforward, though it turned out to be insufficient.

When I appeared on the scene, the discipline's interest in stress—presumably an esoteric topic—was modest, and the concept had not yet been applied to the more ordinary conditions of daily life. The military wanted to know how to select men who would be stress resistant, and to train them to manage stress. The major research questions of the immediately post-World War II period centered on the effects of stress and how they could be explained and predicted. The research style was experimental, reflecting the widely accepted view at the time that the most dependable way to obtain knowledge was in the laboratory.

It soon became apparent, however, that these questions did not have a simple answer. In the 1950s, my colleagues and I, along with many others, soon discovered that stressful conditions did not produce dependable effects; for some persons the stress aroused by a given condition was great, while for others it was small; and under stress conditions, depending on the task, the performance for some was markedly impaired, for others it was improved, and for still others there was no demonstrable effect (e.g. Lazarus & Eriksen 1952).

We concluded that to understand what was happening we had to take into account *individual differences* in *motivational* and *cognitive* variables, which intervened between the stressor and the reaction (Lazarus et al 1952). Our 1952 article, incidently, was one of the two most widely read in that journal (as surveyed by the editor) in that academic year; the other was by Brown & Farber (1951) which, expressing the zeitgeist, was a neobehavioristic analysis of frustration and a treatment of emotion as an intervening variable. Psychology had barely begun to move away from stimulus-response (S-R) models to stimulus-organism-response (S-O-R) models in an early stage of what later was called the cognitive revolution by North Americans. The same mediating variables are now well-established features of current theories of stress and emotion.

I note, parenthetically, that psychology has long been ambivalent about individual differences, opting for the view that its scientific task is to note invariances and develop general laws. Variations around such laws are apt to be considered errors of measurement, though they must be understood if reasonably accurate prediction is to be possible.

Hooke too was interested in individual differences in the elasticity of metals, which were a factor in their resistance to strain. For example, cast iron is hard and brittle and breaks easily, but wrought iron is soft and malleable and bends without breaking. This physical phenomenon is also used as a metaphor for resistance to psychological stress. Thus, the capacity of metals to resist deformation presaged interest in individual differences in the resiliency of people under stress.

The analogy is evident today in the vigorous study of the personality traits and coping processes that help some people resist the deleterious effects of stress better than others. Some of the personality traits that appear to be associated with resilience include constructive thinking (Epstein & Meier 1989), hardiness (Maddi & Kobasa 1984; see also Orr & Westman 1990), hope (Snyder et al 1991), learned resourcefulness (Rosenbaum 1990), optimism—shades of Horatio Alger and Norman Vincent Peale—(Scheier & Carver 1987), self-efficacy (Bandura 1982), and sense of coherence (Antonovsky 1987).

The study of stress has been plagued by an inconsistent and potentially confusing use of terms to denote the variables of the stress process. In the medical tradition, for example, stress is treated as a set of psychological and physiological reactions to noxious agents; Selye used *stressor* to denote the agent, stress to denote the reaction; sociologists speak of stress as the disturbing agent (e.g. social disequilibrium; Smelser 1963) and of *strain* as the collective reaction (e.g. a panic or riot).

Despite these different usages, however, certain essential meanings are always involved. Whatever words are used to describe the stress process, four concepts must always be considered: 1. a causal external or internal agent, which Hooke called a load and others call stress or a stressor. In my own analyses, I emphasize the person-environment relationship and relational meaning (defined below); 2. an evaluation (by a mind or a physiological system) that distinguishes what is threatening or noxious from what is benign; 3. coping processes used by the mind (or body) to deal with stressful demands; and 4. a complex pattern of effects on mind and body, often referred to as the stress reaction.

Because my focus is psychological rather than physiological stress, I should digress briefly to point up the distinction. Early on, the two kinds of stress were unified under homeostatic concepts—and in the related concept of *activation*. Stress represented a deviation from some norm or steady state. The principle of homeostasis was initially described by Claude Bernard, and its mechanisms were later elaborated further by Walter Cannon (1939), as most psychologists know.

An address by Hans Selye to the American Psychological Association in 1950 stimulated great interest in the overlaps between physiological and psychological stress. Selye (1956/1976) shifted attention from the catecholamines of the adrenal medulla, which Cannon had focused on, to the steroids of the adrenal cortex. Selye's General Adaptation Syndrome (GAS) emphasized that any agent noxious to the tissues (a stressor) would produce more or less the same orchestrated physiological defense (stress reaction). The GAS may be thought of as the physiological analogue of the psychological concept of coping.

Psychological stressors were said also to produce the GAS. Yet in research that has not gotten widespread attention, Mason et al (1976) presented data suggesting that corticosteroid secretion may be more or less specific to psychological stress and not particularly responsive to physiological stresses such as heat, exercise, and hunger. Although there are important overlaps between them, psychological stress and physiological stress require entirely different levels of analysis (see Lazarus 1966; Lazarus & Folkman 1984). What generates physiological stress—that is, what is noxious to tissues—is not the same as what is stressful ("noxious") psychologically.

Indeed, the differences between physiological and psychological stress are profound and center on an issue that psychologists have long had great difficulty dealing with, namely, personal meaning. The key question is how to define a load or stressor psychologically. I deal, below, with the question of what an individual considers a harm, threat, challenge, or benefit. Notice that in speaking of several kinds of states relevant to psychological stress and emotion (namely, harm, threat, challenge, and benefit) I abandon the early idea that stress is merely a form of activation. Such a unidimensional concept—degree of stress—ignored qualitative differences.

There have been two influential qualitative expansions of the stress concept. First, although Selye (1956/1976) had originally postulated a general, nonspecific physiological response to any stressor, late in his life (1974) he drew a health-centered distinction between eustress and distress. *Eustress* was the good kind of stress because it was associated, presumably, with positive feelings and healthy bodily states; *distress* was the bad kind, associated with negative feelings and disturbed bodily states.

Unfortunately, Selye did not tell us clearly what the differences were, psychologically and physiologically. We might guess, of course, that, consistent with his views about the GAS, the differences would involve adrenal corticosteroids, some of which are protective (anabolic) while others are destructive (catabolic). The recent explosion of interest in, and the development of technology for measuring, immune response variables and processes offer additional means of distinguishing the two kinds. For example, eustress may enhance immune system competence while distress may impair it.

Second, I had early on (Lazarus 1966) drawn a distinction among three kinds of stress, harm, threat, and challenge (Lazarus 1966, 1981; Lazarus & Launier 1978; Lazarus & Folkman 1984). *Harm* refers to psychological damage that had already been done—e.g. an irrevocable loss. *Threat* is the anticipation of harm that has not yet taken place but may be imminent. *Challenge* results from difficult demands that we feel confident about overcoming by effectively mobilizing and deploying our coping resources.

These different kinds of psychological stress states are presumably brought about by different antecedent conditions, both in the environment and within the person, and have different consequences. For example, threat is an unpleasant state of mind that may seriously block mental operations and impair functioning, while challenge is exhilarating and associated with expansive, often outstanding performance. To the extent that we take these variations seriously, stress cannot be considered in terms of a single dimension such as activation. As will be seen below, such a recognition involves considering diverse emotional states, some negative, some positive.

THE COGNITIVE MEDIATIONAL APPROACH: APPRAISAL

Definition of the psychologically noxious has been the central theme of my theoretical and research efforts from the beginning. Allow me to summarize my research in this area before turning to the parallel problem of the cognitive mediation of the emotions—my current main concern.

Although a number of influential early writers adopted the view that psychological stress is dependent on cognitive mediation (e.g. Arnold 1960; Grinker & Spiegel 1945; Janis 1958; Mechanic 1962), the cognitive movement in North American psychology did not get fully under way until the 1970s. This view is centered on the concept of appraisal, which is the process that mediates—I would prefer to say *actively negotiates*—between, on the one hand, the demands, constraints, and resources of the environment and, on the other, the goal hierarchy and personal beliefs of the individual.

I believe the programmatic efforts of my colleagues and me in the 1960s (e.g. Lazarus 1966, 1968; Lazarus et al 1970) helped convince many of those still wedded to an input-output conceptualization (along with many newcomers to the scene) that appraisal played a significant role in stress reactions. A powerful tide in psychology—eventually becoming a tidal wave that seems to have swept old epistemologies aside—has moved us from behaviorism toward a much freer outlook in the United States. Our psychologists, the main exception being Skinner (1953, 1990), have become less hesitant about referring to what goes on in the mind; we are now less reluctant to explain human and animal actions and reactions in terms of thought processes.

My colleagues and I employed a simple experimental paradigm designed to create psychological stress as naturalistically as possible in the laboratory. We had subjects watch stressful films while we periodically sampled their subjective reports of stress and continuously recorded their autonomic nervous system activity (primarily as reflected in heart rate and skin conductance).

Although a number of films were used in this research, two were particularly important. One presented a series of subincision operations—a male rite of passage among the Arunta of Australia. The other, a film designed to teach woodworking personnel how to avoid shop accidents, depicted such bloody accidents as a worker being fatally impaled on a board thrust from a circular saw and a worker getting his finger cut off.

We used recorded speech passages to orient viewers before the films were shown. Their purpose was to influence the way subjects construed what was happening in the movie (e.g. Lazarus & Alfert 1964; Speisman et al 1964). These passages were based on ego-defense theory, which posited certain themes people used to protect themselves from threat.

One passage, for example, mimicked *denial*—"The people in the film are not hurt or distressed by what is happening," or "These accidents didn't really happen but were staged for their effect." Another mimicked intellectualization or *distancing*—"This is an interesting anthropological study of aboriginal customs," or "The accidents portrayed in this film provide the basis for instructions about how to avoid injuries in a woodworking shop." A third emphasized the main *sources of threat* in the film—"Many of the people you see in this film suffer severe pain and infection from these rituals." The effects of these experimental treatments were compared with each other and with a control condition that involved no attempt to influence the way subjects construed what was happening.

These orientation passages had powerful effects on self-reports of distress and on psychophysiological stress reactions (heart rate and skin conductance). Denial and distancing passages markedly lowered these reactions compared with the control; the threat passage raised them. The tendency of the passages to reduce stress levels could be predicted on the basis of differences among viewers' cognitive styles.

In an attempt to understand what was happening, I shifted from an emphasis on ego defenses to a general concept of *appraisal* as the cognitive mediator of stress reactions. I began to view appraisal as a universal process in which people (and other animals) constantly evaluate the significance of what is happening for their personal well-being. In effect, I considered psychological stress to be a reaction to personal harms and threats of various kinds that emerged out of the person-environment relationship. But more of this below.

In subsequent experiments, we had subjects await a source of stress for different periods—e.g. an electric shock that was anticipated but never actually occurred (Folkins 1970; Monat et al 1973), or a bloody accident (on film) that had been foreshadowed by a flashback (Nomikos et al 1968). These and other psychophysiological studies showed that the degree of stress reaction depended on evaluative thoughts (appraisal and coping). In turn the contents of these thoughts, such as "How bad will it be," depended on how long they had to wait for the harmful confrontation. A strong empirical case was being made that appraisal and coping processes shaped the stress reaction, and that these processes, in turn, were influenced by variables in the environment and within the person.

Such reasoning was consistent with the expansion in the 1960s and 1970s of cognitive mediational views in psychology generally. The outlook was anticipated by many illustrious figures in North American psychology, including Asch, Harlow, Heider, Kelly, McClelland, Murphy, Rotter, and White, as well as their intellectual mentors, Lewin and Murray, and still others who worked within the psychoanalytic framework. We often forget too that this outlook dominated classical Greek and European thought, a point I return to below. In any event, psychologists could now seriously and programmatically ask what must be going on in the mind to influence people to act and react as they do.

Nor is this way of thinking pure phenomenology. Because of different goals and beliefs, because there is often too much to attend to, and because the stimulus array is often ambiguous, people are selective both in what they pay attention to and in what their appraisals take into account. Even when an individual's appraisal deviates from the norm it may still result in a good match between the appraisal and reality. There are many realities rather than a single one, and deviance is not necessarily pathology.

COPING WITH STRESS

As the cognitive mediational outlook developed further, the coping process gained in importance too (Lazarus 1966; Lazarus et al 1974). Because psychological stress defines an unfavorable person-environment relationship, its essence is process and change rather than structure or stasis. We alter our circumstances, or how they are interpreted, to make them appear more favorable—an effort called coping.

Traditional approaches to coping had emphasized traits or styles—that is, stable properties of personality. In contrast, my own analysis and research (Lazarus 1966, 1981; Lazarus & Folkman 1984; Lazarus & Launier 1978) emphasized coping as *process*—a person's ongoing efforts in thought and action to manage specific demands appraised as taxing or overwhelming. Although stable coping styles do exist and are important, coping is highly *contextual,* since to be effective it must change over time and across different stressful conditions (e.g. Folkman & Lazarus 1985). Empirical evaluation of this idea requires study of the same persons over time and across diverse stressful encounters. The Berkeley Stress and Coping Project, which got under way in the late 1970s and continued to the late 1980s (see Lazarus & Folkman 1987 for a review), addressed the contextual side of coping in a number of field studies.

Coping affects subsequent stress reactions in two main ways: First, if a person's relationship with the environment is changed by coping actions the conditions of psychological stress may also be changed for the better. My colleagues and I called this *problem-focused coping.* If we persuade our neighbor to prevent his tree from dropping leaves on our grass, we overcome the original basis of whatever harm or threat their dropping caused us.

Other coping processes, which we called *emotion-focused coping,* change only the way we attend to or interpret what is happening. A threat that we successfully avoid thinking about, even if only temporarily, doesn't bother us. Likewise, reappraisal of a threat in nonthreatening terms removes the cognitive basis of the stress reaction. For example, if a person can reinterpret a demeaning comment by his/her spouse as the unintended result of personal illness or job stress, the appraisal basis for reactive anger will dissipate. Denial and distancing are powerful techniques in the control of psychological stress because they enable a person to appraise an encounter as more benign. In short, whether the change is in external conditions or in one's construal of them, coping influences psychological stress via appraisal; appraisal is always the mediator.

We created a procedure for measuring the coping process in diverse stressful contexts. *The Ways of Coping Questionnaire* (Folkman & Lazarus 1988b) consists of 67 statements about thoughts and actions. An interviewer can use these interactively, or a subject can respond to them in a self-administered procedure. The questionnaire asks whether and to what extent a person had used certain thoughts and actions in a particular stressful encounter.

By asking about thoughts and actions we avoided having our subjects make inferences about their coping. Instead, we enabled observers' inferences based on a factor analysis yielding eight factor scales, each representing a different coping strategy. The procedure was designed to permit repeated measurements on the same subjects over time and in different stress contexts (see, e.g., Folkman & Lazarus 1985; Folkman et al 1986a; Folkman et al 1986b).

A number of replicable findings about coping emerged from this work, the most important of which can be summarized as follows:

1. Coping is complex, and people use most of the basic strategies (factors) of coping in every stressful encounter. (Are specific coping strategies tied to specific stress contents, or does one strategy follow another in a sort of trial-and-error process? The answer is likely both.)

2. Coping depends on appraisal of whether anything can be done to change the situation. If appraisal says something can be done, problem-focused coping predominates; if appraisal says nothing can be done, emotion-focused coping predominates. Here we have rediscovered the Alcoholics Anomymous epigram, that people should try to change the noxious things that can be changed, accept those that cannot, and have the wisdom to know the difference.

3. When the type of stressful encounter is held constant—e.g. work-, health-, or family-related stress—women and men show very similar coping patterns, despite public predjudices to the contrary.

4. Some strategies of coping are more stable than others across diverse stressful encounters while others are linked to particular stressful contexts. For example, thinking positively about the situation is relatively stable and depends substantially on personality, whereas seeking social support is unstable and depends substantially on the social context.

5. Coping strategies change from one stage of a complex stressful encounter to another. If we lump together the stages in a complex encounter we gain a false picture of the coping process.

6. Coping acts as a powerful mediator of emotional outcomes; positive outcomes are associated with some coping strategies, negative outcomes with others. Our data from a nonprospective study suggested this (Folkman & Lazarus 1988a), and Bolger (1990) has confirmed it in a prospective study in which the coping process was measured independently and before the emotional outcome.

7. The utility of any coping pattern varies with the type of stressful encounter, the type of personality stressed, and the outcome modality studied (e.g. subjective well-being, social functioning, or somatic health). What works in one context may be counterproductive in another. Thus, when there is nothing to do but wait until grades are announced, distancing helps to reduce distress and dysfunction; but when effort should be mobilized to study for a future exam, the same strategy leads the person to abandon the effort to prepare, with the same lowered distress but a later performance disaster (Folkman & Lazarus 1985).

REGARDING STRESS AS A SUBSET OF THE EMOTIONS

Psychological stress should be considered part of a larger topic, the emotions. This theoretical consolidation, while posing some difficulties, has important positive consequences: First, though belonging together, the literature on psychological stress and the literature on emotions have generally been treated as separate. Social and biological scientists interested in the emotions are often unaware of a relevant stress literature, and vice versa. Because psychological stress theory is tantamount to a theory of emotion, and because the two literatures share overlapping ideas, the two fields might usefully be conjoined as the field of emotion theory. Second, we have already progressed from unidimensional (activation) to a multi-dimensional (e.g. harm, threat, challenge) concept of stress. In contrast, recognition of 15 or so specific emotions instead of the several dimensions of stress greatly increases what we can say about an individual's coping and adaptation. Knowing, for example, that in a given encounter (or as a consistent pattern across encounters) this individual feels angry, anxious, guilty, sad, happy, or hopeful tells us much more than knowing merely that he/she is harmed, threatened, or challenged. Use of stress as a source of information about an individual's adaptation to environmental pressures is extremely limited compared with the use of the full array of emotions.

An explosion of interest in the emotions is evident in all the relevant scientific disciplines, each of which looks at emotion from a somewhat different perspective and at different levels of analysis. Many conceptually oriented books on the topic have been appearing, most of them since 1980, including readers by Calhoun & Solomon (1984), Harré (1986), Izard et al (1984), Plutchik & Kellerman (1980, 1983, 1986, 1989), and Scherer & Ekman (1984), and theoretical monographs by Averill (1982), Frijda (1986), De Sousa (1987), Gordon (1987), Izard (1971, 1977), Kemper (1978), Mandler (1984), Ortony et al (1988), and Tomkins (1962, 1963), and myself (Lazarus 1991c).

Readers will appreciate the historical implications of this modern explosion of interest more fully if they also understand that 60 years ago academic psychologists seemed ready to abandon the concept of emotion. Allow me to backtrack to the period when the stress concept was in growing favor but emotion was in the doghouse. In 1933, Meyer made the following arrogant and hardly prescient statement about emotion:

> Why introduce into science an unneeded term, such as emotion, when there are already scientific items for everything we have to describe? ... I predict: the "will" has virtually passed out of our scientific psychology today; the "emotion" is bound to do the same. In 1950 American Psychologists will smile at both these terms as curiosities of the past.

When I came on the academic scene in 1948, Duffy (1941a,b; 1960) was arguing with great success that there was nothing special about emotion because it denoted "all of life," that is, the ordinary adaptational activities by means of which an organism maintained its internal equilibrium in the face of threatened disruption from internal and external pressures.

Adaptational responses, she said, have direction, are reactions to relationships, and invoke energy mobilization. Therefore, we should abandon the concept of emotion and substitute activation in its place. Was there any psychologically significant difference between a person running to his/her house on a whim and a person, seeing a fire, running the same way in a panic? Her answer was no. She wrote (1941a:287–88), for example, that

> all behavior is motivated. Without motivation there is no activity … . The responses called "emotional" do not appear to follow different principles of action from other adjustive responses of the individual. Changes in internal or external conditions, or in the interpretation of these conditions, always result in internal accommodations. The responses made are specifically adjustive to the situation and are not subject to classification into such categories as "emotional" and "non-emotional." … All responses—not merely "emotional" responses—are adjustive reactions attempting to adapt the organism to the demands of the situation. The energy level of response varies with the requirements of the situation as interpreted by the individual. Diffuse internal changes (especially in the viscera) are involved in the production of these changes in energy level. But continuous visceral activity, with accompanying changes in energy level, is a function of life itself, not merely a function of a particular condition called "emotion."

At the time, Duffy's theme seemed reasonable and sound to me, though I now reject her position. Those, such as I, who study the psychological process of emotion contend that there is a world of difference between a non-emotional and an emotional event. Although there are behavioral and physiological overlaps, the ways whim-motivated and alarm-motivated actions are organized psychologically are quite different. One's house being on fire elicits motives, beliefs, appraisals, and coping processes different from those elicited in whimsy, and some emotion theorists would wager that panic has its own special physiological response pattern. Once aroused, emotion is a system of its own. Duffy's question and response are reminiscent of Skinner's claim that from a behaviorist's point of view there is no difference between the tears of eye irritation and the tears of emotional distress.

Why did the stress concept survive and flourish in an epistemological climate so hostile to the emotions? The initial noncognitive, nonmediational, S-R view of psychological stress was suggested by Hooke's engineering analysis. This view was carried over into analyses of stress prior to the so-called cognitive revolution. A good example of the carryover was the frequent use in the 1960s and 1970s of life events lists for measuring stress, which emphasized such objective environmental changes as death of a spouse, divorce, and loss of a job as stressors. However, by the 1970s much of North American psychology had begun to change and was now receptive—though still somewhat ambivalently—to a cognitive mediational approach to stress and the emotions.

This historical account does not suggest that the study of stress is no longer useful. Rather, the concept of emotion includes that of stress, and both are subject to appraisal and coping theory. As a topic, stress is more limited in scope and depth than the emotions, as I try to show below.

A COGNITIVE-MOTIVATIONAL-RELATIONAL THEORY OF EMOTION

The topic of the emotions provides many more categories of reaction than does that of stress, as many as there are emotions that we are willing to acknowledge and study (itself a controversial subject). I believe that we can identify 15 different emotions, more or less (Lazarus 1991b,c). There are roughly 9 so-called negative emotions: anger, fright, anxiety, guilt, shame, sadness, envy, jealousy, and disgust, each a product of a different set of troubled conditions of living, and each involving different harms or threats. And there are roughly 4 positive emotions: happiness, pride, relief, and love. To this list we probably could add three more whose valence is equivocal or mixed: hope, compassion, and gratitude. (Below I suggest the "core" relational themes for each of these emotions).

What gives this multiplicity of emotions great analytic power is that each emotion arises from a different plot or story about relationships between a person and the environment; feeling angry has its own special scenario, and so does feeling anxious, guilty, ashamed, sad, proud, and so forth. Notice that this way of thinking complicates but enriches the job of understanding and predicting. If it is true that each emotion is brought about by a different appraisal of the personal significance of an adaptational encounter, then we learn different adaptationally relevant things from each about what is happening and about the psychological characteristics of the person who is reacting.

Emotion theorists and researchers must now tackle many issues—too many to examine adequately here. I spend the remainder of this essay on the one that has powered much of my research, namely, the achievement of *relational meaning* through the process of appraisal. This, as I said, is the fundamental puzzle for students of both psychological stress and the emotions. Although I have addressed the problem recently (Lazarus 1991a–c), the proposed solutions are still fluid and a number of other emotion researchers are also struggling to resolve it.

If one takes the position, as I do, that the particular emotion experienced depends on one's thoughts about an encounter, then these thoughts can most fruitfully be conceptualized at two related but different levels of abstraction, one molar, the other molecular. I begin with the molar level.

Table 1 Emotions and their core relational themes

Emotion	Core relational theme
anger	a demeaning offense against me and mine
anxiety	facing uncertain, existential threat
fright	an immediate, concrete, and overwhelming physical danger
guilt	having transgressed a moral imperative
shame	failing to live up to an ego-ideal
sadness	having experienced an irrevocable loss
envy	wanting what someone else has
jealousy	resenting a third party for the loss of, or a threat to, another's affection or favor
disgust	taking in or being too close to an indigestible object or (metaphorically speaking) idea
happiness	making reasonable progress toward the realization of a goal
pride	enhancement of one's ego-identity by taking credit for a valued object or achievement, either one's own or that of someone or group with whom one identifies
relief	a distressing goal-incongruent condition that has changed for the better or gone away
hope	fearing the worst but wanting better
love	desiring or participating in affection, usually but not necessarily reciprocated
compassion	being moved by another's suffering and wanting to help

Relational Meaning: Core Relational Themes

I said above, without explanation, that emotions are always a response to relational meaning. The relational meaning of an encounter is a person's sense of the harms and benefits in a particular person-environment relationship. To speak of harms and benefits is to allude to motivational as well as cognitive processes; hence the complex name of the theory, which includes the terms cognitive, motivational, and relational.

Personality variables and those that characterize the environment come together in the appraisal of relational meaning. An emotion is aroused not just by an environmental demand, constraint, or resource but by their juxtaposition with a person's motives and beliefs. The process of appraisal negotiates between and integrates these two sets of variables by indicating the significance of what is happening for a person's well-being. This is an extension of the cognitive mediational principle in psychological stress theory—namely, that what causes the stress reaction is not the environmental "stressor" alone but also its significance as appraised by the person who encounters it.

Although one can decompose molar relational meaning into separate, molecular personality and environmental variables (e.g. as hostile actions by another or a goal one is striving for), relational meaning results from a higher or more synthetic level of analysis. At that level the separate variables are lost in favor of a new relational concept—e.g. feeling demeaned, sensing an uncertain threat, feeling failure to live up to an ego-ideal, feeling attainment of what one wants, sensing enhancement of one's self, or suffering an irrevocable loss. Our penchant for reductive analysis in psychology often leaves us without the ability to see how the separate variables are synthesized into molar ones. (For a classic discussion of the difference between reductive analysis and synthesis or transaction, see Dewey & Bentley 1949; see Lazarus & Launier 1978 for another).

Two spouses, A and B, construct different meanings from the same argumentative encounter. For A, the relational meaning of what is happening is that he/she has been demeaned or slighted; this meaning motivates a desire to repair the wounded self-esteem. For B, on the other hand, the argument's relational meaning is that the marital relationship itself has been threatened. The emotion experienced by B is anger, by A anxiety.

If we would demonstrate that relational meaning is the cognitive foundation of emotion, we must define and measure this meaning—address it empirically. I call the *core relational theme* the relational meaning in each emotion (Lazarus 1991b,c). Each emotion involves a different core relational theme. In Table 1 I suggest core relational themes for the emotions discussed above.

The Separate Appraisal Components

A number of different but overlapping proposals have been advanced about the molecular appraisal components underlying each emotion—see, for example, Frijda (1986), Lazarus (1991c), Reisenzein & Hofmann (1990), Roseman (1984, 1991), Scherer (1984), Smith & Ellsworth (1985, 1987), and Weiner (1986)—and these earlier efforts have been reviewed by Lazarus & Smith (1988) and Smith & Lazarus (1990), Smith & Ellsworth (1985), and others.

Although their language often differs, these proposals share a number of appraisal components, which suggests the beginnings of a common theoretical ground. Most of these systems assume that one key appraisal component is motivational; to have an emotion requires an active goal in an encounter; if no goal is at stake there can be no emotion. Most also assume that the valence of an emotion depends on whether the conditions of the encounter are viewed as favorable to goal attainment (thereby begetting a positive emotion) or unfavorable (thereby begetting a negative emotion). In most proposals, too, assignment of responsibility is factored into certain emotions—that is, whether a harm or benefit is attributed to the self or another. The accountability of others is an important component in the appraisal leading to anger, while self-accountability is important in pride, guilt, and shame.

In my treatment of the appraisal pattern for anger, I have adopted a somewhat controversial position. I regard anger as resulting from an individual's appraisal of injury to self-esteem. Blame is a key appraisal component of anger. The angry person locates responsibility in an external agent—i.e. decides that the person who caused the injury could have refrained from doing so. In contrast with the traditional frustration-aggression hypothesis (cf Berkowitz 1989), I suggest that a person who could not have acted otherwise is not blameworthy, and hence is not the object of anger. There is no malevolence or slight in such a situation, and if there is anger it will be directed elsewhere on the basis of complex social attributions. Research addressing the role of imputed intentions in the generation of anger has not yet adequately resolved the theoretical question.

Three additional points should be made about appraisal and relational meaning. First, the two levels of analysis, core relational themes and individual appraisal components, are complementary ways of conceptualizing and assessing the particular relational meaning in an emotion. One is synthetic and molar, the other analytic and molecular. A single appraisal component provides only part of this meaning. In the case of anger, for example, the relational meaning cannot be determined from a sense of frustration alone. The analyst has to observe a pattern composed of several appraisal components. Not only does the subject have to feel thwarted, his/her self-esteem has to have been demeaned, responsibility has to have been attributed, and the responsible person has to have been presumed in control of his/her actions. In short, this analysis can synthesize the complex relational meaning (a demeaning offense against me or mine) only after at least four appraisal decisions have been distinguished (out of a possible total of six; see Lazarus 1991c).

Second, disagreements about the details of the appraisal pattern for each emotion should not obscure the considerable agreement about the appraisal pattern required for most emotions, based on a long history of observation and speculation. The current ferment in appraisal theory and research reflects serious attempts to evaluate some of the disagreements empirically.

Third, among appraisal theorists only Scherer (1984) regards the process of appraising as a sequential search of each appraisal question, thereby implying a conscious and deliberate process of decision-making. Although it conflicts with traditional usage among cognitive psychologists, a view of the evaluative process of appraisal as often nonvolitional and unconscious may be emerging.

There is a resurgence of interest in a way of achieving meaning that is not analytic and distant, but immediate and personal. Concepts such as being-in-the-situation (Heidegger; see Guignon 1984; Taylor 1985), embodied intelligence (Merleau-Ponty 1962), tacit knowledge (Polanyi 1966), and resonance (Shepard 1984; see also Trevarthen 1979 on intersubjectivity) illustrate this way of thinking. We sense things about our relationship to the environment without being able to verbalize them. Our emotions often reflect this ephemeral kind of knowing and evaluating (Lazarus & Smith 1988), as well as the more deliberate and analytic processes studied in modern cognitive psychology (see, for example, Lazarus 1991a; and Varela et al 1991).

Despite current notions that emotions and reason are separate and opposing functions and that people are inherently irrational, I now believe that the emotions have an implacable logic. The task of theory is to determine that logic for each emotion. One may reason poorly and attain a sound conclusion; or one may reason well, and come to an unsound conclusion. These forms of irrationality, if you will, are not the same. Although intense emotions may impair or disrupt reasoning, I believe that most of the time people are rational, given their goals and belief premises.

What could be more logical than the principle that if our goals are thwarted we react with a negative emotion, or that if we are making satisfactory progress toward a goal we react with positive emotion? This reaction may not always be wise, but there is nothing irrational about it. What is more logical than the principle that emotions result from how we evaluate the significance of events to our well-being? It may be foolish to want certain things, or to believe certain things, but it is not illogical to emote on the basis of how we are faring in attaining these goals.

Coping and Emotion

Coping shapes emotion, as it does psychological stress, by influencing the person-environment relationship and how it is appraised. Coping involves both (a) attempts to change the person-environment realities behind negative emotions (problem-focused coping) and (b) attempts to change either what is attended to or how it is appraised (emotion-focused coping). However, inclusion of emotion in the study of coping provides a much richer perspective. One might consider, for example, the sociocultural and intrapsychic implications of having reacted with one or another of the 15 or so emotions. Thus if one expresses anger in a context where anger is rejected by the community, the emotion itself must be coped with—e.g. by inhibition or denial.

With the burgeoning of interest in the emotions has come the realization that coping theory must become more concerned than formerly with the motivational implications of person-environment relationships, which underlie the different emotions. The point can be illustrated by reference to recent research by Laux & Weber (1991), who have been studying how marital partners cope both with angry interchanges and with joint threats that produce anxiety.

Two main patterns have been observed: First, the coping manifested by both parties in an argument is different from that in an anxiety encounter. During an encounter involving anger, more effort is expended in repairing wounded self-esteem than is expended in an anxiety encounter. In anger, such efforts of reparation include attacking the other, escalating anger, defending the self, and posturing. In anxiety encounters, more efforts are made to reassure the other and to preserve the relationship.

Second, even within an anger encounter, the way a marital partner copes differs with his/her differing general goals and situational intentions. If the partner is preoccupied with preserving a relationship threatened by anger, anger escalation is avoided. The partner threatened by damage to the relationship from anger may suppress and conceal his/her anger. I expect this partner would also find excuses not to take offense (emotion-focused coping). On the other hand, the partner whose intention is to repair a wounded self-esteem is more apt to deliver comeuppance. We will understand the coping process better when we understand the general goals and situational intentions, as well as the emotions, of the parties in encounters.

FINAL THOUGHTS

The philosophical history of the emotions has been essentially cognitive from ancient times to the present. Aristotle, who lived in the 4th century BC, might be called the first cognitive theorist of the emotions, writing in *Rhetoric* (1941:1380) that "Anger may be defined as a belief that we, or our friends, have been unfairly slighted, which causes in us both painful feelings and a desire or impulse for revenge." This statement contains the basics of an appraisal theory—for example, in its connecting a belief, desire, or motivation to an impulse for revenge (what today is often called an action tendency). With respect to how anger is aroused, Aristotle asks us to consider "(1) what the state of mind of angry people is, (2) who the people are with whom they usually get angry, and (3) on what grounds they get angry with them. It is not enough to know one or even two of these points; unless we know all three, we shall be unable to arouse anger in anyone. The same is true of the other emotions."

Here Aristotle speaks of the state of mind, and of a cognitively mediated provocation to anger. He seems to be pointing the analysis of emotion toward the researchable conditions behind the arousal of emotions. Quite modern sounding, it seems to me.

Averill's (1982) treatment of historical teachings about anger, particularly his description of the views of Seneca, Lactantius, Aquinas, and Descartes, leaves little doubt that cognitive mediation of the emotions has been a preeminent concept. And lest the reader think that ancient or medieval cognitive-motivational-relational views went into hiding until recently, I quote G. C. Robertson (1877:413), a 19th-century English philosopher who wrote—in a fashion reminiscent of *Rashomon*—the following:

> Four persons of much the same age and temperament are travelling in the same vehicle. At a particular stopping-place it is intimated to them that a certain person has just died suddenly and unexpectedly. One of the company looks perfectly stolid. A second comprehends what has taken place, but is in no way affected. The third looks and evidently feels sad. The fourth is overwhelmed with grief which finds expression in tears, sobs, and exclamations. Whence the difference of the four individuals before us? In one respect they are all alike: an announcement has been made to them. The first is a foreigner, and has not understood the communication. The second has never met with the deceased, and could have no special regard for him. The third had often met with him in social intercourse and business transactions, and been led to cherish a great esteem for him. The fourth was the brother of the departed, and was bound to him by native affection and a thousand ties earlier and later. From such a case we may notice that in order to [experience an emotion] there is need first of some understanding or apprehension; the foreigner had no feeling because he had no idea or belief. We may observe further

that there must secondly be an affection of some kind; for the stranger was not interested in the occurrence. The emotion flows forth from a well, and is strong in proportion to the waters; is stronger in the brother than in the friend. It is evident, thirdly, that the persons affected are in a moved or excited state. A fourth peculiarity has appeared in the sadness of the countenance and the agitations of the bodily frame. Four elements have thus come forth to view.

The attempt to abandon emotion as a topic for scientific study—either by subsuming it within other concepts or by arguing that, being nonmaterial, emotion requires no explanation—seems to me to have been an historical aberration. This aberration, in the form of radical behaviorism, occurred during the early development of academic psychology, which was—except in North America—overly concerned with being ultrascientific in the image of the natural sciences. It was not a reflection of the main lines of thought that had existed for centuries and that have been restored in the last few decades (see also Reisenzein & Schönpflug 1992 for an account of Stumpf's late 19th-century cognitive theory of emotion, which has been given virtually no previous attention).

I entered academic psychology at the height of this movement which, as Deese (1985:31) put it, was dedicated to "the abolition of mind." Psychology was separated from the philosophy departments of modern Western European and North American universities, within which it had traditionally been included, and psychologists were enjoined (this I vividly remember) to avoid "armchair" speculation in the interests of being empirical scientists. Only in recent years have most psychologists once again been willing to see value in philosphical analyses, to take on large-scale theory, to take seriously observations that are not obtained through laboratory experiment, to engage problems of subjective meaning, and to avoid the sterile scientism of the recent past.

The political and social changes my generation has lived through have been profound—the Great Depression, World War II, the advent of rockets, jet planes, atomic energy, and television. Today we observe with awe the profound political changes in Eastern Europe after the collapse of the Soviet Empire, as well as tranformations in Asia and the Middle East. And we are correctly told that even the near future is impossible to predict with confidence.

We have lived through similar monumental changes in the way psychology and its cognate social sciences go about their scientific business. These changes have been no less extraordinary than the political and social ones. They are manifest in the problems being studied and the mindset for studying them. I have tried to reflect them in a small way in my discussion of stress and the emotions. Research and theory on the emotions are beneficiaries of this changing epistemology. Though fads and fashions in psychology have waxed and waned rapidly in the recent past, I believe the emotions are too central to human adaptation for the current enthusiasm to disappear soon. I would certainly like to be around to know.

Literature Cited

Antonovsky, A. 1987. *Unraveling the Mystery of Health: How People Manage Stress and Stay Well.* San Francisco: Jossey-Bass

Aristotle. 1941. Rhetoric. In *The Basic Works of Aristotle,* ed. R. McKeon. New York: Random House

Arnold, M. B. 1960. *Emotion and Personality,* Vols. 1, 2. New York: Columbia Univ. Press

Averill, J. R. 1982. *Anger and Aggression: An Essay on Emotion.* New York: Springer-Verlag

Bandura, A. 1982. Self-efficacy mechanism in human agency. *Am. Psychol.* 44:1175–84

Berkowitz, L. 1989. Frustration-aggression hypothesis: examination and reformulation. *Psychol. Bull.* 106:59–73

Bolger, N. 1990. Coping as a personality process: a prospective study. *J. Pers. Soc. Psychol.* 59:525–37

Brown, J., Farber, I. E. 1951. Emotions conceptualized as intervening variables with suggestions toward a theory of frustration. *Psychol. Bull.* 48:465–95

Calhoun, C., Solomon, R. C., ed. 1984. *What Is an Emotion? Classic Readings in Philosophical Psychology.* New York: Oxford Univ. Press

Cannon, W. B. 1939. *The Wisdom of the Body.* New York: W. W. Simon. 2nd ed. First edition, 1932

Deese, J. 1985. *American Freedom and the Social Sciences.* NY: Columbia Univ. Press

De Sousa, R. 1987. *The rationality of emotions.* Cambridge, MA: MIT Press

Dewey, J., Bentley, A. F. 1949. *Knowing and the known.* Chapters 4–5, pp. 103–43. Boston: Beacon Press

Duffy, E. 1941a. An explanation of "emotional" phenomena without the use of the concept "emotion." *J. Gen. Psychol.* 25:283–93

Duffy, E. 1941b. The conceptual categories of psychology: a suggestion for revision. *Psychol. Rev.* 48:177–203

Duffy, E. 1960. *Activation and Behavior.* New York: Wiley

Epstein, S., Meier, P. 1989. Constructive thinking: a broad coping variable with specific components. *J. Pers. Soc. Psychol.* 57:332–50

Folkins, C. H. 1970. Temporal factors and the cognitive mediators of stress reaction. *J. Pers. Soc. Psychol.* 14:173–84

Folkman, S., Lazarus, R. S. 1985. If it changes it must be a process: study of emotion and coping during three stages of a college examination. *J. Pers. Soc. Psychol.* 48:150–70

Folkman, S., Lazarus, R. S. 1988a. Coping as a mediator of emotion. *J. Pers. Soc. Psychol.* 54:466–75

Folkman, S., Lazarus, R. S. 1988b. *Manual for the Ways of Coping Questionnaire.* Palo Alto, CA: Consulting Psychologists Press

Folkman, S., Lazarus, R. S., Dunkel-Schetter, C., DeLongis, A., Gruen, R. 1986a. The dynamics of a stressful encounter: cognitive appraisal, coping, and encounter outcomes. *J. Pers. Soc. Psychol.* 50:992–1003

Folkman, S., Lazarus, R. S., Gruen, R., DeLongis, A. 1986b. Appraisal, coping, health status, and psychological symptoms. *J. Pers. Soc. Psychol.* 50:572–79

Frijda, N. H. 1986. *The Emotions.* Cambridge: Cambridge Univ. Press

Gordon, R. M. 1987. *The Structure of Emotions.* Cambridge: Cambridge Univ. Press

Grinker, R. R., Spiegel, J. P. 1945. *Men under Stress.* New York: McGraw-Hill

Guigon, C. 1984. Moods in Heidegger's being and time. In *What Is an Emotion? Classical Readings in Philosophical Psychology,* ed. C. Calhoun, R. C. Solomon. New York: Oxford Univ. Press

Harré, R., ed. 1986. *The Social Construction of Emotions.* Oxford: Basil Blackwell

Hinkle, L. E. Jr. 1973. The concept of "stress" in the biological and social sciences. *Sci. Med. Man.* 1:31–48

Izard, C. E. 1971. *The Face of Emotion.* New York: Appleton-Century-Crofts

Izard, C. E. 1977. *Human Emotions.* New York: Plenum

Izard, C. E., Kagan, J., Zajonc, R. B., ed. 1984. *Emotions, Cognition, and Behavior.* New York: Cambridge Univ. Press

Janis, I. L. 1958. *Psychological Stress: Psychoanalytic and Behavioral Studies of Surgical Patients.* New York: Wiley

Kemper, T. D. 1978. *A Social Interaction Theory of Emotions.* New York: Wiley

Laux, L., Weber, H. 1991. Presentation of self in coping with anger and anxiety: an intentional approach. *Anxiety Res.* 3:233–55

Lazarus, R. S. 1966. *Psychological Stress and the Coping Process.* New York: McGraw-Hill

Lazarus, R. S. 1968. Emotions and adaptation: conceptual and empirical relations. In *Nebraska Symposium on Motivation,* ed. W. J. Arnold, pp. 175–266. Lincoln: Univ. Nebraska Press

Lazarus, R. S. 1981. The stress and coping paradigm. In *Models for Clinical Psychopathology,* ed. C. Eisdorfer, D. Cohen, A. Kleinman, P. Maxim, pp. 177–214. New York: Spectrum

Lazarus, R. S. 1991a. Cognition and motivation in emotion. *Am. Psychol.* 46:352–67

Lazarus, R. S. 1991b. Progress on a cognitive-motivational-relational theory of emotion.

Am. Psychol. 46:819–34

Lazarus, R. S. 1991c. *Emotion and Adaptation.* New York: Oxford Univ. Press

Lazarus, R. S., Alfert, E. 1964. The short-circuiting of threat. *J. Abnorm. Soc. Psychol.* 69:195–205

Lazarus, R. S., Averill, J. R., Opton, E. M. Jr. 1970. Toward a cognitive theory of emotions. In *Feelings and Emotions,* ed. M. Arnold, pp. 207–32. New York: Academic

Lazarus, R. S., Averill, J. R., Opton, E. M. Jr. 1974. The psychology of coping: issues of research and assessment. In *Coping and Adaptation,* ed. G. V. Coehlo, D. A. Hamburg, J. E. Adams, pp. 249–315. New York: Basic Books

Lazarus, R. S., Deese, J., Osler, S. F. 1952. The effects of psychological stress upon performance. *Psychol. Bull.* 49:293–317

Lazarus, R. S., Eriksen, C. W. 1952. Effects of failure stress upon skilled performance. *J. Exp. Psychol.* 43:100–5

Lazarus, R. S., Folkman, S. 1984. *Stress, Appraisal, and Coping.* New York: Springer

Lazarus, R. S., Folkman, S. 1987. Transactional theory and research on emotions and coping. *Eur. J. Personality* 1:141–69

Lazarus, R. S., Launier, R. 1978. Stress-related transactions between person and environment. In *Perspectives in Interactional Psychology,* ed. L. A. Pervin, M. Lewis, 287–327. New York: Plenum

Lazarus, R. S., Smith, C. A. 1988. Knowledge and appraisal in the cognition-emotion relationship. *Cognit. Emotion* 2:281–300

Lumsden, D. P. 1981. Is the concept of "stress" of any use, anymore? In *Contributions to Primary Prevention in Mental Health: Working Papers,* ed. D. Randall. Toronto: Toronto Natl. Off. Can. Mental Health Assoc.

Maddi, S. R., Kobasa, S. C. 1984. *The Hardy Executive: Health Under Stress.* Pacific Grove, CA: Brooks/Cole

Mandler, G. 1984. *Mind and Body: Psychology of Emotion and Stress.* New York: Norton

Mason, J. W., Maher, J. T., Hartley, L. H., Mougey, E., Perlow, M. J., Jones, L. G. 1976. Selectivity of corticosteroid and catecholamine response to various natural stimuli. In *Psychopathology of Human Adaptation,* ed. G. Serban, pp. 147–71. New York: Plenum

Mechanic, D. 1962. *Students under Stress: A Study in the Social Psychology of Adaptation.* New York: The Free Press. Reprinted 1978, Univ. Wisconsin Press

Merleau-Ponty, M. 1962. *Phenomenology of Perception,* transl. C. Smith. London: Routledge & Kegan Paul

Meyer, M. F. 1933. That whale among the fishes—the theory of emotions. *Psychol. Rev.* 40:292–300

Monat, A., Averill, J. R., Lazarus, R. S. 1973. Anticipatory stress and coping under various conditions of uncertainty. *J. Pers. Soc. Psychol.* 24:237–53

Nomikos, M. S., Opton, E. M. Jr., Averill, J. R., Lazarus, R. S. 1968. Surprise versus suspense in the production of stress reaction. *J. Pers. Soc. Psychol.* 8:204–8

Orr, E., Westman, M. 1990. Does hardiness moderate stress, and how?: a review. In *Learned Resourcefulness: On Coping Skills, Self-Control, and Adaptive Behavior,* ed. M. Rosenbaum, pp. 64–94. New York: Springer

Ortony, A., Clore, G. L., Collins, A. 1988. *The Cognitive Structure of Emotions.* Cambridge: Cambridge Univ. Press

Plutchik, R., Kellerman, H. 1980, 1983, 1986, 1989. *Emotion: Theory, Research, and Experience,* Vols. 1–4. New York: Academic

Polanyi, M. 1966. *The Tacit Dimension.* Garden City, NY: Doubleday

Reisenzein, R., Hofmann, T. 1990. An investigation of cognitive appraisals in emotion using the repertory grid technique. *Motiv. Emotion* 14:1–26

Reisenzein, R., Schönpflug, W. 1992. Stumpf's cognitive-evaluative theory of emotion. *Am. Psychol.* 47:34–45

Robertson, G. C. 1877. Notes. *Mind: Q. Rev.* 2:413–15

Roseman, I. J. 1984. Cognitive determinants of emotion: a structural theory. In *Review of Personality and Social Psychology: Emotions, Relationships, and Health,* ed. P. Shaver, 5:11–36. Beverly Hills, CA: Sage

Roseman, I. J. 1991. Appraisal determinants of discrete emotions. *Cognit. Emotion* 5:161–200

Rosenbaum, M., ed. 1990. *Learned Resourcefulness: On Coping Skills, Self-Control, and Adaptive Behavior.* New York: Springer

Scheier, M. F., Carver, C. S. 1987. Dispositional optimism and physical well-being: the influence of generalized outcome expectancies on health. *J. Pers.* 55:169–210

Scherer, K. R. 1984. On the nature and function of emotion: a component process approach. See Scherer & Ekman, pp. 293–317

Scherer, K. R., Ekman, P., ed. 1984. *Approaches to Emotion.* Hillsdale, NJ: Erlbaum

Selye, H. 1956/1976. *The Stress of Life.* New York: McGraw-Hill

Selye, H. 1974. *Stress without Distress.* Philadelphia: Lippincott

Shepard, R. N. 1984. Ecological constraints on internal representation: resonant kinematics of perceiving, imagining, thinking, and dreaming. *Psychol. Rev.* 91:417–47

Skinner, B. F. 1953. *Science and Human Behavior.* New York: Macmillan

Skinner, B. F. 1990. Can psychology be a science of mind? *Am. Psychol.* 45:1206–10

Smelser, N. J. 1963. *Theory of Collective Behavior.* New York: The Free Press

Smith, C. A., Ellsworth, P. C. 1985. Patterns of cognitive appraisal in emotion. *J. Pers. Soc. Psychol.* 48:813–38

Smith, C. A., Ellsworth, P. C. 1987. Patterns of appraisal and emotion related to taking an exam. *J. Pers. Soc. Psychol.* 52:475–88

Smith, C. A., Lazarus, R. S. 1990. Emotion and adaptation. In *Handbook of Personality: Theory and Research,* pp. 609–37. New York: Guilford

Snyder, C. R., Harris, C., Anderson, J. R., Holleran, S. A., Irving, L. M., et al. 1991. The will and the ways: development and validation of an individual difference measure of hope. *J. Pers. Soc. Psychol.* 60:570–85

Speisman, J. C., Lazarus, R. S., Mordkoff, A. M., Davison, L. A. 1964. The experimental reduction of stress based on ego-defense theory. *J. Abnorm. Soc. Psychol.* 68:367–80

Taylor, C. 1985. *Philosophical Papers,* Vols. 1, 2. London: Cambridge Univ. Press

Tomkins, S. S. 1962, 1963. *Affect, Imagery, Consciousness,* Vols. 1, 2. New York: Springer

Trevarthen, C. 1979. Communication and cooperation in early infancy. A description of primary intersubjectivity. In *Before Speech: The Beginnings of Human Communication,* ed. M. Bullowa. London: Cambridge Univ. Press

Varela, F. J., Thompson, E., Rosch, E. 1991. *The Embodied Mind: Cognitive Science and Human Experience.* Cambridge, MA: MIT Press

Weiner, B. 1986. *An Attributional Theory of Motivation and Emotion.* New York: Springer-Verlag

Annu. Rev. Psychol. 1993. 44:23–52

MECHANISMS OF SELF-REGULATION: A SYSTEMS VIEW

Paul Karoly

Department of Psychology, Arizona State University, Tempe, Arizona 85287-1104

KEYWORDS: self-guidance, volition, intentional action, goal-directedness, control theory

CONTENTS

INTRODUCTION 23
PARADIGM VARIATIONS AND BASIC MODELS.. 25
   Procedural, Epistemic, and Conceptual Divergence.. 26
   Goal Selection 27
   Goal Cognition.. 28
   Strategic, On-Line Goal Coordination: The Systems Base 29
PROXIMAL VOLITIONAL REGULATORS... 30
   Goal (Standard) Setting 31
   Self-Monitoring... 33
   The Activation and Use of Standards.. 34
   Discrepancy Detection, Self-Evaluative Judgment, Self-Consequation 35
   The Implementation of Discrepancy-Reduction Skills.. 36
   Self-Efficacy.. 37
METASKILLS AND BOUNDARY CONDITIONS.. 38
   Metaskills.. 39
   Boundary Conditions... 41
SELF-REGULATORY FAILURE: CONCEPTS AND DYNAMICS 42
FINAL COMMENT 44

INTRODUCTION

At the turn of the century, when the nascent discipline of psychology sought to appraise consciousness in both its mentalistic (James 1892) and physiologic (Wundt 1910) manifestations, the "problem of volition" emerged as a central

0066-4308/93/0201-0023$02.00

issue. James's ideas about the complex and multilevel relations among thought, affect, will, self, and attention were informed by his medical training, his unificationist leanings, and his wariness of the dualities and fruitless debates of the past. James's *will,* like Freud's (1923) *ego,* became the object of "scientific" scrutiny, a dynamic state "variable" to be analyzed as well as localized within a larger system, rather than a static organismic quality or faculty invoked post hoc as a pseudoexplanation. Notably ambitious, the Jamesian, Wundtian, and to a lesser extent the Freudian and Neo-Freudian agendas and their methods of investigation were eventually eclipsed and undermined by the rise of positivism, mechanism, and reductionism, and by the general sense that the elimination of concepts like consciousness and volition enabled significantly more parsimonious but no less powerful explanations of psychological phenomena. Further, by equating volition with "free will," the psychology of self-determination was written off as blatantly nonscientific (cf Howard & Conway 1986; Secord 1984; Silver 1985; Westcott 1985).

Whether we are currently in the midst of a "conative revolution," a Kuhnian paradigm shift, or a natural recycling of conservable ideas is not clear; but the empirical analysis of voluntary action management, or *self-regulation,* is a healthy and growing enterprise as psychology moves into the 21st century. The resurgence of interest in the presumably measurable and manipulable capacity for self-guidance undoubtedly has multiple roots, including the demise of logical positivism; the successes of cognitive psychology in explicating the processes involved in the retrieval and storage of information; the importation of concepts from digital computing, cognitive neuroscience, cybernetics, and artificial intelligence into applied psychology; the broadening of psychodynamic models and their integration within mainstream psychology; and the liberalization of American learning theory that began in the 1950s. Cultural, economic, and political forces have likewise been at work during the last few decades of the 20th century, creating a climate conducive to personal and societal expressions of individualism, responsibility, autonomy, and freedom of choice (Mahoney 1991; Westcott 1988).

The reintroduction of self-regulation and related concepts into contemporary psychology has not been restricted to a single subdiscipline.[1] Self-regulatory constructs and models are highly visible in such domains as personality (Cantor & Zirkel 1990; Carver & Scheier 1981; Mischel 1973; Mischel et al 1989; Singer & Bonanno 1990), motivation/emotion (Bandura 1991; Deci 1980; Gollwitzer 1990; Heckhausen & Kuhl 1985; Kuhl & Kazen-Saad 1988), social psychology (Beckmann & Irle 1985; Fiske & Taylor 1991; Higgins et al

---

1

Among the terms used (often interchangeably) to denote a capacity for self-regulation are freedom, autonomy, agency, responsibility, maturity, ego-strength, willpower, self-control, choice, purposiveness, self-direction, voluntary action, self-sufficiency, morality, consciousness, free will, independence, conscientiousness, self-discipline, intentional action, self-intervention, intrinsic motivation, self-determination, and volition.

1986; Koestner et al 1992; Markus & Wurf 1987), clinical/abnormal (Glasser 1984; Hilgard 1986; Josephs 1992; Kanfer & Schefft 1988; Karoly & Kanfer 1982; Marlatt & Gordon 1985; Meichenbaum 1985; Semmer & Frese 1985; Shapiro 1965; Watson & Tharp 1989), developmental psychology (Brandtstädter 1989; Kopp 1982; Power & Chapieski 1986; Zivin 1979), health psychology/behavioral medicine (Brownell 1991; Ewart 1991; Goodall & Halford 1991; Holroyd & Creer 1986; Karoly 1991a,b), education (Ames & Ames 1989; Brown 1987; Newman 1991; Pintrich & Garcia 1991), industrial-organizational psychology (Cervone et al 1991; Kanfer & Kanfer 1991; Locke & Latham 1990; Wood et al 1990), and experimental psychology (Libet 1985; Logan & Cowan 1984; MacKay 1984; Norman & Shallice 1986; Pribram 1976; Stelmach & Hughes 1984; Weimer 1977), among others.

Expectable divergences in content emphasis and preferred investigatory methods mark the contemporary psychologies of self-regulation. These sub-disciplines share, however, an aspiration to transcend longstanding philosophical debates over the conditions under which the proximate causes of action may be identified (cf Brand 1984; Lennon 1990). To achieve their empirical objectives, self-regulation researchers of all persuasions employ operational and context-specific definitions and an a priori partitioning of regulatory processes, outcomes, and putative mediators. Despite an absence of paradigmatic consensus, the following multi-element definition can be offered as a conceptual roadmap and organizational aid:

> Self-regulation refers to those processes, internal and/or transactional, that enable an individual to guide his/her goal-directed activities over time and across changing circumstances (contexts). Regulation implies modulation of thought, affect, behavior, or attention via deliberate or automated use of specific mechanisms and supportive metaskills. The processes of self-regulation are initiated when routinized activity is impeded or when goal-directedness is otherwise made salient (e.g. the appearance of a challenge, the failure of habitual action patterns, etc). Self-regulation may be said to encompass up to five interrelated and iterative component phases: 1. goal selection, 2. goal cognition, 3. directional maintenance, 4. directional change or reprioritization, and 5. goal termination.

Self-regulatory skills and processes, as presently conceived, are related to, but remain conceptually distinct from beliefs, attributions, preferences concerning freedom of choice or desirability of control, general intellective capabilities, and biochemical or neurophysiological systems of internal state regulation (homeostasis).

PARADIGM VARIATIONS AND BASIC MODELS

By far the largest empirical literature on mechanisms of self-regulation concerns various aspects of the goal execution sequence (i.e. maintenance, change, and/or termination of action). To be fully appreciated, however, the major regulatory functions should be considered in the context of the theories that proclaim them, the paradigms that contain them, and the surrounding superstructure provided by the less frequently studied (but nonetheless influential) components or phases of the regulatory cycle.

Procedural, Epistemic, and Conceptual Divergence

Investigators of human self-guidance processes can be distinguished not only on the basis of their theoretical (or metatheoretical) allegiances and their investigatory objectives within the regulatory cycle but also by (a) their preference for controlled laboratory simulations vs naturalistic or correlational designs; (b) the degree of their interest in social-contextual modifiers, individual differences, maturation, biological parameters, or other factors potentially interacting with "core" mechanisms; (c) their focus upon basic or normative vs applied or "clinical" phenomena; and (d) their choice of dependent measures, including short-term task performance, extended activity patterns ("self-help", "independent living", "medical compliance"), and the dynamics of self/performance appraisal associated with self-generated motivation (e.g. patterns of self-reward, attributions of self-efficacy, ratings of intrinsic interest, and the like).

Further, in contrast to the experimental anatomization of a psychological process that preserves the temporal integrity of the targeted phenomenon, as in the decomposition of reaction time (Sternberg 1969), investigators of human self-governance have generally opted for the strategy of segmenting and isolating regulatory phases or subfunctions. No research program has ever tackled the entire sequence from goal choice to goal attainment for obvious practical reasons and because the component processes tend to be indexable at different levels, nonrecursive, and difficult to identify in vivo. However, an unfortunate consequence of the artificial (but artful) parsing of a complex, contextually embedded stream of events is the tendency for mechanisms to be analyzed singly (overlooking possible compound effects), via unique paradigmatic renderings, in relation to only a subset of potential outcomes, and with regard to but a portion of the complete regulatory cycle. The difficult trip that many regulatory variables and assessment modes experience in transport between the laboratory and clinic and the absence of a seamless integration of hypothesized causal mechanisms may be traced, at least in part, to prevailing analytic technologies.

Models of self-regulation have sprung from a variety of sources—philosophical exegeses, clinical insights, laboratory studies, and the tenets and ramifications of control-systems engineering—making for an interesting, if not wholly compatible, mix of interpretive metaphors. Theories can be roughly divided into those that address off-line preparation for action via goal selection and schematic organization and those that address on-line goal pursuit via diverse aspects of performance monitoring and evaluation (phases 1 and 2 vs phases 3, 4, and 5 of the process described above).

Goal Selection

The achievement of any personal objective is logically predicated upon the selection of at least a tentative directional path (or set of paths) from among diverse and sometimes conflicting alternatives—but with the important recognition that deciding upon, intending, wishing for, or anticipating an outcome does not alone guarantee its accomplishment (Heckhausen 1991; Heckhausen & Kuhl 1985). Nevertheless, goals remain the quintessential psychological construct—symbolic structures with presumptive causal significance. Unfortunately, many investigators implicitly foreclose the analysis of variations in the preparatory or representational components of motivation by assigning goals to research participants or by operationalizing them narrowly and in relation to proximal determinants.

For example, social psychological approaches to *intention* or *commitment* (e.g. Fishbein & Ajzen 1975; Kiesler 1971) focus not on the unconstrained choice of goal paths but on the factors (typically interpersonal) that compel the actor to follow through on his/her stated intentions. Some operant perspectives (Dulany 1961; Kanfer & Karoly 1972) have centered upon the conditionability of intentions rather than upon their natural emergence (although most radical behaviorists still deny that intentions can ever serve as action motivators). Although the content of children's motivational action patterns has been the subject of social-learning based studies, the specific target of socialization has tended to be either prosocial (moral) or self-constraining goals (delay of gratification, resistance to temptation) often operationalized in a laboratory context and likewise randomly assigned to participants (Mischel & Mischel 1976). Within educational psychology, efforts are under way to classify goal contents (Ford & Nichols 1987, 1991) and to examine the impact of goal types (e.g. self-set vs other-set, intrinsic vs extrinsic, or performance vs mastery goals) upon outcomes such as learning, sustained interest, or the maintenance of effort/performance (cf Deci & Ryan 1985; Dweck 1986; Harackiewicz et al 1984; Lepper & Hodell 1989). However, the study of goals as dependent variables remains infrequent.

Recently, Cantor & Fleeson (1991) addressed what they termed the *goal definition* process, asserting that differential goal selection has been ignored by theorists and researchers in favor of the more readily examined performance-centered subprocesses and mechanisms that seem to function as "goal independent general purpose modules." Cantor & Fleeson speculate that sources of influence, both self-relevant (needs and motives) and contextual (cues to age-graded or normative expectancies), serve to shape the definitional (goal selection) process [see also Markus & Wurf's (1987) discussion of the role of self-definition in self-regulation].

Goal Cognition

Assuming that goal choice is driven (at least partially) by the power of personal identity and the ubiquity of sociocultural forces, and that real time goal pursuit is managed by various on-line processing mechanisms (to be discussed), individuals must additionally be presumed to possess a relatively stable and potentially retrievable *mental model, action schema,* or *script* by means of which active goals are propositionally specified, evaluated, and organized as well as stored. The striving-referent thoughts, appraisals, construals, or abstracting qualities are here collectively labelled *goal cognition*— an emergent domain of empirical investigation (e.g. Cantor & Zirkel 1990; Emmons 1986, 1989; Karoly 1991b; Little 1983; Snyder et al 1991).

Goal cognition has been found to predict various indexes of mental and physical health status in the absence of any formal assessment of people's declarative knowledge base, instrumental skill repertoire, or instantiation of specific goal-coordination mechanisms (cf Emmons 1992; Emmons & King 1988; King & Emmons 1990; Omodei & Wearing 1990; Palys & Little 1983; Ruehlman & Wolchik 1988).

Goal representations or construals also serve a higher-order *governing function* (Ford 1987); that is, by virtue of their content, level of abstraction, and structural organization, they can store, organize, transform, and activate information about self, world, and self-world transactions so as to potentially aid in the mobilization of goal-directed behaviors. A key content feature of goal construal involves motivational or value *preference,* i.e. the specification of what is personally desirable or undesirable. Wants, passions, wishes, hopes, strivings, and the like represent commonplace goal-construal elements with clear affective connections. Of all the things one can develop passionate aversions or attachments to, only some motivational preferences are targeted for action. These are called *commitments,* a second important class of goal-representational content. Finally, although one may prefer an outcome or its absence and be committed cognitively to attaining it, one may not work to achieve or avoid it unless there is an anticipation or expectancy that serves to trigger selective preparation and the expenditure of effort (cf Bandura 1986; Ford 1987; Kuhl & Kazen-Saad 1988). The best-known and most systematically researched anticipatory goal representation is self-efficacy, defined by Bandura (1986) as involving "people's judgments of their capabilities to organize and execute courses of action required to attain designated types of performances" (p. 391).

Over the years, investigators interested in measuring not only goal types but the organizational attributes of goal representation have orchestrated assessment systems that access the value-preference, commitment, and anticipatory features of goal cognition. Klinger (1977), for example, fashioned a detailed procedure for explicating goal-directed strivings, which he labeled *current concerns.* Using both interview and questionnaire procedures, Klinger and his colleagues (Klinger et al 1981) require subjects to list goals and rate them along dimensions such as level of commitment, time availability, expectancy of success, and the like. Little's (1983, 1989) Personal Projects Analysis (PPA) system involves an elicitation of goals, followed by a rating procedure incorporating 17 goal-construal dimensions that cluster into the following five factors: efficacy, meaning, structure, stress, and community. Little's factors reflect a multifaceted mental modeling process wherein projects (defined as a set of interrelated acts, extended over time, intended to achieve or maintain a desired state) are construed as variably worthwhile (meaning), capable of progressing (efficacy), organized (structure), demanding (stress), and visible/supportable by others (community). A number of active investigators (including Emmons and Cantor and their associates) employ similar protocols for the assessment of goal-construal content.

Level of abstractness of goal construal is yet another dimensional attribute that has been postulated to influence the success of the regulatory cycle (Carver & Scheier 1990; Emmons 1992; Powers 1973; Vallacher & Wegner 1989). Little (1989), for example, has sought to capture the hierarchical nature of goals (personal projects) through what he calls "phrasing level analysis." He notes the distinction between the intention to "return my neighbor's ladder" and the goal of "liberating my people" as marking the extremes for an individual, and then discusses the tradeoff between meaning and manageability that needs to occur in order that psychological well-being be maintained. Substituting the concept of *personal strivings* for projects, Emmons (1992) has shown that, in fact, high-level strivers experience greater psychological distress but less physical illness than their low-level-striving peers, who report less negative affect but a greater number of physical symptoms.

Finally, the structural relations among the goals in one's experiential "active file" have long been of interest to theoreticians, particularly as regards incompatibility or conflict (cf Lewin 1926, 1935; Miller 1944; Murray 1938). Several contemporary investigators have assessed the internal conflict among goals for individuals as well as the conflict between the goals of social dyads and have discerned behavioral and emotional consequences associated with incompatibility, ambivalence, and active goal hindrance (e.g. Emmons & King 1988; King & Emmons 1990; McKeeman & Karoly 1991; Ruehlman & Wolchik 1988).

Strategic, On-Line Goal Coordination: The Systems Base

That countless regulatory objectives have occupied the attention of social and behavioral scientists over the years attests (*a*) to the importance our society places on the individual's potential to decide, act, feel, express, think, perceive, and change as his/her intentions/needs dictate, and (*b*) to the equally compelling awareness that barriers, both internal and external, limit the actualization of this potential.[2] Although humanistic psychology has underscored the generative power of self-determination and aptly characterized its experiential nature (e.g. Maslow 1971; May 1953), the task of demystifying and systematically unpacking the cognitive/perceptual and behavioral operations underlying goal directedness has fallen to the more experimentally minded. In attempting to build models of self-regulation, researchers and theoreticians have largely focussed on the pragmatics of post-decisional action management (phases 3–5 of the regulatory cycle, noted above)—the so-called *goal-striving* portion of the motivational loop (cf Lewin et al 1944).

Based upon a century-old insight attributed to William James (cf Powers 1989), that humans are "unique" in nature because they can produce consistent ends by variable means, a number of contemporary (post-1960) models of dynamic self-regulation have been developed under the imprimatur of cognitive theory, control/systems science, cognitive social learning, or European action theory. All presume that on-line regulation is a dynamic process, continuous and holistic rather than linear, built upon the operation of feedback (knowledge of results) and feedforward (standard-produced disequilibrium), sensitivity to action-produced environmental changes, the accessibility of goal representations, and a capacity for the selective mobilization of energy, attention, and relational judgment. The output of any regulatory process is dependent upon the uptake of information and its relatively unconstrained flow within the person and between the person and his/her social world. Goals exist within such a framework as reference values or standards of comparison (e.g. Bandura 1986; Carver & Scheier 1981, 1990; Ewart 1991; Ford 1987; Hyland 1988; Kanfer & Hagerman 1981; Kanfer & Karoly 1972; Miller et al 1960; Powers 1973). The theories differ in the way the components are configured and in which elements are emphasized. Yet all converge in their allegiance to a multi-element, closed-loop, mediational perspective on human self-guidance.

PROXIMAL VOLITIONAL REGULATORS

Ford's (1987) "living systems" perspective, an excellent synthesis of many regulatory models, offers *negative feedback control* as the primary organizing metaphor and specifies six interrelated functional capabilities to serve as the constituents of goal-directed, self-organizing, adaptive systems.

2

Included among the clinical or applied targets of volitional self-regulation are the coordination of skilled behaviors such as studying, simple and complex job performances, and interpersonal transactions; the management of stress, anxiety, or other affective experiences; the control of attentional/cognitive processes that presumably mediate action (e.g. thoughts, images, verbal cues); the modulation of somatic experiences or symptoms, such as sleep, pain, energy level, and body awareness; and the gaining of indirect jurisdiction over the experiential correlates of behavior, thought, and emotional control—such as quality of life, perceived freedom, and the sensed availability of time.

The goal or purpose toward which the actor is directed is called the feedforward, command, set-point, or *directive* function. When engineers use the term, they are discussing a value or objective programmed dispassionately into a machine. In living-systems terms, the directive function is the product of goal-choice socialization and the vagaries of goal cognition (discussed above). Insofar as proximal goal guidance is concerned, the directive function reduces to a standard or criterion for the performance of a specific act or set of acts. Although the overall "goal" may involve "Getting into graduate school," it must be skillfully translated into subgoals whose defining structural properties (e.g. difficulty, specificity) determine the likelihood that the next functional component, the *comparator,* will be engaged.

The comparator, or *regulating function,* addresses the fit between the current status of the regulatory objective and the desired status. The system has access to information about the current status of things owing to an *information collection function* that feeds the data back to the comparator. The comparator is therefore designed so as to match two signals: the set point (command) signal that is fed forward from the directive function ("This is what I desire") and the feedback signal delivered by the information collection function ("This is what I've achieved thus far").

Should a mismatch be detected between the two signals, the discrepancy information is fed forward to a *control function* that selects a course of action and then to an *action function* that produces environmental effects. Finally, because every activity expends energy, the system must have a source of power, labeled the *arousal function.*

It should be clear that the regnant principle of self-regulation, *negative feedback control,* is more aptly viewed as a complex set of interrelated mechanisms (including feedforward) whose coordinated functioning is a prerequisite of adaptive flexibility. No consensus yet exists about the necessary and sufficient volitional regulators. I outline next the mechanisms currently thought essential to negative feedback control (broadly construed).[3]

Goal (Standard) Setting

Several theoretical accounts of self-regulation emphasize the view that its analysis can occur at distinct levels of explanation (e.g. Carver & Scheier 1990; Locke & Latham 1990; Powers 1973) and that the most practical is the action-centered, efficient-cause level. To predict current performance, one must focus upon task-specific goal content (specificity, difficulty, complexity,

---

[3]
The need to construe "negative feedback control" in broad terms is dictated by the desire not only to achieve explanatory comprehensiveness but also to avoid groundless criticisms of control theory as being monolithically tied to discrepancy reduction as its core and only motive principle (cf Locke & Latham 1990). Clearly, the constant presence and reprioritization of preferences and hoped-for possibilities introduce disequilibrium into the control system alongside the equilibrating structure afforded by negative feedback (discrepancy-reducing) mechanisms (Appley 1991; Bandura 1988).

and conflict) and goal intensity (factors influencing task engagement or commitment, such as expectancy and self-efficacy). This is the perspective offered by Locke & Latham's (1990) *goal-setting theory,* perhaps the leading self-regulation model in contemporary industrial-organizational psychology. Goals are said to affect job performance by channeling attention, mobilizing on-task effort (in proportion to task difficulty), sustaining performance over time, and stimulating strategic planning. However, their facilitative effects can be moderated by such factors as availability of feedback, task complexity, commitment, ability, and knowledge. Bandura's (1986) social-cognitive theory likewise emphasizes the "goal properties" of specificity, challenge, proximity, strength of commitment, and degree of participation in goal selection. The influence of the various goal-setting variables is usually complex and interactive, with some relationships yielding consistent findings (e.g. specific, difficult goals to which one is committed produce higher-quality performances than do vague, easy goals toward which one is not attracted) and others being less clear (proximal goals mobilize performance accomplishment/persistence to a greater degree than do distal goals in some studies, fail to differ from distal goals in others, and yield inferior effects in still other experiments) (cf Tubbs 1986).

For present purposes, several points can be made about the goal- or standard-setting literature. First, it helps to bridge the ostensibly distinct domains of goal selection/goal cognition (the off-line, higher-order processes that serve as distal volitional regulators) and goal striving. The schematic *goal construals assessed* by Little, Cantor, Emmons, and others in longitudinal or field studies concerned with predicting mental health, well-being, stress, or activity choices resemble the sorts of *goal properties manipulated* by goal-setting researchers studying performance in classrooms and work settings (cf Kanfer & Kanfer 1991; Lee et al 1989; Schunk 1991).

However, because goal cognition derives from sources other than direct performance feedback (socialization, self-identity, "needs" for consistency and self-esteem) and involves value preferences and symbolic transformations of experience, there need not be a perfect correspondence between the representational domain (how one thinks about goals) and the executional domain (how effectively or hard one works under the immediate influence of task demands and instructions). Indeed, the distinctiveness of the two domains helps explain the difficulty people often encounter in clinical self-change efforts (Kuhl & Kazen-Saad 1988). Research and theorizing at the interface of the representational and executional models, such as Bandura's (1986) work on self-efficacy, Eisenberger's (1992) studies of "learned industriousness," and R. Kanfer & Ackerman's (1989) work on attentional resource allocation, may help to clarify the sometimes tenuous connections between distal and proximal elements in the self-regulatory stream.

Self-Monitoring

An adapting organism is constantly collecting, transforming, and utilizing information within an "open system" context—a process that allows for growth, change, and self-regulation (Ford 1987). Goal-directed organisms selectively attend to and perceive information that bears upon their directive or command functions; that is, goals (intentions, projects, concerns, etc) drive our perceptions of our mental and sensory states and of our self/environment transactions (Klinger 1977). This status check upon internal events and the results of expressive or instrumental activity is called, in a somewhat oversimplified fashion, *self-observation, self-monitoring,* and on occasion (when the individual keeps a written account of what has occurred) *self-recording* (Kanfer & Karoly 1972; Kazdin 1974; McFall 1977; Nelson 1977). Perhaps a better term would be information, input, or disturbance monitoring. In any case, it is clear that systematic, self-consciously guided movement toward or away from a goal or subgoal cannot occur in the absence of deliberate attention to qualitative and quantitative aspects of ongoing performance.

Of course, not all goal-directed movement need be conscious or deliberate. Indeed, when skills are overlearned or automatized, self-regulation is not an issue and self-monitoring is potentially disruptive. Self-monitoring is, therefore, often the first stage in multistage models of self-regulation (e.g. Bandura 1986; Kanfer & Karoly 1972; Kanfer & Hagerman 1981) as it signals a temporary disengagement from automaticity, or a transition from "mindlessness" to "mindfulness" (Langer 1989). Note, however, that when Bandura (1986) declares that "self-observation is not simply a mechanical tracking or registry process" he is alerting us to the multiple antecedents of self-monitoring and its myriad effects, while cautioning us against any literal interpretation of regulatory stages, steps, or sequences (such as self-monitoring → self-evaluation → self-reward). Among the potential determinants of self-observation, in addition to such obvious ones as response failure, sudden environmental change, or social prompts, are moods, self-conceptions, values, and self-attentional proclivities, as well as the effects of supposed postmonitoring mechanisms, such as self-evaluations and -attributions. Among the multiple consequences of self-observation are the collection of goal-relevant information, the enhancement of motivation, and the triggering of self-reflective (judgmental) responses that may alter the occurrence of monitored events or the accuracy with which they are enumerated (cf Bandura 1986; Kanfer & Karoly 1972; Kazdin 1974; Nelson 1977).

When behavioral models predominated in self-regulation research, self-monitoring was usually directed at specific target responses (such as the number of cigarettes smoked or the number of homework pages completed). However, people can monitor not only what they do, but also the environmental vs self-directed influences on their behavior (Kanfer & Hagerman 1981), the *rate* at which they are approaching their goals (a process called *metamonitoring;* cf Carver & Scheier 1990), and the somatic (affective, arousal-based) consequences of goal pursuit (Pennebaker et al 1985).

The Activation and Use of Standards

Having a goal (or a specific performance level to which one aspires) and being able systematically to surveil goal-relevant activities do not alone provide the impetus to self-regulated modulation of thought, affect, or behavior. Before the all-important comparison of the feedforward and the feedback signals can occur in human control systems, the goal or standard must be triggered, activated, or called up from long-term memory. Unlike mechanical servo-mechanisms whose instructions (goals) are unambiguous, fixed, and un-conflicted, human beings are best viewed as pluralistic (multiple-minded as opposed to single-minded) computational systems whose purposes can be assigned to distinct modules that can either compete or cooperate with one another, can be arranged either in a serial or parallel fashion, and can exist in either an activated or a deactivated state at any given time (Navon 1989; Simon 1967). Unless we wish to postulate a homunculus that activates and supervises an enormous and ever-changing agenda of intentions, we must conclude that most goals are "in a queue" as Simon (1967) suggests, waiting to be called into service by the proper environmental circumstance, an internal motive, or via communication with the dominant goal(s) of the moment.

What circumstances, specifically, activate intentional or strategic proposi-tions (goals) presumably stored in working memory? In most experimental research, standards are triggered by clear and compelling instructions and/or incentives and the social demand characteristics intrinsic to the setting (Greenwald 1982). In less-contrived settings, certain external features and internal events can also trigger a mental consideration of one's self-aspects, including but certainly not restricted to one's salient goals. Inspired by the work of Duval & Wicklund (1972), Carver & Scheier (1981, 1990) assumed (*a*) that attention fluctuates between the outside world and the self, (*b*) that certain stimuli such as audiences, mirrors, or physiological arousal direct attention toward the self, and (*c*) that once a person is focused upon him/her-self (regardless of what induced the self-focused attention) there is a tendency to compare his or her present state against a behavioral standard. In a series of experiments, Carver & Scheier demonstrated that, in control-theory terms, self-focused attention can *activate the relevant comparator* and, all else being equal, *promote self-regulation* by encouraging discrepancy-reduction efforts.[4]

Laboratory studies of self-regulation generally allow for little variation in the types of standards that subjects access. If, for example, the experimental

---

4

Of course all else is seldom equal; thus, when subjects are fearful or have low self-confidence about performance, a heightened self-focus engages the comparator and precipitates withdrawal (or giving-up) rather than task persistence (Carver & Scheier 1990). Bear in mind also that self-focus in the Carver/Scheier model activates the comparator, not the standard per se (which is usually triggered by situational relevancy cues).

task involves anagram solution, then subjects access intellectual standards rather than standards of athletic or sexual performance. In many contexts outside the laboratory, the cues, demands, or "opportunity structures" are such that the "appropriate" goal or standard is readily called into service. However, some situations are ambiguous and/or multidimensional, potentially activating multiple and possibly incompatible standards while accentuating individual differences in on-line standard (goal) selection and representation. In this regard, the work of Higgins and associates (1987; Higgins & Moretti 1988; Higgins et al 1986) is instructive. Higgins and his colleagues propose at least three distinct types of self-evaluative standards: factual points of reference, imagined possibilities (see also Markus & Nurius 1986), and acquired guides, the last of which involves the sorts of personal or normative self-relevant anchors usually discussed in the self-regulatory literature. Further, different standards can be employed at different stages in the process of evaluation, yielding different emotions. Finally, these investigators assert that either non-normative *selection* of standards from the above-noted types or the nonnormative *use* of standards (i.e. application of the right type of standard but at the wrong stage of information processing) may form the basis for aberrant self-relevant beliefs, e.g. (delusions).

Discrepancy Detection, Self-Evaluative Judgment, Self-Consequation

A pivotal regulatory operation occurs when an activated personal standard is juxtaposed against the knowledge of one's current performance (gathered via self-monitoring or direct external feedback)—namely, the process of comparison and discrepancy detection. The evaluative reactions that follow are believed to be central to self-motivation, and depend upon the joint availability of standards and knowledge of results (e.g. Bandura & Cervone 1983).[5] Evaluative, "matching-to-standard" reactions are believed capable of guiding behavior not only through their invocation of prescriptive requirements (the feedforward or directive function), but also by their recruitment of effort and energy (when performance falls below expected levels of excellence) and self-satisfaction and pride (when standards are met or surpassed). Social learning conceptions of self-motivation (Bandura 1986; Kanfer & Karoly 1972) presume further that the conditional discrimination of criterion matching precipitates self-reward, whereas the failure to match occasions self-punishment (cf also Grimm 1983; Spates & Kanfer 1977).

   However, self-evaluations or detected discrepancies do not act as reflexive "autoregulators" of action. Although from a purely engineering (cybernetic) perspective, the standard of correctness is "physically embodied as a perfectly

---

5
   We can assume, for the moment, that people are always motivated to compare standards with feedback and are always willing to recognize and own up to discrepancies, should they exist. These assumptions, which hold for well-constructed mechanical systems, may not be justified under conditions considered below, in the section on Self-Regulatory Failure.

real physical reference signal inside the control system" (Powers 1986:152), in human self-regulators the rule-generation and rule-following routines are variable and subject to moderating influences. Recognition of the complexities inherent in the supposedly straightforward process of standard matching (*a*) may help reconcile control-theory formulations with those (e.g. Ellis 1976; Orth & Thebarge 1984) that proclaim self-evaluation to be intrinsically pathogenic, (*b*) underscores the importance of affective processes in self-regulation, and (*c*) paves the way for systematic analyses of self-regulatory failure.

Illustrative of the sensitivity of self-reactive judgment to contextual influences are the following sorts of findings: (*a*) that the degree of increase in effortful behavior following feedback regarding substandard performance is greater for individuals high in self-efficacy than in those low in self-efficacy (Bandura & Cervone 1983); (*b*) that performance in achievement situations varies with whether the standards are self-set or externally determined (Schunk 1989); (*c*) that the degree of mismatch or displacement between performance and standard affects effort and self-appraisal (Bandura & Cervone 1986); (*d*) that the effects of negative evaluation following substandard performance on complex tasks are opposite to those found on simple tasks—namely performance/effort is reduced (Cervone et al 1991); (*e*) that satisfaction is related not only to the absolute level of discrepancy between performance and standard but also to the rate at which the performance changes over time (Carver & Scheier 1990; Hsee & Abelson 1991); and (*f*) that social comparisons can affect the self-reward process, as, for example, when self-reward after successful performance is diminished if others are known to have performed better, and self-punishment after poor performance is diminished if others are known to have performed worse (Karoly & Decker 1979).

The Implementation of Discrepancy-Reduction Skills

In a self-regulating machine such as a thermostatically driven air conditioner or a guided missile, the action function is, as Powers would say, a physical embodiment—a built-in component designed either to operate effectively or be repaired/replaced. In humans, the action function is learned, is subject to interference or deterioration, and can hardly be expected to "kick in" automatically when needed. Most laboratory studies of self-regulation have involved either motor tasks or problem-solving tasks well within the physical or intellectual capabilities of the participants. When difficult or novel tasks are employed, ability must be considered in concert with motivational parameters (R. Kanfer & Ackerman 1989).

In the realm of goal-directedness, "regulation" denotes trajectory correction operations that help either to "stay the course" against obstacles or to recalculate it (often against such powerful contravening contingencies as temptation by an addictive substance). Closing the gap between intention and execution therefore often requires the recruitment of dynamic and diverse discrepancy-reduction mechanisms.[6]

Among the active cognitive-behavioral mechanisms considered useful (with no presumption of necessity or sufficiency) in correcting standard-feedback mismatch are (a) attentional resource allocation (R. Kanfer & Ackerman 1989; Norman & Shallice 1986); (b) effort mobilization (Wright & Brehm 1989); (c) planning and problem solving (Berger 1988; Hayes-Roth & Hayes-Roth 1979; Sternberg 1982); (d) verbal self-cueing (Bem 1967; Hartig & Kanfer 1973; Kanfer et al 1975; Meichenbaum 1977); (e) facilitative cognitive sets or expectations (Bandura 1986; Gollwitzer et al 1990; Rosenbaum 1990); (f) stimulus control or milieu selection (Kanfer & Gaelick-Buys 1991; Thoresen & Mahoney 1974), and (g) mental control/thought suppression (Wegner & Schneider 1989).

Self-Efficacy

In addition to goal-setting and self-evaluative reactions, social-cognitive theory (Bandura 1986) invokes self-efficacy judgments as a third mechanism underlying cognitively based motivation. The theory of self-efficacy (Bandura 1977), a member of a family of conceptual models concerned with personal effectiveness, mastery, or control (cf Maddux 1991; Maddux & Stanley 1986), postulates that broad-based knowledge and specific monitoring and discrepancy-reduction skills are insufficient to insure goal-based performance—as witnessed by the fact that people often do not do what they are perfectly capable of doing. Self-referent thought is believed to mediate the relation between wanting/knowing and action. The belief in domain-specific personal efficacy, in contrast to beliefs about performance consequences (outcome expectancies), is the self-referent, generative capability that stands out as a singularly powerful self-motivating force. Recognizing that efficacy estimates arise (partly) from performance accomplishments does not detract from their putative role as action regulators; thus self-efficacy judgments can serve as predictors and/or dependent variables in research.

Over the years, Bandura and others have demonstrated the significant contribution of self-efficacy judgments to such diverse outcomes as the regulation of approach/avoidance and/or distress responses to fearful stimuli (Bandura et al 1982; Biran & Wilson 1981; Gattuso et al 1992; Ozer & Bandura 1990), smoking cessation/relapse (Condiotte & Lichtenstein 1981; Godding & Glasgow 1985; Haaga & Stewart 1992; Owen & Brown 1991), the perception and tolerance of physical pain (Baker & Kirsch 1991; Bandura et al 1987; Jensen

---

6

Early social-learning models (Bandura 1969; Kanfer & Karoly 1972) depicted the primary task of self-regulation as the taking over ("internalization") of external contingencies. Standards of conduct were viewed as "socially transferable and conditionable," with failure to adhere to them the result of the nonoperation of covert reinforcement practices. Thus, a discrepancy between standard and performance could be rectified by self-generated punishment for inappropriate actions and/or self-reinforcement of behavior-goal correspondence.

et al 1991; Litt 1988; Manning & Wright 1983; Vallis & Bucher 1986), the use of decisional strategies and the control of performance in complex organizational tasks (Bandura & Jourden 1991; Cervone et al 1991), and the process of stress coping and its immunologic correlates (Bandura et al 1988; Wiedenfeld et al 1990), among others. Although not without its critics (Corcoran 1991; Eastman & Marzillier 1984; Kirsch 1985; Powers 1991), the theory of self-efficacy has generated a considerable body of research that has illuminated the role of one major type of self-referent thought (operating in concert with other regulatory mechanisms) across an impressive array of applied domains.

The social-cognitive construct of "self-referent thought" may, however, be somewhat limiting, in that attributions concerning personal mastery do not encompass the full range of schematic goal-relevant cognition. Along with expectancies, values, or goal preferences, beliefs regarding one's instrumental competence represent a type of "guiding" or anticipatory function that Ford (1987) has labeled *directive*. Yet, if we assume that individuals likewise evolve a set of beliefs or attributions concerning their skilled use of other goal-coordination mechanisms (constituting the regulatory, control, action, or arousal functions), then shouldn't these also be assessed and linked (in a domain-specific rather than traitlike fashion) to on-line patterns of behavior, thought, and emotional expressivity? Goal-centered action schemata that have been suggested, in addition to those reflected in the multiple, control-theory functions articulated by Ford (1987), include Read & Miller's (1989) mediating structures [goals, plans (strategies), beliefs (about the world), and resources] and those in Kuhl & Kazen-Saad's (1988) "five-systems model," incorporating the motivational preference system, the executional preference system, the volitional system, the emotional system, and semantic memory (in which all intentional and action-schematic representations are stored). In short, an empirical warrant exists for examining not only self-efficacy but also the complete spectrum of *goal-referent thinking,* including knowledge, attitudes, and attributions relevant to all proximal volitional regulators. Whether beliefs about monitoring, planning, self-evaluation, and the like are mere proxies for efficacy beliefs or have incremental utility as intention-action moderators remains to be determined.

METASKILLS AND BOUNDARY CONDITIONS

Not only do the proximal negative-feedback control mechanisms of human self-regulation need to be contextualized within the purview of the self-contained executive control system of which they are a part, but they likewise require referencing in terms of the multiple, simultaneously operating, and hierarchically organized subsystems responsible for the realization of intelligent (flexible) adaptation in the world. Although self-regulation is distinct from "intelligence," it is nonetheless dependent upon collateral competencies that aid in the computation and recomputation of goal trajectories across changing environments and over time. I call these computational superstructures *metaskills*.

Metaskills

Because we can most effectively describe self-regulation in terms of phases and can most readily examine it via isolation of subfunctions, we might tend to think of the natural regulatory process as a relatively straightforward, sequential combination of constituent parts. Yet such a model would fail dismally to account for how we reach for a glass of water and bring it to our lips, let alone how we manage to study for an examination, lose 30 pounds, or write an *Annual Review* chapter (cf Bullock & Grossberg 1988; Kosslyn & Koenig 1992). The coordination of complex action is now believed to occur across multiple levels of computation whose functional outputs include (but are not limited to) the conscious, reasoning-centered, and potentially trainable regulatory skills discussed above.

Some computational superstructures are more obvious than others. For example, a goal or performance standard can only drive a comparator process if it is encoded as a perceptual signal, stored, and replayed at the proper time. Hence, memory and retrieval are clearly regulatory metaskills (Kuhl & Kazen-Saad 1988; Powers 1973; Wyer & Srull 1986). For most cognitive and instrumental discrepancy-reduction programs to function there must also exist a declarative knowledge base (facts) from which to build event schemas or action scripts (Singer & Salovey 1991). And, to the degree that flexibility and efficiency of goal directedness are desired, the control system should reflect a structural division of labor (specialization) on the one hand and decentralized (or distributed) processing on the other. The statement, above, that goals are "in a queue" should not be taken to imply that they are literally lined-up. Their organization is best seen as hierarchial (Carver & Scheier 1990; Mahoney 1991; Powers 1973). The functional status of one's regulatory hierarchy is not fixed, and depends, in part, on automatic or preconscious activation patterns and on the outcomes of low-level behavioral pursuits (Bargh 1990; Kimble & Perlmuter 1970; Vallacher & Wegner 1985). In a hierarchy, goals must both compete for expression and cooperate by communicating information across levels. This process is facilitated by what has been called *attention work* (Navon 1989), a process that represents yet another metaskill. Clearly, deficits in memory, attention, or knowledge will compromise the effectiveness of the proximal volitional regulators (as will the effects of automatic or inaccessible cognitive operators).

Some metaskills may not come to mind as readily when the negative feedback loop metaphor serves as our sole heuristic guide. Originating in a more experiential and person/environment-interaction analytic mode, social-cognitive theory (e.g. Bandura 1986) postulates several "basic capabilities" as essential to human functioning, including forethought, self-reflectiveness, the capacity to use symbols (images and language), the capacity to learn vicariously, and, of course, the capacity to self-regulate. Volitional freedom, or the exercise of self-influence, requires the availability of all of these capacities acting in concert—a fact that the "machine analogy" sometimes causes us to overlook.

William James believed that holding the desired end state (or goal) "fast before the mind" was a prime animator of action and the all-important bridging element linking the present with the future (cf Cross & Markus 1990). The ability to envision vividly an intended outcome, to create a possible future that connects with the present as well as the past, to anticipate obstacles to symbolic, temporal projections, and to resist actively the episodic intrusions of reality into the realm of imagination is a superordinate mental capacity that should not be assigned to the neverland of *ceteris paribus*.

Forethought (and correlative constructs, such as perspective taking, planning, event simulation, mental control, mental rehearsal, daydreaming, problem solving, or creative imagination) can be assessed and empirically linked to a host of outcomes that include tolerance of delay in the receipt of reward (e.g. Patterson & Mischel 1975), the generation of positive or negative emotions (Cottle & Klineberg 1974; Wohlford 1966; Velten 1968), self-efficacy estimation (Cervone 1989), coping with stress (Taylor & Schneider 1989), behavioral compliance (Gregory et al 1982), and other key aspects of goal directedness.

In their provocative discussion of "event simulation," Taylor & Schneider (1989) suggest that the imaginal evocation of future events can serve as a means of controlling emotions. Further, change or maintenance of mood can be a mechanism of behavior control (cf Showers & Cantor 1985). Thus, we are reminded of yet another metaskill: affect regulation (or "emotional intelligence"; see Salovey & Mayer 1990).

Despite a plethora of theories of emotion and emotive experience, a viewpoint is emerging within which affect is naturally linked to goal-directed behavior. Essentially, it is asserted that diverse feeling states arise as a result of success, failure, frustration, slowing, or delay in the pursuit of goals (e.g. Carver & Scheier 1990; Emmons & Diener 1986; Frijda 1986; Higgins 1987; Lazarus 1991; Sloman 1987). Assuming the general utility of goal discrepancy-affect models, one can expect that individual goal trajectories will give rise to positive and/or negative arousal states that will on occasion become the targets of regulatory efforts, effectively transforming self-regulation into a high workload, dual-task (or multi-task) situation (Wickens 1984). The management of interpersonal emotional displays, emotional arousal, and/or emotional dynamics via cognitive, image-oriented, and/or instrumental means in order either to dampen (or forestall) the intrusive or biasing effects of mood or to accelerate or maximize the strategic goal-energizing effects of affect is an emerging topic of contemporary theory and research (cf Brewin 1989; Friedman & Miller-Herringer 1991; Frijda 1986; Kirsch et al 1990; Salovey & Mayer 1990; Taylor 1991; Wright & Mischel 1982).

Boundary Conditions

Two types of boundedness are worthy of brief consideration. First, *inferential boundaries* are the epistemic limits imposed by natural language habits and/or the surface implications of extant models. Consider, for example, the all-but-universal expectation that, whatever else self-regulation entails, it is something that the individual must accomplish alone. However, the transactional-process definition offered earlier underscores the importance of recognizing the social embeddedness of self-regulation. For example, the pursuit of goals often involves other people (in fact, exciting others' reactions may constitute one's objective); thus, goal attainment is a culture-specific social problem-solving process. To self-regulate, we often seek to "manipulate" or influence others, while, to be a responsive participant in a social exchange, we likewise must regulate ourselves. The cycle of self/social influence and dependence too often remains vaguely implicit in contemporary information-processing models of self-regulation. Cognitive conceptions also tend to elevate the rational, the conscious, and the structural, no doubt because of their reliance upon the dominant computational-representational metaphor (cf Mahoney 1991). However, we must acknowledge the potential for counterfactual and nonmaximal decision-making, bounded rationality, automaticity, and dynamical processes, especially as they bear upon a second type of boundary—the *operational* or functional kind.

Operational boundaries refer to theoretically salient or plausible limits on the realization of self-regulation. For example, persons high in self-efficacy and in possession of the requisite skills will not consistently work toward goals in the absence of incentives. Nor can individuals be expected to persist in goal-directed behavior in the face of powerful counterinfluences by significant others.

Individual differences in people's interpretation of the situational enablers of regulatory activity, their sensitivity to goal-relevant feedback, their exposure to exemplars and context-specific rules of conduct, their attributional habits under conditions of success and failure, their ability to tolerate boredom and stimulus overload, and their ability to "protect" a current intention from being temporarily or permanently displaced by competing motivational tendencies all represent plausible moderators of self-directiveness (cf Bandura 1986; Deci & Ryan 1985; Kuhl 1985; Weiner 1990). A life-span developmental perspective affords an even keener appreciation of the functional boundaries on the enactment of self-regulation by highlighting the age-, phase-, or context-specific emergence of individual differences in componential abilities such as those involved in the representation of self, environment, and their covariation; the selection of realistic goals; the use of absolute vs comparative and self vs other standards of competence evaluation; the awareness of social demands or expectancies; the instantiation of introspection and metacognition; and the creation of anticipatory images and an appreciation of the temporal connectedness (continuity) of past, present, and future (Cottle & Klineberg 1974; Brandstädter 1989; Feltz & Landers 1983; Harter 1990; Karoly 1977; Kopp 1982; Ruble & Frey 1991). Finally, constitutionally derived differences in affectivity and its modulation (temperament), emerging and shifting over the life span, serves as yet another limiting factor on the voluntary control of action and attention (Rothbart & Posner 1985).

SELF-REGULATORY FAILURE: CONCEPTS AND DYNAMICS

People are capable of self-regulating, but they do not do so in a formulaic, dispassionate, unwavering, or fully self-contained manner. This statement broadly summarizes the present review to this point. Further, a critical appraisal of the literature on self-regulatory training of various sorts (Karoly & Kanfer 1982; Kirschenbaum 1987) suggests that people's efforts at self-management, even when professionally assisted, do not always yield successful short- or long-term outcomes. The need for greater empirical attention to the problem of self-regulatory failure is now widely acknowledged. Unfortunately, a wealth of theoretically plausible avenues of dysfunction and the unavailability of a proven troubleshooting algorithm effectively situate contemporary investigators and interventionists under a somewhat rickety signpost that reads "Mechanic On Duty." Nonetheless, if a prescriptive science of self-regulation is someday to be achieved, it may well emanate from a seat-of-the-pants fine-tuning of the models and mechanisms outlined in this chapter, in concert with some creative tinkering and conceptual reformulation. I next consider briefly the psychology of self-regulatory failure, hoping to blend realism and optimism in the proper proportion.

In the absence of general theoretical consensus, either within or between psychological subdisciplines, discussions of regulatory failure (like discussions of self-regulation itself) hinge upon the investigator's assumptions. Learning theorists would, for example, search for failure mechanisms in the same "locale" as they would expect to find normative control mechanisms—in the relation between a target behavior and its environmental contingencies. Psychoanalytic thinkers would, for their part, explore the relational matrix of early childhood and its current representation in adult character structure. Adhering broadly to a control (cybernetic) framework, I view the contours of regulatory failure and its putative causes in the following manner. Insofar as formal categories of miscarried self-regulation are concerned, patterns of goal-directed activity (aimed either at behavior maintenance or change) can fail to be initiated, can terminate (disengage) prematurely, or can persist beyond their useful or necessary lifespan. Explanatory mechanisms can be construed as involving (*a*) subfunction deficiencies; (*b*) disruptions in cross-function communication; (*c*) the pursuit of inappropriate or self-defeating standards or goals; (*d*) the absence (or underdevelopment) of supportive metaskills; (*e*) the encroachment of natural or imposed boundary conditions; or (*f*) some combination of these.

Our most valuable insights into the nature of self-regulatory failure come, I believe, from controlled experiments expressly designed to examine system-based dysfunction, despite the obvious sacrifice of verisimilitude that such designs entail. Much contemporary theory about failure mechanisms is based, however, on the results of clinical intervention efforts aimed at enhancing self-regulatory skills in children or adults and upon studies of "naturalistic" success or failure in self-initiated behavior change. When the analysis of self-regulatory breakdown is secondary or indirect, there is little possibility for the precise identification of causal mechanisms or their interaction. In fact, most clinical studies neglect to assess pre- to post-treatment changes in metaskills or in the specific proximal regulators presumably taught during the intervention phase (or they rely on retrospective reports). And even if focal skills and metaskills are assessed before and after training, the difficulties involved in tracking moment-to-moment person/environment exchanges (relatively molecular transitional events and reactions) would foster largely post hoc guesswork about the reciprocally emergent (transactional) sources of failure (Karoly 1980; Kirschenbaum 1987).

To date, most analyses of failed self-regulation have sought to examine the parameters of premature disengagement from goal pursuit (also known as giving up, relapse, recidivism, resistance, or the maintenance/generalization problem). Notwithstanding a growing interest in commitment disruptions, as reflected in directive-function deficits or internal conflicts (cf Cantor et al 1987; Emmons & King 1988; Kuhl & Kazen-Saad 1988) and some attention to excessive goal pursuit or perseveration (Drigotas & Rusbult 1992; Heckhausen & Beckmann 1990), the lion's share of empirical attention has been directed at untimely goal abandonment presumably brought about by (*a*) short-circuiting of the comparator (defensive self-evaluation), (*b*) dysfunctional standard setting, (*c*) deficient or excessive self-monitoring (self-focus) in combination with negative expectancies, and (*d*) control system overload.

Above I highlighted the sensitivity and complexity of self-reactive judgment and raised the possibility that the comparator (the matching-to-standard process) might on occasion be circumvented. That is, although a standard at a given level in a goal hierarchy is activated and knowledge of substandard performance is clearly available, the individual may nonetheless elect to distort or reinterpret this information and, thereby, fail to initiate the necessary self-correctives. Such a pattern, which I will term *defensive evaluative avoidance* (DEA), appears most likely when the regulatory objective is a difficult, high-stakes, self-relevant, socially discernible outcome set at a level that may exceed the individual's abilities or efficacy/outcome expectations. By engaging in DEA, the person can, in the short run, safeguard a standard match at a higher level in the goal hierarchy while averting the unpleasant emotion associated with failure recognition. For example, a student receiving a grade of

"D" on an examination can attribute his/her "failure" to the teacher's "evil motives" rather than acknowledge his/her own role in the outcome. As a result, a higher-order principle of self-esteem maintenance is achieved, self-deprecatory emotions are precluded, and the aspired-to-standard (getting an "A") is preserved. The cost of DEA, on the other hand, is a self-imposed moratorium on self-knowledge expansion, skills-building, and ultimately goal attainment (Bandura 1986; Baumeister & Scher 1988; Kanfer & Hagerman 1981; Snyder et al 1983).

Several mechanisms of DEA have been explored in addition to externalizing attributions, including rationalization, downward social comparison, self-handicapping (prearranging incompetent performance), self-deception, and compensatory self-inflation (Baumeister 1991; Fiske & Taylor 1991). A relatively new and intriguing formulation, focusing on retreat from responsibility and threatened identity, is *accountability theory* (Schlenker et al 1991). Asserting that accountability "makes self-regulation possible," Schlenker et al (1991) introduce four elements that affect conditional self-evaluation, including (*a*) the prescription (the goal or standard, in control theory terminology), (*b*) the event (the self-monitored feedback), (*c*) a set of identity images (specifications of the sort of person one is or aspires to be), and (*d*) an evaluating audience. The addition of the latter two elements provides salient self-referential and interpersonal anchors that help concretize the nature of "accountability avoidance strategies" such as selective audience exposure, apologies, and the use of excuses and post hoc justifications.

Another momentarily self-serving but ultimately goal-defeating type of self-reaction involves the lowering of standards in the face of failure. As a means of artificially dealing with a standard-performance mismatch, the lowering of standards can occasion decreased motivation (effort), a sacrifice of enjoyment, a decrease in self-esteem, and a counter-intentional increase in dysphoria (Ahrens & Abramson 1991; Bandura 1986; Locke & Latham 1990).

A third disengagement mechanism centers on the self-monitoring/self-awareness subfunction of negative feedback control. Whereas a standard-performance discrepancy can be reduced productively by improving one's performance, an individual can alternatively elect to withdraw from a self-aware state. Several theoretical models (Carver & Scheier 1981; Duval & Wicklund 1972; Duval et al 1992; Hull & Levy 1979) postulate that, in the presence of a salient standard, self-awareness facilitates the matching-to-standard process. However, when expectancy of success is slight and the self-vs-standard discrepancy large, the individual tends to withdraw mentally and/or physically from the task. To complicate matters, excessive self-focus (as opposed to reduced self-awareness) can likewise precipitate adaptive disruptions. Depressed individuals, for example, demonstrate a self-focusing style in which self-awareness is heightened after failure and diminished after success (cf Pyszczynski et al 1991).

Finally, an arousal- or workload-based strain on cognitive capacity can impair information-processing and self-regulation. Because individuals pursue multiple goals over prolonged periods characterized by uncertainty, it is not unreasonable to expect that the complexities and attentional demands of "just one more" self-regulated task can precipitate dysfunctions that will reverberate throughout the system (Hockey 1986; Kanfer & Stevenson 1985). We are here reminded that goal-directed thought is not an absolute good; people must on occasion let go of their end-state cognition in order to enjoy the spontaneity and flow of their lives (Apter 1982; Csikszentmihalyi 1990).

FINAL COMMENT

Self-regulation has, until relatively recently, defied experimental analysis, perhaps because of its uncertain epistemological status. In its modern cast, the topic of self-regulation has captured the creative imagination of a variety of researchers. The empirical results of their work, however satisfying, should be viewed with an appreciation of their recency, their loose ends or unfinished agenda, their restricted phenomenal range, and their limited pragmatic yield to date. As a concept akin to "getting one's life together," self-regulation has not achieved a simple or uniform paradigmatic embodiment, nor should we expect this in the foreseeable future.

Nevertheless, the prospects for strong theoretical and operational advancement are excellent, as model-builders from diverse subdisciplines of psychology increasingly take up the challenge of exploring goal-directedness in slow but steadily more faithful approximations of its emergent and multilayered complexity.

Literature Cited

Ahrens, A. H., Abramson, L. Y. 1991. Changes in personal standards and dysphoria: a longitudinal approach. *Cogn. Ther. Res.* 15:47–68

Ames, C., Ames, R., eds. 1989. *Research on Motivation in Education:* Vol. 3, *Goals and Cognitions.* San Diego: Academic

Appley, M. H. 1991. Motivation, equilibration, and stress. See Dienstbier 1991, pp. 1–67

Apter, M. J. 1982. *The Experience of Motivation: The Theory of Psychological Reversals.* London: Academic

Baker, S. L., Kirsch, I. 1991. Cognitive mediators of pain perception and tolerance. *J. Pers. Soc. Psychol.* 61:504–10

Bandura, A. 1969. *Principles of Behavior Modification.* New York: Holt, Rinehart & Winston

Bandura, A. 1977. Self-efficacy: toward a unifying theory of behavior change. *Psychol. Rev.* 84:191–215

Bandura, A. 1986. *Social Foundations of Thought and Action: A Social Cognitive Theory.* Englewood Cliffs, NJ: Prentice-Hall

Bandura, A. 1988. Self-regulation of motivation and action through goal systems. See Hamilton et al 1988, pp. 37–61

Bandura, A. 1991. Self-regulation of motivation through anticipatory and self-reactive mechanisms. See Dienstbier 1991, pp. 69–164

Bandura, A., Cervone, D. 1983. Self-evaluative and self-efficacy mechanisms governing the motivational effects of goal systems. *J. Pers. Soc. Psychol.* 45:1017–28

Bandura, A., Cervone, D. 1986. Differential engagement of self-reactive influences in cognitive motivation. *Organ. Behav. Hum. Decis. Process.* 38:92–113

Bandura, A., Cioffi, D., Taylor, C. B., Brouillard, M. E. 1988. Perceived self-efficacy in coping with cognitive stressors and opioid activation. *J. Pers. Soc. Psychol.*

55:479–88

Bandura, A., Jourden, F. J. 1991. Self-regulatory mechanism governing the impact of social comparison on complex decision making. *J. Pers. Soc. Psychol.* 60:941–51

Bandura, A., Reese, L., Adams, N. E. 1982. Microanalysis of action and fear arousal as a function of differential levels of perceived self-efficacy. *J. Pers. Soc. Psychol.* 43:5–21

Bandura, A., Taylor, C. B., Gauthier, J., Gossard, D. 1987. Perceived self-efficacy and pain control: opioid and nonopioid mechanisms. *J. Pers. Soc. Psychol.* 53:563–71

Bargh, J. A. 1990. Auto-motives: preconscious determinants of social interaction. See Higgins & Sorrentino 1990, pp. 93–130

Baumeister, R. F. 1991. *Escaping the Self.* New York: Basic Books

Baumeister, R. F., Scher, S. J. 1988. Self-defeating behavior patterns among normal individuals: review and analyses of common self-destructive tendencies. *Psychol. Bull.* 104:3–22

Beckmann, J., Irle, M. 1985. Dissonance and action control. In *Action Control: From Cognition to Behavior,* ed. J. Kuhl, J. Beckmann, pp. 129–50. Berlin: Springer-Verlag

Bem, S. L. 1967. Verbal self-control: the establishment of effective self- instruction. *J. Exp. Psychol.* 74:485–91

Berger, C. R. 1988. Planning, affect, and social action generation. In *Communication, Social Cognition, and Affect,* ed. L. Donohew, H. Sypher, E. T. Higgins, pp. 93–116. Hillsdale, NJ: Erlbaum

Biran, M., Wilson, G. T. 1981. Treatment of phobic disorders using cognitive and exposure methods: a self-efficacy analysis. *J. Consult. Clin. Psychol.* 49:886–99

Brand, M. 1984. *Intending and Acting: Toward a Naturalized Action Theory.* Cambridge, MA: MIT Press

Brandtstädter, J. 1989. Personal self-regulation of development: cross-sequential analyses of development-related control beliefs and emotions. *Dev. Psychol.* 25:96–108

Brewin, C. R. 1989. Cognitive change processes in psychotherapy. *Psychol. Rev.* 96:379–94

Brown, A. 1987. Metacognition, executive control, self-regulation, and other more mysterious mechanisms. In *Metacognition, Motivation, and Understanding,* ed. F. Weinert, R. Kluwe, pp. 65–116. Hillsdale, NJ: Erlbaum

Brownell, K. D. 1991. Personal responsibility and control over our bodies: when expectation exceeds reality. *Health Psychol.* 10:303–10

Bullock, D., Grossberg, S. 1988. Neural dynamics of planned arm movements: emergent invariants and speed-accuracy properties during trajectory formation. *Psychol. Bull.* 95:49–90

Cantor, N., Fleeson, W. 1991. Life tasks and self-regulatory processes. See Maehr & Pintrich 1991, pp. 327–69

Cantor, N., Norem, J. K., Niedenthal, P. M., Langston, C. A., Brower, A. M. 1987. Life tasks, self-concept ideals and cognitive strategies in a life transition. *J. Pers. Soc. Psychol.* 53:1178–91

Cantor, N., Zirkel, S. 1990. Personality, cognition, and purposive behavior. See Pervin 1990, pp. 135–64

Carver, C. S., Scheier, M. F. 1981. *Attention and Self-regulation: A Control Theory Approach to Human Behavior.* New York: Springer-Verlag

Carver, C. S., Scheier, M. F. 1990. Principles of self-regulation: action and emotion. See Higgins & Sorrentino 1990, pp. 3–52

Cervone, D. 1989. Effects of envisioning future activities on self-efficacy judgments and motivation. An availability heuristic interpretation. *Cogn. Ther. Res.* 13:247–61

Cervone, D., Jiwani, N., Wood, R. 1991. Goal-setting and the differential influence of self-regulatory processes on complex decision-making performance. *J. Pers. Soc. Psychol.* 61:257–66

Condiotte, M., Lichtenstein, E. 1981. Self-efficacy and relapse in smoking cessation. *J. Consult. Clin. Psychol.* 49:648–58

Corcoran, K. 1991. Efficacy, "skills," reinforcement, and choice behavior. *Am. Psychol.* 46:155–57

Cottle, T. J., Klineberg, S. L. 1974. *The Present of Things Future.* New York: The Free Press

Cross, S. E., Markus, H. 1990. The willful self. *Pers. Soc. Psychol. Bull.* 16:726–42

Csikszentmihalyi, M. 1990. *Flow: The Psychology of Optimal Experience.* New York: Harper & Row

Deci, E. L. 1980. *The Psychology of Self-Determination.* Lexington, MA: Lexington

Deci, E. L., Ryan, R. M. 1985. *Intrinsic Motivation and Self-Determination in Human Behavior.* New York: Plenum

Dienstbier, R. A., ed. 1991. *Perspectives on Motivation.* Lincoln, NE: Univ. Nebraska Press

Drigotas, S. M., Rusbult, C. E. 1992. Should I stay or should I go? A dependence model of breakups. *J. Pers. Soc. Psychol.* 62:62–87

Dulany, D. E. 1961. Hypotheses and habits in verbal "operant conditioning." *J. Abnorm. Soc. Psychol.* 63:251–63

Duval, S., Wicklund, R. A. 1972. *A Theory of Objective Self-Awareness.* New York: Academic

Duval, T. S., Duval, V. H., Mulilis, J. 1992. Effects of self-focus, discrepancy between self and standard, and outcome expectancy favorability on the tendency to match self to standard or to withdraw. *J. Pers. Soc. Psychol.* 62:340–48

Dweck, C. S. 1986. Motivational processes affecting learning. *Am. Psychol.* 41:1040–48

Eastman, C., Marzillier, J. 1984. Theoretical difficulties in Bandura's self-efficacy theory. *Cogn. Ther. Res.* 8:213–29

Eisenberger, R. 1992. Learned industriousness. *Psychol. Rev.* 99:248–67

Ellis, A. 1976. RET abolishes most of the human ego. *Psychother. Ther. Res. Pract.* 13:343–48

Emmons, R. A. 1986. Personal strivings: an approach to personality and subjective well-being. *J. Pers. Soc. Psychol.* 51:1058–68

Emmons, R. A. 1989. The personal striving approach to personality. See Pervin 1989, pp. 87–126

Emmons, R. A. 1992. Abstract versus concrete goals: personal striving level, physical illness, and psychological well-being. *J. Pers. Soc. Psychol.* 62:292–300

Emmons, R. A., Diener, E. 1986. A goal-affect analysis of everyday situational choices. *J. Res. Pers.* 20:309–26

Emmons, R. A., King, L. A. 1988. Conflict among personal strivings: immediate and long-term implications for psychological and physical well-being. *J. Pers. Soc. Psychol.* 54:1040–48

Ewart, C. K. 1991. Social action theory for a public health psychology. *Am. Psychol.* 46:931–46

Feltz, D., Landers, D. 1983. The effects of mental practice on motor skill learning and performance: a meta-analysis. *J. Sport Psychol.* 5:25–57

Fishbein, M., Ajzen, I. 1975. *Belief, Attitude, Intention, and Behavior.* Reading, MA: Addison-Wesley

Fiske, S. T., Taylor, S. E. 1991. *Social Cognition.* New York: McGraw-Hill. 2nd ed.

Ford, D. H. 1987. *Humans as Self-Constructing Living Systems: A Developmental Perspective on Behavior and Personality.* Hillsdale, NJ: Erlbaum

Ford, M. E., Nichols, C. W. 1987. A taxonomy of human goals and some possible applications. In *Humans as Self-constructing Living Systems: Putting the Framework to Work,* ed. M. E. Ford, D. H. Ford, pp. 289–311. Hillsdale, NJ: Erlbaum

Ford, M. E., Nichols, C. W. 1991. Using goal assessments to identify motivational patterns and facilitate behavioral regulation of achievement. See Maehr & Pintrich 1991, pp. 51–84

Freud, S. 1923. *The Ego and the Id.* New York: Norton

Frese, M., Sabini, J., eds. 1985. *Goal-directed Behavior: The Concept of Action in Psychology.* Hillsdale, NJ: Erlbaum

Friedman, H. S., Miller-Herringer, T. 1991. Nonverbal display of emotion in public and in private: self-monitoring, personality, and expressive cues. *J. Pers. Soc. Psychol.* 61:766–75

Frijda, N. H. 1986. *The Emotions.* Cambridge: Cambridge Univ. Press

Gattuso, S. M., Litt, M. D., Fitzgerald, T. 1992. Coping with gastrointestinal endoscopy: self-efficacy enhancement and coping style. *J. Consult. Clin. Psychol.* 60:133–39

Glasser, W. 1984. *Control Theory: A New Explanation of the How We Control Our Lives.* New York: Harper & Row

Godding, P. R., Glasgow, R. E. 1985. Self-efficacy and outcome expectancy as predictors of controlled smoking status. *Cogn. Ther. Res.* 9:583–90

Gollwitzer, P. 1990. Action phases and mind sets. See Higgins & Sorrentino 1990, pp. 53–92

Gollwitzer, P. M., Heckhausen, H., Steller, B. 1990. Deliberative and implemental mindsets: cognitive tuning toward congruous thoughts and information. *J. Pers. Soc. Psychol.* 59:119–27

Goodall, T. A., Halford, W. K. 1991. Self-management of diabetes mellitus: a critical review. *Health Psychol.* 10:1–8

Greenwald, A. G. 1982. Ego task analysis: an integration of research on ego-involvement and self-awareness. In *Cognitive Social Psychology,* ed. A. H. Hastorf, A. M. Isen, pp. 109–47. New York: Elsevier/North Holland

Gregory, L. W., Cialdini, R. B., Carpenter, K. M. 1982. Self-relevant scenarios as mediators of likelihood estimates and compliance: Does imagining make it so? *J. Pers. Soc. Psychol.* 43:89–99

Grimm, L. G. 1983. The relation between self-evaluation and self-reward: a test of Kanfer's self-regulation model. *Cogn. Ther. Res.* 7:245–50

Haaga, D. A., Stewart, B. L. 1992. Self-efficacy for recovery from a lapse after smoking cessation. *J. Consult. Clin. Psychol.* 60:24–28

Hamilton, V., Bower, G. H., Frijda, N., eds. 1988. *Perspectives on Emotion and Motivation.* Dordrecht: Kluwer

Harackiewicz, J. M., Manderlink, G., Sansone, C. 1984. Rewarding pinball wizardry: effects of evaluation and cue value on intrinsic interest. *J. Pers. Soc. Psychol.* 47:287–300

Harter, S. 1990. Developmental differences in the nature of self-representations: implications for the understanding, assessment, and treatment of maladaptive behavior. *Cogn. Ther. Res.* 14:113–42

Hartig, M., Kanfer, F. H. 1973. The role of verbal self-instructions in children's resistance to temptation. *J. Pers. Soc. Psychol.* 25:259–67

Hayes-Roth, B., Hayes-Roth, F. 1979. A cognitive model of planning. *Cogn. Sci.* 3:275–310

Heckhausen, H. 1991. *Motivation and Action.*

Berlin: Springer-Verlag

Heckhausen, H., Beckmann, J. 1990. Intentional action and action slips. *Psychol. Rev.* 97:36–48

Heckhausen, H., Kuhl, J. 1985. From wishes to action: the dead ends and short cuts on the long way to action. See Frese & Sabini 1985, pp. 134–59

Higgins, E. T. 1987. Self-discrepancy: a theory relating self and affect. *Psychol. Rev.* 94:319–40

Higgins, E. T., Moretti, M. M. 1988. Standard utilization and the social-evaluative process: vulnerability to types of aberrant beliefs. In *Delusional Beliefs,* ed. T. Oltmanns, B. A. Maher, pp. 110–37. New York: Wiley

Higgins, E. T., Sorrentino, R. M., eds. 1990. *Handbook of Motivation and Cognition,* I Vol. 2. New York: Guilford

Higgins, E. T., Strauman, T., Klein, R. 1986. Standards and the process of self-evaluation: multiple effects from multiple stages. See Sorrentino & Higgins 1986, pp. 23–63

Hilgard, E. R. 1986. *Divided Consciousness: Multiple Controls in Human Thought and Action.* New York: Wiley

Hockey, G. R. J. 1986. A state control theory of adaptation and individual differences in stress management. In *Energetics and Human Information Processing,* ed. G. R. J. Hockey, A. W. K. Gaillard, M. G. H. Coles. Dordrecht: Martinus Nijhoff

Holroyd, K. A., Creer, T. L., eds. 1986. *Self-Management of Chronic Disease.* Orlando, FL: Academic

Howard, G. S., Conway, C. G. 1986. Can there be an empirical science of volitional action? *Am. Psychol.* 41:1241–51

Hsee, C. K., Abelson, R. P. 1991. Velocity relation: satisfaction as a function of the first derivative of outcome over time. *J. Pers. Soc. Psychol.* 60:341–47

Hull, J. G., Levy, A. S. 1979. The organizational functioning of the self: an alternative to the Duval and Wicklund model of self-awareness. *J. Pers. Soc. Psychol.* 37:756–68

Hunt, J. McV., ed. 1944. *Personality and the Behavior Disorders.* New York: Ronald Press

Hyland, M. E. 1988. Motivational control theory: an integrative perspective. *J. Pers. Soc. Psychol.* 55:642–51

James, W. 1892. *Psychology: A Briefer Course.* New York: Holt

Jensen, M. P., Turner, J. A., Romano, J. M., Karoly, P. 1991. Coping with chronic pain: a critical review of the literature. *Pain* 47:249–83

Josephs, L. 1992. *Character Structure and the Organization of the Self.* New York: Columbia Univ. Press

Kanfer, F. H., Gaelick-Buys, L. 1991. Self-management methods. In *Helping People Change,* ed. F. H. Kanfer, A. P. Goldstein.

New York: Pergamon. 4th ed.

Kanfer, F. H., Hagerman, S. 1981. The role of self-regulation. In *Behavior Therapy for Depression,* ed. L. P. Rehm. New York: Academic

Kanfer, F. H., Karoly, P. 1972. Self-control: a behavioristic excursion into the lion's den. *Behav. Ther.* 3:398–416

Kanfer, F. H., Karoly, P., Newman, A. 1975. Reduction of children's fear of the dark by competence-related and situational threat-related verbal cues. *J. Consult. Clin. Psychol.* 43:251–58

Kanfer, F. H., Schefft, B. K. 1988. *Guiding the Process of Therapeutic Change.* Champaign, IL: Research Press

Kanfer, F. H., Stevenson, M. K. 1985. The effects of self-regulation on concurrent cognitive processing. *Cogn. Ther. Res.* 9:667–84

Kanfer, R., Ackerman, P. L. 1989. Motivation and cognitive abilities: an integrative aptitude-treatment interaction approach to skill acquisition. *J. Appl. Psychol.* 74:657–90

Kanfer, R., Kanfer, F. H. 1991. Goals and self-regulation: applications of theory to work settings. See Maehr & Pintrich 1991, pp. 287–326

Karoly, P. 1977. Behavioral self-management in children: concepts, methods, issues, and directions. In *Progress in Behavior Modification,* ed. M. Hersen, R. M. Eisler, P. M. Miller, 5:197–262. New York: Academic

Karoly, P. 1980. Self-management problems in children. In *Behavioral Assessment of Childhood Disorders,* ed. E. J. Mash, L. G. Terdal. New York: Guilford

Karoly, P. 1991a. Self-management in health care and illness prevention. See Snyder & Forsyth 1991, pp. 579–606

Karoly, P. 1991b. Goal systems and health outcomes across the life span: a proposal. In *New Directions in Health Psychology Assessment,* ed. H. E. Schroeder. New York: Hemisphere

Karoly, P., Decker, J. 1979. Effects of personally and socially referenced success and failure upon self-reward and self-criticism. *Cogn. Ther. Res.* 3:399–405

Karoly, P., Kanfer, F. H., eds. 1982. *Self-Management and Behavior Change: From Theory to Practice.* New York: Pergamon

Kazdin, A. E. 1974. Self-monitoring and behavior change. In *Self-Control: Power to the Person,* ed. M. J. Mahoney, C. E. Thoresen. Monterey, CA: Brooks/Cole

Kiesler, C. A. 1971. *The Psychology of Commitment.* New York: Academic

Kimble, G. A., Perlmuter, L. C. 1970. The problem of volition. *Psychol. Rev.* 77:361–84

King, L. A., Emmons, R. A. 1990. Conflict over emotional expression: psychological and physical correlates. *J. Pers. Soc. Psychol.* 58:864–77

Kirsch, I. 1985. Self-efficacy and expectancy: old wine with new labels. *J. Pers. Soc. Psychol.* 49:824–30

Kirsch, I., Mearns, J., Catanzaro, S. J. 1990. Mood regulation expectancies as determinants of dysphoria in college students. *J. Couns. Psychol.* 37:306–12

Kirschenbaum, D. S. 1987. Self-regulatory failure: a review with clinical implications. *Clin. Psychol. Rev.* 7:77–104

Klinger, E. 1977. *Meaning and Void.* Minneapolis, MN: Univ. Minnesota Press

Klinger, E., Barta, S. G., Maxeiner, M. 1981. Current concerns: assessing therapeutically relevant motivation. In *Assessment Strategies for Cognitive-Behavioral Interventions,* ed. P. C. Kendall, S. D. Hollon. New York: Academic

Koestner, R., Bernieri, F., Zuckerman, M. 1992. Self-regulation and consistency between attitudes, traits, and behaviors. *Pers. Soc. Psychol. Bull.* 18:52–59

Kopp, C. B. 1982. Antecedents of self-regulation: a developmental perspective. *Dev. Psychol.* 18:199–214

Kosslyn, S. M., Koenig, O. 1992. *Wet Mind: The New Cognitive Neuroscience.* New York: Free Press

Kuhl, J. 1985. Volitional mediators of cognition-behavior consistency: self-regulatory processes and action versus state orientation. See Kuhl & Beckmann 1985, pp. 101–28

Kuhl, J., Beckmann, J., eds. 1985. *Action Control: From Cognition to Behavior.* Berlin: Springer-Verlag

Kuhl, J., Kazen-Saad, M. 1988. A motivational approach to volition: activation and de-activation of memory representations related to uncompleted intentions. See Hamilton et al 1988, pp. 63–85

Langer, E. J. 1989. *Mindfulness.* Reading, MA: Addison-Wesley

Lazarus, R. S. 1991. *Emotion and Adaptation.* New York: Oxford Univ. Press

Lee, T. W., Locke, E. A., Latham, G. 1989. Goal setting theory and job performance. See Pervin 1989, pp. 291–326

Lennon, K. 1990. *Explaining Human Action.* La Salle, IL: Open Court

Lepper, M. R., Hodell, M. 1989. Intrinsic motivation in the classroom. See Ames & Ames 1989, pp. 73–105

Lewin, K. 1926. Intention, will and need. *Psychol. Forsch.* 7:330–85

Lewin, K. 1935. *A Dynamic Theory of Personality.* New York: McGraw-Hill

Lewin, K., Dembo, T., Festinger, L., Sears, P. S. 1944. Level of aspiration. See Hunt 1944, pp. 333–78

Libet, B. 1985. Unconscious cerebral initiative and the role of conscious will in voluntary action. *Behav. Brain Sci.* 8:529–66

Litt, M. D. 1988. Self-efficacy and perceived control: cognitive mediators of pain tolerance. *J. Pers. Soc. Psychol.* 54:149–60

Little, B. R. 1983. Personal projects: a rationale and method for investigation. *Environ. Behav.* 15:273–309

Little, B. R. 1989. Personal projects analyses: trivial pursuits, magnificent obsessions and the search for coherence. In *Personality Psychology: Recent Trends and Emerging Directions,* ed. D. M. Buss, N. Cantor. New York: Springer-Verlag

Locke, E. A., Latham, G. P. 1990. *A Theory of Goal-Setting and Task Performance.* Englewood Cliffs, NJ: Prentice-Hall

Logan, G. D., Cowan, W. B. 1984. On the ability to inhibit thought and action: a theory of an act of control. *Psychol. Rev.* 91:295–327

MacKay, D. M. 1984. Evaluation: the missing link between cognition and action. In *Cognition and Motor Processes,* ed. W. Prinz, A. F. Sanders. Berlin: Springer-Verlag

Maddux, J. E. 1991. Self-efficacy. See Snyder & Forsyth 1991, pp. 57–78

Maddux, J. E., Stanley, M. 1986. Self-efficacy theory in contemporary psychology: an overview. *J. Soc. Clin. Psychol.* 4:249–55

Maehr, M. L., Pintrich, P. R., eds. 1991. *Advances in Motivation and Achievement,* Vol. 7. Greenwich, CT: JAI Press

Mahoney, M. J. 1991. *Human Change Processes.* New York: Basic Books

Manning, M. M., Wright, T. L. 1983. Self-efficacy expectancies, outcome expectancies, and persistence of pain control in childbirth. *J. Pers. Soc. Psychol.* 45:421–31

Markus, H., Nurius, P. 1986. Possible selves. *Am. Psychol.* 41:954–69

Markus, H., Wurf, E. 1987. The dynamic self-concept: a social psychological perspective. *Annu. Rev. Psychol.* 38:299–337

Marlatt, G. A., Gordon, J. R., eds. 1985. *Relapse Prevention: Maintenance Strategies in the Treatment of Addictive Disorders.* New York: Guilford

Maslow, A. 1971. *The Farther Reaches of Human Nature.* New York: Viking

May, R. 1953. *Man's Search for Himself.* New York: Norton

McFall, R. M. 1977. Parameters of self-monitoring. In *Behavioral Self-Management,* ed. R. B. Stuart. New York: Brunner/Mazel

McKeeman, D., Karoly, P. 1991. Interpersonal and intrapsychic goal-related conflict reported by cigarette smokers, unaided quitters, and relapsers. *Addict. Behav.* 16:543–48

Meichenbaum, D. 1977. *Cognitive-Behavior Modification.* New York: Plenum

Meichenbaum, D. 1985. *Stress Inoculation Training.* New York: Pergamon

Miller, G. A., Galanter, E., Pribram, K. H. 1960. *Plans and the Structure of Behavior.* New York: Henry Holt

Miller, N. E. 1944. Experimental studies of conflict. See Hunt 1944, pp. 431–65

Mischel, W. 1973. Toward a cognitive social learning reconceptualization of personality.

Psychol. Rev. 80:252–83

Mischel, W., Mischel, H. N. 1976. A cognitive social-learning approach to morality and self-regulation. In *Moral Development and Behavior,* ed. T. Lickona. New York: Holt, Rinehart & Winston

Mischel, W., Shoda, Y., Rodriguez, M. L. 1989. Delay of gratification in children. *Science* 244:933–38

Murray, H. A. 1938. *Explorations in Personality.* New York: Oxford Univ. Press

Navon, D. 1989. The importance of being visible: on the role of attention in a mind viewed as an anarchic intelligence system. I. Basic tenets. *Eur. J. Cogn. Psychol.* 1:191–213

Nelson, R. O. 1977. Methodological issues in assessment via self-monitoring. In *Behavioral Assessment,* ed. J. D. Cone, R. P. Hawkins. New York: Brunner/Mazel

Newman, R. S. 1991. Goals and self-regulated learning: What motivates children to seek academic help. See Maehr & Pintrich 1991, pp. 151–83

Norman, D. A., Shallice, T. 1986. Attention to action: willed and automatic control of behavior. In *Consciousness and Self-Regulation: Advances in Research and Theory,* ed. R. J. Davidson, G. E. Schwartz, D. Shapiro, 4:1–18. New York: Plenum

Omodei, M. M., Wearing, A. J. 1990. Need satisfaction and involvement in personal projects: toward an integrative model of subjective well-being. *J. Pers. Soc. Psychol.* 59:762–69

Orth, J. E., Thebarge, R. W. 1984. Helping clients reduce self-evaluative behavior: Consider the consequences. *Cogn. Ther. Res.* 8:13–18

Owen, N., Brown, S. L. 1991. Smokers unlikely to quit. *J. Behav. Med.* 14:627-36

Ozer, E. M., Bandura, A. 1990. Mechanisms governing empowerment effects: a self-efficacy analysis. *J. Pers. Soc. Psychol.* 58:472–86

Palys, T. S., Little, B. R. 1983. Perceived life satisfaction and the organization of personal project systems. *J. Pers. Soc. Psychol.* 44:1221–30

Patterson, C. J., Mischel, W. 1975. Plans to resist distraction. *Dev. Psychol.* 11:369–78

Pennebaker, J. W., Gonder-Frederick, L., Cox, D. J., Hoover, C. W. 1985. The perception of general vs. specific visceral activity and the regulation of health-related behavior. In *Advances in Behavioral Medicine,* ed. E. S. Katkin, S. B. Manuck. Greenwich, CT: JAI Press

Pervin, L. A., ed. 1989. *Goal Concepts in Personality and Social Psychology.* Hillsdale, NJ: Erlbaum

Pervin, L. A., ed. 1990. *Handbook of Personality: Theory and Research.* New York: Guilford

Pintrich, P. R., Garcia, T. 1991. Student goal orientation and self-regulation in the college classroom. See Maehr & Pintrich

1991, pp. 371–402

Power, T. G., Chapieski, M. L., 1986. Childrearing and impulse control in toddlers: a naturalistic investigation. *Dev. Psychol.* 22:271–75

Powers, W. T. 1973. *Behavior: The Control of Perception.* Chicago, IL: Aldine

Powers, W. T. 1986. Intentionality: no mystery. *Behav. Brain Sci.* 9:152–53

Powers, W. T. 1989. An outline of control theory. In *Living Control Systems: Selected Papers of William T. Powers,* ed. R. S. Marken. Gravel Switch, KY: Control Systems Group

Powers, W. T. 1991. Commentary on Bandura's 'Human Agency.' *Am. Psychol.* 46:151–53

Pribram, K. H. 1976. Self-consciousness and intentionality. In *Consciousness and Self-Regulation: Advances in Research,* ed. G. E. Schwartz, D. Shapiro, 1:51–100. New York: Plenum

Pyszczynski, T., Hamilton, J. C., Greenberg, J., Becker, S. E. 1991. Self-awareness and psychological dysfunction. See Snyder & Forsyth 1991, pp. 138–57

Read, S. J., Miller, L. C. 1989. Interpersonalism: toward a goal-based theory of persons in relationships. See Pervin 1989, pp. 413–72

Rosenbaum, M. 1990. A model for research on self-regulation: reducing the schism between behaviorism and general psychology. In *Unifying Behavior Therapy,* ed. G. H. Eifert, I. M. Evans. New York: Springer

Rothbart, M. K., Posner, M. J. 1985. Temperament and the development of self-regulation. In *Neuropsychology of Individual Differences: A Developmental Perspective,* ed. H. Hartlage, C. F. Telzrow. New York: Plenum

Ruble, D. N., Frey, K. S. 1991. Changing patterns of comparative behavior as skills are acquired: a functional model of self-evaluation. In *Social Comparison: Contemporary Theory and Research,* ed. J. Suls, T. A. Wills. Hillsdale, NJ: Erlbaum

Ruehlman, L. S., Wolchik, S. A. 1988. Personal goals and interpersonal support and hindrance as factors in psychological distress and well-being. *J. Pers. Soc. Psychol.* 55:293–301

Salovey, P., Mayer, J. D. 1990. Emotional intelligence. *Imag. Cogn. Pers.* 9:185–211

Schlenker, B. R., Weigold, M. F., Doherty, K. 1991. Coping with accountability: self-identification and evaluative reckonings. See Snyder & Forsyth 1991, pp. 96–115

Schunk, D. H. 1989. Self-efficacy and cognitive skill learning. See Ames & Ames 1989, pp. 13–44

Schunk, D. 1991. Goal-setting and self-evaluation: a social-cognitive perspective on self-regulation. See Maehr & Pintrich 1991, pp. 85–113

Secord, P. F. 1989. Determinism, free will and self-intervention: a psychological perspective. *New Ideas Psychol.* 2:25–33

Semmer, N., Frese, M. 1985. Action theory in clinical psychology. See Frese & Sabini 1985, pp. 296–310

Shapiro, D. 1965. *Neurotic Styles.* New York: Basic Books

Showers, C., Cantor, N. 1985. Social cognition: a look at motivated strategies. *Annu. Rev. Psychol.* 36:275–305

Silver, M. 1985. "Purposive behavior" in psychology and philosophy: a history. See Frese & Sabini 1985, pp. 3–17

Simon, H. 1967. Motivational and emotional controls of cognition. *Psychol. Rev.* 74:29–39

Singer, J. L., Bonanno, G. A. 1990. Personality and private experience: individual variations in consciousness and in attention to subjective phenomena. See Pervin 1990, pp. 419–44

Singer, J. L., Salovey, P. 1991. Organized knowledge structures and personality: person schemas, self-schemas, prototypes, and scripts. In *Person Schemas and Maladaptive Interpersonal Patterns,* ed. M. J. Horowitz. Chicago: Univ. Chicago Press

Sloman, A. 1987. Motives, mechanisms, and emotions. *Cogn. Emot.* 1:217–33

Snyder, C. R., Forsyth, D. R., eds. 1991. *Handbook of Social and Clinical Psychology: The Health Perspective.* New York: Pergamon

Snyder, C. R., Harris, C., Anderson, J. R., Holleran, S. A., Irving, L. M., et al. 1991. The will and the ways: development and validation of an individual-differences measure of hope. *J. Pers. Soc. Psychol.* 60:570–85

Snyder, C. R., Higgins, R., Stucky, R. J. 1983. *Excuses: Masquerades in Search of Grace.* New York: Wiley

Sorrentino, R.M., Higgins, E. T., eds. 1986. *Handbook of Motivation and Cognition.* New York: Guilford

Spates, C. R., Kanfer, F. H. 1977. Self-monitoring, self-evaluation, and self-reinforcement in children's learning: a test of a multistage self-regulation model. *Behav. Ther.* 8:9–16

Stelmach, G. E., Hughes, B. G. 1984. Cognitivism and future theories of action: some basic issues. In *Cognition and Motor Processes,* ed. W. Prinz, A. F. Sanders. Berlin: Springer-Verlag

Sternberg, R. J. 1982. Reasoning, problem solving, and intelligence. In *Handbook of Human Intelligence,* ed. R. J. Sternberg. Cambridge, MA: Cambridge Univ. Press

Sternberg, S. 1969. Memory-scanning: mental processes revealed by reaction-time experiments. *Am. Sci.* 57:421–57

Taylor, S. E. 1991. Asymmetrical effects of positive and negative events: the Mobilization-Minimization Hypothesis. *Psychol. Bull.* 110:67–85

Taylor, S. E., Schneider, S. K. 1989. Coping and the simulation of events. *Soc. Cogn.*

7:174–94

Thoresen, C. E., Mahoney, M. J. 1974. *Behavioral Self-Control.* New York: Holt, Rinehart & Winston

Tubbs, M. E. 1986. Goal-setting: a meta-analytic examination of the empirical evidence. *J. Appl. Psychol.* 71:474–83

Vallacher, R. R., Wegner, D. M. 1985. *A Theory of Action Identification.* Hillsdale, NJ: Erlbaum

Vallacher, R. R., Wegner, D. M. 1989. Levels of personal agency: individual variation in action identification. *J. Pers. Soc. Psychol.* 57:660–71

Vallis, T. M., Bucher, B. 1986. Self-efficacy as a predictor of behavior change: interaction with type of training for pain tolerance. *Cogn. Ther. Res.* 10:79–94

Velten, E. 1968. A laboratory task for induction of mood states. *Behav. Res. Ther.* 6:473–82

Watson, D. L., Tharp, R. G. 1989. *Self-Directed Behavior: Self-Modification for Personal Adjustment.* Pacific Grove, CA: Brooks/Cole

Wegner, D. M., Schneider, D. J. 1989. Mental control: the war of the ghosts in the machine. In *Unintended Thought,* ed. J. S. Uleman, J. A. Bargh. New York: Guilford

Weimer, W. B. 1977. A conceptual framework for cognitive psychology: motor theories of the mind. In *Perceiving, Acting, and Knowing: Toward an Ecological Psychology,* ed. R. Shaw, J. Bransford. Hillsdale, NJ: Erlbaum

Weiner, B. 1990. Attribution in personality psychology. See Pervin 1990, pp. 465–85

Westcott, M. R. 1985. Volition is a nag. In *Affect, Conditioning, and Cognition: Essays on the Determinants of Behavior,* ed. F. Brush, J. Overmier. Hillsdale, NJ: Erlbaum

Westcott, M. R. 1988. *The Psychology of Human Freedom.* New York: Springer-Verlag

Wickens, C. D. 1984. *Engineering Psychology and Human Performance.* Columbus, OH: Charles E. Merrill

Wiedenfeld, S. A., O'Leary, A., Bandura, A., Brown, S., Levine, S., Raska, K. 1990. Impact of perceived self-efficacy in coping with stressors on components of the immune system. *J. Pers. Soc. Psychol.* 59:1082–94

Wohlford, P. F. 1966. Extension of personal time, affective states, and expectation of personal death. *J. Pers. Soc. Psychol.* 3:559–66

Wood, R. E., Bandura, A., Bailey, T. 1990. Mechanisms governing organizational productivity in complex decision-making environments. *Organ. Behav. Hum. Decis. Process.* 46:181–201

Wright, J., Mischel, W. 1982. Influence of affect on cognitive social learning person variables. *J. Pers. Soc. Psychol.* 43:901–14

Wright, R. A., Brehm, J. W. 1989. Energization and goal attractiveness. See Pervin 1989, pp. 169–210

Wundt, W. 1910 [1901]. *Principles of Physiological Psychology.* New York: Macmillan

Wyer, R. S., Srull, T. K. 1986. Human cognition in its social context. *Psychol. Rev.* 93:322–59

Zivin, G., ed. 1979. *The Development of Self-Regulation Through Private Speech.* New York: Wiley

Annu. Rev. Psychol. 1993. 44:53–85

PSYCHONEUROIMMUNOLOGY: CONDITIONING AND STRESS

Robert Ader and Nicholas Cohen

Department of Psychiatry and Microbiology and Immunology, University of Rochester School of Medicine and Dentistry, Rochester, New York 14642

KEYWORDS: psychoneuroimmunology, conditioning, stress

CONTENTS

INTRODUCTION 53
CONDITIONED MODULATION OF IMMUNITY 54
    Effects of Conditioning on Humoral and Cell-Mediated Immunity.................... 55
    Effects of Conditioning on Nonimmunologically Specific Reactions 59
    Antigen as Unconditioned Stimulus 60
    Biologic Impact of Conditioned Changes in Immunity...................................... 61
    Conditioning in Human Subjects 61
STRESS AND IMMUNITY.. 63
    Effects of Stress on Disease.. 64
    Effects of Stress on Humoral and Cell-Mediated Immunity 66
    Effects of Stress on Nonimmunologically Specific Reactions............................ 69
MEDIATION OF BEHAVIORALLY INDUCED IMMUNE CHANGES............................ 71
SUMMARY 76

INTRODUCTION

During the past 10–15 years, psychoneuroimmunology—the study of the interactions among behavior, neural and endocrine function, and immune processes—has developed into a bona fide field of interdisciplinary research (Ader 1981a, 1991a). Previously unknown and unsuspected connections between the brain and the immune system provide a foundation for the now numerous observations both (*a*) that the manipulation of neural and endocrine functions alters immune responses, and the antigenic stimulation that induces an immune response results in changes in neural and endocrine function and (*b*) that behavioral processes are capable of influencing immunologic reactiv-

53

0066-4308/93/0201-0053$02.00

ity and, conversely, the immune status of an organism has consequences for behavior. This new research indicates that the nervous and immune systems, the two most complex systems involved in the maintenance of homeostasis, represent an integrated mechanism contributing to the adaptation of the individual and the species. Psychoneuroimmunology emphasizes the functional significance of the relationship between these systems—not in place of, but in addition to the more traditional disciplinary analysis of the mechanisms governing functions within a single system.

The range of phenomena that bears on the relationship between behavior and immunity is quite broad, and no attempt will be made to provide even a cursory summary of all this literature. We focus here on animal studies of the effects of conditioning and stress in the modulation of immune function. There are several more or less programmatic lines of research in humans that the reader may wish to explore. These deal with the immunologic correlates of emotional states (primarily depression), personality traits as modulators of immune function, and the effects of stress on immune function. Few generalizations are possible based on currently available data. Although there is no definitive evidence for the implied chain of events, the hypothesis that immune function may mediate the effects of psychosocial factors on the susceptibility to or progression of some disease processes remains tenable. We confine this review, however, to the experimental literature on the modulation of immunity by stress and conditioning. Other recent reviews (e.g. S. Cohen & Williamson 1991; Geiser 1989; Kemeny et al 1992; O'Leary 1990) have dealt with personality and emotional factors and immunity and/or disease. Some of these have included an introductory outline of the immune system; an extensive treatment of immune function can be found in any of several recent texts (e.g. Stites & Terr 1991).

CONDITIONED MODULATION OF IMMUNITY

Immune responses, like other physiological processes, can be modified by classical conditioning. Conditioned modulation of host defense mechanisms and antigen-specific immune responses were first explored by Russian investigators and followed the Pavlovian conditioning principles and procedures of the day (Metal'nikov & Chorine 1926, 1928). Typically, multiple pairings of a conditioned stimulus (CS; e.g. heat, tactile stimulation) were paired with injections of a foreign protein, the unconditioned stimulus (UCS); subsequent presentation of the CS alone was reported to elicit conditioned increases both in a variety of nonspecific defense responses and in antibody production. There were English language reviews of this literature (Hull 1934; Kopeloff 1941), but they apparently attracted little attention, probably owing to the nascent state of immunology at the time and to the fact that by today's standards most of these early animal experiments were inadequately described, poorly designed, lacked appropriate control groups, and constituted little more than preliminary observations. Although the data on specific antibody responses were not convincing, the studies of nonspecific cellular events (e.g. changes in leukocyte number, phagocytosis, inflammatory responses) were consistent and provided provocative evidence that conditioning could modulate host defenses. A detailed review (and some reanalyses) of these data was provided by Ader (1981b).

Effects of Conditioning on Humoral and Cell-Mediated Immunity

One of the hallmarks of the immune system's defense of the organism against foreign, "nonself" material (antigens) is its specificity—its ability to recognize precisely and then eliminate only the antigens it has confronted. These activities are carried out by a variety of white blood cells (leukocytes). Prominent among these are T and B lymphocytes that are capable of clonal proliferation in response to antigens and retaining the "memory" of that encounter. Humoral or antibody-mediated immunity involves the exposure of antigens to bone marrow–derived B cells. These cells effect the ultimate production of antibodies that protect the organism against extracellular microorganisms and reinfection. Cell-mediated immunity is provided by thymus-derived T cells that protect against intracellular parasitic and viral infections. An integrated immune response to antigens, however, involves complex interactions among specialized subpopulations of T cells (i.e. helper, suppressor, cytotoxic), B cells, other white blood cells such as macrophages, and substances (cytokines) that are secreted by activated leukocytes. A variety of techniques have been developed to measure these cellular interactions in vitro. The essence of psychoneuroimmunology, however, is the recognition that in vivo these reactions occur within a neuroendocrine milieu that is demonstrably sensitive to the organism's perception of and adaptation to events occurring in its environment.

HUMORAL IMMUNITY   Current interest in conditioned changes in immunologic reactivity began with a study by Ader & Cohen (1975). Using a taste aversion conditioning paradigm, a saccharin-flavored drinking solution, the CS, was paired with an injection of cyclophosphamide (CY), an immunosuppressive UCS. All rats were subsequently immunized with sheep red blood cells (SRBC). Antibody titers were measured in conditioned animals that were injected with CY on the day of immunization (to define the unconditioned immunosuppressive effects of CY), in conditioned animals that were not reexposed to the CS (to assess the influence of prior conditioning and the residual effects of CY), and in conditioned animals that were reexposed to the CS on the day of immunization and/or three days later (the critical experimental group). Subgroups of (nonconditioned) animals were injected with CY following the drinking of plain water before immunization and were subsequently provided with the presumably neutral saccharin solution whenever a comparable subgroup of conditioned animals received saccharin. A placebo-treated group was injected with vehicle after consuming saccharin or water before immunization and was exposed to saccharin after immunization. As expected, conditioned animals showed an aversion to the saccharin solution that had been paired with CY. Conditioned animals that were reexposed to the CS at the time of, and/or three days after, immunization also showed an attenuated anti-SRBC antibody response relative either to conditioned animals that were not reexposed to saccharin or to nonconditioned animals that were similarly exposed to saccharin. These results were interpreted as reflecting a conditioned immunosuppressive response. The acquisition and the experimental extinction of a conditioned suppression and/or enhancement of antibody- and cell-mediated immune responses as well as nonspecific host defenses have now been observed under a variety of experimental conditions. Only a brief overview of this research is provided here; more detailed reviews are available elsewhere (Ader & Cohen 1985, 1991).

In the conditioned taste aversion paradigm, animals learn to avoid flavored solutions previously paired with the noxious or illness-inducing effects of a variety of (pharmacologic) agents; that is, they reduce their consumption of the CS solution. Therefore, to obviate the conflict ("stress") induced by having either to drink a solution paired with illness or to remain thirsty—and to equate total fluid consumption among differentially treated animals—conditioning can be assessed with a two-bottle preference procedure that permits the animal to choose between plain water and the flavored CS solution. Under these conditions, conditioned alterations of humoral (e.g. Ader et al 1982; Bovbjerg et al 1987b; N. Cohen et al 1979) and cell-mediated (Bovbjerg et al 1982, 1984) immune responses are still obtained. The available literature reveals no consistent relationship between conditioned behavioral (aversive) responses and conditioned immune changes in the taste aversion learning paradigm; taste aversions can be expressed without concomitant changes in humoral immunity, and conditioned changes in immune function can be obtained without observable conditioned avoidance responses (Ader & Cohen 1975; Ader et al 1987; Bovbjerg et al 1987b; Gorczynski 1987; Gorczynski et al 1984; Rogers et al 1976; Schulze et al 1988; Wayner et al 1978). Moreover, reexposure to the CS before rather than after immunization with SRBC also depresses in vivo antibody production (Ader et al 1982; Schulze et al 1988; Kusnecov et al 1988). The latter results suggest that an antigen-activated immune system is not necessary for the conditioning of an immunosuppressive response.

Conditioned immunomodulatory effects are not confined to the use of CY or the taste aversion conditioning situation. Conditioned changes in various parameters of immunologic reactivity have been observed using other immunomodulating substances (e.g. Ader & Cohen 1981; King et al 1987; Kusnecov et al 1983; see also Hiramoto et al 1987; Husband et al 1987). It is not even necessary to use immunopharmacologic agents as UCSs; evidence for a conditioned suppression of antibody-mediated responses has been obtained using electric shock as the UCS (Sato et al 1984; Zalcman et al 1989, 1991b).

There have been a few studies in which there were no observable conditioned effects (Krank & MacQueen 1988; MacQueen & Siegel 1989). For theoretical reasons (see Eikelboom & Stewart 1982), these experiments were conducted with the expectation of observing "paradoxical" or compensatory conditioned responses (responses opposite in direction to the unconditioned response). In conditioned animals reexposed to a CS previously paired with CY, the anti-SRBC antibody response was higher than the response of conditioned animals that were not reexposed to the CS and the response of animals that experienced unpaired CS-UCS presentations, but the responses of conditioned animals reexposed to the CS did not differ from those of a saline-treated control group. Such results may permit one to infer the existence of a conditioned enhancement of antibody production based on the failure to observe immunosuppression, but, as the investigators acknowledge, no direct evidence of compensatory conditioning was obtained. There is no obvious explanation for the difference between these results and those in the rest of the literature on conditioned immunologic changes.

Evidence for the existence of the compensatory conditioning of host defense reactions, however, can be derived from studies on the role of conditioning in the development of pharmacological tolerance to repeated injections of polyinosinic-polycytidylic acid (poly I:C; Dyck et al 1986, 1987). In keeping with a conditioning analysis of the development of tolerance to some other pharmacologic agents (Siegel 1983), tolerance to the enhancing effects of poly I:C on natural killer cell activity is abrogated by unreinforced exposures to the CS; preexposure to the CS interferes with the development of tolerance; and tolerance is attenuated when poly I:C is injected in the absence of environmental cues previously paired with injections of the drug.

CELL-MEDIATED IMMUNITY The immunosuppressive effects of CY can also be used to condition changes in cell-mediated responses. In the studies by Bovbjerg et al (1982, 1984), (Lewis × Brown Norwegian)F_1 rats were injected with Lewis strain spleen cells to induce a local graft vs host (GvH) response.[1] The basic experimental protocol used by Ader & Cohen (1975) was modified so that: (*a*) there was a 7-week interval between conditioning of the F_1 hybrid hosts and injecting them with donor cells (at which time there were no detectable residual effects of CY), and (*b*) experimental animals were reexposed to the CS in the context of reexposure to a minimally effective injection of CY. (The Lewis × Brown Norwegian)F_1 rats were first conditioned by pairing saccharin consumption and CY and were subsequently injected ("grafted") with splenic leukocytes

---

[1]
When splenic leukocytes from an inbred strain of Lewis rats are injected into the footpad of hybrid (Lewis × Brown Norwegian)F_1 rats, the grafted cells recognize the host as "foreign," and a local inflammatory reaction (the GvH response) ensues and can be measured by weighing the popliteal lymph node that drains the injection site.

from Lewis strain donors. On the day of grafting and on the following two days they were reexposed to the CS; on the day after grafting they were also given a low dose injection of CY. While low-dose injections of CY on Days 0, 1, and 2 dramatically suppressed the local GvH response, a single injection on Day 1 caused only a modest decrease in the response. However, a single low-dose injection of CY plus reexposure to the CS previously paired with CY significantly suppressed the GvH response relative to control groups that received only the single low-dose injection of CY. As expected, unreinforced exposures to the CS during the 7-week interval between conditioning and induction of the GvH response resulted in extinction of the conditioned immunosuppressive response. Experimental extinction, one hallmark of a conditioned response, has also been reported for other conditioned immunologic effects (Dyck et al 1986; Gorczynski et al 1982; see also Lysle et al 1988).

Cyclophosphamide can enhance as well as suppress immunologic reactivity. In the case of a delayed-type hypersensitivity (DTH)[2] reaction to SRBC, low-dose treatment with CY at the time of sensitization can enhance DTH in response to a subsequent challenge with the same antigen (Turk & Parker 1982); CY treatment of sensitized animals just before antigenic challenge decreases the DTH response (Gill & Liew 1978; Rodinone et al 1983). Although CY decreases the DTH reaction to an initial antigenic challenge, the response to subsequent challenges is enhanced (Bovbjerg et al 1986). Bovbjerg et al (1987a) did not observe any conditioning effects when sensitized animals, previously conditioned with CY, were reexposed to the CS before their initial challenge. However, reexposing conditioned animals to the CS before two subsequent antigenic challenges resulted in enhanced DTH responses. The conditioned enhancement could be a consequence of a selective conditioned immunosuppressive effect on suppressor cells (Gill & Liew 1978; Mitsuoka et al 1979). Another drug, levamisole, has been purported to selectively depress cytotoxic/suppressor T cells. Thus, the conditioned elevation of the T-helper:T-suppressor-subset ratio in animals reexposed to a CS previously paired with levamisole (Husband et al 1987) could be the phenomenological expression of a conditioned immunosuppressive response. Such an interpretation would be consonant with data suggesting that T cell–dependent reactions are especially sensitive to conditioning.

As in the case of antibody-mediated immune responses, conditioned changes involving cell-mediated immunity are not confined to the use of the taste aversion conditioning model. Mice exposed to a novel environment plus a distinctive taste in conjunction with rotation on a turntable (the UCS) show a decreased ability to reject allogeneic skin grafts when reexposed to the compound CS at the time of and following the antigenic challenge (Gorczynski 1992). In addition, when conditioned females (mated with nonconditioned

---

2

DTH is an in vivo inflammatory reaction mediated by sensitized T cells that is evoked by contact with the antigen with which the animal had been immunized.

males) were reexposed to the CS on Days 13, 16, and 19 of gestation, there was a depression of humoral and cell-mediated immunity in their unmanipulated offspring.

Effects of Conditioning on Nonimmunologically Specific Reactions

In addition to studying antibody- and cell-mediated immunity, immunologists also study the nonimmunologically specific in vitro actions of natural killer cells and mitogens. These are among the most frequently used measures in behavioral experiments. Natural killer (NK) cells are large granular lymphocytes that nonspecifically attack and destroy certain virus-infected cells and tumor cells and may be involved in preventing tumor metastasis.

T and/or B lymphocytes can be induced to proliferate in vitro by stimulation with various lectins (chemical substances obtained from plants), and the lymphoproliferative response to such mitogens has been used to indicate an alteration of the physiological state of T or B cells in a particular lymphoid compartment (e.g. spleen, lymph nodes, peripheral blood). Changes in mitogenic responsiveness, however, do not necessarily reflect an organism's ability to respond to antigens in vivo or in an immunologically specific manner.

In a comprehensive series of experiments, Lysle and his colleagues (1988, 1990a,b, 1991, 1992b) characterized the conditioned suppression of a variety of nonspecific responses in rats reexposed to cues previously paired with stressful stimulation. Compared to nonconditioned animals, to conditioned animals exposed to novel environmental cues, and to animals exposed to cues explicitly unpaired with the UCS, animals reexposed to auditory (or visual) cues paired with electric shock stimulation showed a reliable suppression of lymphoproliferative responses to concanavalin A (Con A) and phytohemagglutinin (PHA) (two T cell mitogens), lipopolysaccharide (LPS) (a B cell mitogen), interleukin-2 (IL-2)[3] production, and NK cell activity. As expected, exposure to the CS before conditioning retarded development of the conditioned response, and unreinforced exposures to the CS resulted in experimental extinction (Lysle et al 1988). In addition, the conditioned responses varied as a function of both the timing of reexposure to the CS in relation to the time of conditioning and the immune compartment from which the cells were obtained (Lysle et al 1990a,b; Lysle & Maslonek 1991). In splenic lymphocytes there was a depressed response to T and B cell mitogens; in whole blood, there was a suppression of the response to Con A and PHA, but not to LPS;

---

[3]
Macrophages and activated lymphocytes produce soluble products (cytokines), such as interleukin-1 (IL-1), IL-2, interferons, and tumor necrosis factor that are involved in the proliferation, differentiation, and effector functions of lymphocytes. In addition, they serve as "immunotransmitters" in the sense that some, if not all of them have effects within the central nervous system and stimulate the release of hormones.

cells obtained from mesenteric lymph nodes showed no effects of CS reexposure.

Using either a taste or odor aversion conditioning paradigm or a stressor as the UCS, other studies have also observed the conditioned suppression of lymphoproliferative responses both to mitogenic stimulation (Drugan et al 1986; Kusnecov et al 1988; Neveu et al 1986, 1987), NK cell activity (Gorczynski et al 1984; Hiramoto et al 1987; Lysle & Maslonek 1991; O'Reilly & Exon 1986), and total white blood cell count (Klosterhalfen & Klosterhalfen 1987). The conditioned enhancement of NK cell activity has also been reported (Hiramoto et al 1987; Solvason et al 1988, 1991). However, some of these latter studies suffer from major design flaws, and others have been unable to repeat these observations (Ader & Cohen 1991).

In a recent study, Coussons et al (1992) paired exposure to a distinctive environmental setting with injections of morphine (which unconditionally suppresses several nonspecific immune responses). Reexposure to the environmental cues resulted in a conditioned suppression of splenic and peripheral blood lymphocyte response to T and B cell mitogens, splenic NK cell activity, and IL-2 production. These results are of additional interest in relation to the issue of compensatory conditioning discussed above. The conditioned response mimicked the unconditioned response rather than inducing an opposite or compensatory response; induction of such a compensatory response, however, characterizes some of the other behavioral and physiological effects of morphine (e.g. Siegel 1976, 1983).

As is the case with antibody-mediated responses, the above studies uncovered no consistent relationship between conditioned behavioral responses and conditioned changes in nonspecific defense reactions (Klosterhalfen & Klosterhalfen 1987; Kusnecov et al 1988; Neveu et al 1986, 1987; Solvason et al 1988).

Antigen as Unconditioned Stimulus

In behavioral terms, an antigen is an unconditioned stimulus for activation of the immune system and has been used as the UCS in a few studies. A conditioned release of histamine, a nonspecific mediator of an allergic reaction, occurred in response to a CS associated with the injection of the antigen, bovine serum albumin (Dark et al 1987; Peeke et al 1987; Russell et al 1984), and an increase in mast cell protease II was observed in sensitized rats reexposed to environmental cues previously paired with exposure to egg albumin (MacQueen et al 1989). With respect to an immune response, per se, Gorczynski and his colleagues (Gorczynski et al 1982) repeatedly grafted mice with allogeneic skin under a constant set of environmental conditions. When these mice were given sham transplantations, there was an increase in the number of precursor cytotoxic T lymphocytes. Subsequent unreinforced exposures to the graft procedures resulted in extinction of the conditioned response. These experiments are among the relatively few that have addressed conditioned immune responses as distinct from conditioned immunopharmacologic effects.

Biologic Impact of Conditioned Changes in Immunity

Although highly reproducible, the effects of conditioning in modulating immune responses have been "relatively" small, and a recurring question has been whether behaviorally induced alterations in immunocompetence have any biological or clinical significance. So far, only a few studies have addressed this issue. In a study using mice that develop a systemic lupus-erythematosus-like autoimmune disease (Ader & Cohen 1982), conditioned stimuli were substituted for half of the weekly treatments with active immunosuppressive drug (CY). The onset of autoimmune disease in the genetically susceptible (NZB × NZW)F₁ mice was thereby delayed using a cumulative dose of CY that was not, by itself, sufficient to alter the progression of the lupus-like disease. Also, in lupus-prone mice that had previously been given weekly treatments with CY (paired with the taste of saccharin), reexposure to the CS after discontinuation of active drug treatment prolonged survival relative to conditioned mice that received neither active drug nor reexposure to the CS (Ader 1985). Analogous results were obtained in studies of adjuvant-induced arthritis in rats using either CY or cyclosporin as the UCS (Klosterhalfen & Klosterhalfen 1983, 1990) and electric shock as the UCS (Lysle et al 1992a), and in a study in which reexposure to a CS previously paired with CY accelerated mortality among conditioned animals inoculated with a syngeneic plasmacytoma (Gorczynski et al 1985).

Recently the therapeutic potential of conditioning was examined in different transplantation models in an effort to prolong graft survival. A/J recipient mice typically reject allogeneic skin grafts from BALB/c or C57BL/6 donors within two weeks. A low-dose injection of CY on the day of grafting, however, prolongs graft survival. In mice conditioned by the pairing of saccharin and CY, reexposure to the CS alone on the day of grafting and at 5-day intervals thereafter also prolonged survival of the skin allograft (Gorczynski 1990). In another recent study (Grochowicz et al 1991), reexposure of transplant recipient rats to a CS previously paired with cyclosporin A extended the survival of a heterotopic heart transplant. Experiments such as these hint at the potential clinical significance of conditioned alterations in immune function.

Conditioning in Human Subjects

"As early as 1557, Amatus Lusitanus related the case of a Dominican monk, who, whenever he perceived the odor of roses or *saw them at a distance,* was immediately seized with syncope and fell unconscious to the ground" (Mackenzie 1896:51, italics added). Mackenzie described his ability to provoke asthmatic symptoms by presenting an artificial rose to an allergic patient, which "forcibly illustrates the role of purely psychical impressions in awakening the paroxysms of the disease familiarly known as 'rose cold'" (Mackenzie

1896:45). The literature contains descriptions of several similar cases of what may represent conditioning phenomena (Hill 1930; Smith & Salinger 1933; Dekker et al 1957). Laboratory studies in humans (Dekker et al 1957; Khan 1977) and animals (e.g. Ottenberg et al 1958) confirm the clinical suggestions that exposure to symbolic, nonallergenic stimuli (CSs) previously associated with allergens are capable of inducing asthmatic symptoms in some subjects.

More recent data provide preliminary evidence that conditioning may be able to modify immune responses in human subjects. In a study by Ikemi & Nakagawa (1962), four subjects received cutaneous stimulation with a methylene blue solution (the CS) containing the extract of a Japanese lacquer tree that unconditionally induced eczema within 24 hr. After an unspecified number of CS-UCS pairings, the CS alone elicited a skin reaction in all four subjects. Smith & McDaniels (1983) also tried to condition a DTH response in human subjects. Healthy volunteers underwent tuberculin skin testing six times at monthly intervals. In a counterbalanced manner, the "blinded" research nurse administered tuberculin obtained from a green vial to one arm and saline drawn from a red vial to the other arm. On the test trial, the contents of the colored vials were switched; neither the experimenter nor the subject was aware that tuberculin had now been put into the red vial, saline into the green. Saline administered to the arm that had previously been treated with tuberculin did not evoke a skin reaction, but there was a significant diminution of the erythema and induration elicited by tuberculin in the arm previously injected with saline. This finding is remarkably similar to that reported by Moynihan et al (1989) in mice.

The failure of saline to evoke a skin reaction could be instructive, particularly for the strategy underlying such research. First of all, the immunologic mechanisms that could dampen an immunologically specific response are not necessarily the same as those that might elicit or enhance that same response. In the case of immunoenhancement, an immunogenic stimulus may be required, even if it alone is not sufficient to elicit a discernible reaction. A more reasonable paradigm for the behavioral modification of an immune response, then, may require the application of a minimally effective immunogenic stimulus—one barely able to elicit a measurable response but sufficient to initiate some early event in the immunologic cascade that leads to a typical immune reaction. If "subthreshold" stimulation is capable of being potentiated by an alteration of the neural and/or endocrine environment in which immune responses occur, one might be more likely to observe a behaviorally induced alteration in immunologic reactivity under immunogenic stimulus conditions that actually approximate natural conditions. Thus, in the present example, a sensory stimulus (e.g. saline) that does not affect the immune system directly may not suffice to elicit a tuberculin-induced skin reaction. But the superimposition of an immunologically neutral stimulus previously paired with activation of the immune system or the response induced by what would ordinarily be a subthreshold immunogenic stimulus may be sufficient to elicit a discernible immune response. This basic strategy was used by Bovbjerg et al (1982, 1984) who demonstrated that the combination of a CS for immunosuppression and a low dose of CY depressed a GvH response to a significantly greater degree than the low dose of CY was able to accomplish alone.

The anticipatory nausea that occurs in 25–75% of patients undergoing repeated chemotherapy for cancer appears to reflect a classically conditioned response (Andrykowski et al 1985, 1988; Andrykowski & Redd 1987; Carey & Burish 1988; Morrow & Dobkin 1988; Redd & Andrykowski 1982). Bovbjerg et al (1990) studied women who had experienced at least three sessions of chemotherapy to determine if cancer patients who displayed antic-ipatory nausea and vomiting during the course of chemotherapy would also show anticipatory immunosuppressive changes. Peripheral blood was obtained at the patients' homes 3–8 days before a scheduled chemotherapy session and again in the hospital just before the intravenous drug infusion. No differences in NK cell activity or in cell counts or cell subset numbers were observed, but in vitro proliferation in response to the T-cell mitogens PHA and Con A were significantly lower prior to chemotherapy than the responses measured in the home environment. There was no evidence that the decreased mitogen re-sponses were related to anticipatory nausea or to the increased anxiety that occurred in the hospital. This observation of anticipatory immunosuppression is entirely consistent with the proposition that chemotherapy patients who receive an immunosuppressive drug under a relatively constant set of environ-mental conditions would show conditioned changes in immune function as well as in behavior. The extent to which these behavioral and immune re-sponses reflect the same underlying mechanisms—or, as the animal literature suggests, represent independently conditioned responses—remains to be de-termined and might prove important in the clinical management of chemother-apy patients.

STRESS AND IMMUNITY

In the present context, "stress" refers to any natural or experimentally con-trived circumstances that (intuitively, at least) pose an actual or perceived threat to the psychobiological integrity of the individual. In nonhuman ani-mals, environmental conditions that are apparently perceived as a threat to the organism, and to which the organism cannot adapt, are accompanied by both transient and relatively long-lasting psychophysiologic changes. We presume that these changes contribute to the development of disease, especially if the organism is at the same time exposed to potentially pathogenic stimuli. As described below, however, the stress response is not uniformly detrimental to the organism.

Effects of Stress on Disease

Studies in humans have implicated psychosocial factors in the susceptibility to and/or the progression of a variety of pathophysiologic processes including bacterial, allergic, and autoimmune diseases that involve alterations in immunologic defense mechanisms. Specific examples include Epstein-Barr virus infections, respiratory infections, streptococcal infections, asthma, and arthritis. Comprehensive treatments of this subject have been provided recently by S. Cohen & Williamson (1991) and Weiner (1977, 1991). Most of the experimental work has been conducted with animals and indicates that a variety of behavioral manipulations or stressors can influence susceptibility to a variety of disease states in a variety of species. However, the stressors used do not all produce the same effects. The impact and direction of the effects of stressful stimulation depend upon the disease process to which the organism is concurrently subjected. For example, physical restraint in rodents increases susceptibility to infection with herpes simplex virus (Bonneau et al 1991a,b; Rasmussen et al 1957) and the Maloney sarcoma virus (Seifter et al 1973), has no effect on the response to an experimentally induced lymphoma (Greenberg et al 1984), and decreases susceptibility to allergic encephalomyelitis (Levine et al 1962). Likewise, electric shock stimulation increases susceptibility to Coxsackie B virus but decreases susceptibility to malaria (Friedman et al 1965) and to the spontaneous development of leukemia in AKR mice (Plaut et al 1981). Using the same disease outcome (e.g. encephalomyocarditis virus), electric shock stimulation decreases susceptibility but the stimulation of handling has no effect (Friedman et al 1969); and, while both electric shock and handling decrease susceptibility to collagen-induced arthritis, a different stressor, auditory stimulation, increases susceptibility (Rogers et al 1980a,b).

Analogous results are observed in studies on the development and progression of tumors in animals (Justice 1985; Sklar & Anisman 1981). Psychosocial factors can influence the development and/or growth of tumors, but the direction of the effects depends on the tumor model chosen for study. The results also depend on the quality, quantity, and duration of the stressor; the temporal relationship between exposure to the stressor and the introduction of pathogenic stimulation; socioenvironmental conditions (e.g. whether animals are housed individually or in groups); and a variety of host factors (e.g. species, strain, and sex). Further, the observed effects depend on the outcome measures and sampling parameters selected for study. As described below, the effects of stressful stimulation on immune function parallel those on stressful stimulation and disease susceptibility. It seems evident—or, at least likely—that the ability to predict the outcome of studies of the pathophysiologic effects of stressful stimulation depends upon a more detailed understanding of the interaction between responses unconditionally elicited by specific kinds of potentially pathogenic stimulation and the pattern of psychophysiological responses (including immunologic responses) induced by specific forms of stressful stimulation.

While illustrations like those above document the effects of stressors on the response to pathogenic agents, they do not provide evidence that these effects are mediated by behaviorally induced alterations in immune function. Too frequently, however, studies of the effects of stressors on tumor development or metastasis are cited as evidence of the influence of stress or behavioral interventions on immune function—even in the absence of any measure of immune function. And even when simultaneous measures of immune function are being measured, it is not always clear that the indexes chosen for study are related to the pathophysiologic process under study. It is not yet clear that behaviorally induced perturbations in immune function can influence or mediate the effects of psychosocial factors on the development or progression of disease in humans, but provocative data are now being obtained (e.g. Glaser et al 1987; Kemeny et al 1992), especially in relation to the experimental inoculation of respiratory viruses (Broadbent et al 1984; S. Cohen et al 1991; Totman et al 1980).

More recent animal studies, however, are including biologically relevant measures of immune function. Feng et al (1991), for example, infected mice with influenza virus and observed a delay in the production of virus-specific antibody levels in animals subjected to restraint. There were no detectable differences in the magnitude of the humoral response ultimately attained, however—a finding that could be related to an interaction between the temporal relationship of restraint and infection and the virulence of the pathogen (Chao et al 1990). At a clinical level, psychosocial factors have been related to the manifestation of latent herpes virus infection (e.g. Glaser et al 1987). Bonneau et al (1991a), studying the effects of a stressor on the murine response to herpes simplex virus (HSV), found that repeated, prolonged periods of physical restraint (16 hr/day for a varying number of days around the time of inoculation) suppressed NK cell activity and the primary development of HSV-specific cytotoxic T lymphocytes. Also, higher titers of infectious HSV at the site of infection were recovered from restrained than from unrestrained mice. Similar results were obtained by Kusnecov et al (1992) using overnight exposure to intermittent electric shock stimulation (1 shock every 30 min, on average) on the day preceding and for eight days following virus infection. In another study (Bonneau et al 1991b), restraint inhibited the in vitro activation and/or migration of HSV-specific cytotoxic T lymphocytes from previously primed mice—i.e. activation of HSV-specific memory cells was inhibited by the physiological changes induced by the stressor. Other examples relate to neoplastic disease (Ben-Eliyahu et al 1991; Brenner et al 1990). Using a tumor model in which lung metastasis is thought to be controlled by NK cells, Ben-Eliyahu and his colleagues (1991) found that, depending upon when the stressor was imposed in relation to the effect of NK cells on the metastatic process, forced swimming decreased NK cell activity and resulted in a two-fold increase in lung metastases.

Effects of Stress on Humoral and Cell-Mediated Immunity

Unlike the measurement of hormone levels or nonspecific defense reactions that can be gauged by sampling factors circulating in blood, urine, saliva, etc, the assessment of immune responses, such as most of those described above in the context of disease susceptibility, requires that experimental subjects be immunized. This additional variable adds layers of complexity to the characterization of the effects of behavioral and other interventions on immune function and the mediation of these effects. In addition to the quality and quantity of environmental stimulation and the temporal relationship between a stressor and immunization, one must, for example, consider the nature as well as the concentration of antigen and the "cascade" of immune events that eventuate in the production of antibody or a cell-mediated inflammatory response. This complexity is reflected in much of the data describing the effects of stressful stimulation on different aspects of immune function.

The relevance of the concentration of antigen used for immunization in studies of stress has been noted in the past (Solomon et al 1974). In our view, studies that address immune function per se use what might be described as suprathreshold levels of antigenic stimulation—concentrations of antigen calculated to induce a "robust" primary and secondary response. To the extent that behaviorally induced neuroendocrine changes are capable of modulating immune responses, the use of high levels of antigenic stimulation are not comparable to the levels of antigen exposure experienced by the organism under natural conditions and could be counterproductive as a research strategy designed to elaborate behaviorally induced alterations in immunocompetence. For these reasons, Moynihan et al (1990a) studied the effects of a stressor (electric shock) on the response to low-dose antigenic stimulation. An immunizing dose of as little as 1 μg of the protein antigen keyhole limpet hemacyanin (KLH) was insufficient to elicit a detectable primary response but was sufficient to prime mice. When shock was administered for seven days before and after immunization or only on one day, 24 hr after priming, mice exposed to the stressor showed a depressed antibody response to challenge with a second injection of 1 μg of KLH relative to control mice that were simply placed into the shock apparatus or that remained unmanipulated. When mice were challenged with a higher dose of KLH (5 μg) there were no group differences. It is thus possible that concentrations of antigen that unconditionally elicit robust immune responses could mask the effects of behavioral interventions.

For the most part, antibody production is suppressed by stressful stimulation. Although differential housing (frequently mislabeled as "crowding" or "isolation") may not qualify as a stressor, the manner in which animals are housed or a change in housing conditions is sufficient to influence primary and/or secondary antibody responses to several different antigens (e.g. Cunnick et al 1991; Edwards & Dean 1977; Edwards et al 1980; Glenn & Becker 1969; Rabin et al 1987a,b; Rabin & Salvin 1987; Solomon 1969; Vessey 1964). Antibody responses are also suppressed when submissive, intruder, and attacked and defeated rats are subsequently immunized (Beden & Brain 1982, 1984; Fauman 1987; Fleshner et al 1989; Ito et al 1983). A recent review of these data has been provided by Bohus & Koolhaas (1991). Even the odors emitted by mice subjected to stressful stimulation are sufficient to influence antibody production in conspecific recipients. In one study (Zalcman et al 1991a,b), the antibody response to SRBC was suppressed in mice placed into an apparatus vacated by conspecifics that had been exposed to a presumed stressor; in another study (Cocke et al 1992), immunization with KLH following prolonged exposure to alarm signals emitted by conspecifics undergoing concurrent stimulation enhanced antibody responses in the group-housed recipients.

Antibody responses are influenced by early separation experiences. In rats, brief handling and separation from the mother increased both primary and secondary antibody responses to flagellin, a bacterial antigen (Solomon et al 1968). In mice, early separations from the mother resulted in a decreased anti-SRBC antibody response (Michaut et al 1981), and separation from the mother and rearing environment influenced the antibody response of monkeys to an antigenic challenge (e.g. Coe et al 1985, 1988).

Okimura and his colleagues (Okimura & Nigo 1986; Okimura et al 1986b,c) found that serum antibody titers and the number of antibody-forming splenic cells of mice were depressed if physical restraint (12 hr/day on two consecutive days) was imposed after, but not before, immunization with SRBC, a T-cell dependent antigen. Both adrenalectomy and chemical sympathectomy blocked the stressor-induced immunosuppression. The response to a hapten (TNP) conjugated to a type 2 T cell–independent carrier (Ficoll) was not influenced by restraint, but there was enhanced antibody production in response to a type 1 T cell–independent antigen (LPS). In this case, adrenalectomy, but not sympathectomy, blocked the enhanced response. The differential sensitivity of type 1 and type 2 T cell-independent antigens, which activate different populations of B cells, is of additional interest in relation to the differential effects of conditioning on the response to these antigenic stimuli (see N. Cohen et al 1979; Schulze et al 1988; Wayner et al 1978).

Both primary and secondary antibody responses are suppressed when rats are subjected to inescapable electric shock stimulation daily beginning before and continuing after immunization with KLH (Laudenslager et al 1988). Rotating mice after but not before immunization with SRBC also depressed the immune response to SRBC (Esterling & Rabin 1987). In contrast, avoidance conditioning depressed the antibody response to SRBC relative to yoked animals that experienced unavoidable shock and an apparatus control group (Mormede et al 1988). The degree to which rats could avoid or escape shock influenced the immune response, but not in the hypothesized direction. Zalc-man and his colleagues (1988) subjected mice to a single session of footshock 0, 24, 48, 72, or 95 hr after immunization with SRBC. Both the number of antibody-forming cells and serum anti-SRBC antibody titers were depressed, but only in mice subjected to the stressor 72 hr after immunization, suggesting that there is a critical period for this acute stressor, at least, on antibody production. Based on changes in norepinephrine activity within the central nervous system that result from this same schedule of electric shock treatment (Anisman et al 1987; Zacharko & Anisman 1988), Zakman et al expected that "controllability" would have influenced the immune response. There were, however, no differences between mice that were and were not able to escape the electric shock.

A seemingly innocuous form of stimulation with the immediate and long-term ability to influence antibody production is the handling of animals. Moy-nihan et al (1990b) found that antibody production in response to KLH was attenuated in adult mice that were immunized after a 2-week period of daily handling. Raymond et al (1986) found that, depending on strain, rats that were simply handled during the neonatal period had suppressed antibody titers in response to subsequent immunization with SRBC. In response to flagellin administration, adult rats handled during infancy showed an enhanced anti-body response. In related research, Taylor & Ross (1989) found that neonatal restraint (1 hr/day during the first 10 days of life) suppressed antibody re-sponses to immunization with pneumococcal polysaccharide in adult rats. In adult animals, the same restraint imposed for 3 weeks followed by a 3-week interval before immunization had no discernible effects.[4] Moynihan and her associates (Moynihan et al 1989) subjected mice to a different number of intraperitoneal (ip) injections of saline or just handling during the 2-week period before the animals were injected with antigen. Daily handling as well as the repeated ip injections of saline attenuated the production of antibody in response to KLH relative to a group of unmanipulated mice. Whether there was an attenuated response in the manipulated animals or an exaggerated response in the unmanipulated animals cannot be determined. Whether the difference is a reflection of conditioning processes also remains to be deter-mined. In either case, methodological questions arise about the control or "resting" state of immunized animals.

With respect to cell-mediated immune responses, animals subjected to stressors tend to show delayed skin graft rejection (Wistar & Hildemann 1960) and suppressed DTH responses (Okimura et al 1986a). In a series of experi-ments by Blecha and his colleagues (1982a,b), restraint, heat, and cold, three commonly used stressors, had different effects on two different cell-mediated

---

4

The limited data available suggest that an exploration of the long-term effects of early life experiences on immune function would be a fruitful avenue of research (Ader 1983; O'Grady & Hall 1991).

immune responses. Restraint imposed before sensitization or challenge suppressed the delayed cutaneous hypersensitivity response to SRBC. Exposure to cold for two days after sensitization also depressed the DTH response, whereas exposure to cold for eight days increased the DTH response. Heat exposure invariably increased the hypersensitivity response. Contact hypersensitivity to dinitrofluorobenzene was increased by each of these stressors. Further, adrenalectomy or treatment with metapyrone abrogated the stressor-induced suppression of DTH but had no effect on the stressor-induced enhancement of the contact sensitivity response. Again, the literature provides little justification for generalizing from one stressor to another—or from one aspect of immune function to another.

Another immunologically relevant reaction to stressors is a suppression of macrophage function (Pavlidis & Chirigos 1980; Jiang et al 1990; Okimura et al 1986a; Qunidos et al 1986; Zwilling et al 1990), which may be mediated by a stressor-induced depression of IFN production (Glaser et al 1986; Sonnenfeld et al 1992). The expression of class II major histocompatibility complex antigens by macrophages (glycoproteins that, together with processed antigen, are presented to and recognized by lymphocytes) was decreased by physical restraint (Zwilling et al 1990) and cold water exposure (Jiang et al 1990); in the study by Sonnenfeld et al (1992), electric shock suppressed IFN-gamma production and the expression of class II antigens which could, in turn, influence antibody- and cell-mediated immunocompetence.

Effects of Stress on Nonimmunologically Specific Reactions

As in the case of antibody- and cell-mediated immunity, the effects of stressors on nonspecific defense reactions are generally suppressive, but not uniformly so (Croiset et al 1987; Lysle et al 1990a,b; Monjan & Collector 1977; Rinner et al 1992; Weiss et al 1989b).

The differential housing of rodents results in differences in lymphoproliferative responses to mitogens, NK cell activity, and IL-2 production (Ghoneum et al 1987; Jessop et al 1988; Rabin et al 1987a,b; Rabin & Salvin 1987), the direction and magnitude of the effects being determined by species, strain, sex, and duration of housing. Other agonistic social interactions can also reliably influence the response to T and B cell mitogens, NK cell activity, and IL-2 production in fish as well as rodents (Bohus & Koolhaas 1991; Faisal et al 1989; Ghoneum et al 1988; Hardy et al 1990; Raab et al 1986). In addition to changes in antibody production, Cocke et al (1992) also found reduced splenic NK cell cytotoxicity in mice exposed to the odors emitted by footshocked conspecifics.

In general, the in vitro response of laboratory rodents to T cell mitogens in splenic and/or peripheral blood lymphocytes decreases following relatively acute exposure to a variety of stressors such as restraint, noise, and swimming (Jiang et al 1990; Monjan & Collector 1977; Rinner et al 1992; Zha et al

1992), and as a result of separation experiences (Ackerman et al 1988). The effects of separation experiences from mothers or peers in several nonhuman primate species can have long-lasting effects (Coe et al 1989; Friedman et al 1991; Gust et al 1992; Laudenslager et al 1985, 1990). Increases and decreases in lymphocyte proliferation have also been observed in handled animals, depending on the amount of handling and the age at which it is experienced (Lown & Dutka 1987; Moynihan et al 1990b; Rinner et al 1992). Similarly, NK cell activity is frequently, but not invariably, depressed following acute exposure to a variety of stressors (Aarstad et al 1983; Jiang et al 1990; Moynihan et al 1990a; Okimura et al 1986a; Steplewski & Vogel 1986; Steplewski et al 1985).

Electric shock stimulation has been the most frequently used stressor in studies of nonspecifically stimulated defense reactions and thus provides the more systematic data. Keller and his associates (1981) found that, with increasing intensities of electric shock over a period of 18 hr, there was a corresponding decrease in the proliferation of peripheral blood lymphocytes in response to PHA, even when the assay was based on a constant number of cells to correct for the stressor-induced decrease in the total number of circulating lymphocytes. Less reliable effects were found in the response of splenic lymphocytes, although Weiss et al (1989b), using the same paradigm, found a significant suppression of lymphoproliferation of both splenic and blood lymphocytes. Under these conditions, they also found a decline in IL-2 and interferon (IFN) production. Batuman et al (1990) obtained essentially the same results varying the number of days of electric shock stimulation and measuring the response to both Con A and PHA. The proliferative response to B cell mitogens (pokeweed mitogen and LPS) was not influenced by the stressful stimulation. These investigators also noted a decrease in the total number of splenic and peripheral blood lymphocytes, particularly of CD8+ cells. In addition, IL-2 production was diminished after as little as one day of exposure to the 3-hr period of stimulation.

Lysle et al (1987) also found that a single session of approximately 1 hr of stressful stimulation during which rats received 8 or 16 (but not 4) signaled footshocks was sufficient to depress the proliferative response of splenic and peripheral blood lymphocytes to Con A stimulation. After five days of stimulation, the response of spleen but not blood cells had recovered. Similar effects were obtained by Cunnick et al (1988). Thus, whether one varies the intensity of electric shock, the number of sessions of stimulation, or the number of shocks per session, the magnitude of this form of stressful stimulation is related to the magnitude of the changes in at least some measures of cellular host defenses in some immune compartments. However, results obtained by Livnat et al (1985) and Lysle et al (1990b) with electric shock and by Weiss et al (1989b) with qualitative and quantitative differences in stressful stimulation suggest that this relationship may not be linear.

The ability to predict or control the effects of stressful stimulation has become a major focus of stress-related research and, as a result, the effects obtained by Laudenslager et al (1983) indicating that inescapable but not escapable footshock depressed mitogen responsiveness in rats has been cited frequently. Less frequently cited, however, is the report by these investigators (Maier & Laudenslager 1988) of their inability to reproduce these effects. In contrast to the effects on antibody production, however, Mormede and his colleagues (1988) found that "control" did influence the response to mitogens. Rats subjected to inescapable or unsignaled electric shock stimulation showed a suppression of the lymphoproliferative response to T-cell mitogens. Also, preliminary data obtained by Shavit et al (1983) indicated that inescapable but not escapable shock suppressed splenic NK cell activity in rats. In another preliminary study (Irwin & Custeau 1989), however, signaled electric shock resulted in a more pronounced suppression of NK cell activity than unsignaled shock.[5]

Electric shock stimulation also suppresses NK cell activity (Cunnick et al 1988; Keller et al 1988; Lysle et al 1990a; Lysle & Maslonek 1991; Shavit et al 1984; Weiss et al 1989b), the kinetics of which are strain dependent in mice (Zalcman et al 1991a). Shavit and his colleagues (1984, 1986) found that intermittent electric shock stimulation, which induces an opioid-mediated analgesia, also depresses NK cytotoxicity, whereas continuous shock, which results in a nonopioid analgesia, has no such effect.

MEDIATION OF BEHAVIORALLY INDUCED IMMUNE CHANGES

There are no definitive data on the mediation of behaviorally conditioned or stressor-induced changes in either specific or nonspecific defense system responses. It is clear that different immunologic and neuroendocrine mechanisms are involved in mediating the effects of different behavioral interventions on different immune responses measured in different compartments of the immune system.

The available data suggest that the effects of conditioning could be mediated by a preferential effect on T cells. Conditioned suppression of lymphoproliferative responses in rats and mice, for example, has been observed in response to T-cell mitogens but not (or less reliably) in response to B-cell mitogens (Kusnecov et al 1988; Lysle et al 1990b, 1991; Neveu et al 1986). Adoptive transfer experiments also suggest that conditioning may be mediated by T cell changes (Gorczynski 1987). Splenocytes from conditioned or experimentally naive animals were transferred into (irradiated) naive or conditioned animals that were or were not subsequently reexposed to the CS.

---

[5]
    Studies of stressor control in human subjects (Sieber et al 1991; Weisse et al 1990) yield imilar contrasting effects.

The observed increases or decreases in the antibody-forming cell response to SRBC depended on the donor cells and the conditioning treatment experienced by the recipient. The separate transfer of enriched T and B cells into naive or conditioned mice suggested that conditioning effects were attributable to the adoptively transferred T cells (Gorczynski 1991). The question of whether conditioning can modulate the antibody response to different types of T-cell independent antigens has not been resolved (N. Cohen et al 1979; Schulze et al 1988; Wayner et al 1978).

Stressful stimulation also seems to have greater effects on T cell than on B cell function (e.g. Batuman et al 1990; Lysle et al 1990b; Mormede et al 1988; Moynihan et al 1990b). Several investigators have demonstrated conditioned and stressor-induced decreases in IL-2 production that might account for the suppression of T cell proliferation (e.g. Batuman et al 1990; Ghoneum et al 1988; Hardy et al 1990; Kandil & Borysenko 1988; Weiss et al 1989b). However, adding IL-2 to incubated lymphocytes did not normalize the stressor-induced suppression of lymphoproliferation (Weiss et al 1989a). These investigators did find that electric shock decreased the expression of IL-2 receptors on lymphocytes, suggesting that a compromised ability to respond to IL-2 may contribute to stressor-induced immunosuppression (and, via neural and/or endocrine pathways, conditioned antibody- and/or cell-mediated immune responses, as well).

The in vitro T cell effects of behavioral interventions appear to be differentially expressed by splenic and blood lymphocytes in the case of both conditioning (Lysle et al 1990a; Lysle & Maslonek 1991) and stressful stimulation (Cunnick et al 1988; Keller et al 1983, 1988; Lysle et al 1987; Rinner et al 1992). This could reflect the trafficking of lymphocytes and a resulting difference in the kinetics of the response in these two compartments (Cunnick et al 1988; Lysle et al 1987); it could also relate to differences in the manner in which splenic and peripheral blood lymphocytes were cultured. However, the fact that there is noradrenergic innervation of the spleen (Felten et al 1987) and that the stressor-induced suppression of splenic but not blood lymphocyte proliferation is blocked by β-adrenergic antagonists (Cunnick et al 1990) suggests the operation of different mediating mechanisms.

With respect to neuroendocrine influences, it is reasonable to hypothesize that conditioned alterations of immunologic reactivity could be mediated by conditioned neuroendocrine changes, but data collected thus far are inconsistent with the proposition that such effects are mediated simply by nonspecific, stressor-induced changes in hormone levels. As reviewed elsewhere (Ader & Cohen 1991), an extensive literature and other recent studies (e.g. Roudebush & Bryant 1991) directly contradict or are inconsistent with predictions that would follow from a "stress mediation" hypothesis of the effects of conditioning or that conditioning effects are adrenal dependent. An elevation in glucocorticoids is a common (and sometimes defining) characteristic of a stress response, and exogenously administered glucocorticoids are generally (but not uniformly) immunosuppressive (Munck & Guyre 1991). Nonetheless, an endogenous elevation in adrenocortical steroids in response to different stressors cannot be invoked to account for most of the stressor-induced changes in immunocompetence.

In terms of antigen-specific immune responses, Okimura et al (1986b) found that adrenalectomy blocked the suppression of antibody responses to SRBC in rats that had been subjected to restraint, but adrenalectomy did not influence the immunosuppressive effects of rotation (Esterling & Rabin 1987). In studies using electric shock (Laudenslager et al 1988; Mormede et al 1988), no relationship between corticosterone levels and suppressed antibody production in rats was seen. Blecha et al (1982b) found that adrenalectomy attenuated the suppression of a DTH response in restrained mice but did not affect the restraint-induced enhancement of contact hypersensitivity. With respect to nonspecific reactions, electric shock in rats induced a lymphopenia that was adrenal dependent (Keller et al 1981); the stressor-induced suppression of mitogen responsiveness, however, was unaffected by adrenalectomy (Keller et al 1983). The suppressed lymphoproliferative response of splenic T lymphocytes, in particular, has been shown consistently to be independent of stressor-induced adrenal activity (e.g. Lysle et al 1990b; Monjan & Collector 1977; Mormede et al 1988; Rabin et al 1987a,b; Weiss et al 1989b). The stressor-induced suppression of NK cell activity and IL-2 production are not blocked by adrenalectomy (e.g. Weiss et al 1989b).

Both conditioned and stressor-induced alterations of immune and nonspecific defense responses have been attributed to the actions of catecholamines. Gorczynski & Holmes (1989), for example, reported that both chlorpromazine and amitriptyline abolished conditioned immunosuppressive responses based on the pairing of a gustatory stimulus with CY. Lysle et al (1992a) reported that the β-adrenergic antagonist propranolol blocked the effects of conditioned stressor effects on the development of adjuvant-induced arthritis; but propranolol itself may be capable of attenuating inflammatory responses (Kaplan et al 1980). Cunnick and her colleagues (1990) found that propranolol and nadolol (a β-adrenergic antagonist that does not cross the blood-brain barrier) blocked the electric shock–induced suppression of splenic but not peripheral blood lymphocytes to Con A stimulation. Propranolol also blocked attenuation of the lymphoproliferative response of splenic lymphocytes to a CS previously paired with electric shock (Luecken & Lysle 1992). Neither propranolol nor nadolol influenced the conditioned suppression of B cell mitogenesis of peripheral blood lymphocyte responses or IL-2 production, but both antagonists attenuated the conditioned suppression of IFN-gamma. The peripherally acting β-adrenergic receptor antagonist also blocked the suppression of IFN-gamma production induced by electric shock stimulation (Sonnenfeld et al 1992).

Using a different stressor (repeated exposure to cold), Carr et al (1992) described an enhancement of splenic antigen-specific antibody production

and, at the same time, suppressed or unaltered serum levels of im-
munoglobulins. In this instance, phentolamine blocked the effects of cold
exposure and propranolol potentiated the effects of the stressor. While little is
known of the immunologic effects of catecholamines in vivo, it is relevant to
note that Zalcman et al (1991a) were unable to detect any meaningful relationship between the depression of brain levels of norepinephrine and the suppression of NK cell activity induced by one hour of uncontrollable electric shock
stimulation. It is evident that any involvement of catecholamines in the mediation of stressor-induced alterations of immunity is determined by interactions
involving the nature of the immune response and the compartment in which it
is measured and the neurochemical concomitants of the adaptive responses
induced by the nature of the stressor.

Opioids acting within the central nervous system have also been implicated
in the mediation of conditioned and stressor (electric shock)-induced alterations of nonspecific defense responses. Cunnick and her colleagues (1988)
found that naltrexone, an opioid receptor antagonist, blocked a shock-induced
suppression of splenic NK cell activity but did not obviate suppression of the
splenic lymphocyte response to T cell mitogens. Lysle et al (1992b) found that
naloxone (in doses higher than those used by Cunnick et al) blocked the
conditioned suppression of NK cell activity and the depressed response to both
T and B cell mitogens. Although the association between an olfactory CS and
poly I:C was unaffected, subsequent enhancement of NK cell activity in response to reexposure to the CS also could be blocked by naltrexone (Solvason
et al 1989). N-methylnaltrexone, a quaternary form of naltrexone that does not
cross the blood-brain barrier, did not interfere with these conditioned responses.

That the effects of stressful stimulation on NK cell activity may be mediated by centrally acting opioids is suggested by the observations that the
immunosuppression induced by electric shock was prevented by pretreatment
with naltrexone but not by the peripheral actions of N-methylnaltrexone, and
that a dose-dependent suppression of NK cell activity could be induced by
morphine (Shavit et al 1984). However, Shavit et al (1986) found that NK cell
activity was suppressed to the same extent following 4, 14, or 30 daily sessions of electric shock stimulation, whereas tolerance to the immunosuppressive effects of morphine developed after 14 sessions. Also, a stressor-induced
suppression of NK cell activity was observed in both morphine-naive and
morphine-tolerant rats. Thus, the suppression of NK cell activity in response
to morphine and to stressful stimulation is not mediated by precisely the same
mechanisms. Of related interest is the report that serum obtained from mice or
rats subjected to physical restraint (Zha et al 1992) and electric shock (Weiss
et al 1989a) contained one or more factors that could suppress the
lymphoproliferative response of peripheral blood lymphocytes from unmanipulated animals. Neither adrenalectomy nor naltrexone treatment altered
this effect (Zha et al 1992).

It may also be relevant that some studies have uncovered different changes in mitogenesis and/or NK cell activity in animals subjected to avoidable or unavoidable, escapable or inescapable, or signaled or unsignaled electric shock (Irwin & Custeau 1989; Mormede et al 1988; Shavit et al 1983), despite the fact that each of these stressful situations would fit the criterion for an opioid-mediated analgesia that might be expected to suppress NK cell activity. Other studies (e.g. Cunnick et al 1988; Keller et al 1988; Odio et al 1987) have noted a dissociation between the effects of the same stressor, electric shock (albeit of different magnitudes, intensity, and duration), on NK cell and mitogen responses, both of which have been observed to be blocked by naltrexone treatment in one study (Lysle et al 1992b). There is abundant evidence that opioids, for which there are receptors on lymphocytes (Blalock 1988), can influence immune functions. It is not likely, however, that centrally acting opioids are the sole mediator of either conditioned or stressor-induced alterations of immunocompetence.

The fact that some agonistic or antagonistic neurochemical or pharmacologic intervention can block or mimic the immunologic effects of reexposure to a CS or stressful stimulation does not, in itself, constitute an explanation of the behaviorally induced effects. It suggests only that such a pathway is one (of perhaps several) means by which such an effect could occur. Indeed, the complexity of the multiple communication channels between the brain and the immune system provides any number of other pathways through which behaviorally induced alterations in immunity could be mediated. It is beyond the scope of this review, however, to detail these interactions (see Ader et al 1991a); nor, because of the paucity of behavioral data, should we speculate on their role in the psychophysiologic regulation of immunity. These interactions can, however, be summarized as follows.

Primary (thymus, bone marrow) and secondary (spleen, lymph nodes, gut-associated lymphoid tissues) lymphoid organs are innervated by the sympathetic nervous system (Felten & Felten 1991), and lymphoid cells bear receptors for many neuroendocrine and neurotransmitter signals that have demonstrable immunomodulating effects (Blalock 1992). Moreover, microglia cells of the central nervous system can produce cytokines (e.g. Carr 1992; Guillian et al 1986). Conversely, lymphocytes can produce neuroendocrine factors such as proopiomelanocortin-derived peptides (Blalock 1988). Also, cytokines produced by macrophages and activated lymphocytes are signal molecules ("immunotransmitters") that can energize the hypothalamo-pituitary-adrenal axis (e.g. Besedovsky & del Rey 1991). This network provides the structural foundation for and (in combination, perhaps) the mediation of various kinds of relevant observation: that lesioning or electric stimulation of areas within the hypothalamus results in alterations in immune function (Felten et al 1991), and peak antibody production is associated with changes in the electrical activity within the hypothalamus (Besedovsky et al 1977); that hypophysectomy and changes in circulating levels of hormones and neurotransmitters can influence immune responses (e.g. Berczi & Nagy 1991; Ader et al 1990), and that immunologic reactions alter circulating levels of hormones and neurotransmitters (e.g. Besedovsky & del Rey 1991); and that behavioral manipulations (e.g. Pavlovian conditioning, stressful stimulation) can, as described above, modulate antigen-specific and nonspecific immune responses, that the physiological effects of products of an activated immune system can be conditioned (Dyck et al 1990), and that immunologic dysregulations have behavioral consequences (Ader et al 1991b).

We cannot yet specify the mechanisms underlying the functional relationship between the nervous system and the immune system—mechanisms illustrated by conditioned and stressor-induced modulations of different components of immunological defenses. In fact, for the most part we cannot yet specify the functional significance of the neuroanatomical, neurochemical, and neuroendocrine connections between the brain and the immune system. Only in recent years, however, has the autonomy of the immune system been seriously questioned. Behavioral research has played a central and enabling role in provoking studies of interactions between the central nervous system and the immune system, and now represents only one of several lines of research that provide converging support for an integrated approach to an understanding of adaptive processes.

SUMMARY

The acquisition and extinction of the conditioned suppression or enhancement of one or another parameter of antigen-specific and nonspecific defense system responses have been documented in different species under a variety of experimental conditions. Similarly, stressful stimulation influences antigen-specific as well as nonspecific reactions. Moreover, both conditioning and stressful stimulation exert biologically meaningful effects in the sense that they can alter the development and/or progression of what are presumed to be immunologically mediated pathophysiologic processes. These are highly reproducible phenomena that illustrate a functional relationship between the brain and the immune system. However, the extent to which one can generalize from one stressor to another or from one parameter of immunologic reactivity to another is limited. Few generalizations are possible because the direction and/or magnitude of the effects of conditioning and "stress" in modulating immune responses clearly depend on the quality and quantity of the behavioral interventions, the quality and quantity of antigenic stimulation, the temporal relationship between behavioral and antigenic stimulation, the nature of the immune response and the immune compartment in which it is measured, the time of sampling, a variety of host factors (e.g. species, strain, age, sex), and interactions among these several variables. It seems reasonable to assume that the immunologic effects of behaviorally induced neural and endocrine responses depend on (interact with) the concurrent immunologic events upon which they are superimposed. Conversely, the efficacy of immunologic defense mechanisms seems to depend on the neuroendocrine environment on which they are superimposed. We seek to determine when and what immunologic (or neuroendocrine) responses could be affected by what neuroendocrine (or immunologic) circumstances. We therefore need studies that provide a parametric analysis of the stimulus conditions, the neuroendocrine and/or immunologic state upon which they are superimposed, and the responses that are being sampled.

The neural or neuroendocrine pathways involved in the behavioral alteration of immune responses are not yet known. Both conditioning and stressor-induced effects have been hypothesized to result from the action of adrenocortical steroids, opioids, and catecholamines, among others. Indeed, all of these have been implicated in the mediation of some immunologic effects observed under some experimental conditions. We assume that different conditioning and stressful environmental circumstances induce different constellations of neuroendocrine responses that constitute the milieu within which ongoing immunologic reactions and the response to immunologic signals occur. Based on the complexity of the network of connections and regulatory feedback loops between the brain and the immune system, these processes appear to involve both neural and endocrine signals to the immune system and signals from the immune system that are received by the nervous system and provoke further neural and endocrine adjustments. Considering the variety of immunologic processes involved, it does not seem likely—or biologically adaptive—that there would be any single mediator of the diverse effects of either conditioning or stressful stimulation. It does not seem likely, however, that the ultimate elaboration of the mechanisms underlying behaviorally induced alterations of immune function will have important clinical and therapeutic implications.

ACKNOWLEDGMENTS

Preparation of this review was supported by a USPHS Research Scientist Award (K05 MH-06318) to R.A.

Literature Cited

Aarstad, H. J., Gaudernack, G., Seljelid, R. 1983. Stress causes reduced natural killer cell activity in mice. *Scand. J. Immunol.* 18:461–64

Ackerman, S. H., Keller, S. E., Schleifer, S. J., Shindledecker, R. D., Camerino, M., et al. 1988. Premature maternal separation and lymphocyte function. *Brain Behav. Immun.* 2:161–65

Ader, R., ed. 1981a. *Psychoneuroimmunology.* New York: Academic

Ader, R. 1981b. A historical account of conditioned immunobiologic responses. See Ader 1981a, pp. 321–54

Ader, R. 1983. Developmental psychoneuroimmunology. *Dev. Psychobiol.* 16:251–67

Ader, R. 1985. Conditioned immunopharmacologic effects in animals: implications for a conditioning model of pharmacotherapy. In *Placebo: Theory, Research, and Mechanisms,* ed. L. White, B. Tursky, G. Schwartz, pp. 306–23. New York: Guilford

Ader, R., Cohen, N. 1975. Behaviorally conditioned immunosuppression. *Psychosom. Med.* 37:333–40

Ader, R., Cohen, N. 1981. Conditioned immunopharmacologic responses. See Ader 1981a, pp. 185–228

Ader, R., Cohen, N. 1982. Behaviorally conditioned immunosuppression and murine systemic lupus erythematosus. *Science* 215:1534–36

Ader, R., Cohen, N. 1985. CNS-immune system interactions: conditioning phenomena. *Behav. Brain Sci.* 8:379–426

Ader, R., Cohen, N. 1991. The influence of conditioning on immune responses. See Ader et al 1991a, pp. 611–46

Ader, R., Cohen, N., Bovbjerg, D. 1982. Conditioned suppression of humoral immunity in the rat. *J. Comp. Physiol. Psychol.* 96:517–21

Ader, R., Cohen, N., Grota, L. J. 1987. Adrenocortical steroids in the conditioned suppression and enhancement of immune responses. In *Hormones and Immunity*, ed. I. Berczi, pp. 231–46. London: MTP

Ader, R., Felten, D. L., Cohen, N. 1990. Interactions between the brain and the immune system. *Annu. Rev. Pharmacol. Toxicol.* 30:561–602

Ader, R., Felten, D. L., Cohen, N. 1991a. *Psychoneuroimmunology.* New York: Academic. 2nd ed.

Ader, R., Grota, L. J., Moynihan, J. A., Cohen, N. 1991b. Behavioral adaptations in autoimmune disease-susceptible mice. See Ader et al 1991a, pp. 685–708

Andrykowski, M. A., Jacobsen, P. B., Marks, E., Gorfinkle, K., Hakes, T. B., et al. 1988. Prevalence, predictors and course of anticipatory nausea in women receiving adjuvant chemotherapy for breast cancer. *Cancer* 62:2607–13

Andrykowski, M. A., Redd, W. H. 1987. Longitudinal analysis of the development of anticipatory nausea. *J. Consult. Clin. Psychol.* 55:36–41

Andrykowski, M. A., Redd, W. H., Hatfield, A. 1985. The development of anticipatory nausea: a prospective analysis. *J. Consult. Clin. Psychol.* 53:447–54

Anisman, H., Irwin, J., Bowers, W., Ahluwalia, P., Zacharko, R. M. 1987. Variations of norepinephrine concentrations following chronic stressor application. *Physiol. Biochem. Behav.* 26:653–59

Batuman, O. A., Sajewski, D., Ottenweller, J. E., Pitman, D. L., Natelson, B. H. 1990. Effects of repeated stress on T cell numbers and function in rats. *Brain Behav. Immun.* 4:105–17

Beden, S. N., Brain, P. F. 1982. Studies on the effect of social stress on measures of disease resistance in laboratory mice. *Aggressive Behav.* 8:126–29

Beden, S. N., Brain, P. F. 1984. Effects of attack-related stress on the primary immune response to sheep red blood cells in castrated mice. *IRCS Med. Sci.* 12:675

Ben-Eliyahu, S., Yirmiya, R., Liebeskind, J. C., Taylor, A. N., Gale, R. P. 1991. Stress increases metastatic spread of a mammary

tumor in rats: evidence for mediation by the immune system. *Brain Behav. Immun.* 5:193–205

Berczi, I., Nagy, E. 1991. Effects of hypophysectomy on immune function. See Ader et al 1991a, pp. 339–75

Besedovsky, H. O., del Rey, A. 1991. Physiological implications of the immune-neuroendocrine network. See Ader et al 1991a, pp. 589–608

Besedovsky, H. O., Sorkin, E., Felix, D., Haas, H. 1977. Hypothalamic changes during the immune response. *Eur. J. Immunol.* 7:323–25

Blalock, J. E. 1988. Production of neuroendocrine peptide hormones by the immune system. Prog. Allergy 43:1–13

Blalock, J. E., ed. 1992. *Neuroimmunoendocrinol. Chem. Immunol.* 52

Blecha, F., Barry, R. A., Kelley, K. W. 1982a. Stress-induced alterations in delayed-type hypersensitivity to SRBC and contact sensitivity to DNFB in mice. *Proc. Soc. Exp. Biol. Med.* 169:239–46

Blecha, F., Kelley, K. W., Satterlee, D. G. 1982b. Adrenal involvement in the expression of delayed-type hypersensitivity to SRBC and contact sensitivity to DNFB in stressed mice. *Proc. Soc. Exp. Biol. Med.* 169:247–52

Bohus, B., Koolhaas, J. M. 1991. Psychoimmunology of social factors in rodents and other subprimate vertebrates. See Ader et al 1991a, pp. 807–30

Bonneau, R. H., Sheridan, J. F., Feng, N., Glaser, R. 1991a. Stress-induced suppression of herpes simplex virus (HSV)-specific cytotoxic T lymphocyte and natural killer cell activity and enhancement of acute pathogenesis following local HSV infection. *Brain Behav. Immun.* 5:170–92

Bonneau, R. H., Sheridan, J. F., Feng, N., Glaser, R. 1991b. Stress-induced effects on cell mediated innate and adaptive memory components of the murine immune response to herpes simplex virus infection. *Brain Behav. Immun.* 5:274–95

Bovbjerg, D., Ader, R., Cohen, N. 1982. Behaviorally conditioned suppression of a graft-vs-host response. *Proc. Natl. Acad. Sci. USA* 79:583–85

Bovbjerg, D., Ader, R., Cohen, N. 1984. Acquisition and extinction of conditioned suppression of a graft-vs-host response in the rat. *J. Immunol.* 132:111–13

Bovbjerg, D., Ader, R., Cohen, N. 1986. Longlasting enhancement of the delayed-type hypersensitivity response to heterologous erythrocytes in mice after a single injection of cyclophosphamide. *Clin. Exp. Immunol.* 66:539–50

Bovbjerg, D., Cohen, N., Ader, R. 1987a. Behaviorally conditioned enhancement of delayed-type hypersensitivity in the mouse. *Brain Behav. Immun.* 1:64–71

Bovbjerg, D., Kim, Y. T., Siskind, G. W., Weksler, M. E. 1987b. Conditioned suppression of plaque-forming cell response with cyclophosphamide. *Ann. NY Acad. Sci.* 496:588–94

Bovbjerg, D. H., Redd, W. H., Maier, L. A., et al. 1990. Anticipatory immune suppression and nausea in women receiving cyclic chemotherapy for ovarian cancer. *J. Consult. Clin. Psychol.* 5:153–57

Brenner, G. J., Cohen, N., Ader, R., Moynihan, J. A. 1990. Increased pulmonary metastases and natural killer cell activity in mice following handling. *Life Sci.* 47:1813–19

Broadbent, D. E., Broadbent, M. H. P., Phillpotts, R., Wallace, J. 1984. Some further studies on the prediction of experimental colds in volunteers by psychological factors. *J. Psychosom. Res.* 28:511–23

Carey, M. P., Burish, T. G. 1988. Etiology and treatment of the psychological side effects associated with cancer chemotherapy: a critical review and discussion. *Psychol. Bull.* 104:307–25

Carr, D. J. J. 1992. Neuroendocrine peptide receptors on cells of the immune system. *Neuroimmunoendocrinol. Chem. Immunol.* 52:84–105

Carr, D. J. J., Wooley, T. W., Blalock, J. E. 1992. Phentolamine but not propranolol blocks the immunopotentiating effect of cold stress on antigen specific IgM production in mice orally immunized with sheep red blood cells. *Brain Behav. Immun.* 6:50–63

Chao, C. C., Peterson, P. K., Filice, G. A., Pomeroy, C., Sharp, B. M. 1990. Effects of immobilization stress on the pathogenesis of acute murine toxoplasmosis. *Brain Behav. Immun.* 4:162–69

Cocke, R., Moynihan, J. A., Cohen, N., Grota, L. J., Ader, R. 1992. Exposure to conspecific alarm chemosignals alters immune responses in BALB/c mice. *Brain Behav. Immun.* 6: In press

Coe, C. L., Lubach, G. R., Ershler, W. B., Klopp, R. G. 1989. Influence of early rearing on lymphocyte proliferation response in juvenile rhesus monkeys. *Brain Behav. Immun.* 3:47–60

Coe, C. L., Rosenberg, L. T., Levine, S. 1988. Effect of maternal separation on the complement system and antibody responses in infant primates. *Int. J. Neurosci.* 40:289–302

Coe, C. L., Weiner, S. G., Rosenberg, L. T., Levine, S. 1985. Endocrine and immune responses to separation and maternal loss in nonhuman primates. In *The Psychobiology of Attachment and Separation,* ed. M. Reite, T. Field, pp. 163–200. New York: Academic

Cohen, N., Ader, R., Green, N., Bovbjerg, D. 1979. Conditioned suppression of a thymus-independent antibody response. *Psychosom. Med.* 41:487–91

Cohen, S., Tyrell, D. A. J., Smith, A. P. 1991. Psychological stress and susceptibility to the common cold. *N. Engl. J. Med.* 325:606–12

Cohen, S., Williamson, G. M. 1991. Stress and infectious disease in humans. *Psychol. Bull.* 109:5–24

Coussons, M. E., Dykstra, L. A., Lysle, D. T. 1992. Pavlovian conditioning of morphine-induced alterations of immune function. *J. Neuroimmunol.* In press

Croiset, G., Heijnen, C. J., Veldhuis, H. D., de Wied, D., Ballieux, R. E. 1987. Modulation of the immune response by emotional stress. *Life Sci.* 40:775–82

Cunnick, J. E., Cohen, S., Rabin, B. S., Carpenter, A. B., Manuck, S. B., Kaplan, J. R. 1991. Alterations in specific antibody production due to rank and social instability. *Brain Behav. Immun.* 5:357–69

Cunnick, J. E., Lysle, D. T., Armfield, A., Rabin, B. S. 1988. Shock-induced modulation of lymphocyte responsiveness and natural killer activity: differential mechanisms of induction. *Brain Behav. Immun.* 2:102–13

Cunnick, J. E., Lysle, D. T., Kucinski, B. J., Rabin, B. 1990. Evidence that shock-induced suppression is mediated by adrenal hormones and peripheral β-adrenergic receptors. *Pharmacol. Biochem. Behav.* 36:645–51

Dark, K., Peeke, H. V. S., Ellman, G., Salfi, M. 1987. Behaviorally conditioned histamine release. *Ann. NY Acad. Sci.* 496:578–82

Dekker, E., Pelser, H. E., Groen, J. 1957. Conditioning as a cause of asthmatic attacks. *J. Psychosom. Res.* 2:97–108

Drugan, R. C., Mandler, R., Crawley, J. N., Skolnick, P., Barker, J. L., et al. 1986. Conditioned fear induced rapid immunosuppression in the rat. *Neurosci. Abstr.* 12:337

Dyck, D. G., Driedger, S. M., Nemeth, R., Osachuk, T. A. G., Greenberg, A. H. 1987. Conditioned tolerance to drug-induced (Poly I:C) natural killer cell activation: effects of drug-dosage and context-specificity parameters. *Brain Behav. Immun.* 1:251–66

Dyck, D. G., Greenberg, A. H., Osachuk, T. 1986. Tolerance to drug-induced (Poly I:C) natural killer (NK) cell activation: congruence with a Pavlovian conditioning model. *J. Exp. Psychol. Anim. Behav. Proc.* 12:25–31

Dyck, D. G., Janz, L., Osachuk, T. A. G., Falk, J., Labinsky, J., Greenberg, A. H. 1990. The Pavlovian conditioning of IL-1-induced glucocorticoid secretion. *Brain Behav. Immun.* 4:93–104

Edwards, E. A., Dean, L. M. 1977. Effects of crowding of mice on humoral antibody formation and protection to lethal antigenic challenge. *Psychosom. Med.* 39:19–24

Edwards, E. A., Rahe, R. H., Stephens, P. M., Henry, J. P. 1980. Antibody response to bovine serum albumin in mice: the effects of psychosocial environmental change. *Proc. Soc. Exp. Biol. Med.* 164:478–81

Eikelboom, R., Stewart, J. 1982. Conditioning of drug-induced physiological responses. *Psychol. Rev.* 89:507–28

Esterling, B., Rabin, B. S. 1987. Stress-induced alteration of T-lymphocyte subsets and humoral immunity in mice. *Behav. Neurosci.* 101:115–19

Faisal, M., Chiapelli, F., Ahmed, I. I., Cooper, E. L., Weiner, H. 1989. Social confrontation "stress" in aggressive fish is associated with an endogenous opioid-mediated suppression of proliferative responses to mitogens and nonspecific cytotoxicity. *Brain Behav. Immun.* 3:223–33

Fauman, M. A. 1987. The relation of dominant and submissive behavior to the humoral immune response in BALB/c mice. *Biol. Psychiatry* 22:771–76

Felten, D. L., Ackerman, K. D., Wiegand, S. J., Felten, S. Y. 1987. Noradrenergic sympathetic innervation of the spleen: I. Nerve fibers associate with lymphocytes and macrophages in specific compartments of the splenic white pulp. *J. Neurosci. Res.* 18:28–36

Felten, D. L., Cohen, N., Ader, R., Felten, S. Y., Carlson, S. L., Roszman, T. 1991. Central neural circuits involved in neural-immune interactions. See Ader et al 1991a, pp. 3–25

Felten, S. Y., Felten, D. L. 1991. Innervation of lymphoid tissue. See Ader et al 1991a, pp. 27–69

Feng, N., Pagniano, R., Tovar, A., Bonneau, R. H., Glaser, R., Sheridan, J. F. 1991. The effect of restraint stress on the kinetics, magnitude, and isotype of the humoral immune response to influenza virus infection. *Brain Behav. Immun.* 5:370–82

Fleshner, M., Laudenslager, M. L., Simons, L., Maier, S. F. 1989. Reduced serum antibodies associated with social defeat in rats. *Physiol. Behav.* 45:1183–87

Friedman, E. M., Coe, C. L., Ershler, W. B. 1991. Time-dependent effects of peer separation on lymphocyte proliferation response in juvenile squirrel monkeys. *Dev. Psychobiol.* 24:159–73

Friedman, S. B., Ader, R., Glasgow, L. A. 1965. Effects of psychological stress in adult mice inoculated with Coxsackie B viruses. *Psychosom. Med.* 27:361–68

Friedman, S. B., Glasgow, L. A., Ader, R. 1969. Psychosocial factors modifying host resistance to experimental infections. *Ann. NY Acad. Sci.* 164:381–92

Geiser, D. S. 1989. Psychosocial influences on human immunity. *Clin. Psychol. Rev.* 9:689–715

Ghoneum, M., Faisal, M., Peters, G., Ahmed, I. I., Cooper, E. L. 1988. Suppression of natural cytotoxic cell activity by social aggressiveness in *Tilapia. Dev. Comp. Immunol.* 12:595–602

Ghoneum, M., Gill, G., Assanah, P., Stevens, W. 1987. Susceptibility of natural killer cell activity of old rats to stress. *Immunology* 60:461–65

Gill, H. K., Liew, F. Y. 1978. Regulation of delayed-type hypersensitivity. III. Effects of cyclophosphamide on the suppressor cells for delayed-type hypersensitivity to sheep erythrocytes in mice. *Eur. J. Immunol.* 8:172–76

Glaser, R., Rice, J., Sheridan, J., Fertel, R., Stout, J., et al. 1987. Stress-related immune suppression: health implications. *Brain Behav. Immun.* 1:7–20

Glaser, R., Rice, J., Speicher, C. E., Stout, J. C., Kiecolt-Glaser, J. K. 1986. Stress depresses interferon production by leukocytes concomitant with a decrease in natural killer cell activity. *Behav. Neurosci.* 100:675–78

Glenn, W. G., Becker, R. E. 1969. Individual versus group housing in mice: immunological response to time-phased injections. *Physiol. Zool.* 42:411–16

Gorczynski, R. M. 1987. Analysis of lymphocytes in, and host environment of, mice showing conditioned immunosuppression to cyclophosphamide. *Brain Behav. Immun.* 1:21–35

Gorczynski, R. M. 1990. Conditioned enhancement of skin allografts in mice. *Brain Behav. Immun.* 4:85–92

Gorczynski, R. M. 1991. Conditioned immunosuppression: analysis of lymphocytes and host environment of young and aged mice. See Ader et al 1991a, pp. 647–62

Gorczynski, R. M. 1992. Conditioned stress responses by pregnant and/or lactating mice reduce immune responses of their offspring after weaning. *Brain Behav. Immun.* 6:87–95

Gorczynski, R. M., Holmes, W. 1989. Neuroleptic and anti-depressant drug treatment abolishes conditioned immunosuppression in mice. *Brain Behav. Immun.* 3:312–19

Gorczynski, R. M., Kennedy, M., Ciampi, A. 1985. Cimetidine reverses tumor growth enhancement of plasmacytoma tumors in mice demonstrating conditioned immunosuppression. *J. Immunol.* 134:4261–66

Gorczynski, R. M., Macrae, S., Kennedy, M. 1982. Conditioned immune response associated with allogeneic skin grafts in mice. *J. Immunol.* 129:704–9

Gorczynski, R. M., Macrae, S., Kennedy, M. 1984. Factors involved in the classical conditioning of antibody responses in mice. In *Breakdown in Human Adaptation to "Stress:" Towards a Multidisciplinary Approach*, ed. R. E. Ballieux, J. F. Fielding, A. L'Abbate, pp. 704–12. Hingham, MA: Martinus Nijhof

Greenberg, A. H., Dyck, D. G., Sandler, L. S.,

Pohajdak, B., Dresel, K. M., Grant, D. 1984. Neurohormonal modulation of natural resistance to a murine lymphoma. *J. Natl. Cancer Inst.* 72:653–59

Grochowicz, P., Schedlowski, M., Husband, A. J., King, M. G., Hibberd, A. D., Bowen, K. M. 1991. Behavioral conditioning prolongs heart allograft survival in rats. *Brain Behav. Immun.* 5:349–56

Guilian, D., Baker, T. J., Shih, L.-C. N., Lachman, L. B. 1986. Interleukin-1 of the central nervous system is produced by ameboid microglia. *J. Exp. Med.* 164:594–604

Gust, D. A., Gordon, T. P., Wilson, M. E., Brodie, A. R., Ahmed-Ansari, A., McClure, H. M. 1992. Removal from natal social group to peer housing affects cortisol levels and absolute numbers of T cell subsets in juvenile rhesus monkeys. *Brain Behav. Immun.* 6:189–99

Hardy, C., Quay, J., Livnat, S., Ader, R. 1990. Altered T lymphocyte response following aggressive encounters in mice. *Physiol. Behav.* 47:1245–51

Hill, L. E. 1930. *Philosophy of a Biologist.* London: Arnold

Hiramoto, R. N., Hiramoto, N. S., Solvason, H. B., Ghanta, V. K. 1987. Regulation of natural immunity (NK activity) by conditioning. *Ann. NY Acad. Sci.* 496:545–52

Hull, C. L. 1934. The factor of conditioned reflex. In *A Handbook of General Experimental Psychology,* ed. C. Murchison. Worcester: Clark Univ.

Husband, A. J., King, M. G., Brown, R. 1987. Behaviorally conditioned modification of T cell subset ratios in rats. *Immunol. Lett.* 14:91–94

Ikemi, Y., Nakagawa, S. 1962. A psychosomatic study of contagious dermatitis. *Kyushu J. Med. Sci.* 13:335–50

Ito, Y., Mine, K., Ago, Y., Nakagawa, T., Fujiwara, M., Ueki, S. 1983. Attack stress and IgE antibody response in rats. *Pharmacol. Biochem. Behav.* 19:883–86

Irwin, J., Custeau, N. 1989. Stressor predictability and immune function. *Soc. Neurosci. Abstr.* 15:298

Jessop, J. J., Gale, K., Bayer, B. M. 1987. Enhancement of rat lymphocyte proliferation after prolonged exposure to stress. *J. Neuroimmunol.* 16:261–71

Jessop, J. J., Gale, K., Bayer, B. M. 1988. Time-dependent enhancement of lymphocyte activation by mitogens after exposure to isolation or water scheduling. *Life Sci.* 43:1133–40

Jiang, C. G., Morrow-Tesch, J. L., Beller, D. S., Levy, E. M., Black, P. H. 1990. Immunosuppression in mice induced by cold water stress. *Brain Behav. Immun.* 4:278–91

Justice, A. 1985. Review of the effects of stress on cancer in laboratory animals: importance of time of stress application and type of tumor. *Psychol. Bull.* 98:108–38

Kandil, O., Borysenko, M. 1988. Stress-induced decline in immune responsiveness in C3H/HeJ mice: relation to endocrine alterations and tumor growth. *Brain Behav. Immun.* 2:32–49

Kaplan, R., Robinson, C. A., Scavulli, J. F., Vaughan, J. H. 1980. Propranolol and the treatment of rheumatoid arthritis. *Arthritis Rheum.* 23:253–55

Keller, S. E., Schleifer, S. J., Liotta, A. S., Bond, R. N., Farhoody, N., Stein, M. 1988. Stress-induced alterations of immunity in hypophysectomized rats. *Proc. Natl. Acad. Sci. USA* 85:9297–9301

Keller, S. E., Weiss, J. M., Schleifer, S. J., Miller, N. E., Stein, M. 1981. Suppression of immunity by stress: effects of a graded series of stressors on lymphocyte stimulation in the rat. *Science* 213:1397–400

Keller, S. E., Weiss, J. M., Schleifer, S. J., Miller, N. E., Stein, M. 1983. Stress-induced suppression of immunity in adrenalectomized rats. *Science* 221:1301–4

Kemeny, M. E., Solomon, G. F., Morley, J. E., Bennett, T. L. 1992. Psychoneuroimmunology. In *A Comprehensive Textbook of Neuroendocrinology,* ed. C. B. Nemeroff. In press

Khan, A. U. 1977. Effectiveness of biofeedback and counterconditioning in the treatment of bronchial asthma. *J. Psychosom. Res.* 21:97–104

King, M. G., Husband, A. J., Kusnecov, A. W. 1987. Behaviourally conditioned immunosuppression using anti-lymphocyte serum: duration of effect and role of corticosteroids. *Med. Sci. Res.* 15:407–8

Klosterhalfen, S., Klosterhalfen, W. 1987. Classically conditioned cyclophosphamide effects on white blood cell counts in rats. *Ann. NY Acad. Sci.* 496:569–77

Klosterhalfen, S., Klosterhalfen, W. 1990. Conditioned cyclosporine effects but not conditioned taste aversion in immunized rats. *Behav. Neurosci.* 104:716–24

Klosterhalfen, W., Klosterhalfen, S. 1983. Pavlovian conditioning of immunosuppression modifies adjuvant arthritis in rats. *Behav. Neurosci.* 97:663–66

Kopeloff, N. 1941. *Bacteriology in Neuropsychiatry.* Springfield: Charles C Thomas

Krank, M. D., MacQueen, G. M. 1988. Conditioned compensatory responses elicited by environmental signals for cyclophosphamide-induced suppression of antibody production in mice. *Psychobiology* 16:229–35

Kusnecov, A. V., Grota, L. J., Schmidt, S. G., Bonneau, R. H., Sheridan, J. F., et al. 1992. Decreased herpes simplex viral immunity and enhanced pathogenesis following stressor administration in mice. *J. Neuroimmunol.* 38:129–38

Kusnecov, A. V., Husband, A. J., King, M. G. 1988. Behaviorally conditioned suppression of mitogen-induced proliferation and immunoglobulin production: effect of time span between conditioning and reexposure to the conditioned stimulus. *Brain Behav. Immun.* 2:198–211

Kusnecov, A. V., Sivyer, M., King, M. G., Husband, A. J., Cripps, A. W., Clancy, R. L. 1983. Behaviorally conditioned suppression of the immune response by antilymphocyte serum. *J. Immunol.* 130:2117–20

Laudenslager, M. L., Capitanio, J. P., Reite, M. 1985. Possible effects of early separation experiences on subsequent immune function in adult macaque monkeys. *Am. J. Psychiatry* 142:862–64

Laudenslager, M. L., Fleshner, M., Hofstadter, P., Held, P. E., Simons, L., Maier, S. F. 1988. Suppression of specific antibody production by inescapable shock: stability under varying conditions. *Brain Behav. Immun.* 2:92–101

Laudenslager, M. L., Held, P. E., Boccia, M. L., Reite, M. L., Cohen, J. J. 1990. Behavioral and immunological consequences of brief mother-infant separation: a species comparison. *Dev. Psychobiol.* 23:247–64

Laudenslager, M. L., Ryan, S. M., Drugan, R. C., Hyson, R. L., Maier, S. F. 1983. Coping and immunosuppression: Inescapable but not escapable shock suppresses lymphocyte proliferation. *Science* 221:568–70

Levine, S., Strebel, R., Wenk, E. J., Harman, P. J. 1962. Suppression of experimental allergic encephalomyelitis by stress. *Proc. Soc. Exp. Biol. Med.* 109:294–98

Livnat, S., Irwin, J., Ader, R., Gallo, K. L., Anisman, H. 1985. Immunologic reactivity following acute and chronic stress. *Soc. Neurosci. Abstr.* 11:861

Lown, B. A., Dutka, M. E. 1987. Early handling enhances mitogen responses of splenic cells in adult C3H mice. *Brain Behav. Immun.* 1:356–60

Luecken, L. J., Lysle, D. T. 1992. Evidence for the involvement of beta-adrenergic receptors in conditioned immunomodulation. *J. Neuroimmunol.* In press

Lysle, D. T., Cunnick, J. E., Fowler, H., Rabin, B. S. 1988. Pavlovian conditioning of shock-induced suppression of lymphocyte reactivity: acquisition, extinction, and preexposure effects. *Life Sci.* 42:2185–94

Lysle, D. T., Cunnick, J. E., Kucinski, B. J., Fowler, H., Rabin, B. S. 1990a. Characterization of immune alterations induced by a conditioned aversive stimulus. *Psychobiology* 18:220–26

Lysle, D. T., Cunnick, J. E., Rabin, B. S. 1990b. Stressor-induced alteration of lymphocyte proliferation in mice: evidence for enhancement of mitogen responsiveness. *Brain Behav. Immun.* 4:269–77

Lysle, D. T., Luecken, L. J., Maslonek, K. A. 1992a. Suppression of the development of adjuvant arthritis by a conditioned aversive stimulus. *Brain Behav. Immun.* 6:64–73

Lysle, D. T., Luecken, L. J., Maslonek, K. A. 1992b. Modulation of immune function by a conditioned aversive stimulus: evidence for the involvement of endogenous opioids. *Brain Behav. Immun.* 6:179–88

Lysle, D. T., Lyte, M., Fowler, H., Rabin, B. S. 1987. Shock-induced modulation of lymphocyte reactivity: suppression, habituation, and recovery. *Life Sci.* 41:1805–14

Lysle, D. T., Maslonek, K. A. 1991. Immune alterations induced by a conditioned aversive stimulus: evidence for a time-dependent effect. *Psychobiology* 19:339–44

Mackenzie, J. N. 1896. The production of the so-called "rose cold" by means of an artificial rose. *Am. J. Med. Sci.* 91:45–57

MacQueen, G. M., Marshall, J., Perdue, M., Siegel, S., Bienenstock, J. 1989. Pavlovian conditioning of rat mucosal mast cells to secrete rat mast cell protease II. *Science* 243:83–85

MacQueen, G. M., Siegel, S. 1989. Conditional immunomodulation following training with cyclophosphamide. *Behav. Neurosci.* 103:638–47

Maier, S. F., Laudenslager, M. L. 1988. Inescapable shock, shock controllability, and mitogen-stimulated lymphocyte proliferation. *Brain Behav. Immun.* 2:87–91

Metal'nikov, S., Chorine, V. 1926. Rôle des réflexes conditionnels dans l'immunité. *Ann. L'Inst. Pasteur* 40:893–900

Metal'nikov, S., Chorine, V. 1928. Rôle des réflexes conditionnels dans la formation des anticorps. *C. R. Soc. Biol.* 102:133–34

Michaut, R.-J., Dechambre, R.-P., Doumerc, S., Lesourd, B., Devillechabrolle, A., Moulias, R. 1981. Influence of early maternal deprivation on adult humoral immune response in mice. *Physiol. Behav.* 26:189–91

Mitsuoka, A., Morikawa, S., Baba, M., Harada, T. 1979. Cyclophosphamide eliminates suppressor T cells in age-associated central regulation of delayed hypersensitivity in mice. *J. Exp. Med.* 149:1018–28

Monjan, A. A., Collector, M. I. 1977. Stress-induced modulation of the immune response. *Science* 196:307–8

Mormede, P., Dantzer, R., Michaud, B., Kelley, K., Le Moal, M. 1988. Influence of stressor predictability and behavioral control on lymphocyte reactivity, antibody responses, and neuroendocrine activation in rats. *Physiol. Behav.* 43:577–83

Morrow, G. R., Dobkin, P. L. 1988. Anticipatory nausea and vomiting in cancer patients undergoing chemotherapy treatment: prevalence, etiology and behavioral interventions. *Clin. Psychol. Rev.* 8:517–56

Moynihan, J. A., Ader, R., Grota, L. J., Schachtman, T. R., Cohen, N. 1990a. The effects of stress on the development of immunological memory following low-dose antigen priming in mice. *Brain Behav. Immun.* 4:1–12

Moynihan, J., Brenner, G., Koota, D., Breneman, S., Cohen, N., Ader, R. 1990b. The effects of handling on antibody production, mitogen responses, spleen cell number, and lymphocyte subpopulations. *Life Sci.* 46:1937–44

Moynihan, J., Koota, D., Brenner, G., Cohen, N., Ader, R. 1989. Repeated intraperitoneal injections of saline attenuate the antibody response to a subsequent intraperitoneal injection of antigen. *Brain Behav. Immun.* 3:90–96

Munck, A., Guyre, P. M. 1991. Glucocorticoids and immune function. See Ader et al 1991a, pp. 447–513

Neveu, P. J., Crestani, F., Le Moal, M. 1987. Conditioned immunosuppression: a new methodological approach. *Ann. NY Acad. Sci.* 496:595–601

Neveu, P. J., Dantzer, R., Le Moal, M. 1986. Behaviorally conditioned suppression of mitogen-induced lymphoproliferation and antibody production in mice. *Neurosci. Lett.* 65:293–98

Odio, M., Brodish, A., Ricardo, M. J. 1987. Effects on immune responses by chronic stress are modulated by aging. *Brain Behav. Immun.* 1:204–15

O'Grady, M. P., Hall, N. R. S. 1991. Long-term effects of neuroendocrine-immune interactions during early development. See Ader et al 1991a, pp. 561–72

Okimura, T., Nigo, Y. 1986. Stress and immune responses I. Suppression of T cell functions in restraint-stressed mice. *Jpn. J. Pharmacol.* 40:505–11

Okimura, T., Ogawa, M., Yamauchi, T. 1986a. Stress and immune responses III. Effect of restraint stress on delayed type hypersensitivity (DTH) response, natural killer (NK) activity, and phagocytosis in mice. *Jpn. J. Pharmacol.* 41:229–35

Okimura, T., Ogawa, M., Yamauchi, T., Satomi-Sasaki, Y. 1986b. Stress and immune responses IV. Adrenal involvement in the alteration of antibody responses in restraint-stressed mice. *Jpn. J. Pharmacol.* 41:237–45

Okimura, T., Satomi-Sasaki, Y., Ohkuma, S. 1986c. Stress and immune responses II. Identification of stress-sensitive cells in murine spleen cells. *Jpn. J. Pharmacol.* 40:513–25

O'Leary, A. 1990. Stress, emotion, and human immune function. *Psychol. Bull.* 108:363–82

O'Reilly, C. A., Exon, J. H. 1986. Cyclophosphamide-conditioned suppression of the natural killer cell response in rats. *Physiol. Behav.* 37:759–64

Ottenberg, P., Stein, M., Lewis, J., Hamilton, C. 1958. Learned asthma in the guinea pig. *Psychosom. Med.* 20:395–400

Pavlidis, N., Chirigos, M. 1980. Stress-induced impairment of macrophage tumoricidal function. *Psychosom. Med.* 42:47–54

Peeke, H. V. S., Ellman, G., Dark, K., Salfi, M., Reus, V. I. 1987. Cortisol and behaviorally conditioned histamine release. *Ann. NY Acad. Sci.* 496:583–87

Plaut, S. M., Esterhay, R. J., Sutherland, J. C., Wareheim, L. E., Friedman, S. B., et al. 1981. Psychological effects on resistance to spontaneous AKR leukemia in mice. *Psychosom. Med.* 42:72

Qunidos, G., Ruis de Gordioa, J. C., Burgos, A., Ponton, J., Cisterna, R. 1986. Fasting and immobilization stress cause a decrease in phagocytosis in male rats. *Arch. Immunol. Ther. Exp.* 34:573–76

Raab, A., Dantzer, R., Michaud, B., Mormede, P., Taghzouti, K., et al. 1986. Behavioral, physiological, and immunological consequences of social status and aggression in chronically coexisting resident-intruder dyads of male rats. *Physiol. Behav.* 36:223–28

Rabin, B. S., Lyte, M., Epstein, L. H., Caggiula, A. R. 1987a. Alteration of immune competency by number of mice housed per cage. *Ann. NY Acad. Sci.* 469:492–500

Rabin, B. S., Lyte, M., Hamill, E. 1987b. The influence of mouse strain and housing on the immune response. *J. Neuroimmunol.* 17:11–16

Rabin, B. S., Salvin, S. B. 1987. Effect of differential housing and time on immune reactivity to sheep erythrocytes and *Candida*. *Brain Behav. Immun.* 1:267–75

Rasmussen, A. F. Jr., Marsh, J. T., Brill, N. Q. 1957. Increased susceptibility to herpes simplex in mice subjected to avoidance-learning stress or restraint. *Proc. Soc. Exp. Biol. Med.* 96:183–89

Raymond, L. N., Reyes, E., Tokuda, S., Jones, B. C. 1986. Differential immune response in two handled inbred strains of mice. *Physiol. Behav.* 37:295–97

Redd, W. H., Andrykowski, M. A. 1982. Behavioral interventions in cancer treatment: controlling aversive reactions to chemotherapy. *J. Consult. Clin. Psychol.* 50:1018–29

Rinner, I., Schauenstein, K., Mangge, H., Porta, S. 1992. Opposite effects of mild and severe stress on in vitro activation of rat peripheral blood lymphocytes. *Brain Behav. Immun.* 6:130–40

Rodinone, S. N., Giovanniello, O. A., Barrios, H. A., Nota, N. R. 1983. Effect of fractional cyclophosphamide dosage on sheep red blood cell-delayed-type hypersensitivity response in mice. *J. Immunol.* 1130:1600–3

Rogers, M. P., Reich, P., Strom, T. B., Carpenter, C. B. 1976. Behaviorally conditioned immunosuppression: replication of a recent study. *Psychosom. Med.* 38:447–52

Rogers, M. P., Trentham, D. E., Dynesius, R. A., Reich, P., David, J. R. 1980a. Exacerbation of type II collagen-induced arthritis by auditory stress. *Clin. Res.* 28:508

Rogers, M. P., Trentham, D. E., McCune, W. J., Ginsberg, B. I., Rennke, H. G., et al. 1980b. Effect of psychological stress on the induction of arthritis in rats. *Arthritis Rheum.* 23:1337–42

Roudebush, R. E., Bryant, H. U. 1991. Conditioned immunosuppression of a murine delayed type hypersensitivity response: dissociation from corticosterone elevation. *Brain Behav. Immun.* 5:308–17

Russell, M., Dark, K. A., Cummins, R. W., Ellman, G., Callaway, E., Peeke, H. V. S. 1984. Learned histamine release. *Science* 225:733–34

Sato, K., Flood, J. F., Makinodan, T. 1984. Influence of conditioned psychological stress on immunological recovery in mice exposed to low-dose x-irradiation. *Radiat. Res.* 98:381–88

Schulze, G. E., Benson, R. W., Paule, M. G., Roberts, D. W. 1988. Behaviorally conditioned suppression of murine T-cell dependent but not T-cell independent antibody responses. *Pharmacol. Biochem. Behav.* 30:859–65

Seifter, E., Rettura, G., Zisblatt, M., Levinson, S., Levine, N., et al. 1973. Enhancement of tumor development in physically stressed mice incubated with an oncogenic virus. *Experientia* 29:1379–82

Shavit, Y., Lewis, J. W., Terman, G. W., Gale, R. P., Liebeskind, J. C. 1984. Opioid peptides mediate the suppressive effect of stress on natural killer cell cytotoxicity. *Science* 223:188–90

Shavit, Y., Ryan, S. M., Lewis, J. W., Laudenslager, M. L., Terman, G. W., et al. 1983. Inescapable but not escapable stress alters immune function. *Physiologist* 26:A64

Shavit, Y., Terman, G. W., Lewis, J. W., Zane, C. J., Gale, R. P., Liebeskind, J. C. 1986. Effects of footshock stress and morphine on natural killer lymphocytes in rats: studies of tolerance and cross-tolerance. *Brain Res.* 372:382–85

Sieber, W. J., Rodin, J., Larson, L., Ortega, S., Cummings, N. et al. 1992. Modulation of human natural killer cell activity by exposure to uncontrollable stress. *Brain Behav. Immun.* 6:141–56

Siegel, S. 1976. Morphine analgesia tolerance: Its situation specificity supports a Pavlovian model. *Science* 193:323–25

Siegel, S. 1983. Classical conditioning, drug tolerance, and drug dependence. In *Research Advances in Alcohol and Drug Problems,* ed. Y. Israel, F. B. Gaser, H. Kalant, R. E. Popham, W. Schmidt, R. G. Smart, pp. 207–46. New York: Plenum

Sklar, L. S., Anisman, H. 1981. Stress and cancer. *Psychol. Bull.* 89:369–406

Smith, G. H., Salinger, R. 1933. Hypersensi-

tiveness and the conditioned reflex. *Yale J. Biol. Med.* 5:387–402

Smith, G. R., McDaniels, S. M. 1983. Psychologically mediated effect on the delayed hypersensitivity reaction to tuberculin in humans. *Psychosom. Med.* 45:65–70

Solomon, G. F. 1969. Stress and antibody response in rats. *Int. Arch. Allergy* 35:97–104

Solomon, G. F., Amkraut, A. A., Kasper, P. 1974. Immunity, emotions and stress. *Ann. Clin. Res.* 6:313–22

Solomon, G. F., Levine, S., Kraft, J. K. 1968. Early experience and immunity. *Nature* 220:821–22

Solvason, H. B., Ghanta, V. K., Hiramoto, R. N. 1988. Conditioned augmentation of natural killer cell activity. Independence from nociceptive effects and dependence on interferon-β. *J. Immunol.* 140:661–65

Solvason, H. B., Ghanta, V., Soong, S.-J., Hiramoto, R. N. 1991. Interferon interaction with the CNS is required for the conditioning of the NK cell response. *Prog. Neuroendocrinimmunol.* 4:258–64

Solvason, H. B., Hiramoto, R. N., Ghanta, V. K. 1989. Naltrexone blocks the expression of the conditioned elevation of natural killer cell activity in BALB/c mice. *Brain Behav. Immun.* 3:247–62

Sonnenfeld, G., Cunnick, J. E., Armfield, A. V., Wood, P. G., Rabin, B. S. 1992. Stress-induced alterations in interferon production and class II histocompatibility antigen expression. *Brain Behav. Immun.* 6:170–78

Steplewski, Z., Vogel, W. H. 1986. Total leukocytes, T cell subpopulation, and natural killer (NK) cell activity in rats exposed to restraint stress. *Life Sci.* 38:2419–27

Steplewski, Z., Vogel, W. H., Ehya, H., Poropatich, C., Smith, J. M. 1985. Effects of restraint stress on inoculated tumor growth and immune response in rats. *Cancer Res.* 45:5128–33

Stites, D. P., Terr, A. I. 1991. *Basic and Clinical Immunology.* Norwalk, CT: Appleton & Lange

Taylor, C. E., Ross, L. L. 1989. Alteration of antibody response to pneumococcal polysaccharide type III in rats by neonatal immobilization stress. *Brain Behav. Immun.* 3:160–70

Totman, R., Kiff, J., Reed, S. E., Craig, J. W. 1980. Predicting experimental colds in volunteers from different measures of recent life stress. *J. Psychosom. Res.* 24:155–63

Turk, J. L., Parker, D. 1982. The effect of cyclophosphamide on immunological control mechanisms. *Immunol. Rev.* 65:99–113

Vessey, S. H. 1964. Effects of grouping on levels of circulating antibodies in mice. *Proc. Soc. Exp. Biol. Med.* 115:252–55

Wayner, E. A., Flannery, G. R., Singer, G. 1978. The effects of taste aversion conditioning on the primary antibody response to sheep red blood cells and *Brucella abor-*

tus in the albino rat. *Physiol. Behav.* 21:995–1000

Weiner, H. 1977. *Psychobiology and Human Disease.* New York: Elsevier

Weiner, H. 1991. Social and psychobiological factors in autoimmune disease. See Ader et al 1991a, pp. 955–1011

Weiss, J. M., Sundar, S. K., Becker, K. J. 1989a. Stress-induced immunosuppression and immunoenhancement: cellular changes and mechanisms. In *Neuroimmune Networks: Physiology and Disease,* ed. E. J. Goetzl, N. H. Spector, pp. 193–206. New York: Liss

Weiss, J. M., Sundar, S. K., Becker, K. J., Cierpial, M. A. 1989b. Behavioral and neural influences on cellular immune responses: effects of stress and interleukin-1. *J. Clin. Psychiat.* 50:43–53

Weisse, C. S., Pato, C. N., McAllister, C. G., Littman, R., Breier, A., et al. 1990. Differential effects of controllable and uncontrollable acute stress on lymphocyte proliferation and leukocyte percentages in humans. *Brain Behav. Immun.* 4:339–51

Wistar, R. T., Hildemann, W. H. 1960. Effect of stress on skin transplantation immunity in mice. *Science* 131:159–60

Zacharko, R. M., Anisman, H. 1988. Pharmacological, biochemical and behavioral analyses of depression: animal models. In *Animal Models of Affective Disorders,* ed. G. Koob, C. L. Ehlers, D. J. Kupfer, pp. 204–38. Chicago: Univ. Chicago Press

Zalcman, S., Irwin, J., Anisman, H. 1991a. Stressor-induced alterations of natural killer cell activity and central catecholamines in mice. *Pharmacol. Biochem. Behav.* 39:361–66

Zalcman, S., Kerr, L., Anisman, H. 1991b. Immunosuppression elicited by stressors and stressor-related odors. *Brain Behav. Immun.* 5:262–73

Zalcman, S., Minkiewicz-Janda, A., Richter, M., Anisman, H. 1988. Critical periods associated with stressor effects on antibody titers and on the plaque-forming cell response to sheep red blood cells. *Brain Behav. Immun.* 2:254–66

Zalcman, S., Richter, M., Anisman, H. 1989. Alterations of immune functioning following exposure to stressor-related cues. *Brain Behav. Immun.* 3:99–109

Zha, H., Ding, G., Fan, S. 1992. Serum factors induced by restraint stress in mice and rats suppresses lymphocyte proliferation. *Brain Behav. Immun.* 6:18–31

Zwilling, B. S., Brown, D., Christner, R., Faris, M., Hilberger, M., et al. 1990. Differential effect of restraint stress on MHC class II expression by murine peritoneal macrophages. *Brain Behav. Immun.* 4:330–38

Annu. Rev. Psychol. 1993. 44:87–116

PSYCHOLOGY IN CHINA: A Review Dedicated to Li Chen

Zhong-Ming Wang

Department of Psychology, Hangzhou University, Hangzhou 310028, People's Republic of China

KEYWORDS: cross-cultural psychology, developing country, China

CONTENTS

CULTURAL AND HISTORICAL BACKGROUND 87
   Psychological Thinking and Practice in Ancient China 88
   The Development of Psychology in China 89
PROFESSIONAL ORGANIZATIONS AND PSYCHOLOGY TRAINING PROGRAMS ... 91
   Professional Associations and Journals 91
   Research Institutes and Training Programs 92
SOME RECENT PSYCHOLOGICAL RESEARCH AND APPLICATIONS 94
   Experimental Psychology and Physiological Psychology 94
   Psychological Testing and Measurement 96
   Developmental Psychology 97
   Educational and School Psychology 100
   Managerial Psychology 102
   Engineering Psychology 104
   Medical and Clinical Psychology 105
   Social and Sports Psychology 106
   Cross-Cultural Psychology 106
PSYCHOLOGY IN TAIWAN AND HONG KONG 108
CONCLUSIONS AND NEW DIRECTIONS 109

CULTURAL AND HISTORICAL BACKGROUND

In the last decade, psychology has made rapid progress in China under the momentum of recent Chinese economic reform and open-to-the-world policy. Around ten years ago, several excellent review articles about Chinese psychology were published at home (Lin Z. X. & Fang Z. 1980; Kuang P. Z. et al

87

0066-4308/93/0201-0087$02.00

1980; Executive Committee of Chinese Psychological Society 1982) and abroad (Brown 1981; Ching C. C. 1980, 1984) that summarized the short history and development of psychology and suggested future trends in various areas of the discipline in China. Chinese psychologists are now taking an active part in teaching, research, and applications of psychology. Some Chinese models of psychology have emerged, and psychological principles have been applied to education, management, technological innovations, medical care, and social life. In this chapter, I briefly summarize the historical development of psychology in China and then focus on some current psychological research closely linked to the Chinese cultural and social context.

Psychological Thinking and Practice in Ancient China

The early influence of Chinese culture on world psychology has been recognized in the psychological literature (e.g. Murphy & Kovach 1972). The study and discussion of psychological issues have had a long history in China. Ancient Chinese literature offers a rich body of psychological insights applied to work situations and daily life. The modern study of psychology in China is rooted in this tradition.

HUMAN NATURE AND KNOWLEDGE   Ancient Chinese society treasured the human factor. Confucius (551–479 BC) proposed a common heritage of human nature upon which personal development and mental change could be based through education. According to Confucius, intelligence had four aspects: a cognitive state, an attitude, an ability, and a liquidity of thinking. In discussing the relationship between knowledge (cognition) and action, Xuncius (298–238 BC) argued for a kind of consistency or interdependence between knowledge and action. Liu Z. (1660–1730), a minority scholar, examined the brain functions and hypothesized the corresponding parts of the brain for mental activities such as thinking, judgment, recognition, and remembering (Pan S. & Gao J. F. 1983; Gao J. F. 1985).

INTERACTIONS BETWEEN HUMANS AND THE ENVIRONMENT   Ancient Chinese literature taught that humans should master the environment. Liu Y. X. (772–842) emphasized the close interaction between humans (considered as groups and societies) and the environment. Later, it was widely recognized that the human mind was a product combining inherited personality and learned habits. This conception resembles the modern viewpoint of psychological development.

MENTAL AND MEDICAL REHABILITATION   In the first Chinese encyclopedia of medicine, *Medical Principles of The Yellow Emperor,* published about 2000 years ago, the psychological effects of brain pathology were noted, and a biological-psychological-social model dominated approaches to medical and mental rehabilitation. Some principles of Chinese traditional rehabilitation were adopted in ancient medical diagnosis and treatment: balance between ying and yang; interdependence between cultivating the positive and eliminating the negative; accommodating mind and body to nature; exercising mental spirit (*Qi*); adapting movement with static rehabilitation; mediating main and collateral channels as a network; and integrating nursing (Chen K. J. 1988).

PSYCHOLOGICAL MEASUREMENT AND THE CIVIL SERVICE EXAMINATION SYSTEM   The roots of psychological testing can be traced back to the concepts and practices of ancient China, especially the civil service examination system that prevailed in the Chinese empire for some 3000 years (Anastasi 1990). About 1000 years ago, both the "seven cleverness board" (a geometric shape formation test) and the "nine connected rings" (a problem-solving test) were popular Chinese puzzles for testing visual-spatial perception, divergent thinking, and creativity (Zhang H. C. 1988). Various methods for measuring talent and behavior were popular, such as observing traits from behavioral changes, identifying intelligence by response speed, eliciting personality across situations, and measuring mental attributes through interviews (Lin C. T. 1980). The civil service examination system started during the Sui dynasty (581–618) and became well-structured in the Tang dynasty (618–907). It consisted of three parts: regular examinations, including rehearsals of classical works and policy-making essays; a committee examination before the emperor, using interviews on planning and administrative suggestions; and a martial examination including riding, arrow shooting, load-carrying, and martial arts. This personnel examination system has three special characteristics: multi-level screening; public competition for candidates; and comprehensive examinations. The system lasted for hundreds of years and still affects the modern practices of personnel assessment and examination in China.

HUMAN RESOURCE MANAGEMENT   Human resources management formed a significant part of ancient Chinese thinking and social life. Written in about 500 BC, Sun Tzu's classic book *The Art of War* emphasized the moral, intellectual, and circumstantial elements over the physical; careful planning based on sound information in reaching speedy decisions; the moral, emotional, and intellectual qualities of the good general; and especially Sun's strategic and tactical doctrines for managing military force and conducting military operations. On the effective utilization of labor, Mo D. (479–381 BC) argued that evaluation of workload and performance should determine compensation. Mo was the first to propose the idea of division of labor processes (Wang Z. M. 1990e). His fascinating ideas have influenced our modern theories and practice of human resource management.

The Development of Psychology in China

A BRIEF HISTORY OF PSYCHOLOGY DURING THE 1920s AND 1940s   Psychology as an experimental science started somewhat late in China. Around the turn of this century, some Chinese universities started to offer psychology courses while many psychology textbooks were translated and published in China. The first psychological laboratory was set up at Peking University in 1917; Chen D. Q. (1918) published the first Chinese psychology textbook, *Principles of Psychology*. In the early 1920s both the first psychology department and the Chinese Psychological Association of China were founded in Nanjing. The first Chinese psychological journal, *Psychology,* then began publication. Meanwhile, several Chinese scholars returned from abroad to teach and do research in psychology. Western theories of psychology were introduced, and psychological research was carried out in areas such as child development, testing, and learning aspects of the use of Chinese characters. For example, Chen H. Q. (1925) did a longitudinal case study and systematically observed the psychological development of an infant from age of 1.5 months to age 2.7 years. Chen L. (1935) published *Essentials of Industrial Psychology,* the first Chinese book in this area, and conducted field studies in Chinese factories after his doctoral study under the supervision of Charles Spearman at University College London. Later, Chen's study (1948) on the differentiation and integration of the G factor was widely quoted and recognized as a landmark in understanding intellectual development. Still, the general development of psychology during the 1930s and 1940s was slow in China.

DEVELOPMENTS FROM THE 1950s THROUGH THE 1970s   After the founding of the People's Republic of China, the major goal for Chinese psychologists was to develop psychology under the guidance of Marxist dialectical materialism and in the socialist context. Mental activities were viewed as reflections primarily of social reality. During the 1950s, Soviet psychology (e.g. the study of Pavlov's theories) had a great influence on psychology in China. In the late 1950s, critical evaluation of Western psychological schools was undertaken nationwide. In the early 1960s, some basic psychological studies were conducted concerning perception, conceptual development, memory, and physiological psychology (Ching C. C. 1984). Many psychologists participated in studies of such practical issues as reform and simplification of Chinese ideograms, programmed instruction, group therapy for patients, industrial rationalization, technical training, and display design for power stations. The publication of three important Chinese textbooks in the early 1960s reflected a significant development of teaching and research in psychology: *General Psychology* (Cao R. C. 1963), *Educational Psychology* (Pan S. 1964), and *Child Psychology* (Zhu, Zi-Xian 1962). Unfortunately, the study of psychology suffered greatly during the 10-year Cultural Revolution (1966–1976). Psychology was then attacked as a so-called bourgeois pseudoscience. Chen's study on color-form abstraction in children's conceptual development became the first target of the attack upon psychology under the Cultural Revolution (Brown 1981; Chen L. & Wang A. S. 1965, 1979). Research and teaching institutions were dissolved. Like other disciplines, psychology lost almost a generation of scholars.

RAPID DEVELOPMENTS SINCE 1978   The recent (since 1978) Chinese economic reform program with its open-to-the-world policy has brought the 'Springtime of Science' to psychology. The Chinese Psychological Society has resumed its academic activities; research in, and applications of, psychology have been carried out all over China. Psychologists have played important roles in Chinese socialist modernization. A summary of the development of psychology in China over the past 70 years would emphasize 1. the guidance of dialectical and historic materialism and the implementation of the Double Hundreds Flower Policy (encouraging hundreds of achievements and hundreds of schools of thought) for psychology; 2. the promotion of peaceful social environment and necessary working conditions for psychology; 3. the training of psychologists and the learning of new ideas and methods in psychological research and applications; 4. the popularization of scientific knowledge of psychology; 5. the cooperation among Chinese psychologists and the coordination among national and local professional organizations; and 6. the international exchange and collaborations based on studies in China (Lin Z. X. & Zhao L. R. 1992).

As a result of the rapid developments in psychological research and teaching, thousands of Chinese psychology books have been published in the last decade. Among them, to list just a few, are *Experimental Psychology* (He B. Y. et al 1983), *Fundamentals of Psychology* (Zhang Z. S. & Sheng D. L. 1987), *Cognitive Psychology* (Peng D. L. 1990), *Developmental Psychology of Thinking* (Zhu, Zi-Xian & Lin C. D. 1986), *Educational Psychology* (Shao R. Z. 1986), *History of Chinese Psychology* (Gao J. F. 1985), *Statistics in Psychology and Education* (Zhang H. C. & Men Q. M. 1981), *Research Methods in Psychology* (Wang Z. M. 1990b), *Prospectus of Industrial Psychology* (Chen L. 1983), *Psychology of Industrial Management* (Chen L. 1988a), *Managerial Psychology* (Lu S. Z. et al 1985), *Work and Personnel Psychology* (Wang Z. M. 1988a), *Engineering Psychology* (Zhu Zu-Xiang 1990), *Physiological Psychology* (Kuang P. Z. 1987), and *Abnormal Psychology* (Chen Z. G. 1985). Several influential Chinese dictionaries and encyclopedias of psychology have been published, such as *Chinese Dictionary of Psychology* (Zhu Zi-Xian 1989) and *Chinese Concise Encyclopedia of Psychology* (Jing Q. C. 1991).

PROFESSIONAL ORGANIZATIONS AND PSYCHOLOGY TRAINING PROGRAMS

Professional Associations and Journals

THE CHINESE PSYCHOLOGICAL SOCIETY AND CHINESE JOURNALS   The predecessor of the Chinese Psychological Society was the Psychological Association of China (PAC) which was founded in Nanjing in 1921. Zhang Y. X. was elected as the president of PAC. However, the PAC was active only for four years due to the unstable social situation in China. In 1937, the Chinese Psychological Society (CPS) was established in Naning. Lu Z. W. was elected as the CPS president and the journal *Acta Psychologica Sinica* was published. But the professional activity of CPS was soon stopped because of the Anti-Japanese War. After the founding of the People's Republic of China, the CPS was reestablished in 1955 and had more than 2,900 members by 1991; two-thirds of them are developmental and educational psychologists. The CPS is under the leadership of the Chinese National Association of Science and Technology and, since 1980, has been a member of the International Union of Psychological Science. Since 1955, three famous Chinese psychologists have served as presidents of the CPS: Pan S. (from 1955 to 1984), Jing Q. C. (from 1984 to 1989), both from the Academia Sinica, and the present CPS president, Wang S. (from 1989) of Peking University (Lin Z. X. & Zhao L. R. 1992). The CPS now has 11 special committees (divisions) of psychology, including educational psychology, developmental psychology, fundamental theory of psychology, medical psychology, general-experimental psychology, industrial psychology, sports psychology, physiological psychology, psychology of school management, judicial psychology, and psychological measurement. It has three working committees: scientific popularization, academic affairs, and international academic exchange. Several journals of psychology are published in China, such as *Acta Psychologica Sinica, Psychological Sciences* (named *Information on Psychological Science* before 1991), *Chinese Journal of Applied Psychology, Psychological Development and Education,* and *New Explorations in Psychology.* There is also a *Chinese Mental Health Journal.* Each province has its psychological association. For years the CPS has played a leading role in conducting psychological research, promoting regional and inter-area cooperation, organizing conferences, publishing psychological works, encouraging psychological applications, and developing international collaborations.

OTHER PROFESSIONAL ORGANIZATIONS   The Chinese Social Psychological Association, founded in 1982, is one of the main professional organizations in psychology. Since 1985 the Chinese Society of Behavioral Sciences has been active in the study and application of managerial psychology in enterprises and other organizations. The Chinese Ergonomics Society, founded in 1989, has several divisions closely linked with psychology—e.g. cognitive ergonomics, environmental ergonomics, transportation ergonomics, and managerial ergonomics. In addition, the Chinese Educational Association has a division of child and educational psychology. The Chinese Association of Mental Health also actively involves educational and clinical psychologists. Many Chinese psychologists are members of several professional associations.

Research Institutes and Training Programs

RESEARCH INSTITUTES   The largest research institute in psychology in China is the Institute of Psychology at the Academia Sinica in Beijing. Founded in 1951, it has now six sections: 1. developmental psychology and animal psychology;

2. vision, audition, memory, and artificial intelligence; 3. physiological and pathological psychology; 4. fundamental psychological theory; 5. aviation psychology, managerial psychology, and ergonomics; and 6. references and publications. Some other research institutes around the country include the Institute of Child Psychology at Beijing Normal University and the Institute of Industrial Psychology at Hangzhou University. Several psychological research units are affiliated with other disciplines such as education, physiology, sociology, and engineering. Since 1990, both the National Key Program of Industrial Psychology (offering BA, MA and PhD degrees) and the National Key Laboratory of Industrial Psychology have been established at Hangzhou University, specialized in Display Design, Human-Computer Interaction, Managerial Decision Making, and Human Performance. Recent research funds for psychology have mostly come from the Chinese National Science Foundation (CNSF), the Chinese National Foundation of Social Sciences, and the State Education Commission. The 33 project grants supported by CNSF during 1982–1987 were related to Chinese characters, Chinese psycho-linguistics, visual display design, learning disabilities, perception, eye movement and cognitive process, the psycho-physiological mechanisms of emotion, interface design for Chinese computers, personality and mental disorders, early intervention for mentally retarded children, thinking and personality of supernormal children, mental-load, and the effects of shiftwork (Gu J. K. 1988). Many psychologists have also undertaken projects for companies or governmental agencies.

TEACHING PROGRAMS   At present there are six psychology departments in Chinese universities—at Peking University, Beijing Normal University, Hangzhou University, East China Normal University (Shanghai), Shanxi Normal University (Xian), and South China Normal University (Guangzhou)— each with certain special features. For instance, the Psychology Department at Peking University is strong in the areas of clinical, physiological, and cognitive psychology. The Department at Beijing Normal University has more specialists in educational psychology, psychological testing, and child psychology. The Department at Hangzhou University is oriented toward industrial psychology and school psychology. In addition, there are more than 20 psychology programs at various normal universities and teachers' colleges. Indeed, psychology courses are taught at most colleges and universities in China.

The present Chinese degrees system started in the late 1970s. The structure of training in psychology in China has four levels. The first comprises short training courses and distance education. The Institute of Psychology at Academia Sinica in Beijing offers a correspondence course in psychology that enrolls thousands of employees. At Hangzhou University, short training courses on managerial psychology have been conducted for several hundreds of managers and supervisors from various industries and government organizations. The second level of psychology training involves college programs and university BA programs. The third level comprises the master's degree programs that last two or three years, while the fourth is composed of the 3-year doctoral programs now available at universities in Beijing, Shanghai, Hangzhou, and Guangzhou. The institute of Psychology at Academia Sinica runs both master's and doctoral programs. Students graduated from psychology programs are working at colleges, universities, research institutes, hospitals, enterprises, and governmental departments.

SOME RECENT PSYCHOLOGICAL RESEARCH AND APPLICATIONS

Experimental Psychology and Physiological Psychology

GENERAL DEVELOPMENT   When psychology restored its momentum in China in the late 1970s, both experimental and physiological psychologists took the lead in research. Wang S. (1979) examined modes of haptic perception and length discrimination in terms of encoding of length information; Zheng Z. Y. et al (1980) studied information-processing of binocular stereoscopic vision; Luo S. D. et al (1979) did a series of experiments on adult albino rats and showed the effects of pancreatic trypsin and ribonuclease upon memory and learning; and Jiao S. L. et al (1979) tested the luminance of visual field and contrast sensitivity. Later, Jing Q. C. et al (1987) made extensive studies on human vision and proposed a macro-theory of perception emphasizing the importance of both stimulus and reference information in perception. While studies on perception are still active (e.g. Wang S. & Zhang M. 1990), the main interests of research in experimental psychology have recently shifted to areas such as cognitive processing of Chinese characters and language (e.g. Yu B. L. et al 1990; Zhang J. J. et al 1990; Miao X. C. & Sang B. 1991; Tan L. H. & Peng D. L. 1991), cognitive strategies and levels of processing (e.g. Wang Z. M. 1990d; Zhu Y. et al 1991), and knowledge acquisition and representation (e.g. Wang Z. M. 1991b). In the area of emotions, Meng Z. L. (1987) studied the effects of different emotions on intellectual performance. Meanwhile, studies of brain-chemistry and brain functions are popular in physiological psychology (e.g. Kuang P. Z. et al 1988; Long D. & Li X. T. 1990; Zhang D. R. &Chen Lin 1991). Many physiological psychologists are involved in areas such as the neurological and neuroanatomical mechanisms of memory and learning, electrophysiology, and pathology in emotion and sleep.

CHINESE CHARACTERS AND LANGUAGE   In the 1920s Liu T. F. did perhaps the earliest studies on the relationship among the pronunciation, orthographic shapes, and semantics of Chinese characters and found that the effects of shapes upon semantic comprehension were stronger than those of pronunciation. Using an eye-movement monitoring camera, Eugene Shen found that the fixation duration was shorter in reading laterally printed (left–right) than vertically printed (top-down) materials while the number rate of characters in each fixation duration was higher for the latter (Gao J. F. 1985). Later, Ai W. (1948) noticed that the association between the shapes and the meanings of Chinese characters was retained longer than the shape-pronunciation association. These studies provided a good base for the recent research on the psychology of Chinese characters.

Many recent studies have focused upon the short-term memorability of Chinese characters. Yu B. L. & Jing Q. C. (1984) found a modest effect of familiarity upon character chunking and a larger short-term memory (STM) span under serial than under simultaneous input. Subvocal oral articulation was suggested as a necessary condition for the retention of Chinese characters in STM. It was reported that STM capacity differed between visual and auditory modalities (Zhang W. T. & Peng R. X. 1984). In an experiment on the priming effect in reading Chinese characters, Zhang H. C. & Shu H. (1989) showed a significant priming effect when both the pronunciation and the shape of the prime characters were similar to those of the target, suggesting a pronunciation-associated path in the Chinese lexicon. Chen Y. M. & Peng R. X. (1990) found both a general time pattern in the verification process of Chinese sentences and a significant effect of the placement of the negation constituent on sentence-comprehension time. As an effective means of Chinese language learning, the alphabetic pronunciation system, *pinyin*, has been popular on the mainland—has indeed become part of the Chinese language system there. A different kind of *pinyin* is used in Taiwan, and no *pinyin* system is used in Hong Kong. Chen M. J. & Yuen J. C.K. (1991) studied the effects of both Chinese scripts (simplified vs traditional) and *pinyin* on verbal processing among children from the mainland, Taiwan, and Hong Kong, using tasks of pseudohomophone-naming, similarity judgment (pronunciation vs appearance), and lexical decision. *Pinyin* training facilitated the extraction of phonological information for pronunciation. The mainland children were more responsive to visual information but less precise in word recognition.

COGNITIVE STRATEGIES AND KNOWLEDGE REPRESENTATION   Wang A. S. et al (1988) found that children made both knowledge errors and strategy errors in problem-solving; children used four types of problem-solving strategy depending on their level of cognitive development. In a simulated experiment, Wang Z. M. (1990d) showed that both the effective utilization of decision information and the use of cognitive strategies were largely dependent upon the structure of the information display. More recently, Wang Z. M. & Zhong J. A. (1992) demonstrated that type of decision-support information greatly affected subjects' information search patterns and modified their cognitive strategies during the decision-making process. Wang Z. M. (1991b) carried out a knowledge elicitation experiment and showed that experts' knowledge of computer systems was structured as a network connecting key concepts of the domain whereas novices' knowledge tended to be in a single chain linking various key concepts. Based on these studies, a process model of multi-level decision support was built up with the compatibility between types of user knowledge networks and levels of decision support as its key concept.

Psychological Testing and Measurement

GENERAL DEVELOPMENT   In recent years, psychological testing has become a popular practice and an active research area in China. Most research has been done through nationwide collaborations involving psychologists from 20–60 institutions. Two categories of tests have been developed or adapted in China: 1. intelligence and ability tests, including Wechsler Adult and Children Intelligence Scales (WAIS-RC and WISC-CRS) (Li D. et al 1987), Chinese Binet-Simon Test, Raven's Standard Progressive Matrices, and some Chinese tests such as Clinical Memory Test (Xu S. L. & Wu Z. Y. 1986), Children's Cognitive Ability Scale (Lu J. & Xu F. 1988) and the Creativity Test (Zheng R. C. & Xiao B. L. 1983); and 2. personality and neuropsychological tests, including Minnesota Multiphasic Personality Inventory (MMPI), Eysenck Personality Questionnaire (EPQ), California Personality Inventory, Cattell-16PF, Luria-Nebraska and Halstead-Reitan Neuro-Psychological Test Batteries, Thematic Apperception Test, Torrance Tests of Creative Thinking, and the Anxiety Test. With a 5-year effort, Hong D. H. et al (1989) developed the Chinese Adolescent Non-Intellectual Personality Inventory and its national norms with a sample of 9050 students. This test includes six subscales: aspiration, independence, self-confidence, persistence, motivation to learn, and self-consciousness. In addition, psychological scales have been developed for personnel selection and assessment (e.g. Lu H. J. 1986; Xu L. C. 1987). However, while various psychological tests are used increasingly in schools, hospitals, and other organizations, it is widely realized that more attention should be paid to the theoretical constructs behind various tests, the development of Chinese test theories, test administration, and the training of testing techniques.

ADAPTATION AND MODIFICATION OF WESTERN TESTS   Much effort has been exerted to adapt some popular Western diagnosis, selection, and counseling tests and to develop Chinese equivalents. Chen Z. G. (1983) conducted an item analysis on the Chinese version of the Eysenck Personality Questionnaire with a sample of 643 subjects aged 25–35 years old. The results showed that the four scales were generally satisfactory, though some items were unsuitable to the Chinese context. Gong Y. X. (1984) carried out a project of adaptation and norm study on the Chinese EPQ with samples of 3941 students (7–15 years old) and 2517 adults. In a regional collaborative project, WAIS was also revised with a sample of 3021 subjects in 23 provinces of China (Gong Y. X. 1983). Zhang H. C. & Wang X. P. (1989) reported an adaptation study on the Raven's test, a test with high adaptability to different cultures. Altogether, 5108 people (aged 5–70) were sampled to establish the Chinese norms. The results of the item analysis showed an acceptable test difficulty level and no significant sex differences except in the 40–49 age group. In the clinical area, the MMPI was revised and adapted by a group of psychologists from 39 institutions and hospitals (Song W. Z. et al 1982, 1985). Referring to a Hong Kong version of the Chinese MMPI, the present Chinese MMPI with 14 subscales was tested among 1791 normal subjects and 1301 schizophrenia patients aged 16–55. Some items were modified to adapt to the Chinese cultural and social context. The results showed that this Chinese MMPI was generally suitable with an acceptable level of reliability, validity, and discriminability. Still, the criteria for the validity scale had to be modified. For instance, even some items from the Hong Kong version of MMPI were unsuitable for the mainland context, and there appeared to be a special Chinese response set (e.g. more modest, unsociable, self-underestimating). In a recent review of 26 studies on the clinical applications of the MMPI in China, Cheung F. M. & Song W. Z. (1989) concluded that the MMPI profiles among Chinese psychiatric patients differed significantly from those of normal controls and from the Chinese norms, and that the concordance rates between MMPI profiles and clinical diagnoses were good. They noted that establishment of the validity of the Chinese norm in clinical interpretation would require additional studies.

METHODOLOGICAL ISSUES   With the recent developments in psychological testing, Chen L. (1982, 1990, 1991) called strongly for comprehensive item analysis, correct use of tests, and test theory development in China. Adaptation and design of Chinese psychological tests involve several critical methodological issues. First, validations of most Chinese tests have been weak. Although large samples were adopted for establishing Chinese norms, most studies used very small samples for evaluating the reliability and/or validity of tests. In reviewing the problems in revising Western tests in China, Tan J. L. (1986) suggested that regional rather than national norms be used, given the diversity of sub-cultural and socio-economic contexts in different regions of the country. Greater effort must be made to validate various psychological tests in the Chinese context, especially the cultural suitability of items, including careful item analysis and more effective criteria. After a pilot test of the Wechsler Preschool and Primary Scale of Intelligence, Zhu Y. M. et al (1984) suggested we pay more attention to the modification of some WPPSI items based on Chinese cultural context and language characteristics. Second, more research should be done to link testing with psychological counseling. The purpose of diagnosis is to educate people with behavioral problems or psychological deficits (Chen L. 1982), and to help job placement and even organization development.

Developmental Psychology

GENERAL DEVELOPMENT   In an early review of developmental psychology in China, Liu F. (1982) of the Institute of Psychology at Academia Sinica summarized the research work during 1977–1982 in the following six areas: conceptual development, language development, development in thinking, personality and moral development, gifted children, and mentally retarded children. Along with continuous progress in those six areas in recent years, several other areas of Chinese developmental psychology have been active, especially those of children's social and personality development, family environment, and aging. Some theoretical models of child development have been proposed. Some useful tools for screening and diagnosis have been developed, and educational programs have been put into effect (Zhu Zi-Xian & Lin C. D. 1991). One area that has been active recently is that of meta-cognition. Dong Q. (1989) examined the meta-cognition in reading among 400 students aged 10–17 and showed rapid development of meta-knowledge and monitoring skills as the age increased. In a brief summary of recent studies on aging in China, Xu S. L. et al (1988) reported that the age differences in memory and associative learning across ages 20–90 depended on task type. For example, inter-age group comparisons of 30–40, 40–50, and 60–70 year olds showed significant similar declines over age in performance of a picture free-recall task, whereas in the performance of a logical story recall task, a smaller decline was found among 65–80 year olds. In terms of associative learning, the aged performed much worse in the task of nonlogical than in that of logical relation association. In addition, strategy training of the aged had positive effects on word recall and math performance; the exercise of Chinese *QiGong* (similar to meditation) improved the memory of middle-aged and older patients.

NATIONWIDE COLLABORATIVE RESEARCH   The nationwide collaborative efforts in research have effectively organized developmental psychologists in large projects that greatly facilitate progress in teaching, research, and applications in such a large country in the last decade. Liu F. (1982) organized a research group of more than 50 developmental psychologists from 12 cities of China to investigate the cognitive developmental stages of thousands of children aged 5–16. The results of this project showed children's conceptual developments in number series (Zuo M. L. et al 1984), length cognition (Liu J. H. et al 1984), probabilities (Zhang Z. J. et al 1985), and volume (Sheng J. X. et al 1984). Since the early 1980s, UNICEF has actively supported several large projects on child psychology throughout the country. Among others, the 6-year UNICEF project at Hangzhou University has focused on children's physical growth, intellectual development, and, recently, the diagnosis and training of slow learners and mentally retarded children. In another collaborative project, Zha Z. X. (1986) worked with developmental psychologists from 15 regions of China on the psychological development of 700 gifted children. Compared with the control group of ordinary children, the gifted showed much better results in logical and creative thinking, curiosity, observation ability, persistence, self-confidence, memory, and school performance. In summarizing the findings of ten years of research, Zha Z. X. (1990) suggested we use the term 'supernormal' instead of 'gifted' to include both intelligence (or creativity) and non-intellectual personality traits when referring to children with extraordinary abilities. Five principles for identifying the supernormal children were formulated: dynamic comparison, multi-indicator multi-method screening, qualitative and quantitative evaluation, test of intellectual and non-intellectual factors, and identification through training and education. Zhu Zi-Xian (1990) at Beijing Normal University headed a 7-year cooperative project on the psychological development and education of children and adolescents, in which more than 200 psychologists from about 50 institutions joined. Both cross-sectional and longitudinal studies were carried out in 23 provinces and regions in China. This nationwide project has produced systematic data on such aspects of the psychological development and education of children and adolescents as perception, attention, memory, language, thinking, mathematical ability, emotion, personality, self-consciousness, and moral sense. In addition, the relationships between family education and psychological development were carefully studied.

PSYCHOLOGICAL DEVELOPMENT OF MINORITY CHILDREN   China is a large country composed of 56 nationalities. The psychological development of minority children has been an important topic in education and psychology. Niu J. & Zhang S. F. (1983) measured learning abilities among 1437 children of Han, Bai, and Dai nationalities, using tests of synonyms, mathematical reasoning, problem-solving, and language analogy ability. The results showed no significant difference in learning ability between Han and minority children, though social-cultural differences across regions were influential. Zhao M. J. et al (1989) studied the semantic comprehension ability among 450 children aged 7–9 from Han nationality and minorities of Tibet, Dong-Xiang, BoNan, Yuku, and Kazak in the northwest of China. Although some differences were shown among groups of 7-year-olds who had just entered schools, less difference was found among all groups of 9-year-old children in their ability to understand the Chinese Mandarin language (a second language for minority children). Zhang Z. & Zuo M. L. (1990) found little difference in problem-solving strategies between Han and minority children within the same region. These studies have useful implications for the understanding of psychological development among minority children as well as the improvement of bilingual educational programs for the minority areas. It was suggested that regional, social, and cultural factors play more important roles than nationality in children's cognitive and social developments. Many recent studies have shown that within the same or similar regional and social settings the psychological characteristics of Han and minority children differ little. It would be interesting to find out how psychological, cultural, social, and economic factors interactively affect the development of minority children.

PSYCHOLOGICAL STUDIES ON ONLY-CHILDREN   The only-child has been a hot topic in psychological studies in China since the national family planning and birth control program was implemented in the mid-1980s. One common approach in this area is to compare psychological development between only-children and children with siblings. In a study that sampled 964 children from city and suburb areas, Chen K. W. (1985) asked both teachers and parents to evaluate children's behavioral characteristics (e.g. honesty, sociability, self-control, independence, and conformity) and found little difference between only-children and other children from cities, but some significant differences between city and suburban children. In a joint survey on Chinese school children, Falbo et al (1989) found that the differences between only-children and other children were small but statistically significant, with the only-children having higher scores in achievement and physical size. However, further analysis showed that while the urban only-child scored achievement advantages, the only-child in rural peasant families did not. The only-children didn't have undesirable personalities, as judged by teachers and mothers. An interaction among social, educational, and psychological factors seems to affect differences in the development of only-children and other children.

Two methodological issues in sampling should be noted in studies of only-children. First, the family planning and birth control program has been more extensively implemented in cities than remote areas. There may be fewer children with siblings in the cities, and the social norms for family planning there might be different. Besides, the only-children are mostly younger—i.e. have grown up under better educational and living conditions in recent years. Second, the sample sizes in these studies were usually small. As a result, there might be significant differences in regional, social, and chronological backgrounds among different samples of children. Longitudinal studies are needed in examining the psychological development of the only-children.

DIAGNOSIS AND TRAINING OF MENTALLY RETARDED CHILDREN   The psychological development of mentally retarded children has been a concern of various institutions in China, using different programs of diagnosis, training, and intervention. Wang W. J. et al (1988) carried out a two-month program for motor-coordination training of mentally retarded children in Hangzhou, which proved to be effective in promoting children's motor development. Mao Y. Y. (1989) conducted a 1-year program of early intervention for mentally retarded preschool children in Beijing and proved its positive effects: modifying mental and behavioral dysfunctions as well as improving preschool learning. In the area of mentally retarded children, it is noted that a longitudinal paradigm of research should be also adopted for diagnosis and treatment with a more comprehensive assessment of the effects of treatments and training programs.

Educational and School Psychology

GENERAL DEVELOPMENT   Recent research in educational and school psychology has been carried out primarily in the educational setting and has been closely linked with the practice of various educational reform programs. It is also influenced by some early ideas about instruction in China—e.g. the concept of proceeding by steps, teaching according to pupils' mental make-ups, combining rehearsal with understanding, and promoting pupils' interests and attention to instruction. Most studies of instruction overlapped with research in developmental psychology. In a recent analysis of 2274 studies during 1979–1988 in developmental and educational psychology involving 362,665 subjects, Shi S. H. (1990) found that 48.9% of the studies were application-oriented whereas 8% were designed to test hypotheses. (The rest were more or less repetitions or adaptations of previous studies or instruments.) While field survey and measurement remained the main approaches in this area, the review and citation of relevant and recent literature were relatively weak. During the past decade three active areas in educational and school psychology stood out: 1. psychology of instruction and curriculum design, focusing on cognitive skills and instruction in Chinese language and math word problems; 2. psychology of adolescent moral development, and in the motivation of learning; 3. psychology of teams and school management, relating to team behavior, program evaluation, and performance appraisal. An effort has been made recently to extend educational psychology to the family and community context. As a new trend in the training of Chinese psychologists, Chen L. (1992) outlined the program of school psychology as a profession in terms of psychological testing, counseling, and pre-vocational guidance.

CURRICULUM DESIGN AND INSTRUCTION   A significant aspect of educational, school, and developmental psychology is the design and implementation of educational programs with psychological principles. Lin C. D. (1983) reported an educational experiment on the development of thinking ability among primary school children in solving word problems through multi-solution math operations. Compared with those in the control groups, students in the experimental classes were better able to generate multiple solutions, were more flexible in divergent thinking, and generally performed better. On children's mathematical thinking in primary schools, Zhang M. L. & Liu J. H. (1991) conducted a collaborative research project and implemented with success a new program of elementary school math using restructured textbooks in 2500 experimental classes nationwide. Recently the interaction of aptitude and instructional treatment has become a new area of research in educational psychology in China.

MORAL DEVELOPMENT AND THE MOTIVATION OF LEARNING   The development of morals and values has been emphasized in China. Chen X. Y. & Shi R. H. (1987) conducted a field study with children from kindergarten and primary schools, and with adolescents from middle schools. It was reported that young children modeled themselves after teachers and followed peer groups while adolescents showed strong peer group conformity but less teacher-modeling behavior. In a survey among 945 middle-school students and 1180 university students in the southern part of China using a Chinese version of Rokeach's Value Survey (Rokeach 1973), Huang X. T. et al (1989) found that among terminal values, a sense of accomplishment, true friendship, self-respect, and national security were ranked the most important values, while inner harmony, a comfortable life, an exciting life, and salvation were the least important; among instrumental values, being ambitious, capable, and broad-minded were ranked very high, while being clean, self-controlled, and obedient ranked very low. Social recognition, independence, and mature love were valued more highly with increasing age. To some extent, these results suggested that the value system among Chinese adolescents was quite different from that found in adolescents abroad. However, no validation was reported for the Chinese version of the Value Survey instrument. In another study, using a Chinese version of the Allport, Vernon, & Lindzey value scale (see Bond 1986), Peng K. P. & Chen Z. G. (1989) found that the order of value orientations among 690 university students from high to low was Political, Esthetic, Theoretical, Economic, Social, and Religious; this order agreed with results from Taiwan and Hong Kong but differed from that found in Western countries.

With respect to the motivation and interests of learning, Zhao H. T. (1987) made a survey among 1200 students from primary and middle schools and found an age-correlated differentiation in subject interests and extra-curricular readings, especially between science and arts. To facilitate students' achievement motivation, attributional training programs were implemented based upon Weiner's theoretical framework (Weiner 1979). Sui's recent study (1991) showed that among middle-school students academic achievement motivation was significantly correlated with performance, effort was the most important factor in attributions, and attributional training had positive effects on achievement motivation. Wang Z. M.(1986) proved that the attributional patterns were largely contingent on the goal structures (individual vs team) of the task.

SCHOOL TEAMS AND PERFORMANCE APPRAISAL   The psychology of teams is an important topic in Chinese psychology. Huang X. T. et al (1984) studied 133 small groups in universities and showed that a positive team climate affected students' self-concepts. Among recent studies on the evaluation of school performance, Li W. (1988) tested a performance-appraisal system involving 62 middle-school math teachers and 1937 students. In Hangzhou, we are working on a project to evaluate and predict the team effectiveness of university teachers, using the team knowledge structure and team-job fit as main predictors. A useful assessment of principals' behavior and teachers' motivation has been carried out nationwide (Jing 1990).

Managerial Psychology

GENERAL DEVELOPMENT   In China, organizational psychology is known as managerial psychology. Managerial psychology and engineering psychology are two main branches of industrial psychology in China. Other aspects of industrial psychology include personnel psychology, work psychology, and consumer psychology. Managerial psychology has a rather short history and is closely linked with the recent Chinese economic reform and its emphasis on human resources management (Xu L. C. 1986, 1990; Wang Z. M. 1989a, 1993). Research in this area has been conducted primarily in organizational settings. Recent studies of managerial psychology have focused upon four areas: work motivation and employees' needs, group process and structures, leadership assessment, and organizational decision-making and organization development (Xu L. C. & Wang Z. M. 1991; Wang Z. M. 1991a).

WORK MOTIVATION AND GROUP PROCESS   Topics of recent studies on work motivation include the needs structure of Chinese employees (e.g. Xu L. C. 1987; Wang Z. M. 1988a), achievement motivation and its correlates (e.g. Li X. Y. 1988; Chen Q. 1991; Miner et al 1991), team and individual reward systems (Wang Z. M. 1986), and Chinese models of motivation. Xu L. C. & Chen L. (1987) showed that social needs were ranked highest while wages and bonuses were the second important needs among workers. Based on a series of quasi-experiments, Wang Z. M. (1986, 1988b) found that compared with the individual-only responsibility system (contract system), attributional training was more effective under an individual-team-combined work system, in enhancing both motivation and performance among employees. Yu W. Z. (1989) proposed an employee-motivation strategy combining social and material incentives. A general finding was that a multi-reward structure was more effective than a single incentive system for the Chinese work force.

Given the Chinese tradition of a group approach in both work and social life, group behavior has been an important aspect of managerial psychology. Teng's experiment (1989) revealed a general pattern of decision-making in small groups that resembles the pattern found in Western studies (e.g. Davis 1973), though Chinese subjects more often preferred the majority model of decision-making. Using attributions and subsequent goal-setting as indicators, Wang Z. M. (1986, 1988b) found that the goal structure played a crucial role in facilitating or hindering group attributions (e.g. team cooperation) and sense of collectivism among employees. Recent studies showed that team labor contract systems may improve morale and participation, and may lead to higher performance and job satisfaction in the enterprises (e.g. Yu W. Z. 1988a, Wang Z. M. 1988b, Zhong J. A. 1989).

LEADERSHIP AND DECISION MAKING   A significant development in leadership psychology in China is related to theories and techniques for leadership assessment and job analysis (e.g. Xu L. C. 1987, 1989; Lu H. J. 1986; Wu L. L. 1986; Xie X. F. & Lu S. Z. 1990). In the adaptation of a Japanese two-dimensional scale of performance and maintenance (PM) for leadership assessment in enterprises, Lin W. Q. et al (1987) found that a unique moral character (a 'C factor' representing honesty, integrity, and commitment, etc) appeared to be the third dimension of leadership behavior among Chinese managers, in addition to performance and maintenance. A CPM scale was then developed for leadership assessment in China. Recent research in organizational decision-making has focused on two aspects: 1. cognitive process and decision information utilization (e.g. Wang Z. M. 1990d; Wang Z. M. & Wang Y. B. 1991; Wang Z. M. & Zhong J. A. 1992); and 2. power sharing and participation (e.g. Xu L. C. 1990; Wang Z. M. & Heller 1991). Wang Z. M. (1989c) has proposed a process model illustrating the effects of influence/power-sharing on both competence utilization and managerial transparency (two-way communication and sound psychological climate for goal-pursuing), which in turn lead to changes in organizational uncertainty, performance, satisfaction, and managerial success.

ORGANIZATIONAL DEVELOPMENT AND CULTURE   The economic reform has facilitated organizational development (OD) in China, especially in management systems (e.g. Xu L. C.et al 1985; Wang Z. M. & Fan B. N.1990), technological innovations (e.g. Wang Z. M. & He G. B. 1991), and organizational culture (e.g. Wang Z. M. & Sheng J. P. 1990). Chen L. (1989) summarized the OD approach in China in three aspects: developing systems of Management By Objectives, cultivating the sense of masters of organizations, and promoting participative management. Wang Z. M. (1990a) reported an action research project in 16 Chinese enterprises, showing the joint effectiveness of three OD strategies: 1. expertise strategy, focusing upon personnel training and user support; 2. system strategy, emphasizing structural development and systems networking; and 3. participation strategy, enhancing higher involvement, commitment, and positive organizational culture. In a recent study among 25 Sino-foreign joint ventures, these OD strategies also proved useful. Both the nationality of foreign partnership and the locus of decision-making affected the organizational culture (role perception, values, orientation of individualism vs collectivism, etc) (Wang Z. M. 1992).

Engineering Psychology

GENERAL DEVELOPMENT   In a review of 30 years of industrial psychology in China, Peng R. X. (1980) called for research on ergonomic standardization, personnel selection, signal display, managerial psychology, and the man-machine interface. In the last decade, a series of new studies were conducted to formulate the Chinese national ergonomic standards. Recently Zhu Zu-Xiang (1990) published a comprehensive textbook of engineering psychology summarizing some recent research findings. Wang Z. M. (1990c) edited a special issue on 'Ergonomics in China,' including representative papers from industrial psychology. Most studies are made in areas such as visual displays and signal design (e.g. Yang G. X. et al 1984; Zhu Zu-Xiang & Wu J. M. 1990), the human-computer interface (e.g.Wang Z. M.1989b), cognitive strategies and decision support (Wang A. S.& Liu X.1990; Wang Z. M.1990d), and workload and occupational stress (e.g. Zhu Zu-Xiang & Zhang Z. J. 1990).

VDT DISPLAYS AND HUMAN-COMPUTER INTERACTION   Owing to the rapid development and application of Chinese computer systems, VDT displays and human-computer interaction have become active areas in psychological research in China. On the one hand, many experiments have provided psychological parameters for the design of Chinese computers—e.g. illuminance and visual performance (Ge L. Z. & Zhu Z. X. 1987), contrast threshold and color signals (Xu B. H. 1988), VDT luminance contrast (Zhang H. Z. & Jing Q. C. 1988), target size, and color coding (Xu W. & Zhu Z. X. 1990). On the other hand, several studies focused on conceptions of computers (e.g. Allwood & Wang Z. M. 1990) and on modeling human-computer interaction for Chinese computers. In 40 Chinese enterprises Wang Z. M. (1989b) found close interactions among users, tasks, and organizational factors in the relationship between human and computer systems. A LISREL model of the human-computer interface hierarchy was built up with three facets: computer expertise, system connectivity (networking), and organizational climate (participation). The interaction among the three facets determined the degree of interface uncertainty and facilitated the level of human-computer dialog. This characterization of the organizational level of human-computer interface provides an organizational perspective in cognitive ergonomics and the design and implementation of computer systems (Barber & Laws 1989).

OCCUPATIONAL STRESS AND WORKLOAD Li D. M. et al (1990) found that shiftwork nurses at intensive care units usually had high mental workloads while shiftwork nurses at general wards had high physical workload. Significant changes in performance of mathematical symbol and counting before and after shiftwork were demonstrated, indicating that shiftwork might influence attention, memory, and reaction times. Other studies found that long-term exposure to stable noise had a negative effect upon some brain functions and work performance (Li S. Z. et al 1985; He C. D. et al 1986).

Medical and Clinical Psychology

GENERAL DEVELOPMENT Recent studies in medical and clinical psychology in China concern mainly four areas: psychotherapy and counselling; psycho-pathology of neurosis, psychosis, and high-blood pressure patients; psychology of acupuncture; and psycho-diagnosis of mentally retarded children (Li X. T. et al 1980). A significant development in this field has been the popularization of the psycho-medical-social model of medicine in China. Some Western psychotherapeutic methods (behavior modification, group therapy, Gestalt therapy, psychoanalysis, etc) have been introduced and tried among people with psychological problems.

CHINESE PSYCHOTHERAPY The effectiveness of Chinese therapies (e.g. *QiGong* and *TaiJi*) and of traditional medical treatment has been a topic in clinical and medical psychology. *QiGong* is considered an effective means of medical treatment and mental health. Sun F. L. et al (1984) found positive effects of three kinds of *QiGong* among patients achieving a quiet state, as measured by EEG power spectrum and coherence. Using the Eysenck Personality Questionnaire (EPQ) and the Type A Behavior Pattern Questionnaire, Tang C. M. et al (1989) tested personality traits among people aged about 65 who had practiced *QiGong*. Compared with elders who never had *QiGong,* the *QiGong* group showed significant positive effects of practicing *QiGong* on the neuroticism dimension of EPQ and on Type A behavior. Although *QiGong* as a traditional therapy has been popular in China, San H. H. et al (1990) cautioned against problems and psychological disorders due to misuse or abuse of *QiGong* therapy and called for careful guidance of *QiGong* practice.

EFFECTS OF ACUPUNCTURE AND TRADITIONAL MEDICINE   The psychological correlates of acupuncture have interested psychologists in China. Wang J. S. et al (1979) observed several thousands of cases receiving acupuncture anaesthesia over 15 years and found that psychological factors (e.g. cognition, attention, emotion, confidence, past experience, and cooperation with doctors) played active roles in the effects of needling (heart rate, blood pressure, breath, subjective feeling, etc), the analgesia of acupuncture, and the efficacy of acupuncture. In a study among patients for lung resection under acupuncture anesthesia, Xu S. L. et al (1979) showed that both the emotional states (e.g. facial expression, gestures, verbal responses) before needle insertion and the psycho-physiological indicators were highly correlated with the effect of acupuncture anesthesia. Acupuncture may induce hints or distractions that in turn affect the pain threshold (Shi R. H. & Yang Z. L. 1980).

Social Psychology and Sports Psychology

GENERAL DEVELOPMENT   Social psychology has developed later than other branches of psychology in China. Many social psychological issues have been investigated in relation to topics in developmental, educational, and managerial psychology such as attitudes, attributions, group dynamics, and group conformity. Recent social psychological topics in China include attitudes in economic reform (Yu W. Z. et al 1988), consumer behavior, youth socialization, and psychology of minorities. In judicial psychology, studies have been done on the characteristics of criminality and juvenile delinquency, and on strategies for their modification. In sports psychology, studies have been carried out in areas of contest anxiety, athletes' intelligence and personality (e.g. Zhu P. L. & Fang X. C. 1988; Qiu Y. J. 1986), a tactical thinking model for basketball players (Zhou G. 1988), coach leadership behavior (Chen H. Y. 1988), and psychological training. As a nationwide project, psychological assessment and follow-up counseling were carried out among 704 athletes in 1987. Yang X. H. & Wei C. L. (1990) ran a representation training program (similar to a mental imaging program) among artistic gymnastics students and showed its positive effects on motor skill learning, error correction, coordination, and sense of rhythm.

Cross-Cultural Psychology

A number of cross-cultural studies have been undertaken in various areas in the belief that through cross-cultural comparisons one might elucidate the similarities and differences in general human psychological processes and understand the relationships between individual variables, on the one hand, and cultural/socioeconomic variables on the other. Many cross-cultural studies were carried out jointly by Chinese and foreign psychologists in areas such as test anxiety (Ye R. M. & Rocklin 1988), role conflict (Smith et al 1990), and implicit leadership theory (Lin W. Q. et al 1991). Others were done in China by non-Chinese specialists in relation to organization culture and productivity (Nevis 1983), management participation (Laaksonen 1988), and management reform (Warner 1987). Given the difficulties involved with cross-cultural studies done through short one-way visits, and the cultural-linguistic problems in the conventional back-translation method for measurement instruments, Wang Z. M. (1989c) developed a technique of parallel translation and joint-team validation for designing comparable and equivalent instruments for cross-cultural studies. It includes 1. independent-parallel translations by Chinese researchers and 2. joint-team discussion and modifications by Chinese and foreign scholars. This methodology has proved effective in several cross-cultural projects.

Some recent cross-cultural studies have focused on individual psychological characteristics. Harvey et al (1990) tested the individual differences between 600 Chinese and 720 Canadian adolescents in imaginary and verbal styles of thinking; they found highly consistent superiority of imaginary styles of thinking over verbal ones. However, when the tasks were related to social context, cultural variables became significant. Allwood & Wang (1990) compared the concepts about computers held by Chinese and Swedish students. Chinese students harbored greater optimism about the effects of computers on society and perceived humans and computers to be more alike than did the Swedish students who had had more experience in computer use. Wang Z. M. & Peterson (1988) did some experiments on reward allocation among 140 children and adults. Half of each group were Chinese and half Australian. Age-related patterns and attributions of reward allocation depended primarily upon the social practice in one's own country. Xu L. C. (1989) did a comparative study showing that despite much similarity between Chinese and Japanese cultures, leadership behaviors in the two countries were quite different. The factor of moral character proved to be a unique dimension of Chinese leadership behavior. As part of a 6-year cross-cultural joint research project, Wang Z. M. & Heller (1991) compared samples of Chinese and British managerial decision styles and management power-sharing practices. While cultural differences could be assumed to be large, management practices in the two countries exhibited structural similarities due to the existence of similar organizational contingencies. A cross-cultural-socioeconomic perspective might be useful in cross-cultural studies related to social function or organizational context.

PSYCHOLOGY IN TAIWAN AND HONG KONG

PSYCHOLOGICAL ORGANIZATIONS   The Taiwan Psychological Association was established in 1964. It publishes the journal *Acta Psychologica Taiwanica* and organizes annual conferences on psychology in Taiwan. The Taiwan Psychological Testing Society started in 1951; its members are mainly school teachers. The Association of Mental Health in Taiwan has members from psychiatry, psychology, social work, and other disciplines (Zhang R. J. 1987). Psychology departments in Taiwan's universities are variously specialized in experimental psychology, comparative psychology, psychological testing, and business psychology. There are several institutions of psychological service for the mentally and physically handicapped—e.g. Taipei Rehabilitation Institution and College of Education. The Hong Kong Psychological Society was founded in 1968 and is a member of the International Union of Psychological Science. In recent years, many psychological tests from abroad [e.g. the Raven Test, CPI test, MMPI, Cattell's 16 PF, and Developmental Indicators for the Assessment of Learning (DIAL-R)] have been translated and widely adapted in schools and military services. Tests have also been developed in Taiwan—e.g. Ke's Personality Scale for mental health (Zhao L. R. 1981). The psychology of the Chinese language is one of the main areas of study in Taiwan and Hong Kong, including issues of digit span, disorders in reading and writing, perceptual separability and cohesive processes, skills in handwriting, and sentence comprehension (e.g. Kao & Hoosain 1984; Kao 1986). Studies in other areas include self-serving bias in attributions (Wan K. C. & Bond 1982), cultural collectivism and reward allocation (Leung & Bond 1984), student stress and coping strategies (Dyal & Chan 1985), cultural variations in abacus skill (Miller & Stigler 1987), moral judgment (Ma H. K. 1989), and cultural patterns in individualism and collectivism (Triandis et al 1990)—some of these done by psychologists abroad. Many Chinese textbooks on psychology have been published outside the mainland—e.g. *Personnel Psychology* (Hwang M. T. Z. 1976), *Industrial Psychology* (Lin R. M. 1980), and *Educational Psychology* (Hu B. Z. 1985).

PSYCHOLOGY OF CHINESE PEOPLE   The study of the psychology of Chinese people, especially personality in the Chinese context, has been active in Taiwan and Hong Kong (e.g. Yang K. S. & Lee P. H. 1971; Bond 1986; Redding & Wong 1986). Yang K. S. (1986) presented an extensive review on Taiwan personality and concluded that the Chinese motivational pattern was relatively strong on abasement, social-oriented achievement, change, endurance, intraception, nurturance, and order. Chinese students' dominant orientation on the relational modality was individualism rather than collectivism, and their orientation on the time modality was to future rather than past or present perspectives.

People had relatively high authoritarian attitudes and low Machiavellian and internal-control attitudes. These results revealed some changes of Chinese personality under societal modernization. Zhao Z. Y. & Yang C. F. (1989) asked Hong Kong college students to rate personality traits in determining the performance of three occupations. The response profiles were correlated with the desirability index of the trait terms, indicating a cognitive bias of semantic desirability in questionnaire items upon person perception studies. Bond & Hwang (1986) summarized some Chinese theoretical models of social behavior [including Hsu's *Ren* approach, Yang's social orientation, and Hwang's model of resource distribution (*Guanxi*)] and discussed their implications for further studies on Chinese people.

CONCLUSIONS AND NEW DIRECTIONS

Recent developments have shown several characteristics of the Chinese approach in psychology. First, recent Chinese psychological research and applications have been closely linked with the social and cultural developments in China—economic and organizational reform, the design and use of Chinese computers, implementation of the family planning program, the developments of minority educational programs and special education projects, the popularization of psychotherapy and traditional Chinese medicine, and the changes in values and attitudes under the new social development. Second, many studies have been conducted in relation to the Chinese cultural context. Chinese cultural traditions play important roles in current psychological research and applications, and in the interpretation of results. Early Chinese thinking about human nature, about the human-environment interaction, about the relationship between knowledge and action, and about mental rehabilitation has influenced the theoretical development and practice of modern psychology in China. More important, materialistic dialectics has guided recent psychological research in China. Testing causality through action and experiments, along with an emphasis on psychological process, has long been a part of psychological methodology in China (Jing Q. C. 1987; Wang Z. M. 1990b). Third, new Chinese models of psychological theory together with a nationwide collaborative research approach have provided a solid foundation for further development of psychology in China. Such a foundation has special practical implications for psychological research in other developing countries.

Recent studies have revealed some new directions in psychology in China. First, more systematic theoretical development and conceptualization are under way in psychological research and applications in China. In addition to the recent theoretical achievements, more attention is being paid to the development of theoretical models based on Chinese findings of empirical research. Chen L. (1988b) suggested a holistic approach for psychological research and organizational studies which has provided a new theoretical framework for psychological research in China. Second, a 'methodological optimization' has been going on in Chinese psychological research. Instead of cross-sectional comparisons, a longitudinal paradigm is recognized as an important approach for further studies in areas of developmental, educational, and managerial psychology. Also, it is expected that more controlled experiments rather than general surveys will be carried out in various fields of psychology; more careful sampling and strict validations will be adopted in the development of psychological testing and measurements as well as in cross-cultural studies in China. Given that Chinese psychologists are at present relatively few, the nationwide collaborative approach will greatly facilitate research, teaching, and applications of psychology. Third, more emphasis has been put on the link between theoretical studies and practical applications of psychology (Wang S. 1990). Chinese psychologists are playing more important roles in solving practical problems related to the new developments in economic reform, high technology, education, and social life. Fourth, a cross-cultural socioeconomic perspective (Wang Z. M. 1993) should further help us to understand the psychology of Chinese people in the context of global economic and technological developments.

ACKNOWLEDGMENT

This chapter was encouraged and supported by Professor Ward Edwards at the University of Southern California, Professor Ben Schneider at the University of Maryland, and Professor Don Davis at Old Dominion University, USA, when I visited those universities as a Fulbright Scholar in 1990. The chapter is dedicated, on his 90th birthday, to Professor L. Chen, my mentor at Hangzhou University, who has given us invaluable insight, courage, and knowledge in pursuing new development of psychology in China. I would like to thank my colleagues and students at Hangzhou University for their help in my preparation of this chapter.

Literature Cited

Ai, W. 1948. *On Chinese Characters*. Shanghai: Chinese Book Publisher (in Chinese)

Allwood, C. M., Wang, Z. M. 1990. Conceptions of computers among students in China and Sweden. *Comput. Hum. Behav.* 6:185–99

Anastasi, A. 1990. *Psychological Testing*, p. 5. New York: Macmillan. 6th ed.

Barber, P. J., Laws, J. V. 1989. Editorial preface: getting the measure of cognitive ergonomics. *Ergonomics* 32(11):i–v

Bond, M. H., ed. 1986. *The Psychology of the Chinese People*. Hong Kong: Oxford Univ. Press

Bond, M. H., Hwang, K. K. 1986. The social psychology of Chinese people. See Bond 1986, pp. 213–66

Brown, L. B. 1981. *Psychology in Contemporary China*. Oxford: Pergamon Press

Cao, R. C. 1963. *General Psychology*. Beijing: People's Educ. Press (in Chinese)

Chen, D. Q. 1918. *Principles of Psychology*. Shanghai: Commercial Press (in Chinese)

Chen, H. Q. 1925. *Studies on Child Psychology*. Shanghai: Commercial Press (in Chinese)

Chen, H. Y. 1988. Leadership behavior of coaches of the first-class women basketball teams in China. *Acta Psychol. Sinica* 20:400–7 (in Chinese)

Chen, K. J. 1988. *Chinese Traditional Medicine of Rehabilitation*. Beijing: People's Hygiene Press (in Chinese)

Chen, K. W. 1985. A comparative study on behavioral characteristics and family education between only-children and children with siblings. *Soc. Invest. Study* 6 (in Chinese)

Chen, L. 1935. *Essentials of Industrial Psy-*

chology. Shanghai: Chinese Commercial Press (in Chinese)

Chen, L. 1948. A factor study of a test battery at different education levels. *J. Genet. Psychol.* 73:187–99

Chen, L. 1982. Opinions on testing. *Info. Psychol. Sci.* 3:1–4 (in Chinese)

Chen, L. 1983. *Prospectus of Industrial Psychology*. Hangzhou: Zhejiang People's Press (in Chinese)

Chen, L., ed. 1988a. *Psychology of Industrial Management*. Shanghai: Shanghai People's Press (in Chinese)

Chen, L. 1988b. Macroergonomics in industrial modernization. *Chin. J. Appl. Psychol.* 1:1–4 (in Chinese)

Chen, L. 1989. Organization development in China: Chinese version. *Chin. J. Appl. Psychol.* 1:1–5 (in Chinese)

Chen, L. 1990. Theoretical analysis of the validity of ability tests. *Chin. J. Appl. Psychol.* 1:1–4 (in Chinese)

Chen, L. 1991. On item response theory. *Psychol. Sci.* 1:1–5 (in Chinese)

Chen, L. 1992. School psychology as a profession. *Chin. J. Appl. Psychol.* 1:1–5 (in Chinese)

Chen, L., Wang, A. S. 1965. A developmental study of color and form abstraction in children. *Acta Psychol. Sinica* 10:154–62 (in Chinese)

Chen, L., Wang, A. S. 1979. Hold on to scientific experimentation in psychology. *Acta Psychol. Sinica* 11:10–16 (in Chinese)

Chen, M. J., Yuen, J. C. K. 1991. Effects of pinyin and script type on verbal processing: comparisons of China, Taiwan, and Hong Kong experience. *Int. J. Behav. Dev.* 14:429–48

Chen, Q. 1991. The measurement and analysis of achievement motivation among managers. *Chin. J. Appl. Psychol.* 1:38–45 (in Chinese)

Chen, X. Y., Shi, R. H. 1987. An experimental study of two factors affecting students' moral behavior. *Acta Psychol. Sinica* 19:57–62 (in Chinese)

Chen, Y. M., Peng, R. X. 1990. An experimental study on sentence comprehension. *Acta Psychol. Sinica* 22:225–31 (in Chinese)

Chen, Z. F. 1983. Item analysis of Eysenck Personality Questionnaire tested in Beijing-District. *Acta Psychol. Sinica* 15:211–18 (in Chinese)

Chen, Z. G. 1985. *Abnormal Psychology*. Beijing: People's Hygiene Press (in Chinese)

Cheung, F. M., Song, W. Z. 1989. A review on the clinical applications of the Chinese MMPI. *Psychol. Ass.: J. Consult. Clin. Psychol.* 1:230–37

Ching, C. C. 1980. Psychology in the People's Republic of China. *Am. Psychologist* 35:1084–89

Ching, C. C. 1984. Psychology and the four modernizations in China. *Int. J. Psychol.* 19:57–63

Davis, J. H. 1973. Group decision and social interaction: a theory of social decision schemes. *Psychol. Rev.* 80:97–125

Dong, Q. 1989. The development of meta-cognition among children aged 10–17. *Psychol. Dev. Educ.* 4:11–17 (in Chinese)

Dyal, J. A., Chan, C. 1985. Stress and distress: a study of Hong Kong Chinese and Euro-Canadian students. *J. Cross-Cult. Psychol.* 16:447–66

Executive Committee of Chinese Psychological Society. 1982. Retrospect and prospect of 60 years of psychology in China. In commemoration of the 60th anniversary of the founding of the Chinese Psychological Society. *Acta Psychol. Sinica* 14:127–38 (in Chinese)

Falbo, T., Poston, D. L., Ji, G., Jiao, S., Jing, Q., et al. 1989. Physical, achievement and personality characteristics of Chinese children. *J. Biosoc. Sci.* 21:483–95

Fallon, B. J., Pfister, H. P., Brebner, J. 1989. *Advances in Industrial Organizational Psychology*. North-Holland: Elsevier

Gao, J. F., ed. 1985. *History of Chinese Psychology*. Beijing: People's Educ. Press (in Chinese)

Ge, L. Z., Zhu, Z. X. 1987. Effects of task background illumination, task contrast and the size of visual task detail on the visual performance. *Acta Psychol. Sinica* 19:270–81 (in Chinese)

Gong, Y. X. 1983. Revision of Wechsler's Adult Intelligence Scale in China. *Acta Psychol. Sinica* 15:362–70 (in Chinese)

Gong, Y. X. 1984. Eysenck Personality Questionnaire revised in China. *Info. Psychol. Sci.* 4:11–18 (in Chinese)

Gu, J. K. 1988. Projects in psychology during 1982–1987 supported by the National Science Foundation. *Acta Psychol. Sinica* 20:335–36 (in Chinese)

Harvey, C. R., Zhu, M. S., Miao, X. C. 1990. A cross-cultural study of Chinese and Canadian early and middle adolescents' performance in the individual differences. *Info. Psychol. Sci.* 1:1–6 (in Chinese)

He, B. Y., Zhang, H. C., Chen, S. Y. 1983. *Experimental Psychology*. Beijing: Peking Univ. Press (in Chinese)

He, C. D., Wang, A. F., Ke, W. Q., Zhao, G. S., Feng, G. Q., Zhao, Y. 1986. An analysis of the effects of occupational long-term exposure to stable noise on workers' EEG. *Info. Psychol. Sci.* 1:23–25 (in Chinese)

Hong, D. H., Zhou, J. J., Wang, Y. H., Xu, Z. J. 1989. The Chinese Adolescent Non-intellectual Personality Inventory. *Info. Psychol. Sci.* 2:13–17 (in Chinese)

Hu, B. Z. 1985. *Educational Psychology*. Taipei: San-Ming Press (in Chinese)

Huang, X. T., Shi, K., Wang, X. S. 1984. A psychological study of inter-personal relations in college classes. *Acta Psychol. Sinica* 16:455–65 (in Chinese)

Huang, X. T., Zhang, J. F., Zhang, S. L. 1989.

Investigation on the values of Chinese of five cities adolescent students. *Acta Psychol. Sinica* 21:274–83 (in Chinese)

Hwang, M. T. Z. 1976. *Personnel Psychology.* Taipei: San-Ming Press (in Chinese)

Jiao, S. L., Ching, C. C., Yu, B. L. 1979. Changes in luminance of visual field and contrast sensitivity. *Acta Psychol. Sinica* 11:47–54 (in Chinese)

Jing, Q. C. 1987. *Psychology in China.* In *Concise Encyclopedia of Psychology,* ed. R. J. Corsini. New York: Wiley

Jing, Q. C. 1990. A report on the 4th Executive Committee of Chinese Psychological Society. *Info. Psychol. Sci.* 1:58–60 (In Chinese)

Jing, Q. C., ed. 1991. *Chinese Concise Encyclopedia of Psychology.* Cangsa: Wunan Educ. Press (in Chinese)

Jing, Q. C., Jiao, S. L., Ji, G. P. 1987. *Human Vision.* Beijing: Sci. Press (in Chinese)

Kao, H. S. R. 1986. *The Psychology of Handwriting.* Taipei: Dongda Book Company (in Chinese)

Kao, H. S. R., Hoosain, R., eds. 1984. *Psychological Studies of the Chinese Language.* Hong Kong: The Chinese Language Society of Hong Kong

Kuang, P. Z. 1987. *Physiological Psychology.* Beijing: Scientific Press (in Chinese)

Kuang, P. Z., Luo, S. D., Liu, S. X. 1980. Thirty years' of physiological psychology in China. *Acta Psychol. Sinica* 12:144–51 (in Chinese)

Kuang, P. Z., and Associates. 1988. The effects of piracetam, huperzine A, gynostemma pentaphyllum makino, helicid and anisodine on open field behavior in rats. *Acta Psychol. Sinica* 20:205–14 (in Chinese)

Laaksonen, O. 1988. *Management in China: During and after Mao in Enterprises, Government, and Party.* Berlin: Walter de Gruyter

Leung, K., Bond, M. H. 1984. The impact of cultural collectivism on reward allocation. *J. Pers. Soc. Psychol.* 54:793–803

Li, D., Jin, Y., Zhu, Y. M., Tang, C. H. 1987. Report on the norm of Wechsler Intelligence Scale for Children–China Revised (WISC-CR) in Shanghai. *Acta Psychol. Sinica* 19:136–44 (in Chinese)

Li, D. M., Zhou, Y., Chen, S. K., Wang, S. X., Sun, F. L. 1990. A comparative study of hospital nurses' intelligent activities before and after their work shifts. *Info. Psychol. Sci.* 4:29–31 (in Chinese)

Li, S. Z., Cai, F., Dai, X. H., Guo, Y. W. 1985. Effects of industrial noise on human abilities of STM and attention. *Info. Psychol. Sci.* 6:45–50 (in Chinese)

Li, W. 1988. A method of psychological appraisal of the quality of class teaching. *Acta Psychol. Sinica* 20:392–99 (in Chinese)

Li, X. T., Xu, S. L., Kuang, P. Z. 1980. Thirty years of Chinese medical psychology. *Acta Psychol. Sinica* 12:135–43 (in Chinese)

Li, X. Y. 1988. A preliminary study on employees' needs and motivation in enterprises. *Behav. Sci.* 4:5–12 (in Chinese)

Lin, C. D. 1983. The development of thinking flexibility of operation in school children. *Acta Psychol. Sinica* 15:419–28 (in Chinese)

Lin, C. T. 1980. A sketch on the methods of mental testing in ancient China. *Acta Psychol. Sinica* 12:75–80 (in Chinese)

Lin, R. M. 1980. *Industrial Psychology.* Taipei: Zen-Weng Press (in Chinese)

Lin, W. Q., Chen, L. (Long), Wang, D. 1987. The construction of the CPM scale for leadership assessment. *Acta Psychol. Sinica* 19:199–207 (in Chinese)

Lin, W. Q., Fang, L. L., Khanna, A. 1991. The study of implicit leadership theory in China. *Acta Psychol. Sinica* 23:236–42 (in Chinese)

Lin, Z. X., Fang, Z. 1980. Thirty years' developments in Chinese experimental psychology. *Acta Psychol. Sinica* 12:9–15 (in Chinese)

Lin, Z. X., Zhao, L. R. 1992. Seventy years of Chinese Pcychological Society. *Acta Psychol. Sinica* 24:217–22 (in Chinese)

Liu, F. 1982. Developmental psychology in China. *Acta Psychol. Sinica* 14:1–10 (in Chinese)

Liu, J. H., Li, H. Y., Cao, Z. F., Sheng, J. X., Zhou, R. 1984. Development of length concept among 5–12-year-olds in the five regions in China. *Info. Psychol. Sci.* 2:8–12 (in Chinese)

Long, D., Li, X. T. 1990. The hemispheric cooperation in man after callosotomy of the trunk of the corpus collosum. *Acta Psychol. Sinica* 22:421–27 (in Chinese)

Lu, H. J. 1986. A study of the situational simulation method in appraisal and selection of managers. *Info. Psychol. Sci.* 2:43–48 (in Chinese)

Lu, J., Xu, F. 1988. The construction of diagnosing scale of cognitive abilities for children. *Chin. J. Appl. Psychol.* 2:1–7 (in Chinese)

Lu, S. Z., Wu, L. L., Zheng, Q. Q., Wang, Z. M. 1985. *Managerial Psychology.* Hangzhou: Zhejiang Educ. Press (in Chinese)

Luo, S. D., Li, D. M., Sun, L. H. 1979. Brainchemical study of memory and learning. *Acta Psychol. Sinica* 11:65–76 (in Chinese)

Ma, H. K. 1989. Moral orientation and moral judgment in adolescents in Hong Kong, Mainland China, and England. *J. Cross-Cult. Psychol.* 20:152–77

Mao, Y. Y. 1989. An early intervention program for mentally retarded preschool children in Beijing. *Acta Psychol. Sinica* 21:237–46 (in Chinese)

Meng, Z. L. 1987. Influence of different emotions on mental performance. *Info. Psychol. Sci.* 4:1–6 (in Chinese)

Miao, X. C., Sang, B. 1991. A further study of the semantic memory of Chinese words. *Psychol. Sci.* 1:6–9 (in Chinese)

Miller, K., Stigler, J. W. 1987. Counting in Chinese: cultural variation in a basic cognitive skill. *Cogn. Dev.* 2:279–305

Miner, J. B., Chen, C. C., Yu, K. C. 1991. Theory testing under adverse conditions: motivation to manage in the People's Republic of China. *J. Appl. Psychol.* 76:343–49

Murphy, G., Kovach, J. K. 1972. *Historical Introduction to Modern Psychology.* New York: Harcourt Brace Jovanovich. 3rd ed.

Nevis, E. C. 1983. Using an American perspective in understanding another culture: toward a hierarchy of needs for the People's Republic of China. *J. Appl. Behav. Sci.* 19:249–64

Niu, J., Zhang, S. F. 1983. Survey on learning ability of 1400 students of Han, Bai and Dai nationality in Kunming, Dehong and Dali city in Yunnan province. *Acta Psychol. Sinica* 15:395–401 (in Chinese)

Pan, S. 1964. *Educational Psychology.* Beijing: People's Educ. Press (in Chinese)

Pan, S., Gao, J. F., eds. 1983. *The Study of Chinese Ancient Psychological Thinking.* Nanchang: Jiangxi People's Press (in Chinese)

Peng, D. L. 1990. *Cognitive Psychology.* Beijing: Beijing Normal Univ. Press (in Chinese)

Peng, K. P., Chen, Z. G. 1989. Chinese value orientation in university students. *Acta Psychol. Sinica* 21:149–55 (in Chinese)

Peng, R. X. 1980. Thirty years of industrial psychology in China. *Acta Psychol. Sinica* 12:16–21 (in Chinese)

Qiu, Y. J. 1986. A preliminary study on personality among Chinese excellent running athletes. *Info. Psychol. Sci.* 3:20–26 (in Chinese)

Redding, G., Wong, G. Y. Y. 1986. The psychology of Chinese organizational behavior. See Bond 1986, pp. 267–95

Rokeach, M. 1973. *The Nature of Human Values.* New York: Free Press

San, H. H., Yan, W. W., Yan, H. Q. 1990. Mental hygiene problems of QiGong. *Info. Psychol. Sci.* 6:41–43 (in Chinese)

Shao, R. Z. 1986. *Educational Psychology.* Shanghai: Shanghai Educ. Press (in Chinese)

Sheng, J. X., Liu, F., Sun, C. S., Zhao, S. W. 1984. Research on the development of "volume" concept of 5–17 years old children and youth. *Acta Psychol. Sinica* 16:155–64 (in Chinese)

Shi, R. H., Yang, Z. L. 1980. A comparison of effects of acupuncture and suggestion on the pain threshold. *Acta Psychol. Sinica* 12:341–47 (in Chinese)

Shi, S. H. 1990. Analysis of the development in research of developmental and educational psychology during 1979–1988 in China. *Acta Psychol. Sinica:* 22:322–28 (in Chinese)

Smith, P. B., Peterson M. F., Wang Z. M. 1990. Leadership as the management of role conflict. Presented at 22nd Int. Congr. Appl. Psychol. Kyoto, Japan

Song, W. Z., and Associates. 1982. The revision, employment and evaluation of MMPI in China. *Acta Psychol. Sinica* 14:449–58 (in Chinese)

Song, W. Z., and Associates. 1985. Analysis of results of MMPI of normal Chinese subjects. *Acta Psychol. Sinica* 17:346–55 (in Chinese)

Stevenson, H. W., Jing, Q. C. 1984. Issues in cognition. Proc. Joint Conf. Psychol.: Natl. Acad. Sci. & Chinese Acad. Sci. Washington, DC: Natl. Acad. Sci. and APA

Sui, G. Y. 1991. The training of achievement motivation and attribution in middle school students. *Psychol. Sci.* 4:21–26 (in Chinese)

Sun, F. L., Wang, J. S., and Associates. 1984. An analysis on EEG power spectrum and coherence during quiet state in QiGong. *Acta Psychol. Sinica* 16:422–27 (in Chinese)

Tan, J. L. 1986. Problems in revising Western psychological tests such as WAIS. *Acta Psychol. Sinica* 18:333–41 (in Chinese)

Tan, L. H., Peng, D. L. 1991. Visual recognition processes of Chinese characters: a research to the effect of grapheme and phoneme. *Acta Psychol. Sinica* 23:278–83 (in Chinese)

Tang, C. M., Wang, J. M., Lu, Z. Y., Wei, X., Sun, L. H. 1989. Effects of Gi-Gong on personality in the elderly. *Acta Psychol. Sinica* 21:354–58 (in Chinese)

Teng, G. R. 1989. Decision-making in small groups: the influence of member status differences and task type on group consensus. *Acta Psychol. Sinica* 21:76–85 (in Chinese)

Triandis, H. C., McCusker, C., Hui, C. H. 1990. Multimethod probes of individualism and collectivism. *J. Pers. Soc. Psychol.* 59:1006–20

Wan, K. C., Bond, M. H. 1982. Chinese attributions for success and failure under public and anonymous conditions of rating. *Acta Psychol. Taiwanica* 24:23–31

Wang, A. S., Liu, X. 1990. Cognitive strategies in solving covariance-problems in process control. *Ergonomics* 33:891–908

Wang, A. S., Qiu, Z. L., Qian, X. Y. 1988. Cognition in an elementary motor system. *Acta Psychol. Sinica* 20:23–30 (in Chinese)

Wang, J. S., Xin, D. G., Sun, C. H., Lin, S. H. 1979. The role played by the psychological factors in the clinical mechanism of acupuncture anaesthesia. *Acta Psychol. Sinica* 11:88–97 (in Chinese)

Wang, S. 1979. Modes of haptic perception and length discrimination. *Acta Psychol. Sinica* 11:55–64 (in Chinese)

Wang, S. 1990. On further development of psychology in China. *Info. Psychol. Sci.* 1:61–63 (In Chinese)

Wang, S., Zhang, M. 1990. Tactile discrimination of distance between two end-points of a curved line. *Acta Psychol. Sinica* 22:135–40 (in Chinese)

Wang, W. J., He, S. J., Sun, C. F. 1988. An experimental study on the motor coordination training for mentally-retarded children. *Chin. J. Appl. Psychol.* 2:28–39 (in Chinese)

Wang, Z. M. 1986. Worker's attribution and its effects on performance under different responsibility systems. *Chin. J. Appl. Psychol.* 2:6–10 (in Chinese)

Wang, Z. M. 1988a. *Work and Personnel Psychology.* Hangzhou: Zhejiang Educ. Press (in Chinese)

Wang, Z. M. 1988b. The effects of responsibility system change and group attributional training on performance: a quasi-experiment in Chinese factories. *Chin. J. Appl. Psychol.* 3:7–11 (in Chinese)

Wang, Z. M. 1989a. Human resource management in China: recent trends. In *Human Resource management: An International Comparison*, ed. R. Pieper, pp. 195–210. Berlin: Walter de Gruyter

Wang, Z. M. 1989b. The human-computer interface hierarchy model and strategies in system development. *Ergonomics* 32:1391–400

Wang, Z. M. 1989c. Participation and skill utilization in organizational decision making in Chinese enterprises. See Fallon et al 1989

Wang, Z. M. 1990a. Action research and O. D. strategies in Chinese enterprises. *Organ. Dev. J.* 8(1):66–70

Wang, Z. M. 1990b. *Research Methods in Psychology.* Beijing: People's Educ. Press (in Chinese)

Wang, Z. M., ed. 1990c. *Ergonomics. Spec. Issue: Ergonom. in China* 33(7)

Wang, Z. M. 1990d. Information structures and cognitive strategies in decision making on systems development. *Ergonomics* 33:907–16

Wang, Z. M. 1990e. Recent developments in ergonomics in China. *Ergonomics* 33:853–65

Wang, Z. M. 1991a. Recent developments in industrial and organizational psychology in People's Republic of China. In *International Review of Industrial and Organizational Psychology*, ed. C. Cooper, R. T. Robertson, pp. 1–15. London: Wiley

Wang, Z. M. 1991b. New approach to elicitation and acquisition of decision knowledge and rules. *Chin. J. Appl. Psychol.* 1:23–29 (in Chinese)

Wang, Z. M. 1992a. Managerial psychological strategies for Sino-foreign joint-ventures. *J. Manage. Psychol.* 7(3):10–16

Wang, Z. M. 1993. Culture, economic reform and the role of industrial and organizational psychology in China. In *Handbook of Industrial and Organizational Psychology*, ed. M. D. Dunnette, L. M. Hough, Vol. 4. Palo Alto: Consulting Psychologists Press,

Inc. 2nd ed. In press

Wang, Z. M., Fan, B. N. 1990. The task structure and information processing requirements of decision making on director responsibility systems in Chinese enterprises. *Chin. J. Appl. Psychol.* 1:13–18 (in Chinese)

Wang, Z. M., He, G. B. 1991. The information structure and decision support strategies for hi-tech decision-making in Chinese enterprises. *Chinese J. Appl. Psychol.* 2:22–29 (in Chinese)

Wang, Z. M., Heller, F. A. 1991. Some China-UK comparisons on top management decision making across cultures. Presented at Symp. Organ. Decis. Making across Cult. Debrecen, Hungary

Wang, Z. M., Peterson, C. C. 1988. Patterns and attributional correlates in reward allocation between Chinese and Australian children and adults. *Abstr. 24th Int. Congr. Psychol.* 5: F862

Wang, Z. M., Sheng, J. P. 1990. The managerial decision-making and the performance appraisal system for Sino-foreign joint-ventures. *Chin. J. Appl. Psychol.* 4:29–37 (in Chinese)

Wang, Z. M., Wang, Y. B. 1991. The network structure of information and decision support strategies in personnel decision making. *Chin. J. Appl. Psychol.* 3:18–25 (in Chinese)

Wang, Z. M., Zhong, J. A. 1992. The effects of decision support information on decision making patterns in systems development. *Ergonomics* 35: In press

Warner, M. 1987. *Management Reforms in China.* London: Frances Pinter

Weiner, B. 1979. A theory of motivation for some classroom experiences. *J. Educ. Psychol.* 71:3–25

Wu, L. L. 1986. A job analysis of management cadres in enterprises. *Chin. J. Appl. Psychol.* 3:12–16 (in Chinese)

Xie, X. F., Lu, S. Z. 1990. Examination of the assessment method for cadres. *Chin. J. Appl. Psychol.* 1:5–12 (in Chinese)

Xu, B. H. 1988. Contrast threshold in identification of color light signals under different illuminating lights. *Chin. J. Appl. Psychol.* 3:31–37 (in Chinese)

Xu, L. C. 1986. Development on organizational behavior study in China. *Acta Psychol. Sinica* 18:343–48 (in Chinese)

Xu, L. C. 1987. Recent development in organizational psychology in China. In *Advances in Organizational Psychology: An International Review*, ed. B. Bass, pp. 242–51. New York: Sage

Xu, L. C. 1989. Comparative study of leadership between Chinese and Japanese managers based upon PM theory. See Fallon et al 1989

Xu, L. C. 1990. Applied psychology in China. *Appl. Psychol. Int. Rev.* 39:255–64

Xu, L. C., Chen, L. (Long), Wang, D., Xue, A. Y. 1985. The role of psychology in enterprise management. *Acta Psychol. Sinica* 17:339–45 (in Chinese)

Xu, L. C., Chen, L. (Long). 1987. *Managerial Psychology*. Beijing: People's Daily Press (in Chinese)

Xu, L. C., Wang, Z. M. 1991. New development in organizational psychology in China. *Appl. Psychol. Int. Rev.* 40 1:3–14

Xu, S. L., and Associates. 1979. Patients' emotional state on entering the operation room, its relationship to the effect of acupuncture anesthesia and to some psychophysiological functions. *Acta Psychol. Sinica* 11:77–87 (in Chinese)

Xu, S. L., Wu, Z. Y. 1986. The construction of the Clinical Memory Test. *Acta Psychol. Sinica* 18:100–8 (in Chinese)

Xu, S. L., Wu, Z. Y., Sun, C. H., Wu, Z. P. 1988. Some studies in the psychology of aging. *Info. Psychol. Sci.* 4:5–10 (in Chinese)

Xu, W., Zhu, Z. X. 1990. The effects of target size and luminance on color coding in a CRT display. *Acta Psychol. Sinica* 22:260–66 (in Chinese)

Yang, G. X., Jiang, J. Z., Ci, G. X., Yu, W. Z. 1984. The influence of color upon the rate of detection of instrumental visual display. *Acta Psychol. Sinica* 16:70–74 (in Chinese)

Yang, K. S. 1986. Chinese personality and its change. See Bond 1986, pp. 106–70

Yang, K. S., Lee, P. H. 1971. Likability, meaningfulness, and familiarity of 557 Chinese adjectives for personality trait description. *Acta Psychol. Taiwanica* 13:36–57

Yang, X. H., Wei, S. L. 1990. The representation training in instructions of artistic gymnastics. *Chin. J. Appl. Psychol.* 3:33–36 (in Chinese)

Ye, R. M., Rocklin, T. 1988. A cross-cultural research on test anxiety. *Info. Psychol. Sci.* 3:25–29

Yu, B. L., Feng, L., Cao, H. Q. 1990. Visual perception of Chinese characters: effects of perceptual task and Chinese character attributes. *Acta Psychol. Sinica* 23:141–48 (in Chinese)

Yu, B. L., Jing, Q. C. 1984. STM capacity for Chinese words and phrases under simultaneous presentations. See Stevensen & Jing 1984, pp. 317–29

Yu, W. Z. 1988a. The motivational function of group structure under labor contract systems. *Behav. Sci.* 3:8–10 (in Chinese)

Yu, W. Z. 1989. *Managerial Psychology*. Lanzhou: Gansu People's Press (in Chinese)

Yu, W. Z., Wu, L. J., Huang, H. L. 1988. People's tolerance to psychological pressure under economic reform. *Info. Psychol. Sci.* 5:36–40 (in Chinese)

Zha, Z. X. 1986. A five-year study of the mental development of supernormal children. *Acta Psychol. Sinica* 18:123–32 (in Chinese)

Zha, Z. X. 1990. A ten year study of the mental development of supernormal children. *Acta Psychol. Sinica* 22:113–26 (in Chinese)

Zhang, D. R., Chen, L. 1991. Naming asymmetry: a Chinese case with staged callosal section. *Acta Psychol. Sinica* 23:285–91 (in Chinese)

Zhang, H. C. 1988. Psychological measurement in China. *Int. J. Psychol.* 23:101–17

Zhang, H. C., Men, Q. M. 1981. *Statistics in Psychology and Education*. Lanzhou: Gansu People's Press (in Chinese)

Zhang, H. C., Shu, H. 1989. Phonetic similar and graphic similar priming effects in pronouncing Chinese characters. *Acta Psychol. Sinica* 21:284-89 (in Chinese)

Zhang, H. C., Wang, X. P. 1989. Standardization research on Raven's Standard Progressive Matrices in China. *Acta Psychol. Sinica* 21:113–21 (in Chinese)

Zhang, H. Z., Jing, Q. C. 1988. Effects of illuminance and VDT luminance contract on visual performance. *Acta Psychol. Sinica* 20:243–52 (in Chinese)

Zhang, J. J., Zhang, H. C., Peng, D. L. 1990. The semantic retrieval of Chinese characters in the classifying process. *Acta Psychol. Sinica* 23:397–405 (in Chinese)

Zhang, M. L., Liu, J. H. 1991. An experiment to promote the development of children's mathematical thinking. *Appl. Psychol.: Int. Rev.* 40:27–35

Zhang, R. J. 1987. A review of the development of psychology in Taiwan district. *Acta Psychol. Sinica* 19:302–6 (in Chinese)

Zhang, W. T., Peng, R. X. 1984. STM capacity for Chinese words and idioms with visual and auditory presentations. See Stevensen & Jing 1984, pp. 331–44

Zhang, Z., Zuo, M. L. 1990. The development of children's strategy in problem-solving. *Info. Psychol. Sci.* 2:21–26 (in Chinese)

Zhang, Z. J., Liu, F., Zhao, S. W., Sun, C. S., Zuo, M. L., Chen, A. F. 1985. A study of experiments on children aged 5–15 in grasping the concept of probability. *Info. Psychol. Sci.* 6:1–6 (in Chinese)

Zhang, Z. S., Sheng, D. L. 1987. *Fundamentals of Psychology*. Beijing: Educ. Sci. Press (in Chinese)

Zhao, H. T. 1987. An investigation of young people's interest in learning. *Info. Psychol. Sci.* 5:28–33 (in Chinese)

Zhao, L. R. 1981. Psychology in the Taiwan Province. *Acta Psychol. Sinica* 13:364–68 (in Chinese)

Zhao, M. J., Wan, M. G., Ma, N. Q. 1989. A comparative study of semantic comprehension among Han, Tibetan, Dongxiang, Bonan, Yuku and Kazak children aged 7–9. *Acta Psychol. Sinica* 21:207–15 (in Chinese)

Zhao, Z. Y., Yang, C. F. 1989. Semantic desirability as a systematic distortion in person perception studies. *Acta Psychol. Sinica* 21:332-36 (in Chinese)

Zheng, R. C., Xiao, B. L. 1983. A study on the creativity of high school students. *Acta*

Psychol. Sinica 15:445–52 (in Chinese)

Zheng, Z. Y., Zhao, G. M., Qi, X. L., Zhang, C. X. 1980. The information processing of binocular stereoscopic vision. I. The relationship between binocular disparity and spatial frequency spectrum. *Acta Psychol. Sinica* 12:195–204 (in Chinese)

Zhong, J. A. 1989. Perceptions of job characteristics and satisfaction. *Chin. J. Appl. Psychol.* 2:14–21 (in Chinese)

Zhou, G. 1988. A computer simulation of tactic thinking of basketball athletes. *Acta Psychol. Sinica* 20:291–98 (in Chinese)

Zhu, P. L., Fang, X. C. 1988. The intelligence of master athletes. *Acta Psychol. Sinica* 20:283–90 (in Chinese)

Zhu, Y., Wang, H. B., Fan, J., Zhou, A. B. 1991. Levels of processing, declarative retrieval strategies and implicit memory. *Acta Psychol. Sinica* 23:264–71 (in Chinese)

Zhu, Y. M., Lu, S. Y., Tang, C. H., Song, J., Gao, E. S., Gu, X. Y. 1984. The WPPSI and its trial test in Shanghai. *Info. Psychol. Sci.* 5:22–29 (in Chinese)

Zhu, Zi-Xian. 1962. *Child Psychology.* Beijing: People's Educ. Press (in Chinese)

Zhu, Zi-Xian, ed. 1989. *The Chinese Dictionary of Psychology.* Beijing: Beijing Normal Univ. Press (in Chinese)

Zhu, Zi-Xian, ed. 1990. *Psychological Development and Education of Chinese Children and Adolescence.* Beijing: Chinese Excellence Press (in Chinese)

Zhu, Zi-Xian, Lin, C. D. 1986. *Developmental Psychology of Thinking.* Beijing: Beijing Normal Univ. Press (in Chinese)

Zhu, Zi-Xian, Lin, C. D. 1991. Research and application in Chinese child psychology. *Appl. Psychol.: Int. Rev.* 40:15–25

Zhu, Zu-Xiang, ed. 1990. *Engineering Psychology.* Shanghai: East-China Normal Univ. Press (in Chinese)

Zhu, Zu-Xiang, Wu, J. M. 1990. On the standardization of VDT's proper and optimal contrast range. *Ergonomics* 33:925–33

Zhu, Zu-Xiang, Zhang, Z. J. 1990. Maximum acceptable repetitive lifting workload by Chinese subjects. *Ergonomics* 33:875–84

Zuo, M. L., Liu, J. X., Zhou, R., Li, H. Y., Chen, A. F. 1984. A study on the development of concept of number series among 5–11 years old children in five districts in China. *Acta Psychol. Sinica* 16:174–81 (in Chinese)

Annu. Rev. Psychol. 1993. 44:117–54
Copyright © 1993 by Annual Reviews Inc.

ATTITUDES AND ATTITUDE CHANGE

James M. Olson

Department of Psychology, University of Western Ontario, London, Ontario, Canada N6A 5C2

Mark P. Zanna

Department of Psychology, University of Waterloo, Waterloo, Ontario, Canada N2L 3G1

KEYWORDS: persuasion, beliefs, prejudice, stereotypes, values

CONTENTS

INTRODUCTION 118
ATTITUDE STRUCTURE 118
   Definitions of Attitude 119
   Affective, Cognitive, and Behavioral Correlates of Attitudes............................... 120
   Attitude Attributes.. 122
   Measurement of Attitudes... 123
VALUES AND ATTITUDES 125
   Value-Attitude Relations.. 125
   Functions of Attitudes: Value Expression Versus Object Appraisal 125
ATTITUDE FORMATION 127
   Conditioning of Attitudes 127
   Heritability of Attitudes 128
ATTITUDES AND INFORMATION-PROCESSING.. 129
   Selective Interpretation 129
   Selective Memory... 130
ATTITUDES AND BEHAVIORS 131
   Theory of Reasoned Action 131
   Alternative Models of the Attitude-Behavior Relation... 132
   Effects of Behavior on Attitudes 133
PERSUASION... 135
   Elaboration-Likelihood and Heuristic-Systematic Models of Persuasion 135
   Message Reception 136

0066-4308/93/1201-0117$02.00

Source Characteristics 138
Message Characteristics 138
Recipient Characteristics 140
STEREOTYPES AND PREJUDICE 141
Stereotypes 141
Prejudice 143
CONCLUSIONS 145

INTRODUCTION

Attitudes and attitude change remain among the most extensively researched topics by social psychologists. Our task is to review the attitudes literature from 1989 to 1991. Some papers published or in press early in 1992 (prior to the due date for our manuscript) are also included.

We were overwhelmed by the number of articles and chapters on attitudes that appeared in the three-year period of our review. We were forced to exclude several hundred relevant papers to meet space limitations. For example, we excluded many fascinating applications of attitudes research to social problems (e.g. health promotion; effects of salient events on attitudes). We also excluded studies that focused on advertising and research examining the influence of the media on attitudes and behaviors. Studies of group influence (e.g. minority influence), intergroup relations (e.g. social identity theory), and self-presentation were also largely excluded despite their relevance to attitude processes; some of these topics have been reviewed recently elsewhere in this series (e.g. Schlenker & Weigold 1992). Even with these exclusions, we had to be highly selective in citing the relevant articles that remained. We focused on the papers that we found most interesting, provocative, and informative about underlying processes.

The level of activity in the attitudes literature is underscored by the number of books that have appeared recently. In addition to numerous texts for undergraduates (e.g. Milburn 1991; O'Keefe 1990; Oskamp 1991; Rajecki 1990; Reardon 1991; Zimbardo & Leippe 1991), specialized books have appeared on attitude measures (Robinson et al 1991), social judgment (Eiser 1990), propaganda (Pratkanis & Aronson 1991), and prejudice (Mackie & Hamilton 1992; Zanna & Olson 1992). The most noteworthy addition to the literature is an extraordinary book by Eagly & Chaiken (1992), which provides a comprehensive review and analysis of the attitudes literature; we refer readers to this scholarly book for elaboration of many issues raised in our review.

ATTITUDE STRUCTURE

In the last decade, structural issues have become a central interest of attitude researchers (see McGuire 1985; Pratkanis et al 1989), as indicated by the emergence of sections on attitude structure in the two preceding reviews of attitudes published in this series (Chaiken & Stangor 1987; Tesser & Shaffer

1990). Although a few researchers have examined how attitudes toward different topics are interrelated (e.g. the relationship of political expertise and consistency among political attitudes: see Judd & Downing 1990), attention has focused on questions of intra-attitudinal structure.

Definitions of Attitude

The most basic structural question about attitudes concerns the nature of the concept itself. Despite the long history of research on attitudes, there is no universally agreed-upon definition. Influential theorists variously define attitudes primarily in terms of evaluation (e.g. "a psychological tendency that is expressed by evaluating a particular entity with some degree of favor or disfavor," Eagly & Chaiken 1992), affect (e.g. "the affect associated with a mental object," Greenwald 1989 p. 432), cognition (e.g. "a special type of knowledge, notably knowledge of which content is evaluative or affective," Kruglanski 1989 p. 139), and behavioral predispositions (e.g. "a state of a person that predisposes a favorable or unfavorable response to an object, person, or idea" Triandis 1991 p. 485).

Notwithstanding these differences, we think that most attitude theorists agree that (a) evaluation constitutes a central, perhaps predominant, aspect of attitudes, (b) attitudes are represented in memory, and (c) affective, cognitive, and behavioral antecedents of attitudes can be distinguished, as can affective, cognitive, and behavioral consequences of attitudes.

ATTITUDES AS EVALUATIONS   Most theorists implicate evaluation in their definitions of attitudes. Eagly & Chaiken (1992) argue that attitudes do not form until individuals respond evaluatively to an entity and that, once formed, attitudes predispose evaluative responses when the attitude object is subsequently encountered. Eagly & Chaiken also note that evaluative responses can be overt or covert and cognitive, affective, or behavioral.

ATTITUDES AS REPRESENTATIONS IN MEMORY   A second common assumption among attitude researchers is that attitudes are represented in memory. For example, attitudes have been characterized as knowledge structures (e.g. Anderson & Armstrong 1989; Kruglanski 1989) and as associative networks of interconnected evaluations and beliefs (e.g. Fazio 1990; Pratkanis & Greenwald 1989). These perspectives imply that elicitation of one attitude or belief will make closely related attitudes and beliefs more accessible through a process of spreading activation. In a clever demonstration of this idea, Tourangeau et al (1991) timed respondents as they indicated agreement or disagreement with statements about abortion and welfare. These statements had previously been scaled for their topical similarity (reflecting similarity on dimensions independent of evaluation). Agree/disagree judgments were faster when an item followed a topically related item.

One model that nicely integrates the representational and evaluative features of attitudes is the *sociocognitive model* proposed by Pratkanis & Greenwald (1989). According to these authors, an attitude is represented in memory by (*a*) an object label, (*b*) an evaluative summary, and (*c*) a knowledge structure supporting the evaluation. Using principles of social cognition, Pratkanis & Greenwald describe how attitudes provide simple strategies for problem-solving, organize memory for events, and maintain self-worth. These authors view attitudes as cognitive representations of evaluations, which serve a fundamental role in relating an individual to the social world.

Breckler & Wiggins (1989a) define attitudes explicitly as "mental and neural representations." They point out that representations take various forms and that the same object can be represented in multiple ways. For example, an individual's attitude toward sour milk consists of verbal knowledge (e.g. evaluative words and labels) and nonverbal responses to the olfactory stimulation of sour milk itself; these components may be stored in distinct symbolic systems. This representational perspective underscores that verbal, self-report measures of attitudes may not capture the full range of the concept, especially its nonverbal (often affective) component.

Affective, Cognitive, and Behavioral Correlates of Attitudes

The tripartite view of attitudes has been influential from the very beginning of research on this concept (see McGuire 1985). Rather than assuming that all attitudes necessarily have affective, cognitive, and behavioral components, however, recent researchers have focused on these domains as correlates of attitudes. For example, Zanna & Rempel (1988) argued that attitudes can be based upon, or develop from, affective information (as in the case of conditioning), cognitive information (as in the case of knowledge-based evaluations), and behavioral information (as in the case of self-perception inferences from prior actions). Eagly & Chaiken (1992) explain how attitudes can generate affective responses (e.g. liking for an object), cognitive responses (e.g. attributions for the target's actions), and behavioral responses (e.g. overt actions toward the target).

Thus, the affective-cognitive-behavioral framework provides a useful heuristic for thinking about both the antecedents and consequences of attitudes, but these domains will not necessarily all apply to a given attitude. Indeed, consistency among affective, cognitive, and behavioral correlates of attitudes is an empirical issue.

EVALUATION VERSUS AFFECT IN ATTITUDES   Breckler & Wiggins (1989b, 1991) have distinguished between affect and evaluation in the structure of attitudes. Their procedure involves asking subjects to rate the attitude object on a series of bipolar adjective scales (e.g. bad/good, wise/foolish), once according to how the object makes them feel ("affect") and once according to how the object is ("evaluation," though based principally on cognitive beliefs about the object). These ratings do not yield equivalent values. Rather, affect and evaluation correlate uniquely with self-ratings of liking for the object (which Breckler & Wiggins call the global attitude). Also, affect sometimes does a better job of predicting self-report behaviors than does evaluation (e.g. in the domain of blood donation). The authors conclude from their studies that affect and evaluation constitute distinct attitude components.

We prefer to maintain the view of attitudes as evaluative judgments that are stored in memory (as previously articulated), of which affect is one possible source. Nevertheless, Breckler & Wiggins have identified attitude domains where overall evaluations do not fully capture subjects' affective reactions to the objects. Because affect can drive psychological processes and behavior, it has unique predictive utility beyond summary evaluative judgments in these domains.

AFFECT VERSUS COGNITION IN ATTITUDES   Whether attitudes are based on affective or cognitive information seems to be important. Edwards (1990) induced subjects to form either affect-based or cognition-based attitudes, for example by having subjects either taste a new soft drink before reading about its features or read about the features before tasting it. Subjects were then exposed either to an affective or a cognitive means of persuasion, for example the drink's mildly aversive odor or a written description of several negative features of the drink. For affect-based attitudes, subjects showed more attitude change when the persuasive appeal employed an affective approach; cognition-based attitudes were equally influenced by each type of appeal. In contrast to these findings, Millar & Millar (1990) classified subjects as possessing either affect-based or cognition-based attitudes (e.g. liking a beverage because it makes you feel refreshed vs liking it because it is low in calories) and found that persuasive appeals were more effective when they adopted the perspective that did not match the presumed basis of the attitude (e.g. when an affective appeal attacked a cognition-based attitude).

Two methodological differences between these studies seem most pertinent to explaining the divergent results. First, Millar & Millar studied relatively well-formed attitudes; hence, subjects were probably able to counterargue more effectively messages that matched their attitude than mismatched messages. Second, the appeals used by Millar & Millar were all argument-based, providing information either about others' emotional or rational reactions to the object; these authors did not give subjects a new, personal affective experience concerning the object (as Edwards did when she exposed subjects to an aversive odor). Combining these points, we suspect that, for well-established attitudes, rational and emotional *arguments* will yield "mismatch" effects (as in Millar & Millar 1990). On the other hand, new affective *experiences* will be generally powerful sources of influence, perhaps especially for affect-based attitudes (as in Edwards 1990).

Another issue related to the distinction between affect-based and cognition-based attitudes, which again has generated apparently divergent results, concerns the effects of introspection on attitude-behavior consistency. Wilson and colleagues (Wilson 1990; Wilson et al 1989) have shown that asking subjects to think about the reasons for their attitudes produces attitude expressions that are less predictive of behavior. In contrast, Millar, Tesser, and colleagues (e.g. Millar & Tesser 1989; Tesser et al 1992) have found that asking subjects to think about their attitudes can produce more confident and extreme attitudes, which seem to predict behavior better. Of course, thinking about the reasons underlying one's attitude is not the same as thinking about one's attitude; the former instructions can bring to mind incomplete or inaccurate explanations that induce temporary shifts of opinion (Wilson 1990), whereas the latter instructions may evoke attitude-consistent thoughts that polarize evaluations, especially when underlying values are consistent with the attitude (Liberman & Chaiken 1991). Also, when the relevant behaviors are "consummatory" (driven by feelings and emotions) rather than "instrumental" (driven by cognitions), thinking about the reasons underlying one's attitudes might be especially disruptive of attitude-behavior consistency (Millar & Tesser 1992).

Attitude Attributes

Several characteristics of attitudes have been shown to be associated with noteworthy effects, such as biased interpretation of attitude-relevant information, resistance to persuasion, and strong prediction of behavior.

ACCESSIBILITY   Fazio and colleagues (see Fazio 1990 for a review) have collected data showing that the ease or speed with which evaluations can be retrieved from memory predicts the influence of those attitudes on subsequent perceptions of and actions toward the attitude object. Highly accessible attitudes are more likely to bias interpretation of relevant information and shape behavior in a direction consistent with the attitude.

Fazio argues that when object-evaluation associations are strong, the mere presentation of the attitude object can automatically activate the evaluation. For example, he has used a priming paradigm to show that the presentation of highly accessible attitude objects makes subsequent judgments about evaluatively congruent adjectives faster. Recently, Bargh et al (1992) found that the strength of this automatic activation effect correlated not only with the accessibility of an attitude for a particular individual, but also with the normative accessibility of an attitude across subjects (i.e. with the mean latency of all subjects' responses to an attitude item). These findings may reflect, however, the covariation of normative and idiosyncratic accessibility (see Fazio 1992).

STRENGTH   Attitude strength has been increasingly studied over the last few years, as indicated by the forthcoming volume on this topic edited by Petty &

Krosnick (1992). Strong attitudes serve as important sources of identity, resist most attempts at change, and exert widespread effects on perception and behavior. Krosnick & Abelson (1992) argue cogently that strength should be routinely measured in attitudes research. These authors review research on five dimensions that presumably reflect attitude strength: extremity, intensity, certainty, importance, and knowledge. Attitude strength has also been related to accessibility: Krosnick (1989) found that attitudes that people consider personally important are reported more quickly than unimportant attitudes. Of course, whether importance underlies accessibility or vice versa is unclear.

AMBIVALENCE   Ambivalent attitudes are conflicted evaluations—attitudes that contain both positive and negative elements. To the extent that positive and negative elements are equal and extreme, greater ambivalence is present (see Thompson et al 1992). In an interesting program of research, Katz and colleagues (e.g. Hass et al 1991; Katz & Hass 1988) studied the consequences of ambivalent racial attitudes. These authors propose that many members of majority groups have conflicting attitudes toward minorities, consisting of feelings of both aversion and friendly concern. Consequently, majority group evaluations of minority group members tend to be more polarized (both positively and negatively) than evaluations of their own members. Hass et al (1991) found that, indeed, a measure of attitude ambivalence predicted polarized cross-racial evaluations.

Measurement of Attitudes

The most common technique for measuring attitudes continues to be global self-reports, such as ratings of the attitude object on bipolar evaluative dimensions (good-bad, favorable-unfavorable, etc). An excellent summary of attitude measurement techniques is provided by Himmelfarb (1992). Attitude researchers are also employing varied methodologies to test theories, including meta-analytic techniques (e.g. Johnson & Eagly 1989) and computer simulation (e.g. Nowak et al 1990). In a cogent critique of the use of multiplicative composites, Evans (1991) pointed out that tests of theoretical models containing multiplicative terms should not use those composites in subsequent correlational analyses. For example, tests of Fishbein & Ajzen's 1975 theory of reasoned action (where attitudes are expectancy-value products) should enter the components of the attitudes into hierarchical regression analyses to predict subsequent variables (e.g. behavioral intentions).

NEW TECHNIQUES   Several new techniques for measuring attitudes have appeared recently. Bassili & Fletcher (1991) designed a methodology for recording response times in telephone interviews, which holds promise for assessing such qualities as attitude accessibility. Methods that allow for tailored or individually adapted surveys have also been introduced (Balasubramanian &

Kamakura 1989; Singh et al 1990), which pose only those scale items that are most informative about respondents' attitudes, thereby maximizing both the efficiency and quality of the survey. Indirect assessments of attitudes, such as implicit measures of memory, can document both conscious and unconscious effects of attitudes (Banaji & Greenwald 1992; Dovidio & Fazio 1992).

In the psychophysiological domain, Cacioppo and colleagues (Cacioppo et al 1989; Cacioppo & Tassinary 1990) continue their innovative work on physiological manifestations of thoughts, feelings, and behaviors. With respect to attitudes, these researchers have focused on facial EMG in structured situations as a means of assessing individuals' affective and evaluative responses.

RESPONSE EFFECTS   Respondents' answers to attitude and opinion items in surveys are influenced by a variety of methodological factors. Perhaps most obviously, the way questions are worded can affect responses. Relatively minor variations in question wording have been shown to substantially alter expressed support for such issues as government spending (Rasinski 1989) and treatment of criminals (Zamble & Kalm 1990). The response scales offered to subjects can also influence their answers. For example, Gray (1990) found much greater belief in scientifically unsubstantiated phenomena when subjects were asked to rate the degree of their belief or unbelief in each phenomenon than when they were asked to indicate with checkmarks those phenomena they believed in. Schwarz (1990) has outlined several ways that response categories constitute a source of information for respondents, including providing a frame of reference for judgments.

Answers to an item can also be affected by the preceding items. Question order or context effects have received much attention recently, often within the framework of either social judgment theory (see Sarup et al 1991 for an interesting test of this theory) or representational network models of attitude structure (Ottati et al 1989; Tourangeau et al 1989). For example, Schwarz and colleagues (e.g. Schwarz et al 1990; Schwarz et al 1991b) have studied assimilation and contrast effects in attitude measurement. When preceding questions in a survey activate information that is part of the relevant information for answering a current question (e.g. when judgments of present marital satisfaction precede judgments of present life satisfaction), then assimilation typically occurs, such that answers to the current question move in the direction of answers to the preceding question. On the other hand, when information activated by a prior question is outside of the data relevant to the current question (e.g. when judgments of life satisfaction 10 years ago precede judgments of present life satisfaction), then contrast effects can occur, because the activated information serves as a standard of comparison or reference point for anchoring the response scale.

VALUES AND ATTITUDES

Value-Attitude Relations

Values are generally conceptualized as higher-order evaluative standards, referring to desirable means and ends of action (e.g. Rokeach 1973). As such, values are viewed as potential determinants of preferences and attitudes. For example, values have been shown to predict attitudes toward nuclear weapons (Kristiansen & Matheson 1990), attitudes toward the unemployed (Heaven 1990), and beliefs in a just world (Feather 1991).

If values are abstract standards, then their influence on behavior may typically be mediated by more proximal factors. Using an expectancy-value framework, Feather (1990) has provided data suggesting that values affect behavior by influencing individuals' evaluations of the consequences of actions. Values can influence perceived valences both of alternative ways of behaving and of expected outcomes of the actions.

The best-known scale for measuring values is the Rokeach Value Survey (Rokeach 1973), which distinguishes between instrumental and terminal values (see Crosby et al 1990 for a recent factor analysis of the RVS). Schwartz and colleagues (Schwartz & Bilsky 1990; Schwartz et al 1992) have developed a comprehensive value survey that distinguishes broad content domains of values (e.g. achievement, security, conformity). Research in 20 countries has provided evidence of cross-cultural generality for 10 of the content domains. Also, analyses indicate that two fundamental dimensions underlie the content domains: openness to change versus conservation (whether the values motivate behavior along unpredictable vs predictable paths) and self-enhancement versus self-transcendence (whether the values motivate self-interested actions or promote the welfare of others; see also Triandis et al 1990). Interestingly, Rokeach's distinction between instrumental and terminal values (means vs ends) has not emerged as an underlying dimension in Schwartz's research.

Functions of Attitudes: Value Expression Versus Object Appraisal

A theoretical approach that explicitly addresses the connection between values and attitudes is the functional view of attitudes. From this perspective, attitudes fulfill psychological needs for the individual. Two primary functions of attitudes have received the most attention in recent work: value expression and object appraisal. Value expressive attitudes communicate important values and/or seek social approval (this latter, social approval aspect is sometimes labelled separately as the social adjustive function). Thus, these attitudes serve both private and public identity concerns (Eagly & Chaiken 1992; Shavitt 1989). The object appraisal function derives from the previously-discussed representational nature of attitudes. Attitudes facilitate the categorization of objects and events. This function is presumably fulfilled by most attitudes, but especially by strong and accessible attitudes (Fazio 1990; Pratkanis & Greenwald 1989).

Various strategies have been used to explore how certain attitudes operate to serve corresponding personal needs (see Eagly & Chaiken 1992; Shavitt 1989; Tesser & Shaffer 1990). Attitudes toward certain kinds of objects (e.g. perfume) are more likely to serve value expressive needs than are attitudes toward other objects (e.g. coffee; Shavitt 1990). Under certain situational conditions, such as time pressure, attitudes are more likely to serve object appraisal needs (Sanbonmatsu & Fazio 1990). Some personality variables are associated with particular attitude functions (e.g. self-monitoring, see Kristiansen & Zanna 1991; Snyder & DeBono 1987).

Shavitt (1990) investigated the responsiveness of attitudes fulfilling different functions to congruent versus incongruent persuasive appeals. Subjects read advertisements for products that primarily serve either social identity (similar to value expressive) or utilitarian (similar to object appraisal) needs. The advertisements focused either on how the product reflects important values or on the qualities of the product (social identity vs utilitarian appeals). Subjects expressed stronger preference for products advertised in a manner that matched the attitude's underlying function.

Jamieson & Zanna (1989) showed that the object appraisal function of attitudes is moderated by self-monitoring. Subjects read summaries of court cases dealing with affirmative action or capital punishment and were asked to render judgments. Some subjects were given only three minutes per case to complete this task, whereas others had unlimited time. When subjects had unlimited time, their judgments were generally unrelated to their attitudes toward affirmative action or capital punishment, presumably because they were instructed to be impartial and to base their decisions on the merits of the cases. Under time pressure, however, low self-monitors rendered judgments that were strongly related to their attitudes.

Pryor and colleagues (Pryor et al 1989; Pryor et al 1991) propose that attitudes toward persons with AIDS can serve both instrumental and symbolic functions. The instrumental function reflects perceptions of the possible consequences of interacting with such persons (similar to object appraisal). The symbolic function reflects judgments about homosexual promiscuity (similar to value expression). Education campaigns that stress the minimal risks associated with interacting with infected persons may be effective only for individuals whose attitudes fulfill the instrumental function (see Pryor et al 1991). In a similar vein, Snyder & Miene (1992) argue that stereotypes of the elderly can fulfill different functions and that the success of intervention strategies depends on matching those functions.

ATTITUDE FORMATION

A relatively neglected question in the attitudes literature has been *when* attitudes form. Researchers are now beginning to identify conditions that foster crystalization of evaluations, including expecting to interact with the attitude object (Gerard & Orive 1987), being asked about one's attitude (Fazio 1987), and having a lot of knowledge about an issue (Judd & Downing 1990). These analyses underscore the important functions attitudes fulfill in orienting people to the social environment.

A more widely examined question has been *how* attitudes form. For example, repeated exposure to a stimulus results in heightened positive evaluations (Zajonc 1968), although boredom is a limiting condition on this "mere exposure effect" (see Bornstein et al 1990). In an informative review and meta-analysis of the mere exposure literature, Bornstein (1989) identified numerous predictors of the strength of exposure effects, including stimulus complexity and exposure duration. Other interesting work on attitude formation has addressed long-standing topics such as conditioning and new topics such as the heritability of attitudes.

Conditioning of Attitudes

Pairing neutral attitude objects with positive (or negative) stimuli should evoke more positive (or negative) evaluations of the object through classical and/or instrumental conditioning. Recent research has identified boundary conditions for conditioning and explored implications of attitudinal conditioning for seemingly unrelated judgments. Cacioppo et al (1992) paired electric shock with neutral words and nonwords; conditioning was stronger for nonwords, suggesting that prior knowledge about objects can dilute the evaluative consequences of conditioned affect. Kuykendall & Keating (1990) paired positive or negative words with the country names Brazil and Turkey; subjects' judgments about the favorability of the economic conditions in the two countries were affected. Perdue et al (1990) showed that nonsense syllables previously paired with ingroup pronouns (we, us) were rated more favorably than control syllables or syllables paired with outgroup pronouns.

In an intriguing study, Krosnick et al (1992) obtained evidence of subliminal conditioning of attitudes. Subjects viewed slides of a young woman engaged in everyday activities such as getting into a car. Immediately preceding each slide was a subliminal presentation of an affect-arousing photograph, either positive or negative in valence (e.g. kittens, a face on fire). Subjects exposed to positive affect-inducing photos expressed more favorable attitudes toward the woman than did subjects exposed to negative affect-inducing photos. These data suggest that perceivers do not have to be consciously aware of unconditioned stimuli in order for conditioning to occur. It should be noted, however, that a priming interpretation of these findings may be possible, such that induced mood altered subjects' interpretations of the woman's actions (see Eagly & Chaiken 1992).

Heritability of Attitudes

The field of behavioral genetics has begun to exert an influence on social psychologists, including attitude researchers. A fascinating, though controversial, question that has been addressed concerns the heritability of social attitudes. On the face of it, questions about the heritability of attitudes toward capital punishment or abortion may seem absurd, but such reactions may reflect a faulty assumption that genetic findings imply that specific genes directly produce complex social behaviors (which is unlikely). Instead, genetic findings may be traceable to such indirect factors as biological differences in body chemistry, inborn temperament differences, and innate intellectual abilities (see Tesser 1992; Oskamp 1991).

Based on a twin study methodology, Arvey et al (1989) estimated that approximately 30% of the observed variance in job satisfaction was attributable to genetic factors. In other words, subjects' attitudes towards their jobs were assumed to be partly inherited. Eaves et al (1989) report the findings from numerous studies of the heritability of social attitudes, which produced heritability estimates ranging from zero to more than 50% of the observed variance. Some of the most "heritable" attitude items related to the treatment of criminals (perhaps reflecting biologically based differences in aggressiveness or assertiveness), whereas items relating to socialism tended to be among those most heavily influenced by family environments.

In a stimulating paper, Tesser (1992) argues that heritability has important implications for attitude researchers. In a series of studies, he shows that attitudes identified by other researchers as high in heritability produce faster response latencies from subjects and less conformity to alleged normative information than do low heritability attitudes. Also, similarity to a stranger on highly heritable attitudes evokes greater liking than does similarity on low heritability attitudes. Tesser concludes that highly heritable attitudes are "stronger" (e.g. more accessible, more resistant to change), perhaps because they have a biological substrate that makes change uncomfortable and motivates psychological protection mechanisms around them.

We agree with Tesser that genetic perspectives on attitudes deserve attention and are confident that his provocative analysis will stimulate research. At the same time, we have some concerns about the use of heritability estimates in attitude research. First, heritability coefficients say nothing directly about the operation of genes within individuals (Eaves et al 1989; Weizmann et al 1990), being dependent on environmental and genetic variability within the population under study (see Cropanzano & James 1990 for a related critique of Arvey et al's 1989 genetic analysis of work attitudes). In fact, any characteristics on which natural selection has operated so strongly as to produce universality will have low heritabilities, because the degree of genetic variability will be restricted. Second, we wonder about the role of intellectual abilities in past findings; perhaps attitudes that appear to be heritable are those that correlate with intelligence. To our knowledge, researchers have not partialled out the effects of intelligence when examining the heritability of social attitudes; we think such data are essential in order to validate the notion of biological substrates underlying attitudes.

Despite these concerns, we welcome a genetic perspective on attitudes and believe that it raises many interesting questions for existing theories. Behavioral genetic methods can be used to examine environmental influences as well as genetic ones (e.g. Caspi et al 1992), and sophisticated evolutionary psychologists stress the interplay of environmental and genetic factors in the determination of behavior (e.g. Caporael & Brewer 1991).

ATTITUDES AND INFORMATION-PROCESSING

Attitudes can exert profound effects on perceivers' judgments of their social world. Indeed, theorists have argued that attitudes and beliefs can influence every step of the information-processing sequence, including attention, encoding, comprehension, interpretation, elaboration, and memory (e.g. Eagly & Chaiken 1992; Fazio 1990; Hamilton et al 1990; Kunda 1990; but see Jussim 1991 for an alternative perspective).

Selective Interpretation

Attitudes can affect the labelling of information, the interpretation of actions, and predictions about future behaviors (e.g. Anderson & Kellam 1992; Hilton & von Hippel 1990). For example, "enemy" images of the former Soviet Union generated negative labels and attributions of self-serving intent for USSR actions (Sande et al 1989; Silverstein & Flamenbaum 1989).

In an interesting study, Friedrich et al (1989) investigated the "naturalistic fallacy," which is the tendency to infer moral guides from empirical findings (e.g. to infer that sugared-food advertising should be restricted because children exposed to such advertising have been found to choose sugared over nutritious foods). Subjects read descriptive summaries of social science research. Immediately and seven weeks later, subjects responded to several items assessing inferences that the findings "prove" that certain actions need to be taken. Subjects' attitudes toward the issues addressed in the empirical research predicted the occurrence of the naturalistic fallacy on the immediate test and especially on the delayed test, suggesting a causal effect of attitudes on the fallacy. When subjects' attitudes were consistent with the direction of the studies' findings, they were more likely to draw inferences about moral prescriptions.

Liberman & Chaiken (1992) exposed coffee drinkers and nondrinkers to high or low threat messages on the health consequences of caffeine. Coffee drinkers expressed less belief in the seriousness of the threat than did nondrinkers, irrespective of the threat contained in the message. No evidence was obtained for defensive inattention by coffee drinkers. Instead, coffee drinkers appeared to process the threatening parts of the messages in a biased fashion, actively discounting and counterarguing threats to the self.

The mechanisms underlying selective interpretation were investigated by Houston & Fazio (1989). Subjects evaluated the convincingness and methodological rigor of two alleged studies on capital punishment, one concluding that the death penalty is a deterrent to murder and the other coming to the opposite conclusion. Subjects' own attitudes toward the death penalty predicted how they evaluated these studies, such that the study supporting subjects' views was judged superior to the study contradicting their views. This pattern occurred only when subjects' attitudes toward the death penalty were highly accessible, however.

Selective Memory

One of the oldest ideas in the attitude literature is that people find information supporting their attitudes easier to learn and remember than information contradicting their attitudes (for a review, see Eagly & Chaiken 1992). Researchers have found that preferential recall of attitude-consistent information is more likely when the underlying attitude has a unipolar rather than bipolar structure (see Pratkanis & Greenwald 1989). For example, attitudes toward music tend to be unipolar and to produce selective memory, whereas attitudes toward nuclear power tend to be bipolar and to produce heightened recall of both consistent and inconsistent information.

Ross (1989) has documented the role of attitudes in reconstructive memory. When subjects' attitudes are altered by experimental manipulations, their recall or reconstruction of information in memory is affected. For example, persuading subjects that too much toothbrushing is harmful results in estimates of less frequent previous toothbrushing. Ross argues that people possess intuitive theories that (a) attitudes are stable and (b) behavior is consistent with attitudes. Thus, when attitudes are altered by a persuasive message, people incorrectly assume that they always believed what they now believe and that their previous actions were consistent with their current attitude.

Echabe & Rovira (1989) demonstrated the practical relevance of understanding selective memory. Subjects' attitudes towards AIDS divided into two major subgroups: conservative-blaming and liberal representations. Subjects were given technical information about AIDS and tested for recall of the information two weeks later. Subjects showed better recall of information congruent with their representation of AIDS and distorted incongruent information to make it more compatible with their attitude.

ATTITUDES AND BEHAVIORS

The utility of the attitude concept rests on the assumption that attitudes influence behaviors. Researchers continue to elucidate the conditions that enhance or reduce consistency between attitudes and behaviors (e.g. Lord et al 1991). For example, Shavitt & Fazio (1991) showed that attitude expressions can be influenced by momentarily salient characteristics of the attitude object, thereby potentially reducing the predictive utility of those expressions for subsequent behavior (unless the salient characteristics happen to be those that normally guide the individuals' evaluations).

Theory of Reasoned Action

In their theory of reasoned action, Fishbein & Ajzen (1975) proposed that attitudes and subjective norms combine to determine behavioral intentions, which in turn cause volitional behaviors. This theory remains the dominant theoretical framework in the attitude-behavior literature. Not only is it used to predict behavior in many contexts, but inevitably it serves as the standard to which new ideas and theories are compared.

Recent applications of the theory of reasoned action have been diverse. The theory has been used successfully to predict intentions or behaviors in various domains, including smoking (Norman & Tedeschi 1989), seat belt use (Stasson & Fishbein 1990), applying for a nursing program (Strader & Katz 1990), and performing testicular self-exams (Steffen 1990).

CRITICISMS OF THE THEORY OF REASONED ACTION   Many researchers have criticized the theory of reasoned action (for a summary, see Eagly & Chaiken 1992). We will mention only those issues that have received empirical attention during the period covered by our review.

The role of external variables, especially prior behavior, continues to be an issue of debate (e.g. Sutton & Hallett 1989; Eiser et al 1989). It appears that the effects of external variables and prior behaviors are not always fully mediated by the attitudinal and normative components of the model (Bauman et al 1989; Granberg & Holmberg 1990).

Warshaw & Davis (1985) argued that behavioral expectations are better predictors of behavior than are behavioral intentions, because expectations take into account the probability of successful completion of the action (e.g. intending vs expecting to hit a home run). Consistent with this reasoning, Gordon (1989) found that expectations were better predictors of students' academic performances than were intentions. In a related vein, Nederhof (1989) showed that the certainty of subjects' intentions moderated the intention-behavior relation, such that more certain intentions were better predictors of behavior. Kendzierski (1990) distinguished decision making from decision implementation. The intention to exercise physically was more likely to be implemented when individuals had engaged in planning than when they had not.

Bagozzi & Yi (1989) examined whether the clarity of intentions moderated the attitude-behavior relation. They found that when intentions were well formed, intentions completely mediated the effects of attitudes on behavior (as predicted by the theory of reasoned action). When intentions were poorly formed, however, attitudes had a direct effect on behavior, unmediated by intentions. Using similar logic, Bagozzi et al (1990) tested whether the level of effort required for a behavior moderated the attitude-behavior relation. In a field experiment involving homework projects for students, these authors found that when the behavior required substantial effort, intentions completely mediated the effects of attitudes on behavior. In contrast, when the behavior required little effort, attitudes had a direct effect on behavior, unmediated by intentions, presumably because minimal deliberate planning was necessary.

The relative importance of attitudes versus subjective norms in predicting behavior has also received recent attention. Skinner & Cattarello (1989) found that behavioral commitment (operationalized as the length of time an individual has engaged in a behavior) moderated the relative predictive utility of attitudes versus norms. As commitment increased, norms became increasingly important relative to attitudes. The authors speculate that behavioral commitment is associated with the development of a peer culture that comes to control behavior independently of attitudes. Grube & Morgan (1990) investigated possible *contingent consistency* interactions between attitudes and norms, based on the idea that attitudes will affect behavior only (or mainly) when the environment is seen to support the attitude (the theory of reasoned action treats attitudes and subjective norms as independent predictors of intentions). Among students aged 12 to 18, attitudes toward substance use (drinking, smoking, drug use) and perceived substance use by friends consistently interacted to predict behavioral measures.

Alternative Models of the Attitude-Behavior Relation

Given the range of criticisms leveled against the theory of reasoned action, it is not surprising that several alternative theories have been proposed. Some of these models have been developed to explain behavior within specific domains (e.g. see Fisher & Fisher 1992 for a model of AIDS preventive behaviors). Other models, including those described below, have been proposed as general theories of attitude-behavior relations.

MODE MODEL   Fazio (1990) proposed the MODE model (reflecting an emphasis on *m*otivation and *o*pportunity as *de*terminants of how attitudes influence behavior). Fazio argued that when individuals are highly motivated to think deliberatively about an attitude object and when they have the opportunity to do so, attitudes will affect behaviors in the manner outlined in the theory of reasoned action (see Sanbonmatsu & Fazio 1990). When either motivation or opportunity is missing, however (which may be the norm rather than the exception), Fazio suggests that only highly accessible attitudes will guide behaviors (see Fazio et al 1989). Thus, Fazio distinguished between deliberative and automatic effects of attitudes on behavior. The MODE model provides a compelling analysis of how attitudes can spontaneously affect actions.

THEORY OF PLANNED BEHAVIOR   The competing model that has received the most attention was proposed by one of the original authors of the theory of reasoned action. Ajzen's (1985) theory of planned behavior adds perceived behavioral control (a concept similar to self-efficacy) as a third predictor of intentions, independent from attitudes and subjective norms. The addition of perceived control was designed to expand the model to incorporate behaviors not fully under volitional control.

Although some researchers comparing the predictive powers of the theories of reasoned action and planned behavior have concluded that the older theory performs just as well as the newer one (e.g. Fishbein & Stasson 1990; Hinsz & Nelson 1990), most comparisons of the two models have found a predictive advantage for the theory of planned behavior (e.g. Beck & Ajzen 1991; Brubaker & Fowler 1990; Madden et al 1992; Schlegel et al 1992). In a review of relevant studies, Ajzen (1991) concluded that the evidence supports the revised model and that adding further variables to the model (such as moral obligation or past behavior) would improve its predictive power only slightly.

EAGLY & CHAIKEN'S COMPOSITE MODEL   In our opinion, another serious contender for pre-eminence among attitude-behavior theories is a composite model of the attitude-behavior relation proposed by Eagly & Chaiken (1992). Although this model has not yet been tested empirically, it seems comprehensive and integrative. For example, Eagly & Chaiken include both attitudes toward objects and attitudes toward behaviors in their model — a unique aspect of the theory. They propose that attitudes toward objects can influence attitudes toward behaviors in a relatively "spontaneous" fashion (e.g. paralleling the automatic influences outlined in Fazio's 1990 MODE model). Eagly & Chaiken also include habit in their model, both as a possible antecedent of attitudes (e.g. self-perception) and as a direct determinant of behavior. Other features of the model include self-identity considerations as possible antecedents of attitudes toward behaviors, and greater consideration of multiple paths between concepts (e.g. attitudes toward behaviors can potentially affect behavior directly, unmediated by intentions, following Bagozzi & Yi 1989; Bagozzi et al 1990).

Effects of Behavior on Attitudes

An important insight provided by social psychology is that behavior affects attitudes, not just the reverse. We will review two explanations of how actions can affect attitudes: self-perception and dissonance.

SELF-PERCEPTION THEORY   Bem (1972) proposed that when internal states (attitudes, emotions) are weak or ambiguous, individuals must infer these states from knowledge about their overt behavior and the circumstances in which the behavior occurred. Recent studies of self-perception have examined the effects of rewards on intrinsic motivation (the "overjustification effect," e.g. Enzle et al 1991) and inferences of emotional states (e.g. Olson 1990). Kellerman et al (1989) showed that opposite sex strangers who were induced to exchange mutual unbroken gaze for two minutes reported increased feelings of passionate attraction. Damrad-Frye & Laird (1989) found that subjects reported feeling bored when they were distracted from a listening task by extraneous noise that was not loud enough to be perceived as distracting, compared to subjects who were not distracted at all or who were distracted by an obviously loud noise; the first group of subjects presumably inferred that the task must be boring from their inability to pay attention.

Olson (1992) examined the role of self-perception processes in evaluations of humor. All subjects read two sets of jokes; a "laugh track" was played through their headphones for one set but not the other. Subjects had been told that the laugh track would either increase, decrease, or have no effect on their mirth. In a subsequent free time period, subjects had access to the two books from which the two sets of jokes had been taken. As predicted, subjects who were told that the laugh track would increase mirth spent most of their time reading the book whose jokes had not been accompanied by the laugh track — a discounting effect. Subjects who were told that the laugh track would decrease mirth spent most of their time reading the book whose jokes were accompanied by the laugh track — an augmentation effect.

DISSONANCE THEORY   Despite contrasting laments that dissonance theory either has been prematurely abandoned (e.g. Berkowitz & Devine 1989) or should be permanently retired (e.g. Schlenker 1992), creative work continues to appear under the dissonance rubric (e.g. Joule 1991; Losch & Cacioppo 1990). Axsom (1989) clarified the role of dissonance reduction in psychotherapy. In two studies using effort justification procedures, snake phobic and speech anxious subjects showed behavioral improvement when they willingly agreed to undergo effortful "therapies," compared to low effort and/or low freedom conditions.

Scher & Cooper (1989; Cooper & Scher 1992) proposed a conceptual revision to dissonance theory. These authors argue that dissonance is aroused whenever individuals feel responsible for aversive outcomes, whether the behavior that produced those outcomes is consistent or inconsistent with their attitudes. For example, Scher & Cooper (1989) asked student subjects to write an essay strongly opposing an increase in tuition fees (a position they supported). When these subjects were led to believe that their essay would have a "boomerang" effect on an important decision making group (i.e. that it would make the target group more in favor of increased tuition fees), they reported being more favorable toward increased tuition fees themselves. This apparent dissonance reduction following proattitudinal behavior suggests that aversive consequences play an important role in motivating attitude change.

PERSUASION

The single largest topic within the attitudes literature is persuasion: attitude change resulting from exposure to information from others. Such exposure typically occurs via written or spoken messages, delivered by a source to a recipient.

Elaboration-Likelihood and Heuristic-Systematic Models of Persuasion

Two dual-process theories dominate current research on persuasion: Petty & Cacioppo's (1986) elaboration-likelihood model and Chaiken's heuristic-systematic model (Chaiken 1987; Chaiken et al 1989). In both models, individuals are assumed to process a message carefully when they are motivated and able to do so. Under these circumstances (the "central route" to persuasion or "systematic processing"), argument strength will be a primary determinant of whether persuasion occurs, and attitude change that does occur will be relatively enduring or stable. When individuals are unable or unmotivated to process carefully (the "peripheral route" or "heuristic processing," although these terms are not interchangeable — see Chaiken & Stangor 1987; Eagly & Chaiken 1992), cues, heuristics, and other processes besides consideration of message arguments will determine whether persuasion occurs. Any attitude change that does result from heuristic processing will often be temporary or unstable. Although one or another type of processing can dominate, Chaiken et al (1989) do not view systematic and heuristic processing as mutually exclusive. For example, heuristics like source credibility can affect perceivers even when they are processing carefully.

DETERMINANTS OF PROCESSING STRATEGIES   Various factors affect individuals' motivation and ability to process a message carefully, thereby determining which processing strategy will dominate (for reviews, see Eagly & Chaiken 1992; Petty & Cacioppo 1986; Tesser & Shaffer 1990). For example, Burnkrant & Unnava (1989) induced some subjects to use a self-referent processing strategy by encouraging them within the message to remember their own experiences with the attitude object; these subjects were more influenced by argument strength than were subjects not exposed to the self-referencing manipulation, presumably because self-referencing motivated greater elaboration. Maheswaran & Chaiken (1991) tested the *sufficiency principle* from the heuristic-systematic model, which is that perceivers will engage only in whatever amount of deliberation is necessary to provide them with "sufficient" judgmental confidence. Subjects in this research exhibited greater systematic processing when a task was important rather than unimportant (presumably, important tasks generate higher sufficiency thresholds); more interestingly, subjects exhibited systematic processing even when the task was unimportant if the message was incongruent (rather than congruent) with their prior expectations, presumably because incongruency undermined actual confidence.

Involvement and Persuasion   In their original forms, both the elaboration-likelihood and heuristic-systematic models implied that as issue importance or involvement increased for a message recipient, careful message-based processing should increase as well. Consistent with this reasoning, Petty & Cacioppo (1986) reviewed numerous studies where cogent messages produced more persuasion under high than low "issue involvement," whereas specious messages resulted in less persuasion under high than low involvement. Johnson & Eagly (1989), however, distinguished between *outcome-relevant involvement* (where the issue will affect the outcomes of the perceiver) and *value-relevant involvement* (where the issue is relevant to the perceiver's important values). Based on a meta-analysis of past studies, Johnson & Eagly concluded that whereas outcome-relevant involvement had the effects described by Petty & Cacioppo (1986), value-relevant involvement was associated with reduced persuasion (though especially for weak rather than strong arguments). In a reply, Petty & Cacioppo (1990) argued that the studies alleged to have manipulated "value-relevant" involvement by Johnson & Eagly had confounded involvement with other variables that might have inhibited persuasion, such as prior attitudes and knowledge.

Whether involvement should be conceptualized as a unitary or multidimensional construct in terms of its effects on persuasion is not yet clear (see Eagly & Chaiken 1992; Johnson & Eagly 1990; Petty & Cacioppo 1990). Research directly examining this issue is sure to appear in the next few years. Partly in response to the concerns raised by Johnson & Eagly (1989), Chaiken et al (1989) expanded the heuristic-systematic model to provide a general model of social influence, including motives other than accuracy. Specifically, these authors proposed that perceivers can have the additional goals of (*a*) defending or confirming preferred attitude positions and (*b*) expressing socially acceptable attitudes. As with the accuracy goal, these goals can generate either systematic or heuristic processing, i.e. extensive consideration of relevant information or reliance on simple heuristics.

Message Reception

In 1968, McGuire argued that persuasion requires both reception of a message (attention and comprehension) and yielding to the conclusions. Reflecting the information-processing perspective in current persuasion research, there has been a revival of interest in the role of message encoding and reception (e.g. McCann et al 1991; Rhodes & Wood 1992; Zanna 1992). For example, Ratneshwar & Chaiken (1991) found that comprehension moderated the influence of source credibility on attitudes. When recipients could not easily comprehend a message, they used source credibility to infer level of agreement with the recommendations. On the other hand, when comprehensibility was high, source credibility did not affect subjects' attitudes.

Mackie & Asuncion (1990) examined how recall of message content affected persuasion. These authors distinguished *on-line* from *memory-based* attitude change. Some subjects were given tasks to perform during message exposure that inhibited cognitive elaboration; subsequent attitude change for these subjects was related to their recall of message content. Other subjects elaborated on the message as it was presented; subsequent attitude change for these subjects was not related to recall, presumably because evaluations were formed during exposure to the message (and, indeed, attitude judgments were made more quickly by these subjects).

Rhodes & Wood (1992) conducted a meta-analysis testing the prediction that self-esteem would be curvilinearly related to persuasibility. McGuire (1968) hypothesized that low self-esteem individuals have difficulty with message reception due to anxiety or lack of attention, whereas high self-esteem individuals tend not to yield to influence attempts. Thus, intermediate levels of self-esteem should be associated with the greatest persuasibility. The results of the meta-analysis supported this prediction.

Several fascinating studies have examined how perceivers process assertions. Arkes et al (1991) showed that simply repeating a statement causes it to be judged more true, compared to nonrepeated control statements, presumably because familiarity is used as one basis for judging validity (this effect is similar to Jacoby et al's 1989 demonstration that previous exposure to a name increases its judged fame). Gilbert et al (1990) proposed that all assertions are initially represented as true and that false information must then be "unaccepted." Consistent with this reasoning, subjects who were interrupted while processing a false statement were more likely to identify it incorrectly as true than were uninterrupted subjects, whereas interruption did not increase the erroneous identification of true statements as false. Gruenfeld & Wyer (1992) used a "conversational logic" perspective to examine perceivers' beliefs in assertions. One of the rules governing social communication is the *informativeness principle:* recipients assume that communicators intend their statements to convey new information. To the extent that an assertion meets this assumption, it should increase recipients' beliefs in the validity of the assertion. However, if an assertion is redundant with recipients' prior knowledge (e.g. "President Reagan is not an alcoholic"), then recipients will wonder why it was offered and may suspect that the communicator actually possesses information disconfirming what he or she has asserted. Such suspicions could generate a boomerang effect (e.g. to cause suspicion that President Reagan might have a drinking problem). The results of several studies supported this analysis.

Source Characteristics

What kinds of sources are most likely to be persuasive? Recent research has identified a variety of nonverbal characteristics that are associated with persuasiveness, including vocal pleasantness and facial expressiveness (Burgoon et al 1990). People with a babyish facial appearance are perceived as more trustworthy (Brownlow & Zebrowitz 1990). Speed of speech can also influence persuasiveness, although this depends on whether the message generates favorable or unfavorable thoughts (e.g. whether it is proattitudinal or counterattitudinal). Based on reasoning from the elaboration-likelihood model, Smith & Shaffer (1991) predicted and found that rapid speech inhibits the generation of unfavorable thoughts to a counterattitudinal message and thereby enhances agreement, whereas rapid speech inhibits the generation of favorable thoughts to a proattitudinal message and thereby reduces agreement.

In an interesting pair of studies, Carli (1990) found that women who spoke tentatively (with frequent disclaimers, hedges, etc) were more persuasive with men than were women who spoke assertively, presumably because men found tentative female speakers to be more trustworthy and likeable (though also less competent and knowledgeable). In contrast, tentative language reduced the effectiveness of women speaking to other women, presumably because women found tentative female speakers to be less likeable, believeable, competent, and knowledgeable. Language had no influence on perceptions of male speakers or their effectiveness with either men or women.

Cialdini et al (1992) explored the implications of the reciprocity norm for persuasion. These authors found that people will express more agreement with persuaders who have previously yielded to them than with previously noncompliant persuaders. Moreover, such reciprocity-induced public attitude change can translate into private acceptance when the arguments are strong and subjects can attribute their agreement to the cogency of the arguments.

People are usually more influenced by ingroup than outgroup sources (Wilder 1990), although weak arguments can undermine this effect (Mackie et al 1990). Presumably, perceivers process ingroup messages carefully, which can expose weak arguments, whereas outgroup messages are given little thought.

Message Characteristics

Message characteristics often interact with other variables to influence persuasion, as has been shown recently for the use of rhetorical questions (Howard 1990), direct versus indirect verbal claims (Yi 1990), and message repetition (Anand & Sternthal 1990). For example, Cacioppo & Petty (1989) showed that three (vs one) exposures to auditory messages increased the effectiveness of appeals based on strong arguments but decreased the effectiveness of appeals based on weak arguments, presumably because repeated exposure allowed greater elaboration on the messages.

Elaboration is also an important factor in the effectiveness of other message characteristics, including the use of humor (Chattopadhyay & Basu 1990) and discounting appeals (Schul & Mazursky 1990). McGill & Anand (1989) found that vivid information exerts greater influence on attitudinal judgments than nonvivid information only when recipients elaborate extensively on the message. Also, positively framed messages (describing benefits gained from a product) are more effective than negatively framed messages (describing benefits lost by not using a product) when elaboration is minimal, but the reverse is true when elaboration is extensive (Maheswaran & Meyers-Levy 1990).

In a fascinating set of studies, Janiszewski (1990a, 1990b) explored how subconscious or incidental processing of information can affect persuasion. Based on hemispheric processing theories, Janiszewski begins his analysis with the assumption that pictorial information primarily engages the right hemisphere, whereas verbal information primarily engages the left hemisphere. In addition, nonattended stimuli in the right visual field (i.e. stimuli placed to the right of the visual focus of attention) will be sent to the left hemisphere, whereas nonattended stimuli in the left visual field will be sent to the right hemisphere. Finally, nonattended information will receive greater elaboration if it is sent to the hemisphere that is not primarily engaged with attentive tasks. Based on these assumptions, Janiszewski (1990a) proposed that a simple brand name (which can be subconsciously processed equally well by either hemisphere) will receive greater subconscious processing and therefore be better liked when it is placed to the right rather than to the left of dominant pictorial information (e.g. a photograph) but to the left rather than to the right of dominant verbal information (e.g. a slogan). The results of several experiments supported this reasoning.

FEAR APPEALS   Fear appeals have probably received more research attention than any other message characteristic. The dominant theoretical framework in this literature is Rogers's (1983) protection motivation theory, which proposes that threatening messages will be effective to the extent that they convince recipients that (a) the problem is serious, (b) the recipient is susceptible to the problem, (c) the recommendations will effectively avoid the problem, and (d) the recipient is capable of performing the recommmendations. Recent research within this framework has supported its utility for understanding the influence of messages on a variety of issues, including earthquake preparedness (Mulilis & Lippa 1990), condom use (Struckman-Johnson et al 1990), and informing children about sexual abuse (Campis et al 1989). Some personality groups may not respond in the predicted fashion to threatening messages, however (e.g. depressed recipients; Self & Rogers 1990).

Recent work holds promise for linking protection motivation theory with the general dual-process models of persuasion. Gleicher & Petty (1992) led some subjects to be concerned about crime on campus. These subjects processed a message about crime prevention carefully when it contained information that might reassure them about the problem, but exhibited only superficial processing when their fear had already been reassured and the message might serve to raise doubts. Interestingly, similar patterns of processing of the message about crime prevention obtained when fear was aroused on an unrelated topic (illness on campus), suggesting that fear arouses a general protection motivation that can affect processing of all safety-related messages.

Recipient Characteristics

Both chronic dispositions and situationally-induced states of message recipients can influence the success of persuasive messages (e.g. DeBono & Telesca 1990; Hutton & Baumeister 1992). Tyler & Schuller (1991) studied aging and found that older adults (e.g. over 50) exhibited as much attitude change in response to personal experiences as did younger adults (e.g. 18-25). These authors concluded that people remain open to attitude change throughout their lives, a conclusion that differs from some authors' views (e.g. Krosnick & Alwin 1989). In the consumer domain, Bearden et al (1989) have developed a measure of general susceptibility to interpersonal influence, which might have applicability to some persuasive communication settings.

Meyers-Levy & Sternthal (1991) have made the provocative suggestion that women, compared to men, have a lower threshold for elaborating on message cues. Thus, cues may be better recalled and exert more influence on judgments for women than men, unless the cues either are so subtle that they prompt no attention at all or are so powerful that they exceed both genders' attention thresholds. Results from two experiments supported this reasoning. For example, women were more affected than men by two pieces of information about the taste of a toothpaste when both pieces appeared together in a message; when the two cues about taste were separated in the message (in order to push them below the attention threshold), neither gender was affected by them.

MOOD AND PERSUASION   Much attention has recently been directed to understanding the influence of recipient mood on persuasion (for reviews of this work, see Eagly & Chaiken 1992; Petty et al 1991; Schwarz et al 1991a). Numerous researchers have found that people in good moods process messages less systematically than people in neutral moods (e.g. Bless et al 1990; Mackie & Worth 1989; but see Smith & Shaffer 1992). For example, good moods typically reduce cognitive elaboration and blunt the importance of argument strength (Bless et al 1990; Mackie & Worth 1989). Whether these effects of positive mood are attributable to motivational or capacity mechanisms is unclear, however. Mackie & Worth (1989) concluded that a capacity explanation is more plausible (e.g. good moods reduce the ability to elaborate by eliciting positive thoughts, which take up the limited cognitive capacity available), because giving subjects in a good mood unlimited time to process a message eliminated differences between mood conditions (i.e. subjects in a good mood who were given unlimited time processed the message just as systematically as did neutral mood subjects). Other theorists have concluded that a motivational explanation is more compelling (e.g. people in a good mood don't want to ruin their mood by expending cognitive effort), because telling subjects to pay attention to the message can eliminate mood effects (Bless et al 1990). As with many ability versus motivation debates, we suspect that both capacity and motivational mechanisms can produce the effect.

An approach congenial with this last point has been taken by Petty et al (1991), who proposed that affect (e.g. mood, fear, conditioned arousal) can influence persuasion in various ways. Under conditions of low elaboration (e.g. issues of low personal relevance), Petty et al suggested that affect serves as a peripheral cue, and attitudes will move in the direction of the affect (e.g. positive affect causing positive evaluations). Under conditions of moderate elaboration, Petty et al suggested that, consistent with Mackie & Worth (1989), positive affect reduces cognitive elaboration. Under conditions of high elaboration (e.g. very important issues), Petty et al suggested that affect can bias elaboration in a manner consistent with the state (e.g. make positive information accessible) and serve as an argument in its own right (e.g. "I love my wife").

STEREOTYPES AND PREJUDICE

A major reason why social psychologists originally became interested in the concept of attitudes was its relevance to stereotypes and prejudice, which involve beliefs about, evaluations of, and feelings toward groups of people. Stereotypes and prejudice have been studied for many years, but there has been a recent surge of interest in this topic (e.g. Mackie & Hamilton 1992; Zanna & Olson 1992). Part of this increased interest may be attributable to the conceptual links being drawn between intra-individual attitude processes and inter-group perceptions (e.g. Brewer 1992; Dovidio & Gaertner 1992).

Stereotypes

Stereotypes have been defined both as shared, consensual beliefs about a group and as individual perceivers' beliefs about a group (see Gardner 1992). Recent studies have clarified the content of many consensual stereotypes, including the physical attractiveness stereotype (Eagly et al 1991; Feingold 1992) and gender stereotypes (Biernat 1991; Dion & Schuller 1991).

DEVELOPMENT OF STEREOTYPES   Processes underlying the development of stereotypes have received attention in several recent studies. For example, Maass et al (1989) collected data showing that people encode and communicate desirable behaviors by ingroup members and undesirable behaviors by outgroup members at a more abstract level (e.g. in terms of traits) than undesirable behaviors by ingroup members and desirable behaviors by outgroup members.

Maass et al speculate that language contributes to the transmission and persistence of social stereotypes.

Hoffman & Hurst (1990) proposed a rationalization hypothesis for stereotypes, whereby divisons of labor between groups cause the attribution of intrinsic personality differences that are consistent with the social roles. Two experiments showed that subjects formed stereotypes about fictional groups based on the group members' typical roles and that the stereotypes affected judgments even when a target's personal role was specified. The authors speculate that gender stereotypes may serve to rationalize existing sexual divisions of labor.

Perhaps the most studied possible cause of stereotypes has been illusory correlations, whereby the co-occurrence of unusual behaviors and minority group status is overestimated. Because unusual behaviors are often undesirable, such biases could generate negative stereotypes about minority groups. Illusory correlation effects are robust (see Mullen & Johnson 1990 for a review). The psychological mechanisms underlying illusory correlations are a matter of debate, however. Hamilton & Gifford (1976) proposed a distinctiveness explanation, whereby infrequent events (unusual behaviors, minority group status) are more salient and receive deeper processing. Fiedler (1991) argued that information loss and regression effects may underlie the phenomenon, based on demonstrations of illusory correlations in conditions that seem incompatible with distinctiveness (e.g. even zero-frequency events can be overestimated despite their null distinctiveness). Moreover, Smith (1991) showed that a computer simulation of a quantitative model of long-term memory reproduced the illusory correlation effect despite the absence of distinctiveness-based encoding or retrieval biases. Smith proposed that exemplar-based memory processes, which are influenced by the total frequencies (not only the proportions) of events, might account for the phenomenon. Finally, Schaller & Maass (1989) found illusory correlation effects mainly for uninvolved observers of groups, whereas group members exhibited ingroup favoritism (more favorable evaluations of their own group). These findings underscore that motivational factors can influence stereotype formation independently of cognitive factors (see also Schaller 1991).

WHEN DO PERCEIVERS USE STEREOTYPES?   The issue of when perceivers rely on category information (stereotypes) to make judgments about individuals is both theoretically interesting and practically important. Fiske & Neuberg (1990) have proposed a continuum of impression formation ranging from category-based to individuated processing (see also Brewer 1988; Dovidio & Gaertner 1992). Perceivers are assumed initially to make category-based judgments about targets; if personal relevance is high and if available information about the target is inconsistent with category-based expectations, then piecemeal processing (based on specific attributes of the target) can occur. Ruscher et al (1991) showed that factors such as competitive interdependence affect the degree of piecemeal processing, presumably by affecting perceivers' motivation to form accurate impressions (for other factors influencing stereotype use, see Paulhus et al 1992; Kaplan et al 1992).

Several researchers have documented that perceivers rely more on stereotypes when their processing capacities are reduced. For example, Pratto & Bargh (1991) manipulated the speed at which information was presented to subjects; impressions were more stereotypic when subjects did not have time to integrate individuating information. Similarly, Stangor & Duan (1991) showed that requiring perceivers to engage in multiple tasks while encoding information about social groups inhibited recall of behaviors inconsistent with group expectancies. Gilbert & Hixon (1991) showed that cognitive busyness can interfere with the activation of stereotypes (presumably because activation requires cognitive effort), but if a stereotype is activated, cognitive busyness heightens its influence on judgments (presumably because perceivers have insufficient capacity to consider individuating information). In a clever pair of studies, Bodenhausen (1990) found that subjects exhibited more pronounced stereotypic biases in their judgments when tested at a nonoptimal, as opposed to optimal, time of day (e.g. in the morning for "night people"). Presumably, circadian variations in arousal levels influence perceivers' motivation and/or ability to process individuating information.

Prejudice

Prejudice is usually defined as unfavorable evaluations of and negative affect toward members of a group (see Gardner 1992 for alternate definitions). As such, prejudice is often assumed to develop from unfavorable stereotypes of the group and to predict discriminatory behavior toward group members. Some researchers have investigated how perceivers decide that others are prejudiced against a group (e.g. Rodin et al 1990), or the psychological consequences of being a victim of prejudice and discrimination (e.g. Crocker & Major 1992; Lalonde & Cameron 1992; Taylor et al 1992). More common, though, has been research on the determinants and consequences of prejudice within individuals.

DETERMINANTS OF PREJUDICE   Prejudiced attitudes and behaviors develop with age (e.g. Lerner & Grant 1990) and are associated with such personal characteristics as authoritarianism (Altemeyer 1992) and certain kinds of religiosity (Batson & Burris 1992). Social conditions can induce perceived threat and thereby increase authoritarianism and prejudice (Doty et al 1991).

Several researchers have addressed the role of affective or emotional factors in prejudice. For example, work on ambivalence in racial attitudes (e.g. Hass et al 1991) assumes that polarized evaluations of minority group members reflect the simultaneous presence of both sympathy and aversion in majority group members' attitudes. Fiske & Ruscher (1992) suggested that outgroups are spontaneously assumed to hinder one's goals; this negative interdependence arouses negative affect, which can trigger prejudice and discrimination. Esses et al (1992b) examined the influence of moods on the stereotyping of ethnic groups. In several experiments, induced negative moods increased the expression of negative intergroup stereotypes, presumably because perceivers interpreted their stereotypes in more unfavorable terms.

Finally, the relative predictive utility of cognitive versus affective determinants of prejudice has also been explored. Stangor et al (1992) compared the importance of stereotypic beliefs about groups (e.g. traits associated with groups) and affective feelings toward groups (e.g. whether the groups make you feel hopeful, respectful, afraid, disgusted, etc) as predictors of global evaluations and social distance measures. Emotional responses consistently predicted attitudes and social distance more strongly than did cognitive stereotypes. In the most comprehensive examination of this issue, Esses et al (1992a) examined stereotypic beliefs, affective feelings, and symbolic beliefs (beliefs that social groups violate or uphold cherished values) as predictors of overall attitudes. Again, stereotypic beliefs did not predict intergroup attitudes strongly. Both emotions and symbolic beliefs had better predictive power, but were particularly relevant within specific personality subgroups. Symbolic beliefs were the strongest predictors of intergroup attitudes for highly authoritarian individuals, whereas emotions predicted attitudes best for individuals low in authoritarianism.

A NEW RACISM?   The just-mentioned notion of symbolic beliefs raises a controversial issue in the prejudice literature, namely whether a new form of racism has evolved, replacing conscious beliefs in racial differences and endorsement of segregation. Dovidio, Gaertner, and colleagues (e.g. Dovidio et al 1989) propose that a new, relatively subtle form of racism is now common, which they term *aversive racism.* These authors argue that the historically racist culture of the United States has led most majority group members to develop feelings of superiority; most individuals also have convictions of racial fairness and equality, however. These conflicting feelings restrain overtly racist actions, but when negative responses can be rationalized on the basis of some factor other than race, they will emerge. This analysis focuses on subtle racism among liberals.

Sears and colleagues (e.g. Sears 1988; Sears & Funk 1991) argue that old-fashioned racism has been replaced by something they term *symbolic racism.* These authors hypothesize that minority groups are seen to violate traditional American values; racism reflects a mixture of strong anti-minority affect with endorsement of race-neutral values like the Protestant work ethic. This analysis focuses on subtle racism among conservatives.

The concepts of aversive and symbolic racism have been criticized, both on conceptual and empirical grounds. For example, Sniderman et al (1991) obtained evidence suggesting that the violation of traditional values has little to do with expressions of discrimination. Devine (1989) found that low-prejudice subjects consciously inhibited racial stereotypes when making judgments about minority group members; when subjects were unaware that a stereotype had been subliminally activated, however, even low-prejudice subjects exhibited stereotypic judgments. Devine concluded that liberal, low-prejudice persons must deliberately inhibit implicitly-held stereotypes, consistent with both the aversive racism perspective and ambivalence models of racial attitudes. In subsequent research, Devine et al (1991) found that many individuals are aware of discrepancies between how they think minority group members *should* be treated and how they think they *would* treat such persons. Devine et al interpreted these data as supporting ambivalence models and disconfirming aversive racism, because the latter view assumes that negative reactions to minorities are excluded from conscious awareness.

REDUCING PREJUDICE   Whether modern racism is qualitatively different from old-fashioned racism or is simply the same old prejudice packaged in different ways, the problem of reducing racial enmity remains paramount. We believe that social psychologists have much to offer in this domain and expect that the topic of prejudice reduction will receive increased empirical attention over the next few years.

The technique that has been most widely suggested and studied is contact with members of outgroups. Correlational evidence certainly makes contact appear beneficial, although favorable attitudes might motivate contact rather than the reverse. Contact with homosexuals is associated with more favorable beliefs and attitudes toward this group among heterosexuals (e.g. Whitely 1990), and prejudiced, authoritarian individuals report less contact in general with members of outgroups (Altemeyer 1992).

Intergroup contact must satisfy certain requirements in order to reduce prejudice, however, including that the groups cooperate and be of equal status (see Fiske & Ruscher 1992; Gaertner et al 1990). These requirements are inherent parts of Cook's (1990) technique for reducing prejudice and Aronson's (1990) jigsaw method for fostering positive racial attitudes in desegregated classrooms, both of which have been shown to be effective. In a recent experiment, Desforges et al (1991) had undergraduate subjects interact with an alleged former mental patient; the interactions involved either scripted cooperative learning (Dansereau 1988), jigsaw cooperative learning, or individual study. Both scripted and jigsaw cooperative learning (which differ only in particulars) led to more favorable attitudes among initially prejudiced subjects, whereas individual study produced no changes in attitudes.

CONCLUSIONS

We are impressed with the continuing vitality of the attitudes literature. The attitude concept remains useful for understanding a wide variety of phenomena, and theoretical models of attitude processes show increasing sophistication as researchers integrate knowledge from related fields, such as social cognition and intergroup relations.

Among the noteworthy trends in the attitudes literature is an increasing view of attitudes as cognitive representations, with evaluation as a central element. Interest in attitude attributes, including strength, importance, and ambivalence, is also growing steadily. The psychophysical or social judgment approach is more popular than ever before.

We find a few emerging topics and perspectives particularly welcome. First, we are delighted by the renewed interest in attitude formation; researchers have traditionally focused on how existing attitudes change, but many important attitude phenomena occur early in the formative process. Second, we are excited by possible integrative models of the attitude-behavior relation, including the theory of planned behavior and Eagly & Chaiken's composite model. Third, the continuing development of the dual-process models in the persuasion literature has been remarkable. Fourth, we laud renewed attention to message reception processes in persuasion. Finally, we are happy about resurgent interest in the topic of prejudice and are confident that research can yield truly significant advances both in understanding and treatment of this social problem.

ACKNOWLEDGMENTS

This review was prepared while both authors were supported by research grants from the Social Sciences and Humanities Research Council of Canada. We thank Victoria M. Esses and Neal J. Roese for their comments on a previous draft.

Literature Cited

Ajzen, I. 1985. From intentions to actions: a theory of planned behavior. In *Action-Control: From Cognition to Behavior,* ed. J. Kuhl & J. Beckman, pp. 11–39. Heidelberg: Springer

Ajzen, I. 1991. The theory of planned behavior. *Organizational Behav. and Hum. Decision Processes* 50:1–33

Altemeyer, B. 1992. Reducing prejudice in right-wing authoritarians. See Zanna & Olson 1992, In press

Anand, P., Sternthal, B. 1990. Ease of message processing as a moderator of repetition effects in advertising. *J. Marketing Res.* 27:345–53

Anderson, C. A., Kellam, K. L. 1992. Belief preserverance, biased assimilation, and covariation detection: the effects of hypothetical social theories and new data. *Pers. Soc. Psychol. Bull.* In press

Anderson, N. H., Armstrong, N. A. 1989. Cognitive theory and methodology for studying marital interaction. In *Dyadic Decision*

Making, ed. D. Brindberg & D. Jaccard, pp. 3–49. New York: Springer-Verlag

Arkes, H. R., Boehm, L. E., Xu, G. 1991. Determinants of judged validity. *J. Exp. Soc. Psychol.* 27:576–605

Aronson, E. 1990. Applying social psychology to desegregation and energy conservation. *Pers. Soc. Psychol. Bull.* 16:118–32

Arvey, R. D., Bouchard, T. J., Segal, N. L., Abraham, L. M. 1989. Job satisfaction: environmental and genetic components. *J. Appl. Psychol.* 74:187–92

Axsom, D. 1989. Cognitive dissonance and behavior change in psychotherapy. *J. Exp. Soc. Psychol.* 25:234–52

Bagozzi, R. P., Yi, Y. 1989. The degree of intention formation as a moderator of the attitude-behavior relationship. *Soc. Psychol. Q.* 52:266–79

Bagozzi, R. P., Yi, Y., Baumgartner, J. 1990. The level of effort required for behaviour as a moderator of the attitude-behaviour relation. *Eur. J. Soc. Psychol.* 20:45–59

Balasubramanian, S. K., Kamakura, W. A.

1989. Measuring consumer attitudes toward the marketplace with tailored interviews. *J. Marketing Res.* 26:311–26

Banaji, M. R., Greenwald, A. G. 1992. Implicit stereotyping and prejudice. See Zanna & Olson 1992, In press

Bargh, J. A., Chaiken, S., Govender, R., Pratto. F. 1992. The generality of the automatic attitude activation effect. *J. Pers. Soc. Psychol.* 62:893–912

Bassili, J. N., Fletcher, J. F. 1991. Response-time measurement in survey research: a method for CATI and a new look at non-attitudes. *Public Opin. Q.* 55:329–44

Batson, C. D., Burris, C. T. 1992. Personal religion: depressant or stimulant of prejudice and discrimination? See Zanna & Olson 1992, In press

Bauman, K. E., Fisher, L. A., Koch, G. G. 1989. External variables, subjective expected utility, and adolescent behavior with alcohol and cigarettes. *J. Appl. Soc. Psychol.* 19:789–804

Bearden, W. O., Netemeyer, R. G., Teel, J. E. 1989. Measurement of consumer susceptibility to interpersonal influence. *J. Consum. Res.* 15:473–81

Beck, L., Ajzen, I. 1991. Predicting dishonest actions using the theory of planned behavior. *J. Res. Pers.* 25:285–301

Bem, D. J. 1972. Self-perception theory. *Adv. Exp. Soc. Psychol.* 6:1–62

Berkowitz, L., Devine P. G. 1989. Research traditions, analysis, and synthesis in social psychological theories: the case of dissonance theory. *Pers. Soc. Psychol. Bull.* 15:493–507

Biernat, M. 1991. Gender stereotypes and the relationship between masculinity and femininity: a developmental analysis. *J. Pers. Soc. Psychol.* 61:351–65

Bless, H., Bohner, G., Schwarz, N., Strack, F. 1990. Mood and persuasion: a cognitive response analysis. *Pers. Soc. Psychol. Bull.* 116:331–45

Bodenhausen, G. V. 1990. Stereotypes as judgmental heuristics: evidence of circadian variations in discrimination. *Psychol. Sci.* 1:319–22

Bornstein, R. F. 1989. Exposure and affect: overview and meta-analysis of research, 1968–1987. *Psychol. Bull.* 106:265–89

Bornstein, R. F., Kale, A. R., Cornell, K. R. 1990. Boredom as a limiting condition on the mere exposure effect. *J. Pers. Soc. Psychol.* 58:791–800

Breckler, S. J., Wiggins, E. C. 1989a. On defining attitude and attitude theory: once more with feeling. See Pratkanis et al 1989, pp. 407–27

Breckler, S. J., Wiggins, E. C. 1989b. Affect versus evaluation in the structure of attitudes. *J. Exp. Soc. Psychol.* 25:253–71

Breckler, S. J., Wiggins, E. C. 1991. Cognitive responses in persuasion: affective and evaluative determinants. *J. Exp. Soc. Psychol.* 27:180–200

Brewer, M. B. 1988. A dual process model of impression formation. In *Advances in Social Cognition,* ed. R. S. Wyer, Jr. & T. K. Srull, 1:1–36. Hillsdale, NJ: Erlbaum

Brewer, M. B. 1992. The social psychology of prejudice: getting it all together. See Zanna & Olson 1992, In press

Brownlow, S., Zebrowitz, L. A. 1990. Facial appearance, gender, and credibility in television commercials. *J. Nonverbal Behav.* 2:51–60

Brubaker, R. G., Fowler, C. 1990. Encouraging college males to perform testicular self-examination: evaluation of a persuasive message based on the revised theory of reasoned action. *J. Appl. Soc. Psychol.* 17:1411–22

Burgoon, J. K., Birk, T., Pfau, M. 1990. Nonverbal behaviors, persuasion, and credibility. *Hum. Commun. Res.* 17:140–69

Burnkrant, R. E., Unnava, H. R. 1989. Self-referencing: a strategy for increasing processing of message content. *Pers. Soc. Psychol. Bull.* 15:628–38

Cacioppo, J. T., Marshall-Goodell, B. S., Tassinary, L. G., Petty, R. E. 1992. Rudimentary determinants of attitudes: classical conditioning is more effective when prior knowledge about the attitude stimulus is low than high. *J. Exp. Soc. Psychol.* 28:207–33

Cacioppo, J. T., Petty, R. E. 1989. Effects of message repetition on argument processing, recall, and persuasion. *Basic Appl. Soc. Psychol.* 10:3–12

Cacioppo, J. T., Petty, R. E., Tassinary, L. G. 1989. Social psychophysiology: a new look. *Adv. Exp. Soc. Psychol.* 22:39–91

Cacioppo, J. T., Tassinary, L. G. 1990. Inferring psychological significance from physiological signals. *Amer. Psychol.* 45:16–28

Campis, L. K., Prentice-Dunn, S., Lyman, R. D. 1989. Coping appraisal and parents' intentions to inform their children about sexual abuse: a protection motivation theory analysis. *J. Soc. Clin. Psychol.* 8:304–16

Caporael, L. R., Brewer, M. B. 1991. Reviving evolutionary psychology: biology meets society. *J. Soc. Issues* 47(3):187–95

Carli, L. L. 1990. Gender, language, and influence. *J. Pers. Soc. Psychol.* 59:941–51

Caspi, A., Herbener, E. S., Ozer, D. J. 1992. Shared experiences and the similarity of personalities: a longitudinal study of married couples. *J. Pers. Soc. Psychol.* 62:281–91

Chaiken, S. 1987. The heuristic model of persuasion. See Zanna, Olson, & Herman 1987, pp. 3–39

Chaiken, S., Liberman, A., Eagly, A. H. 1989. Heuristic and systematic information processing within and beyond the persuasion context. In *Unintended Thought,* ed. J. S.

Uleman & J. A. Bargh, pp. 212–52. New York: Guilford Press

Chaiken, S., Stangor, C. 1987. Attitudes and attitude change. *Annu. Rev. Psychol.* 38:575–630

Chattopadhyay, A., Basu, K. 1990. Humor in advertising: the moderating role of prior brand evaluation. *J. Marketing Res.* 27:466–76

Cialdini, R. B., Green, B. L., Rusch, A. J. 1992. When tactical pronouncements of change become real change: the case of reciprocal persuasion. *J. Pers. Soc. Psychol.* 63:30–40

Cook, S. W. 1990. Toward a psychology of improving justice: research on extending the equality principle to victims of social injustice. *J. Soc. Issues* 46(1):147–61

Cooper, J., Scher, S. J. 1992. Actions and attitudes: the role of responsibility and aversive consequences in persuasion. In *The Psychology of Persuasion,* ed. T. Brock & S. Shavitt. San Francisco: W. H. Freeman. In press

Crocker, J., Major, B. 1992. Reactions to stigma: the moderating role of justifications. See Zanna & Olson 1992, In press

Cropanzano, R., James, J. 1990. Some methodological considerations for the behavioral genetic analysis of work attitudes. *J. Appl. Psychol.* 75:433–39

Crosby, L. A., Bitner, M. J., Gill J. D. 1990. Organizational structure of values. *J. Bus. Res.* 20:123–34

Damrad-Frye, R., Laird, J. D. 1989. The experience of boredom: the role of the self-perception of attention. *J. Pers. Soc. Psychol.* 57:315–20

Dansereau, D. F. 1988. Cooperative learning strategies. In *Learning and Study Strategies: Issues in Assessment, Instruction, and Evaluation,* ed. C. E. Weinstein, E. T. Goetz, & P. A. Alexander, pp. 103–20. San Diego, CA: Academic Press

DeBono, K. G., Telesca, C. 1990. The influence of source physical attractiveness on advertising effectiveness: a functional perspective. *J. Appl. Soc. Psychol.* 20:1383–95

Desforges, D. M., Lord, C. G., Ramsey, S. L., Mason, J. A., Van Leeuwen, M. D. et al 1991. Effects of structured cooperative contact on changing negative attitudes toward stigmatized social groups. *J. Pers. Soc. Psychol.* 60:531–44

Devine, P. G. 1989. Stereotypes and prejudice: their automatic and controlled components. *J. Pers. Soc. Psychol.* 56:5–18

Devine, P. G., Monteith, M. J., Zuwerink, J. R., Elliot, A. J. 1991. Prejudice with and without compunction. *J. Pers. Soc. Psychol.* 60:817–30

Dion, K. L., Schuller, R. A. 1991. The Ms. stereotype: its generality and its relation to managerial and marital status stereotypes. *Canad. J. Behav. Sci.* 23:25–40

Doty, R. M., Peterson, B. E., Winter, D. G. 1991. Threat and authoritarianism in the United States, 1978–1987. *J. Pers. Soc. Psychol.* 61:629–40

Dovidio, J. F., Fazio, R. H. 1992. New technologies for the direct and indirect assessment of attitudes. See Tanur 1992, pp. 204–37

Dovidio, J. F., Gaertner, S. L. 1992. Stereotypes and evaluative intergroup bias. See Mackie & Hamilton 1992, In press

Dovidio, J. F., Mann, J., Gaertner, S. L. 1989. Resistance to affirmative action: the implications of aversive racism. In *Affirmative Action in Perspective,* ed. F. A. Blanchard & F. J. Crosby, pp. 83–102. New York: Springer-Verlag

Eagly, A. H., Ashmore, R. D., Makhijani, M. G., Longo, L. C. 1991. What is beautiful is good, but...: a meta-analytic review of research on the physical attractiveness stereotype. *Psychol. Bull.* 110:109–28

Eagly, A. H., Chaiken, S. 1992. *The Psychology of Attitudes.* San Diego, CA: Harcourt Brace Janovich

Eaves, L. J., Eysenck, H. J., Martin, N. G. 1989. *Genes, Culture, and Personality: An Empirical Approach.* London: Academic Press

Echabe, A. E., Rovira, D. P. 1989. Social representations and memory: the case of AIDS. *Eur. J. Soc. Psychol.* 19:543–51

Edwards, K. 1990. The interplay of affect and cognition in attitude formation and change. *J. Pers. Soc. Psychol.* 59:202–16

Eiser, J. R. 1990. *Social Judgment.* Buckingham: Open University Press

Eiser, J. R., Morgan, M., Gammage, P., Gray, E. 1989. Adolescent smoking: attitudes, norms and parental influence. *Br. J. Soc. Psychol.* 28:193–202

Enzle, M. E., Roggeveen, J. P., Look, S. C. 1991. Self- versus other-reward administration and intrinsic motivation. *J. Exp. Soc. Psychol.* 27:468–79

Esses, V. M., Haddock, G., Zanna, M. P. 1992a. Values, stereotypes, and emotions as determinants of intergroup attitudes. See Mackie & Hamilton 1992, In press

Esses, V. M., Haddock, G., Zanna, M. P. 1992b. The role of mood in the expression of intergroup stereotypes. See Zanna & Olson 1992, In press

Evans, M. 1991. The problem of analyzing multiplicative composites. *Amer. Psychol.* 46:6–15

Fazio, R. H. 1987. Self-perception theory: a current perspective. See Zanna, Olson, & Herman 1987, pp. 129–50

Fazio, R. H. 1990. Multiple processes by which attitudes guide behavior: the MODE model as an integrative framework. *Adv. Exp. Soc. Psychol.* 23:75–109

Fazio, R. H. 1992. Variability in the likelihood of automatic attitude activation: a data reanalysis and commentary on the paper by Bargh, Chaiken, Govender, and Pratto. *J. Pers. Soc. Psychol.* In press

Fazio, R. H., Powell, M. C., Williams, C. J.

1989. The role of attitude accessibility in the attitude-to-behavior process. *J. Consum. Res.* 16:280–88

Feather, N. T. 1990. Bridging the gap between values and actions: recent applications of the expectancy-value model. In *Handbook of Motivation and Cognition: Foundations of Social Behavior,* ed. E. T. Higgins & R. M. Sorrentino, 2:151–92. New York: Guilford Press

Feather, N. T. 1991. Human values, global self-esteem, and belief in a just world. *J. Pers.* 59:83–106

Feingold, A. 1992. Good-looking people are not what we think. *Psychol. Bull.* 111:304–41

Fiedler, K. 1991. The tricky nature of skewed frequency tables: an information loss account of distinctiveness-based illusory correlations. *J. Pers. Soc. Psychol.* 60:24–36

Fishbein, M., Ajzen, I. 1975. *Belief, Attitude, Intention, and Behavior: An Introduction to Theory and Research.* Reading, MA: Addison-Wesley

Fishbein, M., Stasson, M. 1990. The role of desires, self-predictions, and perceived control in the prediction of training session attendance. *J. Appl. Soc. Psychol.* 20:173–98

Fisher, J. D., Fisher, W. A. 1992. Changing AIDS risk behavior. *Psychol. Bull.* 111:455–74

Fiske, S. T., Neuberg, S. L. 1990. A continuum of impression formation, from category-based to individuating processes: influences of information and motivation on attention and interpretation. *Adv. Exp. Soc. Psychol.* 23:1–74

Fiske, S. T., Ruscher, J. B. 1992. Negative interdependence and prejudice: whence the affect? See Mackie & Hamilton 1992, In press

Friedrich, J., Kierniesky, N., Cardon, L. 1989. Drawing moral inferences from descriptive science: the impact of attitudes on naturalistic fallacy errors. *Pers. Soc. Psychol. Bull.* 15:414–25

Gaertner, S. L., Mann, J. A., Dovidio, J. F., Murrell, A. J., Pomare, M. 1990. How does cooperation reduce intergroup bias? *J. Pers. Soc. Psychol.* 59:692–704

Gardner, R. C. 1992. Stereotypes as consensual beliefs. See Zanna & Olson 1992, In press

Gerard, H. B., Orive, R. 1987. The dynamics of opinion formation. *Adv. Exp. Soc. Psychol.* 20:171–200

Gilbert, D. T., Hixon, J. G. 1991. The trouble of thinking: activation and application of stereotypic beliefs. *J. Pers. Soc. Psychol.* 60:509–17.

Gilbert, D. T., Krull, D. S., Malone, P. S. 1990. Unbelieving the unbelievable: some problems in the rejection of false information. *J. Pers. Soc. Psychol.* 59:601–13

Gleicher, F., Petty, R. E. 1992. Expectations of reassurance influence the nature of fear-stimulated attitude change. *J. Exp. Soc. Psychol.* 28:86–100

Gordon, R. A. 1989. Intention and expectation measures as predictors of academic performance. *J. Appl. Soc. Psychol.* 19:405–15

Granberg, D., Holmberg, S. 1990. The intention-behavior relationship among U.S. and Swedish voters. *Soc. Psychol. Q.* 53:44–54

Gray, T. 1990. Questionnaire format and item context affect level of belief in both scientifically unsubstantiated and substantiated phenomena. *Canad. J. Behav. Sci.* 22:173–80

Greenwald, A. G. 1989. Why attitudes are important: defining attitude and attitude theory 20 years later. See Pratkanis et al 1989, pp. 429–40

Grube, J. W., Morgan, M. 1990. Attitude-social support interactions: contingent consistency effects in the prediction of adolescent smoking, drinking, and drug use. *Soc. Psychol. Q.* 53:329–39

Gruenfeld, D. H., Wyer, R. S. Jr. 1992. The semantics and pragmatics of social influence: how affirmations and denials affect beliefs in referent propositions. *J. Pers. Soc. Psychol.* In press

Hamilton, D. L., Gifford, R. K. 1976. Illusory correlation in interpersonal perception: a cognitive basis of stereotypic judgments. *J. Exp. Soc. Psychol.* 12:392–407

Hamilton, D. L., Sherman, S. J., Ruvolo, C. M. 1990. Stereotype based expectancies: effects on information processing and social behavior. *J. Soc. Issues* 46(2):35–60

Hass, R. G., Katz, I., Rizzo, N., Bailey, J., Eisenstadt, D. 1991. Cross-racial appraisal as related to attitude ambivalence and cognitive complexity. *Pers. Soc. Psychol. Bull.* 17:83–92

Heaven, P. C. L. 1990. Human values and suggestions for reducing unemployment. *Br. J. Soc. Psychol.* 29:257–64

Hilton, J. L., von Hippel, W. 1990. The role of consistency in the judgment of stereotype-relevant behaviors. *Pers. Soc. Psychol. Bull.* 16:430–48

Himmelfarb, S. 1992. The measurement of attitudes. See Eagly & Chaiken 1992, pp. 23–87

Hinsz, V. B., Nelson, L. C. 1990. Testing models of turnover intentions with university faculty. *J. Appl. Soc. Psychol.* 20:68–84

Hoffman, C., Hurst, N. 1990. Gender stereotypes: perception or rationalization? *J. Pers. Soc. Psychol.* 58:197–208

Houston, D. A., Fazio, R. H. 1989. Biased processing as a function of attitude accessibility: making objective judgments subjectively. *Soc. Cogn.* 7:51–66

Howard, D. J. 1990. Rhetorical question effects on message processing and persuasion: the role of information availability and the elicitation of judgment. *J. Exp. Soc. Psychol.* 26:217–39

Hutton, D. G., Baumeister, R. F. 1992. Self-awareness and attitude change: seeing one-self on the central route to persuasion. *Pers. Soc. Psychol. Bull.* 18:68–75

Jacoby, L. L., Kelly, C., Brown, J., Jasechko, J. 1989. Becoming famous overnight: limits on the ability to avoid unconscious influences of the past. *J. Pers. Soc. Psychol.* 56:326–38

Jamieson, D. W., Zanna, M. P. 1989. Need for structure in attitude formation and expression. See Pratkanis et al 1989, pp. 383–406

Janiszewski, C. 1990a. The influence of print advertisement organization on affect toward a brand name. *J. Consum. Res.* 17:53–65

Janiszewski, C. 1990b. The influence of non-attended material on the processing of advertising claims. *J. Marketing Res.* 27:263–78

Johnson, B. T., Eagly, A. H. 1989. Effects of involvement on persuasion: a meta-analysis. *Psychol. Bull.* 106:290–314

Johnson, B. T., Eagly, A. H. 1990. Involvement and persuasion: types, traditions, and the evidence. *Psychol. Bull.* 107:375–84

Joule, R. 1991. Practicing and arguing for abstinence from smoking: a test of the double forced compliance paradigm. *Eur. J. Soc. Psychol.* 21:119–29

Judd, C. M., Downing, J. W. 1990. Political expertise and the development of attitude consistency. *Soc. Cogn.* 8:104–24

Jussim, L. 1991. Social perception and social reality: a reflection-construction model. *Psychol. Rev.* 98:54–73

Kaplan, M. F., Wanshula, L. T., Zanna, M. P. 1992. Time pressure and information integration in social judgment: the effect of need for structure. In *Time Pressure and Stress in Human Judgment and Decision Making,* ed. O. Svenson & J. Maule. New York: Plenum. In press

Katz, I., Hass, R. G. 1988. Racial ambivalence and American value conflict: correlational and priming studies of dual cognitive structures. *J. Pers. Soc. Psychol.* 55:893–905

Kellerman, J., Lewis, J., Laird, J. D. 1989. Looking and loving: the effects of mutual gaze on feelings of romantic love. *J. Res. Pers.* 23:145–61

Kendzierski, D. 1990. Decision making versus decision implementation: an action control approach to exercise adoption and adherence. *J. Appl. Soc. Psychol.* 20:27–45

Kristiansen, C. M., Matheson, K. 1990. Value conflict, value justification, and attitudes toward nuclear weapons. *J. Soc. Psychol.* 130:665–75

Kristiansen, C. M., Zanna, M. P. 1991. Value relevance and the value-attitude relation: value-expressiveness versus halo effects. *Basic Appl. Soc. Psychol.* 12:471–83

Krosnick, J. A. 1989. Attitude importance and attitude accessibility. *Pers. Soc. Psychol Bull.* 15:297–308

Krosnick, J. A., Abelson, R. P. 1992. The case for measuring attitude strength in surveys. See Tanur 1992

Krosnick, J. A., Alwin, D. F. 1989. Aging and susceptibility to attitude change. *J. Pers. Soc. Psychol.* 57:416–25

Krosnick, J. A., Betz, A. L., Jussim, L. J., Lynn, A. R., Stephens, L. 1992. Subliminal conditioning of attitudes. *Pers. Soc. Psychol. Bull.* 18:152–62

Kruglanski, A. W. 1989. *Lay Epistemics and Human Knowledge: Cognitive and Motivational Bases.* New York: Plenum

Kunda, Z. 1990. The case for motivated reasoning. *Psychol. Bull.* 108:480–98

Kuykendall, D., Keating, J. P. 1990. Altering thoughts and judgements through repeated association. *Br. J. Soc. Psychol.* 29:79–86

Lalonde, R. N., Cameron, J. E. 1992. Behavioural responses to discrimination: a focus on action. See Zanna & Olson 1992, In press

Lerner, M. J., Grant, P. R. 1990. The influences of commitment to justice and ethnocentrism on children's allocations of pay. *Soc. Psychol. Q.* 53:229–38

Liberman, A., Chaiken, S. 1991. Value conflict and thought-induced attitude change. *J. Exp. Soc. Psychol.* 27:203–16

Liberman, A., Chaiken, S. 1992. Defensive processing of personally relevant health messages. *Pers. Soc. Psychol. Bull.* In press

Lord, C. G., Desforges, D. M., Ramsey, S. L., Trezza, G. R., Lepper, M. R. 1991. Typicality effects in attitude-behavior consistency: effects of category discrimination and category knowledge. *J. Exp. Soc. Psychol.* 27:550–75

Losch, M. E., Cacioppo, J. T. 1990. Cognitive dissonance may enhance sympathetic tonus, but attitudes are changed to reduce negative affect rather than arousal. *J. Exp. Soc. Psychol.* 26:289–304

Maass, A., Salvi, D., Arcuri, L., Semin, G. 1989. Language use in intergroup contexts: the linguistic intergroup bias. *J. Pers. Soc. Psychol.* 57:981–93

Mackie, D. M., Asuncion, A. G. 1990. On-line and memory-based modification of attitudes: determinants of message recall-attitude change correspondence. *J. Pers. Soc. Psychol.* 59:5–16

Mackie, D. M., Hamilton, D. L., eds. 1992. *Affect, Cognition, and Stereotyping: Interactive Processes in Group Perception.* New York: Academic. In press

Mackie, D. M., Worth, L. T. 1989. Processing deficits and the mediation of positive affect in persuasion. *J. Pers. Soc. Psychol.* 57:27–40

Mackie, D. M., Worth, L. T., Asuncion, A. G. 1990. Processing of persuasive in-group messages. *J. Pers. Soc. Psychol.* 58:812–22

Madden, T. J., Ellen, P. S., Ajzen, I. 1992. A comparison of the theory of planned behavior and the theory of reasoned action. *Pers. Soc. Psychol. Bull.* 18:3–9

Maheswaran, D., Chaiken, S. 1991. Promoting systematic processing in low-motivation settings: effect of incongruent information on processing and judgment. *J. Pers. Soc. Psychol.* 61:13–25

Maheswaran, D., Meyers-Levy, J. 1990. The influence of message framing and issue involvement. *J. Marketing Res.* 27:361–67

McCann, C. D., Higgins, E. T., Fondacaro, R. 1991. Primacy and recency in communication and self-persuasion: how successive audiences and multiple encodings influence subsequent evaluation judgments. *Soc. Cogn.* 9:47–66

McGill, A. L., Anand, P. 1989. The effect of vivid attributes on the evaluation of alternatives: the role of differential attention and cognitive elaboration. *J. Consum. Res.* 16:188–96

McGuire, W. J. 1968. Personality and attitude change: an information processing theory. In *Psychological Foundations of Attitudes*, ed. A. G. Greenwald, T. C. Brock, T. M. Ostrom, pp. 171–96. San Diego, CA: Academic Press

McGuire, W. J. 1985. Attitudes and attitude change. In *Handbook of Social Psychology*, ed. G. Lindzey, E. Aronson, 2:233–346. New York: Random House. 3rd ed.

Meyers-Levy, J., Sternthal, B. 1991. Gender differences in the use of message cues and judgments. *J. Marketing Res.* 28:84–96

Milburn, M. A. 1991. *Persuasion and Politics: The Social Psychology of Public Opinion.* Pacific Grove, CA: Wadsworth

Millar, M. G., Millar, K. U. 1990. Attitude change as a function of attitude type and argument type. *J. Pers. Soc. Psychol.* 59:217–28

Millar, M. G., Tesser, A. 1989. The effects of affective-cognitive consistency and thought on the attitude-behavior relation. *J. Exp. Soc. Psychol.* 25:189–202

Millar, M. G., Tesser, A. 1992. The role of beliefs and feelings in guiding behavior: the mis-match model. In *Construction of Social Judgment*, ed. L. Martin, A. Tesser. Hillsdale, NJ: Erlbaum. In press

Mulilis, J., Lippa, R. 1990. Behavioral change in earthquake preparedness due to negative threat appeals: a test of protection motivation theory. *J. Appl. Soc. Psychol.* 20:619–38

Mullen, B., Johnson, C. 1990. Distinctiveness-based illusory correlations and stereotyping: a meta-analytic integration. *Br. J. Soc. Psychol.* 29:11–28

Nederhof, A. J. 1989. Self-involvement, intention certainty and attitude-intention consistency. *Br. J. Soc. Psychol.* 28:123–33

Norman, N. M., Tedeschi, J. T. 1989. Self-presentation, reasoned action, and adolescents' decisions to smoke cigarettes. *J. Appl. Soc. Psychol.* 19:543–58

Nowak, A., Szamrej, J., Latane, B. 1990. From private attitude to public opinion: a dynamic theory of social impact. *Psychol. Rev.* 97:362–76

O'Keefe, D. J. 1990. *Persuasion: Theory and Practice.* Newbury Park, CA: Sage

Olson, J. M. 1990. Self-inference processes in emotion. See Olson & Zanna 1990, 6:17–41

Olson, J. M. 1992. Self-perception of humor: evidence for discounting and augmentation effects. *J. Pers. Soc. Psychol.* 62:369–77

Olson, J. M., Zanna, M. P. 1990. *Self-Inference Processes: The Ontario Symposium, Vol. 6.* Hillsdale, NJ: Erlbaum

Oskamp, S. 1991. *Attitudes and Opinions.* Englewood Cliffs, NJ: Prentice-Hall. 2nd ed.

Ottati, V. C., Riggle, E. J., Wyer, R. S. Jr., Schwarz, N., Kuklinski, J. 1989. Cognitive and affective bases of opinion survey responses. *J. Pers. Soc. Psychol.* 57:404–15

Paulhus, D. L., Martin, C. L., Murphy, G. 1992. Some effects of arousal on sex stereotyping. *Pers. Soc. Psychol. Bull.* 18:325–30

Perdue, C. W., Dovidio, J. F., Gurtman, M. B., Tyler, R. B. 1990. "Us" and "them": social categorization and the process of intergroup bias. *J. Pers. Soc. Psychol.* 59:475–86

Petty, R. E., Cacioppo, J. T. 1986. The elaboration likelihood model of persuasion. *Adv. Exp. Soc. Psychol.* 19:123–205

Petty, R. E., Cacioppo, J. T. 1990. Involvement and persuasion: tradition versus integration. *Psychol. Bull.* 107:367–74

Petty, R. E., Gleicher, F., Baker, S. M. 1991. Multiple roles for affect in persuasion. In *Emotion and Social Judgments*, ed. J. P. Forgas, pp. 181–200. Oxford: Pergamon Press

Petty, R. E., Krosnick, J. A. 1992. *Attitude Strength: Antecedents and Consequences.* Hillsdale, NJ: Erlbaum. In press

Pratkanis, A. R., Aronson, E. 1991. *Age of Propaganda: The Everyday Use and Abuse of Persuasion.* New York: W. H. Freeman

Pratkanis, A. R., Breckler, S. J., Greenwald, A. G., eds. 1989. *Attitude Structure and Function.* Hillsdale, NJ: Erlbaum

Pratkanis, A. R., Greenwald, A. G. 1989. A sociocognitive model of attitude structure and function. *Adv. Exp. Soc. Psychol.* 22:245–85

Pratto, F., Bargh, J. A. 1991. Stereotyping based on apparently individuating information: trait and global components of sex stereotypes under attention overload. *J. Exp. Soc. Psychol.* 27:26–47

Pryor, J. B., Reeder, G. D., McManus, J. A. 1991. Fear and loathing in the workplace: reactions to AIDS-infected co-workers. *Pers. Soc. Psychol. Bull.* 17:133–39

Pryor, J. B., Reeder, G. D., Vinacco, R. Jr., Kott, T. L. 1989. The instrumental and symbolic functions of attitudes toward persons with AIDS. *J. Appl. Soc. Psychol.* 19:377–404

Rajecki, D. W. 1990. *Attitudes.* Sunderland, MA: Sinauer

Rasinski, K. A. 1989. The effect of question wording on public support for government spending. *Public Opin. Q.* 53:388–94

Ratneshwar, S., Chaiken, S. 1991. Comprehension's role in persuasion: the case of its moderating effect on the persuasive impact of source cues. *J. Consum. Res.* 18:52–62

Reardon, K. K. 1991. *Persuasion in Practice.* Newbury Park, CA: Sage

Rhodes, N., Wood, W. 1992. Self-esteem and intelligence affect influenceability: the mediating role of message reception. *Psychol. Bull.* 111:156–71

Robinson, J. P., Shaver, P. R., Wrightsman, L. S., eds. 1991. *Measures of Personality and Social Psychological Attitudes.* San Diego, CA: Academic Press

Rodin, M. J., Price, J. M., Bryson, J. B., Sanchez, F. J. 1990. Asymmetry in prejudice attribution. *J. Exp. Soc. Psychol.* 26:481–504

Rogers, R. W. 1983. Cognitive and physiological processes in fear appeals and attitude change: a revised theory of protection motivation. In *Social Psychophysiology,* ed. J. T. Cacioppo, R. E. Petty, pp. 153–76. New York: Guilford

Rokeach, M. 1973. *The Nature of Human Values.* New York: Free Press

Ross, M. 1989. Relation of implicit theories to the construction of personal histories. *Psychol. Rev.* 96:341–57

Ruscher, J. B., Fiske, S. T., Miki, H., Van Manen, S. 1991. Individuating processes in competition: interpersonal versus intergroup. *Pers. Soc. Psychol. Bull.* 17:595–605

Sanbonmatsu, D. M., Fazio, R. H. 1990. The role of attitudes in memory-based decision making. *J. Pers. Soc. Psychol.* 59:614–22

Sande, G. N., Goethals, G. R., Ferrari, L., Worth, L. T. 1989. Value-guided attributions: maintaining the moral self-image and the diabolical enemy-image. *J. Soc. Issues* 45(2):91–118

Sarup, G., Suchner, R. W., Gaylor, G. 1991. Contrast effects and attitude change: a test of the two-stage hypothesis of social judgment theory. *Soc. Psychol. Q.* 54:364–72

Schaller, M. 1991. Social categorization and the formation of group stereotypes: further evidence for biased information processing in the perception of group-behavior correlations. *Eur. J. Soc. Psychol.* 21:25–35

Schaller, M., Maass, A. 1989. Illusory correlation and social categorization: toward an integration of motivational and cognitive factors in stereotype formation. *J. Pers. Soc. Psychol.* 56:709–21

Scher, S. J., Cooper, J. 1989. Motivational basis of dissonance: the singular role of behavioral consequences. *J. Pers. Soc. Psychol.* 56:899–906

Schlegel, R. P., d'Avernas, J. R., Zanna, M. P., DeCourville, N. H., Manske, S. R. 1992. Problem drinking: a problem for the theory of reasoned action? *J. App. Soc. Psychol.* 22:358–85

Schlenker, B. R. 1992. Of shape shifters and theories. *Psychol. Inquiry.* In press

Schlenker, B. R., Weigold, M. F. 1992. Interpersonal processes involving impression regulation and management. *Annu. Rev. Psychol.* 44:

Schul, Y., Mazursky, D. 1990. Conditions facilitating successful discounting in consumer decision making. *J. Consum. Res.* 16:442–51

Schwartz, S. H., Bilsky, W. 1990. Toward a theory of the universal content and structure of values: extensions and cross-cultural replications. *J. Pers. Soc. Psychol.* 58:878–91

Schwartz, S. H., Roccos, S., Sagiv, L. 1992. Universals in the content and structure of values: theoretical advances and empirical tests in 20 countries. *Adv. Exp. Soc. Psychol.* In press

Schwarz, N. 1990. What respondents learn from scales: the informative functions of response alternatives. *Int. J. Public Opin. Res.* 2:274–85

Schwarz, N., Bless, H., Bohner, G. 1991a. Mood and persuasion: affective states influence the processing of persuasive communications. *Adv. Exp. Soc. Psychol.* 24:161–99

Schwarz, N., Munkel, T., Hippler, H. 1990. What determines a 'perspective'? Contrast effects as a function of the dimension tapped by preceding questions. *Eur. J. Soc. Psychol.* 20:357–61

Schwarz, N., Strack, F., Mai, H. 1991b. Assimilation and contrast effects in part-whole question sequences: a conversational logic analysis. *Public Opin. Q.* 55:3–23

Sears, D. O. 1988. Symbolic racism. In *Eliminating Racism: Profiles in Controversy,* ed. P. A. Katz, D. A. Taylor, pp. 53–84. New York: Plenum Press

Sears, D. O., Funk, C. L. 1991. The role of self-interest in social and political attitudes. *Adv. Exp. Soc. Psychol.* 24:1–91

Self, C. A., Rogers, R. W. 1990. Coping with threats to health: effects of persuasive appeals on depressed, normal, and antisocial personalities. *J. Behav. Med.* 13:343–57

Shavitt, S. 1989. Operationalizing functional theories of attitude. See Pratkanis et al 1989, pp. 311–37

Shavitt, S. 1990. The role of attitude objects in attitude functions. *J. Exp. Soc. Psychol.* 26:124–48

Shavitt, S., Fazio, R. H. 1991. Effects of attribute salience on the consistency between attitudes and behavior predictions. *Pers. Soc. Psychol. Bull.* 17:507–16

Silverstein, B., Flamenbaum, C. 1989. Biases

in the perception and cognition of the actions of enemies. *J. Soc. Issues* 45(2):51–72

Singh, J., Howell, R. D., Rhoads, G. K. 1990. Adaptive designs for Likert-type data: an approach for implementing marketing surveys. *J. Marketing Res.* 27:304–21

Skinner, W. F., Cattarello, A. M. 1989. Understanding the relationships among attitudes, group norms, and behavior using behavioral commitment: a structural equation analysis of marijuana use. *J. Appl. Soc. Psychol.* 19:1268–91

Smith, E. R. 1991. Illusory correlation in a simulated exemplar-based memory. *J. Exp. Soc. Psychol.* 27:107–23

Smith, S. M., Shaffer, D. R. 1991. Celerity and cajolery: rapid speech may promote or inhibit persuasion through its impact on message elaboration. *Pers. Soc. Psychol. Bull.* 17:663–69

Smith, S. M., Shaffer, D. R. 1992. The effects of good moods on systematic processing: "Willing but not able, or able but not willing?" *Motivation & Emotion.* In press

Sniderman, P. M., Piazza, T., Tetlock, P. E., Kendrick, A. 1991. The new racism. *Am. J. Polit. Sci.* 35:423–47

Snyder, M., DeBono, K. G. 1987. A functional approach to attitudes and persuasion. See Zanna et al 1987, pp. 107–25

Snyder, M., Miene, P. 1992. On the functions of stereotypes and prejudice. See Zanna & Olson 1992, In press

Stangor, C., Duan, C. 1991. Effects of multiple task demands upon memory for information about social groups. *J. Exp. Soc. Psychol.* 27:357–78

Stangor, C., Sullivan, L. A., Ford, T. E. 1992. Affective and cognitive determinants of prejudice. *Soc. Cogn.* In press

Stasson, M., Fishbein, M. 1990. The relation between perceived and preventive action: a within-subject analysis of perceived driving risk and intentions to wear seatbelts. *J. Appl. Soc. Psychol.* 20:1541–57

Steffen, V. J. 1990. Men's motivation to perform the testicle self-exam: effects of prior knowledge and an educational brochure. *J. Appl. Soc. Psychol.* 20:681–702

Strader, M. K., Katz, B. M. 1990. Effects of a persuasive communication on beliefs, attitudes, and career choice. *J. Soc. Psychol.* 130:141–50

Struckman-Johnson, C. J., Gilliland, R. C., Struckman-Johnson, D. L., North, T. C. 1990. The effects of fear of AIDS and gender on responses to fear-arousing condom advertisements. *J. Appl. Soc. Psychol.* 20:1396–410

Sutton, S., Hallett, R. 1989. Understanding seat-belt intentions and behavior: a decision-making approach. *J. Appl. Soc. Psychol.* 19:1310–25

Tanur, J. M., ed. 1992. *Questions about Questions: Inquiries into the Cognitive Bases of Surveys.* New York: Russell Sage

Taylor, D. M., Wright, S. C., Porter, L. E. 1992. Dimensions of perceived discrimination: the personal/group discrimination discrepancy. See Zanna & Olson 1992, In press

Tesser, A. 1992. On the importance of heritability in psychological research: the case of attitudes. *Psychol. Rev.* In press

Tesser, A., Martin, L., Mendolia, M. 1992. The role of thought in changing attitude strength. See Petty & Krosnick 1992, In press

Tesser, A., Shaffer, P. 1990. Attitudes and attitude change. *Annu. Rev. Psychol.* 41:479–523

Thompson, M. M., Zanna, M. P., Haddock, G. 1992. Let's not be indifferent about (attitudinal) ambivalence. See Petty & Krosnick 1992, In Press

Tourangeau, R., Rasinski, K. A., Bradburn, N. 1989. Belief accessibility and context effects in attitude measurement. *J. Exp. Soc. Psychol.* 25:401–21

Tourangeau, R., Rasinski, K. A., D'Andrade, R. 1991. Attitude structure and belief accessibility. *J. Exp. Soc. Psychol.* 27:48–75

Triandis, H. C. 1991. Attitude and attitude change. In *Ency. Hum. Biol.* 1:485–96. San Diego, CA: Academic Press

Triandis, H. C., McCusker, C., Hui, C. H. 1990. Multimethod probes of individualism and collectivism. *J. Pers. Soc. Psychol.* 59:1006–20

Tyler, T. R., Schuller, R. A. 1991. Aging and attitude change. *J. Pers. Soc. Psychol.* 61:689–97

Warshaw, P. R., Davis, F. D. 1985. Disentangling behavioral intention and behavioral expectation. *J. Exp. Soc. Psychol.* 21:213–28

Weizmann, F., Wiener, N. I., Wiesenthal, D. L., Ziegler, M. 1990. Differential K theory and racial hierarchies. *Can. Psychol.* 31:1–13

Whitely, B. E. Jr. 1990. The relationship of heterosexuals' attributions for the causes of homosexuality to attitudes towards lesbians and gay men. *Pers. Soc. Psychol. Bull.* 16:369–77

Wilder, D. A. 1990. Some determinants of the persuasive power of in-groups and out-groups: organization of information and attribution of independence. *J. Pers. Soc. Psychol.* 59:1202–13

Wilson, T. D. 1990. Self-persuasion via self-reflection. See Olson & Zanna 1990, 6:43–67

Wilson, T. D., Dunn, D. S., Kraft, D., Lisle, D. J. 1989. Introspection, attitude change, and attitude-behavior consistency: the disruptive effects of explaining why we feel the way we do. *Adv. Exp. Soc. Psychol.* 22:278–343

Yi, Y. 1990. Direct and indirect approaches to advertising persuasion. Which is more effective?. *J. Bus. Res.* 20:279–91

Zajonc, R. B. 1968. Attitudinal effects of mere exposure. *J. Pers. Soc. Psychol.* 9 (2, pt. 2)

Zamble, E., Kalm, K. L. 1990. General and specific measures of public attitudes toward sentencing. *Canad. J. Behav. Sci.* 22:327–37

Zanna, M. P. 1992. Message receptivity: a new look at the old problem of open- vs. closed-mindedness. In *Advertising Exposure, Memory, and Choice,* ed. A. Mitchell. Hillsdale, NJ: Erlbaum. In press

Zanna, M. P., Olson, J. M., eds. 1992. *The Psychology of Prejudice: The Ontario Sym-posium,* Vol. 7. Hillsdale, NJ: Erlbaum. In press

Zanna, M. P., Olson, J. M., Herman, C. P. , eds. 1987. *Social Influence: The Ontario Sym-posium,* Vol. 5. Hillsdale, NJ: Erlbaum

Zanna, M. P., Rempel, J. K. 1988. Attitudes: a new look at an old concept. In *The Social Psychology of Knowledge,* ed. D. Bar-Tal, A. W. Kruglanski, pp. 315–34. New York: Cambridge University Press

Zimbardo, P. G., Leippe, M. R. 1991. *The Psy-chology of Attitude Change and Social In-fluence.* New York: McGraw-Hill

Annu. Rev. Psychol. 1993. 44:155–94

SOCIAL COGNITION AND SOCIAL PERCEPTION

Susan T. Fiske

Department of Psychology, University of Massachusetts, Amherst, Massachusetts 01003

KEYWORDS: impressions, traits, accuracy, expectancy, categories, goals

CONTENTS

ACCURACY: PEOPLE ARE GOOD-ENOUGH PERCEIVERS.. 156
   Accurate Ratings 157
   Accurate Memory: Expectancy-Congruent versus -Incongruent Information 159
STRUCTURES: PEOPLE MAKE MEANING 162
   Trait Descriptors as Rich Categories 162
   Stereotypes as Complex Portraits 165
   Using Stories and Simulations to Make Meaning 170
GOALS AND CONTROL: THINKING IS FOR DOING.. 171
   Motivated Tacticians and the Revival of Goals 172
   Increasing the Costs of Being Wrong (Accuracy-Oriented Motives) 172
   Increasing the Costs of Being Indecisive (Expectancy-Confirming Motives) 175
   Automaticity and Control 178
CONCLUSION.. 182

"My thinking is first and last and always for the sake of my doing, and I can only do one thing at a time" (James 1890/1983:960). The pragmatics of social cognition, foreseen by James, developed by Bruner, Heider, Asch, Tagiuri, and Jones (for reviews, see S. Fiske 1992; Jones 1990), is finally returning to its proper place at the core of the enterprise. I would argue that we are

0066-4308/93/0201-0155$02.00

relatively faithful to these roots, although we sometimes fail to acknowledge them. Researchers today are tackling important recurring themes raised by the pragmatics of social perception. People try to make sense of each other in order to guide their own actions and interactions. Given these concerns, (a) perceivers must be accurate enough for current purposes, (b) they must create informative but workable structures, and (c) the entire process must be highly sensitive to people's goals, sets, motives, and needs. Each of these themes is alive and well in the current, thriving literatures on social perception and social cognition.

In this chapter I review current work on social cognition and social perception in light of the pragmatic perspective. The review represents at best a snapshot of the present held up against a single daguerreotype from the distant past, with nothing in-between to show how the ideas developed (for that, see S. Fiske 1992). Space constraints required clear inclusion criteria for the material covered: articles published between 1989 and 1991 in major journals have priority; book chapters and other journal articles are cited less often. Entire theories are relegated to single sentences, and research programs to phrases. Space limitations also forced the exclusion of relevant material on social cognitive approaches to attribution, intergroup relations, human inference, the self, and affect. Nevertheless, the abundance of relevant work is a sign of the field's prosperity.

ACCURACY: PEOPLE ARE GOOD-ENOUGH PERCEIVERS

"All ways of conceiving a concrete fact, if they are true ways at all, are equally true ways" (James 1890/1983:959). Accuracy is not absolute; it depends on one's purpose. "That theory will be most generally believed which, besides offering us objects able to account satisfactorily for our sensible experience, also offers those which are most interesting, those which appeal most urgently to our aesthetic, emotional, and active needs" (James 1890/1983:940).

The pragmatic approach suggests that people are good-enough perceivers. Developing the implications of James's pragmatics for person perception, Swann (1984) argues that person perceivers tend to believe whatever is accurate for their everyday purposes, in light of their interaction goals, within their habitual contexts, with their usual partners; he calls this tendency "circumscribed accuracy." The pragmatic approach acknowledges the possible utility for social interaction of both perceivers' theories and the data given by the situation, suggesting that people strike a workable balance (e.g. Higgins & Bargh 1987; Jussim 1991). It emphasizes the interplay of external and internal structures, with feedback in both directions resulting in good-enough perceptions that allow people to navigate their social environments (Zebrowitz 1990).

More broadly, pragmatism and adaptivity fit with a relative approach to standards for accuracy. That is, accuracy is always a judged correspondence between some judgment and some standard; because standards are themselves someone's judgments (however well-argued, however consensual), they are not absolute (Kruglanski 1989a,b). Either a person's own standards or an observer's standards may be relevant. The same is true of the specifically pragmatic argument that people's judgments are accurate if they are useful. Utility may be defined by external or internal standards: the achievement of some observable goal or the attainment of subjective satisfaction. In either case, judged utility (correspondence between a perception and a standard) depends on one's purpose. This approach differs from those emphasizing error (e.g. Gilovich 1991; L. Ross & Nisbett 1991), but it does not claim that perceivers are always successfully adaptive.

Accurate Ratings

PERSONALITY IMPRESSION RATINGS   The testing of accuracy traditionally occurs in the arena of personality impression ratings: Can a person "accurately" judge another person's personality? Although early person perception researchers studied individual differences in rating accuracy, "it all came to a crashing halt" (Kenny & Albright 1987:390) with Cronbach's famous critique of simple discrepancy scores, which advocated instead breaking accuracy down into components. After a hiatus of three decades, the current resurgence of accuracy research takes the componential approach further. It also focuses on when and how, not whether, people are accurate, and emphasizes the interpersonal dimensions of social perception.

As a central example, the Social Relations Model (e.g. Kenny & Albright 1987) separately examines accuracy on a trait across a set of judges and targets, distinguishing contributions of a constant (general elevation of the ratings), the judge (response set), the target (individual accuracy), and the relationship (dyadic accuracy). For the well-acquainted, perceptions are determined more by the target than by the perceiver (Malloy & Albright 1990), but for the less well acquainted, accuracy is determined by the unique dyadic relationship (Ickes et al 1990; Park & Flink 1989).

Consensus is often a proxy for accuracy (e.g., Funder 1987), but consensus is not a necessary or sufficient condition for accuracy (Kenny 1991). A relatively observable trait, such as extraversion, facilitates consensus for the zero-to-moderately-acquainted (e.g. Kenny et al 1992; Paunonen 1989; Park & Judd 1989; see also Watson 1989). Acquaintance can improve observer consensus with targets and the targets' peers (Colvin & Funder 1991; Paunonen 1989, 1991; Stinson & Ickes 1992) but it need not do so (Kenny 1991). Consensus could increase with acquaintance if (a) the observers see a constant proportion of behaviors that overlap, relative to those they observe separately; as they observe more overlapping behavior, the relative weight of their own idiosyncratic initial impression decreases. And acquaintance could increase consensus if (b) the observed behavior shows some consistency, because then reliability increases. Prior work has focused on degrees of acquaintance and behavioral consistency as determining consensus, but Kenny's Consensus-Accuracy Model adds to these both overlap in behaviors observed and similarity in meaning systems (e.g. the disposition to which a particular behavior is attributed).

Acquaintance, the degree of involvement during interactions (Ickes et al 1990), and the observability of relevant cues together can affect consensus accuracy. All of these share the feature of increasing opportunities to observe the other person, which seems to increase consensus, under certain conditions. The same principle of increased observations holds for aggregration across situations (e.g. Moskowitz 1990).

Increasing opportunities to observe requires more than merely extending a single observation in time; people are remarkably accurate at observing brief slices of behavior, with no advantage given to longer observations (Ambady & Rosenthal 1992). People are also remarkably accurate at perceiving, for example, dominance and warmth from photographs and voices, where accuracy is indicated by consensus with the target or with acquaintances (Berry 1990, 1991b).

Good-enough accuracy, or at least substantial consensus, has obvious utility for smoothing social interaction. Speakers elaborate their messages to fit their listeners' perspectives and knowledge (Fussell & Krauss 1989a,b), and people are fairly accurate at estimating others' knowledge (Fussell & Krauss 1991). Perspective-taking in turn improves the listener's comprehension (Krauss & Fussell 1991). Taking account of the other person's situation and the psychological meaning of behavior also improves predictive accuracy (e.g. Funder & Colvin 1991; Shoda et al 1989). In a manner consistent with a pragmatic viewpoint, then, perceivers' trait ratings seem to be accurate enough for many interaction purposes.

EXPECTANCY EFFECTS   If perceivers are so accurate, why are expectancy effects so persistent? A substantial literature attests to the evidence for unintended effects of perceiver expectancies on target behavior (for reviews, see Harris 1991; Rosenthal 1991). In the case of teacher expectancies, this seems to operate through differences in climate, amount of teacher input, and student output opportunities. How can person perceivers fall prey to such expectancies and simultaneously be relatively accurate much of the time?

One answer is that people are relatively accurate but not perfect; they use both expectancies and data to form impressions. Jussim (1989) argues, for example, that although teachers do at times generate self-fulfilling prophecies, they are often quite accurate in their perceptions of student performance. However, to the extent that a judge's particular expectancies are socially disapproved (e.g. stereotypes; Crosby & Clayton 1990; Hamilton et al 1990b), any amount of influence by that expectancy may be socially undesirable (see other applications in Jussim & Eccles 1990).

Another answer to the question of how expectancy effects can coexist with accuracy is that expectancy effects diminish with time. Acquaintance can both improve impression accuracy and undermine expectancies (Raudenbush 1984). Finally, of course, expectancy effects are moderated by many variables (see the section below on goals).

NEGATIVITY EFFECTS   What effect upon accuracy has the human tendency to overreact to negative information? Researchers have moved beyond merely identifying negativity effects; now they have begun both to apply negativity effects (e.g. to political perception; Klein 1991) and to explain them.

Several notable efforts have been made to explain the phenomenon. (*a*) Taylor's (1991) mobilization-minimization hypothesis argues that people respond to negative stimuli first by mobilizing physiologically, cognitively, emotionally, and socially, and then by minimizing such stimuli (Taylor 1989), dampening their impact. (*b*) Skowronski & Carlston's (1989) natural object categorization model assumes that negative information is perceived to be highly diagnostic. (*c*) Coovert & Reeder (1990; see below) propose that, depending on the behavior domain, the positive or negative end may receive more weight. And (*d*) moving beyond impression formation, Peeters & Czapinski (1990; Peeters 1991) propose a generalized positivity bias in approach behaviors, offset by acute sensitivity to the negative.

Running through all of these theories (at least implicitly) is a pragmatic argument that negativity biases in initial reactions may further the person's goals, whether ultimate survival or short-term detection and control of interpersonal damage (see S. Fiske 1992 for more depth). People initially overemphasize negative information because it is useful to do so. Indeed, evidence indicates that negative information is automatically alerting (Pratto & John 1991), and acute stress deploys vigilance for threatening stimuli (Mogg et al 1990).

Accurate Memory: Expectancy-Congruent versus -Incongruent Information

Pragmatic accuracy issues have been neglected in much of person memory research (for one exception, see Zuroff 1989). The field has focused on building plausible models of memory for social information (e.g. Srull & Wyer 1989; for a review, see S. Fiske & Taylor 1991 Ch. 8). As shown next, empirical tests have emphasized memory for expectancy-consistent and -inconsistent information. But even here lurks a pragmatic accuracy question: Do people pass over and forget inconsistencies, leaving their expectancies intact, or do they focus on and remember the inconsistency, thereby apparently showing more accuracy? And which is the more useful strategy?

For more than a decade, person memory research had demonstrated preferential memory for expectancy-incongruent information. The consistently proposed mediating mechanism had been that people's on-line (i.e. immediate) effort to resolve inconsistencies increased the number of retrieval routes for expectancy-incongruent information (e.g. Srull & Wyer 1989). The oft-replicated advantage of incongruence seemed to fly in the face of the emphasis in schema and stereotype theories on confirmatory biases, leaving an unresolved paradox in the literatures.

Then, more recently, the usual advantage of incongruence seemed to evaporate, given any changes that complicate the basic experimental paradigm in person memory research (see below); this apparent evaporation has led some to question the generalizability of previous person memory models—for example, to cases in which information is acquired in a social rather than artificial and isolated context (Wyer et al 1990; Wyer et al 1992). The field's history and recent developments are admirably covered in a meta-analysis by Stangor & McMillan (1992), to which the reader is referred for more detail (cf. Rojahn & Pettigrew 1992).

Recognition effects depend first on which stage of information processing is measured. Corrected recognition measures show the robust advantage of expectancy-incongruent information, which fits the idea that information is encoded with attention to incongruency. (Eliminating response biases presumably isolates such encoding effects.) In contrast, expectancy-congruent information is preferentially recognized if measures are not corrected for response biases such as guessing; this fits the idea that schema-based processes predominate during response.

Turning to the free recall measures that most frequently characterize person memory studies, the direction of the effect depends entirely on expectancy strength; strong, pre-existing expectancies show a congruency advantage in free recall, whereas experimentally induced, weaker expectancies show an incongruency advantage. The importance of expectancy strength was anticipated in previous narrative reviews (S. Fiske & Neuberg 1990; Higgins & Bargh 1987; Ruble & Stangor 1986) and is supported by specific empirical tests (e.g. Stangor & Ruble 1989).

The "standard" person memory advantage for expectancy-incongruent information thus seems limited to the narrow set of circumstances under which it was first established: As noted, free recall and experimentally induced expectancies are necessary; but also required are evaluative plus descriptive inconsistency (not just descriptive), individual (not group) targets, an explicit impression-formation goal (rather than memorizing or evaluating), no interpolated tasks, and location of the whole process within a single experimental session (Stangor & McMillan 1992). In general, complicating the basic experimental paradigm (i.e. by eliminating any of these circumstances) seems to eliminate the incongruency advantage in recall. Creating more demanding conditions (e.g. Hamilton et al 1989; Stangor & Duan 1991) that characterize more realistic settings also eliminates the incongruency advantage.

Fortunately, person memory research is expanding beyond the original experimental conditions. When people are motivated on-line to understand and explain incongruency, it is more memorable; attributional difficulty enhances recall (Hamilton et al 1990a), as do individual differences in uncertainty orientation (Driscoll et al 1991) and need for cognition (Lassiter et al 1991). Some social memory advantages accrue to women (M. Ross & Holmberg 1992; Skowronski et al 1991), who apparently think about (and explain) relationship events to a greater extent than men do. Within ongoing relationships, people may specialize in different domains of memory (Wegner et al 1991). Real-world settings are also necessitating new measures and moderators (Hansen 1989; Skowronski et al 1991).

Person memory research sprang originally from a concern with person perception processes. Researchers abandoned the fruitless either/or debate concerning algebraic vs Gestalt models of impression formation (S. Fiske & Taylor 1991 Ch. 4, Leyens & Fiske 1992) and turned to the cognitive representation of people, as indicated by the structure of memory (Hamilton 1989). It is debatable whether person memory researchers are studying the cognitive processes implied by the original Gestalt-inspired studies (e.g. Asch 1946) or even the algebraic models (N. Anderson 1989). For example, person memory researchers have only recently reconfirmed the Gestalt tenet that individuals are the most likely unit of organization in social memory (Mullen & Copper 1989; Sedikides & Ostrom 1988, 1990).

Nevertheless, person memory research has progressed from the "whether" stage (i.e. asking whether or not people preferentially remember incongruent information) to the "which-when" stage (asking when people preferentially remember congruent and incongruent information). The pattern of effects supports a fairly well-adapted social perceiver: Incongruency has an advantage, primarily at encoding, when perceivers are motivated to understand it or when expectations are weak, which alerts the person to potential cognitive threats at an early stage in important settings. Congruency has an advantage in retrieval and responding or when expectations are strong, which allows the person to maintain and use well-supported structures, especially when unmotivated by immediate needs to be careful. Indeed this pattern mimics the pattern observed for negativity effects: an initial alert at first encounter (which allows coping with the negative or unexpected), followed by a reconfirmation of the normal baseline. Pursuit of this parallel between negativity and incongruency effects might be useful. In general, more work is needed on attentional and encoding processes, the types of on-line explanations that people make, and how the unexpected or unwanted is integrated into existing structures. All of these processes depend on the purposes for which people are acquiring the new information. If the usual process involves explanation and understanding, then how do these meaning-making processes operate?

STRUCTURES: PEOPLE MAKE MEANING

> There are two general points in reasoning. First, an extracted character is taken as equivalent to the entire datum from which it comes; and, second, the character thus taken suggests a certain consequence more obviously than it was suggested by the total datum as it originally came ... . The extracted characters are more general than the concretes, and the connections they may have are, therefore, more familiar to us, having been more often met in our experience ... . The other reason why the relations of the extracted characters are so evident is that their properties are so few, compared with the properties of the whole, from which we derived them (James 1890/1983:966–67).

People make meaning by abstracting relevant essential structures, which then substitute for the original. The familiarity and simplicity of the abstracted structure then make it workable for everyday undertakings. In person perception, the simple, familiar "extracted characters" are most likely to be traits, stereotypes, and stories.

Trait Descriptors as Rich Categories

Research in personality is coming together with that in social psychology (social cognition in particular). Disciplinary boundaries are blurring, as both sets of researchers explore the ways traits are structured and used in the perception of personality. Current work in social cognition views traits as one of many structures people use to make sense of other people. In this view (Leyens & Fiske 1992; Wyer & Lambert 1992), traits are semantic concepts that influence how information is assembled and used. Traits are rich semantic structures in which breadth (inclusion) varies inversely with information (specific behavioral description); people use the highest level of abstraction that still describes behavior, moving to more specific levels with unfamiliarity and inconsistency (John et al 1991).

The most popular and enduring taxonomy of personality trait descriptors is the Five-Factor Model, focusing on extraversion, agreeableness, conscientiousness, neuroticism (stability), and openness (intelligence) (for reviews, see Digman 1990; John 1990; Wiggins & Pincus 1992). The model generalizes, for example, over time (since at least D. Fiske 1949); over different sets of English adjectives (Goldberg 1990), German ones (Angleitner et al 1990), Tagalog ones (Church & Katigbak 1989), and with some recombination, Chinese ones (Yang & Bond 1990); over real people vs conceptual judgments (Peabody & Goldberg 1989); and to ratings of behavior (if total act frequency is removed; Botwin & Buss 1989). Given its apparent utility in describing the structure of trait descriptors, it seems downright odd that social psychologists rarely use and cite this taxonomy.

Social psychologists have tended to rely instead on two- or three-factor models. One explanation lies in the nature of the tasks given subjects. For example, research on implicit personality theory typically asks subjects to judge traits by their similarity or likelihood of going together, without necessarily referring to a concrete person (Van der Kloot & Willemsen 1991; Van Mechelen 1991), whereas the personality literature almost always refers to descriptions of self or other.

A perhaps more important explanation lies in the fact that many social models emphasize expressly interpersonal traits. To be fair, such interpersonal traits are those most important to people in daily interactions. For example, Bales's (1970) model was derived from self-analytic small groups; it focuses essentially on three of the five factors mentioned above: dominance, agreeableness, and conscientiousness. Similarly, Wiggins's circumplex model in effect focuses on extraversion and agreeableness, defined in terms of dominance and nurturance (McCrae & Costa 1989; Trapnell & Wiggins 1990; Wiggins & Pincus 1992). It is ironic that social psychologists have typically limited themselves to the most interpersonal dimensions, given that person perception research itself neglects the interpersonal by isolating perceivers from real targets (de la Haye 1991; Leyens 1991).

Whatever the structure of traits, people think about each other in trait terms for a reason. James's "extracted characters" have the utility of allowing inferences from simple and familiar principles. As extracted characters, prototypical traits are stable, long-lasting, and internally caused, so they "permit people to predict the future from the past" (Chaplin et al 1988:541); indeed, attribution theories have long held this to be the underlying motivation behind people's search for dispositional causes (Pittman & Heller 1987). People thus perceive others in trait terms in order to facilitate their own goals.

Not coincidentally, people also perceive others' traits as reflections of others' goals (Borkenau 1990; Read et al 1990; Read & Miller 1989); for example, a behavior's perceived ability to accomplish a goal predicts its judged prototypicality for a trait category. Perhaps knowledge about other people is represented by action-oriented actor schemata, whose dominant element is the other person's goals cast in the form of a story (Trzebinski 1989).

Related goal-oriented understandings of person perception come out of work by personality theorists oriented toward social cognitive explanations. Mischel's (e.g. 1990) view of person perception is doubly pragmatic: People use goals as important dispositional categories, and whether people emphasize goals per se or traits depends on their own purposes. Other researchers take an even more explicitly pragmatic view, focusing on "the creative, forward-looking thoughts about self, others, and tasks that individuals have, and on the ways in which those intentions are constructed and negotiated in a broad sociocultural context" (Cantor & Zirkel 1990:136). How people construe their social worlds, then set and implement goals, forms the basis of social intelligence (people's adaptive repertoire relevant to life tasks; Cantor & Kihlstrom 1989); it includes social concepts, interpretive processes, self-knowledge, and goal management strategies.

People presumably describe others in terms of traits because they think trait adjectives help them to predict others' behavior. Recent work recognizing the importance of subjective trait interpretation also indicates the importance of personality traits in meaning-making, but it tends to draw an unflattering portrait of the pragmatic outcomes of doing so. The core idea here builds on Asch, Bruner, and other early cognitivists, namely that a person's own actively constructed representation of the situation is crucial (Griffin & Ross 1991; L. Ross & Nisbett 1991). In this view, people are led astray by their failures to acknowledge the central role of their own and others' idiosyncratic interpretations in predicting behavior (Dunning et al 1990; Gilovich 1990; Griffin et al 1990; Vallone et al 1990).

While people generally do think traits predict behavior, additional complications obtain. First, some cultures rely less on trait descriptors than others do (J. Miller 1984). Second, when people adopt an internal, trait-oriented norm, they describe others more evaluatively (Beauvois & Dubois 1991), which fundamentally changes social interactions. Third, traits themselves differ in the types of expected trait-behavior relations (Reeder et al 1992): Only frequency-based traits show a direct relationship with behavior (a talkative person talks a lot). For morality traits, the relationship is asymmetrical, restricting the socially desirable end, in that an honest person can behave only honestly, whereas a dishonest person can behave either honestly or dishonestly. For capacity traits, the asymmetry restricts the socially undesirable end, in that an incapable person can behave only incapably, whereas a capable person can behave either capably or incapably. Finally, attitudes and motives may show no relationship to behavior because such dispositions are not always expressed openly.

Perceivers also use personality trait terms in order to communicate efficiently with others. The pragmatic goals of the perceiver and the influences of the social context come together explicitly in linguistic models of trait usage. Semin & Fiedler (1991; Fiedler & Semin 1992), for example, argue that language is a practical activity in a social context. Language assumes an intent to communicate; this goal influences the level of abstraction that people both perceive and use (the interplay is dialectic; Semin 1989). Communicating efficiently and cooperatively encourages the use of abstractions, which then shape the interpretation of subsequent behaviors (Fiedler et al 1989), at least for observers (Fielder & Semin 1989); this top-down bias reverses toward the concrete when validity is questioned (cf John et al 1991). Similarly, when people use greater abstraction for negative outgroup and positive ingroup behavior, they imply that these endure, confirming biases (Maass et al 1989; see other work on language and stereotypes by Hamilton et al 1992; Semin & Rubini 1990).

So far, the research provides scant evidence of traits' richness. However, a typological approach to person perception explicitly considers person types and views traits as interacting to form complex Gestalts (C. Anderson & Sedikides 1991). More work is needed on the processes by which traits fit together within person types—an issue raised when Asch asked how people make sense of trait incongruency (Casselden & Hampson 1990). The rich typology approach, which fits so well with the original Gestalt approaches to trait impression formation, has ironically been one focus of research on stereotyping, treated next.

Stereotypes as Complex Portraits

SOCIAL CATEGORY MODELS   Compared to traits, stereotypes or person types have richer associations, more visual features, more distinctive characteristics, and operate more efficiently (Andersen et al 1990). One recent model of impression formation (Brewer 1988) suggests that typing operates in terms of pictoliteral prototypes (i.e. specific, configural images). This Dual-Process Model distinguishes among four levels of processing: immediate, automatic identification, within a multidimensional space; typing; individuation according to subtypes or exemplars; and personalization according to individual schemas and propositional networks. Levels of processing are determined by stimulus characteristics, needs or goals, and similarity between perceiver and target (for commentary, see Srull & Wyer 1988).

The Continuum Model also distinguishes more category-based or stereotypic processes from more attribute-based or individuating processes (e.g. S. Fiske & Neuberg 1990). Immediate, automatic reactions are category based; goals and stimulus configuration jointly determine whether the perceiver goes beyond that initial impression (e.g. Neuberg 1989; Pavelchak 1989; Ruscher & Fiske 1990; Ruscher et al 1991). Attention allows the perceiver to gather more information, either confirming the initial category, subcategorizing, or individuating the other person. Where the perceiver stops along this continuum of impression formation depends on the explicitly pragmatic criterion of how much it matters to the perceiver to have a sense of accuracy about the other.

Both models give priority to relatively category-based processes—i.e. to considering when people form complex impressions. Neither model addresses the stop rule—i.e. how people decide that they have enough information to form an impression. The "social judgeability" approach (Leyens et al 1992; Schadron & Yzerbyt 1991) holds that people make judgments when they believe the information they have is of a socially acceptable quality and quantity. Addressing lay theories about judgment, this pragmatic stance holds that impression formation processes, including stereotypes, should be judged by their social value, rather than by some normative standard of accuracy (Leyens 1990). Similarly, Oakes & Turner (1990) argue that stereotypes do not limit but rather enrich social understanding; this follows Bruner's view that categorization provides meaning for raw perceptual experience. Categorization models of stereotyping thus focus on the pragmatic implications for perceivers, who use the stereotypes as a rich resource for making sense of their

social world; people use stereotypes to the extent they seem to have explanatory value, given information, motivation, and social norms.

BASIC CATEGORIES   What then are the core categories that people use to
portray other people? Some characteristics are visually and immediately accessible; the top three are gender (Hoffman & Hurst 1990; Swim et al 1989), age
(Brewer & Lui 1989), and race (Devine 1989; Hewstone et al 1991). Mounting
evidence suggests, however, that subtypes constitute the basic-level categories
that perceivers habitually use. People have in mind specific types of the elderly
(Brewer et al 1981), women (Deaux et al 1985; Eagly et al 1992), and blacks
(Devine & Baker 1991). People also use subtypes that combine gender and race
(Stangor et al 1992), age and race (Hamilton et al 1992), as well as ethnicity and
domain (e.g. as a neighbor vs a marital partner; Hagendoorn & Kleinpenning
1991; Kleinpenning & Hagendoorn 1991). The pragmatic argument is explicit
here: Subtypes are more useful because they seem to convey the most about
dispositions of the other (Stangor et al 1992); as always, the useful level of
categorization strikes a balance between being distinctive and inclusive. One
implication of subtyping is that individuals who disconfirm a global stereotype
can be "fenced off" (Allport 1954), leaving the overall stereotype intact
(Hewstone et al 1992a,b, Johnston & Hewstone 1992).

If age, race, and gender are important by virtue of being visually conspicuous, then appearance in general should be an important basis for stereotypes.
A meta-analytic review of the physical attractiveness stereotype indicates that
it is moderately strong for perceived social competence; weaker for perceived
potency, adjustment, and intellect; and negligible for integrity and interpersonal concern (Eagly et al 1991).

One specific type of appearance has recently provoked considerable research: the degree to which a person's face is babyish. The premise underlying
this work is explicitly anti-cognitive (Zebrowitz 1990) but highly pragmatic.
In the direct perception view, perceivers see baby-faced others (whether infants or adults) as affording opportunities for nurturance. Extending this adaptive perception, baby-faced adults are seen as submissive, naive, warm,
innocent, and not shrewd. Babyish appearance contributes to perceived physical attractiveness, gender stereotypes, hiring decisions, perceived credibility,
judicial decisions, and parental discipline (Berry 1991a, Brownlow &
Zebrowitz 1990; Friedman & Zebrowitz 1992; Zebrowitz & McDonald 1991;
Zebrowitz & Montepare 1991; Zebrowitz et al 1991a,b).

A pragmatic approach must argue that perceivers use categories to accomplish social goals, which by definition operate within relationships. A. Fiske et
al (1991) suggest that spontaneous categorizations follow four elementary
types of social relationships (communal sharing, authority ranking, equality
matching, and market pricing; A. Fiske 1991). Perceivers confuse other people
who fall within the same relationship category and to a lesser extent within
gender; age and race less consistently elicit confusion of one person with

another. As another example of the importance of relationships, dominance ranking can occur within seconds of when people meet, even before any verbal exchanges (Kalma 1991). The target's status then guides memory: It may cause a person to infer that another is assertive, for example, and misremember accordingly (Holtgraves et al 1989).

Still another basis for categorization is derived from unique relationships with significant others and a target's perceived similarity to the significant other. Representations of significant others are associatively rich, distinctive, and accessible, facilitating inferential leaps upon encountering a similar other (Andersen & Cole 1990). This phenomenon, known as transference, fits well with social cognitive theories of mental representation (S. Fiske 1982; Singer 1985).

INDIVIDUATION: EXEMPLARS AND TARGET CASES   In direct contrast to category theories are those emphasizing concrete representations. The exemplar model of social judgment (Smith 1990; Smith & Zárate 1992) posits that specific past experiences inform judgments about similar new experiences. First, single-case exemplars reside in memory and influence judgments with or without awareness. Second, the exemplar's impact on judgment depends on perceived similarity to the target. Finally, social and motivational factors determine attention to features that in turn determine perceived similarity. Categorization and stereotyping then follow from differential attention to stimulus dimensions and subsequent exemplar retrieval. Any stimulus person may be categorized in multiple ways (race, gender, age, occupation, or some combination). The speed of accessing a particular category (i.e. a particular set of exemplars) then predicts stereotyping (Zárate & Smith 1990).

In this view, categorization is merely a convenient way of saying that one particular sort of exemplar (e.g. females) predominated in retrieval. To illustrate, an exemplar model can explain some basic tenets of categorization, namely accentuating perceived between-category differences (Krueger 1991) and increasing perceived variability in familiar groups (Linville et al 1989). This model does not dispute that people can and do use abstract schematic or prototypic representations. The link between category and individual instance is mutual; each cues the other (Schul & Burnstein 1990). People's use of concrete exemplars or abstract prototypes depends on many factors—for example, whether they first encounter individual group members or prototypical descriptions (Smith & Zárate 1990; see also Schul & Burnstein 1990). Attention to category-defining vs individuating attributes determines their relative weight in judgments.

Several researchers have argued that individuating target case information outweighs category-based information; in this view, people underuse base-rate information and rely almost entirely on individuating information (for a review of base rates and the dilution effect, see S. Fiske & Taylor 1991:355–57, 359–62). More generally, Weisz & Jones (1992) have recently suggested that target-based expectancies influence impressions more than do category-based expectancies. Even when they are of equal predictive strength, target-based expectancies are more resistant to disconfirming information. Whereas category-based expectancies are probabilistic (most Xs are y), target-based expectancies assume substantial consistency within an individual. Target-based expectancies (individuating effects) seem robust (e.g. Denhaerinck et al 1989).

Nevertheless, recent research identifies several qualifications to this generalization. The underuse of base-rate information may depend on an experimental paradigm in which (a) the individuating information is presented second, implying according to conversational convention that it is of more critical importance than the just-prior base-rate information (Krosnick et al 1990); (b) the information has been intentionally provided by the experimenter, as opposed to (for example) randomly provided by a computer, again providing conversational cues to its importance (Schwarz et al 1991); (c) the individuating information, although not diagnostic in this instance, is typically diagnostic across many social judgment tasks (Hilton & Fein 1989); (d) similarly, the case cue has a constant and high numerical value (e.g. odds well above 50%) (Lynch & Ofir 1989); and (e) the base rate (stereotype) itself is derived with uncertainty, rather than from innumerable everyday experiences (Nelson et al 1990).

DIAGNOSTICITY AND MEANING-MAKING   The extent to which people use categories or more individuating information depends on what they see as diagnostic (informative) for their current purposes. Categorization first and foremost allows people to differentiate each other by group. Dimensions that most distinguish between groups (showing large between-group differences and low within-group variability) become most stereotypically associated with a group (Ford & Stangor 1992). People use categories both to contrast individual members of different categories and to accentuate average differences between whole groups (Krueger 1991, 1992; Krueger & Rothbart 1990; Krueger et al 1989).

Categorization also allows the outgroup homogeneity effect, whereby outgroups are seen as less variable than the ingroup (Mullen & Hu 1989). Greater familiarity with the ingroup allows perceivers to differentiate more and perceive greater variability across group members (Linville et al 1989), as group members are seen to be more dispersed around the group mean (Park & Judd 1990; Park et al 1991). People think in terms of subgroups for ingroups more than outgroups (Park & Judd 1990; Mackie & Worth 1989), whereas outgroup stereotypicality is exaggerated (Judd et al 1991; but see Simon & Pettigrew 1990).

Perceivers also use social categories to make sense of individual pieces of category-relevant information. Categorization allows ambiguous behavior to be assimilated to a stereotype (Hilton & von Hippel 1990). Although assimilation and contrast may operate simultaneously (Biernat et al 1991; Eiser et al

1991; Manis et al 1991), assimilation seems the cognitively easier default option when there is no reason to discredit the categorization (Martin & Achee 1992; Martin et al 1990; Schwarz & Bless 1992). People use real-world group membership to remember stereotype-relevant material (Cano et al 1991), sometimes distorting it to support their expectancies (Echabe & Rovira 1989).

People use categories to make inferences, too. For example, traits that distinguish one national group from another facilitate inferences from trait to nationality, whereas traits that show high within-group homogeneity facilitate inferences from nationality to trait (Diehl & Jonas 1991). Another type of inference, much more thoroughly studied, entails perceivers seeing an illusory correlation between group membership and behavior, based on shared distinctiveness; that is, people exaggerate the co-occurence of a rare category (i.e. minority group membership) and a rare behavior (i.e. negative acts; see Hamilton & Sherman 1989; Mullen & Johnson 1990, for reviews). Distinctiveness-biased encoding, the traditional explanation, has recently been both supported (C. Johnson & Mullen 1992) and criticized (Fiedler 1991; Smith 1991).

Moreover, illusory correlation is located in a broader context; it is moderated by the addition of a third group (Sherman et al 1989) and by perceivers' own group membership (Maass & Schaller 1991; Schaller 1991; Schaller & Maass 1989). Similarly, people use stereotypes that are meaningful within a particular social milieu (Lalonde & Gardner 1989). Thus, categorization does not merely serve cognitive purposes; it operates within a social and motivational context.

Above all, categorization has important evaluative implications. Attitudes toward men and women, for example, correspond to the evaluative meanings of people's stereotypes about them (Eagly & Mladinic 1989). Indeed, category-based affect may outweigh category-based stereotypes in determining discriminatory responses, despite the predominance of cognitive factors often lately implied (Stangor et al 1991). If a group is homogeneous, people use a member's typicality as a basis for evaluation (Lambert & Wyer 1990).

Because category-based stereotypes have negative evaluative implications and behavioral sequelae, many researchers have investigated strategies to undermine them. For example, some current suggestions include crossed categorization (Vanbeselaere 1991); more inclusive recategorization (Gaertner et al 1989); category members who are atypical in one respect (Hewstone 1989; Mackie et al 1992); and highly motivated perceivers (e.g. S. Fiske & Neuberg 1990).

Thus basic categories include gender, race, and age (as well as their subtypes); appearance; and relationships. Individuating representations include exemplars and target case information, which people use depending on how diagnostic (informative) it seems regarding the relevant judgment. Category membership may be more or less salient to perceivers in judgment situations (e.g. Oakes et al 1991). Nevertheless, categories are useful for distinguishing among people, for interpreting information, and for evaluating others. In all these ways, categories provide meaning for social perceivers.

Using Stories and Simulations to Make Meaning

One strand of current work holds that "we organize our experience and our memory of human happening mainly in the form of narrative …[,] a version of reality whose acceptability is governed by convention and 'narrative necessity' rather than by empirical verification and logical requiredness" (Bruner 1991:4; 1990). Isolated research efforts have also examined the role of narrative reasoning in social explanation; for example, when people try combining apparently contradictory concepts (Harvard-educated and carpenter), they do so by using causal descriptors and emergent attributes (Kunda et al 1990). In effect, faced with surprising combinations for which they do not possess ready-made structures, people create brief stories that provide enabling and temporal links among otherwise puzzling bits of information. Five lines of research suggest the importance of stories in social understanding. Identifying them here as pointers, I do not review them in detail.

1. Standard narrative explanations and causal sequences may be stored as causal knowledge structures or event prototypes containing the typical explanations for events such as theft (Lalljee et al 1992) or defecting from one's country (Sedikides & Anderson 1992; see also Read et al 1989).

2. A host of findings (Koehler 1991) indicates that explaining or imagining a possibility makes it seem more likely; people construct plausible scenarios that could make the hypothetical come true (e.g. C. Anderson & Kellam 1991). If the event is held to be provisionally true and is easily explained, then it seems all the more possible.

3. People also explain past events and assess how normal (probable) or unusual (improbable) they were by generating counterfactuals (what might have been). If it is easy to imagine alternative scenarios that would undo the event, then people view the outcome as retrospectively abnormal. The more mutable and abnormal the event, the stronger people's emotional reactions to it. Current research examines the operation of counterfactual simulations: Events become more normal (less coincidental, less suspicious) the easier it is to imagine similar events (D. Miller et al 1989; but see Kirkpatrick & Epstein 1992). Close counterfactuals (what almost happened) rest on a strong propensity perceived to be present in the episode itself, indicating a set of causal forces that seem urgently and intensely to culminate in particular focal outcomes (Kahneman & Varey 1990). For example, before a game one team might have a greater prior disposition to win, but events during the game (e.g. a growing lead) give one or the other team the perceived propensity to win in that situation.

Some details concerning counterfactual simulations are emerging. For example, (*a*) later events are seen as more mutable and therefore causal and blameworthy (D. Miller & Gunasegaram 1990); (*b*) retrospective mental addition (a factor increasing the likelihood of the event) is easier than mental subtraction (Dunning & Parpal 1989); (*c*) the default or normal event is easier to imagine, so atypical events and category members require more explanation (D. Miller et al 1991); and (*d*) ease of imagining alternatives influences blame (Wells & Gavanski 1989), but the ease of imagining alternative outcomes may depend on a match between exceptional events and outcomes or between normal events and outcomes (Gavanski & Wells 1989). In short, people trying to explain an event construct stories (mentally simulate counterfactuals) that determine the event's ensuing meaning and their own emotions.

4. Current work in real-world decision-making prominently includes mental-model approaches that construct representations consistent with the given information, in order to reach and test conclusions (Galotti 1989). To take a social example, the Story Model argues for the importance of narrative construction in complex judgments. In juror decision-making, an initial step entails the construction of a story to account for the trial evidence, in accord with world knowledge and narrative structure (Hastie & Pennington 1991; Pennington & Hastie 1991). The best story is the one that covers the most evidence and is coherent (consistent, plausible, complete). This story then helps jurors to reach a verdict.

5. Current work on how people cope with negative life events also emphasizes the importance of stories that people construct. Mental simulation, the cognitive (re)construction of scenarios, includes the rehearsal of actual past and probable future events, fantasies about imagined alternatives, and mixtures of real and hypothetical events (Taylor & Schneider 1989). Like other narratives, simulations somehow seem true; they also function as plans, prompt affect, set expectations, and lead to behavioral confirmation; all of these may aid coping with stressful life events. The search for meaning operates by other means than narrative constructions, but many of the identified efforts to construct explanations share elements of narrative truth-making. Needless to say, victims' search for explanation and understanding may result in positive illusions (Taylor 1989) or simply shattered assumptions (Janoff-Bulman 1992); but in both cases the search for meaning entails assimilating the event (Collins et al 1990). Such events threaten basic assumptions about personal invulnerability, control, self-worth, and not least, life's meaning. Related work on problems in close relationships also indicates the importance of story-like explanations for difficult life events (Harvey et al 1989). Meaning-making through schema (re)construction underscores the importance of constructed life narratives (cf Pennebaker 1989a,b).

GOALS AND CONTROL: THINKING IS FOR DOING

"This whole function of conceiving, of fixing, and holding fast to meanings, has no significance apart from the fact that the conceiver is a creature with partial purposes and private ends" (James 1890/1983:456, original's italics omitted).

Motivated Tacticians and the Revival of Goals

Researchers in person perception and social cognition are returning to the core Jamesian notion, namely that one must consider the perceiver's purposes. This return constitutes a new phase of social cognition research; the perceiver is no longer a cognitive miser mainly concerned with conserving scarce mental resources but instead a motivated tactician choosing among a number of possible strategies, depending on current goals (S. Fiske & Taylor 1991). Several separate theories divide goals into those promoting accuracy vs those prompting immediate decisions: Kruglanski (1989a, 1990) describes epistemic motivations characterized by avoiding or seeking closure; S. Fiske (S. Fiske & Neuberg 1990; S. Fiske & Taylor 1991) has split person perception goals into those that tend to increase the costs of being wrong and those that increase the costs of being indecisive; Stangor & Ford (1992) identify expectancy-confirm-ing vs accuracy-oriented processing orientations in the development of stereo-types and prejudice; Gollwitzer (e.g. 1990) describes open-minded, delibera-tive vs action-oriented, implementational mindsets; Hilton & Darley (1991) distinguish between an assessment set and an action set in interaction goals; Snyder (1992) identifies behavioral (dis)confirmation motivations as empha-sizing either accuracy concerns or stability and predictability; from a develop-mental perspective, Ruble (1993; Ruble & Stangor 1986) argues for initial information seeking and later more rigid application of concepts (Stangor & Ford 1992; Stangor & Ruble 1989). Space prevents an adequate description of these theories (see S. Fiske 1992), but all contrast accuracy-oriented or open-minded motivation with confirmatory or closure-seeking motivation. These models are not alone in making this distinction; for example, attitude models of systematic and heuristic processing (Chaiken et al 1989) or central and peripheral processing (Petty & Cacioppo 1986) make a similar motivational distinction. How serviceable is the distinction? The literature indicates that it is at best rough and ready. The core point, however, is that some motivations make people more concerned with feeling or appearing accurate, whereas others prompt fast decisions and action.

Increasing the Costs of Being Wrong (Accuracy-Oriented Motives)

People have a surprising amount of control over their impression formation processes. When motivated by something as simple as an experimenter's instruction to be as accurate as possible, perceivers gather more information and alter their expressive behavior, which influences targets to behave in expectancy-disconfirming ways, and perceivers form more data-driven im-pressions (Neuberg 1989, 1992). Perceivers told to categorize a target form different impressions than do uninstructed perceivers (Pavelchak 1989). Personality feedback and situational norms can act as indirect instructions (S. Fiske & Von Hendy 1992; cf Blanchard et al 1991). People can be more accuracy oriented (individuating) if so instructed, but they can also categorize more if so motivated. Similarly, the experimenter can make an unprejudiced self-concept accessible by highlighting discrepancies between how one should and would respond to an outgroup member (Devine et al 1991).

The social structure can motivate people to be more accurate. Outcome dependency (relying on another person for an outcome) motivates people to attend to expectancy-incongruent information and make dispositional inferences about it (for a review see Riley & Fiske 1991); the motivation stems from the correlated outcomes per se, for negatively correlated outcomes (competitions between individuals) have the same effect (Ruscher & Fiske 1990). Outcome dependency, especially when extremely asymmetrical, deprives the less powerful person of control, leading to information seeking in an attempt to regain control or at least prediction (Dépret & Fiske 1992).

Cooperative interdependence can result in expectancy-disconfirming attitudes that generalize to the group as a whole (Desforges et al 1991). Cooperative interdependence may operate by cognitively transforming two groups into one (Gaertner et al 1990). But it also has affective consequences, promoting empathy, whereas competition promotes counterempathy (i.e. opposite emotions; Lanzetta & Englis 1989). Outcome dependency seems to make people work harder at whatever task they undertake; it increases observer consensus on trait judgments (Flink & Park 1991), perhaps because observers have all worked harder at being accurate; and outcome dependency has similar behavioral consequences, increasing task effort and activity (Harris 1990).

Outcome dependency presumably motivates people to increase their accuracy because they want to be able to predict (and perhaps control) their own outcomes by predicting (and perhaps influencing) the other person. Having an explicit goal of behavioral prediction makes people rely more on their own interaction with a target and less on prior expectancies (Matheson et al 1991). Their impressions also become more variable than those of subjects who have an impression formation goal; interdependence similarly makes people's impressions more variable (Ruscher & Fiske 1990) as people idiosyncratically integrate expectancies and data. The behavioral prediction goal apparently leads people to consolidate their perceptions early on, and then to update them as the interaction continues.

Being in a subordinate role means by definition that one's outcomes depend asymmetrically on those with more power. Subordinate status raises concerns about control, leading subordinates to attend to those in power in order to predict and perhaps influence them (Dépret & Fiske 1992). Indeed, subordinates are more attuned to how leaders view them than vice versa (Snodgrass 1992). This does not mean that subordinates will necessarily be more accurate; they have their own hopes and expectations about leaders (Holtgraves et al 1989).

In a similar way, being stigmatized makes one's outcomes contingent on the actions of those not so marked; people subject to a stigmatizing master status (those who deviate either positively or negatively from the norm) are especially sensitive in interaction if their potential stigma is invisible (e.g. rape or incest victimization, wealth, unusual talent). Compared to people not potentially stigmatized, they recall more information about the interaction situation, and they more often take their interaction partner's perspective (Frable et al 1990). These people are concerned with controlling information about themselves, so attention to their partner is pragmatic. The valence of the stigma determines how they use their observations in actual interaction. On the other hand, the visibly stigmatized, whose concern is to manage an already-revealed stigma, do not gather as much information as nonstigmatized individuals; such people do not remember their partner's side of the conversation. Similarly, solos (people who believe themselves to be visibly unlike all the others in a group) worry about impression management, so they remember less about the interaction (Lord & Saenz 1985). However, if such a person is put in the powerful position of judge, the solo's information-gathering capacities are restored (Saenz & Lord 1989).

Being outcome dependent or stigmatized puts one at least partly under another person's control—in these instances under the control of one's immediate interaction partner. Perceivers can also cede control to third parties outside the immediate interaction. When they are accountable to third parties (i.e. when they are under pressure to justify their impressions) they gather and apply a wider range of information (for a review see Tetlock 1991), whether or not it is actually effective (Tetlock & Boettger 1989). Accountability encourages flexible processing of multiple cues only if people do not know the views of their audience and have not made previous public commitments to a particular judgment; given either a known audience or prior commitments, people instead try to match those standards (Tetlock et al 1989). Accountability makes people expend more effort (Martin et al 1990).

One theme running through the research discussed here is control deprivation (Pittman & Heller 1987) and its pragmatic consequences. Whether one is outcome dependent, subordinate, visibly stigmatized, or accountable, one's outcomes are contingent on the nature and actions of others; observational sensitivity helps to predict others' reactions and consequently one's own outcomes. Control-deprived people more carefully and accurately encode all kinds of information (Pittman & D'Agostino 1989)—a finding consonant with the effects (discussed above) of interdependence on attentional strategies.

Because depression includes significant perceptions of lost control, it also facilitates more detailed, effortful, and complex attentional processes. Depressives are more motivated than others to seek diagnostic (i.e. informative) information about other people (Gleicher & Weary 1991; Hildebrand-Saints &

Weary 1989), are more likely to engage in on-line piecemeal (attribute-based) information processing (Weary 1992), are more motivated to make attributions (Flett et al 1989), generate more inferences about others (Gleicher & Weary 1991), are more likely to generate inferences that combine disparate items of information (Gleicher & Weary 1991), and make more complex attributions (Flett et al 1989; Marsh & Weary 1989). Depression entails uncertainty about one's ability to predict and control one's social environment. It makes sense that an important concomitant (or perhaps cause) of depression is rumination about unattained goals (Martin et al 1992). Depressives assert quickly (perhaps automatically) that negative events are likely and positive events unlikely (Andersen et al 1992).

Thus the social environment can increase the costs of being inaccurate in social perception. Factors such as outcome dependency, subordinate status, stigma, accountability, and depression can cause social perceivers to be more accurate, attentive, detailed, complex, and effortful. However, each of these factors can also increase people's overuse of misleading or irrelevant information. Thus it would be wrong to say that (e.g.) interdependence, accountability, and so on necessarily make people more accurate. People can be motivated to worry more about being accurate, but the strategies they then use may or may not be more effective. Such strategies are likely to work often enough: Attention to more information, particularly to what perceivers believe to be the most significant information, along with expenditure of more information-gathering effort, gives people a sense of being more accurate and can often (but not always) make people more accurate.

Increasing the Costs of Being Indecisive (Expectancy-Confirming Motives)

Certain circumstances in the social environment can also increase the costs of remaining open and undecided. Under these circumstances, information search is curtailed, inconsistencies are ignored or seen as affirming, and snap judgments are justified. Perceivers evidently lack the resources needed to engage in more effortful processes. Like overworked government bureaucrats, social perceivers only bother to gather information on a "need-to-know basis."

Perhaps the most striking demonstration of this phenomenon is people's propensity to stereotype when they are at the low point of their circadian cycles—i.e. when their motivation or ability to search and think carefully is at its lowest (Bodenhausen 1990). Time pressure also encourages stereotyping (e.g. Heaton & Kruglanski 1991; Jamieson & Zanna 1989; Kaplan et al 1992; Kruglanski & Webster 1991); even when people have integrated the individuating information, under time pressure they may not be able to use it appropriately (Pratto & Bargh 1991). Noise distracting enough to be capacity reducing has similar effects (Kruglanski & Webster 1991).

Pressure to implement a decision (i.e. being action-oriented) also forces people to operate more narrowly, confirming their decision and concentrating on how to execute it (Gollwitzer 1990; Gollwitzer & Kinney 1989; Gollwitzer et al 1990a,b). Because questions and doubts would inhibit action, the postdecision, preaction phase favors information relevant to when, where, and how to act; information that promotes the chosen goal; and both optimistic analysis of goal desirability and partial analysis of its feasibility. In effect, action orientation discourages open-mindedness not only in the judgment at hand but also in other judgments made while in the same mindset. The mind focused on action has little "room" for alternative perspectives.

The mind focused on interpersonal interaction seems likewise to lack the resources needed to process complexities or qualifications. Anticipated inter-action causes perceivers to organize information about their prospective part-ner and to recall that person more accurately, at least in single-target settings (Devine et al 1989; Sedikides et al 1991); but enhanced memory of the other person may be of a rather limited dispositional sort. Focused on planning their part in the interaction, people are likely to stay with an initial relatively automatic dispositional characterization of the other, failing to correct for situational constraints (Osborne & Gilbert 1992). If the prospective interaction involves an extremely active role, an unfamiliar goal, or a novel partner—i.e. much preparatory effort—people stay with their initial automatic characteriza-tions. Being cognitively busy also increases the likelihood of using an acti-vated stereotype, although busyness can decrease the likelihood that the stereotype is activated in the first place (Gilbert & Hixon 1991). Social per-ceivers who are busy in general do not use situational information to correct their spontaneous dispositional inferences (for a review see Gilbert 1989). However, the situational information is encoded and even remembered: If people have a chance to think about their partners afterwards, when they are not busy, they retroactively correct their dispositional inferences (Gilbert & Osborne 1989). Cognitively busy people simply do not use all the information at their disposal, and the prototypically busy person is one anticipating a difficult interaction. Pressure to implement a goal or to engage in a difficult interaction promotes use of summarized, simplified, packaged information. People given goals to form simple and straightforward impressions likewise prefer and recall expectancy-confirming information (Stangor & Ford 1992). In the same way, having to commmunicate with another person typically requires neat summaries, not all the gory and inconvenient details (for a review see S. Fiske & Taylor 1991: Ch. 4). Thus a communication mindset encourages the use of categories and abstractions, in effect making would-be communicators less complex and less data driven than people who do not expect to communicate. The information used by communicators is also influ-enced by the nature of the intended audience; communicators shape their messages and even their private opinions to suit the audience (McCann et al 1991; Sedikides 1990; Wilder & Shapiro 1991).

During an interaction, people focus on what they are going to say or do next (Gilbert et al 1988). Especially right before their own conversational turns, people start thinking about what they are about to say and so cannot remember their partner's concurrent conversation, a phenomenon called the next-in-line effect. On the brink of their own conversational turns, people apparently fail to elaborate mentally on their partner's words (Bond et al 1991). Socially anxious people are especially likely to fail in elaborative encoding of their partners' conversations (Bond & Omar 1990). Compared to nonanxious controls, people made temporarily anxious also use less information about, and fail to individuate, an exceptional outgroup member (Wilder & Shapiro 1989a,b). When people are preoccupied, whether by temporary performance anxiety or long-term state anxiety, they form simpler impressions.

Being insecure, like being anxious, diminishes the resources at hand for thinking hard about others. Insecurity prompts doubts, which use up capacity. Insecurity increases the rated consistency of contradictory traits (Wicklund & Braun 1990), thereby creating a simpler, less taxing impression. Insecurity can lead to self-protective withdrawal from effort—essentially a self-reduction of capacity to think about others (Pittman & D'Agostino 1989). Members of groups whose high collective self-esteem is threatened can withdraw effort from careful impression formation and rely on simple ingroup favoritism (Crocker & Luhtanen 1990). Depressed self-esteem motivates simplistic intergroup discrimination (Hogg & Sunderland 1991; for a review of related research see Hogg & Abrams 1990). Under threat, individual self-esteem can be maintained by simple attributions to group prejudice (Crocker & Major 1989; Crocker et al 1991) or by psychologically distancing oneself from the dimension being evaluated (Crocker & Major 1989; Tesser et al 1989). Emotional arousal plays a role in such phenomena (Tesser et al 1989), so there may be an as-yet-unexplored link between (a) threats to self-esteem, anxiety, and arousal and (b) capacity limitations on social perception (S. Fiske & Emery 1992).

Self-protection involves more than resource limitation, of course. Motivated to protect their self-esteem, people often reason in fairly complex ways. For example, people construct self-serving conclusions with justifications based on evidence at hand (W. Klein & Kunda 1992; Kunda 1990); and their prototypes for favored social groups contain self-descriptive attributes, whereas prototypes for disliked groups avoid self-descriptive attributes (Dunning et al 1991). Nevertheless, given plentiful evidence that capacity limitations simplify strategies of impression formation, it would be useful to study the role of limited resources in the defense of self-esteem (S. Fiske & Emery 1992).

Capacity limitations—brought on by time pressure to decide or to act, by cognitive busyness, by preparing for a difficult social interaction, by a communication mindset, by anxiety, and by threats to self-esteem—serve to simplify social cognitive strategies. What, then, are the effects of capacity expansion?

Experts are best identified by their sheer knowledge in a domain (S. Fiske et al 1990; Zaller 1990). Experts in general skillfully detect common patterns, which they represent cognitively as compact schemas rather than a jumble of data; expert social perceivers have this same skill (Dawson et al 1989; Judd & Downing 1990). Experts process relevant information more efficiently than novices (S. Fiske et al 1990; McGraw & Pinney 1990). Compared to novice strategies, expert strategies are less often simply confirmatory—a finding predicted by experts' greater capacity (Borgida & DeBono 1989; Fletcher et al 1992). Experts are less likely than novices to forget the gaps in their knowledge over time (Sanbonmatsu et al 1991). On the other hand, experts have numerous opinions (Krosnick & Milburn 1990), and they may tend to maintain their established expectations when not motivated to be careful (Stangor & Ford 1992).

Some individuals are more cognitively rigid than others. People high on dimensions of order and achievement show more expectancy bias than those assessed as low on these dimensions (Harris 1989). Individual differences in need for structure correspond to greater consistency in ratings of other people (Jamieson & Zanna 1989; Neuberg 1992). High need for structure exacerbates the effects of time pressure (Kaplan et al 1992).

The costs of indecision increase whenever resources are reduced through time pressure, need to implement action, anticipation of interaction, anticipation of communication, anticipation of one's interaction turn, being insecure or incompetent, self-protection, being a novice, or being cognitively rigid. Perceivers are pragmatic: They make good-enough social decisions and stay with them when capacity is strained. As indicated in the previous section, because they are pragmatic, perceivers use more effort in reaching a decision when their goals are jeopardized by lack of ability to predict or control. Current perspectives thus portray perceivers as motivated tacticians, choosing strategies that suit the immediate circumstances of their capacities and their need to know. We know less about how such motives are triggered, but work on automatic processing bears on this question (Bargh 1992).

Automaticity and Control

A pragmatic viewpoint suggests that cognitive efficiency would be maximized if often-used social constructs and often-executed social processes were automatic. Recent social cognition research explores and endorses this idea. The most comprehensive framework for understanding varieties of automaticity results from Bargh's (1989) distinctions among (*a*) preconscious automaticity, in which one is aware of neither the instigating stimulus nor the ensuing process; (*b*) postconscious automaticity, in which one is aware of the stimulus, but not its process effects; and (*c*) goal-dependent automaticity, in which one is aware of the stimulus, but its effects on processing depend on one's overall goal. Goal-dependent automaticity may have unintended effects ("spontaneous processes" Uleman 1989) or intended effects. Uleman (1989) extends the continuum of automaticity to include rumination, which involves having a goal thwarted (Martin & Tesser 1989), being aware of the stimulus, being aware of its effects on one's thought processes, but being unable to terminate the process. On the far end of this continuum, of course, is fully intentional thinking—awareness and control with respect to all the components (see below) (S. Fiske 1989).

Preconscious automaticity occurs without awareness of stimulus or process, without conscious interference, and without ability to end the process. Subliminal perception, chronically accessible constructs, and preconscious affect exemplify this phenomenon (Bargh 1989). Devine's (1989) recent experiment subliminally primed racial constructs, which then facilitated stereotypic interpretations of ambiguous material. The preconscious automatic effects occurred regardless of perceivers' separately measured levels of prejudice. Prejudice did, however, predict more controlled processes. Another example comes from work on advantages in preconscious processing of affect-laden stimuli, occurring when the stimulus words are frequent and expected in context (Kitayama 1990).

Postconscious automaticity, with awareness of the stimulus but not its effects, is studied more commonly than preconscious automaticity in social cognition research. Priming and mood research provide the main examples. Subjects are well aware of the construct-activating or mood-inducing stimulus but are not aware of its effect on their judgments. Work on postconscious automaticity continues apace in construct accessibility research. Effects are so robust and widely applicable that Sedikides & Skowronski (1991) suggest a Law of Cognitive Structure Activation: Ambiguous stimuli are encoded as instances of the structure most active in memory and most semantically similar (see commentaries in *Psychological Inquiry*, Vol. 2). The synapse model of knowledge accessibility (Higgins 1989) holds that a construct's rate of activation decay is inversely proportional to its prior activation frequency. Depending on delay, either recency or frequency may predict construct accessibility.

Most priming research focuses either on recent or on frequent activation, not both. Work on recent activation indicates the importance of encoding processes: For example, prime-relevant dimensions influence subsequent evaluations, an effect probably mediated by differential attention (Sherman et al 1990). Primes processed at encoding are more likely to elicit assimilation, while primes recalled at judgment function as a standard and are more likely to elicit contrast (Philippot et al 1991). Other work indicates the importance of primes as subtle guides to interpretation at encoding or as blatant standards for contrast at judgment (Martin & Achee 1992; Martin et al 1990; Schwarz & Bless 1992). Effects of recent priming are evident in significant domains: assessments of the President as a function of media issue coverage (Krosnick & Kinder 1990), stereotyping based on age (Perdue & Gurtman 1990), stereotyping based on gender (Banaji & Greewald 1992), sexual-harassment-like responses as a function of pornography (McKenzie-Mohr & Zanna 1990), and judgments of antisocial behavior as a function of antisocial rock music videos

(Hansen & Hansen 1990). Priming frequency (chronicity) effects are reported for voting choice (Lau 1989) and trust in government (Erber & Lau 1990).

Salience effects also illustrate postconscious automaticity (see S. Fiske & Taylor 1991: Ch. 7) to the extent that they require conscious focus on a particular stimulus but without awareness, intent, or control over its effects on subsequent judgments. Salient stimuli dominate and polarize judgments. For example, someone who gestures animatedly will seem noticeable, novel, changing, intense, and complex (Sullins 1989). Salient talkers are more likely to be chosen as leaders (Mullen et al 1989), all else being equal. Like priming effects, the effects of salience on judgment require that the target information be ambiguous (J. Johnson et al 1989). Group composition, a naturally occurring form of salience, focuses attention on members of the rarer group (Mullen 1991), exaggerating positive ingroup and negative outgroup biases (Mullen et al 1992). Minority groups overestimate their own consensus (Mullen & Hu 1988) and see themselves as relatively homogeneous (Mullen & Hu 1989). More generally, rare events generate polarized judgments (Ditto & Jemmott 1989).

In *goal-dependent automaticity with unintended effects,* the perceiver is aware of the stimulus but not necessarily of its effects on cognitive processes; such effects nevertheless require some cognitive capacity and depend on the perceiver's goal. Thus, for example, inferring a trait from a written description of behavior seems to occur spontaneously at encoding; it occurs without intent or awareness, is subjectively effortless, and is difficult to disrupt with a concurrent task. This process does use some cognitive capacity, can be inhibited by goals that bypass the detection of meaning (Newman & Uleman 1989, 1990; Uleman et al 1992), and can be altered by other goals (e.g. D'Agostino 1991); thus its occurrence may not be inevitable. Trait inference is therefore described as spontaneous (without intent or awareness) but controllable. While interpretation of these data is still controversial, it seems notable that dispositional judgments are faster than situational judgments (Bassili & Racine 1990); the latter require more attention (Lupfer et al 1990) and are more vulnerable to disruption (see Gilbert 1989 for a review). Traits inferred as part of the behavior categorization process (Bassili 1989a,b,c; Lupfer et al 1990) can prime subsequent judgments (Moskowitz & Roman 1992). Spontaneous or at least rapid dispositional inference makes pragmatic sense, to the extent traits are perceived to predict behavior (Newman 1991).

Indeed, dispositional inference may be a special case of a more general characteristic of belief systems: In understanding a proposition (e.g. a spontaneous dispositional attribution), one first believes it true, then only subsequently qualifies it (e.g. situational correction) (Gilbert 1991, 1992; Gilbert et al 1990). This is not to say that dispositional inferences are fully automatic. For example, categorization of obscured behavior can be difficult, which makes the categorization and characterization phase consume more capacity (Gilbert et al 1992). Similarly, stereotypic categorization and associated inferences may be inhibited when perceivers are busy (Gilbert & Hixon 1991). Moreover, in some circumstances—e.g. category-inconsistent behavior—situational attributions may be even faster than dispositional ones (Macrae & Shepherd 1991).

Other types of processes also illustrate goal-dependent automaticity with unintended effects. People can learn a pattern of covariation without awareness and then unintentionally apply it with increasing frequency to new ambiguous stimuli, thereby self-perpetuating their initial bias (Hill et al 1989, 1990); such a process may account for depressive encoding biases (Hill et al 1991). The evidence does not yet indicate the extent to which this phenomenon is goal dependent or uses up cognitive capacity; if neither, it may instead exemplify postconscious automaticity.

Goal-dependent automaticity with intended effects is perhaps best illustrated in the process of practice (Smith 1990). That processing efficiency is improved by practice is evident in the speed-up and readiness of such specific social inferences as attributions, use of certain traits, and stereotypic inferences (e.g. Smith et al 1992). The speed-up is procedural, i.e. process-specific, not just target-specific or task-specific.

Moving to less automatic processes, *rumination* results from frustration of conscious or unconscious goals and continues until the frustrated goal is identified (Martin & Tesser 1989). Rumination has both automatic and controlled components, in that one is aware of one's repetitive thoughts and their focus but feels unable to terminate the process. Rumination or any kind of mere thought can polarize attitudes (Tesser et al 1992) and mobilize behavior, if the cognitive or affective orientation of the thoughts matches the corresponding behavior (Millar & Tesser 1992). If types of thought and behavior do not match, thought (e.g. cognitively oriented) can undermine consistency between (e.g. more affectively-driven) attitudes and behavior (Wilson & Schooler 1991).

The fact that people find it singularly difficult to suppress their thoughts (Wegner 1989) suggests that such thoughts have automatic determinants. People who attempt to suppress their thoughts in an unfocused way later fall victim to a rebound, thinking the suppressed thoughts more often than controls. Focused distraction techniques reduce this rebound effect (Wegner & Schneider 1989). Suppressing an exciting (arousing) thought leads not only to rebound effects but also to physiological reactivity when the thought does intrude (Wegner et al 1990). Similarly, suppressing a thought while in a particular mood not only leads to exaggerated rebound when the same mood is reinstated but also triggers the prior mood when the thought intrudes (Wenzlaff et al 1991). Such effects of thought suppression on mood and physiology corroborate the salutary effects of confession over inhibition of one's disturbing thoughts (Pennebaker 1989a,b). Mental control operates in the service of social control, largely to meet the demands of social interaction

(Wegner & Erber 1992). (For a varied collection of work on mental control see Wegner & Pennebaker 1992.)

Finally, *fully intentional thinking* requires perceived choice (a perception or potential perception of alternatives) and the deployment of attention to the chosen alternative (S. Fiske 1989). This description of intent builds explicitly on James's view of the will (James 1890/1983) as well as on subsequent cognitive and social views of intent. Because attention is important to the definition of intent, it is necessary to determine the degree to which people control their search and attentional processes in social settings.

People allocate social attention in a controllable, strategic fashion. When motivated to be accurate, people attend to the most informative, expectancy-disconfirming information (e.g. Neuberg & Fiske 1987; Ruscher & Fiske 1990). Even when not specially motivated, people think more systematically in response to inconsistency (Maheswaran & Chaiken 1991). People attend more carefully to someone who is initially inconsistent with expectations (Hilton et al 1991). Because inconsistent information is more informative and carries more weight in initial information seeking, people use less of it and make a judgment sooner (Yzerbyt & Leyens 1991). Although people often attend strategically to the most diagnostic (informative) information, they may remain biased when faced with a single plausible hypothesis and no salient alternatives (McDonald 1990), when it is socially adaptive to seek confirmation (Leyens 1989), or when they are affectively invested in a particular outcome (Holton & Pyszczynski 1989; Sanitioso & Kunda 1991). All else being equal, people prefer diagnostic strategies over confirmatory ones (Devine et al 1990).

CONCLUSION

I have argued here that people construct the meaning of their social environments well enough to enable effective actions—in James's terms, their "thinking" is good enough to serve their "doing." People's use of expectancies and data suits their purposes, given that they are also alert for incongruent and negative information. People use rich personality traits along five dimensions because they believe that traits reflect other people's goals and largely predict their behavior; people believe that such prediction in turn facilitates their own goals. People use stereotypes (which may be richer than traits) in much the same way, but also to distinguish among people according to criteria relevant to the context. People narrate complex stories in an attempt to account for events of minor incongruency or major importance. Certain goals cause people to emphasize the accuracy of their social perception while other goals cause them to favor immediate good-enough decisions. A surprising amount of social cognition and perception happens automatically; but people are not numb robots, and they control many of their strategies, through the allocation of attention, according to their goals. William James could hardly have asked for a better understanding of pragmatic thinking, 100 years down the road.

ACKNOWLEDGEMENTS

This review was facilitated by NIH grant MH41801 and by a sabbatical from the University of Massachusetts at Amherst. For suggesting that she return to William James for inspiration, the author thanks Tory Higgins, and for their comments, the author wishes to thank James Averill, Icek Ajzen, John Bargh, Barbara Fiske, Donald Fiske, Ronnie Janoff-Bulman, David Kenny, Jacques-Philippe Leyens, Beth Morling, Paula Pietromonaco, Charles Stangor, and Shelley Taylor.

Literature Cited

Allport, G. W. 1954. *The Nature of Prejudice.* Reading, MA: Addison-Wesley. 537 pp.

Ambady, N., Rosenthal, R. 1992. Thin slices of expressive behavior as predictors of interpersonal consequences: a meta-analysis. *Psychol. Bull.* 111:256–74

Andersen, S. M., Cole, S. W. 1990. "Do I know you?": the role of significant others in general social perception. *J. Pers. Soc. Psychol.* 59:384–99

Andersen, S. M., Klatzky, R. L., Murray, J. 1990. Traits and social stereotypes: efficiency differences in social information processing. *J. Pers. Soc. Psychol.* 59:192–201

Andersen, S. M., Spielman, L. A., Bargh, J. A. 1992. Certainty of future suffering as perceptual fluency: automaticity in depressed individuals' predictions about future life events. *J. Pers. Soc. Psychol.* In press

Anderson, C. A., Kellam, K. L. 1991. Belief perseverance, biased assimilation, and co-variation detection: the effects of hypothetical social theories and new data. *Pers. Soc. Psychol. Bull.* In press

Anderson, C. A., Sedikides, C. 1991. Thinking about people: contributions of a typological alternative to associationistic and dimensional models of person perception. *J. Pers. Soc. Psychol.* 60:203–17

Anderson, N. H. 1989. Functional memory and on-line attribution. See Bassili 1989a, pp. 175–220

Angleitner, A., Ostendorf, F., John, O. P. 1990. Towards a taxonomy of personality descriptors in German: a psycho-lexical study. *Eur. J. Pers.* 4:89–118

Asch, S. E. 1946. Forming impressions of personality. *J. Abnorm. Soc. Psychol.* 41:1230–40

Bales, R. F., ed. 1970. *Personality and Interpersonal Behavior.* New York: Holt, Rinehart and Winston. 561 pp.

Banaji, M. R., Greenwald, A. G. 1992. Implicit stereotyping and prejudice. See Zanna & Olson 1992. In press

Bargh, J. A. 1992. Auto-motives: preconscious determinants of social interaction. See Higgins & Sorrentino 1990, pp. 93–130

Bargh, J. A. 1989. Conditional automaticity: varieties of automatic influence in social perception and cognition. See Uleman & Bargh 1989, pp. 3–51

Bar-Tal, D., Graumann, C. F., Kruglanski, A. W., Stroebe, W., eds. 1989. *Stereotyping and Prejudice: Changing Conceptions.* New York: Springer-Verlag. 273 pp.

Bassili, J. N. 1989a. *On-line Cognition in Person Perception.* Hillsdale, NJ: Erlbaum

Bassili, J. N. 1989b. Traits as action categories versus traits as person attributes in social cognition. See Bassili 1989a, pp. 61–89

Bassili, J. N. 1989c. Trait encoding in behavior identification and dispositional inference. *Pers. Soc. Psychol. Bull.* 15:285–96

Bassili, J. N., Racine, J. P. 1990. On the process relationship between person and situation judgments in attribution. *J. Pers. Soc. Psychol.* 59:881–90

Beauvois, J.-L., Dubois, N. 1991. Internal/external orientations and psychological information processing. *Eur. Bull. Cognit. Psychol.* 11:193–212

Berry, D. S. 1990. Taking people at face value: evidence for the kernel of truth hypothesis. *Soc. Cognit.* 8:343–61

Berry, D. S. 1991a. Attractive faces are not all created equal: joint effects of facial babyishness and attractiveness on social perception. *Pers. Soc. Psychol. Bull.* 17:523–31

Berry, D. S. 1991b. Accuracy in social perception: contributions of facial and vocal information. *J. Pers. Soc. Psychol.* 61:298–307

Biernat, M., Manis, M., Nelson, T. E. 1991. Stereotypes and standards of judgement. *J. Pers. Soc. Psychol.* 60:485–99

Blanchard, F. A., Lilly, T., Vaughn, L. A. 1991. Reducing the expression of racial prejudice. *Psychol. Sci.* 2:101–05

Bodenhausen, G. V. 1990. Stereotypes as judgmental heuristics: evidence of circadian variations in discrimination. *Psychol. Sci.* 1:319–22

Bond, C. F., Omar, A. S. 1990. Social anxiety, state dependence, and the next-in-line effect. *J. Exp. Soc. Psychol.* 26:185–98

Bond, C. F., Pitre, U., Van Leeuwen, M. D. 1991. Encoding operations and the next-in-line effect. *Pers. Soc. Psychol. Bull.* 17:435–41

Borgida, E., DeBono, K. G. 1989. Social hypothesis testing and the role of expertise. *Pers. Soc. Psychol. Bull.* 15:212–21

Borkenau, P. 1990. Traits as ideal-based and goal-derived social categories. *J. Pers. Soc. Psychol.* 58:381–96

Botwin, M. D., Buss, D. M. 1989. Structure of act-report data: Is the five-factor model of personality recaptured? *J. Pers. Soc. Psychol.* 56:988–1001

Brewer, M. B. 1988. A dual process model of impression formation. *Adv. Soc. Cognit.* 1:1–36

Brewer, M. B., Dull, V., Lui, L. 1981. Perceptions of the elderly: stereotypes as prototypes. *J. Pers. Soc. Psychol.* 41:656–70

Brewer, M. B., Lui, L. N. 1989. The primacy of age and sex in the structure of person categories. *Soc. Cognit.* 7:262–74

Brownlow, S., Zebrowitz, L. A. 1990. Facial appearance, gender, and credibility in television commercials. *J. Nonverbal Behav.* 14:51–59

Bruner, J. S. 1990. *Acts of Meaning.* Cambridge, MA: Harvard Univ. Press

Bruner, J. S. 1991. The narrative construction of reality. *Crit. Inquiry* 18:1–21

Cano, I., Hopkins, N., Islam, M. R. 1991. Memory for stereotype-related material—a replication study with real-life social groups. *Eur. J. Soc. Psychol.* 21:349–57

Cantor, N., Kihlstrom, J. F. 1989. Social intelligence and cognitive assessments of personality. *Adv. Soc. Cognit.* 2:1–59

Cantor, N., Zirkel, S. 1990. Personality, cognition, and purposive behavior. See Pervin 1990, pp. 135–64

Casselden, P. A., Hampson, S. E. 1990. Forming impressions from incongruent traits. *J. Pers. Soc. Psychol.* 59:353–62

Chaiken, S., Liberman, A., Eagly, A. H. 1989. Heuristic and systematic information processing within and beyond the persuasion context. See Uleman & Bargh 1989, pp. 212–52

Chaplin, W. F., John, O. P., Goldberg, L. R. 1988. Conceptions of states and traits: dimensional attributes with ideals as prototypes. *J. Pers. Soc. Psychol.* 54:541–57

Church, A. T., Katigbak, M. S. 1989. Internal, external, and self-report structure of personality in a non-Western culture: an investigation of cross-language and cross-cultural generalizability. *J. Pers. Soc. Psychol.* 57:857–72

Collins, R. L., Taylor, S. E., Skokan, L. A. 1990. A better world or a shattered vision? Changes in life perspectives following victimization. *Soc. Cognit.* 8:263–85

Colvin, C. R., Funder, D. C. 1991. Predicting personality and behavior: a boundary on the acquaintanceship effect. *J. Pers. Soc. Psychol.* 60:884–94

Coovert, M. D., Reeder, G. D. 1990. Negativity effects in impression formation: the role of unit formation and schematic expectations. *J. Exp. Soc. Psychol.* 26:49–62

Crocker, J., Luhtanen, R. 1990. Collective self-esteem and ingroup bias. *J. Pers. Soc. Psychol.* 58:60–67

Crocker, J., Major, B. 1989. Social stigma and self-esteem: the self-protective properties of stigma. *Psychol. Rev.* 96:608–30

Crocker, J., Voelkl, K., Testa, M., Major, B. 1991. Social stigma: the affective consequences of attributional ambiguity. *J. Pers. Soc. Psychol.* 60:218–28

Crosby, F., Clayton, S. 1990. Affirmative action and the issue of expectancies. *J. Soc. Issue* 46:61–80

D'Agostino, P. R. 1991. Spontaneous trait inferences: effects of recognition instructions and subliminal priming on recognition performance. *Pers. Soc. Psychol. Bull.* 17:70–77

Dawson, V. L., Zeitz, C. M., Wright, J. C. 1989. Expert-novice differences in person perception: evidence of experts' sensitivities to the organization of behavior. *Soc. Cognit.* 7:1–30

Deaux, K., Kite, M. E., Lewis, L. L. 1985. Clustering and gender schemata: an uncertain link. *Pers. Soc. Psychol. Bull.* 11:387–97

de la Haye, A. M. 1991. Problems and procedures: a typology of paradigms in interpersonal cognition. *Eur. Bull. Cognit. Psychol.* 11:279–304

Denhaerinck, P., Leyens, J. Ph., Yzerbyt, V. 1989. The dilution effect and group membership: an instance of the pervasive impact of outgroup homogeneity. *Eur. J. Soc. Psychol.* 19:243–50

Dépret, E. F., Fiske, S. T. 1992. Social cognition and power: some cognitive consequences of social structure as a source of control deprivation. See Weary et al 1992. In press

Desforges, D. M., Lord, C. G., Ramsey, S. L., Mason, J. A., Van Leeuwen, M. D., et al. 1991. Effects of structured cooperative contact on changing negative attitudes toward stigmatized social groups. *J. Pers. Soc. Psychol.* 60:531–44

Devine, P. G. 1989. Stereotypes and prejudice: their automatic and controlled components. *J. Pers. Soc. Psychol.* 56:5–18

Devine, P. G., Baker, S. M. 1991. Measurement of racial stereotype subtyping. *Pers. Soc. Psychol. Bull.* 17:44–50

Devine, P., Ostrom, T., Hamilton, D., eds. 1992. *Social Cognition: Contributions to Classical Issues in Social Psychology.* New York: Springer-Verlag. In press

Devine, P. G., Hirt, E. R., Gehrke, E. M. 1990. Diagnostic and confirmation strategies in trait hypothesis testing. *J. Pers. Soc. Psychol.* 58:952–63

Devine, P. G., Monteith, M. J., Zuwerink, J. R., Elliot, A. J. 1991. Prejudice with and without compunction. *J. Pers. Soc. Psychol.* 60:817–30

Devine, P. G., Sedikides, C., Fuhrman, R. W. 1989. Goals in social information processing: the case of anticipated interaction. *J. Pers. Soc. Psychol.* 56:680–90

Diehl, M., Jonas, K. 1991. Measures of national stereotypes as predictors of the latencies of inductive versus deductive stereotypic judgements. *Eur. J. Soc. Psychol.* 21:317–30

Digman, J. M. 1990. Personality structure: emergence of the five-factor model. *Annu. Rev. Psychol.* 41:417–40

Ditto, P. H., Jemmott, J. B. 1989. From rarity to evaluative extremity: effects of prevalence information on evaluations of positive and negative characteristics. *J. Pers. Soc. Psychol.* 57:16–26

Driscoll, D. M., Hamilton, D. L., Sorrentino, R. M. 1991. Uncertainty orientation and recall of person descriptive information. *Pers. Soc. Psychol. Bull.* 5:494–500

Dunning, D., Milojkovic, J. D., Ross, L., Griffin, D. W. 1990. The overconfidence effect in social prediction. *J. Pers. Soc. Psychol.* 58:568–81

Dunning, D., Parpal, M. 1989. Mental addition versus subtraction in counterfactual reasoning: on assessing the impact of personal actions and life events. *J. Pers. Soc. Psychol.* 57:5–15

Dunning, D., Perie, M., Story, A. L. 1991. Self-serving prototypes of social categories. *J. Pers. Soc. Psychol.* 61:957–68

Eagly, A. H., Ashmore, R. D., Makhijani, M. G., Longo, L. C. 1991. What is beautiful is good, but … : a meta-analytic review of research on the physical attractiveness stereotype. *Psychol. Bull.* 110:109–28

Eagly, A. H., Makhijani, M. G., Klonsky, B. G. 1992. Gender and the evaluation of leaders: a meta-analysis. *Psychol. Bull.* 111:3–22

Eagly, A. H., Mladinic, A. 1989. Gender stereotypes and attitudes toward women and men. *Pers. Soc. Psychol. Bull.* 15:543–58

Echabe, A. E., Rovira, D. P. 1989. Social representations and memory: the case of AIDS. *Eur. J. Soc. Psychol.* 19:543–51

Eiser, J. R., Martijn, C., Van Schie, E. 1991. Categorization and interclass assimilation in social judgement. *Eur. J. Soc. Psychol.* 21:493–505

Erber, R., Lau, R. R. 1990. Political cynicism revisited: an information-processing reconciliation of policy-based and incumbency-based interpretations of changes in trust in government. *Am. J. Polit. Sci.* 34:236–53

Fiedler, K. 1991. The tricky nature of skewed frequency tables: an information loss account of distinctiveness-based illusory correlations. *J. Pers. Soc. Psychol.* 60:24–36

Fiedler, K., Semin, G. R. 1992. Attribution and language as a socio-cognitive environment. See Semin & Fiedler 1992. In press

Fiedler, K., Semin, G. R. 1989. Relocating attributional phenomena within a language-cognition interface: the case of actors' and observers' perspectives. *Eur. J. Soc. Psychol.* 19:491–508

Fiedler, K., Semin, G. R., Bolten, S. 1989. Language use and reification of social information: top-down and bottom-up processing in person cognition. *Eur. J. Soc. Psychol.* 19:271–95

Fiske, A. P. 1991. *Structures of Social Life.* New York: Free Press. 480 pp.

Fiske, A. P., Haslam, N., Fiske, S. T. 1991. Confusing one person with another: what errors reveal about the elementary forms of social relations. *J. Pers. Soc. Psychol.* 60:656–74

Fiske, D. W. 1949. Consistency of the factorial structures of personality ratings from different sources. *J. Abnorm. Soc. Psychol.* 44:329–44

Fiske, S. T. 1982. Schema-triggered affect: applications to social perception. In *Affect and Cognition: The 17th Annual Carnegie Symposium on Cognition*, ed. M. S. Clark, S. T. Fiske, pp. 55–78. Hillsdale, NJ: Erlbaum

Fiske, S. T. 1989. Examining the role of intent: toward understanding its role in stereotyping and prejudice. See Uleman & Bargh 1989, pp. 253–83

Fiske, S. T. 1992. Thinking is for doing: portraits of social cognition from daguerreotype to laserphoto. *J. Pers. Soc. Psychol.* In press

Fiske, S. T., Emery, E. J. 1992. Lost mental control and exaggerated social control: social-cognitive and psychoanalytic speculations. See Wegner & Pennebaker 1992. In press

Fiske, S. T., Lau, R. R., Smith, R. A. 1990. On the varieties and utilities of political expertise. *Soc. Cognit.* 8:31–48

Fiske, S. T., Neuberg, S. L. 1990. A continuum of impression formation, from category-based to individuating processes: influences of information and motivation on attention and interpretation. *Adv. Exp. Soc. Psychol.* 23:1–74

Fiske, S. T., Taylor, S. E. 1991. *Social Cognition.* New York: McGraw-Hill. 717 pp.

Fiske, S. T., Von Hendy, H. M. 1992. Personality feedback and situational norms can control stereotyping processes. *J. Pers. Soc. Psychol.* 62:577–96

Fletcher, G., Rosanowski, J., Rhodes, G., Lange, C. 1992. Accuracy and speed of causal processing: experts versus novices in social judgment. *J. Exp. Soc. Psychol.* 28:320–38

Flett, G. L., Pliner, P., Blankstein, K. R. 1989. Depression and components of attributional complexity. *J. Pers. Soc. Psychol.* 56:757–64

Flink, C., Park, B. 1991. Increasing consensus in trait judgments through outcome dependency. *J. Exp. Soc. Psychol.* 27:453–67

Ford, T. E., Stangor, C. 1992. The role of diagnosticity in stereotype formation: perceiving group means and variances. *J. Pers. Soc. Psychol.* In press

Frable, D. E. S., Blackstone, T., Scherbaum, C. 1990. Marginal and mindful: deviants in social interactions. *J. Pers. Soc. Psychol.* 59:140–49

Friedman, H., Zebrowitz, L. A. 1992. The contribution of typical sex differences in facial maturity to sex-role. *Pers. Soc. Psychol. Bull.* 18:430-38

Funder, D. C. 1987. Errors and mistakes: evaluating the accuracy of social judgment. *Psychol. Bull.* 101:75–90

Funder, D. C., Colvin, C. R. 1991. Explorations in behavioral consistency: properties of persons, situations, and behaviors. *J. Pers. Soc. Psychol.* 60:773–94

Fussell, S. R., Krauss, R. M. 1991. Accuracy and bias in estimates of others' knowledge. *Eur. J. Soc. Psychol.* 21:445–54

Fussell, S. R., Krauss, R. M. 1989a. Understanding friends and strangers: the effects of audience design on message comprehension. *Eur. J. Soc. Psychol.* 19:509–25

Fussell, S. R., Krauss, R. M. 1989b. The effects of intended audience on message production and comprehension: reference in a common ground framework. *J. Exp. Soc. Psychol.* 25:203–19

Gaertner, S. L., Mann, J. A., Dovidio, J. F., Murrell, A. J., Pomare, M. 1990. How does cooperation reduce intergroup bias? *J. Pers. Soc. Psychol.* 59:692–704

Gaertner, S. L., Mann, J., Murrell, A., Dovidio, J. F. 1989. Reducing intergroup bias: the benefits of recategorization. *J. Pers. Soc. Psychol.* 57:239–49

Galotti, K. M. 1989. Approaches to studying formal and everyday reasoning. *Psychol. Bull.* 105:331–51

Gavanski, I., Wells, G. L. 1989. Counterfactual processing of normal and exceptional events. *J. Exp. Soc. Psychol.* 25:314–25

Gilbert, D. T. 1992. Assent of man: mental representations and the control of belief. See Wegner & Pennebaker 1992. In press

Gilbert, D. T. 1991. How mental systems believe. *Am. Psychol.* 46:107–19

Gilbert, D. T. 1989. Thinking lightly about others: automatic components of the social inference process. See Uleman & Bargh 1989, pp. 189–211

Gilbert, D. T., Hixon, J. G. 1991. The trouble of thinking: activation and application of stereotypic beliefs. *J. Pers. Soc. Psychol.* 60:509–17

Gilbert, D. T., Krull, D. S., Pelham, B. W. 1988. Of thoughts unspoken: social inference and the self-regulation of behavior. *J. Pers. Soc. Psychol.* 55:685–94

Gilbert, D. T., Malone, P. S., Krull, D. S. 1990. Unbelieving the unbelievable: some problems in the rejection of false information. *J. Pers. Soc. Psychol.* 59:601–13

Gilbert, D. T., McNulty, S. E., Giuliano, T. A., Benson, J. E. 1992. Blurry words and fuzzy deeds: the attribution of obscure behavior. *J. Pers. Soc. Psychol.* 62:18–25

Gilbert, D. T., Osborne, R. E. 1989. Thinking backward: some curable and incurable consequences of cognitive busyness. *J. Pers. Soc. Psychol.* 57:940–49

Gilovich, T. 1990. Differential construal and the false consensus effect. *J. Pers. Soc. Psychol.* 59:623–34

Gilovich, T. 1991. *How We Know What Isn't So: The Fallibility of Human Reason in Everyday Life.* New York: Free Press. 216 pp.

Gleicher, F., Weary, G. 1991. Effect of depression on quantity and quality of social inferences. *J. Pers. Soc. Psychol.* 61:105–14

Goldberg, L. R. 1990. An alternative "description of personality": the big five-factor structure. *J. Pers. Soc. Psychol.* 59:1216–29

Gollwitzer, P. M. 1990. Action phases and mind-sets. See Higgins & Sorrentino 1990, pp. 53–92

Gollwitzer, P. M., Heckhausen, H., Ratajczak, H. 1990a. From weighing to willing: approaching a change decision through preor postdecisional mentation. *Organ. Behav. Hum. Decision Processes* 45:41–65

Gollwitzer, P. M., Heckhausen, H., Steller, B. 1990b. Deliberative and implemental mind-sets: cognitive tuning toward congruous thoughts and information. *J. Pers. Soc. Psychol.* 59:1119–27

Gollwitzer, P. M., Kinney, R. F. 1989. Effects of deliberative and implemental mind-sets on illusion of control. *J. Pers. Soc. Psychol.* 56:531–42

Griffin, D. W., Ross, L. 1991. Subjective construal, social inference, and human misunderstanding. *Adv. Exp. Soc. Psychol.* 24:319–59

Griffin, D. W., Ross, L., Dunning, D. 1990. The role of construal processes in overconfident predictions about the self and others. *J. Pers. Soc. Psychol.* 59:1128–39

Hagendoorn, L., Kleinpenning, G. 1991. The contribution of domain-specific stereotypes to ethnic social distance. *Br. J. Soc. Psychol.* 30:63–78

Hamilton, D. L. 1989. Understanding impression formation: What has memory research contributed? In *Memory: Interdisciplinary Approaches,* ed. P. Soloman, G. Goethals, C. Kelley, B. Stephens, 11:221–42. New York: Springer-Verlag

Hamilton, D. L., Driscoll, D. M., Worth, L. T. 1989. Cognitive organization of impressions: effects of incongruency in complex representations. *J. Pers. Soc. Psychol.* 57:925–39

Hamilton, D. L., Gibbons, P. A., Stroessner, S. J., Sherman, J. W. 1992. Stereotypes and language use. See Semin & Fiedler 1992. In press

Hamilton, D. L., Grubb, P. D., Acorn, D. A., Trolier, T. K., Carpenter, S. 1990a. Attribution difficulty and memory for attribution-relevant information. *J. Pers. Soc. Psychol.* 59:891–98

Hamilton, D. L., Sherman, S. J. 1989. Illusory correlations: implications for stereotype theory and research. See Bar-Tal et al 1989, pp. 59–82

Hamilton, D. L., Sherman, S. J., Ruvolo, C. M. 1990b. Stereotype-based expectancies: effects on information processing and social behavior. *J. Soc. Issues* 46:35–60

Hansen, C. H. 1989. Priming sex-role stereotypic event schemas with rock music videos: effects on impression favorability, trait inferences, and recall of a subsequent male-female interaction. *Basic Appl. Soc. Psychol.* 10:371–91

Hansen, C. H., Hansen, R. D. 1990. Rock music videos and antisocial behavior. *Basic Appl. Soc. Psychol.* 11:357–69

Harris, M. J. 1991. Controversy and culmination: meta-analysis and research on interpersonal expectancy effects. *Pers. Soc. Psychol. Bull.* 17:316–22

Harris, M. J. 1990. Effect of interaction goals on expectancy confirmation in a problem-solving context. *Pers. Soc. Psychol. Bull.* 16:521–30

Harris, M. J. 1989. Personality moderators of interpersonal expectancy effects: replication of Harris and Rosenthal (1986). *J. Res. Pers.* 23:381–97

Harvey, J. H., Agostinelli, G., Weber, A. L. 1989. Account-making and the formation of expectations about close relationships. *Rev. Pers. Soc. Psychol.* 10:39–62

Hastie, R., Pennington, N. 1991. Cognitive and social processes in decision making. In *Perspectives on Socially Shared Cognition,* ed. L. Resnick, J. Levine, S. Teasley, pp. 308–27. Washington DC: Am. Psychol. Assoc.

Heaton, A. W., Kruglanski, A. W. 1991. Person perception by introverts and extraverts under time pressure: effects of need for closure. *Pers. Soc. Psychol. Bull.* 17:161–65

Hewstone, M. 1989. Changing stereotypes with disconfirming information. See Bar-Tal et al 1989, pp. 207–23

Hewstone, M., Hantzi, A., Johnston, L. 1991. Social categorization and person memory: the pervasiveness of race as an organizing principle. *Eur. J. Soc. Psychol.* 21:517–28

Hewstone, M., Hopkins, N., Routh, D. A. 1992a. Cognitive models of stereotype change:(1) generalization and subtyping in young people's views of the police. *Eur. J. Soc. Psychol.* 22:219-34

Hewstone, M., Johnston, L., Aird, P. 1992b. Cognitive models of stereotype change: (2) perceptions of homogeneous and heterogeneous groups. *Eur. J. Soc. Psychol.* 22:235-50

Higgins, E. T. 1989. Knowledge accessibility and activation: subjectivity and suffering from unconscious sources. See Uleman & Bargh 1989, pp. 75–123

Higgins, E. T., Bargh, J. A. 1987. Social cognition and social perception. *Annu. Rev. Psychol.* 38:369–425

Higgins, E. T., Sorrentino, R. M., eds. 1990. *Handbook of Motivation and Cognition: Foundations of Social Behavior,* Vol. 2. New York/London: Guilford. 621 pp.

Hildebrand-Saints, L., Weary, G. 1989. Depression and social information gathering. *Pers. Soc. Psychol. Bull.* 15:150–60

Hill, T., Lewicki, P., Czyzewska, M., Boss, A. 1989. Self-perpetuating development of encoding biases in person perception. *J. Pers. Soc. Psychol.* 57:373–87

Hill, T., Lewicki, P., Czyzewska, M., Schuller, G. 1990. The role of learned inferential encoding rules in the perception of faces: effects of nonconscious self-perpetuation of a bias. *J. Exp. Soc. Psychol.* 26:350–71

Hill, T., Lewicki, P., Neubauer, R. M. 1991. The development of depressive encoding dispositions: a case of self-perpetuation of biases. *J. Exp. Soc. Psychol.* 27:392–409

Hilton, J. L., Darley, J. M. 1991. The effects of interaction goals on person perception. *Adv. Exp. Soc. Psychol.* 24:235–67

Hilton, J. L., Fein, S. 1989. The role of typical diagnosticity in stereotype-based judgements. *J. Pers. Soc. Psychol.* 57:201–11

Hilton, J. L., von Hippel, W. 1990. The role of consistency in the judgement of stereotype-relevant behaviors. *Pers. Soc. Psychol. Bull.* 16:430–48

Hilton, J. L., Klein, J. G., von Hippel, W. 1991. Attention allocation and impression formation. *Pers. Soc. Psychol. Bull.* 17:548–59

Hoffman, C., Hurst, N. 1990. Gender stereotypes: perception or rationalization. *J. Pers. Soc. Psychol.* 58:197–208

Hogg, M. A., Abrams, D. 1990. Social motivation, self-esteem and social identity. In *Social Identity Theory: Constructive and Critical Advances,* ed. D. Abrams, M. A. Hogg, pp. 28–47. New York: Harvester-Wheatsheaf

Hogg, M. A., Sunderland, J. 1991. Self-esteem and intergroup discrimination in the minimal group paradigm. *Br. J. Soc. Psychol.* 30:51–62

Holtgraves, T., Srull, T. K., Socall, D. 1989. Conversation memory: the effects of speaker status on memory for the assertiveness of conversation remarks. *J. Pers. Soc. Psychol.* 56:149–60

Holton, B., Pyszczynski, T. 1989. Biased information search in the interpersonal domain. *Pers. Soc. Psychol. Bull.* 15:42–51

Ickes, W., Stinson, L., Bissonnette, V., Garcia, S. 1990. Naturalistic social cognition: empathic accuracy in mixed-sex dyads. *J. Pers. Soc. Psychol.* 59:730–42

James, W. 1890/1983. *The Principles of Psy-*

chology. Cambridge, MA: Harvard Univ. Press. 1302 pp.

Jamieson, D. W., Zanna, M. P. 1989. Need for structure in attitude formation and expression. In *Attitude Structure and Function,* ed. A. R. Pratkanis, S. J. Breckler, A. G. Greenwald, pp. 383–406. Hillsdale, NJ: Erlbaum

Janoff-Bulman, R. 1992. *Shattered Assumptions: Towards a New Psychology of Trauma.* New York: The Free Press. 256 pp.

John, O. P. 1990. The "big five" factor taxonomy: dimensions of personality in the natural language and in questionnaires. See Pervin 1990, pp. 66–100

John, O. P., Goldberg, L. R., Hampson, S. E. 1991. The basic level in personality-trait hierarchies: studies of trait use and accessibility in different contexts. *J. Pers. Soc. Psychol.* 3:348–61

Johnson, C., Mullen, B. 1992. Evidence for the accessibility of paired distinctiveness in distinctiveness-based illusory correlation in stereotyping. *Pers. Soc. Psychol. Bull.* In press

Johnson, J. D., Jackson, L. A., Smith, G. J. 1989. The role of ambiguity and gender in mediating the effects of salient cognitions. *Pers. Soc. Psychol. Bull.* 15:52–60

Johnston, L., Hewstone, M. 1992. Cognitive models of stereotype change: (3) subtyping and the perceived typicality of disconfirming group members. *J. Exp. Soc. Psychol.* 28:360-86

Jones, E. E. 1990. *Interpersonal Perception.* New York: W. H. Freeman. 313 pp.

Judd, C. M., Downing, J. W. 1990. Political expertise and the development of attitude consistency. *Soc. Cognit.* 8:104–24

Judd, C. M., Ryan, C. S., Park, B. 1991. Accuracy in the judgment of in-group and outgroup variability. *J. Pers. Soc. Psychol.* 61:366–79

Jussim, L. 1991. Social perception and social reality: a reflection-construction model. *Psychol. Rev.* 98:54–73

Jussim, L. 1989. Teacher expectations: self-fulfilling prophecies, perceptual biases, and accuracy. *J. Pers. Soc. Psychol.* 57:469–80

Jussim, L., Eccles, J. S., eds. 1990. Expectancies and social issues. *J. Soc. Issues* 46:1–201

Kahneman, D., Varey, C. A. 1990. Propensities and counterfactuals: the loser that almost won. *J. Pers. Soc. Psychol.* 59:1101–10

Kalma, A. 1991. Hierarchisation and dominance: assessment at first glance. *Eur. J. Soc. Psychol.* 21:165–81

Kaplan, M. F., Wanshula, L. T., Zanna, M. P. 1992. Time pressure and information integration in social judgment: the effect of need for structure. In *Time Pressure and Stress in Human Judgment and Decision Making,* ed. O. Svenson, J. Maule. New York: Plenum. In press

Kenny, D. A. 1991. A general model of consensus and accuracy in interpersonal perception. *Psychol. Rev.* 98:155–63

Kenny, D. A., Albright, L. 1987. Accuracy in interpersonal perception: a social relations analysis. *Psychol. Bull.* 102:390–402

Kenny, D. A., Horner, C., Kashy, D. A., Chu, L. 1992. Consensus at zero acquaintance: replication, behavioral cues, and stability. *J. Pers. Soc. Psychol.* 62:88–97

Kirkpatrick, L. A., Epstein, S. 1992. Cognitive-experiential self-theory and subjective probability: further evidence for two conceptual systems. *J. Pers. Soc. Psychol.* In press

Kitayama, S. 1990. Interaction between affect and cognition in word perception. *J. Pers. Soc. Psychol.* 58:209–17

Klein, J. G. 1991. Negativity effects in impression formation: a test in the political arena. *Pers. Soc. Psychol. Bull.* 17:412–18

Klein, W. M., Kunda, Z. 1992. Motivated person perception: constructing justifications for desired beliefs. *J. Exp. Soc. Psychol.* 28:145-60

Kleinpenning, G., Hagendoorn, L. 1991. Contextual aspects of ethnic stereotypes and interethnic evaluations. *Eur. J. Soc. Psychol.* 21:331–48

Koehler, D. J. 1991. Explanation, imagination, and confidence in judgment. *Psychol. Bull.* 110:499–519

Krauss, R. M., Fussell, S. R. 1991. Perspective-taking in communication: representations of others' knowledge in reference. *Soc. Cognit.* 9:2–24

Krosnick, J. A., Kinder, D. R. 1990. Altering the foundations of support for the president through priming. *Am. Polit. Sci. Rev.* 84:497–512

Krosnick, J. A., Li, F., Lehman, D. R. 1990. Conversational conventions, order of information acquisition, and the effect of base rates and individuating information on social judgments. *J. Pers. Soc. Psychol.* 59:1140–52

Krosnick, J. A., Milburn, M. A. 1990. Psychological determinants of political opinionation. *Soc. Cognit.* 8:49–72

Krueger, J. 1992. On the overestimation of between-group differences. *Eur. Rev. Soc. Psychol.* 3. In press

Krueger, J. 1991. Accentuation effects and illusory change in exemplar-based category learning. *Eur. J. Soc. Psychol.* 21:37–48

Krueger, J., Rothbart, M. 1990. Contrast and accentuation effects in category learning. *J. Pers. Soc. Psychol.* 59:651–63

Krueger, J., Rothbart, M., Sriram, N. 1989. Category learning and change: differences in sensitivity to information that enhances or reduces intercategory distinctions. *J. Pers. Soc. Psychol.* 56:866–75

Kruglanski, A. W. 1989a. *Lay Epistemics and Human Knowledge.* New York: Plenum. 281 pp.

Kruglanski, A. W. 1989b. The psychology of being "right": the problem of accuracy in social perception and cognition. *Psychol. Bull.* 106:395–409

Kruglanski, A. W. 1990. Motivations for judging and knowing: implications for causal attribution. See Higgins & Sorrentino 1990, pp. 333–68

Kruglanski, A. W., Webster, D. M. 1991. Group members' reactions to opinion deviates and conformists at varying degrees of proximity to decision deadline and of environmental noise. *J. Pers. Soc. Psychol.* 61:212–25

Kunda, Z. 1990. The case for motivated reasoning. *Psychol. Bull.* 108:480–98

Kunda, Z., Miller, D. T., Claire, T. 1990. Combining social concepts: the role of causal reasoning. *Cognit. Sci.* 14:551–77

Lalljee, M., Lamb, R., Abelson, R. P. 1992. The role of event prototypes in categorization and explanation. *Eur. Rev. Soc. Psychol.* 3. In press

Lalonde, R. N., Gardner, R. C. 1989. An intergroup perspective on stereotype organization and processing. *Br. J. Soc. Psychol.* 28:289–303

Lambert, A. J., Wyer, R. S. 1990. Stereotypes and social judgment: the effects of typicality and group heterogeneity. *J. Pers. Soc. Psychol.* 59:676–91

Lanzetta, J. T., Englis, B. G. 1989. Expectations of cooperation and competition and their effects on observers' vicarious emotional responses. *J. Pers. Soc. Psychol.* 56:543–54

Lassiter, G. D., Briggs, M. A., Slaw, R. D. 1991. Need for cognition, causal processing, and memory for behavior. *Pers. Soc. Psychol. Bull.* 17:694–700

Lau, R. R. 1989. Construct accessibility and electoral choice. *Polit. Behav.* 11:5–32

Leyens, J. Ph. 1989. Another look at confirmatory strategies during a real interview. *Eur. J. Soc. Psychol.* 19:255–62

Leyens, J. Ph. 1990. Intuitive personality testing: a social approach. (The 1989 Jos Jaspars Memorial Lecture). In *Fundamentele Sociale Psychologie,* ed. J. Extra, A. van Knippenberg, J. van der Pligt, M. Poppe, Vol. 4. Tilburg: Tilburg Univ. Press

Leyens, J. Ph. 1991. Prolegomena for the concept of implicit theories of personality. *Eur. Bull. Cognit. Psychol.* 11:131–36

Leyens, J. Ph., Fiske, S. T. 1992. Impression formation: something old, something new, and even something borrowed. See Devine et al 1992. In press

Leyens, J. Ph., Yzerbyt, V. Y., Schadron, G. 1992. The social judgeability approach to stereotypes. *Eur. Rev. Soc. Psychol.* 3. In press

Linville, P. W., Salovey, P., Fischer, G. W. 1989. Perceived distributions of the characteristics of in-group and out-group members: empirical evidence and a computer simulation. *J. Pers. Soc. Psychol.* 57:165–88

Lord, C. G., Saenz, D. S. 1985. Memory deficits and memory surfeits: differential cognitive consequences of tokenism for tokens and observers. *J. Pers. Soc. Psychol.* 49:918–26

Lupfer, M. B., Hutcherson, H. W., Clark, L. F. 1990. Impact of context on spontaneous trait and situational attributions. *J. Pers. Soc. Psychol.* 58:239–49

Lynch, J. G., Ofir, C. 1989. Effects of cue consistency and value on base-rate utilization. *J. Pers. Soc. Psychol.* 56:170–81

Maass, A., Salvi, D., Arcuri, L., Semin, G. 1989. Language use in intergroup contexts: the linguistic intergroup bias. *J. Pers. Soc. Psychol.* 57:981–93

Maass, A., Schaller, M. 1991. Intergroup biases and the cognitive dynamics of stereotype formation. *Eur. Rev. Soc. Psychol.* 2:189–209

Mackie, D. M., Allison, S. T., Worth, L. T., Asuncion, A. G. 1992. The generalization of outcome-biased counter-stereotypic inferences. *J. Exp. Soc. Psychol.* 28:43–64

Mackie, D. M., Worth, L. T. 1989. Differential recall of subcategory information about in-group and out-group members. *Pers. Soc. Psychol. Bull.* 15:401–13

Macrae, C. N., Shepherd, J. W. 1991. Categorical effects on attributional inferences: a response-time analysis. *Br. J. Soc. Psychol.* 30:235–45

Maheswaran, D., Chaiken, S. 1991. Promoting systematic processing in low-motivation settings: effect of incongruent information on processing and judgment. *J. Pers. Soc. Psychol.* 61:13–25

Malloy, T. E., Albright, L. 1990. Interpersonal perception in a social context. *J. Pers. Soc. Psychol.* 58:419–28

Manis, M., Nelson, T. F., Biernat, M. 1991. Comparison and expectancy processes in human judgement. *J. Pers. Soc. Psychol.* 61:203–11

Marsh, K. L., Weary, G. 1989. Depression and attributional complexity. *Pers. Soc. Psychol. Bull.* 15:325–36

Martin, L. L., Achee, J. W. 1992. Beyond accessibility: the role of processing objectives in judgment. See Martin & Tesser 1992. In press

Martin, L. L., Crelia, R. A., Seta, J. J. 1990. Assimilation and contrast as a function of people's willingness and ability to expend effort in forming an impression. *J. Pers. Soc. Psychol.* 59:27–37

Martin, L. L., Tesser, A., eds. 1992. *The Construction of Social Judgment.* Hillsdale: Erlbaum. In press

Martin, L. L., Tesser, A. 1989. Toward a motivational and structural theory of ruminative thought. See Uleman & Bargh 1989, pp. 306–26

Martin, L. L., Tesser, A., McIntosh, W. D. 1992. Wanting but not having: the effects of unattained goals on thoughts and feelings. See Wegner & Pennebaker 1992. In press

Matheson, K., Holmes, J. G., Kristiansen, C. M. 1991. Observational goals and the integration of trait perceptions and behavior: behavioral prediction versus impression formation. *J. Exp. Soc. Psychol.* 27:138–60

McCann, C. D., Higgins, E. T., Fondacaro, R. A. 1991. Primacy and recency in communication and self-persuasion: how successive audiences and multiple encodings influence subsequent evaluative judgments. *Soc. Cognit.* 9:47–66

McCrae, R. R., Costa, P. T. 1989. The structure of interpersonal traits: Wiggins's circumplex and the five-factor model. *J. Pers. Soc. Psychol.* 56:586–95

McDonald, J. 1990. Some situational determinants of hypothesis-testing strategies. *J. Exp. Soc. Psychol.* 26:255–74

McGraw, K. M., Pinney, N. 1990. The effects of general and domain-specific expertise on political memory and judgment. *Soc. Cognit.* 8:9–30

McKenzie-Mohr, D., Zanna, M. P. 1990. Treating women as sexual objects: look to the (gender schematic) male who has viewed pornography. *Pers. Soc. Psychol. Bull.* 16:296–308

Millar, M. G., Tesser, A. 1992. The role of beliefs and feelings in guiding behavior: the mis-match model. See Martin & Tesser 1992. In press

Miller, D. T., Gunasegaram, S. 1990. Temporal order and the perceived mutability of events: implications for blame assignment. *J. Pers. Soc. Psychol.* 59:1111–18

Miller, D. T., Taylor, B., Buck, M. L. 1991. Gender gaps: who needs to be explained? *J. Pers. Soc. Psychol.* 61:5–12

Miller, D. T., Turnbull, W., McFarland, C. 1989. When a coincidence is suspicious: the role of mental stimulation. *J. Pers. Soc. Psychol.* 57:581–89

Miller, J. G. 1984. Culture and the development of everyday social explanation. *J. Pers. Soc. Psychol.* 46:961–78

Mischel, W. 1990. Personality dispositions revisited and revised: a view after three decades. See Pervin 1990, pp. 111–34

Mogg, K., Mathews, A., Bird, C., Macgregor-Morris, R. 1990. Effects of stress and anxiety on the processing of threat stimuli. *J. Pers. Soc. Psychol.* 59:1230–37

Moskowitz, D. S. 1990. Convergence of self-reports and independent observers: dominance and friendliness. *J. Pers. Soc. Psychol.* 58:1096–106

Moskowitz, G. B., Roman, R. J. 1992. Spontaneous trait inferences as self–generated primes: implications for conscious social judgment. *J. Pers. Soc. Psychol.* 62:728-38

Mullen, B. 1991. Group composition, salience, and cognitive representations: the phenomenology of being in a group. *J. Exp. Soc. Psychol.* 27:297–323

Mullen, B., Hu, L. 1988. Social projection as a function of cognitive mechanisms: two meta-analytic integrations. *Brit. J. Soc. Psychol.* 27:333-356

Mullen, B., Salas, E., Driskell, J. E. 1989. Salience, motivation, and artifact as contributions to the relation between participation rate and leadership. *J. Exp. Soc. Psychol.* 25:545–59

Mullen, B., Brown, R., Smith, C. 1992. In-group bias as a function of salience, relevance, and status: an integration. *Eur. J. Soc. Psychol.* 22:103–22

Mullen, B., Copper, C. 1989. The privileged position of person categories: a comment on Sedikides and Ostrom. *Soc. Cognit.* 7:373–88

Mullen, B., Hu, L. 1989. Perceptions of ingroup and outgroup variability: a meta-analytic integration. *Basic Appl. Soc. Psychol.* 10:233–52

Mullen, B., Johnson, C. 1990. Distinctiveness-based illusory correlations and stereotyping: a meta-analytic integration. *Br. J. Soc. Psychol.* 29:11–28

Nelson, T. E., Biernat, M. R., Manis, M. 1990. Everyday base rates (sex stereotypes): potent and resilient. *J. Pers. Soc. Psychol.* 59:664–75

Neuberg, S. L. 1989. The goal of forming accurate impressions during social interactions: attenuating the impact of negative expectancies. *J. Pers. Soc. Psychol.* 56:374–86

Neuberg, S. L. 1992. Stereotypes, prejudice, and expectancy confirmation. See Zanna & Olson 1992. In press

Neuberg, S. L., Fiske, S. T. 1987. Motivational influences on impression formation: outcome dependency, accuracy-driven attention, and individuating processes. *J. Pers. Soc. Psychol.* 53:431-44

Newman, L. S. 1991. Why are traits inferred spontaneously? A developmental approach. *Soc. Cognit.* 9:221–53

Newman, L. S., Uleman, J. S. 1990. Assimilation and contrast effects in spontaneous trait inference. *Pers. Soc. Psychol. Bull.* 16:224–40

Newman, L. S., Uleman, J. S. 1989. Spontaneous trait inference. See Uleman & Bargh 1989, pp. 155–88

Nisbett, R. E., Smith, M. 1989. Predicting interpersonal attraction from small samples: a reanalysis of Newcomb's acquaintance study. *Soc. Cognit.* 7:67–73

Oakes, P. J., Turner, J. C. 1990. Is limited information processing capacity the cause of social stereotyping? *Eur. Rev. Soc. Psychol.* 1:112–35

Oakes, P. J., Turner, J. C., Hasalm, A. 1991. Perceiving people as group members: the role of fit in the salience of social categorizations. *Br. J. Soc. Psychol.* 30:125–44

Osborne, R. E., Gilbert, D. T. 1992. The preoccupational hazards of social life. *J. Pers. Soc. Psychol.* 62:219–28

Park, B., Flink, C. 1989. A social relations

analysis of agreement in liking judgments. *J. Pers. Soc. Psychol.* 56:506–18

Park, B., Judd, C. M. 1989. Agreement on initial impressions: differences due to perceivers, trait dimensions, and target behaviors. *J. Pers. Soc. Psychol.* 56:493–505

Park, B., Judd, C. M. 1990. Measures and models of perceived group variability. *J. Pers. Soc. Psychol.* 59:173–91

Park, B., Judd, C. M., Ryan, C. S. 1991. Social categorization and the representation of variability information. *Eur. Rev. Soc. Psychol.* 2:211–45

Paunonen, S. V. 1989. Consensus in personality judgments: moderating effects of target-rater acquaintanceship and behavior observability. *J. Pers. Soc. Psychol.* 56:823–33

Paunonen, S. V. 1991. On the accuracy of ratings of personality by strangers. *J. Pers. Soc. Psychol.* 61:471–77

Pavelchak, M. A. 1989. Piecemeal and category-based evaluation: an idiographic analysis. *J. Pers. Soc. Psychol.* 56:354–63

Peabody, D., Goldberg, L. R. 1989. Some determinants of factor structures from personality-trait descriptors. *J. Pers. Soc. Psychol.* 57:552–67

Peeters, G. 1991. Evaluative inference in social cognition: the roles of direct versus indirect evaluation and positive-negative asymmetry. *Eur. J. Soc. Psychol.* 21:131–46

Peeters, G., Czapinski, J. 1990. Positive-negative asymmetry in evaluations: the distinction between affective and informational negativity effects. *Eur. Rev. Soc. Psychol.* 1:33–60

Pennebaker, J. W. 1989a. Confession, inhibition, and disease. *Adv. Exp. Soc. Psychol.* 22:211–44

Pennebaker, J. W. 1989b. *Opening Up: The Healing Power of Confiding in Others.* New York: William Morrow and Company, Inc. 249 pp.

Pennington, N., Hastie, R. 1991. A cognitive theory of juror decision making: the story model. *Cardozo Law Rev.* 13:5001–39.

Perdue, C. W., Gurtman, M. B. 1990. Evidence for the automaticity of ageism. *J. Exp. Soc. Psychol.* 26:199–216

Pervin, L. ed. 1989. *Goal Concepts in Personality and Social Psychology.* New Jersey: Erlbaum

Pervin, L. ed. 1990. *Handbook of Personality: Theory and Research.* New York: Guilford Press

Petty, R. E., Cacioppo, J. T. 1986. The elaboration likelihood model of persuasion. *Adv. Exp. Soc. Psychol.* 19:123–205

Philippot, P., Schwarz, N., Carrera, P., De Vries, N., Van Yperen, N. W. 1991. Differential effects of priming at the encoding and judgment stage. *Eur. J. Soc. Psychol.* 21:293–302

Pittman, T. S., D'Agostino, P. R. 1989. Motivation and cognition: control deprivation and the nature of subsequent information processing. *J. Exp. Soc. Psychol.* 25:465–80

Pittman, T. S., Heller, J. F. 1987. Social motivation. *Annu. Rev. Psychol.* 38:461–89

Pratto, F., Bargh, J. A. 1991. Stereotyping based on apparently individuating information: trait and global components of sex stereotypes under attention overload. *J. Exp. Soc. Psychol.* 27:26–47

Pratto, F., John, O. P. 1991. Automatic vigilance: the attention-grabbing power of negative social information. *J. Pers. Soc. Psychol.* 61:380–91

Raudenbush, S. W. 1984. Magnitude of teacher expectancy effects on pupil IQ as a function of the credibility of expectancy induction: a synthesis of findings from 18 experiments. *J. Ed. Psychol.* 76:85–97

Read, S. J., Druian, P. R., Miller, L. C. 1989. The role of causal sequence in the meaning of actions. *Br. J. Soc. Psychol.* 28:341–51

Read, S. J., Jones, D. K., Miller, L. C. 1990. Traits as goal-based categories: the importance of goals in the coherence of dispositional categories. *J. Pers. Soc. Psychol.* 58:1048–61

Read, S. J., Miller, L. C. 1989. Inter-personalism: toward a goal-based theory of persons in relationships. See Pervin 1989, pp. 412–72

Reeder, G. D., Pryor, J. B., Wojciszke, B. 1992. Trait behavior relations in social information processing. See Semin & Fiedler 1992. In press

Riley, T., Fiske, S. T. 1991. Interdependence and the social context of impression formation. *Eur. Bull. Cognit. Psychol.* 11:173–92

Rojahn, K., Pettigrew, T. F. 1992. Memory for schema-relevant information: a meta-analytic resolution. *Brit. J. Soc. Psychol.* 31:81–109

Rosenthal, R. 1991. Teacher expectancy effects: a brief update 25 years after the pygmalion experiment. *J. Res. Educ.* 1:3–12

Ross, L., Nisbett, R. E. 1991. *The Person and the Situation: Perspectives of Social Psychology.* New York: McGraw-Hill. 286 pp.

Ross, M., Holmberg, D. 1992. Do wives have more vivid memories than their husbands of events in their relationships? *J. Soc. Pers. Relat.* In press

Ruble, D. N. 1993. A phase model of transitions: cognitive and motivational consequences. *Adv. Exp. Soc. Psychol.* 26: In press

Ruble, D. N., Stangor, C. 1986. Stalking the elusive schema: insights from developmental and social-psychological analyses of gender schemas. *Soc. Cognit.* 4:227–61

Ruscher, J. B., Fiske, S. T. 1990. Interpersonal competition can cause individuating processes. *J. Pers. Soc. Psychol.* 58:832–43

Ruscher, J. B., Fiske, S. T., Miki, H., Van Manen, S. 1991. Individuating processes in competition: interpersonal versus intergroup. *Pers. Soc. Psychol. Bull.* 17:595-605

Saenz, D. S., Lord, C. G. 1989. Reversing roles: a cognitive strategy for undoing memory deficits associated with token status. *J. Pers. Soc. Psychol.* 56:698–708

Sanbonmatsu, D. M., Sansone, C., Kardes, F. R. 1991. Remembering less and inferring more: effects of time of judgment on inferences about unknown attributes. *J. Pers. Soc. Psychol.* 61:546–54

Sanitioso, R., Kunda, Z. 1991. Ducking the collection of costly evidence: motivated use of statistical heuristics. *J. Behav. Decision Making* 4:161–78

Schadron, G., Yzerbyt, V. Y. 1991. Social judgeability: another framework for the study of social inference. *Eur. Bull. Cog. Psychol.* 11:229–58

Schaller, M. 1991. Social categorization and the formation of group stereotypes: further evidence for biased information processing in the perception of group-behavior correlations. *Eur. J. Soc. Psychol.* 21:25–35

Schaller, M., Maass, A. 1989. Illusory correlation and social categorization: toward an integration of motivational and cognitive factors in stereotype formation. *J. Pers. Soc. Psychol.* 56:709–21

Schul, Y., Burnstein, E. 1990. Judging the typicality of an instance: should the category be accessed first? *J. Pers. Soc. Psychol.* 58:964–74

Schwarz, N., Bless, H. 1992. Constructing reality and its alternatives: an inclusion/exclusion model of assimilation and contrast effects in social judgement. See Martin & Tesser 1992. In press

Schwarz, N., Strack, F., Hilton, D., Naderer, G. 1991. Base rates, representativeness, and the logic of conversation: the contextual relevance of "irrelevant" information. *Soc. Cognit.* 9:67–84

Sedikides, C. 1990. Effects of fortuitously activated constructs versus activated communication goals on person impressions. *J. Pers. Soc. Psychol.* 58:397–408

Sedikides, C., Anderson, C. A. 1992. Causal explanations of defection: a knowledge structure approach. *Pers. Soc. Psychol. Bull.* 18:420–29

Sedikides, C., Devine, P. G., Fuhrman, R. W. 1991. Social perception in multitarget settings: effects of motivated encoding strategies. *Pers. Soc. Psychol. Bull.* 17:625–32

Sedikides, C., Ostrom, T. M. 1988. Are person categories used when organizing information about unfamiliar sets of persons? *Soc. Cognit.* 6:252–67

Sedikides, C., Ostrom, T. M. 1990. Persons as privileged categories: a rejoinder to Mullen and Copper. *Soc. Cognit.* 8:229–40

Sedikides, C., Skowronski, J. J. 1991. The law of cognitive structure activation. *Psychol. Inquiry* 2:169–84

Semin, G. R. 1989. The contribution of linguistic factors to attribute inferences and semantic similarity judgements. *Eur. J. Soc. Psychol.* 19:85–100

Semin, G., Fiedler, K., eds. 1992. *Language and Social Cognition.* London/New York: Sage Publications. In press

Semin, G. R., Fiedler, K. 1991. The linguistic category model, its bases, applications and range. *Eur. Rev. Soc. Psychol.* 2:1–30

Semin, G. R., Rubini, M. 1990. Unfolding the concept of person by verbal abuse. *Eur. J. Soc. Psychol.* 20:463–74

Sherman, S. J., Hamilton, D. L., Roskos-Ewoldsen, D. R. 1989. Attenuation of illusory correlation. *Pers. Soc. Psychol. Bull.* 15:559–71

Sherman, S. J., Mackie, D. M., Driscoll, D. M. 1990. Priming and the differential use of dimensions in evaluation. *Pers. Soc. Psychol. Bull.* 16:405–18

Shoda, Y., Mischel, W., Wright, J. C. 1989. Intuitive interactionism in person perception: effects of situation-behavior relations on dispositional judgments. *J. Pers. Soc. Psychol.* 56:41–53

Simon, B., Pettigrew, T. F. 1990. Social identity and perceived group homogeneity: evidence for the ingroup homogeneity effect. *Eur. J. Soc. Psychol.* 20:269–86

Singer, J. L. 1985. Transference and the human condition: a cognitive-affective perspective. *Psychoanal. Psychol.* 2:189–219

Skowronski, J. J., Betz, A. L., Thompson, C. P., Shannon, L. 1991. Social memory in everyday life: recall of self-events and other-events. *J. Pers. Soc. Psychol.* 60:831–43

Skowronski, J. J., Carlston, D. E. 1989. Negativity and extremity biases in impression formation: a review of explanations. *Psychol. Bull.* 105:131–42

Smith, E. R. 1990. Content and process specificity in the effects of prior experiences. *Adv. Soc. Cognit.* 3:1–60

Smith, E. R. 1991. Illusory correlation in a simulated exemplar-based memory. *J. Exp. Soc. Psychol.* 27:107–23

Smith, E. R., Stewart, T. L., Buttram, R. T. 1992. Inferring a trait from a behavior has long-term, highly specific effects. *J. Pers. Soc. Psychol.* 62:753–59

Smith, E. R., Zárate, M. A. 1990. Exemplar and prototype use in social categorization. *Soc. Cognit.* 8:243–62

Smith, E. R., Zárate, M. A. 1992. Exemplar-based model of social judgement. *Psychol. Rev.* 99:3–21

Snodgrass, S. E. 1992. Further effects of role versus gender on interpersonal sensitivity. *J. Pers. Soc. Psychol.* 62:154–58

Snyder, M. 1992. Motivational foundations of behavioral confirmation. *Adv. Exp. Soc. Psychol.* 25:67–114

Srull, T. K., Wyer, R. S., Jr. eds. 1988. *Advances in Social Cognition,* Vol. 1. Hillsdale, NJ: Erlbaum

Srull, T. K., Wyer, R. S. 1989. Person memory and judgment. *Psychol. Rev.* 96:58–83

Stangor, C., Duan, C. 1991. Effects of multiple task demands upon memory for information about social groups. *J. Exp. Soc. Psychol.* 27:357–78

Stangor, C., Ford, T. E. 1992. Accuracy and expectancy-confirming processing orientations and the development of stereotypes and prejudice. *Eur. Rev. Soc. Psychol.* 3. In press

Stangor, C., Lynch, L., Duan, C., Glass, B. 1992. Categorization of individuals on the basis of multiple social features. *J. Pers. Soc. Psychol.* 62:207–18

Stangor, C., McMillan, D. 1992. Memory for expectancy-congruent and expectancy-incongruent information: a review of the social and social developmental literatures. *Psychol. Bull.* 111:42–61

Stangor, C., Ruble, D. 1989. Strength of expectancies and memory for social information: What we remember depends on how much we know. *J. Exp. Soc. Psychol.* 25:18–35

Stangor, C., Sullivan, L. A., Ford, T. E. 1991. Affective and cognitive determinants of prejudice. *Soc. Cognit.* 9:359–80

Stinson, L., Ickes, W. 1992. Empathic accuracy in the interactions of male friends versus male strangers. *J. Pers. Soc. Psychol.* In press

Sullins, E. S. 1989. Perceptual salience as a function of nonverbal expressiveness. *Pers. Soc. Psychol. Bull.* 15:584–95

Swann, W. B. Jr. 1984. Quest for accuracy in person perception: a matter of pragmatics. *Psychol. Rev.* 91:457–77

Swim, J., Borgida, E., Maruyama, G., Myers, D. G. 1989. Joan McKay versus John McKay: do gender stereotypes bias evaluations? *Psychol. Bull.* 105:409–29

Taylor, S. E. 1991. Asymmetrical effects of positive and negative events: the mobilization-minimization hypothesis. *Psychol. Bull.* 110:67–85

Taylor, S. E. 1989. *Positive Illusions: Creative Self-Deception and the Healthy Mind.* New York: Basic Books. 301 pp.

Taylor, S. E., Schneider, S. K. 1989. Coping and the simulation of events. *Soc. Cognit.* 7:174–94

Tesser, A., Martin, L., Mendolia, M. 1992. The role of thought in changing attitude strength. In *Attitude Strength: Antecedents and Consequences,* ed. R. E. Petty, J. A. Krosnick. Hillsdale, NJ: Erlbaum. In press

Tesser, A., Pilkington, C. J., McIntosh, W. D. 1989. Self-evaluation maintenance and the mediational role of emotion: the perception of friends and strangers. *J. Pers. Soc. Psychol.* 57:442–56

Tetlock, P. E. 1991. An alternative metaphor in the study of judgment and choice: people as politicians. *Theor. Psychol.* 1:451–75

Tetlock, P. E., Boettger, R. 1989. Accountability: a social magnifier of the dilution effect. *J. Pers. Soc. Psychol.* 57:388–98

Tetlock, P. E., Skitka, L., Boettger, R. 1989. Social and cognitive strategies for coping with accountability: conformity, complexity, and bolstering. *J. Pers. Soc. Psychol.* 57:632–40

Trapnell, P. D., Wiggins, J. S. 1990. Extension of the interpersonal adjective scales to include the big five dimensions of personality. *J. Pers. Soc. Psychol.* 59:781–90

Trzebinski, J. 1989. The role of goal categories in the representation of social knowledge. See Pervin 1989, pp. 363–411

Uleman, J. S. 1989. A framework for thinking intentionally about unintended thought. See Uleman & Bargh 1989, pp. 425–49

Uleman, J. S., Bargh, J. A., ed. 1989. *Unintended Thought.* New York: Guilford. 481 pp.

Uleman, J. S., Newman, L., Winter, L. 1992. Can personality traits be inferred automatically? Spontaneous inferences require cognitive capacity at encoding. *Consciousness Cognit.* 1:77–90

Vallone, R. P., Lin, S., Ross, L., Griffin, D. W. 1990. Overconfident prediction of future actions and outcomes by self and others. *J. Pers. Soc. Psychol.* 58:582–92

Van der Kloot, W. A., Willemsen, T. M. 1991. The measurement, representation and predictive use of implicit theories. *Eur. Bull. Cognit. Psychol.* 11:137–53

Van Mechelen, I. 1991. Symptom and diagnosis inference based on implicit theories of psychopathology: a review. *Eur. Bull. Cognit. Psychol.* 11:155–71

Vanbeselaere, N. 1991. The different effects of simple and crossed categorizations: a result of the category differentiation process or of differential category salience. *Eur. Rev. Soc. Psychol.* 2:248–78

Watson, D. 1989. Strangers' ratings of the five robust personality factors: evidence of a surprising convergence with self-report. *J. Pers. Soc. Psychol.* 57:120–28

Weary, G. 1992. Depression, control motivation, and the processing of information about others. See Weary et al 1992. In press

Weary, G., Gleicher, F., Marsh, K., eds. 1992. *Control Motivation and Social Cognition.* New York: Springer-Verlag. In press

Wegner, D. M. 1989. *White Bears and Other Unwanted Thoughts: Suppression, Obsession, and the Psychology of Mental Control.* New York: Viking. 207 pp.

Wegner, D. M., Erber, R. 1992. Social foundations of mental control. See Wegner & Pennebaker 1992. In press

Wegner, D. M., Pennebaker, J. W., eds. 1992. *Handbook of Mental Control.* Englewood Cliffs, NJ: Prentice-Hall. In press

Wegner, D. M., Erber, R., Raymond, P. 1991. Transactive memory in close relationships. *J. Pers. Soc. Psychol.* 61:923–29

Wegner, D. M., Schneider, D. J. 1989. Mental control: the war of the ghosts in the machine. See Uleman & Bargh 1989, pp. 287–305

Wegner, D. M., Shortt, J. W., Blake, A. W., Page, M. S. 1990. The suppression of exciting thoughts. *J. Pers. Soc. Psychol.* 58:409–18

Weisz, C., Jones, E. E. 1992. Expectancy disconfirmation and dispositional inference: latent strength of target-based and category-based expectancies. *Pers. Soc. Psychol. Bull.* In press

Wells, G. L., Gavanski, I. 1989. Mental simulation of causality. *J. Pers. Soc. Psychol.* 56:161–69

Wenzlaff, R. M., Klein, S. B., Wegner, D. M. 1991. The role of thought suppression in the bonding of thought and mood. *J. Pers. Soc. Psychol.* 60:500–8

Wicklund, R. A., Braun, O. L. 1990. Creating consistency among pairs of traits: a bridge from social psychology to trait psychology. *J. Exp. Soc. Psychol.* 26:545–58

Wiggins, J. S., Pincus, A. L. 1992. Personality: structure and assessment. *Annu. Rev. Psychol.* 43:473–504

Wilder, D. A., Shapiro, P. 1989a. Effects of anxiety on impression formation in a group context: an anxiety-assimilation hypothesis. *J. Exp. Soc. Psychol.* 25:481–99

Wilder, D. A., Shapiro, P. N. 1989b. Role of competition-induced anxiety in limiting the beneficial impact of positive behavior by an out-group member. *J. Pers. Soc. Psychol.* 56:60–69

Wilder, D. A., Shapiro, P. N. 1991. Facilitation of outgroup stereotypes by enhanced ingroup identity. *J. Exp. Soc. Psychol.* 27:431–52

Wilson, T. D., Schooler, J. W. 1991. Thinking too much: introspection can reduce the quality of preferences and decisions. *J. Pers. Soc. Psychol.* 60:181–92

Wyer, R. S., Budesheim, T. L., Lambert, A. J. 1990. Cognitive representation of conversations about persons. *J. Pers. Soc. Psychol.* 2:218–38

Wyer, R. S., Lambert, A. J. 1992. The role of trait constructs in person perception: an historical perspective. See Devine et al 1992. In press

Wyer, R. S., Lambert, A. J., Budesheim, T. L., Gruenfeld, D. H. 1992. Theory and research on person impression formation: a look to the future. See Martin & Tesser 1992. In press

Yang, K., Bond, M. H. 1990. Exploring implicit personality theories with indigenous or imported constructs: the Chinese case. *J. Pers. Soc. Psychol.* 58:1087–95

Yzerbyt, V. Y., Leyens, J. Ph. 1991. Requesting information to form an impression: the influence of valence and confirmatory status. *J. Exp. Soc. Psychol.* 27:337–56

Zaller, J. 1990. Political awareness, elite opinion leadership, and the mass survey response. *Soc. Cognit.* 8:125–53

Zanna, M. P., Olson, J. M., eds. *Psychology of Prejudice: The Ontario Symposium*, Vol. 7. New Jersey: Erlbaum. In press

Zárate, M. A., Smith, E. R. 1990. Person categorization and stereotyping. *Soc. Cognit.* 2:161–85

Zebrowitz, L. A. 1990. *Social Perception.* Pacific Grove, CA: Brooks/Cole

Zebrowitz, L. A., Kendall-Tackett, K., Fafel, J. 1991a. The influence of children's facial maturity on parental expectations and punishments. *J. Exp. Child Psychol.* 52:221–38

Zebrowitz, L. A., McDonald, S. M. 1991. The impact of litigants' babyfacedness and attractiveness on adjudications in small claims courts. *Law Hum. Behav.* 15:603–23

Zebrowitz, L. A., Montepare, J. M. 1991. Impressions of babyfaced males and females across the lifespan. *Dev. Psychol.* In press

Zebrowitz, L. A., Tenenbaum, D. R., Goldstein, L. H. 1991b. The impact of job applicants' facial maturity, gender, and academic achievement on hiring recommendations. *J. Appl. Soc. Psychol.* 21:525–48

Zuroff, D. C. 1989. Judgments of frequency of social stimuli: how schematic is person memory? *J. Pers. Soc. Psychol.* 56:890–98

Annu. Rev. Psychol. 1993. 44:195–229

ORGANIZATIONAL BEHAVIOR: Linking Individuals and Groups to Organizational Contexts

Richard T. Mowday

Graduate School of Management, University of Oregon, Eugene, Oregon 97403-1208

Robert I. Sutton

Department of Industrial Engineering and Engineering Management, Stanford University, Stanford, California 94305

KEYWORDS: micro OB, macro OB, organizational psychology

CONTENTS

THE ORGANIZATIONAL CONTEXT AS AN INFLUENCE ON GROUPS AND
     INDIVIDUALS 198
   Context as Opportunity and Constraint 198
   Context as a Distal or Proximate Influence 201
   Context as Similar and Dissimilar 205
WHEN CONTEXTS HAVE MINIMAL INFLUENCE 208
INDIVIDUALS AND GROUPS AS INFLUENCES ON ORGANIZATIONAL
     CONTEXTS.. 209
   Powerful Individuals as an Influence on Organizations 210
   Powerful Groups as an Influence on Organizations 215
   Aggregate Member Thoughts, Feelings, and Behaviors as Influences on
    Organizations 215
THE INTERACTIONS OF INDIVIDUALS AND GROUPS WITH THEIR
     ORGANIZATIONAL CONTEXTS 217
   The Homeless 218
   Air Disaster 218
   Nuclear Power Plant 219
HOW CAN WE PUT ORGANIZATIONS BACK INTO ORGANIZATIONAL
     BEHAVIOR? 220
   Methodological Implications 220
   Substantive Implications 222

195

0066-4308/93/0201-0195$02.00

Charles O'Reilly's (1991) *Annual Review of Psychology* chapter concluded that the field of micro organizational behavior (OB) was in a fallow period. His review of work published between 1987 and early 1990 focused on research pertinent to the same five areas treated in Terry Mitchell's (1979) review: motivation, work attitudes, job design, turnover and absenteeism, and leadership. O'Reilly (1991:431) used Mitchell's categories so that he could make judgments about "what, if anything, [had] changed in the intervening decade." O'Reilly (1991) found that these five areas remained the most frequently researched in micro OB and that much of the work in this field had "reached a point of diminishing returns" (O'Reilly 1991:431). Instead of the lively conceptual debates evident in the 1970s, he discovered that most studies focused on subtle conceptual refinements, on determining the boundary conditions for well-established theories, and on methodological issues. As a result, he concluded that although useful research was being done, the intellectual excitement he observed in recent work in macro organizational behavior was not evident on the micro side.

This review considers research in organizational behavior through early 1992, focusing on work since 1990. Our review of the five traditional areas covered in O'Reilly's (1991) chapter also revealed that novelty and intellectual excitement were largely absent. Most papers in these areas continued to offer incremental conceptual advances or focused on methodological rather than conceptual issues.

O'Reilly (1991) did conclude, however, there was cause for optimism when one looked beyond the five traditional areas at work that linked micro and macro organizational behavior. He found that, although modest in volume compared to the traditional areas, the most exciting new research considered how the organizational context shaped individual and group behavior. The field of micro organizational behavior has traditionally been dominated by a strong contextual focus, notably in the areas of job design and leadership. But O'Reilly's (1991) assertions, along with Cappelli & Sherer's (1991) recent review, indicate that much of the field has moved away from a contextual focus as other research areas have gained prominence.

Organizational behavior researchers have relied more heavily on cognitive approaches in recent years. Cappelli & Sherer (1991:97) asserted that "OB has systematically abandoned contextual arguments in order to remain consistent with theoretical developments in the field of psychology," a trend also noted in Ilgen & Klein's (1988) *Annual Review of Psychology* chapter. The use of cognitive approaches has opened fruitful new research streams. Because social context is rarely considered in such work, however, or is portrayed in a simplified way, much research published in organizational behavior journals no longer reflects the field's distinctive competence. We agree with Cappelli & Sherer's (1991:97) assertion that "What is unique about behavior in organizations is presumably that being in the organization—the context of the organization—somehow shapes behavior, and it is impossible to explore that uniqueness without an explicit consideration of the context." This trend has diverted attention from research on how individuals shape the organizational context, another aspect of the field's distinctive competence (Schneider 1987; Staw & Sutton 1992). Thus, a preoccupation with cognitive processes can blur the distinction between organizational behavior and psychology. At its worst, this preoccupation can lead to theory and research that portrays organization members as cognitive stick figures whose behavior is unaffected by emotions or interactions with subordinates, peers, or superiors.

There is also a key methodological difference between the contextual research O'Reilly (1991) found exciting and the traditional approach to studying organizational contexts. Cappelli & Sherer (1991) point out that organizational researchers have typically used perceptual measures of contextual variables as correlates of self-reported attitudes and intentions. A distressingly large proportion of the contextual research reviewed in Cummings's (1982) chapter (and of other research that has appeared since) used such designs and thus likely reported relationships inflated by correlated measurement error. Unfortunately, it is difficult to know whether such observed relationships tell us more about the context or about the respondent. The studies we found more convincing and interesting measured the context more directly, either by using samples with systematic variation in context features, measuring contexts objectively, or collecting perceptions of the context from a set of informants who were separate from the respondents reporting reactions to the context. Other interesting studies relied on compelling qualitative data to induce new theory linking individuals and groups to their organizational contexts.

This perspective led us to focus this chapter outside the traditional five areas and on studies unlikely to generate inflated relationships between contextual variables and group and individual variables. We also reviewed several interdisciplinary and disciplinary journals from areas such as sociology and anthropology that are outside the mainstream of micro organizational behavior. We found much work that relied partly or wholly on psychological perspectives to explain how the organizational context influences individuals and groups. Many of these papers used creative approaches to build and test interesting new theories. We also found much promising theory and research on how individuals and groups influence organizational contexts. Thus, when we turned our attention to work on the organizational context as a cause and consequence of behavior in organizations, we found the intellectual excitement that O'Reilly (1991) and others felt the field had lost.

As a result, this chapter is broader in scope and more eclectic—in both method and theory—than prior chapters. We do not provide a comprehensive listing of all relevant articles published in organizational behavior between 1990 and 1992 because doing so would require listing hundreds of citations without discussing any in sufficient depth. Instead, following Frost & Stablein's (1992) book, *Doing Exemplary Research,* we focus on a limited number of publications that illustrate desirable standards for building and testing theory about the links between individuals and groups and their organizational contexts.

We proceed by summarizing exemplary research on the organizational context as an influence on groups and individuals. We next provide a briefer review of exemplary work on how individuals and groups influence the organizational context. Theory building and research of this kind uses states and processes within individuals and groups to explain organizational outcomes and processes. We then review three interesting studies that illustrate reciprocal influences between individuals and groups and their organizational contexts. We conclude by considering the implications of taking research on organizational context more seriously.

THE ORGANIZATIONAL CONTEXT AS AN INFLUENCE ON GROUPS AND INDIVIDUALS

This section of our review is organized around three perspectives that illustrate how the context can influence individuals and groups. Few precise definitions of the organizational context are evident in the literature. But the reviews by Cappelli & Sherer (1991) and Cummings (1981) suggest that the context encompasses stimuli and phenomena that surround and thus exist in the environment external to the individual, most often at a different level of analysis. Consistent with this view, previous reviews of the context take a substantive approach that emphasizes how specific context features such as internal labor markets and technology influence individual outcomes.

Instead of organizing our review around specific contextual variables, we identify three perspectives that explicate how the organizational context is presented to and is experienced by individuals and groups. These perspectives build on the earlier work of psychologists (Mischel 1977), sociologists (Blau 1987; Huber 1990) and organizational behavior researchers (Pfeffer 1991; Staw 1985). First, we review work that portrays the context as an opportunity or a constraint on behavior. Second, we consider contextual features as distal or proximate stimuli. Third, we examine research that considers the similarity or dissimilarity between individuals and groups and features of their organizational context.

Context as Opportunity and Constraint

Sociologists have portrayed context in terms of the opportunities and constraints it presents to individuals and groups (Blau 1987; Huber 1990). Huber's (1990:2) presidential address to the American Sociological Association issued this challenge: "Macrotheory must account for patterns of social relations not on the basis of motives but on the basis of external constraints and opportunities for social relations created by population composition and the structure of positions in the social environment."

Organizational behavior researchers have relied more heavily on individual characteristics such as motives and needs to explain behavior than on contextual dimensions such as opportunity and constraint. Many of us are not accustomed to thinking about our work in terms of the latter dimensions, but the distinction between opportunities and constraints is often implicit in micro organizational behavior. Job-enrichment techniques (Hackman & Oldham 1980), for instance, can be viewed as methods for enhancing individual and group opportunities. In contrast, goal setting (Locke & Latham 1990) can be viewed as a control device that directs and thus constrains behavior (Staw & Boettger 1990). Several recent studies illustrate the value of distinguishing between opportunity and constraint.

OPPORTUNITY   Hassard & Porter's (1990) analysis of the role eunuchs played in administering early civilizations demonstrates how the interpretation of behavior can change when the context is viewed as an opportunity rather than a constraint. Castration had previously been described as a technique used by those in power to insure civil servants' loyalty and commitment—as a control mechanism that eliminated both family feelings and offspring whose interests might compete with the emperor's. Hassard & Porter (1990) provide an alternative interpretation based on the simple observation that castration was often voluntary, particularly during the Chinese Ming Dynasty. Hassard & Porter (1990) point out that voluntary castration provided otherwise unavailable opportunities for upward mobility. In a society where an expensive education provided the usual entré to the Confucian civil service, otherwise capable poor men who became eunuchs could attain powerful positions and wealth as administrators, a group almost as powerful as Confucian scholars. Hassard & Porter gained insight by viewing as an opportunity a phenomenon commonly considered to be a constraint.

Staw & Boettger's (1990) work on task revision likewise benefits from using the distinction between opportunity and constraint as a research lens. Task revision occurs when a person's actions differ from the actions he or she is expected to take. Poor performance often results when people deviate from role expectations, but task revision may enhance performance when expectations are flawed. Staw & Boettger (1990) instructed students to revise a paragraph in a recruiting brochure for their business school. The paragraph contained inaccurate information about the school. In the experiment, (*a*) inaccurate information was either made salient or not, and (*b*) subjects were asked either generally to do their best or to achieve the specific goal of correcting grammar. Evidence of task revision was interpreted from the use of inaccurate information and inclusion of new and more accurate ideas. Students for whom the inaccurate information was made salient inserted more new ideas, and students in the "do your best" (versus specific goal) condition engaged in more task revision. Thus, the specific goal appeared to constrain role innovation. A second experiment determined, however, that this constraint depended on goal content. Task revision occurred more frequently when goals focused on information content and less often when goals focused attention on grammar. The researchers concluded that goal setting, because of its powerful effects on directing behavior, can be a constraint that reduces performance on improperly specified tasks.

A field experiment by Greenberg (1990) also illustrates how contextual changes can create opportunities that influence behavior. He monitored theft in two plants in a company that imposed a temporary 15% pay cut on employees. The pay cut was announced with a vague, incomplete, and impersonal explanation in one plant, a thorough and emotionally sensitive explanation in another plant. No pay cut was implemented in a third plant, which served as a control. Theft rates increased in both plants where pay cuts occurred, but dramatically so in the plant where the explanation was inadequate. Self-reported pay equity also decreased in the plant where an inadequate explanation was given, but not as much in the plant where an adequate explanation was given and not at all in the control plant. After pay was restored to previous levels, the theft rate and perceived inequity declined in the plant where an inadequate explanation was given. Thus, in a manner consistent with equity theory (Adams 1965), employees who experienced inequity saw theft as an opportunity to restore the imbalance created by the pay cut.

CONSTRAINT   Two ethnographic studies by Palmer (1990, 1991) focused on how the context in which people behave constrains their actions. Both studies focus on lobstermen in isolated fishing communities in Maine. Lobstermen fish for a "common property resource" under conditions where one person's good fortune comes at others' expense. Palmer studied deceptive communication among lobstermen who competed for this resource and studied cooperation in organizing the 1989 boat tie-up to combat falling lobster prices. Palmer (1990) predicted that deceptive communication concerning fishing conditions would be prevalent but found far less deception than expected. He attributed this unexpected finding to close social relationships in these small fishing communities. Deceptive communication had great potential cost because, if discovered, it could damage long-term familial and business relationships. Palmer concluded that trust was the only insurance against others' poaching one's traps. Thus, the social fabric of these small communities constrained behavior that might otherwise have been in the lobstermen's best interests.

Palmer's (1991) second study analyzed the organization of a boat tie-up to protest falling lobster prices. The context constrained organizing. Much successful organization occurred within fishing communities, but the physical and social distance between communities hampered coordination. Lobstermen had few acquaintances in other communities, and communication was hindered by boat radios that only transmitted short distances. Moreover, such barriers hampered efforts to end the tie-up after a price increase was negotiated.

Murnighan & Conlon's (1991) study of British string quartets also illustrates how context can constrain behavior. The authors documented how the task facing these quartets influenced the resolution of the group paradoxes identified by Smith & Berg (1987). These paradoxes, including leadership versus democracy and confrontation versus compromise, must be managed by the quartets within the constraints imposed by the group task of producing music. Interviews indicated that, compared to the less successful quartets, more successful quartets did not try to resolve—or even openly discuss—the conflicts inherent in their social context. Successful quartets avoided conflict by playing more than they talked during rehearsals—partly because, as one member put it, "We have a little saying in quartets—either we play or we fight" (Murnighan & Conlon 1991:177–78). Also, compared to less successful quartets, more successful quartets had implicit but well-established rules constraining talk about sensitive issues.

Rafaeli & Sutton's research on expressed emotion also shows how the context constrains behavior. Sutton & Rafaeli's (1988) initial study of 576 convenience stores found that, although corporate executives expected clerks to display positive emotions to all customers, this norm was followed less often during busy than during slow times. A context that presented clerks with numerous customers and long lines encouraged efficient processing of customers and thus constrained friendly displays. This finding was replicated in a sample of Israeli grocery store clerks (Rafaeli & Sutton 1990).

Sutton's (1991) qualitative study of bill collectors sheds further light on how the context constrains expressed emotion. He found that organizational norms encouraged collectors to convey urgency (arousal with a hint of irritation) to debtors. The organization supported these norms by selecting intense and slightly hostile new collectors, socializing new collectors to be urgent (and discouraging other expressions), and tying such expressive behavior to rewards and punishments. The general norm was constrained contingent on debtor demeanor, which was used as a cue about whether the urgent demeanor should be retained, modified, or replaced. For example, very anxious debtors were to be greeted more warmly. Sad, friendly, or indifferent debtors were to receive more irritable, even angry treatment. When the debtor was angry, collectors were expected to convey calm rather than urgency. Thus, the normative context, which included general and specific expectations, constrained which emotions were displayed.

Context as a Distal or Proximate Influence

Staw (1985) argued that the proximity between independent and dependent variables is a key dimension separating "flashy" and "controversial" studies from mundane studies. Claims about relationships between phenomena farther apart in distance or time are inherently more interesting, and sometimes harder to believe, than those about relationships between spatially or temporally more proximate phenomena.

Barley's (1990) study of how technical change influenced the radiology occupation illustrates different ways in which contextual proximity can shape our understanding of organizations. He studied how the introduction of new medical diagnostic technology (e.g. computed tomography scanning) changed role relationships in the radiology departments at two hospitals. The technology that altered relationships in radiology departments arose in the distal computer industry. In contrast, the interpersonal relationships that Barley (1990) analyzed were proximate. X-ray technicians trained in the old technology tended to interact among themselves rather than with technicians who operated the newer, more sophisticated machines. Thus contextual change occurring at a great distance from these organizations had profound effects on behavior within them.

The view that such "technically occasioned social change" influenced relationships between distant variables is also suggested by Barley's (1990:70) findings that such change created a

> series of reverberations that spread across levels of analysis much like ripples on the surface of a pond. When introduced into a work setting, new technologies initially modify tasks, skills, and other nonrelational aspects of roles. These modifications, in turn, shape role relations. Altered role relations either transform or buttress the social networks that constitute occupational and organizational structures. Ultimately, shifting networks should either sustain or modify institutions, since the latter represent blueprints for ongoing action.

Barley (1990) also documented that the change in technology had implications that spanned levels of analysis, ranging from the micro (individual skills and abilities) to the dyadic (interaction patterns), the departmental (structure), and the organizational (status structure).

Barley's study also illustrates the effects of temporal distance between variables. Computerized radiological technology was developed in the 1970s and slowly diffused into hospitals as machines and trained operators became available. A snapshot of radiology departments in the 1970s would have revealed that status, power, and expertise increased with radiologists' tenure. In contrast, a snapshot in the 1980s would have revealed the opposite pattern: Only newly trained radiologists and technologists were expert in the sophisticated diagnostic techniques that patients, doctors, and hospitals demanded. Barley's (1990) temporal view provides insight that a cross-sectional study at either point in time would have missed.

The dimensions of distance and time are further illustrated by other recent research on how context shapes behavior.

DISTANCE   Rafaeli's (1989) study of the dynamics among cashiers, customers, coworkers, and managers in Israeli grocery stores illustrates how the distance dimension helps to clarify contextual influences. Managers had the most legitimate influence over cashiers' behavior, with customers having little or no legitimate influence. Rafaeli (1989:256) argued, however, that customers were in a far better position to influence the cashier's behavior. The customers' influence derived from "physical proximity, the amount of time customers and cashiers spend together, the amount of feedback customers give, the amount of information they provide, and the critical role cashiers attribute to customers."

Rafaeli & Sutton's (1991) efforts to distinguish variations among emotional contrast strategies ("good cop, bad cop" strategies) also illustrate how the distance dimension can be used to characterize the social context. Their qualitative and inductive study of Israeli police interrogators and American telephone bill collectors indicated that some of these strategies entailed confronting the criminal suspect or recalcitrant debtor with both the good cop and the bad cop at the same time (good cop and bad cop both proximal), other strategies entailed alternating the presence of the good cop and bad cop (alternating the proximity of good cop and bad cop), and still other strategies involved the good cop's use of a hypothetical or expected bad cop whom the suspect or debtor never actually encountered (good cop proximal, bad cop distal). Although all of these strategies might lead to compliance, the techniques that involved closer interactions with the bad cop were more likely than the others to be used on recalcitrant suspects and debtors.

A pair of studies that adopted the social-information-processing approach found that attitudes formed by organization members are influenced strongly by people with whom they have frequent contact. Rice & Aydin (1991) reported that attitudes toward a new data processing system were similar to the attitudes of the employee's supervisor and others who interacted with the employee. The effects of these proximal information sources were found even after controlling for the effects of system usage, occupational characteristics, and mean attitude levels in employees' work groups. Rentsch (1990) reported that people interacting with each other shared similar interpretations of events and that members of different interaction groups attached qualitatively different meaning to similar organizational events. Galaskiewicz & Burt (1991) also found evidence of contagion in the evaluation of nonprofit agencies as potential recipients of corporate gifts. Such evaluations of worthiness depended less on the opinions of managers who came into contact with each other than on the opinions of other managers holding structurally equivalent positions in other organizations but with whom they did not interact frequently. Thus contextual influences can be conceptualized in both physical and psychological terms.

Kahn's (1990) innovative study of personal engagement and disengagement at work illustrates the concept of psychological distance. Recognizing that the more traditional areas of study (e.g. organizational commitment and job involvement) represent average levels of engagement across time, Kahn (1990:692) argued that "people are constantly bringing in and leaving out various depths of themselves during the course of their work days." The degree to which individuals invest in their roles can wax and wane throughout the day. Using ethnographic research methods, Kahn identified several psychological conditions for engagement (self-proximal) and disengagement (self-distal), including psychological meaningfulness, safety, and availability.

Finally, Ancona's (1990) study of five consulting teams suggests that the extent to which steps are taken to increase or decrease distance from the organizational context may influence performance. Teams that used a strategy of "informing" (concentrating on internal activities until they were ready to tell outsiders of their intentions) were least successful. Teams that used a strategy of "probing" (concentrating on extensive interactions with outsiders to discover their needs) were most successful. Teams that used a strategy of "parading" (placing simultaneous emphasis on internal activities and gaining external visibility) were more successful than "informing" teams but less successful than "probing" teams. Ancona's (1990) findings suggest that teams were more successful to the extent that they took steps to decrease social distance from their organizational contexts.

TEMPORAL   Repeated calls for more longitudinal research in organizational behavior underscore the importance of the temporal dimension in contextual influences. For example, the innovative new journal *Organization Science* devoted a special issue to longitudinal research (August, 1990) that clarifies the challenges and virtues of such designs.

Several recent studies of newcomers in organizations used longitudinal designs. For example, Allen & Meyer (1990) reported that socialization methods discussed by Van Maanen & Schein (1979) were negatively related to role innovation 6 and 12 months later. These same methods were positively related to organizational commitment at 6 months, but such significant effects had disappeared after 12 months. Lee et al (1992) measured the "commitment propensity" of high school students intending to enter the United States Air Force Academy. The construct of commitment propensity, composed of prior exposure to military values, expectations, and behavioral commitments surrounding the decision to join, was related to initial organizational commitment at entry which, in turn, was related to turnover for up to four years. Cadets entering the academy with lower commitment were more likely to leave than cadets entering with higher commitment. The authors speculated that high- and low-commitment new cadets brought differing frames of reference to the academy that may have caused them to interpret events differently. For instance, a reprimand from an upper-class cadet could be viewed as arbitrary harassment or as information useful to learning the ropes of the organization.

The temporal dimension is also illustrated by Eden's (1990) study of the stress and strain provoked by the shutdown and reopening of an Israeli university computer system. A new computer system was installed during the Passover vacation. Eden (1990) expected both stress and strain to be highest during the shutdown and immediately following the vacation, owing to the backlog of work and new system bugs. Stress, measured as work demands and quantitative and qualitative overload, followed the predicted pattern. Stress increased during the shutdown, decreased during vacation, and increased again when people returned to face a backlog of work. However, the same pattern was not observed for strain (e.g. anxiety, psychosomatic complaints, and blood pressure). Strain was high during the shutdown and after the return to work, but during the vacation period strain did not decrease significantly, remaining above the level characteristic of routine work. The strain provoked by this stressful experience apparently continued even in the absence of the objective stress. This study suggests that strain measured at one point in time may have its origin in events taking place earlier. It thus illustrates the importance to researchers of developing a historical appreciation of the contexts they study.

Finally, Hackett et al's (1989) study of absenteeism has methodological implications for the temporal dimension. Studies of this phenomenon typically measure employee attitudes and other perceptions of their work at one juncture and then track absences from work over the following 6–12 months. This practice can blur the meaning of observed relationships because absences occurring just after the survey administration may be more strongly related to survey measures than absences occurring months later. In contrast, in a study of absenteeism among nurses, Hackett et al (1989) used an idiographic and longitudinal design. Nurses completed questionnaires each day about such potential predictors of their absence from work as feeling ill, tiredness, or having a sick family member. Absence data were also gathered each day. This design enabled investigators to determine whether nurses differed in the predominant reasons they were absent and to identify factors accounting for the most absences across nurses. The findings they reported have greater credibility than most absenteeism studies because the independent variables were measured in close temporal proximity to the dependent variable.

Context as Similar and Dissimilar

The simple observation that organization members do not think, feel, or behave in isolation helps us to understand organizational behavior (Pfeffer 1991). A person's location in the social context influences his/her contacts and experiences within the organization. Recent research on social context has focused on how behavior in organizations is predicted by the degree of similarity among individuals who compose them.

RELATIONAL DEMOGRAPHY   As O'Reilly (1991) noted, Pfeffer's (1983) observation that organizations are fundamentally relational entities has encouraged researchers to examine the implications of similarity and dissimilarity among group members. Similarity can be measured along numerous dimensions. Most researchers have adopted a sociological approach and focused on demographic variables. Pfeffer (1983) argued that the demographic composition of groups and organizations (relational demography) has implications for behavior above and beyond average levels of group demographic characteristics.

Research inspired by Pfeffer's (1983) predictions has found that such demographic characteristics as age, tenure, education, and gender influence outcomes such as employee turnover (McCain et al 1983), social integration (O'Reilly et al 1989), supervisor-subordinate relations (Tsui & O'Reilly 1989), and communication patterns (Zenger & Lawrence 1989). More recently, Tsui et al (1991) reported higher levels of intragroup gender and race differences are associated with (a) more absenteeism and (b) less psychological commitment and intention to stay in the organization.

In contrast, Cox et al (1991) compared the performance of ethnically diverse groups (composed of Asians, Blacks, Hispanics, and Anglos) to homogeneous Anglo groups performing the Prisoner's Dilemma task. They found greater cooperation in ethnically diverse groups than in all-Anglo groups, which was accentuated when a norm of cooperation was introduced. Unfortunately, this study did not compare levels of cooperation in ethnically homogeneous non-Anglo groups with that in the all-Anglo groups. In view of predictions about increasing diversity in the American workforce, the importance of such research will grow (Cox 1990).

Jackson et al (1991) published one of the most comprehensive and insightful recent studies of this kind. They recognized that sociological approaches to relational demography complemented psychological theory on interpersonal attraction. They contended that Pfeffer's (1983) arguments from demography and Schneider's (1987) attraction-selection-attrition (ASA) model led to similar predictions. Pfeffer (1983) was primarily concerned with group- and organization-level explanatory variables such as homogeneity, cohesiveness, and interaction patterns. Schneider (1987) was primarily concerned with the individual-level process of attraction to similar others as a determinant of homogeneity in organizations. The processes of attraction, selection, and attrition increase homogeneity in organizations because those inside the organization attract and select others like themselves and those who differ from most others in the organization tend to leave.

Schneider (1987) emphasized similarity of personality, values, and interests; Pfeffer (1983) emphasized similarity of demographic characteristics. The essential arguments of the two scholars are nevertheless consistent. Both authors focus on the negative reactions provoked in organizations by dissimilarities among members: Schneider (1987) notes that dissimilar people will either be excluded from selection or driven out after selection; Pfeffer (1983) argues that an organization composed of dissimilar people will experience high levels of conflict and turnover, and that individuals in such organizations will have less positive attitudes. Pfeffer (1991) has also explained the tendency toward homogeneous organizational composition by drawing on Kanter's (1977) notion of "homosocial reproduction." Pfeffer's (1991) argument that demographic similarity facilitates trust and communication closely parallel Schnedier's explanations of why people are attracted to similar others.

Jackson et al (1991) tested and (generally) confirmed a number of hypotheses consistent with both the ASA model and relational demography in a study of top management teams from bank holding companies. Executives within firms were more similar to each other demographically than they were to executives from other firms. Dissimilarity with respect to education level, college curriculum, and industry experience predicted turnover—a finding consistent with arguments based on relational demography.

This study is important both because it is rigorous and because it links psychological and sociological approaches. Its findings also have important implications for groups and organizations that intend to increase personnel diversity. Individual preferences and organizational personnel practices may have led to relative homogeneity in the past. As the composition of the workforce changes, however, organizations will likely become less homogeneous, raising questions about how to avert both the possible increase in turnover suggested by Jackson et al's (1991) study and the decreased commitment suggested by Tsui et al's (1991) study.

Research on relational demography has been influential, but Lawrence (unpublished working paper, UCLA Grad. Sch. Manage.) argues that many of the intervening processes hypothesized to link group composition to outcome variables have not been examined empirically. It has been hypothesized, for instance, that group composition influences conflict, communication frequency, social norms, and social integration. Researchers have rarely measured these intervening variables; when the links between group composition and intervening variables have been studied, the observed relationships have generally been weak (B. S. Lawrence, unpublished working paper, UCLA Grad. Sch. Manage.).

INDIVIDUAL-ORGANIZATION FIT   A series of studies on individual-organization fit (Chatman 1991; Caldwell & O'Reilly 1990; O'Reilly et al 1991) used a new approach to assess person-organization fit that enabled a more refined understanding of how and why newcomers do—or do not—adjust to organizational roles. Past research on person-organization fit was hampered by the lack of comparison dimensions that were equally appropriate for measuring the values held by an organization member and the values prevalent in his or her organization. The new measurement tool, the Organizational Culture Profile, allows individuals, jobs, and organizations to be described along identical value dimensions.

Chatman's (1991) ambitious study of new accountants used this method to examine the determinants and consequences of person-organization fit, both at time the individual enters the organization and after a period of socialization. Fit at entry—or similarity between individual and organizational values—was correlated with individual characteristics and time spent with existing members, while fit a year later was influenced by participating in work-related social functions and time spent with a mentor. Person-organization fit, both the kind evident at entry and the kind resulting from socialization, predicted subsequent attitudes and turnover, suggesting that selection and socialization are substitutable processes.

WHEN CONTEXTS HAVE MINIMAL INFLUENCE

We have thus far assumed that the context is a powerful influence on individuals and groups in organizations, an assumption consistent with the situationalist approach (Davis-Blake & Pfeffer 1989). We do not deny, however, that individual characteristics also play an important role in shaping behavior. Indeed, despite prior assertions that organizations are typically strong situations that overwhelm individual personality variables, even Pfeffer's (1992) recent book proposes that individual attributes such as energy, focus, sensitivity, and flexibility help people wield power effectively. The organizational context may have little or no influence when individuals or groups are buffered from or simply ignore contextual forces.

Kaprow (1991) analyzed why firefighters in New York City have successfully resisted "proletarianization"—the bureaucratization of work through regulations, rules, and procedures that cause people to lose control of their jobs. Kaprow (1991) argued that firefighters had maintained control over their work because of the mystique created by its inherent danger and because much of their work takes place in the firehouse, which is off-limits to outsiders. Heroic acts shielded the members of this occupation from external changes. Kaprow (1991) concluded, however, that increasing government regulation and changes in firefighting technology make it only a matter of time until "proletarianization" occurs.

Stevenson & Gilly's (1991) study illustrates the limited effectiveness of one organization's efforts to control information flow. They investigated a hospital that had established formal procedures for handling patient complaints. Prior to the study, employees were reminded of these procedures, and certain official "patient concern personnel" were identified for them to contact in the event of a complaint. The researchers then studied the handling of simulated patient problems, which the hospital employees could either solve or forward to another person. The hospital's informal communication network was used more often than the formal complaint-handling system—a finding that held even among managers presumed to know about and to support the formal procedures. Thus, one dimension of organizational context, location in a social structure, had greater influence than another dimension, the formal control system.

Nelson & Sutton's (1990) study reminds us that taken-for-granted conclusions about contextual influences may require modification. They studied the relationship between work demands and distress symptoms among newcomers to three organizations. Most stress research is cross-sectional. Here a cross-sectional study might have found relationships between work demands and distress symptoms, thus focusing attention on the stressful work context. In contrast, Nelson & Sutton's (1990) longitudinal design allowed them to follow subjects from a point before they entered the organization to a point nine months after they started work. Distress symptoms at nine months were more strongly predicted by distress symptoms reported before entry into the organization than by work demands at six months. Work demands were a significant predictor of distress symptoms, but the variance attributable to prior distress symptoms was four times larger; in addition such prior distress predicted perceived work demands at 6 months. Whether newcomers entering with distress symptoms actually experienced the environment differently or simply maintained a consistent level of distress independent of the work context is not clear from this study, but these results are reminiscent of Staw et al's (1986) finding that affective disposition early in life predicted job attitudes nearly 50 years later.

Finally, in a conceptual paper designed to encourage research on a ne-glected topic, Gersick & Hackman (1990) discussed the nature, antecedents, and consequences of habitual routines in task performing groups. Defining habitual routines as groups' repeated engagement in "a functionally similar pattern of behavior in a given stimulus situation without explicitly selecting it over alternative ways of behaving" (Gersick & Hackman 1990:69), they note that routines are often dysfunctional when groups respond to a familiar stimu-lus but in a different context. Habitual routines insulate the group from contex-tual changes because, confronted by a familiar stimulus, these changes are not noticed or are miscoded by the group.

All four papers illustrate that the presence of contextual variables does not mean they will shape behavior. The context must act on, be noticed by, and be construed as important by individuals and groups before it can influence their behavior. Discovering that contextual variables are present but don't appear to be influential is often as important from a research perspective as confirming their power.

INDIVIDUALS AND GROUPS AS INFLUENCES ON ORGANIZATIONAL CONTEXTS

We have thus far considered how individuals and groups are influenced by the organizational context, a focus consistent with past reviews (Cummings 1982). But the organizational context can also be viewed as a consequence of individual or group behavior. We found much exemplary work that used psychological perspectives alone or in combination with other disciplines to explain how individuals and small groups influence organizations. Staw & Sutton's (1992) effort to map the subfield they labeled "macro organizational psychology" suggests at least three general ways that members' cognitions, emotions, and behaviors can shape processes and outcomes at the organizational level. These three means can also be extended to explain how groups influence organizations.

First, autonomous individuals or groups may take actions that reflect their own preferences but may claim that such actions reflect organizational policies and procedures (Staw 1991). In such instances, Staw writes, individuals are only "dressing up like organizations," and explanations of such so-called organizational actions must rely on theory and research on individual rather than organizational action. Staw's (1991) perspective suggests it might also be interesting to study small groups that act without the endorsement or support of the larger organization while claiming to act in accordance with organization-wide preferences, policies, or procedures. This first means has not—to our knowledge—been studied explicitly but is an area where novel and useful work can occur.

The other two general ways individuals influence organizational contexts have been the subject of much recent theory building and testing. The second occurs when powerful individuals (or groups) take actions that influence organizational structures, processes, and performance. The third occurs because the aggregation of individual thoughts, feelings, and behaviors—and the aggregation of group attributes—can influence the organization as a whole.

Powerful Individuals as an Influence on Organizations

There has been much debate over the past 20 years about whether leaders have a large or small impact on organizational attributes and outcomes (Bass 1990). Although this debate is far from resolved, a consensus seems to be emerging that leaders have at least a modest influence, especially when the organization is small and young. For example, Miller & Droge (1986) found that CEO need for achievement was a stronger predictor of structural variables including centralization, formalization, and integration in smaller and younger firms than in larger and older firms. And, although Pfeffer's (1977) earlier writings asserted that leaders have little influence over organizational performance, Pfeffer & Davis-Blake's (1986) study of coaching changes in National Basketball Association teams indicated that new coaches' past performance affected the win-loss records of their new teams. It was reasonable to expect such effects because basketball teams have a small number of players and a single coach typically makes constant and intensive efforts to influence player performance during games.

Our review uncovered two general paths through which powerful individuals, especially leaders, influence organizational attributes, processes, and outcomes: by making decisions that affect the organization; and by shaping the thoughts, feelings, and actions of people inside and outside the organization.

DECISIONS THAT AFFECT THE ORGANIZATION   Research conducted from a behavioral decision-making perspective has identified numerous shortcomings in human information processing and judgment, including escalation of commitment to a failing course of action, overconfidence in judgment, limited perspective, and problem-framing. Several recent articles suggest that such cognitive shortcomings affect the decisions made by top managers that, in turn, affect the organization.

Zajac & Bazerman (1991) present a particularly convincing argument that individual cognitive shortcomings can be used to explain poor strategic decisions in organizations, including overcapacity, new business failures, and acquisition premiums (i.e. buying new businesses at excessive costs). For example, Zajac & Bazerman (1991) explain why there are often "irrational bidders" (Porter 1980:355) when two or more firms compete to buy the same company: Just as in laboratory experiments, excessive amounts are paid because none of the overconfident partners to the negotiation realizes that he or she is bidding against others who are similarly overconfident. Zajac & Bazerman's (1991) perspective illustrates how leaders' cognitive limits can lead to decisions that change organizational size (e.g. it may become larger as a result of acquisition), mission (e.g. it may enter new markets), and performance (e.g. debts are serviced to pay acquisition premiums).

Staw et al's (1981) influential threat-rigidity model suggested that distress can hinder leaders' cognitive processes and cause them to make poor decisions. D'Aveni & MacMillan (1990) studied letters written by the leaders of 57 bankrupt companies and 57 matched firms that did not declare bankruptcy. They found that during the five years leading up to their companies' fates, the leaders of the firms that went bankrupt tended to deny or ignore the lack of demand for their products or services; they focused narrowly on the demands of creditors and on making internal organizational changes. In contrast, the leaders of matched firms that did not declare bankruptcy paid equal attention to internal and external factors, concerning themselves both with sources of input (such as creditors) and with output factors (such as customer needs and changes in demand). When a crisis of lack of demand occurred, leaders of the surviving firms (but not of the doomed firms) tended to pay increased attention to output factors. D'Aveni & MacMillan (1990) interpret these results as evidence that financial threats cause perceptual narrowing and an inability to focus on long-term planning. The papers by Zajac & Bazerman (1991) and D'Aveni & MacMillan (1990) suggest that psychological perspectives on dysfunction in individual decision-making may provide a useful basis for future work on how top managers' decisions influence organizations.

LEADER INFLUENCE ON PARTICIPANTS INSIDE AND OUTSIDE THE ORGANIZATION
The notion that leaders influence others' thoughts, feelings, and actions is ubiquitous in the vast leadership literature. Yet, as Bass (1990) notes, only a small proportion of this literature considers how leaders influence organizations and institutions. Most studies focus on how leaders influence individual followers or small groups. A modest but interesting body of recent work considers how

leaders influence the followers and external constituents who compose organizations.

Schein (1990) drew on his extensive consulting experience and earlier writings to identify how a founder's beliefs, values, and assumptions determine how things should and should not be done in an organization. Schein shows, for instance, that the founder's actions can be enduring determinants of assumptions about how employees should be controlled, rewarded, hired, promoted, and fired, as well as assumptions about how to cope with critical incidents and crises. Schein argued that the leader's influence, including the founder's, typically wanes after such aspects of organizational culture become institutionalized.

One of the most influential perspectives on leadership suggests that a leader's most important task is to provide "explanations, rationalizations, and legitimation for the activities undertaken in organizations" (Pfeffer 1981:4). This perspective has spawned research that applies aspects of attribution theory to CEO explanations for corporate performance (Bettman & Weitz 1983; Salancik & Meindl 1984; Staw et al 1983). These papers suggest that CEOs generally (but not always) used self-serving attributions for organizational performance, attributing good performance to internal factors and poor performance to external factors. Moreover, these self-serving attributions may have had the desired impact on shareholders because they were associated with subsequent increases in stock prices (Staw et al 1983). Several recent papers elaborate the means through which leaders' interpretations shape how their organizations are construed.

Marcus & Goodman (1991) examined stock market reactions to top managers' announcements during different kinds of crisis. Their study was framed in terms of economic theories on agency and signaling, but it provides insights into the conditions under which leaders' self-serving attributions help or hurt a firm's reputation. Marcus & Goodman's hypotheses focused on the consequences of leaders' admissions that their organization was responsible for causing and repairing a problem (labeled "accommodative signals") versus assertions that the organization was not responsible or that the problem didn't exist (labeled "defensive signals"). Their findings suggest that defensive signals (i.e. self-serving attributions) following accidents such as airplane crashes or oil spills had a positive impact on stock prices. Marcus & Goodman suggest that such findings occurred because it was plausible to argue that "the company could not have foreseen or prevented what has taken place and that the accident does not reflect underlying inadequacies in either the company, its management, or its way of doing business" (p. 286). In contrast, their findings suggest that when internal scandals occurred, use of accommodative signals (i.e. accepting responsibility) rather than defensive signals was associated with the higher subsequent stock prices. The authors attribute this second finding to the difficulty of claiming such acts as the bribing of public officials are impossible to prevent or don't reflect managerial inadequacies.

A pair of papers integrated psychological (e.g. impression management) and sociological (e.g. institutional, population ecology, resource dependence theory) perspectives to help explain how leaders take symbolic action in their efforts to protect and enhance organizational legitimacy. Ashforth & Gibbs (1990:177) argued that when leaders make visible attempts to manage their organization's images (e.g. General Motors' investigation of Ralph Nader after his criticism of the Corvair) risk being viewed as manipulative and as "protesting too much." Ashforth & Gibbs (1990) contend that such efforts can backfire and reduce legitimacy when organizations are viewed as "clumsy" (unethical, heavy-handed, or insensitive), "nervous" (dogmatic, intolerant, or evasive), or "overacting" (exaggerating strengths or reacting too strongly to faults).

Elsbach & Sutton's (1992) case studies of two radical social movement organizations, ACT UP and Earth First!, blended insights from impression management and institutional theories. They analyzed eight illegitimate actions attributed to members of these organizations to develop a process model of how official spokespersons use verbal interpretations to shift attention away from members' illegitimate actions and toward the organization's socially desirable goals. The content of such interpretations often included references to organizational structures or procedures that have been discussed in depth by institutional theorists (e.g. Meyer & Rowan 1977). For example, institutional theorists assert that organizations often decouple illegitimate or controversial actions from legitimate and socially acceptable structures. The excuses used by Earth First! and ACT UP spokespersons routinely included claims that the organization could not be blamed for members' unlawful actions (e.g. disabling logging equipment) because such actions were conducted by autonomous (i.e. decoupled) individuals or groups without the organization's knowledge or endorsement.

Research on "transformational" leaders continued to move forward, along with related work on "charismatic," "visionary," and "inspirational" leaders (Bass 1990). For instance, Westley (1991) drew on published sources to explain how rock star Bob Geldof used "visionary" leadership to organize the Live Aid concert, a global rock music telethon that raised $100 million for Ethiopian famine relief. Westley (1991) demonstrated how Geldof's personal background, reputation, interpersonal skills, and knowledge of the music industry allowed him to take advantage of a moment in history when the structure of the music industry could be used to mobilize and coordinate rock stars for fund raising throughout the world. The emotions aroused by rock music further enhanced Geldof's ability to gain commitment to the enterprise.

Biggart's (1989) qualitative research on direct sales organizations suggests that having a charismatic founder who can create excitement, commitment, and effort in followers is essential to organizational success. Most of the organizations that Biggart (1989) studied had charismatic founders who used their emotional expressiveness, linguistic ability, confidence, and vision to inspire followers and build their corporations. For example, Mary Kay Ash of Mary Kay Cosmetics used both personal attention and inspirational songs to instill felt and displayed enthusiasm in the 150,000 women who sold her cosmetics.

House et al's (1991) study of United States presidents provides intriguing quantitative data on the influence of charismatic leaders on followers. The researchers used information from presidential biographies and other sources coded by independent raters to measure charisma, operationalized as self-confidence, strong ideological conviction, high expectations of followers, and consideration. This measure of charisma also reflected followers' reactions to the leader, including affect, mission involvement, extra effort, agreement, and self-confidence. Charisma explained substantial amounts of variance in presidential performance in economic, domestic, and foreign affairs. A separate measure of charisma based on editorials appearing in the *New York Times* the day after each president's inaugural address explained similar amounts of variance in these performance measures, thus adding greater credibility to the conclusions.

Finally, recent literature suggests two important cautions for work on charismatic or transformational leaders. First, the literature on organizations, with few exceptions (e.g. Howell & Frost 1988; Howell & Avolio 1992), portrays charismatic leaders as having a desirable impact on followers' well-being, organizational performance, and society as a whole. Lindholm's (1990) well-crafted book explores the dark side of charisma by weaving together views from philosophers, anthropologists, sociologists, and psychologists to show that charismatic relationships between leaders and followers often lead to destructive ends (e.g. the phenomena of Adolf Hitler and Nazi Germany). Lindholm's perspective suggests that organizational researchers should reconsider their assumptions about charismatic leaders—who may, for example, encourage employees to sacrifice personal lives for the organization or commit unethical acts that benefit the organization but harm others.

Second, Meindl (1990) proposed that too much attention has been devoted to the attributes and actions of charismatic leaders and not enough to charismatic leadership as an outcome of social psychological forces among followers and observers. He argues that attributional tendencies cause followers and observers, including theorists, to romanticize leaders; such followers and observers overemphasize leaders' personal qualities and actions, giving them too much credit for organizational effectiveness and too much blame for organizational failure. Meindl (1990) contends that "charismatic experiences" occur not because leaders influence followers but because followers influence one another (cf Hollander 1992). He proposed that the charismatic effects described by House (1977) and others (e.g. exertion of extra effort, attraction to the leader, heightened self-esteem) spread from one follower to another through a process of social contagion. Effects attributed to charismatic leaders may tell us more about followers and observers than about leaders, a research lead Chen & Meindl (1991) pursued in a study of how the press portrayed Donald Burr, CEO of People Express Airlines.

Powerful Groups as an Influence on Organizations

The notion that psychological mechanisms may explain how groups of leaders, as well as individual leaders, influence their organizations is implied in much of the literature reviewed above. For example, Zajac & Bazerman (1991) and D'Aveni & MacMillan (1990) suggest that the thoughts of a powerful member, or members, can affect the organization as a whole. But a number of recent studies examined the impact of powerful groups on organizations more explicitly.

Eisenhardt (1989b) developed a model of the relative effectiveness of teams that made fast versus slow decisions in "high velocity" environments. This model was grounded in data from eight microcomputer firms. She found that teams making faster decisions used more information and considered more alternatives compared to slow teams, and that fast decision-making was associated with superior financial performance in this environment. Eisenhardt's (1989b) inferences were confirmed by Judge & Miller's (1991) study of firms in the biotechnology, hospital, and textile industries.

Eisenhardt & Schoonhoven (1990) conducted a longitudinal study of factors that influenced growth in 98 of the 102 semiconductor firms founded in the United States between 1978 and 1985. They found that organizations had greater sales growth when top management teams were composed of people who had worked together more in the past, when they were larger, and when they were composed of people with varying amounts of industry experience. The impact of these variables on growth increased over time, an interesting finding in light of group dynamics research suggesting that groups can't work effectively on tasks until interpersonal issues among members are resolved (Tuckman 1965), and in light of the work reviewed above emphasizing the importance of demographic homogeneity in work groups.

Aggregate Member Thoughts, Feelings, and Behaviors as Influences on Organizations

Schneider's (1987) provocative presidential address to the Society for Industrial and Organizational Psychology argued:

> We have been seduced into thinking that organizational structures and processes are the causes of the attitudes, feelings, experiences, meanings, and behaviors that we observe there. We attribute cause not to the people attracted to, selected by, and remaining within organizations, but to the signs of their existence in the organization: to structure, process, and technology.

> Enough is enough. We are psychologists and behavioral scientists; let us seek explanation in people, not in the results of their behavior. The people make the place (p. 451).

Schneider asserts that the aggregate characteristics and behaviors of individuals exert important influences on organizations. Several recent papers are consistent with his view that "the people make the place."

Interesting work on organizational learning and memory appeared in the February 1991 issue of *Organization Science,* published in honor of James March's distinguished career. Much of this work considered how, in the aggregate, the cognitions and actions of individual members influence the organization as a whole. In his own paper in this issue (1991:71), on "exploration of new possibilities" versus "exploitation of old certainties," March considers how the kinds of people hired by the organization ("slow learners" versus "fast learners"), the rate of socialization of newcomers, and turnover influence stability and change in the organization's code (i.e. language, beliefs, and practices). In organizations that hire a higher proportion of people who learn the organization's code slowly, that socialize newcomers less actively, and that have a higher turnover rate among people who know the code, the level of exploration of new possibilities is likely to be higher. March argues that much exploration will occur because fewer members of the organization are able and willing to rely on the code to get their work done; a greater proportion of members are thus likely to try alternative approaches. In contrast, March asserts, when an organization hires a high proportion of people who learn the code quickly, takes steps to teach the code quickly to newcomers, and has low turnover among people who know the code, the level of exploitation is likely to be higher. Exploitation results because the organization is composed of a high proportion of people who are able and willing to rely on the code to accomplish tasks. March suggests that all organizations need to strike a balance between exploration and exploitation. He also proposes that organizations composed largely of people disposed toward exploitation will be more effective in the short run, but less effective in the long run, than organizations composed largely of people disposed toward exploration.

The notion that the cognitions and actions of individual members can, in aggregate, influence the organization is also considered in Walsh & Ungson's (1991:78) review and integration of the literature on organizational memory. Not only is an organization's memory an individual-level phenomenon, but much (although not all) of an organization's memory resides in the heads of its members. Thus Walsh & Ungson propose that an organization's culture is an aggregation of individuals' shared beliefs. Because individuals remember information and maintain records as memory aids, an organization's memory is determined partly by the aggregation of such information; and it is also individual members who "largely determine what information will be acquired and retrieved from other memory stores."

Finally, recent research also suggests that the aggregation of members' emotions can reflect organizational attributes that are in turn related to other significant organizational variables. In a study of retail stores George (1990) found that measures of individuals' felt emotion could be aggregated and transformed into useful measures of positive and negative affective tone. She found less prosocial behavior in stores where employees reported having more negative feelings. Absenteeism also was lower in stores where employees reported more positive feelings.

THE INTERACTIONS OF INDIVIDUALS AND GROUPS WITH THEIR ORGANIZATIONAL CONTEXTS

Our presentation of recent literature is divided into two broad categories: 1. the organizational context as an influence on individuals and groups and 2. individuals and groups as an influence on organizations. This scheme is useful for organizing the literature, but it does not account for the complex interplay between the context and the individuals and groups operating within it. A more accurate characterization involves reciprocal relationships in which the causal arrow points in both directions.

The complex interplay between the context and individuals is typically not evident in traditional than in current organizational behavior research. This deficiency has several interrelated causes. First, a theory builder's task is made more difficult when he or she tries to develop a model that includes reciprocal relationships between context and individuals or groups. As a result, many theorists may decide—often wisely—that the increased accuracy gained by the inclusion of reciprocal relationships does not offset the parsimony lost. Second, partly because most of our theories do not include reciprocal relationships, most of the hypotheses tested in studies of the relationships between contexts and individuals or groups concern unidirectional relationships between variables. For instance, a researcher may focus specifically on the influence of task characteristics on individual attitudes. The nature of this research question dictates the underlying causal relationships and may blind researchers to the possibility that individuals often redefine and otherwise change their specific tasks (Staw & Boettger 1990). Third, studies that capture complex interactions are frequently more formidable undertakings because variables of interest must often be monitored over lengthy periods. The cross-sectional study has been the staple of traditional organizational behavior research. Longitudinal investigations, while honored in theory, are less often pursued in practice.

The three studies we feel best illustrate the complex interplay between the context, on the one hand, and individuals and groups, on the other, use a case methodology and rely heavily on archival data. Given the difficulties involved in monitoring such relationships across time, these design choices are not accidental. In addition to illustrating complex interactions, each of these studies focuses on an important organizational or societal problem.

The Homeless

Dutton & Dukerich (1991) investigated the interplay between a major contextual change and the image and identity of the Port Authority of New York and New Jersey. The contextual change involved the growing numbers of homeless people using the Port Authority's bus terminal and subsequently other facilities such as the airports and World Trade Center. Organization identity was defined as members' beliefs about the organization's enduring, distinctive, and central characteristics. Image was defined as how members thought people outside the organization saw the organization.

A complex interplay between context and individuals occurred as the Port Authority adapted to the growing numbers of homeless people. This contextual change was defined in words consistent with the Port Authority's identity as a "professional organization with a uniquely technical expertise, ill-suited to social service activities" (p. 526). This identity narrowed the interpretation of the problem (a police-security issue) and the individual actions that were taken as a result (removing the homeless from the facilities by enforcing anti-loitering laws). Public reaction to the growing problem and the Port Authority's strategy caused a reassessment. Over time, the problem was reinterpreted as a business problem requiring a moral solution. This led to the establishment of a homeless project team within the organization and a search for more humane alternative solutions.

Thus, the organization's identity strongly influenced how members interpreted the homeless problem. The study also revealed that

> Over time, actions taken on issues reposition an organization in its environment by modifying tasks, allocation of resources, and assignments of personnel. The pattern of action on issues can therefore reinforce or, potentially, transform the organization's identity and image through individuals' sense making efforts, and the process of adaptation continues (Dutton & Dukerich 1991:543).

Interpretations of the homelessness problem led to individual actions that reshaped the organization's image and subsequently led to different interpretations and actions. This study illustrates that organizations adapt to change through a process that entails reciprocal relationships between the context and organization members over time. These reciprocal relationships would be difficult to detect in the short term and would be impossible to discover using a more traditional cross-sectional design.

Air Disaster

The organizational reactions to the problem of the homeless examined by Dutton & Dukerich (1991) took place over seven years. In contrast, the events surrounding the Tenerife air disaster that Weick (1990) studied took place in a matter of minutes. The disaster involved the collision of a Pan Am 747 and a KLM 747 on the ground at Tenerife airport that killed 583 people. Weick's analysis emphasized the interplay of contextual features, which created stress for cockpit and air-traffic-control crews by interrupting their routines. Weick (1990) argued that a stressful setting caused various crews to fall back on their most familiar and well-rehearsed response routines. Weick applied Mandler's (1982) theory of stress to argue that contextual events interrupted routine operating procedures, causing high levels of arousal. This arousal caused cognitive information-processing capabilities to diminish, leading to the "omission of important cues for task performance and an increase in cognitive inefficiency" (Weick 1990:578). As a result, the flight and air-traffic-control crews made the wrong responses, leading to the deadly crash. This is an example of the context influencing individuals and groups, who responded in ways that changed the context as events unfolded. An interesting aspect of Weick's analysis is the distinction he draws between individual and group responses. He draws on Hage (1980) to argue that most relationships at the individual level of analysis, including those between stress and performance, are curvilinear; but as the level of analysis becomes more macro, relationships become more linear. As a result, a well-functioning, highly integrated cockpit crew might have responded to the increased stress with increased performance. Weick suggests, however, that such integration was not evident in the crews he studied, and thus they behaved more like individuals than teams.

Nuclear Power Plant

J. Ross and B. M. Staw (unpublished working paper, UCB Haas Sch. Bus.) examined the decision to build and operate the Shoreham Nuclear Power Plant by top management of the Long Island Lighting Company. They document how the interplay between top management's actions and the organizational and political context created by these actions led the company to spend over 5 billion dollars on a plant initially estimated to cost 75 million. The plant never became fully operational and is being decommissioned.

Ross and Staw propose that commitment to this losing course of action was initially launched by psychological factors operating on top management, including excessive optimism and social comparisons to other power company executives who had been able to build and operate such plants successfully. Once executives began trying to convince regulatory agencies, local governments, and the public that this was a worthwhile project, norms favoring consistency encouraged them to continue pushing for the project.

Ross and Staw also document how the top managers' decision to go forward created an organizational and political context that made it even more difficult to stop the project. The numerous planners, operators, technical support staff, and other employees hired to build and operate the plant became a powerful internal constituency, who pressured top management to maintain commitment to the project. Executives also recruited a number of external political allies from the nuclear power industry and government who supported nuclear power. Ross and Staw note that once these groups were organized and legitimated, they became not an asset but a constraint on top managers' decision-making, pressuring them to go forward with the project even after continuing financial losses threatened the company. This case study illustrates how top managers' initial actions may create an organizational and political context that subsequently constrains their behavior.

HOW CAN WE PUT ORGANIZATIONS BACK INTO ORGANIZATIONAL BEHAVIOR?

The central theme of this chapter is that our understanding of organizational behavior can be enhanced by devoting greater attention to the links between individuals and groups and their organizational contexts. This theme, while not new (Cummings 1981) or unique (Cappelli & Sherer 1991), has important implications for how we conduct research and for the issues we investigate. We outline several methodological and substantive implications that flow from a stronger contextual orientation in the field.

Methodological Implications

IMMERSION IN THE CONTEXT   As the field of organizational behavior has developed, researchers may have grown more distant from the very phenomena they wish to investigate. Many of the early influential writings were based on intensive observation and experience in organizations (e.g. Barnard 1938; Dalton 1959; Festinger et al 1956; Roethlisberger & Dickson 1939; Selznick 1949). A reading of contemporary journals, though, suggests we have evolved into a field that often requires minimal, if any, contact with organizations. The inspiration for many studies comes from controversies in the scholarly literature rather than observed phenomena in organizations. Studies in leading journals are often based on laboratory investigations using students as subjects. When investigators move into the field, it is often to administer questionnaires to anonymous respondents. And such research often entails sending packets of questionnaires to company representatives for distribution to respondents, who return them by mail. In short, "organizational behavior" is often studied without going near the organization and without talking to any of its members.

Removing researchers from the context has costs, both in terms of the depth of understanding researchers can achieve and with respect to the stimulation that leads to new areas of inquiry. It is no coincidence that some of the most influential studies in recent years have been those in which investigators have become immersed in the phenomena they wish to investigate. Several of these studies have been reviewed here. As further evidence, it is instructive to examine Frost & Stablein's (1992) selection of studies as models of exemplary research. In contrast to typical mainstream organizational behavior research, these studies are characterized by comprehensive analysis of archival data (Barley et al 1988; Baron et al 1986), actual participation in the organizations being studied (Sutton & Rafaeli 1988), and ongoing, extensive interaction between researcher and subjects (Gersick 1988; Meyer 1982). Of the seven "exemplary" studies Frost & Stablein (1992) highlighted, only one—a project with a largely methodological orientation—involved a laboratory investigation.

The need for more systematic investigation of the context was also suggested by James et al (1992). In a critique of the assumptions underlying meta-analytic techniques in validity generalization, they noted that inferring situational influences from residual variance could be misleading. They concluded that the best approach to developing an understanding of the role played by the situation was to undertake systematic investigations in which such influences were predicted, situations sampled, and situational influences measured directly.

The need for immersion in the context is perhaps greatest in cross-cultural or comparative research. There is increasing interest in determining whether organizational behavior theory and research findings largely developed by North American scholars generalizes to other cultures (Doktor et al 1991). Progress in this area is unlikely, however, if research is conducted through short visits to other cultures during which questionnaires are distributed to convenience samples. Instead, Boyacigiller & Adler (1991) advocate more qualitative and idiographic research that can only be accomplished when scholars invest considerable time within the cultural context they wish to understand.

If we wish to be more serious about bringing the context back into organizational behavior, we as researchers must be willing to immerse ourselves in the context. The increasing number of qualitative studies appearing in our leading journals may suggest a trend in this direction.

MEASUREMENT   Beyond immersion in the context, it is important to reconsider traditional approaches to incorporating contextual features in our research. Most studies in micro organizational behavior, when they consider the context, measure it by assessing individuals' perceptions. Research on job design, for instance, has relied almost exclusively on job incumbent perceptions of task characteristics (Spector & Jex 1991). A similar conclusion could be drawn about research in almost all the major topic areas in the field of organizational behavior. One consequence of the increasing cognitive orientation of micro organizational behavior (Ilgen & Klein 1988) has been reliance on perceptual measures as a primary research tool. We believe, as do others (Cappelli & Sherer 1991), that exclusive reliance on perceptual measures of the context may produce a distorted view of the world.

Our concern extends beyond the view often expressed by reviewers that response-response correlations cannot be interpreted unambiguously because of common methods variance. Measurement error is another important concern. It is often unclear whether perceptual measures tell us more about the perceiver or about the object of the perception (cf James & James 1989; James & Tetrick 1986). As Cappelli & Sherer (1991:84) note,

> If we only have the cognitive response—perceptions of the environment without information on the objective environment—we cannot tell whether differences in those responses are due to different information, different dispositions, or differences in the way the information is processed (cognition). In other words, it is not clear what the perceptual variable means because it is not clear what it really measures.

There is mounting evidence that the characteristics of individuals influence both individual reactions to environments and how environments are construed. Isen & Baron (1991) summarize research suggesting that positive affect influences cognitive processes. Lee et al (1992) and Nelson & Sutton (1990) found that the characteristics individuals brought to an organization influenced their perception of key contextual features. Additional research is needed on how individual characteristics affect perceptions of organizational features. Until such evidence is available, it would be wise to treat perceptual data with more skepticism than in the past. A more appropriate research strategy would be to collect multiple measures of the context. In addition to the perceptions of incumbents, we must explore the perceptions of others in the environment (peers, superiors) and collect more objective measures. Unfortunately, when this is done we often find that there is little consensus among observers of the same setting or event (Gerhart 1990; Spector & Jex 1991). This problem, which is easily overlooked when data comes from only one source, must be squarely addressed if we are to make greater progress in understanding contextual influences.

Substantive Implications

DISCIPLINARY INFLUENCES   The dominant theoretical and methodological influence on the development of micro organizational behavior has come from the discipline of psychology. It is time to reach beyond psychology to other disciplines that may make useful contributions to our thinking about organizations. This is not meant to suggest that psychology is no longer a useful source of theory and methods for the study of organizations. Continuing contributions from psychology must be supplemented with theory and methods from other disciplines such as sociology, economics, history, and political science.

Pfeffer (1991) summarizes specific ways in which sociological perspectives emphasizing that organizations are relational entities can contribute to the study of micro organizational behavior. Specifically, he argues that a focus on structural effects can lead to new research questions in such traditional areas as job attitudes, turnover, and job performance. For instance, Pfeffer (1991) suggests viewing job attitudes as a consequence of social contagion processes, an approach that places greater emphasis on investigating who individuals come into contact with than on such other features of the work environment as task characteristics or pay. Research by Rentsch (1990) and Rice & Aydin (1991), reviewed above, supports Pfeffer's arguments.

Sociological perspectives also may offer new insights into how the context shapes stress and emotion, two areas that have been studied extensively by organizational researchers. Barley & Knight (1992) note that most stress research is based on a model in which an objective stressor (e.g. hours worked) leads to a subjective stressor (e.g. role overload) that in turn leads to strain (e.g. anxiety or elevated blood pressure). Adopting a sociological approach, these authors attempt to understand the unexplained variance in subjective stressors and reported strain by focusing on the cultural and social context. For example, they propose that members of quasi-professions such as social workers, nurses, air traffic controllers, and school teachers use claims that their jobs are stressful as rhetorical tools in their effort to gain occupational legitimacy: "Claims of stress may be used to galvanize a sense of consciousness and solidarity among an occupation's members. Moreover, by repeatedly proclaiming exposure to stressful work, an occupation may construct a publicly credible rationale for why it should be allowed such privileges as higher pay and the right to self-regulate" (Barley & Knight 1992:19).

Sociological perspectives on emotion incorporate the social context in two ways typically not considered by organizational researchers working within a psychological perspective (cf. Franks & McCarthy 1989). First, a sociological perspective emphasizes that the emotions expressed by people are often socially constructed, reflecting cultural or organizational norms. Hochschild (1983) adopted this perspective, recognizing that organization members' expressed emotions are not always a reflection of their feelings. Second, while the psychological perspective emphasizes that emotions such as sympathy, love, jealousy, gratitude, and anger reside as states within people, sociologists are more likely to argue that such emotions stem from and are properties of social relationships between people.

The influence of economic theory on OB at both the macro and micro levels is increasing. For instance, O'Reilly et al's (1988) investigation of executive compensation applied a tournament model from economics to make predictions. The agency theory of the firm (Eisenhardt 1989a) has been applied to issues ranging from performance-contingent compensation systems (Eisenhardt 1988; Conlon & Parks 1990) to the diffusion of poison-pill defense strategies (Davis 1991). In an interesting approach to a traditional topic, Frank (1988) applies economic thinking to an analysis of the role of emotions in minimizing self-interested behavior. His arguments are relevant to several research areas in organizational behavior, including rational decision making and social loafing.

As highly specialized journals proliferate, reading by individual researchers becomes narrower. In the face of burgeoning literature, highly focused reading is a simple survival tactic for those wishing to stay current in their fields. Moreover, this trend has influenced doctoral training at major research institutions, which now tends to be more specialized in either the micro or macro areas. While understandable, the trend toward specialization is regrettable. It poses a barrier to increased understanding of organizations and the individuals and groups that compose them, as well as to communication among researchers from different disciplines who share common research interests.

RECONCEPTUALIZING THE CONTEXT   The traditional approach to thinking about the context has been heavily influenced by rational design considerations and bureaucratic theory. Cummings's (1982) review chapter, for example, covered such familiar areas as structure, technology, and control systems with respect to their influence on micro variables. But if we are to move beyond simple assertions that the context is important, we need to articulate more clearly how contextual influences operate. For instance, Mischel (1977) distinguished between strong and weak situations in terms of their influence on encoding information, expectancies about appropriate responses, incentives for responding, and required response skills. We found it useful to think of contextual influences in terms of the various ways they present themselves to individuals and groups. Our dimensions of opportunity versus constraint, proximity versus distance, and similarity versus dissimilarity do not constitute a complete or integrated theory of the organizational context. But these dimensions might prove useful components of such a theory. This chapter suggests that each provides insight into how settings shape individual and group behavior.

Moreover, the dimensions proposed here may help organizational theorists understand how more traditional macro variables influence individual behavior. For example, an organizational structure may be characterized as centralized or decentralized, but the impact of centralization may depend on whether the decisions made by top managers are construed as a constraint on individual autonomy or as creating an opportunity for individuals to focus their attention on tasks they consider more interesting and important than making such decisions.

In a similar vein, leadership is a contextual influence that may be studied from perspectives somewhat different from those of the past. The traditional approach to studying leadership involved identifying specific styles or characteristics thought important to effectiveness. For instance, the field began with the styles of consideration and initiating structure, moving more recently to research on charisma and visionary, transformational leaders. It is useful to recognize, however, that leadership is often a distal contextual influence. Most members of large organizations, rarely if ever, come into contact with executives and instead may find that the leader's distal attempts at influence are mediated by more proximal mid-level managers. Steckler (1991) used the analogy of a thunderstorm to note that organizational units are sometimes subject to "sudden deluges of information and action in the unit's environment," often emanating from top leaders. Taking the analogy one step further to consider the role of mid-level managers, she argued that some act as "umbrellas" to buffer those engaged in producing goods and services from the storm. Other mid-level managers serve as "funnels" that directly pass along, sometimes even amplify, pressures from the environment and thus create a crisis atmosphere characterized by constantly shifting priorities. Conceptualizing contextual influences along a distal-vs-proximal dimension helps sharpen our understanding of the environment in which organization members operate and opens new and potentially important areas for inquiry.

Finally, the major theme of this review is that organizational behavior needs to weave the context more systematically into its traditional areas of research. As Charles O'Reilly (personal communication) has pointed out, the real problem may be that our field has lost sight of the phenomena we seek to understand. Goal displacement may have occurred as the field has matured. The origins of organizational behavior are rooted in a phenomenological interest in administrative practice (March 1965). As research progressed, theories have been proposed to explain organizational behavior, and methods have been developed that permit increasingly rigorous investigations.

Our review of the current literature, however, suggests that the focus of research and writing in our field is increasingly on theory and method, and less on the stuff of organizational life. Much published research is motivated by the desire to test and extend theory, resolve theoretical debates, and apply new, more sophisticated methodologies to old theoretical problems. As a result, we sometimes forget that theory and method are only tools to help us understand organizations and their members. When we look back on our review, the studies we found most compelling were those focusing on organizational phenomena such as how effective groups interact with their external environment or why otherwise skilled and experienced pilots take actions resulting in major disasters.

We believe the field needs to return to a focus on organizational phenomena. This effort will be aided by the immersion of researchers in organizational contexts. It may also move the field in useful directions that will counter the common criticism that much organizational behavior research is irrelevant to the well-being of organizations and their members.

ACKNOWLEDGMENTS

Support provided by the University of Washington and Stanford University is appreciated. We appreciate comments on drafts of the chapter provided by Kathleen Eisenhardt, Thomas Lee, Terence Mitchell, Charles O'Reilly, Jeffrey Pfeffer, Barry Staw, and Nicole Steckler. We thank Lorna Peden for providing valuable computer assistance.

Literature Cited

Adams, J. S. 1965. Inequity in social exchange. *Adv. Exp. Soc. Psychol.* 2:267–99

Allen, N. J., Meyer, J. P. 1990. Organizational socialization tactics: a longitudinal analysis of links to newcomers' commitment and role orientation. *Acad. Manage. J.* 33:847–58

Ancona, D. G. 1990. Outward bound: strategies for team survival in an organization. *Acad. Manage. J.* 33:334–65

Ashforth, B. E., Gibbs, B. W. 1990. The double-edge of organizational legitimation. *Org. Sci.* 1:177–94

Barley, S. R. 1990. The alignment of technology and structure through roles and networks. *Admin. Sci. Q.* 35:61–103

Barley, S. R., Knight, D. B. 1992. Toward a cultural theory of stress complaints. *Res. Org. Behav.* 14:1–48

Barley, S. R., Meyer, G. W., Gash, D. C. 1988. Culture of culture: academics, practitioners, and the pragmatics of normative control. *Admin. Sci. Q.* 33:24–60

Barnard, C. I. 1938. *The Functions of the Executive.* Cambridge: Harvard Univ. Press. 334 pp.

Baron, J. N., Dobbin, F. R., Jennings, P. D. 1986. War and peace: the evolution of modern personnel administration in U. S. industry. *Am. J. Soc.* 92:350–83

Bass, B. M. 1990. *Bass & Stogdill's Handbook of Leadership.* New York: Free Press. 1182 pp.

Bettman, J. R., Weitz, B. A. 1983. Attributions in the boardroom: causal reasoning in corporate annual reports. *Admin. Sci. Q.* 28:165–83

Biggart, N. W. 1989. *Charismatic Capitalism: Direct Selling Organizations in America.* Chicago: Univ. Chicago Press. 223 pp.

Blau, P. 1987. Contrasting theoretical perspectives. In *The Micro-Macro Link,* ed. J. Alexander, B. Giesen, R. Muench, N. Smelser, pp. 71–85. Univ. Calif. Press

Boyacigiller, N., Adler, N. J. 1991. The parochial dinosaur: organizational science in a global context. *Acad. Manage. Rev.* 16:262–90

Caldwell, D. F., O'Reilly, C. A. 1990. Measuring person-job fit with a profile-comparison process. *J. Appl. Psychol.* 75:648–57

Cappelli, P., Sherer, P. D. 1991. The missing role of context in OB: the need for a meso-level approach. *Res. Org. Behav.* 13:55–110

Chatman, J. A. 1991. Matching people and organizations: selection and socialization in public accounting firms. *Admin. Sci. Q.* 36:459–84

Chen, C. C., Meindl, J. R. 1991. The construction of leadership images in the popular press: the case of Donald Burr and People Express. *Admin. Sci. Q.* 36:521–51

Conlon, E. J., Parks, J. M. 1990. Effects of monitoring and tradition on compensation arrangements: an experiment with principal-agent dyads. *Acad. Manage. J.* 33:603–22

Cox, T. H. 1990. Problems with research by organizational scholars on issues of race and ethnicity. *J. Appl. Behav. Sci.* 26:5–23

Cox, T. H., Lobel, S. A., McLeod, P. L. 1991. Effects of ethnic group cultural differences on cooperative and competitive behavior on a group task. *Acad. Manage. J.* 34:827–47

Cummings, L. L. 1981. Organizational behavior in the 1980s. *Decis. Sci.* 12:365–77

Cummings, L. L. 1982. Organizational behavior. *Annu. Rev. Psychol.* 33:541–79

Dalton, M. 1959. *Men Who Manage.* New York: Wiley. 318 pp.

D'Aveni, R. A., MacMillan, I. 1990. Crisis and the content of managerial communications: a study of the focus of attention of top managers in surviving and failing firms. *Admin. Sci. Q.* 35:634–57

Davis, G. F. 1991. Agents without principles? The spread of the poison pill through inter-corporate network. *Admin. Sci. Q.* 36:583–613

Davis-Blake, A., Pfeffer, J. 1989. Just a mirage: the search for dispositional effects in organizational research. *Acad. Manage. Rev.* 14:385–400

Doktor, R., Tung, R. L., Von Glinow, M. A. 1991. Incorporating international dimensions in management theory building. *Acad. Manage. R.* 16:259–61

Dutton, J. E., Dukerich, J. M. 1991. Keeping an eye on the mirror: image and identity in organizational adaptation. *Acad. Manage. J.* 34:517–54

Eden, D. 1990. Acute and chronic job stress, strain, and vacation relief. *Org. Behav. Hum. Decis. Process.* 45:175–93

Eisenhardt, K. M. 1988. Agency and institutional theory explanations: the case of retail sales compensation. *Acad. Manage. J.* 31:488–511

Eisenhardt, K. M. 1989a. Agency theory: an assessment and review. *Acad. Manage. Rev.* 14:57–74

Eisenhardt, K. M. 1989b. Making fast strategic decisions in high-velocity environments. *Acad. Manage. J.* 32:543–76

Eisenhardt, K. M., Schoonhoven, C. B. 1990. Organizational growth: linking founding team, strategy, environment, and growth among U. S. semiconductor ventures, 1978–1988. *Admin. Sci. Q.* 35:504–29

Elsbach, K. D., Sutton, R. I. 1992. Acquiring organizational legitimacy through illegitimate actions: a marriage of institutional and impression management theory. *Acad. Manage. J.* In press

Festinger, L., Riecken, H. W., Schachter, S. 1956. *When Prophecy Fails.* Minneapolis: Univ. Minnesota Press. 256 pp.

Frank, R. H. 1988. *Passion within Reason: The Strategic Role of the Emotions.* New York: W. W. Norton. 304 pp.

Franks, D. D., McCarthy, E. D. 1989. *The Sociology of Emotions: Original Essays and Research Papers.* Greenwich, CT: JAI Press

Frost, P., Stablein, R., eds. 1992. *Doing Exemplary Research.* Newbury Park: Sage. 321 pp.

Galaskiewicz, J., Burt, R. S. 1991. Interorganization contagion in corporate philanthropy. *Admin. Sci. Q.* 36:88–105

George, J. M. 1990. Personality, affect, and behavior in groups. *J. Appl. Psychol.* 75:107–16

Gerhart, B. 1990. Voluntary turnover and alternative job opportunities. *J. Appl. Psychol.* 75:467–76

Gersick, C. J. G. 1988. Time and transition in work teams: toward a new model of group development. *Acad. Manage. J.* 31:9–41

Gersick, C. J. G., Hackman, J. R. 1990. Habitual routines in task performing groups. *Org. Behav. Hum. Decis. Proc.* 47:65–97

Greenberg, J. 1990. Employee theft as a reaction to underpayment inequity: the hidden cost of pay cuts. *J. Appl. Psychol.* 75:561–68

Hackett, R. D., Bycio, P., Guion, R. M. 1989. Absenteeism among hospital nurses: an idiographic-longitudinal analysis. *Acad. Manage. J.* 32:424–53

Hackman, J. R., Oldham, G. R. 1980. *Work Redesign.* Reading: Addison-Wesley. 330 pp.

Hage, J. 1980. *Theories of Organizations.* New York: Wiley. 558 pp.

Hassard, J., Porter, R. 1990. Cutting down the workforce: eunuchs and early administrative management. *Org. Stud.* 11:555–67

Hochschild, A. R. 1983. *The Managed Heart.* Berkeley/ Los Angeles: Univ. Calif. Press. 307 pp.

Hollander, E. P. 1992. The essential interdependence of leadership and followership. *Curr. Dir. Psychol. Sci.* 1:71–5

House, R. J. 1977. A 1976 theory of charismatic leadership. In *Leadership: The Cutting Edge,* ed. J. G. Hunt, L. L. Larsen, pp. 189–273. Carbondale, IL: S. Illinois Press

House, R. J., Spangler, W. D., Woycke, J. 1991. Personality and charisma in the U. S. presidency: a psychological theory of leader effectiveness. *Admin. Sci. Q.* 36:364–96

Howell, J. M., Avolio, B. J. 1992. The ethics of charismatic leadership: submission or liberation. *Acad. Manage. Exec.* 2:43–54

Howell, J. M., Frost, P. J. 1988. A laboratory study of charismatic leadership. *Org. Behav. Hum. Decis. Process.* 43:243–69

Huber, J. 1990. Macro-micro links in gender stratification. *Am. Soc. Rev.* 55:1–10

Ilgen, D. R., Klein, H. J. 1988. Organizational behavior. *Annu. Rev. Psychol.* 40:327–51

Isen, A. M., Baron, R. A. 1991. Positive affect as a factor in organizational behavior. *Res. Org. Behav.* 13:1–53

Jackson, S. E., Brett, J. F., Sessa, V. I., Cooper, D. M., Julin, J. A., Peyronnin, K. 1991. Some differences make a difference: individual dissimilarity and group heterogeneity as correlates of recruitment, promotions, and turnover. *J. Appl. Psychol.* 76:675–89

James, L. A., James, L. R. 1989. Integrating work environment perceptions: explorations into the measurement of meaning. *J. Appl. Psychol.* 74:739–51

James, L. R., Tetrick, L. E. 1986. Confirmatory analytic tests of three causal models relating job perceptions. *J. Appl. Psychol.* 71:77–82

James, L. R., Demaree, R. G., Mulaik, S. A., Ladd, R. T. 1992. Validity generalization in the context of situational models. *J. Appl. Psychol.* 77:3–14

Judge, W. Q., Miller, A. 1991. Antecedents and outcomes of decision speed in different environmental contexts. *Acad. Manage. J.* 34:449–63

Kanter, R. M. 1977. *Men and Women of the Corporation.* New York: Basic Books. 348 pp.

Kahn, W.A. 1990. Psychological conditions of personal engagement and disengagement at work. *Acad. Manage. J.* 33:692–724

Kaprow, M. L. 1991. Magical work: firefighters in New York. *Hum. Org.* 50:97–103

Lee, T. W., Ashford, S. J., Walsh, J. P., Mowday, R. T. 1992. Commitment propensity, organizational commitment, and voluntary turnover: a longitudinal study of organizational entry processes. *J. Manage.* 18:15–32

Lindholm, C. 1990. *Charisma.* Cambridge, MA: Basil Blackwell. 238 pp.

Locke, E. A., Latham, G. 1990. *A Theory of Goals and Performance.* Englewood Cliffs: Prentice Hall. 413 pp.

Mandler, G. 1982. Stress and thought processes. In *Handbook of Stress,* ed. L. Goldberge, S. Breznitz, pp. 88–104. New York: Free Press

March, J. G. 1965. *Handbook of Organizations.* Chicago: Rand-McNally. 1247 pp.

March, J. G. 1991. Exploration and exploitation in organizational learning. *Org. Sci.* 2:71–87

Marcus, A. A., Goodman, R. S. 1991. Victims and shareholders: the dilemmas of presenting corporate policy during a crisis. *Acad. Manage. J.* 34:281–305

McCain, B. R., O'Reilly, C. A., Pfeffer, J. 1983. The effects of departmental demography on turnover. *Acad. Manage. J.* 26:626–41

Meindl, J. R. 1990. On leadership: an alternative to conventional wisdom. *Res. Org. Behav.* 12:159–204

Meyer, A. 1982. Adapting to environmental jolts. *Admin. Sci. Q.* 27:515–37

Meyer, J. W., Rowan, B. 1977. Institutionalized organizations: formal structure as myth and ceremony. *Am. J. Sociol.* 83:340–63

Miller, D., Droge, C. 1986. Psychological and traditional determinants of structure. *Admin. Sci. Q.* 31:539–60

Mischel, P. L. 1977. The interaction of person and situation. In *Personality at the Crossroads,* ed. D. Magnusson, N. S. Endler, pp. 333–52. Hillsdale, NJ: Lawrence Erlbaum

Mitchell, T. R. 1979. Organizational behavior. *Annu. Rev. Psychol.* 30:243–81

Murnighan, J. K., Conlon, D. E. 1991. The dynamics of intense work groups: a study of British string quartets. *Admin. Sci. Q.* 36:165–86

Nelson, D. L., Sutton, C. 1990. Chronic work stress and coping: a longitudinal study and suggested new directions. *Acad. Manage. J.* 33:859–69

Porter, M. E. 1980. *Corporate Strategy.* New York: Free Press. 396 pp.

O'Reilly, C. A. 1991. Organizational behavior: where we've been, where we're going. *Annu. Rev. Psychol.* 42:427–58

O'Reilly, C. A., Caldwell, D. F., Barnett, W. P. 1989. Work group demography, social integration, and turnover. *Admin. Sci. Q.* 34:21–37

O'Reilly, C. A., Chatman, J. A., Caldwell, D. F. 1991. People and organizational culture: a profile comparison approach to assessing person-organization fit. *Acad. Manage. J.* 34:487–516

O'Reilly, C. A., Main, B. G., Crystal, G. S. 1988. CEO compensation as tournament and social comparison: a tale of two theories. *Admin. Sci. Q.* 33:257–74

Palmer, C. T. 1990. Telling the truth (up to a point): radio communication among Maine lobstermen. *Hum. Org.* 49:157–63

Palmer, C. T. 1991. Organizing the coast: information and misinformation during the Maine lobstermen's tie-up of 1989. *Hum. Org.* 50:194–202

Pfeffer, J. 1977 The ambiguity of leadership. *Acad. Manage. Rev.* 2:104–12

Pfeffer, J. 1981. Management as symbolic action. *Res. Org. Behav.* 3:1–52

Pfeffer, J. 1983. Organizational demography. *Res. Org. Behav.* 5:299–357

Pfeffer, J. 1991. Organization theory and structural perspectives on management. *J. Manage.* 17:789–803

Pfeffer, J. 1992. *Managing with Power.* Boston: Harvard Business School Press. 391 pp.

Pfeffer, J., Davis-Blake, A. 1986. Administrative succession and organizational performance. How administrator experience mediates the succession effect. *Acad. Manage. J.* 29:72–83

Rafaeli, A. 1989. When cashiers meet customers: an analysis of the role of supermarket cashiers. *Acad. Manage. J.* 32:245–73

Rafaeli, A., Sutton, R. I. 1990. Busy stores and demanding customers: How do they affect the expression of positive emotion? *Acad. Manage. J.* 33:623–37

Rafaeli, A., Sutton, R. I. 1991. Emotional contrast strategies as means of social influence: lessons from bill collectors and interrogators. *Acad. Manage. J.* 34:749–75

Rentsch, J. R. 1990. Climate and culture: interaction and qualitative differences in organizational meanings. *J. Appl. Psychol.* 75:668–81

Rice, R. E., Aydin, C. 1991. Attitudes toward new organizational technology: network proximity as a mechanism for social information processing. *Admin. Sci. Q.* 36:219–44

Roethlisberger, F. J., Dickson, W. J. 1939. *Management and the Worker.* Cambridge: Harvard Univ. Press. 615 pp.

Salancik, G. R., Meindl, J. R. 1984. Corporate attributions as strategic illusions of management control. *Admin. Sci. Q.* 29:238–54

Schein, E. H. 1990. Organization culture. *Am. Psychol.* 45:109–19

Schneider, B. 1987. The people make the place. *Pers. Psychol.* 40:437–53

Selznick, P. 1949. *TVA and the Grass Roots.* Berkeley/ Los Angeles: Univ. Calif. Press. 274 pp.

Smith, K., Berg, D. 1987. *Paradoxes of Group Life.* San Francisco: Jossey-Bass. 281 pp.

Spector, P. E., Jex, S. M. 1991. Relations of job characteristics from multiple data sources with employee affect, absence, turnover intentions, and health. *J. Appl. Psychol.* 76:46–53

Staw, B. M. 1985. Repairs on the road to relevance and rigor: some unexplored issues in publishing in organizational research. In *Publishing in the Organizational Sciences,* ed. L. L. Cummings, P. Frost, pp. 96–107. Homewood: Richard D. Irwin

Staw, B. M. 1991. Dressing up like an organization: when psychological theories can explain organizational action. *J. Manage.* 17:805–19

Staw, B. M., Bell, N. E., Clausen, J. A. 1986. The dispositional approach to job attitudes: a lifetime longitudinal test. *Admin. Sci. Q.* 31:56–77

Staw, B. M., Boettger, R. D. 1990. Task revision: a neglected form of work performance. *Acad. Manage. J.* 33:534–59

Staw, B. M., McKechnie, P. I., Puffer, S. M. 1983. The justification of organizational performance. *Admin. Sci. Q.* 28:582–600

Staw, B. M., Sandelands, L. E., Dutton, J. E. 1981. Threat-rigidity effects in organizational behavior: a multilevel analysis. *Admin. Sci. Q.* 26:501–24

Staw, B. M., Sutton, R. I. 1992. Macro organizational psychology. In *Social Psychology in Organizations: Advances in Theory and Research,* ed. J. K. Murnighan. Englewood Cliffs, NJ: Prentice Hall. In press

Steckler, N. A. 1991. Thunderstorms, umbrellas, and funnels: the impact of middel-management communications on lower-management politicking. Presented at Annu Meet. Acad. Manage., 51st, Miami

Stevenson, W. B., Gilly, M. C. 1991. Information processing and problem solving: the migration of problems through formal positions and networks of ties. *Acad. Manage. J.* 34:918–28

Sutton, R. I. 1991. Maintaining norms about emotional expression: the case of bill collectors. *Admin. Sci. Q.* 36:245–68

Sutton, R. I., Rafaeli, A. 1988. Untangling the

relationship between displayed emotions and organizational sales: the case of convenience stores. *Acad. Manage. J.* 31:461–87

Tsui, A. S., Egan, T., O'Reilly, C. A. 1991. Being different: relational demography and organizational attachment. *Proc. Acad. Manage.,* pp. 183–87

Tsui, A. S., O'Reilly, C. A. 1989. Beyond simple demographics: the importance of relational demography in superior-subordinate dyads. *Acad. Manage. J.* 32:402–23

Tuckman, B. 1965. Developmental sequence in small groups. *Psychol. Bull.* 63:384–99

Van Maanen, J., Schein, E. H. 1979. Toward a theory of organizational socialization. *Res. Org. Behav.* 1:209–64

Walsh, J. P., Ungson, G. R. 1991. Organizational memory. *Acad. Manage. Rev.* 16:57–91

Weick, K. E. 1990. The vulnerable system: an analysis of the Tenerife air disaster. *J. Manage.* 16:571–93

Westley, F. 1991. Bob Geldof and Live Aid: the affective side of global social innovation. *Hum. Relat.* 44:1011–37

Zajac, E. J., Bazerman, M. H. 1991. Blind spots in industry and competitor analysis: implications of interfirm (mis)perceptions for strategic decisions. *Acad. Manag. Rev.* 16:37–56

Zenger, T. R., Lawrence, B. S. 1989. Organizational demography: the differential effects of age and tenure distributions on technical communications. *Acad. Manage. J.* 32:353–76

Annu. Rev. Psychol. 1993. 44:231–63

ENGINEERING PSYCHOLOGY IN A CHANGING WORLD

William C. Howell

Human Resources Directorate, Armstrong Laboratory, Brooks Air Force Base, Texas 78235-5000

KEYWORDS: human factors, ergonomics, applied experimental psychology, complex skills

CONTENTS

BACKGROUND AND INTRODUCTION 231
   Driving Forces.. 234
UNDERSTANDING AND COPING WITH COMPLEX TASK DEMANDS...................... 237
   Background 237
   Cognitive Task Analysis and Knowledge Elicitation 238
   Situation Awareness 241
   Mental Workload and Related Phenomena 244
   Naturalistic and Group Decision Making... 247
   Displays and HCI... 249
ACCOMMODATING AND EXPLOITING INDIVIDUAL DIFFERENCES 250
   Background 250
   Theoretical Developments.. 251
   Illustrative Research Topics.. 252
   Aging.. 252
   Customized Training 254
SUMMARY AND CONCLUSIONS 257

BACKGROUND AND INTRODUCTION

Engineering psychology remains something of an enigma to most psychologists despite nearly a half century of solid performance. Thus, virtually every previous reviewer has felt obliged to begin with a definition and an explanation of how engineering psychology differs from the closely related domains of human factors or human-factors engineering and ergonomics. The modal view is that engineering psychology is a core applied research component of the other disciplines, all of which are concerned with improving the design of systems that involve people. Its chief role is to provide information on human performance capabilities, limitations, and tendencies that can be used in making systems safer, more efficient, more accurate, and less aggravating for the operator.

Because its origins and principal methodologies are found in experimental psychology, it has always been closely linked to that specialty and indeed is often called applied experimental psychology. However, experimental psychology has changed dramatically over the years and no longer confines itself to basic issues on a narrow range of traditional topics using traditional experimental designs. Research psychologists of many stripes have developed an interest in systems applications. Therefore, finding a special niche in the research literature for engineering psychology is becoming as difficult as finding people who identify themselves as engineering psychologists!

This fact poses an obvious problem for the reviewer. No longer is the field's content confined to a few well-established sources; relevant material can appear anywhere. In fact, most of the material in this review is explored in much greater depth elsewhere in the *Annual Review of Psychology* under headings such as cognitive processes, decision making, cognitive development, instructional psychology, and organizational psychology. The relevance of social, developmental, educational, organizational, and differential branches of psychology has become increasingly apparent because of the growing importance of interpersonal, age-related, instructional, contextual, and individual-differences factors in system design.

In the last review, Gopher & Kimchi (1989) noted that "contemporary work in engineering psychology is marked by a deep interest in high-level cognitive functions and knowledge compilation" (p. 432). This is still true but is by no means the distinguishing feature it once was (Hoffman & Deffenbacher 1992). Now that the cognitive perspective is so pervasive in psychology, and system designers are beginning to realize the need for other kinds of psychological information, engineering psychology may well be disappearing as an identifiable specialty. If so, it is disappearing not because attempts to establish the discipline's basic tenets have failed, but because engineering psychology has succeeded so well. One no longer needs to explain why "user friendliness" is important, or how thinking of human mental processes in the metaphor of machines is useful. The language of engineering psychology has become the language of psychology.

Despite the blurring of distinctions that once set engineering psychology apart, it is still meaningful to differentiate among research efforts in terms of their proximity to system-design issues (Chapanis 1991). Some are clearly driven more by application potential than by sheer intellectual curiosity, and given the rapid pace at which both technology and society are changing, a psychological presence as close as possible to the point where systems originate is more important than ever. Although designers have been slow to absorb

Table 1   A summary of major system design issues and the forces driving them

Driving force	Applied issues
Technology	
computerization	HCI (interface, software)
automation	skill maintenance, workload transition monitoring, troubleshooting function allocation, task design
task complexity/speed	cognitive demands, scheduling, workload, stress
information display	coding, design, quality distribution
general	"technostress" organizational consequences
Society	
demography	special populations, system requirements
skill/education trends	talent shortfall (training, aiding, selection implications)
geopolitical change	military requirements, simulation, logistics support (e.g., maintenance) technology transfer
litigation/consumerism	human error, safety (workplace, environment, consumer products)

this message, human performance requirements are becoming increasingly visible in a variety of systems contexts. Booher's (1990) volume, which includes some explicit guidance for implementing the MANPRINT version of this philosophy, is an important case in point. If proximity to system design rather than content domain or dominant theoretical paradigm is accepted as a plausible basis for defining the field as it exists today, then it seems reasonable to review engineering psychology in terms of prominent system-design issues. And because these issues are driven largely by trends in technology and society—forces that dictate the kinds of systems and system requirements that are likely to evolve—a look at some of the major driving forces is useful. Table 1 illustrates some of the applied issues receiving considerable attention in current literature together with the major trends that are forcing those issues and should continue to do so well into the twenty-first century.

In Table 1, issues are arranged in rough correspondence to principal driving forces, but there is obviously not a 1:1 correspondence across any of the columns: issues have multiple causes, and neither the specific issues nor the specific drivers are independent of one another.

Work represented in this review is sampled chiefly from these domains. After a brief discussion of the driving forces and their significance, current work on selected issues is examined in greater depth. I do not attempt to cover all the important issues nor to provide an exhaustive review of the recent literature on any of them. Rather, the goal is to show how a sample of important design questions is being addressed through a variety of psychological approaches, some rather nontraditional, with both basic and applied objectives. In organizing the chapter according to applied issues, I do not mean to suggest that the field has abandoned theory or fundamental research in favor of the quick and dirty. Indeed, if anything, the opposite is true (Wickens 1992).

Driving Forces

Two main trends are particularly relevant in setting the course for system-design issues: technological and social change. Let us examine briefly the principal forces associated with each.

TECHNOLOGICAL INNOVATION   Technology now moves so fast that a piece of hardware or software can be well on its way to obsolescence by the time it is incorporated into an operational system. As a result, options available to the designer are growing at a remarkable pace, and the cost of certain key components, notably those related to computational power and display capabilities, are dropping rapidly. For example, innovations in image generation and display techniques led to a reduction in the cost of high-performance aircraft simulators from nearly $100 million to $.5 million a copy (Galatowitsch 1991). Moreover, with the evolution of fiber-optic helmet-mounted displays, reliable head-tracking and eye-tracking devices, data gloves, and the ever-declining cost of computing power, pilots may soon be able to carry their simulators with them to wherever they are deployed and maintain their skills in their spare time.

As illustrated in Table 1, innovation is occurring on several fronts particularly relevant for the engineering psychologist. Many, of course, involve computer hardware and software developments that have significant ramifications for human-computer interaction (HCI). Attendant issues are so many and varied that HCI has emerged as a discipline of its own. Its archival publications include *HCI,* which has been in existence for six years, *Computers in Human Behavior,* which is about the same age, and the *SIGCHI Bulletin,* which has a much longer history. From a psychological perspective, the principal focus of HCI has been on perceptual and cognitive issues: how should interfaces and software be designed for maximum usability? However, the scope of HCI implications is beginning to spread into the affective, social, and organizational domains as well (Eason 1991).

Closely related to computer development, but including such additional components as robotics and artificial intelligence (AI) applications, automation continues to pose massive unresolved problems to which psychologists are becoming increasingly attracted (Gies 1991). These range from longstanding questions of how best to allocate functions and exercise supervisory control to the more recent concern over so-called macroergonomic issues that involve social and organizational factors (Robertson 1991).

The next two areas of technological innovation distinguished in Table 1 obviously depend on the first two, yet are sufficiently unique in their respective psychological implications to merit individual attention. Somewhat paradoxically, machines that can do more, and do it faster, provide the basis for systems that are increasingly demanding of the human operator, particularly in terms of cognitive requirements. Public awareness of this fact arose in the aftermath of the Three-Mile Island accident in 1978 (Rubinstein & Mason 1979) and has been reinforced by periodic disasters (e.g. Chernobyl, the Vincennes incident, various commercial air collisions) since. Consequently, research addressing the issues related to task complexity and speed requirements continues at a remarkable pace and has taken on a few new twists as discussed in the section on specific issues below.

Similarly, advances in display technology continue to drive research on how best to represent and present information to the operator, but in a much broader context than the traditional knobs-and-dials focus of yesteryear. Virtual reality, for example, in which the individual can experience the environment visually rather than through a tactile interface such as a keyboard or mouse, offers immense possibilities as well as a host of questions that are only beginning to be explored (Barcus et al 1991). Once again, the evolution of computer networking, videoconferencing, groupware, and other technologies that help link people together in novel ways raises several interpersonal or social-psychological design issues. Are there, for example, more and less effective ways to represent information that must be shared by different specialists comprising a team (Converse et al 1991; Cannon-Bowers et al 1992)?

A final set of applied issues driven by technological change is best thought of as general side effects. Perhaps the most vivid example of this category is the widely publicized case of afflictions attributed to the massive transition to computer workstations (VDT induced ailments, Carpal-Tunnel Syndrome, etc). Research has intensified in an effort to understand—and insofar as possible anticipate—adverse organismic and psychological effects associated with new technologies (Brod 1984; Hudinburg 1989; Nicholson 1991). In addition, however promising technological changes may be, they must ultimately be assimilated into the larger sociotechnical system of the workplace or the organization if that potential is to be realized. Assimilation is neither easy to accomplish nor risk free (Howell 1991; Offerman & Gowing 1990; Turnage 1990; Zedeck 1992).

SOCIAL CHANGE   Less prominent in the engineering psychological literature, but of at least equal significance, are trends in society. In an extremely provocative paper, Moray (1991) argues that the human-factors discipline will never progress much beyond merely scratching the surface of systems problems until we engage more global issues (e.g. population growth, water shortages, environmental destruction, terrorism, etc).

The first two categories of social change noted in Table 1 involve trends featured in a highly influential Hudson Institute report (Johnston & Packer 1987) on U.S. labor force projections. The population is aging, education levels are declining, and the workforce is becoming more diversified (especially in ethnicity and gender). At the same time, skill requirements prompted by the technological advances described earlier are increasing in many occupations. Taken together, these observations point to a serious projected shortfall in talent.

Naturally, the applied-psychology literature is starting to reflect these trends. For example, aging has become a prominent topic in the human-factors literature, and training requirements are taking on new significance in industrial and military contexts (Goldstein & Gilliam 1990; Griffin 1992).

The massive changes in world geopolitics and resulting reduction in military tension among superpowers have greatly shifted the military policies of most industrialized nations (Cheney 1991; Powell 1992). Among those of greatest significance for engineering psychology are changes in the requirements for and anticipated deployment of weapons systems and an increased sensitivity to cost. First, the future emphasis will shift from the creation and production of new weapon systems to the modification and maintenance of old ones. Second, military forces will be smaller, more mobile, and more flexible, capable of mobilizing the required mix of personnel and materiel quickly at any trouble spot on the globe, carrying out a unique mission with skill and precision, and then moving out quickly. Third, cost and environmental considerations will limit the opportunity to conduct realistic combat-training exercises. And finally, more emphasis will be placed on transferring the results of military and other government-sponsored R&D to commercial use (Schriesheim 1990). This latter development is also driven by another geopolitical trend: the USA's declining position in the world economy.

The collective impact of these trends on the kinds of issues to which psychologists will be asked to direct their attention is profound. Consider, for example, the logistics maintenance problem. Rather than taking an airplane or tank to a well equipped base or logistics center staffed with a cadre of highly specialized technicians, the military will often have to take broadly skilled technicians with minimal equipment to some primitive, remote site where they will perform many of the same functions as their specialized counterparts. This need calls for a restructuring of maintenance tasks and a redefinition of skill requirements, increased reliance on computer-based diagnostic aids and logistics support (e.g. technical data, inventory control), and an ability to provide rapid on-site training in order to maintain or refine the requisite skills (Galatowitsch 1991).

We will have to develop a whole new generation of aiding and training tools and accompanying principles in order to meet the decentralization and flexibility requirements. Questions regarding simulation-fidelity requirements, training schedules and strategies, transfer effects, and a host of other longstanding issues are being revisited as a result. The long recognized potential of affordable, individualized, computer-based instruction is also beginning to be exploited and will undoubtedly expand with the growth in our understanding of its cognitive underpinnings (see below).

The final category of social change shown in Table 1 is applicable primarily to the United States with its growing penchant for litigation and the heightened public awareness of environmental, workplace, and consumer-product safety issues. Safety has always been considered an important goal in the human-factors philosophy and has received considerable attention from the practice community over the years. But for those engaged in engineering psychological research, safety has never achieved the prominence of performance or reliability as a dependent variable, except by implication. More importantly, it has generated very little interest in theory development, the articulation of the underlying constructs and processes that relate design (and other) variables to safe or unsafe behavior. One would expect the growing demand for safety in design to stimulate interest in such research, and indeed this appears to be happening (Hale & Glendon 1987; Miller 1988; Wickens 1992).

UNDERSTANDING AND COPING WITH COMPLEX TASK DEMANDS

Background

As noted earlier, concern over the increasing cognitive requirements of advanced systems has preoccupied engineering psychologists for some time. At a basic research level, this concern has expressed itself primarily in work prompted by consensus models of human cognition (e.g. working memory characteristics, attention models, organization of knowledge in long-term memory, etc). The aim has been to expand our understanding of these fundamental mechanisms and thereby build toward an understanding of human performance in the more complex setting of real-world tasks. At an applied level, the concern has focused on issues such as how to measure mental workload, organize and display information, and decide which task components should be automated. Only recently have researchers paid attention to the generic properties of complex tasks that make them problematic or to the manner in which people deal with such tasks, with varying degrees of success.

By contrast, knowledge engineers and HCI specialists have addressed such issues in their attempt to improve the operability of semiautomated systems (Klein 1990). Their approach has generally involved techniques such as knowledge elicitation from subject-matter experts, cognitive-task analysis, and modeling. In other words, they and engineering psychologists have been approaching the complex-task problem from exactly opposite directions. Hammond et al (1991) describe this distinction as a "tension between two research philosophies" (p. 111) in contrasting artificial intelligence (AI) and psychological perspectives on analogical reasoning.

Perhaps the most promising and exciting development since the last review has been an emerging interest among psychological researchers in the more task-oriented perspective of the knowledge engineer. Without abandoning the link with basic cognitive theory, proponents of this paradigm shift seek to understand the cognitive demands of complex tasks in their natural setting. Several important papers have appeared recently explaining and illustrating this philosophy. Adams et al (1991) present a comprehensive review of the relevant theoretical issues and introduce a framework for understanding human cognitive processing in the complex, multitask situation. In their view, the critical neglected area involves "the performance and management of multiple threads of cognitive activity: How do humans manage requirements to perform a stack of tasks that vary dynamically in relative priority and that cannot be performed together?" (p. 7). Building on "fragments of theory" from J. J. Gibson as well as Neisser, schema theory, and connectionist theory (neural networks) together with the most salient empirical evidence, Adams et al lay out systematically the cognitive domain that must be explored in order to understand and deal effectively with the multitask-management situation. They advocate an iterative modeling and experimentation approach as the most expeditious route to this goal.

Others have echoed or practiced this general philosophy in the context of research on scheduling (Sanderson 1989; Moray et al 1991), attention alloca-tion (Gopher 1992), workload management (Hart 1989), interface design (McNeese & Zaff 1991), situation awareness (Sarter & Woods 1991), supervi-sory control (Kirlik, Miller & Jagacinski 1992, unpublished report), and deci-sion making (Lipshitz 1992). Indeed, even those who have exemplified the more traditional (molecular) laboratory approach have begun complementary molar efforts (Wickens et al 1989). And finally, a succinct National Research Council (NRC) report summarizes the status of human-performance modeling in complex systems (Baron et al 1990), and another NRC volume explores in greater depth models of component human-performance functions (from vi-sion to decision making) that are applicable to helicopter piloting (Elkind et al 1989).

Though still in its infancy, the paradigm shift and complex-task orientation has generated a fair amount of research over the past few years. In the present section, therefore, I examine a small sampling from this growing literature on complex task issues.

Cognitive Task Analysis and Knowledge Elicitation

A fundamental difficulty facing those who would apply cognitive theory and principles to system design lies in the extraction of essential cognitive infor-mation from human beings (Gott 1989; Klein 1990). Long recognized as a critical problem in the design of "expert systems" (Feigenbaum & McCorduck

1984), it is equally serious for those seeking to adapt displays, software, or training to the user's mental representation of the task. One must first have some way of describing accurately what that representation is; options for doing so are limited, and each has its drawbacks (Hall et al 1990). By and large all are derived from the traditional strategies of self-report, psychometrics, and inference from behavior.

Still, refinements and specific adaptations of these approaches have resulted in several extraction techniques that have proven useful for various design applications. Progress has been particularly evident during the past few years despite the fact that a great deal of confusion surrounds the nature of that which elicititation techniques seek to measure—typically, mental models (Rouse & Morris 1986). Wilson & Rutherford (1989) present an excellent review of the literature on mental models in which they argue that the human-factors and psychology communities have used (and perhaps need to use) the concept in quite different ways for different purposes—essentially, specific design applications vs conceptualization of basic processes. They caution, among other things, against overgeneralization from the more applied usage, suggesting that what it reveals is often limited to parts or aspects of a mental model that are predetermined by the elicitation methods used and by prior assumptions made.

Knowledge elicitation is also governed by one's theory of human cognition. Techniques tend to focus on particular kinds of knowledge, such as procedural vs declarative, that presumably exist in certain general forms such as production rules or semantic networks or schemata of some sort. Hence in devising or selecting a technique, elicitors are likely to make assumptions about the relation of the problem or task domain to cognitive structure (Kitto & Boose 1989). This process seems a bit circular: one seeks to describe how people represent task features mentally using tools dictated by those very models. However, the circularity is partially resolved by the growing evidence in support of the assumed cognitive architectures. Anderson's (1983, 1987, 1992) ACT theory, for example, which represents cognitive skill in terms of production rules, has received broad support from various lines of research (e.g. Just & Carpenter 1987; Kieras & Bovair 1986; Singley & Anderson 1989; Bovair et al 1990).

Several attempts have been made recently to organize elicitation techniques into some form of taxonomy with implications for differential application (Geiwitz et al 1988; Olson & Biolsi 1991; Shadbolt & Burton 1989; McGraw & Harbison-Briggs 1989). Moreover, McClosky et al (1991) demonstrated empirically that a structured interview technique is better suited for divergent planning and scheduling tasks while a similarity-judgment approach is better for convergent categorization and evaluation tasks.

The most comprehensive and analytic of the taxonomic effort appears in a report by Cooke (1992), which incorporates and distinguishes among all the others. In addition to such well-known approaches as process tracing, task analysis, observation, and interview, it discusses a host of common and not-so-common structural techniques (e.g. structural modeling, clustering techniques) and decision analysis tools, all from the standpoint of conceptual basis and appropriate use.

Space limitations permit only a brief discussion of a few notable examples from these compendia of options: the theory-based production-system approach, a novel process-tracing methodology (PARI), a promising structural modeling technique (Pathfinder), and a specific application involving multiple methods.

The production-system approach deals mainly with how people do and should think through particular (usually well-structured) kinds of problems. In its various forms, it has proven particularly useful in HCI and intelligent tutoring applications, often focusing on comparisons of novice (or student) and expert mental models (Regian & Shute 1992). Because a major goal is to represent knowledge in terms of production rules that can be modeled and tested against human performance, the emphasis is on procedural or strategic rather than declarative knowledge (indeed, the transition from declarative to procedural representation is taken as a goal of learning), and the approach is driven by cognitive theory.

Many task situations, of course, are not well structured, and declarative knowledge is what often distinguishes the novice from the expert (Glaser et al 1985; Soloway 1986). The PARI methodology was developed to analyze cognitive task characteristics for poorly structured problems, as represented by fault-diagnosis or troubleshooting tasks, and to include strategic and declarative as well as procedural knowledge in the process (Hall et al 1990). Based on a variant of the thinking-aloud or verbal protocol-analysis approach typical in expert-systems research, PARI involves a dialogue between experts focused on solving carefully chosen problems, and content analysis of their interactions by trained observers using a structured classification procedure (e.g. actions and the sequence of precursors). Consisting of nine distinct stages, PARI is a costly but, based on evidence to date, highly effective approach for purposes such as development of training for maintenance personnel (Gott 1989). In particular, it provides information of a kind and in a form that permits the shaping of generalized "device models" in technicians, thereby enabling them to deal effectively with unfamiliar or rare malfunctions as well as to adapt more readily to device modifications. In view of the technological driving forces discussed at the outset of this review, these benefits could well outweigh the costs inherent in the method.

Pathfinder is an algorithmic scaling technique that uses relatedness judgments from human subjects (experts or novices) to produce a representation of their mental models in terms of a network structure (Cooke 1992). Concepts are represented as nodes and associations between them as links weighted according to strength (link length). In contrast to the production-system approach, Pathfinder has been used predominantly to represent declarative knowledge, although in one application it also included procedural material (McDonald & Schvaneveldt 1988). Although Pathfinder is still a new approach, models generated using it have proven meaningful or valid in several empirical tests, including the prediction of free-recall order, dimensional judgment time, and category judgment time in laboratory studies (Gillan et al 1992); expert-novice differences in a variety of real-world tasks; and several other applications (Cooke 1992).

Our final example from the knowledge-elicitation literature is a multifaceted approach that was applied to a specific design problem: creation of an interactive AI aid for combat pilots to reduce their cognitive load during tactical fighter missions in high-performance aircraft (the Pilot's Associate or PA). The objective was to obviate the notorious "brittleness" of such expert systems through development of a user-oriented (natural) knowledge structure derived using a combination of Integrated Computer-Aided Manufacturing Definition (IDEF) modeling, concept mapping, and design storyboarding techniques (McNeese & Zaff 1991; McNeese et al 1990). The IDEF approach is a standard (engineering) task-analysis method whereas the concept-mapping approach is an interview-based, graphically structured knowledge-elicitation tool. Storyboarding is a technique for translating concepts into prototypes with which the subject-matter expert can directly interact (Andriole 1989).

McNeese's approach generates two models of the task concurrently (the IDEF or designer's model and the conceptual or expert's model) and then applies both in the interactive mode afforded by storyboarding using experienced pilots as subjects. Like PARI, this is a cumbersome and expensive process, but with systems as complex and significant as the PA, it may well prove to be a wise investment in the long run. Nevertheless, evidence on the effectiveness of such multiperspective, labor-intensive approaches relative to simpler ones is primarily logical and anecdotal at this point.

Situation Awareness

Most of the properties of emerging tasks that worry human-factors professionals are embodied in a concept (or set of concepts) currently receiving a great deal of attention, particularly within the aviation community, under the label situation awareness (SA). While definitions vary, the essential idea is that an operator must keep track of a lot of information from a variety of sources over time and organize or interpret this information to behave appropriately.

Neither the concept nor the measurement of SA has yet been adequately developed, although everyone who uses the term seems confident of his or her particular interpretation and of its importance: clearly, success in maintaining a grasp of complex situations contributes significantly to the safety and performance of manned systems (Carroll 1992; Regal et al 1988). If, in fact, the concept turns out to have unique meaning as one or more demonstrably valid constructs, then it can probably be improved through design, selection, training, or all three (Adams et al 1991). The international scope of SA issues was highlighted by a NATO AGARD (Advisory Group for Aerospace Research and Development) symposium devoted exclusively to this topic that was held in Copenhagen in 1988.

Several recent reports have explored in depth both the potential and the problems inherent in the SA concept. Collectively, they provide a good review of progress to date and future directions. Sarter & Woods (1991) examine the conceptual and measurement problems with particular emphasis on the temporal dimension, which, in their view, is critical and has been neglected in previous research. They note similarities and differences between the SA and mental-model concepts, concluding that (at least in the human-factors or expert-systems sense discussed earlier) mental models are an essential part of SA but are lacking in the "continuously changing open system" character that is its most unique feature. However, because most attempts to measure SA have focused on the static information used to define mental models, the concepts as typically measured are very similar (Crane 1993).

Other critical reviews have appeared in reports by Berniger & Hancock (1989), Fracker (1991a,b), Fracker & Davis (1991), Endsley (1989), Tenney et al (1992), Companion (1990), and Whitaker & Klein (1988). Conceptual distinctions have been drawn between spatial awareness, identity awareness, responsibility or automation awareness, and temporal awareness (Harwood et al 1988); between situation assessment (a process) and its awareness product (Tenney et al 1992); between momentary and reflective SA; and among Level I (perception of situational elements), Level II (information integration), and Level III (projection of future states) processes (Endsley 1988). It remains to be seen, however, how many of these represent valid and useful distinctions.

The work by Tenney et al (1992) and by Fracker (1988, 1991a) constitute the most serious efforts to fit the various constructs into a coherent theoretical framework. Both draw heavily on research and theory from cognitive psychology, especially in the memory and attention areas, although Tenney et al also emphasize theories of perception and comprehension (J. J. Gibson, Neisser, schema theory, etc) to account for the more active, knowledge-driven aspects of the SA phenomenon. Neither group, however, claims to have progressed much beyond an initial conceptualization, and both recognize the need for empirical verification. Tenney et al (1992) advocate a model-based approach (as noted earlier) while Fracker (1991a,b; Fracker & Davis 1991) relies on traditional experimentation (hypothesis testing) for validating SA constructs and on psychometric techniques for establishing the reliability and criterion-referenced validity of SA measures.

Both Tenney et al and Fracker recognize that different purposes call for different measurement techniques, suggesting that no single measure can capture the multiple facets of SA. Measurement issues, of course, are fundamentally intertwined with issues of conceptualization, as Fracker & Davis (1991) emphasize in their analysis of the content and construct validity of various SA measures. In fact, the main thrust of Fracker's empirical work has been to evaluate the three principal types of available measures: explicit techniques (e.g. memory probes, think-aloud protocols), implicit or surrogate measures (e.g. signal detection sensitivity indexes, theory-based performance measures), and subjective measures (e.g. direct and comparative ratings). He does not deal with the model-based approach proposed by Tenney et al, since no one has yet actually carried it out, but clearly this would fall into his implicit category. To date, the most widely used measures have been the explicit ones exemplified by Endsley's (1988) SAGAT (Situation Awareness Global Assessment Technique), an approach in which a complex, dynamic scenario is interrupted and the operator's stored knowledge of specific events is probed.

Not surprisingly, neither SAGAT nor any of the other current measures fared particularly well in Fracker's empirical (psychometric) analysis. Reliability and content validity proved particularly problematic, although the ability to predict task performance on the basis of SA measures (predictive validity) was encouraging. Given the complexity of the SA concept, the fact that SA measurement is still in its infancy, and the limited scope of the only systematic attempt to evaluate SA measures, there does seem to be cause for optimism.

Considerably less heartening, however, is the fact that pressures to find some usable measure and rush it into application for selection, training, or design purposes is growing (Carroll 1992). Such pressures often result in the entrenchment of techniques that are difficult to replace even when later proven to be seriously deficient. Measurement in the absence of understanding is always a risky proposition, and particularly so for a domain with the practical significance of SA.

Despite its conceptual murkiness, SA has been the object of several recent empirical studies. For example, Kass et al (1991) found that training subjects to recognize muzzle-flash patterns under reduced complexity of the stimulus environment led to better performance in a complex battlefield simulation (SIMNET) than did training under realistic complexity. The results were taken as support for a theory of skill-based SA (Companion et al 1990).

Several studies addressed the individual-differences aspect of SA. Bolstad (1991) developed a battery of 14 tests based on assumptions regarding the attributes presumed to underlie SA, and validated it against SAGAT measures of SA. Although the evaluation was admittedly preliminary with a very small sample ($N = 21$), the top five predictors produced promising correlations (0.39–0.72). This work, incidentally, illustrates the cause for concern expressed earlier. Suppose further development of this battery does produce defensible prediction of SAGAT measures. SAGAT is at best a deficient index of SA (Hughes et al 1990; Sarter & Woods 1991), and a refined version of this battery could become an accepted operationalization of SA, with selection and training programs built around it, all in advance of any clear validation of an SA construct (or constructs).

Much the same could be said for a 10-dimensional subjective rating index (SART), which was developed primarily for application in system design (Selcon & Taylor 1989). In this case, however, one can at least be confident that the index has some ecological validity given that it was constructed from the judgments of experienced aircrew personnel. Moreover, a recent study suggests that what it measures is sensitive to task-difficulty manipulation and somewhat independent of subjective workload (Selcon et al 1991). Two other studies also looked at SA and workload measures concurrently (Sullivan & Blackman 1991; Hughes et al 1990), but neither provides much insight into the relation between the constructs. In fact, Hughes et al found that a workload measure (SWORD) was a useful practical tool for measuring SA, whereas in this particular instance, the SA measure (SAGAT) was problematic. Clearly, much remains to be done before the conceptual underpinnings of the two kinds of measures are fully explicated.

Mental Workload and Related Phenomena

Increases in the mental demands of work threaten system performance and operator well-being over both the short and long term. This fact is both obvious and well substantiated by research concerned with vigilance, mental workload, stress, effort, timesharing, and a host of related topics, including SA. Although it undoubtedly shares a limited set of biological and psychological (especially cognitive) mechanisms, the research has tended to organize itself along phenomenal lines. As a result, commonalities in underlying processes, and indeed among the phenomena themselves, have rarely been explored in depth. Nor have hypotheses generated in one context typically been tested in others. But that may be changing.

For most of the 1980s, the measurement of mental workload and the implications of multiple-resource theories of attention for task interference (largely via the dual-task paradigm) held sway. These were properly featured in both the 1985 (Wickens & Kramer) and the 1989 (Gopher & Kimchi) *Annual Review of Psychology* chapters. Those summaries are still fairly current, and excellent updates are available in Lysaght et al (1989) for workload and in Damos (1991) for multiple-task performance. Wickens (1992) covers both, together with underlying theoretical issues, in Chapter 9 of his revised text. Because activity in these areas seems to be waning in the 1990s, present coverage is limited to a sampling of recent work that appears to portend trends.

As noted earlier, there is renewed interest in the top-down or controlled aspect of attention. An influential series of studies by Hirst & Kalmar (1987) posed problems for the traditional view of multiple resources as reservoirs (the fuel metaphor) and suggested alternative metaphors, including a skill conceptualization. Gopher (1992) reached a similar conclusion after reviewing the evidence on the strategic control of attention, which, though impressive, has rarely been the focus of experiments on attention. He and others have identified a popular video game, *Space Fortress,* as an excellent operationalization of that skill, and, after demonstrating its transfer to pilot-training performance, have gotten it incorporated into the regular training of the Israeli Air Force (Gopher et al 1993). Adams et al (1991) also emphasize strategic mechanisms in pointing out limitations in the dual-task paradigm, and multiple-resource researchers themselves have begun exploring skill or strategic facets of dual-task performance (Tsang & Wickens 1988; Goettl 1991; Wickens 1992). Ongoing projects at the United Kingdom's MRC Applied Research Unit continue this laboratory's tradition of leadership in the conceptualization of attention mechanisms, and the current emphasis of their research bears directly on the controlled aspects. What is particularly exciting about this work is the attempt to gather converging evidence from a variety of neurophysiological and psychological research paradigms on one evolving model of attentional control (Baddeley & Weiskrantz 1992). Baddeley's (1992a,b) conception of a "central executive" component that controls phonological and visuo-spatial components of working memory is an important part of this model, as is Duncan & Humphries' (1989) filtering model that posits template-matching and goal-weighting processes to account for selective visual search (Duncan 1992). Shallice's work on the cognitive effects of frontal-lobe lesions in human patients (see Shallice & Burgess 1992), and studies of Alzheimer's patients (Baddeley et al 1992), contribute supporting physiological evidence.

Theoretical and methodological issues surrounding the multiple resource model of attention still generate discussion. Tsang & Velazquez (1991) use Navon's "optimum-maximum" method to demonstrate tradeoffs in dual-task performance predicted by resource theory. Goettl & Joseph (1991), on the other hand, report only "modest" performance tradeoffs between two tracking tasks using the same method. They suggest that subjects may elect not to spend "free resources" on the concurrent task, a conclusion that is consistent with the strategic perspective on dual-task performance noted earlier.

Whatever its limitations, the multiple-resource model remains an extremely useful framework for expanding our understanding of how people perform multiple tasks. It neither obviates other models (metaphors), nor prevents concurrent exploration of the complex-task domain using other approaches (see, e.g. Oatman 1989). Moreover, it serves as a sensitive device for exploring the effects of organismic and environmental variables on human performance. Rodgers & Holding (1991), for example, used Performance Operating Characteristic (POC) measures to chart circadian trends in performance efficiency.

In the mental-workload domain, emphasis has shifted from narrowly focused measurement issues to more fundamental theoretical questions, including the relation of workload to other constructs. For example, Moray et al (1991) report subjective workload effects in a scheduling task, along with efficiency and strategy measures, as a function of time pressure and rule knowledge. Rule knowledge proved of little value in either reducing subjective workload or improving performance under increasing time pressure. Matthews & Margetts (1991) show that the self-reported stress or arousal level generated within the dual-task paradigm controls the proportion of attentional resources invested in higher-priority task components.

Becker et al (1991) continue to find evidence that subjective workload is correlated with performance on vigilance tasks as variables known to control performance are manipulated. Hence vigilance decrements are not the result of declining arousal, but rather are related to increasing subjective workload. Further, Galinski et al (1990) show that sensory alternation, which should attenuate vigilance decrements if pathway inhibition is the causal mechanism, fails to do so, although it does attenuate the event-rate effect (i.e. lower performance with more nontarget events), all of which seems to indicate once again that vigilance is not the simple phenomenon it was once hoped to be (Hancock & Warm 1989; Warm et al 1991).

A related aspect of the workload problem that is just beginning to stimulate interest is the transition from light to heavy loads: for example, when an automated process goes awry or an emergency arises and the task changes from monitoring to controlling (Huey & Van Cott 1991). Wickens (1991) presents interim conclusions from a major Army-sponsored study of this problem emphasizing the human-factors, training, and vigilance perspectives, respectively. Collectively, this report and others in the same symposium constitute more of an agenda for needed research than a set of confident answers. Moreover, the focus is almost exclusively on the multiperson (crew, team) setting, which is certainly prominent but is not the only context in which this transition could threaten system performance.

Workload-measurement issues also seem a bit broader than in the past. Vidulich et al (1991) evaluated the subjective workload dominance technique (SWORD) as a means of predicting the workload associated with alternative display designs by comparing projective vs retrospective measures for experienced operators with those for students. Dramatically different pre-post correlations for the two subject groups validated SWORD for its intended use. Nygren (1991) examined the psychometric properties of the two most commonly used subjective indexes (SWAT and TLX) and found them to be quite different. He concluded that both are useful, but for measuring different aspects of workload.

Physiological indexes besides those involving the EEG, such as cardiac and respiratory measures (Backs et al 1991) and vocal-stress measures (Jones 1991), continue to be of interest, but have progressed little since the last review. Work reported by Posner & Petersen (1990) and Posner (1992), however, suggests real progress toward understanding the neurosystems that serve attention and its relation to cognitive operations. Use of positron emission tomography (PET) scanning with animal, normal, and brain-damaged subjects has produced evidence in support of multiple attention systems (a posterior network located in the parietal lobes, a vigilance network in the right frontal lobes, and an anterior network in the anterior cingulate) that amplify and regulate activity produced by particular cognitive tasks. As a more complete picture of these mechanisms emerges, interest in physiological indicants of all attentional phenomena—vigilance, workload, multiple-resource predictions, and so on—should grow.

As noted at the outset of this section, efforts aimed at integrating the various constructs and phenomena that have been invoked to account for performance changes associated with demanding tasks are beginning to emerge. Nowhere is this more evident than in Wickens' (1992) treatment of attention, time-sharing, workload, and stress. Other noteworthy works center around the most global (and least well understood) of these concepts, stress. Task demands have always held a prominent place in the compendia of stressors. However, task requirements constitute but a part of the overall stress associated with incorporation of advanced technologies into the workplace (Hockey et al 1989). The term *technostress* has been coined in reference to these broader effects (Brod 1984; Hudinburg 1989; Nicholson 1991). An important volume edited by Cooper & Payne (1988) explores a variety of conceptual, methodological, and practical issues, including those of an organizational nature, associated with stress at work. Ironson (1992) reviews the evidence on the relationship of occupational stress to personal and organizational outcomes, and proposes a global model to account for the rather complex pattern of effects. Ivancevich et al (1990) discuss interventions.

At a more basic level, Hancock & Warm (1989) present a dynamic model of stress in which they attempt to link vigilance, workload, and other task-related variables, together with organismic stressors such as noise and heat, to underlying psychological and physiological constructs. In the process, they offer a viable alternative to the horribly flawed, yet widely accepted, concept of a simple arousal mechanism. The essence of their position is that stress involves "… a reduction of available attentional capacity (psychological adaptability) and an increase in physiological strain that has to be compensated for by regulatory systems (physiological adaptability)" (p. 533). If nothing else, the Hancock & Warm model is valuable because it emphasizes the need to integrate current knowledge and future research on these clearly related facets of modern work.

Naturalistic and Group Decision Making

Research on judgment and decision making, undertaken from both normative and descriptive perspectives for both practical and scientific purposes, continues to grow at a seemingly exponential rate. Because it constitutes a field of its own covered regularly in the *Annual Review of Psychology* and is well represented by dedicated journals (e.g. *Organizational Behavior and Human Decision Processes, Journal of Behavioral Decision Making*) the general topic is not addressed here (see Yates 1990; Stevenson et al 1990 for recent overviews).

Work in one particular area, however, has had a significant impact on decision research and theory as it relates to the design of modern systems. This task domain focuses on the problem faced by real decision makers in complex, usually multiperson systems characterized by high levels of uncertainty, information load, time pressure, and decision importance (i.e. "stress"), so it is obviously appropriate to the present discussion. The term *naturalistic* was coined to differentiate this general task domain, and the approach advocated for studying it, from the more traditional axiomatic and heuristic paradigms used in laboratory research (Klein et al 1992).

Both the theoretical and methodological underpinnings of naturalistic decision research draw heavily from the same cognitive literature discussed earlier in the context of expert knowledge and SA. The basic idea is that experienced decision makers reduce the task situation to manageable proportions by converting it into a pattern-recognition problem (Coury et al 1989). This cognitive strategy, which is viewed as entirely different from the more analytic approach implied by traditional decision models, has been articulated by Klein (1989) as the recognition-primed decision (RPD) model. Interviews and other knowledge elicitation techniques have been used in studying fire-fighters, tank commanders, and commanders of wildland forest-fire teams from the RPD perspective (Klein 1989, 1990). A forthcoming book (Klein et al 1992) is devoted entirely to work stimulated by the growing popularity of the naturalistic approach and its underlying philosophy. A major U.S. Navy program on tactical decision-making under stress (TADMUS) is adapting the naturalistic methodology, along with others, in a massive effort to understand—and improve—team performance in situations similar to the unfortunate Vincennes incident (Cannon-Bowers et al 1991a).

Proponents of naturalistic decision-making research are careful to point out the link between this conceptualization of the decision process and such theoretical precursors as Hammond's cognitive continuum theory, which introduced the qualitative distinction between intuitive and analytic decision processes; Rasumssen's skill-rule-knowledge trichotomy; and Beach & Mitchell's image theory (Lipshitz 1992) (see Beach 1990, for a good account of image theory). Thus, although many of the basic ideas have been around for a while and the methodology is hardly new, naturalistic decision making weaves several of these threads together into a fresh approach to the study of decision processes in situations that matter and have heretofore been largely inaccessible to available techniques.

A great deal of the decision making in modern systems is done collectively with the help of sophisticated interface, communication, and aiding technologies (Swezey & Salas 1991; Orasanu & Salas 1992). Here as elsewhere, however, the technology leads the psychology substantially, and knowledge is lacking on a wide variety of critical system-design issues. A recent workshop report provides an excellent summary of these issues together with suggested directions for future research (Harris 1990). A report and annotated bibliography by Dierolf & Richter (1990), though focused on concurrent engineering teams, represents a fairly comprehensive collection of the relevant literature.

One particularly troublesome aspect of team decision making in naturalistic settings is that having multiple operators adds to the already high stress levels typical of these situations, and does so in a variety of ways (Driskill & Salas 1991a,b). Absence of a generally accepted model of team decision making (Morgan & Bowers 1990) makes it difficult even to speculate on how interpersonal, personality, cognitive, organizational, and other variables might operate to enhance or degrade team performance. Nevertheless, Weaver et al (1991) and Orasanu (1990) lay some conceptual groundwork for the investigation of such potential stress moderators. And, of course, empirical validation of hypothesized stress-reduction interventions is a major objective of the TADMUS project. The findings from this research should provide at least some insight into the underlying processes.

In summary, team decision making is receiving considerable attention at present, but mostly in terms of conceptual and methodological preparation for, rather than execution of, the necessary research. The difficulties inherent in such work are clearly massive. On the other hand, knowledge of component aspects of the team-decision situation is available from diverse sources (the social, cognitive, decision, individual-differences, training, and expert-systems literatures), and efforts are underway to draw it together in ways that will direct a meaningful attack on the whole.

Displays and HCI

Display-design issues, particularly as they relate to the computer interface, have dominated the recent human-factors literature like no others. They have generated a body of psychological research that is too large and heterogeneous to summarize coherently. Thus, rather than reviewing the work itself, I merely comment on its collective features as it relates to the topic of complex-task demands. Much of it, in fact, arose in direct response to these demands.

The first noteworthy feature, which largely accounts for the heterogeneity, is the task (and even system) specificity of the research. Relatively few new general principles have surfaced since the last review, or for that matter, since the *Handbook of Human Perception and Performance* (Boff et al 1986), although many of the specific studies draw heavily on perceptual and cognitive theory and extend it. For example, Wickens & Andre (1990) examined the impact of color proximity, spatial proximity, and "objectness" (format) on information integration and focused attention in a task designed to simulate the multiple-indicator requirements of a light aircraft. In another study, the Wickens group explored some of the same proximity/integration issues in a process-control context (Jones et al 1990). Though addressing a specific set of questions in each instance, these studies continued a systematic line of investigation derived from basic concepts in pattern perception and attention allocation. Martin et al (1987) showed that highlighting displayed information with color results in processing that draws virtually nothing from attentional capacity (or is fully automated, depending on one's theoretical preference).

The task specificity of current display research is a natural consequence of the well-established fact that performance reflects the interaction of displays with tasks (Gopher & Kimchi 1989). What this implies is that defining, measuring, and classifying complex tasks is as essential to effective display design as it is to the other topics addressed in the present section.

A second common feature of this literature is its orientation toward issues posed by advanced display capabilities. At present, these include effective use of color (e.g. Pastoor 1990; Travis et al 1990), graphics (e.g. Sanderson et al 1989; Schaubroeck & Muralidhar 1991), stereoscopic imaging (e.g. Tzelgov et al 1990; Yeh & Silverstein 1990), synthetic speech (e.g. Ralston et al 1991), and virtual-world imagery (e.g. Flach et al 1990), to cite but a few. An excellent overview of emerging principles and remaining questions in one of these areas, color usage, is available in a recent NRC workshop report (Kinney & Huey 1990). Knowledge in some of the other areas is not yet sufficient to justify similar treatment, although with the current level of research activity in each, that time may not be far off.

A final commonality apparent in the display/HCI literature is its continuing drift away from the more peripheral (sensory) to the more central (cognitive) aspects of displayed information. This drift reflects several trends, including the improved quality of display signals, the increased potential for overloading the operator, and the explosion of knowledge regarding human cognition. Despite this movement, however, the more peripherally oriented work still has a place in the design arena, primarily with respect to questions of cost/benefit. For example, a number of studies have explored the image-quality factors responsible for reduced reading performance with CRT displays (Jorna & Snyder 1991). Improved quality on any relevant dimension is achievable, but at a cost. The question then becomes what are the relative cost/improvement functions for various approaches?

ACCOMMODATING AND EXPLOITING INDIVIDUAL DIFFERENCES

Background

Traditionally, engineering psychology has focused on general principles of human performance rather than individual differences. Design is for the average, "normal" adult or trained system operator. However, the forces cited in Table 1, coupled with the fact that psychometricians and others who have traditionally favored the individual-differences perspective are converging on the same cognitive territory as engineering psychologists, have stimulated a growing interest in design for targeted populations, or even for individuals. Thus the distinguishing characteristics of older drivers, skilled fighter pilots, and particular kinds of trainees become important, not only for selection purposes, but in order to tailor system design and training to their special needs. The shifting emphasis from hardware to software makes such customization increasingly feasible. And the growing importance of cognitive-task demands means that constructs such as working memory, attentional resources, and automatization of skill are becoming as meaningful to the test developer and instructional designer as they are to the human-factors professional.

Once again, space permits only a sampling of the areas in which an individual-differences perspective is emerging. Reviews of material particularly relevant to engineering psychology may be found in Ackerman & Humphries (1990), Detterman (1991), and Fleishman & Mumford (1989). Orlansky et al (1990) review the most current military research in selection and classification, much of which concerns cognitive measures, improved performance criteria, and computer-based testing.

Theoretical Developments

Two massive programs undertaken by the U.S. Army and U.S. Air Force respectively promise to yield a step-function increment in the measurement of critical predictors. The Army program (Project A) included comprehensive measurements and follow-up on many thousands of recruits. Using a fairly standard (largely empirical) psychometric approach, it has resulted in several important generalizations including a comprehensive modeling of the Army job performance domain and a Longitudinal Research Data Base (LRDB) that will enable continued investigation for years to come (Orlansky et al 1990; Sackett 1990).

The Air Force Learning Abilities Measurement Program (LAMP), now almost a decade old, has also involved thousands of subjects, but from a more limited and nontraditional perspective. It focuses on taxonomizing the cognitive underpinnings of learning, and its approach combines theory-driven with standard psychometric research methods (Kyllonen 1991). As knowledge of cognitive structures and processes grows, the taxonomy is expanded, new tests are devised, and the expanded battery is validated against learning criteria (Kyllonen & Christal 1989). Thus, for example, constructs such as working memory, processing speed, and declarative knowledge have yielded demonstrably valid test items for predicting learning rates in courses such as basic electricity, computer programming, and avionics. Moreover, evidence has surfaced suggesting the differential efficiency of specific instructional strategies for specific cognitive aptitude profiles (Shute 1992) (see below). And recent developments from the cognitive literature, such as the idea that working memory comprises multiple components (Baddeley 1992b) or that attention allocation and time-sharing (Gopher 1992) constitute measurable skills, suggest candidate items for a revised test battery. Subsequent validation, of course, would strengthen the theoretical arguments together with all their practical implications.

Illustrative Research Topics

One can find studies addressing individual-differences issues in almost every corner of the engineering-psychology domain. Here are a few diverse illustrations. Westman (1990) shows that a trait called *hardiness* moderates the relationship between stress and performance: military officers who score higher on this self-report index report lower stress and outperform their less "hardy" peers. People apparently also differ in their preferred level of job demands, and such preferences moderate pacing-performance relationships (Parkes et al 1990).

Several studies cite important individual differences in information processing strategies observed in the context of display design (Purcell & Coury 1988; Coury & Pietras 1989), decision making (Shanteau & Harrison 1991), SA (Bolstad 1991), problem solving (Carpenter et al 1992), vigilance (Koelega et al 1989), cockpit management (Chambers & Whitmore 1991; Orasanu 1991), decision-support systems (Ramamurthy et al 1992), and a host of other applied research topics. As noted earlier, the possibility of systematic aptitude-treatment interactions is central to the idea of customized training (Shute 1992), and systematic changes in the particular abilities that control skill development at different stages of learning further complicate the picture (Fleishman & Mumford 1989; Murphy 1989). Also noted earlier, the skill-metaphor or strategic view of attention carries with it a strong individual-differences implication (Gopher 1992).

Finally, personality and other noncognitive variables are showing up increasingly as potential moderators in studies of system design-performance functions. For example, Weaver et al (1991) examine a number of such variables in their review of team decision making under stress; Arthur et al (1991) find meta-analytic evidence for the role of two personality variables in vehicular accidents; Schaubroeck & Muralidhar (1991) note the possibility of a "cognitive complexity" moderator in display-format effectiveness; and Wickens (1992) cites evidence that "locus of control" and "extraversion" may mediate stress effects.

Aging

Chronological age is often treated as an individual-differences variable (formally, as a mediator or moderator) in studies of displays, controls, or other system-design features (e.g. Barber 1990). For many years, a valid complaint was that the cognitive and behavioral aspects of the aging process are poorly understood, making designing for the older operator difficult (Smith 1990). Less common was the equally defensible proposition that, while undeniably important, chronological age may be a poor surrogate for actual skill changes (Fozard & Popkin 1978; Guide & Gibson 1991; Waller 1991).

Our understanding of how capabilities and system requirements change with age may still be far from complete, but not for want of attention (Light 1991). Few topics are as prominent in today's human-factors literature as aging—obviously a reflection of the general impact that demographic trends are having on all areas of behavioral and social research (Longergan 1991). Over the past three years, more than a dozen age-related articles have appeared in *Human Factors* alone, together with three entire special issues of the journal. One special issue (Czaja 1990) includes a useful overview of the history and current status of aging research as it relates to human-factors applications (Smith 1990), together with papers on such important topics as how experience moderates cognitive deficits (Salthouse 1990) and where the gaps are in anthropometric data on the elderly (Kelly & Kroemer 1990). The issue also reports on some promising approaches to studying how older people function in performing everyday tasks (Lawton 1990; Clark et al 1990).

Also included are two articles on the topic to which the second and third special issues (Barr & Eberhard 1991, 1992) are devoted exclusively: the older driver. This disproportionate emphasis on one particular skill, driving, is both representative of the current literature and easy to justify. More older drivers on the road coupled with age-related decrements in critical functions such as vision (Klein 1991) and response speed (Vercruyssen 1991) clearly imply a growing risk to public safety. Furthermore, we must understand the specifics of that risk in order to advise public policy, whether the policy be aimed at improved highway design (Mast 1991), vehicle design, selection/test procedures, or perhaps even training (Shinar & Schieber 1991).

Unfortunately, the accumulating evidence suggests that the picture is anything but simple, even for the most fundamental issue of all: the existence of a clear and important causal link between age and risk (Barr 1991; Laux 1991). Part of the problem is the aforementioned deficiency in the chronological-age index itself, and part undoubtedly reflects the fact that people tend to compensate in various ways for their eroding skills (Ball & Owsley 1991; Waller 1991). Absence of a clear actuarial case, however, in no way diminishes the need for research on the aging driver.

In reviewing the recent work on aging, one is struck by a most encouraging trend. The research and those engaged in it seem to be drawing increasingly closer to the theoretical mainstream in their exploration of age effects. For example, Rogers & Fisk (1990) examined age as a factor in the maintenance and modification of "automatic" skill components and found that older subjects have difficulty inhibiting such overlearned processes. Brouwer et al (1991) showed divided-attention deficits in older drivers using multiple-resource theory and the dual-task paradigm as the framework for their experimentation. Brogums (1991) used a version of Fitts' Law to describe psychomotor changes with age in a sample of 1318 subjects, reporting that much of the decline in speed is attributable to shifts in the speed-accuracy trade-off. Greatorex (1991) tested the proposition that reaction-time (RT) decrements in older subjects are attributable to age-related arousal changes but concluded—based on task-dependent changes in the shape of the RT distribution—that multiple factors are involved. And finally, Ball & Owsley (1991) developed and have attempted to test a theoretical model of the cognitive information-processing system of the older driver, while Sterns & Doverspike (1989) have reviewed the training implications of aging from the perspective of learning processes.

Customized Training

Design and training are alternative, but highly interactive, strategies for improving system performance and safety (Rouse 1990). For one thing, training requirements should constitute an important part of the specifications for any system design. For another, training is itself best regarded from a system perspective (Goldstein 1989): a training system requires as much care in its design as an operational system does, and perhaps more care should be given its inherently dynamic properties.

Nowhere is the immense potential of advanced technology more apparent than in the realm of training-system design, and nowhere is that potential more needed than in meeting the skill requirements of advanced technology. Widely (and probably justly) criticized in past decades for its faddishness and pedestrian quality, training research and practice enters the 1990s on a wave of enthusiasm prompted as much by its newly formed links with cognitive, social, industrial/organizational, and instructional theory as by space-age technology (Salas 1991).

Since the general topic has been reviewed recently elsewhere (Tannenbaum & Yukl 1992; Goldstein 1989, 1991; Salas 1991), I limit discussion to one noteworthy area of training-system design: customization and automation of instruction (computer-based instruction or training, CBI or CBT, respectively). After more than a half-century of largely unfulfilled promise, automated instruction geared to the individual learner is finally coming of age.

Ever since Sidney Pressey conceived of the idea and B. F. Skinner popularized it, automated instruction aimed at the individual level has promised to revolutionize education. Although theorists disagreed on many aspects of implementation, and programmed instruction (PI) rather than automated delivery became the focus of attention, the advantages of tailoring instruction to the needs and progress of the individual student were compelling, and remain so today. Empirical studies reported by Bloom (1984) strengthened the theoretical case by suggesting a two-sigma mean advantage for the tutorial over the group-instruction mode.

Practical drawbacks, however, such as the difficulty and cost of developing good programs, particularly where complex material and pedagogy is involved, plagued implementation of PI and, subsequently, CBI. Moreover, as the artificial intelligence necessary to assess and address the momentary state of the learner and thereby offer a true tutoring capability was added to CBI, the development problem only grew worse. Not only could "courses offering a minimum of individualization and graphical elaboration...require several hundred hours for every hour of instruction produced" (Towne & Munro 1991, p. 325), but it was unclear what specific pedagogy should be used. And in complex domains such as technical maintenance skills, where expert knowledge is not easily defined or captured as we saw earlier, even the course content was problematic.

Recent progress on several fronts is beginning to make inroads against these difficulties. Towne & Munro (1991) present a succinct review of current approaches to the development of authoring software, some of which—notably simulation-based, general-purpose authoring systems such as RAPIDS—promise to cut development costs of intelligent tutoring systems (ITSs) dramatically.

As for the problem of identifying what to train (the nature and proper representation of to-be-learned content), developments in cognitive theory, task analysis, and knowledge elicitation (see earlier discussion) are beginning to have a significant impact. An excellent review by Cannon-Bowers et al (1991b) summarizes the leading theoretical perspectives and their evolving implications for training technique, not all of which have yet been realized. Foremost among these implications is the idea that cognitive theory provides a powerful means of conceptualizing present and desired mental states as well as the progression of skill development, thereby enabling meaningful analysis of both to-be-learned tasks/skills/content and diagnosis of momentary progress toward goal attainment.

Patrick (1991) explores the analytic implications in depth, and Annett (1991) reviews the perspectives on skill acquisition. Both reviews appear in an important volume, *Training for Performance,* edited by Morrison (1991). Another edited volume (Regian & Shute 1992) presents current perspectives on cognitive diagnosis. Yet another pair of collections provides an excellent overview of the current status of the (ITS) field, one from a more conceptual perspective (Polson & Richardson 1988) and the other from a more practical perspective (Psotka et al 1988). Finally, a new journal, the *Journal of the Learning Sciences,* joins the growing list of serials in which AI, cognitive science, cognitive and educational psychology, cognitive anthropology, education, and education technology or various combinations thereof converge on the important issues in training.

Turning to the question of how to provide individualized training, the tutoring-strategy issue, the picture is still quite murky. Techniques for explaining and demonstrating concepts, correcting student errors, or otherwise promoting the process of learning in ITSs still seem more in the realm of art than science. The knowledge base simply does not exist to indicate when, for example, the student should be given a principle or allowed to discover it. In fact, it is not even clear what all the alternative strategies are.

The cognitive literature does suggest some strategic principles (Ackerman & Kyllonen 1991), and their relative effectiveness likely varies with content domain, skill level, and task features. Most importantly, their effectiveness may also vary with characteristics of the individual student—the cognitive abilities to which the previously mentioned LAMP program is directed. Growing evidence that the aptitude-treatment interaction may be considerably more robust than was previously thought makes this a particularly fertile area for further research (Shute 1992). And, of course, for potential ITS application, tailoring strategies to the particular background-knowledge and cognitive-skill profile of the individual student, as well as to the content domain and all the other factors, would represent the ultimate in customization. The U.S. Air Force has just initiated a large basic research program with this general objective in mind. A companion to LAMP, its acronym is STAMP (Schooling and Training Approaches Measurement Program), and it is scheduled to be fully underway by 1993.

Because this review highlights individualization, the reader should not conclude that it is the only facet of training research that has shown dramatic progress over the past few years. Simulation (Alluisi 1991), embedded and distributed training (Witmer & Knerr 1991; Sheppe & Hayes 1991), part-task and automaticity training (Fisk & Rogers 1991; Lintern 1991b), the organizational context of training (Goldstein & Gilliam 1990), team training (Tannenbaum et al 1992), and transfer issues (Holding 1991; Lintern 1991a) are other topics that have either been revived or introduced in response to emerging system requirements and the driving forces discussed at the beginning of this chapter.

Several underlying themes emerge as one reviews this proliferating literature on training. First, the reorientation from a behavioral to a cognitive emphasis is now fairly complete within the research community but is understandably lagging in many areas of the practice community. For instance, skill training in industry is still driven primarily by behavioral-task analysis and an industrial-engineering mentality rather than principles for promoting automatic processing, mental-model development, metacognition, or other cognitive conditions (Howell & Cooke 1989). And in areas such as team training, in which building "shared mental models" is being proposed as an important objective, knowledge is still too primitive even to think about applications (Cannon-Bowers et al 1992).

A second theme is the resurgence of interest in all forms of simulation and the consequent rediscovery of all the longstanding issues that have surrounded the concept and its implementation for decades (i.e. fidelity requirements, transfer effects, part-whole training strategies, appropriate performance measures, and so on). Andrews (1988) discusses some of these issues in drawing an important functional distinction between simulators and training devices. The former are designed to afford opportunities for practice, hence require high levels of objective and perceptual fidelity, whereas the latter are designed to promote learning, hence require understanding and optimization of conditions for skill acquisition. Recognizing the difference clarifies several often-confused research and application questions (e.g. the kind and level of fidelity required). Unfortunately, despite the renewed interest in the topic, and an improved appreciation for what needs to be known to make these studies more effective, simulation research has yet to resolve many of these issues (Tannenbaum & Yukl 1992).

Finally, there is a growing awareness in the literature of the importance of the context within which training occurs and is eventually put to use, an area in which organizational researchers can contribute. A study by Rouillier & Goldstein (1991), for example, demonstrates that the organizational climate into which training is inserted has a major impact on how well it transfers to actual job performance.

SUMMARY AND CONCLUSIONS

Technological innovation is driving rapid change in the tasks faced by human operators, often in the direction of increased complexity and cognitive demands. Thus, much of the current work in engineering psychology, or more precisely, the entire domain of applied cognitive psychology, is oriented toward understanding these demands and how best to cope with them. Techniques for analyzing and describing complex tasks from the cognitive perspective of the novice as well as the expert are critical but still evolving. New topics (such as situation awareness) join old ones (such as mental workload, vigilance, and stress) as research foci, and others (such as decision making and display issues) are being reoriented to deal with the complexities and capabilities of advanced systems. While still somewhat fractionated, these efforts do seem to be converging on some common conceptual territory.

Changes in society are driving other research trends, many of which involve individual differences—a perspective not typically associated with engineering psychology. Psychometric, experimental, and physiological research efforts are coming together to validate certain cognitive constructs and measures. Applications of this knowledge to problems associated with aging and training are among the foremost growth areas in engineering psychology.

ACKNOWLEDGMENT

Preparation of this manuscript was supported by the Human Resources Directorate, Armstrong Laboratory, Brooks Air Force Base, Texas 78235-5000.

Literature Cited

Ackerman, P. L., Humphries, L. G. 1990. Individual differences theory in industrial and organizational psychology. *Handb. Indust. Org. Psychol.* 1:223–82

Ackerman, P. L., Kyllonen, P. C. 1991. Trainee characteristics. See Morrison 1991, pp. 193–229

Adams, M. J., Tenney, Y. J., Pew, R. W. 1991. *Strategic Workload and the Cognitive Management of Advanced Multi-task Systems.* BBN Rep. No. 7650. Cambridge, MA: BBN Systems & Technologies

Alluisi, E. A. 1991. The development of technology for collective training: SIMNET, a case history. See Salas 1991, pp. 343–62

Anderson, J. R. 1983. *The Architecture of Cognition.* Cambridge, MA: Harvard Univ. Press. 345 pp.

Anderson, J. R. 1987. Production systems, learning, and tutoring. In *Production System Models of Learning and Development,* ed. D. Klahr, P. Langley, R. Neches, pp. 437–58. Cambridge, MA: MIT Press

Anderson, J. R. 1992. General principles for an intelligent tutoring architecture. See Regian & Shute 1992. In press

Andrews, D. H. 1988. The relationship between simulators, training devices and learning: a behavioral view. *Educ. Technol.* 1:48–53

Andriole, S. J. 1989. *Storyboard Prototyping for Systems Design.* Fairfax, VA: QED Information Science

Annett, J. 1991. Skill acquisition. See Morrison 1991, pp. 13–51

Arthur, W. Jr., Barrett, G. V., Alexander, R. A. 1991. Prediction of vehicular accident involvement: a meta-analysis. *Hum. Perform.* 4:89–105

Backs, R. W., Ryan, A. M., Wilson, G. F. 1991. *Proc. Hum. Factors, 35th Annu. Meet.,* pp. 1495–99. Santa Monica: Hum. Factors Soc.

Baddeley, A. D. 1992a. Is working memory working? The fifteenth Bartlett Lecture. *Q. J. Exp. Psychol.* 44A:1–31

Baddeley, A. D. 1992b. Working memory. *Science* 255:556–59

Baddeley, A. D., Bressi, S., Della Salla, S., Logie, R., Spinnler, H. 1992. The decline of working memory in Alzheimer's Disease: a longitudinal study. *Brain.* In press

Baddeley, A. D., Weiskrantz, L., eds. 1992. *Attention: Selection, Awareness, and Control. A Tribute to Donald Broadbent.* Oxford: Oxford Univ. In press

Ball, K., Owsley, C. 1991. Identifying correlates of accident involvement for the older driver. *Hum. Factors* 33:583–95

Barber, A. V. 1990. Visual mechanisms and predictors of far field visual task performance. *Hum. Factors* 32:217–33

Barcus, G. S., Barcus, T. T., Dunn-Roberts, R. R. 1991. *Proc. Interservice/Indust. Train. Syst. Conf., 13th, Orlando,* pp. 487–93

Baron, S., Kruser, D. S., Huey, B. M., eds. 1990. *Quantitative Modeling of Human Performance in Complex, Dynamic Systems.* Washington, DC: Natl. Acad. Press. 96 pp.

Barr, R. A. 1991. Recent changes in driving among older adults. *Hum. Factors* 33:597–600

Barr, R. A., Eberhard, J. W., eds. 1991. Safety and mobility of elderly drivers Part I. *Hum. Factors* (Spec. Issue) 33

Barr, R. A., Eberhard, J. W., eds. 1992. Safety and mobility of elderly drivers, Part II. *Hum. Factors* (Spec. Issue). In press

Beach, L. R. 1990. *Image Theory.* New York: Wiley

Becker, A. B., Warm, J. S., Dember, W. N., Hancock, P. A. 1991. *Proc. Hum. Factors, 35th Annu. Meet.,* pp. 1491–94. Santa Monica: Hum. Factors Soc.

Berniger, D. B., Hancock, P. A. 1989. *Proc. Int. Symp. Aviat. Psychol., 5th, Columbus, Ohio*

Bloom, B. S. 1984. The 2 sigma problem: the search for methods of group instruction as effective as one-on-one tutoring. *Educ. Res.* 13:3–16

Boff, K. R., Kaufman, L., Thomas, J. P., eds. 1986. *Handbook of Human Perception and Performance.* New York: Wiley

Bolstad, C. A. 1991. *Proc. Hum. Factors, 35th Annu. Meet.,* pp. 52–56. Santa Monica, CA: Hum. Factors Soc.

Booher, H. R., ed. 1990. *MANPRINT: An Approach to Systems Integration.* New York: van Nostrand Reinhold. 612 pp.

Bovair, S., Kieras, D. E., Polson, P. G. 1990. The acquisition and performance of text-editing skill: a cognitive complexity analysis. *Hum. Comput. Interact.* 5:1–48

Brod, C. 1984. *Technostress: The Human Cost of the Computer Revolution.* Reading, MA: Addison-Wesley

Brogmus, G. E. 1991. *Proc. Hum. Factors, 35th Annu. Meet.,* pp. 208–16. Santa Monica: Hum. Factors Soc.

Brouwer, W. H., Waterink, W., VanWolffelaar, P. C., Rothengatter, T. 1991. Divided attention and experienced young and older drivers: lane tracking and visual analyses in a dynamic driving simulator. *Hum. Factors* 33:573–82

Cannon-Bowers, J. A., Salas, E., Converse, S. 1992. Shared mental models in expert team decision making. In *Current Issues in Individual and Group Decision Making,* ed. N. J. Castellan, Jr. Hillsdale, NJ: Erlbaum

Cannon-Bowers, J. A., Salas, E., Grossman, J. D. 1991a. *Improving tactical decision making under stress: research directions and applied implications.* Presented at Int. Appl. Military Psychol. Symp., Stockholm

Cannon-Bowers, J. A., Tannenbaum, S. I., Salas, E., Converse, S. A. 1991b. Toward an integration of training theory and technique. See Salas 1991, pp. 281–92

Carpenter, P. A., Just, M. A., Shell, P. 1992. What one intelligence test measures: a theoretical account of the processing in the Raven Progressive Matrices Test. *Psychol. Rev.* In press

Carroll, L. A. 1992. Desperately seeking SA. *TAC Attack* March:1–2

Chambers, R. M., Whitmore, M. 1991. *Proc. Hum. Factors, 35th Annu. Meet.,* pp. 996–1000. Santa Monica: Hum. Factors Soc.

Chapanis, A. 1991. To communicate the human factors message, you have to know what the message is and how to communicate it. *Hum. Factors Soc. Bull.* 34(11):1–4

Cheney, D. 1991. *America's New Defense Policy. Air Force Update.* Washington, DC: Secretary of the Air Force, Office of Public

Affairs

Clark, M. C., Czaja, S. J., Weber, R. A. 1990. Older adults and daily living task profiles. *Hum. Factors* 32:537–49

Companion, M. 1990. *Training Technology for Situational Awareness: Annual Technical Project Report.* Orlando, FL: Inst. Simulation and Training

Companion, M. A., Corso, G. M., Kass, S. J., Herschler, D. A. 1990. *Situational Awareness: An Analysis and Preliminary Model of the Cognitive Process.* (IST-TR-89–5). Orlando, FL: Univ. Central Fla., Inst. Simulation and Training

Converse, S. A., Cannon-Bowers, J. A., Salas, E. 1991. *Proc. Hum. Factors, 35th Annu. Meet.*, pp. 1417–21. Santa Monica: Hum. Factors Soc.

Cooke, N. J. 1992. Eliciting semantic relations for empirically-derived networks. *Int. J. Man-Mach. Stud.* In press

Cooper, C. L., Payne, R. 1988. *Causes, Coping, and Consequences of Stress at Work.* London: Wiley

Coury, B. G., Boulette, M. D., Smith, R. A. 1989. Effects of uncertainty and diagnosticity on classification of multidimensional data with integral and separable displays of system status. *Hum. Factors* 31:551–69

Coury, B. G., Pietras, C. M. 1989. Alphanumeric and graphic displays of dynamic process monitoring and control. *Ergonomics* 32:1373–89

Crane, P. M. 1993. Theories of expertise as models for understanding situation awareness. *Mil. Psychol.* In press

Czaja, S. J., ed. 1990. Aging. *Hum. Factors* (Spec. Issue) 32

Damos, D. L., ed. 1991. *Multiple-Task Performance.* London: Taylor & Francis

Detterman, D., ed. 1991. *Current Topics in Human Intelligence: Theories of Intelligence.* Norwood, NJ: Ablex

Dierolf, D. A., Richter, K. J. 1990. *IDA Pap. P-2516.* Alexandria, VA: Inst. Defense Analysis

Driskell, J. E., Salas, E. 1991a. Group decision making under stress. *J. Appl. Psychol.* 76:473–78

Driskell, J. E., Salas, E. 1991b. Overcoming the effects of stress on military performance: human factors, training, and selection strategies. In *Handbook of Military Psychology,* ed. R. Gal, A. D. Mangelsdorff. New York: Wiley

Duncan, J. 1992. Selection of input and goal in the control of behavior. See Baddeley & Weiskrantz 1992. In press

Duncan, J., Humphries, G. W. 1989. Visual search and stimulus similarity. *Psychol. Rev.* 96:433–58

Eason, K. D. 1991. Ergonomic perspectives on advances in human-computer interaction. *Ergonomics* 34:721–41

Elkind, J. I., Card, S. K., Hochberg, J., Huey, B. M., ed. 1989. *Human Performance Models for Computer-Aided Engineering.*

Washington, DC: Natl. Acad. Press. 309 pp.

Endsley, M. R. 1988. *Proc. Hum. Factors, 32nd Annu. Meet.,* Santa Monica: Hum. Factors Soc.

Endsley, M. R. 1989. *A methodology for objective measurement of situation awareness.* Presented at AGARD Symp. Situation Awareness in Aerospace Operations, Copenhagen

Feigenbaum, E. A., McCorduck, P. 1984. *The Fifth Generation: Artificial Intelligence and Japan's Computer Challenge to the World.* NY: New American Library

Fisk, A. D., Rogers, W. A. 1991. Recombination of automatic processing components: the effects of transfer, reversal, and conflict situations. *Hum. Factors* 33:267–80

Flach, J. M., Hagen, B. A., O'Brien, D., Olson, W. A. 1990. Alternative displays for discrete movement control. *Hum. Factors* 32:685–95

Fleishman, E. A., Mumford, M. D. 1989. Abilities as causes of individual differences in skill acquisition. *Hum. Perform.* 2:201–23

Fozard, J. L., Popkin, S. J. 1978. Optimizing adult development: ends and means of an applied psychology of aging. *Am. Psychol.* 33:975–89

Fracker, M. L. 1988. *Proc. Hum. Factors, 32nd Annu. Meet.,* pp. 102–6. Santa Monica: Hum. Factors Soc.

Fracker, M. L. 1991a. *AL Tech. Rep. 1991–0127.* Armstrong Lab., Wright-Patterson AFB, Ohio

Fracker, M. L. 1991b. *AL Tech. Rep. 1991–0128.* Armstrong Lab., Wright-Patterson AFB, Ohio

Fracker, M. L., Davis, S. A. 1991. *AL Tech. Rep. 1991–0091.* Armstrong Lab., Wright-Patterson AFB, Ohio

Galatowitsch, S. 1991. The Human Resources Directorate: exploring the man/machine interface. *Def. Electron.* 23:32–45

Galinsky, T. L., Warm, J. S., Dember, W. N., Weiler, E. M., Scerbo, M. W. 1990. Sensory alternation and vigilance performance: the role of pathway inhibition. *Hum. Factors* 32:717–28

Geiwitz, J., Klatzky, R. L., McCloskey, B. P. 1988. *Knowledge Acquisition for Expert Systems: Conceptual and Empirical Comparisons.* Santa Barbara, CA: Anacapa Sciences

Gies, J. 1991. Automating the worker. *Invent. Technol.* 6(Winter):56–63

Gillan, D. J., Breedin, S. D., Cooke, N. J. 1992. Network and multidimensional representations of the declarative knowledge of human-computer interaction design experts. *Int. J. Man-Mach. Stud.* In press

Glaser, R., Lesgold, A., Lajoie, S., Eastman, R., Greenberg, L., et al. 1985. *Cognitive Task Analysis to Enhance Technical Skills Training and Assessment.* (Contract No. F41689–83-C-0029). Brooks AFB, TX: Air Force Hum. Resources Lab.

Goettl, B. P. 1991. Tracking strategies and cognitive demands. *Hum. Factors* 33:169–83

Goettl, B. P., Joseph, J. 1991. *Proc. Hum. Factors, 35th Annu. Meet.,* pp. 1486–90. Santa Monica: Hum. Factors Soc.

Goldstein, I. L., ed. 1989. *Training and Development in Work Organizations: Frontiers of Industrial and Organizational Psychology.* San Francisco: Jossey-Bass

Goldstein, I. L. 1991. Training in work organizations. *Handb. Indust. Org. Psychol.* 2:507–619

Goldstein, I. L., Gilliam, P. 1990. Training system issues in the year 2000. *Am. Psychol.* 45:134–43

Gopher, D. 1992. The skill of attention control: acquisition and execution of attention strategies. In *14th Symp. Int. Assoc. Study of Attention and Performance,* ed. D. Meyer, S. Kornblum. Hillsdale, NJ: Erlbaum. In press

Gopher, D., Kimchi, R. 1989. Engineering psychology. *Annu. Rev. Psychol.* 40:431–55

Gopher, D., Weil, M., Bareket, T. 1993. Fidelity revisited: the transfer of skill from a computer game trainer to actual flight. *Hum. Factors.* In press

Gott, S. P. 1989. Apprenticeship instruction for real-world tasks: the coordination of procedures, mental models and strategies. In *Review of Research in Education,* ed. E. Z. Rothkopf, 15:97–169. Washington, DC: Am. Educ. Res. Assoc.

Greatorex, G. L. 1991. *Proc. Hum. Factors, 35th Annu. Meet.,* pp. 193–97. Santa Monica: Hum. Factors Soc.

Griffin, L. 1992. Simulation and training: a well-protected piece of the DoD budget pie? *Def. Electron.* April:45–49

Guide, P. C., Gibson, R. S. 1991. *Proc. Hum. Factors, 35th Annu. Meet.,* pp. 180–84. Santa Monica: Hum. Factors Soc.

Hale, A. R., Glendon, A. I. 1987. *Individual Behavior in the Control of Danger.* Amsterdam: Elsevier

Hall, E. M., Gott, S. P., Pokorny, R. A. 1990. *AFHRL Tech. Pap. 90.* Hum. Resources Lab: Brooks AFB, Tex.

Hammond, K. J., Seifert, C. M., Gray, K. C. 1991. Functionality and analogical transfer: a hard match is good to find. *J. Learn. Sci.* 1:111–52

Hancock, P. A., Warm, J. S. 1989. A dynamic model of stress and sustained attention. *Hum. Factors* 31:519–37

Harris, D. H., ed. 1990. *Distributed Decision Making: Report of a Workshop.* Washington, DC: Natl. Acad. Press. 61 pp.

Hart, S. G. 1989. Crew workload management strategies: a critical factor in system performance. *Proc. Int. Symp. Aviat. Psychol., 5th, Columbus, Ohio,* pp. 22–27

Harwood, K., Barnett, B., Wickens, C. 1988. Situational awareness; a conceptual and methodological framework. In *Proc. 11th Symp. Psychol. in the DoD,* ed. F. E.

McIntire. Colorado Springs, CO: U.S. Air Force Academy

Hirst, W., Kalmar, D. 1987. Characterizing attentional resources. *J. Exp. Psychol. Gen.* 116:68–81

Hockey, G. R. J., Briner, R. B., Tattersall, A. J., Wiethaff, M. 1989. Assessing the impact of computer workload on operator stress: the role of system controllability. *Ergonomics* 11:1401–18

Hoffman, R. R., Deffenbacher, K. A. 1992. A brief history of applied cognitive psychology. *Appl. Cogn. Psychol.* 6:1–48

Holding, D. 1991. Transfer of training. See Morrison 1991, pp. 93–125

Howell, W. C. 1991. Human Factors in the workplace. *Handb. Indust. Org. Psychol.* 2:209–69

Howell, W. C., Cooke, N. J. 1989. Training the human information processor: a look at cognitive models. See Goldstein 1989, pp. 121–82

Hudinburg, R. A. 1989. Psychology of computer use: VII. Measuring technostress: computer-related stress. *Psychol. Rep.* 64:767–72

Huey, B. M., Van Cott, H. P. 1991. *Proc. Hum. Factors, 35th Annu. Meet.,* pp. 974–75. Santa Monica: Hum. Factors Soc.

Hughes, E. R., Hassoun, J. A., Ward, G. F., Rueb, J. D. 1990. *ASD Tech. Rep. 90–5009.* Aeronautical Systems Div. Wright-Patterson AFB, Ohio

Ironson, G. 1992. Work, stress, and health. See Zedeck 1992, pp. 33–69

Ivancevich, J. M., Matteson, M. T., Freedman, S. M., Phillips, J. S. 1990. Worksite stress management interventions. *Am. Psychol.* 45:252–61

Johnston, W. B., Packer, A. E. 1987. *Workforce 2000: Work and Workers for the 21st Century.* Indianapolis, IN: Hudson Inst. 117 pp.

Jones, P. M., Wickens, C. D., Deutsch, S. J. 1990. The display of multivariate information: an experimental study of an information integration task. *Hum. Perform.* 3:1–17

Jones, W. A. Jr. 1991. *Voice stress analysis in a simulated AWACS environment.* Presented at South Texas Symp. Hum. Factors and Ergonomics

Jorna, G. C., Snyder, H. L. 1991. Image quality determines differences in reading performance and perceived image quality with CRT and hard-copy displays. *Hum. Factors* 33:459–69

Just, M. A., Carpenter, P. A. 1987. *The Psychology of Reading and Language Comprehension.* Boston: Allyn & Bacon

Kass, S. J., Herschler, D. A., Companion, M. A. 1991. Training situational awareness through pattern recognition in a battlefield environment. *Mil. Psychol.* 3:105–12

Kelly, P. L., Kroemer, K. H. E. 1990. Anthropometry of the elderly: status and recommendations. *Hum. Factors* 32:571–95

Kieras, D. E., Bovair, S. 1986. The acquisition of procedures from text: a production system analysis of transfer of training. *J. Mem. Lang.* 25:507–24

Kinney, J. S., Huey, B. M., ed. 1990. *Application Principles for Multicolored Displays.* Washington, DC: Natl. Acad. Press. 62 pp.

Kitto, C. M., Boose, J. H. 1989. Selecting knowledge acquisition tools and strategies based on application characteristics. *Int. J. Man-Mach. Stud.* 31:149–60

Klein, G. A. 1989. Recognition-primed decisions. *Adv. Man-Mach. Syst. Res.* 5:47–92

Klein, G. A. 1990. Knowledge engineering: beyond expert systems. *Inf. Decis. Technol.* 16:27–41

Klein, G. A., Orasanu, J., Calderwood, R., eds. 1992. *Decision Making in Action: Models and Methods.* Norwood, NJ: Ablex. In press

Klein, R. 1991. Age-related eye disease, visual imparement, and driving in the elderly. *Hum. Factors* 33:507–19

Koelega, H. S., Brinkman, J. A., Hendriks, L., Verbaten, M. N. 1989. Processing demands, effort, and individual differences in four different vigilance tasks. *Hum. Factors* 31:45–62

Kyllonen, P. C. 1991. CAM: A theoretical framework for cognitive abilities measurement. See Detterman 1991

Kyllonen, P. C., Christal, R. E. 1989. Cognitive modeling and learning abilities: A status report on LAMP. In *Testing: Theoretical and Applied Issues,* ed. R. Dillon, J. W. Pellegrino. San Francisco: Freeman

Laux, L. F. 1991. *Proc. Hum. Factors, 35th Annu. Meet.,* pp. 164–66. Santa Monica: Hum. Factors Soc.

Lawton, M. P. 1990. Aging and performance of home tasks. *Hum. Factors* 32:527–36

Light, L. L. 1991. Memory and aging: four hypotheses in search of data. *Annu. Rev. Psychol.* 42:333–76

Lintern, G. 1991a. An informational perspective on skill transfer in human-machine systems. *Hum. Factors* 33:251–66

Lintern, G. 1991b. See Morrison 1991, pp. 167–91

Lipshitz, R. 1992. Converging themes in the study of decision making in realistic settings. See Klein et al 1992. In press

Longergan, E. T., ed. 1991. *Extending Life, Enhancing Life.* Washington, DC: Natl. Acad. Press

Lysaght, R. J., Hill, S. G., Dick, A. O., Plamondon, B. D., Wherry, R. J., et al, 1989. *ARI Tech. Rep. 851.* U.S. Army Res. Inst., Alexandria, Va.

Martin, D. W., McDonald, D. R., Patton, C. R. 1987. The benefit/cost of VDT highlighting. In *Advances in Human Factors/Ergonomics, IOA: Social, Ergonomic and Stress Aspects of Work with Computers,* ed. G. Salvendy, S. L. Sauter, J. J. Hurrell Jr. Amsterdam: Elsevier

Mast, T. 1991. *Proc. Hum. Factors, 35th Annu. Meet.,* pp. 167–71. Santa Monica: Hum. Factors Soc.

Matthews, G., Margetts, I. 1991. Self-report arousal and divided-attention: a study of performance operating characteristics. *Hum. Perform.* 4:107–25

McClosky, B. P., Geiwitz, J., Kornell, J. 1991. *Proc. Hum. Factors, 34th Annu. Meet.,* pp. 114–18. Santa Monica: Hum. Factors Soc.

McDonald, J. E., Schvaneveldt, R. W. 1988. The application of user knowledge to interface design. In *Cognitive Science and Its Applications for Human-Computer Interaction,* ed. R. Guindon, pp. 289–338. Hillsdale, NJ: Erlbaum

McGraw, K. L., Harbison-Briggs, K. 1989. *Knowledge Acquisition: Principles and Guidelines.* Englewood Cliffs, NJ: Prentice Hall

McNeese, M. D., Zaff, B. S. 1991. *Proc. Hum. Factors, 35th Annu. Meet.,* pp. 1181–85. Santa Monica: Hum. Factors Soc.

McNeese, M. D., Zaff, B. S., Peio, K. J., Snyder, D. E., Duncan, J. C., et al. 1990. *AAMRL-TR-90–060.* Armstrong Aerospace Med. Res. Lab., Wright-Patterson AFB, Ohio

Miller, C. O. 1988. System safety. In *Human Factors in Aviation,* ed. E. L. Wiener, D. C. Nagel, San Diego: Academic

Moray, N. 1991. *Technosophy and humane factors: the future of ergonomics.* Presented at Int. Ergonomic Assoc. Meet., Paris

Moray, N., Dessouky, M. I., Kijowski, B. A., Adapathya, R. 1991. Strategic behavior, workload, and performance in task scheduling. *Hum. Factors* 33:607–29

Morgan, B. B. Jr., Bowers, C. A. 1990. *Teamwork stress and its implications for team decision making.* Presented at Conf. Team Decision Making Organ., Univ. Maryland, College Park, Md.

Morrison, J. E., ed. 1991. *Training for Performance.* New York: Wiley. 311 pp.

Murphy, K. R. 1989. Is the relationship between cognitive ability and job performance stable over time? *Hum. Perform.* 2:183–200

Nicholson, P. 1991. *Proc. Hum. Factors, 35th Annu. Meet.,* pp. 923–24. Santa Monica: Hum. Factors Soc.

Nygren, T. E. 1991. Psychometric properties of subjective workload measurement techniques: implications for their use in the assessment of perceived mental workload. *Hum. Factors* 33:17–33

Oatman, L. C. 1989. *HEL Tech. Note 14–89.* U.S. Army Hum. Eng. Lab., Aberdeen Proving Ground, MD.

Offerman, L. R., Gowing, M. K. 1990. Organizations of the future. *Am. Psychol.* 45:95–108

Olson, J. R., Biolsi, K. J. 1991. Techniques for representing expert knowledge. In *Toward a General Theory of Expertise,* ed. K. A. Ericsson, J. Smith, pp. 240–85. Cambridge:

Cambridge Univ. Press

Orasanu, J. M. 1990. *Cogn. Sci. Lab. Rep. 46.* Cogn. Sci. Lab., Princeton Univ., Princeton, NJ

Orasanu, J. 1991. *Proc. Hum. Factors, 35th Annu. Meet.,* pp. 991–95. Santa Monica: Hum. Factors Soc.

Orasanu, J., Salas, E. 1992. Team decision making in complex environments. See Klein et al 1992. In press

Orlansky, J., Grafton, F., Martin, C. J., Alley, W., Bloxom, B. 1990. *IDA Doc. D-715.* Inst. Defense Analysis, Alexandria, Va.

Parkes, K. R., Styles, E. A., Broadbent, D. E. 1990. Work preferences as moderators of the effects of paced and unpaced work on mood and cognitive performance: a laboratory simulation of mechanized letter sorting. *Hum. Factors* 32:197–216

Pastoor, S. 1990. Legibility and subjective preference for color combinations in text. *Hum. Factors* 32:157–71

Patrick, J. 1991. Types of analysis for training. See Morrison 1991, pp. 127–66

Polson, M. C., Richardson, J. J., ed. 1988. *Intelligent Tutoring Systems.* Hillsdale, NJ: Erlbaum. 280 pp.

Posner, M. I. 1992. Attention as a cognitive and neural system. *Curr. Dir. Psychol. Sci.* 1:11–14

Posner, M. I., Petersen, S. E. 1990. The attention system of the human brain. *Annu. Rev. Neurosci.* 13:25–42

Powell, C. L. 1992. *The National Military Strategy.* Washington, DC: The Pentagon

Psotka, J., Massey, L. D., Mutter, S. A., ed. 1988. *Intelligent Tutoring Systems: Lessons Learned.* Hillsdale, NJ: Erlbaum. 310 pp.

Purcell, J. A., Coury, B. G. 1988. *Proc. Hum. Factors, 32nd Annu. Meet.,* pp. 1366–70. Santa Monica: Hum. Factors Soc.

Ralston, J. R., Pisoni, D. B., Lively, S. E., Greene, B. G., Mullennix, J. W. 1991. Comprehension of synthetic speech produced by rule: word monitoring and sentence-by-sentence listening times. *Hum. Factors* 33:471–91

Ramamurthy, K., King, W. R., Premkumar, G. 1992. User characteristics—DSS effectiveness linkage: an empirical assessment. *Int. J. Man-Mach. Stud.* 36:496–505

Regal, D. M., Rogers, W. H., Boucek, G. P. 1988. *Proc. Aerospace Technol. Conf. and Expo., Anaheim, Calif.*

Regian, J. W., Shute, V. J., eds. 1992. *Cognitive Approaches to Automated Instruction.* Hillsdale, NJ: Erlbaum. In press

Robertson, M. M. 1991. *Proc. Hum. Factors, 35th Annu. Meet.,* pp. 925–29. Santa Monica: Hum. Factors Soc.

Rodgers, M. D., Holding, D. 1991. Dual-task efficiency throughout the day. *Hum. Perform.* 4:187–98

Rogers, W. A., Fisk, A. D. 1990. Age-related differences in the maintenance and modification of automatic processes: arithmetic Stroop interference. *Hum. Factors* 33:45–56

Rouillier, J. Z., Goldstein, I. L. 1991. *Determinants of the climate for transfer of training.* Presented at Annu. Meet. Soc. Indust. Org. Psychol., St. Louis

Rouse, W. B. 1990. Training and aiding personnel in complex systems. See Booher 1990, pp. 237–55

Rouse, W. B., Morris, N. B. 1986. On looking into the black box: prospects and limits in the search for mental models. *Psychol. Bull.* 100:349–63

Rubinstein, T., Mason, A. F. 1979. The accident that shouldn't have happened: an analysis of Three Mile Island. *IEEE Spectrum* Nov:33–57

Sackett, P. R., ed. 1990. Project A: the U.S. Army selection and classification project. *Personnel Psychol.* (Spec. Issue) 43

Salas, E., ed. 1991. Training theory, methods, and technology. *Hum. Factors* 33

Salthouse, T. A. 1990. Influence of experience on age differences in cognitive functioning. *Hum. Factors* 32:551–69

Sanderson, P. M. 1989. The human planning and scheduling role in advanced manufacturing systems: an emerging human factors domain. *Hum. Factors* 31:635–66

Sanderson, P. M., Flach, J. M., Buttigieg, M. A., Casey, E. J. 1989. Object displays do not always support better integrated task performance. *Hum. Factors* 31:183–98

Sarter, N. B., Woods, D. D. 1991. Situation awareness: a critical but ill-defined phenomenon. *Int. J. Aviat. Psychol.* 1:45–57

Schaubroeck, J., Muralidhar, K. 1991. A meta-analysis of the relative effect of tabular and graphic display formats on decision-making performance. *Hum. Perform.* 4:127–45

Schriesheim, A. 1990. Toward a golden age for technology transfer. *Issues Sci. Technol.* Winter:52–58

Selcon, S. J., Taylor, R. M. 1989. *Proc. AGARD AMP Symp. Situational Awareness in Aerospace Operations, CP478.* Seuilly-sur Seine: NATO AGARD

Selcon, S. J., Taylor, R. M., Koritsas, E. 1991. *Proc. Hum. Factors, 35th Annu. Meet.,* pp. 62–66. Santa Monica, CA: Hum. Factors Soc.

Shadbolt, N., Burton, A. M. 1989. Knowledge elicitation. In *Evaluation of Human Work: Practical Ergonomics Methodology,* ed. J. Wilson, N. Corlett. London: Taylor & Francis

Shallice, T., Burgess, P. 1992. Higher-order cognitive impairments and frontal lobe lesions in man. In *Frontal Lobe Function and Injury,* ed. H. Levin, H. M. Eisenberg, A. L. Benton. Oxford: Oxford Univ. Press

Shanteau, J., Harrison, P. 1991. The perceived strength of an implied contract: can it withstand financial temptation? *Org. Behav. Hum. Decis. Process.* 49:1–21

Sheppe, M. L., Hayes, W. A. 1991. *Proc. Interservice/Indust. Train. Syst. Conf.,*

13th, Orlando, Fla., pp. 499–506

Shinar, D., Schieber, F. 1991. Visual requirements for safety and mobility of older drivers. *Hum. Factors* 33:507–19

Shute, V. J. 1992. Aptitude-treatment interactions and cognitive skill diagnosis. See Regian & Shute 1992. In press

Singley, M. K., Anderson, J. R. 1989. *The Transfer of Cognitive Skill.* Cambridge, MA: Harvard Univ. Press

Smith, D. B. D. 1990. Human factors and aging: an overview of research needs and application opportunities. *Hum. Factors* 32:509–26

Soloway, E. M. 1986. Learning to program = learning to construct mechanisms and explanations. *CACM* 29:850–58

Sterns, H. L., Doverspike, D. 1989. Aging and the training and learning process. See Goldstein 1989, pp. 299–332

Stevenson, M. K., Busemeyer, J. R., Naylor, J. C. 1990. Judgement and decision-making theory. *Handb. Indust. Org. Psychol.* 1:283–374

Sullivan, C., Blackman, H. S. 1991. *Proc. Hum. Factors, 35th Annu. Meet.,* pp. 57–59. Santa Monica: Hum. Factors Soc.

Swezey, R. W., Salas, E., eds. 1991. *Teams: Their Training and Performance.* Norwood, NJ: Ablex

Tannenbaum, S. I., Beard, R. L., Salas, E. 1992. Team building and its influence on team effectiveness. In *Issues and Research in Industrial/Organizational Psychology,* ed. K. Kelley. Amsterdam: Elsevier. In press

Tannenbaum, S. I., Yukl, G. 1992. Training and development in work organizations. *Annu. Rev. Psychol.* 43:399–441

Tenney, Y. J., Adams, M. J., Pew, R. W., Huggins, A. W. F., Rogers, W. H. 1992. *A Principled Approach to the Measurement of Situation Awareness in Commercial Aviation.* NASA: Contract Report 445

Towne, D. M., Monro, A. 1991. Simulation-based instruction of technical skill. *Hum. Factors* 33:325–41

Travis, D. S., Bowles, S., Seton, J., Peppe, R. 1990. Reading from color displays: a psychophysical model. *Hum. Factors* 32:147–56

Tsang, P. S., Velazquez, V. L. 1991. *Proc. Hum. Factors, 35th Annu. Meet.,* pp. 1481–85. Santa Monica: Hum. Factors Soc.

Tsang, P. S., Wickens, C. D. 1988. The structural constraints and strategic control of resource allocation. *Hum. Perform.* 1:45–72

Turnage, J. J. 1990. The challenge of new workplace technology for psychology. *Am. Psychol.* 45:171–78

Tzelgov, J., Henik, A., Dinstein, I., Rabany, J. 1990. Performance consequences of two types of stereo picture compression. *Hum. Factors* 32:173–82

Vercruyssen, M. 1991. *Proc. Hum. Factors, 35th Annu. Meet.,* pp. 188–92. Santa Monica: Hum. Factors Soc.

Vidulich, M. A., Ward, G. F., Schueren, J. 1991. Using the subjective workload dominance (SWORD) technique in projective workload assessment. *Hum. Factors* 33:677–91

Waller, P. F. 1991. The older driver. *Hum. Factors* 33:499–505

Warm, J. S., Dember, W. N., Gluckman, J. P., Hancock, P. A. 1991. *Proc. Hum. Factors, 35th Annu. Meet.,* pp. 980–81. Santa Monica: Hum. Factors Soc.

Weaver, J. L., Morgan, B. B. Jr., Adkins-Holmes, C. 1991. *Technical Report.* Orlando, FL: Naval Training Systems Cent.

Westman, M. 1990. The relationship between stress and performance: the moderating effect of hardness. *Hum. Perform.* 3:141–55

Whitaker, L. A., Klein, G. A. 1988. *Proc. 11th Symp. Psychol. in the DoD,* ed. F. E. McIntire. Colorado Springs, CO: U.S. Air Force Academy

Wickens, C. D. 1991. *Proc. Hum. Factors, 35th Annu. Meet.,* pp. 976–79. Santa Monica: Hum. Factors Soc.

Wickens, C. D. 1992. *Engineering Psychology and Human Performance.* New York: Harper Collins. 550 pp. 2nd ed.

Wickens, C. D., Andre, A. D. 1990. Proximity compatibility and information display: effects of color, space, and objectness on information integration. *Hum. Factors* 32:61–77

Wickens, C. D., Kramer, A. 1985. Engineering psychology. *Annu. Rev. Psychol.* 36:307–48

Wickens, C. D., Larish, I., Contorer, A. 1989. In *Proc. 33rd Annu. Meet. Hum. Factors Soc.,* pp. 96–100. Santa Monica: Hum. Factors Soc.

Wilson, J. R., Rutherford, A. 1989. Mental models: theory and application in human factors. *Hum. Factors* 31:617–34

Witmer, B. G., Knerr, B. W. 1991. *Proc. Interservice/Indust. Train. Syst. Conf., 13th, Orlando,* pp. 63–70

Yates, J. F. 1990. *Judgment and Decision Making.* Englewood Cliffs, NJ: Prentice-Hall. 430 pp.

Yeh, Y., Silverstein, L. D. 1990. Limits of fusion and depth judgment in stereoscopic color displays. *Hum. Factors* 32:45–60

Zedeck, S., ed. 1992. *Work, Families, and Organizations.* San Francisco: Jossey-Bass. 475 pp.

Annu. Rev. Psychol. 1993. 44:265–315

THINKING

Keith J. Holyoak and Barbara A. Spellman

Department of Psychology, University of California, Los Angeles, California 90024

CONTENTS

INTRODUCTION 265
CONFLUENCE OF SYMBOLIC AND CONNECTIONIST PARADIGMS 266
    Two Contrasting Paradigms 266
    Systematicity and Symbols 269
    Soft Constraint Satisfaction in Reasoning 273
    Reflexive Reasoning Using Dynamic Binding 275
IMPLICIT THINKING AND COGNITIVE EVOLUTION 278
    Acquisition of Implicit Knowledge 278
    Access and Use of Implicit Knowledge 282
    Evolutionary History and Adaptation 286
    What Is Explicit Thinking For? 289
CONTENT IN THINKING, THINKING IN CONTEXT 290
    Thinking vs Theorem Proving 290
    Relevance and Pragmatic Reasoning 293
    The Context of Learning and the Content of Transfer 297
    Vivid Representations for Reasoning 300
CONCLUSION 307

INTRODUCTION

Reviewing an active field of research is a bit like writing an unauthorized mid-career biography. Your subject is not about to reveal its secrets to you, or even to stand still long enough to allow a coherent story to be constructed. The task is made especially difficult when the topic is as amorphous as thinking. As Oden put it in his prior review for this series, "Thinking, broadly defined, is nearly all of psychology; narrowly defined, it seems to be none of it"

0066-4308/93/0201-0265$02.00

(1987:203). Sometimes thinking is construed as a synonym for all "intelligent information processing," and sometimes it is construed as the umbrella term for a range of processes associated with "high-level" cognition, such as reasoning, categorization, and judgment and decision making. We emphasize the latter conception of thinking, but our chapter is not organized around those traditional subtopics, each of which has been reviewed in its own right (see Medin & Smith 1984; Payne et al 1992; Rips 1990). Rather, we are guided by a piece of folk psychology. Rips & Conrad (1989) found that lay people believe that virtually all "everyday" mental activities (e.g. reasoning and remembering) are kinds of thinking, and that thinking is a part of each kind of mental activity. In keeping with the perceived ubiquity of thinking in cognition, we review a number of general themes that have emerged in recent research on the topic, drawing a sprinkling of examples from work in a variety of subareas.

In surveying the field of thinking, three recent trends seem particularly noteworthy. 1. The rise of the connectionist paradigm has led to a critical reexamination of assumptions concerning the symbolic nature of human thinking. 2. Cognitive psychologists are taking seriously the notion that human thinking may be based on two very different systems; and there have been increased efforts to use evolutionary arguments, as well as biological evidence, to constrain cognitive theories. 3. Theoretical efforts have been directed at explaining how thinking is constrained by the content of what is thought about, and by the context in which thinking takes place. Our review is organized around these three themes, which are interconnected in various ways.

CONFLUENCE OF SYMBOLIC AND CONNECTIONIST PARADIGMS

Two Contrasting Paradigms

Our first theme is not simply the rise of connectionism, but rather the meeting and merging of two theoretical streams that have been channeled into the analysis of thinking. Human thinking (along with language) has generally been viewed as the *sine qua non* of symbolic mental activity. Since the cognitive revolution in the mid-20th century, thinking has been characterized as the product of a "physical symbol system." In 1990, Simon concluded that "The physical symbol system hypothesis has been tested so extensively over the past 30 years that it can now be regarded as fully established, although over less than the full gamut of activities that are called 'thinking'" (p. 3).

This sanguine assessment has been challenged, however, by those who have developed alternative "subsymbolic" paradigms, such as Hofstadter (1984), Rumelhart, McClelland, and the PDP Research Group (1986), and Smolensky (1988). Connectionist models, the most common instantiations of the subsymbolic approach, [1] consist of networks of relatively simple processing units connected by links. Processing involves a series of cycles of activity; on each cycle, units take on new states of activation as a function of their own prior activations, the activations of units to which they are connected, and the weights (excitatory or inhibitory) on the interconnecting links. Typical connectionist models embody some or all of four central ideas. First, control is distributed over the network of units, rather than localized in a central "executive." Second, knowledge is to varying extents distributed over sets of units, rather than identified with single units. Third, decision making is based on parallel constraint satisfaction, by which successive cycles of processing tend to converge on an activation pattern that best satisfies the constraints embodied in the weights on links. At convergence, the units with highest activations tend to support each other and inhibit their competitors. Fourth, learning consists of incremental revision of weights on the basis of either feedback concerning the performance of the network or internal constraints on weight patterns.

These characteristics of connectionist models contrast with the prototypical features of serial production systems, the style of model most closely associated with the symbolic approach to modeling cognition (Newell 1973). In a "classical" production system, knowledge is encoded locally in "condition-action" rules, perhaps coupled with a declarative semantic network (e.g. Anderson 1983). A central executive selects a single rule to fire on each processing cycle. When the condition of a rule is matched and that rule is selected to fire, then the action specified by that rule will be taken. The global behavior of a production system is more naturally characterized as serial generation of an action sequence, rather than parallel satisfaction of multiple constraints. Learning primarily consists of the addition of new productions, a process that requires the intervention of an executive controller that decides what new rules to build and when to build them (e.g. Anderson 1987; Rosenbloom et al 1991). It should be emphasized that some production systems developed in recent years, such as CAPS (Just & Carpenter 1992) and SOAR (Rosenbloom et al 1991), depart from the "classical" architecture in important ways; nonetheless, the above contrast captures in broad strokes the differences between the models associated with each of the two paradigms.

The symbolic and connectionist paradigms bear a rough but interesting correspondence to two different perspectives on thinking that have coexisted (with some degree of tension) over this century. The symbolic paradigm was shaped in large part by Newell & Simon's (1972) treatment of problem solving. Their approach primarily focused on "well-defined" problems, for which the problem solver knows at the outset what goal is to be achieved, what the

---

[1]
    Other types of subsymbolic models include classifier systems (Holland et al 1986; see Druhan & Mathews 1989, for a psychological application), and models based on flexible semantic networks such as Hofstadter's (1984; Hofstadter & Mitchell, 1993) Copycat model of analogy.

starting state is, and what operators are potentially relevant to achieving a solution. Problems that meet this description (such as proving geometry theorems or solving logical puzzles) approximately satisfy a "closed world" assumption: The pool of knowledge relevant to their solution, although possibly large, is nonetheless circumscribed. Newell & Simon characterized explicit thinking as conscious serial search through a specifiable space of possibilities, based in large part on heuristics that evaluate incremental progress toward goal attainment. In addition, they stressed the role of rapid recognition processes that match external inputs against knowledge stored in long-term memory (Chase & Simon 1973). Production systems emerged as the model that most directly embodied Newell & Simon's characterization of thinking.

In contrast, the earlier Gestalt psychologists, such as Duncker (1945) and Wertheimer (1945), stressed the solution of problems that are less well defined, and hence do not satisfy the closed world assumption. In working on a particular new "target" problem, for example, a reasoner may be reminded of a better-understood analogous "source" problem, perhaps drawn from a substantially different knowledge domain. The source analog may then suggest new goals or operators that might be used to solve the target problem. Because the bounds within which a potentially useful source analog may be found are not clearly circumscribed, analogical thinking can violate the closed-world assumption. More generally, Gestaltists emphasized that thinking may involve parallel integration of knowledge based on mechanisms that are largely unconscious, sometimes producing a "restructuring" of the problem representation.

The theoretical ideas of the Gestaltists were notoriously vague, and Simon (1986; Kaplan & Simon 1990) has shown that the symbolic paradigm can accommodate many of the empirical phenomena associated with such Gestalt concepts as "intuition" and "insight." Nonetheless, some alternative approach might provide a computational realization of the Gestalt perspective on thinking. As Rock & Palmer (1990) have pointed out, there is some affinity between Gestalt theory and current connectionist models. In particular, connectionist networks perform "soft" constraint satisfaction (i.e. each constraint has some influence on the overall behavior of the network, but is not as inviolate as a hard-and-fast rule). A constraint network based on partially convergent and partially discrepant knowledge may yield a coherent interpretation of a situation, so that "the whole is different from the sum of its parts."[2]

2

The broad current interest in connectionism within psychology is in part attributable to the fact that, in different ways, it captures some of the flavor of both Gestalt psychology and behaviorism, the main intellectual rivals that dominated early 20th-century psychology. Roughly, parallel constraint satisfaction is reminiscent of Gestalt ideas, while learning by incremental weight adjustment over distributed representations is reminiscent of associationist conceptions of learning (see Estes 1991, for the latter perspective). Current cognitive psychologists generally hold basic conceptions of cognition that have been shaped to a large extent by reactions to the Gestaltist and associationist legacies. As a consequence, connectionism offers something for almost everyone to love and/or hate, in a mixture that is a function of selective focus and intellectual predispositions.

These two perspectives on thinking tend to bring with them different views of the relationship between "high-level" thinking and the broader spectrum of information processing, which includes perceptual and motor components. The symbolic approach has dealt most directly with "central" cognition, either leaving aside the problem of modeling input and output processing, or attempting to press models of high-level cognition downwards to serve also as models of perception and action (e.g. Anderson 1983; Rosenbloom et al 1991). Even theorists who acknowledge that "one thing wrong with much theorizing about cognition is that it does not pay much attention to perception on the one side or motor behavior on the other" (Newell 1990:159) are wont to find themselves, for the pragmatic reason that peripheral processes are highly complex, "committing this same sin" (p. 160).

In contrast, Gestalt psychologists emphasized that high-level thinking is in many ways akin to perception. Similar views have been expressed by recent proponents of the subsymbolic approach, such as Hofstadter (1984; Hofstadter & Mitchell, 1993). Lakoff (1993) reviews a wide range of linguistic evidence suggesting that human understanding of such abstract concepts as time, categories, and causality is based on metaphors derived from perceptuomotor experience. (See Mandler 1992 for a discussion of the implications of this view for cognitive development.) Perceptual and motor processes, as well as basic memory processes, clearly evolved long before high-level human cognition. A general principle of evolutionary biology is that mechanisms that initially evolved to serve one function may later be coopted to serve other functions (a type of change termed "exaptation"). Thus from an evolutionary perspective, it is reasonable to conjecture that the mechanisms of high-level cognition have important links to those that evolved earlier to support perception and action. As we note below, recent analyses of "implicit" cognition have drawn attention to the evolutionary development of human thinking (e.g. Reber, 1992). Connectionist models, which have been developed primarily in the context of work on perception and motor control (e.g. Jordan & Rosenbaum 1989), tend to encourage "outer to inner" theorizing, in which models of peripheral processes are extended in attempting to account for more central processes, rather than the reverse.

Systematicity and Symbols

It is unlikely, however, that connectionism will undermine the traditional view that human thinking requires a symbol system. The most fundamental argument for the necessity of symbolic representations was presented by Fodor & Pylyshyn (1988; Fodor & McLaughlin 1990). They pointed out that knowledge is systematic in the sense that the ability to think particular thoughts seems to imply the ability to think certain related thoughts. For example, if a person understands the meaning of the concepts "love," "boy," and "girl," and can understand the proposition "The boy loves the girl," then it would seem extremely bizarre if the person were nonetheless unable to understand the proposition "The girl loves the boy." More generally, it seems characteristic of thinking that if each concept in a set of potential constituent concepts is understood, and a relation structure (such as a frame for a predicate and its arguments) can be instantiated by one assignment of the constituent concepts, then the thinker can also instantiate the relation structure with other permissible assignments of the concepts. The need to represent this kind of systematic relational information was part of the motivation for Minsky's (1975) concept of frames, a type of symbolic relation structure that continues to be influential in modeling human cognition (Barsalou & Hale, 1992).

Systematic reasoning with composable constituents requires symbols. Newell (1990) describes the workings of a representational system: It can encode an external situation and external transformations; it can internally apply the encoded transformation to the encoded situation; and it can decode the result back to the environment—thereby predicting the external result of applying the transformation. (See Palmer 1978 for an earlier discussion of the nature of representations.) A representational system must be sufficiently flexible to predict the effects of all the distinct external situations and transformations that are important to the organism. Newell argues that as the diversity of the knowledge that an organism must represent and manipulate increases, it becomes increasingly difficult to find specialized representational systems to provide appropriate encodings. In what Newell terms "the Great Move," evolution developed a representational system that enables more complex representations to be composed from simpler ones.

This representational system must be able to share knowledge across many different contexts, because it will be impossible (owing to physical limits of the storage system) to store all the information potentially required for every task in a form in which it is immediately available. A "symbol" is fundamentally a locally available code that can provide access to distal information relevant to a task. In a symbol system, information acquired in one task context has the potential to be made available in a different task context. This is exactly what is required for systematic reasoning with composable constituents. In our example above, we can understand both "The boy loves the girl" and "The girl loves the boy" because the concepts "girl" and "boy" are represented in a manner that keeps each distinct from both the "lover" and "beloved" contexts; both are therefore available for use in either context. When multiple task contexts permit access to a shared pool of knowledge, by virtue of constituency relations, performance in one context will be systematically related to performance in others. The ability to use systematic relational knowledge across contexts enables analogical reasoning about novel situations (Falkenhainer et al 1989; Holyoak & Thagard 1989).

Systematicity is also a key feature of rules of inference, such as "If X sells Y to Z, then Z owns Y." Smith et al (1992) propose several empirical criteria that may reveal when some knowledge used in human reasoning is coded as abstract rules. One criterion, which applies for at least some well-established rules, is that it seems just as easy to draw inferences about unfamilar instantiations—including nonsense ones—as about familiar ones. Thus if we are told that "Henry sold the floogle to Sam," we immediately conclude that Sam now owns the floogle, whatever a floogle might be. The inference follows directly from the role that "floogle" plays in the argument structure of the rule, without any requirement that floogles resemble familiar objects that have been transferred from one owner to another.

Systematicity of relational correspondences (i.e. of correspondences between the arguments of multi-place predicates) also plays a role in judgments of perceptual similarity (Goldstone et al 1991). For example, suppose people are shown three pairs of geometric shapes, with each pair arranged vertically. One pair consists of two identical triangles, one of identical squares, and one of identical circles. People tend to evaluate the pair of triangles as more similar to the pair of squares than to the pair of circles. But if a square is now added as a third form below the two items in each of the pairs, the evaluation of similarity reverses: Two triangles and a square are viewed as less similar to three squares then to two circles and a square. This similarity reversal reflects differences in relational correspondences: Both the first and the third triad can readily be represented as "two same forms plus a square," whereas the middle triad is most naturally represented as "three squares." Thus the first and third triads match better in terms of relational correspondences. Goldstone et al demonstrated not only that systematic relations matter to similarity, but also that relational matches matter more (relative to matches of one-place predicates, such as "square") as the overall relational overlap between two complex figures increases. Their findings are difficult to interpret in terms of feature models of similarity (most notably Tversky's 1977 contrast model) that do not specify a role for systematic relational correspondences in similarity judgments. (Connectionist models that are implementations of feature models also fail to capture relational aspects of similarity.)

If thinking depends on symbol systems, as the arguments of Fodor & Pylyshyn (1988) and Newell (1990) imply, connectionist models of thinking face the formidable challenge of implementing symbolic processing within the constraints imposed by the simplicity of units and links (e.g. Dyer 1991). As McCarthy (1988) has observed, the representational power of connectionist models is generally restricted to unary (i.e. one-place) predicates applied to a single fixed object. An adequate model of human thinking, however, requires representations with at least the logical power of the first-order polyadic predicate calculus (Stenning & Oaksford, 1993): That is, it must be able to express relations among multiple objects that fill particular roles associated with the arguments of predicates (e.g. the "lover" and the "beloved" roles associated with the predicate "love"). Accordingly, a crucial requirement for systematic reasoning is a solution to the "binding problem": the need to keep track of what roles are being played by each constituent. (For example, distinguishing "John loves Mary" from "Mary loves John" requires a way to encode which object fills which argument slot.) Humans can obviously make such distinctions and can code binding information in long-term memory (although it takes longer to recognize previously encountered role bindings than simply to recognize recurrences of objects; Ratcliff & McKoon 1989).

Simple connectionist representations, however, lack constituency relations. Unlike symbolic representations in which links between elements typically define meaningful relationships, the links in connectionist models merely serve to transmit activation between units. As a result, connectionist models do not guarantee systematicity of thinking in principle; in practice, most current connectionist models fail to deal with anything like the systematic knowledge involved in everyday human reasoning. For example, binding information is conspicuously absent in connectionist models such as that used by Rumelhart et al (1986) to represent a "room schema." In their model, a "kitchen," for example, would be represented by a vector of features (i.e. unary predicates) such as "has refrigerator," "has stove," "has sink," and so on. Lacking any capability of expressing multi-place predicates and their role bindings, the model is unable to distinguish a "normal" kitchen from a room with a refrigerator in the sink with a stove piled on top of it.[3] Thus, a key theoretical challenge facing the connectionist approach to meaning is to show how distributed representations of individual concepts could function symbolically as constituents of more complex relation structures. (See Farah & McClelland 1991 for an analysis of neurological data consistent with the possibility that individual concepts have distributed representations in semantic memory.)

The fact that human cognition has both symbolic and subsymbolic aspects encourages various attempts to integrate the approaches. A number of suggestions for hybrid "symbolic-connectionist" models have been offered (e.g. Dyer 1991; Holyoak 1991; Minsky 1991). These models can be divided roughly into two classes. One class of models maintains a core of "traditional" symbolic machinery (e.g. discrete propositions and rules) to represent relation structures, while adding connectionist-style mechanisms for "soft" constraint satisfaction. The second class of models seeks to develop connectionist representations of relation structures by introducing techniques for handling the binding of objects to roles. We review examples of each of these approaches to integrating the two theoretical perspectives.

3

Connectionist models typically introduce units that respond selectively to combinations (e.g. conjunctions) of inputs, allowing the expression of Boolean operations. Such capability (equivalent to introducing the operators "and," "or," etc) is sometimes characterized as capturing "relational" information (e.g. Estes 1991). However, Boolean operations on a finite set of elements do not suffice to represent relation structures based on multi-place predicates. A typical connectionist model might be able to roughly represent the propositional conjunction "room has sink and room has stove" by including a unit that becomes active just in case both the "room has sink" and "room has stove" units are on. But Boolean operations on propositions do not distinguish "stove is beside sink in room" from "stove is on top of sink in room," "sink is on top of stove in room," and so on. This broader ability to represent argument bindings for multi-place predicates is lacking in typical connectionist representation schemes.

Soft Constraint Satisfaction in Reasoning

The generation and evaluation of beliefs—the central task of induction—has a holistic quality that has posed grave difficulty for theoretical treatments. Tweney (1990) identified the complex interrelatedness of hypotheses as a major challenge for computational theories of scientific reasoning. Fodor (1983) has taken the pessimistic position that little progress is to be expected in understanding central cognition because the facts relevant to any belief cannot be circumscribed (i.e. we do not operate within a closed world) and the degree of confirmation of any hypothesis is sensitive to properties of the whole system of beliefs. As Quine (1961:41) put it, "our statements about the external world face the tribunal of sense experience not individually but only as a corporate body." A psychological theory of induction must identify mechanisms that can cope with the holistic quality of hypothesis evaluation (Holland et al 1986).

One mechanism with the requisite properties is parallel constraint satisfaction, a basic capability of connectionist models. In a connectionist network, local computations involving individual units interact to generate stable global patterns of activity over the entire network. Models that perform "soft" constraint satisfaction over units corresponding to relation structures can attempt to capitalize on the complementary strengths of symbolic representation and connectionist processing. Such symbolic-connectionist models can make inferences based on incomplete information, which standard symbolic systems are often unable to do, using knowledge that distributed connectionist systems cannot readily represent. Models of this sort have been used to account for psychological data concerning text comprehension, analogical reasoning, and evaluation of explanations.

Kintsch (1988) has developed a symbolic-connectionist model to deal with the resolution of ambiguities during text comprehension. His "construction-integration" model has four main components: 1. initial parallel activation of memory concepts corresponding to words in the text, together with formation of propositions by parsing rules; 2. spreading of activation to a small number of close associates of the text concepts; 3. inferring additional propositions by inference rules; and 4. creating excitatory and inhibitory links, with associated weights, between units representing activated concepts and propositions, and allowing the network to settle. The entire process is iterative. A small portion of text is processed, the units active after the settling process are maintained, and then the cycle is repeated with the next portion of text. In addition to accounting for psycholinguistic data on text comprehension, the construction-integration model has been extended to simulate levels of expertise in planning routine computing tasks (Mannes & Kintsch 1991).

Symbolic-connectionist models have been developed to account for two of the basic processes in analogical reasoning—retrieving useful analogs from memory and mapping the elements of a known situation (the source analog) and a new situation (the target analog) to identify useful correspondences. Because analogical mapping requires finding correspondences on the basis of relation structure, most distributed connectionist models lack the requisite representational tools to do it. Purely symbolic models have difficulty avoiding combinatorial explosion when searching for possible analogs in a large memory store and when searching for optimal mappings between two analogs. The two symbolic-connectionist models—the ACME model of Holyoak & Thagard (1989), which does analogical mapping, and the ARCS model of Thagard et al (1990), which does analogical retrieval—operate by taking symbolic, predicate-calculus-style representations of situations as inputs, applying a small set of abstract constraints to build a network of units representing possible mappings between elements of two analogs, and then allowing parallel constraint satisfaction to settle the network into a stable state in which asymptotic activations of units reflect degree of confidence in possible mappings. The constraints on mapping lead to preferences for sets of mapping hypotheses that yield isomorphic correspondences, link similar elements, and map elements of special importance. These same constraints (with differing relative impacts) operate in both the mapping and retrieval models. The mapping model has been applied successfully to model human judgments about complex naturalistic analogies (Spellman & Holyoak 1992) and has been extended to account for data concerning analogical transfer in mathematical problem solving (Holyoak et al, 1993). A similar constraint-satisfaction model has been proposed by Goldstone & Medin (1993) to account for the role of relational correspondences in similarity judgments.

Thagard (1989, 1992) has shown that the problem of evaluating competing explanations can be addressed by a symbolic-connectionist model of explanatory coherence, ECHO. The model takes as inputs symbolic representations of basic explanatory relations between propositions corresponding to data and explanatory hypotheses. The system then builds a constraint network linking units representing the propositions, using a small number of very general constraints that support explanations with greater explanatory breadth (more links to data), greater simplicity (fewer constitutent assumptions), and greater correspondence to analogous explanations of other phenomena. Relations of mutual coherence (modeled by symmetrical excitatory links) hold between hypotheses and the data they explain; relations of competition (inhibitory links) hold between rival hypotheses. Parallel constraint satisfaction settles the network into an asymptotic state in which units representing the most mutually coherent hypotheses and data are active and units representing inconsistent rivals are deactivated. Thagard (1989) showed that ECHO can model a number of realistic cases of explanation evaluation in both scientific and legal contexts; Schank & Ranney (1991, 1992; Ranney, 1993) have used the model to account for students' belief revision in the context of physics problems; and Read & Marcus-Newhall (1993) have applied the model to the evaluation of explanations of everyday events.

The role of constraint satisfaction in human reasoning may explain a set of reasoning and memory phenomena that have sometimes been interpreted as evidence for "mental models" (Johnson-Laird 1983; Johnson-Laird & Byrne 1991). In syllogistic reasoning tasks, people tend to perform poorly when the premises admit of multiple consistent instantiations; and comprehension of described spatial relations is impaired when the description cannot be mapped onto a single determinate array. As Stenning & Oaksford (1993) and Stenning & Oberlander (1992) have noted, connectionist networks have the property of "self-completion": Given a fragmentary input, they naturally settle into a state representing a coherent, unified interpretation of the input. Although such networks may be massively parallel at the level of unit activity, they nonetheless are radically serial at the level of network states. Thus constraint satisfaction is well-suited to reasoning tasks in which a single unified interpretation of the input is both possible and desirable (i.e. the interpretation corresponds to a unique stable state of the network) but badly suited to reasoning tasks in which a single unified interpretation is not possible (as in coding indeterminate spatial descriptions) or not desirable (as in syllogistic tasks for which identifying an acceptable conclusion depends on all possible consistent instantiations of the premises, rather than a single instantiation). We return to the topic of mental models when we discuss "vivid representations" below.

Reflexive Reasoning Using Dynamic Binding

Whereas the models discussed above involve various hybridizations of connectionist processing mechanisms and symbolic representations, a second class of models attempts to provide pure connectionist-style representations of complex relational knowledge. Achieving this goal requires a mechanism for coding bindings of properties and relations to sets of individuals. In contrast to purely symbolic models (e.g. Anderson 1983) in which bindings are represented by unanalyzed elements of notation (e.g. labeled arcs in a semantic network), the connectionist approach represents bindings by more global properties of network states. One general proposal has been to introduce distributed representations in which both the argument slots associated with a predicate, and the objects that fill the slots, are represented as patterns of activity over pools of shared units. For example, Smolensky (1990) developed a representation of argument bindings based on taking the tensor product of appropriate vectors representing the predicate and each of the fillers of its argument slots. Halford et al (1993) have proposed a model based on tensor-product representations to account for constraints on analogical reasoning, as well as for capacity limits on working memory.

A very different approach, based on mechanisms that neurophysiological evidence suggests may play a role in mammalian vision, involves using oscillations of unit firings to represent transient bindings between objects and the argument slots in propositions and rules. A number of researchers have suggested that temporal synchrony can be used to bind features to object representations in visual perception (Hummel & Biederman 1992; von der Malsburg 1981). Shastri & Ajjanagadde (1993) have developed a detailed computational model that uses temporal dynamics to code the relation structure of propositions and rules. Dynamic bindings in working memory are represented by units firing in phase. Consider a proposition such as "John gave the book to Mary." On a single phase, a unit representing the object John will fire in synchrony with a unit representing the "giver" role; in a different phase the unit for Mary will fire in synchrony with a unit for the "recipient" role. The system is object-based, in the sense that each time slice is occupied by the firing of a single active object unit together with units for all the argument roles that the object fills. Bindings are systematically propagated to make inferences by means of links between units for argument slots. For example, in a rule stating that "If someone receives something, then they own it," the "recipient" role in the antecedent of the rule will be connected to the "owner" role in the consequent. Accordingly, if Mary is dynamically bound to the "recipient" role (by phase locking firing of the "Mary" and "recipient" units), then Mary will become bound to the "owner" role as well (i.e. the unit for Mary will fire in phase with units for *both* relevant roles). Shastri & Ajjanagadde show that their model can answer questions based on inference rules in time that is linear with the length of the inference chain but independent of the number of rules in memory—the most efficient performance pattern theoretically possible.

Shastri & Ajjanagadde (1993) note a number of interesting psychological implications of their dynamic binding model. In particular, they distinguish between two forms of reasoning, which they term "reflexive" and "reflective." Reflexive reasoning is based on spontaneous and efficient inferences drawn in the course of everyday understanding, whereas reflective reasoning is the deliberate and effortful deliberation required in conscious planning and problem solving. It is intriguing that humans are far better at text comprehension than, for example, syllogistic reasoning, even though the formal logical complexity of the former task is much greater than that of the latter (Stenning & Oaksford, 1993). In terms of the Shastri & Ajjanagadde model, text comprehension mainly involves reflexive reasoning, whereas syllogistic inference requires reflective reasoning. Fluent comprehension draws upon a rich network of stored rules, which are used in conjunction with the input to establish a coherent, elaborated model of the situation. Reflexive reasoning of the sort involved in ordinary comprehension relies on dynamic binding of objects to argument slots in preexisting rules. These rules have been encoded into long-term memory, with appropriate interconnections between their arguments. In contrast, reflective reasoning requires manipulation of knowledge in the absence of relevant prestored rules. An arbitrary deductive syllogism (e.g. " If all artists are beekeepers, and some beekeepers are chemists, what follows?") is unrelated to any stored rules; rather, understanding the premises requires setting up de novo "rules" (e.g. "If someone is an artist, then that person is a beekeeper") for each problem.

Shastri & Ajjanagadde's model predicts that reflexive reasoning will be constrained by limits on the number of multiply instantiated predicates, as well as by patterns of variable repetition across the arguments of a rule. The model also makes predictions about the limits of the information that can be active simultaneously in working memory. Although the number of active argument units is potentially unlimited, the number of objects that can be reasoned about in a single session is limited to the number of distinct phases available (because only one object unit may fire in a single phase). Given plausible assumptions about the speed of neural activity, this limit on the number of active objects can be calculated as being five or fewer. This figure is strikingly similar to Miller's (1956) estimate of short-term memory capacity and is consistent with work by Halford & Wilson (1980) indicating that adults cannot simultaneously represent relations involving more than four elements. For example, recent empirical evidence (described by Halford et al, 1993) confirms a limit that will be recognized by anyone who has worked with statistical interactions: The most complex statistical relation that people can deal with in working memory is a 3-way interaction (which involves three independent variables and one dependent variable, for a total of four dimensions). Experimental studies of people's memory for bindings between individuals and properties have revealed similar capacity limits, as well as error patterns consistent with distributed representations of bindings (Stenning & Levy 1988; Stenning et al 1988). Recent work has extended the temporal-synchrony approach to other forms of reasoning. Hummel & Holyoak (1992) have shown that the principles embodied in Holyoak & Thagard's (1989) ACME model of analogical mapping can be captured by a model that encodes propositional structure by temporal synchrony.

An interesting feature of the synchrony approach is that the need to minimize "cross talk" between the constituents of relation structures encourages postulating specific types of serial processing at the "micro" level of temporal phases. For example, in the Shastri & Ajjanagadde model only one object is allowed to fire in each time slice. It is also noteworthy that their model combines localist representations of concepts with distributed control, and thus exemplifies a theoretical "middle ground" between traditional production systems and fully distributed connectionist networks. It is possible that attempts to develop connectionist models of symbol systems will cast new light on the limits of parallel information processing. In addition, connectionist models may provide more effective implementations of the flexible recognition processes based on long-term memory that appear crucial to expertise (Chase & Simon 1973). More generally, the confluence of the symbolic and connectionist paradigms seems likely to deepen our understanding of the kinds of computations that constitute human thinking.

IMPLICIT THINKING AND COGNITIVE EVOLUTION

One interpretation of the contrast between connectionist and symbolic approaches to thinking is that human knowledge depends on two distinct cognitive systems. In fact, many theorists of diverse persuasions have been led to propose cognitive dichotomies, which have been given a rather bewildering array of labels: unconscious vs conscious, procedural vs declarative, automatic vs controlled, reflexive vs reflective, and many others. These distinctions do not always divide cognition along the same lines, nor are particular cognitive functions necessarily associated uniquely with particular halves of the dichotomy (Kihlstrom 1987). Nonetheless, there are tantalizing similarities among the proposed dichotomies. In particular, the first member of each pair is generally viewed as involving unconscious mental processes, a topic that has seen a recent resurgence of interest among experimental psychologists (see *American Psychologist* 47(6) for reviews from various perspectives).

We discuss some of the evidence for a gross cognitive dichotomy, which we term (following Reber, 1992) implicit vs explicit cognition. Reber argues that this dichotomy can be understood in terms of the evolutionary constraints that have molded human cognition, a type of argument that has attracted considerable attention lately (Anderson 1990). We therefore also review the broader issues raised by the use of evolutionary and adaptationist arguments in analyses of cognition.

Acquisition of Implicit Knowledge

The fact that at least some of our knowledge is conscious, explicit, and verbalizable is incontrovertible. At the same time, motor skills provide clear examples of knowledge that can be acquired without awareness and maintained in some implicit form that is not readily verbalized (e.g. Pew 1974). The more controversial claim is that some of the knowledge that underlies higher-level thinking tasks is also implicit in much the same ways as are motor skills. Implicit knowledge, as we use the term here, has a number of important characteristics. It is (*a*) knowledge about covariations in the environment, (*b*) learned by exposures to stimuli exhibiting the covariations, (*c*) obtainable without intention or awareness (although in some cases similar knowledge might be obtained explicitly), and (*d*) demonstrated by improved performance on tasks that seem to require thinking (e.g. generalization and prediction); but it is knowledge that does not have a fully explicit representation in that (*e*) it is not fully verbalizable and (*f*) it is not manipulable in the sense that it cannot be re-represented explicitly to serve as input to other procedures.

We begin by considering evidence concerning the acquisition of implicit knowledge—that is, implicit *learning*. Implicit learning may well be related to implicit memory, a topic that has received much attention in recent years (see Richardson-Klavehn & Bjork 1988; Roediger 1990; and Schacter et al 1993 for reviews). Work on implicit memory, however, typically focuses on the effect of specific events on subsequent task performance, whereas work on implicit learning focuses on the cumulative impact of multiple events involving different (although related) stimuli, emphasizing the acquisition of knowledge about overall regularities in the stimuli rather than about the details of single learning events. Implicit learning has been demonstrated in the laboratory using many different techniques which, until recently, have been explored in relative isolation. Seger (1992) has provided an integrated review of three major methodologies: artificial-grammar learning, learning to control the behavior of dynamic systems, and sequence-learning tasks.

In the typical artificial-grammar learning procedure (see Reber 1989 for a review of the extensive work from his laboratory, which began with the seminal study of Reber 1967), the experimenter constructs a finite-state grammar that generates "grammatical" letter-strings. In the learning phase, subjects are exposed to some of those strings; they may be told to observe or memorize the strings or, in an intentional learning task, to observe and try to figure out the rules that govern the regularities in the strings. In the test phase subjects are typically asked to make "grammaticality" judgments for both old and novel strings. They are told that the strings they have seen were generated according to rules; they are then asked to judge whether or not various test strings follow those rules. In addition, they are often asked to verbalize their knowledge about the grammar and explain how they made their grammaticality judgments. Two consistent results have emerged from these studies: 1. subjects can usually distinguish grammatical from nongrammatical letter strings at an above-chance although far-from-perfect level, and 2. subjects cannot fully articulate the rules they are using to make those judgments.

In dynamic systems tasks, subjects are asked to learn to control the output of a rule-governed system by manipulating input into the system. For example, subjects may be asked to try to control the output of a simulated sugar production factory by typing in the number of workers the company should employ to reach a specified level of production. On each trial the subject types in a number and then is told how much sugar will be produced. The rules underlying the system are linear equations (sometimes with a random error factor added) and always depend on either the previous or current input or output. Berry & Broadbent (1984) used rules of the form: output = 2 × current input − previous output + error. In that study, subjects were able to learn to control the system but were not able to verbalize how they did so. Berry & Broadbent (1988) and Hayes & Broadbent (1988) compared performance on a task with one of two underlying rules—a "salient" rule (output = current input − 2 + error) and a "nonsalient" rule (output = previous input − 2 + error). Under standard learning conditions, subjects receiving the first rule were better able to control the system, were more likely to be able to state the relationship between the variables of the task in protocols, and were more accurate on a questionnaire asking what they could do to control the system given specific circumstances.

Dynamic systems tasks and artificial grammar tasks are similar in that (*a*) subjects seem to acquire knowledge through exposure to repeated exemplars, and (*b*) subjects' performance exceeds their ability to verbalize their knowledge. The tasks differ, however, in that subjects in the dynamic systems tasks are explicitly trying to achieve an objective goal (to maintain production at a specific level). Thus it seems likely that all subjects in the dynamic systems task, unlike subjects in the artificial-grammar task, are intentionally seeking the systems' underlying rules.

In sequence-learning tasks, subjects' implicit knowledge is usually demonstrated by a decrease in reaction time to events generated by underlying rules relative to events generated randomly—without the subject being able to articulate the rule or make explicit predictions about subsequent events (e.g. Cohen et al 1990; Stadler 1989; Willingham et al 1989; but Kushner et al 1991; see Seger 1992). In a study by Nissen & Bullemer (1987), for example, subjects were to press a corresponding button after each in a series of flashes of light. Subjects showed a decrease in reaction time to push buttons when the pattern of flashes was repeated relative to random light sequences. These results are similar to those obtained in the Hebb (1961) digits task, in which subjects echo strings of digits, some of which are repeated. Subjects make fewer errors on repeated strings than on other strings, a result that has been shown to hold regardless of subjects' level of awareness of the repetition (McKelvie 1987). In other sequence-learning tasks (e.g. Lewicki et al 1988), subjects show a decrease in reaction time when responding to targets whose position is predictable from the positions of items in earlier trials. When questioned, however, subjects report no knowledge of the sequences underlying the task.

Evidence of implicit learning also comes from studies of "intuitive physics." As they interact with the physical world, humans acquire knowledge about the complex rule-governed behavior of moving objects. (See Wellman & Gelman 1992 for a recent review of developmental aspects.) People often make systematic errors in predicting (by verbalizing or drawing) the future motion of physical objects as they exit from curvilinear tubes, are released from strings constraining their motion, or are dropped from moving carriers. Yet implicit knowledge of physical rules is demonstrated when subjects view contrived videotapes showing what objects would look like following the paths that subjects predict (Kaiser et al 1985; Shanon 1976; but see McCloskey & Kohl 1983). Even 6-year-old subjects recognize that these trajectories "look wrong" (Kaiser & Proffitt 1984). Such recognition only occurs, however, for the physics of objects that behave like point masses (such as the examples described above); for more complex motion involving multidimensional relationships (e.g. rotating objects), subjects have great difficulty in distinguishing possible from impossible motions while viewing simulations of ongoing events (Proffitt et al 1990). In addition, explicit knowledge (such as that produced by training in physics) often does not increase the accuracy of predictions (e.g. Proffitt et al 1990).

The fact that people apparently acquire implicit knowledge of only certain types of physical regularities is consistent with other evidence indicating that there are limits or constraints on which covariations can be learned implicitly (Seger 1992). A variety of factors apparently contributes to those limitations, of which two major classes are (a) the "simplicity" of the rules underlying the covariations, and (b) biases—both innate and learned—that favor learning certain kinds of covariation.

Some rules may be too difficult to learn implicitly. There may be limits on our ability to detect covariations over spatial and temporal distances (e.g. Broadbent et al 1986; Cleeremans & McClelland 1991), or between a large number of interacting variables (e.g. Proffitt et al 1990). Other rules may be, in a sense, "too easy" to learn implicitly. If a covariation is sought and discovered consciously, then it becomes explicit: Performance is more accurate, the rule is more likely to be verbalizable, and there is no dissociation between verbalization and performance. Explicit learning can be encouraged by instructions to search for rules underlying the covariations in the exemplars; however, such instructions only seem to improve performance when the rules are, in fact, discoverable. Reber et al (1980) found that instructions interacted with the way the learning exemplars were presented. When the exemplar presentation made the underlying rules more obvious, subjects instructed to search for rules performed better than those not so instructed (also Servan-Schreiber & Anderson 1990). In contrast, when the presentation of exemplars was unstructured, subjects who were told to search for rules performed worse than those given more implicit instructions, because the rule-seeking subjects induced nonrepresentative rules. Similarly, Berry & Broadbent (1988) found that intentional instructions helped subjects' performance in the easy "salient" condition but impaired the performance of those in the "nonsalient" condition.

Humans seem to be biased to learn certain types of regularities more readily than others. In category learning, for example, subjects more easily learn categories with unimodal than with bimodal distributions (Flannagan et al 1986). In cue-probability learning, subjects perform better with linear than with nonmonotonic functions; for psychophysical functions, humans find it easiest to learn functions that are linear in logarithmic space (Koh & Meyer 1991). When exposed to stimuli that exhibit nonpreferred regularities, people's judgments early in learning are biased toward the preferred form of regularity; with additional exposure, however, people eventually learn the actual pattern, overcoming their entering bias.

In tasks involving sequence learning, the early items in a series appear to be especially significant, perhaps because they serve to mark the beginning of a new pattern. In the Hebb digits task, changing the first two digits (but not just the first one, or just the last one or two) eliminates learning (Schwartz & Bryden 1971). Servan-Schreiber & Anderson (1990) found that subjects who memorized three-chunk letter strings by building a larger chunk out of the first two smaller chunks were more accurate at grammaticality judgments than subjects who memorized the strings by chunking the second two smaller chunks.

In addition, implicit learning is sometimes affected by the semantic content of the stimuli. The same underlying rule may be learned better when presented with some stimuli than with others. Stanley et al found that subjects performed better in a dynamic systems task when the cover story involved controlling the friendliness of a person rather than the sugar production of a factory, even though the underlying rule was the same in both cases (also Berry & Broadbent 1984). Such content effects suggest that prior knowledge can modulate implicit learning, perhaps by biasing subjects to attend to particular features or to expect particular types of regularities. (We discuss other content effects observed in thinking tasks in a later section.)

Access and Use of Implicit Knowledge

An important characteristic of implicit knowledge, demonstrated in several of the learning studies reviewed above, is that subjects cannot verbalize all of their knowledge. It is clear, however, that at least some useful knowledge is often verbalizable. In an artificial-grammar learning task, Mathews et al (1989) told some subjects that after each test trial they should explain to an "unseen partner" how they made the grammaticality decision. These explanations were later played to another group of subjects as the latter made grammaticality judgments without any prior training or feedback. Such yoked subjects performed better than chance, but not as well as the original subjects, suggesting that some but not all knowledge is verbalizable. Stanley et al (1989) obtained similar results for yoked subjects in a dynamic systems task. Note, however, that the lower performance of the yoked subjects might be attributable either to (*a*) the inability of the original subjects to articulate all of their knowledge, or to (*b*) the inability of the yoked subjects to implement the transmitted knowledge successfully.

In general, it would be difficult to show conclusively that knowledge is inaccessible to consciousness, because the methodology for assessing access to implicit knowledge is inevitably open to challenge. Various methods that do not rely on verbalization of rules have been used to elicit subjects' implicit knowledge; often these methods reveal accessible covariation-based or fragmentary knowledge that can account for much or all of the subjects' performance. In artificial-grammar tasks, classification performance can be accounted for by: subjects' ability to indicate grammatical or ungrammatical parts of letter strings (Dulany et al 1984); knowledge of bigrams or trigams (Perruchet & Pacteau 1990, 1991; Perruchet et al 1992); knowledge of chunks (Servan-Schreiber & Anderson 1990); or knowledge of sequential letter dependencies—i.e. the ability to decide, when presented a string of letters, whether each letter in the grammar, if presented next, would create a grammatical string (Dienes et al 1991). Similar arguments have been levied against the sequence learning tasks (Perruchet et al 1990). Most recently, Perruchet & Amorim (1992) showed that in a sequence-learning task, subjects' conscious ability explicitly to generate and recognize parts of the sequences paralleled their improvement on the reaction-time task. One critique that may be leveled against some methods used to elicit implicit knowledge is that the procedure itself may change the representation of the knowledge from implicit to explicit (Reber et al 1985); certainly knowledge that is initially implicit may eventually be re-represented in some more explicit form (Karmiloff-Smith 1990; also Berry & Broadbent 1988). On the other hand, these studies offer insight into two important and unresolved questions: (a) How unconscious is the learning and (b) is what is being learned abstract rules or something less complex?

Nonetheless, evidence still suggests that subjects' ability to consciously access implicit knowledge typically lags behind their ability to use it. Rubin et al (1993) had subjects study and recall a series of five highly similar ballads, and then attempt to compose a ballad of their own. These subjects were also asked to write down the rules and generalizations that characterized the ballads they had studied. The ballads by the subjects followed more than half of the objective regularities in the studied ballads, but the subjects could only state about one quarter of these rules. Moreover, the correlation between the implicit regularities observed in the composed ballads and the explicitly stated rules was low and statistically nonsignificant. Further support for a dissociation between implicit and explicit knowledge comes from studies of people solving various types of "insight" problems, which reveal that subjects often reach correct conclusions even though they either fail to report they are nearing a solution (Metcalfe 1986; Metcalfe & Wiebe 1987) or are unable to verbalize why their conclusion is correct and lack confidence in it (Bowers et al 1990).

Another important issue relevant to accessing and using implicit knowledge concerns the range of related cases to which such knowledge can be applied. Although it is typical to find generalization to new cases drawn from the same basic pool as those used during training, more distant transfer is not readily obtained. Berry & Broadbent (1988) trained subjects on one dynamic systems task and then measured their performance on a second task involving the same underlying rule. The semantic cover story of the transfer task was either superficially similar or dissimilar to that of the learning task. Subjects in the superficially similar condition improved their performance as much as control subjects (who continued to perform the same task); however, subjects in the superficially dissimilar condition showed no such transfer. Furthermore, subjects who were given a hint that the underlying equation in the transfer task was the same as that in the learning task were not helped: In fact, subjects in the similar condition performed *worse* when given such a hint. By contrast, such a hint generally aids transfer in explicit tasks involving analogical transfer across semantic contexts; in the latter case, subjects seem only to need reminding of knowledge available to them (e.g. Gick & Holyoak 1980). Lack of transfer has also been demonstrated for intuitive physics problems: Subjects are accurate when making predictions about familiar problems but do not transfer their knowledge to make correct predictions on an unfamiliar problem with the same underlying structure (Kaiser et al 1986).

There is, however, evidence of remote transfer in studies using the artificial-grammar task: Subjects who are trained on an artificial grammar using one set of letters perform well on test items generated by structurally isomorphic grammars based on new letters (Mathews et al 1989; Reber 1969). Reber (1989) and Mathews (1990) have argued, on the basis of such evidence for remote transfer, that implicit knowledge is abstract in the sense that the person has learned rules about the structure of the stimuli independent of its physical instantiation. It is possible, however, that such transfer effects are due to shared relational features that were associated with grammaticality during learning of the initial grammar (e.g. a run of three "same" letters near the middle of the string, or the presence of certain "fragments" as discussed above, might indicate grammaticality; see Seger 1992). Although such relational features are arguably abstract to some degree (Mathews 1990), learning covariations based on such features might not indicate general sensitivity to relational structure. It is also possible that transfer between isomorphic grammars depends at least in part on analogical reasoning between studied exemplars and transfer items (Brooks & Vokey 1991), or possibly between studied chunks and transfer items. However, exemplars need not be explicitly remembered. Knowlton et al (1992) found that amnesic patients were able to classify letter strings according to the rules of an artificial grammar as well as control subjects, even though the patients' ability to recognize the studied exemplars was impaired.

The transfer issue may well prove central in assessing potential models of implicit learning. In particular, subsymbolic models based on classifier systems (Druhan & Mathews 1989) and on connectionist learning algorithms (Dienes 1992; Kushner et al 1991) have been successful in accounting for many aspects of human performance in learning artificial grammars. The subsymbolic models readily account for the difficulty that people have in fully verbalizing their knowledge of stimulus regularities, which in the models is largely contained in low-level patterns (of strengths of classifier rules, or weights on links in a distributed connectionist network). However, none of these models can account for transfer between isomorphic grammars based on entirely different sets of letters. If such transfer could be explained on the basis of a limited set of relational features, or by additional explicit processes operating in the transfer task, then it might be possible to characterize the limits of implicit learning in terms of the capabilities of current subsymbolic models; if not, more sophisticated learning models will be required. The limits of transfer based on implicit learning clearly warrant further investigation.

The kind of covariational information that can be learned implicitly appears to be statistical in nature. The question then arises as to the conditions under which such information will be accessed and used in tasks that require making intuitive predictions. The classic work of Kahneman & Tversky (see Kahneman et al 1982) produced many compelling illustrations of people's failures to use statistical information of the sort that could plausibly be acquired by implicit learning. In particular, people commonly underutilize base rates and sample frequencies in making judgments about the likelihood of individual events. Hasher & Zacks (1984) argued that the encoding of event frequency is based on an automatic or implicit process that takes place largely without awareness. Although there has been some dispute about the extent to which frequency encoding satisfies various proposed criteria for automaticity, people are generally accurate in picking up such information (e.g. Sanders et al 1987). The evidence for implicit frequency encoding leads to the following puzzle: If the encoding of frequency is automatic, then one would expect the encoding of base rates, which are simply relative frequencies, to be automatic also. Why, then, have countless studies shown that subjects neglect base-rate information when making various inferences?

In fact, the paradox may be more apparent than real. In almost all studies showing base-rate neglect, subjects are provided with summary information about base rates, rather than with an opportunity to learn information about each individual event comprising the set of events. The base-rate information is thus presented explicitly; no implicit learning occurs. Generally, in experiments in which base-rate information is derived from real-life experience (Christensen-Szalanski & Bushyhead 1981), or learned from presentation of exemplars (Manis et al 1980), subjects use that information effectively. The procedure of giving summary information can be contrasted with the typical category-learning experiment in which subjects are presented with individual exemplars of the categories, are asked to make category judgments, and then are given feedback. When subjects learn to predict membership in categories that occur with different frequencies, they learn to use base rates accurately during the study trials (Estes et al 1989; Gluck & Bower 1988; Medin & Edelson 1988). However, subsequent transfer trials, in which subjects are asked either to indicate category membership or to estimate the probability that a category was correct given a cue, often reveal some apparent misuse of base-rate information.

The findings from category learning experiments suggest that base-rate use has two components: acquisition, which might be done implicitly and is quite accurate (perhaps based on learning feature-to-category conditional probabilities); and access, which (depending on the type of test) may well be explicit and under more conscious control. When acquisition and test both tap implicit knowledge (e.g. during learning trials), subjects generally use base rates accurately; however, it seems that when engaged in more explicit tasks, subjects must be "reminded" to use base rates. In such tasks, people tend to focus on the strength or extremity of the individuating evidence about the case, with insufficient regard for its weight or credibility; base rates and sample size are special cases of the latter type of information (Griffin & Tversky 1992). Explicitly presented base rates have greater impact when they have strong causal implications (Ajzen 1977; Bar-Hillel & Fischhoff 1981; Tversky & Kahneman 1980), when people bring a scientific rather than a clinical orientation to a problem (Zukier & Pepitone 1984), when subjects watch a random sampling process or operate in a domain in which revision of base-rate information is common (Gigerenzer et al 1988), or when conversational context suggests that base-rate information is more relevant than individuating information (Krosnick et al 1990; Schwarz et al 1991). The situations in which subjects tend to use base-rate information are similar to those in which subjects are more likely to invoke other elements of appropriate statistical reasoning (Nisbett et al 1983). We discuss further examples of contextual variations in the use of reasoning strategies in a later section.

In the absence of cues of the above types, statistical knowledge is more likely to be evoked when subjects make judgments about an aggregated set of cases rather than individual cases (Tversky & Kahneman 1983). In particular, people are typically overconfident in evaluating the accuracy of their own beliefs taken one at a time, yet quite well calibrated in judging their overall accuracy for a set of beliefs (Gigerenzer et al 1991; Griffin & Tversky 1992). Without some "reminder" cue, people tend to base their decisions on their assessment of individual events, rather than estimates about a population of similar events (Kahneman & Lovallo, 1993; Tversky & Kahneman 1982). It follows that people are often overconfident in their decisions even though at some level they "know better." Such examples support the general possibility of dissociation between the acquisition and use of implicit knowledge.

Evolutionary History and Adaptation

Another theme in recent work on thinking, closely related to evidence for implicit cognition, concerns the use of evolutionary arguments to support cognitive analyses. The evolution of human cognition is, of course, largely a matter of conjecture. As Lewontin (1990) wrote, in a cautionary introduction to the topic, "If it were our purpose ... to say what is actually known about the evolution of human cognition, we could stop at the end of this sentence" (1990:229). Lewontin pointed out that different types of evolutionary arguments must be distinguished. Here we focus on two types: those based on the evolutionary connections among species, and those based on the adaptive significance of cognitive characteristics. Of these, the former has the virtue of being more closely tied to observable evidence.

There are many reasons to suspect that implicit cognition is phylogenetically older than the explicit variety (Rozin 1976; Sherry & Schacter 1987)—certainly, basic covariation detection is within the cognitive capacity of many species, whereas the writing of review articles is practiced, as far as we know, by *Homo sapiens* alone. Based on the assumption that implicit cognition evolved long before high-level consciousness, Reber (1992) argues that certain principles of evolutionary biology—von Baer's pre-Darwinian laws of embryological development and Wimsatt's (1986) "developmental lock" model of evolutionary change—can be used to derive a number of predictions about the general character of implicit cognition. The major predictions Reber derives are that: 1. implicit systems should be more *robust* than explicit systems, operating despite injuries, diseases and other disorders; 2. implicit processes should be more *age independent,* revealing fewer differences than explicit processes in both infancy and old age; 3. implicit processes should be *IQ independent*; 4. more generally, implicit processes should show *lower population variance* than explicit processes; and 5. implicit processes should show *across-species commonalities.* Reber cites empirical evidence in support of each of these predicted characteristics of implicit cognition.

In addition to deriving predictions based on evolutionary history, Reber (1992) and others have proposed reasons it would be adaptive to have two basic cognitive systems—one to passively pick up covariations among significant environmental stimuli, and another to selectively integrate and control information from many different sources. Others, most notably Anderson (1990), have made much more general appeals to arguments based on adaptation. Anderson argues that psychologists can best develop theories of human cognition by making the assumption that human cognition is optimally adapted to the environment. He terms his research program "rational analysis," taking care to distinguish two meanings of the term "rational": 1. "the normative sense, as used in philosophy, in which human behavior is matched against some model that is supposed to represent sound reasoning ... [and 2.] the adaptive sense, as used in economics, in which the behavior is said to be optimized with respect to achieving some evolutionarily relevant goals" (1990:250–51). It is in this latter sense that Anderson argues human behavior is rational.

Developing a theory using Anderson's program of rational analysis involves six steps (Anderson 1990:29): 1. Specify the goals of the cognitive system; that is, what the system is trying to optimize. 2. Develop a formal model of the environment to which the system is adapted; that is, the environment in which the cognitive system evolved. 3. Make minimal assumptions about computational limits and abilities of the system, including the costs incurred in achieving optimal performance. 4. Derive what the optimal behavioral function should be, given Steps 1–3. 5. Examine the empirical literature to see whether the predictions of the behavioral functions are confirmed. 6. If the predictions are off, try reexamining and revising the assumptions in Steps 1–3.

There is considerable potential for slipperiness in executing this program, especially in Steps 1–3, as has been noted both by Anderson himself (Anderson 1990:30) and others (see commentary on Anderson 1991a in *Behavioral and Brain Sciences,* Vol. 14; also Lewontin 1990). Step 3 is especially problematic because we know little about the environment(s) in which cognition evolved. Thus if the predictions of rational analysis fail, it may be all too tempting to go back and redefine the environment. It is always possible to invent an environment in which a behavior would be adaptive (Dawkins 1987; Simon 1991).

Anderson (1990) demonstrates the use of his method in analyzing memory (also Anderson & Milson 1989), categorization (also Anderson 1991b), causal inference, and problem solving. In practice, his rational approach involves Bayesian analysis, making various simplifying assumptions to avoid the computational intractibility of unconstrained Bayesian inference (see Pearl 1988 for an artificial-intelligence approach along broadly similar lines). With some minor tinkering, Anderson's analysis of memory predicts many major memory findings; the optimized categorization model also predicts a large number of laboratory phenomena. In both cases Anderson's models are nearly equivalent to more mechanistic models that had been proposed previously, and inherits their weaknesses as well as their strengths (e.g. his categorization model, like other similarity-based models, does not provide any constraints on which features are used to represent objects, nor does it account for theory-based influences on categorization; see Medin 1989).

Anderson's program has so far been less successful in dealing with other topics. In particular, rational analysis provides few insights into problem solving, as Anderson admits. He believes that this failing "is more a comment on the state of the literature on problem solving than on the theory" (1990:229). As Anderson points out, most studies of problem solving have been concerned with games and puzzles, which have little adaptive value when compared to the sorts of problems that people confront in real life. More naturalistic problems might include choosing a birthday card, getting the car fixed, or deciding whether to buy an expensive zoom lens. (Of course, none of the latter examples is any more likely than are puzzle problems to have exerted great selection pressure during human evolution.) There is reason to suspect, however, that the limitations of rational analysis in dealing with general problem solving arise for a more basic reason. Problem-solving performance reveals much more pronounced individual differences (often due to the relative efficacy of different strategies) than do tasks that more specifically tap memory retrieval, categorization, or causal inference. In fact, problem-solving skill seems to meet none of Reber's (1992) predicted criteria for implicit knowledge—it is not robust, and it is quite variable across age, IQ, and within as well as across species. The other cognitive functions that Anderson analyzes, which at least in primitive forms are doubtlessly phylogenetically older than general problem solving, seem to have a more implicit than explicit character (although Anderson does not address the implicit/explicit distinction). It is possible that implicit systems, which have undergone longer evolutionary refinement, are in general better optimized to the environment than is explicit cognition and therefore more amenable to rational analysis (S. Kosslyn and S. J. Gould, personal communication). Indeed, given the greater inherent computational complexity of the functions that explicit cognition attempts to compute (which are almost certainly intractible in the general case), it is unlikely that even a few more billion years of evolution will make much difference.

What Is Explicit Thinking For?

In many ways we have painted a more attractive picture of implicit thinking than of its younger explicit sibling. Implicit knowledge is acquired with little effort and is often accurate, perhaps even optimized in some sense. Explicit knowledge, by contrast, takes hard mental work to achieve and might seem barely worth the effort—it often flouts the dictates of rationality, even wantonly ignoring the accurate statistical knowledge that the implicit system has patiently accumulated. What, then, is explicit thinking for?

One answer (at the risk of seeming facetious) is that it enables us to draw a picture of a person with two heads. If the answer seems absurd, consider: For how long would the implicit system have to absorb covariations passively before its knowledge would enable us to draw such a picture? Longer than a lifetime, no doubt. Drawing a two-headed person requires more than the simple reproduction of patterns observed in the environment; it requires the creation of something we have never seen. We may use our experience, however limited, with drawing other objects, such as people with the more typical quota of heads; but to make the required transformation, the usual procedure for drawing a person must itself be manipulated in the process. And to be manipulated in this way, the procedure must be represented explicitly.

The role of internal representations in creative drawing has been explored by Karmiloff-Smith (1990), from whom we have borrowed our example. As she points out (also Rutkowska 1987), a procedure can have two functions: 1. it can be activated to generate an output; and 2. it can itself be manipulated or reorganized by other procedures. In terms of the implicit vs explicit distinction, only a procedure that has an explicit representation can serve as "data" for another procedure, and hence be transformed. According to Karmiloff-Smith (1986, 1990), it is characteristic of cognitive development that procedures initially represented implicitly, such that they can accomplish routine tasks, must be re-represented at a more explicit level before they can be manipulated to accomplish novel tasks.

Karmiloff-Smith (1990) found evidence of a developmental progression in children's abilities to draw such novel objects as a two-headed man—evidence that supports her theoretical claims. When given this task, 5-year-old children were likely to draw a normal man first, then add a second head with an entire second body attached. By age 8–10, however, children had acquired the ability to systematically interrupt their routine drawing procedure, insert two heads symmetrically tilted away from the upright, and then continue drawing the rest of the man. Whereas for the younger children the drawing procedure seemed to be represented as a fixed sequence, for the older children it seemed to have a more abstract part-whole structure, allowing the routine to be interrupted and novel parts to be inserted.

The re-representation of procedures from an implicit to an explicit form is the opposite of the progression assumed in Anderson's (1983, 1987) conception of knowledge compilation, a process that transforms explicit declarative knowledge into an implicit procedural representation. We return to this contrast below when we discuss expertise and knowledge transfer. For now, we note that Karmiloff-Smith's concept of explicit representation appears to imply a capacity for systematic manipulation of knowledge of much the same sort as we discussed earlier when we considered the relationship between connectionist and symbolic representations.

A more general answer to our opening question, then, is that explicit thinking is required for some important forms of creative thought (Boden 1990). (This is not to deny, however, that implicit processes may also play important roles in creativity.) Such a function would suggest that the explicit system ought *not* to be adapted to the environment in which it evolved—at least not in the sense of Anderson's (1990) rational analysis. Let the implicit system become adapted to the environment; the explicit system can help us adapt the environment to us. Explicit representations of knowledge allow us to imagine what is not the case, but might be, and how we might make it so.

CONTENT IN THINKING, THINKING IN CONTEXT

Our third theme is an extension of a topic we encountered in the previous section: the role played in thinking by prior knowledge and contextual cues. Across a wide variety of tasks, the manner in which individuals reason and solve problems is intimately related to the content of what is being thought about as well as to the context in which the thinking takes place. Indeed, content and context are themselves interwined, since the context of thinking— for example, the actions of other individuals and the goals of the reasoner—directly influences the content of thought. Conversely, the content of thought— for example, the internal representation of a problem situation—may trigger goals that alter the effective context in which the thinker is operating. The implications of content and context effects are a focus of current theoretical debates.

Thinking vs Theorem Proving

Cognitive scientists all agree that thinking is properly construed as computation. At the same time, the most vigorous debates in the field concern the questions of what kinds of computation underlie human thinking, and what kinds of representations are used. Various theorists have championed representations for reasoning and problem solving based on stored cases, schemas, rules of varying degrees of generality, constructed semantic models of individuals, and quasi-spatial or image-like structures. The "classical" view has been that thinking is much like the conventional procedures for proving theorems in a formal system, such as a logic. The derivation of inferences, in this proof-theoretic view, depends on the serial application of exceptionless formal rules of inference to internal "statements" expressed in a "language of thought" (Fodor 1983). The classical account implies that reasoning depends on rules that manipulate internal representations on the basis of their syntactic form, rather than their semantic content.[4] Fodor & Pylyshyn have emphasized the centrality of the proof-theoretic approach to cognitive science: "It would not be unreasonable to describe Classical Cognitive Science as an extended attempt to apply the methods of proof theory to the modelling of thought" (1988:29-30).

It is now clear that the conventional proof-theoretic approach is seriously limited in its ability to account for human thinking (Oaksford et al 1990). Two empirical problems present themselves. First, everyday commonsense reasoning is based on defeasible (i.e. "defeatable") inferences, such that conclusions derived from premises can be overturned by subsequent information. For example, suppose we have a rule-like belief that Tom leaves for work in his car every morning at 8 AM. If we see Tom pulling out of the driveway at 8 AM sharp, we will probably conclude that he is going to work. However, we are likely to retract this conclusion if we later remember that it is actually a holiday or if we hear that Tom's wife delivered a baby at the local hospital at 9:00 AM, and so on. The list of exceptions to most rule-like regularities is indefinitely long, thwarting attempts to code the exceptions exhaustively into rules. Thus although there have been many attempts to formalize commonsense reasoning in versions of nonmonotonic logics (i.e. logics in which inferences may be subtracted, as well as added, with the addition of new premises), these efforts have met with limited success (Minsky 1991; Oaksford et al 1990).

The second problem with the proof-theoretic approach is that everyday reasoning is highly content dependent. As we observed in our earlier discussion of connectionist approaches to thinking, people are often poor at solving deductive problems based on arbitrary content (like syllogisms), yet they easily use knowledge stored in long-term memory to make inferences that

---

4

The terms "formal" and "syntactic" have multiple usages in cognitive science. As has often been noted (e.g. Rips 1990), any computational system is necessarily "formal" and "syntactic" in the sense that the procedures are specified in terms of the form of the representations over which they operate. In principle, any aspect of semantic or pragmatic content could be used by a theorist to define the forms that determine the range of applicability for inferential procedures. Accordingly, any computational model of reasoning (including, if they are made explicit, those based on pragmatic schemas and mental models; see below) is necessarily formal in this basic sense. This point has often been misunderstood (see Stenning 1992). Those psychological theories that we refer to as based on "formal rules," however, place strong constraints on what aspects of meaning are required to define the form of representation. Such theories postulate that only the meanings of the "logical terms" included in logics that have been proposed by logicians (e.g. connectives, quantifiers, and modals) are required to define the forms to which inference rules apply.

contribute to a coherent interpretation of a situation. That is, the psychological difficulty of inferences seems to depend more on the relationship between the content of the premises and prior knowledge than on the logical form of the reasoning involved.

The defeasibility of commonsense inferences is closely connected to their content specificity. For example, studies of reasoning about propositional connectives, such as "if," reveal that the content of premises can affect the conclusions drawn. For example, Byrne (1989) gave one group of subjects premises such as the following:

1. If she has an essay to write then she will study late in the library.
2. She has an essay to write.

Almost all subjects (96%) in this group drew the conclusion supported by the formal inference rule *modus ponens,* namely

3. She will study late in the library.

Another group of subjects also received premises 1 and 2 but in addition received

1'. If the library stays open then she will study late in the library.

Only 38% of the latter subjects drew conclusion 3, indicating that introduction of premise 1' blocked application of *modus ponens* based on premises 1 and 2.

Although Byrne (1989; Johnson-Laird & Byrne 1991) interpreted her results as indicating that people do not "follow rules" such as *modus ponens* when reasoning, this conclusion is overstated (Politzer & Braine 1991). The most obvious interpretation of Byrne's results, as she herself noted, is simply that the addition of premise 1' causes subjects to implicitly alter their interpretation of premise 1, reinterpreting the antecedent as a conjunction of two clauses, "she has an essay to write" and "the library is open." Once the premise is tacitly altered, *modus ponens* does not apply (cf Henle 1962). Other results indicate that people are reluctant to apply *modus ponens* to conditional statements when the antecedent is interpreted as a probabilistic cause, such as, "If a person smokes, then that person will get lung cancer" (Cummins et al 1991). Cheng & Nisbett (1993) argue that causal regularities of the form "If *cause* then *effect*" (a major subclass of conditionals) are treated as expressions of probabilistic contingencies. It seems that people generally treat conditional rules not as deterministic and inviolate but as expressions of "default" regularities, assumed to hold unless overridden by other information (cf Oaksford & Chater, 1993). Certain general inference rules, such as *modus ponens,* may, in fact, be used in reasoning, as some theorists argue (e.g. Braine & O'Brien 1991; Rips 1989; Smith et al 1992); however, if the content triggers knowledge that overrides the stated premises, application of the inference rule may be blocked. The theoretical challenge is to provide a model that accounts for people's facility in making plausible but defeasible inferences (e.g. Osherson et al 1990). It seems unlikely that a successful model of everyday reasoning will resemble standard methods for constructing proofs using exceptionless formal rules. [See Stenning & Oaksford (1993) for a discussion of the relationship between logic and reasoning.]

Relevance and Pragmatic Reasoning

A crucial question for theories of thinking concerns *relevance*: How do people access and exploit knowledge relevant to their goals when drawing inferences, making decisions, or solving problems? The problem of determining relevance emerges in many guises. In the area of deductive reasoning, psychological theories based entirely on formal logics have been unable to explain how everyday inference is constrained by intuitions about the relevance of premises to conclusions. For example, an apparent constraint on the use of the English connective "if" is that the antecedent should be relevant to the consequent. But when "if" is interpreted in terms of the material conditional in propositional logic, the sentence "If the moon is made of green cheese, then 13 is a prime number" is considered to be true (because any conditional with either a false antecedent or a true consequent is true). The "schema for Conditional Proof" that Braine & O'Brien (1991) adapt from natural-deduction logic to form a core component of their psychological theory of "if" implies that any sentence of the form "If p then q" is true whenever q is already known to be true, even when p is irrelevant to q. Often, however, people find such irrelevant conditionals peculiar. And even premises that are relevant to making a deductive inference may fail to be relevant to explanation, as an example from Hempel (1965) demonstrates. Suppose we are given the premises

> All members of the Greenbury School Board are bald.
> Horace is a member of the Greenbury School Board.

We can readily deduce that Horace is bald. However, if asked to explain *why* Horace is bald, we are unlikely to say it is because he is a member of the school board. So far, no formal theory has satisfactorily solved the problem of defining relevance.

People's inferential procedures are also influenced by their current beliefs about the content of the premises. In deductive inference tasks, for example, reasoners are more likely to accept an invalid conclusion that is consistent with their beliefs than an invalid conclusion that they do not believe is true (and hence are motivated to refute) (Evans et al 1983; Markovits & Nantel 1989; Oakhill et al 1989). In hypothesis testing, the reasoner's current hypothesis will guide selection of cases chosen to be examined. People have a strong preference for "positive" tests—that is, for examining cases in which either the hypothesized condition for the target outcome, or the target outcome itself, is known to hold. As Klayman & Ha (1987, 1989) have argued, positive testing need not indicate an irrational bias toward confirmation of one's hypotheses. In many realistic cases, positive testing actually maximizes the possibility that the tested hypothesis will be disconfirmed. More generally, focus on confirmation vs disconfirmation may vary dynamically as the reasoner collects evidence over time. Successful hypothesis testing, in studies both of scientific inference and of medical diagnosis, often involves an initial focus on confirmation followed by more critical examination of "loose ends" or apparent anomalies, which may lead to hypothesis revision (Dunbar, 1993; Mynatt et al 1978; Patel & Groen 1991). In cases of "pathological science," however, scientists with strong attachment to their hypotheses may actively avoid collecting or recognizing disconfirming evidence (Rousseau 1992). In a review of evidence for motivated reasoning, Kunda (1990) argues that motivation to arrive at particular conclusions enhances the use of strategies (such as biased memory search) likely to lead to the desired conclusion.

Content effects and intuitions of relevance have been studied extensively over the past quarter century using Wason's (1966) "selection task" (see Evans 1989 for a review). The selection task involves giving subjects a conditional rule in the form "If p then q." Subjects are shown one side of each of four cards, which respectively show the cases corresponding to p, not-p, q, and not-q. They are told that the cards show the value of p (i.e. p or not-p) on one side and the value of q on the other. Their task is to decide which of the cards must be turned over to check whether the rule is false. The "correct" choice, according to standard propositional logic, is to select the p card (which might have not-q on its back) and the not-q card (which might have p on its back), because these are the only two possibilities that would falsify the rule. Subjects seldom make the correct choice when the conditional rule has arbitrary content (e.g. "If a card has an 'A' on one side, then it must have a '4' on the other"). Rather, they tend to make various errors, of which the most common is to select the cards corresponding to p and q (i.e. "A" and "4"). In contrast, for certain comparable rules that can be interpreted as expressing permission or obligation relations, such as "If a person is to drink alcohol, then they must be at least 21 years old," the p and not-q cases are selected much more frequently (see, for example, D'Andrade 1982; Cheng & Holyoak 1985; Cosmides 1989; Girotto et al 1989b; Johnson-Laird et al 1972; Light et al 1990; Manktelow & Over 1991; Politzer & Nguyen-Xuan 1992).

To explain the influence of content on reasoning in the selection task and other tasks (such as linguistic rephrasing) involving inference with conditionals, Cheng & Holyoak (1985) suggested that thematic content evokes pragmatic reasoning schemas: sets of rules that deal with situations defined in terms of recurring classes of goals and relationships to these goals. Pragmatic reasoning schemas fall into broad categories, of which prominent varieties are those dealing with causal inferences (Cheng & Nisbett, 1993; Tversky & Kahneman 1980) and those dealing with inferences based on the concepts of permission and obligation (Cheng & Holyoak 1985; Cheng et al 1986). The pragmatic schema theory predicts that performance on the selection task will depend on which schema (if any) is evoked by the content and context of the stated rule. For example, the "drinking age" rule just mentioned will tend to evoke a "permission schema," which applies when a precondition must be satisfied if a regulated action is to be taken. If a rule is interpreted as a conditional permission, the schema will focus attention on the case in which the action is taken (e.g. someone who drinks alcohol should be checked to be sure the age precondition has been met) and that in which the precondition has not been met (e.g. someone who is under age should be checked to be sure they are not drinking alcohol), because these two cases might reveal a violation. These are in fact the p and $not\text{-}q$ cases—the selections dictated by standard logic. Accordingly, problems that evoke the permission schema show a dramatically greater frequency of these "correct" selections.

In addition to explaining patterns of facilitation for rules with concrete thematic content, Cheng & Holyoak (1985) demonstrated that facilitation could be obtained even for an abstract permission rule, "If one is to take action 'A', then one must first satisfy precondition 'P'" (also see Cheng & Holyoak 1989; Girotto, et al, 1992). The fact that people can reason reliably about rules with novel content or abstract content fulfills two of the major empirical criteria for rule use proposed by Smith et al (1992). In addition, the ability to reason about regulations has been demonstrated in children as young as 6 years old (Girotto et al 1988; Legrenzi & Murino 1974; Light et al 1989).

As Cheng & Holyoak (1985) noted, evocation of a pragmatic schema will not necessarily lead to selection of the "logically correct" cases. The perceived relevance of cases may vary both across schemas (because different schemas may encourage different inferences) and within schemas (because the context may alter the mapping of the elements of the stated conditional onto components of the schema). Moreover, a single conditional may be potentially mapped onto multiple schemas. Subjects who are encouraged to take different perspectives on a rule may interpret the rule in terms of different schemas, each of which yields a distinct response pattern (Politzer & Nguyen-Xuan 1992). Politzer & Nguyen-Xuan's analysis can account for other demonstrations that subjects' perspectives guide their evaluation of conditional regulations (Cosmides 1989; Gigerenzer & Hug 1992; Manktelow & Over 1991).

It has been suggested that people only have one special case of the permission schema—that in which someone who receives a rationed benefit must pay a cost (Cosmides 1989). In fact, however, many findings are inconsistent with this restriction (e.g. Cheng & Holyoak 1989; Girotto et al 1989a; Manktelow & Over 1990; Politzer & Nguyen-Xuan 1992). For example, Manktelow & Over (1990) found facilitation in the selection task for the conditional precaution, "If you clean up spilt blood, then you must wear rubber gloves," where there was no suggestion that cleaning up spilt blood was a rationed benefit for which one must pay a cost. Although Cosmides (1989) reported failing to obtain facilitation with some conditional rules, none of them was unambiguously cast as a permission situation for subjects (Cheng & Holyoak 1989; Pollard 1990).

The influence of content on reasoning extends well beyond the domain of social regulations. Work on causal reasoning—both inductive and deductive—reveals that people have inference procedures that are to some extent specialized for reasoning about cause and effect relations (e.g. Cheng & Nisbett, 1993; Cheng & Novick 1990, 1991, 1992; Hilton & Slugoski 1986; Kahneman & Miller 1986; Tversky & Kahneman 1980). One line of research has investigated the conditions under which people base causal judgments on the contingency between potential causal factors and an effect, where the contingency is defined as the proportion of events for which the effect occurs when a factor is present vs absent. Contingency is therefore sensitive not only to information about what occurs when the causal factor is present, but also to information about what happens in its absence. For example, in evaluating whether smoking causes cancer, information about nonsmokers who do not develop cancer is relevant. Cheng & Novick (1990) found that people's causal attributions could be reliably predicted from a contingency computation—as long as the set of events over which contingency is computed was taken into account (also Novick, Fratianne & Cheng, 1992). A number of apparent biases in causal attribution, such as a bias to attribute effects to a person rather than a situation, can be attributed to the fact that experimenters have not been fully aware of the information their subjects were using to compute contingency (Cheng & Novick 1992). Often people do not compute contingency over all possible cases, but rather some subset of cases—the *focal set* (Cheng & Novick 1990)—that they consider pragmatically relevant in the context. Variations in focal sets have been shown to account for people's intuitions about the distinction between causes and enabling conditions (Cheng & Novick 1991). For example, people will typically perceive a lightning strike as the cause of a forest fire, but they will view the presence of oxygen as merely an enabling condition, even though the lightning and the oxygen (along with other factors, such as the presence of combustible material) were individually necessary and jointly sufficient to yield the fire. In another context, for example that of a special oxygen-free laboratory, oxygen will be considered the cause of a fire that breaks out when it seeps into the lab. The distinction between causes and conditions thus depends on pragmatic contextual influences, rather than simply on the formal properties of necessity and sufficiency.

The application of causal schemas is also constrained by factors other than contingency, most notably temporal directionality: People assume that causes must precede their effects (Bullock et al 1982; Tversky & Kahneman 1980). Waldmann & Holyoak (1992) have shown that when a causal context is imposed on a task of classification learning, the pattern of performance differs radically across a predictive context, in which the cues are interpreted as possible causes of a common effect, and a diagnostic context, in which the cues are interpreted as possible effects of a common cause. In particular, competition among cues during learning is reduced or eliminated when they are perceived as joint effects of a common cause, rather than as alternative causes of a common effect. These differing patterns of cue competition suggest that people have a natural tendency to induce contingencies from causal factors to effects, rather than the reverse, even when the order in which information is presented is "effect followed by cause."

Taken as a whole, work on pragmatic reasoning indicates that thinking is heavily constrained by semantic and pragmatic content, and that the effects of broad classes of content are interpretable in terms of schemas that are relatively abstract, although less so than rules of formal logic. The forms of inference generated by the two classes of schemas that have received closest scrutiny—causal and regulation schemas—are very different, reflecting the differing goals associated with these domains. Whereas causal schemas serve to guide informative prediction, diagnosis, and explanation, the permission and obligation schemas govern assessment of conformity with contractual agreements and maintenance of freedom of choice for individuals within the limits of established regulations. Each schema provides a unique set of inference rules that embodies relevance relations appropriate for the pertinent goals.

The Context of Learning and the Content of Transfer

The issue of relevance arises again in connection with the transfer of knowledge from the context of learning to other related situations. Essentially by definition, transfer is based on the perception that prior knowledge is relevant to the current context. Transfer is in turn intimately related to the nature of expertise: We typically think of an "expert" as someone who is particularly good at recognizing the relevance of domain knowledge to new problems.

Expertise, however, may come in two qualitatively distinct varieties, only one of which promotes transfer across contexts. Hatano & Inagaki (1986; Hatano 1988) have drawn a distinction between routine and adaptive expertise; Salomon & Perkins (1989) elucidate a related distinction between "low-road" and "high-road" mechanisms of transfer. Routine expertise is characterized by rapid and accurate solution of well-practiced types of problems; adaptive expertise is characterized by flexible transfer of knowledge to novel types of problems and the ability to invent new procedures derived from expert knowledge. In terms of the distinctions drawn earlier, routine expertise may be based on implicit knowledge of procedures, whereas adaptive expertise may depend on more explicit and abstract representations. Of course, it is possible for a single individual to demonstrate both forms of expertise. Current production-system models of learning, with their emphasis on the acquisition of more specialized production rules through knowledge compilation, can be characterized as attempts to explain routine expertise (e.g. Anderson 1987; Rosenbloom et al 1991). These models have been directed primarily at accounting for stable superior performance on representative tasks, for which reproductive methods and specific knowledge are in fact central. Indeed, such theories are often described as models of "skill acquisition," which as Wenger (1987) has pointed out, is not coextensive with expertise: "Whereas skill acquisition can be tested by straightforward performance measures, expertise is a much more subtle notion ... . [It] must also be evaluated by the capacity to handle novel situations, to reconsider and explain the validity of rules, and to reason about the domain from first principles ... " (p. 302).

Hatano & Inagaki (1986) suggest that the key to adaptive expertise—which involves facility in the recognition of relevance relations across contexts—is the development of a deeper and more explicit understanding of the target domain (cf Karmiloff-Smith 1990). Such understanding is heavily dependent on the conditions under which learning takes place. Understanding is more likely to result when the task is variable and in some degree unpredictable rather than stereotyped, and when the task is explored freely without heavy pressure to achieve an immediate goal (Sweller 1988). Understanding can result from sensitivity to internally generated feedback, such as surprise at a predictive failure, perplexity at noticing alternative explanations of a phenomenon, and discoordination due to lack of explanatory links between pieces of knowledge that apparently should be related. Understanding is also fostered by social support and encouragement of deeper comprehension, and by efforts to explain a task to others or to oneself. For example, Chi et al (1989) found that better students of physics, as measured by transfer performance, took a more active approach to learning from worked examples of word problems than did weaker students. The better students continually tried to explain *why* the steps of the illustrated solutions were required.

Analogical transfer—transfer of structural knowledge between specific situations—demonstrates an important bridge between context-bound and abstract knowledge. Theories of analogical thinking must attempt to explain when and how a novel target situation will evoke potentially useful source analogs stored in memory. The issue of how relevance relations can be recognized is thus central to analogical transfer. As we noted earlier, one general proposal (Thagard et al 1990) is that analog retrieval is governed by three types of constraints on the mappings between elements of the target and those of potential source analogs: semantic similarity (i.e. preference for mappings between taxonomically related concepts), isomorphism (i.e. preference for one-to-one mappings in which corresponding elements consistently fill parallel roles), and pragmatic centrality (i.e. preference for mappings involving elements deemed to be especially important to goal attainment). Empirical evidence suggests that for novices in a knowledge domain, retrieval is dominated by semantic similarity but that isomorphism also plays a role (e.g. Holyoak & Koh 1987; Keane 1988; Ratterman & Gentner 1987; Ross 1987, 1989; Seifert et al 1986; Wharton et al 1992). Access is improved if the source and target have similar goal structures. Schank (1982) placed particular emphasis on the importance to the reminding process of encodings that are influenced by goal failures. Recent evidence indicates that an initial goal failure experienced in connection with a source problem increases the likelihood that it will be retrieved in the context of a subsequent target problem in which an analogous impasse is reached (Gick & McGarry 1992; Read & Cesa 1991).

An important component of the development of expertise appears to be the induction of more abstract knowledge structures, such as rules and schemas, that serve to "highlight" problem-relevant aspects of situations, including less salient relations that are crucial to finding solutions (e.g. Chi et al 1981; Sweller 1988). In a kind of bootstrapping, analogical reasoning between problem examples fosters schema induction, schematic knowledge yields more expert transfer across superficially different content domains, and expertise permits more effective processing of novel analogs (Brown 1989; Catrambone & Holyoak 1989; Gick & Holyoak 1983; Novick 1988; Novick & Holyoak 1991; Ross & Kennedy 1990). Transfer of problem-solving procedures appears to be limited by the diversity of the content represented in the learning context, and by the structural parallels between the concepts in the acquired schema and the concepts that the learner uses to represent the target domain (Bassok 1990).

In addition to laboratory studies of learning and transfer, related lines of research have examined these processes in naturalistic contexts, investigating the roles of social and cultural contexts in guiding thinking. The work on cultural constraints in learning includes detailed studies of apprenticeship learning (Lave & Wenger 1991). Other research examines the differences between skills (such as mathematical strategies) as they emerge from formal instruction vs informal cultural practices (e.g. Carraher et al 1985, 1988; Lave 1988; Saxe 1982, 1988, 1991; Stevenson & Stigler 1992).

The "cultural practice" model offered by the Laboratory of Comparative Human Cognition (LCHC 1983) fostered the extreme view that thinking is simply a collection of cognitive skills, each independently acquired in a specific social context and inextricable from that context. This view, a version of what is sometimes termed "situated cognition," has led some people to conclude that it is not possible to understand thinking in terms of the individual's cognitive processes [see Vera & Simon (1993) for a critical discussion]. Early evidence from laboratory studies indicating that spontaneous cross-domain analogical transfer is difficult to obtain with novices (e.g. Gick & Holyoak 1980) was taken as evidence that transfer inevitably depends on the social organization of experience: *"Transfer is arranged by the social and cultural environment.* This shift of focus does not so much solve the transfer problem as it dissolves it" (LCHC 1983:341; italics in original).

Such extreme "situationism" provides an overly restrictive picture of the impact of culture and context on thinking. There are in fact important variations in the degree to which culturally embedded learning impedes or promotes flexible transfer. Hatano (1988) exemplifies the distinction between routine and adaptive expertise with a cross-cultural contrast between two forms of mathematical calculation skills: use of the abacus in Japan and other Asian cultures (e.g. Hatano & Osawa 1983), and the "street math" of Brazilian children working as vendors. Expertise in use of the abacus leads to extremely rapid calculations and to increased digit span; however, such knowledge cannot be readily generalized to repair "buggy" pencil-and-paper arithmetic procedures (Amaiwa 1987) or to use nonconventional abacuses with different base values. In contrast, unschooled Brazilian children who acquire arithmetic skills in the context of selling merchandise on the street can adapt general components of their procedures, such as decomposition and regrouping, to solve novel problems both on the street and in classroom mathematics (Saxe 1991). Hatano suggests that the primary difference between the two skills is that representations of number relations on the abacus are impoverished in meaning, whereas those used in street math are semantically transparent, analogous to actual activities dealing with goods and money. In addition, abacus use is basically a solitary skill in which speed and accuracy are the dominant goals, whereas street math is a social enterprise in which transparency to the customer is more important than speed.

In general, as Guberman & Greenfield (1991) have argued, sociocultural studies of everyday cognition provide evidence that dovetails nicely with laboratory research on learning and transfer. The extent of transfer varies enormously as a function of the content and context of learning. In both formal and informal settings, degree of transfer depends on the induction of abstract schemas, which is fostered by such factors as diversity of learning contexts, free exploration of the results produced by applying problem-solving operators, and perceived similarity of goal structures across examples.

Vivid Representations for Reasoning

The role of content in reasoning is intimately related to debates about the nature of the representational systems available for human thinking. Few if any issues in psychology or cognitive science have been debated as vigorously as the question of whether (or when) people think in "images" or "propositions." The debate peaked in the 1970s (Kosslyn et al 1979; Kosslyn & Pomerantz 1977; Pylyshyn 1973), stimulating a great deal of important empirical research but also, owing to the lack of theoretical clarity, causing some psychologists to become pessimistic about the very possibility of evaluating competing cognitive models (Anderson 1978). After a relative lull of a decade or so, basic questions about distinctions among types of human representations are now being reopened. Several lines of research bear upon these issues, including studies of imagery and the use of diagrams in problem solving, logical analyses of graphical representations, and theoretical proposals about "mental models."

We use the term *vivid representations* to refer to representations of the general sort just mentioned. The psychological character of these representations remains a matter for investigation, and so we use the term informally. It is inspired, however, by Levesque's (1986) characterization of "vivid knowledge" in logical systems—a conception not tied to spatial representations. The key idea is that reasoning is often facilitated when it can make use of representations in which information is definite rather than vague (Stenning & Oberlander 1992). In a vivid representation, a finite number of objects are represented and each is associated with definite values for all relevant properties and relations.

Representational systems vary in the degree of vagueness they permit. Imagine a simple world consisting solely of three animals (a fox, a pig, and a hen) standing in three positions, ordered from left to right. We might describe the current state of this world using sentences such as "The fox is left of the pig" and "The pig is left of the hen." Note the proposition expressed by the first sentence leaves the location of the hen unspecified, while the second is vague about the fox. From this sentential representation we can draw no further inferences in the absence of explicit inference rules. Such paucity of immediate inferences characterizes what we might term *pallid* representations.

In contrast, to illustrate a vivid representation let us represent this same simple world using a system quite different from sentences: an imagined horizontal line with three positions on it. Suppose we establish correspondences between the positions of the animals in the world and locations on the line. Each complete assignment of animal positions to line locations will constitute a model of this simple world. Now we can assess whether various propositions are true in particular models. Let the letters F, H and P stand for the positions of the fox, hen, and pig, respectively. There will be three models in which it is true that the fox is left of the pig (F P H, F H P, H F P) and three models in which it is true that the pig is left of the hen (P H F, P F H, F P H). The two sets of models have only one model in common, F P H; i.e. there is only one model in which both propositions are true. (Finding this unique model need not require exhaustive search of all the possibilities; rather, one might first represent the animals as described by the initial premise, and then add the third animal introduced in the second premise in a way that maintains consistency with the first premise.) Thus from two propositions, each of which fixes the relative position of two objects, we can deduce the absolute position of all three, as well as an additional relative ordering (the fox is left of the hen).

Note these inferences do not require use of any explicit rules: The deductions follow from the basic structure of the represented world (the finite number of animals in a restricted set of possible arrangements). If there is a unique model in which both premises are true, and we succeed in identifying it, we receive the inferences about the absolute locations of the objects as a "bonus." Such inferences will remain implicit in the model until some "read-out" procedure interprets it. Read-out procedures for models bear some resemblance to inference rules; however, there is one highly significant difference.

Whereas inference rules operate on given premises to yield conclusions, read-out procedures operating on a model completely blur the distinction between "premises" and "conclusions." Thus once the model F P H has been established as the representation of the stated propositions (and assuming the initial sentential representation of the premises has been lost), then the same read-out procedures would be required to derive from the model the fact that the fox is left of the pig (an initial premise) and the fact that the fox is left of the hen (an inferred conclusion). In fact, empirical studies of reaction time to make judgments of relative order for items in a memorized linear series have revealed that some valid inferences (based on relations between items far apart in the series) can be judged to be true more quickly than premises based on relations between adjacent items (e.g. Potts 1974). Such evidence that conclusions can be more accessible than premises is difficult to explain in terms of the operation of inference rules but is consistent with read-out mechanisms applied to imagined arrays. [See McGonigle & Chalmers (1986) for a discussion of the conditions under which a distinction in memory between premises and conclusions is maintained or lost.]

In general, a vivid representational system is one that *compels* specification of certain information and that specifies interdependencies between properties and relations so that a partially specified input can yield a definite model. In such a system, to think a certain thought may not only entail that you *can* think some other related thought (as in Fodor & Pylyshyn's 1988 concept of systematicity) but that you *are* thinking it. To form a model, it is necessary to have enough information to assign each represented object to a unique symbol in the model and to establish values for objects with respect to all relevant predicates. A wide range of evidence indicates that indeterminancy is in fact often highly detrimental to both memory and inference (Mani & Johnson-Laird 1982; McGonigle & Chalmers 1986). In addition, capacity limits on the number of objects that can be maintained in working memory imply that humans can only reason with vivid representations based on very small numbers of objects.

The fact that a vivid representational system promotes definiteness (by requiring that all variables be bound to values) does not prevent it from allowing abstraction (Stenning & Oberlander 1992). Abstraction may arise in several ways. First, a crucial aspect of the general characterization of a representational system is that it involves specifying which aspects of the represented world are relevant. Thus if only a subset of the objects and properties in the world is selected as relevant to the model, the model is allowed to be abstract—it need only be definite with respect to the selected subset of possible information. Second, vagueness can be represented by forming multiple models, each of which corresponds to a single determinate state of affairs, such that the set of models exhausts the possibilities. Third, vagueness of a property might be represented within a single model by introducing probability distributions of property values. Finally, the system may be augmented by explicit sentential statements: Representational vividness can be viewed as a continuum rather than a strict categorical distinction. Levesque succinctly captures the inherent trade-off between pallid and vivid representational systems: "... [T]he representational expressiveness of a language ... is not so much in what it allows you to say, but in what it allows you to *leave unsaid.* ... The more that is left unsaid, the more possibilities are allowed by what is said" (1988:370; italics in original). We would add the following: when more possibilities are allowed, fewer inferences can be made immediately.

The kinds of relation structures often assumed to underlie knowledge-based human thinking (e.g. schemas) are generally viewed as having properties that foster vivid representations. A schema specifies the relevant properties to be modeled, thus guiding relevant abstraction. Once a situation has been mapped into a schema, each relevant object will typically take on a definite value—either a determinate value or one generated as a default by the schema itself—with respect to each schema-relevant property. As Stenning & Oberlander (1992) point out, connectionist-style constraint satisfaction tends to naturally generate vivid representations in which a partially specified input may "complete itself," thus automatically performing a kind of default reasoning.

The fact that general representational concepts, such as schemas and connectionist networks, provide properties associated with vivid representations implies that vivid representations are not strictly tied to spatial imagery alone. Indeed, Stenning & Oberlander (1992) argue that the contrast between "images" and "propositions" is fundamentally misleading. In psychological discussions, "propositions" are often equated with sentences—if not natural-language sentences, then sentences in a language of the predicate-calculus or LISP-string style. But from the point of view of logic, propositions are abstract objects that can have truth values with respect to a represented world, and are not tied to any specific representational system. Under this usage, the information conveyed by a graph is just as propositional as that conveyed by a sentence. Thus the central issues for cognitive psychologists do not concern whether imagery is somehow nonpropositional but whether representational systems differ in the range of propositions they can express and the nature of the procedures they provide for drawing inferences. (Of course, imagistic and sentential representations may have different neural underpinnings.)

Although vivid representations are not necessarily imagistic, quasi-spatial representations certainly provide prominent examples of the vivid variety. A great deal of research indicates that people can manipulate visuospatial representations to make certain types of inferences, such as judgments of the similarity of rotated objects (Shepard & Metzler 1971), or of the shape formed by the two-dimensional projection of a rotated three-dimensional object (Pinker & Finke 1980; for a recent review see Finke 1989). Image-based inferences may also play a role in various forms of creative thinking (Finke 1990). There is considerable evidence that graphical and imagistic representations provide expressive and inferential power that differs from that afforded by sentential representations; for certain types of problems, the former type of system conveys distinct advantages. Larkin & Simon (1987) discuss the case of external diagrams of the sort used to capture relationships in physical space (e.g. pulley problems), in an ideal space (e.g. geometry problems), or in nonspatial domains that nonetheless can be mapped onto spatial displays (e.g. supply and demand functions in economics). They emphasize that diagrams organize information by location in a plane, and that information required for inferencing is therefore often present and explicit at a single location. Both recognition of meaningful elements and control of search (i.e. matching of elements to inference rules) are likely to be enhanced when using vivid visuospatial rather than pallid sentential representations. Recognition benefits from the highly specialized procedures available to the human visual system; search benefits because multiple elements that must be matched to a rule are typically found in close spatial proximity.

Because external diagrams are effective for certain types of problem solving, it is natural to expect that internal memory representations of a quasi-spatial nature would also prove useful. Koedinger & Anderson (1990) describe a simulation model of expert theorem proving in geometry based on quasi-spatial schemas. Each schema is a cluster of geometry facts associated with a prototypical geometric image. Schemas enable efficient forward search from given information to the goal, a central characteristic of expert performance in this domain. Koedinger & Anderson found that the schema-based model could account for the steps that experts skipped mentioning in verbal protocols. The main steps experts did tend to mention corresponded to "whole-statements" (the overall conclusion supported by the configuration, such as the fact that two triangles with certain properties are congruent). Thus schemas seem to serve as "macro-operators," shortening the number of steps required to execute a procedure. It is interesting, however, that current production-system models of the formation of macro-operators (Anderson 1987; Rosenbloom et al 1991) were unable to account for how such geometry macro-operators could be learned. In these production-system models, macro-operators are formed by conjoining consecutive production rules that are applied to achieve the same goal. In contrast, the geometry schemas involve macro-operators organized around objects and aggregations of objects in the domain. Other evidence suggests that induction of problem schemas is better fostered by free exploration of the search space (e.g. investigating the effects of applicable operators on objects) than by direct pursuit of specific goals (Sweller 1988; Sweller et al 1983).

The work of Johnson-Laird and his colleagues on "mental models" illustrates how vivid representations in working memory can be used in reasoning (e.g. Johnson-Laird 1983; Johnson-Laird & Byrne 1991; Johnson-Laird, Byrne, et al, 1992; Johnson-Laird et al 1989). In the mental-models framework, deductive reasoning is viewed as the construction and manipulation of models derived from the premises. The most compelling examples of the approach involve spatial reasoning. Consider the following two sets of premises:

Problem I Premises	Problem II Premises
A is on the right of B.	B is on the right of A.
C is on the left of B.	C is on the left of B.
D is in front of C.	D is in front of C.
E is in front of B.	E is in front of B.

For both sets of premises, one can ask the same question: What is the relation between D and E? For Problem I, it is possible to construct a single determinate model:

```
C    B    A
D    E
```

yielding the conclusion that D is left of E. In contrast, Problem II requires two distinct models:

```
C    A    B    and    A    C    B
D         E                D    E
```

but both models support the conclusion that D is left of E. The two problems not only have the same answer, they are identical except for the first premise in each set. Moreover, the initial premise is in both cases irrelevant to the conclusion, because the relation between D and E depends only on the relation between C and B and not on the location of A. Although the problems are closely matched in form and content, the mental-models theory predicts that Problem I should be easier than Problem II because the first premise leads to multiple models for the latter problem. A study by Byrne & Johnson-Laird (1989) provided support for this prediction. Subjects were significantly more accurate for cases such as Problem I that had a valid conclusion based on a single model than for cases such as Problem II that had a valid conclusion based on multiple models (61% vs 50% correct). Indeterminate problems with no valid conclusion, which should theoretically require exhaustive scrutiny of multiple models, were much more difficult (18% correct). For such spatial deductive tasks it would be difficult to devise a proof-theoretic model that could account for the observed patterns of human reasoning performance.

Johnson-Laird and his colleagues have also proposed that people construct models in order to reason with syllogisms and propositional connectives. More complex assumptions are required to apply the mental-model approach to these more abstract tasks. It is assumed that sets of individuals or situations are mapped onto tokens in the model, thus eliminating variables; and that people tend to establish initial "default" models for the various logical terms (e.g. the quantifiers "all" and "some," and connectives such as "and" and "if"). Under some circumstances, it is assumed that people will "flesh out" their initial representation by constructing further possible models. Various symbolic devices are also postulated—e.g. special symbols to indicate negations, to denote which sets have been exhaustively considered, and to signify whether further models remain to be explored. The most general prediction of the approach is that problem difficulty will increase with the number of models that must be considered to arrive at a logically correct conclusion.

The overall success of the mental-models approach in this domain is so far mixed. On the positive side, several novel predictions of the model were confirmed in the Johnson-Laird et al (1992) study (e.g. deductions from exclusive disjunctions proved easier than those from inclusive disjunctions, as expected given the assumption that fewer models are required in the former case). Other inference phenomena are accounted for by auxillary assumptions. For example, to explain why people do not usually restate premises when drawing conclusions, Johnson-Laird et al assume that people keep track of the stated premises. Since a mental model (like vivid representations in general) does not preserve the identity of premises, some other representational system must presumably be helping out.

Other phenomena place greater strain on the theory. If mental models are intended to be vivid representations in the sense we have discussed, then the application of the approach to propositional reasoning is based on questionable assumptions. Johnson-Laird et al introduce a notation that allows for objects that are not fully specified—what they call an "implicit model." Of course, for vivid representations the notion of an "implicit model" is an oxymoron: The basic requirement for a vivid model is that it be fully definite. Given such problems, Johnson-Laird et al's account of propositional reasoning does not convincingly refute the view that formal inference rules such as *modus ponens* play some role in explaining human inference patterns. In any case, such a conclusion seems extremely unlikely given the highly evolved linguistic abilities of humans. Humans are presumably capable of reasoning both with pallid sentential representations, for which inference rules are well suited, and with more vivid representations.

Moreover, the mental-models approach to deductive reasoning is itself fundamentally based on formal procedures for representing arbitrary situations involving logical terms, just as are formal-rule theories. The procedures are directed at the manipulation of tokens rather than syntactic rules, but the two approaches are equally formal (in the sense of making minimal reference to semantic content; see footnote 4). Accordingly, theories based on mental models, like those based solely on formal rules, are unable to account for content effects in reasoning except by adding auxillary assumptions (often unacknowledged) about when people retrieve relevant counterexamples, schematic knowledge about types of situations, and so on (e.g. Johnson-Laird & Byrne 1992).

Thus although vivid representations undoubtedly play an important role in human thinking, an adequate theory must specify much more than procedures for manipulating symbolic tokens in mental models. The construction of mental models in working memory must be guided by retrieval of relevant knowledge structures from long-term memory, and the use of models requires read-out procedures that can make use of information implicit in the models. Moreover, as Stenning & Oaksford (1993) have argued, it would be desirable to show how initial default models in working memory emerge as a consequence of more primitive computational mechanisms, such as procedures for dynamic binding of objects to roles (e.g. Shastri & Ajjanagadde, 1993). In a constraint-satisfaction model of binding, only one set of consistent bindings of objects to roles (i.e. one vivid model) can be maintained at one time. This basic processing limitation offers an explanation of why it is that if multiple models must be considered to solve a deductive problem, each must be considered serially, yielding a concomitant increment in problem difficulty.

CONCLUSION

There can be no real "conclusion" to a review of a field in progress, any more than to a mid-career biography. What conclusions we have reached were largely laid out at the beginning of the chapter in our selection of central themes—the confluence of symbolic and connectionist perspectives on thinking, the relationship between implicit and explicit cognition, and the theoretical implications of the impact of content and context on thinking. These themes amount to our "best guess" about the trajectory of current research on thinking. There are hopeful signs that topics previously investigated in isolation from one another—for example, dynamic binding and vivid representations, implicit learning and neuropsychological organization, and sociocultural learning contexts and knowledge transfer—may prove deeply related. How these confluences will change the study of thinking remains to be seen.

ACKNOWLEDGMENTS

Preparation of this article was supported by Contract MDA 903-89-K-0179 from the Army Research Institute. We are grateful to the many researchers who kindly provided us with material to review, and we apologize for the fact that space limitations and the vagaries of the topics we selected precluded treatment of many significant papers. We thank Patricia Cheng, John Hummel, Carol Seger, Keith Stenning, and Michael Waldmann for helpful discussions as well as comments on earlier drafts. Requests for reprints should be sent to K. J. Holyoak, Department of Psychology, University of California, Los Angeles, CA 90024-1563.

Literature Cited

Ajzen, I. 1977. Intuitive theories of events and the effects of base rate information on prediction. *J. Pers. Soc. Psychol.* 35:303–14

Amaiwa, S. 1987. Transfer of substraction procedures from abacus to paper and pencil. *Jpn. J. Educ. Psychol.* 35:41–48 (In Japanese with English summary)

Anderson, J. R. 1978. Arguments concerning representations for mental imagery. *Psychol. Rev.* 85:249–77

Anderson, J. R. 1983. *The Architecture of Cognition.* Cambridge, MA: Harvard Univ.

Anderson, J. R. 1987. Skill acquisition: compilation of weak-method problem solutions. *Psychol. Rev.* 94:192–210

Anderson, J. R. 1990. *The Adaptive Character of Thought.* Hillsdale, NJ: Erlbaum

Anderson, J. R. 1991a. Is human cognition adaptive? *Behav. Brain Sci.* 14:471–517

Anderson, J. R. 1991b. The adaptive nature of human categorization. *Psychol. Rev.* 98:409–29

Anderson, J. R., Milson, R. 1989. Human memory: an adaptive perspective. *Psychol. Rev.* 96:703–19

Bar-Hillel, M., Fischhoff, B. 1981. When do base rates affect predictions? *J. Pers. Soc. Psychol.* 41:671–81

Barsalou, L. W., Hale, C. R. 1992. Components of conceptual representation: from feature lists to recursive frames. In *Categories and Concepts: Theoretical Views and Inductive Data Analysis,* ed. I. Van Mechelen, J. Hampton, R. Michalski, P. Theuns. San Diego, CA: Academic.

Bassok, M. 1990. Transfer of domain-specific problem-solving procedures. *J. Exp. Psychol.: Learn., Mem., Cognit.* 16:522–33

Berry, D. C., Broadbent, D. E. 1984. On the relationship between task performance and associated verbalizable knowledge. *Q. J. Exp. Psychol.* 36A:209–31

Berry, D. C., Broadbent, D. E. 1988. Interactive tasks and the implicit-explicit distinction. *Br. J. Psychol.* 79:251–72

Boden, M. A. 1990. *The Creative Mind: Myths and Mechanisms.* New York: Basic Books

Bowers, K. S., Regehr, G., Balthazard, C., Parker, G. 1990. Intuition in the context of discovery. *Cognit. Psychol.* 22:72–110

Braine, M. D. S., O'Brien, D. P. 1991. A theory of *if*: a lexical entry, reasoning program, and pragmatic principles. *Psychol. Rev.* 98:182–203

Broadbent, D. E., FitzGerald, P., Broadbent, M. H. P. 1986. Implicit and explicit knowledge in the control of complex systems. *Br. J. Psychol.* 77:33–50

Brooks, L. R., Vokey, F. R. 1991. Abstract analogies and abstracted grammars: comments on Reber (1989) and Mathews et al. 1989. *J. Exp. Psychol.: Gen.* 120:316–23

Brown, A. L. 1989. Analogical learning and transfer: What develops? In *Similarity and Analogical Reasoning,* ed. S. Vosniadou, A. Ortony, pp. 369–412. Cambridge: Cambridge Univ. Press

Bullock, M., Gelman, R., Baillargeon, R. 1982. The development of causal reasoning. In *The Developmental Psychology of Time,* ed. W. J. Friedman, pp. 209–53. San Diego: Academic

Byrne, R. M. J. 1989. Suppressing valid inferences with conditionals. *Cognition* 31:61–83

Byrne, R. M. J., Johnson-Laird, P. N. 1989. Spatial reasoning. *J. Mem. Lang.* 28:564–75

Carraher, T. N., Carraher, D. W., Schliemann, A. D. 1985. Mathematics in the streets and in the schools. *Br. J. Dev. Psychol.* 3:21–29

Carraher, T. N., Carraher, D. W., Schliemann, A. D. 1988. Mathematical concepts in everyday life. In *Children's Mathematics,* ed. G. B. Saxe, M. Gearhart, pp. 71–88. San Francisco: Jossey Bass

Catrambone, R., Holyoak, K. J. 1989. Overcoming contextual limitations on problem-solving transfer. *J. Exp. Psychol.: Learn., Mem., Cognit.* 15:1147–56

Chase, W. G., Simon, H. A. 1973. Perception in chess. *Cognit. Psychol.* 4:55–81

Cheng, P. W., Nisbett, R. E. 1993. A pragmatic constraint on causal deduction. In *Rules for Reasoning: Implications for Cognitive Science and Education,,* ed. R. E. Nisbett. Hillsdale, NJ: Erlbaum. In press

Cheng, P. W., Holyoak, K. J. 1985. Pragmatic reasoning schemas. *Cognit. Psychol.* 17:391–416

Cheng, P. W., Holyoak, K. J. 1989. On the natural selection of reasoning theories. *Cognition* 33:285–313

Cheng, P. W., Novick, L. R. 1990. A probabilistic contrast model of causal induction. *J. Pers. Soc. Psychol.* 58:545–67

Cheng, P. W., Novick, L. R. 1991. Causes versus enabling conditions. *Cognition* 40:83–120

Cheng, P. W., Novick, L. R. 1992. Covariation in natural causal induction. *Psychol. Rev.* 99:365–82

Cheng, P. W., Holyoak, K. J., Nisbett, R. E., Oliver, L. M. 1986. Pragmatic versus syntactic approaches to training deductive reasoning. *Cognit. Psychol.* 18:293–328

Chi, M. T. H., Bassok, M., Lewis, M. W., Reimann, P. Glaser,, R. 1989. Self-explanations: how students study and use examples in learning to solve problems. *Cognit. Sci.* 13:145–82

Chi, M. T. H., Feltovich, P. J., Glaser, R. 1981. Categorization and representation of physics problems by experts and novices. *Cognit. Sci.* 5:121–52

Christensen-Szalanski, J. J. J., Bushyhead, J. B. 1981. Physicians' use of probabilistic information in a real clinical setting. *J. Exp. Psychol.: Hum. Percept. Perform.* 7:928–35

Cleeremans, A., McClelland, J. L. 1991. Learning the structure of event sequences. *J. Exp. Psychol.: Gen.* 120:235–53

Cohen, A., Ivry, R. I., Keele, S. W. 1990. Attention and structure in sequence learning. *J. Exp. Psychol.: Learn., Mem., Cognit.* 16:17–30

Cosmides, L. 1989. The logic of social exchange: Has natural selection shaped how humans reason? Studies with the Wason selection task. *Cognition* 31:187–276

Cummins, D. D., Lubart, T., Alksnis, O., Rist, R. 1991. Conditional reasoning and causation. *Mem. Cognit.* 19:274–82

D'Andrade, R. 1982. Reason versus logic. Paper presented at the Symp. Ecol. Cognit.: Biol., Cult., Hist. Perspect., Greensboro, NC

Dawkins, R. 1987. *The Blind Watchmaker.* New York: Norton

Dienes, Z. 1992. Connectionist and memory-array models of artificial grammar learning. *Cognit. Sci.* 16:41–80

Dienes, Z., Broadbent, D., Berry, D. 1991. Implicit and explicit knowledge bases in artificial grammar learning. *J. Exp. Psychol.: Learn., Mem., Cognit.* 17:875–87

Druhan, B., Mathews, R. 1989. THIYOS: a classifier system model of implicit knowledge of artificial grammars. In *Proceedings of the Eleventh Annual Conference of the Cognitive Science Society,* pp. 66–73. Hillsdale, NJ: Erlbaum

Dulany, D. E., Carlson, R. A., Dewey, G. I. 1984. A case of syntactical learning and judgment: how conscious and how abstract? *J. Exp. Psychol.: Gen.* 113:541–55

Dunbar, K. 1993. Concept discovery in a scientific domain. *Cognit. Sci.* In press

Duncker, K. 1945. On problem solving. *Psychol. Monogr.* 58(270)

Dyer, M. G. 1991. Symbolic neuroengineering for natural language processing: a multilevel research approach. In *Advances in Connectionist and Neural Computation Theory.* Vol. 1: *High Level Connectionist Models,* J. Barnden, J. Pollack, pp. 32–86. Norwood, NJ: Ablex

Estes, W. K. 1991. Cognitive architectures from the standpoint of an experimental psychologist. *Annu. Rev. Psychol.* 42:1–28

Estes, W. K., Campbell, J. A., Hatsopoulos, N., Hurwitz, J. B. 1989. Base-rate effects in category learning: a comparison of parallel network and memory storage-retrieval models. *J. Exp. Psychol.: Learn., Mem., Cognit.* 15:556–71

Evans, J. St. B. T. 1989. *Bias in Human Reasoning: Causes and Consequences.* Hove, UK: Erlbaum

Evans, J. St. B. T., Barnston, J. L., Pollard, P. 1983. On the conflict between logic and belief in syllogistic reasoning. *Mem. Cognit.* 11:295–306

Falkenhainer, B., Forbus, K. D., Gentner, D. 1989. The structure-mapping engine: algorithm and examples. *Artif. Intell.* 41:1–63

Farah, M. J., McClelland, J. L. 1991. A computational model of semantic memory impairment: modality specificity and emergent category specificity. *J. Exp. Psychol.: Gen.* 120:339–57

Finke, R. A. 1989. *Principles of Mental Imagery.* Cambridge, MA: MIT Press

Finke, R. A. 1990. *Creative Imagery: Discoveries and Inventions in Visualization.* Hillsdale, NJ: Erlbaum

Flannagan, M. J., Fried, L. S., Holyoak, K. J. 1986. Distributional expectations and the induction of category structure. *J. Exp. Psychol.: Learn., Mem., Cognit.* 12:241–56

Fodor, J. A. 1983. *The Modularity of Mind.* Cambridge, MA: MIT Press

Fodor, J. A., McLaughlin, B. P. 1990. Connectionism and the problem of systematicity: why Smolensky's solution doesn't work. *Cognition* 35:183–204

Fodor, J. A., Pylyshyn, Z. W. 1988. Connectionism and cognitive architecture: a critical analysis. In *Connections and Symbols,* ed. S. Pinker, J. Mehler, pp. 3–71. Cambridge, MA: MIT Press

Gick, M. L., Holyoak, K. J. 1980. Analogical problem solving. *Cognit. Psychol.* 12:306–55

Gick, M. L., Holyoak, K. J. 1983. Schema induction and analogical transfer. *Cognit. Psychol.* 15:1–38

Gick, M. L., McGarry, S. J. 1992. Learning from mistakes: Inducing analogous solution failures to a source problem produces later successes in analogical transfer. *J. Exp. Psychol.: Learn., Mem., Cognit.* 18:623–39

Gigerenzer, G., Hug, K. 1992. Domain-specific reasoning: social contracts, cheating, and perspective change. *Cognition* 43:127–71

Gigerenzer, G., Hell, W., Blank, H. 1988. Presentation and content: the use of base rates as a continuous variable. *J. Exp. Psychol.: Hum. Percept. Perform.* 14:513–25

Gigerenzer, G., Hoffrage, U., Kleinbölting, H. 1991. Probabilistic mental models: a Brunswikian theory of confidence. *Psychol. Rev.* 98:506–28

Girotto, V., Blaye, A., Farioli, F. 1989a. A reason to reason: pragmatic basis of children's search for counterexamples. *Euro. Bull. Cognit. Psychol.* 9:227–321

Girotto, V., Gilly, M., Blaye, A., Light, P. H. 1989b. Children's performance in the selection task: plausibility and familiarity. *Br. J. Psychol.* 80:79–95

Girotto, V., Light, P. H., Colburn, C. J. 1988. Pragmatic schemas and conditional reasoning in children. *Q. J. Exp. Psychol.* 40A:469–82

Girotto, V., Mazzocco, A., Cherubini, P. 1992. Judgments of relevance in deonic reasoning: a reply to Jackson and Griggs. *Q. J. Exp. Psychol.* In press

Gluck, M. A., Bower, G. H. 1988. From conditioning to category learning: an adaptive network model. *J. Exp. Psychol.: Gen.* 117:227–47

Goldstone, R. L., Medin, D. L. 1993. Similarity, interactive activation, and mapping: an overview. See Holyoak & Barnden 1993. In press

Goldstone, R. L., Medin, D. L., Gentner, D. 1991. Relational similarity and the non-independence of features in similarity judgments. *Cognit. Psychol.* 23:222–62

Griffin, D., Tversky, A. 1992. The weighing of evidence and the determinants of confidence. *Cognit. Psychol.* 24:411–35

Guberman, S. R., Greenfield, P. M. 1991. Learning and transfer in everyday cognition. *Cognit. Dev.* 6:233–60

Halford, G. S., Wilson, W. H. 1980. A category theory approach to cognitive development. *Cognit. Psychol.* 12:356–441

Halford, G. S., Wilson, W. H., Guo, J., Wiles, J., Stewart, J. E. M. 1993. Connectionist implications for processing capacity limitations in analogies. See Holyoak & Barnden 1993. In press

Hasher, L., Zacks, R. T. 1984. Automatic processing of fundamental information: the case of frequency of occurrence. *Am. Psychol.* 39:1372–88

Hatano, G. 1988. Social and motivational bases for mathematical understanding. In *Children's Mathematics,* ed. G. B. Saxe, M. Gearhart, pp. 55–70. San Francisco: Jossey-Bass

Hatano, G., Inagaki, K. 1986. Two courses of expertise. In *Child Development and Education in Japan,* ed. H. Stevenson, H. Azuma, K. Hakuta, pp. 262–72. San Francisco: Freeman

Hatano, G., Osawa, K. 1983. Digit memory of grand masters in abacus-derived mental calculation. *Cognition* 15:95–110

Hayes, N. A., Broadbent, D. E. 1988. Two modes of learning for interactive tasks. *Cognition* 23:80–108

Hebb, D. O. 1961. Distinctive features of learning in the higher animal. In *Brain Mechanisms and Learning,* ed. J. F. Delafresnaye. London: Oxford Univ.

Hempel, C. 1965. *Aspects of Scientific Explanation.* New York: Free Press

Henle, M. 1962. On the relation between logic and thinking. *Psychol. Rev.* 69:366–78

Hilton, D. J., Slugoski, B. R. 1986. Knowledge-based causal attribution: the abnormal conditions focus model. *Psychol. Rev.* 93:75–88

Hofstadter, D. R. 1984. *The Copycat Project: An Experiment in Nondeterministic and Creative Analogies.* Cambridge, MA: MIT A. I. Lab. Memo 755

Hofstadter, D. R., Mitchell, M. 1993. An overview of the Copycat project. See Holyoak & Barnden 1993. In press

Holland, J. H., Holyoak, K. J., Nisbett, R. E., Thagard, P. R. 1986. *Induction: Processes of Inference, Learning, and Discovery.* Cambridge, MA: MIT Press

Holyoak, K. J. 1991. Symbolic connectionism: toward third-generation theories of expertise. In *Toward a General Theory of Expertise: Prospects and Limits,* ed. K. A. Ericsson, J. Smith, pp. 301–35. Cambridge: Cambridge Univ. Press

Holyoak, K. J., Barnden, J. A., eds. 1993. *Advances in Connectionist and Neural Computation Theory.* Vol. 2: *Analogical Connections.* Norwood, NJ: Ablex. In press

Holyoak, K. J., Koh, K. 1987. Surface and structural similarity in analogical transfer. *Mem. Cognit.* 15:332–40

Holyoak, K. J., Thagard, P. 1989. Analogical mapping by constraint satisfaction. *Cognit. Sci.* 13:295–355

Holyoak, K. J., Novick, L. R., Melz, E. R. 1993. Component processes in analogical transfer: mapping, pattern completion, and adaptation. See Holyoak & Barnden 1993. In press

Hummel, J. E., Biederman, I. 1992. Dynamic binding in a neural network for shape recognition. *Psychol. Rev.* 99:480–517

Hummel, J. E., Holyoak, K. J. 1992. Indirect analogical mapping. In *Proceedings of the 14th Annual Conference of the Cognitive Science Society,* pp. 516–21. Hillsdale, NJ: Erlbaum

Jacobs, R. A., Jordan, M. I., Barto, A. G. 1991. Task decomposition through competition in a modular connectionist architecture: the what and where vision tasks. *Cogn. Sci.* 15:219–50

Johnson-Laird, P. N. 1983. *Mental Models: Towards a Cognitive Science of Language, Inference, and Consciousness.* Cambridge, MA: Harvard Univ. Press

Johnson-Laird, P. N., Byrne, R. M. J. 1991. *Deduction.* Hillsdale, NJ: Erlbaum

Johnson-Laird, P. N., Byrne, R. M. J. 1992. Modal reasoning, models, and Manktelow and Over. *Cognition* 43:173–82

Johnson-Laird, P. N., Byrne, R. M. J., Schaeken, W. 1992. Propositional reasoning by model. *Psychol. Rev.* 99:418–39

Johnson-Laird, P. N., Byrne, R. M. J., Tabossi, P. 1989. Reasoning by model: the case of multiple quantification. *Psychol. Rev.* 96:658–73

Johnson-Laird, P. N., Legrenzi, P., Legrenzi, S. M. 1972. Reasoning and a sense of reality. *Br. J. Psychol.* 63:395–400

Jordan, M. I., Rosenbaum, D. A. 1989. Action. In *Foundations of Cognitive Science,* ed. M. I. Posner, pp. 727–67. Cambridge, MA: MIT Press

Just, M. A., Carpenter, P. A. 1992. A capacity theory of comprehension: individual differences in working memory. *Psychol. Rev.* 99:122–49

Kahneman, D., Lovallo, D. 1993. Timid choices and bold forecasts: a cognitive perspective on risk taking. *Manage. Sci.*

Kahneman, D., Slovic, P., Tversky, A. 1982. *Judgment Under Uncertainty: Heuristics and Biases.* Cambridge: Cambridge Univ. Press

Kahneman, D., Miller, D. T. 1986. Norm theory: comparing reality to its alternatives. *Psychol. Rev.* 93:136–53

Kaiser, M. K., Proffitt, D. R. 1984. The development of sensitivity to causally-relevant dynamic information. *Child Dev.* 55:1614–

24
Kaiser, M. K., Proffitt, D. R., Anderson, K. 1985. Judgments of natural and anomalous trajectories in the presence and absence of motion. *J. Exp. Psychol.: Learn., Mem., Cognit.* 11:795–803

Kaiser, M. K., Jonides, J., Alexander, J. 1986. Intuitive reasoning about abstract and familiar physics problems. *Mem. Cognit.* 14:308–12

Kaplan, C. A., Simon, H. A. 1990. In search of insight. *Cognit. Psychol.* 22:374–419

Karmiloff-Smith, A. 1986. From meta-processess to conscious access: evidence from children's metalinguistic and repair data. *Cognition* 23:95–147

Karmiloff-Smith, A. 1990. Constraints on representational change: evidence from children's drawing. *Cognition* 34:57–83

Keane, M. 1988. *Analogical Problem Solving.* Chichester: Ellis Horwood

Kihlstrom, J. F. 1987. The cognitive unconscious. *Science* 237:1445–52

Kintsch, W. 1988. The role of knowledge in discourse comprehension: a construction-integration model. *Psychol. Rev.* 95:163–82

Klayman, J., Ha, Y. 1987. Confirmation, disconfirmation, and information in hypothesis testing. *Psychol. Rev.* 94:211–28

Klayman, J., Ha, Y. 1989. Hypothesis testing in rule discovery: strategy, structure and content. *J. Exp. Psychol.: Learn., Mem., Cognit.* 15:596–604

Knowlton, B. J., Ramus, S. J., Squire, L. R. 1992. Intact artificial grammar learning in amnesia: dissociation of classification learning and explicit memory for specific instances. *Psychol. Sci.* 3:172–79

Koedinger, K. R., Anderson, J. R. 1990. Abstract planning and perceptual chunks: elements of expertise in geometry. *Cognit. Sci.* 14:511–50

Koh, K., Meyer, D. E. 1991. Function learning: induction of continuous stimulus-response relations. *J. Exp. Psychol.: Learn., Mem., Cognit.* 17:811–36

Kosslyn, S. M., Pomerantz, J. R. 1977. Imagery, propositions, and the form of internal representations. *Cognit. Psychol.* 9:52–76

Kosslyn, S. M., Pinker, S., Smith, G. E., Schwartz, S. P. 1979. On the demystification of mental imagery. *Behav. Brain Sci.* 2:535–81

Krosnick, J. A., Li, F., Lehman, D. R. 1990. Conversational conventions, order of information acquisition, and the effect of base rates and individuating information on social judgments. *J. Pers. Soc. Psychol.* 59:1140–52

Kunda, Z. 1990. The case for motivated reasoning. *Psychol. Bull.* 108:480–98

Kushner, M., Cleeremans, A., Reber, A. 1991. Implicit detection of event interdependencies and a PDP model of the process. In *Proceedings of the 13th Annual Confer-ence of the Cognitive Science Society,* pp. 215–20. Hillsdale, NJ: Erlbaum

Laboratory of Comparative Human Cognition. 1983. Culture and cognitive development. In *Handbook of Child Psychology:* Vol. 1. *History, Theories and Methods,* ed. P. H. Mussen, pp. 295–356. New York: Wiley

Lakoff, G. 1993. What is metaphor? See Holyoak & Barnden 1993. In press

Larkin, J., Simon, H. A. 1987. Why a diagram is (sometimes) worth ten thousand words. *Cognit. Sci.* 11:65–100

Lave, J. 1988. *Cognition in Practice: Mind, Mathematics and Culture in Everyday Life.* New York: Cambridge Univ. Press

Lave, J., Wenger, E. 1991. *Situated Learning: Legitimate Peripheral Participation.* New York: Cambridge Univ.

Legrenzi, P., Murino, M. 1974. Falsification at the pre-operational level. *Ital. J. Psychol.* 1:361–68

Levesque, H. 1986. Making believers out of computers. *Artif. Intell.* 30:81–108

Levesque, H. 1988. Logic and the complexity of reasoning. *J. Philos. Logic* 17:355–89

Lewicki, P., Hill, T., Bizot, E. 1988. Acquisition of procedural knowledge about a pattern of stimuli that cannot be articulated. *Cognit. Psychol.* 20:24–37

Lewontin, R. C. 1990. The evolution of cognition. In *Invitation to Cognitive Science: Thinking,* 3:239–46. Cambridge, MA: MIT

Light, P. H., Blaye, A., Gilly, M., Girotto, G. 1989. Children's reasoning on conditional promises and permissions. *Cognit. Dev.* 5:369–83

Light, P. H., Girotto, V., Legrenzi, P. 1990. Children's reasoning on conditional promises and permissions. *Cognit. Dev.* 5:369–83

Mandler, J. M. 1992. How to build a baby: II. Conceptual primitives. *Psychol. Rev.* In press

Mani, K., Johnson-Laird, P. N. 1982. The mental representation of spatial descriptions. *Mem. Cognit.* 10:81–87

Manis, M., Dovenalina, I., Avis, N. E., Cardoze, S. 1980. Base rates can affect individual predictions. *J. Pers. Soc. Psychol.* 38:287–98

Manktelow, K. I., Over, D. E. 1990. Deontic thought and the selection task. In *Lines of Thought: Reflections on the Psychology of Thinking,* ed. K. J. Gilhooly, M. Keane, R. Logie, G. Erdos, pp. 153–64. Chichester: Wiley

Manktelow, K. I., Over, D. E. 1991. Social roles and utilities in reasoning with deontic conditionals. *Cognition* 39:85–105

Mannes, S. M., Kintsch, W. 1991. Routine computing tasks: planning as understanding. *Cognit. Sci.* 15:305–42

Markovits, H., Nantel, G. 1989. The belief-bias effect in the production and evaluation of logical conclusions. *Mem. Cognit.* 17:11–

17

Mathews, R. C. 1990. Abstractness of implicit grammar knowledge: comments on Perruchet and Pacteau's analysis of synthetic grammar learning. *J. Exp. Psychol.: Gen.* 119:412–16

Mathews, R. C., Buss, R. R., Stanley, W. B., Blanchard-Fields, F., Cho, J., Druhan, B. 1989. Role of implicit and explicit processing in learning from examples: a synergistic effect. *J. Exp. Psychol.: Learn., Mem., Cognit.* 15:1083–1100

McCarthy, J. 1988. Epistemological challenges for connectionism. Commentary to "On the proper treatment of connectionism" by P. Smolensky. *Behav. Brain Sci.* 11:44

McCloskey, M., Kohl, D. 1983. Naive physics: the curvilinear impetus principle and its role in interactions with moving objects. *J. Exp. Psychol.: Learn., Mem., Cognit.* 9:146–56

McGonigle, B., Chalmers, M. 1986. Representations and strategies during inference. In *Reasoning and Discourse Processes,* ed. T. F. Myers, E. K. Brown, B. McGonigle. London: Academic

McKelvie, S. J. 1987. Learning and awareness in the Hebb digits task. *J. Gen. Psychol.* 114:75–88

Medin, D. L. 1989. Concepts and conceptual structure. *Am. Psychol.* 44:1469–81

Medin, D. L., Edelson, S. M. 1988. Problem structure and the use of base-rate information from experience. *J. Exp. Psychol.: Gen.* 117:68–85

Medin, D. L., Smith, E. E. 1984. Concepts and concept formation. *Annu. Rev. Psychol.* 35:113–38

Metcalfe, J. 1986. Premonitions of insight predict impending error. *J. Exp. Psychol.: Learn., Mem., Cognit.* 12:623–34

Metcalfe, J., Wiebe, D. 1987. Intuition in insight and non-insight problem solving. *Mem. Cognit.* 15:238–46

Miller, G. A. 1956. The magical number seven, plus or minus two: some limits on our capacity for processing information. *Psychol. Rev.* 63:81–97

Minsky, M. 1975. A framework for representing knowledge. In *Metaphor and Thought,* ed. P. H. Winston. Cambridge: Cambridge Univ. Press

Minsky, M. 1991. Logical versus analogical or symbolic versus connectionist or neat versus scruffy. *AI Mag.* 12(2):34–51

Mynatt, C. R., Doherty, M. E., Tweney, R. D. 1978. Consequences of confirmation and disconfirmation in a simulated research environment. *Q. J. Exp. Psychol.* 30:395–406

Newell, A. 1973. Production systems: models of control structures. In *Visual Information Processing,* ed. W. G. Chase, pp. 463–526. New York: Academic

Newell, A. 1990. *Unified Theories of Cognition.* Cambridge, MA: Harvard Univ. Press

Newell, A., Simon, H. A. 1972. *Human Problem Solving.* Englewood Cliffs, NJ: Prentice-Hall

Nisbett, R. E., Krantz, D. H., Jepson, C., Kunda, Z. 1983. The use of statistical heuristics in everyday inductive reasoning. *Psychol. Rev.* 90:339–63

Nissen, M. J., Bullemer, P. 1987. Attentional requirements of learning: evidence from performance measures. *Cognit. Psychol.* 19:1–32

Novick, L. R. 1988. Analogical transfer, problem similarity, and expertise. *J. Exp. Psychol.: Learn., Mem., Cognit.* 14:510–20

Novick, L. R., Holyoak, K. J. 1991. Mathematical problem solving by analogy. *J. Exp. Psychol.: Learn., Mem., Cognit.* 17:398–415

Novick, L. R., Fratianne, A., Cheng, P. W. 1992. Knowledge-based assumptions in causal attribution. *Soc. Cognit.* 10:299–332

Oakhill, J., Johnson-Laird, P. N., Garnham, A. 1989. Believability and syllogistic reasoning. *Cognition* 31:117–40

Oaksford, M., Chater, N. 1993. Reasoning theories and bounded rationality. In *Rationality,* ed. K. I. Manktelow, D. E. Over. London: Routledge . In Press

Oaksford, M., Chater, N., Stenning, K. 1990. Connectionism, classical cognitive science and experimental psychology. *AI Soc.* 4:73–90

Oden, G. C. 1987. Concept, knowledge and thought. *Annu. Rev. Psychol.* 38:203–28

Osherson, D. N., Smith, E. E., Wilkie, O., Lopez, A., Shafir, E. 1990. Category-based induction. *Psychol. Rev.* 97:185–200

Palmer, S. 1978. Fundamental aspects of cognitive representation. In *Cognition and Categorization,* ed. E. Rosch, B. B. Lloyd, pp. 259–302. Hillsdale, NJ: Erlbaum

Patel, V. L., Groen, G. J. 1991. The general and specific nature of medical expertise: a critical look. In *Toward a General Theory of Expertise: Prospects and Limits,* ed. K. A. Ericsson, J. Smith, pp. 93–125. Cambridge: Cambridge Univ. Press

Payne, J. W., Bettman, J. R., Johnson, E. J. 1992. Behavioral decision research: a constructive processing perspective. *Annu. Rev. Psychol.* 43:87–131

Pearl, J. 1988. *Probabilistic Reasoning in Intelligent Systems: Networks of Plausible Inference.* San Mateo, CA: Morgan Kaufmann

Perruchet, P., Amorim, M.-A. 1992. Conscious knowledge and changes in performance in sequence learning: evidence against dissociation. *J. Exp. Psychol.: Learn., Mem., Cogn.* 18:785–800

Perruchet, P., Gallego, J., Pacteau, C. 1992. A reinterpretation of some earlier evidence for abstractiveness of implicitly acquired knowledge. *Q. J. Exp. Psychol.* 44A:193–

210

Perruchet, P., Gallego, J., Savy, I. 1990. A critical reappraisal of the evidence for unconscious abstraction of deterministic rules in complex experimental situations. *Cognit Psychol.* 22:493–516

Perruchet, P., Pacteau, C. 1990. Synthetic grammar learning: implicit rule abstraction or explicit fragmentary knowledge? *J. Exp. Psychol.: Gen.* 119:264–75

Perruchet, P., Pacteau, C. 1991. The implicit acquisition of abstract knowledge about artificial grammar: some methodological and conceptual issues. *J. Exp. Psychol.: Gen.* 120:112–16

Pew, R. W. 1974. Levels of analysis in motor control. *Brain Res.* 71:393–400

Pinker, S., Finke, R. A. 1980. Emergent two-dimensional patterns in images rotated in depth. *J. Exp. Psychol.: Hum. Percept. Perform.* 6:244–64

Politzer, G., Braine, M. D. S. 1991. Responses to inconsistent premises cannot count as suppression of valid inferences: comment on Byrne. *Cognition* 38:103–8

Politzer, G., Nguyen-Xuan, A. 1992. Reasoning about promises and warnings: Darwinian algorithms, mental models, relevance judgments or pragmatic schemas? *Q. J. Exp. Psychol.* 44A:401–21

Pollard, P. 1990. Natural selection for the selection task: limits to the social exchange theory. *Cognition* 36:195–204

Potts, G. R. 1974. Storing and retrieving information about ordered relationships. *J. Exp. Psychol.* 103:431–39

Proffitt, D. R., Kaiser, M. K., Whelan, S. M. 1990. Understanding wheel dynamics. *Cognit. Psychol.* 22:342–73

Pylyshyn, Z. 1973. What the mind's eye tells the mind's brain: a critique of mental imagery. *Psychol. Bull.* 80:1–24

Quine, W. V. O. 1961. *From a Logical Point of View.* New York: Harper Torchbooks. 2nd ed.

Ranney, M. 1993. Explorations in explanatory coherence. In *Designing Intelligent Learning Environments: From Cognitive Analysis to Computer Implementation,* ed. E. Bar-On, B. Eylon, Z. Schertz. Norwood, NJ: Ablex. In press

Ratcliff, R., McKoon, G. 1989. Similarity information versus relational information: differences in the time course of retrieval. *Cognit. Psychol.* 21:139–55

Ratterman, M. J., Gentner, D. 1987. Analogy and similarity: determinants of accessibility and inferential soundness. In *Proceedings of the Ninth Annual Conference of the Cognitive Science Society,* pp. 22–34. Hillsdale, NJ: Erlbaum

Read, S. J., Cesa, I. L. 1991. This reminds me of the time when …: expectation failures in reminding and explanation. *J. Exp. Soc. Psychol.* 27:1-25

Read, S. J., Marcus-Newhall, A. 1993. The role of explanatory coherence in social explanations. *J. Pers. Soc. Psychol.* In press

Reber, A. S. 1967. Implicit learning of artificial grammars. *J. Verb. Learn. Verb. Behav.* 6:855–63

Reber, A. S. 1969. Transfer of syntactic structure in synthetic languages. *J. Exp. Psychol.* 81:115–19

Reber, A. S. 1989. Implicit learning and tacit knowledge. *J. Exp. Psychol.: Gen.* 118:219–35

Reber, A. S. 1992. The cognitive unconscious: an evolutionary perspective. *Consciousness Cognit.* 1:93–133

Reber, A. S., Allen, R., Regan, S. 1985. Syntactical learning and judgment, still unconscious and still abstract: comment on Dulaney, Carlson, and Dewey. *J. Exp. Psychol.: Gen.* 114:17–24

Reber, A. S., Kassin, S. M., Lewis, S., Cantor, G. 1980. On the relationship between implicit and explicit modes in the learning of a complex rule structure. *J. Exp. Psychol.: Hum. Learn. Mem.* 6:492–514

Richardson-Klavehn, A., Bjork, R. A. 1988. Measures of memory. *Annu. Rev. Psychol.* 39:475–543

Rips, L. J. 1989. The psychology of knights and knaves. *Cognition* 31:85–116

Rips, L. J. 1990. Reasoning. *Annu. Rev. Psychol.* 41:321–53

Rips, L. J., Conrad, F. G. 1989. Folk psychology of mental activities. *Psychol. Rev.* 96:187–207

Rock, I., Palmer, S. 1990. The legacy of Gestalt psychology. *Sci. Am.* 263(6):84–90

Roediger, H. L. III. 1990. Implicit memory: retention without remembering. *Am. Psychol.* 45:1043–56

Rosenbloom, P. S., Laird, J. E., Newell, A., McCarl, R. 1991. A preliminary analysis of the Soar architecture as a basis for general intelligence. *Artif. Intell.* 47:289–325

Ross, B. H. 1987. This is like that: the use of earlier problems and the separation of similarity effects. *J. Exp. Psychol.: Learn., Mem., Cognit.* 13:629–39

Ross, B. H. 1989. Distinguishing types of superficial similarities: different effects on the access and use of earlier problems. *J. Exp. Psychol.: Learn., Mem., Cognit.* 15:456–68

Ross, B. H., Kennedy, P. T. 1990. Generalizing from the use of earlier examples in problem solving. *J. Exp. Psychol.: Learn., Mem., Cognit.* 16:42–56

Rousseau, D. L. 1992. Case studies in pathological science. *Am. Sci.* 80:54–63

Rozin, P. 1976. The evolution of intelligence and access to the cognitive unconsious. *Progr. Psychobiol. Physiol. Psychol.* 6:245–80

Rubin, D. C., Wallace, W. T., Houston, B. C.

1993. The beginnings of expertise for ballads. *Cogn.it Sci.* In press

Rumelhart, D. E., Smolensky, P., McClelland, J., Hinton, G. E. 1986. Schemata and sequential thought processes in PDP models. In *Parallel Distributed Processing: Explorations in the Microstructure of Cognition,* ed. J. L. McClelland, D. E. Rumelhart, and the PDP Research Group, 2:7–57. Cambridge, MA: MIT Press

Rumelhart, D. E., McClelland, J. L., and the PDP Research Group, eds. 1986. *Parallel Distributed Processing: Explorations in the Microstructure of Cognition.* Cambridge, MA: MIT Press. 2 vols.

Rutkowska, J. C. 1987. Computational models and developmental psychology. In *Computation and Development,* pp. 187–215. Chichester: Wiley

Salomon, G., Perkins, D. N. 1989. Rocky roads to transfer: rethinking mechanisms of a neglected phenomenon. *Educ. Psychol.* 24:113–42

Sanders, R. E., Gonzalez, E. G., Murphy, M. D., Liddle, C. L., Vitina, J. R. 1987. Frequency of occurrence and the criteria for automatic processing. *J. Exp. Psychol.: Learn., Mem., Cognit.* 13:241–50

Saxe, G. B. 1982. Developing forms of arithmetic operations among the Oksapmin of Papua New Guinea. *Dev. Psychol.* 18:583–94

Saxe, G. B. 1991. *Culture and Cognitive Development: Studies in Mathematical Understanding.* Hillsdale, NJ: Erlbaum

Schacter, D. L. 1987. Implicit memory: history and current status. *J. Exp. Psychol.: Learn., Mem., Cognit.* 13:501–18

Schacter, D. L., Chiu, C.-Y. P., Ochsner, K. N. 1993. Implicit memory: a selective review. *Annu. Rev. Neurosci.* 16:159–82

Schank, P., Ranney, M. 1991. The psychological fidelity of ECHO: modeling an experimental study of explanatory coherence. In *Proceedings of the 13th Annual Conference of the Cognitive Science Society,* pp. 892–97. Hillsdale, NJ: Erlbaum

Schank, P., Ranney, M. 1992. Assessing explanatory coherence: a new method for integrating verbal data with models of on-line belief revision. In *Proceedings of the 14th Annual Conference of the Cognitive Science Society,* pp. 599–604. Hillsdale, NJ: Erlbaum

Schank, R. C. 1982. *Dynamic Memory.* New York: Cambridge Univ. Press

Schwartz, M., Bryden, M. P. 1971. Coding factors in the learning of repeated digit sequences. *J. Exp. Psychol.* 87:331–34

Schwarz, N., Strack, F., Hilton, D., Naderer, G. 1991. Base-rates, representativeness, and the logic of conversation: the contextual relevance of "irrelevant" information. *Soc. Cognit.* 9:67–84

Seger, C. A. 1992. Implicit learning. Tech. Rep. UCLA-CSRP-92-3, Cogn. Sci. Res. Progr., Univ. Calif., Los Angeles

Seifert, C. M., McKoon, G., Abelson, R. P., Ratcliff, R. 1986. Memory connections between thematically similar episodes. *J. Exp. Psychol.: Hum. Learn. Mem.* 12:220–31

Servan-Schreiber, E., Anderson, J. R. 1990. Learning artificial grammars with competitive chunking. *J. Exp. Psychol.: Learn., Mem., Cognit.* 16:592–608

Shanon, B. 1976. Aristotelianism, Newtonianism and the physics of the layman. *Perception* 5:241–43

Shastri, L., Ajjanagadde, V. 1993. From simple associations to systematic reasoning: a connectionist representation of rules, variables and dynamic bindings. *Behav. Brain Sci.* 16

Shepard, R. N., Metzler, J. 1971. Mental rotation of three-dimensional objects. *Science* 171:701–3

Sherry, D. F., Schacter, D. L. 1987. The evolution of multiple memory systems. *Psychol. Rev.* 94:439–54

Simon, H. A. 1986. The information processing explanation of Gestalt phenomena. *Comput. Hum. Behav.* 2:241–55

Simon, H. A. 1990. Invariants of human behavior. *Annu. Rev. Psychol.* 41:1–19

Simon, H. A. 1991. Cognitive architectures and rational analysis: comment. In *Architectures for Intelligence: The 22nd Carnegie Mellon Symposium on Cognition,* ed. K. VanLehn. Hillsdale, NJ: Erlbaum

Smith, E. E., Langston, C., Nisbett, R. E. 1992. The case for rules in reasoning. *Cognit. Sci.* 13:145–82

Smolensky, P. 1988. On the proper treatment of connectionism. *Behav. Brain Sci.* 11:1–74

Smolensky, P. 1990. Tensor product variable binding and the representation of symbolic structure in connectionist systems. *Artif. Intell.* 46(1–2):159–216

Spellman, B. A., Holyoak, K. J. 1992. If Saddam is Hitler then who is George Bush? Analogical mapping between systems of social roles. *J. Pers. Soc. Psychol.* 62:913–33

Stanley, W. B., Mathews, R. C., Buss, R. R., Kotler-Cope, S. 1989. Insight without awareness: on the interaction of verbalization, instruction and practice in a simulated process control task. *Q. J. Exp. Psychol.* 41A:553–78

Stadler, M. A. 1989. On learning complex procedural knowledge. *J. Exp. Psychol.: Learn., Mem., Cognit.* 15:1061–69

Stenning, K. 1992. Distinguishing conceptual and empirical issues about mental models. In *Models in the Mind,* ed. Y. Rogers, A. Rutherford, P. Biddy. San Diego: Academic

Stenning, K., Levy, J. 1988. Knowledge-rich solutions to the binding problem: a simulation of some human computational mechanisms. *Knowledge Based Systems* 1:143–52

Stenning, K., Oaksford, M. 1993. Rational reasoning and human implementations of logics. In *Rationality*, ed. K. I. Manktelow, D. E. Over. London: Routledge. In Press

Stenning, K., Oberlander, J. 1992. A cognitive theory of graphical and linguistic reasoning: logic and implementation. Res. Pap. HCRC/RP-20, Hum. Commun. Res. Cent., Univ. Edinburgh

Stenning, K., Shepherd, M., Levy, J. 1988. On the construction of representations for individuals from descriptions in text. *Lang. Cognit. Proc.* 2:129–64

Stevenson, H. W., Stigler, J. W. 1992. *The Learning Gap: Why Our Schools Are Failing and What We Can Learn from Japanese and Chinese Education.* New York: Summit

Sweller, J. 1988. Cognitive load during problem solving: effects on learning. *Cognit. Sci.* 12:257–86

Sweller, J., Mawer, R., Ward, M. 1983. Development of expertise in mathematical problem solving. *J. Exp. Psychol.: Gen.* 112:639–61

Thagard, P. 1989. Explanatory coherence. *Behav. Brain Sci.* 12:435–67

Thagard, P. 1992. *Conceptual Revolutions.* Princeton: Princeton Univ. Press

Thagard, P., Holyoak, K. J., Nelson, G., Gochfeld, D. 1990. Analog retrieval by constraint satisfaction. *Artif. Intell.* 46:259–310

Tversky, A. 1977. Features of similarity. *Psychol. Rev.* 84:327–52

Tversky, A., Kahneman, D. 1980. Causal schemas in judgments under uncertainty. In *Progress in Social Psychology*, pp. 49–77. Hillsdale, NJ: Erlbaum

Tversky, A., Kahneman, K. 1980. Causal schemas in judgments under uncertainty. See Tversky & Kahneman 1980, pp. 49–72

Tversky, A., Kahneman, K. 1983. Extensional versus intuitive reasoning: the conjunction fallacy in probability judgment. *Psychol. Rev.* 90:293–315

Tweney, R. D. 1990. Five questions for computationalists. In *Computational Models of Scientific Discovery and Theory Formation,* ed. J. Shrager, P. Langley, pp. 471–84. San Mateo, CA: Morgan Kaufmann

Vera, A. H., Simon, H. A. 1993. Situated action: a symbolic interpretation. *Cognit. Sci.* In press

von der Malsburg, C. 1981. The correlation theory of brain function. Internal Rep. 81–2. Dep. Neurobiol., Max-Planck-Inst. Biophys. Chem., Göttingen

Waldmann, M. R., Holyoak, K. J. 1992. Predictive and diagnostic learning within causal models: asymmetries in cue competition. *J. Exp. Psychol.: Gen.* 121:222–36

Wason, P. C. 1966. Reasoning. In *New Horizons in Psychology,* ed. B. M. Foss, Vol. 1. Harmondsworth, UK: Penguin

Wellman, H. M., Gelman, S. A. 1992. Cognitive development: foundational theories of core domains. *Annu. Rev. Psychol.* 43:337–75

Wenger, E. 1987. *Artificial Intelligence and Tutoring Systems: Computational and Cognitive Approaches to the Communication of Knowledge.* Los Altos, CA: Morgan Kaufmann

Wertheimer, M. 1945. *Productive Thinking.* New York: Harper Row

Wharton, C. M., Holyoak, K. J., Downing, P. E., Lange, T. E., Wickens, T. D. 1992. The story with reminding: Memory retrieval is influenced by analogical similarity. In *Proceedings of the 14th Annual Conference of the Cognitive Science Society,* pp. 588–93. Hillsdale, NJ: Erlbaum

Willingham, D. B., Nissen, M. J., Bullemer, P. 1989. On the development of procedural knowledge. *J. Exp. Psychol.: Learn., Mem., Cognit.* 15:1047–60

Wimsatt, W. C. 1986. Developmental constraints, generative entrenchment, and the innate-acquired distinction. In *Integrating Scientific Disciplines,* ed. W. Bechtel, pp. 185–208. Dordrecht: Martinus-Nijhoff

Zukier, H., Pepitone, A. 1984. Social roles and strategies in predicting: some determinants of the use of base rate information. *J. Pers. Soc. Psychol.* 47:349–60

Annu. Rev. Psychol. 1993. 44:317–42

MAMMALIAN BRAIN SUBSTRATES OF AVERSIVE CLASSICAL CONDITIONING

David G. Lavond, Jeansok J. Kim, and Richard F. Thompson

Departments of Psychology and Biological Sciences, Neuroscience Program, University of Southern California, Los Angeles, California 90089-2520

KEY WORDS: learning and memory, cerebellum, brainstem, plasticity, amygdala

CONTENTS

INTRODUCTION 318
RELATION OF NONSPECIFIC AND SPECIFIC AVERSIVE CLASSICAL
    CONDITIONING 320
BRAIN SUBSTRATES FOR NONSPECIFIC FEAR CONDITIONING............................ 321
    Evidence from Lesion Studies 321
    Evidence from Recording and Stimulation Studies 323
    Evidence from Pharmacological Studies 323
    Brain Areas Other than the Amygdala.. 324
    Evidence Against Amygdala 326
    Conclusion 326
BRAIN SUBSTRATES FOR SPECIFIC CONDITIONED RESPONSES 327
    Evidence from Stimulation and Recording 327
    Evidence from Lesions: the Conditioned-Response Path.................................... 328
    Cerebellar Cortex.. 328
    The Previously Neutral Stimulus: Lesions of the Conditioned-Stimulus Path ... 329
    The Reinforcing Stimulus: Lesions and the Unconditioned-Stimulus Path........ 330
    The Locus of Plasticity.. 331
    Current Issues 331
    Alternative Loci for Conditioning 333
SUMMARY 334

0066-4308/93/0201-0317$02.00

INTRODUCTION

Considerable progress has been made in the past few years in identifying structures and systems in the mammalian brain that subserve processes of associative learning and memory (see Thompson 1992 for an overview; see also the chapter by Squire et al in this volume). This is particularly so for aversive classical conditioning. This method has important advantages for neurobiological analysis over the use of operant/instrumental tasks (see Disterhoft et al 1977; Kandel 1976; Thompson et al 1976). By restricting learning to basic classical conditioning, recent searches for engrams or memory traces have been successful and, at the same time, realistically limited in that they do not attempt to account for all forms of learning. For classical conditioning, the engram must (*a*) be a locus of convergence for the conditioned and unconditioned stimulus systems and (*b*) produce a unique output that is a function of proper (contingent) pairing of these systems.

In this review, we examine results over the past few years on studies using an aversive unconditioned stimulus.[1] This research demonstrates that memory traces for simple forms of conditioning can be localized. In particular, the amygdala plays a critical role in what we classify as nonspecific or fear-conditioned responses. These are responses such as changes in heart rate, blood pressure, pupillary dilation, freezing, and/or startle that seem to be generalized responses, the sorts of behaviors that have been characterized as the first phase of conditioning in two-process models (e.g. Prokasy 1972; Rescorla & Solomon 1967). On the other hand, the cerebellum plays a critical role in what we classify as specific conditioned responses. These are responses that involve somatic motor movements such as an eye blink or leg flexion that can be characterized as specifically adaptive to avoid the unconditioned stimulus. These behaviors fit into the second phase of two-process models. As discussed in the following pages, the nonspecific and specific response systems appear to be anatomically and functionally dissociable.

One should keep three important points in mind while reading this review. First, we restrict our discussion to the simplest substrates of aversive conditioning. The basic premise is that once we understand a simple form of conditioning then more complex behaviors will be more tractable to study. Second, clearly not all learning occurs within the structures focused on in this review; at the very least the hippocampus and the cerebral cortex certainly play important roles in more complex learning, as well as being influenced in aversive classical conditioning. Third, the evidence for localization does not depend upon a single technique. Lesion experiments are critical for determining the necessary role of a structure, but lesions alone cannot tell us what, why, or how

---

[1]
    We apologize to the many excellent investigators whose work we could not include because of space limitations. We did not cover taste-aversion learning because it was recently reviewed in an *Annual Review of Neuroscience* chapter (Chambers 1990).

that structure plays a role. Similarly, recording studies alone cannot tell us whether a locus is essentially involved in a function or merely informed of a function located elsewhere. The two are commonly confused. The results of lesion, recording, stimulation, reversible inactivation, and neurochemical experiments converge into a coherent story of the localization of engrams or memory traces.

The literature contains some confusion regarding the nature of memory traces (see e.g. Bloedel et al 1991; Woody 1986). The essential memory trace, together with its associated circuitry, is necessary and sufficient for the basic aspects of a given form of learning (e.g. acquisition and retention). Other brain structures may also form memory traces, defined as long lasting changes in synaptic excitability or efficacy, but these may not be essential for the basic learning. Thus, in eye-blink conditioning, long-lasting increases in synaptic efficacy and associated changes in receptor binding develop in neurons in the hippocampus (Berger & Thompson 1978; Berger et al 1986; Disterhoft et al 1986; Tocco et al 1991). The hippocampus is not necessary for basic associative learning and memory (Enser 1976; Mauk & Thompson 1987; Norman et al 1977; Schmaltz & Theios 1972) but plays an important modulatory role in more complex aspects of this learning, for example in discrimination reversal and long-interval trace conditioning (Berger & Orr 1983; Moyer et al 1990; Solomon et al 1986b).

These higher order memory traces would seem to play important roles in the adaptive behavior of the organism. In a similar vein, aversive classical conditioning can modify the receptive-field properties of neurons in sensory systems. Particularly striking are the studies of Weinberger and associates (Bakin & Weinberger 1990; Diamond & Weinberger 1984, 1986; Edeline & Weinberger 1991; Weinberger 1982; Weinberger et al 1984) showing that neurons in secondary areas of auditory thalamus and cortex shift their best frequencies toward the frequency of the conditioning stimulus. Such changes might increase conditioned stimulus activation of the essential memory trace circuitry. The motor area of the cerebral cortex provides yet another example. Classical eye-blink conditioning results in marked and persisting increases in excitability of pyramidal neurons in motor cortex (Woody et al 1976, 1991). However, the cerebral cortex is not necessary for either learning or memory of the conditioned eye-blink response (Oakley & Russell 1972, 1977; but see Woody et al 1974 for glabellar tap conditioning). The possible modulatory role of motor cortex in eye-blink conditioning is not yet known.

The obvious point here is that the organism can learn, remember, and perform the basic learned response following destruction of nonessential memory trace systems, but destruction of the essential memory trace system abolishes the ability of the organism to do these. If the essential memory trace (or systems that form the mandatory afferents and efferents for the trace) are completely destroyed, the memory (or at least the ability to perform the learned response) will be completely and permanently abolished. However, destruction of the essential memory trace (or mandatory circuitry) ought not to alter the organism's ability to perform the unlearned (reflex) response. The latter of course assumes that essential memory traces are not embedded in the essential reflex circuitry, an outcome that is true at least for eye-blink and heart-rate conditioning. However, we hasten to add (as noted above) that the lesion method, per se, cannot localize the essential memory trace, only the essential circuitry.

RELATION OF NONSPECIFIC AND SPECIFIC AVERSIVE CLASSICAL CONDITIONING

When Teuber (1955) proposed that a test of "double dissociation" be a criterion for localization of function he had in mind the results of the experiment by Harlow et al (1952), which showed that frontal-lobe lesions resulted in a delayed response deficit whereas temporal-lobe lesions resulted in deficits of concept formation, and not the other way. For the most part, that criterion has been too stringent; many aspire to show a double dissociation in brain memory systems but few actually do. Recently, however, Supple and colleagues (Supple et al 1989; Supple & Leaton 1990) demonstrated a double dissociation between nonspecific and specific conditioned responses. They found that cerebellar vermal lesions prevent heart-rate conditioning but not eyelid conditioning, and confirmed that lateral cerebellar lesions prevent eyelid conditioning but not heart-rate conditioning (Lavond et al 1984a). That is, a lesion that prevents the formation of nonspecific learning has no effect on specific learning, and vice versa. Importantly, Supple & Leaton (1990) report that the vermal lesion affects the conditioned autonomic response without affecting the unconditioned autonomic response.

There are several important implications. First, the fact that associations can still be formed with either lesion suggests that learning is a function of the response system that is reinforced. Nonspecific learning includes heart-rate and other autonomic response systems that are affected by vermal lesions, whereas specific learning such as an eye blink are affected by lateral cerebellar lesions. Second, because the time courses for conditioning of the two response systems are normally very different (e.g. Powell et al 1974; Schneiderman et al 1962, 1966), the double dissociation suggests that associations are represented locally rather than globally and diffusely. Third, the dissociation further implies that two-process models of conditioning that require sequential learning of nonspecific and then specific behaviors are basically incorrect, because specific learning occurs without nonspecific learning. Thus, multiple brain sites may learn different things about a learning situation, and learning in one site is independent of learning that occurs elsewhere, but the memories can interact. An ensemble of engrams may represent an integrated behavior. Indeed, Wagner and associates have developed an elegant theoretical analysis

(AESOP) showing how what we term specific and nonspecific memory systems can interact to yield adaptive behavior (Wagner & Brandon 1989). Interestingly, Wagner's earlier SOP theory (1981), concerned with discrete response learning, shows a striking correspondence to the essential cerebellar circuitry (see below and Wagner & Donegan 1989). Fourth, the observations of selective effects on conditioned but not unconditioned responses and the fact that learning appears normal in the unlesioned response system implies that the results are specific to conditioning rather than to a generalized performance deficit. Below we examine additional evidence for the localization of each of these two forms of conditioning.

BRAIN SUBSTRATES FOR NONSPECIFIC FEAR CONDITIONING

Initially neutral stimuli such as tones, lights, or experimental chambers, when paired with aversive unconditioned stimuli such as electric shock, can rapidly become conditioned stimuli that can elicit numerous fear-conditioned responses. Several lines of evidence point to the amygdala as a critical neural substrate for this type of emotional learning. The amygdala is one of the principal structures of the limbic system (Isaacson 1974), and it seems to be situated such that it has access to both sensory inputs and response outputs (see LeDoux 1987). In brief, various sensory information enters the amygdala through its basal and lateral nuclei (Amaral 1987). These nuclei are reciprocally connected with the central nucleus via intraamygdaloid projections. The central nucleus appears to be the major amygdaloid output structure that projects to various autonomic and somatomotor pathways involved in fear expression (LeDoux et al 1988; Rosen et al 1991; Schwaber et al 1982). A variety of experimental manipulations of the amygdala, as well as its afferents and efferents, can affect fear learning. In this section, we examine evidence that the amygdala is the site of conditioned stimulus–unconditioned stimulus convergence for formation of fear conditioning.

Evidence from Lesion Studies

Amygdala lesions, in particular of the central nucleus, reduce or abolish various conditioned fear-related behaviors in several mammalian species. In rats, acquisition and retention of fear responses such as increase in blood pressure (Iwata et al 1986a), fear-potentiated startle (Hitchcock & Davis 1986, 1987), reduction in pain sensitivity (Helmstetter et al 1988), and defensive freezing (Blanchard & Blanchard 1972; Iwata et al 1986a) are all attenuated by the lesion. Amygdalectomy is also known to disrupt inhibitory/passive avoidance responses (Grossman et al 1975; Liang et al 1982; Nagel & Kemble 1976), but not appetitive conditioned responses (Cahill & McGaugh 1990). In rabbits, the amygdala lesion impairs learned deceleration in heart rate (bradycardia) (Gentile et al 1986; Kapp et al 1979). In cats, reversible cryogenic ("cooling") blockade of the central amygdaloid nucleus decreases conditioned blood pressure and respiratory responses (J. X. Zhang et al 1986). In addition to acquired fear responses, amygdala lesions also impair innate fear responding. For example, rats typically engage in defensive freezing in the presence of predators such as cats. However, animals with amygdala lesions tend not to freeze in response to the cat (Blanchard & Blanchard 1972). Amygdala lesions also reduce reactivity to the footshock unconditioned stimulus and block shock sensitization of startle (Hitchcock et al 1989). That amygdalectomy impairs both the conditioned and unconditioned fear responses indicates that the amygdala receives information about both conditioned stimuli and unconditioned stimuli. As mentioned in the introduction, fear conditioning results in diffuse or nonspecific conditioned fear responses. It has been suggested that conditioned stimuli activate a "central fear motivational state" rather than a series of "discrete conditioned responses" (e.g. Bolles & Fanselow 1980). The fact that lesions affect conditioned responses in a range of response systems strongly supports this notion.

Selective lesions of structures afferent to the amygdala can affect conditioning to specific sensory stimuli. For instance, lesioning of the medial geniculate nucleus of the thalamus, which sends auditory information directly to the lateral amygdaloid nucleus (LeDoux et al 1990), blocks the formation of the tone-footshock, but not light-footshock, association as measured by conditioned freezing and blood-pressure responses (LeDoux et al 1986) and the fear-potentiated startle response (Campeau & Davis 1991). Similarly, hippocampal lesions affect context-footshock association but not tone-footshock association (Kim & Fanselow 1992; Phillips & LeDoux 1992). Note that in tone fear conditioning, the medial geniculate nucleus also projects to the auditory cortex, which in turn projects to the amygdala (LeDoux 1987). This corticoamygdala pathway is not essential (LeDoux et al 1984), but is sufficient (Romanski & LeDoux 1991), for auditory fear conditioning. On the efferent side, lesions confined to the hypothalamic and brainstem areas to which the central amygdaloid nucleus projects affect specific conditioned fear responses (Francis et al 1981; Hitchcock et al 1989; Iwata et al 1986b). In a representative set of studies, LeDoux and his colleagues showed that lesions of the lateral hypothalamus and ventral region of the periaqueductal gray matter abolished blood-pressure and freezing conditioned responses, respectively (LeDoux et al 1988). However, the lateral hypothalamus lesion did not affect freezing, and the periaqueductal gray lesions did not alter blood pressure. Thus, the lateral hypothalamus and the ventral periaqueductal gray matter appear to be efferent mediators for specific fear responses. This double dissociation of conditioned stimuli and conditioned responses, as a result of lesions made in structures that are afferent and efferent to the amygdala, further indicates that the amygdala is a critical mediator of fear learning.

Evidence from Recording and Stimulation Studies

Electrophysiological studies reveal that neurons in the central nucleus of the amygdala respond to both conditioned and unconditioned fear stimuli (Pascoe & Kapp 1985a) and undergo plastic changes during fear conditioning (Applegate et al 1982). Using a differential conditioning paradigm, Pascoe & Kapp (1985b) reported that cells in the central nucleus exhibited increases in extracellular single unit activity to a tone that signaled the paraorbital shock. In contrast, a different tone that did not signal the shock elicited little or no change in unit activity. The bradycardia response paralleled the neuronal response in that it was observed only during the reinforced tone presentation. Moreover, the unit activity in the amygdala correlated with the bradycardia amplitude.

Electrical or chemical stimulation of specific regions in the amygdala (e.g. the central nucleus) elicits fear responses that tend to mimic conditioned responses. In rats, amygdala stimulation enhances both acoustically and electrically (Rosen & Davis 1988, 1990) elicited startle responses and produces cardiovascular changes that are similar to those evoked by a tone-conditioned stimulus (Iwata et al 1987). The freezing response has also been reported with stimulation of the amygdala (Weingarten & White 1978). In rabbits, somatic and autonomic changes associated with the conditioned stimulus occur following stimulation in the amygdala (Applegate et al 1983). These stimulation studies suggest that the amygdala directly influences fear responses. In some cases, however, stimulation of the amygdala can hinder fear conditioning. For example, immediate posttraining stimulation of the amygdala produces amnesia that interferes with avoidance learning (Gold et al 1975; McDonough & Kesner 1971).

Evidence from Pharmacological Studies

Immediate posttraining pharmacological manipulations in the amygdala are known to impair or facilitate fear conditioning. Gallagher & Kapp (1978) found that the opioid receptor antagonist naloxone enhanced the acquisition of conditioned fear when infused into the amygdala immediately after training. In contrast, intraamygdala administration of the opioid agonist levorphanol attenuated fear learning (Gallagher et al 1981). Subsequent studies indicate that the memory-enhancing effect of opioid antagonists is mediated in part by blocking the endogenously released opioids from inhibiting the release of norepinepherine in the amygdala (see McGaugh 1989). For instance, posttraining intraamygdala administrations of the noradrenergic antagonist propranolol impaired the retention of an inhibitory avoidance response (Gallagher et al 1981) and blocked the memory-enhancing effect of naloxone (McGaugh et al 1988). Moreover, posttraining intraamygdala injections of norepinepherine enhanced retention in an inhibitory avoidance task (Liang et al 1986). Interactions of noradrenergic, opiate, and perhaps other neurochemical systems (e.g. γ-

aminobutyric acid) in the amygdala may modulate fear conditioning (McGaugh 1989).

Recent studies suggest that the N-methyl-D-aspartate (NMDA) class of excitatory amino acid receptors plays an important role in fear conditioning. Administration of DL-2-amino-5-phosphonovalerate (APV), an NMDA antagonist, into the amygdala completely blocks the acquisition of the fear-potentiated startle response to a light stimulus (Miserendino et al 1990) as well as to a tone stimulus (Campeau et al 1992). A similar effect was observed when APV was microinfused into the basolateral nucleus (a region rich in NMDA receptors), but not the central nucleus (a region sparse in NMDA receptors), of the amygdala using contextual fear conditioning and freezing (Fanselow et al 1991). The drug APV, however, does not impair the performance of previously acquired fear responses such as freezing and startle (Kim et al 1991; Miserendino et al 1990). Moreover, APV blocks fear conditioning only when administered prior to the time that conditioned stimulus–unconditioned stimulus association occurs, but not immediately following conditioned stimulus–unconditioned stimulus association (Kim et al 1991). These findings suggest that NMDA receptors in the amygdala may be specifically involved in the fear-learning process. The NMDA receptors are also critical for the induction, but not expression, of long-term potentiation (LTP), an experimentally induced alteration in synaptic efficacy. Because LTP has several attributes that resemble classical conditioning, it has been proposed as a synaptic mechanism underlying associative learning (for reviews, see Teyler & DiScenna 1987; Thompson 1986). Because APV affects fear conditioning and LTP in similar manners, i.e. blocks acquisition/induction but not performance/expression, LTP has been proposed as a possible synaptic mechanism that mediates fear learning (Kim et al 1991; Miserendino et al 1990). Recently, Clugnet & LeDoux (1990) demonstrated LTP in the auditory conditioned-stimulus pathway from the thalamus (the medial division of the medial geniculate nucleus) to the amygdala. This auditory projection to the amygdala is also known to be glutaminergic (Farb et al 1989). LTP has also been demonstrated in the basolateral amygdala region using a brain-slice preparation (Chapman et al 1990a).

Brain Areas Other than the Amygdala

Most of the evidence presented so far indicates that the amygdala is critical for the learning of fear-conditioned responses. However, it is not clear whether the amygdala is the storage site for long-term fear memory. The site of learning is not necessarily the site of memory storage. For example, fear retention is abolished if the amygdala is lesioned shortly after training but not several days after training (Liang et al 1982). Intraamygdala infusion of a local anesthetic agent lidocaine yields a similar outcome in that it impairs inhibitory avoidance responding when given before a 1-day but not a 21-day retention test (Liang 1991). These results suggest that the long-term fear memory is not stored in the amygdala. The insular cortex that receives and relays sensory, such as visual (Turner & Zimmer 1984), information to the amygdala may have some role in the storage of fear memory. Davis and his colleagues found that lesioning of the most posterior aspect of the insular cortex blocked retention of the fear-potentiated startle response to the conditioned light stimulus (Davis 1990; Rosen et al 1989). Similarly, reversible inactivation of the insular cortex by a sodium-channel blocker tetrodotoxin impairs retention of an inhibitory avoidance response in rats (Bermudez-Rattoni et al 1991). Also, the hippocampus may be involved in fear memory (Kim & Fanselow 1992). In rats, contextual fear is completely abolished when the hippocampus is lesioned shortly after conditioning. However, animals retain a considerable amount of contextual fear when a long delay is imposed between the time of conditioning and the time of hippocampectomy. Hence, the hippocampus appears to have a transient role in fear-context memory. Interestingly, auditory fear is not affected by the hippocampal lesion at any time (Kim & Fanselow 1992; Phillips & LeDoux 1992). Finally, as noted earlier, lesions of the cerebellar vermis also abolish the conditioned heart-rate response in rat (Supple & Leaton 1990). In general, the amygdala appears to play a critical role in the acquisition of conditioned fear but may not be the locus of the permanent fear engram, at least in contextual fear.

Evidence Against Amygdala

If the amygdala is the neural substrate underlying fear conditioning, then lesioning it should block learning completely. But the evidence seems to conflict. For example, in inhibitory/passive avoidance studies, the effect of amygdala lesions is not always consistent. While some have found reliable lesion effects (e.g. Liang et al 1982; Nagel & Kemble 1976), others have not (e.g. Bresnahan et al 1976; Molino 1975). In one recent study, chemical lesions of the amygdala had no effect on passive avoidance learning (Selden et al 1991). McGaugh and his colleagues also showed that even though amygdala lesions affect fear conditioning, animals can learn and retain fear when they are overtrained (Parent et al 1992). Rats that received more training prior to lesions exhibited far greater retention of acquired fear in an inhibitory avoidance task. Furthermore, animals with amygdalectomy can learn an inhibitory avoidance task when trained extensively. Most of the conflicting findings regarding amygdala lesions and fear conditioning are from studies of inhibitory/passive avoidance responding, which are tasks with an instrumental component. Perhaps, different or additional fear system(s) may be involved in this type of avoidance learning.

Conclusion

An accumulating body of data points to the amygdala as a mediator of fear conditioning. However, the amygdala is comprised of several heterogeneous nuclei, and it is unclear where actual fear learning occurs. Clearly more studies are necessary to pinpoint the critical region. Also, while a considerable amount of work has focused on the conditioned-stimulus pathways, far less is known about the unconditioned-stimulus pathways. Because the unconditioned stimulus is typically a painful stimulus such as electric shock, careful examination of the pain pathways might provide valuable information. Considering the data presented so far, the amygdala is clearly involved in fear conditioning. However, the fear memory trace may, at least in part, reside elsewhere (the neocortex perhaps?).

BRAIN SUBSTRATES FOR SPECIFIC CONDITIONED RESPONSES

Since 1980, Thompson and colleagues have gathered evidence for the role of the cerebellum in developing specific conditioned responses (see recent review by Thompson 1990). This research has capitalized on the large amount of behavioral data developed by Gormezano (1972; Gormezano et al 1983) for conditioning of the rabbit nictitating-membrane response. Typically, rabbits are trained to give an eye blink (conditioned response) to a warning tone (conditioned stimulus) that predicts a puff of air to the cornea (unconditioned stimulus). This research brings together evidence from lesions, recordings, and stimulation that indicates the cerebellum is critically involved in conditioning, in agreement with many other reports implicating the cerebellum in motor learning and in a variety of other aspects of behavior (Albus 1971; Berntson & Micco 1976; Berntson & Torello 1982; Dow & Moruzzi 1958; Eccles et al 1967; Ito 1970, 1980; Leiner et al 1986; Marr 1969; Thach et al 1992; Watson 1978). Figure 1 summarizes our current understanding of the circuit for classical conditioning of the eyeblink response.

Evidence from Stimulation and Recording

Evidence that the cerebellum is involved (but not that it is essential) in forming the association for classical conditioning comes from recording and stimulation studies. Stimulation of the interpositus nucleus of the cerebellum evokes a discrete eye blink before any conditioning (McCormick & Thompson 1984). The best location for evoking a response is in the ventral aspect of the interpositus nucleus (Chapman et al 1988; McCormick & Thompson 1984). The basic constraint here requires that the site of plasticity be hard wired and that conditioning modify the threshold for the conditioned stimulus to evoke the motor response. Recordings of the cells in the interpositus and in the overlying cerebellar cortex show activity during a trial that predicts the occurrence and form of the learned behavioral responses (McCormick & Thompson 1984). Cells in the interpositus increase their activity (Berthier & Moore 1990; Foy et al 1984), while Purkinje cells in the cortex decrease their activity (Thompson 1990; but see also Berthier & Moore 1986), which is consistent with the inhibitory projection from cortex to the interpositus. Within the interpositus, the best model of unit activity is found in its ventral aspect.

Direct stimulation of the inputs to the cerebellum can substitute for the conditioned and unconditioned stimuli. Instead of using an external tone, one can stimulate the mossy fibers from the lateral pons to the cerebellum as a conditioned stimulus (Steinmetz et al 1985). It is now known that the pons receives auditory projections from the auditory system (Steinmetz et al 1987; J.K. Thompson et al 1991) and projects to the interpositus nucleus (Steinmetz & Sengelaub 1988). Subjects who learn when trained with lateral pontine stimulation show immediate transfer of training when an auditory stimulus is substituted for electrical stimulation (Steinmetz 1990). Similarly, stimulation

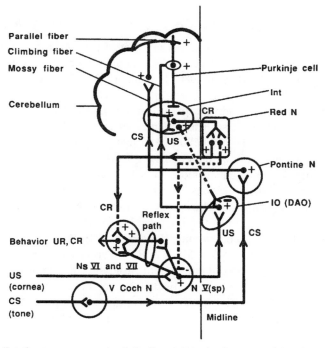

Figure 1   Putative memory trace circuit for discrete behavioral responses learned as adaptation to aversive events. The US (corneal airpuff) pathway consists of somatosensory projections to the dorsal accessory inferior olive (DAO) and its climbing fiber projections to the cerebellum (to its cortex and to the interpositus nucleus). The CS (tone) pathway consists of auditory projections to the cerebellum. The efferent CR (eyelid closure) pathway projects from the interpositus nucleus (Int) of the cerebellum to the red nucleus (Red N) and via the descending rubral pathway to act ultimately on motor neurons. The red nucleus exerts inhibitory control over the transmission of somatic sensory information about the US to the inferior olive (10), and there is also a direct inhibitory pathway from the interpositus nucleus to the inferior olive, such that when an eye-blink CR occurs there is inhibition of US activation of climbing fibers. Evidence to date is most consistent with storage of the memory traces in the interpositus nucleus and cerebellar cortex. Synaptic action is indicated as excitatory (plus) or inhibitory (minus). Additional abbreviations: N V(sp), spinal fifth cranial nucleus; NVI, sixth cranial nucleus; N VII, seventh cranial nucleus; V Coch N, ventral cochlear nucleus. Adapted from Thompson 1986.

of climbing fibers from the inferior olive substitutes for an air-puff unconditioned stimulus (Mauk et al 1986). Finally, subjects learn conditioned responses when both lateral pons and inferior olive stimulation are used for
training without any external stimuli (Steinmetz et al 1989). These systems are
sufficient for learning.

Stimulation of the interpositus and of the red nucleus in the correct topography produces eye blinks (Chapman et al 1988; McCormick & Thompson
1984). When either stimulation is paired with a tone as the conditioned stimulus then no conditioned responses develop. However, learning is substantially
faster when tones and air puffs are used after previous interpositus stimulation
(Chapman et al 1988). This observation implies that some conditioning actually occurred during stimulation of the interpositus.

Evidence from Lesions: the Conditioned-Response Path

Evidence that the cerebellum is necessary (not just involved or informed) in
the formation of the association for classical conditioning comes from lesion
experiments (G. A. Clark et al 1984; Lavond et al 1985; Lincoln et al 1982;
McCormick et al 1981; Steinmetz et al 1992; Yeo et al 1982; 1985a). Lesion of
the interpositus nucleus prevents new learning and abolishes a previously
learned conditioned response. The deficit is selective to the side of the lesion
(unlike the neocortex, the cerebellum represents the same side of the body).
Learning occurs normally on the opposite side, demonstrating that the lesion
has not disrupted some general motivational system. The lesion effect is restricted to the conditioned response; the unconditioned response is not affected
by the lesion (see below). And as we have noted above, the lesion prevents
classical conditioning of only discrete, adaptive somatic responses to an aversive stimulus. Heart-rate conditioning (Lavond et al 1984a) and a treadle press
operant response (L. Holt, M. D. Mauk & R. F. Thompson, unpublished data)
are not prevented. Reflex facilitation seems to involve the brainstem (Nowak
& Gormezano 1988) and is not affected by cerebellar lesions (Weisz &
LoTurco 1988). After much experimental work (see Thompson 1990 review),
the conditioned response pathway has now been defined as projecting from
interpositus to red nucleus to premotor and/or to the cranial motor nuclei
responsible for the eye blink (oculomotor, trochlear, abducens, accessory abducens, facial cranial nuclei) (Rosenfield et al 1985; Rosenfield & Moore
1983).

Cerebellar Cortex

Researchers have disagreed about the results of lesions of the cerebellar cortex
(see Yeo et al 1984, 1985b). We have consistently found conditioned responses after large cerebellar cortical lesions (R. E. Clark et al 1990; Lavond
& Steinmetz 1989; Lavond et al 1987; Logan 1991; Logan et al 1989; McCormick & Thompson 1984; Woodruff-Pak et al 1985). We have examined differences in lesion size, in training parameters and paradigms, and in type of rabbit

used in these experiments, and we typically see conditioned responses unless there is ancillary damage to the interpositus nucleus. The evidence supports an important role for the cerebellar cortex in amplifying and in timing of the conditioned response (McCormick 1983; Perrett et al 1991). After cerebellar cortical lesions, conditioned responses take much longer to acquire and they are small and inconsistent, while unconditioned responses are larger than in the intact animal.

Most likely the cerebellar cortex is critically involved in facilitating acquisition and in improving the size, shape, and timing of conditioned responses (i.e. the cerebellar cortex learns something), but the cerebellar cortex does not appear to be essential for basic classical conditioning with normal training parameters because conditioned responses can be trained or retained after large cortical lesions that include and extend well beyond lobules HVI and HVII. Yeo and colleagues have reported that the effects of HVI lesions are not permanent, indicating that HVI is important for retention and performance but not essential for reacquisition (Harvey et al 1990). On the other hand, Yeo recently wrote "If the lesion is extended to include the adjacent medial parts of ansiform lobe (HVII), the conditioning deficits are permanent, though there may be continued low levels of responding" (Yeo 1991, p. 294). We interpret this to mean that in Yeo's hands the conditioned response is much impaired and does not recover, but is not completely abolished. We note again that appropriate interpositus lesions completely and permanently abolish the conditioned response.

The cerebellar cortex has not been completely lesioned in any of these studies. The interpositus receives projections from a parasagittal cortical zone that includes a projection from the anterior lobe, which often is not damaged in these studies. In addition, there are intracortical cerebellar connections outside of this zone. Finally, Welker and associates (Shambes et al 1978) have shown that there are multiple fractured somatotopies in cerebellar cortex. The engram may be multiply represented in cerebellar cortex, and lesions to date might not have included all of the critical tissue.

We (R. F. Thompson and D. G. Lavond) agree that the cerebellum and its associated circuitry are essential (necessary and sufficient) for classical conditioning of discrete, adaptive, somatic, conditioned responses to aversive stimuli and that the cerebellar cortex plays an extremely important role in classical conditioning. Thompson believes that the engram is represented in the interpositus and multiply in cerebellar cortex. Lavond believes that cortex is important for some aspects of this learning but not essential for the basic association.

The Previously Neutral Stimulus: Lesions of the Conditioned-Stimulus Path

Lesions of the middle cerebellar peduncle (conveying mossy fibers to the cerebellum) abolish conditioned responses to all modalities of peripheral stimuli and to pontine stimulation used as a conditioned stimulus (Lewis et al 1987; Solomon et al 1986a). Bilateral lesions of the lateral pons selectively abolish conditioned responses to a tone-conditioned stimulus but not to a light (Steinmetz et al 1987). This demonstrates a new pathway for auditory information to reach the cerebellum, and at the same time shows that the locus of learning itself has not been destroyed because conditioned responses persist to the light stimulus. It is now well established that auditory nuclei project to the pons (Kandler & Herbert 1991; J. K. Thompson et al 1986, 1988) and that the pons sends mossy fiber collaterals to the interpositus nucleus (Steinmetz & Sengelaub 1988; J. K. Thompson et al 1991).

The Reinforcing Stimulus: Lesions and the Unconditioned-Stimulus Path

The inferior olivary projection of climbing fibers to the interpositus has never been controversial. On one hand, lesion of the inferior olive has been reported to immediately abolish conditioned responses (Yeo et al 1986). On the other, lesion of the inferior olive results in behavioral extinction when the subjects are still presented with paired conditioned and unconditioned stimuli for eyeblink conditioning (McCormick et al 1985) and for limb-flexion conditioning (Voneida et al 1990). The discrepancy may result from differences in lesion size [the larger lesion of Yeo et al may cause massive Purkinje cell firing that disrupts its projection to the interpositus (see Benedetti et al 1984)] or from time of testing after the lesion (McCormick et al tested soon after the lesion). The extinction result would be consistent with the stimulation data (see above), indicating that the olive projects information about the unconditioned stimulus to the interpositus. Extinction also demonstrates that the memory trace cannot be in the inferior olive.

The inferior olive projection to the cerebellum may reinforce information about the unconditioned stimulus to the site of learning. This suggestion is supported by recordings during conditioning. Before learning, neuronal unit activity recorded in the olive exhibits no responses to the conditioned stimulus but shows a clear evoked increase in unit activity at the onset of the unconditioned stimulus (arguing that the memory trace is not in the olive). This evoked neuronal activity decreases on paired trials as animals learn and perform the conditioned response, but the evoked activity is still fully present on unconditioned stimulus–alone test trials (Sears & Steinmetz 1991).

By the same token, before training, Purkinje neurons (which receive the olivary projection) show a complex spike evoked by the onset of the unconditioned stimulus. In trained animals, this evoked complex spike is virtually absent on paired trials when the animal gives a conditioned response but occurs normally on unconditioned stimulus–alone test trials (Krupa et al 1991; Thompson 1990). This observation led us to hypothesize (Donegan et al 1989) that the olive's climbing fiber projection could function as an error-correcting algorithm in classical conditioning (Rescorla & Wagner 1972), for example by way of the direct GABAergic descending pathway from the interpositus to the inferior olive (Nelson & Mugnoini 1989). That is, as learning develops, the learning-induced increase in neuronal activity in the interpositus would result in increased inhibition of the olive, thus preventing climbing-fiber activation by unconditioned-stimulus onset from reaching the cerebellum. Such a mechanism could account for the behavioral phenomenon of blocking.

The Locus of Plasticity

We do not yet have definitive proof that the cerebellum is the locus of essential plasticity associated with eyelid conditioning, but the evidence leading to that conclusion is very strong.

Chapman and associates (1990b; Chapman 1988) injected the local anesthetic lidocaine to create a temporary lesion into either the red nucleus or the interpositus nucleus in well-trained animals. Either injection temporarily abolished conditioned responses. Learning-related unit activity in the red nucleus was abolished during interpositus anesthesia. However, learning-related unit activity in the interpositus continued during red nucleus anesthesia. This result implies that the memory is projected from interpositus to red nucleus.

In recent work, a reversible lesion created by cooling has shown that the cerebellum is essential for the formation of memory (Lavond et al 1990). When the interpositus is cooled during 5 days of acquisition training, the animal exhibits no behavioral learned responses and no learning-related unit activity occurs in the red nucleus (the major cerebellar projection target). When cooling is terminated and training continues, the subjects acquire learning as if they were completely naive. However, when the same procedure is used with cooling of the red nucleus, which also prevents behavioral learned responses during cooling, the interpositus develops a learning-related unit model during cooling. Then when cooling is terminated, there is immediate or rapid acquisition and savings (R. E. Clark et al 1991; R. E. Clark & Lavond 1992). Similar cooling of cerebellar cortical lobule HVI above the interpositus nucleus does not prevent learning (A.A. Zhang et al 1990).

Together, these results implicate the interpositus nucleus as the site of plasticity necessary for conditioning and rule out the red nucleus as that locus (but see below). However, both lidocaine and cooling may also affect fibers of passage to the cerebellar cortex, so these results do not rule out involvement of the cortex. Both results support the conclusion that the cerebellum is critically involved in conditioning.

Current Issues

Welsh & Harvey (1989b) tried to accomplish a similar result by injecting lidocaine into the interpositus in subjects who already knew a light-conditioned stimulus while acquiring a response to a tone-conditioned stimulus. These authors reported learning to the tone despite interpositus anesthesia. The cooling probe experiments contradict this observation (Clark et al 1991). In current work, we find that infusions of lidocaine in the critical region of the cerebellum during training in naive animals completely prevents learning and the animals subsequently learn with no savings. Cannula location and drug dose (concentration) are critically important. With appropriate cannula locations, complete prevention of acquisition is a consistent finding (Nordholm et al 1992).

Welsh & Harvey (1989a) also question the cerebellar hypothesis because they report that conditioned responses still occur with cerebellar lesions. They pooled the results of complete and incomplete lesions (see Welsh's 1986 thesis). Many of their lesions are incomplete. In the few cases of complete lesions, their animals did not show conditioned responses. We have not seen any evidence of learning when we periodically test over a period of up to 8 months after the lesion (Lavond et al 1984b), when Welsh & Harvey's paradigm is replicated exactly (Steinmetz et al 1992; Thompson et al 1987), nor when the subjects are trained postlesion for 200 days (Steinmetz & Steinmetz 1991).

Welsh & Harvey also claim that interpositus lesions that abolished the conditioned response produced a performance deficit rather than a memory deficit; that is, the lesion effect on the conditioned response was secondary to its effect on the unconditioned response. Actually, Welsh & Harvey reported that effective lesions of the interpositus (those lesions that abolished the conditioned response) had no effect on the amplitude of the unconditioned response at all stimulus intensities they used. They claimed to have shown a very small effect on reflex topography at very low intensities. But they did not in fact even demonstrate this because they did not report prelesion unconditioned responses; to demonstrate a deficit in reflex performance one must compare lesion effects on conditioned and unconditioned responses in the same animals both before and after the lesion. When this comparison is made it shows that lesions that permanently abolish the conditioned response have no persisting effect on any property of the unconditioned response over a wide range of unconditioned-stimulus intensities (Ivkovich et al 1990; Steinmetz et al 1992).

In marked contrast, lesions of motor nuclei that produce massive and permanent impairment of reflex performance have much less effect on conditioned responses (Disterhoft et al 1985; Ivkovich et al 1991; Steinmetz et al 1992). Finally, large lesions of cerebellar cortex that markedly impair or abolish the conditioned response result in an increase in reflex amplitude (Logan 1991; Yeo 1991). There is thus a double dissociation between lesion effects on the conditioned and unconditioned responses; the "performance" argument is decisively negated (see also Ivry & Baldo 1992). Supple & Leaton (1990) also reported no effect of vermal lesions on unconditioned heart-rate responses.

Bloedel and associates (Kelly et al 1990) also argue against a role for the cerebellum in conditioning. They claim to have established conditioning in subjects who are decerebrated and decerebellated. However, they reported results from only a very few of the many animals they ran, used methods of measurement that would count spontaneous responses as conditioned responses, and did not run any of the control groups essential to rule out nonassociative processes such as sensitization or pseudoconditioning. Indeed, the training procedures they used (9-s intertrial interval) do not result in any learning at all in normal rabbits (Nordholm et al 1991). Yeo (1991) trained acute, decerebrate rabbits with more reasonable procedures and reported that cerebellar lesions completely abolished conditioned responses that were established in the decerebrate.

The responses described by Bloedel and associates seem to result from sensitization (see discussion in Nordholm et al 1991). To demonstrate that the memory trace is stored in the brainstem (i.e. not in the cerebellum) in normal animals, one must train them in the normal state and show (with appropriate control groups) that they retain the conditioned response after decerebration and decerebellation. In fact, Mauk & Thompson (1987) showed just the opposite result several years ago: Normal animals were trained and then decerebrated; they retained the eye-blink conditioned response only if the cerebellum and red nucleus (part of the conditioned-response pathway) were not damaged.

Alternative Loci for Conditioning

Besides the cerebellum, alternative suggestions for the locus of the engram for classical conditioning have included the red nucleus (Tsukahara 1981, 1982), the supratrigeminal nucleus (Desmond & Moore 1983), the trigeminal nucleus (Bracha et al 1990), the reticular formation near the pars oralis of the trigeminal nucleus (Harvey et al 1985), and perhaps the motor nuclei themselves (e.g. facial nucleus, Woody 1986). Only Tsukahara presents convincing evidence for any of these suggestions.

The data from stimulation (Chapman et al 1988), from lidocaine injections (Chapman 1988), and from the cooling probe studies (e.g. R. E. Clark et al 1991) argue strongly against the red nucleus as the site for the essential plasticity. In Tsukahara's experiment, he paired stimulation of the pyramidal tract as a conditioned stimulus with shock to the forearm in the cat. He then tested thresholds of corticobulbar (pyramidal) and interpositobulbar (superior cerebellar peduncle) projections to the red nucleus, finding that the corticobulbar synapses showed plasticity. His finding may depend upon his method of inducing the conditioned stimulus path and might have little to do with learning to natural stimuli. Nevertheless, his experiments do demonstrate plasticity in the red nucleus, and the cerebellar hypothesis is complemented by (not contradicted by) the possibility that additional modification of the basic engram occurs in the red nucleus.

The trigeminal nuclear complex needs further evaluation as a potential site for plasticity. In the case of the supratrigeminal nucleus, Desmond & Moore (1983) conceive of its contributions as parallel to the cerebellum rather than instead of a cerebellar engram. The implication of the reticular formation in classical conditioning is based upon a single anatomy experiment (Harvey et al 1985). As far as we know, there is no recording, stimulation, or lesion data to support that hypothesis. Nevertheless, we recently cooled that region during acquisition training. We found that conditioned responses developed normally during cooling (A. A. Zhang et al 1990).

Learning could conceivably occur in the motor nuclei responsible for the actual behavioral learned response. Neural responses in the abducens region involved in the nictitating membrane reflex, for example, are influenced by auditory stimuli (Cegavske et al 1979). The eye-blink response involves several facial and extrinsic eye muscles and cranial motor nuclei. We recently cooled the facial nucleus and monitored EMG activity from the orbicularis oculi muscles. During cooling, no conditioned or unconditioned responses were observed. As soon as cooling was terminated, both responses were immediately present (A. A. Zhang & Lavond 1991). This result indicates that cooling effectively inactivated the facial nucleus but did not prevent the formation of the memory expressed by the facial nucleus. Woody (1986) reviews evidence that cells in the facial nucleus are more excitable after conditioning or random presentations of the stimuli, and may facilitate learning. Our evidence demonstrates that the site of learning is located upstream and that memory is expressed by coordinated projections to many motor nuclei.

We must emphasize that none of this discussion implies that plasticity in these alternative locations may not occur and contribute to final performance. As we have elaborated above (see Introduction) some engrams are essential for forming the association between conditioned and unconditioned stimuli and the conditioned response, and other nonessential engrams are important for shaping and timing the final learned response. We would also emphasize that our evidence arguing for the cerebellum as the site of the essential memory trace for aversive classical conditioning of discrete responses is completely consistent with, and strongly supportive of, current views of the role of the cerebellum in the adaptive coordination of movement (Thach et al 1992).

SUMMARY

In this review, we have examined recent studies that have successfully identified neural circuits necessary for nonspecific and specific conditioned responses. This success is due in large part to the advantages of the classical conditioning paradigm for controlling stimuli and responses. Clearly, this research does not attempt to account for all forms of memory. The power of this approach is demonstrated by the distinction between essential and nonessential memory traces or engrams. Essential memory traces represent the circuitry responsible for forming the association in classical conditioning. Nonessential memory traces do not represent the essential association, but they are important for facilitating, adapting, and modifying the final performance of the learned behavior.

The search for the engram for any learned behavior has been viewed with skepticism by some investigators who quote Karl Lashley: "This series of experiments has yielded a good bit of information about what and where the memory is not. It has discovered nothing directly of the real nature of the engram" (1950, pp. 477–78). However, these authors neglect to quote Lashley fully, for even he was less pessimistic about that search than is normally recognized. He continued, "I sometimes feel, in reviewing the evidence on the localization of the memory trace, that the necessary conclusion is that learning just is not possible. It is difficult to conceive of a mechanism which can satisfy the conditions set for it. Nevertheless, in spite of such evidence against it, *learning does sometimes occur*" (1950, pp. 477–78, emphasis added). Learning does indeed occur, and its neurobiological substrates can be localized.

ACKNOWLEDGMENTS

This review was supported by National Science Foundation grant BNS-8906612 to D. G. L., by National Institute of Aging postdoctoral training grant (AG00093) for J. J. K.; and by National Science Foundation (BNS-8106648), Office of Naval Research (N0001483K0238), and McKnight Foundation grants to R. F. T.

Literature Cited

Albus, J. S. 1971. A theory of cerebellar function. *Math. Biosci.* 10:25–61

Amaral, D. G. 1987. Memory: anatomical organization of candidate brain regions. See Plum 1987, pp. 211–94

Applegate, C. D., Frysinger, R. C., Kapp, B. S., Gallagher, M. 1982. Multiple unit activity recorded from the amygdala central nucleus during Pavlovian heart rate conditioning in the rabbit. *Brain Res.* 238:457–62

Applegate, C. D., Kapp, B. S., Underwood, M., McNall, C. L. 1983. Autonomic and somatomotor effects of amygdala central nucleus stimulation in awake rabbits. *Physiol. Behav.* 31:353–60

Bakin, J. S., Weinberger, N. M. 1990. Classical conditioning induces CS-specific receptive field plasticity in the auditory cortex of guinea pig. *Brain Res.* 536:271–86

Benedetti, F., Montarolo, P. G., Rabacchi, S. 1984. Inferior olive lesion induces long-lasting functional modification in the Purkinje cells. *Exp. Brain Res.* 55:368–71

Berger, T. W., Berry, S. D., Thompson, R. F. 1986. Role of the hippocampus in classical conditioning of aversive and appetitive behaviors. In *The Hippocampus,* ed. R. L. Isaacson, K. H. Pribram, pp. 203–29. New York: Plenum

Berger, T. W., Orr, W. B. 1983. Hippocampectomy selectively disrupts discrimination reversal conditioning of the rabbit nictitating membrane response. *Behav. Brain Res.* 8:49–68

Berger, T. W., Thompson, R. F. 1978. Neuronal plasticity in the limbic system during classical conditioning of the rabbit nictitating membrane response. I. The hippocampus. *Brain Res.* 145:323–46

Bermudez-Rattoni, F., Introini-Collison, I. B., McGaugh, J. L. 1991. Reversible inactivation of the insular cortex by tetrodotoxin produces retrograde and anterograde amnesia for inhibitory avoidance and spatial learning. *Proc. Natl. Acad. Sci.* 88:5379–82

Berntson, G. G., Micco, D. J. 1976. Organization of brain stem behavioral systems. *Brain Res. Bull.* 1:471–83

Berntson, G. G., Torello, M. W. 1982. The paleocerebellum and the integration of behavioral function. *Physiol. Psych.* 10:2–12

Berthier, N. E., Moore, J. W. 1986. Cerebellar Purkinje cell activity related to the classically conditioned nictitating membrane response. *Exp. Brain Res.* 63:341–50

Berthier, N. E., Moore, J. W. 1990. Activity of deep cerebellar nuclear cells during classical conditioning of nictitating membrane extension in rabbits. *Exp. Brain Res.* 83:44–54

Black, A. H., Prokasy, W. F., eds. 1972. *Classical Conditioning.* Vol. 2. *Current Research and Theory.* New York: Appleton-Century-Crofts

Blanchard, D. C., Blanchard, R. J. 1972. Innate and conditioned reactions to threat in rats with amygdaloid lesions. *J. Comp. Physiol. Psychol.* 81:281–90

Bloedel, J. R., Bracha, V., Kelly, T. M., Wu, J. Z. 1991. Substrates for motor learning: does the cerebellum do it all? *Ann. N.Y. Acad. Sci.* 627:305–18

Bolles, R. C., Fanselow, M. S. 1980. A perceptual-defensive-recuperative model of fear and pain. *Behav. Brain Sci.* 3:291–323

Bracha, V., Wu, J. Z., Cartwright, M., Bloedel, J. R. 1990. Selective effects of lidocaine microinjections into the region of the spinal trigeminal nucleus on the conditioned and unconditioned responses of the rabbit nictitating membrane reflex. *Soc. Neurosci. Abstr.* 16:474

Bresnahan, J. C., Meyer, P. M., Baldwin, R. B., Meyer, D. R. 1976. Avoidance behavior in rats with lesions in the septum, fornix longus, and amygdala. *Physiol. Psychol.* 4:333–40

Cahill, L., McGaugh, J. L. 1990. Amygdaloid complex lesions differentially affect retention of tasks using appetitive and aversive reinforcement. *Behav. Neurosci.* 104:532–43

Campeau, S., Davis, M. 1991. Lesions of the auditory thalamus block acquisition and expression of aversive conditioning to an auditory but not a visual stimulus measured with the fear potentiated startle paradigm. *Soc. Neurosci. Abstr.* 17:658

Campeau, S., Miserendino, M. J. D., Davis, M. 1992. Intra-amygdala infusion of the N-methyl-D-aspartate receptor antagonist AP5 blocks retention but not expression of fear-potentiated startle to an auditory conditioned stimulus. *Behav. Neurosci.* In press

Cegavske, C. F., Patterson, M. M., Thompson, R. F. 1979. Neuronal unit activity in the abducens nucleus during classical conditioning of the nictitating membrane response in the rabbit, *Oryctolagus cuniculus. J. Comp. Physiol. Psychol.* 93:595–609

Chambers, K. C. 1990. A neural model for conditioned taste aversions. *Annu. Rev. Neurosci.* 13:373–85

Chapman, P. F. 1988. *An analysis of the critical neural circuits for the conditioned eyeblink response in the rabbit.* PhD dissertation, Stanford University, Stanford, Calif.

Chapman, P. F., Kairiss, E. W., Keenan, C. L., Brown, T. H. 1990a. Long-term synaptic potentiation in the amygdala. *Synapse* 6:271–78

Chapman, P. F., Steinmetz, J. E., Sears, L. L., Thompson, R. F. 1990b. Effects of lidocaine injection in the interpositus nucleus and red nucleus on conditioned behavioral and neuronal responses. *Brain Res.* 537:140–56

Chapman, P. F., Steinmetz, J. E., Thompson, R. F. 1988. Classical conditioning does not occur when direct stimulation of the red nucleus or cerebellar nuclei is the unconditioned stimulus. *Brain Res.* 442:97–104

Clark, G. A., McCormick, D. A., Lavond, D. G., Thompson, R. F. 1984. Effects of lesions of cerebellar nuclei on conditioned behavioral and hippocampal neuronal responses. *Brain Res.* 291:125–36

Clark, R. E., Brown, D. J., Thompson, R. F., Lavond, D. G. 1990. Reacquisition of classical conditioning after removal of cerebellar cortex in Dutch Belted rabbits. *Neurosci. Abstr.* 16:271

Clark, R. E., Lavond, D. G. 1992. Reversible lesions of the red nucleus during acquisition and retention of a classically conditioned behavior in rabbits. *Soc. Neurosci. Abstr.* In press

Clark, R. E., Zhang, A. A., Lavond, D. G. 1991. Cooling red nucleus or interpositus nucleus during acquisition of a classically conditioned eyeblink response in the rabbit. *Int. NIBS Conf. Synaptic Plasticity, Nov. 5, 1991, Los Angeles*

Clugnet, M. C., LeDoux, J. E. 1990. Synaptic plasticity in fear conditioning circuits: induction of LTP in the lateral nucleus of the amygdala by stimulation of the medial geniculate body. *J. Neurosci.* 10:2818–24

Davis, M. 1990. Pharmacological and anatomical analysis of fear conditioning. In *Neurobiology of Drug Abuse: Learning and Memory,* ed. L. Erinoff, pp. 126–62. Rockville, MD: National Institute on Drug Abuse

Desmond, J. E., Moore, J. W. 1983. A supratrigeminal region implicated in the classically conditioned nictitating membrane response. *Brain Res. Bull.* 10:765–73

Diamond, D. M., Weinberger, N. M. 1984. Physiological plasticity of single neurons in auditory cortex of the cat during acquisition of the pupillary conditioned response: II. Secondary field (AII). *Behav. Neurosci.* 98:189–210

Diamond, D. M., Weinberger, N. M. 1986. Classical conditioning rapidly induces specific changes in frequency receptive fields of single neurons in secondary and ventral ectosylvian auditory cortical fields. *Brain Res.* 372:357–60

Disterhoft, J. F., Coulter, D. A., Alkon, D. L. 1986. Conditioning-specific membrane changes of rabbit hippocampal neurons measured in vitro. *Proc. Natl. Acad. Sci.* 83:2733–37

Disterhoft, J. F., Kwan, H. H., Lo, W. D. 1977. Nictitating membrane conditioning to tone in the immobilized albino rabbit. *Brain Res.* 137:127–44

Disterhoft, J. F., Quinn, K. J., Weiss, C., Shipley, M. T. 1985. Accessory abducens nucleus and conditioned eye retraction/nictitating membrane extension in rabbit. *J. Neurosci.* 5:941–50

Donegan, N. H., Gluck, M. A., Thompson, R. F. 1989. Integrating behavioral and biological models of classical conditioning. See Hawkins & Bower 1989, pp. 109–56

Dow, R. S., Moruzzi, G. 1958. *The Physiology and Pathology of the Cerebellum.* Minneapolis: Univ. Minn. Press

Eccles, J. C., Ito, M., Szentagothai, J. 1967. *The Cerebellum as a Neuronal Machine.* New York: Springer-Verlag

Edeline, J. M., Weinberger, N. M. 1991. Subcortical adaptive filtering in the auditory system: associative receptive field plasticity in the dorsal medial geniculate body. *Behav. Neurosci.* 105:154–75

Enser, D. 1976. *A study of classical nictitating membrane conditioning in neodecorticate, hemidecorticate and thalamic rabbits.* PhD thesis, Univ. Iowa, Iowa City

Fanselow, M. S., Kim, J. J., Landeira-Fernandez, J. 1991. Anatomically selective blockade of Pavlovian fear conditioning by application of an NMDA antagonist to the amygdala and periaqueductal gray. *Soc. Neurosci. Abstr.* 17:659

Farb, C. F., LeDoux, J. E., Milner, T. A. 1989. Glutamate is present in medial geniculate body neurons that project to lateral amygdala and in lateral amygdala presynaptic terminals. *Soc. Neurosci. Abstr.* 15:890

Foy, M. R., Steinmetz, J. E., Thompson, R. F. 1984. Single unit analysis of cerebellum during classically conditioned eyelid response. *Soc. Neurosci. Abstr.* 10:122

Francis, J., Hernandez, L. L., Powell, D. A. 1981. Lateral hypothalamic lesions: effects on Pavlovian cardiac and eyeblink conditioning in the rabbit. *Brain Res. Bull.* 6:155–63

Gallagher, M., Kapp, B. S. 1978. Manipulation of opiate activity in the amygdala alters memory processes. *Life Sci.* 23:1973–78

Gallagher, M., Kapp, B. S., McNall, C. L., Pascoe, J. P. 1981. Opiate effects in the amygdala central nucleus alters rabbit heart rate conditioning. *Pharm. Biochem. Behav.* 14:497–505

Gentile, C. G., Jarrell, T. W., Teich, A. H., McCabe, P. M., Schneiderman, N. 1986. The role of amygdaloid central nucleus in differential Pavlovian conditioning of bradycardia in rabbits. *Behav. Brain Res.* 20:263–76

Gold, P. E., Hankins, L., Edwards, R. M., Chester, J., McGaugh, J. L. 1975. Memory interference and facilitation with posttrial amygdala stimulation: effect on memory varies with footshock level. *Brain Res.* 86:509–13

Gormezano, I. 1972. Investigations of defense and reward conditioning in the rabbit. See Black & Prokasy 1972, pp. 151–81

Gormezano, I., Kehoe, E. J., Marshall, B. S. 1983. Twenty years of classical conditioning research with the rabbit. In *Progress in Psychobiology and Physiological Psychology*, ed. J. M. Sprague, A. N. Epstein, pp. 198–275. New York: Academic

Grossman, S. P., Grossman, L., Walsh, L. 1975. Functional organization of the rat

amygdala with respect to avoidance behavior. *J. Comp. Physiol. Psychol.* 88:829–50

Harlow, H. F., Davis, R. T., Settlage, P. H., Meyer, D. R. 1952. Analysis of frontal and posterior association syndrome in brain-damaged monkeys. *J. Comp. Physiol. Psychol.* 45:419–29

Harvey, J. A., Gormezano, I., Cool-Hauser, V. A. 1985. Relationship between heterosynaptic reflex facilitation and acquisition of the nictitating membrane response in control and scopolamine-injected rabbits. *J. Neurosci.* 5:596–602

Harvey, J. A., Yeo, C. H., Welsh, J. P., Romano, A. G. 1990. Recoverable and non-recoverable deficits in conditioned responses (CRs) after cerebellar cortical lesions. *Soc. Neurosci. Abstr.* 16:268

Hawkins, R. D., Bower, G. H., eds. 1989. *The Psychology of Learning and Motivation.* New York: Academic

Helmstetter, F. J., Leaton, R. N., Fanselow, M. S., Calcagnetti, D. J. 1988. The amygdala is involved in the expression of conditioned analgesia. *Soc. Neurosci. Abstr.* 14:1227

Hitchcock, J. M., Davis, M. 1986. Lesions of the amygdala, but not of the cerebellum or red nucleus, block conditioned fear as measured with the potentiated startle paradigm. *Behav. Neurosci.* 100:11–22

Hitchcock, J. M., Davis, M. 1987. Fear-potentiated startle using an auditory conditioned stimulus: effect of lesions of the amygdala. *Physiol. Behav.* 39:403–8

Hitchcock, J. M., Sananes, C. B., Davis, M. 1989. Sensitization of the startle reflex by footshock: blockade by lesions of the central nucleus of the amygdala or its efferent pathway to the brainstem. *Behav. Neurosci.* 103:509–18

Isaacson, R. L. 1974. *The Limbic System.* New York: Plenum. 3rd ed.

Ito, M. 1970. Neurophysiological aspects of the cerebellar motor control system. *Int. J. Neurol.* 7:162–76

Ito, M. 1980. *The Cerebellum and Neural Control.* New York: Raven

Iwata, J., Chida, K., LeDoux, J. E. 1987. Cardiovascular responses elicited by stimulation of neurons in the central amygdaloid nucleus in awake but not anesthetized rats resemble conditioned cardiovascular responses. *Brain Res.* 418:183–88

Iwata, J., LeDoux, J. E., Meeley, M. P., Arneric, S., Reis, D. J. 1986a. Intrinsic neurons in the amygdaloid field projected to by the medial geniculate body mediate emotional responses conditioned to acoustic stimuli. *Brain Res.* 383:195–214

Iwata, J., LeDoux, J. E., Reis, D. J. 1986b. Destruction of intrinsic neurons in the lateral hypothalamus disrupts cardiovascular but not behavioral conditioned emotional responses. *Brain Res.* 368:161–66

Ivkovich, D., Lavond, D. G., Logan, C. G., Thompson, R. F. 1990. Measurements of reflexive intensities over the course of classical conditioning. *Soc. Neurosci. Abstr.* 16:271

Ivkovich, D., Logan, C. G., Thompson, R. F. 1991. Accessory abducens lesions produce performance deficits without permanently affecting conditioned responses. *Soc. Neurosci. Abstr.* 16:271

Ivry, R. B., Baldo, J. V. 1992. Is the cerebellum involved in learning and cognition? *Curr. Opin. Neurobiol.* 2:212–16

Kandel, E. R. 1976. *Cellular Basis of Behavior.* San Francisco: Freeman

Kandler, K., Herbert, H. 1991. Auditory projections from the cochlear nucleus to pontine and mesencephalic reticular nuclei in the rat. *Brain Res.* 562:230–42

Kapp, B. S., Frysinger, R., Gallagher, M., Haselton, J. 1979. Amygdala central nucleus lesions: effects on heart rate conditioning in the rabbit. *Physiol. Behav.* 23:1109–17

Kelly, T. M, Zuo, C. C., Bloedel, J. R. 1990. Classical conditioning of the eyeblink reflex in the decerebrate-decerebellate rabbit. *Behav. Brain Res.* 38:7–18

Kim, J. J., DeCola, J. P., Landeira-Fernandez, J., Fanselow, M. S. 1991. N-methyl-D-aspartate receptor antagonist APV blocks acquisition but not expression of fear conditioning. *Behav. Neurosci.* 105:126–33

Kim, J. J., Fanselow, M. S. 1992. Modality-specific retrograde amnesia of fear. *Science* 256:675–77

Krupa, D. J., Weiss, C., Thompson, R. F. 1991. Air puff evoked Purkinje cell complex spike activity is diminished during conditioned responses in eyeblink conditioned rabbits. *Soc. Neurosci. Abstr.* 17:322

Lashley, K. S. 1950. In search of the engram. *Soc. Exp. Biol. Symp.* 4:454–82

Lavond, D. G., Hembree, T. L., Thompson, R. F. 1985. Effect of kainic acid lesions of the cerebellar interpositus nucleus on eyelid conditioning in the rabbit. *Brain Res.* 326:179–82

Lavond, D. G., Kanzawa, S. A., Esquenazi, V., Clark, R. E., Zhang, A. A. 1990. Effects of cooling interpositus during acquisition of classical conditioning. *Soc. Neurosci. Abstr.* 16:270

Lavond, D. G., Lincoln, J. S., McCormick, D. A., Thompson, R. F. 1984a. Effect of bilateral lesions of the dentate and interpositus cerebellar nuclei on conditioning of heart-rate and nictitating membrane/eyelid responses in the rabbit. *Brain Res.* 305:323–30

Lavond, D. G., McCormick, D. A., Thompson, R. F. 1984b. A nonrecoverable learning deficit. *Physiol. Psychol.* 12:103–10

Lavond, D. G., Steinmetz, J. E. 1989. Acquisition of classical conditioning without cerebellar cortex. *Behav. Brain Res.* 33:113–64

Lavond, D. G., Steinmetz, J. E., Yokaitis, M. H., Thompson, R. F. 1987. Reacquisition of classical conditioning after removal of cerebellar cortex. *Exp. Brain Res.* 67:569–93

LeDoux, J. E. 1987. Emotion. See Plum 1987, pp. 419–59

LeDoux, J. E., Farb, C., Ruggiero, D. A. 1990. Topographic organization of neurons in the acoustic thalamus that project to the amygdala. *J. Neurosci.* 10:1043–54

LeDoux, J. E., Iwata, J., Cicchetti, P., Reis, D. J. 1988. Different projections of the central amygdaloid nucleus mediate autonomic and behavioral correlates of conditioned fear. *J. Neurosci.* 8:2517–29

LeDoux, J. E., Iwata, J., Pearl, D., Reis, D. J. 1986. Disruption of auditory but not visual learning by destruction of intrinsic neurons in the rat medial geniculate body. *Brain Res.* 371:395–99

LeDoux, J. E., Sakaguchi, A., Reis, D. J. 1984. Subcortical efferent projections of the medial geniculate nucleus mediate emotional responses conditioned to acoustic stimuli. *J. Neurosci.* 4:683–98

Leiner, H. C., Leiner, A. L., Dow, R. S. 1986. Does the cerebellum contribute to mental skills? *Behav. Neurosci.* 100:443–54

Lewis, J. L., LoTurco, J. J., Solomon, P. R. 1987. Lesions of the middle cerebellar peduncle disrupt acquisition and retention of the rabbit's classically conditioned nictitating membrane response. *Behav. Neurosci.* 101:151–57

Liang, K. C. 1991. Pretest intra-amygdala injection of lidocaine or glutamate antagonists impairs retention performance in an inhibitory avoidance task. *Soc. Neurosci. Abstr.* 17:486

Liang, K. C., Juler, R., McGaugh, J. L. 1986. Modulating effects of posttraining epinephrine on memory: involvement of the amygdala noradrenergic system. *Brain Res.* 368:125–33

Liang, K. C., McGaugh, J. L., Martinez, J. L., Jensen, R. A. Jr., Vasquez, B. J., Messing, R. B. 1982. Post-training amygdaloid lesions impair retention of an inhibitory avoidance response. *Behav. Brain Res.* 4:237–49

Lincoln, J. S., McCormick, D. A., Thompson, R. F. 1982. Ipsilateral cerebellar lesions prevent learning of the classically conditioned nictitating membrane/eyelid response. *Brain Res.* 242:190–93

Logan, C. G. 1991. *Cerebellar cortical involvement in excitatory and inhibitory classical conditioning.* PhD dissertation, Stanford Univ., Stanford, Calif.

Logan, C. G., Lavond, D. G., Thompson, R. F. 1989. The effects of combined lesions of cerebellar cortical areas on acquisition of the rabbit conditioned nictitating membrane response. *Soc. Neurosci. Abstr.* 15:640

Marr, D. 1969. A theory of cerebellar cortex. *J. Physiol. (London)* 202:437–70

Mauk, M. D., Steinmetz, J. E., Thompson, R. F. 1986. Classical conditioning using stimulation of the inferior olive as the unconditioned stimulus. *Proc. Natl. Acad. Sci.* 83:5349–53

Mauk, M. D., Thompson, R. F. 1987. Retention of classically conditioned eyelid responses following acute decerebration. *Brain Res.* 493:89–95

McCormick, D. A. 1983. *Cerebellum: essential involvement in a simple learned response.* PhD dissertation, Stanford Univ., Stanford, Calif.

McCormick, D. A., Lavond, D. G., Clark, G. A., Kettner, R. E., Rising, C. E., Thompson, R. F. 1981. The engram found? Role of the cerebellum in classical conditioning of nictitating membrane and eyelid responses. *Bull. Psychon. Soc.* 18:103–5

McCormick, D. A., Steinmetz, J. E., Thompson, R. F. 1985. Lesions of the inferior olivary complex cause extinction of the classically conditioned eyeblink response. *Brain Res.* 359:120–30

McCormick, D. A., Thompson, R. F. 1984. Cerebellum: essential involvement in the classically conditioned eyelid response. *Science* 223:296–99

McDonough, J. H. Jr., Kesner, R. P. 1971. Amnesia produced by brief electrical stimulation of amygdala or dorsal hippocampus in cats. *J. Comp. Physiol. Psychol.* 77:171–78

McGaugh, J. L. 1989. Involvement of hormonal and neuromodulatory systems in the regulation of memory storage. *Annu. Rev. Neurosci.* 12:255–87

McGaugh, J. L., Introini-Collison, I. B., Nagahara, A. H. 1988. Memory-enhancing effects of posttraining naloxone: involvement of beta-noradrenergic influences in the amygdaloid complex. *Brain Res.* 446:37–49

Miserendino, M. J. D., Sananes, C. B., Melia, K. R., Davis, M. 1990. Blocking of acquisition but not expression of conditioned fear-potentiated startle by NMDA antagonists in the amygdala. *Nature* 345:716–18

Molino, A. 1975. Sparing of function after infant lesions of selected limbic structures in the rat. *J. Comp. Physiol. Psychol.* 89:868–81

Moyer, J. R., Deyo, R. A., Disterhoft, J. F. 1990. Hippocampectomy disrupts trace eye-blink conditioning in rabbits. *Behav. Neurosci.* 104:243–52

Nagel, J. A., Kemble, E. D. 1976. Effects of amygdaloid lesions on the performance of rats in four passive avoidance tasks. *Physiol. Behav.* 17:245–50

Nelson, B. J., Mugnoini, E. 1989. Origins of GABAergic inputs to the inferior olive. In *The Olivocerebellar System in Motor Control,* ed. P. Strata, pp. 86–107. New York: Springer-Verlag

Nordholm, A. F., Lavond, D. G., Thompson, R. F. 1991. Are eyeblink responses to tone in the decerebrate, decerebellate rabbit conditioned responses? *Behav. Brain Res.* 44:27–34

Nordholm, A. F., Thompson, J. K., Standley, S., Tocco, G., Dersarkissian, C., Thompson, R. F. 1992. Lidocaine infusion in a

critical region of cerebellum completely prevents learning of the conditioned eyeblink response. *Soc. Neurosci. Abstr.* In press

Norman, R. J., Buchwald, J. S., Villablanca, J. R. 1977. Classical conditioning with auditory discrimination of the eyeblink in decerebrate cats. *Science* 196:551–52

Nowak, A. J., Gormezano, I. 1988. Reflex facilitation (RF) and classical conditioning of the rabbit's nictitating membrane response (NMR) to electrical stimulation of brainstem structures as an unconditioned stimulus (UCS). *Soc. Neurosci. Abstr.* 14:3

Oakley, D. A., Russell, I. S. 1972. Neocortical lesions and classical conditioning. *Physiol. Behav.* 8:915–26

Oakley, D. A., Russell, I. S. 1977. Subcortical storage of Pavlovian conditioning in the rabbit. *Physiol. Behav.* 18:931–37

Parent, M. B., Tomaz, C., McGaugh, J. L. 1992. Increased training in an aversively motivated task attenuates the memory impairing effects of posttraining NMDA-induced amygdala lesions. *Behav. Neurosci.* In press

Pascoe, J. P., Kapp, B. S. 1985a. Electrophysiological characteristics of amygdaloid central nucleus neurons in the awake rabbit. *Brain Res. Bull.* 14:331–38

Pascoe, J. P., Kapp, B. S. 1985b. Electrophysiological characteristics of amygdaloid central nucleus neurons during Pavlovian fear conditioning in the rabbit. *Behav. Brain Res.* 16:117–33

Perrett, S. P., Ruiz, B. P., Mauk, M. D. 1991. Cerebellar cortex ablation disrupts extinction of conditioned eyelid responses. *Soc. Neurosci. Abstr.* 17:870

Phillips, R. G., LeDoux, J. E. 1992. Differential contribution of amygdala and hippocampus to cued and contextual fear conditioning. *Behav. Neurosci.* 106:274–85

Plum, F., ed. 1987. *Handbook of Physiology,* Vol. 5, *Higher Functions of the Brain.* Baltimore: Williams and Wilkins

Powell, D. A., Lipkin, M., Milligan, W. L. 1974. Concomitant changes in classically conditioned heart rate and corneoretinal potential discrimination in the rabbit (*Oryctolagus cuniculus*). *Learn. Motiv.* 5:532–47

Prokasy, W. F. 1972. Developments with the two-phase model applied to human eyelid conditioning. See Black & Prokasy 1972, pp. 119–47

Rescorla, R. A., Solomon, R. L. 1967. Two-process learning theory: relationships between Pavlovian conditioning and instrumental learning. *Psychol. Rev.* 74:151–82

Rescorla, R. A., Wagner, A. R. 1972. A theory of Pavlovian conditioning: variations in the effectiveness of reinforcement and non-reinforcement. See Black & Prokasy 1972, pp. 64–99

Romanski, L. M., LeDoux, J. E. 1991.

Equipotentiality of thalmo-amygdala and thalmo-cortico-amygdala circuits in auditory fear conditioning. *Soc. Neurosci. Abstr.* 17:658

Rosen, J. B., Davis, M. 1988. Enhancement of acoustic startle by electrical stimulation of the amygdala. *Behav. Neurosci.* 102:195–202

Rosen, J. B., Davis, M. 1990. Enhancement of electrically elicited startle by amygdaloid stimulation. *Physiol. Behav.* 48:343–49

Rosen, J. B., Hitchcock, J. M., Miserendino, M. J. D., Davis, M. 1989. Lesions of the perirhinal cortex block fear-potentiated startle. *Soc. Neurosci. Abstr.* 15:305

Rosen, J. B., Hitchcock, J. M., Sananes, C. B., Miserendino, M. J. D., Davis, M. 1991. A direct projection from the central nucleus of the amygdala to the acoustic startle pathway: anterograde and retrograde tracing studies. *Behav. Neurosci.* 105:817–25

Rosenfield, M. E., Dovydaitis, A., Moore, J. W. 1985. Brachium conjuntivum and rubrobulbar tract: brain stem projections of red nucleus essential for conditioned nictitating membrane response. *Physiol. Behav.* 34:751–59

Rosenfield, M. E., Moore, J. W. 1983. Red nucleus lesions disrupt the classically conditioned nictitating membrane response in the rabbit. *Behav. Brain Res.* 10:393–98

Schmaltz, L. W., Theios, J. 1972. Acquisition and extinction of a classically conditioned response in hippocampectomized rabbits (*Oryctolagus cuniculus*). *J. Comp. Physiol. Psychol.* 79:328–33

Schneiderman, N., Fuentes, I., Gormezano, I. 1962. Acquisition and extinction of the classically conditioned eyelid response in the albino rabbit. *Science* 136:650–52

Schneiderman, N., Smith, M. C., Smith, A. C., Gormezano, I. 1966. Heart rate classical conditioning in rabbits. *Psychon. Sci.* 6:241–42

Schwaber, J. S., Kapp, B. S., Higgins, G. A., Rapp, P. R. 1982. Amygdaloid and basal forebrain direct connections with the nucleus of the solitary tract and the dorsal motor nucleus. *J. Neurosci.* 2:1424–38

Sears, L. L., Steinmetz, J. E. 1991. Dorsal accessory inferior olive activity diminishes during acquisition of the rabbit classically conditioned eyelid response. *Brain Res.* 545:114–22

Selden, N. R. W., Everitt, B. J., Jarrard, L. E., Robbins, T. W. 1991. Complementary roles for the amygdala and hippocampus in aversive conditioning to explicit and contextual cues. *Neuroscience* 42:335–50

Shambes, G. M., Gibson, J. M., Welker, W. 1978. Fractured somatotopy in granule cell tactile areas of rat cerebellar hemispheres revealed by micromapping. *Brain Behav. Evol.* 15:94–140

Solomon, P. R., Lewis, J. L., LoTurco, J. J., Steinmetz, J. E., Thompson, R. F. 1986a. The role of the middle cerebellar peduncle in acquisition and retention of the rabbit's classically conditioned nictitating membrane response. *Bull. Psychon. Soc.* 24:75–78

Solomon, P. R., Vander Schaff, E. F., Thompson, R. F., Weisz, D. G. 1986b. Hippocampus and trace conditioning of the rabbit's classically conditioned nictitating membrane response. *Behav. Neurosci.* 100:729–44

Steinmetz, J. E. 1990. Neuronal activity in the rabbit interpositus nucleus during classical NM-conditioning with pontine-nucleus-stimulation CS. *Psychol. Sci.* 1:378–82

Steinmetz, J. E., Lavond, D. G., Ivkovich, D., Logan, C. G., Thompson, R. F. 1992. Disruption of classical eyelid conditioning after cerebellar lesions: Damage to a memory trace system or a simple performance deficit? *J. Neurosci.* In press

Steinmetz, J. E., Lavond, D. G., Thompson, R. F. 1985. Classical conditioning of the rabbit eyelid response with mossy fiber stimulation as the conditioned stimulus. *Bull. Psychon. Soc.* 23:245–48

Steinmetz, J. E., Lavond, D. G., Thompson, R. F. 1989. Classical conditioning in rabbits using pontine nucleus stimulation as a conditioned stimulus and inferior olive stimulation as an unconditioned stimulus. *Synapse* 3:225–33

Steinmetz, J. E., Logan, C. G., Rosen, D. J., Thompson, J. K., Lavond, D. G., Thompson, R. F. 1987. Initial localization of the acoustic conditioned stimulus projection system to the cerebellum essential for classical eyelid conditioning. *Proc. Natl. Acad. Sci.* 84:3531–35

Steinmetz, J. E., Sengelaub, D. R. 1988. Direct projections from the lateral pontine nucleus to the anterior interpositus nucleus: a potential CS pathway for classical conditioning. *Soc. Neurosci. Abstr.* 14:782

Steinmetz, J. E., Steinmetz, S. S. 1991. Rabbit classically conditioned eyelid responses fail to reappear after interpositus lesions and extended postlesion training. *Soc. Neurosci. Abstr.* 17:323

Supple, W. F., Archer, L., Kapp, B. S. 1989. Lesions of the cerebellar vermis severely impair acquisition of Pavlovian conditioned bradycardic responses in the rabbit. *Soc. Neurosci. Abstr.* 15:640

Supple, W. F., Leaton, R. N. 1990. Lesions of the cerebellar vermis and cerebellar hemispheres: effects on heart rate conditioning in rats. *Behav. Neurosci.* 104:934–47

Teuber, H. L. 1955. Physiological psychology. *Annu. Rev. Psychol.* 6:267–96

Teyler, T. J., DiScenna, P. 1987. Long-term potentiation. *Annu. Rev. Neurosci.* 10:131–61

Thach, W. T., Goodkin, H. P., Keating, J. G. 1992. The cerebellum and the adaptive coordination of movement. *Annu. Rev. Neurosci.* 15:403–42

Thompson, J. K., Lavond, D. G., Thompson, R.

F. 1986. Preliminary evidence for a projection from the cochlear nucleus to the pontine nuclear region. *Soc. Neurosci. Abstr.* 12:754

Thompson, J. K., Spangler, W. J., Thompson, R. F. 1991. Differential projections of pontine nuclei to interpositus nucleus and lobule HVI. *Soc. Neurosci. Abstr.* 17:871

Thompson, J. K., Thompson, R. F., Weiss, C., Lavond, D. G. 1988. Pontine projections of cochlear nuclei using anterogade HRP or PHA-L. *Soc. Neurosci. Abstr.* 14:782

Thompson, R. F. 1986. The neurobiology of learning and memory. *Science* 233:941–47

Thompson, R. F. 1992. Memory. *Curr. Opin. Neurobiol.* 2:203–8

Thompson, R. F. 1990. Neural mechanisms of classical conditioning in mammals. *Philos. Trans. R. Soc. London Ser. B* 329:161–70

Thompson, R. F., Berger, T. W., Cegavske, C. F., Patterson, M. M., Roemer, R. A., et al 1976. The search for the engram. *Am. Psychol.* 31:209–27

Thompson, R. F., Steinmetz, J. E., Chapman, P. F. 1987. Appropriate lesions of the interpositus nucleus completely and permanently abolish the conditioned eyelid/NM response in the rabbit. *Soc. Neurosci. Abstr.* 13:801

Tocco, G., Devgan, K. K., Hauge, S. A., Weiss, C., Baudry, M., Thompson, R. F. 1991. Classical conditioning selectively increases AMPA/Quisqualate receptor binding in rabbit hippocampus. *Brain Res.* 559:331–36

Tsukahara, N. 1981. Synaptic plasticity in the mammalian central nervous system. *Annu. Rev. Neurosci.* 4:351–79

Tsukahara, N. 1982. Classical conditioning mediated by the red nucleus in the cat. See Woody 1982, pp. 223–31

Turner, B. H., Zimmer, J. 1984. The architecture and some of the interconnections of the rat's amygdala and lateral periallocortex. *J. Comp. Neurol.* 227:540–57

Voneida, T., Christie, D., Boganski, R., Chopko, B. 1990. Changes in instrumentally and classically conditioned limb-flexion responses following inferior olivary lesions and olivocerebellar tractotomy in the cat. *J. Neurosci.* 10:3583–93

Wagner, A. R. 1981. SOP: a model of automatic memory processing in animal behavior. In *Information Processing in Animals: Memory Mechanisms,* ed. N. E. Spear, R. R. Miller, pp. 5–47. Hillsdale, NJ: Lawrence Erlbaum

Wagner, A. R., Brandon, S. E. 1989. Evolution of a structured connectionist model of Pavlovian conditioning (AESOP). In *Contemporary Learning Theories: Pavlovian Conditioning and the Status of Traditional Learning Theory,* ed. S. B. Klein, R. R. Mowrer, pp. 149–90. Hillsdale, NJ: Lawrence Erlbaum

Wagner, A. R., Donegan, N. H. 1989. Some relationships between a computational model (SOP) and a neural circuit for Pavlovian (rabbit eyeblink) conditioning. See Hawkins & Bower 1989, pp. 157–203

Watson, P. J. 1978. Nonmotor functions of the cerebellum. *Psychol. Bull.* 85:944–67

Weinberger, N. M. 1982. Sensory plasticity and learning: the magnocellular medial geniculate nucleus of the auditory system. See Woody 1982, pp. 697–710

Weinberger, N. M., Hopkins, W., Diamond, D. M. 1984. Physiological plasticity of single neurons in auditory cortex of the cat during acquisition of the pupillary conditioned response: I. Primary field (AI). *Behav. Neurosci.* 98:171–88

Weingarten, H., White, N. 1978. Exploration evoked by electrical stimulation of the amygdala in rats. *Physiol. Psychol.* 6:229–35

Weisz, D. J., LoTurco, J. J. 1988. Reflex facilitation of the nictitating membrane response remains after cerebellar lesions. *Behav. Neurosci.* 103:203–9

Welsh, J. P. 1986. *The effect of nucleus interpositus lesions on retention of the rabbit's classically conditioned nictitating membrane response.* MS thesis, Univ. Iowa, Iowa City

Welsh, J. P., Harvey, J. A. 1989a. Cerebellar lesions and the nictitating membrane reflex: performance deficits of the conditioned and unconditioned response. *J. Neurosci.* 9:299–311

Welsh, J. P., Harvey, J. A. 1989b. Intra-cerebellar lidocaine: dissociation of learning from performance. *Soc. Neurosci. Abstr.* 15:639

Woody, C. D., ed. 1982. *Conditioning: Representation of Involved Neural Functions.* New York: Plenum

Woody, C. D. 1986. Understanding the cellular basis of memory and learning. *Annu. Rev. Psychol.* 37:433–93

Woody, C. D., Gruen, E., Birt, D. 1991. Changes in membrane currents during Pavlovian conditioning of single cortical neurons. *Brain Res.* 539:76–84

Woody, C. D., Knispel, J. D., Crow, T. J., Black-Clewarth, P. A. 1976. Activity and excitability of current of cortical auditory receptive field neurons of awake cats as affected by stimulus association. *J. Neurophysiol.* 39:1045–61

Woody, C. D., Yarowsky, P., Owens, J., Black-Clewarth, P., Crow, T. 1974. Effect of lesions of coronal motor areas on acquisition of conditioned eye blink in the cat. *J. Neurophysiol.* 37:385–94

Woodruff-Pak, D. S., Lavond, D. G., Thompson, R. F. 1985. Trace conditioning: abolished by cerebellar nuclear lesions but not lateral cerebellar cortex aspirations. *Brain Res.* 348:249–60

Yeo, C. H. 1991. Cerebellum and classical conditioning of motor responses. *Ann. NY Acad. Sci.* 627:292–305

Yeo, C. H., Hardiman, M. J., Glickstein, M.

1984. Discrete lesions of the cerebellar cortex abolish the classically conditioned nictitating membrane response of the rabbit. *Behav. Brain Res.* 13:261–66

Yeo, C. H., Hardiman, M. J., Glickstein, M. 1985a. Classical conditioning of the nictitating membrane response of the rabbit. I. Lesions of the cerebellar nuclei. *Exp. Brain Res.* 60:87–98

Yeo, C. H., Hardiman, M. J., Glickstein, M. 1985b. Classical conditioning of the nictitating membrane response of the rabbit. II. Lesions of the cerebellar cortex. *Exp. Brain Res.* 60:99–113

Yeo, C. H., Hardiman, M. J., Glickstein, M. 1986. Classical conditioning of the nictitating membrane response of the rabbit. IV. Lesions of the inferior olive. *Exp. Brain Res.* 63:81–92

Yeo, C. H., Hardiman, M. J., Glickstein, M., Russell, I. S. 1982. Lesions of cerebellar nuclei abolish the classically conditioned nictitating membrane response. *Soc. Neurosci. Abstr.* 8:22

Zhang, A. A., Clark, R. E., Lavond, D. G. 1990. Cooling cerebellar HVI lobule does not abolish conditioned responses. *Soc. Neurosci. Abstr.* 16:270

Zhang, A. A., Lavond, D. G. 1991. Effects of reversible lesion of reticular or facial neurons during eyeblink conditioning. *Soc. Neurosci. Abstr.* 17:869

Zhang, J. X., Harper, R. M., Ni, H. 1986. Cryogenic blockade of the central nucleus of the amygdala attenuates aversively conditioned blood pressure and respiratory responses. *Brain Res.* 386:136–45

Annu. Rev. Psychol. 1993. 44:343–81

INDIVIDUALITY AND DIVERSITY: Theory and Research in Counseling Psychology

Nancy E. Betz

Department of Psychology, The Ohio State University, 1885 Neil Avenue, Columbus, Ohio 43210

Louise F. Fitzgerald

Departments of Psychology and Educational Psychology, University of Illinois, 1310 South Sixth Street, Champaign, Illinois 61820

KEYWORDS: gender, racial/ethnic minorities, gay, lesbian, bisexual

CONTENTS

GENDER ISSUES: RESEARCH RELEVANT TO COUNSELING WOMEN 346
   Career Development.. 346
   Eating Disorders.. 350
   Sexual Violence... 352
   Therapist Attitudes and Behaviors.. 355
GENDER ISSUES: RESEARCH RELEVANT TO COUNSELING MEN........................... 357
   Male Socialization: The Hazards of Being Male 357
   Men in Therapy: A Difficult Relationship.. 358
   Assessment: The Measure of Man... 360
   Male Violence: The Missing Variable? 361
RACIAL, ETHNIC, AND CULTURALLY DIVERSE POPULATIONS 362
   Counseling and Psychotherapy with Diverse Populations 362
   Multicultural Issues in Training 364
   Research Comment.. 366
RESEARCH ON COUNSELING ISSUES WITH GAY, LESBIAN, AND
   BISEXUAL INDIVIDUALS.. 367
   From Pathology to Diversity 367
   Defining Sexual Orientation 368
   Therapist and Client Attitudes 369
   Research on Gay and Lesbian Lifestyles 371
POSTSCRIPT 373

343

The individual-differences tradition in counseling psychology is … a generalized expectation that each person is different and unique, … a belief that individual differences are matters of degree and not kind, … a confidence in the compensatory capabilities of human beings, … a tolerance for deviation, … awareness of bias, … [and] an abiding respect for the individual.

R. V. Dawis (1992)

The beginnings of counseling psychology can be traced to the psychology of individual differences and the attendant technology of applied psychometrics or psychological measurement (Dawis 1992; Whitely 1984). In one of a series of special reviews commissioned in honor of the centennial of the American Psychological Association (APA), Dawis describes the history and development of the individual-differences tradition in counseling psychology, noting its beginnings in the laboratories of Galton and Cattell, the applied contributions of Binet and the Army psychologists of WWI, and the definitive contributions of what Dawis modestly labels the "Minnesota tradition."

Differential psychology has not, of course, been without its darker side; much of its celebrated focus on individuality and the liberatory ability of psychological assessment to identify talent among the socially disenfranchised has borne a decided within-group focus, the group of course consisting of white men of Western European descent. The use of individual-differences theory and research to rationalize oppressive social arrangements by supplying a person-centered explanation for the disadvantaged status of Blacks, women, and other minority groups has been documented by Gould (1981), Shields (1975), Russett (1989), and others, and apparently continues in some quarters to this day [see, for example, Gordon et al (1988) and Gottfredson (1988), more generally].

Still, neither the politics nor polemics have been one-sided, and as Dawis (1992) has noted, "criticism of individual-differences research on intelligence by persons with strong ideological ties has tainted such research to the extent that many practitioners have been effectively discouraged from using any individual-differences findings at all" (p. 17). He notes that the need to come to terms with cultural pluralism or diversity, transcend ethnocentrism, and develop cultural empathy overshadows other challenges faced by the discipline today. His reading of this issue is a pessimistic one, as he concludes that individual-differences research bearing on cultural diversity has to date had little impact on counseling-psychology practice.

We agree that the issues of diversity and cultural pluralism are prominent ones for counseling psychology, but our reading of the research is more optimistic. Indeed, it seems to us that diversity is one of the most (if not the most) vigorous areas of practice-related theory and research today. Research addressing the counseling needs of women and of racial/ethnic minority groups has burgeoned in the past 10 years, followed more recently by interest in the specific needs of men and of gay, lesbian, and bisexual individuals. In addition, two other major individual-differences variables, age and disability status, are beginning to appear in the literature, although these continue to receive much less attention than they deserve.

This focus on diversity is also paralleled more generally within psychology. The 1990 and 1991 APA convention programs included diversity themes, and the APA is publishing Goodchilds' (1992) *Psychological Perspectives on Diversity in America.* Journals devoted to what are sometimes (misleadingly) called "special groups" are well established (e.g. *Psychology of Women Quarterly, Journal of Multicultural Counseling and Development*), and the APA has published an important discussion of ethnic and cultural considerations in graduate training (Myers et al 1991).

To reflect the importance and vigor of this perspective in counseling (and psychology more generally), our review focuses on recent work pertaining to the influence of variables such as gender, race, ethnicity, and sexual orientation on counseling and career psychology. We consider these to be stimulus variables as well as organismic or person variables. Much of their influence derives from their social-stimulus value and its importance for individual experience.

Because of the nature of our subject, our coverage of journals is of necessity somewhat broader than has been true of previous reviews. We cover, of course, the core journals in counseling psychology: the *Journal of Counseling Psychology, The Counseling Psychologist,* and the *Journal of Vocational Behavior.* In addition, we have selectively examined the *American Psychologist, Journal of Counseling and Development, Journal of Consulting and Clinical Psychology, Psychotherapy, Orthopsychiatry, Career Development Quarterly, Journal of College Student Development,* and *Measurement and Evaluation in Counseling and Development,* as well as journals relevant to specific groups (e.g. *Psychology of Women Quarterly, Sex Roles,* and *Journal of Multicultural Counseling and Development*). Our review aims to be critical and integrative, rather than exhaustive, for we seek to discover questions as well as answer them as we review what is currently known of diversity and pluralism, which we view as the intellectual heir to the individual-differences tradition in counseling psychology.

We begin by noting several major published or forthcoming works. In 1990, Gelso & Fassinger (1990) noted an explosion within counseling psychology of high quality integrative reviews on specific topics, a trend that continued in the late 1980s and early 1990s. Edited volumes by Watkins & Schneider (1991) and Watkins & Campbell (1990) appeared, as did several major new books (Atkinson & Hackett 1988; Gelso & Fretz 1992). The area of career psychology continued to grow with the appearance of several new books (Brown & Brooks 1990; Spokane 1991) and the continuation of the Walsh & Osipow series on *Advances in Vocational Psychology* (e.g. Walsh & Osipow 1988, 1990). The second edition of the *Handbook of Counseling Psychology* (Brown & Lent 1992) also appeared. To commemorate the 20th anniversary of the founding of the *Journal of Vocational Behavior,* the 1991 volumes contained reviews of 20 years of research in various areas of vocational behavior. Finally, to acknowledge the centennial of the APA, a special series of reviews were published in the *Journal of Counseling Psychology* in 1992. These articles cover the individual-differences tradition in counseling psychology (Dawis 1992), applications of social psychology to counseling psychology (Strong et al 1992), applications of personality and developmental theories (Gelso & Fassinger 1992), and the sociocultural context of the field (Howard 1992).

GENDER ISSUES: RESEARCH RELEVANT TO COUNSELING WOMEN

The psychology of gender and its implications for counseling may well be the fastest-growing area within counseling psychology today. Although we have separated research related to counseling women from that related to counseling men, we are cognizant of the current preference of many in this area to refer to a "psychology of gender" and "gender issues in counseling" (e.g. Gilbert 1992; Gilbert & Osipow 1991). Such terminology emphasizes the conceptualization of gender as a social psychological construction and reflects its importance as a stimulus variable influencing individuals' interactions with others (Gilbert 1992).

We focus in the present section on three of the most vigorous and programmatic areas of research relevant to counseling women: career development, mental-health issues primarily affecting women (in this case, eating disorders and sexual violence), and factors influencing the process and outcome of counseling with female clients.

Career Development

Our coverage here is brief, not only because of space limitations but also because research on career development/vocational behavior is reviewed annually in two major journals, the *Journal of Vocational Behavior* and *Career Development Quarterly*. Following Crites (1969), Betz & Fitzgerald (1987), and others, we have organized the research on women's career development appearing between 1989 and 1991 under the headings of career choice and career adjustment, and emphasized work that is theory-based and programmatic.

CAREER CHOICE   Recent research in this area continued to focus on individual and background variables related to women's aspirations and career salience/commitment, including vocational interests (e.g. Douce & Hansen 1990; Lapan et al 1990), values (Scozzaro & Subich 1990; Tinsley & Tinsley 1989), personality variables (Matsui et al 1991; Mazen & Lemkau 1990), and family factors (Fitzpatrick & Silverman 1989). As is typically the case, few of these studies have been integrative in nature; thus, Fassinger's (1990) use of structural-equation modeling to examine how multiple background and individual variables were related to constructs describing the nature of career orientation and preferences is noteworthy.

Two important lines of research concerning the role played by gender in the career decision-making process continued to influence the field. The first of these is Gottfredson's (1981) theory concerning the influence of occupational gender-typing on the circumscription of career options and subsequent compromises in career choice. Second, Hackett & Betz's (1981) proposal that gender-role socialization influences women's career choices primarily because it leads to lowered career-related self-efficacy expectations (originally from Bandura 1977) generated considerable research.

The heuristic value of Gottfredson's (1981) theory has recently been increased by several methodological improvements related to assessing its constructs. With respect to circumscription, Leung & Harmon (1990) provided a measure of the zone of acceptable alternatives, and Hesketh et al (1989) operationalized the range of acceptability for occupational sex type, prestige, and interests. Leung & Plake (1990) and Hesketh et al's (1990b) use of pair comparisons (of fuzzy ratings) and Henderson et al (1988) and Holt's (1989) refinement of ranking methods provided means of studying the compromise process that take into account the nonindependence of sex type, prestige, and interests (most glaringly, the linkage of feminine sex-typing with lower-prestige occupations) (Hesketh et al 1990a).

Results based on these assessment methods have demonstrated a need for modifications in Gottfredson's theory. For example, contrary to the postulate that the range of vocational alternatives is circumscribed with increasing age, Leung & Harmon (1990) reported that the number of acceptable alternatives actually increased from early childhood through adolescence, stabilizing about age 18. In addition, several variables appear to moderate both the nature and extent of circumscription. Research findings consistently suggest that sex type may limit boys' choices more than girls, who are much more likely to prefer and choose counter-stereotypic careers than are boys (Hannah & Kahn 1989; Henderson et al 1988; Leung & Harmon 1990). Leung & Harmon found that the range of alternatives varies as a function of gender-role orientation, with androgynous individuals most flexible with respect to both occupational sex type and prestige preferences. Henderson et al (1988) found that ability was more closely related to prestige preferences than was social background (SES).

Gottfredson's (1981) postulate that when career-choice compromises are necessary individuals will sacrifice first their interests (field of work), then their desired prestige levels, and last their preferred sex type, also has not been consistently supported (Holt 1989). If anything, sex type may be the least rather than the most important factor. The research of Hesketh and her colleagues (Hesketh et al 1990a,b) has consistently suggested that individuals of both sexes are more willing to compromise on sex type and prestige than interests, and Leung & Plake (1990) reported that sex type was compromised before prestige except when men were forced to choose between a high-prestige feminine occupation and a low-prestige masculine occupation. Leung et al (1991) reported that family approval was more important than prestige, which was, in turn, more important than sex type.

Based on their research, Hesketh et al (1990b) propose that interests are the most salient factor in the ultimate career-choice process; contrary to Gottfredson's original developmental formulation, their research suggests that concepts acquired later (interests) in development incorporate elements of the earlier concepts (sex type) and are thus more salient because they are more inclusive. This reformulation of the theory provides a more optimistic view of possibilities for restoration of options to individuals who may earlier have rejected them, thus supporting the opportunity-vs-socialization hypothesis (see Cole & Hanson 1975). Although the validity of much of Gottfredson's theory is questionable, it continues to have considerable heuristic value for examining the processes of choice circumscription and compromise.

Hackett & Betz (1981) originally proposed low career self-efficacy expectations as an explanation for women's continued underrepresentation in male-dominated career fields; however, most career self-efficacy research in the past three years (see Hackett & Lent 1992 for a review) has concerned the general applicability of career-related cognitions of efficacy to the vocational development of both sexes. The research of Matsui and her colleagues (Matsui et al 1989; Matsui et al 1991) on Japanese college students and employed women has provided evidence for the cross-cultural generalizability of career self-efficacy. In addition, continued work on mathematics self-efficacy (e.g. Lent et al 1991) and the relationship between efficacy expectations and vocational interests (Lent et al 1989; Hackett et al 1990) has potential importance for understanding women's continued underrepresentation in scientific and technical careers (Betz 1991).

Although these two approaches continued to dominate the field during the years under reivew, research also examined the utility of Holland's (1985) theory for women (e.g. Celmer & Winer 1990; Mazen 1989). In addition, Scott & Hatalla (1990) tested the "accident theory" of vocational choice (e.g. Crites 1969), that is, the postulation that unforeseen circumstances or events, including what Bandura (1982) called "chance encounters" (p. 748) may importantly influence educational and/or occupational decisions and behaviors. In a sample of 94 women, 63% indicated that "unexpected personal events" had played a significant role in their career development; whether such a percentage would characterize a sample of men is an interesting question. Finally, several important longitudinal studies appeared during the review period, most notably Harmon's (1989) examination of cross-sectional and longitudinal data to compare developmental vs historical explanations for changes in women's career aspirations, and Jenkins' (1989) examination of the relationship of occupational aspirations to women's actual employment 14 years later.

CAREER ADJUSTMENT   Emphases in the area of women's career adjustment included the interaction of work and family roles (e.g. Loerch et al 1989) and the adjustment of women in nontraditional-career fields, especially management (Cox & Harquail 1991; Long 1989, 1990). In addition, one of the fastest-growing areas of research related to career adjustment concerned a particularly serious barrier to women's success and satisfaction in educational and career pursuits: sexual harassment. Recent work focused on providing more systematic description and measurement of experiences of harassment, including the development and programmatic study of the sexual experiences questionnaire (SEQ) (Fitzgerald et al 1988; as fully described in Beere 1990a). The SEQ measures the five dimensions of sexual-harassment behaviors originally postulated by Till (1980) and ordered on a rough continuum of severity: gender harassment (i.e. gender-related insults and putdowns), seduction, sexual bribery, sexual coercion, and sexual imposition. Factor analyses using both college-student and employed samples indicate that individuals generally do perceive five separate types of harassment (Fitzgerald & Ormerod 1991); however, the actual experience of harassment seems to comprise three major dimensions (gender harassment, seductive or sexual behavior, and sexual coercion) (Fitzgerald et al 1988). Multidimensional scaling of pair comparisons of harassment stimulus situations yielded the familiar five types, embedded within a two-dimensional solution (type and severity), with gender harassment emerging as a distinct construct (Fitzgerald & Hesson-McInnis 1989). The importance of this work arises from the systematic attention given to theory and sound methods of scale construction, issues which had previously been relatively ignored in this area.

A related area of work has examined by whom and when a particular behavior will be perceived as harassing. Lee & Heppner (1991) have developed a measure of sensitivity to both sexual and nonsexual harassing behaviors [see Beere (1990a) for descriptions of existing instruments]. Consistent with earlier research, most recent work confirms that women are more likely than men to perceive a given incident as harassing (Fitzgerald & Ormerod 1991), especially when it involves gender harassment, including sexist jokes and demeaning comments. Those with more liberal gender-role ideologies are also more likely to perceive a given incident as harassment relative to more traditional individuals (Brooks & Perot 1991; Malovich & Stake 1990). Also, severity, explicitness, and the degree of prior relationship between harasser and victim influence appraisal, although whether or not a faculty member had explicit decision-making power over a student was unrelated to harassment perceptions in a university setting (Fitzgerald & Ormerod 1991).

Perceptions of harassment are especially important because they may influence emotional and behavioral consequences. The impact of sexual harassment on women's lives is nothing less than traumatic (Koss 1990), but the nature of responses may influence not only the emotional and career outcomes for the woman but the consequences for the perpetrator as well. For example, Brooks & Perot (1991) examined a model designed to predict the reporting of sexual harassment in a large sample of women faculty and graduate students. Feminist ideology and frequency of behavior were positively related to perceived offensiveness of behavior, which, in turn, was directly related to the likelihood of reporting. Malovich & Stake (1990) reported that nontraditional gender-role attitudes were related to a tendency to blame the perpetrator (as opposed to the victim) and to preference for confrontive vs compliant responses.

Another potentially productive line of research involves examination of environmental, organizational, or situational variables that may serve to sustain sexual-harassment behaviors (Baker 1989). In two studies, higher levels of sexual harassment were associated with low numbers of women in the work group (Baker 1989) and, in universities, with more permissive departmental norms concerning sexual contact between faculty and students (Bond 1988). More generally, what is needed at this time are integrative models postulating how characteristics of the victim, harassing behavior, and organizational context influence coping responses as well as the ways in which these influence educational, career, and psychological outcomes for the victim. Fitzgerald & Ormerod (in press) propose one such integrative model, which should prove heuristically useful; additional models as well as prospective designs and those permitting causal analysis are badly needed.

Eating Disorders

Within the counseling research literature, eating disorders have probably received more research attention in the past three to five years than any other disorder, probably because counseling psychology has always been closely associated with higher education—given the prevalence of eating disorders among college women (Mintz & Betz 1988), such attention is thus not surprising. In addition to anorexia and bulimia nervosa, chronic dieting, purging, obsession with food, and poor body image are pervasive problems among American women. Although recent studies indicate that between 2% and 18% of college women now meet *Diagnostic and Statistical Manual* (DSM-III-R) criteria for bulimia, a large majority of the remainder exhibit one or more symptoms of disordered eating (Mintz & Betz 1988). The problem is severe enough to justify the assertion that, at least among middle-class women, disordered eating appears to be the rule rather than the exception (Gilbert 1992). The importance of this topic is evidenced by the appearance of the *International Journal of Eating Disorders* in 1982 and the frequent development of new measures of body image and eating attitudes and behaviors—Beere (1990b) lists 17 measures of body image and appearance and 20 of eating attitudes and behaviors.

Considerable research attention has recently been directed at the assessment and differentiation of levels of this disorder and of psychological characteristics predictive of subclinical vs clinical forms. Consistent differences in pathology are found when individuals who fully meet DSM-III-R criteria for bulimia are compared to chronic dieters, bingers, and normal eaters. The most frequent and important finding is of significantly greater pathology (including depression, negative cognitions and attributions, anxiety, and low self-esteem) among bulimics vs other groups (Klemchuk et al 1990; Mintz & Betz 1988; Etringer et al 1989; Laessle et al 1989). Also important are findings of lower levels of perceived problem-solving and coping ability (Etringer et al 1989), more difficulty with interpersonal relationships (Thelen et al 1990), and disturbed family interactions (Humphrey 1989).

Klemchuk et al (1990) found that a group of college women reporting extreme body dissatisfaction but without binge/purge symptoms could be differentiated from a bulimic group by their much poorer psychological adjustment, as indicated by several scales of the eating disorders inventory (EDI) (Garner et al 1983). In a somewhat similar vein, Laessle et al (1989), also using the EDI, suggest applying the two-component model of anorexia (from Garner et al 1984) to the conceptualization of bulimia nervosa. The components include: (a) intense concern over weight, body image, and appearance, with a concomitant tendency to lose control over eating, and (b) a pathological constellation of characteristics including ineffectiveness, interpersonal distrust, and distorted interoceptive awareness. Based on this work, Klemchuk et al suggested using the EDI to identify and differentiate chronic dieters (or other subclinical groups) with severe body dissatisfaction from bulimics. Different interventions would be suggested for these groups; however, discerning the roles, if any, such body dissatisfaction and chronic severe dieting play in the subsequent development of bulimia nervosa is critical. Findings such as those of Thelen et al (1990) that a subclinical bulimic group showed fewer rather than more symptoms over a 19-month follow-up period suggest the possibility that it is in the presence of other problems that female obsession with food and appearance turns into full-blown bulimia.

Studies of this type are often plagued by methodological difficulties, most usually inappropriate suggestions of causality, small Ns, elevated experiment-wise error, and the assumption that university students, when used as a comparison group to patients, are disease-free (researchers rarely actually assess symptomatology and eliminate disordered control-group subjects). In addition, more attention to theoretical issues and use of longitudinal research or structural-modeling procedures are needed to explicate the complex relationships of negative cognitions, depression, and interpersonal ineffectiveness to bulimia.

Also critical is attention to the potentially causal role played by societal emphasis on beauty and thinness as a measure of women's worth (Gilbert 1992). Mintz & Betz (1988) reported that the extent of disordered eating in 682 college students was strongly associated with the tendency to endorse sociocultural norms regarding female attractiveness and thinness as a measure of worth. The sociocultural emphasis on beauty and thinness as the sine qua non of female value may be causally related not only to bulimia and disordered eating but to associated features of depression, low self-esteem, and ineffectiveness. Research into these connections is badly needed. In addition, some writers have suggested an association between childhood sexual abuse (whose victims are most often female) and the subsequent development of eating disorders (Root & Fallon 1988). As these authors suggest, incest may cause not only disordered eating behavior but the associated features of depression and troubled interpersonal relationships as well. Other researchers, employing object-relations concepts to understand the development of eating disorders, reported that dependency conflicts and functional impairment along with a general diminished sense of individuality were related to bulimic behaviors and pursuit of thinness (Friedlander & Siegel 1990); Heesacker & Niemeyer (1990) found that higher levels of disordered eating were related to measures of "insecure attachment" and "social incompetence," ambivalent and painful interpersonal relationships, fear of abandonment, and almost desperate longings for closeness.

Although this area of the literature is developing rapidly, we need more comprehensive formulations of the etiology of eating disorders, formulations that have implications not only for treatment but also for the prevention of these disorders. Given that age of onset is usually adolescence and young adulthood, preventive efforts directed at these groups should have high research priority. Cognitive-behavioral treatments have considerable efficacy in the treatment of bulimia nervosa (Agras et al 1989; Garner et al 1987; Fairburn 1988; Craighead & Agras 1991) and binge behavior (Telch et al 1990). Fairburn (1988) reviews the status of psychological treatments, and Craighead & Agras (1991) review cognitive-behavioral and pharmacological treatments. Recent research has compared cognitive-behavioral to response prevention treatments (Agras et al 1989), and compared brief group psychoeducation vs no treatment for bulimics (Davis et al 1990). In the latter study, the increasingly used criterion of "clinically significant change" (e.g. Jacobson & Revenstorf 1988) rather than only "statistical significance" was employed. Clinically significant change is defined as change that renders the treated subjects more similar on major dependent variables to normal than to afflicted subjects. In Davis et al's study, statistically significant change was observed on all dependent variables, both symptom measures (e.g. binge/purge behavior), and associated personality dysfunctions (e.g. depression, ineffectiveness), but only the former measures showed clinically significant change in a reasonably large number of subjects. The analysis and reporting of clinically significant change should be encouraged in future treatment research.

Sexual Violence

Women are disproportionately the targets of sexual violence, and the mental-health effects and counseling implications of this violence have become a major research priority (Frazier & Cohen 1992; Koss 1990). In addition to sexual harassment, covered in a previous section, recent research has focused on the prevalence and consequences of rape, including acquaintance rape, and of childhood sexual abuse, including incest. McCann et al (1988) reviews the long-term effects of rape, incest, and other types of trauma and victimization, which include, but are not limited to, fear and anxiety, which is often generalized beyond the attack situation; low self-esteem; depression; loss of a sense of control in one's life; anger; sexual dysfunction; and difficulties in intimate relationships, especially those with men.

Recent research has examined variables mediating the effects of sexual assault on subsequent functioning, on relating treatments to theories of the effects of sexual assault, and on therapists' attitudes toward sexual assault and the implications of these for treatment. Both circumstantial and individual-differences variables have been examined as mediators of the psychological effects of assault. The circumstantial variables of severity of abuse and degree of closeness to the offender have also received research attention. More severe victimization, including repeated rapes within one incident, is consistently related to more negative psychological outcomes (Wyatt et al 1990; Wyatt & Newcomb 1990). Closeness to the offender was related to negative outcomes of incest in Wyatt & Newcomb's (1990) study but not in that of Draucker (1989). Koss et al (1988) compared the experiences of victims of stranger rape with those of victims of rapes by acquaintances ranging in closeness from nonromantic acquaintances to casual dates, steady dates, spouses, and family members, and found similar degrees of adverse psychological reactions. The most violent rapes, however, were those by strangers or, poignantly, family members or spouses.

The most potent individual-differences mediator of rape outcome appears to be the tendency toward self-blame, which shows a significant relationship to continued negative outcomes such as depression (e.g. Frazier 1991) and negative attitudes toward sex and intimacy (Wyatt et al 1990). Wyatt & Newcomb (1990) reported that self-blame and nondisclosure predicted negative outcomes following incest as well. Their research (Wyatt & Newcomb 1990; Wyatt et al 1990) is based on a model postulating both direct and mediated effects of circumstantial variables, in which the mediators were individual-differences/response variables. This and other such integrative models hold considerable promise for understanding the consequences of rape. For example, the model proposed by McCann et al (1988) postulates that schemas regarding safety, trust, power, esteem, and intimacy are negatively affected by violence or trauma, which in turn negatively affects adaptation; their work has much potential for understanding the effects of violence and the treatment of survivors.

Koss & Burkhart (1989) caution, however, that the tendency to blame oneself also allows the maintenance of the illusion of personal control, which is vital to the recovery of assault survivors; therefore, therapist discouragement of self-blame must be accompanied by strategies that restore a sense of personal control and mastery. Ozer & Bandura (1990) addressed this issue and demonstrated that a mastery program modeling control over sexually coercive and assaultive situations led to significant increases in coping self-efficacy. Although interpreted cautiously, follow-up data indicated that of women who had completed the program and were later assaulted, 95% (an unusually high proportion) successfully evaded the assault.

There has also been recent interest in factors that may heighten the risk of rape to any individual woman. Consistent with previous research in this area, the data of Koss & Dinero (1989), in a study of a nationally representative sample of 2,723 college women, supported the predictive power of prior (usually childhood) sexual abuse and vulnerability-enhancing factors, i.e. greater sexual activity and alcohol use. These variables, along with more liberal sex-role attitudes, accounted for virtually all the discriminating power of a high-risk profile describing women significantly more likely to be raped (37% vs 14% of those not fitting it). However, it is important to note that in the vast majority of instances, rape victims were no different from nonvictims on critical risk variables; thus, it is inappropriate to seek explanations for rape in victims' behavior.

Little research has focused on the comparative efficacy of different treatments, variables influencing treatment response, or, most importantly, ways in which treatment components relate to theories of the posttrauma adaptation process (see Dye & Roth 1991). Recent comparative outcome research includes that of Alexander & Follette and their colleagues. Alexander et al (1989) compared two group treatments, as well as a wait-list control, in the treatment of adult survivors of incest; significant reductions in depression and distress at both treatment conclusion and follow-up were reported by the treated subjects in comparison to the controls, although the maintenance of gains at follow-up may have resulted at least partially from the large number of subjects seeking individual therapy after group treatment concluded. In a subsequent study, Follette et al (1991) noted that women with less education, currently married women, women with lower initial levels of adjustment, and those who had experienced oral-genital abuse or intercourse (vs "simply" fondling or genital touching) made smaller gains in group therapy treatment. Dye & Roth (1991) reviewed research concerning the efficacy of cognitive-behavioral, group, and psychoanalytic treatment with incest survivors, concluding that there is evidence for the efficacy of the former two approaches, but not the latter.

In attempts to connect treatment to theory, several researchers have conceptualized the psychological sequelae of rape as post-traumatic stress disorder (PTSD), included in the DSM-III-R since 1980. Foa et al (1991) compared stress inoculation training (SIT), prolonged exposure (PE), supportive counseling, and a wait-list control, reporting that SIT was superior in reducing PTSD symptoms at posttreatment, whereas PE was superior at follow-up. Although some researchers find the concept of PTSD useful, Koss & Burkhart (1989) note that sexual assault differs from other traumatic events in that rape is an interpersonal event—"a malevolent, personally directed event ... directed, focused, intentional harm involving the most intimate interpersonal act" (p. 31)—and one embedded in a societal belief system based on victim-blaming. Given the essential differences between sexual assault and other forms of victimization, a high priority for research should be to develop a better understanding of the long term cognitive-emotional responses associ-ated with sexual assault (Koss & Burkhart 1989). This priority implies a need for longitudinal research, as well as retrospective studies, in addition to the more typical investigations conducted within a year or so after the assault.

Therapist Attitudes and Behaviors

In addition to a focus on concerns that either uniquely or predominantly affect women, work has continued on how counselors view and treat women clients. Following the report of the APA Task Force on Sex Bias and Sex Role Stereotyping (1975), researchers attempted to examine the existence of the four kinds of therapist bias, i.e. fostering of traditional sex roles, bias in expectations of and devaluation of women, sexist use of psychoanalytic con-cepts, and response to women as sex objects, including seduction of female clients. With the exception of the last category, research evidence for the existence of sex bias in psychotherapy has provided few clear-cut conclusions (e.g. Stricker & Shafran 1983).

One factor that does not seem to be in doubt, however, is the continuing occurrence and harmful effects of sex between therapists and clients. Because samples in both case-study and survey-research methodologies can be as-sumed to be self-selecting, although not in known ways (see Williams 1992), estimates of prevalence and extent of harm apply to these volunteer samples rather than to the population at large. However, in Pope's (1990) review of research, 1 out of 10 male and 1 out of 50 female therapists report erotic contact with patients; overall, 90% of therapist-patient sexual activity involves male therapists and female clients. Gilbert (1992) noted that sexual intimacy between therapists and clients accounted for 25% of all ethics violations in 1988, more than twice the number reported for any other category of the ethical principles. There is mounting evidence that this practice is harmful to clients, both present and former (see e.g. Pope 1988). Pope & Vetter (1991) reported that female patients felt harmed by such relationships 90% of the time when the relationships occurred prior to termination of therapy and 80% of the time after termination. Findings such as these have led to a statement in the ethical principles that it is unethical for a therapist to have sexual intimacies with a current or former client. Williams (1992) suggests the need for com-prehensive tracking of ethics complaints filed with various sources (e.g. ethics committees, licensing boards, and civil and criminal courts) as a means of observing changes over time in the prevalence of this behavior.

More productive than further research on therapist bias is work based on theoretical statements related to the mechanism by which client gender influ-ences counselor behavior and on statements that examine client and counselor gender interactions. For example, Fisher (1989) suggests that a productive focus of research attention involves the view of gender as a stimulus variable influencing the processing of information about people, most importantly, patients. This approach might be useful in the continuing examination and rectification of possible biases in the assignment of women and men to DSM-III-R diagnostic categories. Fisher (1989) also reviewed research suggesting that female-female counselor-client pairings are most consistently effective, and that same-gender pairs in general achieve greater therapeutic gains. Although use of therapist/client gender pairings, both same and cross-gender, in research is important, it will be most profitable if theories of the mechanisms by which these pairings affect process and outcome variables can be articulated. Fisher (1989) reported that regardless of client sex, female therapists tended to blame themselves for problems in the therapeutic relationship, whereas male therapists tended to blame their patients. Because patient-blaming was related to a lack of improvement, this suggests one explanation for the lesser effectiveness of male therapists. Patient-blaming constitutes, in essence, a gender-related individual-differences variable (Cook 1990) that could prove useful on an explanatory, as well as a predictive, level.

Another productive area for research is an evaluation of feminist therapeutic approaches. Generally speaking, feminist therapeutic approaches (e.g. Enns & Hackett 1990; Good et al 1990) share several common emphases with the Division 17 Principles for the Counseling/Psychotherapy of Women (APA, Ad Hoc Committee on Women, Division 17, 1979), which were subsequently endorsed by all other APA Divisions concerned with psychotherapeutic treatment (Gilbert & Osipow 1991). These principles emphasize, among other things, transcendence of traditional gender roles in counselors' expectations of clients and models of mental health, cognizance of the effects of gender-role socialization and sociocultural expectations on women's development and functioning, and the necessity of being knowledgeable about the vast individual differences among women, including such variables as race/ethnicity, sexual/affectional preference, age, and disability.

Glidden & Tracey (1989) examined the feminist therapy postulate that clients should not be blamed for societally caused problems using Brickman et al's (1982) model of attributions in counseling, which suggested two dimensions of attributions: the source for the problem (labeled blame) and the source of a solution (labeled control). Feminist therapies would externalize blame (to society) while internalizing control, that is, they emphasize personal responsibility for the solution. Glidden & Tracey (1989) exposed female college students to videotapes portraying counseling for issues of weight and body image—one tape focused on external attributions (society's unrealistic expectations of women) and the other focused on personal causes (poor eating habits related to a negative self-image). Contrary to the expectation that women with profeminist beliefs would be more receptive to feminist approaches in counseling (McNamara & Rickard 1989), nontraditional gender-role attitudes were correlated with preference for the personal explanation, while the sociocultural explanation was preferred by traditional women (probably, as suggested by the authors, because each group profited from an explanation somewhat novel to them). In a carefully designed study, Enns & Hackett (1990) compared the reactions of 150 feminist and nonfeminist college women to videotaped portrayals of liberal-feminist, radical-feminist, and nonsexist-humanistic female counselors. Results indicated that both feminist and nonfeminist women preferred the feminist counselors for career and sexual assault–harassment concerns, and that the counselors were equally preferred for personal-interpersonal concerns. The more positive reactions of these participants to feminist counselors, compared with results reported in some earlier studies, likely resulted from the naturalistic videotape portrayals vs the more usual written announcements or descriptions of counseling services.

Although these studies represent a beginning, further comparative process and outcome research is needed. Enns & Hackett (1990) suggest, in addition, the use of naturalistic investigations of client reactions to feminist counselors, more rigorous use of such potential moderators as feminist beliefs and identity development, and the comparison of feminist therapies to other directive approaches such as cognitive-behavioral therapies. In this regard, one should note that feminism is not in itself a theoretical approach, but rather a perspective congruent with any nonbiologically based theory of intervention, e.g. cognitive-behavioral, Gestalt, client-centered, etc. Thus, feminist and cognitive-behavioral approaches could well be integrated by a given therapist.

GENDER ISSUES: RESEARCH RELEVANT TO COUNSELING MEN

In 1978, *The Counseling Psychologist* published an issue devoted to the topic "Counseling Men." Stimulated by the women's movement, as well as by a nascent movement towards men's liberation, this first collection of articles introduced the main themes that continue to characterize the literature in this area today: the prescriptive nature of masculine socialization (with a particular focus on restricted emotionality) and the impact of such socialization on the therapeutic encounter, including men's lesser willingness to participate in psychotherapy.

Male Socialization: The Hazards of Being Male

The Counseling Psychologist collection was followed in 1981 by an influential pair of articles by O'Neil (1981a,b) in which he synthesized this perspective, arguing that the primary outcomes of male socialization in American society are restrictive emotionality; focus on control, power, and competition; homophobia; restrictive sexual and affectionate behavior; and obsession with achievement and success. O'Neil labeled this pattern *masculine gender role conflict* and argued that despite being the normative (and in fact, idealized) version of masculine behavior in American society, it was psychologically dysfunctional for men. A series of studies appearing in the years covered by this review suggest that his analysis has merit.

Sharpe & Heppner (1991) found that scores on the gender-role conflict scale (GRCS), a measure of O'Neil's constructs (O'Neil et al 1986), were positively related to anxiety and depression and negatively related to self-esteem and social intimacy in a sample of college men. Similarly, Good & Mintz (1990) reported that GRCS scores were positively correlated with depression (although the sizes of the effects were very small), and Cook (1990) reviewed the literature on gender and psychological distress, arguing that gender influences not only what is experienced as problematic, but also how psychological distress is manifested.

On a slightly different tack, Stillson et al (1991) reported that male gender-role conflict also predicted physical symptoms as assessed by Osipow & Spokane's (1983) Physical Strain Questionnaire. The relationship between exaggerated commitment to the male role and increased health risk has been the subject of speculation by many writers (see, for example, Pleck 1981; Silverberg 1986); additional supporting data are provided by Eisler and his colleagues (Eisler et al 1988), who reported that scores on their measure of male-role conflict (MGRS) (Eisler & Skidmore 1987) predicted not only increased anger and anxiety, but also poor health habits (e.g. tobacco and alcohol intake, seat-belt use, and other health-risk behaviors).

Eisler & Blalock (1991) have most thoroughly summarized the data relating exaggerated and inflexible masculine role commitment to a variety of psychological and physical health risks. In a thoughtful and persuasive article, these authors propose that such phenomena can be best understood from a cognitively mediated stress-and-coping perspective. They argue that masculine socialization results in what amounts to a cognitive schema in which a variety of gender-linked situations (e.g. those that are competitive, sexually challenging, or that require the expression or acceptance of emotions) are experienced by men as highly stressful. Arguing further that such socialization also limits men's coping repertoires to behaviors that are gender-sanctioned (e.g. drinking, driving fast, aggressive acting out), Eisler & Blalock conclude that masculine gender-role stress is implicated in a variety of psychological and physical problems, from men's higher rates of alcohol/drug dependence and Antisocial Personality Disorder to their higher death rates from automobile accidents and coronary heart disease (Cleary 1987, and others). Evidently, as Harrison (1978) warned some years ago, masculinity can be hazardous to one's health.

Men in Therapy: A Difficult Relationship

The second major theme in the emerging literature on the psychology of men has to do with the impact of male socialization on the psychotherapeutic encounter, particularly men's lesser willingness to participate in therapy. As far back as the original *Counseling Psychologist* collection on counseling men, the consensus in the literature has been that the requirements of the male role appear antithetical to the requirements of a "good" client, i.e. psychological mindedness, willingness to self-disclose, and a capacity for emotional intimacy. Since that time, several books have appeared devoted to men and therapy (Meth & Pasick 1990; Scher et al 1987; Silverberg 1986; Solomon & Levy 1982) as have special issues of various journals (e.g. *Journal of Counseling and Development, Psychotherapy*), all of which sound this theme to a greater or lesser degree.

Although researchers agree on the problem, less consensus surrounds the solution. Thus, one school of thought notes men's documented resistance to expressing emotion (May 1990) and to seeking psychological assistance (Good et al 1989) and argues for some form of training for men to improve their chances for success in therapy and other intimate relationships. This is similar to the approach advocated years ago for the non-YAVIS client discussed by Schofield (1964; see Orne & Wender 1968, Truax & Bloxom 1973). Along this line, Moore & Havercamp (1989) reported an interesting experimental study documenting the success of a 10-week, multimodal group intervention targeted at changing cognitive, affective, and behavioral components of expressiveness in a group of 30- to 50-year-old male volunteers. Utilizing a post-test only design, these researchers reported that the experimental group members were significantly more emotionally expressive as measured by a behavioral task and various other measures. Although the study was impressive for its rigor and promising in its outcome, its generalizability is questionable, as participants were all volunteers who answered an advertisement for a "relationship skills" group. Thus, whether such an intervention would be effective for men who had not felt a need for change is unclear. The second school of thought on this issue subscribes to a bring-the-mountain-to-Mohammed strategy, arguing that if male socialization is inimical to successful participation in psychotherapy, then it is therapy, not men, that must change. An early adherent of this view was Bruch (1978); more recently, Levant (1990) described the success of a structured psychoeducational fathering group as an example of how psychological services could be designed to capitalize on men's greater comfort with rational problem-solving approaches. Similarly, Robertson & Fitzgerald (1992) demonstrated that advertising psychological services in terms congruent with masculine socialization (e.g. problem-solving groups, career advice, self-help groups and the like) was more successful than descriptions in traditional terms in eliciting the interest and willingness of traditional college men to seek help for both personal and vocational problems.

Finally, men's resistance to emotional interaction does not account for all of the variance in their difficulties in successfully engaging the therapeutic encounter. Using a powerful interactive video methodology, Robertson & Fitzgerald (1990) reported that their sample of experienced psychotherapists diagnosed more severe pathology when a depressed male client presented with a nontraditional lifestyle (i.e. preferring the homemaker/parenting role to the breadwinner role), and the therapists were more likely to attribute his depression to this lifestyle even though the client proactively stated that he was satisfied with this aspect of his life. Reminiscent of similar studies of nontraditional women some two decades ago, this investigation reminds us again that psychotherapy continues to be in many ways an essentially conservative institution.

Assessment: The Measure of Man

The increasing acknowledgement of the gendered nature of experience and particularly the emerging interest in men as a specific group has led to the development of several scales designed to assess various aspects of the male psychological experience. The most well known and widely used of these instruments are O'Neil et al's (1986) gender role conflict scale (GRCS) and Eisler's (Eisler & Skidmore 1987) masculine gender role stress scale (MGRS). The GRCS is by far the most well known instrument within the traditional counseling psychology literature, whereas the MGRS has been employed by gender-role researchers more generally as well as within the area of stress, coping, and health.

According to O'Neil et al (1986:335), "gender role conflict is a psychological state where gender roles have negative consequences or impact on a person or others." The GRCS is a 37-item measure scored for four subscales: success, power, and competition (SPC); restricted emotionality (RE); restricted affectionate behavior between men (RA); and work/family conflict (WFC). The SPC subscale consists of 13 items tapping the salience and importance of winning; RE appears to tap distaste for emotionally tinged interactions; and RA equates generally to homophobia (e.g. "Affection with other men makes me tense"). Unlike these three scales, WFC appears to assess what is more generally meant by conflict, and contains six items specifically juxtaposing work demands to other areas of life (e.g. family, leisure, health). Internal consistency and four-week stability coefficients are acceptable, and O'Neil et al report initial validity data that have since been considerably supplemented by numerous investigations, some of which were described above.

The GRCS has proven itself to be a heuristic and fruitful contribution to the empirical literature on the male gender role. At the same time, several aspects of the scale could benefit from clarification. The first is theoretical and has to do with the term gender-role conflict. Although we are sufficiently loyal to the positivist tradition to accept the preeminence of operational definitions, we believe that, with the exception of work/family conflict, the GRCS does not appear to tap conflict as it is generally understood, i.e. as the result of two competing response tendencies. Rather, the other scales appear to assess unambivalent approach or avoidance tendencies (SPC, and RE/RA respectively). Use of the term conflict introduces a certain degree of excess meaning that may not be conceptually justified. On a more technical note, we suggest that the use of separate subscale scores appears based solely on a series of exploratory factor analyses utilizing various (and theoretically incompatible) factor extraction and rotational techniques. A confirmatory factor analysis could both strengthen the model conceptually and provide a stronger empirical base for subscale usage.

The MGRS, on the other hand, is conceptualized quite differently. Eisler & Skidmore (1987) postulate a construct of masculine gender–role stress, defined as the "cognitive appraisal of specific situations as [being] stressful for men" (p. 125); they argue that "men will experience stress when they judge themselves unable to cope with the imperatives of the male role or when a situation is viewed as requiring 'unmanly' or feminine behavior" (p. 125).

Their 40-item scale, based on extensive item-development procedures, yields 5 scores, each assessing stressful aspects of the male role: physical inadequacy (the belief that one is unable to meet standards of physical fitness and sexual prowess), emotional inexpressiveness (high scores reflect the appraisal of emotionally charged situations as stressful), subordination to women (discomfort with situations in which women are more successful or powerful), intellectual inferiority (a somewhat heterogeneous group of items reflecting discomfort in situations that appear to question one's rational abilities, ambition, or decisiveness), and performance failure (concerning potential failure in work-related or sexual situations). Eisler & Blalock's (1991) review provides persuasive evidence for the usefulness of this conceptualization of the traditional male role as a stress factor in men's lives. In addition, other instruments assessing various aspects of the male role have appeared (e.g. Brannon & Juni 1984; Downs & Engleson 1982; and others), suggesting that the literature in this area may be ripe for a thorough review.

Male Violence: The Missing Variable?

The increasing realization that men's experience, like that of women, is a gendered, rather than a universal, nonsituated given, has been one of the more important theoretical advances in the recent literature. In reviewing this work, however, we are struck by the absence of any serious discussion of what could arguably be considered the most problematic aspect of the male role: the socialization of male violence.

Discussions of male socialization and its conflicts and stresses emphasize variables such as emotional restrictiveness and difficulties with intimacy, and generally examine interventions to assist men to live fuller psychological lives. Conspicuous by its absence is any sustained attempt to analyze and intervene in what can only be considered one of the most serious social problems of our age—male violence against women. Although such investigations are beginning to appear in the specialized literature on aggression and victimization— e.g. *Violence and Victims* and *Victimology*—these studies are generally not being conducted by counseling psychologists nor are they written about in the core counseling psychology literature. Of the several major books that have appeared on counseling men, only two devoted a chapter to treating men who batter (Scher et al 1987; Moore & Leafgren 1990), most did not index the term violence, and not one mentioned the topic of rape, despite the fact that, according to the FBI, a man commits rape every six minutes. Studies have found that as many as one-third to one-half of all men report that they would rape if they could be assured that no one would know (Check & Malamuth 1983; Krahe 1988, and others).

Only one empirical study was located that specifically addressed the issue of male sexual aggression (Gilbert et al 1991). Evaluating an intervention based on Petty & Cacioppo's elaboration likelihood model (ELM) (Petty & Cacioppo 1986), Gilbert et al reported success in altering rape-supportive attitudes in college men, changes that persisted at a one-month follow-up. Their work stands as a model of what can be accomplished through carefully designed, theoretically based interventions targeted at this important social problem. Hopefully, more researchers interested in the damaging effects of masculine socialization will begin to follow their example.

RACIAL, ETHNIC, AND CULTURALLY DIVERSE POPULATIONS

Recognition of the profound influence of race, culture, and ethnicity on individuals' life experiences and world view represents nothing less than a sea change in the ways that psychologists view their clients, their research, and their training; indeed, Pedersen (1991) has labeled the multicultural view a "fourth force" in psychology. Second in scope only to the enormous literature on women (and gender more generally) this body of work represents a fundamental transformation of a discipline in which only a few years ago "Even the Rat Was White" (Guthrie 1976). Although we cannot hope to review this literature thoroughly here, this section highlights its major themes with respect to counseling practice, training, and research.

Counseling and Psychotherapy with Diverse Populations

Recent discussions within the cross-cultural counseling literature have been organized around three major topics: racial identity development, acculturation, and counselor-client matching (Heath et al 1988; Atkinson & Thompson 1992). We adopt this framework for our own discussion, noting at the same time the appearance of important contributions in other areas, particularly career development (e.g. Arbona 1990; Leong 1991). For example, the recent emphasis on the career development of non-college-bound youth (Grant Foundation 1988), of whom a significant proportion are minority-group members, is particularly noteworthy.

RACIAL IDENTITY DEVELOPMENT   According to Helms (1990), the term racial identity development refers to a sense of collective identity that develops from an awareness of a shared racial/ethnic heritage. Most often equated with Black racial identity (BRID) (but see Atkinson et al 1989, for a more general model), the theory suggests that a psychological continuum of Black identity is marked at one pole by an acceptance of the dominant culture's devaluation of Blacks and overevaluation of Whites (PreEncounter) moving in a series of stages marked by conflict and reactivity (Encounter, Immersion/Emersion) to a self-affirming inner security and pride in one's blackness (Internalization, Commitment). The process is thought to be life long and recursive (Parham 1989) as individuals recycle through previous periods depending on life experiences and personal readiness; the stages are thought to code a process of self-actualization, and should thus theoretically be related to mental health and personal adjustment. During the period of our review, this perspective generated a major monograph (Parham 1989) and a comprehensive volume of theory and research (Helms 1990), as well as numerous empirical articles (Carter 1990; Carter & Helms 1987; Cheatham et al 1990; Ponterotto et al 1988, and others); earlier influential work includes the development of a widely used measure, BRID (Black racial identity scale) (Parham & Helms 1981), and an interactional model of counseling based on various combinations of counselor/client race and racial identity (Helms 1984).

ACCULTURATIÓN   Ponterotto & Casas (1991) point out that parallel identity work on non-Black immigrant groups has focused on acculturation (Casas 1985a,b; Ponterotto 1987, 1988), the process of change that occurs when an individual of one culture comes in contact with another (Padilla 1980). Although often thought to be unidimensional, (i.e. immigrant groups adopt the culture of the dominant group), bicultural or multicultural socialization models have also appeared, suggesting that individuals can develop ties to more than one culture and that the relative strength of those ties have important psychological implications. Well-known measures of acculturation include the acculturation rating scale for Mexican Americans (ARSMA) (Cuellar et al 1980) and the Suinn-Lew Asian self-identity acculturation scale (SL-ASIA) (Suinn et al 1987), modeled after the ARSMA.

Considerable research has been devoted to attempts to relate level of acculturation to counseling-relevant variables—counselor credibility, expectations about counseling, willingness to see a particular counselor, and so forth—in samples of Hispanics (Kunkel 1990; Pomales & Williams 1989; Ponce & Atkinson 1989) and Asian Americans (Atkinson & Gim 1989; Gim et al 1990; Gim et al 1991, and others). In their recent review of this literature, Atkinson & Thompson (1992) suggest that the research supports the usefulness of the acculturation concept in counseling research, citing support for intuitively logical relationships between acculturation and counselor credibility, preference for an ethnically similar counselor, and so forth.

COUNSELOR-CLIENT MATCH   As has much of the research on cross-cultural counseling, the work on counselor-client match has been criticized for its atheoretical nature. In an important paper marking his receipt of the APA Award for Distinguished Contributions to Science in the Public Interest, Stanley Sue (1988) reviewed 20 years of research examining the role of ethnic match in psychotherapy and concluded that, for the most part, we have been posing the wrong question. He notes that most actual treatment studies have failed to show differential outcomes (i.e. client improvement or well-being) on the basis of either client race/ethnicity or therapist-client ethnic match. Evidence of a race effect is stronger in clinical analog studies; however, such studies of necessity generally use process-dependent variables (e.g. client preferences) and suffer as well from a variety of methodological difficulties. Basing his statements on a conceptual model proposed earlier by Sue & Zane (1987), he argues that therapist ethnicity is a distal variable and, as such, is less likely to be linked to treatment outcome than factors more proximal to the therapeutic encounter. Further, he notes that ethnicity per se reveals little about the attitudes and behaviors of individuals (either therapist or client), although it may code powerful cultural meanings such as attitudes, behaviors, and ways of under-standing the world. Such cultural meanings, being more proximal to the therapy process, are more important to study than ethnicity itself. Sue & Zane suggest that this cultural match is the critical one to examine, and that it can be operationalized in terms of fit between therapist and client views of (*a*) the client's problems, (*b*) the means of solving those problems, and (*c*) the goals for treatment. Akutsu et al (1990) have recently provided empirical support for aspects of the proximal-distal model in a Chinese-American sample.

Atkinson & Thompson (1992) offered a complementary theoretical analy-sis based in the social psychology of source credibility and attitude change—one of the most durable theoretical frameworks in counseling psychology and was introduced first by Strong (1968)—which invokes Simons et al's (1970) distinction between membership-group (ethnic/racial) similarity and attitudi-nal (cultural meaning) similarity. Their review of both previous and more recent research generally supports the greater explanatory power of the latter category, as well as the importance of examining such individual-differences variables (Atkinson et al 1989; Ponterotto et al 1988; Bennett & Big Foot 1991). The emergence of these theoretical frameworks, with their focus on the importance of within-group differences, marks an increase in the sophistica-tion of the cross-cultural counseling literature over its early focus on some-what simplistic racial/ethnic matching models.

Multicultural Issues in Training

The increased recognition of the mental-health needs of minority individuals has focused attention on the role of graduate training programs in preparing psychologists to meet those needs. Although the importance of multicultural issues in training has been acknowledged since at least the Vail Conference two decades ago (Korman 1974), serious attention has been paid only relatively recently to this issue on a national level. This attention has taken two main foci: the recruiting and training of ethnic minority individuals for careers in psychology, and the revision of graduate training curricula to ensure that all psychologists are competent to provide services to persons of diverse ethnic and cultural backgrounds (Myers et al 1991). Myers et al (1991), summarizing the recommendations from the 1988 NIMH-sponsored Conference on Improving Training and Psychological Services for Ethnic Minorities, emphasized the importance of multicultural competency for all psychologists, as well as the critical nature of sustained funding and policy support for recruiting minorities into psychology, developing minority faculty, and devising appropriate training curricula.

The issue of curriculum revision has proven a thorny one. Although there has been some progress in the last decade [(Bernal 1990; see Bernal & Padilla (1982) for an earlier status report and Casas (1984) for a discussion], profound curricular changes are rare. They note the resistance of nonminority faculty to the notion that specialized multicultural knowledge and experience are necessary, as well as the small number of minority faculty available to spearhead such training efforts and the limited empirical information of clinical relevance to ethnic minority populations. Most curricular revisions are of the offer-a-special-course variety (Myers et al 1991; D'Andrea & Daniels 1991), and considerable skepticism surrounds the degree to which training programs are committed to the spirit of the APA accreditation criterion requiring multicultural competency.

Lefly (1985) discusses the relative advantages and disadvantages of additive vs substitutive training models (i.e. the degree to which cross-cultural training should be in addition to vs instead of traditional clinical training), but as Myers et al (1991) point out, either approach risks reifying the special-groups perspective; they argue for an integrative approach in which multicultural issues are considered integral to concepts of mental health and disorder, but note that few if any training programs espouse this perspective although models have been available for some time (e.g. Sue & Zane 1987; LeVine & Padilla 1980; Sue et al 1982). In a similar vein, D'Andrea & Daniels (1991) note that training programs can be characterized in terms of varying levels and stages of multicultural training. They note four stages of multicultural awareness: cultural entrenchment, cross-cultural awakening, cultural integrity, and cultural infusion. The first stage is characterized by an almost complete absence of multicultural training and an ethnocentric perspective, whereas programs in the process of cross-cultural awakening demonstrate some awareness of the inadequacy of traditional approaches for addressing the mental-health needs of culturally diverse populations but offer no systematic alternatives [cf Johnson's (1987) distinction between knowing that and knowing how]. Programs at the stage of cultural integrity generally require students to complete a course focused on multicultural issues (e.g. acquisition of cross-cultural communication skills development of cultural sensitivity, acquisition of culturally relevant knowledge, and/or acquisition of integrative experiential training experiences), an approach that appears to be by far the most common. Finally, programs at the infusion stage extend their efforts by infusing multicultural issues throughout the curriculum, often developing an interdisciplinary model (Copeland 1982). Although the general sense is that the infusion model is the most desirable, educators agree that it is by far the most difficult to implement.

We observe with surprise and some chagrin the relative absence of counseling-psychology participation in the national policy debate on multicultural training and curriculum. With a few notable exceptions, the 1988 NIMH conference participants represented clinical psychology and psychiatry, and none of the model training programs highlighted in the conference report (Myers 1991) were housed within counseling psychology. This is somewhat puzzling, as much of the theory and research on mental-health services for ethnic minorities has developed within the counseling-psychology perspective (see e.g. Atkinson 1985; Atkinson et al 1989; Casas 1984; Helms 1984; Leong 1986; Pedersen 1985; Sue & Sue 1990, to name only a few), and counseling psychologists have long been committed to developing appropriate training models for multicultural counseling (e.g. Carney & Kahn 1984; Copeland 1983; Sue 1978; Sue et al 1982; Pedersen 1978, 1988; Ponterotto & Casas 1987). For example, Division 17's original position paper on cross-cultural counseling competencies (Sue et al 1982) has provided a framework for designing multicultural training curricula for over a decade; additional specific examples from this review period include proposals for individualizing counselor training based on levels of trainee racial identity (Sabnani et al 1991) and Leong & Kim's (1991) description of the intercultural sensitizer as a training technology grounded in cross-cultural psychology. As psychology begins (at last) to engage multicultural training issues in a serious and sustained manner, counseling psychologists must make their voices heard in the national policy dialogue.

Research Comment

The research on multicultural counseling has been extensively analyzed and critiqued, most recently and thoroughly by Ponterotto & Casas (1991), and space does not allow us to do justice to the subject here. We note, however, the continuing dependence of much of this work on (likely nonrepresentative) college-student samples and (fairly weak) analog procedures. [In fact, the great majority of this research does not even employ analog procedures but rather depends on paper-and-pencil surveys of college students, examining questions such as willingness to participate in counseling and for what problems (Ponterotto & Casas 1991)]. Although often elegantly designed, most of this work is simply too far removed from the complexities of psychotherapy to offer much practical assistance to those struggling with the pressing mental-health needs of the minority community. Although we have no particular bone to pick with analog studies per se, and indeed have conducted many of these studies ourselves, we do wish to suggest that researchers should begin to increase the noise-to-signal ratio in these studies, thus increasing their chances for external validity and generalizability. Use of more powerful analogs (e.g. Enns & Hackett 1990), particularly those that are interactive and simulate actual counseling situations (e.g. Robertson & Fitzgerald 1990), represent possible first steps; the use of naturalistic reactions of actual clients to actual therapists in ongoing therapy is another. After all, internal and external validity are tradeoffs, not absolute goals; until we begin to risk a little of the former in pursuit of the latter, we continue to risk the dismissal of this work as an irrelevant, academic enterprise.

RESEARCH ON COUNSELING ISSUES WITH GAY, LESBIAN, AND BISEXUAL INDIVIDUALS

From Pathology to Diversity

Although until recently it was relatively ignored, research on gay/lesbian/bisexual individuals is important for numerous reasons. First, gays/lesbians comprise 10–15% of the population (22 million individuals), with bisexuals constituting as many as 15–35% more (Klein 1978) depending on definitions used. These groups have been referred to as a hidden minority because they are invisible not only to the people around them but to psychologists engaged in research, theory, and practice (Atkinson & Hackett 1988; Fassinger 1991b). Further, they are subject to many of the same kinds of discrimination and harassment experienced by other minority groups in society (Atkinson & Hackett 1988; Fassinger 1991b; Herek 1989). In spite of the oppression they face, gay and lesbian individuals often receive less sympathy and support from others because it is assumed that they are choosing their orientation. No one ever suggests that it is wrong to be black or female, or that a woman or a Black had some choice in the matter, but gay and lesbian individuals frequently encounter such attitudes.

Fassinger (1991b) and Melton (1989), among others, document the continued widespread disapproval and stigmatization of gay men and lesbians in American society and suggest that the AIDS epidemic has contributed to the maintenance/exacerbation and justification of such attitudes. Mental-health professionals are not immune to the effects of societal prejudice, which likely detrimentally affects their clients (Garnets et al 1991). Thus, attention to these issues within psychology is vital.

Morin & Rothblum (1991) document the changes that have occurred within psychology since the destigmatization of homosexuality in 1975. In that year, APA adopted an official policy stating that "homosexuality per se implies no impairment in judgement, stability, reliability, or general social or vocational capabilities" (Conger 1975, p. 633). The APA went further, urging psychologists to take the lead in removing the stigma of mental illness from homosexuality. Although the intervening years have witnessed some positive changes, most notably the shift in research from a focus on homosexuality as a pathology (a search for its causes and its cures) to research focusing on the unique needs and experiences of gay people, in many ways little has changed. A recent study of therapist knowledge and attitudes about gay/lesbian issues indicated the continuing existence of homophobia, heterosexual bias, and misinformation among practicing psychologists (Garnets et al 1991).

Possibly because of the AIDS epidemic [which Morin & Rothblum (1991) contend has accelerated the lesbian and gay civil rights movement], and most definitely because of the work of gay/lesbian psychologists and their supporters, e.g. members of the Society for the Psychological Study of Gay and Lesbian Issues (APA's Division 44), progress is finally being made in bringing the needs of gay and lesbian individuals to light in psychology. The number of articles relevant to gay/lesbian issues published in mainstream journals (vs specialized outlets such as the *Journal of Homosexuality*) has increased markedly in the past five or so years. As examples, the Psychology in the Public Forum sections of the June, 1989 and September, 1991 *American Psychologist* were devoted, respectively, to legal and social policy issues relevant to gay rights (Melton 1989) and to progress in removing the stigma against homosexuality in psychological research, language, and practice (Morin & Rothblum 1991). Special issues on AIDS and/or HIV infection have appeared in many journals, including the *American Psychologist* (Backer et al 1988), the *Journal of Consulting and Clinical Psychology* (Heaton 1990), and *The Counseling Psychologist* (Hoffman 1991). (Due to space limitations, we cannot review the psychological issues surrounding AIDS/HIV infection—interested readers are referred to these special issues.)

Within counseling psychology, progress has also been noteworthy. For example, Gelso & Fassinger (1990) noted that only one study of gay/lesbian issues had appeared in the core counseling psychology journals in the six-year period (1983–1988) covered by their review. Buhrke et al (1992) noted that over the 12-year period from 1978 to 1989, only 43 of 6661 articles (0.65%) in major counseling psychology journals (*Journal of Counseling Psychology, Journal of Consulting and Clinical Psychology, Journal of Counseling and Development,* and *The Counseling Psychologist*) addressed gay/lesbian issues, but of these, 23 were published in 1989 (vs from 0 to 3 per year each of the preceding 11 years). Similarly, in our review of the counseling literature for the years 1988 to 1991, we noted considerable activity in this area. Clearly, interest in these issues is accelerating.

Defining Sexual Orientation

Before proceeding with discussion of specific areas of work, we note that sexual orientation is correctly conceived as a continuous and flexible, rather than categorical and fixed, variable. Beginning with Kinsey et al's (1953) seven-point continuum of behavior ranging from exclusively heterosexual to exclusively homosexual, researchers have begun to realize the complexity and cross-situational variability of individual sexual and affectional behavior (Garnets & Kimmel 1990). Basing their research on the work of Money (1988), Garnets & Kimmel note that sexual orientation is based on, at a minimum, both affectional (emotional) and erotic (sexual) attachments to persons of the same and/or other sex. Garnets & Kimmel define erotic and emotional love for the same sex as homophilia and for the other sex as heterophilia. The relative balance of homophilia and heterophilia defines sexual orientation, and bisexuals would be those individuals possessing high levels of each. They also note, however, that homophilia is not enough to define oneself as gay or lesbian—the individual must also be self-aware and identify with some gay or lesbian community.

This definition has several important implications. First, and most important, is the emphasis on both sexual and emotional attachment. Second, homosexual behavior is not sufficient to define sexual orientation—without both homophilia and self-identification, the behavior is simply sexual behavior. Research indicates numerous instances of cross-orientation sexual behavior. Reinisch et al (1988) reported that 62–74% of self-identified gay men report having had heterosexual intercourse, and 15–26% have been married. A total of 70% of gay men report having had sex with a married man, and of all men, 37% report a same-sex sexual experience. Eighty percent of lesbians have had heterosexual sex, and 20–35% have been married at least once (cf Eldridge 1987). Finally, these definitions are important when considering the ways in which subjects for studies of gay/lesbian individuals are obtained—as discussed later, defining as gay someone who attends a gay event or who has had sex with someone of the same sex is fraught with the possibility of error.

Therapist and Client Attitudes

One area beginning to receive empirical attention is therapists' attitudes toward gay and lesbian clients, and evidence indicates that many practicing psychologists lack both gay-affirmative attitudes and information about gay lifestyles. For example, Rudolph (1989) reviewed research pertaining to counselor attitudes toward homosexuality and reported much negativity as well as internally contradictory attitudes. Rudolph suggests that contradiction is to be expected in the context of a generally gay-affirmative profession existing in a gay-negative society. Hayes & Gelso (1991) reported counselor discomfort with HIV-infected clients, but discomfort with gay vs nongay clients in general was related primarily to counselors' measured homophobia. The APA Task Force on Lesbian and Gay Concerns (Garnets et al 1991) generally followed the methods of the (APA) Task Force on Sex Bias and Sex Role Stereotyping in Psychotherapy (1975) in its attempt to define and categorize specific ways in which negative attitudes and misinformation may be manifest in psychological practice. Of 6580 survey questionnaires mailed, 2544 (39%) were returned. The large majority of respondents were white (96%) and heterosexual (85%), and 58% provided examples (in the form of "critical incidents") of negative treatment of gay or lesbian individuals in therapy. (Of those providing incidents, 23% identified themselves as gay, lesbian, or bisexual.) The report provided a list of the major types of therapist bias and misinformation regarding lesbians and gay men, along with examples, and also solicited from respondents examples of beneficial or exemplary practice. Although this study relies on anecdotal data, it is useful in that systematic description of phenomena (in this case, less-than-effective therapist behaviors with gay clients) must precede more rigorous empirical study and because it by itself could provide practicing psychologists with basic information about the dos and don'ts of effective and ethical practice with gay/lesbian/bisexual individuals.

Like the APA Task Force report, several other recent articles or special issues of journals were designed to educate psychologists and counselors concerning gay issues. For example, the special issue of *The Counseling Psychologist* (Fassinger 1991a) contained review articles pertaining to the counseling needs of gay men (Shannon & Woods 1991), lesbians (Browning et al 1991), counseling-psychology training (Buhrke & Douce 1991), and general theoretical, professional, and ethical issues involved in working with gay individuals in counseling (Fassinger 1991b). The special issue of the *Journal of Counseling and Development* (Dworkin & Gutierrez 1989) also contained many practice-oriented articles. Although review articles are helpful to those who are relatively uninformed concerning gay issues, more empirical work is clearly needed in this area. Research concerning the seeking of psychotherapeutic services by gay men and lesbians and their reactions to therapy is also needed. The evidence, for example, indicates that although two to four times as many gay as nongay people seek counseling, their rates of dissatisfaction with the services they receive are much higher—40–50% as reported by Rudolph (1988). On the other hand, Morgan (1992) reported that lesbians have significantly more positive attitudes toward counseling than do nonlesbians. McDermott et al (1989) report that as many as half of gay/lesbian clients prefer but may not be able to find a gay or lesbian therapist—the effects of this are poorly understood. Gelso & Fassinger (1990) noted that research on premature termination by the client had come to a virtual standstill during the period of their review, but the observation that 10–15% or more of clients are gay or lesbian (whether the counselor knows it or not) may be an important factor in and impetus for further research in this area. Issues related to transference/countertransference with gay and lesbian clients [see Van Wagoner et al (1991) for some discussion] are also neglected.

Also needed are studies of the effects of educational interventions designed to increase counselors' awareness and knowledge of gay/lesbian issues. One such study was that of Rudolph (1989), who evaluated the effects of a three-day workshop on gay/lesbian issues on the attitudes of mental-health professionals. Although the study had a control group, it was quasiexperimental in that participants in the workshop were volunteers. Thus, interpretation of the findings, that in comparison to control subjects, treated subjects became more tolerant of homosexuality and had better ideas concerning effective treatment strategies, must take into account the a priori openness of the subjects to the topic area, not to mention the obvious demand characteristics of the situation.

Research on Gay and Lesbian Lifestyles

As previously mentioned, research prior to the mid 1970s focused primarily on homosexuality as pathology (Garnets & Kimmel 1990), but in the past 15 years, examinations of the unique experiences of gay men and lesbians have begun to appear. A frequently discussed topic in the last few years was models of gay-identity development, that is, the process of coming out as a gay or lesbian. Models recently proposed were those of Troiden (1989) and Fassinger & McCarn (1991). As reviewed by Fassinger & McCarn (1991), these models consist of between three and seven stages describing the process by which one moves from initial awareness of homoerotic or affectional feelings to fully embracing one's identity as a gay person. Problems with such models have been the tendency to assume that identity development is similar in gay men and lesbians and the failure to distinguish between the processes of internal/individual homoerotic identification and political/social identification with the gay/lesbian community. Fassinger & McCarn also object to the assumption in these models that the only route to maturity is an immutable and politicized homoerotic identity and note the failure of existing models to consider diversity in race/ethnicity, class, age, geographic locale, or the possibility of parallel or prior feminist-identity development among lesbians. Finally, few of these models have been subject to rigorous empirical scrutiny.

The model of gay-identity development initially proposed and developed for lesbians (Fassinger & McCarn 1991) was intended to address these problems. It postulates a four-phase model of the occurrence of two parallel and reciprocal processes, those of internal articulation of one's sexual preference and awareness of membership in and identification with an oppressed minority group. Using a card-sort methodology to provide initial validation for the model, Fassinger and colleagues have found preliminary support for the two branches (individual and group membership identity) on diverse samples of 40 lesbians (Fassinger & McCarn 1991) and 50 gay men (R. E. Fassinger, S. R. McCarn & B. Miller, unpublished manuscript). Efforts are currently underway to develop an objectively administered measure of gay/lesbian identity development based on the model.

One rich area for theory development involves models postulating the effects of gender on same-sex relationships. As noted by Eldridge & Gilbert (1990), power and the politics of housework are the major issues affecting heterosexual dual career couples, but in same-gender relationships, where gender roles are not givens, these may not be as salient as other issues. Some empirical research addressed issues facing gay or lesbian couples. An exemplary study was that of Eldridge & Gilbert (1990) using 275 lesbian dual-career couples. The study avoided most problems common to research in this area by virtue of its use of a variety of sources for subjects (thus avoiding the typical reliance on the "friends network" alone), had a return rate of 76%, and represented most of the states and two foreign countries. Thus, although the sample was not random, the chances for generalizability were increased. Extensive descriptive data, particularly needed when traditionally underrepresented populations are under study, as well as predictive findings were reported. Important findings were that these women were in general very satisfied with both their lives and their relationships and reported high levels of self-esteem and career commitment. Interpretation of the findings that emotional intimacy and life satisfaction were most highly predictive of relationship satisfaction is complicated by the correlational nature of the study.

Another recent direction for research involves the recognition that gay men and lesbian women face unique problems in career choice and adjustment, including discrimination and negative stereotyping (Hetherington et al 1989; Hetherington & Orzek 1989). Although, again, most available articles deal with counseling issues stemming from vocational barriers and problems, one empirical study (Etringer et al 1990) examined career indecision as a function of sexual orientation. They found that lesbians showed the least amount of uncertainty, and that lesbians and heterosexual men were most satisfied with their choices.

Recent, and much needed, research efforts focus on the needs of gay males and lesbians who are members of visible minority (racial/ethnic and/or disabled) groups, and who thus face what some authors have referred to as "multiple oppression" (Reynolds & Pope 1991). Research suggests that most racial/ethnic minority groups judge gay/lesbian members harshly, both for religious reasons and because of the desire to pass on the culture to one's children (Carballo-Dieguez 1989). Chan (1989) studied 16 lesbian and 16 gay-male Asian-Americans; these individuals tended to identify more strongly with their gay identity than with their Asian-American identity, but preferred to acknowledge and embrace both identities (made difficult by extreme homophobia and denial among many Asian families). Loiacano (1989) interviewed three lesbian and three gay-male African-Americans and, again, found both the desire for but difficulties in the integration of gay and African-American identities. Although these studies represent a beginning, the sample sizes are much too small to permit generalizability of the findings—efforts to study large samples of ethnically diverse individuals are needed.

Two essentially ignored groups are bisexuals and gay/lesbian parents. As discussed by Fassinger (1991b), bisexuals face many of the same problems faced by gay men and lesbians, but usually confront the additional stresses of dual marginality (from both the gay and nongay communities) and of lack of community-provided social support. Of articles reviewed here, fewer than 1% even mentioned bisexuals, and no empirical studies of bisexuality were found in the period of the review. Buhrke et al's (1992) content analysis of 12 years of research on gay men and lesbians failed to mention bisexuals at all. With regard to gay parenting, not only are one-third of lesbians mothers, and one-fourth of gay men fathers, but many gays, especially lesbians, are now choosing parenthood through adoption and alternative insemination (Fassinger 1991b). Gay parents, like bisexuals, have been a particularly invisible group. Finally, research examining the utility of existing theories of personality, career development, and counseling/therapy to gay/lesbian individuals is needed.

Overall, research on gay-affirmative counseling and on the needs of gay, lesbian, and bisexual individuals is in its infancy. The scant empirical research has been characterized both by its atheoretical nature and by methodological flaws that seriously impair generalizability. Sampling techniques in particular have been flawed. Sample sizes are often very small, and the problems with small sample sizes are often exacerbated by the use of biased sampling techniques such as friendship networks (e.g. the snowball method, where subjects provide the names of other subjects) and solicitation at gay bars or social/political events. Obviously, it is erroneous to assume that all people found at gay bars or events are gay. Not only does this sampling method ignore bisexuals and heterosexuals engaging in same-sex sexual behavior, but it assumes that nongay people do not attend or support gay causes. Actual assessments of the sexual orientation of research participants are essential before the researcher concludes that they are gay or lesbian. Researchers must also distinguish gay men from lesbians, as gender and gender role can be assumed to affect individuals' own experiences, their intimate relationships, and the attitudes toward them held by others (Buhrke et al 1992; Fassinger & McCarn 1991).

POSTSCRIPT

Gelso & Fassinger (1990) noted that counseling psychology has not always lived up to its avowed commitment to diversity; although this is still true, it is happily less true than in the past. We emphasize that, although this problem is most often cast as a moral or ethical issue, it is equally a scientific and epistemological one (cf Sue 1988). We hope that our focus will serve as an impetus for more theory and research related to issues of diversity throughout counseling psychology, for this way we will come to reflect and understand the complexities of our world more fully and accurately, as well as accord to all individuals respect and human dignity. If the individual-differences tradition in counseling psychology stands for anything, it stands for this goal.

ACKNOWLEDGMENTS

The authors thank Ruth E. Fassinger, Frederick T. L. Leong, and Christine S. Smithies for providing critiques of portions of this article, and Karla Brock for extensive assistance with searching and locating the literature.

Literature Cited

Agras, W. S., Schneider, J. A., Arnow, B., Raeburn, S. D., Telch, C. F. 1989. Cognitive-behavioral and response-prevention treatments for bulimia nervosa. *J. Consult. Clin. Psychol.* 57:215–21

Akutsu, P. D., Lin, C. H., Zane, N. W. S. 1990. Predictors of utilization intent of counseling among Asian and White American college students: Controlling for confounds. *J. Couns. Psychol.* 37:445–53

Alexander, P. C., Neimeyer, R. A., Follette, V. M., Moore, M. K., Harter, S. 1989. A comparison of group treatments of women sexually abused as children. *J. Consult. Clin. Psych.* 57:479–83

American Psychological Association. 1975. Report of the task force on sex bias and sex-role stereotyping in psychotherapeutic practice. *Am. Psychol.* 30:1169–75

American Psychological Association, Ad Hoc Committee on Women (Division 17). 1979. Principles for the counseling psychotherapy of women. *Couns. Psych.* 8:21

Arbona, C. 1990. Career counseling research and Hispanics: a review of the literature. *Couns. Psychol.* 18:300–23

Atkinson, D. R. 1985. A meta-review of research on cross-cultural counseling and therapy. *J. Multicul. Couns. Dev.* 13:138–53

Atkinson, D. R., Gim, R. H. 1989. Asian-American cultural identity and attitudes toward mental health services. *J. Couns. Psychol.* 36:209–12

Atkinson, D. R., Hackett, G. 1988. *Counseling Non-Ethnic American Minorities.* Springfield, IL: Thomas

Atkinson, D. R., Morten, G., Sue, D. W. 1989. *Counseling American Minorities: A Cross-Cultural Perspective.* Dubuque, IA: Brown. 3rd ed.

Atkinson, D. R., Thompson, C. E. 1992. Racial, ethnic and cultural variables in counseling. See Brown & Lent 1992.

Backer, T. E., Batchelor, W. F., Jones, J. M., Mays, V. M., eds. 1988. Psychology and AIDS. *Am. Psychol.* 43:835–937

Baker, N. L. 1989. *Sexual harassment and job satisfaction in traditional and nontraditional industrial occupations.* PhD thesis, Calif. School of Prof. Psychol., Los Angeles

Bandura, A. 1977. Self-efficacy: Toward a unifying theory of behavioral change. *Psychol. Rev.* 84:191–214

Bandura, A. 1982. The psychology of chance encounters and life paths. *Am. Psychol.* 37:747-55

Beere, C. A. 1990a. *Gender Roles.* New York: Greenwood

Beere, C. A. 1990b. *Sex and Gender Issues.* New York: Greenwood

Bennett, S., BigFoot, D. S. 1991. American Indian and White college student preferences for counselor characteristics. *J. Couns. Psychol.*

Bernal, M. E. 1990. Minority mental health training: trends and issues. In *Mental Health of Ethnic Minorities,* ed. F. C. Serafica, A. Schwebel, R. Russell, and P. Isaac, pp. 112–37. New York: Praeger

Bernal, M. E., Padilla, A. M. 1982. Status of minority curricula and training in clinical psychology. *Am. Psychol.* 37:780–87

Betz, N. E. 1991. *What Stops Women and Minorities from Choosing and Completing Majors in Science and Engineering?* Washington, DC: Federation of Behavioral, Psychological, and Cognitive Sciences

Betz, N., Fitzgerald, L. F. 1987. *The Career Psychology of Women.* New York: Academic

Bond, M. E. 1988. Division 27 sexual harassment survey. *The Commun. Psychol.* 21:7–10

Brannon, R., Juni, S. 1984. A scale for measuring attitudes toward masculinity. *Psychol. Doc.* 14:6

Brickman, P., Rabinowitz, V. C., Karuza, J., Coates, D., Cohn, E., Kidder, L. 1982. Models of helping and coping. *Am. Psychol.* 37:368–84

Brooks, L., Perot, A. R. 1991. Reporting sexual harassment: Exploring a predictive model. *Psychol. Women* 15:31–48

Brown, D., Brooks, L. 1990. *Career Counseling Techniques.* Needham Heights, MA: Allyn

Brown, S. D., Lent, R. W., eds. 1992. *Handbook of Counseling Psychology.* New York: Wiley. 2nd ed.

Browning, C., Reynolds, A. L., Dworkin, S. H. 1991. Affirmative psychotherapy for lesbian women. *Couns. Psychol.* 19:177–96

Bruch, M. A. 1978. Holland's typology applied to client-counselor interaction: implications for counseling with men. *Couns. Psychol.* 7:26–32

Buhrke, R., Ben-Ezra, L. A., Hurley, M. E., Ruprecht, L. J. 1992. Content analysis and methodological critique of articles concerning lesbian and gay male issues in counseling journals. *J. Couns. Psychol.* 39:91–99

Buhrke, R. A., Douce, L. A. 1991. Training issues for counseling psychologists in working with lesbian women and gay men. *Couns. Psychol.* 19:216–34

Carballo-Dieguez, A. 1989. Hispanic culture, gay male culture, and AIDS: counseling implications. *J. Couns. Dev.* 68:26–30

Carney, C. G., Kahn, K. B. 1984. Building competencies for effective cross-cultural counseling: a developmental view. *Couns. Psychol.* 12:111–19

Carter, R. T. 1990. The relationship between racism and racial identity among White Americans: an exploratory investigation. *J. Couns. Dev.* 69:46–50

Carter, R. T., Helms, J. E. 1987. The relationship between Black value-orientation and racial identity attitudes. *Meas. Eval. Couns. Dev.* 19:185–95

Casas, J. M. 1984. Policy, training and research in counseling psychology: the ethnic/minority perspective. In *Handbook of Counseling Psychology,* ed. S. D. Brown, R. W. Lent, pp. 785–831. New York: Wiley

Casas, J. M. 1985a. A reflection on the status of racial/ethnic minority research. *Couns. Psychol.* 13:581–98

Casas, J. M. 1985b. The status of racial and ethnic-minority counseling: a training perspective. See Pedersen 1985, pp. 267–74

Celmer, V., Winer, J. L. 1990. Female aspirants to the Roman Catholic priesthood. *J. Couns. Dev.* 69:178–83

Chan, C. S. 1989. Issues of identity development among Asian-American lesbians and gay men. *J. Couns. Dev.* 68:16–20

Cheatham, H. E, Slaney, R. B., Coleman, N. C. 1990. Institutional effects on the psychosocial development of African-American college students. *J. Couns. Psychol.* 37:453–58

Check, J. V. P., Malamuth, N. M. 1983. Sex role stereotyping and reactions to depictions of stranger versus acquaintance rape. *J. Pers. Clin. Psychol.* 45:344–56

Cleary, P. D. 1987. Gender differences in stress-related disorders. In *Gender and Stress,* ed. R. C. Barnett, L. Biener, G. K. Baruch, pp. 11–38. New York: Free Press

Cole, N. S., Hanson, G. R. 1975. The impact of interest inventories on career choice. In *Issues of Sex Bias and Sex Fairness in Career Interest Measurement,* ed. E. E. Diamond, pp. 1–18. Washington, DC: Natl. Inst. Educ.

Conger, J. 1975. Proceedings of the APA, Inc. for 1974: minutes of the annual meeting of the council of representatives. *Am. Psychol.* 30:620–51

Cook, E. P. 1990. Gender and psychological distress. *J. Couns. Dev.* 68:371–75

Copeland, E. J. 1982. Minority populations and traditional counseling programs: some alternatives. *Couns. Educ. Supervis.* 21:187–93

Copeland, E. J. 1983. Cross-cultural counseling and psychotherapy: a historical perspective, implications for research and training. *Pers. Guid. J.* 62:10–15

Cox, T. H., Harquail, C. V. 1991. Career paths and career success in the early career stages of male and female MBA's. *J. Vocat. Behav.* 39:54–75

Craighead, L. W., Agras, W. S. 1991. Mechanism of action in cognitive-behavioral and pharmacological interventions for obesity and bulimia nervosa. *J. Couns. Psychol.* 59:112

Crites, J. O. 1969. *Vocational Psychology.* New York: McGraw Hill

Cuellar, I., Harris, L. C., Jasso, R. 1980. An acculturation scale for Mexican-American normal and clinical populations. *Hisp. J. Behav. Sci.* 2:199–217

D'Andrea, M., Daniels, J. 1991. Exploring the different levels of multicultural counseling training in counselor education. *J. Couns. Dev.* 70:78–84

Davis, R., Olmstead, M. P., Rickert, W. 1990. Brief group psychoeducation for bulimia nervosa: assessing the clinical significance of change. *J. Consult. Clin. Psychol.* 58:882–85

Dawis, R. V. 1992. The individual differences tradition in counseling psychology. *J. Couns. Psychol.* 39:7–19

Douce, L. A., Hansen, J. C. 1990. Willingness to take risks and college women's career choice. *J. Vocat. Behav.* 36:258–73

Downs, A. C., Engleson, S. A. 1982. The attitudes toward men scale (AMS): an analysis of the role and status of men and masculinity. JSAS. *Cat. Sel. Doc. Psychol.* 8:35

Draucker, C. B. 1989. Cognitive adaptation of female incest survivors. *J. Consult. Clin. Psychol.* 57:668–70

Dworkin, S. H., Gutierrez, F., eds. 1989. Special issue: Gay, lesbian, and bisexual issues in counseling. *J. Couns. Dev.* 68:1

Dye, E., Roth, S. 1991. Psychotherapy with Vietnam veterans and rape and incest survivors. *Psychotherapy* 28:103–20

Eisler, R. M., Blalock, J. A. 1991. Masculine gender role stress: Implications for the assessment of men. *Clin. Psychol. Rev.* 11:45–60

Eisler, R. M., Skidmore, J. R. 1987. Masculine gender role stress: Scale development and component factors in the appraisal of stressful situations. *Behav. Mod.* 11:123–36

Eisler, R. M., Skidmore, J. R., Ward, C. H. 1988. Masculine gender role stress: Predictor of anger, anxiety, and health-risk behaviors. *J. Pers. Assess.* 52:133–41

Eldridge, N. S. 1987. Gender issues in counseling same-sex couples. *Prof. Psychol.* 18:567–72

Eldridge, N., Gilbert, L. 1990. Correlates of relationship satisfaction in lesbian couples. *Psychol. Women Q.* 14:43–62

Enns, C. Z., Hackett, G. 1990. Comparison of feminist and non-feminist women's reactions to variants of nonsexist and feminist counseling. *J. Couns. Psychol.* 37:33–40

Etringer, B. D., Altmaier, E. M., Bowers, W. 1989. An investigation into the cognitive functioning of bulimic women. *J. Couns. Dev.* 68:216–19

Etringer, B. D., Hetherington, C., Hillerbrand, E. 1990. The influence of sexual orientation on career decision making. *J. Homosex.* 19:103–12

Fairburn, C. G. 1988. The current status of the psychological treatments for bulimia nervosa. *J. Psychosom. Res.* 32:635–45

Fassinger, R. E. 1990. Causal models of career choice in two samples of college women. *J. Vocat. Behav.* 36:225–40

Fassinger, R. E. 1991a. Counseling lesbian women and gay men. *Couns. Psychol.* 19:156

Fassinger, R. E. 1991b. The hidden minority: issues and challenges in working with lesbian women and gay men. *Couns. Psychol.* 19:157–76

Fassinger, R. E., McCarn, S. R. 1991. *Embracing our diversity: an inclusive model of lesbian identity development.* Pres. Assoc. Women. Psychol., 16th, Hartford, CT

Fisher, E. H. 1989. Gender bias in psychotherapy? An analysis of patient and therapist causal explanations. *Psychotherapy* 26:389–401

Fitzgerald, L. F., Hesson-McInnis, M. 1989. The dimensions of sexual harassment: a structural analysis. *J. Vocat. Behav.* 35:309–26

Fitzgerald, L. F., Ormerod, M. 1993. Breaking silence: the sexual harassment of women in academia and the workplace. In *Handbook of the Psychology of Women,* ed. F. Denmark, M. Paludi. New York: Greenwood. In press

Fitzgerald, L. F., Ormerod, A. J. 1991. Perceptions of sexual harassment: The influence of gender and academic context. *Psychol. Women* 15:281–95

Fitzgerald, L. F., et al. 1988. The incidence and dimensions of sexual harassment in academia and the workplace. *J. Vocat. Behav.* 32:152–75

Fitzpatrick, J. L., Silverman, T. 1989. Women's selection of careers in engineering. *J. Vocat. Behav.* 34:266–78

Foa, E. B., Rothbaum, B. O., Risss, D. S., Murdock, T. B. 1991. Treatment of posttraumatic stress disorder in rape victims: A comparison between cognitive-behavioral procedures and counseling. *J. Consult. Clin. Psychol.* 59:715–23

Follette, V. M., Alexander, P. C., Follette, W. C. 1991. Individual predictors of outcome in group treatment for incest survivors. *J.*

Consult. Clin. Psychol. 59:150–55

Frazier, P. 1991. Self-blame as a mediator of post-rape depression symptoms. *J. Soc. Clin. Psychol.* 10:47–57

Frazier, P. A., Cohen, B. B. 1992. Research on the sexual victimization of women: Implications for counselor training. *Couns. Psychol.* 20:141–58

Friedlander, M. L., Siegel, S. M. 1990. Separation-individuation difficulties and cognitive-behavioral indicators of eating disorders among college women. *J. Couns. Psychol.* 37:74–78

Garner, D. M., Olmstead, M. P., Polivy, J. 1983. Development and validation of a multidimensional eating disorder inventory for anorexia nervosa and bulimia. *Int. J. Eating Disord.* 2:15–34

Garner, D. M., Olmstead, M. P., Polivy, J., Garfinkel, P. E. 1984. Comparison between weight-preoccupied women and anorexia nervosa. *Psychosom. Med.* 46:255–66

Garner, D. M., Fairburn, I. G., Davis, R. 1987. Cognitive-behavioral treatment of bulimia nervosa: a critical appraisal. *Behav. Mod.* 11:398–431

Garnets, L., Hancock, K. A., Cochran, S. D., Goodchilds, J., Peplan, L. A. 1991. Issues in psychotherapy with lesbians and gay men. *Am. Psychol.* 46:964–72

Garnets, L., Kimmel, D. 1990. *Lesbian and gay male dimensions in the psychological study of human diversity.* Pres. Annu. Meet. Am. Psych. Assoc., 98th, Boston, Mass.

Gelso, C. J., Fassinger, R. E. 1990. Counseling psychology. *Annu. Rev. Psychol.* 41:355–86

Gelso, C. J., Fassinger, R. E. 1992. Personality, development, and counseling psychology. *J. Couns. Psychol.* 39:275–98

Gelso, C. J., Fretz, B. R. 1992. *Counseling Psychology.* Fort Worth: Holt, Rinehart & Winston

Gilbert, B. J., Heesacker, M., Gannon, L. J. 1991. Changing the sexual aggression-supportive attitudes of men.: a psychoeducational intervention. *J. Couns. Psychol.* 38:197–203

Gilbert, L. A. 1992. Gender and counseling psychology: Current knowledge and directions for research and social action. See Brown & Lent 1992, pp. 383–416

Gilbert, L. A., Osipow, S. H. 1991. Feminist contributions to counseling psychology. *Psychol. Women Q.* 15:537–48

Gim, R. H., Atkinson, D. R., Kim, S. J. 1991. Asian-American acculturation, counselor ethnicity and sensitivity and ratings of counselors. *J. Couns. Psychol.* 38:57–62

Gim, R. H., Atkinson, D. R., Whiteley, S. 1990. Asian-American acculturation, severity of concerns, and willingness to see a counselor. *J. Couns. Psychol.* 37:281–85

Glidden, C. E., Tracey, T. J. 1989. Women's perceptions of personal versus socio-cultural counseling interventions. *J. Couns.*

Psychol. 36:54–62

Good, G. E., Dell, D. M., Mintz, L. B. 1989. Male role and gender role conflict: relations to helpseeking in men. *J. Couns. Psychol.* 36:295–300

Good, G. E., Gilbert, L. A., Scher, M. 1990. Gender aware therapy. *J. Couns. Dev.* 68:376–80

Good, G. E., Mintz, L. B. 1990. Gender role conflict and depression in college men: evidence for compounded risk. *J. Couns. Dev.* 69:17–21

Goodchilds, J. 1992. *Psychological Perspectives on Diversity in America.* Washington, DC: Am. Psychol. Assoc.

Gordon, R. A., Lewis, M. A., Quigley, A. M. 1988. Can we count on muddling through the *g* crisis in employment. *J. Vocat. Behav.* 33:424–51

Gottfredson, L. S. 1981. Circumscription and compromise: a developmental theory of career aspiration. *J. Couns. Psychol.* 28:416–27

Gottfredson, L. S. 1988. Fairness in employment testing. *J. Vocat. Behav.* 32

Gould, S. J. 1981. *The Mismeasure of Man.* New York: Norton

Grant Foundation. 1988. *The Forgotten Half: Non-College Bound Youth in America.* Washington DC: William T. Grant Found.

Guthrie, R. V. 1976. *Even the Rat Was White: A Historical View of Psychology.* New York: Harper & Row

Hackett, G., Betz, N. E. 1981. A self-efficacy approach to the career development of women. *J. Vocat. Behav.* 18:326–39

Hackett, G., Betz, N. E., O'Halloran, S. M., Romac, D. S. 1990. Effects of verbal and mathematics task performance on task and career self-efficacy. *J. Couns. Psychol.* 37:169–77

Hackett, G., Lent, R. W. 1992. Theoretical advances in career psychology. See Brown & Lent 1992, pp. 419–51

Hannah, J. S., Kahn, S. E. 1989. The relationship of socioeconomic status and gender to the occupational choices of grade 12 students. *J. Vocat. Behav.* 34:161–78

Harmon, L. W. 1989. Longitudinal changes in women's career aspirations: developmental or historical? *J. Vocat. Behav.* 35:46–63

Harrison, J. 1978. Warning: the male sex role may be dangerous to your health. *J. Soc. Issues.* 34:65–86

Hayes, J. A., Gelso, C. J. 1991. *Male counselors' discomfort with gay and HIV-infected clients.* Pres. Conf. North Am. Soc. Psychother. Res., Panama City, Fla.

Heath, A. E., Neimeyer, G. J., Pedersen, P. B. 1988. The future of cross-cultural counseling: a Delphi poll. *J. Couns. Dev.* 67:27–30

Heaton, R. K., ed. 1990. Special series: acquired immune deficiency syndrome. *J. Consult. Clin. Psychol.* 58:3–76

Heesacker, R. S., Niemeyer, G. 1990. Assessing object relations and social cognitive correlates of eating disorders. *J. Couns.*

Psychol. 37:419–26

Helms, J. E. 1984. Toward a theoretical model of the effects of race on counseling: a black and white model. *Couns. Psychol.* 12:153–65

Helms, J. E., ed. 1990. *Black and White Racial Identity: Theory, Research and Practice.* New York: Greenwood Press

Henderson, S., Hesketh, B., Tuffin, K. 1988. A test of Gottfredson's theory of circumscription. *J. Vocat. Behav.* 32:37–48

Herek, G. M. 1989. Hate crimes against lesbians and gay men: issues for research and policy. *Am. Psychol.* 44:948–55

Hesketh, B., Durant, C., Pryor, R. 1990a. Career compromise: a test of Gottfredson's theory using a policy-capturing procedure. *J. Vocat. Behav.* 36:97–108

Hesketh, B., Elmslie, S., Kaldor, W. 1990b. Career compromise: an alternative account to Gottfredson's 1981 theory. *J. Couns. Psychol.* 37:49–56

Hesketh, B., Pryor, R., Gleitzman, M. 1989. Fuzzy logic: toward measuring Gottfredson's concept of occupational social space. *J. Couns. Psychol.* 36:103–9

Hetherington, C., Hillerbrand, E., Etringer, B. D. 1989. Career counseling with gay men: issues and recommendations for research. *J. Couns. Dev.* 67:452–54

Hetherington, C., Orzek, A. 1989. Career counseling and life planning with lesbian women. *J. Couns. Dev.* 68:52–57

Hoffman, M. A. 1991. Counseling the HIV-infected client: a psychosocial model for assessment and intervention. *Couns. Psychol.* 19:467–542

Holland, J. L. 1985. *Making Vocational Choices.* New York: Prentice-Hall. 2nd ed.

Holt, P. A. 1989. Differential effect of status and interest in the process of compromise. *J. Couns. Psychol.* 36:42–47

Howard, G. S. 1992. What counseling psychology has become and must yet become. *J. Couns. Psychol.* 39: In press

Humphrey, L. L. 1989. Observed family interactions among subtypes of eating disorders using structural analyses of social behavior. *J. Consult. Clin. Psychol.* 57:206–14

Jacobson, N. S., Revenstorf, D. 1988. Statistics for assessing the clinical significance of psychotherapy techniques: issues, problems, and new developments. *Behav. Assess.* 10:133–45

Jenkins, S. R. 1989. Longitudinal prediction of women's careers: psychological, behavioral, and social-structural influences. *J. Vocat. Behav.* 34:204–35

Johnson, S. D. 1987. Knowing versus knowing how: toward achieving expertise through multicultural training for counseling. *Couns. Psychol.* 15:320–31

Kinsey, A. C., Pomeroy, W. B., Martin, C. E., Gebhard, P. H. 1953. *Sexual Behavior in the Human Female.* Philadelphia: Saunders

Klein, F. 1978. *The Bisexual Option.* New York: Arbor House

Klemchuk, H. P., Hutchinson, E. B., Frank, R. I. 1990. Body dissatisfaction and eating-related problems on the college campus. *J. Couns. Psychol.* 37:297–305

Korman, M. 1974. National conference on levels and patterns of professional training in psychology. *Am. Psychol.* 29:441–49

Koss, M. P. 1990. Changed lives: The psychological impact of sexual harassment. In *Ivory Power,* ed. M. Paludi. Albany: SUNY

Koss, M. P., Burkhart, B. R. 1989. A conceptual analysis of rape victimization: long term effects and implications for treatment. *Psychol. Women Q.* 13:27–40

Koss, M. P., Dinero, T. E. 1989. Discriminant analysis of risk factors for sexual victimization among a national sample of college women. *J. Consult. Clin. Psychol.* 57:242–50

Koss, M. P., Dinero, T. E., Seibel, C. A., Cox, S. L. 1988. Stranger and acquaintance rape: are there differences in the victim's experience? *Psychol. Women Q.* 12:1–24

Kunkel, M. A. 1990. Expectations about counseling in relation to acculturation in Mexican-American and Anglo-American student samples. *J. Couns. Psychol.* 37:286–92

Laessle, R. G., Tuschl, R. J., Waadt, S., Pirke, K. M. 1989. The specific psychopathology of bulimia nervosa: a comparison with restrained and unrestrained (normal) eaters. *J. Consult. Clin. Psychol.* 57:772–75

Lapan, R. T., McGrath, E., Kaplan, D. 1990. Factor structure of the basic interest scales by gender across time. *J. Couns. Psychol.* 37:216–22

Lee, L. A., Heppner, P. P. 1991. The development and evaluation of a sexual harassment inventory. *J. Couns. Dev.* 69:512–17

Lefly, H. 1985. Mental health training across cultures. See Pedersen 1985, pp. 256–66

Lent, R. W., Larkin, K. C., Brown, S. D. 1989. Relation of self-efficacy to inventoried vocational interests. *J. Vocat. Behav.* 34:279–88

Lent, R. W., Lopez, F. G., Bieschke, K. J. 1991. Mathematics self-efficacy: sources and relation to science-based career choice. *J. Couns. Psychol.* 38:424–30

Leong, F. T. L. 1986. Counseling and psychotherapy with Asian-Americans: review of the literature. *J. Couns. Psychol.* 33:196–206

Leong, F. T. L., ed. 1991. Special issue: career development of racial and ethnic minorities. *Career Dev. Q.* 39:195–285

Leong, F. T. L., Kim, H. H. W. 1991. Going beyond cultural sensitivity on the road to multiculturalism: using the intercultural sensitizer as a counseling training tool. *J. Couns. Dev.* 70:112–18

Leung, S. A., Harmon, L. W. 1990. Individual and sex differences in the zone of acceptable alternatives. *J. Couns. Psychol.* 37:153–59

Leung, S. A., Ivey, D., Scheel, M. 1991. *A systematic approach to test Gottfredson's (1981) theory.* Pres. Annu. Meet. Am. Psychol. Assoc., 99th, San Francisco, Calif.

Leung, S. A., Plake, B. S. 1990. A choice dilemma approach for examining the relative importance of sex type and prestige preferences in the process of career choice compromise. *J. Couns. Psychol.* 37:399–406

Levant, R. F. 1990. Psychological services designed for men. *Psychotherapy* 27:309–15

LeVine, E. S., Padilla, A. M. 1980. *Crossing Cultures in Therapy: Pluralistic Counseling for the Hispanic.* Belmont, CA: Wadsworth

Loerch, K. J., Russell, J. E. A., Rush, M. C. 1989. The relationships among family domain variables and work-family conflict for men and women. *J. Vocat. Behav.* 35:288–308

Loiacano, D. K. 1989. Gay identity issues among black Americans: racism, homophobia, and the need for validation. *J. Couns. Dev.* 68:21–25

Long, B. C. 1989. Sex role orientation, coping strategies, and self-efficacy of women in traditional and nontraditional occupations. *Psychol. Women Q.* 13:307–24

Long, B. C. 1990. Relation between coping strategies, sex-typed traits, and environmental characteristics: a comparison of male and female managers. *J. Couns. Psychol.* 37:185–94

Malovich, N. J., Stake, J. E. 1990. Sexual harassment on campus: Individual differences in attitudes and beliefs. *Psychol. Women Q.* 14:63–82

Matsui, T., Ikeda, H., Ohnishi, R. 1989. Relations of sex-typed socializations to career self-efficacy expectations of college students. *J. Vocat. Behav.* 35:1–16

Matsui, T., Ohawa, T., Onglatco, M. L. U. 1991. Personality and career commitment among Japanese female clerical employees. *J. Vocat. Behav.* 38:351–60

May, R. 1990. Finding ourselves: self-esteem, self-disclosure and self-acceptance. In *Problem-Solving Strategies and Interventions for Men in Conflict,* ed. D. Moore, F. Leafgreen, pp. 11–22. Alexandria: Am. Assoc. Couns. Dev.

Mazen, A. 1989. Testing an integration of Vroom's Instrumentality Theory and Holland's Typology on working women. *J. Vocat. Behav.* 35:327–41

Mazen, A., Lemkau, J. P. 1990. Personality profiles of women in traditional and nontraditional occupations. *J. Vocat. Behav.* 37:46–59

McCann, I. L., Sakheim, D. K., Abrahamson, D. J. 1988. Trauma and victimization: A model of psychological adaptation. *Couns. Psychol.* 16:531–94

McDermott, D., Tyndall, L., Lichtenberg, J. L. 1989. Factors related to counselor preference among gays and lesbians. *J. Couns. Dev.* 68:31–35

McNamara, K., Rickard, K. M. 1989. Feminist identity development: implications for feminist therapy with women. *J. Couns. Dev.* 68:184–89

Melton, G. B. 1989. Public policy and private prejudice. *Am. Psychol.* 44:933–40

Meth, R. L., Pasick, R. S. 1990. *Men in Therapy: the Challenge of Change.* New York: Guilford

Mintz, L. B., Betz, N. E. 1988. Prevalence and correlates of eating disordered behavior among college women. *J. Couns. Psychol.* 35:463–71

Money, J. 1988. *Gay, Straight, and In-between: The Sexology of Erotic Orientation.* New York: Oxford Univ. Press

Moore, D., Havercamp, B. E. 1989. Measured increases in male emotional expressiveness following a structured group intervention. *J. Counsel. Dev.* 67:513–17

Moore, D., Leafgren, F. 1990. *Men in Conflict: Problemsolving Strategies and Interventions for Men.* Alexandria, VA: Am. Assoc. Couns. Dev.

Morgan, K. S. 1992. Caucasian lesbians' use of psychotherapy: a matter of attitude? *Psychol. Women Q.* 16:127–30

Morin, S. F., Rothblum, E. D. 1991. Removing the stigma: fifteen years of progress. *Am. Psychol.* 46:947–49

Myers, H. F. 1991. Preface. In *Ethnic Perspectives on Clinical Training and Services in Psychology,* ed. H. F. Myers, P. Wohlford, L. P. Guzman, R. J. Echemendia, pp. x–xiii. Washington DC: Am. Psychol. Assoc,

Myers, H. F., Wohlford, P., Guzman, L. P., Echemendia, R. J., eds. 1991. *Ethnic Minority Perspectives on Clinical Training and Services in Psychology.* Washington, DC: Am. Psychol. Assoc.

O'Neil, J. M. 1981a. Male sex role conflicts, sexism and masculinity: psychological implications for men, women and the counseling psychologist. *Couns. Psychol.* 9:61–80

O'Neil, J. M. 1981b. Patterns of gender role conflict and strain: Sexism and fear of femininity in men's lives. *Pers. Guid. J.* 60:203–10

O'Neil, J. M., Helms, B. J., Gable, R. K., Lawrence, D., Wrightsman, L. S. 1986. Gender role conflict scale: college men's fear of femininity. *Sex Roles* 14:335–50

Orne, M. T., Wender, P. H. 1968. Anticipating socialization for psychotherapy: method and rationale. *Am. J. Psychiat.* 124:1202–12

Osipow, S. H., Spokane, A. 1983. *A Manual for Measures of Occupational Stress, Strain and Coping.* Odessa, FL: Psychol. Assess. Res.

Ozer, E. M., Bandura, A. 1990. Mechanisms governing empowerment effects: a self-efficacy analysis. *J. Pers. Soc. Psychol.* 58:472–86

Padilla, A. M. 1980. *Acculturation: Theory, Models and Some New Findings.* Boulder,

CO: Westview

Parham, T. A. 1989. Cycles of psychological nigrescence. *Couns. Psychol.* 17:187–226

Parham, T. A., Helms, J. E. 1981. The influence of black students' racial attitudes on preferences for counselor's race. *J. Couns. Psychol.* 28:250–57

Pedersen, P. B., ed. 1985. *Handbook of Cross-Cultural Counseling and Therapy.* Westport, CT: Greenwood

Pedersen, P. B. 1978. Four dimensions of cross-cultural skill in counselor training. *Pers. Guid. J.* 56:480–83

Pedersen, P. B. 1988. *A Handbook for Developing Multicultural Awareness.* Alexandria: Am. Assoc. Couns. Dev.

Pedersen, P. B., ed. 1991. Special issue: multiculturalism as a fourth force in counseling. *J. Couns. Dev.* 70:4–250

Petty, R. E., Cacioppo, J. T. 1986. *Communication and Persuasion: Central and Peripheral Routes to Attitude Change.* New York: Springer-Verlag

Pomales, J., Williams, V. W. 1989. Effects of level of acculturation and counseling style on Hispanic students' perceptions of counselor. *J. Couns. Psychol.* 36:79–83

Ponce, F. Q., Atkinson, D. R. 1989. Mexican-American acculturation, counselor ethnicity, counselor style and perceived counselor credibility. *J. Couns. Psychol.* 36:203–8

Ponterotto, J. G. 1987. Counseling Mexican-Americans: a multi-modal approach. *J. Couns. Dev.* 65:308–12

Ponterotto, J. G. 1988. Racial consciousness development among white counselor trainees: a stage model. *J. Multicult. Couns. Dev.* 16:146–56

Ponterotto, J. G., Alexander, C. M., Hinkston, J. A. 1988. Afro-American preferences for counselor characteristics: a replication and extension. *J. Couns. Psychol.* 35:175–82

Ponterotto, J. G., Casas, J. M. 1987. In search of multicultural competence within counselor education programs. *J. Couns. Dev.* 65:430–34

Ponterotto, J. G., Casas, J. M. 1991. *Handbook of Racial/Ethnic Minority Counseling Research.* Springfield, IL: Thomas

Pleck, J. H. 1981. *The Myth of Masculinity.* Cambridge: MIT Press

Pope, K. S. 1988. How clients are harmed by sexual contact with mental health professionals: the syndrome and its prevalence. *J. Couns. Dev.* 67:222–26

Pope, K. S. 1990. Therapist-patient sexual involvement: a review of the research. *Clin. Psychol. Rev.* 10:477–90

Pope, K. S., Vetter, V. A. 1991. Prior therapist-patient sexual involvement among patients seen by psychologists. *Psychotherapy* 28:429–38

Reinisch, J. M., Sanders, S. A., Ziemba-Davis, M. 1988. The study of sexual behavior in relation to transmission of human immunodeficiency virus. *Am. Psychol.* 43:921–27

Reynolds, A. R., Pope, R. L. 1991. The complexities of diversity: exploring multiple oppressions. *J. Couns. Dev.* 70:174–80

Robertson, J. R., Fitzgerald, L. F. 1990. The (mis)treatment of men: effects of client gender-role and life style on diagnosis and attribution of pathology. *J. Couns. Psychol.* 37:3–9

Robertson, J. R., Fitzgerald, L. F. 1992. Overcoming the masculine mystique: preferences for alternative forms of assistance among men who avoid counseling. *J. Couns. Psychol.* 39:240–46

Root, M., Fallon, P. 1988. The incidence of victimization experiences in a bulimic sample. *J. Interpers. Viol.* 3:161–73

Rudolph, J. 1988. Counselors' attitudes toward homosexuality: a selective review of the literature. *J. Couns. Dev.* 67:165–68

Rudolph, J. 1989. Effects of a workshop on mental health practitioners' attitudes toward homosexual and counseling effectiveness. *J. Couns. Dev.* 68:81–85

Russett, C. E. 1989. *Sexual Science: The Victorian Construction of Womanhood.* Cambridge: Harvard Univ. Press

Sabnani, H. B., Ponterotto, J. G., Borodovsky, L. G. 1991. White racial identity development and crosscultural counselor training: a stage model. *Couns. Psychol.* 19:76–102

Scher, M., Stevens, M., Good, G. E., Eichenfield, G. A. 1987. *Handbook of Counseling and Psychotherapy with Men.* Newbury Park, CA: Sage

Schofield, W. 1964. *Psychotherapy: The Purchase of Friendship.* Englewood Cliffs, NJ: Prentice-Hall

Scott, J., Hatalla, J. 1990. The influence of chance and contingency factors on career patterns of college-educated women. *Career Dev. Q.* 39:18–31

Scozzaro, P. P., Subich, L. M. 1990. Gender and occupational sex-type differences in job outcome factor perceptions. *J. Vocat. Behav.* 36:109–19

Shannon, J. W., Woods, W. J. 1991. Affirmative psychotherapy for gay men. *Couns. Psychol.* 19:197–215

Sharpe, M. J., Heppner, P. 1991. Gender role, gender role conflict and psychological wellbeing in men. *J. Couns. Psychol.* 38:323–30

Shields, S. A. 1975. Functionalism, Darwinism and the psychology of women: a study in social myth. *Am. Psychol.* 30:739–54

Silverberg, R. A. 1986. *Psychotherapy for Men: Transcending the Masculine Mystique.* Springfield, IL: Thomas

Simons, H. W., Berkowitz, N. N., Moyer, R. J. 1970. Similarity, credibility and attitude change: a review and a theory. *Psychol. Bull.* 73:1–6

Solomon, K., Levy, N. B., eds. 1982. *Men in Transition: Theory and Therapy.* New York: Plenum

Spokane, A. R. 1991. *Career Intervention.* Englewood Cliffs, NJ: Prentice Hall

Stillson, R. W., O'Neil, J. M., Owen, S. V. 1991. Predictors of adult men's gender-role conflict: race, class, unemployment, age, instrumentality-expressiveness, and personal strain. *J. Couns. Psychol.* 38:458–64

Stricker, G., Shafran, R. 1983. Gender and psychotherapy: a review of the empirical literature. In *Bias in Psychotherapy,* ed. J. Murray, P. R. Abramson, pp. 192–214. New York: Praeger

Strong, S. R. 1968. Counseling: an interpersonal influence process. *J. Couns. Psychol.* 30:202–8

Strong, S. R., Welsh, J. A., Corcoran, J. L., Hoyt, W. T. 1992. Social psychology and counseling psychology. *J. Couns. Psychol.* 39:139–57

Sue, D. W. 1978. Eliminating cultural oppression from counseling: toward a general theory. *J. Couns. Psychol.* 25:419–28

Sue, D. W., Sue, D. 1990. *Counseling the Culturally Different: Theory and Practice.* New York: Wiley. 2nd ed.

Sue, D. W., Bernier, J. E., Durran, A., Feinberg, L., Pedersen, P., et al. 1982. Position paper: cross-cultural counseling competencies. *Couns. Psychol.* 10:45–52

Sue, S. 1988. Psychotherapeutic services for ethnic minorities: Two decades of findings. *Am. Psychol.* 43:301–8

Sue, S., Zane, N. 1987. The role of culture and cultural techniques in psychotherapy: a critique and reformulation. *Am. Psychol.* 42:37–45

Suinn, R. M., Rickard-Figueroa, K., Lew, S., Vigil, P. 1987. The Suinn-Lew Asian Self-Identity Acculturation Scale: an initial report. *Ed. Psychol. Meas.* 47:401–7

Telch, C. F., Agras, W. S., Rossiter, E. M., Wilfley, D., Kenardy, J. 1990. Group cognitive-behavioral treatment for the nonpurging bulimic: an initial evaluation. *J. Consult. Clin. Psychol.* 58:629–35

Thelen, M. H., Farmer, J., Mann, L. M., Pruitt, J. 1990. Bulimia and interpersonal relationships: a longitudinal study. *J. Couns. Psychol.* 37:85–90

Till, F. J. 1980. *Sexual Harassment: A Report on the Sexual Harassment of Students.* Washington, DC: National Advisory Council on Women's Educational Programs

Tinsley, H. E. A., Tinsley, D. J. 1989. Reinforcers of the occupation of homemaker: an analysis of the need-gratifying properties of the homemaker occupation across the stages of the homemaker life cycle. *J. Couns. Psychol.* 36:189–95

Troiden, R. R. 1989. The formation of homosexual identities. *J. Homosexual.* 17:43–73

Truax, C. B., Bloxom, A. L. 1973. Preparing lower-class patients for group therapy: development and evaluation of a role induction film. *J. Consult. Clin. Psychol.* 20:25–37

Van Wagoner, S. L., Gelso, C. J., Hayes, J. A.,

Diemer, R. A. 1991. Countertransference and the reputedly excellent therapist. *Psychotherapy* 28:411–21

Walsh, W. B., Osipow, S. H., eds. 1988. *Advances in Vocational Psychology,* Vol. 2, *The Assessment of Career Decision Making.* Hillsdale, NJ: Erlbaum

Walsh, W. B., Osipow, S. H., eds. 1990. *Advances in Vocational Psychology,* Vol. 3, *Career Counseling.* Hillsdale, NJ: Erlbaum

Watkins, C. E., Jr., Campbell, V. E., eds. 1990. *Testing in Counseling Practice.* Hillsdale, NJ: Erlbaum

Watkins, C. E., Jr., Schneider, L. J. 1991. *Research in Counseling.* Hillsdale, NJ:

Erlbaum

Whiteley, J. M. 1984. Counseling psychology: a historical perspective. *Couns. Psychol.* 12:3–110

Williams, M. H. 1992. Exploitation and inference. *Am. Psychol.* 47:412–21

Wyatt, G. E., Newcomb, M. 1990. Internal and external mediators of women's sexual abuse in childhood. *J. Consult. Clin. Psychol.* 58:758–67

Wyatt, G. E., Notgrass, C. M., Newcomb, M. 1990. Internal and external mediators of women's rape experiences. *Psychol. Women Q.* 14:153–76

Annu. Rev. Psychol. 1993. 44:383–425

INFORMATION PROCESSING MODELS: Microscopes of the Mind

Dominic W. Massaro

Program in Experimental Psychology, University of California, Santa Cruz, California 95064

Nelson Cowan

Department of Psychology, University of Missouri, Columbia, Missouri 65211

KEYWORDS: perception, experimental psychology, psychophysics, cognition, psychological theory

CONTENTS

INFORMATION PROCESSING (IP) APPROACH 384
   Characteristics of the IP Approach 384
   Justifications of the IP Approach 387
   Metatheoretical Issues and IP 389
CHARACTERIZING STAGES OF PROCESSING 394
   Recent Evidence for Stages of Processing 394
   Discrete vs Continuous Representation and Processing 395
   Serial vs Parallel Processing 401
   Attentional and Strategic Effects 404
   Summary 406
ILLUSTRATIVE DOMAINS OF INQUIRY 406
   Psychophysics 406
   Visual Perception 408
   Speech Perception 409
   Reading Written Words 411
   Memory 412
   Decision Making 413
   Summary 413
VARIATIONS ON THE IP FRAMEWORK 414
   Physical Symbol Systems (PSS) 414
   Connectionism 415
   Modularity 417
   Ecological Realism 419
RETROSPECTIVE 419

0066-4308/93/0201-0383$02.00

INFORMATION-PROCESSING (IP) APPROACH

"Information," though difficult to define precisely, refers to representations derived by a person from environmental stimulation or from processing that influences selections among alternative choices for belief or action. "Information processing" (IP) refers to how the information is modified so that it eventually has its observed influence. "IP models" are theoretical descriptions of a sequence of steps or stages through which this processing is accomplished. In this chapter, we (a) reexamine the assumptions and rationale of the IP-modeling approach as it was conceived in the initial work on psychophysics, perception, attention, and memory (Atkinson & Shiffrin 1968; Broadbent 1958; Green & Swets 1966; Sternberg 1969), (b) review the theoretical literature in which clarifications or modifications of the approach are suggested, (c) illustrate some of these points in a discussion of the applications of IP models to various topics within contemporary cognitive psychology, and (d) evaluate the IP approach in comparison to related approaches.

IP models have played a major role in shaping the current dominant understanding of perception and action. In the last *Annual Review* article on IP models Posner & McLeod (1982) saw the IP approach as a search for elementary operations. Their vantage point was contrasted with that of the Newell (1980) and Simon (1979) school, which emphasized simulation of a wide range of mental activity by complex information processing models. Posner & McLeod chose instead to emphasize "fundamental operations that can be used to characterize the human mind" (1982:478).

One can sometimes gain insight into existing metatheory by considering what is taught to psychology students. Today, most courses and textbooks covering such experimental topics as human perception, memory, and thought are called "Cognitive Psychology" or "Cognition," but they most often profess allegiance to the IP approach (Anderson 1990a; Glass & Holyoak 1986; Massaro 1989a; Solso 1991). However, even though IP has had a solid and continuing tradition beginning with Broadbent's (1958) work and progressing through surveys by Neisser (1967), Norman (1969), and Lachman et al (1979), the IP paradigm generally has been neither clearly defined nor contrasted with other metatheories. We seek to fill this void by reviewing the recent literature that allows the metatheory of IP to be articulated and contrasted with other metatheories of psychological inquiry.

Characteristics of the IP Approach

In an important paper, Palmer & Kimchi (1986) described five properties of the IP approach. First, an *informational description* means that the environment and mental processing can be described in terms of the amount and types of information. *Recursive decomposition*, perhaps better described as hierarchical decomposition, denotes the breaking down of one stage of processing into substages. For example, a memory stage can be broken down into acquisition, retention, and retrieval stages; retrieval can be further broken down into memory search and decision; and memory search can be further broken down into access and comparison stages. The *flow continuity* principle states that information is transmitted forward in time. All inputs necessary to complete one operation are available from the outputs that flow into it. Central to the IP approach, as well, is the principle of *flow dynamics,* asserting that each stage or operation takes some time (i.e. that a mental process cannot be instantaneous). Finally, the *physical embodiment* principle is the assumption that information processing occurs in a physical system. Information is embedded in states of the system called representations, and operations used to transform the representations are called processes.

INFORMATION   The use of the term "information" in the IP approach is not identical to the classic information measure. For Shannon (1948), the amount of information in a given message is positively related to how much the message reduces the number of possible outcomes. John von Neumann suggested that Shannon call the measure of information "entropy": Because no one knew what entropy was, Shannon would always have the advantage in debate. Shannon's measure does formally resemble the mathematical definition of entropy (Tribus & McIrvine 1964). Young (1987) tries valiantly to define information in mass-energy terms—the putative nature of all events and objects in a traditional scientific view. The form characteristics are the primary ingredient in information flow, and the energetic events are simply the substrate embodying the form characteristics. Information transmission between successive stages of processing can also be clarified using an example from Young. Consider sound waves setting the tympanic membrane into vibration. The sound waves do not leave the air and go into the membrane (the air molecules retain their identity, although their pattern is likely to be changed by rebounding off the tympanic membrane); rather, the form characteristics of the sound waves flow to the membrane the way waves move a boat in water. This action represents a resonance in which one oscillatory system influences another's activity. This observation is important in thinking about transmission of information from one stage of processing to another. The representation of the preceding stage maintains its integrity even after it has been "transformed" and transmitted to the following stage of processing. For example, the notion that categorization of a visual item necessarily supplants any visual representation is not reasonable. The maintenance of multiple representations has become a landmark of models of short-term memory (e.g. Baddeley 1986; Massaro 1975).

The classic measure of information often does not permit the number of possible outcomes, and hence the amount of information, to be calculated unambiguously. In practice, however, a precise definition is not essential because it becomes clear that one is discussing types of information such as feature values or category assignments that distinguish among potential stimuli or responses in a specific experimental situation (Neisser 1967). Psychologists did not adhere to the restrictive formal definition of Shannon.

It is important for our purposes to distinguish between data and information. Information for us is knowledge within the receiver, whereas data are in the environment. A classic illustration of this distinction is found in this telegram from Myron Tribus's daughter in Paris: PLEASE SEND ME FIFTY DOLLARS AMERICAN EXPRESS NICE LETTER OF EXPLANATION FOLLOWS LOVE LOU. One reader of this cable might expect to receive a nice letter; another would know that Nice is a city on the French Riviera. The reader's knowledge determines the interpretation of the telegram.

This example also weakens the accepted claim that the traditional measure of information is devoid of meaningful content, inasmuch as the meaning determines the nature and number of alternatives. The number of viable alternatives for "NICE" could not be deduced without some consideration of meaning. A similar point was made by MacKay (1969) and reiterated by Gregory (1986). Perhaps Gregory (1986) is correct in regretting that information theory has not played a more central role in the study of information processing.

INFORMATION PROCESSING   The basic notion of IP is that one must trace the progression of information through the system from stimuli to responses. To construct an IP theory one must first postulate certain stages of processing. This is not always easy, and the method of doing so will vary from situation to situation. One generally starts by mapping out a logically necessary sequence of processes, which must include at least stimulus decoding and response selection stages. Then various experimental methods can be used to search for manipulations that differentially affect hypothesized stages. Although an IP model usually describes the mapping from one stage to another, it is generally the case that several different stages can operate at once. For example, in reading aloud, one can pronounce a word while silently reading ahead to identify the next word. Several stages can operate at once; but if a particular input were followed through the system, the operations carried out on it might occur in sequential order (thus the basis of the term "stage"). In this case, the IP model lends itself to powerful analytic devices, such as Donders's subtraction method, Sternberg's (1969) additive factor method (AFM), backward masking, and various mathematical models. In this situation, each of the hypothesized underlying mechanisms of psychological processing can be associated with a separate segment of time between a stimulus and the response to that stimulus. Furthermore, the operations within a stage might be characterized by a mathematical expression.

It should be stressed that not all researchers using the IP approach claim to explain the processes underlying behavior. For example, mental processes have been conceptualized more weakly as intervening variables that permit a parsimonious interpretation of research findings. In this view, IP is purely pragmatic in allowing descriptive and prescriptive accounts that would not be possible without mental processes as intervening variables. Van der Heijden & Stebbins (1990) claim this much less ambitious goal for the IP approach. For these authors, the only reasonable goal of the IP approach is to describe differences in behavior as a function of differences in external and/or internal conditions: A certain behavior under situation A may be expected to be more accurate or faster, for example, than this same behavior under situation B. To achieve even this more limited goal, however, the IP approach must explain the processes causing behavior (Hatfield 1991).

Note that Newell & Simon's metatheory (the Physical Symbol Systems view) is more restrictive than the IP approach we articulate here (see the section below on variations on the IP approach). We do not restrict representations to symbols, let alone discrete symbols, nor do we restrict processes to rule-like operations performed on these symbols. For example, the currency of most memory models usually consists of memory traces, feature vectors, or simply familiarity—continuous representations similar to activation in many connectionist models. Thus, IP psychologists do not necessarily subscribe to Fodor's (1975) notion of a "language of thought." Within IP, processes are not necessarily rules, nor are representations always discrete objects, concepts, or events. This distinction has played an important role in contemporary theory. The recent connectionist view (e.g. Rumelhart & McClelland 1986) is essentially an alternative to the Physical Symbol Systems view but falls within the general IP framework (Massaro 1988, 1990).

Having defined the IP approach, we must further articulate its goals. We therefore evaluate and seek to justify the IP approach as a metatheory for psychological inquiry. We review well-known constraints on psychological inquiry and their implications for research strategy.

Justifications of the Approach

Although many psychologists work within the IP framework, the approach has not often been justified explicitly. Although most existing justifications in our textbooks center around criticisms of behaviorism, IP has adopted many of the best features of the behaviorist's experimental paradigm (van der Heijden & Stebbins 1990). Even the object of inquiry did not change as dramatically during the "cognitive revolution" as many textbooks have suggested. For example, empirical work on attention did not diminish during the heyday of behaviorism, although the concept of attention carried less theoretical value (Lovie 1983). Van der Heijden & Stebbins (1990) review evidence that the IP approach provided few features absent from mainstream experimental psychology. We must nevertheless not underestimate the importance of the attempt by the IP approach to account for the mental processes intervening between stimulus and response. Where behaviorism aimed to understand behavior, the IP approach seeks to elucidate the processes that cause behavior

(Hatfield 1991). As in other natural sciences, the IP approach attempts to understand complex behavior in terms of the interaction of simpler processes.

CONSTRAINTS ON PSYCHOLOGICAL INQUIRY   One way to justify the IP approach is to consider it in light of several constraints on psychological research. The first is that behavior is both variable and complex. By dissecting complex behaviors into simpler component stages, the IP approach may offer the parsimony critical to scientific inquiry. The IP approach is less daunted than other approaches by behavioral variability because it attends to information and information processing of component stages rather than to global behaviors. As an example, individual differences in speech perception may be caused by differences in information at a particular stage of information processing (Massaro 1992).

A second constraint on psychological research stems from our inadequacies as theorists and researchers. As noted several centuries ago by Francis Bacon, we tend to interpret the world as more orderly than it actually is. In addition, scientists, like all humans, have a strong confirmation bias: We actively search for evidence that supports our beliefs, often ignoring contradictory data.

Mitroff (1974) and Wenner & Wells (1990) documented confirmation bias in even the most experienced scientists. In addition, both political maneuvering (Mahoney 1976) and downright cheating sometimes occur in scientific inquiry (Broad & Wade 1982).

A third factor affecting psychological inquiry is the difficulty of determining which of many possible theories best explains a given phenomenon. Consider the competing current theories of language acquisition and use. At issue is whether a child's ability to produce language requires an internalization of rules, or whether it can be explained adequately by reference to associative and generalization mechanisms (MacWhinney & Leinbach 1991; Rumelhart & McClelland 1986; Pinker & Prince 1988; Plunkett & Marchman 1991). In Berko's classic experiment (1958), young children were able to generate plurals of pseudowords they had never heard before. Berko concluded that the children used a rule to achieve the "correct" outcome. As emphasized by Baron (1977), Brooks (1978), and Glushko (1979), however, the children might have performed correctly by generalizing from specific words they already knew. Knowing the plurals of rug, bug, and tug, children might simply generalize that the plural of wug would be wugs.

IMPLICATIONS FOR PSYCHOLOGICAL INQUIRY   Three characteristics consistent with the IP approach can overcome the three constraints just mentioned. First, the research strategies of falsification (Popper 1959) and strong inference (Chamberlin 1965; Platt 1964) should be used. Given the constraints on inquiry, the investigator must develop opposing models and devise an experiment capable of distinguishing between the predictions of the different models.

Contradictory evidence disqualifies a theory—even a theory consistent with many other findings. For example, although the hypothesis that whole word shape had a function in reading was consistent with many findings, it was falsified by means of an IP approach (Adams 1979; Paap et al 1984).

The falsification strategy has been criticized (Feyerabend 1975). One criticism concerns the obvious boundary conditions for any test, but we do not see how this disqualifies a falsification strategy. Newell (1990) argues that researchers should nurture rather than falsify theories. Newell sees falsification as a weak research strategy because it leads not to rejection but only to modification of theories. We argue, on the contrary, that the process of modification allows large subclasses of models to be rejected. Moreover, "modification" is an inappropriate description of the outcome if the contrasting alternatives are specific enough. If an experiment decides between categorical and continuous perception (Massaro 1987), it is difficult to see how one alternative can be modified without being made identical to the other. As long as we are concerned with specific assumptions rather than global theories, falsification, strong inference, and fine-grained analysis should be profitable.

Second, we must develop specific, precise, and simple experiments in order to reveal fundamental regularities in the phenomena we study. Such regularities or laws cannot easily be discerned amid the myriad factors present in complex situations. A New Realist philosophy of science allows for predictability in the laboratory but not in the naturally varying environment (Manicas & Secord 1983). Theories will have predictive power only in the laboratory where complexity can be reduced, measured, and controlled. In many respects, the complexity of the prototypical psychology experiment still exceeds any theory's predictive power.

Third, the IP approach enables the investigator to perform the kind of thorough, systematic, and fine-grained analyses of observations that alone can enable the winnowing of alternative interpretations.

We must attempt actively to eliminate alternative models. In addition, parsimonious models are to be preferred. Collyer (1985) argued that a more complex model (with more free parameters) is not necessarily preferable even if it is more accurate than a simpler model. It is difficult to falsify models so general that they predict a wide range of alternative results. One research strategy permits only models with "discriminating taste" to survive. A model has discriminating taste if it predicts *only* actual results, not the universe of possible results.

Metatheoretical Issues and IP

Several metatheoretical issues must be addressed to help situate the IP approach. The first—identifiability—concerns the feasibility of discriminating among alternative explanations of a set of observations. The second—proximal vs distal causes—concerns the types of evidence most relevant to psychology (to IP models in particular).

IDENTIFIABILITY   What may be a weakness of the IP approach concerns whether various explanatory models can be differentiated by experimental results. The so-called identifiability issue concerns whether a given model of an experimental result can be *identified* as the correct one. The issue arises from the theorems of E. F. Moore (1956) and from subsequent work in formal automata theory (see also Greeno & Steiner 1964). Moore was concerned with the behavior of sequential machines. Observers of machines or people can record only their inputs and outputs. It is not possible to look, so to speak, inside the black box. The question is: To what extent can the accuracy of one model of the inner workings of a black box be distinguished from that of another model, given only a set of input-output observations? Moore proved that any input-output function can be exactly mimicked by some other such function. No explanatory model of an experimental result can exclude all others.

Several prominent investigators have been convinced by this argument. Hintzman (1991), for example, points out how exemplar models of categorization can explain outcomes once thought explicable exclusively by prototype models. Hintzman (1991) advocates the use of formal models in scientific inquiry to overcome non-identifiability. For Anderson (1990b), the identifiability problem places an enormous constraint on "traditional" psychological research concerned with mechanism or process. How can we converge on a given process or mechanism when we can always compose another set of processes to make the same prediction? Anderson's solution is to limit the family of acceptable models to those that are behaviorally optimal. We deal with Anderson's strategy of adaptive rationality in the next section.

Scientific inquiry can potentially choose among apparently nonidentifiable models by extending the empirical data-base, evaluating the models on the basis of parsimony, and testing among viable models using the principles of falsification and strong inference described above. Extending the data-base to include additional measures of performance is a valuable strategy for distinguishing models that make identical input-output predictions of other measures. Consider a series of experiments on how children add two numbers. One model claims that children use a simple lookup table. A second model claims that, at one stage of development, the child recognizes the numbers, chooses the larger one, and then adds the smaller number by counting from the larger to the smaller in successive units (Groen & Parkman 1972). Thus "6 + 3" requires the series "6, 7, 8, 9," whereas "7 + 1" requires only the shorter series "7, 8". Both models predict correct answers to addition problems. However, experiments have been able to falsify the first model of addition by measuring reaction times (RTs) to different problems. The problem "6 + 3" takes about the same amount of time as the problem "4 + 3," as predicted by both the lookup table and counting models. However, these problems take longer than "7 + 1," a result consistent only with the counting model.

Within the IP approach, Townsend (1990) has repeatedly demonstrated that what look like the results of a serial search process in cognition may actually be the results of a parallel search process. A phenomenon such as limited cognitive capacity could cause parallel search to produce the same observable results as serial search. Such demonstrations do not leave the psychologist helpless to pursue the distinction between the two kinds of search, since certain experimental results remain more informative than others. A flat function showing no increase in RT with increases in the number of items is evidence against a serial search. Furthermore, there should be experimental manipulations that can address the role of limited capacity when increasing linear functions are found.

It is also possible to identify parallel processing without manipulating the memory or array set sizes (Schweickert 1978). Egeth & Dagenbach (1991) presented two-element displays in which the visual quality of the elements was independently manipulated, resulting in displays in which 0, 1, or 2 of the items were of high quality. The diagnostic was based on target-absent trials, in which both items would always have to be searched. It was assumed that a high-quality item could be searched in time T, whereas a low-quality item would take $T + \Delta T$ to search. If the search process occurred serially, then it would be expected to take an average of $2 \times (T + \Delta T)$ on low-low trials, $T + (T + \Delta T)$ on low-high or high-low trials, and $2T$ on high-high trials. If the two items could be searched in parallel, then the search would be completed when the slowest item-search was completed—on the average, in time $(T + \Delta T)$ when at least one of the items was of low quality, and in time T when both items were of high quality. Results agreed with the parallel processing predictions when subjects searched arrays consisting of the letters X and O, as well as arrays of T and L in canonical orientation. When the arrays consisted of T and L and the orientation of each letter varied, however, the predictions for serial processing were fulfilled. The difference may have occurred because subjects can perceive well-learned patterns (letters) in parallel but have no well-learned representation of rotated letters. Alternatively, our poorer sensitivity to oblique than to vertical and horizontal lines may account for the difference.

As pointed out by S. Sternberg (personal communication), within the serial model described by Egeth & Dagenbach, it must be assumed that (*a*) *all* operations influenced by legibility are serial and (*b*) there is no additional switching time on trials with two letters differing in visual quality. If either of these two assumptions does not hold, a mechanism that includes an underlying "serial" process might give results matching the parallel model. Conversely, Egeth & Dagenbach warned that their diagnostic is not conclusive for results indicating serial processing. The reason is that a subject using parallel search cannot respond in the target-absent condition until all of the items in the array have been perceived. With variability in the perception times, the more poor-quality items in the display, the slower would be the expected processing time. Thus, a parallel search could give mean RTs similar to those expected from a serial search. Notwithstanding the limits of this diagnostic method, it holds promise and can be broadened. For an example of how RT distributions might be analyzed, see Roberts & Sternberg (in press).

Roberts & Sternberg (in press) apply a falsification and strong-inference strategy within the context of the additive factor method (AFM) to overcome problems of identifiability. They describe three models—a successive stage model, an alternative pathways model, and a cascade model—each of which can predict additive effects of two factors on RTs. The standard stage model assumes serially arranged and separately changeable processes. Roberts & Sternberg (in press) strengthen this stage model by adding the assumption of stochastic independence—the durations of the stages in question are stochastically independent. The alternative pathways model assumes that one process is used on some proportion p of the trials and another process is used on the other $1 - p$ trials. The cascade model assumes that one process provides continuous output to a second process that occurs concurrently. Although these three models are not identifiably different with respect to mean RTs (Ashby 1982; McClelland 1979), they make different predictions about the RT distributions. The results from four diverse experiments were reanalyzed to test the new predictions of the models (see also Ashby & Townsend 1980). The analyses of the RT distributions and their variances falsified the alternate pathways model and cascade model, while supporting the stage model. The success of these analyses provides a boost for the IP approach. The research illustrates the value of a falsification strategy in inquiry, how problems with identifiability can be overcome, and the potential for broadening the domain of inquiry by extending the range of dependent measures and statistical tests used.

Other recent research has made progress in overcoming identifiability problems. In Massaro & Friedman's (1990) analysis, some models that cannot be identified as correct in a task with just two response alternatives made different predictions for four responses. Cohen & Massaro (in press) demonstrated that some models required more free parameters than others. Massaro (1989b) performed a fine-grained analysis on the joint contribution of stimulus information and context in order to distinguish between the Fuzzy Logical Model of Perception (FLMP) and the TRACE model of speech perception. McClelland (1991) then modified TRACE and the class of interactive activation models to bring them into line with the new empirical results. Although the FLMP and interactive activation models now made similar predictions for asymptotic performance, Massaro & Cohen (1991) were able to discriminate between the models by attending to their predictions about the dynamics of information processing. The interactive activation models had difficulty predicting (*a*) substantial context effects, given little processing time, and (*b*) a strong stimulus influence, given substantial processing time. The FLMP, on the other hand, provided a good quantitative description of these results.

In summary, the problem of identifiability is *not* insurmountable. Moore's theorem applies to the situation in which there is only a single experimental result. Rewarding progress can be made by examining additional predictions of the models and additional experimental situations (Townsend & Ashby 1983). Other examples of solutions to the identifiability problem are described below.

PROXIMAL AND DISTAL CAUSATION   A second issue that helps situate the IP approach concerns the causes of behavior. An important distinction made in evolutionary biology is between proximal (occurring nearby—here construed as nearby in time) and distal (temporally distant) influences on behavior (Alcock 1989). Proximal influences (proximal causes) include psychological processes that affect behavior. Distal causes concern the adaptive significance of an observed behavior. As psychologists, we consider primarily proximal influences. For example, what visual features are used in letter recognition, how are these features combined, and how is a decision made on the basis of this information? Distal causes, such as how the ability of the visual system to detect edges evolved, we usually ignore. Research within the IP approach is concerned with ongoing mental processes, whose modulation by proximal causes is most readily observed.

Some psychologists, on the other hand, have considered distal causation as a constraint upon psychological theorizing. As a solution to the identifiability problem Anderson (1990b) proposes selection of the model that assumes optimal adaptation to the environment. In most domains, however, many models can meet optimality criteria (Gigerenzer et al 1988; Massaro & Friedman 1990). Furthermore, optimality and computational constraints are fuzzy concepts that seem to be used without consensus. Recent explanations within evolutionary theory seem to stretch traditional notions of optimal behavior (Anderson 1990b; Cosmides 1989; Real 1991). In addition, Schoemaker (1991) offers several cases where "optimality" does not explain the phenomenon of interest.

Finally, it is likely that not every behavior is optimal. Evolutionists note many behaviors that have no obvious purpose. The questions of interest to psychologists are fundamentally empirical ones not simply answerable in terms of the optimality of models (Nosofsky 1991).

The issue of proximal vs distal causation can be clarified by acknowledging different levels of understanding in inquiry. David Marr described three levels at which any machine carrying out an information-processing task must be understood. In computer terms, the computational level is an abstract description of the problem to be solved, the algorithmic level is the software program to solve the problem, and the implementation level is the computer it is being run on. The computational level concerns the nature of the problem being solved. This entails the information available and the mapping of this information to another kind of information. It is clear that evolutionary history can inform this computational level of analysis. The algorithmic level, which is most compatible with the IP approach, entails the operations that transform the information from one type to another. This level specifies the representations for the input and output and the mapping between them. Understanding proximal causation seems most productive in illuminating the algorithmic level. The implementation or hardware level describes the physical realization of the algorithmic level. Both distal and proximal causation would appear to be relevant to the hardware level.

CHARACTERIZING STAGES OF PROCESSING

Here we present recent evidence that information processing occurs in stages, and then we take up several important issues related to stages of processing. Given a single stimulus, we can distinguish between input and output representations, and between transformation and transmission processes. Each of these representations and processes can be characterized as discrete or continuous. Comparable distinctions apply when multiple stimuli are presented. If multiple codes can co-exist in a stage, they can be processed either in parallel or serially. Finally, strategic and attentional effects can modulate the character of information processing.

Recent Evidence for Stages of Processing

An analysis of information processing performance into separate stages can lead to specific, quantitative predictions for a particular task if one is willing to make certain strong assumptions about the nature of processing. One must, of course, assume that some processing stages between the presentation of a stimulus and the subject's response can be identified. Sanders (1990) identifies seven stages of processing and presents evidence for each of these stages. Massaro (1991) describes a variety of research on perception-action relationships in terms of a similar stage model.

Roberts (1987) provided dramatic evidence for two stages of processing in accounting for response rates under various levels of food deprivation and various schedules of reinforcement in rats, pigeons, and goldfish. Response rates in these animals show selective influences from deprivation time and schedule of reinforcement. These two influences combine multiplicatively to influence response rate. Roberts proposed that the first process generates pulses that are transmitted to the second process, a filter. A response occurs whenever a pulse passes through the filter. Either deprivation time changes the rate of pulses in the generator and reinforcement schedule changes the setting of the filter, or vice versa. This simple theory was made more complex by allowing the occurrence of operant responses that are not under stimulus control. In the tradition of strong inference, Roberts showed how this stage theory gave a better description of the results than alternative theories that violated the assumption underlying the stage theory. This support for stages with different organisms and behaviors is an impressive achievement in psychological inquiry.

Using an IP approach, Theios & Amrhein (1989) illuminated the representation and processes involved in reading words and naming pictures. An IP model sought to explain why subjects took longer to name pictures than to read words. According to this model, picture (and color) naming took longer because it involved two processes (determining the meaning and mapping this meaning into a response) while word naming involved only one. The same model described visual and conceptual comparisons among pictures and words—a successful use of Donders's Subtractive Method. Using this model it was possible to test whether pictures are also perceived more easily than words. According to this model, they were not: Previous findings to the contrary had apparently been based on the fact that the pictures were larger than the words.

Discrete vs Continuous Representation and Processing

As Miller (1988, 1990) has pointed out, if one assumes that processing occurs in stages one must consider separately (a) whether the representational codes input to or output from a particular stage of processing are discrete or continuous, (b) whether the transformation accomplished at a particular stage takes place in a discrete manner or gradually (i.e. continuously), and (c) whether the information is transmitted to the next stage in discrete steps or continuously. These are important issues within the IP approach because some IP models require types of discreteness and some require types of continuity (see below). Miller acknowledges that continuity and discreteness are not dichotomous, but matters of degree. For example, placing a stimulus feature in one of many ordinally arranged categories would probably produce experimental observations indistinguishable from those using continuous coding but far different from those using a binary classification system.

THEORETICAL POSSIBILITIES   Stage models propose four ways in which discrete and continuous information and information processing can occur. In all cases, the *input* to a stage can be continuous or discrete. Second, either of these types of input can be *transformed* in a discrete or continuous fashion. Third, the *transmission* of information from one stage to the next can be discrete or continuous. [Miller (1988) argued that if the transformation is discrete the transmission must also be discrete. However, consider a discrete transformation of 0 to 1 with a transmission that sums the outcome of the transformation over some finite time. The average passed on by the transmission will be 0 until the transformation produces a 1. The transmission will then grow continuously, however, depending on the averaging period.] Finally, regardless of the type of transformation and/or transmission, the *output* of a stage can be discrete or continuous. Sixteen alternatives appear to be possible.

Discrete transmission is usually assumed to apply in the additive factor method (AFM); without it, RT would not necessarily equal the sum of durations of processing at all stages. In addition, application of the AFM is usually assumed to require errorless performance (in which coding is necessarily discrete). However, Schweickert (1985) proved that, with some additional assumptions, factors having additive effects on RT will also have additive effects on log percent correct. This method should encourage investigators to carry out their tests at several points on the speed-accuracy function. Studies with performance significantly below perfect accuracy can be more sensitive to effects of the independent variables of interest. There are other IP models of stages with continuous codes, transformation, and transmission that make specific testable predictions. For example, McClelland's (1979) cascade model assumes that information flows continuously from one stage to the next. Still, the idea of sequential stages is meaningful, and quantitative predictions for reaction time can be derived. Similarly, in the dynamic FLMP (Massaro & Cohen 1991), evaluation and integration transform and transmit information continuously, and yet quantitative predictions of response probability and RT can be made.

In many instances the outcome of identification is necessarily continuous or "fuzzy" because the available category labels describe some stimuli better than others (Massaro 1987). This situation would violate the constant-stage output assumption of the AFM. That is, the output of an identification stage would take on a range of values rather than be limited to one of the response alternatives in the task. This is not a problem for the IP approach in general because continuous outputs are compatible with serially arranged stages of processing that are separately influenced. In the FLMP, for example (Massaro & Friedman 1990), continuous information is obtained from each source and then transmitted to an integration stage. The outcome of the integration stage, also continuous, is transmitted to a decision stage. The stages in the FLMP are sequential and separately changeable even though the outputs of some of them are continuous.

An alternative scheme, intermediate between discrete and continuous, is Miller's (1988) asynchronous discrete coding model. Here successive stages can overlap in time—i.e. information can be transmitted to the next stage before the current stage is complete. However, the transmission of information about each separable code within the stimulus is discrete. As an example, discrete information about the color, shape, and size of an object would be separately transmitted as soon as the processing of each of these dimensions is completed. Several recent studies show discreteness in some situations and continuity in others, a result consistent with Miller's asynchronous discrete model. However, results from other paradigms, such as backward recognition masking and speech identification, falsify the asynchronous discrete model's central assumption that a single feature dimension is transmitted in discrete steps.

EMPIRICAL EVIDENCE   At some stage of processing, information and information processing are best characterized as continuous. In an ingenious pioneering study, Allport (1968) showed that the sensory system makes information available to conscious perception continuously. Sets of lines on an oscilloscope, presented with a short asynchrony between lines, were perceived in a particular overlapping fashion that could only be explained by a continuously moving window of perceived simultaneity. Even though lines were presented one at a time, 11 of 12 were visible at any moment because of the subject's sensory memory. A discrete-moment hypothesis would predict perceived movement of the nonvisible line or "shadow" in a direction opposite of the line presentation sequence, but the shadow instead moved in the same direction as the line presentation sequence, as a continuously moving temporal window of experience would predict. A recent sophisticated study ruled out two general classes of discrete perceptual moment (stimulus-independent, stimulus-triggered) (Ulrich 1987). Most recent inquiries have searched for discreteness using RTs rather than perceptual reports.

Miller & Hackley (1992) have extended Miller's research on response preparation. Miller (1982) had previously showed that a subject's hand can be put in a response-ready state before the subject knows exactly how to respond. The subject was signaled about which hand to use in the response by means of an easily processed feature of the stimulus (e.g. its shape); which finger to use was signaled by a feature that took longer to process (e.g. subtle differences in size). In their work a decade later Miller & Hackley employed the lateralized readiness potential (LRP), a component of the movement-related brain potential, as an additional dependent measure and adopted a slightly different "go/no-go" procedure in which the easier stimulus feature signaled which hand to use if a response was to be made, while the more difficult feature signaled whether or not to make the response at all. Motor preparation, as measured by the LRP, was observed even when the response was ultimately aborted, suggesting that the two critical features of the stimulus were transmitted at different times. In a similar study, Osman et al (1992) found that the two stimulus characteristics were processed concurrently and that preparation of the appropriate response hand began before the "go/no-go" decision was completed. These results are consistent with both the continuous and asynchronous discrete models.

The continuous model predicts that information along a single dimension is transformed and transmitted continuously. The asynchronous discrete model, on the other hand, assumes that information from a single dimension is transmitted only after processing is complete (i.e. discretely). To distinguish between the models, a subsequent experiment used four values of a single attribute, size (with scale values of 8, 10, 16, and 19). An easy judgment about size was enough to decide which hand to make ready (e.g. for some subjects, size 8 would indicate a left-hand reaction and size 19 a right-hand reaction). The two intermediate values signaled that no response was to be made. Visual processing should indicate which hand should be used before indicating whether or not a response should be made. If this information is transmitted to the response stage, a LRP should be observed. That no advanced preparation was observed was interpreted to suggest that a given individual stimulus feature is transmitted all at once rather than continuously. Of course, the size experiment only supports the null hypothesis, and there was a nonsignificant trend toward a readiness potential in that experiment (Miller & Hackley 1992: Figure 6). There is also evidence from other paradigms, such as backward recognition masking, for continuous processing of single stimulus dimensions (see below).

Reeve & Proctor (1984) challenged the logic of Miller's demonstrations of advanced motor preparation. They used a speeded keypress response with the index or middle finger of the left or right hand. Advanced preparation cues in the form of "+" marks above some keys allowed the subject to ready the appropriate hand, to ready the same finger of each hand (e.g. both the left and right index fingers), or to ready two unrelated fingers (e.g. left index and right middle). A control condition carrying no information was also included. Subjects could ready any combination of fingers if given a long enough (e.g. 3-s) preparatory period. Moreover, in an experiment in which the left and right hands were placed on the keyboard in an overlapping fashion, with fingers in the order "right index, left middle, right middle, left index," it was shown that the speed advantage was for preparation of responses to be made in a particular (left or right) spatial portion of the response array, not for the left or right hand per se.

The types of preparation observed in these complex situations (long preparation intervals, lack of spatial separation of hands) might not apply to the simpler situations that Miller has used. Even if they do apply, however, they do not (contrary to Reeve & Proctor's suggestion) negate Miller's conclusions about the continuous passage of information to the motor system. Even if advanced preparation always occurs on the basis of spatial location and not the limb of the effector, it is motor preparation nonetheless, and an easily perceived feature of the stimulus still facilitates that preparation.

Meyer et al (1985) addressed the issue of whether information can be transmitted continuously to a response preparation. They used a choice RT task in which a left-hand response was signaled by an arrow facing in one direction, and a right-hand response by an arrow facing in the other direction. However, a preceding prime stimulus presented on some trials perfectly predicted the RT signal that was to follow (words were followed by right arrows, nonwords by left arrows). The prime was presented either 200 or 700 ms in advance of the arrow. A 700-ms interval consistently permitted the subject to be in a state of readiness, whereas a 200-ms interval did so about half the time. The distribution of responses in the 200-ms condition looked like a hybrid of the distributions in the 700-ms and no-prime conditions, with an early peak coinciding with that of the 700-ms condition, a later peak coinciding with that of the no-prime condition, and tails covering the entire range. This result was taken to suggest that information from the prime was transmitted to the response-preparation process in a discrete all-or-none fashion and that, in the 200-ms condition, subjects were in a prepared state on some trials but not on others. However, the results were different in a situation in which signals were presented at four different locations, signaling a response with the left or right middle or index finger (with a complex mapping of signal to finger). In this situation, the prime stimuli only indicated which hand to use in making the response, not which finger. In contrast to the previous experiment, the 200-ms condition produced an RT distribution with a single, intermediate peak, suggesting continuous transmission of information from the prime. Thus whereas stimulus information sufficient to plan the response was used in a discrete, all-or-none fashion, stimuli providing only partial information about the response produced a continuous buildup of readiness over time.

Support for continuous stimulus evaluation is found in the results of the "speed-accuracy decomposition technique" (Meyer et al 1988a,b), which relies upon a RT task in which subjects are induced sometimes to make hasty decisions following the appearance of a response signal at various intervals. The results were analyzed with a mathematical model in which it is assumed that the formation of complete stimulus information is in a race with a guessing process (based on partial information and response bias) that is initiated when the response signal occurs. Guessing accuracy was found to increase in a continuous fashion for a simple lexical decision task but in a stepwise (3-state) way for a more complex task in which the lexical status of two words were to be compared. However, in the latter situation, the general availability of continuous information for each stimulus item might be obscured when the two items must be compared. A comparison process might wait for discrete information about each of the two items before it begins. Thus, the continuous transformation and transmission of information of one stage might be obscured by a following discrete stage.

The Meyer et al (1988a,b) studies may challenge continuous theories less than would first appear. Ratcliff (1988) showed that even the results believed by Meyer et al to support the discrete model could be explained by a continuous model. An important aspect of the analysis concerns the decision time required under "partial" and "complete" stimulus information. Meyer et al assumed that the decision time would be equivalent in these two cases. Ratcliff, on the other hand, argued that more decision time would be required given "partial" rather than "complete" information. His argument is reasonable given the well-known negative correlation between decision time and stimulus information. Subjects are naturally slower when stimulus information is incomplete. This finding has been described within the context of signal-detection theory—response time is longer to the extent the perceptual observation is close to the criterion separating two responses (Norman & Wickelgren 1969; Thomas & Myers 1972). As an example, RT to a speech stimulus is positively correlated with ambiguity of the speech event (Massaro 1987:Ch. 5). Subjects' longer decision times when given "partial" than when given "complete" information could be responsible for the results taken to support a discrete model.

Abrams & Balota (1991) extended our understanding of IP by adding a behavioral measure of force of a handle movement in the RT paradigm (see also Schweickert, in press). Word frequency influences RT in a lexical decision task; this study showed that it also influences response force (although the effects were small). More forceful responses were found for high-frequency words. A similar result was found in the Sternberg memory search task. Response force reflected the relative evidence for "yes" and "no" responses. These results can be interpreted in several ways. Either the information arriving at the decision process was stronger in some cases than in others (a continuous-coding hypothesis—e.g. more word-like information for high-frequency words) or the information was transmitted to the decision process over different periods (a continuous-transmission hypothesis—e.g. temporally more compact transmission in the case of high-frequency words). Of course, both hypotheses could be true.

Additional evidence for both continuous transformation and transmission processes and continuous output codes is the backward masking of recognition. This task has been valuable for examining the temporal course of perceptual processing of visual (Breitmeyer 1984) as well as auditory (Hawkins & Presson 1986; Kallman & Massaro 1979, 1983) stimuli. A brief target stimulus is followed, after a variable stimulus onset asynchrony (SOA), by a second stimulus (the mask) and then a multiple-choice test of the target's identity. The amount of time for which the target information is available for recognition processing can be carefully controlled by manipulating the duration of the SOA. The accuracy of target identification increases as the SOA lengthens to about 250 ms (Breitmeyer 1984; Cowan 1984, 1988; Kallman & Massaro 1983; Massaro 1975; Turvey 1973), even though the presence of the unrecognized targets can still be detected.

Although two different explanations of backward recognition masking have been offered, both are consistent with the view that information is transmitted continuously from one stage of processing to the next. Consider presentation of a pure tone that must be identified as high or low in pitch. All would argue that here the stimulus code is continuous. Is the code transformed and transmitted in a discrete or continuous fashion? According to Massaro (1972, 1975), the target tone is transduced by the listener's sensory system and retained in a preperceptual sensory store that briefly holds a single event within the sensory modality. Processing of the target is necessary for perceptual recognition. The mask is said to replace the target in the preperceptual auditory store and therefore to terminate any further reliable perceptual processing of the target. An account offered by Hawkins & Presson (1986) differs from this one in that the mask is said to switch attention away from the target rather than replacing it in the sensory store.

In either case, a continuous response output would suggest that transformation and transmission were continuous. Such continuity is indeed observed. No matter whether the discrimination must be made on the basis of a single feature such as pitch (Massaro 1975) or on the basis of multiple features (Moore & Massaro 1973; Kallman & Massaro 1983), steplike masking functions have never been observed, even in individual-subject results. An alternative to this continuity-based explanation would be that the relevant information is all-or-none and that the probability that the discrete information is available on a particular trial is what varies with the SOA. However, backward recognition masking also occurs in experiments in which subjects report the perceived quality of the target using a graduated response scale rather than identifying the target in a multiple-choice situation (Cowan 1987; Idson & Massaro 1977). Such experiments indicate a gradual shift in perceived quality across SOA rather than a change in the proportion of an all-or-none response. For example, Cowan (1987) measured the perceived loudness of targets of 3 intensities and found a general growth of loudness across SOAs for all targets, superimposed on an increasing discriminability of the loudness of targets across SOAs. Still, a closer examination of the distribution of responses (which should be bimodal if transformation and transmission of a discrete code occurred in an all-or-none fashion) would prove helpful (Massaro & Cohen 1983).

As the above discussion suggests, it is important to distinguish between the metatheory of IP and the assumptions made within particular applications of the metatheory (e.g. Sternberg's AFM). It is important to evaluate models with reference to the specific objects processed, the types of processing implicated, and the strategies induced by the task. Continuously formed information sometimes may be transmitted in discrete packages when the task demands discourage the use of partial information and encourage delaying the response until more complete information is available (i.e. the "criterion" amount of information necessary for some level of accuracy).

Serial vs Parallel Processing

Whereas the issue of discreteness vs continuity is relevant to how a single stimulus item is processed in each stage, the issue of serial vs parallel processing concerns the processing of a stimulus array at each stage. Resolving this issue is important because the ultimate goal of a processing model is to determine how the entire stimulus field, not simply an item within that field, is processed. If it uses serial processing, a stage can handle items only one at a time; if it employs parallel processing, it can handle multiple items at the same time. The question of whether serial or parallel processing is used must be settled independently for each processing stage.

Determination of the manner of processing is not a simple task. Early on, in an experiment involving search of a set of items in memory to detect the presence or absence of a probe item, Sternberg (1966) found a linear increase in RT as a function of the number of items in the memory set. The slope of the function for trials in which the probe was a member of the set of items in memory was the same as that for the trials in which it was not a member. Sternberg sought to account for this finding with a model of exhaustive serial search. However, as Townsend (1974) pointed out, a parallel search of the items in memory could also account for the results, provided that the time for each item-search is affected by the number of concurrent searches in a linear fashion. In Ratcliff's (1978) random walk model, for example, evidence of the presence or absence of the probe in the memory set is accumulated relative to all items in the memory set at once, until a decision threshold is reached. A linear increase in RT is one possible outcome that can be predicted by this model.

Ruling out the possibility that a process is serial is easier than excluding the possibility that it is parallel. For example, Schneider & Shiffrin (1977) asked subjects to search a set of 1–4 items presented on the computer screen to determine whether it included any one of 1–4 items held in memory. In a "consistent mapping" condition, the memory set on each trial was drawn from a larger, fixed set of items, and the foils were drawn from a different set. After considerable practice in this condition, response rates were no longer affected by the number of items in either the stimulus set or the memory set. This could occur only if subjects searched for all of the stimulus items in parallel, and is called "automatic processing." This result does not imply that it would hold for larger or unlimited sets, however (Shaw 1984).

In another condition, termed "variable mapping," the items that were the potential targets on some trials (i.e. members of the memory set) could be foils on other trials. This sort of search resulted in a roughly linear increase in the RT as a function of the number of items in either the stimulus set or the memory set, regardless of the amount of practice. This could be accounted for either by a "serial search" or by a parallel search at a rate that is slower when more items are present. The latter is termed a "capacity-limited parallel search," in which the nature of the limitation is left unspecified until there is evidence identifying it.

The traditional serial vs parallel processing distinction may not be the distinction that best captures what is important for IP models. A more fine-grained analysis would be better. Such an analysis would distinguish among fully serial processing (in which items can be processed only one at a time), several degrees of capacity-limited parallel processing (in which multiple items can be processed at once but with some interference between items), and capacity-free parallel processing (in which there is no interference). As an analogy, consider the case of pedestrians crossing a bridge. More important than a determination of whether the pedestrians cross one abreast or several abreast is an estimate of the delay in one pedestrian's passage as a function of the number of others hoping to cross simultaneously. The situation in which two or three people can pass at once is far closer to the one-at-a-time situation than to a 100-at-a-time circumstance. This analogy reveals the value of deter-mining in detail the efficiency of search over a wide range of conditions. Exemplifying this approach, Duncan & Humphreys (1989) observed that both (a) decreasing the similarity between the target and foils and (b) increasing the similarity among the foils increase efficiency. In terms of the bridge analogy, it is as if only some people are permitted to cross the whole bridge, such that passage is more efficient for those whose passage matters most. It would be useful for the bridge travel authority to have a simple means to distinguish the privileged class from others attempting to gain access to the bridge. The Duncan & Humphreys study suggests that the different categories of bridge crossers wear different uniforms, so to speak, to set them apart.

The limited-capacity model may apply even to automatic processing; the width of the bridge may simply vary with the degree of automaticity. Thus, Shaw (1984:111) suggested that automatic and controlled search differ quanti-tatively, not qualitatively. Fisher et al (1988) presented evidence supporting a different type of limited-channel model. Their assumption was that the re-sources devoted to each channel remain constant with changes in the number of stimuli in the display (load) up to a limit of about 4 channels. This model suits the bridge analogy even better than a limited-capacity model because here the most critical factor is thought to be rate of item presentation rather than a capacity to be divided among items.

Clearer distinctions are needed among the limited-capacity and limited-channel explanations. In one experiment, for example, Fisher et al required subjects to search for the digit 5 among letter foils in a series of matrixes of 8 items (high-load condition) or 4 items (low-load condition). In each condition, one matrix rapidly followed another, and in the low-load condition the display alternated between square and diamond arrangements of 4 items. A large load effect was obtained. However, what would happen if the square and diamond arrangements were randomly mixed? Fisher's limited-channel model would predict no added difficulty, because the rate of presentation has not changed and is still relatively low. A capacity-based model, on the other hand, would predict added difficulty, because the location at which the target may appear becomes less predictable.

Once a capacity-limited parallel process has been identified, further work can be focused on determining the nature of the capacity limitation. For example, in the case of consistently vs variably mapped search, Logan (1988) has proposed that the availability of sufficient knowledge in memory plays a critical role. His results from various experiments suggest that, in speeded tasks, there is a race between an algorithm and direct retrieval of the needed information from memory. When a sufficient number of exemplars with the correct stimulus-response mapping exist in memory, direct retrieval usually wins. This occurs after sufficient practice in a task with consistent mapping.

Strayer & Kramer (1990) clarified the nature of processing in Sternberg search tasks. They found that a secondary memory load influenced search rate in a variably mapped condition. When the emphasis on the search task relative to the secondary memory task was manipulated there were tradeoffs in performance in the two tasks. Neither secondary memory load effects nor tradeoffs were obtained following considerable practice in a consistently mapped condition. These results suggest that the search that is presumably used in a variably mapped condition involves holding the search set in a working memory with a limited storage capacity. Considerable practice in a consistently mapped condition changes this type of processing.

Attentional and Strategic Effects

As Shiffrin (1988) noted, "Attention has been used to refer to all those aspects of human cognition that the subject can control … or aspects of cognition having to do with limited resources or capacity, and methods of dealing with such constraints." While under certain circumstances stimulus search and memory search are apparently examples of unconstrained parallel processing, a processing bottleneck typically occurs later in the processing sequence when a response to each target must be selected and executed. Several studies (e.g. Duncan 1980; Sorkin et al 1973) suggest that, in contrast to the type of search in which only one target is present on each trial, there is considerable interference among multiple targets presented simultaneously.

In a study by Pashler (1989), subjects received a tone to be identified as quickly as possible, followed after a variable interval (50, 150, or 650 ms) by a visual array to be searched for a target (of a type that differed between experiments) at the subject's leisure. The array was followed by a mask to make target search and detection difficult. The interval between the tone (stimulus for Task 1) and array (stimulus for Task 2) had little effect on RT in Task 1 or on accuracy in Task 2. In other experiments, the array was not masked, and a speeded response was obtained in both tasks. In that situation, a dramatic impact of intertask interval on the RT for Task 2 was found, even when the first response was manual and the second response vocal. There was little influence of intertask interval on Task 1 RT. These results show that responding to Task 1 delays responding to Task 2, even though the perceptibility of Task 2 stimuli has not been affected.

Of course, it is unlikely that attentional effects are limited to one stage of processing. Johnston & Heinz (1978) showed that subjects can select on the basis of either physical or semantic characteristics, although with a greater cost in terms of performance on a secondary RT task in the case of semantic selection. A response bottleneck did not preclude perceptual limitations in the Pashler (1989) study, either. When Task 1 was a complex visual task (identification of a right-pointing slash among left-pointing slashes), perceptibility was affected along with response processes. Severe interference with Task 2 accuracy was observed. An IP explanation of these observations would identify detection of the physical cue and semantic recognition of the semantic cue as two different stages, and would differentiate the attentional limitations of these two stages.

Pashler (1990), too, argued for several types of attentional limitation. One is a general "bottleneck" or serial constraint on response selection. Superimposed on this general response bottleneck are limitations in more specific resources. One such limitation is a resource used to perceive elements within a complex visual array (Pashler 1989). Another is a short-term memory constraint that may come into play when subjects must make two similar, consecutive responses. Pashler (1990) found that unpredictability in the order of two responses greatly increased the amount of interference between them if both were manual responses, whereas predictability had little effect when one response was manual and one vocal. The residual interference that occurred regardless of response modality or predictability was taken to reflect a response bottleneck, whereas the effect that was dependent on predictability presumably reflected intrusion errors in short-term memory for the two manual responses. These three processing limitations may be localized in what would appear to be distinct stages of information processing (perceptual encoding of the stimulus, response buffering in memory, and response selection).

When attention does *not* have a consistent effect on an assumed stage of processing, that stage may have to be broken into smaller stages, according to the principle of decomposition described by Palmer & Kimchi (1986). For example, considerable evidence has suggested that while perception is partly preattentive, some important perceptual products emerge only in the presence of attention (Cowan 1988; Posner & Snyder 1975; Treisman 1991). Thus the stage termed "perception" may comprise at least two substages (e.g. featural encoding and featural combination) that are affected in different ways by manipulations of attention (also see Massaro 1985).

These considerations indicate a strategy for investigating attention within an IP approach. One should try to identify aspects of processing that are preattentive, and try to identify attentional effects that can be localized in a particular stage. A good example of this approach is a study by Shulman (1991), who found effects of attention (to one of two figures rotating in opposite directions) on the degree of motion aftereffect. A physiological example is the finding that attention to one of several auditory stimulus channels affects the latency of the eyeblink startle reflex (Hackley & Graham 1987). These studies suggest that attention can affect not only response processing but even fairly early stages of stimulus processing. As Kinchla (1992) concludes, selectivity occurs in many processes ranging from early to late stages of IP.

Strategies are controllable aspects of cognition in which control is exercised in order to maximize task performance. Attention and strategies are central to IP research (and to all of experimental psychology) in an important, often unacknowledged way. In our experiments we often require subjects to follow a precise protocol. In tasks with visual displays, we tell subjects to focus on (attend to) the fixation point; in memory tasks, to remember strategically a set of items; and so on. We take it for granted that subjects can follow these instructions to the letter, but we sometimes forget to ensure that they are actually doing so. For example, according to Logan (1988), subjects in the consistently mapped search task might carry it out not by using the presented search set on each trial, as Shiffrin & Schneider (1977) assumed, but by overlearning the entire superset from which each search set was drawn.

Summary

It is possible to use performance accuracy and speed to chart the flow of information through a number of distinct stages of information processing. Investigators have usefully shifted among several levels of analysis in order to capture different aspects of information flow. At a sequential-stage level, investigations have focused on factors that affect distinctly different segments in the chain of processing, treating the basic types of information transfer (e.g. discrete or continuous). Zooming in to a substage level, investigations have examined the responses of the processing system when multiple, concurrent demands are placed on a particular processing stage. Zooming out to a super-stage level, they have examined the strategic and attentional factors that modulate the way stages act and interact. The processing system appears capable of shifting from parallel processing and continuous transmission of information under low-demand conditions, to more serial processing and discrete transmission when necessary to meet special demands such as unfamiliar stimuli or the need for great accuracy of response.

These conclusions are speculative, but substantial empirical and theoretical progress is being made. For example, Yantis et al (1991) have provided a detailed discussion of various ways to analyze response distributions to determine whether subjects are using a single strategy or a mixture of strategies. Schweickert (in press) has summarized recent theoretical work that extracts from the intuitively appealing early concepts about interactions and non-interactions in parallel and serial processing (Sternberg 1975) a more logically complete set of dependencies. For example, factors affecting sequential stages can interact, but stages can be combined into superstages that do not interact. Researchers can usefully apply these concepts to new data, provided they take seriously the need to check the assumptions underlying the theoretical analyses.

ILLUSTRATIVE DOMAINS OF INQUIRY

Psychophysics

It took an engineering approach to appreciate the value of a stage model in psychophysics. Two stages occur between stimulus and response: sensory and decision. The sensory stage's input is the stimulus; its output is some sensory event. This information is made available to the decision stage before a response is made. The output of the decision operation determines the response, but its input is the information given by the outcome of the sensory process rather than by the stimulus itself. Transformation of the stimulus into a sensory experience is determined by both stages. The output of the sensory system—the sensation value—should be a direct function of the characteristics of the stimulus and the state of the sensory system. The operations of the decision stage should be affected by variables that determine the appropriateness of a response—for example, knowledge of the experimental situation, payoffs, attitudes, and motivations. Each process is influenced only by an exclusive set of variables. The rule of the decision process is independent of the operation of the sensory process. Similarly, the sensitivity of the sensory process should be independent of any decision bias induced by the decision process. The value of this distinction goes well beyond psychophysics. We discuss its use in visual perception, speech perception, reading, memory, and judgment. Before doing so, we consider evidence for a belief bias in addition to a decision bias.

BELIEF BIAS AND DECISION BIAS   The preceding two-stage analysis permits independent measures of sensitivity and bias. The former measures operation of the sensory process and the latter operation of the decision process. Although the distinction between sensitivity and bias is important, we must also distinguish between two types of bias. One we term a "belief bias," referring to the way the subject interprets the stimulus. The other we term a "decision bias," referring to the way the subject is inclined to respond, given the payoff matrix that is in place. A subject might go against his/her beliefs for a certain payoff. For example, subjects willingly learn to respond in concordance with false information feedback rather than with their actual experience. In one study, subjects learned to call a loud tone soft and a soft tone loud in order to match the feedback given after each trial (Massaro 1969).

Perhaps because it is difficult to distinguish between the two types of bias, signal-detection theory blurs belief bias and decision bias. However, the distinction can be made in some situations. If a signal-detection analysis is performed on an optical illusion, such as the Müller-Lyer figure, there is reason to believe that the illusion would be primarily reflected in bias and not sensitivity. That is, we would see the Müller-Lyer figure with outgoing wings as longer than a control figure but our ability to discriminate line length would remain intact. In fact, Nevin (1991) found that the illusion is adequately explained by a bias effect without changes in line-length discrimination. Although Nevin calls the bias "response bias," we interpret it as belief bias. The perceiver actually "sees" one line as longer than another, even though they are the same length (a true optical illusion).

Although the distinction between sensitivity and bias is reasonable and has been confirmed by experimental analysis, identification of the type of bias would remain speculative. Luckily, empirical techniques and theoretical analyses now exist that enable us to distinguish belief bias from decision bias. Connine & Clifton (1987) replicated the finding that lexical context can influence a phoneme judgment in speech (Ganong 1980). For example, subjects were more likely to report /t/ in the context -*ype* and /d/ in the context -*ice*. The lexical contribution occurred only within the ambiguous range of the stimulus property distinguishing /t/ and /d/. To address the bias issue, an ingenious follow-up study involved only nonwords. A monetary payoff scheme was imposed to bias the subjects to respond with one alternative or the other. The results of the test revealed a bias similar in magnitude to that found with lexical context. If the lexical effects are belief bias and the payoff effects are decision bias, the response probabilities cannot be taken to reflect this fact. Luckily, the pattern of RTs for the two tasks differed even though the response probabilities did not. When the bias was produced lexically, the RTs of word judgments were faster only for speech stimuli that gave a context effect on response probability. When the bias was produced with a monetary payoff, the RTs were always faster for the bias-consistent alternative even for speech stimuli that gave no effect of payoff on response probability. Given this evidence for two types of bias, it seems reasonable that the lexical effect induced a belief bias and the monetary payoff a decision bias.

Visual Perception

Stages of information processing have been taken most seriously in the field of visual perception (see Banks & Krajicek 1991 for a recent review). Perception is hierarchical; it is traditionally assumed, for example, that there are at least three stages of processing: retinal transduction, sensory cues, and perceived attributes (DeYoe & Van Essen 1988). There is a one-to-many and many-to-one relationship between sensory cues and perceived attributes. As an example, physical motion provides information about both the shape of an object and its movement. Similarly, information about the shape of an object is enriched not only by physical motion, but also by linear perspective, binocular disparity, and shading (e.g. chiaroscuro).

Bennett et al's (1989) "observer theory" has three basic assumptions compatible with most of our current understanding of perception: (*a*) perception is a process of inference, (*b*) perceptual inference is not deductively valid, and (*c*) perceptual inferences are biased. Of course, the first two assumptions go back at least to Helmholtz and require little explanation. The third simply means that the perceptual system reaches some interpretations in preference to others—seeing many two-dimensional projections as three-dimensional, for example. Included in perceptual bias is the minimality principle of Gestalt psychology: We see the simplest possible interpretation of a pattern (Leeuwenberg & Boselie 1988). The three assumptions mentioned here confront the inverse mapping problem: The perceiver's goal is to determine what environmental situation exists, given the current conflux of sensory cues.

Speech Perception

Stimulus information and context contribute to speech perception (Bagley 1900). An important controversial issue is the nature of their joint contribution. Two competing explanations are the TRACE model (McClelland & Elman 1986) and the Fuzzy Logical Model of Perception (FLMP; Massaro 1987, 1991). The first assumes that context modifies lower-level representations (a sensitivity effect); the second assumes independent contributions to a higher-level representation (a bias effect). The distinction between sensitivity and bias has enabled several tests between these alternatives. Simulations have shown that TRACE predicts sensitivity effects whereas the FLMP does not (Massaro 1989b). Using a signal-detection analysis of behavioral results, the contribution of phonological context on phoneme identification was shown to be located in bias and not sensitivity (Massaro 1989b). This result supports the FLMP and contradicts the predictions of the TRACE model. Similar conclusions are warranted for another set of context effects in speech perception.

In the original type of phonemic-restoration study (Warren 1970), a phoneme in a word is removed and replaced with some other stimulus, such as a tone or white noise. Subjects perceive the word as intact and have difficulty indicating what phoneme is missing. Samuel (1981) asked whether failure to spot the missing phoneme is a sensitivity effect or a bias effect, as these effects are defined in signal-detection theory. Signal and noise trials were tested. For noise trials, the phoneme was replaced with white noise. Signal trials contained the same noise superimposed on the original phoneme. Subjects indicated whether or not the original phoneme was present. Sensitivity is reflected in the degree to which the two types of trials can be discriminated, and can be indexed by d' within the context of signal-detection theory. Bias, indexed by β, would be reflected in the overall likelihood of saying that the original phoneme is present.

Samuel compared performance on phonemes in test words to performance on the phoneme segments presented in isolation. A bias was observed in that subjects were more likely to respond that the phoneme was present in the word than in the isolated segment. In addition, subjects discriminated the signal from the noise trials much better in the segment context than the word context. The d' values averaged two or three times larger for the segment context than for the word context. Thus, top-down context from the word appears to have a large negative effect on sensitivity. However, the segment vs word comparison in the Samuel study confounds stimulus contributions with top-down contributions (Massaro 1989b). Forward and backward masking may degrade the perceptual quality of a segment more when presented in a word than when presented alone. In addition, the word context may provide co-articulatory information about the critical phoneme that is not available in the isolated segment. Thus one ought not to conclude that the difference in d' values results from top-down context.

A second study compared a word context to a pseudoword context—e.g. *modern* was compared to *madorn*. The presentations were primed because subjects would not know what sequence of segments makes up a pseudoword. Each word or pseudoword was spoken in intact form (primed) before it was presented as a test item. A d' advantage of primed pseudowords over primed words was observed. Unfortunately, natural speech was used in this experiment, and the pseudowords' durations averaged about 10% longer than those of the words. When words are spoken with a longer duration, as in citation speech, they usually provide a higher-quality speech signal.

In a final experiment, Samuel placed test words in a sentence context. The same test word was either predicted or not by the sentence context. The influence of sentence predictability appears to be a valid comparison because the test stimuli were the same in the predictable and unpredictable contexts. The predictability of the test word significantly influenced bias but not sensitivity. To summarize, sensitivity effects were found only when the stimuli were confounded. Repp (1992) found similar evidence against sensitivity effects in phonemic restoration.

Selective adaptation in speech perception also appears to influence bias and not sensitivity. In selective adaptation, listeners are exposed to a number of repetitions of an "adapting" syllable and then asked to identify syllables from a speech continuum between two speech categories. Relative to the baseline condition of no adaptation, the identification judgments of syllables along the speech continuum are pushed in the direction opposite that of the adapting syllable (a contrast effect). Roberts & Summerfield (1981) employed different adaptors to evaluate unimodal and cross-modal adaptation and found no evidence for cross-modal adaptation. The visual adaptors presented alone produced no adaptation along the auditory continuum. Similarly, equivalent levels of adaptation were found for an auditory adaptor and a bimodal adaptor with the same phonetic information. The most impressive result, however, was the adaptation obtained with the conflicting bimodal adaptor. An auditory /be/ paired with visual /ge/ adaptor is sometimes perceived as /the/, /ve/, or /de/, but seldom as /be/. Even so, this condition produced adaptation equivalent to the auditory adaptor /be/. Thus, the adaptation followed the auditory information and was not influenced by the visual information or the phenomenal experience of the bimodal syllable. This result suggests that there is an acoustic feature-evaluation stage that is unaffected by visual feature processing. The feature-evaluation stage is also immune to a following integration stage that combines features from different modalities to give a phenomenal experience of the speech event.

More generally, top-down effects on sensitivity have yet to be convincingly demonstrated. The context effects can be explained by supposing that stimulus information and context make independent but joint contributions to word recognition. Contrary to interactive activation models (McClelland & Elman

1986), the concept of top-down activation of lower-level representations appears to be unnecessary and wrong (Massaro 1989b).

Reading Written Words

Context effects occur in reading as well as in speech perception. Some of the first experiments in experimental psychology established a word superiority effect (WSE) (Cattell 1886). Letters in a word were more accurately reported than letters in a nonword. Although a variety of uninteresting reasons could be responsible for this result, the IP approach has convincingly demonstrated that word context influences word perception.

Two classes of explanations of the WSE can be distinguished. One explanation, within the context of the FLMP, states that readers given a word have two sources of information, while readers given a nonword have only a single source. Integrating letter information and word context will lead to more accurate performance relative to a nonword or single-letter condition. The interactive activation model (IAM) has a different explanation (McClelland & Rumelhart 1981): The WSE occurs because of activation from the word level to the letter level.

Using an IP approach, Massaro (1979) evaluated these two explanations. A reader was asked to read lowercase letter strings containing an ambiguous test letter with a shape intermediate between that of *c* and *e*. In addition, the test letter was placed in orthographic contexts that supported *e* and *c* to various degrees. The test string was presented for a short duration followed after some short interval by a masking stimulus. Subjects were instructed to identify the test letter on the basis of what they saw. Both the test letter and the context influenced performance in the expected direction. Furthermore, the effect of context was larger for the more ambiguous test letters along the stimulus continuum.

A signal-detection analysis indicated that orthographic context strongly affected bias. The influence of orthographic context was *independent* of the influence of the ambiguous test letter. That is, context did not influence the reader's sensitivity to the differences in the ambiguous letters. Similarly, the test letter did not influence the perceiver's sensitivity to the differences in the orthographic context. Oden (1984) obtained similar results.

This study also evaluated context effects as a function of processing time controlled by backward masking. Both the test letter and the context influenced performance at all masking intervals. The test letter had less effect at the short than at the long processing times. That is, the identification functions covered a larger range across the *e–c* continuum with increases in processing time. Context has a significant effect at all masking intervals. In fact, the context effect was larger for the unambiguous test letters at the short than at the longer masking intervals. This result follows naturally from the trade-off between stimulus information and context in the FLMP. Context has a smaller influence to the extent the stimulus information is unambiguous.

These results falsified stochastic interactive activation (SIAC) models (McClelland 1991). In the FLMP a strong context will not override a relatively weak stimulus, as it can in the SIAC models. Given the latter's assumption of interactive activation, context can sometimes overwhelm stimulus information about the target as additional processing occurs. This prediction is contradicted by both experience and experimental results. We are more likely to notice a misspelling in a word we read carefully. In experiments varying target information, context, and processing time, stimulus effects are larger as processing time increases. SIAC models cannot predict the observed stimulus and context effects with increasing processing time.

Memory

Priming—the influence of earlier information on later performance—is a central interest in memory research. A stage analysis, in the context of signal-detection theory, has illuminated the nature of priming. In a typical task, subjects are presented with a list of study items. Some time later, they are asked to identify test words, each flashed briefly on a screen and masked. The likelihood of correctly identifying the word is greater for words previously studied than for words not previously studied. Ratcliff et al (1989) asked if this advantage would be located in the sensitivity (d') or the criterion (β) component of the signal-detection formulation.

Subjects read sentences containing priming words—e.g. *died*. Priming was positive if the subject was more likely to identify *died* correctly when it was presented later as a test word. A forced-choice task with two alternatives, *died* or *lied,* was used. If the context sentence enhances the *discrimination* of the words within the sentence from other words, then subjects should be better able to discriminate *died* from *lied*. Enhanced discriminability would lead to an increase in d'. The context sentence might also simply increase the overall likelihood of the subject's responding *died*. Both results might also occur.

Ratcliff et al (1989) replicated previous results, showing that the likelihood of correct identification of a test word was greater given priming of the test word by a context sentence. However, the forced-choice task revealed that the effect was on β, not d'. In contrast to the positive effect on β, prior occurrence in a sentence context did not influence d'. The results, therefore, showed that a sentence context biases the perceptual system in the direction of deciding that it sees a particular test item that has been seen in the recent past; the sentence context does not enhance the ability of the perceptual system to discriminate that word from similar words. This perceptual bias is probably advantageous in daily life where words are often repeated in text (or conversation) in contexts where similar words are unlikely. Such a bias can increase the efficiency of processing without significantly increasing processing cost.

Decision Making

Signal-detection theory has been used to clarify the role of prior probability in decision making. Such a use is controversial, owing primarily to the work of Kahneman & Tversky (1972) and the studies of Leon & Anderson (1974), Birnbaum & Mellers (1983), and Gigerenzer et al (1988). Situations can be created in which subjects will ignore prior probability in their decisions. As an example, Kahneman & Tversky create a hypothetical male who is shy, withdrawn, meek, tidy, methodical, and orderly. Subjects rank the likelihood that he is a farmer, salesman, airline pilot, librarian, or physician. Librarian is ranked higher than farmer despite the fact that there are many more farmers than librarians and that there are relatively few male librarians. This result might be interpreted to mean that subjects do not distinguish between prior probabilities—prior probability is uninformative. However, interpretation requires a test to see whether subjects can detect a difference between two *different* prior probabilities when they are also given an influential description.

Nevin (1991) evaluated this question by factorially combining prior probability and description. Presented with descriptions of a male or female as either stereotypically (*a*) shy and withdrawn or (*b*) quiet but strong, subjects were asked to assign as occupations either librarian or airline pilot. As expected, the personality description influenced the likelihood that the person was judged to be a librarian. However, gender also influenced the judgment. Subjects are sensitive to gender differences in occupations, and a strong stereotypic personality description does not overwhelm this sensitivity. Furthermore, when measured within the framework of signal-detection theory, the influence of prior probability was relatively constant across the two different descriptions. Based on these results, we can conclude that the description and the gender of the individual being described provided independent sources of evidence for the person's occupation. Both sources of evidence were influential and one source did not override the other.

Summary

Psychophysical theory has helped us to determine at which information-processing stage a particular variable has an effect. Visual perception is hierarchically structured in terms of stages and influenced by multiple sources of information. In speech perception and reading, a fundamental question concerns how multiple sources of information influence processing. In a simple two-stage model, each source of information is evaluated and passed forward to a stage that integrates these evaluations. Two important questions concern the extent to which crosstalk occurs between the evaluations and whether integration feeds back and influences evaluation. The evidence in both domains indicates a negative answer to both questions. Similarly, the contribution of a priming stimulus in memory can bias later perceptual processing but does not appear to feed down and modify sensory processing. Finally, a biased description of a person does not override information about prior probability of occurrence.

VARIATIONS ON THE IP FRAMEWORK

We support the IP paradigm as a general metatheory for psychological inquiry. We envision other metatheories as variations on the IP framework rather than as alternatives. In many respects, these variations constrain the general framework of IP. We consider four of these variations: Physical Symbol Systems (PSS), Connectionism, Modularity, and Ecological Realism. The first three propose unique architectures that house processing. The fourth denies as much as possible any internal structure. In many respects the differences among variations are modest.

Physical Symbol Systems (PSS)

At the heart of Physical Symbol Systems (PSS) theory are *symbolic architectures,* whose structures underlie computer science (Newell 1990; Newell et al 1989). In this framework, as Harnad (1990) notes, arbitrary *physical tokens* are manipulated by *explicit rules* that are also composed of tokens. The manipulations are based solely on the physical properties of the tokens, not their meaning. All processing entails *rule-based combination* of symbol tokens and strings of tokens. The entire system is *semantically interpretable*; that is, its components all stand for objects or describe states of affairs.

Several assumptions of the PSS framework are more restrictive than those of the IP approach. In the latter, units of information need not be limited to semantically interpretable symbols, inasmuch as subsymbolic and even continuous featural values might be processed. Also, inasmuch as the stages of processing need not conform to the steps that one would observe in the rule-based manipulation of symbols, the IP approach places a greater emphasis on understanding the temporal course of processing in humans. Few mainstream experimental psychologists who adhere to the IP approach work in the PSS framework.

Newell (1990) notes that computation is necessarily local—internal; symbols are therefore needed to represent the external world. Newell's SOAR architecture is the most ambitious PSS to date. He proposes 10 operating principles of the model human processor. This processor is clearly nonmodular, since the operating principles are constant across different processing domains. SOAR uses a production system as its foundation, and functions as a recognize-act system. A fundamental process is search through a problem space that is constructed on the fly. The learning mechanism, called chunking, resolves conflicts among productions by combining (*a*) the conditions involved in the conflict with (*b*) the outcomes to store a new production in memory. Given adherence to the traditional PSS architecture, there doesn't seem to be much room in SOAR for continuous information (fuzziness)—a shortcoming also noted by Lindsay (1991). It should also be noted that pattern recognition is not one of the 10 operating principles. This stands in marked contrast to the apparently central role played by pattern recognition, even in cognitive domains such as chess that have been investigated by advocates of PSS (Chase & Simon 1973).

Connectionism

Connectionism (Rumelhart & McClelland 1986) includes the following features: a set of *processing units* (simulated neurons, computing elements) that are interconnected by *connection weights*. Inputs to the system cause activations that are modulated by the connection weights. Inputs to a unit are combined with its current state according to an *activation rule*. The connection weights are manipulated on the basis of *learning rules,* which are mathematical *functions*. The manipulation is based purely on the value of the activations and the connection weights (not their "meaning"). Inputs to the system are transformed into outputs by the activation rules, which consist of *combining* and recombining activation values. Although some have argued that connectionism does not have explicit representations (Ramsey et al 1991) there is evidence that the system and all its parts are semantically interpretable (P. Verschure 1992). More generally, connectionism does not seem to have departed from the "representationalist strategy" (Cummins 1991). The approach has both semantically structured representations and learning procedures that are characteristic of GOFAI—good old-fashioned artificial intelligence.

Connectionism shares several attributes with the general IP approach (Massaro 1990). Both information processing and connectionism contain both parallel and sequential processing. Traditional IP models have assumed that feature analysis of letters occurs in parallel, and letter recognition is dependent on the output of the feature analysis [e.g. Selfridge's (1959) seminal pandemonium model]. In IP models, certain processes are assumed to be sequential. For example, a short-term memory search might not begin until the test item is recognized (Sternberg 1975). Sequential processing also occurs in connectionist recurrent network models in that top-down activation of lower-level units might not occur until activation of lower-level units activates higher-level units (Anderson et al 1977).

The distinction between local and distributed processing in connectionism parallels to some extent the difference between feature and node theories of memory representation (e.g. Schvaneveldt & Meyer 1973). Node theories place all the information about a pattern within a single representation, whereas feature theories distribute the information across several different representations. Local representation of some concept exists when all of the information about the concept is represented in a single location, whereas distributed representation refers to a representation of the concept that is distributed across several locations or a representation that is not located in one place. In connectionism, local representation corresponds to the case in which information about a pattern is stored in the connections of a single unit reserved for that pattern. Representation is distributed when information about a pattern is stored in the interconnections among many processing units. One class of distributed models can be mimicked by local models, which may blur somewhat the local-distributed distinction (Smolensky 1986). Thus, the local-distributed distinction does not differentiate connectionist and IP paradigms of inquiry. Estes (1991) believes that it will be difficult, if not impossible, to distinguish between local and distributed representation.

Connectionist models have been used to explain behavior at a functional level of description by assuming processes *analogous* to those occurring at a physiological level. Within IP, the feature detectors for letters were viewed as instances of neural units uncovered in electrophysiological research (e.g. Lindsay & Norman 1972). Models are metaphors; the metaphorical aspect of connectionist models is less detectable than that of other models because the connectionist metaphor is glossed neurologically rather than psychologically (Gentner & Grudin 1985). When models are formulated in a connectionist paradigm using "neurological" terms, they may not attract the analytic scrutiny that is necessary for precision, systematization, and empirical evaluation.

The defining characteristic of IP models, if there is one, is their inclusion of a multitude of mental processes operating jointly to produce behavior. Connectionist models, to date, do not assume distinct stages of processing but simply a direct mapping between input and output. To us the distinction between different stages of processing appears necessary to explanations of even the simplest behavior. In reading aloud English text, for example, the visual form of the letters does not predict the pronunciation as well as do the letter names (i.e. categories). Solving this mapping with hidden units camouflages the possibility that distinct processing stages are involved. Although the desired behavior may be produced by a connectionist model, the model does not necessarily elucidate the behavior (McCloskey 1991).

Some claim that connectionism offers an alternative to the physical-symbol-system paradigm (Derthick & Plaut 1986). The latter often uses symbols to embody sensory experience and rules to map experience into action. Connectionism uses activations to embody sensory experience and the modification and transmission of these activations to map experience into action. This aspect of connectionism is consistent with the IP approach: IP theory has a history of nonsymbolic representations including discriminability, familiarity, memory strength, and even activation and inhibition among representations.

Connectionist models with more than two layers of units may be too unconstrained to be informative. Models of this type may be Turing-equivalents capable of mimicking any computable function—any possible result. Hidden-unit models can predict not only observed results but also results that do not occur (Massaro 1988). That is, connectionist models with hidden units can simulate results that have not been observed in psychological investigations and results generated by incorrect process models of performance (Massaro

1988). More recently, it has been shown that a wide class of input-output mappings can be simulated as long as the theorist uses a sufficient number of hidden units and the operational system does not get trapped in a local minimum (Massaro 1988; Hornik et al 1989).

This superpower of connectionist models with hidden units allows the investigator to avoid the traditional framework of psychophysics (specifying the environmental characteristics that are utilized by subjects). If any input can be mapped to the desired output, then the characterization of the input does not matter. Massaro (1988) illustrated how the superpower of connectionist models with hidden units can also camouflage the observation of different stages of processing. Hidden units can simulate the outcomes of intervening stages of processing, but they do not shed light on how the intervening processes work (McCloskey 1991).

Finally, feedforward models with hidden units, as currently instantiated, make no predictions about the time course or dynamics of IP. Kawamoto (in press) has extended these models by adding cascading assumptions as formulated by McClelland (1979). Activation at each layer of units grows gradually and continuously passes its activation on to the next layer. This extension has the potential to predict response choice and RT as a function of the available processing time. An important discovery was that even the simplest networks have several configurations of weights that can solve some problem, such as exclusive or (XOR). Kawamoto found that these different solutions make significantly different predictions about the dynamics of behavior. This result is analogous to the superpower of the static predictions of these same models. Thus, dynamic hidden-layer models also have the potential for being superpowerful in that they can predict several different types of results. The variety of predicted results will most likely exceed the types of actual results, creating a situation in which the theory is too powerful and not falsifiable. We believe that connectionist theory will have to become more stage-like to be falsifiable and to solve mappings between input and output in an informative manner. That is, networks created for each of the prototypical stages uncovered in the IP approach should be informative and testable.

Modularity

Modularity has been offered as another framework for studying the functional level of behavior (Fodor 1983; Gardner 1985). Modularity assumes independent input systems (such as the one responsible for object perception) and more general cognitive processes called central systems. Input systems are *domain specific* in the sense that each uses different information and processes it differently. Input systems resemble stages of information processing in terms of selective influence by variables. Input systems are also *mandatory* because they must operate given the appropriate stimulus. Their most important property is *encapsulation*: Processing is influenced only by information within the input module's domain. Thus, a speech module is influenced only by speech input, not by situational and linguistic context. Input modules are *cognitively impenetrable*—i.e. not subject to volitional control. Input systems have shallow outputs; for example, a language module for lexical access outputs only word meanings. Input systems operate independently of one another and do not communicate. Finally, an input module is associated with specific neural structure.

In contrast to input systems, central systems are influenced by many different variables. Central systems have access to the outputs of all of the input systems and all knowledge in memory. In this dichotomy, input systems are considered to be computational systems, whereas central systems correspond to what the organism "believes." Input systems can be studied as computational systems, whereas central systems cannot. Because so many factors influence central processes, Fodor believes that a scientific account of the latter is not possible (see also Gardner 1985). This conclusion stands in marked contrast to proponents of PSS. Simon & Kaplan (1989) believe that "deep thinking" has proved easier to understand and simulate than hand-eye coordination.

Fodor & Pylyshyn (1981) argue that the process of inference must stop somewhere. That is, the system must be grounded at some level in which inference is not necessary. They propose a trichotomy of levels: transducers, input systems, and central systems. A transducer putatively does not infer: It detects a property P whenever it occurs, and this detection gives rise to state S. State S does not arise if property P does not occur. Bennett et al (1989) provide an illuminating critique of this assumption. Even for the simplest property such as light, however, transducers do not meet this criterion. State S can occur without light as, for example, when the eye is pressed and produces phosphenes. The accepted theory of signal detection is also based on the assumption that inference is central to the detection of outputs from transducers. Thus, inference is also involved in simple "transducer" functions such as light detection. Inference is not deductively valid at all three levels and the buck of inference does not stop. Using this same logic, Bennett et al also demonstrate that the distinction between input systems and central systems is unjustified. Additional evidence is Massaro's (1987) finding of similar processes in speech perception (an input system) and fixation of belief (a central system).

In summary, the modularity approach shares many of the same premises as the IP approach, particularly the assumptions of separable systems for perception and action (Massaro 1987, 1989). However, modularity's distinctions between transducers and input systems and between input systems and central systems appear to be erroneous.

Ecological Realism

Ecological realism appears to be best described in terms of what it denies (Gibson 1966, 1979). This approach rejects the notion that perception is a form of knowing. Ecological realists reject the idea of an ambiguous environment embellished by processes of the perceiver. For them, the perceiver simply extracts *invariants* from the sensory flux. Processing occurs, but intermediate processes are absent, as it is assumed that the important properties of the environment are invariant relations that can simply be "picked up" by the observer. In addition, ecological realists consider processing to be *non-algorithmic*. Gibson suggested that the perceptual system is attuned to pick up environmental properties without computation in a manner resembling the mechanical resonance between one piano string and another. This metaphor makes oscillatory systems and nonlinear dynamic systems attractive explanatory constructs applicable to information processing.

Many ecological realists in psychology view their work as contrary to that of IP-oriented investigators. As we have noted, IP psychologists focus on internal representations and processes whereas neo-Gibsonians place a high priority on understanding the mapping of invariant properties of the environment to perceptual responses (Carello & Turvey 1991). On the other hand, ecological realists do not seem immune to hidden processes and feel free to use such concepts as attention (Gibson 1979). However, ecological realism has not solved the inverse mapping problem in which the environmental situation must be induced from information available to the perceiving system. Thus, ecological realism must confront the role that inductive inference necessarily plays in perception and action. To accomplish this goal, we believe they will find it necessary to adduce internal mental processes.

RETROSPECTIVE

Here we have attempted to (*a*) characterize the IP approach, (*b*) justify it, (*c*) describe important metatheoretical and theoretical issues, and (*d*) compare it to other metatheories. We hope to have demonstrated that the IP approach goes far beyond the mere use of a single technique such as the AFM. The IP approach has its roots in mathematical psychology as well as the experimental method, and the value of its fine-grained analyses is becoming apparent. We have not been able to survey the impressive progress made in the use of anatomical measures as converging indexes of IP (Meyer et al 1988b; Posner & Carr 1992).

Posner & McLeod (1982) distinguished between more global theoretical syntheses and simpler experimental studies. We look forward to a merging of these two enterprises. Theorists should become more sensitive to empirical constraints and experimentalists should direct their inquiries toward tests of theories. That said, has the field advanced over the past decade? While we have documented here how our understanding of information processing has increased over the 10-year period, we suggest that the field's most important progress has been in learning how to ask the right questions and how most fruitfully to pursue the answers. We look forward to the next decade of progress.

ACKNOWLEDGMENTS

The authors' research reported in this paper and the writing of the paper were supported, in part, by grants from the Public Health Service (PHS R01 NS 20314 to Massaro and R01 HD 21338 to Cowan), the National Science Foundation (BNS 8812728 to Massaro), and the graduate division of the University of California, Santa Cruz. The authors thank Steve Hackley, Steve Kitzis, Nancy McCarrell, Dave Meyer, Jeff Miller, Hal Pashler, Gregg Oden, Allen Osman, Roger Ratcliff, Seth Roberts, Rich Schweickert, Saul Sternberg, Jim Townsend, Lex van der Heijden, and Paul Verschure for helpful comments on a draft of this chapter.

Literature Cited

Abrams, R. A., Balota, D. A. 1991. Mental chronometry: beyond reaction time. *Psychol. Sci.* 2:153–57

Adams, M. J. 1979. Models of word recognition. *Cogn. Psychol.* 11:133–76

Alcock, J. 1989. *Animal Behavior.* Sunderland, MA: Sinauer

Allport, D. A. 1968. Phenomenal simultaneity and the perceptual moment hypothesis. *Br. J. Psychol.* 59:395–406

Anderson, J. A., Silverstein, J. W., Ritz, S. A., Jones, R. S. 1977. Distinctive features, categorical perception, and probability learning: Some applications of a neural model. *Psychol. Rev.* 84:413–51

Anderson, J. R. 1990a. *Cognitive Psychology and Its Implications.* New York: Freeman

Anderson, J. R. 1990b. *The Adaptive Control of Thought.* Hillsdale, NJ: Erlbaum

Ashby, F. G. 1982. Deriving exact predictions for the cascade model. *Psychol. Rev.* 89:599–607

Ashby, F. G., Townsend, J. T. 1980. Decomposing the reaction time distribution: Pure insertion and selective influence revisited. *J. Math. Psychol.* 21:93–123

Atkinson, R. C., Shiffrin, R. M. 1968. Human memory: a proposed system and its control processes. In *The Psychology of Learning and Motivation: Advances in Research and Theory,* ed. K. W. Spence, J. T. Spence, 2:89–195. New York: Academic

Baddeley, A. D. 1986. *Working Memory.* Oxford: Oxford Univ. Press

Bagley, W. C. 1900. The apperception of the spoken sentence: a study in the psychology of language. *Am. J. Psychol.* 12:80–130

Banks, W. P., Krajicek, D. 1991. Perception. *Annu. Rev. Psychol.* 42:305–31

Baron, J. 1977. Mechanisms for pronouncing printed words: use and acquisition. In *Basic Processes in Reading: Perception and Comprehension,* ed. D. LaBerge, S. J. Sam-
uels. Hillsdale, NJ: Erlbaum

Bennett, B. M., Hoffman, D. D., Prakash, C. 1989. *Observer Mechanics: A Formal Theory of Perception.* San Diego: Academic

Berko, J. 1958. The child's learning of English morphology. *Word* 14:150–77

Birnbaum, M. H., Mellers, B. A. 1983. Bayesian inference: Combining base rates with opinions of sources who vary in credibility. *J. Pers. Soc. Psychol.* 45:792–804

Breitmeyer, B. G. 1984. *Visual Masking: An Integrative Approach.* New York: Oxford

Broad, W., Wade, N. 1982. *Betrayers of the Truth.* New York: Simon & Schuster

Broadbent, D. E. 1958. *Perception and Communication.* New York: Pergamon

Brooks, L. 1978. Nonanalytic concept formation and memory for instances. In *Cognition and Categorization,* ed. E. Rosch, B. B. Lloyd, pp. 169–211. Hillsdale, NJ: Erlbaum

Carello, C., Turvey, M. T. 1991. Ecological units of analysis and baseball's "illusions." In *Cognition and the Symbolic Processes,* ed. R. R. Hoffman, D. S. Palermo, pp. 371–86. Hillsdale, NJ: Erlbaum

Cattell, J. M. 1886. The time it takes to see and name objects. *Mind* 11:53–65

Chamberlin, T. C. 1965. The method of multiple working hypotheses. *Science* 148:754–59

Chase, W. G., Simon, H. A. 1973. Perception in chess. *Cogn. Psychol.* 4:55–81

Cohen, M. M., Massaro, D. W. 1992. On the similarity of categorization models. In *Probabilistic Multidimensional Models of Perception and Cognition,* ed. F. G. Ashby, pp. 395–447. New York: Academic.

Collyer, C. E. 1985. Comparing strong and weak models by fitting them to computer-generated data. *Percept. Psychophys.* 38:476–81

Connine, C. M., Clifton, C. 1987. Interactive use of lexical information in speech perception. *J. Exp. Psychol.: Hum. Percept. Perform.* 13:291–99

Cosmides, L. 1989. The logic of social exchange: Has natural selection shaped how humans reason? Studies with the Wason selection task. *Cognition* 31:187–276

Cowan, N. 1984. On short and long auditory stores. *Psychol. Bull.* 96:341–70

Cowan, N. 1987. Auditory sensory storage in relation to the growth of sensation and a-coustic information extraction. *J. Exp. Psychol.: Hum. Percept. Perform.* 13:204–15

Cowan, N. 1988. Evolving conceptions of memory storage, selective attention, and their mutual constraints within the human information processing system. *Psychol. Bull.* 104:163–91

Cummins, R. 1991. The role of representation in connectionist explanations of cognitive capacities. In *Philosophy and Connectionist Theory,* ed. W. Ramsey, S. P. Stich, D. E. Rumelhart, pp. 91–114. Hillsdale, NJ: Erlbaum

Derthick, M., Plaut, D. C. 1986. Is distributed connectionism compatible with the physical symbol system hypothesis? *Proc. Cogn. Sci. Soc.,* pp. 639–44

DeYoe, E. A., Van Essen, D. C. 1988. Concurrent processing streams in monkey visual cortex. *Trends Neurosci.* 11:219–26

Duncan, J. 1980. The locus of interference in the perception of simultaneous stimuli. *Psychol. Rev.* 87:272–300

Duncan, J., Humphreys, G. W. 1989. Visual search and stimulus similarity. *Psychol. Rev.* 96:433–58

Egeth, H., Dagenbach, D. 1991. Parallel versus serial processing in visual search: further evidence from subadditive effects of visual quality. *J. Exp. Psychol.: Hum. Percept. Perform.* 17:551–60

Elman, J., McClelland, J. 1986. Exploiting lawful variability in the speech wave. In *Invariance and Variability in Speech Processes,* ed. J. S. Perkell, D. H. Klatt. Hillsdale, NJ: Erlbaum

Estes, W. K. 1991. Cognitive architectures from the standpoint of an experimental psychologist. *Annu. Rev. Psychol.* 42:1–28

Feyerabend, P. K. 1975. *Against Method.* London: NLB

Fisher, D. L., Duffy, S. A., Young, C., Pollatsek, A. 1988. Understanding the central processing limit in consistent-mapping visual search tasks. *J. Exp. Psychol.: Hum. Percept. Perform.* 14:253–66

Fodor, J. 1975. *The Language of Thought.* New York: Crowell

Fodor, J. A. 1983. *Modularity of Mind.* Cambridge, MA: Bradford

Fodor, J. A., Pylyshyn, Z. W. 1981. How direct is visual perception?: some reflections on Gibson's ecological approach. *Cognition* 9:139–96

Ganong, W. F. III. 1980. Phonetic categoriza-tion in auditory word recognition. *J. Exp. Psychol.: Hum. Percept. Perform.* 6:110–25

Gardner, H. 1985. *The Mind's New Science: A History of the Cognitive Revolution.* New York: Basic Books

Gentner, D., Grudin, J. 1985. The evolution of mental metaphors in psychology: a 90-year retrospective. *Am. Psychol.* 40:181–92

Gibson, J. J. 1966. *The Senses Considered as Perceptual Systems.* Boston: Houghton Mifflin

Gibson, J. J. 1979. *The Ecological Approach to Visual Perception.* Boston: Houghton Mifflin

Gigerenzer, G., Hell, W., Blank, H. 1988. Presentation and content: the use of base rates as a continuous variable. *J. Exp. Psychol.: Hum. Percept. Perform.* 14:513–25

Glass, A. L., Holyoak, K. J. 1986. *Cognition.* New York: Random House

Glushko, R. J. 1979. The organization and acti-vation of orthographic knowledge in reading aloud. *J. Exp. Psychol.: Hum. Percept. Perform.* 5:674–91

Green, D. M., Swets, J. A. 1966. *Signal Detection Theory and Psychophysics.* New York: Wiley

Greeno, J. G., Steiner, T. E. 1964. Markovian processes with identifiable states: general considerations and application to all-or-none learning. *Psychometrika* 29:309–33

Gregory, R. L. 1986. *Odd Perceptions.* London: Methuen

Groen, G. J., Parkman, J. M. 1972. A chrono-metric analysis of simple addition. *Psychol. Rev.* 79:329–43

Hackley, S. A., Graham, F. K. 1987. Effects of attending selectively to the spatial position of reflex-eliciting and reflex-modulating stimuli. *J. Exp. Psychol.: Hum. Percept. Perform.* 13:411–24

Harnad, S. 1990. The symbol grounding problem. *Physica D* 42:335–46

Hatfield, G. 1991. Representation in perception and cognition: connectionist affordances. See Ramsey et al 1991, pp. 163–95

Hawkins, H. L., Presson, J. C. 1986. In *Handbook of Perception and Human Performance:* Vol. 2. *Cognitive Processes and Performance,* ed. K. R. Boff, L. Kaufman, J. P. Thomas, pp. 26-1–26-64. New York: Wiley

Hintzman, D. L. 1991. Why are formal models useful in psychology? In *Relating Theory and Data: Essays on Human Memory in Honor of Bennett B. Murdock,* ed. W. E. Hockley, S. Lewandowsky, pp. 39–56. Hillsdale, NJ: Erlbaum

Hornik, K., Stinchcombe, M., White, H. 1989. Multilayer feedforward networks are universal approximators. *Neural Networks* 2:359–66

Idson, W. L., Massaro, D. W. 1977. Perceptual processing and experience of auditory duration. *Sensory Processes* 1:316–37

Johnston, W. A., Heinz, S. P. 1978. Flexibility and capacity demands of attention. *J. Exp. Psychol.: Gen.* 107:420–35

Kahneman, D., Tversky, A. 1972. Subjective probability: a judgment of representativeness. *Cogn. Psychol.* 3:430–54

Kallman, H. J., Massaro, D. W. 1979. Similarity effects in backward recognition masking. *J. Exp. Psychol.: Hum. Percept. Perform.* 5:110–28

Kallman, H. J., Massaro, D. W. 1983. Backward masking, the suffix effect, and preperceptual storage. *J. Exp. Psychol.: Learn. Mem. Cogn.* 9:312–27

Kawamoto, A. H. 1992. Time course of processing in feed-forward connectionist networks. *J. Math. Psychol.* In press

Kinchla, R. A. 1992. Attention. *Annu. Rev. Psychol.* 43:711–42

Lachman, R., Lachman, J. L., Butterfield, E. C. 1979. *Psychology and Information Processing.* Hillsdale, NJ: Erlbaum

Lee, D. N., Raddish, P. E. 1981. Plummeting gannets: a paradigm of ecological optics. *Nature* 293:293–94

Leeuwenberg, E., Boselie, F. 1988. Against the likelihood principle in visual form perception. *Psychol. Rev.* 95:485–91

Leon, M., Anderson, N. H. 1974. A ratio rule from integration theory applied to inference judgments. *J. Exper. Psychol.* 102:27–36

Lindsay, P. H., Norman, D. A. 1972. *Human Information Processing: An Introduction to Psychology.* New York: Academic

Lindsay, R. K. 1991. Symbolic-processing and the SOAR architecture. *Psychol. Sci.* 2:294–302

Logan, G. D. 1988. Toward an instance theory of automation. *Psychol. Rev.* 95:492–527

Lovie, A. D. 1983. Attention and behaviourism—fact and fiction. *Br. J. Psychol.* 74:301–10

MacKay, D. M. 1969. *Information, Mechanism, and Meaning.* Cambridge, MA: MIT Press

MacWhinney, B., Leinbach, J. 1991. Implementations are not conceptualizations: revising the verb learning model. *Cognition* 40:121–57

Mahoney, M. J. 1976. *Scientist as Subject: The Psychological Imperative.* Cambridge: Ballinger

Manicas, P. T., Secord, P. F. 1983. Implications for psychology of the new philosophy of science. *Am. Psychol.* 38:399–413

Massaro, D. W. 1969. The effects of feedback in psychophysical tasks. *Percept. Psychophys.* 6:89–91

Massaro, D. W. 1972. Preperceptual images, processing time, and perceptual units in auditory perception. *Psychol. Rev.* 79:124–45

Massaro, D. W. 1975. *Experimental Psychology and Information Processing.* Chicago: Rand-McNally

Massaro, D. W. 1979. Letter information and orthographic context in word perception. *J. Exp. Psychol.: Hum. Percept. Perform.* 5:595–609

Massaro, D. W. 1985. Attention and perception: an information-integration perspective. *Acta Psychol.* 60:211–43

Massaro, D. W. 1987. *Speech Perception by Ear and Eye: A Paradigm for Psychological Inquiry.* Hillsdale, NJ: Erlbaum

Massaro, D. W. 1988. Some criticisms of connectionist models of human performance. *J. Mem. Lang.* 27:213–34

Massaro, D. W. 1989a. *Experimental Psychology: An Information Processing Approach.* San Diego, CA: Harcourt Brace Jovanovich

Massaro, D. W. 1989b. Testing between the TRACE model and the Fuzzy Logical Model of Perception. *Cogn. Psychol.* 21: 398–421

Massaro, D. W. 1990. The psychology of connectionism. *Behav. Brain Sci.* 13:403–6

Massaro, D. W. 1991. Language processing and information processing. In *Contributions to Information Integration Theory.* Vol. I: *Cognition,* ed. N. H. Anderson, pp. 259–92. Hillsdale, NJ: Erlbaum

Massaro, D. W. 1992. Broadening the domain of the fuzzy logical model of perception. In *Cognition: Conceptual and Methodological Issues,* ed. H. L. Pick Jr., P. Van den Broek, D. C. Knill, pp. 51–84. Washington, DC: Am. Psychol. Assoc.

Massaro, D. W., Cohen, M. M. 1983. Phonological context in speech perception. *Percept. Psychophys.* 34:338–48

Massaro, D. W., Cohen, M. M. 1991. Integration versus interactive activation: the joint influence of sensory information and context in perception. *Cogn. Psychol.* 23:558–614

Massaro, D. W., Friedman, D. 1990. Models of integration given multiple sources of information. *Psychol. Rev.* 97:225–52

Massaro, D. W., Friedman, D. 1991. Book review of *The Adaptive Character of Thought* by John R. Anderson. *Am. J. Psychol.* 104: 467–74

McClelland, J. L. 1979. On the time relations between mental processes: a framework for analyzing processes in cascade. *Psychol. Rev.* 86:287–330

McClelland, J. L. 1991. Stochastic interactive processes and the effect of context on perception. *Cogn. Psychol.* 23:1–44

McClelland, J. L., Elman, J. L. 1986. The TRACE model of speech perception. *Cogn. Psychol.* 18:1–86

McClelland, J. L., Rumelhart, D. E. 1981. An interactive activation model of context effects in letter perception: Part I. An account of basic findings. *Psychol. Rev.* 88:375–407

McCloskey, M. 1991. Networks and theories: the place of connectionism in cognitive science. *Psychol. Sci.* 2:387–95

Meyer, D. E., Osman, A. M., Irwin, D. E., Kounios, J. 1988a. The dynamics of cognition and action: mental processes inferred from speed-accuracy decomposition. *Psy-*

chol. Rev. 95:183–237

Meyer, D. E., Osman, A. M., Irwin, D. E., Yantis, S. 1988b. Modern mental chronometry. *Biol. Psychol.* 26:3–67

Meyer, D. E., Yantis, S., Osman, A. M., Smith, J. E. K. 1985. Temporal properties of human information processing: tests of discrete versus continuous models. *Cogn. Psychol.* 17:445–518

Miller, J. 1982. Discrete versus continuous stage models of human information processing: in search of partial output. *J. Exp. Psychol.: Hum. Percept. Perform.* 8:273–96

Miller, J. 1988. Discrete and continuous models of human information processing: theoretical distinctions and empirical results. *Acta Psychol.* 67:191–257

Miller, J. 1990. Discreteness and continuity in models of human information processing. *Acta Psychol.* 74:297–318

Miller, J., Hackley, S. A. 1992. Electrophysiological evidence for temporal overlap among contingent mental processes. *J. Exp. Psychol.: Gen.* 121:195–209

Mitroff, I. I. 1974. *The Subjective Side of Science.* Amsterdam: Elsevier

Moore, E. F. 1956. Gedanken-experiments on sequential machines. In *Automata Studies,* ed. C. E. Shannon, J. McCarthy. Princeton, NJ: Princeton

Moore, J. J., Massaro, D. W. 1973. Attention and processing capacity in auditory recognition. *J. Exp. Psychol.* 99:49–54

Neisser, U. 1967. *Cognitive Psychology.* New York: Appleton-Century-Crofts

Nevin, J. A. 1991. Signal-detection analysis of illusions and heuristics. In *Signal Detection: Mechanisms, Models, and Applications,* ed. M. L. Commons, J. A. Nevin, M. C. Davison, pp. 257–74. Hillsdale, NJ: Erlbaum

Newell, A. 1980. Physical symbol systems. *Cogn. Sci.* 4:135–83

Newell, A. 1990. *Unified Theories of Cognition.* Cambridge, MA: Harvard Univ. Press

Newell, A., Rosenbloom, P. S., Laird, J. E. 1989. Symbolic architecture for cognition. In *Foundation of Cognitive Science,* ed. M. I. Posner, pp. 93–131. Cambridge, MA: MIT Press

Norman, D. A. 1969. *Memory and Attention: An Introduction to Human Information Processing.* New York: Wiley

Norman, D. A., Wickelgren, W. 1969. Strength theory of decision rules and latency in retrieval from short term memory. *J. Math. Psychol.* 6:192–208

Nosofsky, R. M. 1991. Relation between the rational model and the context model of classification. *Psychol. Sci.* 2:416–21

Nosofsky, R. M. 1992. Similarity scaling and cognitive process models. *Annu. Rev. Psychol.* 43:25–53

Oden, G. C. 1984. Dependence, independence, and emergence of word features. *J. Exp.*

Psychol.: Hum. Percept. Perform. 10:394–405

Osman, A., Bashore, T. R., Coles, M. G. H., Donchin, E., Meyer, D. E. 1992. On the transmission of partial information: inferences from movement-related brain potentials. *J. Exp. Psychol.: Hum. Percept. Perform.* 18:217–32

Paap, K. R., Newsome, S. L., Noel, R. W. 1984. Word shape's in poor shape for the race to the lexicon. *J. Exp. Psychol.: Hum. Percept. Perform.* 10:413–28

Palmer, S. E., Kimchi, R. 1986. The information processing approach to cognition. In *Approaches to Cognition: Contrasts and Controversies,* ed. T. J. Knapp, L. C. Robertson, pp. 37–77. Hillsdale, NJ: Erlbaum

Pashler, H. 1989. Dissociations and dependencies between speed and accuracy: evidence for a two-component theory of divided attention in simple tasks. *Cogn. Psychol.* 21:469–514

Pashler, H. 1990. Do response modality effects support multiprocessor models of divided attention? *J. Exp. Psychol.: Hum. Percept. Perform.* 16:826–42

Pinker, S., Prince, A. 1988. On language and connectionism: analysis of a parallel distributed processing model of language acquisition. *Cognition* 29:73–193

Platt, J. R. 1964. Strong inference. *Science* 146:347–53

Plunkett, K., Marchman, V. 1991. U-shaped learning and frequency effects in a multilayered perceptron: implications for child language acquisition. *Cognition* 38:43–102

Popper, K. 1959. *The Logic of Scientific Discovery.* New York: Basic Books

Posner, M. I., Carr, T. H. 1992. Lexical access and the brain: anatomical constraints on cognitive models of word recognition. *Am. J. Psychol.* 105:1–26

Posner, M. I., McLeod, P. 1982. Information processing models—in search of elementary operations. *Annu. Rev. Psychol.* 33:477–514

Posner, M. I., Snyder, C. R. R. 1975. Attention and cognitive control. In *Information Processing and Cognition,* ed. R. L. Solso. Hillsdale, NJ: Erlbaum

Ramsey, W., Stich, S. P., Rumelhart, D. E., eds. 1991. *Philosophy and Connectionist Theory.* Hillsdale, NJ: Erlbaum

Ratcliff, R. 1978. A theory of memory retrieval. *Psychol. Rev.* 85:59–108

Ratcliff, R. 1988. Continuous versus discrete information processing: modeling accumulation of partial information. *Psychol. Rev.* 95:238–55

Ratcliff, R., McKoon, G., Verwoerd, M. 1989. A bias interpretation of facilitation in perceptual identification. *J. Exp. Psychol.: Learn. Mem. Cogn.* 15:378–87

Real, L. A. 1991. Animal choice behavior and the evolution of cognitive architecture. *Science* 253:980–86

Reeve, T. G., Proctor, R. W. 1984. On the advance preparation of discrete finger responses. *J. Exp. Psychol.: Hum. Percept. Perform.* 10:541–53

Repp, B. H. 1992. Perceptual restoration of a "missing" speech sound: auditory induction or illusion? *Percept. Psychophys.* In press

Roberts, S. 1987. Evidence for distinct serial processes in animals: the multiplicative-factors method. *Animal Learn. Behav.* 15:135–73

Roberts, S., Sternberg, S. 1992. The meaning of additive reaction-time effects: test of three alternatives. In *Attention and Performance. Vol. 14: Synergies in Experimental Psychology, Artificial Intelligence, and Cognitive Neuroscience—A Silver Jubilee,* ed. D. E. Meyer, S. Kornblum. Cambridge, MA: MIT Press

Roberts, M., Summerfield, Q. 1981. Audiovisual presentation demonstrates that selective adaptation in speech perception is purely auditory. *Percept. Psychophys.* 30:309–14

Rumelhart, D. E., McClelland, J. L., eds. 1986. *Parallel Distributed Processing. Vol. 1: Foundations.* Cambridge, MA: MIT Press

Rumelhart, D. E., McClelland, J. L. 1986. On learning the past tense of English verbs: implicit rules or parallel distributed processes? In *Parallel Distributed Processing: Explorations in the Microstructure of Cognition,* ed. D. E. Rumelhart, J. L. McClelland, the PDP Research Group, 2:216–71. Cambridge, MA: MIT Press

Samuel, A. G. 1981. Phonemic restoration: insights from a new methodology. *J. Exp. Psychol.: Gen.* 110:474–94

Sanders, A. F. 1990. Issues and trends in the debate on discrete vs. continuous processing of information. *Acta Psychol.* 74:123–67

Schneider, W., Shiffrin, R. M. 1977. Controlled and automatic human information processing: I. Detection, search, and attention. *Psychol. Rev.* 84:1–66

Schoemaker, P. J. H. 1991. The quest of optimality: a positive heuristic of science? *Behav. Brain Sci.* 14:205–45

Schvaneveldt, R. W., Meyer, D. E. 1973. Retrieval and comparison processes in semantic memory. In *Attention and Performance,* ed. S. Kornblum, pp. 395–409. New York: Academic

Schweickert, R. 1978. A critical path generalization of the additive factor method: analysis of a Stroop task. *J. Math. Psychol.* 18:105–39

Schweickert, R. 1985. Separable effects of factors on speed and accuracy: memory scanning, lexical decision, and choice tasks. *Psychol. Bull.* 97:530–46

Schweickert, R. 1992. Information, time, and the structure of mental events: a twenty-five year review. In *Attention and Performance. Vol. 14: Synergies in Experimental Psychology, Artificial Intelligence, and*

Cognitive Neuroscience—A Silver Jubilee, ed. D. E. Meyer, S. Kornblum. Cambridge, MA: MIT Press

Selfridge, O. G. 1959. Pandemonium: a paradigm for learning. In *Mechanization of Thought Processes,* pp. 511–26. London: Her Majesty's Stationery Office

Shannon, C. 1948. The mathematical theory of communication. *Bell Syst. Tech. J.* 27:379–423, 623–58

Shaw, M. L. 1984. Division of attention among spatial locations: a fundamental difference between detection of letters and detection of luminance increments. In *Attention and Performance. Vol. 10: Control of Language Processes,* ed. H. Bouma, D. G. Bouwhuis. Hillsdale, NJ: Erlbaum

Shiffrin, R. M. 1988. Attention. In *Stevens' Handbook of Experimental Psychology,* ed. R. C. Atkinson, R. J. Herrnstein, G. Lindzey, R. D. Luce, 2:739–811. New York: Wiley

Shiffrin, R. M., Schneider, W. 1977. Controlled and automatic human information processing: II. Perceptual learning, automatic attending, and a general theory. *Psychol. Rev.* 84:127–90

Shulman, G. L. 1991. Attentional modulation of mechanisms that analyze rotation in depth. *J. Exp. Psychol.: Hum. Percept. Perform.* 17:726–37

Simon, H. A. 1979. Information processing models of cognition. *Annu. Rev. Psychol.* 30:363–96

Simon, H. A., Kaplan, C. A. 1989. Foundation of cognitive science. In *Foundation of Cognitive Science,* ed. M. I. Posner, pp. 1–47. Cambridge, MA: MIT Press

Smolensky, P. 1986. Neural and conceptual interpretation of PDP models. In *Parallel Distributed Processing. Vol. 2: Psychological and Biological Models,* ed. J. L. McClelland, D. E. Rumelhart, pp. 390–431. Cambridge: MIT Press

Smolensky, P. 1988. On the proper treatment of connectionism. *Behav. Brain Sci.* 11:1–73

Solso, R. L. 1991. *Cognitive Psychology.* New York: Allyn & Bacon

Sorkin, R. D., Pohlmann, L. D., Gilliom, J. D. 1973. Simultaneous two-channel signal detection. III. 639 and 1400 Hz signals. *J. Acoust. Soc. Am.* 53:1045–50

Sternberg, S. 1966. High-speed scanning in human memory. *Science* 153:652–54

Sternberg, S. 1969. The discovery of processing stages: extensions of Donders' Method. *Acta Psychol.* 30:276–315

Sternberg, S. 1975. Memory scanning: new findings and current controversies. *Q. J. Exp. Psychol.* 27:1–32

Strayer, D. L., Kramer, A. F. 1990. Attentional requirements of automatic and controlled processing. *J. Exp. Psychol. Learn. Mem. Cogn.* 16:67–82

Theios, J., Amrhein, P. C. 1989. Theoretical

analysis of the cognitive processing of lexical and pictorial stimuli: naming, and visual and conceptual comparisons. *Psychol. Rev.* 96:5–24

Thomas, E. A. C., Myers, J. L. 1972. Implications of latency data for threshold and nonthreshold models of signal detection. *J. Math. Psychol.* 9:253–85

Townsend, J. T. 1974. Issues and models concerning the processing of a finite number of inputs. In *Human Information Processing: Tutorials in Performance and Cognition,* ed. B. H. Kantowitz. Hillsdale, NJ: Erlbaum

Townsend, J. T. 1990. Serial vs. parallel processing: Sometimes they look like Tweedledum and Tweedledee but they can (and should) be distinguished. *Psychol. Sci.* 1:46–54

Townsend, J. T., Ashby, F. G. 1983. *Stochastic Modeling of Elementary Psychological Processes.* London: Cambridge Univ. Press

Treisman, A. 1991. Search, similarity, and the integration of features between and within dimensions. *J. Exp. Psychol.: Hum. Percept. Perform.* 17:652–76

Tribus, M., Mclrvine, E. C. 1964. Energy and information. *Sci. Am.* 211:179–88

Turvey, M. T. 1973. On peripheral and central processes in vision: inferences from an information processing analysis of masking with patterned stimuli. *Psychol. Rev.* 80:1–52

Ulrich, R. 1987. Threshold models of temporal-order judgments evaluated by a ternary response task. *Percept. Psychophys.* 42:224–39

van der Heijden, A. H. C., Stebbins, S. 1990. The information-processing approach. *Psychol. Res.* 52:197–206

Venezky, R. L., Massaro, D. W. 1987. Orthographic structure and spelling-sound regularity in reading English words. In *Language Perception and Production: Shared Mechanisms in Listening, Speaking, Reading and Writing,* ed. D. A. Allport, D. G. MacKay, W. Prinz, E. Scheerer, pp. 111–29. London: Academic

Verschure, P. F. M. J. 1992. Taking connectionism seriously: the vague promise of subsymbolism and an alternative. Proc. 14th Annu. Conf. Cogn. Sci. Soc., Bloomington, Indiana, pp. 653–58

Warren, R. M. 1970. Perceptual restoration of missing speech sounds. *Science* 167:392–63

Wenner, A. M., Wells, P. H. 1990. *Anatomy of a Controversy: The Question of a "Language" among Bees.* New York: Columbia Univ. Press

Yantis, S., Meyer, D. E., Smith, J. E. K. 1991. Analyses of multi-nomial mixture distributions: new tests for stochastic models of cognition and action. *Psychol. Bull.* 110:350–74

Young, P. 1987. *The Nature of Information.* New York: Praeger

Annu. Rev. Psychol. 1993. 44:427-52
Copyright © 1993 by Annual Reviews Inc.

A HOLISTIC VIEW OF PERSONALITY: A Model Revisited

David Magnusson and Bertil Törestad

Department of Psychology, Stockholm University, Stockholm, Sweden

KEYWORDS: dynamic models, interaction, development, variable-oriented approach, person-oriented approach

CONTENTS

INTRODUCTION 428
ASPECTS OF INDIVIDUAL PSYCHOLOGICAL FUNCTIONING........................ 428
   The Individual as an Intentional, Active Being.. 429
   The Individual as a Biological Being... 430
   The Individual as a Social Being 431
CHARACTERISTICS OF PERSONALITY RESEARCH.. 431
   Fragmentation 431
   Emphasis on Variables 432
   Prediction 434
   Unidirectional Causality.. 434
   The Dominance of Methods and Statistics over Analysis of the Phenomena..... 435
   Theory vs Empirical Research 435
A HOLISTIC, DYNAMIC MODEL OF PERSONALITY 435
   A Holistic View 436
   Dynamic, Lawful Interaction 437
   Psychological Functioning—A Dynamic Process.. 437
   Levels of Dynamic Processes... 439
PREDICTION VS. UNDERSTANDING AND EXPLAINING LAWFULNESS.................. 440
   Prediction in Dynamic Processes 440
   Prediction as a Goal and Prediction as a Tool.. 442
   The Goal of Scientific Personality Research 442
METHODOLOGICAL IMPLICATIONS OF A HOLISTIC, DYNAMIC MODEL.............. 443
   The Variable-Oriented Approach in a Holistic Perspective 443
   Person-Oriented Analyses 444
   Pattern Analysis.. 445
   Comments 446
CONCLUDING COMMENTS 447

0066/4308/93/0201-0427$2.00

INTRODUCTION

Many attempts have been made to establish the boundaries of personality research by defining personality. In our opinion, there is no personality as such. What exists is a living, active, and purposeful organism, functioning and developing as a total integrated being. Based on this view, personality research is herein defined as the study of how and why individuals think, feel, act, and react as they do—i.e. from the perspective of the individual as a total, integrated organism.

Theoretically, in order to understand how and why an individual functions in a specific way at a given stage of development, two complementary types of theory and model must be distinguished: those that discuss the issue from a current perspective and those that cover it from a developmental perspective.

Developmental personality models (e.g. psychoanalytical and genetic models) analyze and explain current functioning in terms of an individual's developmental history. Such models are concerned with the ontogeny of relevant aspects of the individual, the timing and expression of significant environmental events in his/her past and present, and the ways these factors interact to produce current functioning. Development, in its most general form, refers to any process of progressive change. In biology, development refers to progressive changes in size, shape, and function during the life span of an organism. Consequently, processes that go on without change, within existing structures, do not constitute development. By this definition, development is not synonymous with time. Although time is not equivalent to development, development always has a time dimension.

Models that emphasize the current perspective (such as cognitive and psycho-biological models) analyze and explain why individuals function as they do in terms of their current psychological and biological dispositions. In this approach accounts are framed independently of any developmental processes that may have led to the individual's present state. The two models are complementary and both are needed for a comprehensive account of human nature.

ASPECTS OF INDIVIDUAL PSYCHOLOGICAL FUNCTIONING

Effective empirical analysis is based on careful analysis of the phenomena to be studied. Without a close analytical link to the character of the phenomena, theorizing and empirical research occur in a vacuum, interesting only to those who wish to defend or attack a particular position (Magnusson 1992).

What basic characteristics of individuals' psychological functioning require explanation?

The Individual as an Intentional, Active Being

The individual's selection, interpretation, and use of information from the environment plays a basic role in the way in which he/she functions and develops. A fundamental principle in the individual's inner and outer life is that the perceptual-cognitive system (including world-views and self-perceptions) operates together with concomitant emotions, needs, motives, values, and goals to produce the integrated mental system. By selecting and interpreting information from the external world and transforming this information into inner and outer action, the mental system plays a crucial role in the process of interaction between mental and biological factors within the individual, and in the process of interaction between the individual and his/her environment. Modern theories of perception assign an active, constructive role to the cognitive system involved (Been-Zeev 1988).

Various models have shown how individuals process the overwhelming amount of information that constantly impinges upon them and how these pieces of information are transformed into decisions and actions. These models include such concepts as "categories," "dimensions," "plans," "programs," "semantic networks," "coping strategies" (Anderson 1985), personal projects (Horley et al 1991), and personal strivings (Emmons 1992) as well as the old concept of "schemata" (Bartlett 1932; Alba & Hasher 1983). A fundamental principle of psychological functioning is that the individual is not only a passive receiver of stimulation from the environment to which he/she reacts; he/she is also an active, purposeful agent in relation to the physical and social environment (Endler & Magnusson 1976; Pervin 1983).

The dynamic conception of the mind and mental processes as activities, rather than as an organ receiving and processing information, was advocated early by the so-called "act psychologists" in Europe, such as Brentano (1924 [1874]) and Stumpf (1883). In the United States, James was a proponent of the same view. The intentional character of the individual's way of functioning was stressed by Tolman (1951), among others, and more recently the individual as an active, purposeful agent has been emphasized in action theory (Brandtstädter in press; Strelau 1983; see also Brushlinskii 1987).

During the past few decades interest has been growing in the two parallel modes of information processing—i.e. controlled (conscious, attended to, and thus subject to critical analysis) vs automatic (out of attentional focus and awareness) (Brewin 1986; Bowers 1981; Norman & Shallice 1980; Loftus & Klinger 1992). Continuously ongoing processing of signals impinging on the senses subliminally and/or *out of awareness* gives new importance to the perceptual-cognitive system. At the same time it plays down the central role earlier ascribed to conscious functioning, without necessarily referring to psychoanalytical concepts. Subliminal sensations influence the individual's actions and reactions unconsciously, making personality research a more complex venture, because the relationships between various levels and aspects of psychological functioning do not lend themselves to easy inferences from, for example, self-reports.

The Individual as a Biological Being

An individual's way of functioning psychologically cannot be understood and explained without consideration of the fact that an individual has not only a mind but also a body. That biological factors play a basic role in the individual's way of thinking, feeling, acting, and reacting was long ago expounded in the theory of the four basic temperaments, e.g. the dominance of different body fluids. In 1883, when Wundt made a plea for psychology as an independent scientific discipline, he emphasized the biological basis of psychological phenomena (Wundt 1883 [1948]). In 1899, Angell & Thompson discussed the relation between certain organic processes and consciousness. Later, in his presentation of functional psychology, Angell (1907) stressed the necessity of integrating biological with psychological factors in the model of individual functioning. During recent decades a strong advocate of a biological basis for personality factors has been Eysenck (1990) (see also Gray 1985).

Among those who have stressed the importance of biological factors in personality research are Hettema (1989), who emphasized the role of biological factors for human adaptation; and Kagan (1989) and Strelau (1983), who discussed the biological characteristics of temperament. The reasons for considering biological factors in research on personality development have been summarized by Susman (1989). The rapid developments in neuropsychology, endocrinology, and pharmacology during the last decades have demonstrated the essential role played by physiological factors in the way individuals think, feel, act, and react (Hockey et al 1986). Research in these areas will contribute much to our understanding of how individuals function as totalities.

Since the beginning of the history of differential psychology, the role of genetic factors has been a main issue (Galton 1869). Genetic factors in personality development and functioning have recently been discussed by Loehlin (1992), Plomin (1989), and Scarr (in press), among others. Plomin & Nesselroade (1990) have suggested that genetic factors play a more dominating role during early years than later in life. How concepts from biological theory have been assigned a prominent role in the continuity of social behavior was critically assessed by Cairns & Hood (1983). The results of this research have led to the integration of biological factors in the formulations of what has been designated modern interactionism (Magnusson 1990; Eysenck 1991; Gottlieb 1991).

It is interesting to note the limited extent to which biological factors have been considered in personality models, in spite of the propositions put forward by prominent researchers as mentioned above.

The Individual as a Social Being

A prerequisite for normal individual functioning is healthy relationships to other individuals (Cairns 1979). Contact with others is necessary for the development of speech and language as tools for thought and communication (Camaioni 1989; Tomaselli 1992); for the development of adequate worldviews and self-perceptions (Epstein & Erskine 1983); and for functional, integrated normative and/or moral systems (Wilson et al 1967). The importance of contact with others to mental and physical health has been emphasized in the increasing number of reports from research on social networks (Wills 1984; Wortman & Dunker-Schetter 1987).

CHARACTERISTICS OF PERSONALITY RESEARCH

How does empirical personality research generally approach the central issues?

Fragmentation

As noted by almost all reviewers of personality research in the *Annual Review of Psychology* during the past few decades, a main characteristic of this work is fragmentation. The total space of relevant issues has been compartmentalized into subareas, such as perception, cognition, emotion, behavior, genetics, and physiology, each with its own concepts, methods, and research strategies and with little or no mutual exchange of ideas (Coops 1990; de Groot 1990). We lack a fruitful, iterative process of specialization and integration. Instead, as Toulmin noted in 1981,

> the fragmentation of the behavioral sciences rests—too often—on nothing more than sectarial rivalry and incomprehension. As a result, what has grown up in the behavioral sciences is less a rational and functional division of labor than a state of bureaucratic warfare! Even—given the charismatic character of the leading figures involved—a condition of sectarial hostility (pp. 267–68).

Fragmentation is reflected in the application of three main approaches at a metatheoretical level to the study of individual functioning—the mentalistic, biological, and environmentalistic paradigms. Each has far-reaching implications both for basic research on normal and deviant functioning and for application (Magnusson 1988). According to the mentalistic view, the main explanation for an individual's way of thinking, feeling, acting, and reacting is to be found in the functioning of the mind and can be discussed and explained in terms of intrapsychic mental processes. The biological view identifies biological factors as having a primary influence on human behavior. The environmental approach locates the main causal factors for individual functioning in the environment.

Fragmentation can be described as specialization. Indeed, at one stage a discipline's scientific development is characterized by specialization. However, true scientific development is also characterized by integration among specialties. The most interesting steps forward are taken through integration. When specialization reached a certain level in physics and chemistry, important development took place at the interface of the two disciplines. Currently, the most interesting developments in the natural sciences are taking place at the interface among physics, chemistry, and biology.

The fragmentation of personality research into sub-areas is one of the greatest impediments to scientific progress. The result is that much personality research proceeds in a circle. For scientific progress to take place, specialization is a must. However, essential for further progress in personality theory is a general "model of individual funtioning in humans" that integrates the individual and environmental phenomena that operate simultaneously to influence psychological functioning. The models presented by Fogel & Thelen (1987), Hettema (1989), Kenrick et al (1985), and Magnusson (1990) are examples of striving in this direction.

Emphasis on Variables

Another main characteristic of personality research, from either a current or a developmental perspective, is its emphasis on the analysis of variables. Problems are formulated in terms of variables; and generalizations on the basis of empirical results are made in such terms. This nomothetical approach reflects the search for general principles of psychological functioning. One manifestation of this emphasis is the prevalence of trait-centered or dimensional approaches (Thomae 1988; Weinert & Schneider, in press).

The concentration on variables dominates empirical research on personality consistency, in terms of cross-situational and temporal stability of person-bound factors such as intelligence, aggressiveness, and hyperactivity. This approach is also characteristic of (a) studies of relations among person-bound variables that seek higher-order dimensions—e.g. traits—and (b) studies of relationships between environmental factors (such as childhood circumstances) and person-bound factors. A review of two volumes of *Journal of Personality and Social Psychology* (vols 56 and 58) and of two volumes of *Journal of Personality* (vols 57 and 59) showed that 86% (86/100) and 74% (46/63), respectively, of all articles were organized around the study of variables.

Methodologically, the emphasis on variables has led to the frequent application of various regression models, mainly linear regression models. Using a variable-oriented approach with the application of such models implies two interrelated things: (a) inferences about how an individual functions and develops are drawn from studies of interindividual differences, and (b) the general interrelations among variables, as reflected, for example, in correlation coefficients, are used as a basis for inferences about how the variables actually function in individuals. Relationships among variables and their way of functioning in the totality is then assumed to be the same for all individuals. In a multiple regression equation, each variable has the same weight for all individuals and reflects what is characteristic of the average person.

A special problem arises from the fact that many, not to say most, of the variables studied in personality research are hypothetical variables (Magnusson 1990). Among the articles published in the journals mentioned above, 95% (95/100) and 92% (58/63), respectively, included analyses of hypothetical variables. A hypothetical variable is an abstraction aimed at delineating a certain aspect of the total functioning of the individual, such as intelligence or aggressiveness, or sometimes the environment, such as social class or poverty. What is actually assessed as a measure of this aspect is, of course, defined by the properties of the procedure used for data collection, independent of the wording of the theoretical definition. Hypothetical constructs, which personality research abounds in, run the risk of reification, i.e. to be regarded as tangible and really existing, as when trait psychologists state that traits determine behavior. This view was discussed by Stagner (1948), who concluded "Too many psychologists write as if a trait were an effective cause of behavior. This is quite incorrect and misleading. ... The trait, then, should be considered descriptive, but not explanatory" (p. 144).

Two interrelated, methodological aspects of the frequent use of hypothetical variables are of interest in this connection. One issue is the existence of co-linearity among variables, i.e. the frequent existence of high correlations among independent variables (Darlington 1968). Statistical co-linearity is reflected in intercorrelations, sometimes very high, among operating variables. The high correlations, for example, among aspects of manifest behaviors such as aggressivity and motor restlessness, reflect the fact that they largely overlap with respect to content. This fact implies that the unique contribution of measures of each of these variables, independent of other aspects of behavior, to understanding and explaining why individuals think, feel, act, and react as they do in real life, is limited, sometimes extremely so. This conclusion has been illustrated empirically by Magnusson et al (in press).

Second, the existence and validity of a hypothetical variable are usually determined in studies of interindividual differences [cf Mischel's (1968) discussion of the existence of traits]. This means, among other things, that the psychological significance is assumed to be the same for individuals at all levels of the dimension for the variable under consideration, which implies that individuals differ only quantitatively, not qualitatively with respect to each variable under study.

The variable-oriented approach presents a static model of how an individual functions and develops. An example is the pure trait position, which holds that an individual's way of thinking, feeling, acting, and reacting in a certain situation, with its specific characteristics and psychological significance, can be predicted, explained, and understood by combining values from a set of traits. This view does not consider individual psychological functioning as a dynamic process, nor does it allow for an understanding and explanation of the process of development.

Prediction

In the Newtonian mechanistic view of nature, prediction is a central concept, supporting the search for precise laws. Since the well-known formulation by Watson (1913), that the goal of scientific psychology is to predict and control behavior, a high level of prediction has, most often implicitly, been regarded as the ultimate goal of psychological research (e.g. Smith 1992). High prediction has been accepted as the ultimate criterion of success.

Discussion of the role of prediction as a central concept in personality research is not just a theoretical matter. The concept of prediction as a goal for psychology is closely connected with a mechanistic model of man (Overton & Reese 1973). Associated with this view are the concepts of cause and effect and of independent and dependent variables, as well as analyses of predictor-criterion relations, and interpretation of results in terms of explained variance. In the review of research published in the two journals referred to above, 68% (68/100) and 54% (34/63), respectively, of all articles were focused on prediction and interpretation of the results in terms of explained variance. Research in which the connections between independent and dependent variables and between predictors and criteria are studied as unidirectional, cause-and-effect relationships, is often motivated by the goal of accurate prediction. This view is also reflected in the operationalization of psychological concepts, the choice of variables to be studied, the methods for data treatment and the interpretation of empirical results.

Unidirectional Causality

Related to the concept of prediction is the concept of causality. For a long time relations among variables were almost exclusively discussed in terms of unidirectional causality. This view is reflected in the experimental designs, with the distinctions between independent and dependent variables and between predictors and criteria. The notion of unidirectional causality has been particularly dominant when the relation has been between biological and environmental variables, on the one hand, and various person factors, on the other. In these cases, environmental factors and biological aspects of the individual have been regarded and treated as independent factors, and mental and behavioral aspects of individual functioning as dependent variables. The notion of stimulus-response (S-R) relations has been one of the most influential views in psychology. Many personality models also assume a unidirectional relation between cognitive-motivational factors and behavior. In some areas, e.g. in models for social functioning, a more nuanced view has become prevalent, one that takes into consideration the interactive character of social processes (Bell 1968, 1971; Caspi 1987; Peterson 1979).

The Dominance of Methods and Statistics over Analysis of the Phenomena

The development of new tests and inventories as tools for data collection, and of more sophisticated methods for data treatment, have contributed a great deal to scientific progress in empirical personality research. However, in some personality research there has been a tendency for methods and statistics to take priority over careful analysis of phenomena as a basis for choosing appropriate methods for data collection and data treatment. Methods and statistics are only tools, and their appropriate use depends on the extent to which they are applied in a way that correctly matches the character of the phenomena they are assumed to reflect. Too much research is now evaluated with reference to the technical sophistication of the methods and statistics, rather than with reference to the strength with which it answers relevant questions (Cairns 1986; Magnusson 1992; Roskam 1979; Thomae 1988). In 1988, a main portion of the *Journal of Personality* (56:3) was devoted to the discussion of traits. This discussion was conducted without substantial reference to analyses of the phenomena under investigation. Rather, the main aspects that were discussed were the psychometric properties of scales for measuring traits.

Theory vs Empirical Research

Personality research is characterized by a lack of integration between theory and empirical studies. Generally, the proponents of personality theory and those involved in empirical research work in two different spheres. One can note, for example, how empirical research on the person-situation interaction issue was, for a long time, planned and carried through without reference to the theoreticians who had emphasized for decades the role of situational factors in individual functioning. It appears that development of empirical personality research has been guided more by the development of methods for data collection (tests and inventories) and of new, sophisticated methods for data treatment than by theories based on careful analysis of the phenomena.

A HOLISTIC, DYNAMIC MODEL OF PERSONALITY

The issue is not new in psychology. It is reflected in the old assumption of the four basic temperaments, in the typologies, and in the discussion of an idiographic versus a nomothetical approach to empirical research. James (1890) eloquently expounded the idea of the individual as a whole, and Dewey (1896) warned against the danger of atomistic psychology, which he saw growing out of the Wundt school. In personality research, the holistic view has been advocated by many prominent figures: e.g. Stern (1911), Lewin (1935), Allport (1937), Angyal (1941), and Murray (1938). In recent years, dismay at the lack of consideration given to the implications of the holistic approach in theoretical and empirical research on psychological phenomena has been expressed by almost all contributors to the *Annual Review of Psychology* (see Helson & Mitchell 1978 on personality research; Tyler 1981 on psychological research in general; also Carlson 1984). For research on psychological functioning from a developmental perspective, a holistic view has been advocated by Block (1971), Cairns (1983), Sameroff (1983), Wapner & Kaplan (1983), and Magnusson (1990), among others.

A fundamental proposition in the following discussion is the view that an individual functions and develops as an integrated whole and that individual functioning, both in a current and in a developmental perspective, can be characterized as a dynamic, multi-determined, stochastic process. The reasons for a holistic view on individual functioning have been strengthened by the development of powerful theories and models for dynamic, complex processes in general. Psychological functioning has certain elements in common with dynamic, nonlinear, complex processes, which are the object of interest in general systems theory (von Bertalanffy 1968; Laszlo 1972; Miller 1978), chaos theory (Crutchfield et al 1986; Gleick 1987) and catastrophe theory (Zeeman 1976). The presentation of these theories has had a tremendous influence on empirical research and on the development of measurement models and statistics in the natural and life sciences concerned with dynamical, nonlinear, complex processes such as meteorology, biology, chemistry and ecology (Bothe et al 1987). Chaos theory has been regarded as one of the most powerful theories in this century and has been applied in many scientific disciplines (Hall 1991). Attempts have even been made to apply chaos theory to the functioning of the brain (Basar 1990). However, these theories have so far had very little impact in psychology.

A Holistic View

The point of departure for a holistic analysis of individual functioning is that an individual functions as a totality and that each aspect of the structures and processes (perceptions, cognitions, plans, values, goals, motives, biological factors, conduct, and other aspects) takes on meaning from the role it plays in the total functioning of the individual: "There is a logic and coherence to the person that can only be seen in looking at total functioning" (Sroufe 1979, p. 835). The whole picture has an information value that is beyond what is contained in its specific parts (the doctrine of epigenesis): "Behavior, whether social or nonsocial, is appropriately viewed in terms of an organized system, and its explanation requires a 'holistic analysis'" (Cairns 1979, p. 325).

A key element in the dynamic processes of individual psychological functioning, distinguishing it from other holistic, dynamic processes for which the general models mentioned above were developed, is played by the individual's mental system. This is reflected in the proposals to conceive of personality as a goal-directed, adaptive open system (Allport 1961; Hettema 1979; Schwartz 1987).

Dynamic, Lawful Interaction

Interaction is a fundamental principle in the functioning of open systems, from the macrocosm to the microcosm. It is central at all levels of individual functioning, from the functioning of single cells and how they organize themselves into systems in a lawful manner to fulfill their developmental role in the total organism (Edelman 1987) to the functioning of an individual in relation to his/her environment (Endler & Magnusson 1976).

An example will illustrate how the principle of dynamic interaction characterizes the interplay of psychological and biological factors in the individual and factors in the environment. If a person encounters a situation that he/she experiences as threatening or demanding—for example, an examination or a work task—the cognitive act of interpreting the situation stimulates, via the hypothalamus, the excretion of adrenaline from the adrenal glands, which in turn triggers other physiological processes. This cognitive-physiological interplay is accompanied by emotional states of fear and/or anxiety and/or generally experienced arousal. In the next stage of the process these emotions affect not only the individual's behavior and handling of the environment, but also his/her interpretation of the sequence of changes in the situational conditions and thereby his/her physiological reactions in terms of autonomous reactivity. Thus, the perceptual-cognitive system and the biological system of an individual are involved in a continuous loop of reciprocal interaction. The way this process functions is dependent, among other things, on the character of the environment, particularly the environment as it is perceived and interpreted by the individual. Across time this interplay of biological and mental factors contributes to changes in the structure and functioning of these systems as well as to changes in the structure and functioning of related subsystems, such as the immune system. One possible result is psychosomatic disorders. (See also the review in this volume by Ader & Cohen.)

All factors are involved in the consistently ongoing interplay of various aspects of the total organism. As noted above, in the traditional view, manifest behavior was mainly regarded as the result of cognitive-motivational factors. Animal research has demonstrated how even manifest behavior is involved as an operating, causal factor in the total interaction process of the organism (Cairns et al 1990).

Psychological Functioning—A Dynamic Process

An essential aspect of the processes of psychological functioning is their dynamic character. From a current perspective, the processes take place in the framework of stable structures and operating factors. From a developmental perspective, the character of the total system of interacting factors changes with maturation and experience in the development process. These changes in turn affect the character of the current perspective.

An individual's thoughts, feelings, actions and reactions are aspects of a holistic process characterized by dynamic, *lawful interaction*. This concept includes six basic principles: *multi-determination, interdependence, reciprocity, nonlinearity, temporality* and *integration*. Each of these is stated briefly here.

Multi-determination. All activities of the system involve several underlying factors or conditions.

Interdependence. The principle of interdependence implies that two factors depend on each other without necessarily influencing each other reciprocally.

Reciprocity. Reciprocity is an essential feature of the way biological and psychological factors operate together within the individual and of the way an individual relates to the environment (Bandura 1978).

> The basic principle underlying reciprocal influences in development arising from parent-offspring interaction is that of a moving bi-directional system in which the responses of each participant serve not only as the stimuli for the other but also change as a result of the stimuli exchanges, leading to the possibility of extended response on the part of the other (Bell 1971:822).

As summarized earlier, empirical research has been dominated by the view of unidirection causality. However, in some areas, particularly when the issues concern social relationships, the principle of reciprocity has been accepted and has guided empirical research. Reciprocity among operating factors contributes to developmental change in the functioning of the total system.

Nonlinearity. The principle of nonlinearity refers basically to the interrelations among variables operating at the individual level. It applies already at the cellular level. Information transfer between nerve cells depends on release of a chemical transmitter that acts on specific receptors on the second neuron. This is a nondigital, analog process that is usually nonlinear (Burgen, in press). The principle implies, for example, that the individual effect of hormone A on the dependent hormone B is not necessarily linear; the relation may take on any function within an individual. The same holds true for the interplay of a single individual with his/her environment. For example, individuals' psychological and physiological stress reactions to increasing stimulation from the environment are usually curvilinear. The nonlinear function for the relation between two operating person-bound factors or the relation between the individual and his/her environment may differ among individuals. Thus, choosing an adequate methodology for studying individual differences is crucial.

Temporality. A process can be characterized as a continuous *flow* of interrelated, interdependent events (Pervin 1983). This definition introduces time as a fundamental element in any model for individual functioning. In modern models of dynamic processes, a central concept is the concept of *motion*. Key aspects of biological processes are *rhythm* and *periodicity* (Weiner 1989). In an important but largely neglected article, Faulconer & Williams (1985), drawing on Heidegger, emphasized the importance of annexing temporality in our endeavors to understand individual functioning. Without the principle of temporality, dynamics, so fundamental for the understanding of human functioning and development, are ignored.

Integration. At all levels of the dynamic, holistic processes the operating parts are coordinated in their operations so as to serve the goal of the system to which they belong. This holds for parts of subsystems as well as for the coordination of subsystems in the functioning of the totality. Integration is the principle behind the fact that the total is more than the sum of its parts.

Levels of Dynamic Processes

At all levels the processes of psychological functioning are going on within organized systems guided by lawful principles. The lawfulness of the processes is reflected in the development and functioning of all organized subsystems as well as in the functioning of the organized totality. From the standpoint that an individual's thoughts, feelings, actions and reactions are dependent on the functioning of the individual as a biological being, the characteristic features of biological systems have direct relevance for personality research.

A basic, well-documented principle in the functioning of biological systems is their ability for self-organization (Nicolis & Prigogine 1977; Prigogine & Stengers 1985). Odum's 1983 discussion of energy self-organization in ecology is useful, as is the presentation of models for the immune system by Farmer et al 1987. Also relevant for the discussion of this issue is Edelman's 1987 Theory of Neuronal Group Selection and the way the development of the brain, both with respect to morphology and function, depends on interaction between the organism and the environment.

Within subsystems the operating components organize themselves in a way that maximizes the functioning of each subsystem with respect to its purpose in the total system. At a higher level subsystems organize themselves in order to fulfill their role in the functioning of the totality. Good illustrations of this principle are the development and functioning of the brain, along with its implications for the development and functioning of the cognitive system of an individual, and the functioning of the coronary system (Kaas 1987). In coronary research, factors and operating mechanisms involved in "remodeling" the coronary system have become an important area of scientific study with reference to the self-organizing qualities of this system (Packer et al 1983; Sharpe et al 1991).

Individuals differ to some extent in the way operational factors are organized and function within subsystems, such as the perceptual-cognitive-emotional system, the immune system, the coronary system, and the behavioral system. Individuals also differ in subsystem organization and function. These organizations can be described in terms of patterns of operating factors within subsystems and in terms of patterns of functioning subsystems. Of relevance for this discussion is Weiner's (1989) idea that even the oscillations produced by the natural pacemakers of the heart, the stomach and the brain are patterned. One important implication of this view is that each subsystem must be analyzed in terms of its context in the total functioning of the individual and the total functioning of the person-environment system, and in terms of the manner in which it affects and is affected by other subsystems.

PREDICTION VS UNDERSTANDING AND EXPLAINING LAWFULNESS

As defined in the introduction, the basis of scientific personality research is how and why individuals think, feel, act, and react as they do in life situations. This formulation has consequences for the choice between two contrasting ultimate goals for scientific personality research, namely *prediction* of psychological functioning in a total perspective, on the one hand, and explaining and understanding of the *lawfulness* of psychological functioning, on the other. The term *lawfulness* is used here to describe individual functioning that proceeds according to a set of identifiable principles but is not necessarily predictable (much as chaos theory describes dynamic processes that are lawful but unpredictable).

Prediction in Dynamic Processes

In the theoretical approach summarized so far, the primary interest in personality research is twofold: (*a*) the lawful continuity of the processes involved in the individual's functioning in *current* situations within unchanged structures; and (*b*) the lawful continuity of the processes involved in the changes in the individual's way of functioning from a *developmental* perspective (Magnusson & Törestad 1992). Given the complex, often nonlinear interplay of biological and mental subsystems within the individual, and the complex interplay between the individual and an environment that is operating in a probabilistic, sometimes very uncertain and unpredictable way, it is unrealistic to hope for high prediction of individual molar social behavior from one situation to another or over age spans. To foresee molar social behavior is as difficult for psychologists as it is for meteorologists to predict the weather a week ahead.

In general models for nonlinear dynamical processes, two interrelated aspects contribute to limit the possibilities for accurate prediction. Their existence is relevant to understanding the dynamical processes in personality research.

The first aspect concerns the prerequisites for predictability. These include (*a*) a perfect model, and (*b*) initial conditions that are exactly the same from occasion to occasion. These prerequisites are never met in the dynamic processes of individual functioning, even in a current perspective. A small change in the initial conditions may have dramatic effects on the total process in the long run. It is easy to find examples in individuals' lives of this so-called *butterfly effect.* Events and actions, which at the time of their occurrence may seem totally negligible, may later result in dramatic changes in the life course of individuals. Attention was originally drawn to this characteristic of dynamic systems by Poincaré (1946):

> A very small cause, which escapes us, determines a considerable effect we cannot help seeing, and then we say that the effect is due to chance. If we could know exactly the laws of nature and the situation of the universe at the initial instant, we should be able to predict the situation of this same universe at a subsequent instant .... But it is not always the case; it may happen that slight differences in the initial conditions produce very great differences in the final phenomena; a slight error in the former would make an enormous error in the latter. Prediction becomes impossible, and we have the fortuitous phenomenon.

The second interrelated aspect of the dynamic processes of open systems, applicable also to the processes of individual functioning, is the occurrence and effect of *significant events,* which can act to change the initial conditions and contribute to the butterfly effect. Some seem to occur randomly, but are actually a consequence of the joint occurrence of an individual's readiness for a certain type of action or reaction (a marriage or taking on a new job) and an opportunity offered by the environment (e.g. meeting another person or receiving an offer of a new job) (cf Bandura's 1982 discussion of "chance events"). In other cases, a significant event may be the result of deliberate action by the individual himself/herself or by individuals whose actions influence others. Buying a new house in a certain area with specific characteristics of neighbors, opportunity for jobs, schooling, cultural and leisure time activities and so on, instead of in an area with other characteristics, may have decisive effects on the future of all family members. Sometimes, this effect is not immediately visible but grows slowly to resemble the butterfly effect. In other cases, the effect is more direct and leads to what has been discussed in terms of "turning points" in the development process (Pickles & Rutter 1991). Often, the necessary condition for a significant event to have this effect is that the individual, at the time of its occurrence, is in a state of disequilibrium. The event serves the purpose of restoring the balance of the total system with a new direction of the life course. Under such conditions, significant events in individual life cycles serve the same function as *bifurcations* or singularities in the physical environment according to catastrophe theory.

It is important to point out that prediction is not a prerequisite for scientific analysis of dynamic processes or for explanation and understanding of such processes.

> Satisfactory explanation of the past is possible even when prediction of the future is impossible ... the thesis of this article is that scientific explanation is perfectly possible in the irregular subjects even when prediction is precluded. One consequence of this view is that the impossibility of a Newtonian revolution in the social

sciences, a position that I would maintain on other grounds, is not fatal to their status as sciences. (Scriven 1959:477).[1]

Prediction as a Goal and Prediction as a Tool

It should be emphasized that what we have discussed so far is prediction as a *goal* for personality research, not prediction as a *tool* in a research design. Our argument is against the tendency to make high predictability the primary goal of scientific psychology. Given the character of the processes that are our main interest, pursuit of such a goal is not only futile, it is destructive and hampers real progress. Of course, prediction is a useful conceptual and methodological tool in a research design when such a design is applicable to properly analyzed phenomena. The concept of prediction as a tool also is applicable in numerous practical situations in the application of psychological knowledge; for example, as a basis for personnel selection and for decision making. In such situations, the certainty with which the predictions are made, i.e. the probability with which certain events may occur, is of basic interest.

The Goal of Scientific Personality Research

Empirical research in psychology has derived much of its ideal from the natural sciences, particularly from physics. This is reflected in some of the characteristics of personality research summarized earlier. From that perspective, it is interesting to listen to Francis Crick, who shared the Nobel prize in 1962 for the discovery of the structure of DNA. Crick started his career in physics but moved into research in microbiology and later into cognitive psychology. In his book *What Mad Pursuit,* Crick (1988) discussed biology and physics as two very different kinds of subject:

> Physics is also different because its results can be expressed in powerful, deep and often counterintuitive general laws. There is really nothing in biology that corresponds to special and general relativity, or quantum electrodynamics, or even such simple conservation laws as those of Newtonian mechanics: the conservation of energy, of momentum, and of angular momentum. Biology has its "laws", such as those of Mendelian genetics, but they are often only rather broad generalizations, with significant exceptions of them. The laws of physics, it is believed, are the same everywhere in the universe. This is unlikely to be true in biology. ...
> What is found in biology is mechanisms, mechanisms built with chemical components and that are often modified by other, later, mechanisms added to the earlier ones. While Occam's razor is a useful tool in the physical sciences, it can be a very dangerous implement in biology (p. 138).

---

[1] The scientific status of psychoanalysis as a model for personality is sometimes questioned on the grounds that it cannot predict behavior. According to the standpoint formulated here this argument is not valid, although the scientific status of psychoanalysis may be questioned on other grounds.

Crick's view is relevant to a discussion of the kinds of laws sought in personality research. In this perspective the scientific goals for personality research can be expressed as being (*a*) to identify the factors operating in the processes underlying individuals' thoughts, feelings, actions, and reactions; and (*b*) to identify the mechanisms by which these factors operate, i.e. to answer the classical question: How?

These two tasks are distinctly different and require distinctly different research strategies and methodologies. For example, a large number of empirical studies indicate that low sympathetic physiological activity/reactivity of the nervous system is an operating factor in the development of various kinds of antisocial behavior. However, we still lack research showing the mechanisms by which it operates. In the same way, we know a great deal about the genetic factors behind some psychiatric illnesses but very little, if anything, about how they operate.

With reference to what we said earlier about the gap between theoretical and empirical approaches to personality issues, we can conclude that empirical research has contributed more to the identification of possible operating factors than to the understanding of the mechanisms, while theoretical approaches have been more concerned with the mechanisms guiding the processes. A prerequisite for future success is that these two aspects of personality research become integrated.

METHODOLOGICAL IMPLICATIONS OF A HOLISTIC, DYNAMIC MODEL

A holistic dynamic view of individual functioning will have far-reaching and serious consequences for research strategy and methodology. An essential implication is that research on single aspects, taken out of their context of other related aspects operating at the same time, only has very limited relevance for the understanding and explanation of the total process. This puts a new light on the question of the efficacy of a variable vs a person-oriented approach, in empirical studies of personality issues.

The Variable-Oriented Approach in a Holistic Perspective

The variable-oriented approach to personality issues was described in an earlier section. As noted, in the variable-oriented tradition data treatment often use linear models. These include factor analysis for the study of intervariable relationships, and analysis of variance for the study of cause-effect relations. Such methods range from pair-wise Pearson correlations to methods aiming to test theoretical models for causal relations among variables (LISREL) (Jöreskog 1979). Recent developments of methods for the study of nonlinear relations (e.g. logistic correlations) and of time-series have contributed to make more refined analyses possible (Hosmer & Leweshow 1989).

Variable-oriented research has contributed much to personality research and will continue to do so. Sophisticated analyses along these lines, based on careful description and analysis of the phenomena, form an indispensable part of empirical personality research. The greatest merit of the variable-trait approach—studying interrelations among variables using regression models—is that it contributes to our knowledge about the possible operating factors in the total process. However, three interrelated factors inherent in the model of personality functioning as a holistic, dynamical, nonlinear process must be considered for a meaningful applicability of a variable-trait approach using linear models for the study of personality issues.

The first one is the interdependence of any single aspect of the total dynamic process with other operating factors in the individual. Taken out of the context of other variables, any one variable loses much of its specific psychological significance, which basically is specific to a given individual.

The second factor is the existence of strong interactions among single aspects of individual functioning and among individual and environmental factors across individuals (Hinde & Dennis 1986; Rutter & Quinton 1987). Of course, to a certain extent interactions can be handled within, for example, structural equation modelling, but these possibilities are limited (Bergman 1993).

Third, one reflection of the application of linear models for the treatment of data is the fact that the focus of interest most often is on the study of main effects, in terms of significant correlations or significant differences among means. As discussed earlier, the variable-oriented approach usually implies, among other things, that the results are valid for the average individual and do not account for individual deviations from what is valid across individuals in general. The problems and limitations of this approach were discussed by Lewin (1931). "The concepts of the average child and of the average situation are abstractions that have no utility whatever for the investigation of dynamics" (p. 591).

Person-Oriented Analyses

The main research strategical and methodological consequence of the holistic, interactionistic view of personality is that the traditional variable-oriented research strategies and methodologies should be complemented with a person-oriented approach, (cf Block 1971; Caspi & Bem 1990; Magnusson & Allen 1983; Ozer & Gjerde 1989, among others). In a person-oriented approach, the person is the central unit of analysis. Problems for investigation are formulated in terms of persons, and operationalization is carried out in terms of individual patterns of values for variables relevant to the problem under investigation. The results of studies grouping individuals on the basis of their characteristic patterns of values for relevant factors are interpreted in person terms. A growing number of empirical studies applying a pattern approach on different issues have demonstrated its effectiveness (Baird et al 1990; Bergman & Magnusson 1983; Gustafson & Magnusson 1991; Pulkkinen & Trembley, in press; Magnusson & Bergman 1988; Mumford & Owens 1984).

Pattern Analysis

Partly as a result of the presentation of models for dynamic, complex processes, methods for pattern analyses have become an important tool for research in such disciplines as meteorology, biology, ecology, and chemistry. In the study of individual functioning using pattern analysis, two tasks can be distinguished: *pattern description* and *pattern dynamics*.

PATTERN DESCRIPTION   Pattern description implies the identification of central patterns of operating factors (*a*) at the level of single subsystems (e.g. antisocial behavior), or (*b*) at the level of cooperating subsystems (e.g. perceptual-cognitive-behavioral-physiological subsystems).

In operational terms, pattern description is based on the classification of individuals in homogeneous groups with respect to their patterns of values for the variables relevant to the issue under consideration. This raises the question of how to choose the variables for pattern analysis. In the study of individual functioning the theoretical basis for such a choice is based on the concept of self-organization of subsystems (cf. p. 439) and of the individual as a totality in terms of patterns of operating variables.

Fundamental to the application of pattern analysis is, in most cases, the fact that the number of biologically and psychologically possible organizations of factors within subsystems, and of subsystems within individuals, is limited. This constitutes the theoretical basis for grouping individuals and studying individual differences in terms of their characteristic patterns of values for relevant factors. This is, of course, opposed to the view held by extreme advocates of an ideographic notion, that individuals are totally unique.

One major consequence of this is that the choice of variables used for classification of individuals is based on careful description and analysis of the phenomena involved in the issue under consideration.

A number of methods for pattern description have been presented and applied: multivariate P-technique factor analysis (Cattell et al 1947; Nesselroade & Ford 1987); Q-sort technique (Block 1971; Asendorpf & van Aken 1991); latent profile analysis (LPA) (Gibson 1959; Magnusson et al 1975); configural frequency analysis (CFA) (von Eye 1990; Lienert & zur Oeveste 1985); and cluster analytical techniques (Bergman, in press).

Pattern description is the first step toward an understanding and explanation of the the the lawfulness of individual functioning. Its main merit, distinguishing it from a variable-oriented approach, is that it considers the holistic character of the functioning of subsystems and of the totality. Its limitations are obvious; it does not investigate the dynamics of the processes in individual functioning, neither in a current, nor in a developmental perspective.

PATTERN DYNAMICS   Pattern dynamics include two different measurement models and methods: (*a*) models and methods for the study of dynamic processes in a current perspective, i.e. processes going on within the boundaries of unchanged structures; and (*b*) models and methods for the study of dynamic processes in a developmental perspective, i.e. lawful changes in the patterns and the mechanisms by which changes are initiated and carried through. These types of pattern analysis are needed in order to understand and explain how these processes work.

Comments

Both the tasks of pattern description and of pattern dynamics are full of conceptual, theoretical and methodological problems (Bergman, in press). These have to be solved in order for the analyses to contribute successfully to our understanding and explanations of the lawfulness of the process of individual functioning. We are only in the beginning of developing adequate and effective methods for pattern analyses.

At the present stage of development, most empirical work has been restricted to pattern description. For further success in handling the important issues in this scientific domain, the development of appropriate methods which match the character of the processes we are interested in, and the refining of the theoretical basis for such methods, are among the most important future tasks (Bergman et al 1991). One of these challenges is to develop methods for the analyses of motion and change in the systems, i.e. for dynamic pattern analysis. At present we are much better at describing states than describing and explaining the change from one state to another or from one age to another (Dannefer & Perlmutter 1990).

It should be emphasized that a person-oriented approach is not a new term for a typological approach, which would refer each individual, once and for all, to a certain category. The essential claim in personality research is that analyses of any aspect of individual functioning, in a current and in a developmental perspective, shall be made with reference to the total functioning of the subsystems and their role in the functioning of the individual, and that interpretation of results of the analyses shall be made within the same frame of reference. Here the formulation by Weiss (1969) is appropriate:

> As one of us has tried to illustrate in a recent article (P. W. 1967), the "more" (than the sum of parts) in the above tenet does not at all refer to any measurable quantity in the observed systems themselves; it refers solely to the necessity for the observer to supplement the sum of statements that can be made about separate parts by any such additional statements as will be needed to describe the collective behavior of the parts, when in an organized group. In carrying out this upgrading process, he/she is in effect doing no more than restoring information content that has been lost on the way down in the progressive analysis of the unitary universe into abstracted elements (p. 11).

A person-oriented approach and a variable-oriented approach are conceptually distinct. They are complementary and answer different questions. Determining once and for all which one is the appropriate óne is not possible. This depends upon the character of the problem under investigation. Often a combination of both is the most effective way of using the data for the elucidation of a certain problem.

CONCLUDING COMMENTS

As summarized above, there is a need for a general theoretical framework for personality research. The view of individual functioning as a holistic, dynamical and complex process leads to the conclusion that such a model must include and integrate psychological and biological factors with individual and environmental-situational factors. For a full understanding of how and why individuals think, feel, act, and react as they do, personality theory has to incorporate knowledge from research in many specialized fields: perception, cognition, emotion, values, goals, behavior, genetics, neuropsychology, physiology, endocrinology, genetics, environmental psychology, and other related fields.

The view presented above is essentially a modern interactionistic perspective on individual functioning. Most of the discussion about the relevance of an interactionistic model has referred to empirical results which demonstrate the absence or presence of significant statistical interactions across individuals in experimental designs. However, from the perspective presented here the existence of interactive processes within individuals and between the individual and the environment does not necessarily show up in statistical analyses of individual differences. In order to avoid confusion in future discussions, a clear distinction must be made between *dynamic individual interaction* of complex processes and *statistical interaction* in experimental designs.

The holistic, dynamic interactionistic view has been criticized and it has been argued that this view is too loose and too general and even truistic; it only states that "everything interacts with everything." This has formed the basis for dismissal of the whole paradigm. It is true that one implication of the elaboration of individual psychological functioning, as a holistic, dynamic process, is that everything actually interacts with everything in a very general sense. However, the scientific attitude to this characteristic of our object of interest, namely the total psychological functioning of a person, is not resignation or simplification and distortion of reality in order to make the traditional approaches and methods applicable. The true scientific reaction is rather to conduct careful analyses of the consequences of the characteristics of the organized structures and processes involved, as a basis for the development of appropriate research strategies and methodologies for the study of the complex phenomena. Acceptance of the formulations of general models for nonlinear, dynamic, "chaotic" models in other disciplines concerned with these processes, has had a tremendous, positive influence on research in these disciplines and has sometimes led to totally new directions of research. The interaction processes of psychological functioning, those going on within unchanged structures and those leading to changes in size, shape, and/or function of the organism, take place at all levels in organized systems for individual functioning, in a way that is guided by lawful principles. It is the task and challenge of scientific psychological research to unveil these principles. Thus, a holistic, interactionistic view offers the conditions for systematic analyses of specific aspects of structures and processes and of specific mechanisms operating in current and developmental processes.

As emphasized above, theoretical and empirical research in scientific disciplines concerned with dynamical, complex processes, such as meteorology, chemistry, biology, and ecology, has become vitalized and redirected by the formulation of modern dynamic system theories. The view of individual functioning as a dynamic, multidetermined process includes the key principles of holistic processes and interaction. However, in one important respect individual functioning differs from general models of dynamic processes in these other disciplines: A fundamental aspect of the dynamic complex process of individual functioning is the individual's mental system including his/her self-perceptions and world views. The individual is an active, purposeful agent. This fact implies that the mathematical models developed for the study of nonlinear, chaotic systems are not immediately and directly applicable to the study of individual functioning as a dynamic process. We psychologists must avoid the mistake we made previously, when, in striving to attain the status of a truely scientific discipline, we adopted the research paradigm of physics, with its Newtonian view of nature. It is imperative that we develop research strategies and methods appropriate to the phenomena that are our main concern.

Literature Cited

Alba, J. W., Hasher, L. 1983. Is memory schematic? *Psychol. Bull.* 93:203–31

Allport, G. W. 1937. *Personality: a Psychological Interpretation.* New York: Holt, Rinehart & Winston

Allport, G. W. 1961. *Pattern and Growth in Personality.* New York: Holt, Rinehart & Winston

Anderson, J. R. 1985. *Cognitive Psychology and Memory.* New York: W. H. Freeman

Angell, J. R. 1907. The province of functional psychology. *Psychol. Rev.* 14:61–91

Angell, J. R., Thompson, H. B. 1899. A study of the relations between certain organic processes and consciousness. *Psychol. Rev.* 6:32–46

Angyal, A. 1941. *Foundations for a Science of Personality.* Cambridge MA: Harvard Univ. Press

Asendorpf, J. B., van Aken, M. A. G. 1991.

Correlates of the temporal consistency of personality patterns in childhood. *J. Pers.* 59(4):689–703

Baird, J. C., Berglund, M. B., Berglund, U., Lindvall, T. 1990. Symptom patterns as an early warning signal of community health problems. *Environ. Int.* 16:3–9

Bandura, A. 1978. The self system in reciprocal determinism. *Am. Psychol.* 33:344–58

Bandura, A. 1982. The psychology of chance encounters and life paths. *Am. Psychol.* 37:747–55

Bartlett, F. C. 1932. *Remembering: A Study in Experimental and Social Psychology.* Cambridge: Cambridge Univ. Press

Basar, E., ed. 1990. *Chaos in Brain Function.* Berlin: Springer

Been-Zeev, A. 1988. The schema paradigm in perception. *J. Mind Behav.* 9:487–514

Bell, R. Q. 1968. Reinterpretation of the direction of effects in studies of socialization. *Psychol. Rev.* 75:81–95

Bell, R. Q. 1971. Stimulus control of parent or caretaker by offspring. *Dev. Psychol.* 4:63–72

Bergman, L. R. 1993. Some methodological issues in longitudinal research: looking forward. See Magnusson & Casaer 1993. In press

Bergman, L. R., Eklund, G., Magnusson, D. 1991. Studying individual development: problems and methods. In *Problems and Methods in Longitudinal Research: Stability and Change,* ed. D. Magnusson, L. R. Bergman, G. Rudinger, B. Törestad, pp. 1–28. Cambridge: Cambridge Univ. Press

Bergman, L. R., Magnusson, D. 1983. *The development of patterns of maladjustment.* Rep. Proj. Indiv. Dev. Environ., Dep. Psychol., Stockholm Univ., No. 50

Block, J. 1971. *Lives Through Time.* Berkeley: Bancroft Books

Bothe, H. G., Ebeling, W., Kurzhanski, A. B., Peschel, M., eds. 1987. *Dynamical Systems and Environmental Models.* Berlin: Akademie-Verlag

Bowers, K. S. 1981. Knowing more than we can say leads to saying more than we can know: on being implicitly informed. In *Toward a Psychology of Situations,* ed. D. Magnusson, pp. 179–94. Hillsdale, NJ: Erlbaum

Brandtstädter, J. 1993. Development, aging and control: empirical and theoretical issues. See Magnusson & Casaer 1993. In press

Brentano, E. 1924. Psychologie vom empirischen Standpunkte. Leipzig: F. Meiner (Original published 1874)

Brewin, C. R. 1986. *Cognitive Foundations of Clinical Psychology.* Hillsdale, NJ: Erlbaum

Brushlinskii, A. V. 1987. Activity, action and mind as process. *Sov. Psychol.* 4:59–81

Burgen, A. 1993. Information flow in the nervous system. *Eur. Rev.* In press

Cairns, R. B. 1979. *Social Development: The Origins and Plasticity of Interchanges.* San Francisco: Freeman Cooper

Cairns, R. B. 1983. The emergence of developmental psychology. In *Handbook of Child Psychology,* ed. P. H. Mussen, 1:41–101. New York: Wiley. 4th ed.

Cairns, R. B. 1986. Phenomena lost: issues in the study of development. In *The Individual Subject and Scientific Psychology,* ed. J. Valsiner, pp. 79–111. New York: Plenum

Cairns, R. B., Hood, K. E. 1983. Continuity in social development: a comparative perspective on individual difference prediction. In *Life-Span Development and Behavior,* ed. P. B. Baltes, O. G. Brim, 5:302–58. New York: Academic

Cairns, R. B., Gariépy, J. L., Hood, K. E. 1990. Development microevolution, and social behavior. *Psychol. Rev.* 97:49–65

Camaioni, L. 1989. The role of social interaction in the transition from communication to language. In *Transition Mechanisms in Child Development,* ed. A. de Ribaupierre, pp. 109–25. New York: Cambridge Univ. Press

Carlson, R. 1984. What's social about social psychology? Where is the person in personality psychology. *J. Pers. Soc. Psychol.* 47:1304–9

Caspi, A. 1987. Personality in the life course. *J. Pers. Soc. Psychol.* 53(6):1203–13

Caspi, A., Bem, D. J. 1990. Personality continuity and change across the life course. See Pervin 1990, pp. 549–75

Cattell, R. B., Cattell, A. K. S., Rhymer, R. M. 1947. P-technique demonstrated in determining psycho-physiological source traits in a normal individual. *Psychometrika* 12:267–88

Coops, W. 1990. A viable developmental psychology in the nineties by way of renewed respect for tradition. See Drenth et al 1990, pp. 171–93

Crick, F. 1988. *What Mad Pursuit: A Personal View of Scientific Discovery.* New York. Basic

Crutchfield, J. P., Farmer, J. D., Packard, N. H., Shaw, R. B. 1986. Chaos. *Sci. Am.* 252:38–49

Dannefer, D., Perlmutter, M. 1990. Development as a multidimensional process: individual and social constituents. *Hum. Dev.* 33:108–37

Darlington, R. B. 1968. Multiple regression in psychological research and practice. *Psychol. Bull.* 69:161–82

de Groot, A. D. 1990. Unifying psychology: a European view. See Drenth et al 1990, pp. 3–16

Dewey, J. 1896. The reflex arc concept in psychology. *Psychol. Rev.* 3:357–70

Drenth, P. J. D., Sergeant, J. A., Takens, R. J. 1990. *European Perspectives in Psychology,* Vol. 1. Chichester, Sussex: John Wiley

Edelman, G. 1987. *Neural Darwinism: The Theory of Neuronal Group Selection.* New York: Basic

Emmons, R. A. 1992. Abstract versus concrete goals: personal strivings level, physical illness, and psychological well-being. *J. Pers. Soc. Psychol.* 62:292-300

Endler, N. S., Magnusson, D. 1976. Toward an interactional psychology of personality. *Psychol. Bull.* 83:956–79

Epstein, S., Erskine, N. 1983. The development of personal theories of reality from an interactional perspective. See Magnusson & Allen 1983, pp. 133–47

Eysenck, H. J. 1990. Biological dimensions of personality. See Pervin 1990, pp. 244–76

Eysenck, H. J. 1991. Personality, stress, and disease: an interactionist perspective. *Psychol. Inq.* 2:221–32

Farmer, J. D., Kaufmann, A., Packard, N. H., Perelson, A. S. 1987. Adaptive dynamic networks as models for the immune system and autocalytic sets. In *Perspectives in Biological Dynamics and Theoretical Medicine*, ed. S. H. Koslow, A. J. Mandell, M. F. Schlesinger, pp. 118–31. New York: Ann. NY Acad. Sci.

Faulconer, J. E., Williams, R. N. 1985. Temporality in human action: an alternative to positivism and historicism. *Am. Psychol.* 40:1179–88

Fogel, A., Thelen, E. 1987. Development of early expressive and communicative action: reinterpreting the evidence from a dynamic systems perspective. *Dev. Psychol.* 23(6):747–61

Galton, F. 1869. *Hereditary Genius: An Inquiry into its Laws and Consequences.* London: Macmillan

Gibson, W. A. 1959. Three multivariate models: factor analysis, latent structure analysis, and latent profile analysis. *Psychometrica* 24:229–52

Gleick, J. 1987. *Chaos: Making a New Science.* New York: Penguin

Gottlieb, G. 1991. Experiential canalization of behavioral development: theory. *Dev. Psychol.* 27:4–13

Gray, J. A. 1985. Issues in the neuropsychology of anxiety. In *Anxiety and the Anxiety Disorders,* ed. A. H. Tuma, J. D. Maser, pp. 5–25. Hillsdale, NJ: Erlbaum

Gustafson, S., Magnusson, D. 1991. Female life careers. In *Paths Through Life,* ed. D. Magnusson, Vol. 3. Hillsdale, NJ: Erlbaum

Hall, N., ed. 1991. *The New Scientist Guide to Chaos.* London: Penguin Books

Helson, R., Mitchell, V. 1978. Personality. *Annu. Rev. Psychol.* 29:555–85

Hettema, P. J. 1979. *Personality and Adaptation.* Amsterdam: North-Holland

Hettema, P. J., ed. 1989. *Personality and Environment: Assessment of Human Adaptation.* Chichester: Wiley

Hinde, R. A., Dennis, A. 1986. Categorizing individuals: an alternative to linear analysis. *Int. J. Behav. Dev.* 9:105–19

Hockey, G. R., Gaillard, A. W. K., Coles, M. G. H., eds. 1986. *Energetics and Human Information Processing.* Dordrecht: Martinus Nijhoff

Horley, J., Carroll, B., Little, B. R. 1991. A typology of life styles. *Soc. Indicator Res.* 20:383–98

Hosmer, D. W., Leweshow, S. 1989. *Applied Logistic Regression.* New York: Wiley

James, W. 1890. *The Principles of Psychology.* New York: Holt

Jöreskog, K. G. 1979. Statistical estimation of structural models in longitudinal developmental investigations. In *Longitudinal Research in the Study of Behavior and Development,* ed. J. R. Nesselroade, P. B. Baltes, pp. 303–51. New York: Academic

Kaas, H. 1987. The organisation of neocortex in mammals: implications for theories of brain function. *Annu. Rev. Psychol.* 38:129–51

Kagan, J., ed. 1989. *Unstable Ideas: Temperament, Cognition, and Self.* Cambridge, MA: Harvard Univ. Press

Kenrick, D. T., Montello, D. R., MacFarlane, S. 1985. Personality: social learning, social cognition, or sociobiology? In *Perspectives in Personality,* ed. R. Hogan, W. H. Jones, pp. 201–34. Greenwich, CT: JAI

Laszlo, E. 1972. *The Systems View of the World.* New York: Braziller

Lewin, K. 1931. Environmental forces. In *A Handbook of Child Psychology,* ed. C. Murchison, pp. 590–625. Worcester, MA: Clark Univ. Press

Lewin, K. 1935. *A Dynamic Theory of Personality.* New York: McGraw-Hill

Lienert, G. A., zur Oeveste, H. 1985. CFA as a statistical tool for developmental research. *Educ. Psychol. Meas.* 45:301–7

Loehlin, J. C. 1992. *Genes and Environments in Personality Development.* London: Sage

Loftus, E. F., Klinger, M. R. 1992. Is the unconscious smart or dumb? *Am. Psychol.* 47:761–65

Magnusson, D. 1988. Individual development from an interactional perspective. In *Paths Through Life,* ed. D. Magnusson, Vol. 1. Hillsdale, NJ: Erlbaum

Magnusson, D. 1990. Personality development from an interactional perspective. See Pervin 1990, pp. 193–222

Magnusson, D. 1992. Back to the phenomena: theory, methods, and statistics in psychological research. *Eur. Pers.* 6:1–14

Magnusson, D., Allen, V. L. 1983. Implications and applications of an interactional perspective for human development. In *Human Development: An Interactional Perspective,* ed. D. Magnusson, V. L. Allen, pp. 369–87. New York: Academic

Magnusson, D., Andersson, T., Törestad, B. 1993. Methodological implications of a peephole perspective on personality. In *Studying Lives Through Time: Approaches to Personality and Development,* ed. D. Funder, C. Tomlinson-Keasey, R. Parke, K. Widaman. Washington, DC: Am. Psychol. Assoc. In press

Magnusson, D., Bergman, L. R. 1988. Individual and variable-based approaches to longitudinal research on early risk factors. In *Studies of Psychosocial Risk: The Power of Longitudinal Data,* ed. M. Rutter, pp. 45–61. Cambridge: Cambridge Univ. Press

Magnusson, D., Casaer, P., eds. 1993. *Longitudinal Research on Individual Development: Present Status and Future Perspectives.* Cambridge: Cambridge Univ. Press. In press

Magnusson, D., Dunér, A., Zetterblom, G. 1975. *Adjustment: A Longitudinal Study.* Stockholm: Almqvist & Wiksell

Magnusson, D., Törestad, B. 1992. The individual as an interactive agent in the environment. In *Person-Environment Psychology: Models and Perspectives*, ed. W. B. Walsh, K. Craig, R. Price, pp. 89–126. Hillsdale, NJ: Erlbaum

Miller, J. G. 1978. *Living Systems*. New York: McGraw-Hill

Mischel, W. 1968. *Personality and Assessment*. New York: Wiley

Mumford, M. D., Owens, W. A. 1984. Individuality in a developmental context: some empirical and theoretical considerations. *Hum. Dev.* 27:84–108

Murray, H. A. 1938. *Explorations in Personality*. New York: Oxford Univ. Press

Nesselroade, J. R., Ford, D. H. 1987. Methodological considerations in modeling living systems. In *Humans as Self-Constructing Living Systems: Putting the Framework to Work*, ed. M. E. Ford, D. H. Ford, pp. 47–79. Hillsdale, NJ: Erlbaum

Nicolis, G., Prigogine, I. 1977. *Self-Organization in Non-Equilibrium Systems*. New York: Wiley Interscience

Norman, D. A., Shallice, T. 1980. *Attention to Action: Willed and Automatic Control of Behavior. Cent. Hum. Inf. Proc. Rep. 99.* San Diego: Univ. Calif., San Diego

Odum, H. T. 1983. *Systems Ecology: An Introduction*. New York: Wiley

Overton, W. F., Reese, H. W. 1973. Models of development: methodological implications. In *Life-Span Developmental Psychology: Methodological Issues*, ed. J. R. Nesselroade, H. W. Reese, pp. 65–86. New York: Academic

Ozer, D., Gjerde, P. F. 1989. Patterns of personality consistency and change from childhood through adolescence. *J. Pers.* 57:483–507

Packer, M., Medina, N., Yershak, R. N., Meller, J. 1983. Thermodynamic patterns of response during long-term captropil therapy for severe chronic heart failure. *Circulation* 68:803–12

Pervin, L. 1983. The stasis and flow of behavior: toward a theory of goals. In *Nebraska Symposium on Motivation*, ed. M. M. Page, pp. 1–53. Lincoln: Univ. Nebraska Press

Pervin, L. A. 1990. *Handbook of Personality: Theory and Research*. New York: Guilford

Peterson, D. R. 1979. Assessing interpersonal relationships by means of interaction research. *Behav. Assess.* 1:221–76

Pickles, A., Rutter, M. 1991. Statistical and conceptual models of "turning points" in developmental processes. In *Problems and Methods in Longitudinal Research: Stability and Change*, ed. D. Magnusson, L. R. Bergman, G. Rudinger, B. Törestad, pp. 133–66. Cambridge: Cambridge Univ. Press

Plomin, R. 1989. Environment and genes: determinants of behavior. *Am. Psychol.* 4:105–11

Plomin, R., Nesselroade, J. R. 1990. Behavior genetics and behavioral change. *J. Pers.* 58:191–220

Poincaré, H. 1946. *The Foundations of Science*. Lancaster, UK: Science

Prigogine, I., Stengers, I. 1985. *Order Out of Chaos*. New York: Bantam

Pulkkinen, L., Trembley, R. 1993. Patterns of boys' social adjustment in two cultures and at different ages: a longitudinal perspective. *Int. J. Behav. Dev.* In press

Roskam, E. E. 1979. Theorie und Methoden: eine Fallstudie der Forschungsmethodik. *Z. Sozialpsychol.* 10:114–33

Rutter, M., Quinton, D. 1987. Parental mental illness as a risk factor for psychiatric disorders in childhood. In *Psychopathology: An Interactional Perspective*, D. Magnusson, A. Öhman, pp. 199–219. Orlando, FL: Academic

Sameroff, A. J. 1983. Developmental systems: contexts and evolution. In *Handbook of Child Psychology*, ed. P. H. Mussen, 1:237–94. New York: Wiley

Scarr, S. 1993. Genes, experience, and development. See Magnusson & Casaer 1993. In press

Schwartz, C. 1987. Personality and the unification of psychology and modern physics: a system approach. In *The Emergence of Personality*, ed. J. Aronoff, A. I. Robin, R. A. Zucker, pp. 217–54. New York: Springer

Scriven, M. 1959. Explanation and prediction in evolutionary theory. *Science* 130:477–82

Sharpe, N., Smith, H., Murphy, J., Greaves, S., Hart, H., Gamble, G. 1991. Early prevention of left ventricular dysfunction after myocardial infarction with angiotensin-converting-enzyme inhibition. *Lancet* 337:872–76

Smith, L. 1992. On prediction and control: B. F. Skinner and the technological ideal of science. *Am. Psychol.* 47:216–23

Sroufe, L. A. 1979. The coherence of individual development: early care, attachment, and subsequent developmental issues. *Am. Psychol.* 34:834–41

Stagner, R. 1948. *Psychology of Personality*. New York: McGraw-Hill

Stern, W. 1911. *Die differentielle Psychologie in ihren metodischen Grundlagen*. Leipzig: von Hohann A. Barth

Strelau, J. 1983. *Temperament—Personality—Activity*. New York: Academic

Stumpf, C. 1883. *Tonpsychologie*, Vol. 1. Leipzig: S. Hirzel

Susman, L. 1989. Biology—behavior interactions in behavioral development. *Int. Soc. Stud. Behav. Dev. Newsl.* 15:1–3

Thomae, H. 1988. *Das Individuum und seine Welt: eine Persöhnlichkeitstheorie*. Göttingen: Hogrefe

Tolman, E. C. 1951. A psychological model. In *Toward a General Theory of Action*, ed. T. Parsons, E. A. Shils, pp. 279–364. Cambridge, MA: Harvard Univ. Press

Tomaselli, M. 1992. The social bases of language acquisition. *Soc. Dev.* 1:67–87

Toulmin, S. 1981. Toward reintegration: an agenda for psychology's second century. In *Psychology's Second Century: Enduring Issues,* ed. R. A. Kasshau, Ch. N. Cofer, pp. 81–97. New York: Praeger

Tyler, L. E. 1981. More stately mansions—psychology extends its boundaries. *Annu. Rev. Psychol.* 32:1–20

von Bertalanffy, L. 1968. *General System Theory.* New York: Braziller

von Eye, A. 1990. *Introduction to Configural Frequency Analysis: The Search for Types and Antitypes in Cross-Classifications.* New York: Cambridge Univ. Press

Wapner, S., Kaplan, B. 1983. *Toward a Holistic Developmental Psychology.* Hillsdale, NJ: Erlbaum

Watson, J. B. 1913. Psychology as the behaviorist views it. *Psychol. Rev.* 20:158–77

Weiner, H. 1989. The dynamics of the organism: implications of recent biological thought for psychosomatic theory and research. *Psychosom. Med.* 51:608–35

Weinert, F. E., Schneider, W. 1993. Cognitive, social, and emotional development. See Magnusson & Casaer 1993. In press

Weiss, P. A. 1969. The living system. Determinism stratified. In *Beyond Reductionism: New Perspectives in the Life Sciences,* ed. A. Koestler, J. R. Smythies, pp. 11–55. New York: McMillan

Wills, T. A. 1984. Supportive functions of interpersonal relationships. In *Social Support and Health,* ed. S. Cohen, L. Syme, pp. 61–82. New York: Academic

Wilson, J., Williams, N., Sugarman, B. 1967. *Introduction to Moral Education.* Baltimore, MD: Penguin

Wortman, C. B., Dunkel-Schetter, C. 1987. Conceptual and methodological issues in the study of social support. In *Handbook of Psychology and Health,* ed. A. Baum, J. E. Singer, 5:33–67. Hillsdale, NJ: Erlbaum

Wundt, W. 1948. Principles of physiological psychology. In *Readings in the History of Psychology,* ed. W. Dennis, pp. 248–50. New York: Appleton-Century Crofts

Zeeman, E. C. 1976. Catastrophe theory. *Sci. Am.* 234:65–83

Annu. Rev. Psychol. 1993. 44:453–95
Copyright © 1993 by Annual Reviews Inc. All rights reserved

THE STRUCTURE AND ORGANIZATION OF MEMORY

L. R. Squire, B. Knowlton, and G. Musen

Veterans Affairs Medical Center and University of California, San Diego, California 92161

KEYWORDS: declarative memory, nondeclarative memory, amnesia, hippocampus, brain systems

CONTENTS

INTRODUCTION 454
SHORT-TERM MEMORY 454
LONG-TERM MEMORY 457
   Declarative Memory 457
   Episodic and Semantic Memory 459
THE BRAIN SYSTEM SUPPORTING DECLARATIVE MEMORY 461
TIME-LIMITED FUNCTION OF THE BRAIN SYSTEM SUPPORTING
   DECLARATIVE MEMORY 462
THE DEVELOPMENT OF DECLARATIVE MEMORY 464
CAN THE BRAIN SYSTEM SUPPORTING DECLARATIVE MEMORY BE
   SUBDIVIDED? 466
   Forgetting Rates 466
   Spatial Memory 467
   Recall and Recognition 469
NONDECLARATIVE MEMORY 471
   Skills and Habits 471
   Neural Evidence for Distinguishing Skills and Habits from Declarative
      Memory 475
   Conditioning 477
   Priming 478
PERSPECTIVE 482

453

0066-4308/93/0201-0453$2.00

INTRODUCTION

A major goal of psychology is to understand the underlying organization of cognition—that is, to develop formal accounts of cognitive processes, information flow, and representations. Ultimately, one wants to understand cognition not just as an abstraction, or in terms that are simply plausible or internally consistent. Rather, one wants to know as specifically and concretely as possible how the job is actually done. It is often said, working from logical considerations alone, that in describing the function of a complex device one can separate consideration of its formal operations (the software) from consideration of the mechanisms used to implement the operations (the hardware). In the history of cognitive psychology it has been traditional to separate psychological theory from neurobiological detail. Until recently, this approach could be justified by the fact that relevant neurobiological information was simply not available. Yet it is increasingly true that the domains of psychology and neuroscience are reinforcing each other and working hand in hand (Kandel & Squire 1992). Neuroscience has become relevant and useful for elucidating the structure and organization of cognition.

Here we consider recent work on learning and memory from a combined psychology-neuroscience point of view. We focus on the characteristics of various forms of memory, their relationship to each other, and how they are organized in the brain. Although work with normal human subjects has been vital to this line of inquiry, our discussion draws especially on neuropsychological studies of memory-impaired patients and related studies with experimental animals. For recent reviews that emphasize work with normal subjects, see Hintzman (1990), Richardson-Klavehn & Bjork (1988), Schacter et al (1993), and Tulving (1991).

SHORT-TERM MEMORY

One of the oldest and most widely accepted ideas about memory is that short-term memory (STM) can be usefully distinguished from long-term memory (LTM) (James 1890; Waugh & Norman 1965; Glanzer & Cunitz 1966; Atkinson & Shiffrin 1968). That this distinction is prominently reflected in the organization of brain systems is demonstrated by the fact that amnesic patients have intact STM despite severely impaired LTM (Baddeley & Warrington 1970; Drachman & Arbit 1966; Milner 1971). A recent study of amnesic patients has made this proposition even more secure (Cave & Squire 1992a). Verbal STM was assessed with seven separate administrations of the standard digit span test in order to obtain a more precise measure of STM than has previously been available. In addition, nonverbal STM was assessed with four tests, including a test of STM for spatial information. Amnesic patients with hippocampal formation damage had the same average digit span as normal subjects (6.8 digits) and performed entirely normally on the other tests. Thus,

STM is independent of LTM and independent of the structures and connections damaged in amnesia.

An important development has been the separation of STM and LTM in experimental animals, which raises the possibility of investigating the biological basis of STM. In one compelling study (Wright et al 1985), the same recognition memory test consisting of four sequentially presented colored slides was given to pigeons, monkeys, and humans. (The humans viewed patterns from a kaleidoscope, and the pigeons and monkeys viewed pictures.) After a variable delay interval, a probe item was presented that on half the trials matched one of the four list items. Subjects made one response if the probe matched a list item, another if it did not. All three species exhibited primacy and recency effects as indicated by U-shaped serial position functions in which the first and fourth items in the list were remembered better than the second and third items. (The primacy effect refers to the superiority of the first item, and the recency effect refers to the superiority of the last item.) Pigeons exhibited a U-shaped serial position function at delay intervals of 1 and 2 sec, monkeys at delays of 1–10 sec, and humans at delays of 10–60 sec. At shorter delays than these, the primacy effect was absent. At longer delays, the recency effect was absent. The results for all three species require two distinct memory processes—e.g. a transient STM to account for the short-lived recency effect and, to account for the primacy effect, a longer-lasting LTM that emerges as retroactive interference decays during the delay interval.

A strong parallel between humans and experimental animals is also indicated by the finding that hippocampal lesions in rats eliminate the primacy portion of the serial position curve but not the recency portion (Kesner & Novak 1982), just as occurs in amnesic patients (Baddeley & Warrington 1970; Milner 1978). Finally, monkeys with large medial temporal lobe lesions were entirely normal at relearning postoperatively the trial-unique delayed nonmatching to sample task (Mishkin & Delacour 1975) with a delay interval of 1 sec between the sample and the choice (Overman 1990). In contrast, a severe impairment in performance was observed at longer delays. This finding is noteworthy because the usefulness of the delayed nonmatching to sample task for studying memory in monkeys was questioned recently, precisely because this task has not always distinguished STM and LTM (Ringo 1991). This issue was subsequently considered more fully (Alvarez-Royo et al, in press). Monkeys with medial temporal lobe lesions exhibited impaired memory at long retention delays and normal memory at short retention delays, when the delay intervals were presented in mixed order. Moreover, the normal monkeys and the monkeys with lesions exhibited a statistically significant group X retention delay interaction, which could be demonstrated whether the data were analyzed using a percentage correct measure, a d′ (discriminability) measure, or an arcsine transform. Thus, the work with monkeys is fully consistent with the facts of human amnesia and provides an additional illustration of the separation between STM and LTM.

The traditional view of the distinction between STM and LTM has been that the systems operate serially (Atkinson & Shiffrin 1968; Glanzer & Cunitz 1966; Waugh & Norman 1965). Information initially enters STM and subsequently becomes incorporated into a more stable LTM. This view was challenged some years ago (Shallice & Warrington 1970; Warrington & Shallice 1969) based on findings from a carefully studied patient (K.F.). Following a left parietal injury from a motorcycle accident, K.F. had a severely deficient verbal STM, as reflected by a digit span of one item, but nevertheless exhibited normal verbal LTM as measured, for example, by paired-associate learning of words and word-list learning. This pattern of findings led to the proposal that information may not need to enter STM before reaching LTM because the inputs to these two systems are arranged in parallel (Shallice & Warrington 1970; Weiskrantz 1990).

As the result of newer work, the findings from patient K.F. can now be understood fully without postulating parallel STM and LTM stores. STM has come to be viewed as a diverse collection of temporary capacities that are distributed across multiple, separate processing modules (Baddeley & Hitch 1974; Goldman-Rakic 1987; Monsell 1984; Squire 1987). In this view, auditory-verbal STM is a temporary storage system only for phonologically coded information. If one supposes that STM and LTM are serially organized, then one would expect a deficit in auditory-verbal STM to result in a corresponding deficit in LTM, but only to the extent that tests of LTM also depend critically on phonological analysis of verbal material. Findings from recent studies support this perspective.

Baddeley and his colleagues studied a patient (P.V.) who had suffered a cerebrovascular accident involving the left perisylvian region (Baddeley et al 1988). The patient appeared to have a deficit in STM similar to that of patient K.F. Thus, her auditory digit span was two items, but prose recall and free recall of word lists were intact. Yet, when tests of LTM were specially devised that required P.V. to depend on phonological analysis at the time of learning (e.g. visual or auditory presentation of foreign-language word pairs that would be difficult to learn by forming semantic associations), performance was distinctly impaired.

Related evidence on this point came from studies of 4–6-year-old normal children who were selected according to their repetition ability for single nonwords. Children who had low repetition scores for nonwords also had difficulty in a LTM task involving the learning and retention of arbitrary, unfamiliar names for toys (Gathercole & Baddeley 1990). Finally, articulatory suppression (whereby subvocal rehearsal is discouraged by requiring subjects to perform an interfering task) impaired the long-term learning of Russian vocabulary in normal adult subjects but not the learning of native-language paired associates (Papagno et al 1991). These findings all suggest that a deficit in short-term phonological memory leads to a deficit in LTM when the long-term learning also depends on phonological information.

Accordingly, the findings from patients K.F., P.V., and other similar patients with impaired verbal STM can be understood as a selective deficit in one component of STM, and a correspondingly selective deficit in LTM for information that is ordinarily processed by the defective STM component. Such a deficit leaves other components of STM available for the establishment of LTM. This perspective thus holds to the traditional view that STM grades into LTM and is essential for its formation.

LONG-TERM MEMORY

Declarative Memory

One important insight to emerge recently is that LTM is not a single entity but is composed of several different components, which are mediated by separate brain systems. Precursors to this idea can be found in many earlier writings (for reviews, see Schacter 1987; Squire 1987), but it became the subject of wide interest beginning only in the early 1980s as the result of experimental findings with normal adult subjects, amnesic patients, and experimental animals (see, e.g., Cohen & Squire 1980; Graf et al 1984; Jacoby & Witherspoon 1982; Malamut et al 1984; Tulving et al 1982; Warrington & Weiskrantz 1982; for two important earlier proposals, see Hirsh 1974; O'Keefe & Nadel 1978). The major distinction is between conscious memory for facts and events and various forms of nonconscious memory, including skill and habit learning, simple classical conditioning, the phenomenon of priming, and other instances where memory is expressed through performance rather than by recollection (see the section below on Nondeclarative Memory).

Studies of amnesic patients have provided particularly strong evidence for this distinction. These patients fail conventional memory tasks that involve, for example, recall or recognition but nevertheless perform entirely normally on a wide variety of other tasks. Although various terms have been used to describe these kinds of memory, the terms have remarkably similar meanings. Declarative memory (explicit memory, relational memory) is a brain-systems construct, referring to memory that is dependent on the integrity of the hippocampus and anatomically related structures in the medial temporal lobe and diencephalon (Squire & Zola-Morgan 1991; Zola-Morgan & Squire 1993). Nondeclarative (implicit) memory is a heterogeneous collection of separate abilities that can be additionally dissociated from each other (Butters et al 1990; Heindel et al 1989, 1991). These memory abilities depend on brain systems outside of the medial temporal lobe and diencephalon.

A number of important questions have been raised about whether distinctions between kinds of memory can be defined and established outside of the experimental contexts in which they were first developed. For example, the distinction between declarative and nondeclarative (or explicit and implicit) emphasizes the notion of conscious recollection, which is not useful when considering learning and memory in nonhuman animals. It has therefore been important to ask whether terms like declarative and nondeclarative have meaning independent of the concept of conscious recollection and independent of an empirically determined list of what amnesic patients can and cannot do. Recent work has helped to free these terms from such potential circularity by showing that different kinds of memory have different characteristics (for additional discussion see Sherry & Schacter 1987; Squire 1992a).

Declarative memory is fast, it is not always reliable (i.e. forgetting and retrieval failure can occur), and it is flexible in the sense that it is accessible to multiple response systems. Nondeclarative memory is slow (priming is an exception), reliable, and inflexible—that is, the information is not readily expressed by response systems that were not involved in the original learning. Two important experiments have illustrated that declarative and nondeclarative memory differ in flexibility. In the first experiment (Eichenbaum et al 1989), rats with damage to the hippocampal system were trained concurrently on two separate odor discrimination tasks (A+B−, C+D−) that they could eventually perform about as well as normal rats. Thus, both normal rats and rats with lesions came to choose odor A when it was presented in the odor pair AB and odor C when it was presented in the odor pair CD. However, a transfer task showed that something different had been learned by the two groups. Specifically, when rats were presented with recombined odor pairs (AD or CB), the normal rats tended to choose odor A, performing about as well as on the regular learning trials. That is, they were not disrupted by the new combination of stimuli; they were able to use relational information about the odors in a flexible way. In contrast, the rats with lesions behaved as if they were confronting a new problem and performed near chance. In their case, it appeared that the kind of knowledge that had been acquired was inaccessible when the original learning event was not precisely repeated.

A similar result was obtained with monkeys who had lesions of the hippocampus or related structures (Saunders & Weiskrantz 1989). Monkeys first learned which pairs of four objects were rewarded (e.g. AB+ and CD+) and which were not (e.g. AC− and BD−). Specifically, normal monkeys and monkeys with lesions were given a series of two-choice discrimination tasks in which a positive object pair was always presented together with a negative pair (e.g. AB+ and AC−). In this way, monkeys were required to respond on the basis of both objects in each pair (e.g. object A was correct when it appeared with object B but not when it appeared with object C). In a subsequent transfer task, monkeys were tested to determine what they had learned about the associations. One element of a previously rewarded pair was first presented (e.g. object A), and monkeys were immediately given a choice between two other objects (in this example, objects B and C). The normal monkeys selected object B, which had been part of the two-element, rewarded pair (AB), on 70% of the trials; but the monkeys with lesions performed at chance. Thus, what the operated monkeys had learned about the object-reward associations was bound to the original learning situation.

This issue has been addressed to some extent in studies of human learning and memory. In one study, amnesic patients who had gradually (and abnormally slowly) learned computer programming commands had difficulty applying their knowledge to new situations and difficulty answering open-ended questions about what they had learned (Glisky et al 1986a). In another study, in which much less training was given, amnesic patients acquired a limited ability to complete sentences in response to cue words (cued recall) (Shimamura & Squire 1988). In this case, it was shown that the knowledge acquired by the patients was as flexible, as accessible to indirect cues, and as available to awareness as the knowledge acquired by normal subjects. A likely possibility is that these patients relied on residual declarative memory to learn the sentences, while the patients who learned computer commands acquired the information as procedural memory for programming skills. Hyperspecificity appears to be a property of nondeclarative memory (also see Tulving & Schacter 1990), not a property of whatever information amnesic patients are able to acquire. When tasks are amenable to declarative memory strategies, amnesic patients will attempt to learn with their impaired declarative memory system, and whatever they succeed in remembering will be flexible and accessible to awareness.

Episodic and Semantic Memory

Episodic and semantic memory are two types of declarative memory (Tulving 1983, 1991). Episodic memory refers to autobiographical memory for events that occupy a particular spatial and temporal context, and semantic memory refers to general knowledge about the world. Both types of memory are declarative, in the sense that retrieval of information is carried out explicitly and subjects are aware that stored information is being accessed. While it is agreed that episodic memory is severely impaired in amnesia and dependent on the integrity of the brain system damaged in amnesia, the relationship between semantic memory and this brain system has not been so clear. Amnesic patients do have great difficulty acquiring semantic knowledge (Glisky et al 1986a,b; Kovner et al 1983), but they can typically succeed to some extent after much repetition. In one report (Tulving et al 1991), a severely amnesic patient (K.C.) eventually learned to complete arbitrary three-word sentences during a large number of training trials distributed over many months. This occurred despite the apparent absence of any memory at all for specific episodes.

An issue that remains to be addressed is whether episodic memory can truly be absent altogether, in the presence of gradually successful semantic learning, or whether semantic learning succeeds by building on residual episodic memory. Even a small amount of residual episodic memory might, in the fullness of time and after sufficient repetition, develop into serviceable semantic knowledge. When memory is impaired, the ability to acquire new semantic knowledge through repetition will always exceed the ability to acquire episodic memory, because episodic memory is by definition unique to time and place and cannot be repeated (see Ostergaard & Squire 1990).

One proposal is that episodic and semantic memory are dissociated in amnesia (Cermak 1984; Kinsbourne & Wood 1975; Parkin 1982). For example, it has been proposed that amnesia selectively affects episodic memory, that semantic learning is fully intact in amnesia, and that the advantage of normal subjects over amnesic patients in tests of semantic learning is due to the fact that normal subjects can perform these tests by drawing on episodic memory (Tulving 1991). By this view, repeated exposure to factual material can lead gradually and directly to long-term memory storage without requiring the participation of the brain system damaged in amnesia. A problem with this view is that amnesic patients have difficulty with factual information even when the contribution of episodic retrieval is unlikely. Thus, they fail remote memory questions about past public events that occurred more than a decade before the onset of amnesia (Squire et al 1989). This deficit would appear to reflect a failure of semantic memory because it is unlikely that normal subjects gain their advantage over amnesic patients on such remote memory tests by using episodic memory to answer the questions. Can episodic memory materially contribute to one's ability to identify Sara Jane Moore (the woman who attempted the assassination of President Ford) or to recall what dance the Peppermint Lounge was famous for (the Twist)?

A second difficulty turns on the question of how memory systems in humans relate to memory systems in nonhuman animals. If semantic memory is independent of the brain system damaged in amnesia, then experimental animals should be affected by damage to this brain system only to the extent that they use episodic memory to perform tasks. The difficulty is that rats, monkeys, and other animals are severely impaired on a wide variety of memory tasks following damage to the hippocampus and related structures (for reviews, see Sutherland & Rudy 1989; Squire 1992a), and the tasks that are affected involve much more than is usually intended by the term episodic memory (e.g. maze tasks and object recognition tasks). Indeed, episodic memory is usually considered to be either unavailable to nonhuman animals altogether or analogous to particular forms of trial-dependent memory (Olton 1985; Tulving 1985). Thus, one must suppose either that animals use episodic memory extensively, or that in animals some kinds of memory other than episodic memory depend on the hippocampus and related structures.

If the distinction between episodic and semantic memory is not relevant to the function of the brain system damaged in amnesia, the distinction is no less interesting or important. One possibility is that both episodic and semantic memory depend on the brain system damaged in amnesia (i.e. the hippocampus and related structures) and that episodic memory additionally depends on the integrity of the frontal lobes. Patients with frontal lobe damage, who are not amnesic, exhibit a phenomenon termed source amnesia (Janowsky et al 1989b). Source amnesia refers to loss of information about when and where a remembered item was acquired (Evans & Thorn 1966; Schacter et al 1984; Shimamura & Squire 1987). Thus, source amnesia amounts to a loss of auto-biographical involvement with recollected material—i.e. a disturbance of episodic memory. It is important to note that amnesic patients who commit source errors can subsequently demonstrate by multiple-choice testing that they have as much knowledge about the learning event as amnesic patients who do not commit source errors (Shimamura & Squire 1991). Thus, source amnesia appears to reflect a loss of episodic memory, related to frontal lobe dysfunction, which reflects a disconnection between facts and their contexts.

If episodic memory were understood in this way, a number of points would be clarified. First, the biological validity of the distinction between episodic memory and semantic memory is based on the greater contribution that frontal lobe function makes to episodic memory, compared to semantic memory. Second, episodic memory is available to nonhuman animals in a limited way, in the sense that animals do not acquire or express information about past events in the same way that people do—i.e. as recollections of past personal happenings. According to this view, the difference between human episodic memory and that of animals is attributable to the greater size and complexity of the human frontal lobe.

Third, episodic memory can be virtually absent in some severely amnesic patients who can still accomplish some semantic learning (e.g. patient K. C.). Such a condition depends in part on source amnesia, pursuant to frontal lobe pathology, which is superimposed on a severe difficulty in acquiring information about both facts and events. This view suggests two possibilities: 1. patients more amnesic than K. C., but without frontal damage, might be unable to accomplish semantic learning as well as patient K. C.; 2. severely amnesic patients might be able to accomplish some semantic learning as well as a corresponding degree of learning about single past events, albeit at an impaired level, provided they were tested with a method that does not require source memory and is not sensitive to frontal lobe pathology. For example, patients could be tested with multiple-choice methods that asked about what occurred in a specific event without requiring that the patients be able to place themselves autobiographically within the episode.

THE BRAIN SYSTEM SUPPORTING DECLARATIVE MEMORY

During the past decade, an animal model of human amnesia was established in the monkey (Mishkin 1982; Squire & Zola-Morgan 1983; Mahut & Moss 1984). Cumulative work with monkeys based on this animal model, together with findings from rats and new information from memory-impaired patients, has identified in broad outline the structures and connections important for declarative memory. Damage within the medial temporal lobe or the medial thalamus is sufficient to cause severe memory impairment. Within the medial temporal lobe, the important structures are the hippocampus and adjacent, anatomically related cortex (i.e. entorhinal, perirhinal, and parahippocampal cortices) (Squire & Zola-Morgan 1991). Within the diencephalon, the most important structures are in the medial thalamus: the anterior thalamic nucleus, the mediodorsal nucleus, and connections to and from the medial thalamus that lie within the internal medullary lamina. The medial thalamus receives well-described projections from several anatomical components of the medial temporal lobe. It is not clear whether or not the mammillary nuclei (MN) make an important separate contribution to memory functions, although damage to MN has sometimes been reported to produce a small degree of memory impairment (for reviews, see Markowitsch 1988; Victor et al 1989; Zola-Morgan & Squire in press).

Both the medial temporal lobe and the medial thalamus project to the frontal lobe, thereby providing a route by which recollections can be translated into action. Damage to the frontal lobe does not itself cause amnesia (Janowsky et al 1989); but frontal lobe pathology markedly affects cognition (Levin et al 1991), and it substantially alters the nature of the memory impairment when it occurs together with damage to the medial temporal lobe or medial thalamus (Shimamura et al 1991).

Transient amnesic conditions leave patients permanently unable to remember the events that occurred while they were amnesic (Kritchevsky et al 1988). This shows that the medial temporal/diencephalic system is required at the time of learning if an enduring and retrievable long-term (declarative) memory is to be established. How long after learning this brain system remains essential can in principle be determined by examining the phenomenon of retrograde amnesia. In particular, one wants to know which periods are lost from the period before amnesia began. In practice, it has been difficult to settle this matter with memory-impaired patients. First, the moment when amnesia begins is often difficult to establish. Second, there is usually considerable uncertainty about the precise locus and extent of damage in the particular patients being studied. Third, studies of remote memory in patients necessarily rely on retrospective methods and imperfect tests. Despite these difficulties, something useful has been learned about retrograde amnesia through quantitative studies of memory-impaired patients. More recently, the matter has been clarified by prospective studies of retrograde amnesia in mice, rats, and monkeys.

TIME-LIMITED FUNCTION OF THE BRAIN SYSTEM SUPPORTING DECLARATIVE MEMORY

The characteristics of retrograde amnesia vary enormously across different patients and patient groups. For one patient (R.B.), in whom the damage was restricted to the CA1 region of the hippocampus, retrograde amnesia was limited to perhaps one or two years prior to the onset of amnesia (Zola-Morgan et al 1986). Other patients exhibit temporally graded memory loss covering one to two decades (Squire et al 1989). Still other patients, usually ones with severe impairment, exhibit retrograde amnesia that appears extensive and ungraded, covering most of adult life (for reviews, see Butters & Stuss 1989; Squire 1992a). One possibility is that the extent of retrograde memory loss is related simply to the severity of amnesia and to the extent of damage within the medial temporal/diencephalic system. By this view, extended, ungraded retrograde memory loss represents an extreme condition on a continuum of severity. This alternative seems unlikely, because the severity of anterograde amnesia and the severity of remote memory impairment are not always correlated (Barr et al 1990; Shimamura & Squire 1986; Kopelman 1989) and because the severely amnesic patient H.M. is capable of recalling well-formed episodic memories from his early life (Sagar et al 1985). Many of the patients who have been reported to have extended, ungraded remote memory impairment have damage outside of the medial temporal lobe and medial thalamus. Thus, another possibility is that temporally graded retrograde amnesia occurs when damage is limited to the medial temporal lobe or medial thalamus and that extended, ungraded loss occurs only when there is damage outside this system.

Retrograde amnesia exhibits quite similar characteristics in medial temporal lobe amnesia and diencephalic amnesia (Squire et al 1989). The amnesia reflects a loss of usable knowledge, not a loss of accessibility that can be compensated for by providing repeated retrieval opportunities. Moreover, there are no compelling demonstrations that retrograde amnesia can be remediated by simple changes in the test procedures [e.g. asking patients to complete a famous name from a few letters instead of matching the name to a photograph (see Squire et al 1990)].

Retrograde amnesia can in one sense be described as a retrieval deficit. This description fits the observation that most lost memories return following transient amnesia (Benson & Geschwind 1967; Squire et al 1975). Yet, in another sense this description does not capture the nature of the impairment. First, memories acquired just prior to the amnesic episode cannot be recovered. Second, it is not clear that lost memories would return so fully if the system remained dysfunctional for a long time. Third, recent treatments of the medial temporal/diencephalic brain system favor a role for the system in establishing long-term memory that does not fit easily either a storage or a retrieval interpretation (Eichenbaum et al 1992; Halgren 1984; McNaughton & Nadel 1990; Milner 1989; Rolls 1990; Teyler & Discenna 1986; Squire 1992a). For example, the system has been proposed as the storage site for a summary sketch, a conjunction, or an index; and it has been proposed that one critical event is the induction of long-term potentiation (LTP) in the hippocampus at the time of learning.

Prospective studies with experimental animals have addressed long-standing questions concerning the precise shape of retrograde amnesia gradients (see Squire et al 1984). In one study, monkeys learned 100 object pairs prior to removal of the hippocampal formation (Zola-Morgan & Squire 1990). Twenty object pairs were learned at each of 5 preoperative periods (16, 12, 8, 4, and 2 weeks). After surgery, memory was tested by presenting all 100 objects in a mixed order for a single trial. Normal monkeys remembered objects learned recently better than objects learned 12–16 weeks earlier. Operated monkeys exhibited the opposite pattern, remembering objects learned remote from surgery significantly better than objects learned recently. Moreover, memory for remotely learned object pairs was entirely normal. Similar temporal gradients of retrograde amnesia have recently been demonstrated for rats acquiring a context-dependent fear response at different times prior to hippocampal damage (Kim & Fanselow 1992), for rats acquiring a food preference prior to hippocampal or diencephalic damage (Winocur 1990), and for mice acquiring maze habits at different times prior to damage of entorhinal cortex (Cho et al 1991).

These results show that the medial temporal/diencephalic memory system is not a repository of long-term memory. Indeed, in each of the animal experiments it was possible to identify a time after learning when damage to this system had no effect on memory for what had been learned. Thus, information that initially depends on the medial temporal/diencephalic system can eventually become independent of it. Initially, this system participates in the storage and retrieval of declarative memory. As time passes after learning, a process of consolidation and reorganization occurs such that a more permanent memory is established that is independent of the system. Permanent storage is likely to occur in neocortex where information is first processed and held in short-term memory.

A more specific version of this idea states that the medial temporal/diencephalic memory system initially binds together the distributed sites in neocortex that together represent the memory of a whole event (Zola-Morgan & Squire 1990). This low-capacity, fast system permits the acquisition and storage of representations involving arbitrarily different elements, and for a period it provides a basis for retrieving the full representation, even when a partial cue is presented. As time passes, the burden of long-term memory storage is assumed fully by neocortex. The time course of consolidation will vary depending on the species, the strength of initial learning, and the rate of forgetting. The changes can be expected to continue during a significant portion of the lifetime of a memory.

THE DEVELOPMENT OF DECLARATIVE MEMORY

When the notion of multiple memory systems was first developed, it provided a new way to think about the phenomenon of infantile amnesia—i.e. the relative unavailability of memories for events that occurred before the third year of life. The traditional view, as influenced by psychoanalytic theory (Freud 1962), has been that memories are acquired in infancy but are later repressed or become otherwise inaccessible (Neisser 1962; White & Pillemer 1979). Another possibility, based on notions about multiple memory systems, is that the memory system that supports declarative memory develops late and that declarative (conscious) memories are simply not formed early in life (Bachevalier & Mishkin 1984; Douglas 1975; Nadel & Zola-Morgan 1984; Overman 1990; Schacter & Moscovitch 1984).

This newer idea initially found support in the fact that the delayed non-matching to sample task, which in adult humans and nonhuman primates depends on the integrity of medial temporal/diencephalic memory structures, is performed poorly by infant monkeys (Bachevalier & Mishkin 1984) and by human infants (Diamond 1990; Overman 1990). By contrast, habit learning, which does not depend on this same brain system, is possible in monkeys as early as 3 months of age (Bachevalier 1990). Moreover, many of the tasks that can support learning and memory in infants younger than one year can be construed as implicit memory tasks, i.e. as tasks of habituation, conditioning, and skill learning (see Schacter & Moscovitch 1984).

However, recent data have cast doubts on this view (for discussion, see Diamond 1990). One focus of interest has been the visual paired-comparison task (Fantz 1964; Fagan 1970), in which two identical items are presented together followed later by presentation of a familiar item and a novel item. Infants as young as 5 months of age tend to look more at the new item than the old item, thus providing a spontaneous measure of their memory for the previously encountered item. What kind of memory is exhibited here? Does visual paired-comparison depend on implicit (nondeclarative) memory or does it reflect early-developing declarative memory?

There are two relevant findings. First, performance on the visual paired-comparison task is severely impaired in infant monkeys with large bilateral medial temporal lobe lesions (Bachevalier 1990). Second, performance on this task is also severely impaired in human amnesic patients (McKee & Squire 1993). Thus, performance on this task is dependent on the medial temporal/diencephalic structures that are essential for declarative memory. It therefore seems reasonable to suppose that successful performance on the visual paired-comparison task reflects an early capacity for declarative memory. If so, the medial temporal/diencephalic memory system must be functional early in life, and its absence or slow development cannot account for infantile amnesia. The view that declarative memory is available early in life is also consistent with recent demonstrations of long-term-recall-like memory abilities in human infants (Baillargeon & DeVos 1991; Bauer & Mandler 1989; Mandler 1990; Meltzoff 1985). For example, infants younger than one year will reproduce actions involving toys, even one day after viewing a single demonstration of the actions by the experimenter.

If some degree of declarative memory is available to infants, what accounts for infantile amnesia? Recent evidence from nonhuman primates suggests that inferotemporal cortex, a higher-order visual association area in neocortex, is functionally immature early in life and less mature than medial temporal lobe structures (Bachevalier 1990; Bachevalier et al 1986). Thus, what limits the formation and persistence of declarative memory may be, not the maturation of the medial temporal/diencephalic structures that are essential for declarative memory, but rather the gradual maturation of the neocortical areas that are served by these structures and that are believed to be the repositories of long-term memory. This perspective provides points of contact between a neural account of infantile amnesia and accounts founded in cognitive psychology that emphasize the gradual maturation of cognition, the emergence of strategies for organizing information, the development of language, and the growth of individual identity (Neisser 1962; White & Pillemer 1979; Nelson 1988).

CAN THE BRAIN SYSTEM SUPPORTING DECLARATIVE MEMORY BE SUBDIVIDED?

Do the anatomical components of the medial temporal/diencephalic memory system make similar or different contributions to memory? Although it is entirely reasonable, and even likely, that specialization exists within this large system, it has been difficult to find compelling evidence for this idea (for two points of view, see Parkin 1984 and Victor et al 1989). For many years there was confusion on this point. Patients with Korsakoff's syndrome, an example of diencephalic amnesia, differ behaviorally in a number of respects from other amnesic patients, including those with medial temporal lobe lesions. However, it is now clear that amnesic patients with Korsakoff's syndrome typically have frontal lobe pathology (Jacobson & Lishman 1987; Shimamura et al 1988). Their frontal lobe pathology produces certain symptoms that are not essential to memory impairment itself and that can also be found in patients with frontal lobe lesions who are not globally amnesic. For example, frontal lobe pathology produces difficulty in making temporal order judgments (Meudell et al 1985; Milner 1971; McAndrews & Milner 1991; Squire 1982), it impairs metamemory (Janowsky et al 1989a; Shimamura & Squire 1986), and it produces source amnesia (Janowsky et al 1989b; Schacter et al 1984). While these findings concerning the frontal lobes are important, they do not speak to possible differences in the contributions of diencephalic or medial temporal lobe structures to memory function.

Forgetting Rates

With respect to diencephalic and medial temporal lobe brain structures, one early suggestion was that both regions are essential for establishing long-term memory but that medial temporal lobe damage is associated with rapid forgetting (of whatever information enters long-term memory) and that diencephalic damage is associated with a normal rate of forgetting (Huppert & Piercy 1979; Squire 1981). However, the case for medial temporal lobe damage rested on data from a single patient (H.M.), and subsequent testing of the same patient has not confirmed the original impression (Freed et al 1987). In support of these later results, patients with Alzheimer's disease, who have severe memory impairment and prominent pathology in the medial temporal lobe, also exhibited a normal rate of forgetting within long-term memory (Kopelman 1985).

It has recently been possible to study forgetting rates in amnesic patients with confirmed medial temporal lobe lesions or diencephalic lesions (McKee & Squire 1992), using the same procedure used in the original study by Huppert & Piercy (1979). The two groups of patients saw 120 colored pictures, each for 8 sec, and normal subjects saw the same pictures for 1 sec each. This procedure resulted in all three groups' performing equivalently at a 10-min retention delay. The important finding was that performance was also equivalent at retention delays of 2 hr and 1 day. Thus, the two amnesic groups exhibited equivalent (and apparently normal) rates of forgetting. The available data favor the idea that the medial temporal lobe and diencephalic structures damaged in amnesia are part of a single memory system. While it is likely that the two regions make different contributions to the function of the system, convincing evidence for this idea has yet to be demonstrated.

Spatial Memory

The medial temporal/diencephalic memory system, and more commonly the hippocampus proper, has sometimes been considered particularly important for spatial memory (O'Keefe & Nadel 1978). This idea originated in electro-physiological data from rats showing that cells in the hippocampus respond selectively when the animal is in a particular place (Ranck 1973); and also in hippocampal lesion studies, which demonstrated striking deficits in rats performing spatial memory tasks. However, hippocampal cells respond to many properties of the stimulus environment besides spatial location (Berger & Thompson 1978; Eichenbaum et al 1986; Wible et al 1986), and hippocampal lesions impair memory on a variety of nonspatial tasks, including odor discrimination learning in rats (Eichenbaum et al 1988), configural learning in rats (Sutherland & Rudy 1989), object discrimination and delayed nonmatching to sample in monkeys (Zola-Morgan et al 1989), and numerous human memory tests that assess retention of recently learned facts and events (Mayes 1988; Squire 1987). These considerations show clearly that the function of the hippocampus is not exclusively spatial, but the question remains whether the hippocampus and related limbic/diencephalic structures are more important for spatial memory than for other kinds of memory.

One approach has been to assess the status of spatial memory in human amnesia. In one study (Shoqeirat & Mayes 1991) subjects were presented with 16 nameable shapes arranged in a 7×7 grid. The scores of amnesic patients and control subjects were matched on a recognition task for the shapes by increasing the number of presentations given to the patients and by decreasing the delay between study and test. Under these conditions, the amnesic patients performed worse than the control subjects both on tests of free recall for the shapes and on tests of incidental recall for their spatial locations. In a second study (Mayes et al 1991), subjects were shown words in one of the four corners of a computer screen and instructed to remember the words and their locations. Amnesic patients and control subjects were matched on a recognition task for the words by requiring the amnesic patients to retain a shorter list of words, by providing them longer exposure to each word, and by using a shorter retention delay between study and test. Under these conditions, the amnesic patients performed worse than the control subjects in recollecting the locations of the words they had seen.

A complicating feature of these two experiments is that spatial and nonspatial memory were confounded with recall and recognition memory. Also, whenever a match is forced between amnesic patients and control subjects based on just one data point and using just one measure of memory, it is possible that amnesic patients would perform poorly on many other measures. Further, some spatial tasks might be failed because they approximate tests of source memory—e.g. tests in which spatial location provides important context for what is to be remembered. Finally, a recent study of human amnesia found only proportionate impairments of spatial memory relative to recall and recognition memory, using variations of the same tasks just described (MacAndrew & Jones 1993). An additional complication is that many of the amnesic patients in these studies had frontal lobe pathology, which can especially affect recall performance and can cause source amnesia (Janowsky et al 1989; Janowsky et al 1989b; Jetter et al 1986).

In another study, object name recall, object name recognition, and object location memory were tested in patients with confirmed damage to the diencephalon or the hippocampal formation (Cave & Squire 1991). Amnesic patients and normal subjects were matched on both recall and recognition by testing amnesic patients after a 5-min delay and different groups of control subjects after delays from 5 min to 5 weeks. The main finding was that, when the recall and recognition performance of amnesic patients was matched to the recall and recognition performance of control subjects, spatial memory performance was equivalent in the two groups. Taken together, the available data in humans do not provide strong support for the idea that the hippocampus, or other components of the medial temporal/diencephalic memory system, are especially involved in spatial memory. A reasonable alternative is that spatial memory is simply a good example of a broader class of (declarative, relational) memory abilities that are dependent on the integrity of this system (also see Eichenbaum et al 1992; Squire & Cave 1991).

This issue was also explored in monkeys with lesions of the posterior medial temporal lobe that included the hippocampus, the parahippocampal gyrus, and the posterior entorhinal cortex (Parkinson et al 1988). The monkeys were severely impaired in forming associations between objects and places. In addition, they were more severely impaired on this object-place association task than on a recognition memory task for objects (delayed nonmatching to sample). A comparison group with lesions of the anterior medial temporal lobe, which included the amygdala and underlying perirhinal cortex, performed about as well on the recognition task as the monkeys with hippocampal formation lesions, but were only mildly impaired on the spatial task.

Although more work is needed, these results can be interpreted in the light of recent information concerning the anatomical projections from neocortex to the anterior and posterior portions of the medial temporal lobe. Parietal cortex, which processes spatial information, projects posteriorly to parahippocampal cortex but not anteriorly to perirhinal cortex. Inferotemporal cortex, which processes visual pattern information, projects more strongly to perirhinal cortex than to parahippocampal cortex (Suzuki et al 1991). The perirhinal and parahippocampal cortices provide nearly two thirds of the input to entorhinal cortex, which in turn originates most of the afferent projections to the hippocampus. Based on these considerations, spatial memory functions may be associated more with parahippocampal cortex than with perirhinal cortex. Accordingly, posterior medial temporal lobe lesions (i.e. lesions that include parahippocampal cortex) would be expected to disrupt spatial memory more than anterior lesions. By this view, although a specialization for spatial memory might exist in the parahippocampal cortex, and a specialization for visual memory in the perirhinal cortex, no such specialization should be found in the entorhinal cortex or in the hippocampus itself, because these structures receive convergent projections from both the perirhinal and parahippocampal cortices.

Recall and Recognition

Another important question about the function of the brain system that supports declarative memory is whether it is equivalently involved in the two fundamental processes of recall and recognition. By one view, recall and recognition are closely linked functions of declarative memory (Tulving 1983; Hayman & Tulving 1989). Alternatively, recall has been proposed to depend on declarative memory, while recognition depends partly on declarative memory and partly on increased perceptual fluency—i.e. priming (Gardiner 1988; Jacoby 1983; Mandler 1980). By this view, subjects can detect the facility with which they process a test item and can attribute this improved fluency to the fact that the item was recently presented.

Evidence relevant to this issue could come from the study of amnesia, because amnesia spares priming while severely impairing declarative memory.

Accordingly, if recognition performance is supported significantly by implicit (nondeclarative) memory, amnesic patients should perform disproportionately better on recognition tests than on recall tests, in comparison to normal subjects. Two early studies that examined this issue (Hirst et al 1986, 1988) reported that amnesic patients exhibited disproportionate sparing of recognition memory. In these studies, recall and recognition performance were compared at a single performance level.

In another study, amnesic patients and control subjects were compared across a range of retention intervals (15 sec to 8 weeks), and performance was assessed independently by recall, recognition, and confidence ratings for the recognition choices (Haist et al 1992). The results were that recall and recognition were proportionately impaired in the patients, and their confidence ratings were commensurate with the level of impaired performance.

It is not entirely clear what accounts for the different findings by Hirst and his colleagues concerning the relative status of recall and recognition in amnesia. When an attempt was made to reproduce the experimental conditions from the second of these studies (Hirst et al 1988), the findings were not replicated (Haist et al 1992). The explanation may lie in differences in the locus of pathology in the patient populations and differences in the pattern of cognitive deficits present in addition to memory impairment. For example, some of the patients in the studies by Hirst et al (1988) became amnesic from a condition that produces signs of frontal lobe dysfunction, and frontal lobe pathology can affect recall performance more than recognition performance (Janowsky et al 1989; Jetter et al 1986).

The available findings provide little support for the view that recognition memory differs from recall in depending importantly on processes like priming that are intact in amnesia. Some behavioral findings with normal subjects have been taken as evidence that recognition memory regularly and typically depends on priming (i.e. increased fluency). However, the results appear to support this idea only indirectly, and recognition is usually not considered in relation to recall [Graf & Mandler 1984; Jacoby & Dallas 1981; Mandler 1980; Gardiner 1988; Gardiner & Java 1990; Johnston et al 1985; also, see Jacoby 1991 for a different method of assessing in normal subjects the separate contributions of intentional and automatic processes (recollection and familiarity) to recognition performance]. While one cannot rule out a possible contribution of priming-like phenomena to recognition performance under some conditions, another possibility is that implicit (nondeclarative) memory does not ordinarily contribute to performance on the typical recognition memory task. That is, when a recently encountered percept is encountered again, perceptual fluency will be operating and detection will be improved, but these effects need not contribute to overt judgments concerning whether the percept is familiar, in the sense of having been presented previously. Johnston et al (1991) have also concluded that the contribution of perceptual fluency to recognition memory may occur under limited conditions, perhaps when explicit (declarative) memory is weak. More work is needed to understand the dissociations that have been demonstrated in normal recognition memory performance, the implications of these dissociations for conscious and nonconscious forms of memory, and the relationship between recognition performance and free recall.

In summary, the idea developed here is that limbic/diencephalic brain structures are equivalently involved in recall and recognition. Recall and recognition are no doubt different in important ways, and the differential contribution of other brain structures, including the frontal lobe, to recall and recognition will be important in understanding the difference. For example, recognition memory would be expected to depend on processes that can be dissociated from other components of memory processing. Thus, recognition memory should be dissociable from the component of recall that depends on the contribution of the frontal lobe. The experiments reviewed here suggest simply that implicit (nondeclarative) memory probably does not typically support recognition memory performance, at least no more than it also contributes to free recall.

NONDECLARATIVE MEMORY

Whereas declarative memory is a brain-systems construct, a form of memory that is reflected in the operation of an anatomically real neural system and its interaction with neocortex, nondeclarative (or implicit) memory includes several forms of learning and memory abilities and depends on multiple brain systems. Although it is too early to develop a classification scheme for all the nondeclarative forms of memory, one can tentatively distinguish among skills and habits, some forms of conditioning, and the phenomena of priming. Information is emerging about the neural basis of these major types, and this information can be expected to be relevant to the problem of classification.

Skills and Habits

Skills are procedures (motor, perceptual, and cognitive) for operating in the world; habits are dispositions and tendencies that are specific to a set of stimuli and that guide behavior. Under some circumstances, skills and habits can be acquired in the absence of awareness of what has been learned and independently of long-term declarative memory for the specific episodes in which learning occurred. However, many skill-like tasks are also amenable to declarative learning strategies. For example, if a task is sufficiently simple and the information being acquired becomes accessible to awareness, then performance can be enhanced by engaging declarative memory strategies. Examples are available of human learning tasks that result in both declarative and nondeclarative knowledge (Willingham et al 1989), and of tasks that are learned nondeclaratively by monkeys but declaratively by humans (pattern discrimination and the 24-hr concurrent discrimination task; Zola-Morgan & Squire

1984; Malamut et al 1984; Squire et al 1988). Accordingly, identifying the varieties of nondeclarative memory is not straightforward. The most compelling examples have come from dissociations in normal human subjects, findings of fully intact performance in otherwise severely amnesic patients, and findings of fully normal performance in experimental animals with lesions of the hippocampus or related structures.

The earliest evidence that skill learning can proceed independently of long-term declarative memory came from the finding that the severely amnesic patient H.M. was capable of day-to-day improvement on a mirror-drawing task, despite being unable to remember that he had practiced the task (Milner 1962). Later, it was demonstrated that perceptuomotor learning can occur at an entirely normal rate in amnesia (Brooks & Baddeley 1976). During the past decade, it has become clear that motor-skill learning is a small subset of a much broader category of skill-based abilities that also include perceptual and cognitive skills. The perceptual skills that have now been found to be fully intact in human amnesia include mirror reading (Cohen & Squire 1980), speeded reading of normal text (Musen et al 1990), speeded reading of repeated nonwords (Musen & Squire 1991), the ability to resolve random-dot stereograms (Benzing & Squire 1989), and adaptation-level effects based on sampling sets of weights (Benzing & Squire 1989).

One particularly interesting group of experiments has demonstrated implicit learning of a sequence of regularly repeating spatial locations (Cleeremans & McClelland 1991; Lewicki et al 1987; Stadler 1989; Nissen & Bullemer 1987) or words (Hartman et al 1989). The evidence that the learning was implicit is that subjects improved their performance (a) in the absence of awareness that a sequence had been presented; or (b) in the absence of the ability to generate the sequence at the completion of testing. In this case, the sequence was presented once again, and subjects attempted to predict each successive element in the sequence before it appeared. In one study (Nissen & Bullemer 1987) it was also shown that amnesic patients could acquire the sequence at a normal rate. If the sequence tasks are complex enough, they can be attention demanding in the sense that learning is impeded by requiring subjects to perform a competing task (Nissen & Bullemer 1987). Alternatively, simpler versions of such tasks may be acquired automatically without requiring attention (Cohen et al 1990).

One reason for identifying these tasks as skill-based is that patients with Huntington's disease, who have pathological, degenerative changes in the neostriatum, have been found to be deficient in many of these tasks, including mirror reading (Martone et al 1984), adaptation-level effects (Heindel et al 1991), and sequence learning (Knopman & Nissen 1991). In two of the studies just cited, the patients with Huntington's disease performed better than other memory-impaired patients on conventional tasks of recognition memory.

Some tasks that are neither perceptual nor motor can also be acquired implicitly. For example, cognitive tasks have been studied in which subjects attempt to achieve and then maintain a specific target value across trials. On each trial, the response needed to achieve the target value is determined algorithmically by current task conditions. When the relationship is sufficiently obscure, and not amenable to easy discovery or memorization, subjects improve their performance despite having little or no understanding of what they have done (Berry & Broadbent 1984). For example, one task asked subjects to achieve a target level of production in a fictitious sugar factory by determining how many workers should be hired on each trial. In this case, subjects learned the mapping function that related the level of sugar production on the previous trial to the target value. Amnesic patients were entirely intact at the early stages of this task, although normal subjects eventually acquired declarative knowledge about the task structure and outperformed the patients (Squire & Frambach 1990). The important finding is that early-stage acquisition of skilled behavior can sometimes proceed independently of verbal mediation and declarative knowledge.

There are other ways in which subjects can apparently learn regularities in their environment implicitly and then reveal what they have learned in their judgments or choices. In one notable study (Lewicki 1986a), normal subjects saw a few photographs of women, some with short hair and some with long hair. Hair length was systematically associated with narratives that described the women as either kind or capable. (These terms did not appear in the narratives.) A few minutes later, subjects decided (yes or no) whether new photographs depicted someone who was \"kind" or, in other cases, \"capable." Reaction times for yes and no decisions were slower when subjects judged photographs of women whose hair length had previously been associated with the corresponding attribute than when they judged photographs that were discordant with the attribute. It was suggested that processing time is increased whenever subjects have information available about the relevant covariation. In addition to these findings for reaction time, subjects more often judged photographs of women as \"kind" or \"capable" when hair length had been associated with the corresponding narrative than when it had been associated with the other narrative. However, these effects were rather small and were not consistently observed across experiments. Nevertheless, the finding that subjects indicated no awareness that hair length was linked to any attributes raises the possibility that whatever was learned about the covariance between physical features and attributes was learned independently of declarative knowledge. However, in these and similar experiments (Lewicki 1986b), it is difficult to rule out a threshold interpretation based on weak declarative memories that are more or less accessible depending on how memory is tested. For example, in the hair-length experiment, the results could mean simply that as declarative memory weakens, the ability to make judgments based on the learned relationships between stimuli will usually remain in evidence after the ability to report the relationships has reached chance levels.

Artificial grammar learning is an extensively studied problem domain in which subjects acquire knowledge through multiple presentations of unique material. Subjects see letter strings (e.g. BFZBZ) in which the letter order is determined by a finite-state rule system. After the letter strings are presented, subjects are told for the first time that the letter strings were in fact all determined by a complex set of rules. Subjects then attempt to classify new items as being either consistent (grammatical) or inconsistent (nongrammatical) with these rules. Reber (1967, 1989), who introduced this paradigm, suggested that the learning is implicit and independent of conscious access to the training items. For example, subjects can usually provide little information about the basis for their judgments, and telling subjects beforehand about the existence of the rules does not improve classification performance (Reber 1976; Dienes et al 1991). Another point of view has been that artificial grammar learning is based on conscious application of declarative knowledge that is weak and imperfect (Dulany et al 1984; Perruchet & Pacteau 1990). In support of this idea, it has been shown that the ability of subjects to recognize grammatically valid fragments of letter strings (bigrams and trigrams) was sufficient to account for their classification performance (Perruchet & Pacteau 1990).

This issue was clarified by the finding that amnesic patients, who were much poorer than normal subjects at recognizing which letter strings had been presented, were nevertheless able to classify letter strings (grammatical vs nongrammatical) as well as normal subjects (Knowlton et al 1992). This finding supports the view that artificial grammar learning is implicit, and it appears to rule out the idea that the learning is based on consciously accessible rules, declarative memory for permissible letter groups, or direct and conscious comparisons with letter strings that are stored in declarative memory.

Although these possibilities can probably be excluded, several other possibilities remain for how implicit learning of artificial grammars could occur: the implicit acquisition of abstract rules (Reber 1989; Mathews et al 1989), analogic comparisons to individual test items based on acquired (but implicit) associations between the test items and the grammatical category (Brooks & Vokey 1991; Vokey & Brooks 1992), or the acquisition of implicit associations between letter groups (chunks) and the grammatical category (Servan-Schreiber & Anderson 1990).

The ability to classify is more commonly based on natural categories, like chairs and birds, where class membership is defined by experience with exemplars rather than by fixed rules (Rosch 1973). In this case, too, a number of possible mechanisms have been proposed by which category-level knowledge is achieved (for reviews, see Estes 1988, 1991; Smith & Medin 1981). One possibility is that category-level knowledge is acquired in the form of knowledge about prototypes (a representative instance) or knowledge of the statistical characteristics of groups of exemplars, and that this knowledge is represented distinctly from knowledge about the exemplars themselves (Fried

& Holyoak 1984; Posner & Keele 1968; Reed 1972). Another possibility is that category-level knowledge has no special status but is derivative from item memory (Brooks 1978; Hintzman 1986; Medin & Schaffer 1978; Nosofsky 1984). By this view, knowledge about prototypes emerges as a property of the way in which items are stored. Specifically, a test item will be recognized as a good representative of a category because it shares many features with items in storage. Exemplar-based models of category learning can account for important aspects of classification performance such as the ability of subjects to identify the prototype more accurately than the items that were actually presented, even when subjects did not see the prototype itself and when the prototype itself is not actually represented.

A third possibility is illustrated by connectionist models in which the elements of the model are neither features nor items but homogeneous units that can vary in the strengths of their connections with each other (Estes 1991; Gluck & Bower 1988; McClelland & Rumelhart 1985; see the section below on Conditioning). In such models, knowledge about prototypes emerges naturally during the learning process as a result of the fact that multiple instances are stored in a distributed fashion within the network. Models that combine elements of these approaches have also been proposed [e.g. exemplar-based connectionist models (Kruschke 1992; Nosofsky et al 1992)].

Preliminary findings with amnesic patients suggest that prototype learning proceeds in parallel with and independently of declarative memory for specific instances (Knowlton & Squire 1992). If so, it cannot be the case that prototype knowledge is derived from or is in any way dependent on long-term declarative memory for individual instances. Whereas limbic/diencephalic brain structures support memory for individual instances, a different brain system may support the development of category-level knowledge.

One possibility is that learning based either on rules (e.g. artificial grammar learning) or natural categories (e.g. prototype learning) is best classified as habit learning. In both cases, category learning can be viewed as the acquisition of implicit associations between items or features and a category. A growing body of evidence from studies with experimental animals, reviewed below, suggests that the neural substrates of habit learning are different from those of declarative memory.

Neural Evidence for Distinguishing Skills and Habits from Declarative Memory

Recent work suggests that the brain structures important for acquiring skills and habits involve the corticostriatal system—i.e. projections from the neocortex to the caudate and putamen. Patients with Parkinson's disease, who have striatal dysfunction as the result of primary pathology in the substantia nigra pars compacta, were impaired on a cognitive skill task but intact at the declarative memory tasks of recall and recognition (Saint-Cyr et al 1988). Recent results for the delayed nonmatching to sample task and the 24-hr concurrent discrimination task, two memory tasks developed for the monkey, have been especially illuminating. Delayed nonmatching to sample is a test of recognition memory, in which the monkey attempts to select in a two-choice test the object that was *not* presented recently. New pairs of objects are used for each trial. Monkeys initially learn to perform the task across a short delay interval and are then tested at increasing delays that can be 10 min or even longer. In the 24-hr concurrent discrimination task, monkeys are presented with 20 pairs of objects for one trial each day. One of the objects in each pair is always correct. Learning in this task occurs gradually in about 10 days.

In humans, both these tasks are learned declaratively—i.e. subjects memorize the material to be learned—and performance is impaired in amnesic patients (Squire et al 1988). In monkeys, the findings are quite different. Both tasks are impaired by damage to inferotemporal cortex (area TE), a higher-order visual area in neocortex that is essential for processing information about visually presented objects (Mishkin 1982; Phillips et al 1988). However, the two tasks can be differentiated in an important way. Performance on delayed nonmatching to sample is impaired by large medial temporal lobe lesions (Mishkin 1978; Squire & Zola-Morgan 1991), but monkeys with these same lesions learn the 24-hr concurrent discrimination task about as well as normal animals (Malamut et al 1984). In contrast, the 24-hr concurrent task is impaired by damage to the tail of the caudate nucleus, which is a target of cortical projections from area TE, but performance on delayed nonmatching to sample is not affected (Wang et al 1990).

Thus, an interaction between visual area TE and limbic/diencephalic areas is critical for visual recognition memory, but an interaction between TE and the neostriatum is critical for the 24-hr concurrent task. The results are similar for two-choice, visual pattern-discrimination learning, which is unaffected by large medial temporal lobe lesions (Zola-Morgan & Squire 1984) but is impaired by lesions of the caudate nucleus (Divak et al 1967). These differential effects have been interpreted in terms of two qualitatively different memory systems, a system that supports cognitive (or declarative) memory and a second system, involving the caudate and putamen, that supports noncognitive habit memory (Mishkin et al 1984; Phillips et al 1988).

A similar distinction was drawn on the basis of work with rats (Packard et al 1989). A win-shift task, which required animals to remember which arms of a radial maze had been recently visited, was impaired by fornix lesions but not by caudate lesions. Conversely, a win-stay task that required animals to visit arms that were marked by a light was impaired by caudate lesions but not by fornix lesions.

It is tempting to relate these habit-like tasks to habit learning in humans. A complication is that win-stay tasks and the 24-hr concurrent discrimination task are readily learned by humans using their well-developed declarative memory strategies, particularly when the rules governing reward contingencies are simple ones (Squire et al 1988). It is significant that patients with

Huntington's disease are impaired on a number of skill-like tasks involving motor responses, but neuropsychological studies are needed with habit-like tasks that have no motor component. The ability to relate findings from experimental animals and humans should improve as it becomes possible to define tasks in terms of what strategies are being used to learn them rather than in terms of the logical structure of the tasks (see the section, above, on Long-term Memory: Declarative Memory).

Conditioning

Learning of simple conditioned responses of the skeletal musculature or conditioned autonomic responses occurs normally in experimental animals despite complete removal of the hippocampus (Solomon & Moore 1975; Caul et al 1969). Moreover, amnesic patients exhibit progressive learning and 24-hr retention of a conditioned eyeblink response, despite inability to describe the apparatus or what it had been used for (Weiskrantz & Warrington 1979; Daum et al 1989). Thus, although conditioning in humans has been reported to require awareness of the CS-US contingency (Marinkovic et al 1989), the successful conditioning that has been observed in amnesic patients and in decerebrate animals (Norman et al 1977) suggests that awareness is not always necessary for conditioning to occur. However, until control subjects are tested to determine whether the learning in amnesic patients is entirely normal, the possibility remains that an essential part of conditioned performance in humans is due to declarative knowledge about the structure of the task. If so, the limbic/diencephalic structures important for declarative memory could play some role. In any case, other brain structures and connections are known to be critically important (see Thompson 1988 and Lavond et al, in this volume, for eyeblink conditioning; LeDoux 1987 for fear conditioning; Dunn & Everitt 1988 for taste aversion learning).

Limbic/diencephalic structures are not essential when experimental animals acquire a simple conditioned response—i.e. when a single CS and US are used in a standard delay paradigm, CS onset occurs about 250 msec prior to US onset, and CS and US offset occurs together. However, these structures are important for more complex conditioning procedures such as reversal of conditioned discriminations (Berger & Orr 1983), occasion setting (Ross et al 1984), trace conditioning (Moyer et al 1990), or when configural (Sutherland & Rudy 1989) or contextual cues (Winocur et al 1987) are used. An examination of these and other paradigms in human amnesic patients should help to identify fundamental aspects of declarative memory.

Some recent work on classification learning in human subjects has been inspired by theories of animal conditioning. In one paradigm, subjects performed a medical diagnosis task in which each of four different symptoms was probabilistically associated across trials with each of two fictitious diseases (Gluck & Bower 1988; Shanks 1990). On each trial, subjects were presented with a "patient" who exhibited one, two, three, or four symptoms in any combination and tried to guess which disease the "patient" had. In this case, performance could be modeled by a connectionist network that learned according to the Rescorla-Wagner rule, as derived from studies of associative learning in animals (Rescorla & Wagner 1972). Thus, subjects could be viewed as learning to associate each symptom with one of the diseases in much the same way that a CS gradually becomes associated with a US (for other connectionist models of classification learning, see Kruschke 1992; Nosofsky et al 1992).

Other experiments with human subjects using similar tasks have demonstrated the phenomena of blocking, overshadowing, and conditioned inhibition (Chapman & Robbins 1990; Gluck & Bower 1988; Shanks 1991). These phenomena can be understood as resulting from competition among cues for associative strength. According to theories derived from animal conditioning, very predictive cues will successfully compete for the available associative strength at the expense of less predictive cues. Because the framework developed in animal conditioning accounts for these phenomena, and because simple forms of animal conditioning are known to occur independently of limbic/diencephalic brain structures, it is reasonable to expect that human learning of associations between features and categories will also occur independently of these brain structures (so long as the associative rules cannot easily be discovered and memorized).

Although some examples of human classification learning can be illuminated by theories of classical conditioning, the similarities between classification learning and classical conditioning should not be pushed too far. In terms of neural organization, the cerebellum is essential for classical conditioning of skeletal musculature (Thompson 1988; Lavond et al, in this volume), perhaps because precise timing of responses is needed (Ivry & Baldo 1992). For conditioned emotional responses, the amygdala is important. In contrast, when subjects must learn the predictive value of two or more cues, and the predictive relationship is not easily discovered, such learning is probably better viewed as another example of habit learning, just as has been suggested for artificial grammar learning and prototype learning. If so, the neostriatum may be an important substrate for classification learning.

Priming

Priming refers to an improved facility for detecting or identifying perceptual stimuli based on recent experience with them. Priming is currently the most intensively studied example of nondeclarative memory, and a number of reviews are available that consider this topic in some detail (Richardson-Klavehn & Bjork 1988; Shimamura 1986; Schacter 1990; Schacter et al 1993; Tulving & Schacter 1990). The discussion here identifies the key features of priming and considers the phenomenon in the context of brain systems. In a typical experiment, subjects see lists of words, pictures of objects, or nonverbal materials such as novel objects or line drawings. Subsequently, subjects are tested with both old and new items and asked to name words or objects, to produce items from fragments, or to make rapid decisions about new and old items. The finding is that performance is better for old than for new items.

Two lines of evidence show that priming is dissociable from and independent of declarative memory. First, manipulations in normal subjects that markedly affect the strength of declarative memory, such as variations in the extent of elaborative processing carried out at the time of encoding, have little or no effect on priming (for review, see Schacter et al 1993). Second, several examples of priming have been shown to be fully intact in amnesic patients, including word priming as measured by word-stem completion, perceptual identification, and lexical decision (Cermak et al 1985; Graf et al 1984; Smith & Oscar-Berman 1990), visual object priming (Cave & Squire 1992b), and priming of novel objects or line patterns (Gabrieli et al 1990; Musen & Squire 1992; Schacter et al 1991). Amnesic patients provide a favorable way to establish the distinction between priming and declarative memory, because amnesic patients are impaired on conventional recall and recognition tests. If declarative memory significantly supports priming, then amnesic patients should be impaired on tests that measure priming. Finally, it has also been pointed out that measures of priming and measures of declarative memory often exhibit statistical independence (Tulving & Schacter 1990), but this criterion for making inferences about the independence of memory systems has been questioned by a number of authors (Hintzman & Hartry 1990; Ostergaard 1992; Shimamura 1985).

An early view, based especially on work with amnesic patients, was that priming involves the activation of pre-existing memory representations (Diamond & Rozin 1984; Cermak et al 1985, 1991). However, a number of studies with amnesic patients have now demonstrated robust and intact priming of nonwords as well as nonverbal material such as novel objects and line drawings that have no pre-existing representations (Haist et al 1991; Musen & Squire 1992; Schacter et al 1991; Squire & McKee 1992; for other recent studies involving normal subjects, see Bentin & Moscovitch 1988; Kersteen-Tucker 1991; Musen & Treisman 1990; Schacter et al 1991). An exception appears to be the priming of nonwords on lexical-decision tasks, which is weak even in normal subjects (Bentin & Moscovitch 1988; Verfaillie et al 1991; for a report that nonword lexical-decision priming occurs in normal subjects but not in amnesic patients, see Smith & Oscar-Berman 1990).

One of the striking features of priming is that it can sometimes be extraordinarily long-lasting. Word-stem completion priming, which was among the first well-studied examples of priming, disappears within 2 hr, at least when multiple completions are available for each word stem (Squire et al 1987). In contrast, in normal subjects priming of object naming is still present 6 weeks after a single exposure to a picture (Mitchell & Brown 1988); and word-fragment completion priming, when only one solution is available for each fragment, has been demonstrated in normal subjects after a delay of 16 months (Sloman et al 1988). The question of how long priming persists is complicated by the possibility that tests for priming can be contaminated by declarative memory strategies. A contribution from declarative memory has been ruled out in one case by the finding of fully intact object-naming priming in amnesic patients, even 7 days after a single exposure to pictures (Cave & Squire 1992b). Thus, stimuli can result in long-lasting effects on performance that are supported independently of the limbic/diencephalic structures important for declarative memory.

Presentation of stimuli can also influence preferences and judgments about the stimuli, even when the stimuli are exposed so briefly that they cannot later be recognized (Bonnano & Stillings 1986; Kunst-Wilson & Zajonc 1980; Mandler et al 1987). A related phenomenon is that subjects are more likely to judge a proper name as famous if the name has been encountered previously. Dividing attention during the initial presentation of famous and nonfamous names markedly reduced recognition memory scores but had no effect on the fame-judgment effect (Jacoby et al 1989). Moreover, amnesic patients exhibited the fame-judgment effect at full strength (Squire & McKee 1992). These results suggest that priming not only improves the ability to identify stimuli but can also alter judgments about the stimuli.

The kinds of priming discussed so far are perceptual in the sense that the effects are pre-semantic and highly determined by the specific perceptual features of the originally presented item. For example, when pictures of objects are presented and subjects are asked to name them as quickly as possible, the priming effect is greatly attenuated by changing the orientation of the object, adding shading to the object, or changing from one example of an object to another example that has the same name (Bartram 1974; Biederman & Cooper 1991a; Cave & Squire 1992b). Also, in word-priming tasks, priming can be attenuated by changes in sensory modality from study to test and by changes in the voice of the speaker (Graf et al 1985; Jacoby & Dallas 1981; Schacter & Church 1992). Finally, priming effects are sometimes reduced by changes in type case or other surface features of words, although such effects are not always obtained (see Schacter et al 1993).

Although priming effects are highly specific, the representation that supports priming does not retain all the perceptual information in the stimulus. For example, changes in size or left-right mirror reflection of objects did not affect priming, despite the fact that these same changes significantly affected performance on tests of declarative memory (Biederman & Cooper 1991b, 1992; Cooper et al 1992). Because declarative memory was sensitive to these stimulus features, it is difficult to explain priming as depending on the same process or system that supports declarative memory.

Priming effects can also occur on tests that require semantic or conceptual processing, but these effects can be dissociated from and are likely quite different from perceptual priming (Srinivas & Roediger 1990; Tulving & Schacter 1990). For example, conceptually driven priming depends on the extent of elaborative encoding at the time of study (Hamman 1990). Nevertheless, this kind of priming is also independent of declarative memory, as demonstrated by the fact that amnesic patients are fully intact at tests of free-association priming (Shimamura & Squire 1984) and priming of category exemplars (Gardner et al 1973; Graf et al 1985; Schacter 1985).

There has also been interest in whether associative priming effects can occur for previously unrelated pairs of items (Graf & Schacter 1985; Moscovitch et al 1986). Recent work suggests that the most commonly studied paradigm (word-stem completion priming using novel associates as cues) does not yield associative priming in severely amnesic patients (Cermak et al 1988; Mayes & Gooding 1989; Schacter & Graf 1986; Shimamura & Squire 1989). Although the phenomenon as a whole can be dissociated from declarative memory in normal subjects (see Schacter et al 1993), the initial formation of novel associations probably places a critical demand on declarative memory (Shimamura & Squire 1989). In addition, the rapid (one-trial) formation of implicit associations between unrelated word pairs (using a paradigm based on reading speed; Moscovitch et al 1986) has proven difficult to demonstrate within implicit memory (Musen & Squire 1993).

Some information has recently become available about the neural basis of perceptual priming. In divided visual-field studies with normal subjects, word-stem completion priming was greater when word stems were presented to the right hemisphere than to the left (Marsolek et al 1992). This effect was obtained if and only if the study and test items were in the same sensory modality and in the same type case. Thus, the right cerebral hemisphere appears to be more effective than the left at supporting form-specific components of perceptual priming. The left hemisphere may support more abstract components of perceptual priming—e.g. the priming that survives type-case changes and modality changes. These results suggest that the two hemispheres contribute to priming in different ways, and that the results of priming studies can be expected to differ depending on which hemisphere is dominant in performing the task.

A recent study using positron emission tomography (PET) has provided direct evidence for the involvement of right posterior cortex in word priming (Squire et al 1992). Study and test items were presented visually and always in uppercase letters. During word-stem completion priming there was a significant reduction of cerebral blood flow in right extrastriate cortex, in the region of the lingual gyrus, in comparison to a baseline condition in which subjects also completed word stems but none of the possible word completions had been presented for study. This finding suggests a simplifying hypothesis for perceptual priming: After a word has been presented for study, less neural activity is subsequently required to process the same stimulus. The right posterior cortical locus identified by PET in this study is precisely the same region that in earlier studies was activated by the visual features of words (Petersen et al 1990). Words, nonwords, letter strings, and letter-like shapes were all effective at activating this locus.

The PET findings count against earlier proposals that a left-hemisphere word-form area is the locus of word priming (Schacter 1990; Tulving & Schacter 1990). More likely, left or right posterior cerebral cortex is important depending on whether priming is based on more abtract or more form-specific mechanisms. Indeed, we suggest that perceptual priming may occur in any of the more than 30 cortical areas known to be involved in visual information processing (Felleman & Van Essen 1991). Which areas are involved in any particular case would depend on the extent of the match between study and test materials and task demands. Indeed, this diversity of cortical areas potentially relevant to priming may help to explain why so many dissociations have been found among different kinds of verbal priming tests (Keane et al 1991; Srinivas & Roediger 1990; Witherspoon & Moscovitch 1989).

Priming is presumably adaptive because animals evolved in a world where stimuli that are encountered once are likely to be encountered again. Perceptual priming improves the speed and fluency by which organisms interact with familiar stimuli. For example, in the case of visual priming, the posterior visual cortex becomes more efficient at processing precisely those stimuli that have been processed recently. This plasticity occurs well before information reaches the limbic/diencephalic structures important for declarative memory.

PERSPECTIVE

This review has considered several kinds of memory as well as the distinct brain systems that support them. It has sometimes been proposed that distinctions between kinds of memory are best understood as reflecting the different processes that can be used to access a common memory trace (Blaxton 1989; Jacoby 1988; Masson 1989; Roediger 1990). When discussion of this issue is limited to priming, the matter can seem difficult to settle (see Schacter 1990). For example, the same single words can be remembered intentionally, or they can be produced in a priming paradigm. However, when discussion of memory is broadened to include the learning of skills and habits, and conditioning phenomena, the data favor a systems perspective over a processing perspective (for discussion of points of contact between these two views, see Roediger 1990; Schacter 1992; Tulving & Schacter 1990). Indeed, it cannot even be assumed that long-term storage of declarative and nondeclarative memories occurs in the same brain region. Declarative memories require the reciprocal anatomical connections that enable the neocortex to interact with the hippocampus and related structures, and the neocortex is thought to be the final repository of declarative memory. Skills and habits depend on corticostriatal projections, and these projections are not reciprocated by return projections to neocortex from the neostriatum. Accordingly, one possibility is that the storage of information underlying skills and habits occurs at the synapses between cortical neurons and neurons in the neostriatum.

The findings from PET also strongly endorse a brain-systems orientation. Word-stem completion priming was supported significantly by right extrastriate visual cortex. Intentional recall of words using word stems as cues engaged the right hippocampal region significantly more than the priming condition did. (The priming condition also engaged the hippocampal region more than the above-mentioned baseline condition did. Because subjects became aware of the link between word stems and study words during the priming task, some explicit visual recognition probably occurred as the word stems were presented, even though the performance measure in the priming task does not itself depend on declarative memory.)

Recent studies of event-related potentials (ERPs) also suggest that different brain regions are involved in word recall and recognition on the one hand, and word priming, on the other (Paller 1990; Paller & Kutas 1992). For example, the ERP associated with intentional recognition had a different scalp distribution and a different latency from the ERP associated with perceptual identification priming (Paller & Kutas 1992).

It has been noted previously that the finding of task dissociations in normal subjects is an insufficient basis on which to postulate two or more memory systems (Roediger 1990; Schacter 1992). Indeed, as several authors have noted (Graf et al 1984; Jacoby 1991; Roediger 1990; Schacter 1990; Squire 1992b), the proper emphasis is on the processes and strategies that subjects use, not the tasks used to measure memory. Moreover, to support hypotheses about multiple memory systems, evidence is needed that is independent of dissociation experiments. This kind of evidence has come from findings in experimental animals and neurological patients where the contributions to performance of anatomically defined brain systems can be evaluated directly. For example, a consideration of this evidence has led us in this review to suggest that superficially different tasks including artificial grammar learning and classification learning in human subjects, the 24-hr concurrent discrimination task in monkeys, and win-stay, lose-shift maze tasks in rodents all depend on similar underlying computations and might usefully be categorized together under the generic heading of habit learning.

One difficulty with the processing view is that it has been stated rather abstractly, so that it is sometimes difficult to appreciate what would count for or against it. A difficulty with the systems view is that the definition of the term \"system" is uncertain, and it is not always clear from studies of normal subjects when behavioral findings justify postulating a separate memory system. The concept of brain systems, while not entirely free of problems itself, provides a more concrete and in the end a more satisfying basis for thinking about memory systems. This is because a long tradition of anatomical and physiological work on the structure and organization of the brain has concerned itself with the identification and study of separable neural systems, sometimes independently of or in advance of any understanding of their functional significance.

This kind of information provides powerful convergent evidence that becomes extremely compelling when a function identified and characterized from psychological data appears to map onto a neural system that has been defined previously by anatomical and physiological criteria. Indeed, this is approximately what has happened in the case of limbic/diencephalic structures (for declarative memory), the neostriatum (for skills and habits), and the cerebellum (for some forms of conditioning). In any case, it should be clear that the issue is not a philosophical or semantic one about whether a processing or systems view provides the best research approach. The issue is about how memory is actually organized and how the brain accomplishes learning and memory.

A fundamental issue that so far has yielded little biological information concerns the nature and locus of long-term declarative representations. However, one can find a few clues and identify some guiding principles. The brain is highly specialized and differentiated, and it is organized such that different regions of neocortex carry out parallel computations on many different dimensions of external stimuli. Memory for an event, even memory for a single object, is stored in component parts and in a distributed fashion across geographically separate parts of the brain (Mishkin 1982; Squire 1987). Although direct evidence is not available, permanent information storage is thought to occur in the same processing areas that are engaged during learning. By this view, long-term memory is stored as outcomes of processing operations and in the same cortical regions that are involved in the perception and analysis of the events and items to be remembered.

Available information about the organization and structure of knowledge systems suggests a surprising degree of specialization in how information is stored. Cortical lesions in humans can produce remarkably selective losses of category-specific knowledge—e.g. loss of the ability to comprehend the names of small \"indoor" objects with relative preservation of the names of large \"outdoor" objects; or loss of knowledge about inanimate, man-made objects with relative preservation of knowledge about foods and living things (Damasio 1990; Farah et al 1991; Hart et al 1985; Warrington & Shallice 1984; Yamadori & Albert 1973). It has been proposed that these specializations can be understood in terms of the nature of the interaction between the perceiver and objects in the world during the time that objects are learned about (Damasio 1990; Farah & McClelland 1991; Warrington & McCarthy 1987). By this view, the sensory modality that is relevant to learning about an item and the nature of the relevant information (physical or functional) will influence the locus of information storage. For example, information based especially on physical features such as shape and color (e.g. gems, animals) will be stored in different loci from information based more on manual interaction and an understanding of function (e.g. tools and furniture).

What is needed is a way to access neurons within the networks that actually represent long-term declarative knowledge, so that the locus and organization of representations can be studied directly. There are abundant examples, from single-cell recordings of neurons in the temporal lobe of awake monkeys, where neurons change their activity rather quickly in response to behaviorally relevant stimuli (Fuster & Jervey 1981; Miller et al 1991; Riches et al 1991). However, it is difficult to know in these cases what kind(s) of memory the neurons might be involved in. Particularly in experiments that require retention of newly acquired information across delays of less than a minute, neurons that respond either during the delay or when test stimuli are presented at the end of the delay could be related to short-term memory or priming. The question is how would one determine whether or not a neuron being recorded from were part of a network representing information in long-term declarative memory?

One promising approach is suggested by a recent study of paired-associate learning in the awake monkey (Sakai & Miyashita 1991). During extended training, monkeys learned 12 pairs of computer-generated patterns. On each trial, a monkey observed one of the pictures (the cue) and then 4 sec later selected its associate from among two patterns. A reward was delivered if a correct response occurred within 1.2 sec. Neurons were found in the anterior temporal cortex that responded strongly to one of the pictures when that picture served as a cue in the paired-associate test. These same neurons were found to exhibit increased activity during the 4-sec delay on trials when the associate of that picture served as a cue. These neurons were termed \"pair-recall" neurons. Thus, neurons acquired information about the specific pairings of the patterns that were used, and they exhibited activity related to the process of stimulus recall.

These results should make it possible to pursue several interesting experimental questions. Does development of pair-specific neuronal activity require a contribution from the limbic/diencephalic brain system that is essential for declarative memory? What would be the effect of inactivating circuitry within the hippocampus or inactivating efferent projections from entorhinal cortex to neocortex? If the limbic/diencephalic system proved essential, then should pair-recall neurons be viewed as belonging to a network that represents long-term declarative memory of the associations? What is the role of the limbic/diencephalic system in the acquisition of pair-specific activity, its maintenance, and its expression? In other words, how does the limbic/diencephalic system interact with neocortex during learning, consolidation, and retrieval? If it becomes feasible, using this or some other paradigm, to observe directly the development of cortical plasticity related to declarative memory, one can expect the entire discussion of memory systems to be raised to a new level.

In the span of just a few years, the field of memory research has moved from a rather monolithic view of long-term memory to a view that distinguishes several kinds of memory. One system involves limbic/diencephalic structures, which in concert with neocortex provides the basis for conscious recollections. This system is fast, phylogenetically recent, and specialized for one-trial learning—e.g. for the rapid acquisition of associations, propositions, or items in a context. The system is fallible in the sense that it is sensitive to interference and prone to retrieval failure. It is also precious, giving rise to the capacity for personal autobiography and the possibility of cultural evolution.

Other kinds of memory have also been identified—e.g. those involved in skills and habits, priming, conditioning, and perhaps the ability to acquire category-level generic knowledge. Such memories can be acquired, stored, and retrieved without the participation of the limbic/diencephalic brain system. These forms of memory are phylogenetically early, they are reliable and consistent, and they provide for myriad, nonconsious ways of responding to the world. In no small part, by virtue of the nonconscious status of these forms of memory, they create much of the mystery of human experience. Here arise the dispositions, habits, and preferences that are inaccessible to conscious recollection but that nevertheless are shaped by past events, influence our behavior, and are a part of who we are.

ACKNOWLEDGMENTS

Supported by the Medical Research Service of the Department of Veterans Affairs, NIMH Grant MH24600, the Office of Naval Research, the McKnight Foundation, and by postdoctoral fellowships from NIMH (G.M) and the McDonnell-Pew Center for Cognitive Neuroscience (B.K.) Gail Muser is now at the Department of Psychology, Barnard College, Columbia University, New York, New York 10027.

Literature Cited

Alvarez-Royo, P., Zola-Morgan, S., Squire, L. R. 1993. Impairment of long-term memory and sparing of short-term memory in monkeys with medial temporal lobe lesions: a response to Ringo. *Brain Behav. Res.* In press

Atkinson, R. C., Shiffrin, R. M. 1968. Human memory: a proposed system and its control processes. In *Psychology of Learning and Motivation: Advances in Research and Theory,* ed. K. W. Spence, J. T. Spence, pp. 89–195. New York: Academic

Bachevalier, J. 1990. Ontogenetic development of habit and memory formation in primates. See Diamond 1990, pp. 457–84

Bachevalier, J., Mishkin, M. 1984. An early and a late developing system for learning and retention in infant monkeys. *Behav. Neurosci.* 98:770–78

Bachevalier, J., Ungerleider, L. G., O'Neill, J. B., Friedman, D. P. 1986. Regional distribution of [³H]naloxone binding in the brain of a newborn rhesus monkey. *Dev. Brain Res.* 25:302–8

Baddeley, A. D., Hitch, G. J. 1974. Working memory. In *The Psychology of Learning and Motivation: Advances in Research and Theory,* ed. G. A. Bower, pp. 47–90. New York: Academic

Baddeley, A. D., Papagno, C., Vallar, G. 1988. When long-term learning depends on short-term storage. *J. Mem. Lang.* 27:586–95

Baddeley, A. D., Warrington, E. K. 1970. Amnesia and the distinction between long and short-term memory. *J. Verbal Learn. Verbal Behav.* 9:176–89

Baillargeon, R., DeVos, J. 1991. Object permanence in young infants: further evidence. *Child Dev.* 62:1227–46

Barr, W. B., Goldberg, E., Wasserstein, J., Novelly, R. A. 1990. Retrograde amnesia following unilateral temporal lobectomy. *Neuropsychologia* 28:243–56

Bartram, D. J. 1974. The role of visual and semantic codes in object naming. *Cogn. Psychol.* 6:325–56

Bauer, P. J., Mandler, J. M. 1989. One thing follows another: effects of temporal structure on 1- to 2-year-olds' recall of events. *Dev. Psychol.* 25:197–206

Benson, D. F., Geschwind, N. 1967. Shrinking retrograde amnesia. *J. Neurol. Neurosurg.*

Psychiatry 30:539–44

Bentin, S., Moscovitch, M. 1988. The time course of repetition effects for words and unfamiliar faces. *J. Exp. Psychol.: Gen.* 117:148–60

Benzing, W., Squire, L. R. 1989. Preserved learning and memory in amnesia: intact adaptation-level effects and learning of stereoscopic depth. *Behav. Neurosci.* 103:548–60

Berger, T. W., Orr, W. B. 1983. Hippocampectomy selectively disrupts discrimination reversal learning of the rabbit nictitating membrane response. *Behav. Brain Res.* 8:49–68

Berger, T. W., Thompson, R. F. 1978. Neuronal plasticity in the limbic system during classical conditioning of the rabbit nictitating membrane response. I. The hippocampus. *Brain Res.* 145:323–46

Berry, D., Broadbent, D. 1984. On the relationship between task performance and associated verbalizable knowledge. *Q. J. Exp. Psychol.* 36A:209–31

Biederman, I., Cooper, E. E. 1991a. Priming contour deleted images: evidence for intermediate representations in visual object recognition. *Cogn. Psychol.* 23:393–419

Biederman, I., Cooper, E. E. 1991b. Evidence for complete translational and reflectional invariance in visual object priming. *Perception.* 20:585–93

Biederman, I., Cooper, E. E. 1992. Size invariance in visual object priming. *J. Exp. Psychol. Hum. Percept. Perform.* 18:121–33

Blaxton, T. A. 1989. Investigating dissociations among memory measures: support for a transfer appropriate processing framework. *J. Exp. Psychol. Learn. Mem. Cogn.* 15:657–68

Bonnano, G. A., Stillings, N. A. 1986. Preference, familiarity, and recognition after repeated brief exposures to random geometric shapes. *Am. J. Psychol.* 99:403–15

Brooks, D. N., Baddeley, A. 1976. What can amnesic patients learn? *Neuropsychologia* 14:111–22

Brooks, L. R. 1978. Nonanalytic concept formation and memory for instances. In *Cognition and Categorization,* ed. E. Rosch, B. B. Lloyd, pp. 169–211. New York: Wiley

Brooks, L. R., Vokey, J. R. 1991. Abstract analogies and abstracted grammars: comments on Reber (1989) and Mathews et al. (1989). *J. Exp. Psychol.: Gen.* 120:316–23

Butters, N., Heindel, W. C., Salmon, D. P. 1990. Dissociation of implicit memory in dementia: neurological implications. *Bull. Psychonomic Soc.* 28:359–66

Butters, N., Stuss, D. T. 1989. Diencephalic amnesia. In *Handbook of Neuropsychology,* ed. F. Boller, J. Grafman, pp. 107–48. Amsterdam: Elsevier

Caul, W. F., Jarrard, L. E., Miller, R. E., Korn, J. H. 1969. Effects of hippocampal lesions on heart rate in aversive classical conditioning. *Physiol. Behav.* 4:917–22

Cave, C. B., Squire, L. R. 1991. Equivalent impairment of spatial and nonspatial memory following damage to the human hippocampus. *Hippocampus* 1:329–40

Cave, C. B., Squire, L. R. 1992a. Intact verbal and nonverbal short-term memory following damage to the human hippocampus. *Hippocampus* 2:151–63

Cave, C. B., Squire, L. R. 1992b. Intact and long-lasting repetition priming in amnesia. *J. Exp. Psychol. Learn. Mem. Cogn.* 18:509–20

Cermak, L. S. 1984. The episodic-semantic distinction in amnesia. See Squire & Butters 1984, pp. 55–62

Cermak, L. S., Bleich, R. P., Blackford, S. P. 1988. Deficits in implicit retention of new associations by alcoholic Korsakoff patients. *Brain Cogn.* 7:312–23

Cermak, L. S., Talbot, N., Chandler, K., Wolbarst, L. R. 1985. The perceptual priming phenomenon in amnesia. *Neuropsychologia* 23:615–22

Cermak, L. S., Verfaellie, M., Milberg, W., Letourneau, L., Blackford, S. 1991. A further analysis of perceptual identification priming in alcoholic Korsakoff patients. *Neuropsychologia* 29:725–36

Chapman, G. B., Robbins, S. J. 1990. Cue interaction in human contingency judgment. *Mem. Cogn.* 18:537–45

Cho, Y. H., Beracochea, D., Jaffard, R. 1991. Temporally graded retrograde and anterograde amnesia following ibotenic entorhinal cortex lesion in mice. *Soc. Neurosci. Abstr.* 17:1045

Cleeremans, A., McClelland, J. L. 1991. Learning the structure of event sequences. *J. Exp. Psychol.: Gen.* 120:235–53

Cohen, A., Ivry, R. I., Keele, S. W. 1990. Attention and structure in sequence learning. *J. Exp. Psychol. Learn. Mem. Cogn.* 16:17–30

Cohen, N. J., Squire, L. R. 1980. Preserved learning and retention of pattern analyzing skill in amnesia: dissociation of knowing how and knowing that. *Science* 210:207–10

Cohen, N. J., Squire, L. R. 1981. Retrograde amnesia and remote memory impairment. *Neuropsychologia* 19:337–56

Cooper, L. A., Schacter, D. L., Ballesteros, S., Moore, C. 1992. Priming and recognition of transformed three-dimensional objects: effects of size and reflection. *J. Exp. Psychol.: Learn. Mem. Cogn.* 18:43–57

Damasio, A. R. 1990. Category-related recognition defects as a clue to the neural substrates of knowledge. *Trends Neurosci.* 13:95–98

Daum, I., Channon, S., Canavar, A. 1989. Classical conditioning in patients with severe memory problems. *J. Neurol. Neurosurg. Psychiatry* 52:47–51

Diamond, A. 1990. Rate of maturation of the hippocampus and the developmental progression of children's performance on the delayed non-matching to sample and visual paired comparison tasks. In *The Development and Neural Bases of Higher Cognitive Functions,* ed. A. Diamond, pp. 394–426. New York: NY Acad. Sci.

Diamond, R., Rozin, P. 1984. Activation of existing memories in anterograde amnesia. *J. Abnorm. Psychol.* 93:98–105

Dienes, Z., Broadbent, D., Berry, D. 1991. Implicit and explicit knowledge bases in artificial grammar learning. *J. Exp. Psychol. Learn. Mem. Cogn.* 17:875–87

Divak, J., Rosvold, H. E., Szwarcbart, M. K. 1967. Behavioral effects of selective ablation of the caudate nucleus. *J. Comp. Physiol. Psychol.* 63:184–90

Douglas, R. J. 1975. The development of hippocampal function: implications for theory and for therapy. In *The Hippocampus: Neurophysiology and Behavior,* ed. L. Isaacson, K. H. Pribram, pp. 327–61. New York: Plenum

Drachman, D. A., Arbit, J. 1966. Memory and the hippocampal complex. II. Is memory a multiple process? *Arch. Neurol.* 15:52–61

Dulany, D. E., Carlson, R. A., Dewey, G. I. 1984. A case of syntactical learning and judgment: how conscious and how abstract? *J. Exp. Psychol.: Gen.* 113:541–55

Dunn, L. T., Everitt, B. J. 1988. Double dissociations of the effects of amygdala and insular cortex lesions on conditioned taste aversion, passive avoidance, and neophobia in the rat using the excitotoxin ibotenic acid. *Behav. Neurosci.* 102:3–23

Eichenbaum, H., Fagan, A., Mathews, P., Cohen, N. J. 1988. Hippocampal system dysfunction and odor discrimination learning in rats: impairment or facilitation depending on representational demands. *Behav. Neurosci.* 102:331–39

Eichenbaum, H., Kuperstein, M., Fagan, A., Nagode, J. 1986. Cue-sampling and goal-approach correlates of hippocampal unit activity in rats performing an odor discrimination task. *J. Neurosci.* 7:716–32

Eichenbaum, H., Mathews, P., Cohen, N. J. 1989. Further studies of hippocampal representation during odor discrimination learning. *Behav. Neurosci.* 103:1207–16

Eichenbaum, H., Otto, T., Cohen, N. J. 1992. The hippocampus—What does it do? *Behav. Neurol. Biol.* 57:2–36

Estes, W. K. 1988. Human learning and memory. In *Stevens' Handbook of Experimental Psychology,* ed. R. D. Atkinson, R. Herrnstein, G. Lindzey, R. D. Luce, pp. 352–415. New York: Wiley

Estes, W. K. 1991. Cognitive architectures from the standpoint of an experimental psychologist. *Annu. Rev. Psychol.* 42:1-28

Evans, F. J., Thorn, W. A. F. 1966. Two types of posthypnotic amnesia: recall amnesia and source amnesia. *Int. J. Clin. Exp. Hypnosis* 14:162–79

Fagan, J. F. 1970. Memory in the infant. *J.*

Exp. Child Psychol. 9:217–26

Fantz, R. L. 1964. Visual experience in infants. Decreased attention to familiar patterns relative to novel ones. *Science* 146:668–70

Farah, M. J., McClelland, J. L. 1991. A computational model of semantic memory impairment: modality specificity and emergent category specificity. *J. Exp. Psychol.: Gen.* 120:339–57

Farah, M. J., McMullen, P. A., Meyer, M. M. 1991. Can recognition of living things be selectively impaired? *Neuropsychologia* 29:185–93

Felleman, D., Van Essen, D. 1991. Distributed hierarchical processing in primate cerebral cortex. *Cerebral Cortex* 1:1–47

Freed, D. M., Corkin, S., Cohen, N. J. 1987. Forgetting in H. M.: a second look. *Neuropsychologia* 25:461–71

Freud, S. 1962. *Three Essays on the Theory of Sexuality,* pp. 125–273. New York: Basic Books (Originally published 1905)

Fried, L. S., Holyoak, K. J. 1984. Induction of category distributions: a framework for classification learning. *J. Exp. Psychol.: Learn. Mem. Cogn.* 10:234–57

Fuster, J. M., Jervey, J. P. 1981. Inferotemporal neurons distinguish and retain behaviorally relevant features of visual stimuli. *Science* 212:952–55

Gabrieli, J. D. E., Milberg, W., Keane, M. M., Corkin, S. 1990. Intact priming of patterns despite impaired memory. *Neuropsychologia* 28:417–27

Gardiner, J. M. 1988. Recognition failures and free-recall failures: implications for the relation between recall and recognition. *Mem. Cogn.* 16:446–51

Gardiner, J. M., Java, R. I. 1990. Recollective experience in word and nonword recognition. *Mem. Cogn.* 18:23–30

Gardner, H., Boller, F., Moreines, J., Butters, N. 1973. Retrieving information from Korsakoff patients: effects of categorical cues and reference to the task. *Cortex* 9:165–75

Gathercole, S. E., Baddeley, A. D. 1990. The role of phonological memory in vocabulary acquisition: a study of young children learning new names. *Br. J. Psychol.* 81:439–54

Glanzer, M., Cunitz, A. R. 1966. Two storage mechanisms in free recall. *J. Verbal Learn. Verbal Behav.* 5:351–60

Glisky, E. L., Schacter, D. L., Tulving, E. 1986a. Computer learning by memory-impaired patients: acquisition and retention of complex knowledge. *Neuropsychologia* 24:313–28

Glisky, E. L., Schacter, D. L., Tulving, E. 1986b. Learning and retention of computer-related vocabulary in memory-impaired patients: method of vanishing cues. *J. Clin. Exp. Neuropsychol.* 8:292–312

Gluck, M. A., Bower, G. H. 1988. From conditioning to category learning: an adaptive network model. *J. Exp. Psychol.: Gen.* 117:227–47

Goldman-Rakic, P. S. 1987. Circuitry of primate prefontal cortex and regulation of behavior by representational memory. In *Handbook of Physiology,* ed. V. B. Mountcastle, F. Plum, S. R. Geiger, pp. 373–418. Bethesda, MD: Am. Physiol. Soc.

Graf, P., Mandler, G. 1984. Activation makes words more accessible, but not necessarily more retrievable. *J. Verbal Learn. Verbal Behav.* 23:553–68

Graf, P., Schacter, D. L. 1985. Implicit and explicit memory for new associations in normal and amnesic subjects . *J. Exp. Psychol. Learn. Mem. Cogn.* 11:501–18

Graf, P., Shimamura, A. P., Squire, L. R. 1985. Priming across modalities and priming across category levels: extending the domain of preserved function in amnesia. *J. Exp. Psychol. Learn. Mem. Cogn.* 11:386–96

Graf, P., Squire, L. R., Mandler, G. 1984. The information that amnesic patients do not forget. *J. Exp. Psychol. Learn. Mem. Cogn.* 10:164–78

Haist, F., Musen, G., Squire, L. R. 1991. Intact priming of words and nonwords in amnesia. *Psychobiology* 19:275–85

Haist, F., Shimamura, A. P., Squire, L. R. 1992. On the relationship between recall and recognition memory. *J. Exp. Psychol. Learn. Mem. Cogn.* 18:691–702

Halgren, E. 1984. Human hippocampal and amygdala recording and stimulation: evidence for a neural model of recent memory. See Squire & Butters 1984, pp. 165–82

Hammann, S. B. 1990. Level-of-processing effects in conceptually driven implicit tasks. *J. Exp. Psychol. Learn. Mem. Cogn.* 16:970–77

Hart, J., Berndt, R. S., Caramazza, A. 1985. Category-specific naming deficit following cerebral infarction. *Nature* 316:439–40

Hartman, M., Knopman, D. S., Nissen, M. J. 1989. Implicit learning of new verbal associations. *J. Exp. Psychol. Learn. Mem. Cogn.* 15:1070–82

Hayman, C. A. G., Tulving, E. 1989. Contingent dissociation between recognition and fragment completion: the method of triangulation. *J. Exp. Psychol. Learn. Mem. Cogn.* 15:220–24

Heindel, W. C., Salmon, D. P., Butters, N. 1991. The biasing of weight judgments in Alzheimer's and Huntington's disease: a priming or programming phenomenon? *J. Clin. Exp. Neuropsychol.* 13:189–203

Heindel, W. C., Salmon, D. P., Shults, C. W., Walicke, P. A., Butters, N. 1989. Neuropsychological evidence for multiple implicit memory systems: a comparison of Alzheimer's, Huntington's, and Parkinson's disease patients. *J. Neurosci.* 9:582–87

Hintzman, D. 1986. Schema abstraction in a multiple-trace memory model. *Psychol. Rev.* 93:411–28

Hintzman, D. 1990. Human learning and memory: connections and dissociations. *Annu. Rev. Psychol.* 41:109–39

Hintzman, D., Hartry, A. L. 1990. Item effects in recognition and fragment completion: contingency relations vary for different subsets of words. *J. Exp. Psychol. Learn. Mem. Cogn.* 16:955–69

Hirst, R. 1974. The hippocampus and contextual retrieval from memory: A theory. *Behav. Biol.* 12:421–44

Hirst, W., Johnson, M. K., Phelps, E. A., Risse, G., Volpe, B. T. 1986. Recognition and recall in amnesics. *J. Exp. Psychol. Learn. Mem. Cogn.* 12:445–51

Hirst, W., Johnson, M. K., Phelps, E. A., Volpe, B. T. 1988. More on recognition and recall in amnesics. *J. Exp. Psychol. Learn. Mem. Cogn.* 14:758–62

Huppert, F. A., Piercy, M. 1979. Normal and abnormal forgetting in organic amnesia: effect of locus of lesion. *Cortex* 15:385–90

Ivry, R., Baldo, J. 1992. Is the cerebellum involved in learning and cognition? *Curr. Opin. Neurobiol.* 2:212–16

Jacobson, R. R., Lishman, W. A. 1987. Selective memory loss and global intellectual deficits in alcoholic Korsakoff's syndrome. *Psychol. Med.* 17:649–55

Jacoby, L. L. 1983. Remembering the data: analyzing interactive processes in reading. *J. Verbal Learn. Verbal Behav.* 22:485–508

Jacoby, L. L. 1988. Memory observed and memory unobserved. In *Remembering Reconsidered: Ecological and Traditional Approaches to the Study of Memory,* ed. U. Neisser, E. Winograd, pp. 145–177. Cambridge: Cambridge Univ. Press

Jacoby, L. L. 1991. A process dissociation framework: separating automatic from intentional uses of memory. *J. Mem. Lang.* 30:513–41

Jacoby, L. L., Dallas, M. 1981. On the relationship between autobiographical memory and perceptual learning. *J. Exp. Psychol. Learn. Mem. Cogn.* 3:306–40

Jacoby, L. L., Witherspoon, D. 1982. Remembering without awareness. *Can. J. Psychol.* 32:300–24

Jacoby, L. L., Woloshyn, V., Kelley, C. M. 1989. Becoming famous without being recognized: unconscious influences of memory produced by dividing attention. *J. Exp. Psychol.: Gen.* 118:115–25

James, W. 1890. *Principles of Psychology.* New York: Holt

Janowsky, J. S., Shimamura, A. P., Kritchevsky, M., Squire, L. R. 1989. Cognitive impairment following frontal lobe damage and its relevance to human amnesia. *Behav. Neurosci.* 103:548–60

Janowsky, J. S., Shimamura, A. P., Squire, L. R. 1989a. Memory and metamemory: comparisons between patients with frontal lobe lesions and amnesic patients. *Psychobiol-*

ogy 17:3–11

Janowsky, J. S., Shimamura, A. P., Squire, L. R. 1989b. Source memory impairment in patients with frontal lobe lesions. *Neuropsychologia* 27:1043–56

Jetter, W., Poser, U., Freeman, R. B. Jr., Markowitsch, J. H. 1986. A verbal long-term memory deficit in frontal lobe damaged patients. *Cortex* 22:229–42

Johnston, W. A., Dark, W. J., Jacoby, L. L. 1985. Perceptual fluency and recognition judgments. *J. Exp. Psychol.: Learn. Mem. Cogn.* 11:3–ll

Johnston, W. A., Hawley, K. J., Elliot, M. G. 1991. Contribution of perceptual fluency to recognition judgments. *J. Exp. Psychol. Learn. Mem. Cogn.* 17:210–23

Kandel, E. R., Squire, L. R. 1992. Cognitive neuroscience. *Curr. Opin. Neurobiol.* 2:143–45

Keane, M. M., Gabrieli, J. D. E., Fennema, A. C., Growdon, J. H., Corkin, S. 1991. Evidence for a dissociation between perceptual and conceptual priming in Alzheimer's disease. *Behav. Neurosci.* 105:326–42

Kersteen-Tucker, Z. 1991. Long-term repetition priming with symmetrical polygons and words. *Mem. Cogn.* 19:37–43

Kesner, R. P., Novak, J. M. 1982. Serial position curve in rats: role of the dorsal hippocampus. *Science* 218:173–75

Kim, J. J., Fanselow, M. S. 1992. Modality-specific retrograde amnesia of fear. *Science.* 256:675–77

Kinsbourne, M., Wood, F. 1975. Short-term memory processes and the amnesic syndrome. In *Short-term Memory*, ed. D. Deutsch, J. A. Deutsch, pp. 258–91. New York: Academic

Knopman, D. S., Nissen, M. J. 1991. Procedural learning is impaired in Huntington's disease: evidence from the serial reaction time task. *Neuropsychologia* 29:245–54

Knowlton, B. J., Ramus, S. J., Squire, L. R. 1992. Intact artificial grammar learning in amnesia: dissociation of classification learning and explicit memory for specific instances. *Psychol. Sci.* 3:172–79

Knowlton, B. J., Squire, L. R. 1992. Intact prototype learning by amnesic patients: evidence for parallel learning of item-specific and general information. *Soc. Neurosci. Abstr.* 18:386

Kopelman, M. D. 1985. Rates of forgetting in Alzheimer type dementia and Korsakoff's syndrome. *Neuropsychologia* 23:623–38

Kopelman, M. D. 1989. Remote and autobiographical memory, temporal context memory and frontal atrophy in Korsakoff and Alzheimer patients. *Neuropsychologia* 27:437–60

Kovner, R., Mattis, S., Goldmeier, E. 1983. A technique for promoting robust free recall in chronic organic amnesia. *J. Clin. Neuropsychol.* 5:65–71

Kritchevsky, M., Squire, L. R., Zouzounis, J.

1988. Transient global amnesia: characterization of anterograde and retrograde amnesia. *Neurology* 38:213–19

Kruschke, J. K. 1992. ALCOVE: an exemplar-based connectionist model of category learning. *Psychol. Rev.* 99:22–44

Kunst-Wilson, W. R., Zajonc, R. B. 1980. Affective discrimination of stimuli that cannot be recognized. *Science* 207:557–58

LeDoux, J. E. 1987. Emotion. In *Handbook of Physiology: The Nervous System v. Higher Functions of the Nervous System*, ed. F. Plum, pp. 419–60. Betheda, MD: Am. Physiol. Soc.

Levin, H. S., Eisenberg, H. M., Benton, A. L. 1991. *Frontal Lobe Function and Dysfunction.* New York: Oxford Univ. Press

Lewicki, P. 1986a. Processing information about covariations that cannot be articulated. *J. Exp. Psychol.: Learn. Mem. Cogn.* 12:135–46

Lewicki, P. 1986b. *Nonconscious Social Information Processing*, pp. 130–72. New York: Academic

Lewicki, P., Czyzewska, M., Hoffman, H. 1987. Unconscious acquisition of complex procedural knowledge. *J. Exp. Psychol. Learn. Mem. Cogn.* 13:523–30

MacAndrew, S. B. G., Jones, G. V. 1993. Spatial memory in amnesia: Evidence from Korsakoff patients. *Cortex.* In press

Mahut, M., Moss, M. 1984. Consolidation of memory: the hippocampus revisited. See Squire & Butters 1984, pp. 297–315

Malamut, B. L., Saunders, R. C., Mishkin, M. 1984. Monkeys with combined amygdalo-hippocampal lesions succeed in object discrimination learning despite 24-hour intertrial intervals. *Behav. Neurosci.* 98:759–69

Mandler, G. 1980. Recognizing: the judgment of previous occurrence. *Psychol. Rev.* 87:252–71

Mandler, G., Nakamura, Y., Van Zandt, B. J. S. 1987. Nonspecific effects of exposure on stimuli that cannot be recognized. *J. Exp. Psychol. Learn. Mem. Cogn.* 13:646–48

Mandler, J. M. 1990. Recall of events by preverbal children. See Diamond 1990, pp. 485–516

Marinkovic, K., Schell, A. M., Dawson, M. E. 1989. Awareness of the CS-UCS contingency and classical conditioning of skin conductance responses with olfactory CSs. *Biol. Psychol.* 29:39–60

Markowitsch, H. 1988. Diencephalic amnesia: a reorientation towards tracts? *Brain Res. Rev.* 13:351–70

Marsolek, C. J., Kosslyn, S., Squire, L. R. 1992. Form-specific visual priming in the right cerebral hemisphere. *J. Exp. Psychol. Learn. Mem. Cogn.* 18:492–508

Martone, M., Butters, N., Payne, P. 1984. Dissociations between skill learning and verbal recognition in amnesia and dementia. *Arch. Neurol.* 41:965–70

Masson, M. E. J. 1989. Fluent reprocessing as an implicit expression of memory for experience. In *Implicit Memory: Theoretical Issues,* ed. S. Lewandowsky, J. C. Dunn, K. Kirsner, pp. 123–38. Hillsdale, NJ: Erlbaum

Mathews, R. C., Buss, R. R., Stanley, W. B., Blanchard-Fields, F., Cho, J. R., et al. 1989. The role of implicit and explicit processes in learning from examples: a synergistic effect. *J. Exp. Psychol. Learn. Mem. Cogn.* 15:1083–1100

Mayes, A. R. 1988. *Human Organic Memory Disorders.* New York: Oxford Univ. Press

Mayes, A. R., Gooding, P. 1989. Enhancement of word completion priming in amnesics by cuing with previously novel associates. *Neuropsychologia* 27:1057–72

Mayes, A. R., Meudell, P., MacDonald, C. 1991. Disproportionate intentional spatial memory impairments in amnesia. *Neuropsychologia* 29:771–84

McAndrews, M. P., Milner, B. 1991. The frontal cortex and memory for temporal order. *Neuropsychologia* 29:849–60

McClelland, J. L., Rumelhart, D. E. 1985. Distributed memory and the representation of general and specific information. *J. Exp. Psychol.: Gen.* 114:159–88

McKee, R., Squire, L. R. 1992. Equivalent forgetting rates in long-term memory for diencephalic and medial temporal lobe amnesia. *J. Neurosci.* 12:3765–72

McKee, R., Squire, L. R. 1993. On the development of declarative memory. *J. Exp. Psychol.: Learn. Mem. Cognit.* In press

McNaughton, B. L., Nadel, L. 1990. Hebb-Marr networks and the neurobiological representation of action in space In *Neuroscience and Connectionist Theory,* ed. M. Gluck, D. Rumelhart, pp. 1–63. Hillsdale, NJ: Erlbaum

Medin, D. L., Schaffer, M. M. 1978. Context theory of classification learning. *Psychol. Rev.* 85:207–38

Meltzoff, A. N. 1985. Immediate and deferred imitation in fourteen- and twenty-month-old infants. *Child Dev.* 56:62–72

Meudell, P. R., Mayes, A. R., Ostergaard, A., Pickering, A. 1985. Recency and frequency judgments in alcoholic amnesics and normal people with poor memory. *Cortex* 21:487–511

Miller, E. K., Li, L., Desimone, R. 1991. A neural mechanism for working and recognition memory in inferior temporal cortex. *Science* 254:1377–79

Milner, B. 1962. Les troubles de la mémoire accompagnant des lésions hippocampiques bilatérales. In *Physiologie de l'hippocampe,* pp. 257–72. Paris: Cent. Natl. Rech. Sci.

Milner, B. 1971. Interhemispheric differences in the localization of psychological processes in man. *Br. Med. Bull.* 27:272–77

Milner, B. 1978. Clues to the cerebral organization of memory. In *Cerebral Correlates of Conscious Experience, INSERM Symposium,* ed. P. A. Buser, A. Rougeul-Buser, pp. 139–53. Amsterdam: Elsevier

Milner, P. M. 1989. A cell assembly theory of hippocampal amnesia. *Neuropsychologia* 27:23–30

Mishkin, M. 1978. Memory in monkeys severely impaired by combined but not by separate removal of amygdala and hippocampus. *Nature* 273:297–96

Mishkin, M. 1982. A memory system in the monkey. *Philos. Trans. R. Soc. London Ser. B* 298:85–92

Mishkin, M., Delacour, J. 1975. An analysis of short-term visual memory in the monkey. *J. Exp. Psychol. Anim. Behav.* 1:326–34

Mishkin, M., Malamut, B., Bachevalier, J. 1984. Memories and habits: two neural systems. In *Neurobiology of Learning and Memory,* ed. G. Lynch, J. L. McGaugh, N. M. Weinberger, pp. 65–77. New York: Guilford

Mitchell, D. B., Brown, A. S. 1988. Persistent repetition priming in picture naming and its dissociation from recognition memory. *J. Exp. Psychol. Learn. Mem. Cogn.* 14:213–22

Monsell, S. 1984. Components of working memory underlying verbal skills: a "distributed capacities" view. In *International Symposia on Attention and Performance,* ed. H. Bouma, D. Bonnhuis, 10:327–50. Hillsdale, NJ: Erlbaum

Moscovitch, M., Winocur, G., McLachlan, D. 1986. Memory as assessed by recognition and reading time in normal and memory impaired people with Alzheimer's disease and other neurological disorders. *J. Exp. Psychol.: Gen.* 115:331–47

Moyer, J. R., Deyo, R. A., Disterhoft, J. F. 1990. Hippocampectomy disrupts trace eye-blink conditioning in rabbits. *Behav. Neurosci.* 204:243–52

Musen, G., Shimamura, A. P., Squire, L. R. 1990. Intact text-specific reading skill in amnesia. *J. Exp. Psychol. Learn. Mem. Cogn.* 6:1068–76

Musen, G., Squire, L. R. 1993. On the implicit learning of novel associations by amnesic patients and normal subjects. *Neuropsychology.* In press

Musen, G., Squire, L. R. 1992. Nonverbal priming in amnesia. *Mem. Cogn.* 20:441–48

Musen, G., Squire, L. R. 1991. Normal acquisition of novel verbal information in amnesia. *J. Exp. Psychol. Learn. Mem. Cogn.* 17:1095–1104

Musen, G., Treisman, A. 1990. Implicit and explicit memory for visual patterns. *J. Exp. Psychol. Learn. Mem. Cogn.* 16:127–37

Nadel, L., Zola-Morgan, S. 1984. Infantile amnesia: a neurobiological perspective. In *Infant Memory,* ed. M. Moscovitch, pp. 145–72. New York: Plenum

Neisser, U. 1962. Cultural and cognitive discontinuuity. In *Anthropology and Human*

Behavior, ed. T. E. Gladwin, W. Sturtevant. Washington, DC: Anthropol. Soc.

Nelson, K. 1988. The ontogeny of memory for real events. In *Remembering Reconsidered: Ecological and Traditional Approaches to the Study of Memory,* ed. U. Neisser, E. Winograd, pp. 244–77. New York: Cambridge Univ. Press

Nissen, M. J., Bullemer, P. 1987. Attentional requirements of learning: evidence from performance measures. *Cogn. Psychol.* 19:1–32

Norman, R. J., Buchwald, J. S., Villablanca, J. R. 1977. Classical conditioning with auditory discrimination of the eyeblink reflex in decerebrate cats. *Science* 196:551–53

Nosofsky, R. M. 1984. Choice, similarity, and the context theory of classification. *J. Exp. Psychol. Learn. Mem. Cogn.* 10:104–14

Nosofsky, R. M., Kruschke, J. K., McKinley, S. C. 1992. Combining exemplar-based category representations and connectionist learning rules. *J. Exp. Psychol. Learn. Mem. Cogn.* 18:211–33

O'Keefe, J., Nadel, L. 1978. *The Hippocampus as a Cognitive Map.* London: Oxford Univ. Press

Olton, D. S. 1985. Memory: neuropsychological and ethopsychological approaches to its classification. In *Perspectives on Learning and Memory,* ed. L. Nilsson, T. Archer, pp. 95–118. Hillsdale, NJ: Erlbaum

Ostergaard, A. L. 1992. A method for judging measures of stochastic dependence: further comments on the current controversy. *J. Exp. Psychol. Learn. Mem. Cogn.* 18:413–20

Ostergaard, A. L., Squire, L. R. 1990. Childhood amnesia and distinctions between forms of memory. *Brain Cogn.* 14:127–33

Overman, W. H. 1990. Performance on traditional matching to sample, non-matching to sample, and object discrimination tasks by 12- to 32-month-old-children: a developmental progression. See Diamond 1990, pp. 365–94

Overman, W. H., Ormsby, G., Mishkin, M. 1991. Picture recognition vs. picture discrimination learning in monkeys with medial temporal removals. *Exp. Brain Res.* 79:18–24

Packard, M. G., Hirsh, R., White, N. M. 1989. Differential effects of fornix and caudate nucleus lesions on two radial maze tasks: evidence for multiple memory systems. *J. Neurosci.* 9:1465–72

Paller, K. A. 1990. Recall and stem-completion priming have different electrophysiological correlates and are modified differentially by directed forgetting. *J. Exp. Psychol. Learn. Mem. Cogn.* 16:1021–32

Paller, K. A., Kutas, M. 1992. Brain potentials during memory retrieval: neurophysiological support for the distinction between conscious recollection and priming. *J. Cogn. Neurosci.* 4:375–91

Papagno, C., Valentine, T., Baddeley, A. 1991. Phonological short-term memory and foreign-language vocabulary learning. *J. Mem. Lang.* 30:331–47

Parkin, A. J. 1982. Residual learning capability in organic amnesia. *Cortex* 18:417–40

Parkin, A. J. 1984. Amnesic syndrome: a lesion-specific disorder. *Cortex* 20:479–508

Parkinson, J. K., Murray, E., Mishkin, M. 1988. A selective mnemonic role for the hippocampus in monkeys: memory for the location of objects. *J. Neurosci.* 8:4159–67

Perruchet, P., Pacteau, C. 1990. Synthetic grammar learning: implicit rule abstraction or explicit fragmentary knowledge? *J. Exp. Psychol.: Gen.* 119:264–75

Petersen, S. E., Fox, P. T., Snyder, A. Z., Raichle, M. E. 1990. Activation of extrastriate and frontal cortical areas by visual words and word-like stimuli. *Science* 249:1041–44

Phillips, R. R., Malamut, B. L., Bachevalier, J., Mishkin, M. 1988. Dissociation of the effects of inferior temporal and limbic lesions on object discrimination learning with 24-h intertrial intervals. *Behav. Brain Res.* 27:99–107

Posner, M. I., Keele, S. W. 1968. On the genesis of abstract ideas. *J. Exp. Psychol.* 77:353–63

Ranck, J. B. 1973. Studies on single neurons in dorsal hippocampal formation and septum in unrestrained rats. *Exp. Neurol.* 41:461–531

Reber, A. S. 1967. Implicit learning of artificial grammars. *J. Verbal Learn. Verbal Behav.* 6:855–63

Reber, A. S. 1976. Implicit learning of synthetic languages: the role of instructional set. *J. Exp. Psychol. Hum. Learn. Mem.* 2:88–94

Reber, A. S. 1989. Implicit learning and tacit knowledge. *J. Exp. Psychol.: Gen.* 3:219–35

Reed, S. K. 1972. Pattern recognition and categorization. *Cogn. Psychol.* 3:382–407

Rescorla, R. A., Wagner, A. R. 1972. A theory of Pavlovian conditioning: variations in the effectiveness of reinforcement and non-reinforcement. In *Classical Conditioning II: Current Theory and Research,* ed. A. H. Black, W. F. Prokasy, pp. 64–99. Orlando, FL: Academic

Richardson-Klavehn, A., Bjork, R. A. 1988. Measures of memory. *Annu. Rev. Psychol.* 39:475–543

Riches, I. P., Wilson, F. A. W., Brown, M. W. 1991. The effects of visual stimulation and memory on neurons of the hippocampal formation and the neighboring parahippocampal gyrus and inferior temporal cortex of the primate. *J. Neurosci.* 11:1763–979

Ringo, J. L. 1991. Memory decays at the same rate in macaques with and without brain lesions when expressed in d' or arcsine terms. *Behav. Brain Res.* 42:123–34

Roediger, H. L. 1990. Implicit memory: retention without remembering. *Am. Psychol.* 45:1043–56

Rolls, E. 1990. Principles underlying the representation and storage of information in neuronal networks in the primate hippocampus and cerebral cortex. In *Introduction to Neural and Electronic Networks,* ed. S. F. Zornetzer, J. L. Davis, C. Lau, pp. 73–90. San Diego, CA: Academic

Rosch, E. H. 1973. On the internal structure of perceptual and semantic categories. In *Cognitive Development and the Acquisition of Language,* ed. T. E. Moore, pp. 111–44. New York: Academic

Ross, R. T., Orr, W. B., Holland, P. C., Berger, T. W. 1984. Hippocampectomy disrupts acquisition and retention of learned conditional responding. *Behav. Neurosci.* 98:211–25

Sagar, H. H., Cohen, N. J., Corkin, S., Growdon, J. M. 1985. Dissociations among processes in remote memory. In *Memory Dysfunctions,* ed. D. S. Olton, E. Gamzu, S. Corkin, pp. 533–35. New York: NY Acad. Sci.

Saint-Cyr, J. A., Taylor, A. E., Lang, A. E. 1988. Procedural learning and neostriatal dysfunction in man. *Brain* 111:941–59

Sakai, K., Miyashita, Y. 1991. Neural organization for the long-term memory of paired associates. *Nature* 354:152–55

Saunders, H. I., Warrington, E. K. 1971. Memory for remote events in amnesic patients. *Brain* 94:661–68

Saunders, R. C., Weiskrantz, L. 1989. The effects of fornix transection and combined fornix transection, mammillary body lesions and hippocampal ablations on object-pair association memory in the rhesus monkey. *Behav. Brain Res.* 35:85–94

Schacter, D. L. 1985. Priming of old and new knowledge in amnesic patients and normal subjects. *Ann. NY Acad. Sci.* 444:44–53

Schacter, D. L. 1987. Implicit memory: history and current status. *J. Exp. Psychol.: Learn. Mem. Cogn.* 13:501–18

Schacter, D. L. 1990. Perceptual representation systems and implicit memory: toward a resolution of the multiple memory systems debate. See Diamond 1990, pp. 543–71

Schacter, D. L. 1992. Understanding implicit memory: a cognitive neuroscience approach. *Am. Psychol.* 47:559–69

Schacter, D. L., Chiu, C.-Y. P., Ochsner, K. N. 1993. Implicit memory: a selective review. *Annu. Rev. Neurosci.* 16:159–82

Schacter, D. L., Church, B. 1992. Auditory priming: implicit and explicit memory for words and voices. *J. Exp. Psychol. Learn. Mem. Cogn.* 18:915–30

Schacter, D. L., Cooper, L. A., Tharan, M., Rubens, A. B. 1991. Preserved priming of novel objects in patients with memory disorders. *J. Cogn. Neurosci.* 3:118–31

Schacter, D. L., Graf, P. 1986. Preserved learning in amnesic patients: perspectives on research from direct priming. *J. Clin. Exp.*

Neuropsychol. 8:727–43

Schacter, D. L., Harbluk, J. L., McLachlan, D. R. 1984. Retrieval without recollection: an experimental analysis of source amnesia. *J. Verbal Learn. Verbal Behav.* 23:593–611

Schacter, D. L., Moscovitch, M. 1984. Infants, amnesics, and dissociable memory systems. In *Infant Memory,* ed. M. Moscovitch, pp. 173–216. New York: Plenum

Servan-Schreiber, E., Anderson, J. R. 1990. Learning artificial grammars with competitive chunking. *J. Exp. Psychol. Learn. Mem. Cogn.* 16:592–608

Shallice, T., Warrington, E. K. 1970. Independent functioning of verbal memory stores: a neuropsychological study. *Q. J. Exp. Psychol.* 22:261–73

Shanks, D. R. 1990. Connectionism and the learning of probabilistic concepts. *Q. J. Exp. Psychol.* 42A:209–37

Shanks, D. R. 1991. Categorization by a connectionist network. *J. Exp. Psychol. Learn. Mem. Cogn.* 17:433–43

Sherry, D. F., Schacter, D. L. 1987. The evolution of multiple memory systems. *Psychol. Rev.* 94:439–54

Shimamura, A. P. 1985. Problems with the finding of stochastic independence as evidence for multiple memory systems. *Bull. Psychon. Soc.* 23:506–8

Shimamura, A. P. 1986. Priming effects in amnesia: evidence for a dissociable memory function. *Q. J. Exp. Psychol.* 38a:619–44

Shimamura, A. P., Janowsky, J. S., Squire, L. R. 1991. What is the role of frontal lobe damage in memory disorders? In *Frontal Lobe Functioning and Dysfunction,* ed. H. D. Levin, H. M. Eisenberg, A. L. Benton, pp. 173–95. New York: Oxford Univ. Press

Shimamura, A. P., Jernigan, T. L., Squire, L. R. 1988. Korsakoff's syndrome: radiological (CT) findings and neuropsychological correlates. *J. Neurosci.* 8:4400–10

Shimamura, A. P., Squire, L. R. 1984. Paired-associate learning and priming effects in amnesia: a neurospsychological analysis. *J. Exp. Psychol.: Gen.* 113:556–70

Shimamura, A. P., Squire, L. R. 1986. Memory and metamemory: a study of the feeling of knowing phenomenon in amnesic patients. *J. Exp. Psychol. Learn. Mem. Cogn.* 12:452–60

Shimamura, A. P., Squire, L. R. 1987. A neuropsychological study of fact memory and source amnesia. *J. Exp. Psychol.: Learn. Mem. Cogn.* 13:464–73

Shimamura, A. P., Squire, L. R. 1988. Long-term memory in amnesia: cued recall, recognition memory, and confidence ratings. *J. Exp. Psychol. Learn. Mem. Cogn.* 14:763–70

Shimamura, A. P., Squire, L. R. 1989. Impaired priming of new associations in amnesia. *J. Exp. Psychol. Learn. Mem. Cogn.* 15:721–28

Shoqeirat, M. A., Mayes, A. R. 1991. Disproportionate incidental spatial memory and recall deficits in amnesia. *Neuropsychologia* 29:749–69

Sloman, S. A., Hayman, C. A. G., Ohta, N., Law, J., Tulving, E. 1988. Forgetting in primed fragment completion. *J. Exp. Psychol. Learn. Mem. Cogn.* 14:223–39

Smith, E. E., Medin, D. L. 1981. *Categories and Concepts.* Cambridge, MA: Harvard Univ. Press

Smith, M. E., Oscar-Berman, M. 1990. Repetition priming of words and pseudowords in divided attention in amnesia. *J. Exp. Psychol. Learn. Mem. Cogn.* 16:1033–42

Solomon, P. R., Moore, J. W. 1975. Latent inhibition and stimulus generalization of the classically conditioned nictitating membrane response in rabbits *Oryctolagus cuniculus*) following dorsal hippocampal ablation. *J. Comp. Physiol. Psychol.* 89:1192–203

Squire, L. R. 1981. Two forms of human amnesia: an analysis of forgetting. *J. Neurosci.* 1:635–40

Squire, L. R. 1982. Comparisons between forms of amnesia: some deficits are unique to Korsakoff's syndrome. *J. Exp. Psychol. Learn. Mem. Cogn.* 8:560–71

Squire, L. R. 1987. *Memory and Brain.* New York: Oxford Univ. Press

Squire, L. R. 1992a. Memory and the hippocampus: a synthesis from findings with rats, monkeys, and humans. *Psychol. Rev.* 99:195–231

Squire, L. R. 1992b. Declarative and nondeclarative memory: multiple brain systems supporting learning and memory. *J. Cogn. Neurosci.* 4:232–43

Squire, L. R., Butters, N., eds. 1984. *Neuropsychology of Memory.* New York: Guilford

Squire, L. R., Cave, C. B. 1991. The hippocampus, memory, and space. *Hippocampus* 1:329–40

Squire, L. R., Cohen, N. J., Nadel, L. 1984. The medial temporal region and memory consolidation: a new hypothesis. In *Memory Consolidation,* ed. H. Weingartner, E. Parker, pp. 185–210. Hillsdale, NJ: Erlbaum

Squire, L. R., Frambach, M. 1990. Cognitive skill learning in amnesia. *Psychobiology* 18:109–17

Squire, L. R., Haist, F., Shimamura, A. P. 1989. The neurology of memory: quantitative assessment of retrograde amnesia in two groups of amnesic patients. *J. Neurosci.* 9:828–39

Squire, L. R., McKee, R. 1992. Influence of prior events on cognitive judgments in amnesia. *J. Exp. Psychol. Learn. Mem. Cogn.* 18:106–15

Squire, L. R., Ojemann, J. G., Miezin, F. M., Petersen, S. E., Videen, T. O., Raichle, M. E. 1992. Activation of the hippocampus in normal humans: a functional anatomical study of memory. *Proc. Natl. Acad. Sci. USA* 89:1837–41

Squire, L. R., Shimamura, A. P., Graf, P. 1987. The strength and duration of priming effects in normal subjects and amnesic patients. *Neuropsychologia* 25:195–210

Squire, L. R., Slater, P. C., Chace, P. M. 1975. Retrograde amnesia: temporal gradient in very long-term memory following electroconvulsive therapy. *Science* 187:77–79

Squire, L. R., Zola-Morgan, S. 1983. The neurology of memory: the case for correspondence between the findings for man and non-human primate. In *The Physiological Basis of Memory,* ed. J. A. Deutsch, pp. 199–268. New York: Academic

Squire, L. R., Zola-Morgan, S. 1991. The medial temporal lobe memory system. *Science* 253:1380–86

Squire, L. R., Zola-Morgan, S., Cave, C. B., Haist, F., Musen, G., Suzuki, W. A. 1990. Memory: organization of brain systems and cognition. *Cold Spring Harbor Symp. Quant. Biol.* 55:1007–23

Squire, L. R., Zola-Morgan, S., Chen, K. 1988. Human amnesia and animal models of amnesia: performance of amnesic patients on tests designed for the monkey. *Behav. Neurosci.* 11:210–21

Srinivas, K., Roediger, H. L. I. 1990. Classifying implicit memory tests: category association and anagram solution. *J. Mem. Lang.* 29:389–413

Stadler, M. A. 1989. On learning complex procedural knowledge. *J. Exp. Psychol. Learn. Mem. Cogn.* 15:1061–69

Sutherland, R. W., Rudy, J. W. 1989. Configural association theory: the role of the hippocampal formation in learning, memory and amnesia. *Psychobiology* 17:129–44

Suzuki, W., Zola-Morgan, S., Squire, L. R., Amaral, D. G. 1991. Lesions of the perirhinal and parahippocampal cortices in monkeys produce a modality general and long lasting memory impairment. *Soc. Neurosci. Abstr.* 21:399

Teyler, T. J., Discenna, P. 1986. The hippocampal memory indexing theory. *Behav. Neurosci.* 100:147–54

Thompson, R. F. 1988. The neural basis of basic associative learning of discrete behavioral responses. *Trends Neurosci.* 11:152–55

Tulving, E. 1983. *Elements of Episodic Memory.* Cambridge: Oxford Univ. Press

Tulving, E. 1985. How many memory systems are there? *Am. Psychol.* 40:385–98

Tulving, E. 1991. Concepts in human memory. In *Memory: Organization and Locus of Change,* ed. L. R. Squire, N. M. Weinberger, G. Lynch, J. L. McGaugh, pp. 3–32. New York: Oxford Univ. Press

Tulving, E., Hayman, C. A. G., MacDonald, C. A. 1991. Long-lasting perceptual priming and semantic learning in amnesia: a case experiment. *J. Exp. Psychol. Learn. Mem. Cogn.* 17:595–617

Tulving, E., Schacter, D. L. 1990. Priming and human memory systems. *Science* 247:301–

6

Tulving, E., Schacter, D. L., Stark, H. 1982. Priming effects of word-fragment completion are independent of recognition memory. *J. Exp. Psychol. Learn. Mem. Cogn.* 8:336–42

Verfaellie, M., Cermak, L. S., Letourneau, L., Zuffante, P. 1991. Repetition effects in a lexical decision task: the role of episodic memory in alcoholic Korsakoff patients. *Neuropsychologia* 29:641–57

Victor, M., Adams, R. D., Collins, C. 1989. *The Wernicke-Korsakoff Syndrome and Related Neurological Disorders Due to Alcoholism and Malnutrition.* Philadelphia: Davis. 2nd ed.

Vokey, J. R., Brooks, L. R. 1992. Salience of item knowledge in learning artificial grammars. *J. Exp. Psychol.: Learn. Mem. Cogn.* 18:328–44

Wang, J., Aigner, T., Mishkin, M. 1990. Effects of neostriatal lesions on visual habit formation in rhesus monkeys. *Soc. Neurosci. Abstr.* 16:617

Warrington, E. K., McCarthy, R. A. 1987. Categories of knowledge: further fractionations and an attempted integration. *Brain* 110:1273–96

Warrington, E. K., Shallice, T. 1969. The selective impairment of auditory verbal short-term memory. *Brain* 92:885–96

Warrington, E. K., Shallice, T. 1984. Category specific semantic impairments. *Brain* 107:829–54

Warrington, E. K., Weiskrantz, L. 1982. Amnesia: a disconnection syndrome? *Neuropsychologia* 20:233–48

Waugh, N. C., Norman, D. A. 1965. Primary memory. *Psychol. Rev.* 72:89–104

Weiskrantz, L. 1990. Problems of learning and memory: one or multiple memory systems? *Philos. Trans. R. Soc. London Ser. B* 329:99–108

Weiskrantz, L., Warrington, E. K. 1979. Conditioning in amnesic patients. *Neuropsychologia* 17:187–94

White, S. H., Pillemer, D. B. 1979. Childhood amnesia and the development of a socially accessible memory system. In *Functional Disorders of Memory,* ed. J. F. Kihlstrom, F. J. Evans, pp. 29–47. Hillsdale, NJ: Erlbaum

Wible, C. G., Findling, R. L., Shapiro, M.,

Lang, E. J., Crane, S., et al. 1986. Mnemonic correlates of unit activity in the hippocampus. *Brain Res.* 399:97–110

Willingham, D. B., Nissen, M. J., Bullemer, P. 1989. On the development of procedural knowledge. *J. Exp. Psychol. Learn. Mem. Cogn.* 15:1047–60

Winocur, G. 1990. Anterograde and retrograde amnesia in rats with dorsal hippocampal or dorsomedial thalamic lesions. *Behav. Brain Res.* 38:145–54

Winocur, G., Rawlins, J. N. P., Gray, J. A. 1987. The hippocampus and conditioning to contextual cues. *Behav. Neurosci.* 101:617–27

Witherspoon, D., Moscovitch, M. 1989. Stochastic independence between two implicit memory tasks. *J. Exp. Psychol. Learn. Mem. Cogn.* 15:22–30

Wright, A. A., Santiago, H. C., Sands, S. F., Kendrick, D. F., Cook, R. G. 1985. Memory processing of serial lists by pigeons, monkeys and people. *Science* 229:287–89

Yamadori, A., Albert, M. L. 1973. Word category aphasia. *Cortex* 9:112–25

Zola-Morgan, S., Squire, L. R. 1984. Preserved learning in monkeys with medial temporal lesions: sparing of motor and cognitive skills. *J. Neurosci.* 4:1072–85

Zola-Morgan, S., Squire, L. R. 1990. The primate hippocampal formation: evidence for a time-limited role in memory storage. *Science* 250:288–90

Zola-Morgan, S., Squire, L. R. 1993. The neuroanatomy of memory. *Annu. Rev. Neurosci.* 16:547–63

Zola-Morgan, S., Squire, L. R., Amaral, D. G. 1986. Human amnesia and the medial temporal region: enduring memory impairment following a bilateral lesion limited to field CA1 of the hippocampus. *J. Neurosci.* 6:2950–67

Zola-Morgan, S., Squire, L. R., Amaral, D. G. 1989. Lesions of the hippocampal formation but not lesions of the fornix or the mammillary nuclei produce long-lasting memory impairment in monkeys. *J. Neurosci.* 9:898–913

Zola-Morgan, S., Squire, L. R., Mishkin, M. 1982. The neuroanatomy of amnesia: amygdala-hippocampus versus temporal stem. *Science* 218:1337–39

Annu. Rev. Psychol. 1993. 44:497-523

CULTURAL PSYCHOLOGY: WHO NEEDS IT?

Richard A. Shweder

Committee on Human Development, University of Chicago, Chicago, Illinois 60637

Maria A. Sullivan

Department of Psychiatry, Columbia Presbyterian Medical Center, New York, New York 10032

KEYWORDS: psychological anthropology, ethnopsychology, cross-cultural psychology, ethnicity emotions, self

CONTENTS

INTRODUCTION 497
CULTURAL PSYCHOLOGY: SOME CONTEXTS 498
   The Disciplinary Context 499
   The Historical Context 503
   The Institutional Context 504
CULTURAL PSYCHOLOGY: SOME ASSUMPTIONS 505
   The Study of "Experience-Near" Concepts 507
   Cultural Learning as the Refashioning of Inherited Complexity 512
   Universalism Without the Uniformity 514
CONCLUSION: THE DECADE OF ETHNICITY 517

INTRODUCTION

An interdisciplinary subfield called "cultural psychology" has begun to re-emerge at the interface of anthropology, psychology, and linguistics. The aim of cultural psychology is to examine ethnic and cultural sources of psychological diversity in emotional and somatic (health) functioning, self organization, moral evaluation, social cognition, and human development. Its goal is to understand why so many apparently straightforward questions about human psychological functioning (e.g. Are there basic emotions and which ones are they? Is human category learning a feature frequency process, an exemplar

0066-4308/93/0201-0497$02.00

comparison process, or a prototype comparison process? Is moral reasoning equivalent to reasoning about harm, rights, and justice? Under what conditions does classroom learning take place? Is there a mid-life crisis? How fundamental is the fundamental attribution error?) have not resulted in a consensus among qualified scientists, and why so many generalizations about the psychological functioning of one particular population (e.g. the contemporary secularized Western urban white middle class) have not traveled well across sociocultural, historical, and institutional fault lines. Sapir once wrote (1929:209), "the worlds in which different societies live are distinct worlds, not merely the same world with different words attached." The aim of cultural psychology is to understand the varieties of normal human consciousness across those historically and culturally constructed worlds (see Averill 1980; Geertz 1973, 1984b; Harré 1986a; Marriott 1989; Shweder 1991b; Shweder & Much 1987; Stearns & Stearns 1988; Taylor 1989).

The deep historical antecedents of cultural psychology have recently been traced in eye-opening detail by Jahoda 1992 (see also M. Cole 1988, 1990; Shweder 1984, 1990, 1991b). This essay (a) locates cultural psychology in its immediate disciplinary, historical, and institutional contexts; (b) mentions a few core assumptions and problematics of the field; (c) identifies key contributors to an emerging conception of cultural psychology; and (d) outlines some research agendas of the discipline, with selective reference to studies of emotion, self, social cognition, and health. Other contemporary formulations of the aims and assumptions of the field are available (Bruner 1990; M. Cole 1990; D'Andrade 1990; Howard 1985; LeVine 1984, 1990; Lutz 1985a,b; Lutz & White 1986; Markus & Kitayama 1991, 1992; P. Miller et al 1990; Peacock 1984; Rosaldo 1984; Shweder 1984, 1985, 1990, 1991b, 1992a,b; Shweder & Sullivan 1990; Stigler et al 1986; Wertsch 1985, 1991, 1992; White 1992a,b; see also D'Andrade & Strauss 1992; Fiske 1991; Harris 1991; Kurtz 1992; Lucy 1992a,b; Holland & Quinn 1987; Rosenberger 1992; Schwartz et al 1992; Shweder & LeVine 1984; Stigler et al 1990; White & Kirkpatrick 1985; see also the journals *Ethos: Journal of the Society for Psychological Anthropology, Culture, Medicine and Psychiatry* and the *Publications of the Society for Psychological Anthropology* published by Cambridge University Press).

CULTURAL PSYCHOLOGY: SOME CONTEXTS

Cultural psychology is, first of all, a designation for the comparative study of the way culture and psyche make each other up. Second, it is a label for a practical, empirical, and philosophical project designed to reassess the uniformitarian principle of psychic unity and aimed at the development of a credible theory of psychological pluralism. Third, it is a summons to reconsider the methods and procedures for studying mental states and psychological processes across languages and cultures. It is widely recognized that performance differences among human populations may arise from the partial translatability or limited commensurability of stimulus situations and materials (see M. Cole & Scribner 1974; MacIntyre 1985; see also Hollis & Lukes 1982; Wilson 1970). Far less appreciated is the fact that through the methodical investigation of specific sources of incommensurability in particular stimulus situations (so-called thick description) a culture's distinctive psychology may be revealed (Geertz 1973; Shweder 1991b).

The current excitement about the development of a cultural psychology is related to events in three contexts: a disciplinary context, an historical context, and an institutional context.

The Disciplinary Context

There are many stories that can be told about the reemergence of an interdisciplinary concern for the development of a cultural psychology at the interface of anthropology, psychology, and linguistics. Here is one brief tale (for the full story see Shweder 1990 and Shweder & Sullivan 1990).

In the late 1950s experimental work on animal learning and psycho-physics was considered real psychology and ethnographic work on ritual, myth, and kinship real anthropology. Yet the two disciplines had relatively little interaction. General psychology had little interest in the content, meaning, and distribution of human understandings and social practices; instead, the search was for universal psychic structures and the fundamental processes of consciousness. General anthropology had little interest in the person and his or her psychological functioning; its main goal was to document historical and ethnographic variations in collective representations and social institutions.

Today, after thirty years of intellectual diversification in psychology and anthropology (some disparage it as fragmentation, although we view it as progress), there are many opportunities for fruitful conversation between the disciplines. A semiotic agenda has become more prevalent in both fields. The items on the agenda include such questions as "What is meaning such that a situation can have it?" "What is a person such that what a situation means can determine his or her response to it?" "What meanings or conceptions of things have been stored up and institutionalized in everyday practice and discourse in various regions and cultural enclaves of the world?" "In what ways can different meanings have an effect on the organization and operation of individual consciousness?"

In anthropology there has been a resurgence of interest in person-centered ethnography, the study of local psychologies, and discourse-centered conceptions of mind, self, body, gender, motivation, and emotion (Abu-Lugod 1985, 1986; Briggs 1970; Crapanzano 1980; D'Andrade & Strauss 1992; Heelas & Lock 1981; Levy 1973, 1978, 1983, 1991; Obeyesekere 1981; Lutz 1988; Shostak 1983; Weisner 1984; White 1992a). It should be noted, however, that some scholars, for example B. Whiting and J. Whiting, have nurtured the anthropological flame of person-centered ethnography and kept it alive for well over half a century. For them interest in the topic has never waned (see

Whiting 1992; Whiting & Edwards 1985; also Spindler 1980). Research in developmental, social, and cognitive psychology has turned to a series of culture- and meaning-saturated topics such as appraisal, construal, conceptual framing, internal working models, expertise, and domain-specific learning (Barsalou 1991, 1992a,b,c; Bond 1988; Doi 1986; Ellsworth 1991; D. G. Freedman & J. Gorman, unpublished; Goodnow 1990; Kakar 1978, 1982; Lave 1990; Markus & Kitayama 1991; Medin 1989; J. G. Miller & Luthar 1989; Ross & Nisbett 1991; Russell 1989, 1991; Semin 1989; Semin & Fiedler 1988; Smith 1991; Stigler 1984; Wertsch 1985, 1991). Narrative, discourse, and situated learning have become familiar concepts on the intellectual landscape (Bruner 1990; Cohler 1991, 1992; Garvey 1992; Heath 1983; Lave 1990; P. Miller & Sperry 1987; P. Miller et al 1990, 1992; Rogoff 1990; Wertsch 1991). Processes once presumed to be fundamental, and hence fixed and uniform (e.g. the fundamental attribution error, self-aggrandizing motivations, patterns of self-other comparison, and moral reasoning as justice reasoning), have been reframed as local regularities embedded in culturally constructed and institutionally supported forms of self organization (Gilligan 1977, 1982; J. Haidt et al, unpublished; Markus & Kitayama 1991; J. G. Miller 1984; J. G. Miller & Bersoff 1992; Pepitone & Triandis 1987).

The semiotic agenda in anthropology and psychology has been reinforced by work in linguistics and philosophy on discourse and implicit meanings and by debates about the ambiguous and shifting boundary between semantic meanings and pragmatic meanings (P. Cole 1981; Flanagan 1991; Gergen 1986, 1990; Goody 1978; Goodman 1968, 1978; Labov & Fanshel 1977; Lakoff & Johnson 1980a,b; Lakoff 1987; Langacker 1986; MacIntyre 1981; Much 1983; Much & Shweder 1978; Shweder & Much 1987; Silverstein 1979; Taylor 1985; Talmy 1988; Wierzbicka 1985, 1991; Wittgenstein 1968; Wong 1984; Ziff 1972). Semantic meanings (e.g. that "bachelor" means a "marriageable unmarried male") are implications which are necessary, and hence unalterable and invariant, across all possible contexts of application and for all possible speakers. Pragmatic meanings (e.g. that "John is a lion" means that "John is brave"), in contrast, are implications that are dependent on the context and speaker. An influential position has emerged in philosophy, linguistics, and literary theory, which argues that necessary and intrinsic meanings (fixed essences) are few, difficult to locate, and perhaps even nonexistent (Derrida 1976; Fish 1980; Gendlin 1991; Gergen 1990; also see Putnam 1987, who argues against the existence of context-free or intrinsic laws of nature in the physical world). The implications of this pragmatic stance for the study of cultural psychology still need to be traced systematically (although see MacIntyre 1981). Nevertheless cultural psychology has grown up in an intellectual climate suspicious of a one-sided emphasis on fixed essences, intrinsic features, and universally necessary truths—an intellectual climate disposed to revalue processes and constraints that are local, variable, context-dependent, contingent, and in some sense made up.

While researchers in cultural psychology are still alert to the possible existence of cross-cultural empirical generalities, which might be derived from comparative research, new presumptions have emerged, e.g. that cultural and institutional factors particular to a population may have a major impact on the processes of psychological functioning and human development, and that local factors of a particular cultural environment typically interact with more widely distributed factors to produce diverse outcomes. While the possible existence of contingent empirical universals in psychological functioning is not denied in cultural psychology—a respectable cultural psychology is both "anti anti-relativist" (Geertz 1984a) and "anti anti-universalist" (Kilbride 1992)—uniformities in functioning are not privileged as deeper or as more fundamental, basic, or intrinsic truths about the life of the psyche.

Indeed one challenging goal for cultural psychology has been to find a way to document, acknowledge, and honor the reality of population or group differences in cognitive, emotional, motivational, and health functioning and in the patterning of the life course without underestimating our common humanity, without dismissing differences as measurement error, and without falling back on the interpretation of the other as a deficient or underdeveloped version of the self (for this view of the "other" as a deficient version of the self see Hallpike 1979 and Kohlberg 1981). For a critique of certain applications of developmental interpretation see Gilligan (1982), LeVine (1990), Shweder (1982a,b) and Shweder et al (1990).

Within the discipline of anthropology, one important historical watershed in the development of a cultural psychology was the initiative undertaken by the Social Science Research Council in 1980–81 to organize a conference entitled *Conceptions of Culture and its Acquisition.* The conference proceedings, later published under the title *Culture Theory: Essays on Mind, Self and Emotion* (Shweder & LeVine 1984), examined the relevance of a new Geertzian conception of culture for the study of psychological processes and reevaluated some assumptions of earlier forms of psychological anthropology, cognitive anthropology, and culture and personality studies in light of advances in the semiotic conception of the subject or person. That conception of culture (Geertz 1973:89), defined as "an historically transmitted pattern of meanings embodied in symbols, a system of inherited conceptions expressed in symbolic form by means of which men [and women] communicate, perpetuate and develop their knowledge about and attitudes towards life" continues to be influential today in discussions of the cultural psychology of mind, self, and emotion; *Culture Theory,* now in its tenth printing, has become a standard primer for students of cultural psychology.

A second watershed within anthropology was the publication of *Person, Self, and Experience* (White & Kirkpatrick 1985), which contained detailed ethnopsychologies of the culture areas of the Pacific Islands. A third watershed was an important review essay, published in the *Annual Review of Anthropology* (Lutz & White 1986), which catalyzed and legitimized anthropological research on the cultural psychology of the emotions. It was quickly followed by the publication of *Cultural Models in Language and Thought* (Holland & Quinn 1987), which had a similarly invigorating effect on research on the cultural psychology of cognition. (For a systematic overview of the cultural psychology of cognition see D'Andrade 1990; also Hutchins 1980; Nuckolls 1991).

Simultaneously in the field of psychology, H. Markus and R. Nisbett started a seminar at the Institute of Social Research at the University of Michigan entitled "Cultural Psychology," which was influential in defining an intellectual agenda for the internationalization of psychological theory and the pursuit of social psychological research related to ethnicity (see e.g. Markus & Kitayama 1991). Similar seminars and activities had long been a standard feature of intellectual life at the University of California at San Diego in Communications (under the leadership of M. Cole) and in Anthropology (under the leadership of R. D'Andrade, R. Levy, T. Schwartz, M. Spiro, and others), but in the 1980s forums relevant to cultural psychology began to flourish at various institutions around the country, most conspicuously at Harvard University (in Anthropology, Education, and Social Medicine under R. A. LeVine, A. Kleinman, B. Good, and others), at the University of Chicago (in the Committee on Human Development under J. Stigler, G. Herdt, P. Miller, R. Fogelson, S. Kurtz, E. Gendlin, B. Cohler, and others), at the University of California at Los Angeles (in Anthropology and Psychiatry under T. Weisner, E. Ochs, and others), at the University of Pennsylvania (in Psychology under P. Rozin, A. Fiske, and others), and at Emory University (in Anthropology under B. Shore, R. Paul, C. Nuckolls, and others, and more recently in connection with discussions at the Emory Cognition Project on the topic of the conceptual self under the direction of U. Neisser).

By the late 1980s a change in intellectual interest that cut across disciplinary boudaries was taking place. The expression "cultural psychology" was gaining currency (see M. Cole 1990; Howard 1985; Peacock 1984; Shweder & Sullivan 1990) and the designation of a new burgeoning subdiscipline was sparking great interest nationally and internationally. In 1986–87 two international and interdisciplinary symposia drawing together anthropologists and developmental psychologists were held at the University at Chicago and were published under the title *Cultural Psychology: Essays on Comparative Human Development* (see Stigler et al 1990). At the 1989 Biannual Meeting of the Society for Research on Child Development (SRCD), during the "Brunerfest"held in honor of Jerome Bruner, the guest of honor delivered a formal presentation to a standing room only audience in which he declared that much of his scholarly activity throughout his life should properly be called "cultural psychology" (see Bruner 1990); a separate SRCD panel session on cultural psychology also attracted a large enthusiastic audience.) By the time of the arrival of the well-publicized last decade of the 20th century it had become apparent to many social scientists that the 1990s was not only going to be the "decade of the brain," it was going to be the "decade of ethnicity" as well. Indeed, one suspects that the reemergence of cultural psychology is a measure of the culture-sensitive intellectual climate of our times.

The Historical Context

The historical context for the reemergence of cultural psychology can be addressed at both the national and the international level.

Nationally, the current attention of social scientists and policy analysts to ethnic and cultural diversity is largely motivated by the increasing recognition that there is no single population for research in the United States that can be treated as the normative base line for social and psychological functioning or for health and human development. Starting in 1964, US immigration policy resulted in significant changes in the cultural topography of many American cities. For example, between 1970 and 1990 the non-Hispanic white population of New York City dropped from 63% to 43% while there were major increases in the percentage of foreign born residents from Asia, the Caribbean, and Africa. Most major American cities from Los Angeles to Atlanta, from Chicago to Boston have active tribal associations for the Asanti people of Ghana; each community has a King and Queen and an elected group of elders, all anointed by the King of the Asantis in Ghana. Prominent South Asian religious figures now spend more time in temples in Pittsburgh and Queens than in traditional pilgrimage sites in India. A similar story can be told for many other ethnic groups. The United States is becoming a thought-provoking and cosmopolitan place, a land of internationally linked diversity.

Of course there are many complexities, even tensions associated with ethnic diversity in the context of civic norms in the United States. While the legal and political structure of the country, which tends to focus on the individual person as the bearer of rights and privileges, is unlikely to grant formal standing or authority to ethnic groupings, informal social processes have resulted in broad, rough and ready ethnic segmentation at the level of marriage and the family, neighborhoods, work sites, schools, apprenticeships, and patterns of affiliation and social support. Forty percent of plumbers, electricians, and carpenters in New York City trade unions learned their skills from a kin (typically their father) or neighbor. A recent map of Chicago published in *National Geographic Magazine* (May 1991) displays clear residential patterns based on ethnicity and race, with distinct Asian, Afro-American, Hispanic, and non-Hispanic white European neighborhoods.

Work sites and types of occupations can be roughly categorized by ethnicity as well. In New York City the fire department, for example, is predominantly serviced by Americans of Northern European descent (Irish, English, German), while workers in the apparel industry are predominantly Americans and foreign born immigrants of Puerto Rican and Dominican descent. It should be noted, however, that ethnic self-identification is itself a fascinating and complex process. For example, for immigrants to New York from Anglicized countries in the West Indies such as Jamaica, Antigua, or British Giana, a "West Indies" self-identification is something which follows rather than precedes life in Brooklyn, where everyone wants to be represented in the West Indies parade.

Nevertheless, whatever the social, and political implications of this new multiplicity in American society, the fact of ethnic self-consciousness and the persistence of a middle level of social organization that stands between the individual and the state has raised many questions about the reality and social origins of psychological and ethical diversity among populations, and about the limited appropriateness of presumptive universalizing notions of normal psychological functioning, health, and human development. Cultural psychology addresses these questions in a disciplined way and helps us overcome the unwitting ethnocentrism of much social and psychological theory, and the limitations of various question-begging methodologies for research.

A related concern arises on an international scale. A major intellectual problem facing the Western liberal democracies in the contemporary world is to develop an appropriate understanding of cultural diversity. Perhaps thirty or forty years ago it was reasonable to predict that tribes would be replaced by individuals, that religious meanings would be replaced by scientific understandings, and that history was inclined in the direction of a homogenous world culture of capitalist consumers who all spoke Esperanto (or English). Today these are no longer secure (or even reasonable) predictions. Should current trends continue—the global reemergence of primordial ethnic identifications, the decline in the authority of the hegemonic bureaucratic state, the tension between market values and communal values in the world system—public policy debates are likely to hinge on the answer one gives to the problem of diversity. While it is important to acknowledge that diversity is not always a measure of health or well-being, it is crucial to recognize that differences are not necessarily a mark of deficiency or a lower stage of development. On a worldwide scale there may be no single optimal pattern for social and psychological functioning, although further investigation is necessary. Multiple equilibria states for successful health and psychological functioning must be empirically explored. The very idea of multiple equilibria states must be theoretically enriched.

The Institutional Context

Cultural psychology is concerned, in part, with the contexts (disciplinary, historical, and institutional) that support psychological (including cognitive) functioning, and the development of a discipline of cultural psychology is not independent of the institutions that give life to scholarly activities focused on culture, ethnicity, and the internationalization of social and psychological theory. There are indications from agencies such as the National Center for Health Statistics (NCHS), the Census Bureau, the General Accounting Office (GAO), and the National Institute of Mental Health (NIMH) that interest is mounting within our public institutions for research on culture and ethnicity, with special interest in psychological and health processes and the role of local cultural models and norms of communication in the production and interpretation of answers to survey questions. One looks forward to the day when there might be an interdisciplinary National Science Foundation panel dedicated to those topics.

Nevertheless in the reemergence of cultural psychology, private research institutions (the MacArthur Foundation, the Russell Sage Foundation, the Spencer Foundation, the Rockefeller Foundation, the W. T. Grant Foundation, the Social Science Research Council [SSRC], and others) have been the major innovators in the development of the field.

In particular, the MacArthur Foundation Research Network on Successful Mid-Life Development (MIDMAC, chaired by G. Brim), the Research Network on Health-Related Behaviors (chaired by J. Rodin), and the Research Network on Successful Adolescence (chaired by R. Jessor) have supported various activities aimed at making research on health and human development not only interdisciplinary but culturally informed as well. They have sponsored conferences on such topics as *Ethnographic Approaches and Human Development* (organized by R. Jessor and A. Colby) and *Morality and Health* (organized by P. Rozin, A. Brandt, and S. Katz). An important sign of the times is the recent formation at the SSRC of a planning group on "Culture, Health, and Human Development" (co-chaired by A. Kleinman and R. LeVine) and an SSRC–MacArthur Foundation (MIDMAC) working group on ethnic and racial differences in developmental processes in New York City (chaired by L. Aber). The development of a cultural psychology has been relevant to the work of the Russell Sage Foundation on pluralism, immigration, and poverty; in principle, cultural psychology shares many intellectual aims with the international health interest of the Rockefeller Foundation and with the educational interests of the Spencer Foundation. The American Psychological Association recently sponsored the *International Conference on Culture and Emotion* (organized by S. Kitayama and H. Markus), and the Center for Advanced Study in the Behavioral Sciences is undertaking a special project to develop the cultural psychology research agenda. Thus, for a diversity of reasons, in a variety of contexts, cultural psychology seems to be in the air at the permeable boundaries of several disciplines and at the place where social science concerns, social policy concerns, and real life concerns deserve to intersect.

CULTURAL PSYCHOLOGY: SOME ASSUMPTIONS

Our readers are well aware that the social sciences are rife with invidious distinctions and divisive (and arguably false) dichotomies (innate vs learned, internal vs external, quantitative vs qualitative, natural vs cultural, universal vs relative, scientific vs interpretive, essential vs constructed, etc) that greatly facilitate the process of placing things in pigeonholes but all too often do so by short-circuiting the process of intellectual curiosity. In such an intellectual climate it is easy to misunderstand the aims and methods of a renewed cultural psychology: by mistakenly presuming that it is a version of an empty-organism learning theory, or that it is the study of cultural doctrines and ideologies rather than of lived realities, or that it is the voice of parochialism, solipsism, or radical relativism (see some of the concerns and criticisms expressed by Spiro 1984, 1986, 1990, 1992), or that it commits the error of essentializing group differences (see some of the concerns expressed by Gergen 1990; also Clifford & Marcus 1986; Kondo 1992). In order to clarify the aims of cultural psychology we offer three core assumptions of this reemerging field. We do not set forth these assumptions as canons or as orthodoxy but rather as a sample of the kinds of contestable assumptions that define current debates within the field.

We have already offered several initial definitions of the intellectual agenda of cultural psychology. One hallmark is its concern with cultural and ethnic divergences in the processes of consciousness. Cultural psychology endeavors to understand how such divergences relate to acts of interpretation and to the socially constructed meaning or representation of stimulus events. Systematic differences among populations have been found in the areas of attribution theory, categorization and similarity judgments, moral evaluation, processes of school learning, and in the organization of somatic and emotional responses to distress (Angel & Guarnaccia 1981; Angel & Idler 1992; Angel & Thoits 1987; J. Haidt et al, unpublished; Kleinman 1986; Markus & Kitayama 1992; J. G. Miller 1984; J. G. Miller & Bersoff 1992; Peak 1986; Pepitone & Triandis 1987; Shweder et al 1990; Stevenson & Stigler 1992; Stigler & Perry 1990; Tobin 1989).

For example, there are relatively well-documented systematic differences among populations in the organization of emotional and nonemotional (somatic) feeling states (Angel & Guarnaccia 1981; Angel & Idler 1992; Guarnaccia et al 1990; Kleinman 1986; Kleinman & Good 1985; Levy 1973, 1984; Shweder 1985, 1988, 1992a,b). In some populations various distress conditions (e.g. loss, goal blockage) are experienced and reacted to with nonemotional somatic feelings such as fatigue, chest pain, and headache. In other populations the same conditions are experienced and reacted to with emotional feelings such as anger or sadness. These differences in the processing of feeling states are automatic and unconscious, and display group level effects that call for explication in terms of local systems of meaning, value, and practice.

Whether such differences between populations should be conceptualized as the differential somatization of emotions or alternatively as the differential emotionalization of somatic experience is open for debate. Nevertheless, such group differences seem robust and systematic. They are evident, for example, on health surveys. Some populations seem far more likely than others to experience or report physical symptoms. These group differences are also revealed in the magnitude and direction of discrepancy scores between self-ratings of health and the health ratings given by physicians after a physical examination. Puerto Rican and Mexican-American populations in the US, for example, tend to rate themselves as being in far poorer health than is indicated by the ratings of their health made by physicians using the standard of a biomedical examination. Discrepancies between self-ratings and physicians' ratings for Euro-American populations are usually smaller, and when there is a deviation, it tends to be in the other direction (Angel & Guarnaccia 1981; Angel & Idler 1992).

Such population differences raise practical questions about the interpretation of health survey responses to standard questions such as "How would you rate your overall health?" It is not just the interpretation of the words "health" and "overall" that is problematic. The meaning of "your" presents some fascinating problems as well. It is a plausible hypothesis that individuals in some ethnic groups are less willing to state that they are in excellent health or are less able to experience themselves in excellent health when other members of the family are suffering; new research is needed on cultural variations in the degree to which personal health and collective health are experienced as separate issues. Such population differences also raise provocative theoretical questions about the cultural construction of emotional and nonemotional feeling states and about the institutionalization of health norms (see below).

The major goals then of cultural psychology are to spell out the implicit meanings that shape psychological processes, to examine the distribution of these meanings across cultural groups, and to identify the manner of their social acquisition. We now discuss three of the core assumptions of the field: (a) that cultural psychology is the study of "experience-near" concepts, (b) that cultural learning is the refashioning of inherited complexity, and (c) that the study of cultural psychology does not necessitate the blanket denial of universals because cultural psychology is a form of pluralism and pluralism is a special form of universalism. Indeed, an appropriate slogan for the discipline of cultural psychology might well be "universalism without the uniformity."

The Study of "Experience-Near" Concepts

It is assumed in cultural psychology that acts of interpretation and representation can take place so rapidly and unconsciously that they are experienced by informants or subjects as indistinguishable from consciousness itself, thereby creating the naive realist illusion that acts of consciousness are unmediated or direct. In other words to study cultural psychology (e.g. of self, emotion, cognition, etc) in some designated population (e.g. !Kung Bushmen, Oriya Brahmans, or Anglo-American college students) is to carry out a study in a realm where it is possible to "know more than we can tell" (Nisbett & Wilson

1977) and where conceptualization (by which we mean equivalence class formation and constrained inferencing) occurs rapidly, subliminally, and without deliberate or reflective calculation.

Cultural psychology is the study of constituted or compiled experiences (what Geertz has called "experience-near" concepts) in contrast to explicated experiences ("experience-distant" concepts). As Geertz notes (1984b:125): "People use experience-near concepts spontaneously, unselfconsciously, as it were colloquially; they do not, except fleetingly and on occasion, recognize that there are any 'concepts' involved at all." In the study of the cultural psychology of self (emotion, cognition) in an ethnic or cultural group, one must determine the concepts and beliefs implicit in the individuals' self-functioning (emotional functioning, cognitive functioning, etc), regardless of whether the members of the group (correctly or incorrectly) acknowledge those concepts and beliefs or spell them out for themselves.

Precisely how, or indeed whether, concepts and beliefs are implicated in psychological functioning is a controversial issue, and the appeal to implicit representations is not everyone's cup of tea. For the sake of argument we shall assume (following Kirsh 1991:164) that there are many aspects of psychological functioning "that do not presuppose use of a [fully] articulated world model... but which clearly rely on concepts [nonetheless]"; that "when [e.g.] a person composes a sentence, he [or she] is making a subliminal choice among dozens of words in hundreds of milliseconds"; that "there can be no doubt that conceptual representations of some sort are involved, although how this is done remains a total mystery"; and that (again following Kirsh) "if in language, why not elsewhere?" (also see Epstein 1992).

We assume, as well, that one can invoke conceptual representations in the study of psychological functioning even if the psychological system does not always (or even ever) operate on conceptual representations per se as long as a conceptual translation of the psychological system is possible and a conceptual story can be told about how the psychological system is designed, constituted, or compiled.

Consider, for example, Markus & Kitayama's (1991) study of the cultural psychology of the self. The focus of the research is on something called a "conceptual representation of the self." A distinction is drawn between an "independent" and "interdependent" conceptual representation of the self, which Markus & Kitayama believe is useful in interpreting population differences (e.g. US vs Japan), in cognitive performance (e.g. counterfactual reasoning, similarity judgments), emotional experience (e.g. the predominant conditions that elicit many emotions, which emotions are expressed and experienced, and their intensity and frequency), and motivational functioning (e.g. the role of hedonic reward and the extent to which the maintenance of high self-regard becomes an addiction or fundamental motive). (With regard to research on contrastive conceptual representations of the self—independent vs interdependent, egocentric vs sociocentric, individualist vs collectivist—see

Bond et al 1982; Cousins 1989; Doi 1973, 1986; Dumont 1965, 1970; Geertz 1984b; Gilligan 1982; Kim & Choi 1992; Lebra 1976, 1983; Marriott 1976; J. G. Miller & Bersoff 1992; Smith Noricks et al 1987; Roland 1989; Rosaldo 1984; Sampson 1988; Shweder 1984; Shweder & Bourne 1984; Shweder et al 1990; Triandis 1989, 1990).

In other words, Markus & Kitayama's theory of "conceptual representations of the self" concerns thought in action, and their claims about cultural divergences in the conceptual representation of the self are not claims about cross-cultural variations in (official or heterodox) doctrines about the self that are encoded in collective representations, or even about an individual's explicit self-concept, except to the extent that collective representations and explicit self-concepts influence thought in action (as they sometimes do when they become part of a socially or personally enforced system of self-construction and control).

In this context a comment by Neisser (1988) is helpful. In his seminal essay on aspects of the self Neisser writes, with characteristic flare, "There is a remarkable variety in what people believe about themselves, and not all of it is true." We think the proper response, from the point of view of cultural psychology, ought to be [and here we paraphrase and extend a formulation in Kirsh 1991], "That's right! Introspection is a misleading indicator of when concepts and beliefs are causally involved in action and an even worse indicator of which concepts and beliefs are causally involved in action." In other words, no practitioner of cultural psychology should claim that a metaphysical speculation in a theological text must directly reflect the true functioning of the self in the everyday life of its author. One might, however, be inspired by the text to construct a theoretical model of a conceptual representation of the self that may prove useful in accounting for some people's psychological functioning.

The implication of the assumption that cultural psychology is first and foremost the study of experience-near concepts is this: If we study the cultural psychology of self (emotion, cognition, etc), we must construct our own theories about when, which, and how concepts and beliefs may be causally involved in a person's actions and reactions to the world. We must be careful not to confuse the study of the explicated self, which is conceptual all right because all articulated world models must be, with the study of the constituted or compiled self, which is not only conceptual but is (by our definition) that aspect of psychological functioning in which concepts and beliefs are causally involved in action.

In other words, "conceptual representation" designates a theoretical model, constructed by the investigator, that identifies those experience-near concepts that organize and help make sense of the actual psychological functioning of some person or people. Because the focus of research in cultural psychology is on experience-near concepts, the conceptual representations studied in cultural psychology are not necessarily equivalent to the native's explicit model of his or her psychological world. Nevertheless, in principle, one cannot rule out the possibility that, in any particular study, the conceptual representation constructed by the investigator and the native's articulated model of his or her psychological world might converge. In practice they sometimes do.

Thus, for example, a cultural psychology study of a conceptual representation of a self with "permeable boundaries" does not primarily refer to a person's explicit self-concept or to a people's articulated folk concept. Instead it refers to a way of theoretically representing certain aspects of a person's or people's functioning, e.g. that they are vulnerable to spirit attack, trance, or hypnosis; that many personal events (a bad dream, a dark or ignoble thought) are experienced as ego-alien forces or pollutions that have entered the body and can be exorcised or washed away. The status of such theoretical models of the self is analogous to the status of a grammarian's representations of speech performance. Competent speakers of a language may have explicit folk models or theories about the grammar of their language (and those who study ethnolinguistic theories will want to document them), but such folk models are not a primary focus for the grammarian's theory of constituted or compiled language use.

In other words, explicated concepts and beliefs—for example, that the human body may become polluted because it is a temple for the soul (Shweder 1985), that mental life is animated by a god who makes perception and experience possible (Parish 1991), that part of a person cannot be seen and is also part of another world, that good beings are part of that world, that this unseen element enables one to be a good person, that this aspect never dies, that this part of a person connects one to a divine realm (Wierzbicka 1989), or, to switch from a Hindu and Christian to a Buddhist conceptualization of the self, that the sense of self is epiphenomenal and illusory and there really is no self at all (Huebner & Garrod 1991; also see Minsky 1985 for an analogous Buddhist-like conceptualization of artificial intelligence)—are theoretical constructs that have relevance for the study of the constituted or compiled self only to the extent that they illuminate some person or people's lived experience.

The question of the proper unit of analysis for cultural psychology, however, is not so readily resolved, and is thus far more interesting and dynamic than the easy separation of explicit models from constituted actualities or metaphysical musings from hard realities. In certain types of communities, with certain processes of social control, an explicated model (of self, emotion, etc) can be more than a metaphysical speculation or a hazardous personal hypothesis about oneself. With Neisser's cogent comment in mind, one might say that while there is remarkable cross-cultural variety in what people believe about themselves, there are also many processes at work—political processes involving power (sanctioning systems), social communication processes comprising the selective flow of symbols and meanings (for example, story-telling), intra-psychic processes involving self-monitoring and feelings of dignity, esteem, shame, guilt, disgust, pollution, and humiliation—designed to make those beliefs and doctrines true, to compile the constituted self on the model of an explicated self, and to articulate and canonize a representation of a self that is modeled on what has already been constituted or compiled (see e.g. H. Fung, unpublished; Garvey 1992; LeVine 1984, 1990; M. Mahapatra et al, unpublished; P. Miller et al 1990, 1992; Ochs & Schieffelin 1984; Schieffelin & Ochs 1986; Shweder & Much 1987; Shweder et al 1992).

We predict that those who link the study of cultural psychology (the theoretical representation of the experience-near concepts that organize psychological functioning) with the study of ethno-psychology (the documentation of a culture's explicit models of and for psychological functioning; see D'Andrade 1987; Kurtz 1992; M. Sullivan, unpublished; White 1992a) will discover that some of the best theoretical models are derived from the articulated models of those cultures where what is explicated and what is constituted do not live separate lives. It is misleading to think that cultural conceptions must be located either outside the person or inside the person. In an authentic culture, cultural conceptions are likely assembled or reproduced in both places at once, and probably for good psychological reasons. Gibson's (1979) account of "affordances" seems relevant here. Culture and psyche "afford" each other, which is another way of saying they make each other up.

It has been necessary to discuss in detail the assumption that experience-near concepts are the proper unit of analysis for cultural psychology and to consider some of the complexities of that assumption. This emphasis is essential because there is considerable ambiguity in the anthropological literature about the meaning of the expression a "cultural conception of ... ." Where there is ambiguity there is bound to be "cross-talk," misunderstanding, and difficulty in fixing the topic for any debate (e.g. see the transcripts of the colloquy entitled "What is the problem of the self anyway?" in Shweder & LeVine 1984:12–17).

Thus, when some anthropologists write about a cultural conception of the self, they mean the explicated self—in the sense of church doctrine or another's official view of the self. This view is associated with a definition of a culture as a "cognitive system encoded in collective representations" (Spiro 1984:323–25). For Spiro, a cultural conception of the self, emotion, body, or gender is a tradition-laden set of ideas or meanings that can be formulated as a series of propositions and is encoded in collective representations rather than in the thoughts, feelings, or actions of any or all individuals. For Spiro a "cultural conception" of self, of emotion, etc) is definitely not in the head, or in the heart, or in the guts; it is something outside the person. (See also Spiro 1992, although his critique of cross-cultural studies of the self is somewhat vitiated when it is recognized that in cultural psychology a cultural conception refers primarily to the theoretical spelling out of an experience-near concept and not to an explicit ethno-psychological formulation by the native.)

For other anthropologists a cultural conception of the self means the constituted or compiled self. This view is associated with a definition of a culture as precisely those meanings, conceptions, and interpretive schemes that are activated, constructed, or brought on-line through participation in normative social institutions and practices (including linguistic practices). In our own theoretical elaboration of this view (e.g. Shweder 1991b:18), a culture is a subset of "mind"; mind (assumed to be latently available and accessible through each individual's nervous system) is conceptualized as an "etic grid," a heterogeneous and inherently complex collection of all possible or available meanings. A culture, from this analytic perspective, is that subset of possible or available meanings, which by virtue of enculturation (informal or formal, implicit or explicit, unintended or intended) has so given shape to the psychological processes of individuals in a society that those meanings have become, for those individuals, indistinguishable from experience itself. From this point of view, one important aspect of the study of cultural learning is to identify the social, political, and psychological processes that explain how, when, and which meanings are brought "on- and off-line," are turned into local essences, or are kept more or less permanently suppressed. A second aspect of the study of cultural learning is described below.

Cultural Learning as the Refashioning of Inherited Complexity

Cultural psychology assumes that cultural learning is usefully conceptualized as the refashioning of what is inherited, prior, built-in, or given. In human beings, as in other species, learning processes are not incompatible with the existence of an inherited system of complex forms. Indeed, learning may be thought of as the transformation of what is given by the past, and one of the goals of cultural psychology is to develop a theory of how those transformations take place for the semiotic subject of cultural psychology, for whom the culturally and historically activated meaning of a situation or stimulus event is a major constraint on his or her response to it.

Sometimes cultural learning transformations take place because received or inherited forms that lacked meaning have been turned into symbolic forms (i.e. they become vehicles for local systems of signification). We refer to this type of cultural learning as a transformation through symbolization. This process is illustrated by the inversion of affective associations that takes place when English speakers listen to the sound patterns "queep" and "deep" (Whorf 1956:257). "Queep" is a sound pattern that has no meaning and, as a nonsense syllable, elicits a universal set of affective associations: Throughout the world the sound pattern "queep" is experienced in terms of affective tone as fast (not slow), narrow (not wide), sharp (not dull), light (not dark). Yet from a phonetic point of view "deep" and "queep" are very similar sound patterns, and indeed, on a worldwide scale they elicit the same set of associations (fast, narrow, sharp, light) from those peoples for whom both sounds are nonsense sounds. Yet "deep" is not a nonsense sound for English speakers; it is a sound pattern with significance. Uniquely for English speakers the affective associations of the sound pattern "deep" are transformed, indeed inverted, by its meaning. Embedded in or appropriated to the semantics of the English lexicon, "deep" has acquired a parochial or culture-specific set of routine, automatic, and self-involving affective associations as slow, wide, dull, and dark.

A second type of cultural learning transformation takes place when the structures for experience made available within a local cultural world result in the differential activation, maintenance, or loss of available mental or symbolic forms. Following Werker (1989) we shall refer to this type of cultural learning as a "maintenance-loss" transformation. As Werker has shown through her research on listening in infants, infants come into the world with a detailed and elaborated capacity to detect categorical distinctions in sound. They are able to perceive exotic language-specific phonemic distinctions (e.g. the difference between an aspirated and unaspirated "t" sound in Hindi) that do not exist in the ambient language environment of their parents and that their own parents are unable to hear and have difficulty learning.

If this capacity of the infant is kept activated through even a small amount of second language learning during the second year of life (e.g. an American infant with English speaking parents who lives in India for the first 18 months of life and produces a few words of Hindi before returning to America), it is maintained into adulthood. More typically it disappears by the end of the first year of life, with the onset of exclusive single language learning. Here we have a case of apparent "unlearning," where a smaller subset of preexisting forms are kept alive, while a larger subset of preexisting forms become lost, dormant, or difficult to access.

One implication of our examples of cultural learning is that infants do not come into the world innocent or as blank slates. There is no tabula rasa. Cultural learning does not presuppose an empty organism. Infants are complex at birth and already primed with a nervous system that responds in structured ways to "deep" and "queep" as fast, sharp, light, and narrow, and is able to detect a heterogeneous set of exotic language-specific phonemic contrasts. Learning is the transformation of what is given and does not necessarily presuppose that infants come into the world naive or identical. In other words, human beings enter the world already equipped with a complex and heterogeneous array of differentiated interpretive schemes, some of which are activated and transformed throughout the life course.

A second implication of our examples is that there may be aspects of psychological functioning that are empirical universals in infancy but are not cross-cultural universals for adults. We do not mean to suggest that everyone is uniform at birth (see e.g. Freedman 1974; Super 1981 on population differences in neonatal response tendencies). Rather, it is our point that some things that are universally present in infancy are differentially lost or suppressed as a result of cultural learning, and the complexity and sophistication of the inherited past, which semiotic subjects bring with them into the world at birth, can be reworked or refashioned in different ways through participation in the practices (including language and discourse practices) of a local and particularizing cultural world.

Universalism Without the Uniformity

A primary concern of cultural psychology is the divergences in the experience-near concepts that organize and make sense of population differences in normal psychological functioning. It would be a mistake, however, to conclude that because cultural psychology is concerned with the divergent, discretionary, or optional aspects of normal psychological functioning, it denies that within a certain range of environments there may exist widely distributed or even universal features of a normal mental life (see Edgerton 1992). Whether or not there are empirical universals of the mental life, and what they are, is an empirical issue, which implies very little about the existence of an inherent or intrinsic feature of normal psychological functioning (again see Putnam 1987 for a critique of the intrinsic).

One can be an "anti anti-relativist" and an "anti anti-universalist" at the same time. Cultural psychology documents divergent forms of normal psychological functioning and critiques the idea of necessary or intrinsic processes of mind. Cultural psychology does not deny the possibility of empirical or contingent universals, for it is a mistake to assume that the idea of the intrinsic implies a universal distribution or that processes that are widely distributed must be intrinsic.

For example, we suspect that very few researchers would quarrel with LeVine's observation (Shweder & LeVine 1984:14) that "in all cultures there [is] some perception of the self as a continuous entity in time and as, in some sense, the same person. There [is] some kind of distinction between internal experience and external things." In other words, although the boundaries between internal and external may vary in scope and permeability across cultural communities, the concept of an individuated person or self is widely distributed across a broad range of cultural and informational environments, and there may in fact be no place where normal members of the society (religious virtuosos aside) conduct their lives as though they simply merged with one another.

Geertz (1984b:126), for example, whose essay on variations in the self in Bali, Java, and Morocco is both influential and controversial, is often quoted,

> The Western conception of the person as a bounded, unique, more or less integrated motivational and cognitive universe, a dynamic center of awareness, emotion, judgment and action organized into a distinctive whole and set contrastively both against other such wholes and against its social and natural

background, is, however incorrigible it may seem to us, a rather peculiar idea within the context of the world's cultures.

The beginning of the paragraph, however, is rarely quoted:

> But at least some conception of what a human individual is, as opposed to a rock, an animal, a rainstorm, or a god, is, so far as I can see universal.

Dumont, whose relativistic writings on the Western conception of the individual (1965, 1970) have also been influential and controversial, begins *Homo Hierarchicus* by drawing some distinctions. He writes,

> To start with, much imprecision and difficulty arises from failing to distinguish in the "individual": 1- *the empirical agent present in every society* in virtue of which he is the raw material of any sociology. 2- the rational being and *normative subject* of institutions; this is peculiar to us as shown by the value of equality and liberty.

In other words, Geertz and Dumont are not only anti anti-relativist; they are apparently anti anti-universalist as well. So are most researchers in cultural psychology, who believe that the constituted self is variable across temporal and spatial regions of the world, and that it is possible to characterize that variation with theoretical contrasts between independence vs interdependence, individualistic vs communal, egocentric vs socio-centric, autonomy vs community vs divinity, bounded vs permeable, and so forth (see e.g. Gaines 1982; Kim & Choi 1992; Markus & Kitayama 1991; Marriott 1976; J. G. Miller 1984; J. G. Miller & Bersoff 1992; Shweder & Bourne 1984; Shweder et al 1990; Shweder et al 1992; Triandis 1989, 1990). Essences reside in theoretical models. That is a proper place for them, before they are psychologically brought "on-line," only to be maintained or transformed through processes of cultural learning.

That the study of variety in psychological functioning is not burdened by a blanket denial of universals can be demonstrated by the study of the cultural psychology of the emotions. In recent years there has been much excitement in cultural psychology about research on variations in the emotional meanings (e.g. Ifaluk "fago," Pintupi "watjilpa," Newar "lajya," American "happiness," Ilongot "linget") that are brought "on-line" or constructed among different ethnic groups and in different regions of the world (e.g. Abu-Lughod 1985, 1986; Appadurai 1985; Brennis 1990; Briggs 1970; Epstein 1984; Fajans 1983; Geertz 1959; Gerber 1985; Good & Kleinman 1984; Heider 1991; Herdt 1990; Jenkins & Karno 1992; Kapferer 1979; Keeler 1983; Kleinman & Good 1985; Levy 1984; Levy & Wellenkamp 1989; Lutz & White 1986; Lynch 1990; Mesquita & Fridja 1992; Lutz 1982, 1988; P. Miller & Sperry 1987; Myers, 1979a,b; Parish 1991; Rosaldo 1980, 1983, 1984; Rozin & Nemeroff 1990; Russell 1991; Scherer et al 1986; Schieffelin 1976, 1983, 1985; Seymour 1983; Smedslund 1991; Solomon 1984; Stearns & Stearns 1988; Swartz 1988; Wierzbicka 1986, 1990; Wikan 1984, 1989). An approach to the comparative study of emotions is emerging in which, for the sake of establishing translation equivalence, emotions are viewed as complex intentional states that can be decomposed into parameters, components, frames, or "narrative slots" (see e.g. Ellsworth 1991; Lewis 1989; Mesquita & Fridja 1992; Russell 1991; Shweder 1985, 1992a,b; Stein & Levine 1987).

The cultural psychology of the emotions investigates whether cultural groups are alike or different in their emotional functioning by dividing that question into several more specific ones. While the questions or parameters vary somewhat from scholar to scholar, the following are worthy of note:

1. Environmental determinants: Are members of different cultural groups alike or different in the antecedent conditions of the world (e.g. violating a rule, job loss) that elicit somatic and affective feelings?
2. Self-appraisal: Are members of different cultural groups alike or different in the perceived implications for the self (e.g. status loss, fame, goal block-age) of those antecedent conditions of the world?
3. Somatic phenomenology: Are members of different cultural groups alike or different in their somatic reactions (e.g. muscle tension, headaches) to those antecedent conditions of the world?
4. Affective phenomenology: Are members of different cultural groups alike or different in their affective reactions (e.g. feelings of emptiness, calm, expansiveness) to those antecedent conditions of the world?
5. Social appraisal: Are members of different cultural groups alike or different in the extent to which displaying those somatic and affective reactions has been socially baptized a vice or virtue or a sign of sickness or health?
6. Self-management: Are members of different cultural groups alike or differ-ent in the plans for the management of self-esteem that are activated as part of an emotional action routine (e.g. withdrawal, celebration, attack)?
7. Communication: Are members of different cultural groups alike or differ-ent in the iconic or symbolic vehicles (e.g. facial expressions, voice, pos-ture) for expressing the whole cluster of interconnected components (Ques-tions 1–6 above)?

Given this decomposition of an emotion into its narrative slots, the cultural psychology of the emotions becomes, in part, the study of whether the vari-ables from each of those slots display the same pattern of relationships across human groups. Notice, however, that this type of research in cultural psychol-ogy, which is aimed at characterizing differences in emotional functioning across human groups, presupposes the existence of a set of analytic or concep-tual universals, which is the particular meta-language for comparison, in terms of narrative slots such as self-appraisal, social appraisal, and somatic phenom-enology.

These various examples illustrate that one of the goals of theory in cultural psychology is to understand variety in the mental states and processes of others while avoiding the philosophical pitfalls and incoherences of claims of variety without unity. Its aim is to document genuine differences without turning the other into an incomprehensible alien (or "stranger" as Spiro 1990 put it).

There are undoubtedly many ways to reconcile human variety with our common humanity. One way is to argue that what everyone has in common, what unifies and in a sense universalizes us is itself a heterogeneous complex of inherited psychological processes and forms. These processes and forms are activated, institutionalized, and rationalized by various cultures selectively and differentially, but considered as a complex whole and examined theoretically as an etic grid, make the study of cultural psychology possible. From this point of view psychic unity is what makes us imaginable to one another, not what makes us the same (see Shweder 1991a, 1991b:18), and the goal of theory in cultural psychology is to develop a conception of psychological pluralism or group difference psychology that might be described as "universalism without the uniformity." The future of the reemergent discipline of cultural psychology depends on the richness of just such a conception. How this theory of "universalism without the uniformity" will develop and whether it can be made fully convincing remains to be seen.

CONCLUSION: THE DECADE OF ETHNICITY

For a variety of compelling reasons—disciplinary, historical, institutional, theoretical, and empirical—a science concerned with diversity in health, human development, and psychological functioning has reemerged at the interface of anthropology and psychology under the banner of "cultural psychology." The 1990s is the decade of ethnicity. It should also be the decade when anthropologists and psychologists (and linguists and philosophers) unite to deepen our understanding of the varieties of normal human consciousness.

ACKNOWLEDGMENTS

Some ideas for this essay were developed while Shweder was a Visiting Scholar at the Russell Sage Foundation, and with the support of the Health Program of the John D. and Catherine T. MacArthur Foundation. We are grateful to Gilbert Brim for his helpful comments on the manuscript.

Literature Cited

Abu-Lughod, L. 1985. Honor and the sentiments of loss in a Bedouin society. *Am. Ethnol.* 12:245–61

Abu-Lughod, L. 1986. *Veiled Sentiments: Honor and Poetry in a Bedouin Society.* Berkeley: Univ. Calif. Press. 317 pp.

Angel, R., Guarnaccia, P. 1981. Mind, body and culture: somatization among Hispanics. *Soc. Sci. Med.* 12(28):1229–38

Angel, R., Idler, E. L. 1992. Somatization and hypocondriasis: sociocultural factors in subjective experience. *Res. Community Ment. Health* 7:71–93

Angel, R., Thoits, P. 1987. The impact of culture on the cognitive structure of illness. *Cult. Med. Psychiatry* 11:465–94

Appadurai, A. 1985. Gratitude as a social mode in South India. *Ethos* 13:236–45

Averill, J. 1980. A constructivist view of emotion. In *Emotion, Theory, Research and Experience,* ed. R. Plutchik, H. Kellerman. New York: Academic

Barsalou, L. W. 1991. Deriving categories to achieve goals. In *The Psychology of Learning and Motivation: Advances in Research and Theory,* ed. G. H. Bower, 27:1–64. San Diego, Calif.: Academic

Barsalou, L. W. 1992a. Frames, concepts, and conceptual fields. In *Frames, Fields, and Contrasts: New Essays in Semantic and Lexical Organization,* ed. E. Kittay, A. Lehrer, pp. 21–74. Hillsdale, NJ: Erlbaum

Barsalou, L. W. 1992b. Components of conceptual representation: from feature lists to recursive frames. In *Theoretical Views and Inductive Data Analysis,* ed. I. Van Mechelen, J. Hampton, R. Michalski, P. Theuns. San Diego, Calif.: Academic. In press

Barsalou, L. W. 1992c. Structure, flexibility and linguistic vagary in concepts: manifestations of a compositional system of perceptual symbols. In *Theories of Memory,* ed. A. C. Collins, S. E. Gathercole, M. A. Conway. Hillsdale, NJ: Erlbaum

Bond, M. H., ed. 1988. *The cross-cultural challenge to social psychology.* Newbury Park, Calif.: Sage. 337 pp.

Bond, M. H., Leung, K., Wan, K. C. 1982. How does cultural collectivism operate? *J. Cross-cultural Psych.* 13:186–200

Brennis, D. 1990. Shared and solitary sentiments: the discourse of friendship, play and anger in Bhatgaon. In *Language and the Politics of Emotion,* ed. C. Lutz, L. Abu-Lughod, pp. 113–125. New York: Cambridge Univ. Press

Briggs, J. L. 1970. *Never in Anger: Portrait of an Eskimo Family.* Cambridge, Mass.: Harvard Univ. Press. 379 pp.

Bruner, J. S. 1990. *Acts of Meaning.* Cambridge, Mass.: Harvard Univ. Press. 179 pp.

Clifford, J., Marcus, G. E., eds. 1986. *Writing Culture.* Berkeley: Univ. Calif. Press. 305 pp.

Cohler, B. 1991. The life-story and the study of resilience and response to adversity. *J. Narrative and Life-History* 1:169–200

Cohler, B. 1992. Aging, morale, and meaning: the nexus of narrative. In *Voices and Contexts: Towards a Critical Gerontology.* New York: Springer. In press

Cole, M. 1988. Cross-cultural research in the sociohistorical tradition. *Hum. Dev.* 31:137–57

Cole, M. 1990. Cultural psychology: a once and future discipline? In *Cross-cultural Perspectives. Nebraska Symposium on Motivation, 1989,* ed. J. J. Berman. Lincoln: Univ. of Nebraska Press. 227 pp.

Cole, M., Scribner, S. 1974. *Culture and Thought: A Psychological Introduction.* New York: Wiley. 227 pp.

Cole, P. 1981. *Radical Pragmatics.* New York: Academic. 328 pp.

Cousins, S. 1989. Culture and selfhood in Japan and the U. S. *J. Personality Soc. Psychol.* 56:124–31

Crapanzano, V. 1980. *Tuhami: Portrait of a Moroccan.* Univ. Chicago Press. 187 pp.

D'Andrade, R. G. 1987. A folk model of the mind. See Holland & Quinn 1987

D'Andrade, R. G. 1990. Some propositions about the relations between culture and human cognition. See Stigler et al 1990, pp. 65–129

D'Andrade, R. G., Strauss, C., eds. 1992. *Human Motives and Cultural Models.* New York: Cambridge Univ. Press. 238 pp.

Derrida, J. 1976. *Of Gramatology.* Transl. G. C. Spivak. Baltimore, Md.: Johns Hopkins Univ. Press. 354 pp.

Doi, L. T. 1973. *The Anatomy of Dependence.* Tokyo: Kodansha. 170 pp.

Doi, L. T. 1986. *The Anatomy of Self.* Tokyo: Kodansha. 170 pp.

Dumont, L. 1965. The modern conception of the individual: notes on its genesis. *Contrib. Indian Sociol.* 66:13–61

Dumont, L. 1970. *Homo Hierarchicus.* Univ. Chicago Press. 386 pp.

Edgerton, R. B. 1992. *Sick Societies: Challenging the Myth of Primitive Harmony.* New York: Free Press

Ellsworth, P. 1991. Some implications of cognitive appraisal theories of emotion. *Int. Rev. Stud. Emot.* 1:143–61

Epstein, A. L. 1984. *The Experience of Shame in Melanesia.* London: Royal Anthropol. Inst. 58 pp.

Epstein, S. L. 1992. The role of memory and concepts in learning. *Minds and Machines.* 2:239–62

Fajans, J. 1983. Shame, social action, and the person among the Baining. *Ethos* 11:166–80

Fish, S. E. 1980. *Is There a Text in This Class? The Authority of Interpretive Communities.* Cambridge, Mass.: Harvard Univ. Press. 394 pp.

Fiske, A. P. 1991. *Structures of Social Life, The Four Elementary Forms of Human Relations: Communal Sharing, Authority Ranking, Equality Matching, Market Pricing.* New York: Free Press. 480 pp.

Flanagan, O. 1991. *Varieties of Moral Personality: Ethics and Psychological Realism.* Cambridge, Mass.: Harvard Univ. Press. 393 pp.

Freedman, D. G. 1974. *Human Infancy.* Hillsdale, NJ: Erlbaum. 212 pp.

Freedman, D. G., Gorman, J. 1992. Attachment, internal working models and cultural transmission. Manuscript, Committee on Hum. Dev., Univ. Chicago

Fung, H. 1987. Early talk about the past: some sociocultural reflections of two Chinese children's narratives of personal experience. Trial Res. Pap., Univ Chicago

Gaines, A. D. 1982. Cultural definitions, behavior and the person in American psychiatry. In *Cultural Conceptions of Mental Health and Therapy,* ed. A. Marsella, G. White, pp. 167–91. Dordrecht, The Netherlands: Reidel

Garvey, C. 1992. Talk in the study of socialization and development. *Merrill-Palmer Q.* 38(1)

Geertz, C. 1973. *The Interpretation of Cultures.* New York: Basic Books. 470 pp.

Geertz, C. 1984a. Anti anti-relativism. *Am. Anthropol.* 86:263–78

Geertz, C. 1984b. From the native's point of view. See Shweder & LeVine 1984, pp. 123–36

Geertz, H. 1959. The vocabulary of emotion: a study of Javanese socialization processes. *Psychiatry* 22:225–36

Gendlin, E. T. 1991. Thinking beyond patterns: body, language and situation. In *The Presense of Feeling in Thought,* ed. B. den Ouden, M. Moen. New York: Peter Lang

Gerber, E. R. 1985. Rage and obligation: Samoan emotions in conflict. See White & Kirkpatrick 1985, pp. 121–67

Gergen, K. J. 1986. Correspondence vs. autonomy in the language of understanding human action. In *Metatheory in Social Science: Pluralisms and Subjectivities,* ed. D. Fiske, R. A. Shweder, pp.136–62 Chicago: Univ. Chicago Press

Gergen, K. J. 1990. Social understanding and the inscription of self. In *Cultural Psychology,* ed. J. Stigler, R. Shweder, G. Herdt, pp. 569–607. New York: Cambridge Univ. Press

Gibson, J. J. 1979. *The Ecological Approach to Visual Perception.* Boston: Houghton Mifflin. 332 pp.

Gilligan, C. 1977. In a different voice: women's conceptions of the self and of morality. *Harvard Educ. Rev.* 47:481–517

Gilligan, C. 1982. *In a Different Voice: Psychological Theory and Women's Development.* Cambridge, Mass.: Harvard Univ. Press. 184 pp.

Good, B. J., Kleinman, A. M. 1984. Culture and anxiety: cross-cultural evidence for the patterning of anxiety disorders. In *Anxiety and the Anxiety Disorders,* ed. A. H. Tuma, J. D. Maser. Hillsdale, NJ: Erlbaum

Goody, E., ed. 1978. *Questions and Politeness: Strategies in Social Interaction.* New York: Cambridge Univ. Press. 323 pp.

Goodman, N. 1968. *Languages of Art.* Indianapolis: Bobbs Merill. 277 pp.

Goodman, N. 1978. *Ways of Worldmaking.* New York: Hackett. 142 pp.

Goodnow, J. J. 1990. The socialization of cognition: what's involved? See Stigler et al 1990, pp. 259–86

Guarnaccia, P. J., Good, B. J., Kleinman, A. 1990. A critical review of Puerto Rican mental health. *Am. J. Psychiatry* 147:1449–56

Hallpike, C. 1979. *The Foundations of Primitive Thought.* Oxford: Clarendon. 516 pp.

Haidt, J., Koller, S. H., Dias, M. G. 1992. Disgust, disrespect and moral judgement: or, is it wrong to eat your dog? Manuscript, Dept. Psychol., Univ. Pennsylvania

Harré, R. 1986a. An outline of the social constructionist viewpoint. See Harré 1986b, pp. 2–14

Harré, R., ed. 1986b. *The Social Construction of Emotions.* Oxford: Basil Blackwell. 316 pp.

Harris, P. 1991. Uneasy union and neglected children: cultural psychology and its prospects. *Curr. Anthropol.* 32:82–89

Harris, P., Saarni, C. 1989. *Children's Understanding of Emotions.* New York: Cambridge Univ. Press. 385 pp.

Heath, S. B. 1983. *Ways with Words: Language, Life and Work in Communities and Classrooms.* Cambridge Univ. Press. 421 pp.

Heelas, P. L. F., Lock, A. J., eds. 1981. *Indigenous Psychologies: The Anthropology of the Self.* San Diego, Calif.: Academic. 322 pp.

Heider, K. G. 1991. *Landscapes of Emotion: Mapping Three Cultures in Indonesia.* Cambridge Univ. Press. 332 pp.

Herdt, G. 1990. Sambia nosebleeding rites and male proximity to women. See Stigler et al 1990, pp. 366–400

Holland, D., Quinn, N., eds. 1987. *Cultural Models in Language and Thought.* Cambridge Univ. Press. 400 pp.

Hollis, M., Lukes, S. 1982. *Rationality and Relativism.* Cambridge, Mass.: Mass. Inst. Technol. Press. 312 pp.

Howard, A. 1985. Ethnopsychology and the prospects for a cultural psychology. In *Person, Self and Experience: Exploring Pacific Ethnopsychologies,* ed. G. M. White, J. Kirkpatrick, pp. 401–20. Berkeley: Univ. Calif. Press

Huebner, A., Garrod, A. 1991. Moral reasoning in a karmic world. *Hum. Dev.* 34:341–52

Hutchins, E. 1980. *Culture and Inference.* Cambridge, Mass.: Harvard Univ. Press. 143 pp.

Jahoda, G. 1992. *Crossroads Between Culture and Mind: Continuities and Change in Theories of Human Nature.* London: Harvester Wheatsheaf

Jenkins, J., Karno, M. 1992. The meaning of expressed emotion: theoretical issues raised by cross-cultural research. *Am. J. Psychiatry* 149:9–21

Kakar, S. 1978. *The Inner World: A Psychoanalytic Study of Childhood and Society in India.* Oxford Univ. Press. 213 pp.

Kakar, S. 1982. *Shamans, Mystics and Doctors.* Boston: Beacon. 306 pp.

Kapferer, B. 1979. Emotion and feeling in Sinhalese healing rites. *Soc. Anal.* 1:153–76

Keeler, W. 1983. Shame and stage fright in Java. *Ethos* 11:152–65

Kilbride, P. L. 1992. Anti anti-universalism: rethinking cultural psychology as anti anti-relativism. *Rev. Anthropol.* In press

Kim, U., Choi, S. C. 1992. Individualism, collectivism and child development: a Korean perspective. In *Cognitive Development of Minority Children,* ed. P. Greenfield, R. C. Cocking. Hillsdale, NJ: Erlbaum

Kirsh, D. 1991. Today the earwig, tomorrow man? *Artif. Intell.* 47:161–84

Kleinman, A. 1986. *Social Origins of Distress and Disease.* New Haven: Yale Univ. Press. 264 pp.

Kleinman, A., Good, B. 1985. *Culture and Depression: Studies in the Anthropology and Cross-cultural Psychiatry of Affect and Disorder.* Berkeley: Univ. Calif. Press. 535 pp.

Kohlberg, L. 1981. *The Philosophy of Moral Development: Moral Stages and the Idea of Justice,* Vol. 1. New York: Harper & Row. 441 pp.

Kondo, D. 1992. Multiple selves: the aesthetics and politics of artisanal identities. See Rosenberg 1992, pp. 40–66

Kurtz, S. N. 1992. *All the Mothers are One: Hindu India and the Cultural Reshaping of Psychoanalysis.* New York: Columbia Univ. Press. 306 pp.

Labov, W., Fanshel, D. 1977. *Therapeutic Discourse: Psychotherapy as Conversation.* New York: Academic. 392 pp.

Lakoff, G. 1987. *Women, Fire and Dangerous Things: What Categories Reveal About the Mind.* Univ. Chicago Press. 614 pp.

Lakoff, G., Johnson, M. 1980a. The metaphorical structure of the human conceptual system. *Cogn. Sci.* 4:195–208

Lakoff, G., Johnson, M. 1980b. *Metaphors We Live By.* Univ. Chicago Press. 242 pp.

Langacker, R. W. 1986. An introduction to cognitive grammar. *Cogn. Sci.* 10:1–40

Lave, J. 1990. *Cognition in Practice: Mind, Mathematics and Culture in Everyday Life.* New York: Cambridge Univ. Press 214 pp.

Lebra, T. S. 1976. *Japanese Patterns of Behavior.* Honolulu: Univ. Hawaii Press. 295 pp.

Lebra, T. S. 1983. Shame and guilt: a psychocultural view of the Japanese self. *Ethos* 11:192–209

LeVine, R. A. 1984. Properties of culture: an ethnographic view. See Shweder & LeVine 1984, pp. 67–87

LeVine, R. A. 1990. Infant environments in psychoanalysis: a cross-cultural view. See Stigler et al 1990, pp. 454–76

Levy, R. I. 1973. *Tahitians: Mind and Experience in the Society Islands.* Univ. Chicago Press. 547 pp.

Levy, R. I. 1978. Tahitian gentleness and redundant controls. In *Learning Non-Aggression,* ed. A. Montagu, pp. 222–35. Oxford Univ. Press.

Levy, R. I. 1983. Introduction: self and emotion. *Ethos* 11:128–34

Levy, R. I. 1984. Emotion, knowing and culture. See Shweder & LeVine 1984, pp. 214–37

Levy, R. I. 1991. *Mesocosm.* Princeton Univ. Press. 829 pp.

Levy, R., Wellenkamp, J. 1989. Methodology in the anthropological study of emotion. In *The Measurement of Emotion,* ed. R. Plutchnik, H. Kellerman. San Diego: Academic

Lewis, M. 1989. Cultural influences in children's knowledge of emotional scripts. See Harris & Saarni 1989

Lewis, M., Haviland, J. 1992. *Handbook of Emotions.* New York: Guilford

Lucy, J. A. 1992a. *Grammatical Categories and Cognition: A Case Study of the Linguistic Relativity Hypothesis.* New York: Cambridge Univ. Press. 211 pp.

Lucy, J. A. 1992b. *Language Diversity and Thought: A Reformulation of the Linguistic Relativity Hypothesis.* New York: Cambridge Univ. Press. 328 pp.

Lutz, C. 1982. The domain of emotion words on Ifaluk. *Am. Ethnol.* 9:113–28

Lutz, C. 1985a. Ethnopsychology compared to what? Explaining behavior and consciousness among the Ifaluk. See White & Kirkpatrick 1985

Lutz, C. 1985b. Depression and the translation of emotional worlds. See Kleinman & Good 1985, pp. 63–100

Lutz, C. 1988. *Unnatural Emotions: Everyday Sentiments on a Micronesian Atoll and Their Challenge to Western Theory.* Univ. Chicago Press. 273 pp.

Lutz, C., White, G. 1986. The anthropology of emotions. *Annu. Rev. Anthropol.* 15:405–36

Lynch, O. M., ed. 1990. *Divine Passions: The Social Construction of Emotion in India.* Berkeley: Univ. Calif. Press. 312 pp.

MacIntyre, A. 1981. *After Virtue: A Study in Moral Theory.* Univ. Notre Dame Press. 252 pp.

MacIntyre, A. 1985. Relativism, power, and philosophy. Proc. and Addresses Am. Phil. Assoc. In *Relativism: Interpretation and Confrontation,* ed. M. Krausz. Univ. Notre Dame Press

Mahapatra, M., Much, N. C., Shweder, R. A. 1991. Sin and suffering in a sacred town: some Oriya ideas about spiritual debts and moral cause and effect. Manuscript, Committee Hum. Dev., Univ. Chicago

Markus, H. R., Kitayama, S. 1991. Culture and the self: implications for cognition, emotion and motivation. *Psychol. Rev.* 98:224–53

Markus, H. R., Kitayama, S. 1992. The what, why and how of cultural psychology. *Psychol. Inq.* 3(3): In press

Marriott, M. 1976. Hindu transactions: diversity without dualism. In *Transaction and Meaning,* ed. B. Kapferer. Philadelphia: Inst. Study Hum. Issues

Marriott, M. 1989. Constructing an Indian ethnosociology. *Contrib. Indian Sociol.* 23(1):1–39

Medin, D. L. 1989. Concepts and conceptual structure. *Am. Psychol.* 89:1469–81

Mesquita, B., Fridija, N. H. 1992. Cultural

variations in emotions: a review. *Psychol. Bull.* In press

Miller, J. G. 1984. Culture and the development of everyday social explanation. *J. Personality Soc. Psychol.* 46:961–78

Miller, J. G., Bersoff, D. M. 1992. Culture and moral judgement: How are conflicts between justice and interpersonal responsibility resolved? *J. Personality Soc. Psychol.* 62:541–54

Miller, J. G., Bersoff, D. M., Hardwood, R. L. 1990. Perceptions of social responsibilities in India and in the United States: moral imperatives or personal decisions? *J. Personality Soc. Psychol.* 58:33–46

Miller, J. G., Luthar, S. 1989. Issues of interpersonal responsibility and accountability: a comparison of Indians' and Americans' moral judgements. *Soc. Cogn.* 3:237–61

Miller P., Mintz, J., Hoogstra, L., Fung, H., Potts, R. 1992. The narrated self: young children's construction of self in relation to others in conversational stories of personal experience. *Merrill-Palmer Q.* 38(1):45–67

Miller P., Potts, R., Fung, H., Hoogsta, L., Mintz, J. 1990. Narrative practices and the social construction of self in childhood. *Am. Ethnol.* 17:292–311

Miller, P., Sperry, L. 1987. Young children's verbal resources for communicating anger. *Merrill-Palmer Q.* 33:1–31

Minsky, M. 1985. *The Society of Mind.* New York: Simon & Shuster. 339 pp.

Much, N. C. 1983. *The microanalysis of cognitive socialization.* Ph.D. thesis. Univ. Chicago.

Much, N. C., Shweder, R. A. 1978. Speaking of rules: the analysis of culture in breach. In *New Directions for Child Development,* ed. W. Damon. San Francisco: Jossey-Bass

Myers, F. R. 1979a. Emotions and the self: a theory of personhood and political order among Pintupi aborigines. *Ethos* 7:343–70

Myers, F. R. 1979b. The logic and meaning of anger among Pintupi aborigines. *Man* 23:589–610

Neisser, U. 1988. Five kinds of self-knowledge. *Philos. Psychol.* 1:35–59

Nisbett, R. E., Wilson, T. D. 1977. Telling more than we can know: verbal reports on mental processes. *Psychol. Rev.* 84:231–59

Nuckolls, C. 1991. Culture and causal thinking: prediction and diagnosis in a South Indian fishing village. *Ethos* 17:3–51

Obeyesekere, G. 1981. *Medusa's Hair: An Essay on Personal Symbols and Religious Experience.* Univ. Chicago Press. 217 pp.

Ochs, E., Schieffelin, B. 1984. Language acquisition and socialization: three developmental stories. See Shweder & LeVine 1984, pp. 276–320.

Parish, S. 1991. The sacred mind: Newar cultural representations of mental life and the production of moral consciousness. *Ethos* 19(3):313–51

Peacock, J. L. 1984. Religion and life history: an exploration in cultural psychology. In *Text, Play and Story: The Construction and Reconstruction of Self and Society,* ed. E. M. Bruner. Washington: Am. Ethnol. Soc.

Peak, L. 1986. Training learning skills and attitudes in Japanese early educational settings. In *Early Experience and the Development of Competence,* ed. W. Fowler. San Francisco: Jossey-Bass

Pepitone, A., Triandis, H. C. 1987. On the universality of social psychological theories. *J. Cross-cultural Psychol.* 18:471–98

Putnam, H. 1987. *The Many Faces of Realism.* La Salle, Ill.: Open Court. 98 pp.

Rogoff, B. 1990. *Apprenticeship in Thinking: Cognitive Development in Social Context.* New York: Oxford Univ. Press. 242 pp.

Roland, A. 1989. *In search of self in India and Japan.* Princeton Univ. Press. 386 pp.

Rosaldo, M. Z. 1980. *Knowledge and Passion: Ilongot Notions of Self and Social Life.* Cambridge Univ. Press. 286 pp.

Rosaldo, M. Z. 1983. The shame of headhunters and the autonomy of self. *Ethos* 11:135–51

Rosaldo, M. Z. 1984. Toward an anthropology of self and feeling. See Shweder & LeVine 1984, pp. 137–57

Rosenberger, N. R. 1992. *Japanese Sense of Self.* New York: Cambridge Univ. Press. 176 pp.

Ross, L., Nisbett R. 1991. *Person and the Situation.* Philadelphia: Temple Univ. Press. 286 pp.

Rozin, P., Nemeroff, C. 1990. The laws of sympathetic magic. See Stigler et all 1990, pp. 205–32

Russell, J. A. 1989. Culture, scripts and children's understanding of emotion. See Harris & Saarni 1989, pp. 293–318

Russell, J. A. 1991. Culture and the categorization of emotions. *Psychol. Bull.* 110(3):426–50

Sampson, E. E. 1988. The debate on individualism: indigenous psychologies of the individual and their role in personal and societal functioning. *Am. Psychol.* 43:15–22

Sapir, E. 1929. The status of linguistics as a science. *Language* 5:207–14

Scherer, K. R., Walbott, H. G., Summerfield, A. B., eds. 1986. *Experiencing Emotion: A Cross-Cultural Study.* New York: Cambridge Univ. Press. 302 pp.

Schieffelin, B., Ochs, E., eds. 1986. *Language Socialization Across Cultures.* New York: Cambridge Univ. Press. 274 pp.

Schieffelin, E. L. 1976. *The Sorrow of the Lonely and the Burning of the Dancers.* New York: St. Martin's. 243 pp.

Schieffelin, E. L. 1983. Anger and shame in the tropical forest: on affect as a cultural system in Papua, New Guinea. *Ethos* 11:181–91

Schieffelin, E. L. 1985a. The cultural analysis of depressive affect: an example from New

Guinea. See Kleinman & Good 1985, pp. 101–33

Schieffelin, E. L. 1985b. Anger, Grief and Shame: Toward a Kaluli Ethnopsychology. See White & Kirkpatrick 1985, pp. 168–82

Schwartz, T., White, G. M., Lutz, C. 1992. *New Directions in Psychological Anthropology* Cambridge Univ. Press. In press

Semin, G. R. 1989. The contribution of linguistic factors to attribute inferences and semantic similarity judgements. *Eur. J. Soc. Psychol.* 19:85–100

Semin, G. R., Fiedler, K. 1988. The cognitive functions of linguistic categories in describing persons: social cognition and language. *J. Personality Soc. Psychol.* 54:558–67

Seymour, S. 1983. Household structure and status and expressions of affect in India. *Ethos* 11:263–77

Shostak, M. 1983. *Nisa: The life and words of a !Kung woman.* New York: Vintage. 402 pp.

Shweder, R. A. 1982a. Liberalism as destiny. *Contemp. Psychol.* 2:421–4

Shweder, R. A. 1982b. On savages and other children. *Am. Anthropol.* 84:354–66

Shweder, R. A. 1984. Anthropology's romantic rebellion against the enlightenment, or there's more to thinking than reason and evidence. See Shweder & LeVine 1984, pp. 27–66

Shweder, R. A. 1985. Menstrual pollution, soul loss and the comparative study of emotions. See Kleinman & Good 1985, pp. 182–215, See also: Shweder 1991b, pp. 241–68

Shweder, R. A. 1988. Suffering in style. *Cult. Med. Psychiatry* 12:479–97; see also Shweder 1991b. pp. 313–31

Shweder, R. A. 1990. Cultural psychology: What is it? See Stigler et al 1990, pp. 1–43. See also Shweder 1991b, pp. 73–112

Shweder, R. A. 1991a. Commentary. *Hum. Dev.* 34:353–62

Shweder, R. A. 1991b. *Thinking Through Culture: Expeditions in Cultural Psychology.* Cambridge, Mass.: Harvard Univ. Press. 404 pp.

Shweder, R. A. 1992a. The cultural psychology of the emotions. See Lewis & Haviland 1992

Shweder, R. A. 1992b. You're not sick, you're just in love: emotion as an interpretive system. In *Fundamental Issues and Questions About Emotion,* ed. P. Ekman, R. Davidson. In press

Shweder, R. A., Bourne, E. J. 1984. Does the concept of the person vary cross-culturally? See Shweder & LeVine 1984, pp. 158–99. Also see Shweder, 1991b, pp. 113–155

Shweder, R. A., LeVine, R. A. 1984. *Culture Theory: Essays on Mind, Self and Emotion.* Cambridge Univ. Press. 359 pp.

Shweder, R. A., Mahapatra, M., Miller, J. G. 1990. Culture and moral development. In *The Emergence of Moral Concepts in Early Childhood,* ed. J. Kagan, S. Lamb. Univ. Chicago Press. See also Stigler et al 1990, pp. 130–204

Shweder, R. A., Much, N. C. 1987. Determinations of meaning: discourse and moral socialization. In *Moral Development Through Social Interaction,* ed. W. Kurtines, J. Gewirtz, pp. 197–244. New York: Wiley. See also Shweder 1991b, pp. 186–240

Shweder, R. A., Much, N. C., Mahapatra, M. M., Park, L. 1992. The 'Big Three' of morality (autonomy, community and divinity), and the 'Big Three' explanations of suffering, as well. In *Morality and Health,* ed. P. Rozin, A. Brandt, S. Katz. In press

Shweder, R. A., Sullivan, M. 1990. The semiotic subject of cultural psychology. In *Handbook of Personality: Theory and Research,* ed. L. A. Pervin, pp. 399–416. New York: Guilford

Silverstein, M. 1979. Language structure and linguistic ideology. In *The Elements: A Parasession on Linguistic Units and Levels,* ed. P. Clyne, W. Hanks, C. Hofbauer, pp. 193–247. Chicago Linguist. Soc.

Smedslund, J. 1991. The pseudoempirical in psychology and the case for psychologic. *Psychol. Inquiry* 2:325–38

Smith, M. B. 1991. *Value, Self and Society: Toward a Humanistic Social Psychology.* New Brunswick, NJ: Transactions. 289 pp.

Smith Noricks, J., Agler, H. L., Bartholomew, H., Howard-Smith, S., Martin, D., et al 1987. Age, abstract thinking and the American concept of the person. *Am. Anthropol.* 89:667–75

Solomon, R. C. 1984. Getting angry: the Jamesian theory of emotion in anthropology. See Shweder & LeVine 1984, pp. 238–54

Spindler, G. D. 1980. *The Making of Psychological Anthropology.* Berkeley: Univ. Calif. Press. 665 pp.

Spiro, M. E. 1984. Some reflections on cultural determinism and relativism with special reference to emotions and reason. See Shweder & LeVine 1984, pp. 323–46

Spiro, M. E. 1986. Cultural relativism and the future of anthropology. *Cult. Anthropol.* 1:259–86

Spiro, M. E. 1990. On the strange and familiar in recent anthropological thought. See Stigler et al 1990, pp. 47–64

Spiro, M. E. 1992. Is the western conception of the self 'peculiar' within the context of the world's cultures? *Ethos* .In press

Stearns, C. Z., Stearns, P. N., eds., 1988. *Emotion and Social Change: Toward a New Psychohistory.* New York: Holmes & Meier. 231 pp.

Stein, N., Levine, L. J. 1987. Thinking about feelings: the development and organization of emotional knowledge. In *Aptitude, Learning and Instruction,* ed. R. E. Snow, M. J. Farr, pp. 165–97. Hillsdale, NJ:

Erlbaum

Stevenson, H., Stigler, J. 1992. *The Learning Gap.* New York: Summit Books. 236 pp.

Stigler, J. W. 1984. 'Mental abacus': the effect of abacus training on Chinese children's mental calculation. *Cogn. Psychol.* 16:145–76

Stigler, J. W., Chalip, L., Miller, K. 1986. Culture and mathematics learning. *Rev. Res. Educ.* 15:253–306

Stigler, J. W., Perry, M. 1990. Mathematics learning in Japanese, Chinese, and American classrooms. See Stigler et al 1990, pp. 328–56

Stigler, J. W., Shweder, R., Herdt, G., eds. 1990. *Cultural Psychology: Essays on Comparative Human Development.* Cambridge Univ. Press. 625 pp.

Sullivan, M. 1992. Depression and alcoholism among the Irish: popular perceptions of causality. Manuscript, Dept. Psychiatry, Columbia Presbyterian Med. Cent., New York

Super, C. M. 1981. Behavioral development in infancy. In *Handbook of Cross-Cultural Human Development,* ed. R. Monroe, R. Monroe, B. Whiting. New York: Garland

Swartz, M. J. 1988. Shame, culture, and status among the Swahili of Mombasa. *Ethos* 16:21–51

Taylor, C. 1985. *Human Agency and Language.* Cambridge Univ. Press. 294 pp.

Taylor, C. 1989. *Sources of the Self.* Cambridge, Mass.: Harvard Univ. Press. 601 pp.

Talmy, L. 1988. Force dynamics in language and cognition. *Cogn. Sci.* 12:49–100

Tobin, J. J. 1989. *Preschool in Three Cultures: Japan, China and the United States.* New Haven: Yale Univ. Press. 238 pp.

Triandis, H. C. 1989. The self and social behavior in differing cultural contexts. *Psychol. Rev.* 96:508–20

Triandis, H. C. 1990. Cross-cultural studies of individualism and collectivism. *Nebraska Symp. Motiv., 1989,* pp. 41–143. Lincoln: Univ. Nebraska Press

Weisner, T. S. 1984. A cross-cultural perspective: ecological niches of middle childhood. In *The Elementary School Years: Understanding Development During Middle Childhood,* ed. A. Collins, pp. 335–69. Washington: National Academy

Werker, J. 1989. Becoming a native listener. *Am. Sci.* 77:54–59

Wertsch, J., ed. 1985. *Culture, Communication and Cognition: Vygotskian Perspectives.* Cambridge Univ. Press. 102 pp.

Wertsch, J. 1991. *Voices of the Mind: A Sociocultural Approach to Mediated Action.* London: Harvester Wheatsheaf. 169 pp.

Wertsch, J. 1992. Keys to cultural psychology. *Cult. Med. Psychiatry* 16(3):273–80

White, G. M. 1992a. Ethnopsychology. See Schwartz et al 1992

White, G. M. 1992b. Emotions inside out: the anthropology of affect. See Lewis & Haviland 1992

White, G. M., Kirkpatrick, J. 1985. *Person, Self and Experience: Exploring Pacific Ethnopsychologies.* Berkeley: Univ. Calif. Press. 433 pp.

Whiting, J. W. M. 1992. *Culture and Human Development: The Whiting Model.* New York: Cambridge Univ. Press. In press

Whiting, B. B., Edwards, C. P. 1985. *Children of Other Worlds.* Cambridge, Mass.: Harvard Univ. Press. 337 pp.

Whorf, B. L. 1956. *Language, Thought, and Reality: Selected Writings of Benjamin Lee Whorf.* Cambridge, Mass.: Mass. Inst. Technol. Press. 278 pp.

Wierzbicka, A. 1985. *Lexicography and Conceptual Analysis.* Ann Arbor, Mich.: Karoma. 386 pp.

Wierzbicka, A. 1986. Human emotions: universal or culture-specific? *Am. Anthropol.* 88(3):584–94

Wierzbicka, A. 1989. Soul and mind: linguistic evidence for ethnopsychology and cultural history. *Am. Anthropol.* 91(1):41–58

Wierzbicka, A. 1990. The semantics of emotions: fear and its relatives in English. *Aust. J. Linguist. Spec. Issue Semant. Emot.* 10(2):359–75

Wierzbicka, A. 1991. *Cross-cultural pragmatics: the semantics of human interaction.* Berlin: de Gruyter. 502 pp.

Wikan, U. 1984. Shame and honor: a contestable pair. *Man* 19:635–52

Wikan, U. 1989. Illness from fright or soul loss: a North Balinese culture-bound syndrome? *Cult. Med. Psychiatry* 13:25–50

Wilson, B. R. 1970. *Rationality.* Oxford: Basil Blackwell. 275 pp.

Wittgenstein, L. 1968. *Philosophical Investigations.* Transl. G. E. M. Anscombe. New York: Macmillan. 272 pp.

Wong, D. B. 1984. *Moral Relativity.* Berkeley: Univ. Calif. Press. 248 pp.

Ziff, P. 1972. *Understanding Understanding.* Ithaca, NY: Cornell Univ. Press. 146 pp.

Annu. Rev. Psychol. 1993. 44:525-58
Copyright © 1993 by Annual Reviews Inc.

SOCIAL AND COMMUNITY INTERVENTIONS

Murray Levine

Department of Psychology, State University of New York at Buffalo, Buffalo, New York 14260

Paul A. Toro

Department of Psychology, Wayne State University, Detroit, Michigan 48202

David V. Perkins

Department of Psychological Science, Ball State University, Muncie, Indiana 47306

KEYWORDS: seriously mentally ill, homelessness, children's community care, self-help, prevention

CONTENTS

INTRODUCTION 526
   Developments in Community Mental Health 527
COMMUNITY RESOURCES AND ADAPTATION.. 528
   Assertive Community Treatment for the Mentally Ill 528
   Homelessness: Intervention and Policy 530
   Alternatives to Institutional Care for Children and Adolescents 532
   Self–Help Interventions... 537
PREVENTION AND LIFE STYLE CHANGE 541
   Promoting Healthy Behavior 541
   Prevention of Adolescent Parenthood... 543
   SCIs and the Prevention of AIDS... 547
CONCLUSION.. 550

We would like to thank the following individuals who provided comments or other important assistance for this review: Gary R. Bond, Mary Anne Caldwell, Agnes Hatfield, Joan Lafuse, Louis Medvene, Julian Rappaport, and Deborah Salem.

0066-4308/93/0201-525$02.00

525

INTRODUCTION

This year marks the 30th anniversary of the Community Mental Health Centers (CMHC) Act and the 20th anniversary of the *Annual Review of Psychology* chapters on social and community interventions (SCI). The CMHC Act was the impetus for the development of the field of community psychology, as the Swampscott conference noted (Bennett 1966). The CMHC Act provided for community-based services designed to reduce the censuses of state hospitals and to provide treatment to maintain psychiatric patients in the community. The Act also spoke of preventive services. (For a personal history of these developments, see Sarason 1988). Space limitations and the rapid growth of the literature preclude comprehensive reviews in both the areas of treatment and prevention. We have therefore selected a few key topics with implications for public policy.

We rely heavily on the ecological model, initially articulated by Kelly (1966, 1986), and elaborated on and applied to specific social problems by others (e.g. Hall et al 1987, Toro et al 1991). Programs developed in the last two decades increasingly have come to reflect ecological principles. The ecological viewpoint emphasizes person-environment transactions and the adaptations individuals may make in relation to their resources. (Resources is a broad term referring to psychological resources, material goods, and other features of the social environment.) One corollary of the ecological principle of adaptation is that "To be effective, help has to be located strategically to the manifestation of the problem" (Levine & Perkins 1987:93). The concept of transaction implies mutual influences—services are modified to take into account the characteristics of the target population. Ideally, program developers should collaborate with clients and other members of the community in designing and evaluating SCIs. In reality, services tend to be modified in response to their use or lack of use by the target population (Salem 1990). The evolution of many SCIs reflects these principles.

We can classify problems in the field of community mental health into two broad categories. The first category may be termed resource-related. The seriously mentally ill and the population Wilson (1987) calls the "truly disadvantaged"—the homeless, children, and adolescents—have resource-related problems. Members of these populations tend to be concentrated in certain geographic areas and are dependent on others for their survival. Their behavior patterns may be interpreted as adaptations to barriers they encounter in gaining access to resources and as expressions of the personal deficits which make them less effective in competing with others. Some SCIs are directed toward improving coping skills (or reducing deficits) so that members of the target population may adapt more effectively. However, improved coping skills alone may not be sufficient. In addition, many need income, housing, food, medical care, transportation, vocational training, and opportunities for recreation. Improving access to such resources has become a primary mode of treatment in the community for the population of SMIs and for the homeless. In this regard, advocacy efforts by families of the mentally ill and self-help or mutual assistance efforts within the target population represent new attempts to find and utilize resources.

Problems in the second category, risky behavior and life styles, can be treated, or prevented, by a focus on behavior change, but the most effective methods may be those which lead to a change in broad social norms. Changing norms requires the application of large resources over a period of years. Yet change is possible. Examples of successful efforts to introduce normative social change include those aimed at inhibiting the use of controlled substances, reducing risk factors for cardiac illness, changing sexual practices to prevent AIDS, and preventing adolescent parenthood. The extent of change in behavior in these areas is much greater than can possibly be accounted for by individuals being exposed to interventions one at a time.

Developments in Community Mental Health

When CMHCs first started functioning, critics said they failed to innovate or to reach the population in greatest need (e.g. Chu & Trotter 1974). Deinstitutionalization policy (the preference for treating patients in the community rather than in isolated, closed institutions), powered in part by fiscal incentives to shift the financial burden from state to federal budgets, resulted in the placement of thousands of patients into inadequate nursing homes, single room occupancy hotels, and unlicensed board and care homes. Former patients, the elderly, low income people, and members of minority ethnic groups were under-utilizing services provided on the medical model (self-initiated care, obtained in a doctor-patient relationship on a fee-for-service basis, provided by a specially trained professional in a hospital or clinic). (Modifications in the pattern of delivering services may be changing the picture [O'Sullivan et al (1989)]. These problems were exacerbated with gentrification and rising housing costs which pushed many onto the streets, causing public criticism and bringing homelessness to public attention.

Recognizing there was no well-thought-through deinsitutionalization policy, the National Institute of Mental Health developed a community support program to help work with the SMI population (Levine 1981). New programs took to the streets to reach patients who were not otherwise responsive to care (Cohen 1990). As they did, psychosocial rehabilitation models (Anthony et al 1983) began to supersede medical models of care in the United States (Cohen 1990), Canada (Bennett 1987; Cochrane et al 1991; Rioux & Crawford 1990), Australia and New Zealand (Thomas & Veno 1992), and Italy (Francescato & Ghirelli 1988), among other countries. We now turn to an examination of one of these models—assertive community treatment.

COMMUNITY RESOURCES AND ADAPTATION

Assertive Community Treatment for the Mentally Ill

Assertive Community Treatment (ACT), also known as Training in Community Living or the Madison Model, involves intensive case management for individuals with serious mental illness (SMI) who have been recently released from a hospital. The program aims to prevent or reduce the rehospitalization of these individuals and increase their quality of life in the community. ACT had its origins in an innovative inpatient psychosocial treatment program which was adapted for community-based aftercare (Thompson et al 1990). By the early 1970s, ACT had been proposed as an alternative to hospital care for individuals with SMI (Stein & Test 1985), and over the past decade ACT or similar programs have been widely disseminated in many states (e.g. New York; see Surles et al 1991).

CHARACTERISTICS   The supportive services provided by ACT staff are practical in nature and focus directly on basic issues in day-to-day living: domestic skills, medications, finances, housing, and advocacy with other providers. ACT provides a fixed point of responsibility for all client needs and exemplifies a nontraditional process of service delivery (Test 1991). Contact is almost exclusively *in vivo,* and assertive efforts are made to keep clients enrolled in the program. The ratio of staff to clients is small (typically 1:10), and staff members work as a team to increase client autonomy and access to services (e.g. during evening and weekend hours) and to facilitate communication and support among staff (Stroul 1986). Some versions of ACT also maintain a "no close" policy, such that clients who need services are never discharged, even when they are rehospitalized (Witheridge 1989).

ACT is notable for several reasons. It expands the concept of what makes an individual vulnerable to SMI to include nonpsychiatric factors (e.g. deficits in coping skills, problems with finances or housing) and gives explicit emphasis to nonmedical community support interventions. ACT's perspective is ecological and therefore it minimizes the role of formal treatment settings in order to exploit natural settings, with special emphasis on organizing and maintaining a system of social support. ACT is also competence-oriented, i.e. its goal is less to eliminate psychiatric symptoms than to improve the adaptation to community life of highly vulnerable individuals.

Philosophically and conceptually, ACT is sensitive to the risk of rehospitalization. Most of the clients in these programs have had a history of previous hospitalization. By providing support and teaching coping skills within the setting of the client's day-to-day life, ACT directly counteracts the stresses and problems which lead to rehospitalization. Compared to hospitalization, ACT's cost is competitive, but compared with other forms of outpatient care ACT is labor-intensive and thus relatively expensive. Lack of resources and maldistributed resources (e.g. to hospitals rather than community programs) are still problems in many communities (Stein & Test 1985; Torrey 1990). Even outside the mental health system, communities often have shortages of work and housing suitable for individuals with SMI.

Finally, although ACT is described as client-centered and flexible (Witheridge 1989), it is also pragmatic. Ethical questions might thus arise regarding paternalism and coercion in such an assertive, in vivo, "no close" treatment, and guidelines (e.g. regarding the client's right to refuse ACT services) are needed (Diamond & Wikler 1985).

DISSEMINATION   SCIs are inspired in part by the desire to initiate and maintain a significant reduction in the prevalence of an important problem. Successful experimental studies and demonstration projects thus stand as unfinished work until effectively disseminated to new settings and consumers. Among ACT's advantages for dissemination are straightforward conceptual principles, a positive philosophy of intervention, respectable empirical support, and the enthusiasm of researchers.

ACT has been especially recommended for young adults with severe mental illness (Stein & Test 1985), recognized for more than a decade as an especially challenging population (Iscoe & Harris 1984). ACT has also been provided to homeless mentally ill individuals and mentally ill substance abusers (Olfson 1990).

Wider dissemination of ACT will further test its effectiveness. ACT was initially disseminated in rural areas, an ecological context for which its flexible staff role, emphasis on indigenous resources (especially clients' families), and relatively small scale are particularly well-suited (Diamond & Van Dyke 1985). At the other end of the urban-rural continuum, the Thresholds Bridge Program in Chicago stands as a successful adaptation of ACT for very high risk individuals (with histories of multiple hospitalizations or long-standing homelessness) living in an inner-city environment, an ecological context with limited natural resources and a complex, bureaucratic web of discontinuous services (Witheridge & Dincin 1985).

CRITIQUE   Although recognizable versions of ACT go back 25 years or more (Thompson et al 1990), this past decade has seen an acceleration in its adoption as its empirical research base has grown. For example, ACT repeatedly has been shown to reduce both hospital use and costs across a number of different studies performed in different communities and/or by different investigators (e.g. Bond et al 1988, 1990; Gilman & Diamond 1985; Test 1991; Witheridge & Dincin 1985), although other desirable effects (e.g. symptom reduction, improved social relationships, and subjective quality of life) have been less robust (Olfson 1990). Most studies have been descriptive or outcome-oriented, with less attention to the important processes involved in ACT. For example, the possibility that positive results are attributable simply to better compliance with medication under intense ACT conditions has not been ruled out (Taube et al 1990).

Experimental research involving SMI individuals in the community is challenging, since participants can be difficult to track, are exposed to many other influences and helping efforts, and because programs must evolve in response to changing conditions (Mowbray 1990). Investigators should describe in some detail not only the specific characteristics of the intervention under study but also features of the surrounding community context (e.g. the general availability of affordable housing and human services). Other treatment approaches used as controls in evaluating ACT ought to be ones that are reasonable and well-established, and they need to be well-described (Taube et al 1990).

Future research should determine ACT's appropriate place in a comprehensive support system. For example, ACT may best be used as an intense support during episodes of crisis, with less formal client-driven supports readily available at other times. Another possible new direction would involve blending ACT with principles of mutual help by enrolling some clients as ACT staff (Toro 1990).

Homelessness: Intervention and Policy

In the past decade, homelessness has attracted the nation's attention and has come to be perceived as a major social problem (Blau 1992; Institute of Medicine 1988; Kondratas 1991; Lee et al 1991; Rossi 1989; Shinn et al 1990; Shinn & Weitzman 1990; Wright 1989). The Stewart B. McKinney Homeless Assistance Act (Public Law 100–77) was signed into law in July 1987 and retains strong support (Gore 1990; Levine & Rog 1990). Estimates of the extent of homelessness in the United States vary widely in different studies using different measures (Alliance Housing Council 1988; Rossi 1989; Toro & McDonell 1992). Initially, some believed that deinstitutionalization policy was primarily responsible for the visible increase in the homeless population. However, the homelessness problem extends well beyond the population of deinstitutionalized mentally ill patients (Foscarinis 1991). Homelessness may be one of the few social problems for which public sentiment strongly favors policy change (Lee et al 1991; Toro & McDonell 1992).

The existing research has focused on documenting the general characteristics of the homeless, especially their areas of personal deficit (e.g. Fischer et al 1986) with few attempts to evaluate SCIs designed to address the problem. Societal resources have been oriented toward developing shelters, soup kitchens, and other emergency services that provide important humanitarian aid, but these may be perpetuating the problem by making it easier for people to remain homeless (Toro et al 1991). Here we will review a few emerging intervention models that take an ecological perspective.

One group of proposals dealing with the homeless mentally ill suggests that many need asylum in psychiatric hospitals (Bachrach 1987; Bennett et al

1988; Torrey 1988a). The American Psychiatric Association has formally advocated the increased use of mental hospitals for the homeless and a loosening of our now stringent civil commitment laws (Lamb 1984). However, such advocacy for hospitalization flies in the face of a large and convincing body of research on the advantages of various alternative noninstitutional SCIs for the mentally ill (Kiesler 1982). Such proposals also target a relatively small minority of the homeless population (about 15–30% are seriously mentally ill, based on sound diagnostic standards; see Farr et al 1986; Fischer & Breakey 1991; Toro & Wall 1991).

Other proposals advocate more active outreach efforts through the use of mobile teams, drop-in centers, existing shelters, or community mental health centers (Arce & Vergare 1987; Gold Award 1986). Whatever the locale for service provision, such proposals generally advocate the provision and coordination of a broad range of services including intensive case management, job training, money management, and assistance obtaining and maintaining benefits—all vital resources for escaping homelessness. Evaluation of these interventions is difficult to carry out and the area is new. Much of the research is detailed in unpublished manuscripts. In their ongoing evaluation of an intensive case management program for the homeless mentally ill, modeled after ACT, Morse et al (unpublished) have randomly assigned 150 homeless mentally ill persons to experimental vs comparison programs. Preliminary analyses suggest gains among experimental clients relative to the comparison clients on time housed and satisfaction with services, but not on other variables (including psychiatric symptomatology). Toro has developed a similar intensive case management program designed to facilitate a permanent escape from homelessness for clients and is currently evaluating it.

Barrow et al, in an unpublished evaluation of several outreach programs in New York City, found that a high percentage (46%) of mentally ill participants remained homeless at the six-month follow-up, in spite of the special services. The large number of the mentally ill who remain homeless may be due to the limited housing resources available to them—a limit on the success of any intervention program. The best predictors of obtaining housing and remaining housed were socioeconomic background, level of functioning, client-staff agreement on housing goals, and services oriented towards gaining financial entitlements and housing. Psychiatric history, diagnosis, mental health and other social services were not significant predictors. This study points out that, even within a defined group of mentally ill persons (i.e. the homeless mentally ill), services oriented towards basic needs may be more important than mental health services.

Much is being done to adapt existing mental health and other social services and to develop cost-effective solutions to meet the special needs of the homeless (Levine & Rog 1990). Professionally-based emergency-oriented services are very costly and may never be able to reach the large numbers of homeless persons in need. Furthermore, because of the way programs are funded, many services are targeted toward groups showing particular deficits, such as the mentally ill or substance abusers. This focus on deficits may have the effect of diverting our attention from the more basic needs for low income housing and income maintenance required by all homeless persons (Shinn 1992).

Self-help programs run by clients can be cost-effective and potentially accessible to a wide range of homeless persons, including the mentally ill (Long & Van Tosh 1988). Mental health consumers have operated services covering the full range of services typically run by professionals, including meal and clothing programs, drop-in centers, transitional residences, advocacy, outreach, and case management. Unfortunately, no rigorous evaluations of such programs have yet been done and such evaluations may be difficult to arrange given the "hands off" attitudes of many self-help leaders (Jacobs & Goodman 1989; Levy 1984). However, these programs could be attractive to the homeless, many of whom have become disenchanted with existing social and mental health services. In designing interventions for the homeless we must be careful not to set up professionalism as the sole criterion for measuring quality of services.

Alternatives to Institutional Care for Children and Adolescents

Children's services have lagged behind adult services (Joint Commission on the Mental Health of Children 1969; President's Commission on Mental Health 1978; Knitzer 1982). Although the number of adults in mental hospitals declined sharply in the past 40 years, the number of youths in hospitals and in residential care increased (Kiesler et al 1989; Knitzer 1982; Schwartz 1991; US Department of Justice 1989; Weithorn 1988). Children are institutionalized for mental illness, mental retardation, victimization by abuse or neglect, dependency (e.g. orphans, or children whose parents cannot care for them), delinquency, and status offenses. The increase in residential care has complicated causes: increasing reports of child maltreatment; funding for institutional care; growth of private for-profit psychiatric hospitals; and the limited legal rights of children and youth (Weithorn 1988).

Residential care is very expensive (Burns & Friedman 1990) while community care is much less costly (e.g. Jordan & Hernandez 1990; Rosenthal & Glass 1990). The effectiveness of residential care has been questioned (Saxe et al 1987), while at the same time researchers are exploring alternative models which may reduce the use of institutions (Burns & Friedman 1990). Moreover, serious deficiencies in residential care in some places (e.g. Schwartz 1991) have resulted in institutional reform law suits that have the potential for changing whole state systems (Behar 1985; Levine 1986; Soler & Warboys 1990).

EFFECTIVENESS OF RESIDENTIAL CARE   Studies evaluating the effectiveness of the psychiatric hospitalization of youth, or placement in other residential treatment facilities, face formidable methodological problems (Curry 1991). Methodological problems aside, a large majority of youths who are sent to residential care improve while in the institution (Schaefer & Swanson 1988; Small et al 1991). Garrett (1985) reported a meta-analysis of 126 studies of the residential treatment of delinquents. Summing over all forms of treatment (e.g. behavioral, group, family, milieu) and over all measures (e.g. recidivism, measures of adjustment), she reported an effect size of .37. Studies of institutional adjustment reported an effect size of .41.

Yet improvement at the point of discharge has little or no relationship to adaptation in the community. When recidivism was the criterion measure, Garrett (1985) found that effect size for treatment of delinquents was smallest (.17). She reported an effect size of .63 when measures of community adjustment (e.g. attending school, working, living at home) provided the criterion. She didn't examine post-residential outcome in relation to aftercare programs in the community. Lab & Whitehead (1988) examined studies reporting positive, negative, and no difference in recidivism following institutional-residential care for juveniles. Only one of ten comparisons in six studies reported positive effects on recidivism.

Juveniles with mild pathology do better after discharge from residential treatment than those with severe pathology (Goldfine et al 1985). Moreover, post-discharge community support is apparently critical to post-institutional adaptation (Burns & Friedman 1990; Curry 1991; Wells 1991). These findings suggest that those with the least severe pathology may benefit from a policy of sustaining them in the community *before* attempting institutional treatment.

Recently there have been accusations of widespread fraud in charges and unnecessary hospitalization of youth in private, for-profit psychiatric hospitals (Kerr 1991). In order to provide guidelines to insurance companies about when to pay, researchers have examined admission and discharge criteria (Friedman & Street 1985; Wells 1991). Friedman & Street concluded that it is too difficult to develop useful criteria, and that therefore the emphasis should be on "treatment in the least restrictive alternative, in family-focused services, and in community-based programs" (Friedman & Street 1985:234). North Carolina, under court order to improve services for youth, claimed some success following these principles even with violent and severely disturbed children and youths (Behar 1985; Soler & Warboys 1990).

COMMUNITY-BASED CARE   The lag in children's services stimulated the federal Child and Adolescent Service System Program (CASSP) to provide funds to states to develop a community-based approach to this problem. These funds, and private foundation funds (Beachler 1990), encourage states to limit institutional care, to develop community-based care, and to integrate fragmented community service systems (Friedman & Duchnowski 1990).

Community-based care can reduce the numbers sent to hospitals or residential treatment centers, and may reduce recidivism of juvenile delinquents and status offenders (Lab & Whitehead 1988). One of the few well-controlled studies was conducted by Davidson et al (1987). This study, which included a two-year follow up, used college students supervised by graduate students as the key change agents. Working with juveniles referred by a probation depart-ment, the students used a combination of behavioral contracting, advocacy, and family focus techniques. Though the program demonstrated a decrease in the number of subsequent petitions against the youths, treatment and control groups showed no difference in self-reported delinquencies. The youths may not have changed. We speculate that the advocacy portion of the program may have prompted informal resolutions of problems that otherwise would have caused a petition to be filed. Less well-controlled studies using similar thera-peutic methods have reported comparable results, either in reducing recidivism or in reducing the rates of youths placed out of the home (Barton et al 1985; Gordon et al 1988; Hinckley & Ellis 1985; Jordan & Hernandez 1990).

Based on a survey of agencies and unpublished literature, Stroul & Gold-man (1990) found that the cost of home-based care was less than the cost of out-of-home placement, and prevented 70–90% of out-of-home placements. Success rates decreased six months after treatment, but nonetheless 60% of placements were prevented. Although Lab and Whitehead (1988) were gener-ally pessimistic about the effectiveness of juvenile correctional treatment in reducing recidivism, they concluded that diversion programs operating as part of the formal juvenile justice system had the most effect on recidivism. They did not report the effects of diversion programs on other indices of community adjustment.

The best known approach to community-based care is called Homebuilders. The program has been replicated in many communities since 1974 (Kinney et al 1991). The program accepts cases when the referring worker states that a placement is imminent. Homebuilders' social workers serve only two families at a time to allow the worker to provide intensive services and, in keeping with ecological principles, services are delivered in the client's home. Cost per case are comparable to those in standard agencies. Homebuilders asserts that the cost of treatment is $2,700 per year per child. Foster care is three times as expensive. Residential care is three to eight times as expensive as foster care (Kinney et al 1991).

Workers are on call 24 hours a day, seven days a week. There is no waiting list. Cases are accepted on a time-available basis. Social workers spend an average of eight to ten hours per week for four to six weeks, face-to-face with families. They will stay in family homes for several hours, depending on the problem. "We try to accommodate values, style, resources, and energy levels of our clients, and to approach change from many angles, including behav-ioral, cognitive, and environmental" (Kinney et al 1991:28). In keeping with ecological principles, the workers provide concrete services and advocacy, as well as counseling and other forms of therapy. According to Homebuilders, the continuous, intense involvement makes the worker seem more like a supportive friend.

The Homebuilders program has not been systematically evaluated. 73–91% of children were kept out of placement for one year following the initiation of services. The placement rate in institutions of youths the program could not accept (so-called "overflow" cases) was 76–100% (Kinney et al 1991). Other than reducing institutional placement, we have little knowledge about the program's effect on children's adaptation in school or in the neighborhood.

Following the passage of a Colorado law designed to reduce out-of-home placements, Rosenthal & Glass (1990) studied interventions in youths aged 12–17 in a white working class community. Three forms of treatment were offered: (*a*) out-of-home placement in a residential treatment facility, group home, or foster care home; (*b*) day treatment; and (*c*) family therapy. The treatment philosophy did not include efforts to affect the school environment or the peer group. Youths were assigned to treatments by a committee of professionals who evaluated their needs. Within six months out-of-home placement rates dropped and stayed low, especially confinement in the most restrictive placement. Some youths initially placed in day treatment and in family therapy later were placed out of the home. Of the youths who committed offenses while in treatment, those placed out of the home committed the fewest. Those in day treatment had a high rate of recorded offenses both before and after treatment. Those in family therapy had rates lower than those in day treatment, but higher than those in placement. The rate of offenses for the two groups treated in the home actually increased from the 12 months preceding treatment to the 12 months following treatment.

School performance for youths in all three groups was very poor. The number enrolled in regular classes in the two community-based treatment groups steadily declined—probably reflecting drop-out rates as these youths reached school-leaving age. The grade point averages of those who did stay in school were very low. No mention was made of alternative education programs, or programs to give work skill training, or assistance in obtaining employment. Parents who participated in family treatment reported less satisfaction than those whose children had been placed out of the home. They also reported less change in their adolescents. The dollar costs of out-of-home placement were saved, but not the emotional costs to the family.

Some treatment methods may have limited effectiveness because they are not sufficiently comprehensive. One method that does take a comprehensive approach is multisystemic therapy (MST). MST assumes that adolescent substance abuse and other serious antisocial behaviors have multiple causes (Henggeler et al 1991). MST is based on ecological principles and a concern with generalization (using on new problems the insights and coping methods gained in treatment), maintenance (maintaining gains after treatment stops), and transfer of treatment effects (application of gains in new settings) (Paquin & Perry 1990). MST uses intensive family and other interventions to promote behavior change in youths in their natural environment. This is in keeping with Garrett's (1985) conclusion that the most effective forms of treatment for adolescents are family therapy and cognitive behavioral approaches.

Henggeler et al (in press) reported two studies of reasonably large samples of youths referred from juvenile court, who met a definition of "serious and chronic offender." The youths were assigned randomly to MST or to individual counseling (IC). In a four-year follow-up, offenders who completed MST compared with those who completed IC had significantly lower rates of drug-related arrests, though the mean number of hours in treatment was very similar (MST = 24 hr; IC = 28 hr). About 12% of the families refused treatment. In addition, 16% terminated MST prematurely and 25% terminated IC prematurely. Subsequent analyses took attrition into account.

Henggeler et al (1991) reported another study of serious and chronic youthful offenders at risk for out-of-home placement who were referred by the state's division for youth in yoked pairs. One member of each pair was randomly assigned to MST and the other to the usual services offered by the division for youth. MST treatment lasted for an average of 13 weeks (mean contact hours = 33). At a 59-week follow-up, the arrest rate for MST-treated youths was about 50% lower than those receiving usual services; of those arrested, far fewer had been incarcerated (20% vs 68%). A battery of self-report and other assessment instruments confirmed that there was greater improvement in the MST group. However, it was difficult to demonstrate in a hierarchical regression analysis that change in behavior during treatment predicted the likelihood of later arrest, incarceration, or self-reported delinquency.

CONCLUSION   Changes in criminal justice policy and any of several treatment programs can reduce out-of-home placement and recidivism among youths. However, what happens in the long run, after the effect of these immediate interventions has subsided? Home-based, family-based, and community-based services have much to commend them, but we do not as yet have the full story.

Even though treatment programs are taking ecological principles more seriously, and are tailoring treatments to meet client needs, services focused on one aspect of life—say family—may not make up for problems in other areas, such as poor attitudes toward school, inadequate school programs, or the attractions provided by peers and peer group norms. The concept of community support may have to be defined still more broadly if it is to meet the needs of those who are not yet touched by current services. Few programs heed Paquin and Perry's (1990) admonition that in order to enhance the long-term effects of treatment, programs should pay attention to promoting generalization to new behaviors, maintenance over time of the desired improvements, and transfer of positive changes to new environments.

Self-Help Interventions

Costs of treatment and complaints about the adequacy of treatment have stimulated a tremendous growth in the number of self-help groups. The self-help
philosophy has been incorporated into a wide range of more formal SCIs, in
part through services operated by former patients (e.g. Chamberlin 1990). The
self-help philosophy involves many components that are consistent with an
ecological framework. In particular, the self-help movement's response to the
resource problem is to use clients as service providers.

The self-help movement arose more or less spontaneously, although the
NIMH Community Support Program has played a role in its growth. Surgeon
General C. Everett Koop recognized the value of the movement by sponsoring
a 1987 workshop on self-help and public health (Petrakis 1988). Clearing-
houses designed to disseminate information about self-help and to help interested persons start programs (e.g. Madeira 1986, Meissen et al 1991) have had
an effect in promoting the movement.

Quality research on self-help has begun to catch up with the growth in
groups (see Borkman 1991). A large number of uncontrolled studies on the
efficacy of self-help groups have yielded generally positive results (e.g. Raiff
1982, 1984; Videka 1979). Other studies that included matched comparison
groups (e.g. Hinrichsen et al 1985; Hughs 1977) or followed members over
time (e.g. Lieberman & Videka-Sherman 1986) have also obtained positive
results. Several more rigorous studies have evaluated self-help approaches by
randomly assigning members to self-help or similar groups, no treatment
control groups, and/or professionally-operated interventions. Most of these
studies have found significant improvements for the self-help participants or
no difference between self-help and professional interventions (Edmunson et
al 1984; Jensen 1983; Minde et al 1980; Peterson et al 1985; Spiegel et al
1981; Vachon et al 1980). A few studies found professional intervention to be
more effective (Bond et al 1991; Drob et al 1986; Levitz & Stunkard 1974),
although these too are subject to methodological criticisms. Studies oriented
toward understanding the processes through which self-help groups operate
also have become increasingly common. For example, Maton (1988) has
found support for the validity of the often-cited "helper-therapy principle" that
many presume occurs in the self-help context (Reissman 1965).

Here we shall focus on two very different groups dealing with the SMI
population—GROW, and the Alliance for the Mentally Ill (AMI). GROW
follows the Alcoholics Anonymous model. Members are interested mainly in
helping themselves. They avoid involvement in social and political action. The
body of information on GROW is extensive and includes several studies of the
relationship of self-help processes to outcomes.

In addition to providing mutual support, AMI members engage in political
and social action to promote change. AMI "Anti-psychiatry" and ex-patients'

groups have attracted attention (e.g. Chamberlin 1990). However, AMI has been the most successful in influencing mental health policy.

GROW SELF-HELP GROUPS FOR THE MENTALLY ILL GROW is a mutual help organization for persons with mental disorders. It originated in Australia nearly 30 years ago and now operates over 500 groups worldwide, making it one of the world's largest organizations of its kind.

Rappaport and colleagues (Rappaport et al 1985) studied the organization over several years, collecting detailed observational data from over 500 actual group meetings in Illinois and interviewing nearly 300 group members. Many of the research reports are found in unpublished dissertations and in papers read at meetings. The study lacked a randomly assigned control group.

GROW is fully controlled by its members. Its philosophy of personal growth stresses self-control, caring for fellow members, and spiritual beliefs. In practice, this means the development of support networks among members and assistance in helping them adjust to community living. Each local group conducts weekly meetings which usually last two to three hours and adhere to a carefully structured "group method" which allows time for members to raise personal problems, and read and discuss pieces from GROW's extensive body of member-written literature. GROW's international organizational structure helps assure a consistency of approach among groups widely scattered around the world and allows members to develop as leaders.

Most members, especially those who attend GROW meetings more frequently, stabilize or show positive changes over time in one or more major domains. Statistically controlling for background variables, Reischl found associations between frequency of attendance at GROW meetings and the quality of strategies used to cope with stressful incidents. Compared with demographically matched newcomers, members who had attended a group for at least nine months demonstrated a greater number of social relationships, more occupational success, and better mental health functioning (Rappaport et al 1985). Compared in a longitudinal analysis to a carefully matched sample of persons with similar psychiatric histories, GROW members were less likely to be hospitalized in a psychiatric facility.

A number of process analyses have documented the behaviors that occur in GROW group meetings (Roberts et al 1991), how these behaviors and the social climate of these groups compare to other interventions (Toro et al 1987, 1988), and how the dynamics of group behavior and continued attendance relate to eventual outcomes. In keeping with the key role of the "helper therapy principle" (Reissman 1965), new members are quickly engaged in assisting others. Engaging in helping behaviors is a good predictor of continued attendance at GROW meetings. The methods used by GROW for organizational expansion have also been documented (Zimmerman et al 1991). A similar evaluation of GROW groups has been done in Australia (Young & Williams 1989). GROW apparently helps those who participate. However, selection bias as reflected in the dropout rate suggests that only a select group, whose characteristics are not fully understood, may benefit the most.

ALLIANCE FOR THE MENTALLY ILL (AMI)   AMI groups arose in response to the accelerating pace of deinstitutionalization in the 1960s and 70s, which greatly increased the burden of care placed on the families of mentally ill people. At the same time, NIMH's Community Support Program was encouraging client and family participation on community mental health center boards, putting families into direct contact with each other (Mosher & Burti 1989), thus providing fertile ground for new cooperative efforts such as AMI.

National organization   The National Alliance for the Mentally Ill (NAMI) was founded in 1979 with 284 members. A decade later the organization had a national office and an estimated 1050 AMI affiliates in all 50 states, with an overall membership of 130,000 (Hatfield 1991; Lynn Saunders, personal communication). NAMI has been successful in advocating better services in local communities (e.g. crisis intervention, respite programs for families), lobbying for Social Security Disability Income and insurance coverage for individuals with severe mental illness, and expanding legal grounds for the involuntary commitment of persons with mental illness (Backer & Richardson 1989; Hatfield 1987). Using strategies of political action and litigation, NAMI succeeded in reducing the cost of the drug clozapine and convincing at least one state (New York) to include it in its Medicaid program (Hassner 1991). NAMI has also lobbied successfully to have schizophrenia-related programs transferred from the National Institute of Mental Health to the much larger National Institutes of Health, arguing that recognizing schizophrenia as a biologically-based illness would strengthen the case for insurance reimbursement, increase research dollars, and decrease the stigma attached to the disease. In addition, NAMI assisted in establishing the National Alliance for Research on Schizophrenia and Depression (NARSAD), a private research fund awarding about $1 million per year (Hatfield 1991).

Finally, NAMI has undertaken extensive educational efforts to counteract the stigma associated with severe mental illness and increase public support for funding and research. One noteworthy example is NAMI's Curriculum and Training Committee, made up of clinicians and social scientists who are also family members of individuals with severe mental illness.

Local groups   The proliferation of local AMI groups is a new development since Iscoe & Harris (1984) last reviewed this area. Individual AMI chapters are lay consumer groups, with professionals taking no leadership positions unless they have mentally ill relatives. At regular meetings members (who may include individuals with severe mental illness) share common experiences and practical advice, and organize grass-roots advocacy efforts (e.g. strategies for influencing legislatures and councils). Members also receive educational information about mental illness, medications, rehabilitation services, and alternative ways to understand severe mental illness. Much of this information comes from NAMI, which is responsible for disseminating the latest developments in research, treatment, and insurance practices to its affiliates and members.

Many mutual help groups work in part by providing an ideological view or "cognitive antidote" useful in coping with members' core problems (see Levine & Perkins 1987). In AMI groups such cognitive antidotes may include (*a*) a belief that family members of a person with mental illness are not pathogenic and dysfunctional themselves, but instead are normal individuals attempting to cope with abnormal events or circumstances; (*b*) a belief in a biological etiology for schizophrenia and other severe mental illnesses (Johnson 1989), plus a rejection of psychogenic theories placing blame on parents and family members (Lefley 1989); and (*c*) a belief that clients and family members share with professionals the responsibility for improving services for those with severe mental illness.

Empirical research   Research on the process and outcome of participating in AMI groups has lagged far behind their proliferation. The empirical literature consists of surveys and descriptive studies. The group process in AMI meetings may be similar to that in many other mutual help groups in emphasizing catharsis, explanation, and other non-threatening procedures (Biegel & Yamatani 1987). AMI members report increased knowledge about mental illness and credit the organization with giving them practical information for coping with problems [e.g. recognizing signs of decompensation]. Members' acceptance of AMI's ideology, specifically its biological explanation for severe mental illness, may reduce personal guilt and other psychological burdens on families, facilitates more comfortable interactions with their mentally ill children, and may also lead to increased comfort in talking with outsiders about the problem (Medvene & Krauss 1989). We found no studies (e.g. of former members who dropped out) which examined the organization's limitations.

Critique   NAMI is a good example of an SCI. That is, it approaches a significant human problem—severe mental illness—by focusing on its social context (e.g. public attitudes and the politics of mental health care) while also providing practical coping strategies to those directly affected. Its biological view of mental illness notwithstanding, NAMI is ecologically-oriented in favoring community support wherever appropriate over institutionalization (Howe & Howe 1987). NAMI operates effectively at local levels as well as nationally, and functions to empower a historically disadvantaged population (the families of individuals with severe mental illness) by giving them increased knowledge and active support. NAMI has also redressed somewhat the power balance between family members and mental health professionals, whose interests do not always coincide.

In contrast to Alcoholics Anonymous and GROW, which maintain low public profiles, NAMI takes a visible role in aggressively lobbying for a specific political agenda. Furthermore, to preserve its distinct message and the particular interests of its members, NAMI has avoided merging its efforts with those of other mental health advocacy groups.

NAMI is the product of a specific historical and sociopolitical context, and the eventual limits of NAMI's appeal and effectiveness are not yet clear. Membership surveys have suggested that NAMI's current constituency consists primarily of white, upper middle class, well-educated parents (especially mothers) of mentally ill adults (Hatfield 1991; Medvene & Krauss 1989). Efforts are underway to increase the involvement of spouses and siblings of those with mental illness, families with adolescents at risk for severe mental illness, and racial and ethnic minorities (Howe & Howe 1987). However, economic and social disadvantages may deter some of these families, and NAMI may need to consider new strategies as efforts to reach and support them grow.

In summary, NAMI is an impressive special interest group which undeniably meets many important needs of the people it represents. However, systematic empirical research on this mutual help organization is just appearing, and extending support to a more diverse spectrum of families (e.g. those who are economically disadvantaged) is an important current concern.

Conclusion On the whole, mutual help groups show great potential as SCIs because they can be implemented on a large scale at little or no cost (but see Revenson & Cassel 1992). The ability of such groups to affect social policy, as the AMI example illustrates, is also significant. However, some possible limitations need to be considered. Many who attend mutual help groups drop out after a few meetings, although probably not more than drop out of psychotherapy. There may be a tendency over time for the more disturbed to drop out and the less disturbed to continue to come, causing the groups to drift away from their core constituency.

Mutual help will probably never fully displace the need for other services. Much more research is warranted to document the efficacy of the approach.

PREVENTION AND LIFE STYLE CHANGE

Promoting Healthy Behavior

Some social problems are less stigmatizing than mental illness and homelessness, and may be addressed with fewer social resources. In the past few decades, we have seen major progress on several such problems in America. SCIs have played a role in this progress, but many other factors are related to producing change on such a large scale.

The two leading causes of death in America have been, and continue to be, cardiovascular disease (CVD) and cancer (Winett et al 1989; American Cancer Society 1987; American Heart Association 1987). Cigarette smoking, the single most preventable cause of death in America (Surgeon General 1979), is a major risk factor for both CVD and cancer. Other significant risk factors for CVD and/or cancer include: high blood cholesterol, high blood pressure, obesity, heavy use of alcohol, and physical inactivity. In the past few decades, Americans have shown behavioral changes that have reduced all of these risk factors, resulting in corresponding reductions in the incidence of CVD and many cancers (Winett et al 1989). Reductions in Americans' use of drugs as well as alcohol have been documented in recent years (Alcohol, Drug Abuse, and Mental Health Administration 1987).

How have such positive changes in a wide range of health-related behaviors come about in the past few decades? What can be learned from the processes through which such changes have occurred? While we will not here provide a detailed review of the large literature on SCIs and changing behaviors (for excellent reviews, see Gesten & Jason 1987; Winett et al 1989), a careful analysis of large-scale behavioral changes can be very instructive for those concerned with improving the health and well-being of our society. In particular, for those designing and evaluating SCIs such an analysis can suggest how best to target intervention and dissemination efforts.

One of the most widely cited and successful types of SCI aims at reducing the risk for heart disease (e.g. Cohen et al 1986; Egger et al 1983; Farquhar et al 1983; Puska et al 1985). These programs generally operate over several years on a community-wide basis (with target populations ranging from 45,000 to over 400,000). Typically, they make heavy use of the mass media, attempt to change a wide range of behaviors, and evaluate program effectiveness through quasi-experimental designs that compare intervention communities to demographically similar control communities who receive no intervention. As a group, these programs have demonstrated drops of 9–15% in risk for heart disease (Maccoby & Alexander 1980), and shown themselves to be cost effective in reaching large numbers of people. Such programs may achieve their results by targeting multiple health problems (e.g. Health Promotion Resource Center 1987; Winett et al 1989), devising strategies that address multiple levels of the community (e.g. individual, organizational, and political), and using multiple methods to reach the target population (e.g. mass media, small group discussions, face-to-face services). Similar large-scale programs have been applied to reducing smoking, stress, and substance abuse (Gesten & Jason 1987; Winett et al 1989).

We believe that such SCIs, though themselves reaching only a small proportion of the total population, have made important contributions by helping to change the "zeitgeist," thereby affecting social norms about various health-related behaviors. As social norms about a behavior change, more researchers and program developers are attracted to the problem (e.g. substance abuse prevention is very popular and fundable right now), resulting in more SCIs whose effectiveness helps legitimize the changes in social norms that are already occurring. Bidirectional feedback between SCIs targeted toward health-related behaviors and social norms concerning those behaviors is very common. How to encourage such feedback and thereby increase the momentum for solutions to social problems might be the focus of future research.

Prevention of Adolescent Parenthood

Pregnancy is not a disease, but adolescent parenthood is a serious social problem with enduring consequences for the teenager and her child. Unwed teenagers who give birth are more often depressed, have lower achievement in school, are less likely to complete high school, less likely to enter the labor force, and more likely to be welfare dependent than mothers who have their first child at an older age (Hamburg 1986). Many young women use cigarettes, marijuana, and alcohol during their first pregnancies (Abma & Mott 1991). Probably as a function of poor prenatal care, teenagers are more likely than older mothers to have premature and low birth weight babies (Garn et al 1986). Prematurity and low birth weight may be associated with neurological impairment and consequent school and behavioral problems. On the average, children of teenage mothers have poorer adaptations later in life compared to children of women who had their first babies at an older age (Furstenberg et al 1987). Racial and ethnic differences in rates of teenage out-of-wedlock pregnancies and births are important to understand if we are to use ecological principles in planning interventions (Reppucci 1987).

There are several strategic points at which to address the problem. Prevention programs may be directed at reducing sexual activity or at increasing contraception use. Births also may be prevented by abortions. Prenatal care can improve mother and infant health. Finally, we can provide support to young mothers and their children to improve later adaptation.

LOWERING THE RATE OF SEXUAL ACTIVITY   In 1988 in the United States, there were 24.7 million youths between the ages of 13 and 19. The rate of sexual activity among teenagers rises with age. This rate can be measured by the rate of births plus the rate of legal and illegal abortions, and spontaneous miscarriages. About half of all high school seniors have had sexual intercourse. The percentage of sexually active adolescent females increased from 1982 to 1988 (Chilman 1986; Dryfoos 1990; Forrest & Singh 1990).

One approach to reducing the risk of teenage pregnancy is to encourage teenagers to delay sexual involvement. Howard & McCabe (1990) studied such a program. Based on a survey showing that adolescent girls would like to learn to say "No" without hurting the boy's feelings, a four-session program using social inoculation concepts, peer counselors, and experiential learning was followed by a reinforcement session one to three months later. 395 low income African-American youths, exposed to the program in eighth grade, were followed to the end of ninth grade. On a follow-up telephone interview, both boys and girls exposed to the program reported significantly lower rates of sexual activity than youths from 141 matched schools without the program. The program's effect seemed larger with girls who had not yet become sexually active when the program began in eighth grade. About 27% of nonprogram girls started having sex by the end of ninth grade, compared to 17% of girls exposed to the program. Based on hospital records, pregnancies may have been reduced.

Sexuality education, not necessarily focused on abstinence, may have some effect on the short-term postponement of sexual activity, although not all studies report the same result (Dryfoos 1990). The effect may be different depending on gender, race, ethnicity, prior experience with sexuality education, and the type of program (Eisen et al 1990). One program emphasizing abstinence may have backfired: More male participants claimed to have had sexual intercourse by the end of the program than males in a control group (Christopher & Roosa 1990).

A national teenage outreach program in 1986 and 1987 encouraged adolescents to engage in volunteer activities and in related discussion classes which included some sexuality education. Compared with a matched control group, participants had fewer pregnancies and other problem behaviors. It is not clear whether abstinence or better contraceptive use was responsible for the decline in pregnancy (Allen et al 1990).

These somewhat inconsistent, weak, and difficult-to-document effects (Rickel 1989) suggest that much more will have to be done to change norms, if we aim to reduce adolescent sexual activity. Concerns about contracting AIDS may eventually have some effect in reducing sexual activity. Abstinence programs reach a very small fraction of the group at risk. Even if we learn which are the most effective persuasion techniques, using them to reach the entire population at risk is a difficult task, given the controversy about sexuality education programs.

CONTRACEPTION   If an adolescent is sexually active, the risk of pregnancy is reduced by the use of contraception. On average, adolescents are not well informed about reproductive physiology and fertility cycles, but know about the pill and the condom. However, many adolescents have expressed negative attitudes toward contraception. Only 30% of sexually active teenagers "always" use some form of it. These may be youths who are in a stable relationship (Morrison 1985).

Contraception education programs have produced complex, difficult-to-interpret results. These programs increase knowledge of contraception, but increased knowledge alone has little effect on behavior (Dryfoos 1990). The type of program being used seems to make little difference (Eisen et al 1990). Yet the picture is not entirely negative. Those who are exposed to the programs before they become sexually active may be more likely to use contraceptives later. Some school-based clinics serving low income populations have had success promoting the use of contraceptives, though school-wide pregnancy rates remain unaffected (Kirby et al 1991).

In general, contraceptive use at first premarital intercourse has increased from 1965 to 1988 (Mosher & McNally 1991), and this seems to reflect a gradual change in norms. Certainly not all teenagers have been exposed to specific programs. Media campaigns—including posters, TV, and radio ads with hot line numbers—have resulted in increased requests for information about contraception. The prominence of contraceptives displayed in supermarkets may have an effect as well (Dryfoos 1990). It may be possible to accelerate this process. One school district saturated with pregnancy prevention messages—through the schools, the churches, courses for parents, use of media, and a speaker's bureau—reported reduced teenage pregnancy rates compared to neighboring districts (Dryfoos 1990). It is not clear whether sexual activity was less frequent, or contraceptive use increased.

ABORTION   Although the concentration of out-of-wedlock births has increased among teenagers, the overall rate of teenage births has decreased. The rate in 1960 was 89.1 births per thousand women age 15–19. By 1987 the rate had dropped to 51.1. The trend is similar for white and African-American teenagers (Table 82, Bureau of the Census 1990). Most of the decrease in births is probably due to an increase in legal abortions, rather than a decrease in sexual activity or an increase in contraceptive use. Teenagers accounted for 244,000 abortions in 1973, but 416,000 in 1985 (after abortions were legal in all states), even though the number of teenagers in the population declined somewhat over those years. In 1973, the ratio of abortions to abortions plus births (i.e. the proportion of pregnancies terminated by abortion, not including spontaneous miscarriages) was .476 for those less than 15 and .280 for those 15–19. By 1985, the ratios were .624 and .462 respectively (Table 101, Bureau of the Census 1990). Obviously, no one has a specific program to teach about abortions, but once they became legally available, teenagers used them to terminate unwanted pregnancies.

Hodgson vs Minnesota (1990) allows states to have laws requiring adolescents seeking an abortion to obtain parental consent or to notify parents. (A judicial bypass option—i.e. the teenager can go to court and request a judicial order waiving the parental notice of consent provision before notifying the parent—must be included for the statute to pass constitutional muster.) When Massachusetts passed a parental consent law, there was a decline in abortions among Massachusetts teenagers, but abortions to Massachusetts teenagers increased in neighboring states that did not have such a law. Massachusetts teenage mothers may have shown a small increase in births because of the law (Cartoof & Klerman 1986). However, in Minnesota, a much larger state geographically, making alternative resources more difficult to reach, a similar law resulted in a decline in the number of abortions among women 15–17 years old. There was also a decline in the birth rate (Rogers et al 1991). The authors suggest that with access to abortion made more difficult, adolescents might have either reduced sexual activity or taken more precautions to avoid pregnancy. The large differences in effect between the Massachusetts and Minnesota laws reflect variations in the access to resources, and suggest that macroscale ecological effects may be more weighty than any specific intervention.

ASSISTING THE MOTHER   There are programs to care for pregnant adolescents, and to assist adolescent mothers after they have given birth (Stahler & DuCette 1991). Rickel (1989) used college students as peer advocates for pregnant adolescents but did not report a formal evaluation. In another program (Olds 1988), home visits by nurses during pregnancy and in the period after delivery helped high risk young women to make better use of prenatal care services. Under the program rates of premature and low birth-weight infants declined. There was also a sharp reduction in verified cases of child abuse and neglect, and more frequent positive interactions between mothers and children. Few similar programs to assist the teenage mother have been adequately evaluated (Stahler & DuCette 1991).

CHANGE IN ACCESS TO RESOURCES   Specific programs to help teenage mothers may be less important than other social changes. Legislation taking effect in 1975 (Title IX of the Education Amendment Act) forbade schools receiving federal funds from expelling pregnant adolescents or adolescent mothers. Moreover, as social norms changed and the stigma surrounding teenage pregnancy subsided, many schools developed programs to assist pregnant teens and teenage mothers to complete school. Upchurch & McCarthy (1989) reviewed the findings of three national surveys using very large samples of women. High school completion rates for women who had their first child before age seventeen changed from 18.6% in 1958 to 55.5% in 1986. The change was apparent for both whites and African-Americans. In fact, in 1986 more African-American women (60.6%) who had their first child before age 17 completed high school than comparably situated white women (53.7%). Nevertheless, the rates of high school completion for both whites and African-American young mothers lagged far behind the 1986 completion rate for all women of 89.2%. Women who had not had a child, or who delayed bearing their first child until they were older, graduated at higher rates (96.2% and 90.8–92.0% respectively) than those who had their first child before age 17 (55.5%) or before age 19 (74.6%).

CONCLUSIONS   The number of out-of-wedlock births among teenagers is still very high, but the overall rate of teenage births is down. More who have babies complete high school than at any earlier date. These changes cannot be accounted for by specific interventions. Rather, they reflect changes in norms (access to abortion) and in availability of resources (support services for young mothers; legislative protection). Yet the group that Wilson (1987) termed the "truly disadvantaged" still has a high rate of out-of-wedlock births. We need to learn how to reach this group.

Teenage births may be down overall but the rate of teenage pregnancy is still high. Most successful programs to prevent teenage pregnancy tend to be community wide, ensure access to many different services including abortion and contraception, and include comprehensive services especially targeted at youngsters at high risk of pregnancy (Dryfoos 1990). But we probably will not have much effect on teenage pregnancy through these small-scale prevention programs. We won't begin to see a significant decline until norms change within the targeted population, and that won't happen unless many other components of the social system operate in concert to provide comprehensive services and highly redundant messages.

SCIs and the Prevention of AIDS

Acquired Immune Deficiency Syndrome (AIDS) can be understood as a number of different epidemics, distinguishable by modes of transmission and by many personal and environmental risk factors. As this review is being written, it is ten years since AIDS was formally recognized. In the past decade, more than 179,000 persons with AIDS have been reported to public health departments in the United States (Centers for Disease Control 1991).

The goal of AIDS prevention programs is to reduce the incidence of infection by the human immunodeficiency virus (HIV), precursor to AIDS. A vaccine for this purpose has not yet been developed. Even when one becomes available, issues of cost and distribution may limit its impact (Cohen 1991). Testing to detect HIV-infected individuals has been used to promote increases in knowledge and awareness, and to reduce risky behavior in gay men and intravenous drug users (IVDUs) (Higgins et al 1991). But mandatory HIV testing is ineffective and inappropriate as a preventive measure (Coates et al 1988). For the moment we must look to SCIs for the most effective strategies to prevent AIDS. These include media campaigns, individual and small-group interventions, and social reorganization to promote new behavioral norms.

Media campaigns are designed to increase knowledge and awareness of AIDS and to prevent discrimination against persons infected with HIV. One widely-known example was the Surgeon General's distribution of an educational pamphlet to every U.S. household in 1987. This effort was reasonably well-received by the public (Gerbert & Maguire 1989), and has been cited as a likely cause of subsequent nationwide increases in condom sales (Moran et al 1990). However, the expected preventive effect was so slight that no formal evaluation was ever planned (Booth 1988).

A limitation of media campaigns against AIDS is that people must actually use the information provided, and those who make the best use of this kind of information may be at lower risk of HIV infection in the first place. As a result, many media-driven programs are directed at specific groups who are (*a*) at high risk for HIV infection or (*b*) influential with those who are at risk. For example, Crawford et al (1990) developed a media-based intervention designed to facilitate communication about AIDS within urban families, identified as a high risk group. Eighth-grade students in Chicago were given copies of a newspaper supplement about AIDS and encouraged to watch a series of television news segments on AIDS. Children in the intervention group viewed more of the broadcasts, learned more about AIDS, and talked more with their parents about AIDS than did children in the control group. In a study of those influential with high risk individuals, Sheridan et al (1990) reported increased knowledge and decreased fear regarding contact with infected individuals in leaders and members of a major religious organization following a single day-long seminar presenting medical and psychological knowledge about AIDS.

However, directing a given media campaign at more than one group (e.g. both parents and children, as in Crawford et al 1990) is potentially complicated. Messages need to be developmentally appropriate for the targeted group (Lorion 1990), specific to the characteristics placing this group at risk, delivered via the media most likely to reach the group, and explicit in presenting the relevant factual information (Longshore 1990). Furthermore, media campaigns alone are probably not sufficient to halt the spread of HIV infection because the ultimate goal of inhibiting even a single high risk behavior is so stringent. Mistakes at any step (e.g. inappropriate information, ineffective procedures) may cause the entire effort to fail (Winett et al 1990). In any case, lack of relevant knowledge about AIDS is less often a key problem today. Increased knowledge and awareness may not correlate with changes in risky behavior (Flowers et al 1991). Attention has shifted to promoting specific communication and coping skills needed to reduce risk in specially targeted groups.

A popular approach has been small group sessions. For example, Kelly et al (1989) increased knowledge about AIDS and reduced high risk behavior in homosexual men by providing 12 weekly group sessions presenting information, coping strategies, assertion training, and social support for low risk behavior. Valdiserri et al (1989) reported that small group lecture/discussion sessions which dealt with peer acceptance of low risk sex and also provided skills for avoiding high risk situations significantly increased condom use for anal intercourse compared with lecture/discussion sessions alone. Jemmott et al (1992) also reported a reduction in self-reported risky sexual behavior at three months followup in small group discussions with African-American adolescents using African-American group facilitators. AIDS prevention efforts with IVDUs (see Sorensen et al 1991) include treatment to reduce or stop IV drug use (Watters et al 1990), instruction in safe methods for using needles, and education to prevent the initiation of the practice in the first place (Stephens et al 1991), all of which have had some success (Des Jarlais et al 1990).

Although these sundry results appear promising, individual and small group interventions are labor-intensive and require aggressive outreach. Not only do those at risk need to learn new skills (e.g. managing relationships, substituting safe behaviors for risky ones), they also need to practice them under safe conditions in the hope they will use them when it really counts—under the pressure of temptation by sex or drugs. Lapses in safe behavior are frequent (Kelly et al 1991a), and here (in contrast to smoking or drinking abusively) a single lapse can prove fatal. Supportive programs must therefore be maintained indefinitely and include a strong focus on relapse prevention (Ekstrand & Coates 1990). Essential to any long-term solution is the adoption of new norms which support low risk behavior and inhibit unhealthy behavior (Coates 1990).

An additional problem is that it is not always easy to gain access to high risk individuals. Some (e.g. runaways, IVDUs who are not in treatment, the sexual partners of such individuals) are hard to reach, and others are unresponsive or even hostile to intervention efforts. The African-American community, very vulnerable to the inroads of AIDS, is a case in point. The infamous Tuskegee syphilis study, in which African-American men with the disease were followed for years but not given treatment, has evidently left a legacy of distrust in the African-American community about health education efforts to prevent AIDS (Thomas & Quinn 1991).

The scope of HIV infection and the practical limitations of formal programs suggest that efforts built upon informal supports and resources will be critical. In particular, it may be possible to establish new norms both for sexual contact (Catania et al 1991; Ekstrand & Coates 1990) and IV drug use (Des Jarlais et al 1990). For example, Kelly et al (1991b) identified influential members of the gay community in one city and gained their cooperation in promoting risk-reducing behavior. At three- and six-month intervals following this intervention, men in this community reported significant reductions in risky behavior (more use of condoms and fewer men having sex with multiple partners) compared with their pre-test responses and with gay men in two comparison cities.

The enormous challenge posed by HIV infection suggests that multiple approaches (i.e. media-based, skill-oriented, and norm-focused) will be necessary to have the largest and most lasting effects. Programs need to be delivered under natural conditions and as close as possible to where high risk behavior takes place (Joseph & Roman-Nay 1990). They should exploit strategies already favored by the given risk group (McKusick et al 1991). Television and print media are being exploited, but more programs are needed for schools, work sites, and community organizations.

An adequate infrastructure of risk-reducing services (e.g. job programs for those recovering from drug addiction, treatment programs, condoms and other devices to control sexually-transmitted diseases, bleach sterilization kits, needle exchange programs, HIV antibody testing, and counseling) will be needed

(Coates 1990), especially for individuals who are hard to reach (Rugg et al 1990). Given that government institutions may lack ties to or credibility with many risk groups, community-based organizations, peer networks, and other natural or indigenous supports should be used to dispense these services. For all of these reasons, collaborative studies involving representatives of the indigenous community are important.

It is also important to begin disseminating prevention programs to other groups less critically but still signficantly at risk, such as adolescents, persons over 50, persons engaging in high risk behavior who live outside the AIDS epicenters (Coates 1990), and culturally diverse populations (Mays et al 1989). In fact, behavior change campaigns have not even been attempted in many countries where prevalence rates are rapidly growing (Palca 1991).

Ecological factors will challenge our ability to disseminate AIDS prevention programs. Sociodemographic barriers may hamper target individuals' acquisition of AIDS information and limit their exposure to new norms supporting low risk behaviors (e.g. Bertrand et al 1991; McCaig et al 1991; Thomas & Quinn 1991). IVDUs, for example, are a heterogeneous risk group and often lack the kind of social infrastructure that would permit effective grass roots organization, although mutual help programs (reviewed elsewhere in this chapter) are being tried with this group to disseminate information and foster new norms (Joseph & Roman-Nay 1990). In general, we need a better understanding of high risk situations to know how to change behavioral norms (Lorion 1990).

A large amount of conceptual and methodological work on AIDS prevention is under way, and what is learned about sexual behavior in this effort will also have implications for efforts to control other sexually transmitted diseases and efforts to reduce unwanted pregnancy. However, most studies still rely on self-reported changes in knowledge or behavior, and it will be important in future research to assess other outcomes (e.g. HIV and other STD infection rates) as well. An ecological approach requires that the units of analysis should go beyond individuals to include couples, families, and communities. Finally, research occurs in social and political contexts, and neither the methods used nor the knowledge gained are free of distortion by these contexts (Anderson 1991).

CONCLUSION

The community mental health movement has seen considerable development in the treatment and prevention of social health problems. Over time, many programs have implicitly or explicitly developed an ecological orientation. On the treatment side, workers are more willing to reach out to clients, especially the seriously mentally ill, and are willing to see their clients' problems, at least in part, as involving access to resources. Similar viewpoints are being developed toward the "truly disadvantaged"—the homeless, children, and adolescents. We have also seen the development of a mutual help orientation in this field. Former patients and family members are now viewed as important participants in the treatment process. However, taking advantage of these new approaches will require additional investment of public resources (e.g. for low income housing) that can only be made through the political system.

On the prevention side, we have also seen progress. However, in those areas where we have seen sizable changes in behavior, specific interventions cannot be credited for the changes. We believe these behavioral changes have resulted from broad shifts in social norms that were brought about because of massive, redundant messages delivered over many years and through many channels. Yet the primary focus of community psychologists working on SCIs has been on developing specific interventions (Heller 1990). Though this may help us to understand something about techniques, we believe that specific interventions and scientific studies establishing risk factors are most useful because they provide a rationale for action, and because they contribute to the massive redundancy of information as studies are reported in the mass media.

We are learning more about serving the seriously mentally ill and other resource-poor groups, and about mounting prevention programs. We have a much clearer sense of direction, and a clearer sense of the obstacles, than we did thirty years ago when the field of community psychology was born. However, we still have not fully heeded the words of Stanton Coit, one of the pioneers of the settlement house movement:

> If we consider the vast amount of personal attention and time needed to understand and deal effectively with the case of any one man or family that has fallen into vice, crime, or pauperism, we shall see the impossibility of coping with even these evils alone, unless the helpers be both many and constantly at hand (Coit 1891, quoted in Levine & Levine 1992:61).

Literature Cited

Abma, J. C., Mott, F. L. 1991. Substance use and prenatal care during pregnancy among young women. *Fam. Plan. Perspect.* 23:117–22

Alcohol, Drug Abuse, and Mental Health Adm. 1987. ADAMHA update fact sheet. Washington, DC: Public Health Service

Allen, J. P., Philliber, S., Hoggson, N. 1990. School-based prevention of teen-age pregnancy and school drop-out: process evaluation of the national replication of the Teen Outreach program. *Am. J. Community Psychol.* 18:505–24

Alliance Housing Council. 1988. *Housing and Homelessness.* Washington, DC: Natl. Alliance to End Homelessness

Am. Cancer Soc. 1987. *Cancer Facts and Figures—1987.* New York: Am. Cancer Soc.

Am. Heart Assoc. 1987. *Heart Facts.* Dallas, TX: Am. Heart Assoc.

Anderson, W. 1991. The New York needle trial: the politics of public health in the age of AIDS. *Am. J. Public Health* 81:1506–17

Anthony, W. A., Cohen, M. R., Cohen, B. F. 1983. Philosophy, treatment process, and principles of the psychiatric rehabilitation approach. In *Deinstitutionalization. New Directions for Mental Health Services,* No. 17, ed. L. L. Bachrach. San Francisco: Jossey-Bass

Arce, A. A., Vergare, M. J. 1987. Homelessness, the chronically mentally ill, and community mental health centers. *Community Ment. Health J.* 23:8–15

Bachrach, L. L. 1987. Asylum for chronic mental patients. In *Leona Bachrach Speaks: Selected Speeches and Lectures. New Directions for Mental Health,* No. 35, ed. L. L. Bachrach. San Francisco: Jossey-Bass

Backer, T. E., Richardson, D. 1989. Building

bridges: psychologists and families of the mentally ill. *Am. Psychol.* 44:546–50

Barton, C., Alexander, J. F., Waldron, H., Turner, C. W., Warburton, J. 1985. Generalizing treatment effects of functional family therapy: three replications. *Am. J. Fam. Ther.* 13:16–26

Beachler, M. 1990. The mental health services program for youth. *J. Mental Health Adm.* 17:115–21

Behar, L. 1985. Changing patterns of state responsibility: a case study of North Carolina. *J. Clin. Child Psychol.* 14:188–95

Bennett, C. C. 1966. *Community Psychology*. Boston, MA: Boston Univ. Dep. Psychol.

Bennett, E. M., ed. 1987. *Social Intervention: Theory and Practice*. Queenston, Ontario: Edward Mellen

Bennett, M. I., Gudeman, J. E., Jenkins, L., Brown, A., Bennett, M. B. 1988. The value of hospital-based treatment for the homeless mentally ill. *Am. J. Psychiatry* 145:1273–76

Bertrand, J. T., Makani, B., Hassig, S. E., Niwembo, K. L., Djunghu, B. et al. 1991. AIDS-related knowledge, sexual behavior, and condom use among men and women in Kinshasa, Zaire. *Am. J. Public Health* 81:53–58

Biegel, D. W., Yamatani, H. 1987. Help-giving in self-help groups. *Hosp. Community Psychiatry* 38:1195–97

Blau, J. 1992. *The Visible Poor: Homelessness in the United States*. New York: Oxford Univ. Press

Bond, G. R., Miller, L. D., Krumweid, R. D., Ward, R. S. 1988. Assertive case management in three CMHCs: a controlled study. *Hosp. Community Psychiatry* 39:411–17

Bond, G. R., Witheridge, T. F., Dincin, J., Wasmer, D. 1991. Assertive Community Treatment: correcting some misconceptions. *Am. J. Community Psychol.* 19:41–52

Bond, G. R., Witheridge, T. F., Dincin, J., Wasmer, D., Webb, J., DeGraaf-Kaser, R. 1990. Assertive Community Treatment for frequent users of psychiatric hospitals in a large city: a controlled study. *Am. J. Community Psychol.* 18:865–91

Booth, W. 1988. Social engineers confront AIDS. *Science* 242:1237–38

Borkman, T. J., ed. 1991. Special issue: self-help groups. *Am. J. Community Psychol.* 19(5):643–805

Bureau of the Census. 1990. *Statistical abstract of the United States, 1990*. Washington, DC: US Dep. Commer.

Burns, B. J., Friedman, R. M. 1990. Examining the research base for child mental health services and policy. *J. Mental Health Adm.* 17:87–98

Cartoof, V. G., Klerman, L. V. 1986. Parental consent for abortion: impact of the Massachusetts law. *Am. J. Public Health* 76:397–400

Catania, J. A., Coates, T. J., Stall, R., Bye, L., Kegeles, S. et al. 1991. Changes in condom use among homosexual men in San Francisco. *Health Psychol.* 10:190–99

Centers for Disease Control. 1991. *Morb. Mortal. Wkly. Rep.* 40:(7 June)

Chamberlin, J. 1990. The ex-patients' movement: where we have been and where we're going. *J. Mind Behav.* 11:323–36

Chilman, C. S. 1986. Some psychosocial aspects of adolescent sexual and contraceptive behaviors in a changing American society. See Lancaster & Hamburg 1986, pp. 191–217

Christopher, F. S., Roosa, M. W. 1990. An evaluation of an adolescent pregnancy prevention program: is 'Just Say No' enough? *Fam. Relat.* 39:68–72

Chu, F. D., Trotter, S. 1974. *The Madness Establishment: Ralph Nader's Study Group Report on the National Institute of Mental Health*. New York: Grossman

Coates, T. J. 1990. Strategies for modifying sexual behavior for primary and secondary prevention of HIV disease. *J. Consult. Clin. Psychol.* 58:57–69

Coates, T. J., Stall, R. D., Kegeles, S. M., Lo, B., Morin, S. F. et al. 1988. AIDS antibody testing: will it stop the AIDS epidemic? Will it help people infected with HIV? *Am. Psychol.* 43:859–64

Cochrane, J. I., Goering, P., Rogers, J. M. 1991. Vocational programs and services in Canada. *Can. J. Community Mental Health* 10:51–63

Cohen, J. 1991. AIDS vaccine trials: bumpy road ahead. *Science* 251:1312–13

Cohen, N. D., ed. 1990. *Psychiatry Takes to the Streets: Outreach and Crisis Intervention for the Mentally Ill*. New York: Guilford

Cohen, R. Y., Stunkard, A., Felix, M. R. J. 1986. Measuring community change in disease prevention and health promotion. *Prev. Med.* 15:411–21

Crawford, I., Jason, L. A., Riordan, N., Kaufman, J., Salina, D. et al. 1990. A multimedia-based approach to increasing communication and the level of AIDS knowledge within families. *J. Community Psychol.* 18:361–73

Curry, J. F. 1991. Outcome research on residential treatment: implications and suggested directions. *Am. J. Orthopsychiatry* 61:348–57

Davidson, W. S. II, Redner, R., Blakely, C. H., Mitchell, C. M., Emshoff, J. G. 1987. Diversion of juvenile offenders: an experimental comparison. *J. Consult. Clin. Psychol.* 55:68–75

Des Jarlais, D. C., Friedman, S. R., Casriel, C. 1990. Target groups for preventing AIDS among intravenous drug users: 2. The "hard" data studies. *J. Consult. Clin. Psychol.* 58:50–56

Diamond, R. J., Van Dyke, D. 1985. Rural community support programs: the experience in three Wisconsin counties. See Stein & Test, pp. 49–58

Diamond, R. J., Wikler, D. I. 1985. Ethical problems in community treatment of the chronically mentally ill. See Stein & Test, pp. 85–93

Drob, S., Bernard, H., Lifshutz, H., Nierenberg, A. 1986. Brief group psychotherapy for herpes patients: a preliminary study. *Behav. Ther.* 17:229–38

Dryfoos, J. G. 1990. *Adolescents at Risk.* New York: Oxford Univ. Press

Edmunson, E. D., Bedell, J. R., Gordon, R. E. 1984. The community network development project: bridging the gap between professional aftercare and self-help. See Gartner & Reissman 1984, pp. 195–203

Egger, G., Fitzgerald, W., Frape, G., Monaem, A., Rubinstein, P. et al. 1983. Results of large scale media antismoking campaign in Australia: North Coast "Quit for Life" programme. *Br. Med. J.* 287:1125–28

Eisen, M., Zellman, G. L., McAlister, A. L. 1990. Evaluating the impact of a theory-based sexuality and contraceptive education program. *Fam. Plan. Perspect.* 22:261–71

Ekstrand, M. L., Coates, T. J. 1990. Maintenance of safer sexual behaviors and predictors of risky sex: the San Francisco Men's Health Study. *Am. J. Public Health* 80:973–77

Farquhar, J. W., Fortmann, S. P., Wood, P. D., Haskell, W. L. 1983. Community studies of cardiovascular disease prevention. In *Prevention of Coronary Heart Disease,* ed. N. Kaplan, J. Stamler, pp. 170–81. Philadelphia: W. B. Saunders

Farr, R. K., Koegel, P., Burnam, A. 1986. *A Study of Homelessness and Mental Illness in the Skid Row Area of Los Angeles.* Los Angeles: Los Angeles Cty. Dep. Mental Health

Fischer, P. J., Breakey, W. R. 1991. The epidemiology of alcohol, drug, and mental disorders among homeless persons. *Am. Psychol.* 46:1115–28

Fischer, P. J., Shapiro, S., Breakey, W. R., Anthony, J. C., Kramer, M. 1986. Mental health and social characteristics of the homeless: a survey of mission users. *Am. J. Public Health* 76:519–24

Flowers, J. V., Booraem, C., Miller, T. E., Iverson, A. E., Copeland, J. et al. 1991. Comparison of the results of a standardized AIDS prevention program in three geographic locations. *AIDS Educ. Prev.* 3:189–96

Forrest, J. D., Singh, S. 1990. The sexual and reproductive behavior of American women, 1982–1988. *Fam. Plan. Perspect.* 22:206–14

Foscarinis, M. 1991. The politics of homelessness: a call to action. *Am. Psychol.* 46:1232–38

Francell, C. G., Conn, V. S., Gray, D. P. 1988. Families' perceptions of burden of care for

chronic mentally ill relatives. *Hosp. Community Psychiatry* 39:1296–1300

Francescato, D., Ghirelli, G. 1988. *Fondamenti de psicologia di communita.* Roma: Nuova Italia Scientifica

Friedman, R. M., Duchnowski, A. J. 1990. Service trends in the children's mental health system: implications for the training of psychologists. In *Improving Psychological Services for Children and Adolescents with Severe Mental Disorders: Clinical Training in Psychology,* ed. P. R. Magrab, P. Wohlford, pp. 35–41. Washington, DC: Am. Psychol. Assoc.

Friedman, R. M., Street, S. 1985. Admission and discharge criteria for children's mental health services: a review of the issues and options. *J. Clin. Child Psychol.* 14:229–35

Furstenberg, F. F. Jr., Brooks-Gunn, J., Morgan, S. P. 1987. *Adolescent Mothers in Later Life.* New York: Cambridge Univ. Press

Garn, S. M., Pesick, S. D., Petzold, A. S. 1986. The biology of teenage pregnancy: the mother and the child. See Lancaster & Hamburg 1986, pp. 77–93

Garrett, C. J. 1985. Effects of residential treatment on adjudicated delinquents: a meta-analysis. *J. Res. Crime Delinq.* 22:287–308

Gartner, A., Reissman, F., eds. 1984. *The Self-Help Revolution.* New York: Human Sciences

Gerbert, B., Maguire, B. 1989. Public acceptance of the Surgeon General's brochure on AIDS. *Public Health Rep.* 104:130–33

Gesten, E. L., Jason, L. A. 1987. Social and community interventions. *Annu. Rev. Psychol.* 38:427–60

Gilman, S. R., Diamond, R. J. 1985. Economic analysis in community treatment of the chronically mentally ill. See Stein & Test, pp. 77–84

Gold Award: a network of services for the homeless chronically mentally ill. 1986. *Hosp. Community Psychiatry* 37:1148–51

Goldfine, P. E., Heath, G. A., Hardesty, V. A., Berman, H. J., Gordon, B. J., Lind, H. W. 1985. Alternatives to psychiatric hospitalization for children. *Pediatr. Clin. N. Am.* 8:527–35

Gordon, D. A., Arbuthnot, J., Gustafson, K. E., McGreen, P. 1988. Home-based behavioral-systems family therapy with disadvantaged juvenile delinquents. *Am. J. Fam. Ther.* 16:243–55

Gore, A. 1990. Public policy and the homeless. *Am. Psychol.* 45:960–62

Hall, G. B., Nelson, G., Fowler, H. S. 1987. Housing for the chronically mentally disabled: Part I—Conceptual framework and social context. *Can. J. Community Mental Health* 6:65–78

Hamburg, B. A. 1986. Subsets of adolescent mothers: developmental, biomedical, and psychosocial issues. See Lancaster & Hamburg 1986, pp. 115–45

Hassner, V. 1991. Clozapine update and AMI-

NYS strategy. *Alliance Ment. Ill N.Y. State News* (Spring) 30:5, 9

Hatfield, A. B. 1987. The National Alliance for the Mentally Ill: the meaning of a movement. *Int. J. Mental Health* 15:79–93

Hatfield, A. B. 1991. The National Alliance for the Mentally Ill: a decade later. *Community Mental Health J.* 27:95–103

Hatfield, A., ed. 1987. *Families of the Mentally Ill: Meeting the Challenges. New Directions for Mental Health Services*, No. 34. San Francisco: Jossey-Bass

Health Promotion Resource Center. 1987. *A Guide to Comprehensive Integrated Community Health Promotion Programs.* Stanford, CA: Health Promot. Resour. Cent.

Heller, K. 1990. Social and community intervention. *Annu. Rev. Psychol.* 41:141–68

Henggeler, S. W., Broduin, C. M., Melton, G. B., Mann, B. J., Smith, L. A. et al. 1991. Effects of multisystemic therapy on drug use and abuse in serious juvenile offenders: a progress report from two outcome studies. *Fam. Dyn. Addict. Q.* 1:40–51

Henggeler, S. W., Melton, G. B., Smith, L. A. 1993. Multisystemic treatment of serious juvenile offenders: an effective alternative to incarceration. *J. Consult. Clin. Psychol.* In press

Higgins, D. L., Galavotti, C., O'Reilly, K. R., Schnell, D. J., Moore, M. et al. 1991. Evidence for the effects of HIV antibody counseling and testing on risk behaviors. *J. Am. Med. Assoc.* 266:2419–29

Hinckley, E. C., Ellis, W. F. 1985. An effective alternative to residential placement: home-based services. *J. Clin. Child Psychol.* 14:209–19

Hinrichsen, G. A., Revenson, T. A., Shinn, M. 1985. Does self-help help? An empirical investigation of Scoliosis peer support groups. *J. Soc. Issues* 41:65–87

Hodgson v Minnesota. 1990. 110 S. Ct. 2926

Howard, M., McCabe, J. B. 1990. Helping teenagers postpone sexual involvement. *Fam. Plan. Perspect.* 22:21–26

Howe, C. W., Howe, J. W. 1987. The National Alliance for the Mentally Ill: history and ideology. *Int. J. Mental Health* 15:23–34

Hughs, J. M. 1977. Adolescent children of alcoholic parents and the relationship of Alateen to these children. *J. Consult. Clin. Psychol.* 45:946–47

Institute of Medicine. 1988. *Homelessness, Health, and Human Needs.* Washington, DC: Natl. Acad. Press

Iscoe, I., Harris, L. C. 1984. Social and community interventions. *Annu. Rev. Psychol.* 35:333–60

Jacobs, M., Goodman, G. 1989. Psychology and self-help groups: predictions on a partnership. *Am. Psychol.* 44:1–10

Jemmott, J. B. III, Jemmott, J. B., Fong, G. T. 1992. Reductions in HIV risk-associated sexual behaviors among black male adolescents: effects of an AIDS prevention intervention. *Am. J. Public Health* 82:372–77

Jensen, P. S. 1983. Risk, protective factors, and supportive interventions in chronic airway obstruction. *Arch. Gen. Psychiatry* 40:1203–7

Johnson, D. L. 1989. Schizophrenia as a brain disease: implications for psychologists and families. *Am. Psychol.* 44:553–55

Joint Commission on Mental Health of Children. 1969. *Crisis in Child Mental Health: Challenge for the 1970s.* New York: Harper & Row

Jordan, D. D., Hernandez, M. 1990. The Ventura planning model: a proposal for mental health reform. *J. Mental Health Adm.* 17:26–47

Joseph, H., Roman-Nay, H. 1990. The homeless intravenous drug abuser and the AIDS epidemic. In *AIDS and Intravenous Drug Use: Future Directions for Community-Based Prevention Research. Natl. Inst. Drug Abuse Res. Monogr. Ser.* 93, ed. C. Leukefeld, R. Battjes, Z. Amsel, pp. 210–53. Washington, DC: US Dep. Health Human Serv.

Kelly, J. A., Kalichman, S. C., Kauth, M. R., Kilgore, H. G., Hood, H. V. et al. 1991a. Situational factors associated with AIDS risk behavior lapses and coping strategies used by gay men who successfully avoid lapses. *Am. J. Public Health* 81:1335–38

Kelly, J. A., St. Lawrence, J. S., Diaz, Y. E., Stevenson, L. Y., Hauth, A. C. et al. 1991b. HIV risk behavior reduction following intervention with key opinion leaders of population: an experimental analysis. *Am. J. Public Health* 81:168–71

Kelly, J. A., St. Lawrence, J. S., Hood, H. V., Brasfield, T. L. 1989. Behavior intervention to reduce AIDS risk activities. *J. Consult. Clin. Psychol.* 57:60–67

Kelly, J. G. 1966. Ecological constraints on mental health services. *Am. Psychol.* 21:535–39

Kelly, J. G. 1986. Context and process: an ecological view of the interdependence of practice and research. *Am. J. Community Psychol.* 14:581–90

Kerr, P. 1991. Mental hospital chains accused of much cheating on insurance. *The New York Times,* Nov. 24, A-1, 28

Kiesler, C. A. 1982. Public policy and professional myths about mental hospitalization: an empirical reassessment of policy-related beliefs. *Am. Psychol.* 37:1323–39

Kiesler, C. A., Simpkins, C., Morton, T. 1989. The psychiatric inpatient treatment of children and youth in general hospitals. *Am. J. Community Psychol.* 17:821–29

Kinney, J., Haapala, D., Booth, C. 1991. *Keeping Families Together: The Homebuilders Model.* Hawthorne, NY: de Gruyter

Kirby, D., Waszak, C., Ziegler, J. 1991. Six school-based clinics: their reproductive health services and impact on sexual behavior. *Fam. Plan. Perspect.* 23:6–16

Knitzer, J. 1982. *Unclaimed Children: The Failure of Public Responsibility to Chil-*

dren and Adolescents in Need of Mental Health Services. Washington, DC: Children's Defense Fund

Kondratas, A. 1991. Housing policy and homelessness in the United States. Am. Psychol. 46:1226–31

Lab, S. P., Whitehead, J. T. 1988. An analysis of juvenile correctional treatment. Crime Delinq. 34:60–83

Lamb, H. R., ed. 1984. The Homeless Mentally Ill: A Task Force Report of the American Psychiatric Association. Washington, DC: Am. Psychiatric Assoc.

Lancaster, J. B., Hamburg, B. A., eds. 1986. School-Age Pregnancy and Parenthood: Biosocial Dimensions. Hawthorne: de Gruyter

Lee, B. A., Link, B. G., Toro, P. A. 1991. Images of the homeless: public views and media messages. Housing Policy Debate 2:3–36

Lefley, H. P. 1987. The family's response to mental illness in a relative. Int. J. Mental Health 15:3–22

Lefley, H. P. 1989. Family burden and family stigma in major mental illness. Am. Psychol. 44:556–60

Levine, I. S., Rog, D. J. 1990. Mental health services for homeless mentally ill persons: federal initiatives and current service trends. Am. Psychol. 45:963–68

Levine, M. 1981. The History and Politics of Community Mental Health. New York: Oxford Univ. Press

Levine, M. 1986. The role of special master in institutional reform litigation: a case study. Law & Policy 8:275–321

Levine, M., Levine, A. 1992. Helping Children: A Social History. New York: Oxford Univ. Press

Levine, M., Perkins, D. V. 1987. Principles of Community Psychology. New York: Oxford Univ. Press

Levitz, L. S., Stunkard, A. J. 1974. A therapeutic coalition for obesity: behavior modification and patient self-help. Am. J. Psychiatry 131:423–27

Levy, L. 1984. Issues in research and evaluation. See Gartner & Reissman 1984, pp. 155–72

Lieberman, M. A., Videka-Sherman, L. 1986. The impact of self-help groups on the mental health of widows and widowers. Am. J. Orthopsychiatry 53:435–49

Long, L. A., Van Tosh, L. 1988. Program Descriptions of Consumer-Run Programs for Homeless People With a Mental Illness, Vol. 2. Rockville, MD: Progr. Homeless Ment. Ill, Natl. Inst. Mental Health

Longshore, D. 1990. AIDS education for three high-risk populations. Eval. Program Plan. 13:67–72

Lorion, R. P. 1990. Evaluating HIV risk reduction efforts: ten lessons from psychotherapy and prevention outcome strategies. J. Community Psychol. 18:325–36

Maccoby, N., Alexander, J. 1980. Use of media

in lifestyle programs. In Behavioral Medicine: Changing Health Lifestyles, ed. P. O. Davidson, S. M. Davidson. New York: Brunner/Mazel

Madeira, E. 1986. A comprehensive systems approach to promoting mutual aid self-help groups: the New Jersey Self-Help Clearinghouse Model. J. Volunt. Action Res. 15:57–63

Maton, K. I. 1988. Social support, organizational characteristics, psychological well-being, and group appraisal in three self-help populations. Am. J. Community Psychol. 16:53–77

Mays, V. M., Albee, G. W., Schneider, S. F. 1989. Primary Prevention of AIDS: Psychological Approaches. Newbury Park, CA: Sage

McCaig, L. F., Hardy, A. M., Winn, D. M. 1991. Knowledge about AIDS and HIV in the US adult population: influence of local incidence of AIDS. Am. J. Public Health 81:1591–95

McKusick, L., Hoff, C. C., Stall, R., Coates, T. J. 1991. Tailoring AIDS prevention: differences in behavioral strategies among heterosexual and gay bar patrons in San Francisco. AIDS Educ. Prev. 3:1–9

Medvene, L. J., Krauss, D. H. 1989. Causal attributions and parent-child relationships in a self-help group for families of the mentally ill. J. Appl. Soc. Psychol. 19:1413–30

Meissen, G. J., Gleason, D. F., Embree, M. G. 1991. An assessment of the needs of mutual help groups. Am. J. Community Psychol. 19:427–42

Minde, K., Shosenberg, N., Marton, P., Thompson, J., Ripley, J., Burns, S. 1980. Self-help groups in a premature nursery: a controlled evaluation. J. Pediatr. 96:933–40

Moran, J. S., Janes, H. R., Peterman, T. A., Stone, K. M. 1990. Increase in condom sales following AIDS education and publicity, United States. Am. J. Public Health 80:607–8

Morrison, D. M. 1985. Adolescent contraceptive behavior: a review. Psychol. Bull. 98:538–68

Mosher, L. R., Burti, L. 1989. Community Mental Health: Principles and Practice. New York: Norton

Mosher, W. D., McNally, J. W. 1991. Contraceptive use at first premarital intercourse: United States, 1965–1988. Fam. Plan. Perspect. 23:108–16

Mowbray, C. T. 1990. Community treatment for the seriously mentally ill: Is this community psychology? Am. J. Community Psychol. 18:893–902

Olds, D. L. 1988. The prenatal/early infancy project. In 14 Ounces of Prevention, ed. R. H. Price, E. L. Cowen, R. P. Lorion, J. Ramos-McKay, pp. 9–23. Washington, DC: Am. Psychol. Assoc.

Olfson, M. 1990. Assertive Community Treatment: an evaluation of the experimental evidence. *Hosp. Community Psychiatry* 41:634–41

O'Sullivan, M. J., Peterson, P. D., Cox, G. B., Kirkeby, J. 1989. Ethnic populations: community mental health services, ten years later. *Am. J. Community Psychol.* 17:17–30

Palca, J. 1991. The sobering geography of AIDS. *Science* 252:372–73

Paquin, M. J. R., Perry, G. P. 1990. Maintaining successful interventions in social, vocational, and community rehabilitation. *Can. Community Mental Health* 9:39–49

Peterson, G., Abrams, D. B., Elder, J. P., Beaudin, P. A. 1985. Professional versus self-help weight loss at the work site: the challenge of making a public health impact. *Behav. Ther.* 16:213–22

Petrakis, P. L., ed. 1988. *The Surgeon General's Workshop on Self-Help and Public Health.* Washington, DC: USGPO

President's Commission on Mental Health. 1978. *Report to the President,* Vol. I. Washington, DC: USGPO, Stock No. 040-000-00390

Puska, P., Nissinen, A., Tuomilehto, J., Salonen, J. T., Koskela, K. et al 1985. The community-based strategy to prevent coronary heart disease: conclusions from the ten years of the North Karelia Project. *Annu. Rev. Public Health* 6:147–93

Raiff, N. R. 1982. Self-help participation and quality of life: a study of the staff of Recovery, Inc. In *Helping People to Help Themselves: Self-Help and Prevention,* ed. L. D. Borman, L. E. Borck, R. Hess, F. L. Pasquale, pp. 79–89. New York: Haworth

Raiff, N. R. 1984. Some health related outcomes of self-help participation: Recovery, Inc. as a case example of a self-help organization in mental health. See Gartner & Reissman 1984, pp. 183–93

Rappaport, J., Seidman, E., Toro, P. A., McFadden, L. S., Reischl, T. M. et al. 1985. Finishing the unfinished business: collaborative research with a mutual help organization. *Soc. Policy* 15:12–24

Reissman, F. 1965. The "helper-therapy" principle. *Soc. Work* 10:27–32

Reppucci, N. D. 1987. Prevention and ecology: teen-age pregnancy, child sexual abuse, and organized youth sports. *Am. J. Community Psychol.* 15:1–22

Revenson, T. A., Cassel, B. J. 1992. An exploration of leadership in a medical mutual help organization. *Am. J. Community Psychol.* 19:683–98

Rickel, A. U. 1989. *Teen Pregnancy and Parenting.* New York: Hemisphere

Rioux, M. H., Crawford, C. 1990. Poverty and disability: toward a new framework for community mental health. *Can. J. Community Mental Health* 9:97–109

Roberts, L. J., Luke, D. A., Rappaport, J., Seidman, E., Toro, P. A., Reischl, T. M. 1991. Charting uncharted terrain: a behavioral observation system for mutual help groups.

Am. J. Community Psychol. 19:715–37

Rogers, J. L., Boruch, R. F., Stoms, G. B., DeMoya, D. 1991. Impact of the Minnesota parental notification law on abortion and birth. *Am. J. Public Health* 81:294–98

Rosenthal, J. A., Glass, G. V. 1990. Comparative impacts of alternatives to adolescent placement. *J. Soc. Serv. Res.* 13:19–37

Rossi, P. H. 1989. *Down and Out in America: The Origins of Homelessness.* Univ. Chicago Press

Rugg, D. L., O'Reilly, K. R., Galavotti, C. 1990. AIDS prevention evaluation: conceptual and methodological issues. *Eval. Program Plan.* 13:79–90

Salem, D. A. 1990. Community-based services and resources: the significance of choice and diversity. *Am. J. Community Psychol.* 18:909–16

Sarason, S. B. 1988. *The Making of an American Psychologist: An Autobiography.* San Francisco: Jossey-Bass

Saxe, L., Cross, T., Silverman, N., Dougherty, D. 1987. *Children's Mental Health: Problems and Services.* Durham, NC: Duke Univ. Press. (Originally published in 1986 by the Off. Technol. Assess., US Congr., Washington, DC: USGPO)

Schaefer, C. E., Swanson, A. J. 1988. *Children in Residential Care: Critical Issues in Treatment.* New York: Van Nostrand Reinhold

Schwartz, I. J. 1991. Out of home placement of children: selected issues and prospects for the future. *Behav. Sci. Law* 9:189–99

Sheridan, K., Humfleet, G., Phair, J., Lyons, J. 1990. The effects of AIDS education on the knowledge and attitudes of community leaders. *J. Community Psychol.* 18:354–60

Shinn, M. 1992. Homelessness: what is a psychologist to do? *Am. J. Community Psychol.* 20:1–24

Shinn, M., Burke, P. D., Bedford, S. 1990. Homelessness: abstracts of the psychological and behavioral literature 1967-1990. *Bibliographies in Psychology,* Ser. 7. Washington, DC: Am. Psychol. Assoc.

Shinn, M., Weitzman, B. C. 1990. Research on homelessness: an introduction. *J. Soc. Issues* 46:1–12

Small, R., Kennedy, K., Bender, B. 1991. Critical issues for practice in residential treatment: the view from within. *Am. J. Orthopsychiatry* 61:327–38

Soler, M., Warboys, L. 1990. Services for violent and severely disturbed children: the Willie M. litigation. In *Stepping Stones: Successful Advocacy for Children,* ed. S. Dicker, pp. 61–112. New York: Found. Child Dev.

Sorensen, J. L., Wermuth, L. A., Gibson, D. R., Choi, K., Guydisch, J. R. et al. 1991. *Preventing AIDS in Drug Users and Their Sexual Partners.* New York: Guilford

Spiegel, D., Bloom, J. R., Yalom, I. 1981. Group support for patients with metastatic cancer: a randomized prospective outcome study. *Arch. Gen. Psychiatry* 38:527–33

Stahler, G. J., DuCette, J. P. 1991. Evaluating adolescent pregnancy programs: rethinking our priorities. *Fam. Plan. Perspect.* 23:129–33

Stein, L. I., Test, M. A., eds. 1985. *The Training in Community Living Model: A Decade of Experience. New Directions for Mental Health Services,* ed. H. R. Lamb, No. 26. San Francisco: Jossey-Bass

Stephens, R. C., Feucht, T. E., Roman, S. W. 1991. Effects of an intervention program on AIDS-related drug and needle behavior among intravenous drug users. *Am. J. Public Health* 81:568–71

Stroul, B. A. 1986. *Models of Community Support Services: Approaches to Helping Persons with Long-Term Mental Illness.* Boston: Cent. Psychiatric Rehabil.

Stroul, B. A., Goldman, S. K. 1990. Study of community-based services for children and adolescents who are seriously disturbed *J. Mental Health Adm.* 17:61–77

Surgeon General. 1979. *Healthy People.* Washington, DC: US Dep. Health Human Serv.

Surles, R., Blanch, A., Shern, D., Donahue, S. 1992. Case management as a strategy for systems change. *Health Affairs* 11:151–63

Taube, C. A., Morlock, L., Burns, B. J., Santos, A. B. 1990. New directions in research on Assertive Community Treatment. *Hosp. Community Psychiatry* 41:642–46

Test, M. A. 1991. The Training in Community Living model: delivering treatment and rehabilitation services through a continuous treatment team. In *Handbook of Psychiatric Rehabilitation,* ed. R. Liberman. New York: Pergamon Press

Thomas, D., Veno, A., eds. 1992. *Psychology and Social Change.* Palmerston North, New Zealand: Dunmore

Thomas, S. B., Quinn, S. C. 1991. The Tuskegee syphilis study, 1932-1972: implications for HIV education and AIDS risk reduction programs in the black community. *Am. J. Public Health* 81:1498–1505

Thompson, K. S., Griffith, E. E. H., Leaf, P. J. 1990. A historical review of the Madison model of community care. *Hosp. Community Psychiatry* 41:625–34

Toro, P. A. 1990. Evaluating professionally operated and self-help programs for the seriously mentally ill. *Am. J. Community Psychol.* 18:903–8

Toro, P. A., McDonell, D. M. 1992. Beliefs, attitudes, and knowledge about homelessness: a survey of the general public. *Am. J. Community Psychol.* 20:53–80

Toro, P. A., Rapapport, J., Seidman, E. 1987. Social climate comparison of mutual help and psychotherapy groups. *J. Consult. Clin. Psychol.* 55:430–31

Toro, P. A., Reischl, T. M., Zimmerman, M. A., Rappaport, J., Seidman, E. et al. 1988. Professionals in mutual help groups: impact on social climate and members' behavior.

J. Consult. Clin. Psychol. 56:631–32

Toro, P. A., Trickett, E. J., Wall, D. D., Salem, D. A. 1991. Homelessness in the United States: an ecological perspective. *Am. Psychol.* 46:1208–18

Toro, P. A., Wall, D. D. 1991. Research on homeless persons: diagnostic comparisons and practice implications. *Prof. Psychol.: Res. Pract.* 22:479–88

Torrey, E. F. 1988a. *Nowhere to Go: The Tragic Odyssey of the Homeless Mentally Ill.* New York: Harper & Row

Torrey, E. F. 1988b. *Surviving Schizophrenia: A Family Manual.* New York: Harper & Row. Revised ed.

Torrey, E. F. 1990. Economic barriers to widespread implementation of model programs for the seriously mentally ill. *Hosp. Community Psychiatry* 41:526–31

Upchurch, D. M., McCarthy, J. 1989. Adolescent childbearing and high school completion in the 1980s: have things changed? *Fam. Plan. Perspect.* 21:199–208

US Department of Justice. 1989. *Children in Custody, 1975-1985: Census of Public and Private Juvenile Detention, Correctional, and Shelter Facilities.* Washington, DC: Bur. Justice Stat.

Vachon, M. L., Lyall, W. A., Rogers, J., Freedman-Letofsky, K., Freeman, S. J. 1980. A controlled study of self-help intervention for widows. *Am. J. Psychiatry* 137:1380–84

Valdiserri, R. O., Lyter, D. W., Leviton, L. C., Callahan, C. M., Kingsley, L. A., Rinaldo, C. R. 1989. AIDS prevention in homosexual and bisexual men: results of a randomized trial evaluating two risk reduction interventions. *AIDS* 3:21–26

Videka, L. M., ed. 1979. Psychosocial adaptation in a medical self-help group. In *Self-Help Groups for Coping with Crisis: Origins, Processes, Members, and Impact,* ed. L. D. Lieberman, L. D. Borman & Assoc., pp. 362–86. San Francisco: Jossey-Bass

Watters, J. K., Downing, M., Case, P., Lorvick, J., Cheng, Y. et al. 1990. AIDS prevention for intravenous drug users in the community: street-based education and risk behavior. *Am. J. Community Psychol.* 18:587–96

Weithorn, L. A. 1988. Mental hospitalization of troublesome youth: an analysis of skyrocketing admission rates. *Stanford Law Rev.* 40:773–838

Wells, K. 1991. Placement of emotionally disturbed children in residential treatment: a review of placement criteria. *Am. J. Orthopsychiatry* 61:339–47

Wilson, W. J. 1987. *The Truly Disadvantaged: The Inner City, the Underclass, and Public Policy.* Univ. Chicago Press

Winett, R. A., Altman, D. G., King, A. C. 1990. Conceptual and strategic foundations for effective media campaigns for preventing the spread of HIV infection. *Eval. Program Plan.* 13:91–104

558 LEVINE ET AL

Winett, R. A., King, A. C., Altman, D. G. 1989. *Health Psychology and Public Health: An Integrative Approach.* New York: Pergamon Press

Witheridge, T. F. 1989. The Assertive Community Treatment worker: an emerging role and its implications for professional training. *Hosp. Community Psychiatry* 40:620–24

Witheridge, T. F., Dincin, J. 1985. The Bridge: an assertive outreach program in an urban setting. See Stein & Test, pp. 65–76

Wright, J. D. 1989. *Address Unknown: The Homeless in America.* Hawthorne: de Gruyter

Young, J., Williams, C. L. 1989. Group process and social climate of GROW, a community mental health organization. *Aust. NZ J. Psychiatry* 23:117–23

Zimmerman, M. A., Reischl, T. M., Seidman, E., Rappaport, J., Toro, P. A., Salem, D. A. 1991. Expansion strategies of a mutual help organization. *Am. J. Community Psychol.* 19:251–78

Annu. Rev. Psychol. 1993. 44:559-84

SOCIAL-COGNITIVE MECHANISMS IN THE DEVELOPMENT OF CONDUCT DISORDER AND DEPRESSION

Kenneth A. Dodge

Department of Psychology and Human Development, Vanderbilt University, Nashville, Tennessee 37215

KEYWORDS: social information processing, child psychopathology, aggressive behavior, knowledge structures, mental processes

CONTENTS

INTRODUCTION.. 559
   Mental Processes in Social Behavior 560
SOCIAL-INFORMATION-PROCESSING THEORY 560
   Application to Single Behavioral Events 562
   Application to Child Psychopathology 563
   Critique 571
KNOWLEDGE STRUCTURES THAT GUIDE PROCESSING 573
   Relation to Aggressive Behavior 575
   Relation to Depression 577
DEVELOPMENTAL PSYCHOPATHOLOGY OF CONDUCT DISORDER
   AND DEPRESSION 578
CONCLUSION 580

INTRODUCTION

> Just as the physical sciences can be conceived as the study of energy in its many aspects, the behavioral and social sciences can be characterized in terms of their concern with the processing and transformation of information (Estes 1991:1).

This statement by a highly respected experimental psychologist emphasizes the central role that information-processing and information-transformation

0066-4308/93/0201-0559$02.00

theories have come to play in important psychological domains. Progress in child psychopathology over the past decade can be traced to the application of these theories to problems of behavioral maladaptation in childhood (e.g. Garber & Hilsman in press; Huesmann 1989; Ingram 1984; Rubin & Krasnor 1986).

Information-processing theories describe the mental processes that are proximally responsible for the display of a maladaptive behavioral response to a social stimulus (e.g. a depressive response to rejection by a loved one or an aggressive response to a provocation by a peer). Information-transformation theories (e.g. schema theory, working models) describe how information in behavioral episodes is transformed in memory into knowledge structures that guide future processing and account for continuity in behavior across time. These mental process-behavioral response linkages form the building blocks for psychopathological disorders when habitual maladaptive mental processing is linked to habitual deviant behavior.

The goals of this chapter are: (a) to review critically the progress that has been made in the application of social-information-processing theory and schema theory to the child psychopathologic disorders of conduct disorder and depression; (b) to integrate concepts of schema theory with social-information-processing theory into a broad theory of social-cognitive developmental psychopathology; and (c) to suggest how this new theory might be applied to child conduct disorder and depression.

Mental Processes in Social Behavior

The conceptual grounding for theories of mental processes in social behavior comes from experimental psychology and cognitive science. Progress in cognitive science has been achieved through the search for essential cognitive architectures that describe the set of informational structures and symbol-manipulating processing that characterize learning and the relation between stimuli and responses (Estes 1991). Basic architectures have been described in theories of how individuals store and retrieve information in memory (Underwood 1969), search associative memory (Raaijmakers & Shiffrin 1981), automatize search and attention (Schneider & Shiffrin 1977), distribute processing in parallel and hierarchical fashion (Rumelhart & McClelland 1986), and, ultimately, solve problems (Newell & Simon 1972). All of these theories are characterized by a set of sequential processes in which individuals encode, represent, and store information that is later accessed in behavioral responding. Descriptions of how individuals accomplish these tasks form the basis for understanding how individuals interact with their social environment as well.

SOCIAL-INFORMATION-PROCESSING THEORY

Essential features of this architecture as applied to social behavior have been formulated in theories of social information processing (Dodge et al 1986;

McFall 1982; Rubin & Krasnor 1986). These theories describe both the cognitive tasks of perception and problem solving and the emotional tasks of integrating this information with one's goals, motivational state, and arousal regulation. The term "mental process" is meant to include both cognitive and emotional features.

According to these theories, a person's behavioral response to a situational stimulus (such as rejection by a loved one or a provocation by a peer) occurs as a function of a sequence of processing steps. This sequence is conceptualized as an ongoing repetitive process that occurs during ongoing social interactions, in either conscious or nonconscious ways. Within-individual variations in behavioral responding across different stimuli are hypothesized to occur as a function of cue-elicited variations in processing. Likewise, cross-individual differences in behavioral responding to the same stimulus are hypothesized to occur as a function of cross-individual differences in processing.

The first step in this sequence of processing social information is to *encode* relevant aspects of the stimulus array through sensory input, selective attention to social cues, and storage of cue information into short-term memory. The stimulus array at any point in time is so complex and overwhelming that the developing organism learns to attend selectively to certain features (such as facial expression) over other features, in order to respond effectively. Personal-emotional needs (such as self-preservation) and socializing influences (such as a parent's directives) help the developing toddler child learn to attend to features such as others' intent, social norms and rules, and threats (Walden & Ogan 1988).

Once cues are encoded, meaning is applied through the second step of *mental representation.* The child stores in memory a meaningful interpretation of the stimulus rather than iconic traces of the stimulus itself (Schneider 1991). For example, a child who has been left out of a social group (such as a ball team or lunch table gathering) might interpret and store the event either as an act of willful rejection by the peer group or as an inadvertent slip-up. What becomes important is the meaning applied by the child to the encoded stimulus array rather than the topographical features of the event itself. Inevitably, meanings are applied that relate the stimulus to the individual's emotional needs and goals.

The mental representation elicits one or more behavioral and affective responses, through the step of *response accessing.* Mental representations are conditioned (or innately hard-wired) to be associated with numerous possible responses that include verbalizations, motor activities, endocrine secretions, autonomic arousal, and experienced affect (Schneider 1991). For example, a child who interprets an act of social rejection as a threat to overall self-concept might access responses that include crying, loss of appetite, sad affect, and cortisol secretions. Response accessing is known to follow rules (such as "rejection cues crying") (Dodge et al 1986) that are probably stored in the brain as acquired associative networks.

Accessed responses are not necessarily enacted in behavior (that is, we all have had the experience of a withheld impulse), so a fourth step of *response evaluation* is posited to describe an individual's decision making. Responses may be evaluated in terms of moral ("good" versus "bad") acceptability and/or anticipated consequences that could include interpersonal, intrapersonal, and instrumental outcomes. When an accessed response passes threshold criteria of acceptability, it is selected for enactment. If a response is deemed unacceptable, the individual feeds back to further response accessing (this processing is experienced by the individual as problem solving) until an acceptable response is selected (Crick & Ladd 1991).

Not all accessed responses are submitted to scrutiny of evaluation, however. Some responses, such as endocrine secretion, heart-rate changes, and experienced affects, are triggered without evaluation and without the inhibiting control of evaluative restraints (that is, once they are accessed, enactment follows immediately) (Guerra & Slaby 1989). Failure to evaluate can also occur because of developmental immaturity or emotional dysregulation. It is hypothesized here that infants engage in little or no response evaluation and that the evaluative process is acquired with neural development and a growing store of experiences. However, heightened arousal, physiological intemperance (brought on by fatigue, alcohol, or appetitive needs) or matters of emotional importance can lead to temporary failure to consider long-term outcomes adequately in favor of dependence on immediate gratification (Dodge & Somberg 1987). Failing to evaluate accessed responses sufficiently can be termed a problem of impulse control, delay of gratification, or over-emotionality (as in a "passionate" rather than reasoned response), whereas evaluating outcomes fully but in deviant ways can be termed a problem of inappropriate values, inaccurate beliefs, or poor decision-making.

The final step of processing is *enactment,* in which the selected response is transformed into behavior. Behavior here includes verbalizations, motor activity, autonomic activation, neuroendocrine secretions, and any other overt response that is brain-mediated. Many behaviors require rehearsal and practice to be enacted competently, so the concept of skill applies to the task of enactment.

The path from a particular stimulus to its behavioral response is linear in that the processing steps follow sequentially and in necessary order; however, the information-processing system is dynamic and processing occurs at all steps simultaneously (Rumelhart & McClelland 1986). The child is encoding new cues while she or he is accessing responses to a previous cue, and while she or he is enacting a response to an even earlier cue, and so on. The sequential nature applies only to the processing of a single cue, whereas in reality processing more likely occurs in distributed parallel ways.

Application to Single Behavioral Events

Social-information-processing theory is a description of the mental processes implicated in a single event. As such, it is a plausible and extremely powerful heuristic. For example, we can describe an act of aggressive behavior such as hitting a provocative peer in terms of processing operations that might include interpreting the peer's behavior as malicious and failing to consider the long-term consequences of hitting. At this level, the social-information-processing analysis is more a description of *how* a particular behavior comes about than it is an explanation of *why* the behavior occurred. It is a description of the phenomenology of social interaction. This description may be the most important contribution of the social-information-processing analysis.

The relation between processing and behavior is so close that sometimes deviant behaviors are defined in terms of deviant processing. Depression is sometimes operationally defined by helpless attributions and hopeless expectations. Defensive aggression is defined as a reaction to an attribution of threat, and impulsive aggression is defined as an act committed without regard to its likely consequences.

Empirical analyses also support the role of processing in individual deviant acts. Dodge (1980) found that when children attribute hostile intent to a peer provocateur, the probability of a subsequent behavioral response of aggression is .70, whereas when the same children attribute benign intent to a provocateur, the probability of aggression is just .25. Likewise, Bandura (1986) has demonstrated in numerous contexts that aggressive behavior follows from evaluations that aggression will lead to positive outcomes.

Application to Child Psychopathology

Social-information-processing theory can be extended to describe and to explain general patterns of deviant behavior and child psychopathology. The logic is that if a processing action (such as attributing hostile intent) is correlated with a deviant behavior (such as an aggressive act), then a general processing tendency (a bias to attribute hostile intentions) will be correlated with a general behavioral tendency (conduct disorder). Likewise, if specific attributions (of helplessness and hopelessness) lead to specific symptom responses (of cortisol secretions and listlessness), then a general processing tendency (to attribute negative stimuli in helpless and hopeless ways) will be correlated with psychopathology (depression).

Over the past decade, a large body of empirical studies has examined information-processing tendencies in socially or clinically deviant samples of children. These studies generally indicate that both aggressive and depressed children display processing biases and deficits at all stages of processing and in numerous types of social situations, but that the processing patterns of these two groups differ in crucial ways. Contrasting these two groups affords the opportunity to examine which processing tendencies are characteristic of deviance in general and which are specific to particular disorders.

ENCODING   Crucial features of encoding include attention to as many relevant cues as possible and in an unbiased manner. Aggressive children have been found to have difficulties with both patterns. Dodge & Newman (1981) assessed the degree to which children attend to all available relevant cues by allowing children to gather as many cues as they deemed necessary in order to make a behavioral decision. They found that chronically aggressive school children attend to fewer cues than do nonaggressive children. Consequently, the interpretations that these aggressive children make about the social cues are less accurate than when they encode all cues and less accurate than the interpretations of other children.

Not only is the encoding by aggressive children incomplete, it is systematically biased toward sensitivity to hostile cues. Gouze (1987) has found that aggressive children direct their attention selectively toward hostile social cues and have difficulty diverting their attention away from these cues. This pattern of hypervigilance to hostile cues may serve a defensive function for aggressive children, but it also enhances the likelihood that these children will interpret stimuli in hostile ways and will respond aggressively in retaliation. For example, Dodge & Frame (1982) examined the relation between patterns of attention (assessed by free recall of previously presented hostile and nonhostile cues) and subsequent interpretations made by children and found that attention to hostile cues is correlated with hostile attributions about the intent of the stimulus person and subsequent aggressive behavioral response.

Beck (1967) was the first to hypothesize that depressed individuals filter out positive cues and exaggerate attention to negative cues when processing novel stimuli in situations involving affiliative loss or failure. Ingram (1984) and Kuiper & Olinger (1986) followed suit. As Garber & Hilsman (in press) noted, "the depressed individual is primed to perceive and process depressogenic information over other types of information available." Hammen (Hammen & Zupan 1984; Zupan et al 1987) has supported this hypothesis in empirical studies that have shown that depressed children attend to and recall negative self-referent words selectively over positive words, whereas nondepressed children demonstrate an opposite pattern.

Thus, both aggressive and depressed children demonstrate biased encoding, with aggressive children selectively attending to hostile acts directed toward the self (leading to hostile attributions and retaliatory aggression) and depressed children attending to failure, loss, and negative self-reference (presumably leading to self-rumination and other depressive symptoms).

MENTAL REPRESENTATION   The second step of processing involves representation of the encoded cues, including a broad array of features such as attributions of causality, interpretations of intent, social perspective-taking, moral reasoning, inferences about self-worth, and generation of expectations about future events. Again, both aggressive and depressed children demonstrate idiosyncrasies in the manner in which they represent encoded cues.

Socially deviant or unpopular children (including both aggressive and withdrawn children) have been found to display relative deficits in *affective perspective taking* (that is, understanding the emotion of another) (Marcus 1980), *social perspective taking* (that is, understanding the reasoning of another)

(Chandler 1973; Rubin & Maioni 1975), *generation of organized inferences* (Campbell & Yarrow 1961), and *social reasoning* (Pellegrini 1985; Selman 1980). Goldman et al (1980) found that rejected children (who are actively disliked and are, on average, highly aggressive) are twice as inaccurate as withdrawn children and popular children. These findings suggest that aggressive children are inaccurate in their labelling of emotions in others, whereas internalizing problem children are not.

Studies of aggressive children have focused primarily on attributions of others' intent in situations in which the other has provoked the subject. As hypothesized by Feshbach (1970), the probability of an aggressive behavioral response is much more likely when a child attributes hostile intent than when the same child attributes benign intent. Dodge (1980) found that aggressive responses occur 70 percent of the time after a hostile attribution is made, in contrast with 25 percent of the time when a benign attribution is made. He also found that when a provocateur's actual intent is ambiguous, aggressive children are about 50 percent more likely to infer hostile intent than are nonaggressive children, thus accounting for some (but not all) of their increased tendency to behave aggressively.

At least 26 independent studies have demonstrated a similar effect in chronically aggressive children, the effect being termed a "hostile attributional bias" by Nasby et al (1979). This processing bias is displayed by rejected-aggressive elementary school boys (Guerra & Slaby 1989; Lochman 1987; Sancilio et al 1989; Waas 1988) and girls (Feldman & Dodge 1987), aggressive children from European-American backgrounds (Dell Fitzgerald & Asher 1987) as well as those from African-American backgrounds (Dodge & Coie 1987), boys with externalizing problems (McClaskey 1988), rejected-aggressive junior high school children (Dodge & Tomlin 1987), aggressive boys in outpatient clinics (Milich & Dodge 1984), aggressive boys in residential treatment (Nasby et al 1979), aggressive adolescents in a maximum security prison (Dodge et al 1990b), and adolescent offenders incarcerated for violent criminal acts (Slaby & Guerra 1988). Hostile attributional biases have been demonstrated in aggressive children not only in response to hypothetical stimuli but also in response to actual peer provocations under controlled circumstances (Steinberg & Dodge 1983).

Even though hostile attributional bias is a highly robust phenomenon, the magnitude of effect is not always large. Several circumstances moderate this effect. For example, the effect is a personalized tendency, in that aggressive children do not display this bias when they are merely observers to an event, that is, when they are evaluating behavior by one peer toward a second peer (Dodge & Frame 1982; Sancilio et al 1989). Their own emotional involvement is crucial, in that they are more likely to display this bias when they are affectively aroused than when not (Dodge & Somberg 1987). Hostile attributional bias is not related to all kinds of aggressive deviance. It is predictive of angry reactive violence but not proactive kinds of aggressive behavior, such as bullying and coercion, that do not involve anger (Dodge & Coie 1987). It predicts violent crimes but not nonviolent crimes (Dodge et al 1990b).

Because the studies reported here are correlational, it has not been proven that the relation between attributional bias and chronic reactive aggression is causal. It might be that the causal path is actually reversed or that these two variables are linked by a third factor. Three additional kinds of evidence are consistent with a causal relation, however. First, Dodge et al (1990a) found that hostile attributional biases in preschool predict the onset of aggressive behavior problems six months later in kindergarten, suggesting an antecedent relation. Second, experimental manipulation of children's expectations (as hostile or nonhostile) regarding the intent of peers whom they are about to meet leads those children to behave in ways that are consistent with this attribution (Rabiner & Coie 1989). Third, Slaby & Guerra (1988) found that experimental manipulation of hostile attributions through long-term intervention can lead to reductions in aggressive behavior. Thus, several kinds of evidence point toward hostile attributional biases as one mechanism implicated in chronic reactive aggression.

The tendency by aggressive children to interpret others' intentions as hostile extends to stimuli in which the intent of the peer provoking the subject is acually benign. This tendency, called an *intention-cue detection deficit* has been found in aggressive preschoolers (Dodge et al 1990a), aggressive elementary school children (Dodge et al 1984), reactive-aggressive African-American boys (Dodge & Coie 1987), and incarcerated adolescent males (Dodge et al 1990b). This deficit is not due simply to intelligence or general cue detection skill: three studies (Dodge et al 1984, 1990b; Waldman 1988) have covaried out these factors and still found an intention-cue deficit in aggressive children.

An important question for theories of hostile attributional bias is whether this pattern is related to problems other than reactive aggression. For example, hostile attributional biases may place an individual at risk for health problems as well as aggression. Cynical attributional styles(i.e. negative interpretations of others' actions) in 25-year-old law students have been shown to predict later morbidity (due mainly to cardiovascular disease) (Barefoot et al 1989). Waldman (1988) found specificity in the relation between attributional biases and aggression, in that these biases are related to chronic aggression but not to chronic isolation. In the one known study of hostile attributional biases in depressed children, Quiggle et al (1992) found that both depressed children and aggressive children display hostile attributional biases (although other aspects of mental representation, specifically, attributions of causality, distinguish aggressive and depressed children).

The mental representations of depressed children have been the subject of as much investigation as those of aggressive children, but the focus has been on different aspects of representation. Instead of hostile attributional biases, most of the work has addressed the causal attributions (internality, globality, and stability) by depressed children for negative events or the distorted generalizations and expectations for future events that negative stimuli elicit.

The reformulated learned helplessness model of depression (Abramson et al 1978) posits that when faced with a negative affiliative or academic event, an individual who attributes this event to internal, global, and stable causes is more likely to become depressed than an individual without such a processing style. A large body of literature supports this hypothesis, with both adult and child samples (see reviews by Garber & Hilsman in press; and Peterson & Seligman 1984). Children who are socially unpopular and withdrawn tend to attribute their negative outcomes (such as failure or rejection by a peer) to internal causes and their positive outcomes to external causes (Ames et al 1977; Aydin & Markova 1979; Goetz & Dweck 1980). That is, their attributions tend to lay blame on the self.

Likewise, at least 18 studies have found that depressive symptoms are positively correlated with the tendency to attribute positive events to external, specific, and unstable causes and negative events to internal, global, and stable causes (Garber 1987; Nolen-Hoeksma et al 1986). Studies using the Children's Attributional Style Questionnaire (Seligman et al 1984) consistently find this relation in community samples (e.g. Bodiford et al 1988; Seligman et al 1984). Similar findings hold in studies employing other measures of attributional tendencies (e.g. Fincham et al 1987; Quiggle et al in press). Studies of clinical populations indicate a similar attributional style in depressed child inpatients (Asarnow & Bates 1988).

Longitudinal studies indicate that a chronic tendency to attribute negative events to internal, global, and stable causes may predict the onset of depression if and when the child ultimately experiences negative life events such as academic failure (Garber & Hilsman 1992) or peer rejection (Panak & Garber in press), although these findings may be equivocal (Nolen-Hoeksema et al 1986).

Other patterns of distorted mental representations have also been associated with depression in children. Controlled studies indicate that depressed children interpret their own performance more negatively than other children do, even when their actual performance is identical (Garber 1987). Leitenberg et al (1986) found positive correlations between depressive symptoms and cognitive errors such as overgeneralizing from negative events and catastrophizing. Child depression has also been related to self-blaming, negative stimulus appraisal (Moyal 1977; Schwartz et al 1982), distorted thinking (Haley et al 1985), dysfunctional attitudes and automatic negative thoughts (Garber & Hilsman in press).

In sum, both aggressive and depressed children display deviant patterns of mental representation, but these patterns differ. Aggressive children are deficient at interpreting peer intention cues, and their errors are biased in the direction of presumed hostility by others. These hostile attributions lead aggressive children to engage in retaliatory angry aggression. Depressed children also interpret the peers' behavior as hostile, but they attribute blame for peers' behavior to the self, that is, to internal, global, and stable causes. Depressed children also engage in distorted thinking and overgeneralization from negative events. Hypothetically, these attributional patterns and cognitive errors then trigger depressive symptoms.

RESPONSE ACCESS   Once stimulus cues have been encoded and represented mentally, the child accesses one or more possible behavioral responses from long-term memory (or constructs a novel response from those in memory). Researchers have studied both the generativity of children's response search (i.e. how many responses are generated) as well as the quality of responses accessed. In order to distinguish response accessing from other steps of processing, researchers have typically controlled previous processing steps through induction and clear presentation of cues so that biased encoding of interpretation is unlikely. It is hypothesized that children's actual behavioral responding is constrained by their response accessing. If few competent responses and numerous incompetent responses are accessed, deviant behavior is likely.

Shure, Spivack, & colleagues (Shure & Spivack 1980; Shure et al 1973) pioneered the study of generativity of response accessing in aggressive children. They found a negative correlation between the number of responses that a child accesses and the rate of aggressive behavior by that child, with the strength of this association declining as children move from preschool to elementary school age.

As children get older, the quality of response accessing becomes more crucial. Depending on the stimulus, aggressive children may be able to generate as many responses as nonaggressive children, but the types of responses that they access clearly differ from average (Rubin et al 1991). Aggressive children tend to access responses that are statistically atypical and that deviate from peer group norms (Ladd & Oden 1979; Rubin et al 1991). In response to object acquisition dilemmas, aggressive children are more likely than average to generate responses such as bribery and affect manipulation (Rubin et al 1987). In response to friendship or peer group entry initiation dilemmas, they are more likely to generate responses that are verbally coercive, physically aggressive, or bizarrely irrelevant to the task (Dodge et al 1986; Rubin et al 1987). In response to peer provocations, they are more likely to access direct physical aggression as a response (Slaby & Guerra 1988; Waas 1988; Walters & Peters 1980). In peer conflict situations, they generate responses of asking adults to intervene (Asher & Renshaw 1981). Aggressive children also access fewer competent responses in these same situations, including fewer assertive responses (Deluty 1981), fewer mature responses that convey planning ability (Asarnow & Callan 1985), and fewer prosocially effective and relationship-enhancing responses (Asher & Renshaw 1981; Pettit et al 1988). Response accessing deficits by aggressive children may be particularly prominent in situations involving complex solutions or the coordination of multiple goals (Taylor & Gabriel 1989).

Aggressive children are also known to be relatively inflexible in response accessing, in that they are unable to access different kinds of responses if their initial response is not successful (Rubin et al 1991). Richard & Dodge (1982) found that response accessing by aggressive children deteriorates significantly after an initial response is generated and found to be unsuccessful.

Another aspect of response accessing is the affect generated by the mental representation of the encoded cues. Interestingly, aggressive children do not report experiencing more anger than other children do in response to peer provocation stimuli, in spite of their tendency to attribute hostile intent to others and to behave aggressively in this situation (Quiggle et al in press). It may be that aggressive children are not aware of their anger or that they respond aggressively even without any heightened experience of anger. The former possibility is consistent with the hypothesis that these children are unaware of their emotional states (Greenberg et al 1991), and the latter possibility would make sense if most of the aggression by the aggressive children in those samples were of a nonangry, proactive type (in contrast with angry reactive aggression).

Response accessing by depressed children is also deviant. Isolate young children (argued by Rubin et al 1990 to be at risk for depression) access responses that involve appealing to adult authorities for help (Rubin 1982) or are inept and unlikely to be successful (Richard & Dodge 1982). Depressed children are known to access numerous irrelevant responses to problems (Mullins et al 1985) and relatively few assertive responses (Quiggle et al in press).

In addition to accessing deviant behavioral responses, depressed children report experiencing more sadness and anger and less happiness in response to academic failure and social rejection than do nondepressed children (Garber et al 1991). The sadness is consistent with their behavioral responding, but the anger is surprising. It suggests that the mechanisms of depressive symptoms are a complicated combination of self-blame linked with sadness and hostile attributions linked with anger; when combined, depressive symptoms may result.

Thus, both aggressive and depressed children demonstrate deviant response accessing patterns that indicate a dearth of competent behavioral responses, an abundance of behavioral responses that are consistent with their behavioral symptoms, and peculiar affective reactions.

RESPONSE EVALUATION AND SELECTION   Once a response is accessed, it may be evaluated for possible selection and enactment. Dimensions of evaluation known to influence response decisions in children include the *moral acceptability of a response* (how "good" or "bad" the behavior is judged to be), expectations of probable *instrumental* (material gain), *sanctional* (punishment by others such as authority figures), *interpersonal* (liking), and *intrapersonal* (affect about self) outcomes, and *self-efficacy judgments* about the child's ability to enact a response. There are several ways in which deviant processing at this step could lead to deviant behavior. A child might fail to engage in response evaluation altogether (a problem of impulsivity), a child might evaluate the outcomes of deviant behavior in overly positive ways, or the child might lack confidence that if he or she enacted a nondeviant behavior (one that most persons evaluate positively) it would lead to positive outcomes.

Chronically aggressive children have been hypothesized to enact responses without sufficient prior evaluation of their consequences, and anecdotal explanations by aggressive children for their impulsive behavior support this notion (Kendall & Braswell 1985). Slaby & Guerra (1988) found that incarcerated aggressive adolescents generate fewer possible outcomes for their behavior than do nonaggressive adolescents, suggesting insufficient consideration of response outcomes by this group.

Numerous studies indicate that aggressive children evaluate aggression more positively than other children do. They judge aggression as being less morally "bad" (Deluty 1983) and more "friendly" (Crick & Ladd 1991) than other children do. They rate aggression more positively in a global sense than do other children (Asarnow & Callan 1985; Boldizar et al 1989; Quiggle et al in press). They expect more positive instrumental outcomes (Hart et al 1990), fewer negative interpersonal outcomes (Quiggle et al in press), and fewer sanctional outcomes (Perry et al 1986) to accrue for aggressing. They anticipate feeling better about themselves after aggressing (Deluty 1983), and they are more likely than others to expect that engaging in aggression will come easily for them and that inhibiting aggression will be especially difficult for them (Perry et al 1986). Finally, they report that they would be more likely than other children to select aggressive behavior as the best and most appropriate response to peer provocations and social rejection (Garber et al 1991).

As hypothesized, response evaluation tendencies are more strongly related to the display of proactive, instrumental aggressive behavior (such as bullying, coercion, and intimidation) than to reactive angry behavior (Crick & Dodge 1989). As noted earlier, reactive anger is more under the control of processing at the mental representation stage than the response evaluation stage (that is, anger is less a fully evaluated behavioral response than is bullying).

Depressed children evaluate the outcomes of behaviors in different ways than do either aggressive or average children. Depressed children judge the overall quality of withdrawal responses more favorably than do nondepressed children, even though they expect more negative instrumental and fewer positive instrumental outcomes to accrue from withdrawal than do nondepressed children (Garber et al 1991). This paradoxical set of findings indicates the plight of these children: they expect that withdrawal behavior (in which they are likely to engage) will lead to negative instrumental outcomes, but they endorse it as a strategy worth enacting nonetheless. Depressed children report less efficacy for engaging in assertive responses than do nondepressed children, so this alternative is not viable for them (Garber et al 1991).

The response evaluations of depressed children involve not only expectations about the kinds of outcomes that might accrue for various behaviors, but also the degree to which any specific desired outcomes are under the control of the child. According to one theory of depression, "individuals who believe that the locus of control for events is external to themselves and that they have no control over the important consequences that affect them will develop feelings of incompetence, hopelessness, and depression" (Garber & Hilsman in press). Indeed, depressed children, like depressed adults (Benassi et al 1988), display a general tendency toward *external locus of control* (Lefkowitz et al 1980; McCauley et al 1988). These children perceive themselves to lack control of their own desired outcomes (Weisz et al 1987).

When evaluating their own behavior, depressed children are hypothesized to apply overly strict standards (Rehm 1977). Doing so would inevitably lead to expectations that failure is likely, but what is not clear is whether depressed children believe that: (*a*) their outcomes are under their personal control but are very difficult to achieve; or (*b*) outcomes in general are out of anyone's personal control. The former possibility would lead to personalized feelings of failure and perhaps depression, but it would not be consistent with findings of external locus of control in depressed children. The latter possibility is consistent with findings of external locus of control, but it is not clear how such generalized expectations (if the child believes the same is true for all individuals) should lead to depression.

Resolution of this discrepancy may come with the finding that depressed children (and children with suicidal intent) hold the expectation that their behavior will not lead to positive outcomes in the future, either immediately or in the long-term (Kashani et al 1992). Numerous studies have shown that depressed children display hopelessness about future outcomes, in both community samples (Garber et al 1991; Kashani et al 1989) and clinical outpatient and inpatient samples (Asarnow et al 1987; Benfield et al 1988; Garber 1987; Kazdin et al 1983, 1986). In fact, one theory specifically posits a subtype of depression defined by hopelessness (Abramson et al 1989). If a child experiences hopelessness, it may not matter what that child believes about the probable outcomes for other persons' behavior.

ENACTMENT   The step of enactment involves translating response decisions into verbal and motor behaviors in social interaction. Skills acquired through rehearsal, experience, and observation are critical for the competent display of selected behaviors. Enactment skill has been assessed by asking children to act out a prescribed behavior that is selected by an experimenter (as a way of controlling for previous steps of processing), but very few studies have been conducted. Aggressive children have been found to be less skilled at enacting competent peer group entry behaviors than other children (Dodge et al 1986; Gottman et al 1975). No findings are known for depressed children.

Critique

The findings regarding the relation between social-information-processing and deviant child behaviors are impressive in the range of processing patterns implicated and the breadth of deviant behavior patterns described. One common critique has been that the magnitude of correlation for any single processing pattern is small, with correlations on the order of .30 (Dodge et al 1986).

AGGREGATION ACROSS STEPS   However, because processing is multidimensional and multi-componential, correlations between processing and behavior are expected to be small for single steps of processing, but multiple correlations are hypothesized to be large when processing steps are aggregated. Indeed, findings from six samples (three samples from Dodge et al 1986; one from Slaby & Guerra 1988; and two from Weiss et al in press) indicate that processing patterns at different steps provide unique increments in the prediction of deviant behavior, such that an aggregated assessment through multiple correlation yields a much larger magnitude of prediction than an assessment of any single step. Multiple correlations have ranged as high as .94 (Slaby & Guerra 1988).

The strong multiple correlational findings are not surprising when one considers that processing theory is articulated as a description of the mental processes that directly lead to a behavioral response. That is, processing is less of an etiological explanation than it is a description of the phenomenology of behavioral acts. More distal variables (such as socialization patterns or cultural norms) must be considered to understand the etiology of behavior patterns across time.

AGGREGATION ACROSS BEHAVIORS   At the level of the single event, processing patterns ought to account for 100 percent of the variance in behavior (because they describe how behavior comes about), and weaker findings must be attributed to measurement error. At the level of *patterns* of processing and *patterns* of behavior, the correlation will necessarily be weaker, because temporary contextual factors alter behavior in single situations. That is, no matter how narrowly a type of situation is defined, idiosyncratic features (e.g. presence of strangers, mood states, interpersonal histories) will raise the variance across instances of the same situation. Problems arise when aggregating across behavior patterns.

The problem can be framed in terms of the psychiatric diagnosis and classification that is one goal of aggregating across behavioral events. Dimensional analyses of child clinical problems have consistently revealed major dimensions of internalizing and externalizing problems (Achenbach 1985), but these dimensions include heterogeneous sets of acts. Externalizing problems include far more than aggression, with noncompliance, deviance, stealing, and perversion well represented. It is unlikely that a single processing pattern will correlate well with all of these diverse behaviors.

At the categorical level of conceptualizing psychopathology, generalizing from individual acts to psychopathology involves more than summing of acts. It involves constellations of behaviors, with multiple behavior types and criteria of cross-time and cross-situational stability. Studies of processing-behavior linkages indicate that processing patterns in one situation strongly predict specific behaviors within the same type of situation, but they do not strongly predict behavior patterns in other situations, a phenomenon known as situation-specificity (Dodge et al 1986). Yet the classification of disorder requires some degree of cross-situational consistency in behavior. Thus, the processing-behavior link at the broader level will suffer from reduced coherence (operationalized as internal consistency) of measures. Reliability and validity of assessment become major concerns. These factors reduce the likelihood that processing patterns applied as causal factors for individual acts will apply equally well as causal patterns for psychopathology.

AGGREGATION ACROSS PROCESSING TRIALS   On the processing side, summing across responses to multiple stimuli can produce a reasonably coherent processing pattern, with coefficient alphas exceeding .70, as long as the stimuli are of the same situational domain (such as peer provocations or peer group entry situations) (Dodge & Feldman 1990a). However, the coherence breaks down once different types of situations are aggregated (Dodge et al 1986). Also, and more importantly, simply summing across processing responses to multiple testing trials to generate a "pattern" score is not based on any theory of how a predisposition to process information in a particular way is stored in memory, nor how continuity in responding across time is achieved. For example, there is little theoretical meaning to the measured variable of "pattern of hostile attributional bias."

KNOWLEDGE STRUCTURES THAT GUIDE PROCESSING

Thus, there is a press to discover mental structures that are coherent across a range of stimuli and that are posited to be latent constructs that drive processing in any single instance. As Schneider (1991) stated, "information processing is fundamentally 'top-down' or schema driven" (p. 532). Processing provides the theoretical link between these mental structures and behavior, but these mental structures provide the theoretical link between early socializing experiences and processing in a future situation. The role of these latent mental structures is depicted in Figure 1. According to this model, the proximal mechanisms of behavior involve the processing of social information in numerous specific situational episodes. Within an episode, the relation between processing and behavior is very strong, but processing varies somewhat across episodes, just as behavior varies. Guiding processing is a latent knowledge structure that is more consistent. The distinction between processing and knowledge structures is one of proximal versus distal impact on behavior. The distinction in measurement may be analogous to the difference between measuring serotonin at a synaptic site in the brain (the proximal level) and measuring a metabolite of serotonin in cerebrospinal fluid (the distal level).

Social-cognitive theories posit that processing outputs are based on two hypothesized mental constructs, called procedural knowledge and structural knowledge (Schneider 1991). Procedural knowledge consists of the set of memory stores and neural paths that enable an individual to process information in consistent and coherent sequential steps and to apply rules of access from memory. For example, a boy who represents a peer bumping into him as an instance of peer threat might associate this threat with expectations of future harm and might apply a rule of response access that leads to the generation of aggressive retaliation as a possible response. These rules and sequential associations are examples of procedural knowledge.

Structural knowledge broadly consists of the data base, and it refers to the memory stores and knowledge structures generated by past experiences for the individual. As stated earlier and as demonstrated repeatedly in cognitive experiments (Medin 1989), these memory stores rarely consist of iconic traces of actual events; rather, the structure is usually a representation of a category. The representation might be a prototype of an event, sequence, or person, or an exemplar of the same (Schneider 1991). A prototype is some average of past instances, whereas an exemplar is a representation of a single important instance (Hintzman 1986; Linville et al 1989). Different knowledge structures are probably stored in different forms.

Knowledge structures often consist of complex combinations of prototypes and exemplars that cohere around a theme. When these structures color subsequent attention, they are called frames of reference. When they guide interpretation of novel stimuli, they are called schemata, or, if the guiding influence has preference attached to it, they are called attitudes. When they include

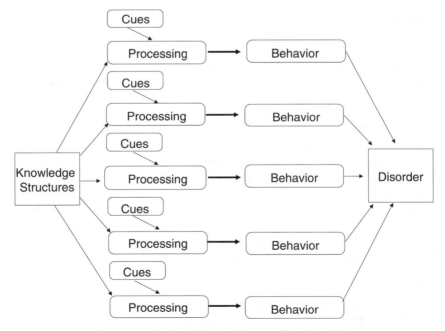

Figure 1   Mental process mechanisms in the development of psychopathology.

sequences of actions, they are known as scripts. When the knowledge is biased, it is called a stereotype. All of these concepts from social psychology are hypothetical constructs formulated to explain how individuals carry in memory representations of past events that "affect the seeking and molding of incoming information" (Schneider 1991, p. 533).

In the social developmental literature, a similar construct has been formulated from attachment research, called a "working model" of relationships (Bowlby 1982). According to attachment theory, the child's early experiences with significant others leads the child to develop in memory working models of how relationships typically proceed. These working models, in turn, guide the child's processing of information in future situations. For example, Crittendon & Ainsworth (1989) hypothesize that early experiences of physical abuse may lead a child to develop a working model of relationships as involving harm to the self, which, in turn, may lead the child to be hypervigilant to future threatening cues.

The relation between knowledge structures and processing patterns has not been made in the child psychopathology literature, partly because of the methodological difficulty in operationalizing each construct independently. Knowledge structures have typically been measured by asking children to recall certain events (e.g. Hammen & Goodman-Brown 1990), to respond to hypothetical stimuli (e.g. Renshaw & Asher 1983), or to characterize their typical ways of responding (e.g. Asarnow & Bates 1988). Similar methods are used to assess processing patterns; indeed, researchers often use assessments of processing to infer latent knowledge structures. Researchers try to distinguish between the two by focusing on the bases of processing to infer knowledge structures. Still, the distinction between knowledge structures and processing is largely a theoretical, rather than empirical, one at this time. Recent innovations in methods used in social cognition research, such as priming, response time assessment, analysis of recall clustering, and protocol analysis, should lead to sharper distinctions in future empirical work.

Over the past decade, researchers have examined the hypotheses that conduct disordered and depressed children carry with them unique knowledge structures. Some structures (such as self-schema) are hypothesized to lead to behavior indirectly, that is, they guide processing in specific instances in a manner that leads to deviant behavior (Derry & Kuiper 1981), whereas others (such as loneliness) are presumably the outcome of repeated deviant behavioral events (Asher & Wheeler 1985).

Relation to Aggressive Behavior

Attempts to find unique knowledge structures in aggressive children have yielded mixed findings, depending on the kind of structure assessed. Review of the literature on perceived self-competence, as measured by Harter's (1982) Perceived Self-Competence Scale, reveals that the evidence does not support a relation between self-concept and aggressive behavior (Crick & Dodge 1989).

Psychodynamic theorists (Keith 1984) argue that aggressive children must carry with them a miserable self-view, but self-defensive mechanisms render the measurement of this view difficult. Processing analyses, as reviewed in this chapter, suggest that aggressive children blame others, rather than the self, for negative outcomes; thus, these children might not harbor a negative self-image (Cairns 1991).

Even though aggressive children do not perceive themselves to be incompetent, they do carry with them feelings of loneliness. Asher et al (1984), Asher & Wheeler (1985), and Cassidy & Asher (1989) all found that socially rejected children (a combination of withdrawn and aggressive children) report higher levels of loneliness than average and popular children. Asher & Williams (1987) distinguished between rejected-aggressive and rejected-withdrawn children and found that both groups report higher loneliness levels than average children. Loneliness is more likely to be a consequence of aggressive interactions with peers than a cause of this behavior, although a growing schema of the world as a lonely place might begin to influence subsequent processing of social cues.

La Greca et al (1988) found that rejected children carry with them a fear of negative evaluation by others, and Taylor & Asher (1989) found that rejected children worry about possible future negative outcomes. These fears and worries might well influence future processing, such as selective attention to negative cues and hostile interpretations of peers' actions.

In an attempt to understand how deviant processing comes about, researchers have studied aggressive children's use of aggressive schemas when interpreting the behavior of others. Dodge & Tomlin (1987) found that average children rely on presented information ("bottom-up" processing) in order to reach social judgments, whereas aggressive children are more likely to call on information from their own past experiences (aggressive-schema-based, or "top-down," processing). Strassberg & Dodge (1987) assessed these aggressive schemas more directly by asking children to provide a running commentary of what was occurring as they watched videotapes of children at play. They noted the categories that children spontaneously use to characterize the behavior of others, hypothesizing that if aggressive children hold aggressive schemas they will evaluate the world with reference to this category. The findings tended to support the hypothesis. Stromquist & Strauman (in press) assessed children's social constructs through open-ended interviews in which they scored the categories that children use in describing others. They found that children with a preponderance of aggression-related constructs engage in high rates of fighting.

The goals and values that aggressive children bring to social situations also influence their processing (particularly at the response evaluation step) and behavior. Taylor & Asher (1989) found a positive correlation between endorsement of performance goals (in contrast with goals of enhancing relationships) and the display of aggressive behavior. Aggressive children have been found to endorse hostile goals (e.g. getting even with a provocateur) and competitive goals (e.g. winning the game rather than preserving a friendship) (Taylor & Gabriel 1989) more frequently than do nonaggressive children. Aggressive children also value aggressive behavior more than other children do. Bandura & Walters (1959) and Cairns & Cairns (1988) report that aggressive children take great pride in their "toughness" and ability to aggress skillfully.

How do such knowledge structures, in the form of goals and values, lead to aggressive behavior? "Such values can predispose adolescents to create confrontations in which they eventually become both antagonists and victims... The beliefs and values are then employed in the organization of their views of relationships, and their instigation of behaviors" (Cairns 1991, p. 263). Although goals and values can influence how information in specific situations is processed at all steps, beginning with selective attention to certain cues, the influence is most obvious at the steps of accessing responses and evaluating responses. In fact, a major problem for research in this area is that some methods of assessing goals and values confound this assessment with assessments of processing itself.

Relation to Depression

The role of knowledge structures has been more prominent in theories of depression than aggression. Beck (1967) proposed that two latent knowledge structures, negative self-concepts and negative self-schema, influence cognitive errors and distortions that arise during processing.

A negative self-concept influences processing in the form of self-deprecating statements, underestimation of one's performance, negatively biased explanations of events, and negative expectations of future outcomes (Garber & Hilsman in press). Numerous studies have examined self-concept in internalizing children. Harter (1982) reported a positive correlation between perceived social competence and peer status. Franke & Hymel (1984) found a negative correlation between perceived self-competence and isolate behavior, but only in girls and not in boys. Ladd & Price (1986) also reported a significant correlation and found that the magnitude of this relation tended to increase across age, suggesting that this knowledge structure becomes formulated as children acquire more experiences. Rubin (1985) found that consistently isolated children report lower-than-average perceived self-competence.

Studies of clinically depressed children reveal a robust finding of lowered self-esteem, with correlations between depression and self-esteem ranging from -.12 to -.75 and averaging -.52 (Garber & Hilsman in press). Low self-esteem characterizes depression in elementary school children (Strauss et al 1984), early adolescents (McGee et al 1986; Windle et al 1986), high schoolers (Battle 1980), child inpatients (Asarnow & Bates 1988), and suicidal children (Asarnow et al 1987).

Also important to Beck's (1967) theory is the concept of negative self-schema, which are organized representations of past experiences and knowledge in critical domains, notably interpersonal loss and achievement failure.

"Schema serve as underlying predispositions that guide the selective processing of information, thereby maintaining the characteristic negative views of the self, world, and future" (Garber & Hilsman in press).

Self-schema have been assessed indirectly, through measures such as biased recall of presented words about oneself and speed of recall of negative versus positive self-referent words. "The schema measure is based on the assumption that enduring mental constructs organize, guide, interpret, and retrieve information about the self in memory" (Hammen & Goodman-Brown 1990, p. 216). Hammen & Zuppan (1984) found that dysphoric children recall fewer positive and more negative self-descriptive words than do nondepressed children. Zupan et al (1987) extended these same findings to depressed offspring of depressed mothers. Thus, it appears that depressed children carry with them a structure in memory that organizes their world in negative self-referent ways.

Schema may be classified not only according to valence (positive versus negative) but also according to domain. That is, some children have well-developed, highly salient schema for interpersonal events, whereas other children have well-developed schema for achievement events. Hammen & Goodman-Brown (1990) assessed such domain-specific schema by asking children to recall past events. They hypothesized, and found, that children with well-developed interpersonal schema (but not well-developed achievement schema) are more vulnerable to depression following the later occurrence of negative interpersonal events than are children without such schema and than are the same children following negative achievement events. Two important conclusions follow from this work. First, knowledge structures may render a child vulnerable to the depression-inducing effects of later negative life events, consistent with a diathesis-stress model of depression (Garber & Hilsman in press). Second, vulnerability-inducing knowledge structures may be idiosyncratic.

DEVELOPMENTAL PSYCHOPATHOLOGY OF CONDUCT DISORDER AND DEPRESSION

The constructs of social information processing patterns and knowledge structures can be integrated into a novel theoretical framework for understanding the etiology of conduct disorder and depression (see Figure 2). According to this framework, early life experiences interact with biologically-based limits on memory and neural functioning to produce ever-evolving knowledge structures. These knowledge structures consist of schema for past life experiences, expectations for future events, and affectively-charged vulnerabilities. When particular social stimuli are encountered, these knowledge structures organize the child's processing (that is, selective attention to particular cues, representation of those cues, accessing of particular responses, evaluation and selection of responses, and response enactment). The product of this schema-driven processing can be deviant behavior. Chronically deviant processing and behavior culminate in the psychiatric diagnosis of psychopathology.

Note that this account integrates both biological and environmental sources of psychopathology. The constructs of knowledge structures and processing patterns describe the mental processes that accompany psychopathological behavior, at distal and proximal levels, respectively. An equally coherent account of this process could be given at a neural level (and, in fact, the integration of accounts at the mental process and neural process levels would be exciting). The origins of these mental processes include both early environmental experiences and genetic or acquired biological predispositions. This account provides a framework for understanding and describing a varied set of events that could lead to psychopathology. Numerous paths to conduct disorder or depression are possible, so a general theory must be flexible.

With regard to conduct disorder, it is hypothesized that early experiences of physical abuse (Dodge et al 1990a), exposure to aggressive models (Bandura 1973), and insecure attachment relationships (Sroufe 1983) lead a child to develop memory structures of the world as a hostile place that requires coercive behavior to achieve desired outcomes. Later, when this child is presented with provocative stimuli (such as peer teasing, rough play, or adult demands), these knowledge structures lead him or her to attend to the hostile aspects of these cues and to interpret these stimuli as a threat to the self. Associative networks in memory lead the child to access aggressive responses to these cues. The child evaluates the probable outcomes of aggressing in this instance as favorable and engages in aggressive behavior. Repeated experiences of this

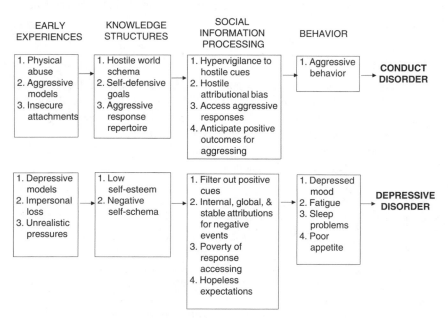

Figure 2   Models of the development of conduct disorder and depression.

sort will strengthen the child's knowledge structures, make this processing pattern more automatized, and lead to conduct disorder.

With regard to depression, early life experiences of either interpersonal loss and instability or pressure to achieve at an unrealistic level (both of which are more likely by living with a depressed parent) may lead a child to develop in memory negative self-schema and low self-esteem. Later, when this child encounters interpersonal loss or failure, these schema lead the child to attend to the negative aspects of these new events and to attribute their causes to internal, stable, and global factors. The child then readily accesses depressive responses from memory and behaves with sad affect, reduced activity level, and other symptoms of depression. The child's negative schema and depressogenic processing patterns prevent external forces (such as family support and contrary cues) from mitigating the depressive symptoms so that the child becomes chronically depressed.

CONCLUSION

These developmental accounts are highly speculative and surely apply to only some children. The heuristic utility of the theory outlined in Figure 2 is that it forces a developmental perspective on psychopathology and provides a framework for integrating both distal and proximal mechanisms of psychopathology. It has provided researchers with a host of hypotheses that have been tested empirically over the past decade. Its value for the field will be decided over the next decade, when researchers and clinicians begin to develop interventions directed at distal prevention and proximal treatment of psychopathologic processes.

ACKNOWLEDGMENTS

The author is grateful for the support of a Research Career Development Award from the National Institute of Child Health and Human Development, Research Grant 42498 from the National Institute of Mental Health, and Research Grant BNS 8908935 from the National Science Foundation. He is indebted to Janice Brown, Nicki Crick, Joan Orrell, David Schwartz, and Zvi Strassberg for key ideas in this chapter.

Literature Cited

Abramson, L. Y., Alloy, L. B., Metalsky, G. I. 1989. Hopelessness depression: a theory-based subtype of depression. *Psychol. Bull.* 96:358–72

Abramson, L. Y., Seligman, M., Teasdale, J. 1978. Learned helplessness in humans: critique and reformulation. *J. Abnorm. Psychol.* 87:49–74

Achenbach, T. M. 1985. *Assessment and Taxonomy of Child and Adolescent Psychopathology.* Newbury Park: Sage

Ames, R., Ames, C., Garrison, W. 1977. Children's causal ascriptions for positive and negative interpersonal outcomes. *Psychol. Rep.* 41:595–602

Asarnow, J. R., Bates, S. 1988. Depression in child psychiatric inpatients: cognitive and attributional patterns. *J. Abnorm. Child Psychol.* 16:601–15

Asarnow, J. R., Callan, J. W. 1985. Boys with peer adjustment problems: social cognitive processes. *J. Consult. Clin. Psychol.* 53:80–87

Asarnow, J. R., Carlson, G. A., Guthrie, D.

1987. Coping strategies, self perceptions, hopelessness, and perceived family environments in depressed and suicidal children. *J. Consult. Clin. Psychol.* 55:361–66

Asher, S. R., Hymel, S., Renshaw, P. D. 1984. Loneliness in children. *Child Dev.* 55:1457–64

Asher, S. R., Renshaw, P. D. 1981. Children without friends: social knowledge and social skill training. In *The Development of Children's Friendships,* ed. S. R. Asher, J. M. Gottman, pp. 273–96. New York: Cambridge Univ. Press

Asher, S. R., Wheeler, V. A. 1985. Children's loneliness: a comparison of rejected and neglected peer status. *J. Consult. Clin. Psychol.* 53:500–5

Asher, S. R., Williams, G. 1987. *New approaches to identifying rejected children at school.* Presented at the Annu. Meet. Am. Educ. Res. Assoc., Washington, DC

Aydin, O., Markova, I. 1979. Attribution tendencies of popular and unpopular children. *Br. J. Soc. Clin. Psychol.* 18:291–98

Bandura, A. 1973. *Aggression: A Social Learning Analysis.* Englewood Cliffs, NJ: Prentice-Hall

Bandura, A. 1986. *Social Foundations of Thought and Action: A Social Cognitive Theory.* Englewood Cliffs, NJ: Prentice-Hall

Bandura, A., Walters, R. H. 1959. *Adolescent Aggression.* New York: Ronald Press

Barefoot, J. C., Dodge, K. A., Peterson, B. L., Dahlstrom, W. G., Williams, R. B. 1989. The Cook-Medley hostility scale: item content & ability to predict survival. *Psychosom. Med.* 51:46–57

Battle, J. 1980. Relationship between self-esteem and depression among high school students. *Percept. Motion Skills* 51:157–58

Beck, A. T. 1967. *Depression: Clinical, Experimental, and Theoretical Aspects.* New York: Harper & Row

Benassi, V. A., Sweeney, P. D., Dufour, C. L. 1988. Is there a relation between locus of control orientation and depression? *J. Abnorm. Psychol.* 97:357–67

Benfield, C. Y., Palmer, D. J., Pfefferbaum, B., Stowe, M. L. 1988. A comparison of depressed and nondepressed disturbed children on measures of attributional style, hopelessness, life stress, and temperament. *J. Abnorm. Child Psychol.* 16:397–410

Bodiford, C. A., Eisenstadt, T. H., Johnson, J. H., Bradlyn, A. S. 1988. Comparison of learned helpless cognitions and behavior in children with high and low scores on the Children's Depression Inventory. *J. Clin. Child Psychol.* 17:152–58

Boldizar, J. P., Perry, D. G., Perry, L. C. 1989. Outcome values and aggression. *Child Dev.* 60:571–79

Bowlby, J. 1982. *Attachment.* New York: Basic Books

Cairns, R. B. 1991. Multiple metaphors for a singular idea. *Dev. Psychol.* 27:23–26

Cairns, R. B., Cairns, B. D. 1988. The

sociogenesis of self concepts. In *Persons in Social Context: Developmental Processes,* ed. D. Olweus, J. Block, M. Radke-Yarrow, pp. 315–42. New York: Academic

Campbell, J. D., Yarrow, M. R. 1961. Perceptual and behavioral correlates of social effectiveness. *Sociometry* 24:1–20

Cassidy, J., Asher, S. R. 1989. *Loneliness and peer relations in young children.* Presented at Bienn. Meet. Soc. Res. Child Dev., Kansas City, KS

Chandler, M. 1973. Egocentrism and antisocial behavior: the assessment and training of social perspective-taking skills. *Dev. Psychol.* 9:326–32

Cicchetti, D., Toth, S., eds. 1991. *Rochester Symposium on Developmental Psychopathology: Internalizing and Externalizing Expressions of Dysfunction,* Vol. 2. Hillsdale, NJ: Erlbaum

Crick, N. R., Dodge, K. A. 1989. *Rejected children's expectations and perceptions of peer interaction.* Paper presented at Annu. Meet. Am. Educ. Res. Assoc., San Francisco

Crick, N. R., Ladd, G. 1991. Children's perceptions of the consequences of aggressive behavior: do the ends justify being mean? *Dev. Psychol.* 26:612–20

Crittenden, P. M., Ainsworth, M. D. S. 1989. Child maltreatment and attachment theory. In *Child Maltreatment: Theory and Research on the Cause and Consequences of Child Abuse and Neglect,* ed. D. Cicchetti, V. Carlson, pp. 254–77. New York: Cambridge Press

Dell Fitzgerald, P., Asher, S. R. 1987. *Aggressive-rejected children's attributional biases about liked and disliked peers.* Paper presented at Annu. Meet. Am. Psychol. Assoc., New York

Deluty, R. H. 1981. Alternative-thinking ability of aggressive, assertive, and submissive children. *Cognit. Ther. Res.* 5:309–12

Deluty, R. H. 1983. Children's evaluation of aggressive, assertive, and submissive responses. *J. Consult. Clin. Psychol.* 12:124–29

Derry, P., Kuiper, N. 1981. Schematic processing and self-reference in clinical depression. *J. Abnorm. Psychol.* 90:125–33

Dodge, K. A. 1980. Social cognition and children's aggressive behavior. *Child Dev.* 51:162–70

Dodge, K. A., Bates, J. E., Pettit, G. S. 1990a. Mechanisms in the cycle of violence. *Science* 250:1678–83

Dodge, K. A., Coie, J. D. 1987. Social information processing factors in reactive and proactive aggression in children's peer groups. *J. Pers. Soc. Psychol.* 53:1146–58

Dodge, K. A., Feldman, E. 1990a. Issues in social cognition and sociometric status. In *Peer Rejection in Childhood,* ed. S. R. Asher, J. D. Coie, pp. 119–55. New York: Cambridge Univ. Press

Dodge, K. A., Frame, C. L. 1982. Social cognitive biases and deficits in aggressive boys.

Child Dev. 53:620–35

Dodge, K. A., Murphy, R. R., Buchsbaum, K. 1984. The assessment of intention-cue detection skills in children: implications for developmental psychopathology. *Child Dev.* 55:163–73

Dodge, K. A., Newman, J. P. 1981. Biased decision making processes in aggressive boys. *J. Abnorm. Psychol.* 90:375–79

Dodge, K. A., Pettit, G. S., McClaskey, C. L., Brown, M. 1986. Social competence in children. *Monogr. Soc. Res. Child. Dev. Ser.* 213(2):51

Dodge, K. A., Price, J. M., Bachorowski, J., Newman, J. P. 1990b. Hostile attributional biases in severely aggressive adolescents. *J. Abnorm. Psychol.* 99:385–92

Dodge, K. A., Somberg, D. 1987. Hostile attributional biases among aggressive boys are exacerbated under conditions of threats to the self. *Child Dev.* 58:213–24

Dodge, K. A., Tomlin, A. 1987. Cue utilization as a mechanism of attributional bias in aggressive children. *Soc. Cognit.* 5:280–300

Estes, W. K. 1991. Cognitive architectures from the standpoint of an experimental psychologist. *Annu. Rev. Psychol.* 42:1–28

Feldman, E., Dodge, K. A. 1987. Social information processing and sociometric status: sex, age, and situational effects. *J. Abnorm. Psychol.* 15:211–27

Feshbach, S. 1970. Aggression. In *Carmichael's Manual of Child Psychology,* ed. P. H. Mussen, 2:159–259. New York: Wiley

Fincham, F. D., Diener, C. I., Hokoda, A. 1987. Attributional style and learned helplessness: relationship to the use of causal schemata and depressive symptoms in children. *Br. J. Soc. Psychol.* 26:1–7

Franke, S., Hymel, S. 1984. *Social anxiety and social avoidance in children: the development of a self-report measure.* Presented at Bienn. Meet. Univ. Waterloo Conf. Child Dev., Waterloo, Ontario, Canada

Garber, J. 1987. *Depression in children: validation of the construct.* PhD thesis. Univ. Minnesota

Garber, J., Hilsman, R. 1992. Cognitions, stress, and depression in children and adolescents. *Child. Adolesc. Psychol. Clin. N. Am.* In press

Garber, J., Quiggle, N. L., Panak, W., Dodge, K. A. 1991. Aggression and depression in children: comorbidity, specificity, and cognitive processing. See Cicchetti & Toth 1991, pp. 225–64

Goetz, T. W., Dweck, C. S. 1980. Learned helplessness in social situations. *J. Pers. Soc. Psychol.* 39:246–55

Goldman, J. A., Corsini, D. A., DeUrioste, R. 1980. Implications of positive and negative sociometric status for assessing the social competence of young children. *J. Appl. Dev. Psychol.* 1:209–20

Gottman, J., Gonso, J., Rasmussen, B. 1975. Social interaction, social competence, and friendship in children. *Child Dev.* 46:709–

18

Gouze, K. R. 1987. Attention and social problem solving as correlates of aggression in preschool males. *J. Abnorm. Child Psychol.* 15:181–97

Greenberg, M. T., Kusche, C. A., Speltz, M. 1991. Emotion regulation, self-control, and psychopathology: the role of relationships in early childhood. See Cicchetti & Toth 1991, pp. 21–55

Guerra, N. G., Slaby, R. G. 1989. Evaluative factors in social problem solving by aggressive boys. *J. Abnorm. Child Psychol.* 17:277–89

Haley, G. M. T., Fine, S., Marriage, K., Moretti, M. M., Freeman, R. J. 1985. Cognitive bias and depression in psychiatrically disturbed children and adolescents. *J. Consult. Clin. Psychol.* 53:535–37

Hammen, C., Goodman-Brown, T. 1990. Self-schemas and vulnerability to specific life stress in children at risk for depression. *Cogn. Res. Ther.* 14:215–27

Hammen, C., Zupan, B. A. 1984. Self-schema, depression, and the processing of personal information in children. *J. Exp. Child Psychol.* 37:598–608

Hart, C. H., Ladd, G. W., Burleson, B. 1990. Children's expectations of the outcomes of social strategies: relations with sociometric status and maternal disciplinary styles. *Child Dev.* 61:127–37

Harter, S. 1982. The perceived competence scale for children. *Child Dev.* 53:89–97

Hintzman, D. 1986. Schema abstraction in a multiple-trace memory model. *Psychol. Rev.* 93:411–28

Huesmann, L. R. 1989. An information processing model for the development of aggression. *Aggress. Behav.* 14:13–24

Ingram, R. E. 1984. Toward an information-processing analysis of depression. *Cogn. Ther. Res.* 8:443–78

Kashani, J. H., Dandoy, A. C., Reid, J. C. 1992. Hopelessness in children and adolescents. *Acta Paedopsychiatr.* 55:33–39

Kashani, J. H., Reid, J. C., Rosenberg, T. K. 1989. Levels of hopelessness in children and adolescents: a developmental perspective. *J. Consult. Clin. Psychol.* 57:496–99

Kazdin, A., French, N., Unis, A., Esveldt-Dawson, K., Shenck, R. 1983. Hopelessness, depression, and suicidal intent among psychiatrically disturbed inpatient children. *J. Consult. Clin. Psychol.* 51:504–10

Kazdin, A., Rodgers, A., Colbus, D. 1986. The hopelessness scale for children: psychometric characteristics and concurrent validity. *J. Consult. Clin. Psychol.* 54:241–45

Keith, C. R., ed. 1984. *The Aggressive Adolescent.* New York: Free Press

Kendall, P. C., Braswell, L. 1985. *Cognitive-Behavioral Therapy for Impulsive Children.* New York: Guilford

Kuiper, N. A., Olinger, J. 1986. Dysfunctional attitudes and a self-worth contingency model of depression. In *Advances in Cognitive-Behavioral Research and Therapy,* ed. P. C. Kendall, 5:115–42. New York: Academic

Ladd, G. W., Oden, S. 1979. The relationship between peer acceptance and children's ideas about helpfulness. *Child Dev.* 50:402–8

Ladd, G. W., Price, J. M. 1986. Promoting children's cognitive and social competence: the relations between parent's perceptions of task difficulty and children's perceived and actual competence. *Child Dev.* 57:446–60

La Greca, A. M., Dandes, S. K., Wick, P., Shaw, K., Stone, W. 1988. Development of social anxiety scale for children: reliability and concurrent validity. *J. Consult. Clin. Psychol.* 17:84–91

Lefkowitz, M. M., Tesiny, E. P., Gordon, N. H. 1980. Childhood depression, family income, and locus of control. *J. Nerv. Ment. Dis.* 168:732–35

Leitenberg, H., Yost, L. W., Carroll-Wilson, M. 1986. Negative cognitive errors in children: questionnaire development, normative data, and comparisons between children with and without self-reported symptoms of depression, low self-esteem, and evaluation anxiety. *J. Consult. Clin. Psychol.* 54:528–36

Linville, P. W., Fischer, G. W., Salovey, P. 1989. Perceived distributions of the characteristics of in-group and out-group members: empirical evidence and a computer simulation. *J. Pers. Soc. Psychol.* 57:165–88

Lochman, J. E. 1987. Self and peer perceptions and attributional biases of aggressive and nonaggressive boys. *J. Consult. Clin. Psychol.* 55:404–10

Marcus, R. F. 1980. Empathy and popularity of preschool children. *Child Study J.* 10:133–45

McCauley, E., Mitchell, J. R., Burke, P., Moss, S. 1988. Cognitive attributes of depression in children and adolescents. *J. Consult. Clin. Psychol.* 56:903–8

McClaskey, C. L. 1988. *Symptoms of ADHD, ADD, and aggression in children: teacher ratings, peer sociometrics, and judgments of hypothetical behavior.* PhD thesis. Indiana Univ.

McFall, R. M. 1982. A review and reformulation of the concept of social skills. *Behav. Assess.* 4:1–33

McGee, R., Anderson, J., Williams, S., Silva, P. 1986. Cognitive correlates of depressive symptoms in 11-year-old children. *J. Abnorm. Child Psychol.* 14:517–24

Medin, D. L. 1989. Concepts and conceptual structure. *Am. Psychol.* 44:1469–81

Milich, R., Dodge, K. A. 1984. Social information processing patterns in child psychiatric populations. *J. Abnorm. Child Psychol.* 12:171–89

Moyal, B. R. 1977. Locus of control, self-esteem, stimulus appraisal, and depressive symptoms in children. *J. Consult. Clin. Psychol.* 45:951–52

Mullins, L. L., Siegal, L. J., Hodges, K. 1985. Cognitive problem-solving and life event correlates of depressive symptoms in children. *J. Abnorm. Child Psychol.* 13:305–14

Nasby, W., Hayden, B., DePaulo, B. M. 1979. Attributional bias among aggressive boys to interpret unambiguous social stimuli as displays of hostility. *J. Abnorm. Psychol.* 89:459–68

Newell, A., Simon, H. A. 1972. *Human Problem Solving.* Englewood Cliffs, NJ: Prentice-Hall

Nolen-Hoeksema, S., Girgus, J. S., Seligman, M. E. P. 1986. Learned helplessness in children: a longitudinal study of depression, achievement, and explanatory style. *J. Pers. Soc. Psychol.* 51:435–42

Panak, W., Garber, J. 1992. The role of aggression, rejection, and attributions in the prediction of depression in children. *Dev. Psychopathol.* 4:145–66

Pellegrini, D. 1985. Social cognition and competence in middle-childhood. *Child Dev.* 56:253–64

Perry, D. G., Perry, L. C., Rasmussen, P. 1986. Cognitive social learning mediators of aggression. *Child Dev.* 57:700–11

Peterson, C., Seligman, M. E. P. 1984. Causal explanations as a risk factor for depression: theory and evidence. *Psychol. Rev.* 91:347–74

Pettit, G. S., Dodge, K. A., Brown, M. M. 1988. Early family experience, social problem solving patterns, and children's social competence. *Child Dev.* 59:107–20

Quiggle, N., Garber, J., Panak, W., Dodge, K. A. 1992. Social information processing in aggressive and depressed children. *Child Dev.* In press

Raaijmakers, J. G. W., Shiffrin, R. M. 1981. Search of associative memory. *Psychol. Rev.* 88:93–134

Rabiner, D. L., Coie, J. D. 1989. The effect of expectancy inductions on rejected children's acceptance by unfamiliar peers. *Dev. Psychol.* 25:450–57

Rehm, L. P. 1977. A self-control model of depression. *Behav. Ther.* 8:787–804

Renshaw, P. D., Asher, S. R. 1983. Children's goals and strategies for social interaction. *Merrill-Palmer Q.* 29:353–74

Richard, B. A., Dodge, K. A. 1982. Social maladjustment and problem solving in school-age children. *J. Consult. Clin. Psychol.* 50:226–33

Rubin, K. H. 1982. Social and social-cognitive developmental characteristics of young isolate, normal, and sociable children. In *Peer Relationships and Social Skills in Childhood,* ed. K. H. Rubin, H. S. Ross, pp. 353–74. New York: Springer-Verlag

Rubin, K. H. 1985. Socially withdrawn children: an "at risk" population? In *Children's Peer Relations: Issues in Assessment and Intervention,* ed. B. Schneider, K. H. Rubin, J. E. Ledingham. New York: Springer-Verlag

Rubin, K. H., Bream, L. A., Rose-Krasnor, L. 1991. Social problem solving and aggression in childhood. In *The Development and Treatment of Childhood Aggression,* ed. D. J. Pepler, K. H. Rubin, pp. 219–48. Hillsdale, NJ: Erlbaum

Rubin, K. H., Krasnor, L. R. 1986. Social-cognitive and social behavioral perspectives on problem solving. *Minn. Symp. Child Psychol.,* 18:1–68

Rubin, K. H., LeMare, L. J., Lollis, S. 1990. Social withdrawal in childhood: developmental pathways to rejection. In *Peer Rejection in Childhood,* ed. S. R. Asher, J. D. Coie, pp. 217–49. New York: Cambridge Univ. Press

Rubin, K. H., Maioni, T. L. 1975. Play preference and its relationship to egocentrism, popularity, and classification skills in preschoolers. *Merrill-Palmer Q.* 21:171–79

Rubin, K. H., Moller, L., Emptage, A. 1987. The preschool behavior questionnaire: a useful index of behavior problems in elementary school-age children. *Can. J. Behav. Sci.* 19:86–100

Rumelhart, D. E., McClelland, J. L. 1986. *Parallel Distributed Processing: Exploration in the Microstructure of Cognition.* Vol. 1: *Foundations.* Cambridge, MA: MIT Press/Bradford Books

Sancilio, M., Plumert, J. M., Hartup, W. W. 1989. Friendship and aggressiveness as determinants of conflict outcomes in middle childhood. *Dev. Psychol.* 25:812–19

Schneider, D. J. 1991. Social cognition. *Annu. Rev. Psychol.* 42:527–61

Schneider, W., Shiffrin, R. M. 1977. Controlled and automatic human information processing: 1. Detection, search, and attention. *Psychol. Rev.* 84:1–66

Schwartz, M., Friedman, R., Lindsay, P., Narrol, H. 1982. The relationship between conceptual tempo and depression in children. *J. Consult. Clin. Psychol.* 52:955–67

Seligman, M. E. P., Peterson, C., Kaslow, M. J., Tanenbaum, R. L., Alloy, L. B., Abramson, L. Y. 1984. Explanatory style and depressive symptoms among children. *J. Abnorm. Psychol.* 93:235–38

Selman, R. 1980. *The Growth of Interpersonal Understanding.* New York: Academic

Shure, M. B., Newman, S., Silver, S. 1973. *Problem solving thinking among adjusted, impulsive, and inhibited Head Start children.* Presented at Meet. East. Psychol. Assoc., New York

Shure, M. B., Spivack, G. 1980. Interpersonal problem-solving as a mediator of behavioral adjustment in preschool and kindergarten children. *J. Appl. Dev. Psychol.* 1:29–44

Slaby, R. G., Guerra, N. G. 1988. Cognitive mediators of aggression in adolescent offenders: 1. Assessment. *Dev. Psychol.* 24:580–88

Sroufe, L. A. 1983. Infant-caregiver attachment and patterns of adaptation in preschool. In *Minnesota Symposia on Child Psychology,* ed. M. Perlmutter, Vol. 16. Hillsdale, NJ: Erlbaum

Steinberg, M. D., Dodge, K. A. 1983. Attributional bias in aggressive adolescent boys and girls. *J. Soc. Clin. Psychol.* 1:312–21

Strassberg, Z., Dodge, K. A. 1987. *Focus of social attention among children varying in peer status.* Presented at the Annu. Meet. Assoc. Adv. Behav. Ther., Boston

Strauss, C. C., Forehand, R., Frame, C., Smith, K. 1984. Characteristics of children with extreme scores on the children's depression inventory. *J. Clin. Child Psychol.* 13:227–31

Stromquist, V. J., Strauman, T. J. 1992. Children's social constructs: II. Nature, assessment, and association with adaptive and maladaptive behavior. *Soc. Cognit.* 9:330–58

Taylor, A. R., Asher, S. R. 1989. Children's goals in game playing situations. Paper presented at the Annu. Meet. Am. Psychol. Assoc., New York

Taylor, A. R., Gabriel, S. W. 1989. *Cooperative versus competitive game-playing strategies of peer-accepted and peer-rejected children in a goal conflict situation.* Presented at Bienn. Meet. Soc. Res. Child Dev., Kansas City, KS

Underwood, B. J. 1969. Attributers of memory. *Psychol. Rev.* 76:559–73

Waas, G. A. 1988. Social attributional biases of peer-rejected and aggressive children. *Child Dev.* 59:969–92

Walden, T., Ogan, T. 1988. The development of social referencing. *Child Dev.* 59:1230–40

Waldman, I. D. 1988. *Relationships between non-social information processing, social perception, and social status in 7- to 12-year-old boys.* PhD thesis. Univ. Waterloo

Walters, J., Peters, R. D. 1980. *Social problem solving in aggressive boys.* Presented at Annu. Meet. Can. Psychol. Assoc., Calgary

Weiss, B., Dodge, K. A., Bates, S. E., Pettit, G. S. 1992. Some consequences of early harsh discipline: child aggression and a maladaptive social information processing style. *Child Dev.* In press

Weisz, J. R., Weiss, B., Wasserman, A. A., Rintoul, B. 1987. Control related beliefs and depression among clinic-referred children and adolescents. *J. Abnorm. Psychol.* 96:58–63

Windle, M., Hooker, K., Lenerz, K., East, P. L., Lerner, J. V., Lerner, R. M. 1986. Temperament, perceived competence, and depression in early and late adolescents. *Dev. Psychol.* 22:384–92

Zupan, B., Hammen, C., Jaenicke, C. 1987. The effects of current mood and prior depressive history on self-schematic processing in children. *J. Exp. Child Psychol.* 43:149–58

Annu. Rev. Psychol. 1993. 44:585–612

SOCIAL FOUNDATIONS OF COGNITION

John M. Levine and Lauren B. Resnick

Learning Research and Development Center, and Department of Psychology, University of Pittsburgh, Pittsburgh, Pennsylvania 15260

E. Tory Higgins

Department of Psychology, Columbia University, New York, NY 10027

KEYWORDS: social roles, mental representation, shared cognition

CONTENTS

INTRODUCTION 586
MERE PRESENCE OF OTHERS 588
    Social Facilitation 588
    Social Loafing 589
    Crowding 590
    Group Composition 590
SOCIAL ROLES, POSITIONS, AND IDENTITIES 591
    Social Roles 591
    Social Positions 592
    Social Identities 592
MENTAL REPRESENTATIONS OF OTHERS 593
    Role-Taking 593
    Reference Groups and Individuals 593
    Social Comparison 594
    Anticipated Interactions with Others 595
SOCIAL INTERACTION AND COGNITIVE CHANGE 596
    Conflict as a Source of Cognitive Growth 596
    Majority and Minority Influence 597
    Group Decision Making 599
COGNITION AS COLLABORATION 599
    Development of Shared Cognitions in Groups 600
    Group Memory 602

0066-4308/93/0201-585$02.00

Communication and Linguistic Interaction 602
CONCLUSION 603

INTRODUCTION

Cognitive psychology has traditionally been a psychology of the individual, seeking to delineate the processes by which individual minds perceive, manipulate, and interpret information. Initially applied to artificial and puzzle-like tasks, cognitive theories have increasingly sought to explain more complex, ill-structured, and "real world" forms of cognitive activity. But even as explanatory ambitions have expanded, the standard metaphors (some treat them as true models) for problem solving and other forms of complex "higher-order" cognitive activity have been the rule-based theories of artificial intelligence in the Newell & Simon (1972) tradition. The rise of blackboard models and connectionist theories (Rummelhart et al 1986) has provided new and enriching metaphors, such as the "society of mind" (Minsky 1986), but the focus has remained on the individual as a solitary and, for the most part, purely intellective being. Although cognitive psychology's increasing engagement with complex tasks has pressed the field toward a consideration of the context of problem solving as an important element in cognition, little attention has been paid to intentions, motivations, social interpretations, or cognitive functioning in interaction with others.

A continuing debate among cognitive psychologists concerns the relative importance of general processes (sometimes called "skills") versus domain-specific knowledge in generating competent performance. Most now agree that "experts" in a domain are characterized by large pools of quickly accessible and highly specific knowledge, that general skills and domain-specific knowledge can to some degree compensate for one another, and that general skills are "weak" compared to domain-specific knowledge but are nonetheless crucial in allowing for novel performances.

Recognition of the importance of domain-specific knowledge took the cognitive psychologist on a first step toward eventual inclusion of social factors as part of cognition. This first step did not specifically implicate social factors but did highlight how particular, how *situated,* cognition always is. In practice, what qualifies as domain–specific is extremely dependent on particulars of the situation—what questions are asked in the experiment, for example, and what other information is given. That, in turn, makes it necessary to attend not only to knowledge elements but also to the conditions of their use—the situations in which cognition takes place.

This focus on situations leads the investigator away from the traditional site of cognitive research, the laboratory where a subject works alone at an experimenter-defined task, to various sites familiar to applied psychologists—the family, the classroom, the playground, and the workplace. At each of these sites one finds a complex social environment containing multiple actors, each with his or her own intentions and interpretations of the situation, who influence one another's knowledge, opinions, and values, and who interact to produce shared cognitive products. This increased interest in situated, or contextualized, cognition has led cognitive scientists to recognize the importance of relations among cognition, motivation, and broader processes of social influence and engagement. Recent work on such topics as mood and memory (Bower 1981), attribution and memory (e.g. Johnson & Sherman 1990), and transfer of situated learning (Greeno et al 1992) reflects this growing interest in socially situated cognitions.

In this chapter we develop a point of view that treats cognition as a fundamentally social activity. In so doing, we expand and elaborate our previous ideas about "socially shared cognition" (Resnick et al 1991) and the "social science of cognition" (Higgins 1992b). Much of the research we discuss here was conducted by social psychologists, and some of it falls under the heading of "social cognition." Critics sometimes complain that the field of social cognition is nothing more than "cognitive psychology with social objects." The implication is that social cognition researchers simply borrow cognitive psychology models originally developed for nonsocial objects and then test their generalizability to social objects. But, as Higgins (1992b) has argued, several cognitive models originated by social psychologists are applicable to cognition in general. These include models of attribution processes, salience effects, knowledge accessibility, and inference and decision making.

Of particular interest in the search for social foundations of cognition is the interface between cognition and motivation (see Higgins & Sorrentino 1990). Cognition as a source of motivation was a fundamental issue in social psychology during the late 1950s and 1960s, as exemplified in various cognitive consistency models (see Abelson et al 1968, for a review) and in the information transmission approach to attitude formation and change (see McGuire 1969). In addition, work by investigators interested in social development (e.g. Dweck & Bempechat 1983; Nicholls 1983) has shown how different self-attributions can motivate different forms of cognitive behavior, demonstrating how motivation can affect the form and substance of cognition as well as the amount of cognitive effort exerted.

Investigators from several disciplines outside psychology are also contributing to our understanding of cognition as a social process. These include anthropologists, who are studying how knowledge and skills are transmitted in traditional cultures and defining the cognitive foundations of cultural differences, and ethnomethodologists, who are investigating the structure of communication and language.

In this chapter, we ignore the boundaries of disciplines and subfields, focusing instead on substantive questions that seem central in understanding cognition as a social process. We are less concerned with evaluating the empirical support for various theories than with presenting ideas that have heuristic utility for an emerging field of inquiry, and we are illustrative rather than exhaustive in citing relevant research.

We consider five ways in which social factors influence both the content of people's cognitions and the processes by which cognitive activities proceed. In the first four sections, we focus primarily on how individual cognition is affected by social factors. Here our emphasis is on "social action" in Max Weber's (1967) sense, namely that the meaning people assign to events is transformed because their actions take others into account. In the fifth section, the cognitive and the social are fused. There we challenge the assumption that cognition is exclusively an individual act, clearly distinguishable from external social processes that may influence it. We explore the proposition that the social and the cognitive are more intimately intertwined than psychologists have typically assumed and that much thinking must be understood as a form of social interaction. In so doing, we review work that treats the social unit (i.e. the dyad or group), rather than the individual, as the focus of analysis.

MERE PRESENCE OF OTHERS

The most rudimentary way in which social factors influence cognition is via the simple presence of other people. Even when their responses are neither observed nor cognitively represented and there is no opportunity for interaction, the fact that others are physically present can affect a person's cognitive activity, sometimes facilitating and sometimes impeding it.

Social Facilitation

Two of the earliest experiments in social psychology (Triplett 1898; Meumann 1904, cited by Cottrell 1972) demonstrated that the presence of either co-actors or a passive audience can enhance performance. These social-facilitation effects elicited a good deal of research attention, but by the early 1960s a confusing picture had emerged. Some studies confirmed that the mere presence of others enhanced performance; others found that passive audiences and co-actors impeded performance.

Zajonc (1965) imposed order on these findings by arguing that the mere presence of others is a source of general arousal. This arousal increases the likelihood that dominant responses will be emitted, which in turn facilitates performance on tasks that require familiar responses and impairs performance on tasks that require novel responses. Evidence that audiences hinder performance when new responses must be learned but help performance after these responses have been acquired (e.g. Hunt & Hillery 1973) is consistent with Zajonc's position.

According to Zajonc's view, the presence of others is likely to elicit accessible cognitions (e.g. common word associations to verbal stimuli), which in turn facilitate performance when these cognitions are correct for the task at hand and impair performance when they are incorrect (cf Matlin & Zajonc 1968). For example, Schmitt et al (1986) had subjects type their own names, either as they normally appear (a simple task) or backwards with ascending numbers interspersed among the letters (a difficult task). In the "alone" condition, subjects worked by themselves; in the "mere presence" condition, they worked in a room with another person who wore a blindfold and earphones. Performance times were faster for the simple task and slower for the difficult task in the mere presence than in the alone condition.

Baron (1986) has proposed an alternative to Zajonc's drive theory based on the idea that the presence of others is a distraction, which leads to attentional conflict. This conflict produces cognitive overload and selective focusing of attention, which causes either performance decrements or increments, depending on the information-processing demands of the task (e.g. Groff et al 1983). (See Geen 1989, for a review of attentional explanations for the effects of others' presence.)

Yet another explanation of social facilitation is that the presence of an audience causes people to focus attention on the self (Duval & Wicklund 1972; Wicklund 1975). This in turn leads to thoughts about discrepancies between the actual self and the ideal self. Such "objective self-awareness" can be thought of as a form of "metacognition" (Brown et al 1983). (See also Schon 1983 on reflection on one's own cognitive work.) Although metacognitive theories typically stress the enhancing effects of being aware of one's cognitive processes, objective self-awareness can either enhance (e.g. Wicklund & Duval 1971) or depress (e.g. Liebling & Shaver 1973) task performance, depending on how it affects motivation and attention (see also Gibbons 1990; Scheier & Carver 1988).

Social Loafing

Fifteen years after Triplett's paper on social facilitation, Ringelmann (1913, summarized by Kravitz & Martin 1986) presented evidence that people working together did not perform as well as expected on the basis of their individual performances. One explanation for this reduced performance is "coordination loss" due to group members' interfering with one another's responses. Subsequent studies eliminated coordination loss as an explanation of reduced group performance by having members work alone but leading them to believe that others were simultaneously working on the same task and that the outputs of all members would be combined. Results indicated that, in this "pseudogroup" situation, individuals expended less effort when they thought they were working in a group than when they thought they were working alone. This decreased effort, labeled "social loafing" (Latane et al 1979), has proven to be a robust phenomenon, occurring on cognitive tasks, such as evaluating written materials and brainstorming (see Harkins & Petty 1983), as well as physical tasks.

Although the belief that others are working on the same task can decrease effort, social loafing is not inevitable. Loafing can be reduced or eliminated by increasing the identifiability and uniqueness of members' task contributions (e.g. Harkins & Petty 1982), the ease of evaluating those contributions (e.g. Harkins & Szymanski 1989), and members' accountability (e.g. Weldon & Gargano 1988). In Weldon & Gargano's study, subjects who performed a multiattribute judgment task were led to believe that (a) they either did or did not share responsibility for their performance (i.e. their output would or would not be combined with that of several others) and (b) they either were or were not accountable for their individual performance (i.e. the experimenter would or would not contact them to learn more about their evaluations). Mathematical models of subjects' judgments indicated that subjects in the shared responsibility/no-accountability condition used less complex judgment strategies than did those working alone. However, this social loafing was reduced when subjects in the shared-responsibility condition felt accountable for their performance. The positive impact of accountability on motivation in groups is also evident in work on cooperative learning (Bossert 1988; Slavin 1983).

Crowding

Another type of mere presence that can influence individual cognitive activity is crowding. Here, the issue is not simply that other people are physically present or even that large numbers of others are present. Instead, crowding involves the subjective sense that "too many" people are occupying a given physical space (Stokols 1972). The perception of crowding is itself socially determined, as indicated by cultural differences in how people perceive and use space (Hall 1966). Crowded situations have several aversive properties, including uncertainty, loss of control, cognitive overload, and behavioral constraints (Paulus & Nagar 1989). It is not surprising, then, that crowding impairs performance, particularly on complex tasks (Baum & Paulus 1987). For example, Paulus et al (1976) found that various ways of producing crowding led to performance decrements on a multiple-level maze task. In addition, crowding may elicit particular types of thoughts and judgments, including perceptions of helplessness, attributions about the behaviors of others, and ideas about how to cope with or escape from the unpleasant situation, which may be distracting and thereby inhibit cognitive performance (cf Baum & Gatchel 1981; Schmidt & Keating 1979; Worchel & Teddlie 1976).

Group Composition

A final type of mere presence that can affect individual cognition is group composition—that is, the mix of people who belong to a group. Group composition has been studied for many years, and the relevant literature is extensive (see Moreland & Levine 1992). Group composition can affect several types of social information processing, including stereotype-related memory and judgment, social projection, and the perception that the ingroup is more heterogeneous than the outgroup (Higgins & King 1981; Mullen 1991). For example, compared to majority members of groups, "token" and minority members (e.g. women in predominantly male groups) attract more attention from others (Lord & Saenz 1985; Taylor et al 1978) and are more aware of the characteristics that distinguish them from others (Cota & Dion 1986; McGuire & Padawer-Singer 1976; see also Frable et al 1990). This visibility, in turn, can distract token members from their task and thereby interfere with their performance (Lord & Saenz 1985).

SOCIAL ROLES, POSITIONS, AND IDENTITIES

Cognitive activity is strongly affected by how people construe the social situation in which they find themselves. Several lines of research in developmental, educational, and cultural psychology suggest that people whose abilities are assessed in particular situations (e.g. laboratory interviews, standardized tests) often do not demonstrate their full capacities. This may occur because a person's beliefs about how he or she ought to behave in the situation do not match the expectations of the assessor (e.g. Cole et al 1971; Siegal 1991). Interest in how people's perceptions of others' expectations affect their own cognitions and behaviors has a long history in social psychology and sociology.

Social Roles

As defined by Sarbin & Allen (1968), role expectations "are comprised of the rights and privileges, the duties and obligations, of any occupant of a social position in relation to persons occupying other positions in the social structure" (p. 497). When a person adopts a role, his or her behavior is constrained by the expectations associated with the role. In addition, the person's cognitions are often influenced by these expectations and the role enactments they elicit.

In an early study of the impact of role enactment on cognition, Jones & deCharms (1958) had subjects listen to an interview between a psychologist and an ex-prisoner of war who had signed propaganda statements during captivity. Subjects were assigned different roles vis-à-vis the ex-prisoner (i.e. member of a judicial board of inquiry, member of a medical-psychological board, potential friend). Results indicated that subjects' attributions of the target's personality characteristics varied markedly depending on the role they were assigned. More recent studies provide additional evidence for the impact of role enactment on cognitions. For example, Anderson & Pichert (1978) found that subjects' assignment to the role of home buyer versus burglar influenced their memory for the properties of a house that they read about. And Zukier & Pepitone (1984) found that assignment to the role of scientist versus clinical counselor influenced subjects' use of base rate information in evaluating a target person.

Social Positions

"Social positions" are defined as socially recognized categories of actors. When a positional category is assigned to a person, the individual is expected to possess particular attributes and is responded to on the assumption that he or she has these attributes (see Stryker & Statham 1985). Whereas some social positions are social roles, which involve normative expectations regarding appropriate behavior and sanctions for violating these expectations, other social positions simply involve probabilistic expectancies about how a person "will" (as opposed to "should") behave. The latter type of social position, like the former type discussed above, can influence cognitive activity.

An interesting consequence of assigning a person to a social position occurs when (a) the individual is assumed to possess certain characteristics that he or she does not possess, (b) others treat the person as though he or she possesses these characteristics, and (c) this treatment causes the person to exhibit the very characteristics he or she was (incorrectly) assumed to possess in the first place. These "self-fulfilling prophecies" (Merton 1957) have at least two kinds of cognitive consequences. First, assigning a person to a social position causes others to have certain cognitions about the person. Second, being treated as though one had a position-related characteristic causes the person to have certain cognitions about himself or herself (e.g. Fazio et al 1981; Snyder & Swann 1978). Both laboratory experiments (e.g. Word et al 1974) and non-laboratory studies (e.g. Rosenthal & Jacobson 1968) have demonstrated the power of self-fulfilling prophecies (see the review by Snyder 1992).

Dispositional inferences (e.g. industrious, aggressive) can also be treated as social positions if these terms are used to identify individuals who share similar characteristics that distinguish them from people in general. These dispositional inferences can have a major impact on subsequent information processing (for reviews, see Higgins & Stangor 1988; Wyer & Srull 1989).

Social Identities

As suggested above, people who are assigned to social positions by others sometimes internalize these positional designations and come to view themselves as the others view them (see Stryker & Statham 1985). Such internalized designations are called "social identities." It is important to note that, although social roles often become social identities, these two types of social positions are conceptually distinct. A person can enact a particular role but not identify with it (e.g. because role performance is forced by external pressure), and a person can identify with a social position (e.g. being short) that does not involve any role responsibilities.

Activation of a social identity can influence both behavior and cognition. For example, Charters & Newcomb (1952) increased the salience of Catholic students' religious identity by emphasizing the common religious identification of everyone in the room and found that this identity activation caused students' opinions to shift toward orthodox Catholic beliefs. Frable et al (1990) found that individuals who have social identities that are statistically rare and socially important (e.g. bisexual, wealthy) are more "mindful" during a dyadic interaction than are their "normal" partners, recalling more detailed information and taking their partner's perspective. Finally, socially categorizing another person as an ingroup versus an outgroup member can substantially affect how this person is perceived and treated (see, for example, Messick & Mackie 1989; Wilder 1986).

MENTAL REPRESENTATIONS OF OTHERS

In many cases, an individual who is not in the physical presence of others has knowledge about their responses or expects to learn about these responses in the future. These mental representations of others can have important effects on the individual's cognitions.

Role-Taking

The ability to take the roles of others is critical to effective role enactment (Mead 1934; Sarbin & Allen 1968). Situational role-taking involves "putting yourself in someone else's shoes" and inferring how you would respond if you were in the other person's situation. Individual role-taking involves "seeing the world through someone else's eyes" and inferring how the other person would respond if he or she were in the same situation as you (Higgins 1981b).

Role-taking ability shows systematic developmental shifts with age (see Flavell et al 1968; Higgins 1981b). As they mature, children become more adept at shifting perspective when asked to process identical input from different viewpoints; older (but not younger) children can represent events differently as a function of the perspective they are asked to adopt (Feffer 1970). Developmental and individual differences in role-taking appear to underlie differences in interpersonal sensitivity, social maturity, and prosocial behavior (Moore & Underwood 1981; Selman 1980).

Reference Groups and Individuals

Individuals' opinions are often influenced by the assumed opinions of groups they deem important. The critical role that reference groups play in social influence has been recognized for some time (see Singer 1981). A reference group may or may not be a membership group—people are sometimes formal members of groups with which they identify and sometimes not. In addition, people are motivated to meet the standards of some (positive) reference groups and to violate those of other (negative) reference groups. Siegel & Siegel (1957) found that both reference groups and membership groups influenced the authoritarianism of students' attitudes. And Carver & Humphries (1981) found that students who associated an opinion with a negative reference group showed less agreement with this position than did students who did not make this association.

Recent research shows that people's susceptibility to social influence depends on their self-categorization as members of a particular group and their conformity to the norms defining that group (Turner & Oakes 1989). Social influence occurs to the extent that (*a*) the source and target are perceived by the target as members of the same group (i.e. as sharing the same social identity) and (*b*) the source's position is viewed by the target as prototypical of the group's position. (See also Mackie et al 1992 and Van Knippenberg & Wilke 1992 for work indicating differential cognitive processing of messages from ingroup and outgroup sources.)

People are also influenced by the assumed responses of *reference individuals* (cf Elkind 1967). For example, several theorists have argued that social facilitation effects are not due to others' "mere presence" but rather to anxiety about how the others will evaluate one's performance (see Geen 1989 for a review of evaluation apprehension and self-presentation theories of social facilitation). And Baldwin et al (1990) have shown that students' evaluations of their own research ideas can be influenced by evoked representations of approving or disapproving faculty members.

Social Comparison

People's self-perceptions and evaluations are influenced by comparing themselves to others, even when no evaluation by these others is expected. Although knowledge about others' characteristics and performances is sometimes obtained from direct observation, often this knowledge is acquired from third parties (e.g. newspaper writers, mutual acquaintances). In both cases, comparison targets typically do not intend to influence the observer and may not even know that a comparison is taking place.

Stimulated by Festinger's classic 1954 paper on social comparison, scores of studies have assessed how self-judgments are affected by comparing one's own and others' abilities, opinions, emotions, and outcomes (see, for example, Higgins 1990; Kruglanski & Mayseless 1990; Levine & Moreland 1987; Suls & Wills 1991). Several trends in contemporary social comparison research suggest links between social and cognitive processes. For example, current research demonstrates that social comparison is itself a cognitive process, in which people actively select comparison targets and construct and distort comparison information to serve their goals. Thus, people sometimes imagine comparison targets who do not exist (e.g. hypothetical others who are worse off than they are) and select comparison dimensions that are likely to satisfy their goals (e.g. dimensions on which they are likely to be superior to others) (e.g. Wood & Taylor 1991). In addition, current investigations emphasize the cognitive consequences of receiving information indicating that one is superior or inferior to others. These consequences include changes in outcome expectations and self-efficacy as well as in achievement striving (e.g. Major et al 1991).

Anticipated Interactions with Others

When people expect to interact with others, they often prepare by engaging in various kinds of anticipatory cognitive activity. This anticipatory activity is likely to differ as a function of the kind of interaction that is expected and the presumed nature of the interaction partners. For example, a person may expect only to receive information, only to transmit information, or to both receive and transmit information. Similarly, a person may know nothing about the interaction partner's position or believe that the partner agrees or disagrees with his or her position. These factors are likely to affect both the amount and type of anticipatory cognitive activity that occurs. Other potentially important determinants of such activity include the person's goals for the upcoming interaction (cf Kruglanski 1989; Kunda 1990), the type of issue on which communication will occur (cf Laughlin & Ellis 1986), the communication modality that will be used (cf Kiesler et al 1984), and the amount of social support that the person expects to receive either during (cf Doms & Van Avermaet 1985) or outside (cf Miller et al 1991) the interaction.

Expecting to present one's position to others and/or expecting to learn about their position can affect cognitive activity. Work by Zajonc (1960) on cognitive tuning revealed that persons who expect to transmit information have more organized and polarized cognitive structures than do those who expect to receive information. Studies by Bargh & Schul (1980) and Benware & Deci (1984) indicated that individuals learn material better when they expect to teach it to others than when they do not have this expectation. Tetlock (1992) found that people who feel accountable to significant others for their decisions deal with this accountability in three ways: by saying what the others want to hear, by preemptively criticizing their own ideas, and by generating justifications for their position. These strategies can have important cognitive consequences, including, in the case of preemptive self-criticism, increased cognitive complexity regarding the topic under consideration. Finally, work by Cialdini & Petty (1981), Fitzpatrick & Eagly (1981), and McFarland et al (1984) on anticipatory attitude change revealed that expecting to receive a counterattitudinal message can produce issue-relevant thought as well as opinion change.

The cognitive impact of anticipated interaction is not restricted to the topic that will be discussed. Several authors have argued that different interaction goals (e.g. accurately assessing a partner's characteristics versus shaping the partner's behavior) can affect cognitions about other people (see reviews by Fiske & Neuberg 1990 and Hilton & Darley 1991). And several studies have shown that anticipated interaction can influence information processing about the people with whom one will interact (e.g. Devine et al 1989; Fiske & Von Hendy 1992; Osborne & Gilbert 1992). Devine et al demonstrated that expecting to interact with a target person, compared with not expecting to do so, produces better recall of information about the person, more individuation of the person in memory, and more accurate name-to-item associations for the person.

SOCIAL INTERACTION AND COGNITIVE CHANGE

Two influential thinkers, Mead (1934) and Vygotsky (1978), have proposed that people's fundamental capacities for thinking, as well as the forms their thinking takes, are created in socially shared cognitive activities. Mead called thought "conversation with the generalized other," suggesting that private thinking is an internalized version of the process of challenge, justification, and revision of ideas that first occurs during argumentation with others (see Hilton 1991 for a theory of how everyday causal explanations are grounded in conversational processes). Except for those interested in interpersonal communication, Mead has been largely ignored by students of cognition. In contrast, Vygotsky, who had similar ideas about thought as internalization of social practice, has profoundly influenced theories of cognitive development. Even biologically oriented developmental theorists, such as Piaget (1950; see also Gelman & Carey 1991), who attribute cognitive development to children's private mental work in grappling with the events and objects in their environments, acknowledge that certain kinds of social interactions stimulate mental effort and promote cognitive change. In addition, within social psychology, work on social influence and group participation also stresses the ways cognitive challenges from others can produce elaborations in individual thinking.

Conflict as a Source of Cognitive Growth

A significant body of research suggests that certain forms of interpersonal disagreement can facilitate intellectual development in children (Azmitia & Perlmutter 1989; Garton 1992; Murray 1983; see also Damon & Phelps 1989 on cognitive growth through cognitive collaboration). Much of this research has been conducted by a group of Genevan psychologists influenced by Piagetian theories of cognitive development (see Doise & Mugny 1984; Perret-Clermont & Nicolet 1988). These investigators assume that social interaction can produce intellectual development if socio-cognitive conflict is generated and resolved. Socio-cognitive conflict occurs when individuals have different responses to the same problem and are motivated to achieve a joint solution. The intellectual development produced by socio-cognitive conflict reflects extensive cognitive restructuring rather than mere imitation, as indicated by subjects' ability to generalize responses from one domain to another, to employ novel arguments that were not mentioned during interaction, and to profit from interaction with peers at the same or lower levels of cognitive development. Evidence suggests that the impact of conflict resolution on intellectual progress is influenced by the intensity and social significance of the conflict, as well as by whether the conflict is resolved through compliance by one of the participants (De Paolis et al 1987; Mugny et al 1984). In addition, the interactants' levels of cognitive development, and their social origin and status, are important (Mackie 1983; Perret-Clermont & Schubauer-Leoni 1981). (For evidence that socio-cognitive conflict does not always function as suggested by Doise and his colleagues, see Roy & Howe 1990 and Tudge 1989.)

Although interpersonal conflict is an important facilitator of cognitive change, such conflict need not involve face-to-face interaction in order to be effective. For example, the large literature on attitude change demonstrates that simply reading or hearing a counterattitudinal message (in the absence of any face-to-face interaction with the communicator) can influence the quantity and quality of individuals' cognitive activity (see Eagly & Chaiken 1984, and Petty & Cacioppo 1986).

Majority and Minority Influence

The stimulative effect of interpersonal disagreement on individual mental activity can be seen in research on majority and minority influence. Beginning with Asch (1951), researchers have sought to understand majority influence, or conformity, by clarifying the circumstances under which people who hold a minority position in a group adopt the position held by the majority (see reviews by Allen 1965; Levine & Russo 1987). More recently, beginning with Moscovici (Moscovici & Faucheux 1972), investigators have tried to understand minority influence, or innovation, by clarifying the conditions under which people holding a majority position adopt the minority position (see reviews by Kruglanski & Mackie 1990; Levine 1989; Moscovici 1985).

An important question regarding both conformity and innovation is whether the position change resulting from disagreement represents public agreement (*compliance*) or private agreement (*conversion*). Moscovici (1980, 1985) has argued that minorities have their primary impact on conversion, whereas majorities have their primary impact on compliance. Evidence regarding minority influence is consistent with this argument, but data regarding majority influence are not as clear (Maass & Clark 1984; Maass et al 1987; Mackie 1987).

From the perspective of socially influenced cognition, conversion is more interesting than compliance. As suggested above, conversion is often defined as private movement toward the influence source's position (e.g. agreement with other group members even though they cannot see one's responses). In addition, conversion is sometimes defined as *delayed* change, which occurs after the influence source is no longer present, and as *indirect* change, which occurs on related issues that were not mentioned by the source (Moscovici 1980; Mugny 1982; Mugny & Perez 1991). A particularly interesting, though controversial, indication of conversion involves changes in chromatic afterimages following exposure to minority responses suggesting that a stimulus of one color is actually another color (e.g. Moscovici & Personnaz 1986; but see Sorrentino et al 1980). This kind of basic perceptual change, when subjects are unaware of the physical laws relating visual images and afterimages, suggests that social influence may sometimes be powerful enough to affect perceptual processes normally considered to be purely physiological.

Another way in which the opinions of others in a group can influence cognitions is by leading individuals to reinterpret information so as to maintain their original position while still minimizing dissonance with the group's opinion. For example, Allen & Wilder (1980) had subjects read several statements (e.g. "I would never go out of my way to help another person if it meant giving up some personal pleasure.") and then give their interpretations of key phrases in each statement (e.g. "go out of my way"). Some subjects subsequently were told that a unanimous group of peers disagreed with their opinions on the statements; other subjects (controls) were not given this information. Allen & Wilder found that the two groups of subjects interpreted the key phrases differently. For example, the phrase "go out of my way" in the above example was interpreted to mean "risk my life" in the unanimous condition and "be inconvenienced" in the control condition. This reinterpretation of a stimulus in order to maintain a position in the face of dissonant information is analogous to the behavior of many science learners when they obtain experimental data that contradict their beliefs. Rather than change their beliefs, they often reinterpret the data or question its correctness (cf Johsua & Dupin 1987; Nissani & Hoefler-Nissani 1992).

Why does exposure to disagreement from others (particularly minorities) produce these cognitive changes? Moscovici (1980, 1985) argues that minorities trigger a "validation" process involving attention to the minority's position and cognitive activity about this position. Nemeth (1986) asserts that minorities stimulate issue-relevant, divergent thinking, which in turn leads to creative responses (see also Maass et al 1987). Interpersonal disagreement can indeed affect cognitive processes, including attention, convergent and divergent thought, and memory (e.g. Nemeth & Kwan 1987; Nemeth et al 1990). Nemeth & Kwan asked subjects to name words embedded in letter strings and informed them that either a majority or a minority of other group members adopted a nonobvious, or dissenting, strategy (i.e. reading the letters backward). When subsequently asked to form all the words they could from several letter strings, subjects exposed to minority dissent used more strategies (forward, backward, mixed) and therefore detected more words than did subjects exposed to majority dissent. These results suggest that a minority can sometimes stimulate more "advanced" cognitive responses than those exhibited in its own behavior. We saw similar effects in the work on socio-cognitive conflict discussed above.

Group Decision Making

Most studies of majority and minority influence do not involve explicit pressure on group members to reach a joint decision. However, such pressure is a defining characteristic of research on group decision making. Although the goal of group decision making is to arrive at a consensual judgment superior to the judgments of individual members, participation in this collective activity can have important cognitive consequences for group members. (We discuss group decision making as a joint cognitive activity below.)

One cognitive consequence for the individual is private opinion change in the direction of the group's final position (e.g. Sande & Zanna 1987). It is generally assumed that such change is more likely if the person is yielding to "informational" rather than "normative" pressure (Deutsch & Gerard 1955). In their work on mock jury deliberations, Stasser & Davis (1981) concluded that changes in members' (private) certainty levels were primarily attributable to informational influence, whereas changes in their (public) verdict preferences were due to normative as well as informational influence (see Stasser et al 1989 for a discussion of consensus models and group decision making). Kaplan (1987) has discussed several variables that increase the probability of informational influence (and hence private opinion change) during group decision making. These include an intellective (factual) issue, private responses, and desire to obtain a correct decision. Although the cognitive mechanisms underlying normative and informational influence are not well understood, the power of informational influence to produce private opinion change may be due, at least in part, to the validation process that Moscovici believes is responsible for conversion to minority opinions.

Other research suggests that engaging in group decision making can lead individuals to adopt the problem-solving strategies that the group used. For example, Laughlin and his colleagues (e.g. Laughlin & Ellis 1986) have demonstrated specific group-to-individual transfer on the same type of problem that the group worked on, whereas Stasson et al (1991) have demonstrated general transfer on different but related problems. And people who work together to resolve "judgment policy" conflicts (regarding how probabilistic cues should be weighted and combined in making inferential judgments) and who receive feedback regarding the correct answer show convergence in their judgment policies, although disagreements often continue because of inconsistent application of these policies (Brehmer 1984; Cook & Hammond 1982).

COGNITION AS COLLABORATION

Outside the laboratory and the school, cognition is almost always collaborative (Resnick 1987). At work and in civic and personal life, each person's ability to function successfully depends upon coordinated cognitive interactions with others, and the cognitive "products" that emerge from these interactions cannot be attributed to single individuals. In studying joint cognition, it is critical to examine both the process and outcomes of cognitive collaboration, treating the group or the dyad, rather than the individual, as the primary unit of analysis.

Development of Shared Cognitions in Groups

Coordinated cognitive activity depends upon *intersubjectivity* (Ickes et al 1990; Rommetveit 1979)—that is, a shared understanding of what is being discussed or worked on. Intersubjectivity, although an intuitively appealing concept, is difficult to operationalize. Its presence is typically inferred from successful coordination of activity by dyad or group members, rather than from direct measurement. Some research, however, has explicitly examined the extent to which shared cognitions are developed by group members.

A classic example is Sherif's (1935) research on norm formation in groups. Sherif investigated how people come to share common perceptions of an ambiguous perceptual stimulus, namely the apparent movement of a stationary point of light in an otherwise dark room (the *autokinetic effect*). The judgments of individual group members converged until a shared estimate of the light's direction and distance of movement was attained, and this socially developed norm continued to influence members' judgments when they later responded alone. Subsequent work has indicated that, once established, such a norm is often maintained over several "generations" during which old members gradually leave the group and new members join (Jacobs & Campbell 1961; Weick & Gilfillan 1971). Going beyond perceptual norms, a large body of work indicates that a group's efforts to transmit its norms are particularly strong when newcomers are involved (Levine & Moreland 1991; Moreland & Levine 1989). Groups are highly motivated to provide newcomers with the knowledge, ability, and motivation they will need to play the role of full member (e.g. Van Maanen & Schein 1979; Wanous 1980). Newcomers are typically receptive to these influence attempts because they feel a strong need to learn what is expected of them (e.g. Louis 1980; Van Maanen 1977).

To the extent that socially shared cognitions are developed during group interaction, we might expect groups to perform better than individuals on various tasks, including learning and concept attainment, creativity, and problem solving. However, this often is not the case (Hill 1982). In a review of research on individual versus group accuracy in judgment tasks, Hastie (1986) concluded that the relative performance of individuals and groups depends heavily on the task. On numerical estimation tasks, group judgment is slightly superior to the average individual judgment. On other tasks (e.g. logical and mathematical brainteaser problems), group judgment is better than the average individual judgment and worse than the best individual judgment, except on "Eureka" problems, where group performance tends to equal that of the most competent member. These findings suggest that "solution demonstrability" is the critical determinant of a group's ability to develop an adequate shared representation, with groups performing best when the task has a correct solution that can be readily demonstrated and communicated to members (cf Laughlin & Ellis 1986).

Information exchange is an important determinant of the effectiveness of joint decision making (e.g. Vinokur et al 1985). However, recent work by Stasser (1992) indicates that groups often do not exchange all the information available to their members. Rather than disseminating unshared information, group discussion tends to be dominated by information that members initially share and that supports their initial preferences.

This overreliance on shared information points to the negative consequences of too much intersubjectivity, which can prevent groups from fully exploiting the cognitive resources of their members (cf Levine & Moreland 1991). An extreme example of this phenomenon is "groupthink," which is defined as extreme concurrence-seeking that produces poor group decisions. Janis (1982) argued that factors such as external threat, high group cohesiveness, and directive leadership produce symptoms of groupthink (e.g. illusions of invulnerability, pressure on dissenters), which in turn undermine members' ability to process information and arrive at sound group decisions (see also McCauley 1989). In a similar vein, Hutchins (1991), using connectionist models of group and individual thinking, showed how the initial distribution of information in a group, together with the patterns of communication among members and the decision rules for integrating information, can either exacerbate or ameliorate problems that exist in individual cognitive systems (e.g. confirmation bias) (see also Tindale 1993).

An ostensible outcome of groupthink is the tendency for groups to pursue unduly risky courses of action. Evidence suggests that, at least under certain circumstances, groups do indeed make decisions more extreme than the average of members' initial positions (e.g. Isenberg 1986). A popular explanation for these group choice shifts (and for group polarization, or the tendency for individuals' opinions to become more extreme after discussion) is persuasive-arguments theory (Burnstein & Sentis 1981). According to this theory, choice shifts occur when people are exposed to novel and persuasive arguments supporting the side they already favor.

The ways groups develop shared cognitions during interaction have also been examined by Hastie & Pennington (1991) in their studies of jury decision making. They found that jurors' demographic characteristics (e.g. gender, age, socioeconomic status) influenced how much they talked during deliberation, that jurors used various social-influence tactics to reach consensus (e.g. factual arguments, appeals to values, direct rewards and punishments), and that juries tended to use one of two deliberation styles—evidence-driven or verdict-driven—to decide cases. Hastie & Pennington's analysis highlights the need to study how a shared interpretation of events is negotiated among individuals (and factions) who have different views of reality.

Group Memory

As the research on groupthink and confirmation bias suggests, maximum intersubjectivity, with all group members possessing exactly the same knowledge and thinking exactly the same way, often fails to capitalize on the total cognitive resources of the group. To ameliorate this problem, groups often evolve mechanisms for distributing cognitive responsibilities, thereby creating an expanded and more efficient cognitive system. Wegner (1987) has studied transactive memory, which he defines as a shared system for encoding, storing, and retrieving information. This system, which develops when people interact over time, is composed of the memory systems of the individuals in the relationship and the communication processes that link these systems (cf Hutchins 1991). Wegner and his colleagues have pointed out several ways in which transactive memory improves information encoding, storage, and retrieval, but they have also shown that, under certain conditions, it can have detrimental effects. For example, Wegner et al (1991) demonstrated that romantic partners exhibited lower recall than did pairs of strangers when the experimenter imposed a particular memory structure (e.g. one person should remember food items, and the other should remember history items), whereas just the opposite pattern emerged when no memory structure was assigned. Apparently transactive memory systems that develop in ongoing relationships can hinder recall when the partners are forced to adopt a new memory structure.

Memory is social in at least two other senses (cf Middleton & Edwards 1990). First, the content of memory is social to the extent that it refers to one's past social actions and experiences (e.g. Duck 1982; Messe et al 1981). Second, the process of memory formation is social to the extent that it is based on symbolic communication with other people. Several studies have examined how interaction affects memory in face-to-face groups (e.g. Clark & Stephenson 1989; Hartwick et al 1982; Vollrath et al 1989). Evidence indicates that three variables play an important role in collaborative recall: the degree of consensus favoring a response alternative, the correctness of the alternative, and members' confidence in their responses (Hinsz 1990).

Communication and Linguistic Interaction

The relations between cognition and communication are complex (cf Billig 1987; Schwarz & Strack 1991; Zajonc & Adelmann 1987), but there is broad agreement that the conventions of conversation both enable and constrain collaborative thought (cf Vygotsky 1962 and Wertsch 1985). Several investigators have examined how particular features of conversation are used to establish and maintain "common ground" (i.e. to coordinate referential meaning) during communication (see Higgins 1981a). Some of this work involves the ways speakers work together to honor conversation principles of the sort that Grice (1975) proposed. For example, Clark and his colleagues (e.g. Clark

& Brennan 1991) have argued that grounding activities are determined by the principle of "least collaborative effort" and that these activities change with both the purpose of the conversation (e.g. identify referents vs register verbatim content) and the medium of the conversation (e.g. face-to-face vs electronic mail).

The importance of the communication medium is also being recognized in the growing body of work on distributed cognition and collaborative mental work (e.g. Galegher et al 1990; Resnick et al 1992; Suchman 1987). This work shows that in conversation, talk, like ideas, is produced jointly. Analysis of the linguistic structure of dialogs shows that much of what is said by each speaker is incomplete and relies for coherence on the contributions of others, along with the physical context.

Taking a sociological perspective on language, ethnomethodologists have argued that language contains specific tools for maintaining social and cognitive coordination, so that it is neither necessary nor desirable for individual contributions to be complete. For example, Schegloff (1991) has shown how conversational "repair" of misperceived utterances maintains both the shared reference and the appropriate social relationship between the conversation partners.

Several investigators have shown that speakers construct their communications to fit the assumed knowledge and social communities of their listeners. According to Krauss & Fussell (1991), communicators use two sources of evidence to construct hypotheses about their shared communicative environments: (*a*) prior beliefs and expectations about others, based on their personal characteristics and social category memberships; and (*b*) feedback obtained from direct interaction with others. Higgins and his colleagues (Higgins 1992a) have found that knowledge of the audience's position on an issue affected what the communicator transmitted about this issue, as well as the communicator's subsequent memory for the original information on the issue. Finally, there is evidence that communicators take into account the different knowledge possessed by different audiences by communicating a hidden message to one audience while simultaneously misleading a second audience (Fleming & Darley 1991).

CONCLUSION

Our selective review, drawing on work in social psychology and in several social sciences, documents the many ways the social and the cognitive interpenetrate and interact in human functioning. The last two sections of our review signal most clearly the future of the new field of *sociocognition* that we believe is emerging. The research discussed there considers social interaction to be a paramount site for the development and practice of cognition. We have distinguished research that treats individual mental activity as the central problem in cognitive research, considering interaction primarily as a stimulus to that private mental work, from research that treats the interacting group as the cognitive unit, considering individuals primarily as contributors to the cognitive work of the group. This distinction—between interaction that *stimulates* cognition and interaction that *constitutes* cognition—may become less crisp as the field continues to develop.

Although some might claim that the brain as the physical site of mental processing requires that we treat cognition as a fundamentally individual and even private activity, we are prepared to argue that all mental activity—from perceptual recognition to memory to problem solving—involves either representations of other people or the use of artifacts and cultural forms that have a social history. Our attention to linguistic processes in cognitive collaboration brings into focus the extent to which cultural inheritances shape even individual cognitive activity (cf Wertsch 1985). The rules of pragmatic discourse (cf Austin 1962; Grice 1975; Searle 1969) vary from culture to culture, as does the vocabulary available for expressing ideas. Other inherited tools, such as scientific instruments and theories, also embody accepted ways of thinking (cf Latour 1987) and thus invisibly shape the course of both individual and group cognitive activity.

Culture, which includes the ways of thought, tools, and artifacts of a group of people, is both socially constructed and socially transmitted (Shweder 1991). It carries the past history of a group into the present and therefore influences how group members understand their social, physical, and spiritual worlds. This point has been powerfully elaborated by Cole (1988; Laboratory of Comparative Human Cognition 1983) and others representing what is called the *sociocultural* perspective on cognition (Greenfield 1984; Lave 1988). A related idea is Moscovici's theory of *social representations,* which are mental schemata or images that people use when making attributions and causal explanations (see Farr & Moscovici 1984; von Cranach et al 1992). As Potter & Wetherell (1987) suggest, social representations are "social" in at least three senses: (*a*) they originate in social interaction and communication, (*b*) they provide a consensual code that facilitates communication, and (*c*) they provide a means of distinguishing between social groups.

In the messy "real world" it is difficult to imagine any situation that is purely cognitive—devoid of emotions, social meanings, social intentions, and social residues in the form of inherited roles and tools. Indeed, the drive to understand cognition in everyday use has stimulated the interest of cognitive psychologists in social processes. Some of the lines of sociocognitive research and theory discussed in this chapter have begun to penetrate everyday contexts in another way. Several techniques have been developed to exploit social relationships as tools for enhancing learning and performance in school and nonschool settings (see Weinstein 1991). Two important techniques are peer tutoring (allen 1976; Cohen et al 1982) and cooperative learning (Bossert 1988; Slavin 1983). Some particularly effective educational interventions have used structured procedures in which students learn to ask questions and provide explanations in small-group settings (e.g. Palincsar & Brown 1984).

Palincsar & Brown's work is part of a broader movement to apply Vygotskian and related theories of situated cognition to education (see Brown et al 1989; Lave & Wenger 1991; Newman et al 1989; and Rogoff 1990). Central to all of these efforts is the notion of learning as apprenticeship (cf Collins et al 1989). For example, Rogoff (1990) uses apprenticeship theory in analyzing how children acquire cognitive skills, such as memory and planning, during interactions with adults and peers. Lave (1988) gives less attention to the instructional aspects of interaction and more attention to how apprentices acquire knowledge and skills by actively participating in socially valued production activities with more experienced workers. Her analysis emphasizes the linkages between acquiring cognitive skills and developing an identity as a member of a social community.

This work on situated cognition and education is testimony to how engagement with real-world problems can blur disciplinary boundaries as well as the formerly sharp distinction between cognition and social behavior. This blurring is welcome because of the theoretical advances it allows. Two historical examples illustrate the theoretical benefits of taking social processes seriously in studying cognition: Efforts to account for the role of social factors in recall led to Bartlett's (1932) theory of *reconstructive memory,* and work on how social values affect perception led to Bruner's (1957) concept of *accessibility.* As the field of sociocognition develops and new conceptions of the relationship between individual and collective cognition emerge, fundamental advances in both social and cognitive sciences are likely.

ACKNOWLEDGMENTS

Preparation of this chapter was supported by funds from the Office of Educational Research and Improvement, Department of Education; the A. W. Mellon Foundation; and the National Institute of Mental Health.

Literature Cited

Abelson, R. P., Aronson, E., McGuire, W. J., Newcomb, T. M., Rosenberg, M. J., Tannenbaum, P. H., eds. 1968. *Theories of Cognitive Consistency: A Source Book.* Chicago: Rand McNally

Allen, V. 1965. Situational factors in conformity. *Adv. Exp. Soc. Psychol.* 2:133–76

Allen, V., ed. 1976. *Children as Teachers: Theory and Research on Tutoring.* New York: Academic

Allen, V. L., Wilder, D. A. 1980. Impact of group consensus and social support on stimulus meaning: mediation of conformity by cognitive restructuring. *J. Pers. Soc. Psychol.* 39:1116–24

Anderson, R. C., Pichert, J. W. 1978. Recall of previously unrecallable information following a shift in perspective. *J. Verb. Learn. Verb. Behav.* 17:1–12

Asch, S. E. 1951. Effects of group pressure upon the modification and distortion of judgments. In *Groups, Leadership, and Men,* ed. H. Guetzkow, pp. 177–90. Pittsburgh: Carnegie Press

Austin, J. 1962. *How to Do Things with Words.* Oxford: Clarendon Press

Azmitia, M., Perlmutter, M. 1989. Social influences on children's cognition: state of the art and future directions. In *Adv. Child Dev. Behav.* 22:89–144

Baldwin, M. W., Carrell, S. E., Lopez, D. F. 1990. Priming relationship schemas: My advisor and the Pope are watching me from the back of my mind. *J. Exp. Soc. Psychol.*

26:435–54

Bargh, J. A., Schul, Y. 1980. On the cognitive benefits of teaching. *J. Educ. Psychol.* 72:593–604

Baron, R. S. 1986. Distraction/conflict theory: progress and problems. *Adv. Exp. Soc. Psychol.* 19:1–40

Bartlett, F. C. 1932. *Remembering: A Study in Experimental and Social Psychology.* New York: Cambridge Univ. Press

Baum, A., Gatchel, R. J. 1981. Cognitive determinants of reaction to uncontrollable events: development of reactance and learned helplessness. *J. Pers. Soc. Psychol.* 40:1078–89

Baum, A., Paulus, P. B. 1987. Crowding. In *Handbook of Environmental Psychology,* ed. D. Stokols, I. Altman, 1:533–70. New York: Wiley

Benware, C. A., Deci, E. L. 1984. Quality of learning with an active versus passive motivational set. *Am. Educ. Res. J.* 21:755–65

Billig, M. 1987. *Arguing and Thinking.* Cambridge: Cambridge Univ. Press

Bossert, S. T. 1988. Cooperative activities in the classroom. *Rev. Res. Educ.* 15:225–50

Bower, G. H. 1981. Mood and memory. *Am. Psychol.* 36:129–48

Brehmer, B. 1984. The role of judgment in small-group conflict and decision-making. In *Progress in Applied Social Psychology,* ed. G. M. Stephenson, J. H. Davis, 2:163–83. Chichester: Wiley

Brown, A. L., Bransford, J. D., Ferrara, R. A., Campione, J. C. 1983. Learning, remembering, and understanding. In *Cognitive Development,* ed. J. H. Flavell, E. M. Markman, pp. 77–166. New York: Wiley

Brown, J. S., Collins, A., Duguid, P. 1989. Situated cognition and the culture of learning. *Educ. Res.* 18:32–42

Bruner, J. S. 1957. On perceptual readiness. *Psychol. Rev.* 64:123–52

Burnstein, E., Sentis, K. 1981. Attitude polarization in groups. See Petty et al 1981, pp. 197–216

Carver, C. S., Humphries, C. 1981. Havana daydreaming: a study of self-consciousness and the negative reference group among Cuban Americans. *J. Pers. Soc. Psychol.* 40:545–52

Charters, W. W., Newcomb, T. M. 1952. Some attitudinal effects of experimentally increased salience of a membership group. In *Readings in Social Psychology,* ed. G. E. Swanson, T. M. Newcomb, E. L. Hartley, pp. 415–20. New York: Holt, Rinehart & Winston. 2nd ed.

Cialdini, R. B., Petty, R. E. 1981. Anticipatory opinion effects. See Petty et al 1981, pp. 217–35

Clark, H. H., Brennan, S. E. 1991. Grounding in communication. See Resnick et al 1991, pp. 127–49

Clark, N. K., Stephenson, G. M. 1989. Group remembering. See Paulus 1989, pp. 357–91

Cohen, P. A., Kulik, J. A., Kulik, C. C. 1982. Educational outcomes of tutoring: a meta-analysis of findings. *Am. Educ. Res. J.* 19:237–48

Cole, M. 1988. Cross–cultural research in the socio-historical tradition. *Hum. Dev.* 31:137–57

Cole, M., Gay, J., Glick, J. A., Sharp, D. W. 1971. The *Cultural Context of Learning and Thinking.* New York: Basic Books

Collins, A., Brown, J. S., Newman, S. 1989. Cognitive apprenticeship: teaching the crafts of reading, writing, and mathematics. In *Knowing, Learning, and Instruction: Essays in Honor of Robert Glaser,* ed. L. B. Resnick, pp. 453–94. Hillsdale: Erlbaum

Cook, R. L., Hammond, K. R. 1982. Interpersonal learning and interpersonal conflict reduction in decision-making groups. See Guzzo 1982, pp. 13–40

Cota, A. A., Dion, K. L. 1986. Salience of gender and sex composition of ad hoc groups: an experimental test of distinctiveness theory. *J. Pers. Soc. Psychol.* 50:770–76

Cottrell, N. B. 1972. Social facilitation. In *Experimental Social Psychology,* ed. C. G. McClintock, pp. 185–236. New York: Holt, Rinehart & Winston

Damon, W., Phelps, E. 1989. Strategic uses of peer learning in children's education. In *Peer Relationships in Child Development,* ed. T. Berndt, A. Ladd, pp. 135–57. New York: Wiley

De Paolis, P., Doise, W., Mugny, G. 1987. Social markings in cognitive operations. In *Current Issues in European Social Psychology,* ed. W. Doise, S. Moscovici, 2:1–46. Cambridge: Cambridge Univ. Press

Deutsch, M., Gerard, H. B. 1955. A study of normative and informational social influences upon individual judgment. *J. Abnorm. Soc. Psychol.* 51:629–36

Devine, P. G., Sedikides, C., Fuhrman, R. W. 1989. Goals in social information processing: the case of anticipated interaction. *J. Pers. Soc. Psychol.* 56:680–90

Doise, W., Mugny, G. 1984. *The Social Development of the Intellect.* Oxford: Pergamon Press

Doms, M., Van Avermaet, E. 1985. Social support and minority influence: the innovation effect reconsidered. In *Perspectives on Minority Influence,* ed., S. Moscovici, G. Mugny, E. Van Avermaet, pp. 53–74. Cambridge: Cambridge Univ. Press

Duck, S. W. 1982. A topography of relationship disengagement and dissolution. In *Personal Relationships 4: Dissolving Personal Relationships,* ed. S. W. Duck. New York: Academic

Duval, S., Wicklund, R. A. 1972. *A Theory of Objective Self-Awareness.* New York: Academic

Dweck, C. S., Bempechat, J. 1983. Children's theories of intelligence: consequences for learning. See Paris et al 1983, pp. 239–56

Eagly, A. H., Chaiken, S. 1984. Cognitive theories of persuasion. *Adv. Exp. Soc. Psychol.* 17:268–359

Elkind, D. 1967. Egocentrism in adolescence. *Child Dev.* 38:1025–34

Farr, R., Moscovici, S., eds. 1984. *Social Representations.* Cambridge: Cambridge Univ. Press

Fazio, R. H., Effrein, E. A., Falender, V. J. 1981. Self-perceptions following social interaction. *J. Pers. Soc. Psychol.* 41:232–42

Feffer, M. 1970. Developmental analysis of interpersonal behavior. *Psychol. Rev.* 77:197–214

Festinger, L. 1954. A theory of social comparison processes. *Hum. Relat.* 7:117–40

Fiske, S. T., Neuberg, S. L. 1990. A continuum of impression formation, from category-based to individuating processes: influences of information and motivation on attention and interpretation. *Adv. Exp. Soc. Psychol.* 23:1–74

Fiske, S. T., Von Hendy, H. M. 1992. Personality feedback and situational norms can control stereotyping processes. *J. Pers. Soc. Psychol.* 62:577–96

Fitzpatrick, A. R., Eagly, A. H. 1981. Anticipatory belief polarization as a function of the expertise of a discussion partner. *Pers. Soc. Psychol. Bull.* 7:636–42

Flavell, J. H., Botkin, P. I., Fry, C. L. Jr., Wright, J. W., Jarvis, P. E., eds. 1968. *The Development of Role-Taking and Communication Skills in Children.* New York: Wiley

Fleming, J. H., Darley, J. M. 1991. Mixed messages: the multiple audience problem and strategic communication. *Soc. Cognit.* 9:25–46

Frable, D. E. S., Blackstone, T., Scherbaum, C. 1990. Marginal and mindful: deviants in social interactions. *J. Pers. Soc. Psychol.* 59:140–49

Galegher, J., Kraut, R. E., Egido, C., eds. 1990. *Intellectual Teamwork: Social and Technological Foundations of Cooperative Work.* Hillsdale: Erlbaum. 542 pp.

Garton, A. F. 1992. *Social Interaction and the Development of Language and Cognition.* Hillsdale: Erlbaum. 155 pp.

Geen, R. G. 1989. Alternative conceptions of social facilitation. See Paulus 1989, pp. 15–51

Gelman, R., Carey, S. eds. 1991. *The Epigenesis of Mind: Essays on Biology and Cognition.* Hillsdale: Erlbaum

Gibbons, F. X. 1990. Self-attention and behavior: a review and theoretical update. *Adv. Exp. Soc. Psychol.* 23:249–303

Greenfield, P. M. 1984. A theory of the teacher in everyday life. In *Everyday Cognition: Its Development in Social Context,* ed. B. Rogoff, J. Lave, pp. 117–38. Cambridge: Harvard Univ. Press

Greeno, J. G., Smith, D. R., Moore, J. L. 1992. Transfer of situated learning. In *Transfer on Trial,* ed. D. Detterman, R. Sternberg.

Norwood: Ablex. In press

Grice, H. P. 1975. Logic and conversation. In *Syntax and Semantics,* ed. P. Cole, J. Morgan, 3:225–42. New York: Seminar Press

Groff, B. D., Baron, R. S., Moore, D. S. 1983. Distraction, attentional conflict, and drivelike behavior. *J. Exp. Soc. Psychol.* 19:359–80

Guzzo, R. A. 1982. *Improving Group Decision Making in Organizations.* New York: Academic

Hall, E. T. 1966. *The Hidden Dimension.* Garden City: Doubleday & Company

Harkins, S. G., Petty, R. E. 1982. Effects of task difficulty and task uniqueness on social loafing. *J. Pers. Soc. Psychol.* 43:1214–29

Harkins, S. G., Petty, R. E. 1983. Social context effects in persuasion: the effects of multiple sources and multiple targets. In *Basic Group Processes,* ed. P. B. Paulus, pp. 149–75. New York: Springer-Verlag

Harkins, S. G., Szymanski, K. 1989. Social loafing and group evaluation. *J. Pers. Soc. Psychol.* 56:934–41

Hartwick, J., Sheppard, B. H., Davis, J. H. 1982. Group remembering: research and implications. See Guzzo 1982, pp. 41–72

Hastie, R. 1986. Review essay: experimental evidence on group accuracy. In *Information Pooling and Group Decision Making,* ed. G. Owen, B. Grofman, pp. 129–57. Westport: JAI Press

Hastie, R., Pennington, N. 1991. Cognitive and social processes in decision making. See Resnick et al 1991, pp. 308–27

Higgins, E. T. 1981a. The "communication game": implications for social cognition and persuasion. In *Social Cognition: The Ontario Symposium,* ed. E. T. Higgins, C. P. Herman, M. P. Zanna, 1:343–92. Hillsdale: Erlbaum

Higgins, E. T. 1981b. Role taking and social judgment: alternative developmental perspectives and processes. In *Social Cognitive Development: Frontiers and Possible Futures,* ed. J. H. Flavell, L. Ross, pp. 119–53. New York: Cambridge Univ. Press

Higgins, E. T. 1992a. Achieving "shared reality" in the communication game: a social action that creates meaning. *J. Soc. Psychol. Lang.* In press

Higgins, E. T. 1992b. Social cognition as a social science: how social action creates meaning. In *The Social Psychology of Mental Health,* ed. D. N. Ruble, P. R. Costanzo, M. E. Oliveri, pp. 241–78. New York: The Guilford Press

Higgins, E. T., King, G. 1981. Accessibility of social constructs: information processing consequences of individual and contextual variability. In *Personality, Cognition, and Social Interaction,* ed. N. Cantor, J. Kihlstrom, pp. 69–121. Hillsdale: Erlbaum

Higgins, E. T., Sorrentino, R. M., eds. 1990. *Handbook of Motivation and Cognition: Foundations of Social Behavior,* Vol. 2.

New York: The Guilford Press

Higgins, E. T., Stangor, C. 1988. Context-driven social judgment and memory: when "behavior engulfs the field" in reconstructive memory. In *The Social Psychology of Knowledge,* ed. D. Bar-Tal, A. W. Kruglanski, pp. 262–98. Cambridge: Cambridge Univ. Press

Hill, G. W. 1982. Group versus individual performance: are N + 1 heads better than one? *Psychol. Bull.* 91:517–39

Hilton, D. J. 1991. A conversational model of causal explanation. In *European Review of Social Psychology,* ed. W. Stroebe, M. Hewstone, 2:51–81. London: Wiley

Hilton, J. L., Darley, J. M. 1991. The effects of interaction goals on person perception. *Adv. Exp. Soc. Psychol.* 24:236–67

Hinsz, V. B. 1990. Cognitive and consensus processes in group recognition memory performance. *J. Pers. Soc. Psychol.* 59:705–18

Hunt, P. J., Hillery, J. M. 1973. Social facilitation in a coaction setting: an examination of the effects over learning trials. *J. Exp. Soc. Psychol.* 9:563–71

Hutchins, E. 1991. The social organization of distributed cognition. See Resnick et al 1991, pp. 283–307

Ickes, W., Stinson, L., Bissonnette, V., Garcia, S. 1990. Naturalistic social cognition: empathic accuracy in mixed-sex dyads. *J. Pers. Soc. Psychol.* 59:730–42

Isenberg, D. J. 1986. Group polarization: a critical review and meta-analysis. *J. Pers. Soc. Psychol.* 50:1141–51

Jacobs, R. C., Campbell, D. T. 1961. The perpetuation of an arbitrary tradition through several generations of a laboratory microculture. *J. Abnorm. Soc. Psychol.* 62:649–58

Janis, I. L. 1982. *Groupthink.* Boston: Houghton Mifflin, 2nd ed.

Johnson, M. K., Sherman, S. J. 1990. Constructing and reconstructing the past and the future in the present. See Higgins & Sorrentino 1990, pp. 482–526

Johsua, S., Dupin, J. J. 1987. Taking into account student conceptions in a didactic strategy: an example in physics. *Cognit. Instruc.* 4:117–35

Jones, E. E., de Charms, R. 1958. The organizing function of interaction roles in person perception. *J. Abnorm. Soc. Psychol.* 57:155–64

Kaplan, M. F. 1987. The influencing process in group decision making. *Rev. Pers. Soc. Psychol.* 8:189–212

Kiesler, S., Siegel, J., McGuire, T. W. 1984. Social psychological aspects of computer-mediated communication. *Am. Psychol.* 39:1123–34

Krauss, H. H., Fussell, S. R. 1991. Constructing shared communicative environments. See Resnick et al 1991, pp. 172–200

Kravitz, D. A., Martin, B. 1986. Ringelmann rediscovered: the original article. *J. Pers.*

Soc. Psychol. 50:936–41

Kruglanski, A. W. 1989. *Lay Epistemics and Human Knowledge.* New York: Plenum

Kruglanski, A. W., Mackie, D. M. 1990. Majority and minority influence: a judgmental process analysis. In *European Review of Social Psychology,* ed. W. Stroebe, M. Hewstone, 1:229–61. London: Wiley

Kruglanski, A. W., Mayseless, O. 1990. Classic and current social comparison research: expanding the perspective. *Psychol. Bull.* 108:195–208

Kunda, Z. 1990. The case for motivated reasoning. *Psychol. Bull.* 108:480–98

Laboratory of Comparative Human Cognition. 1983. Culture and cognitive development. In Handbook of Child Psychology, ed. P. H. Mussen, 1:295–356. New York: Wiley

Latane, B., Williams, K. D., Harkins, S. G. 1979. Many hands make light the work: the causes and consequences of social loafing. *J. Pers. Soc. Psychol.* 37:822–32

Latour, B. 1987. *Science in Action.* Cambridge: Harvard Univ. Press

Laughlin, P. R., Ellis, A. L. 1986. Demonstrability and social combination processes on mathematical intellective tasks. *J. Exp. Soc. Psychol.* 22:177–89

Lave, J. 1988. *Cognition in Practice.* Cambridge: Cambridge Univ. Press

Lave, J., Wenger, E. 1991. *Situated Learning: Legitimate Peripheral Participation.* Cambridge: Cambridge Univ. Press

Levine, J. M. 1989. Reaction to opinion deviance in small groups. See Paulus 1989, pp. 187–231

Levine, J. M., Moreland, R. L. 1987. Social comparison and outcome evaluation in group contexts. In *Social Comparison, Social Justice, and Relative Deprivation: Theoretical, Empirical, and Policy Perspectives,* ed. J. C. Masters, W. P. Smith, pp. 105–27. Hillsdale: Erlbaum

Levine, J. M., Moreland, R. L. 1991. Culture and socialization in work groups. See Resnick et al 1991, pp. 257–79

Levine, J. M., Russo, E. M. 1987. Majority and minority influence. *Rev. Pers. Soc. Psychol..* 8:13–54

Liebling, B. A., Shaver, P. 1973. Evaluation self-awareness and task performance. *J. Exp. Soc. Psychol.* 9:297–306

Lindzey, G., Aronson, E., eds. 1985. *The Handbook of Social Psychology.* Reading: Addison-Wesley, 3rd ed.

Lord, R. G., Saenz, D. S. 1985. Memory deficits and memory surfeits: differential cognitive consequences of tokenism for tokens and observers. *J. Pers. Soc. Psychol.* 49:918–26

Louis, M. R. 1980. Surprise and sense making: what newcomers experience in entering unfamiliar organizational settings. *Adm. Sci. Q.* 25:226–51

Maass, A., Clark, R. D. III. 1984. Hidden impact of minorities: fifteen years of minority influence research. *Psychol. Bull.* 95:428–50

Maass, A., West, S. G., Cialdini, R. B. 1987. Minority influence and conversion. *Rev. Pers. Soc. Psychol.*. 8:55–79

Mackie, D. 1983. The effect of social interaction on conservation of spatial relations. *J. Cross-Cult. Psychol.* 14:131–51

Mackie, D. M. 1987. Systematic and nonsystematic processing of majority and minority persuasive communications. *J. Pers. Soc. Psychol.* 53:41–52

Mackie, D. M., Gastardo-Conaco, M. C., Skelly, J. J. 1992. Knowledge of the advocated position and the processing of in-group and out-group persuasive messages. *Pers. Soc. Psychol. Bull.* 18:145–51

Major, B., Testa, M., Bylsma, W. H. 1991. Responses to upward and downward social comparisons: the impact of esteem-relevance and perceived control. See Suls & Wills 1991, pp. 237–60

Matlin, M. W., Zajonc, R. B. 1968. Social facilitation of word associations. *J. Pers. Soc. Psychol.* 10:435–60

McCauley, C. 1989. The nature of social influence in groupthink: compliance and internalization. *J. Pers. Soc. Psychol.* 57:250–60

McFarland, C., Ross, M., Conway, M. 1984. Self-persuasion and self-presentation as mediators of anticipatory attitude change. *J. Pers. Soc. Psychol.* 46:529–40

McGuire, W. J. 1969. The nature of attitudes and attitude change. In *The Handbook of Social Psychology,* ed. G. Lindzey, E. Aronson, 3:136–314. Reading: Addison-Wesley. 2nd ed.

McGuire, W. J., Padawer-Singer, A. 1976. Trait salience in the spontaneous self-concept. *J. Pers. Soc. Psychol.* 33:743–54

Mead, G. H. 1934. *Mind, Self, and Society.* Chicago: Univ. Chicago Press

Merton, R. K. 1957. *Social Theory and Social Structure.* Glencoe: Free Press

Messe, L. A., Buldain, R. W., Watts, B. 1981. Recall of social events with the passage of time. *Pers. Soc. Psychol. Bull.* 7:33–38

Messick, D. M., Mackie, D. M. 1989. Intergroup relations. *Annu. Rev. Psychol.* 40:45–81

Middleton, D., Edwards, D., eds. 1990. *Collective Remembering.* London: Sage

Miller, N., Gross, S., Holtz, R. 1991. Social projection and attitudinal certainty. See Suls & Wills 1991, pp. 177–209

Minsky, M. L. 1986. *The Society of Mind.* New York: Simon & Schuster

Moore, B., Underwood, B. 1981. The development of prosocial behavior. In *Developmental Social Psychology: Theory and Research,* ed. S. S. Brehm, S. M. Kassin, F. X. Gibbons, pp. 72–95. New York: Oxford Press

Moreland, R. L., Levine, J. M. 1989. Newcomers and oldtimers in small groups. See Paulus 1989, pp. 143–86

Moreland, R. L., Levine, J. M. 1992. The composition of small groups. In *Advances in Group Processes,* ed. E. Lawler, B. Markovsky, C. Ridgeway, H. Walker, 9:237–80. Greenwich: JAI Press

Moscovici, S. 1980. Toward a theory of conversion behavior. *Adv. Exp. Soc. Psychol.* 13:209–39

Moscovici, S. 1985. Social influence and conformity. See Lindzey & Aronson 1985, pp. 347–412

Moscovici, S., Faucheux, C. 1972. Social influence, conformity bias, and the study of active minorities. *Adv. Exp. Soc. Psychol.* 6:149–202

Moscovici, S., Personnaz, B. 1986. Studies on latent influence by the spectrometer method I: the impact of psychologization in the case of conversion by a minority or a majority. *Eur. J. Soc. Psychol.* 16:345–60

Mugny, G. 1982. *The Power of Minorities.* New York: Academic

Mugny, G., De Paolis, P., Carugati, F. 1984. Social regulations in cognitive development. In *Social Interaction in Cognitive Development,* ed. W. Doise, A. Palmonari, pp. 127–46. Cambridge: Cambridge Univ. Press

Mugny, G., Perez, J. A. 1991. *The Social Psychology of Minority Influence.* Cambridge: Cambridge Univ. Press

Mullen, B. 1991. Group composition, salience, and cognitive representations: the phenomenology of being in a group. *J. Exp. Soc. Psychol.* 27:297–323

Mullen, B., Goethals, G. R., eds. 1987. *Theories of Group Behavior.* New York: Springer-Verlag

Murray, F. B. 1983. Learning and development through social interaction and conflict: a challenge to social learning theory. In *Piaget and the Foundation of Knowledge,* ed. L. Liben, pp. 231–47. Hillsdale: Erlbaum

Nemeth, C. 1986. Differential contributions of majority and minority influence. *Psychol. Rev.* 93:23–32

Nemeth, C., Kwan, J. L. 1987. Minority influence, divergent thinking and detection of correct solutions. *J. Appl. Soc. Psychol.* 17:786–97

Nemeth, C. J., Mayseless, O., Sherman, J., Brown, Y. 1990. Exposure to dissent and recall of information. *J. Pers. Soc. Psychol.* 58:429–37

Newell, A., Simon, H. A. 1972. *Human Problem Solving.* Englewood Cliffs: Prentice-Hall

Newman, D., Griffin, P., Cole, M. 1989. *The Construction Zone: Working for Cognitive Change in School.* Cambridge: Cambridge Univ. Press. 169 pp.

Nicholls, J. G. 1983. Conceptions of ability and achievement motivation: a theory and its implications for education. See Paris et al 1983, pp. 211–37

Nissani, M., Hoefler-Nissani, D. M. 1992. Experimental studies of belief dependence of observations and of resistance to conceptual change. *Cognit. Instruc.* 9:97–111

Osborne, R. E., Gilbert, D. T. 1992. The preoccupational hazards of social life. *J. Pers. Soc. Psychol.* 62:219–28

Palincsar, A. S., Brown, A. L. 1984. Reciprocal teaching of comprehension-fostering and comprehension-monitoring activities. *Cognit. Instruc.* 1:117–75

Paris, S. G., Olson, G. M., Stevenson, H. W. eds. 1983. *Learning and Motivation in the Classroom.* Hillsdale: Erlbaum

Paulus, P. B., ed. 1989. *Psychology of Group Influence.* Hillsdale: Erlbaum. 2nd ed.

Paulus, P. B., Annis, A. B., Seta, J. J., Schkade, J. K., Matthews, R. W. 1976. Density does affect task performance. *J. Pers. Soc. Psychol.* 34:248–53

Paulus, P. B., Nagar, D. 1989. Environmental influences on groups. See Paulus 1989, pp. 111–42

Perret-Clermont, A.-N., Nicolet, M. 1988. *Interagir et Connaitre.* Cousset (Fribourg): Delval

Perret-Clermont, A.-N., Schubauer-Leoni, M.-L. 1981. Conflict and cooperation as opportunities for learning. In *Communication in Development,* ed. P. Robinson, pp. 203–33. London: Academic

Petty, R. E., Cacioppo, J. T. 1986. *Communication and Persuasion.* New York: Springer-Verlag

Petty, R. E., Ostrom, T. M., Brock, T. C., eds. 1981. Cognitive Responses in Persuasion. Hillsdale: Erlbaum

Piaget, J. 1950. *The Psychology of Intelligence.* New York: Harcourt Brace

Potter, J., Wetherell, M. 1987. *Discourse and Social Psychology.* London: Sage

Resnick, L. B. 1987. Learning in school and out. *Educ. Res.* 16:13–20

Resnick, L. B., Levine, J. M., Teasley, S. D., eds. 1991. *Perspectives on Socially Shared Cognition.* Washington: Am. Psychol. Assoc.

Resnick, L. B., Salmon, M. H., Zeitz, C. M. 1992. The structure of reasoning in conversation. In *Interazione sociale e conoscenza,* ed C. Pontecorvo. Firenze: La Nuova Italia

Rogoff, B. 1990. *Apprenticeship in Thinking.* New York: Oxford. 242 pp.

Rommetveit, R. 1979. On the architecture of intersubjectivity. In *Studies of Language, Thought, and Verbal Communication,* ed. R. Rommetveit, R. M. Blakar, pp. 93–107. New York: Academic

Rosenthal, R., Jacobson, L. 1968. *Pygmalion in the Classroom.* New York: Holt, Rinehart, & Winston

Roy, A. W. N., Howe, C. J. 1990. Effects of cognitive conflict, socio-cognitive conflict and imitation on children's socio-legal thinking. *Eur. J. Soc. Psychol.* 20:241–52

Rumelhart, D. E., McClelland, J. L., PDP Research Group. 1986. *Parallel Distributed Processing: Explorations in the Microstructure of Cognition,* Vols. 1, 2. Cambridge: Bradford Books/MIT Press

Sande, G. N., Zanna, M. P. 1987. Cognitive dissonance theory: collective actions and individual reactions. See Mullen & Goethals 1987, pp. 49–69

Sarbin, T. R., Allen, V. L. 1968. Role theory. In *Handbook of Social Psychology,* ed. G. Lindzey, E. Aronson, 1:488–567. Reading: Addison-Wesley. 2nd ed.

Schegloff, E. A. 1991. Conversation analysis and socially shared cognition. See Resnick et al 1991, pp. 150–71

Scheier, M. F., Carver, C. S. 1988. A model of behavioral self-regulation: translating intention into action. *Adv. Exp. Soc. Psychol.* 21:303–46

Schmidt, D. E., Keating, J. P. 1979. Human crowding and personal control: an integration of the research. *Psychol. Bull.* 86:680–700

Schmitt, B. H., Gilovich, T., Goore, N., Joseph, L. 1986. Mere presence and social facilitation: one more time. *J. Exp. Soc. Psychol.* 22:242–48

Schon, D. 1983. *The Reflective Practitioner: How Professionals Think in Action.* New York: Basic Books

Schwarz, N., Strack, F., eds. 1991. Social cognition and communication: human judgment in its social context. *Soc. Cognit.* 9 [Special issue]

Searle, J. 1969. *Speech Acts.* Cambridge: Cambridge Univ. Press

Selman, R. L. 1980. *The Growth of Interpersonal Understanding: Developmental and Clinical Analyses.* New York: Academic

Sherif, M. 1935. A study of some social factors in perception. *Arch. Psychol.* No. 187

Shweder, R. A. 1991. *Thinking Through Cultures: Expeditions in Cultural Psychology.* Cambridge: Cambridge Univ. Press

Siegal, M. 1991. A clash of conversational worlds: interpreting cognitive development through communication. See Resnick et al 1991, pp. 23–40

Siegel, A. E., Siegel, S. 1957. Reference groups, membership groups, and attitude change. *J. Abnorm. Soc. Psychol.* 55:360–64

Singer, E. 1981. Reference groups and social evaluations. In *Social Psychology: Sociological Perspectives,* ed. M. Rosenberg, R. H. Turner, pp. 66–93. New York: Basic Books

Slavin, R. E. 1983. When does cooperative learning increase student achievement? *Psychol. Bull.* 94:429–45

Snyder, M. 1992. Motivational foundations of behavioral confirmation. *Adv. Exp. Soc. Psychol.* 25:67–114

Snyder, M., Swann, W. B. Jr. 1978. Hypothesis-testing processes in social interaction. *J. Pers. Soc. Psychol.* 36:1202–12

Sorrentino, R. M., King, G., Leo, G. 1980. The influence of the minority on perception: a note on a possible alternative explanation. *J. Exp. Soc. Psychol.* 16:293–301

Stasser, G. 1992. Pooling of unshared information during group discussion. In *Group Process and Productivity,* ed. S. Worchel, W. Wood, J. A. Simpson, pp. 48–67. Newbury Park: Sage

Stasser, G., Davis, J. H. 1981. Group decision making and social influence: a social interaction sequence model. *Psychol. Rev.* 88:523–51

Stasser, G., Kerr, N. L., Davis, J. H. 1989. Influence processes and consensus models in decision-making groups. See Paulus 1989, pp. 279–326

Stasson, M. F., Kameda, T., Parks, C. D., Zimmerman, S. K., Davis, J. H. 1991. Effects of assigned group consensus requirement on group problem solving and group members' learning. *Soc. Psychol. Q.* 54:25–35

Stokols, D. 1972. On the distinction between density and crowding: some implications for future research. *Psychol. Rev.* 79:275–77

Stryker, S., Statham, A. 1985. Symbolic interaction and role theory. See Lindzey & Aronson 1985, pp. 311–78

Suchman, L. A. 1987. *Plans and Situated Actions: The Problem of Human-Machine Communication.* Cambridge: Cambridge Univ. Press

Suls, J. M., Wills, T. A., eds. 1991. *Social Comparison: Contemporary Theory and Research.* Hillsdale: Erlbaum. 431 pp.

Taylor, S. E., Fiske, S. T., Etcoff, N. L., Ruderman, A. J. 1978. Categorical and contextual bases of person memory and stereotyping. *J. Pers. Soc. Psychol.* 36:778–93

Tetlock, P. E. 1992. The impact of accountability on judgment and choice: toward a social contingency model. *Adv. Exp. Soc. Psychol.* 25:331–76

Tindale, R. S. 1993. Decision errors made by individuals and groups. In *Current Issues in Individual and Group Decision Making,* ed. N. J. Castellan. Hillsdale: Erlbaum. In press

Triplett, N. 1898. The dynamogenic factors in pacemaking and competition. *Am. J. Psychol.* 9:507–33

Tudge, J. 1989. When collaboration leads to regression: some negative consequences of socio-cognitive conflict. *Eur. J. Soc. Psychol.* 19:123–38

Turner, J. C., Oakes, P. J. 1989. Self-categorization theory and social influence. See Paulus 1989, pp. 233–75

Van Knippenberg, D. V., Wilke, H. 1992. Prototypicality of arguments and conformity to ingroup norms. *Eur. J. Soc. Psychol.* 22:141–55

Van Maanen, J. 1977. Experiencing organization: notes on the meaning of careers and socialization. In *Organizational Careers: Some New Perspectives,* ed. J. Van Maanen, pp. 15–45. New York: Wiley

Van Maanen, J., Schein, E. H. 1979. Toward a theory of organizational socialization. In *Research in Organizational Behavior: An Annual Series of Analytical Essays and Critical Reviews,* ed. B. M. Staw, 1:209–64. Greenwich: JAI Press

Vinokur, A., Burnstein, E., Sechrest, L., Wortman, P. M. 1985. Group decision making by experts: field study of panels evaluating medical technologies. *J. Pers. Soc. Psychol.* 49:70–84

Vollrath, D. A., Sheppard, B. H., Hinsz, V. B., Davis, J. H. 1989. Memory performance by decision-making groups and individuals. *Organ. Behav. Hum. Dec. Processes* 43:289–300

von Cranach, M., Doise, W., Mugny, G., eds. 1992. *Social Representations and the Social Bases of Knowledge.* Lewiston, NY: Hogrefe & Huber

Vygotsky, L. 1962. *Thought and Language.* Cambridge: MIT Press

Vygotsky, L. 1978. *Mind in Society.* Cambridge: Harvard Univ. Press

Wanous, J. P. 1980. *Organizational Entry: Recruitment, Selection, and Socialization of Newcomers.* Reading: Addison-Wesley

Weber, M. 1967. Subjective meaning in the social situation. In *Culture and Consciousness: Perspectives in the Social Sciences,* ed. G. B. Levitas, pp. 156–69. New York: Braziller

Wegner, D. M. 1987. Transactive memory: a contemporary analysis of the group mind. See Mullen & Goethals 1987, pp. 185–208

Wegner, D. M., Erber, R., Raymond, P. 1991. Transactive memory in close relationships. *J. Pers. Soc. Psychol.* 61:923–29

Weick, K. E., Gilfillan, D. P. 1971. Fate of arbitrary traditions in a laboratory microculture. *J. Pers. Soc. Psychol.* 17:179–91

Weinstein, C. S. 1991. The classroom as a social context for learning. *Annu. Rev. Psychol.* 42:493–525

Weldon, E., Gargano, G. M. 1988. Cognitive loafing: the effects of accountability and shared responsibility on cognitive effort. *Pers. Soc. Psychol. Bull.* 14:159–71

Wertsch, J. V. 1985. *Vygotsky and the Social Formation of Mind.* Cambridge: Harvard Univ. Press

Wicklund, R. A. 1975. Objective self-awareness. *Adv. Exp. Soc. Psychol.* 8:233–75

Wicklund, R. A., Duval, S. 1971. Opinion change and performance facilitation as a result of objective self awareness. *J. Exp. Soc. Psychol.* 7:319–42

Wilder, D. A. 1986. Social categorization: implications for creation and reduction of intergroup bias. *Adv. Exp. Soc. Psychol.* 19:291–355

Wood, J. V., Taylor, K. L. 1991. Serving self-relevant goals through social comparison.

See Suls & Wills 1991, pp. 23–49

Worchel, S., Teddlie, C. 1976. The experience of crowding: a two-factor theory. *J. Pers. Soc. Psychol.* 34:30–40

Word, C. O., Zanna, M. P., Cooper, J. 1974. The nonverbal mediation of self-fulfilling prophecies in interracial interaction. *J. Exp. Soc. Psychol.* 10:109–20

Wyer, R. S., Srull, T. K. 1989. *Memory and Cognition in its Social Context.* Hillsdale: Erlbaum

Zajonc, R. B. 1960. The process of cognitive tuning and communication. *J. Abnorm. Soc. Psychol.* 61:159–67

Zajonc, R. B. 1965. Social facilitation. *Science* 149:269–74

Zajonc, R. B., Adelmann, P. K. 1987. Cognition and communication: a story of missed opportunities. *Soc. Sci. Info.* 26:3–30

Zukier, H., Pepitone, A. 1984. Social roles and strategies in prediction: some determinants of the use of base-rate information. *J. Pers. Soc. Psychol.* 47:349–60

Annu. Rev. Psychol. 1993. 44:613-44

CHILD CARE RESEARCH: Issues, Perspectives, and Results

Sandra Scarr and Marlene Eisenberg

Department of Psychology, University of Virginia, Charlottesville, Virginia 22903-2477

KEYWORDS: day care, maternal employment, attachment, quality of care, child development

CONTENTS
CONTEXTS OF CHILD CARE RESEARCH 613
DEFINITIONAL ISSUES 615
CHILD CARE AS RISK 618
CHILD CARE OUTCOMES 626
SCIENTIFIC IMPLICATIONS 636
PUBLIC POLICY 637

CONTEXTS OF CHILD CARE RESEARCH

Science has its own ecological niche; it is a creature of its historical times and cultural places (Scarr 1985). The human sciences are particularly embedded in society because they address issues of great societal concern, such as child care. Psychologists who study child care are influenced by political and social events to believe that certain questions are worthy of investigation while others are not. Many possible questions are not even conceived or asked because they are not consonant with the current Zeitgeist.

Political and Societal Context

For child care research, the major political and societal issues revolve around women's participation in society. Should mothers work outside of the home? What will happen to the all-American family if mothers are employed and fathers are not the sole breadwinners? What, if anything, should governments do to foster or discourage maternal employment by addressing their needs for child care? In this context, other value questions arise: Is child care primarily a

0066-4308/93/0201-613$02.00

support service for working parents, or is it primarily intended to meet the developmental needs of children?

Scientific Context

Psychologists have adopted overwhelmingly the latter assumption that child care should, first and foremost, benefit children's development. Research questions, such as "What developmental effects does nonmaternal care have on infants and young children?" are rooted in that assumption. The implication of this question is that if child care does not prove beneficial to children, and especially if separation from mothers is found to be harmful to young children, then maternal employment should be discouraged and the need for child care reduced. Lost in this assumptive question and its implications are the economic necessity of most mothers to be employed, the ragtag assortment of child care arrangements that parents in the United States can afford, and the lack of a governmental network of support for working families, of which child care is just one piece among many widely shared public policies in Europe and elsewhere.

If the first assumption, that child care is primarily a support service for working parents, were taken into account in psychological research, then another question would be primary: "What kind of child care arrangements will make parents happiest and most comfortable in the necessary balance of work and family life?" On the further assumption that happy parents are likely to be better parents, children's interests may also be served by child care services addressing parents' needs. In the 1990s we are beginning to see psychologists turn their attention to the larger political and societal context of child care problems and the embeddedness of child care issues in the family.

Three Waves of Research

The ecology of child care research has undergone some important changes in the past two decades. Three waves of child care research have been identified (Belsky 1984; McCartney & Marshall 1989). In the 1970s, the first wave concentrated on comparisons of maternal and nonmaternal care without consideration of the quality of either setting. The implicit research question was, "How much damage is done to infants and young children by working mothers?" There was no consideration of whether variation in child development depended on variation in kind and quality of care, at home or in other child care settings.

The second wave examined the quality and variety of child care settings and introduced the idea that children's responses to child care may be different (Belsky 1984). In the 1980s, many child care studies actually observed child care in process, evaluated quality of care, and assessed children individually.

The child development field is currently deluged by a third wave of research that includes not only proximal influences on the child, but distal influences as well. McCartney & Marshall (1989) suggest the inclusion of three systems to describe a true ecological study of the child care experience: variation of child care quality and type, family characteristics, and individual differences among children. A richer picture of the ecology of the child care setting and the child's experience of that setting is evolving (Scarr et al 1990). Although considerable attention has been devoted to evaluating child care settings, characteristics of parents and family settings have seldom been integrated into child care research.

The most recent investigations focus on the impact of factors that are distal to the child but of proximal concern to those caring for the child. Research on variables affecting parenting and child development includes studies on the effects of maternal separation anxiety, the selection of child care arrangements, maternal depression, employment stresses, quality of marital relationships, relationships between parents and caregivers, support systems (Hock et al 1988; McBride 1990), and so forth. Staff wages, caregiver education and child care training, director's credentials, and staff turnover are among distal variables studied in child care settings for their effects on the quality of programs and ultimately on children. This chapter will review this most current wave of research.

DEFINITIONAL ISSUES

Much of the controversy concerning child care stems from conflicting ideas about nonmaternal care, maternal employment, and the role of social institutions in American family life (Phillips 1991). Child care may be seen as providing a number of services that are not mutually exclusive: child health and welfare, early education, and support for employed mothers. Because it is possible to provide child welfare services that are educational and allow mothers to work, we will not distinguish purposes of care, but concentrate on research describing the consequences of child care for children and for their families.

Semantic Confusion

Is child care day care? Yes. However, since more than one-fourth of working parents do shift work, child care services are provided in hospitals and other settings during evenings and nights, as well as days. We use the term child care to cover all such services. Equating terms such as "babysitting" with child care trivializes child care and its providers by implying that anyone over 12 years of age can do it, that no special training is needed, and that it is unimportant. Research shows that good child care is not babysitting. Terms such as custodial, communal, and institutional care discredit child care as a supplement to, not a replacement for, parental care. Preschool education is a term in good standing although it does not describe the extended day or parental support offered by child care settings.

Today there is little boundary between early childhood education and child care even though the two services evolved for different purposes—early education as a part-time experience for the benefit of middle-class children and child care for the benefit of poor working class parents.[1] The two fields, however, have not developed on parallel tracks; rather, they have converged and because of modern demographic realities, have almost merged. The resulting service is both educational and caregiving, and the clients are the family unit.

Child Care vs Home Care

As Caldwell notes (1987, p. 4),

> perhaps the most basic misconception about child care is that it is a substitute for rather than a supplement to family care. [This] ... is false on at least two counts: first, it implies the existence of children who do not experience extrafamilial child care; second, it implies that children who have some extrafamilial child care are not primarily home reared. In fact, virtually every child experiences some degree of extrafamily care. Similarly, short of foster home placement, all children who receive child care services are still being reared primarily by their own families.

Settings for Child Care

In addition to their own homes, children are most often cared for in others' homes by relatives and nonrelatives, in child care centers, and in schools with child care programs. As of 1990, approximately half of all preschoolers in the United States with employed mothers were in some form of nonrelative care; the largest group (26%) was center-based care. Child care centers are licensed facilities specially built for or specially adapted for child care; centers often care for 75 to 175 children, divided into age groups. Most states require preservice staff training in child care and/or inservice training. Ratios of children at different ages to caregivers and, in some states, group sizes are regulated. Public school systems now offer after school care for older children, and some are beginning to incorporate preschool child care programs in their buildings. Zigler & Lang (1991) have developed models of school-based child care in Missouri and Connecticut.

Of working parents, 19% used family day care and 4% used in-home care by a sitter or other nonrelative (Hofferth 1992). In most states, family day care homes with six or fewer children do not have to be licensed and are often informal arrangements between untrained caregivers and parents. Unlicensed family day care homes usually have children from infancy to school-age in a

---

[1] In the late nineteenth century, publicly available child care was intended to keep poor children off the streets while their unfortunate mothers worked and to shore up socially pathological families. Thus, child care services were associated with the have-nots of society even though all well-to-do and most middle class families had child care help at home. Public acceptance of professional child care came only in the 1980s, when middle class mothers stayed in the labor force after giving birth (Scarr et al 1989). Terms to describe the service also changed, giving child care the respectability it now enjoys.

single group with one caregiver. Licensed family and group care often has 10 to 20 children in a home, and the family day care provider is assisted by a regulated number of other caregivers. Few states require any training for family care providers.

The other 51% of working parents placed their preschool children with grandparents (30%), or with other relatives (18%). Clearly, there has been an increase in the use of nonrelative care by working parents, yet a slim majority of children remain within the care of their families (Hofferth 1992). Additionally, while there has been research on center-based care, virtually no research has been done on nannies or relative care.

Dimensions of Quality

Determinations of child care quality are based on a number of criteria, but the most commonly agreed upon are health and safety requirements, responsive and warm interaction between staff and children, developmentally appropriate curriculum, limited group size, age-appropriate caregiver-child ratios, adequate indoor and outdoor space, and adequate staff training in either early childhood education or child development (Bredekamp 1989; Kontos & Fiene 1987).

Howes et al (1992) examined thresholds of quality and highlighted the sensitive nature of the child care setting. These investigators found that the addition of even one child to a group made a meaningful difference in quality. Other investigators have found that the quality of the caregiver-child relationship is related to group size (Stith & Davis 1984), caregiver-child ratios (Howes 1983; Howes & Rubenstein 1985), and caregiver training (Roupp et al 1979; Howes 1983; Clarke-Stewart 1987; Rosenthal 1991). Caregivers with specific training in child care and child development provide more sensitive and responsive care than do those without such training. However, overall educational level of caregivers appears to be far less important.

Staff turnover is another common measure of the quality of care. Caregivers lack job prestige, are poorly paid, and have low morale (Whitebook et al 1991; Shiomi 1990). High turnover means that children have fewer opportunities to develop stable, affectionate relationships with caregivers. Stability of care appears to be especially important for infants and toddlers who displayed more appropriate social behaviors when in stable vs unstable care arrangements (Howes & Stewart 1987; Suwalsky et al 1986).

Nonfamilial early childhood environments can promote positive development (Phillips et al 1987a), but a realistic balance must be achieved between consideration of these environments and influences of the family and child characteristics (Ackerman-Ross & Khana 1989). These influences are considered in the next section.

CHILD CARE AS RISK

In 1986 Belsky stated that "entry into care in the first year of life is a 'risk factor' for the development of insecure-avoidant attachments in infancy and heightened aggressiveness, noncompliance, and withdrawal in the preschool and early school years" (p. 7). A response to this statement (Phillips et al 1987b) that cited the embeddedness of child care in other aspects of children's lives, notably families, created the foundation for the current group of child care investigations.

Evolution of Ideas About Risk

In the first wave of psychological research on child care, nonmaternal care was seen as a threat to children's attachment relationship to mother and a possible detriment to cognitive, language, and social development as well. Although the results of studies comparing children at home with mothers with children in high quality center care showed no differences in attachment or any other developmental measures (Caldwell et al 1970; Kagan 1982), concern about child care as a risk factor continued into the second wave of research. In the 1980s, early entry into nonmaternal care and poor quality care were identified as serious risk factors (Belsky & Rovine 1988).

In the second wave of research, degree of risk from poor child care was said to be increased or decreased by characteristics of the child and of the child's home. Gamble & Zigler (1986) note that

> chances for developmental damage increase as a function of the number and magnitude of negative environmental encounters. ... The risk for damage increases if the child who experiences poor infant day care also comes from a highly stressed home environment, or one without an father, etc. We feel that the weight of the evidence gathered on the effects of infant day care supports such a model (p. 29).

Based on a review of child care research, Gamble & Zigler (1986) concluded that: 1. In families facing significant life stresses, substitute care during the first year increases the likelihood of insecure parent-child attachments. 2. An insecure attachment makes the child more vulnerable to the effects of stressful events encountered later. 3. The best predictor of later pathology is a cumulative frequency of stressful life events coupled with an insecure attachment in infancy. This description fits a linear continuum model with the chances for nonoptimal outcomes increasing as a function of the number and magnitude of stressful experiences encountered (p. 35).

In this view, poor child care is part of an additive model of stress (along with male gender, family dysfunction, etc). Good quality care can provide an opportunity to compensate for or ameliorate negative family circumstances. As the second and third waves of research show, good quality child care can enhance development of children from disadvantaged, stressed, and dysfunctional homes.

Child care research has changed perspectives over the past two decades. The major research question has evolved from, "Is nonmaternal care harmful? " to "What effects do differences in quality of care have? " to "What effect does variability in nonmaternal care have for which kind of child from which kind of family?" The literature portrays a reasonably coherent picture of the effects of nonmaternal care of various qualities at various ages for children from different backgrounds. Although the best answer is still, "It depends" (Clarke-Stewart 1992), we now have more information concerning developmental effects of child care for different groups of children.

In this section, we examine research on child care as risk in two parts: (*a*) characteristics of care that pose risks to some or all children and (*b*) characteristics of children that place them at special risk for child care effects.

Risky Child Care

FAMILY PATHOLOGY   Children's development is influenced by poor, abusive, neglectful, and inappropriate care, whether by parents or others (Scarr 1992); thus child care effects must be seen in the larger and more important context of family functioning. Parental psychopathology, especially maternal depression (Teti & Gelfand 1991; Strickland 1992), can disturb children's normal social development. Abusive parents have less securely attached infants (Crittenden 1989). Persistent marital conflicts and conflictive divorces can have devastating effects on children's emotional well-being (Emery 1988).

Fortunately, children can develop multiple attachments that may differ in function, but which may still be of high quality (Kermoian & Leiderman 1986); and children without secure attachments to parents can benefit from secure attachments to caregivers. Two recent studies indicate the possibility of ameliorative effects from out-of-home care for these children. Children have about the same rate of secure attachments to mothers and to caregivers, but there is little or no correlation between security of attachment to mothers and caregivers. Goossens & van Ijzendoorn (1990) measured the child's attachment to the caregiver and additionally assessed the concordance between this rating and ratings of the child's attachment to the mother and the father in order to assess the child's most important attachment connections. Parent-child and caregiver-child relationships were evaluated for 75 infants who had entered care before their seventh month. These relationships were assessed using the Strange Situation (Ainsworth et al 1978), as well as a free-play session. Results indicated that children were generally rated as being more attached to parents than to caregivers. Most importantly, however, was the lack of concordance between parent-child attachment ratings and caregiver-child attachment ratings. This allows for the possibility that poor parent-child relationships may not necessarily be duplicated at the child care center.

Howes & Hamilton (1992a,b) assessed attachment with the Waters and Deane Q-sort for attachment behaviors with mothers and caregivers. They too found little correspondence between quality of attachment to mother and caregivers. They showed, moreover, that warm, responsive interactions between caregiver and child occurred more frequently when the child was rated as securely attached to the caregiver. Thus, for children without secure relationships with mothers, child care provided a positive setting for emotional development.

POOR QUALITY CARE   Poor quality child care puts children's development at risk for poorer language and cognitive scores and lesser ratings of social and emotional adjustment. However, child care is not a uniform intervention and should not be discussed as such—a point that has been emphasized by many researchers in the second wave of child care research (Clarke-Stewart & Fein 1983; Etaugh 1980; Rosenthal 1991; Rutter 1981; Scarr 1984; Belsky et al 1982). Just as home environments are not all the same, child care environments are not all the same, and some are better for children than others (Phillips et al 1987b, p. 19).

Studies that provide data on center quality, family background variables, and child outcomes find that overall quality affects language and cognitive development (Goelman & Pence 1987; McCartney 1984; Wasik et al 1990), social competence, and social adjustment (Phillips et al 1987a). This last study was unique in that it addressed variation in center quality, and both center and family characteristics were evaluated. Child behavior ratings were completed by parents and observers. Observational measures of center quality as well as interviews with center directors provided information about center quality.

Analyses included controls for child's age, family background, and child care experience in predicting developmental status from differences in child care quality. Caregiver-child interaction was found to be a strong predictor of developmental status. Affective and informational verbal interactions between caregivers and children appeared to accelerate verbal and cognitive skills. Parents and caregivers rated children as more considerate, sociable, intelligent, and task oriented when caregivers engaged in more positive verbal interactions with the children. Paradoxically, children's social adjustment was related to poorer quality care, but this finding has not been replicated and is probably sample specific.

These results are supported by numerous studies that found that children with involved and responsive caregivers display more exploratory behaviors (Anderson et al 1981), are more positive (Clarke-Stewart 1987; Holloway & Reichhart-Erickson 1989), and display better peer relations (Howes et al 1992).

FAMILIES WHO USE EXTENSIVE CHILD CARE   One of the first questions to ask about a study of child care effects is, "Are families who use extensive child care, where mother is employed, different from families where mother stays home with young children?" It is impossible to evaluate effects of child care environments without evaluating possible differences between single and married mothers (Eisenberg 1991) and between employed and unemployed mothers (Hoffman 1984); these mothers may differ in their interactions with the child or may differ in personality, intelligence, etc, all of which can be transmitted to the child genetically as well as environmentally. Some investigators find few measurable differences between employed and unemployed mothers in their levels of responsiveness, affect, and degree of social stimulation toward their children (Cleary & Mechanic 1983; Stith & Davis 1984). Other studies have found employed mothers to be less sensitive when they are conflicted about their work status (Alvarez 1985; Farel 1980; Vandell & Ramanan 1992).

Attitudes toward work and work preferences may make a difference in parenting. According to Farel (1980), achievement scores declined in children with mothers who were conflicted about their work status. Children of mothers who wished to be employed, but stayed home, displayed the lowest achievement scores. Children of women who chose to be homemakers, but whose jobs were important for the survival of the family, also suffered some negative consequences. These mothers perceived their children more negatively than did mothers who worked because of personal preference (Alvarez 1985).

Belsky & Rovine (1988) evaluated the effects of family stress and maternal personality characteristics as moderators of mother-child attachment for children cared for by mothers and those cared for by substitute caregivers. Results indicated that infants exposed to more than 20 hours of care per week were more likely to be rated as insecure if they were boys, had nonresponsive mothers, and were rated as difficult by their mothers. The mothers of these infants were also more likely to be less satisfied with their marriages and more job oriented.

Although most studies of child care compare groups of children with more and less child care experience, the groups are usually matched only on age and rough measures of socioeconomic background. Other unmeasured qualities of parents and family life may differ between the groups and show up as differences between children with more and less child care experience. As Hock et al (1988) have shown, maternal separation anxiety is higher among mothers who place their children in care later than earlier, and maternal separation anxiety is likely to be still higher among mothers who do not work outside of the home. Differences in parental characteristics between families who use extensive child care services and those who do not are seldom explored well in child care research.

CORRELATIONS OF FAMILY AND CHILD CARE   Another problem in studies of child care effects on children is a correlation between quality of care selected by parents and parents' personal characteristics. This leads to overestimation of child care effects that belong in part to family differences. For example, parents with more punitive forms of discipline and more authoritarian attitudes toward children were found to choose lower quality care for their children (Bolger 1991;

Scarr et al 1992). With respect to social and emotional development, children from punitive families and poorer quality child care settings are doubly disadvantaged, but the causes are also correlated, and neither the family nor the child care setting deserve sole responsibility.

As of 1986 little was known about the relationship between patterns of parenting and the use of nonmaternal care. Howes & Olenick (1986) investigated compliance and self-regulation in children from high and low quality alternate care and with different family backgrounds. Their findings reveal the importance of antecedent family conditions in models that predict outcomes for children in child care. Children from families with more complexity (single, employed mother, low income) were more likely to be found in lower quality alternate care. Parenting behavior was also found to be predictive of behavior in the center environment. Children in high quality care had parents who were more involved and interested in compliance than parents of children in lower quality care.

POOR FAMILIES AND CARE   Socio-economically disadvantaged families cannot provide the range of developmental opportunities available to children in more advantaged families. Low income families also cannot afford good quality care and are not likely to find subsidized care in the present political climate. Children from low income families receive greater benefits from good quality child care than children from more advantaged homes. For example, entry into licensed child care requires age-appropriate inoculations, which most middle-class children have and most low income children do not. Subsidized child care programs provide inoculations, as well as other health care. Nutrition provided by child care settings is important to the health of many low income children and less essential to more advantaged ones. Social services, parental involvement, and social support are all important parts of child care to low income, especially single-parent families (Feiring et al 1987).

Quality child care can also make a major contribution to the cognitive and language development of socially disadvantaged children. The more intensive and more extensive the program, the greater the results (Breitmayer & Ramey 1986). The effects of intellectually stimulating programs on children from disadvantaged homes far exceed the cognitive benefits to middle-class children, whose homes provide a great deal of intellectual stimulation. This finding provides important supportive evidence for other studies that find that children from stressed or improverished family backgrounds display better cognitive functioning and social skills than disadvantaged children who are cared for by their mothers at home.

The most thorough research on child care-as-intervention are the Frank Porter Graham longitudinal studies, the Abecedarian Project, and Project Care (Breitmayer & Ramey 1986; Haskins 1985; Ramey et al 1983; Ramey et al 1989). Infants were enrolled in intensive and extensive child care programs from six weeks to five years of age. The child care children far exceeded randomly selected control groups on intelligence tests and school achievement. In the preschool years, the child care group scored higher on language assessments (Ramey & Farran 1982) and measures of social competence (Ramey et al 1983).

Unfortunately, fewer low income than high income children are enrolled in child care programs with an educational component. This phenomena, coupled with the high costs of child care and the lack of adequate public support, contributes to "a two-tiered system of care for our youngest children" (Chorvinsky 1982). Those who can benefit most are least likely to receive high quality, educationally oriented child care.

Risky Children

Children can be arrayed along a continuum of vulnerability to insult (Murphy & Moriarty 1976) that results from both internal and external process, both objective and subjective perspectives, and both conscious and unconscious determination (Anthony 1987). Some children may be more vulnerable to the effects of poor care, at home and elsewhere, because of their own characteristics (e.g. age, gender, temperament, disabilities).

INFANT CARE   Nearly all of the child care debate ("Is child care harmful?") has swirled around infant care. No one has proposed that preschool children over the age of three years are likely to be harmed by good quality, nonmaternal care since they benefit from interactions with peers and other adults. Infants under 12 months, or perhaps 24 months (Belsky 1986; Belsky & Rovine 1988; Benn 1986), are said to be emotionally harmed by separation from their mothers. Attachments to mother, measured in the Strange Situation (Ainsworth et al 1978), were less often secure among infants with more extensive nonmaternal care in the first year of life. The importance of this difference in secure attachment is questionable; only 8% fewer infants with extensive early nonmaternal care have secure attachment to mother (47% and 53%; Clarke-Stewart 1987).

Age at entry into nonmaternal care has not proved to have a substantial effect on any aspects of children's development in several studies (Clarke-Stewart 1987; McCartney 1984b; Phillips et al 1987). Because of publication biases against null results, there are probably a large number of studies that could report no effects of age at entry to child care.

More recent studies of this issue have found similar results. Andersson (1989) investigated the impact of early entry into child care on cognitive skills and socio-emotional adjustment. He followed a large sample of Swedish children from their first year through 13 years of age. When tested at age 8, children who had entered high quality center-based care before the age of 1 were found to have received more favorable ratings from caregivers and higher scores on cognitive tests than children who had entered center care later or those who had remained at home. The study controlled for parental marital status, educational levels, occupations, and family income. Similar results were obtained at age 13. Entry into high quality child care centers at the end of the first year continued to show positive effects on children's intellectual, social, and emotional development into their early teens.

Other studies that compared early vs late entry into child care found no differences in attachment behavior, but did find that children in earlier care displayed more positive social interactions than late entry children (Field et al 1988). In another study, Field (1991) followed another early entry group, and found that the length of time in quality care was positively related to number of friends in grade school, number of extracurricular activities, parent ratings of the child's emotional well-being, leadership, popularity, attractiveness, assertiveness, and less aggressiveness. A second group of early entry, full-time care children assessed at the sixth grade indicated the positive progression of these findings. Children who had experienced some child care early in life in centers of varying quality exhibited more assertive behavior than their late entry peers. This is consistent with observations of child behavior at the center itself. These findings suggest that advantages of early entry into quality center care may linger well beyond early years of schooling.

On the other hand, infants are said to be more vulnerable than older children to the bad effects of poor quality care (Gamble & Zigler 1986). Unfortunately, this predicted interaction between child's age at entry into nonmaternal care and quality of care has not been rigorously tested.

GENDER   In many areas of psychology, males are found to have more developmental problems than females. Indeed, Belsky & Rovine (1988) have found gender interactions, as well as maternal care interactions, with early entry into child care. Nearly all of the avoidantly attached infants among those with extensive child care experience in the first year were males. It appears that males may be more vulnerable to nonmaternal care than females. On average, boys are developmentally less mature than girls at any given chronological age, which could explain this difference in reaction; gender may be a proxy for maturity (Mott 1989).

A number of studies have found differences in social competence and cognitive development to be associated with gender: Boys are more vulnerable to child care effects (Howes 1988; Moore 1975; Mott 1991; Zaslow et al 1986; see also Hoffman 1980). However, data are emerging that find some increased acting-out behavior by girls in center-based care as well (Goossens et al 1991).

Not all studies have found gender differences of any type, however. In a study of the relationship between caregivers and child care children, boys were just as likely as girls to experience a positive relationship with mothers and caregivers (Howes & Hamilton 1992a).

The interaction between quality, family characteristics, and gender may be important for the clarification of deficits observed in boys' nonmaternal care. Howes & Olenick (1986) report that boys from families with high levels of stress, with high parental involvement, and in poor quality care were more likely to resist following directions in a directed task, than boys from families without high levels of stress, with parents who allowed them some independence, and who were in high quality care. However, stability of care may help to ameliorate some of these negative effects. Boys who enter care early and stay in that care were more likely to engage in higher level object play than boys who entered later or who changed care (Howes & Stewart 1987).

The literature on the effects of nonmaternal care and gender indicates that boys may be more vulnerable than girls. However, research also indicates that the interaction must be considered between quality, age of entry, and family background characteristics (Mott 1991). A consideration of family variables is also helpful in integrating findings of increased aggression in child care girls within the context of maternal employment literature (Bronfenbrenner & Crouter 1982).

TEMPERAMENT   In Belsky & Rovine's (1988) study, children considered by their mothers to be difficult in temperament were less likely to be securely attached than easier children. Temperament and attachment may be confounded in research (Lamb et al 1985; Vaughn et al 1992); therefore it is difficult to interpret this finding. Attachment and temperament may be theoretically distinct (Sroufe 1985); however, in practice, the regulation of affect observed in the Strange Situation (Ainsworth et al 1978) is probably affected by both attachment and temperament (Vaughn et al 1992).

A temperamental characteristic that can affect emotional responses to child care and the Strange Situation is inhibition. Inhibited children (Kagan 1982), who find novel situations frightening at first, may be more threatened by the Strange Situation than less inhibited children, and they may display more avoidant behavior. Inhibited children may also require a longer time to become familiar and comfortable in a new child care arrangement.

DISABLED CHILDREN   The percentage of handicapped children in the total population of children under age 6 is estimated at between 9.2% and 12.4% (Fewell 1987). Fewell (1987) estimates that approximately 1.3 million families are in need of some child care for young handicapped children. In fact, these families may have more need for child care services because of the extra stress of parenting a handicapped child. Breslau et al (1982) studied 369 families of children with physical handicaps and chronic illnesses to determine the effects of the child's disability on mothers' employment. Mothers' employment was directly related to the severity of the child's handicap—the more severe the handicap, the less likely mother was to work, and the lower the family income. Care for handicapped children is unfortunately not readily available. In a survey of centers in the Washington, DC area, Berk (1985) found that although 58% of the centers polled were willing to accept handicapped children, many required the child to be ambulatory and toilet trained, and some centers charged extra fees.

There is virtually no psychological research on the effects of child care on handicapped children. It is reasonable to hypothesize, however, that children's vulnerability is increased by physical and mental handicaps and by chronic illnesses, so that variations in quality of care may have more effect on such children than on more robust and healthy ones.

INTERACTIONS OF CHILD AND CARE CHARACTERISTICS   In this section we have described what is known about possible interactions between child characteristics and features of child care and family environments. Clearly, further understanding of child care effects depends on the further exploration of person-situation interactions, in which not all children are affected in the same ways by the same treatments.

CHILD CARE OUTCOMES

Centers vs Homes

In one of the earliest investigations of center vs family day care, a number of meaningful differences were found that indicated that family day care may provide the child with higher quality care than center care. A study of 39 4-year-olds from two centers and two family care arrangements found that children in family day care spent more time in structured activities and in groups of larger size than children in center care (Innes et al 1982). Children in family day care interacted more with their caregivers and displayed fewer negative behaviors than children in center-based care. Unfortunately, confounds in this study of age at entry, family background characteristics, and type of care cloud the results.

Increased levels of verbal stimulation in family care compared to center-based care have also been found (Cochran 1977). Not surprisingly, comparisons on reponsiveness dimensions reveal that children at home with mothers experience more warmth and affection than do children in family day care (Rubenstein et al 1977).

A longitudinal study conducted in the United Kingdom that assessed the caregiver-child interactional experience of 246 18-month-olds found a great deal of variability both within and between four different types of child care: home care, relative care, sitter care in the sitter's home, and private care in the child's home (Melhuish et al 1990, 1991). Perhaps the most consistent finding was that children in center-based care engage in more peer-peer behaviors than do children at home with mother or in family day care. This is consistent with findings reported by Clarke-Stewart & Gruber (1984) in which children in center-based care displayed better social skills with peers than children in home care situations.

Other studies have found no real differences between center-based care, family day care, and home care (Moore 1975; Weinraub et al 1988). However, quality of care was not measured in one of these studies (Moore 1975) and is likely a factor in children's behaviors. When quality has been considered, quality of care found in both the family and alternate care arrangements predicts better social competence and personality maturity (Lamb et al 1988).

There were no quality-of-care effects observed in another recent study conducted in Holland on multiple care arrangements (Goossens et al 1991). However, Dutch centers are of rather uniform high quality, so that a quality effect that could be found in other countries did not appear. In the presence of increased variability in quality, differences are found (Golden et al 1978; McCartney et al 1982; Phillips et al 1987b; Schwarz et al 1973).

Other studies find that the quality of care found in both the family and alternate care arrangements predicts better social competence and personality maturity (Lamb et al 1988). These investigators found no group differences in comparisons of center-based care, family day care, and home care by a parent. Individual child outcomes did vary, however, with the quality of care received within each of the three settings. This study points to the importance of quality in both the home and child care settings.

Often no differences are found between children with more and less child care experience. For example, in a study of child care and language perform-ance, comparisons were made between 40 white, middle-class three-year-olds, who were cared for at home, and a group of children who had been in center care since infancy (Ackerman-Ross & Khana 1989). This study found no group difference in auditory or receptive language performance. There was also no real difference in the amount of time parents from the two groups spent interacting with their children.

Employed parents spend about as much time interacting with their young children as do parents who are not employed. Employed parents use their time at home to attend to their children, rather than to housework, sleep, or personal leisure time; they also devote more time to children on weekends than unem-ployed parents (see Scarr et al 1990). Should it be surprising, therefore, if only small differences among children can be attributed to child care experiences, rather than to differences among families?

Cognitive Effects

Perhaps the most consistent finding about child care is that participation in some form of nonmaternal care has either no effect on cognitive development (Belsky & Steinberg 1978; Kagan et al 1978; Scarr 1984) or has positive effects (Andersson 1988; Caldwell & Freyer 1982; Caldwell et al 1970; Clarke-Stewart & Gruber 1984; Howes 1988; Keister 1970; McCartney et al 1985; Ramey et al 1989; Ramey & Farren 1982). However, two recent studies of white, middle class, American samples found that children from advantaged families may be negatively affected by early entry into nonmaternal care (Baydar & Brooks-Gunn 1991; Desai et al 1989), particularly full-time care. The explanation of these discrepant findings lies in the complex interaction between quality, family characteristics, gender, and age at entry as predictors of cognitive development (Howes 1988).

The inclusion of quality measures in predictive models articulates the relationship between cognitive development and nonmaternal care with even more clarity. High quality care has potent positive effects on the cognitive development of children from socially disadvantaged families (Finkelstein 1982; Lally et al 1988; Phillips et al 1987a; Ramey et al 1983; Breitmayer & Ramey 1986), and special intervention programs may facilitate cognitive development even further (Finkelstein 1982; Finkelstein & Wilson 1977; Haskins 1985; Lally et al 1988; Ramey et al 1983). Gender may also affect cognitive development since infant girls perform better on tests of cognitive development than their male peers (Mott 1989).

Andersson (1989) followed a moderately large sample of Swedish children from their first year through year eight. When tested at age eight, children who had entered high quality center-based care before the age of one were found to have received more favorable ratings from caregivers and higher scores on cognitive tests than children who had entered center care later or those who had remained at home.

The inclusion of family characteristics such as socio-economic status, marital status, household composition, and parental intelligence further clarifies cognitive outcomes observed in child care research. A longitudinal study of children in family day care, child care centers, or home care by mothers in Bermuda (Scarr et al 1989) found that children of single mothers who lived with parents or other family members were more similar to children living with both parents than they were to children of single mothers living alone. It was the latter group that displayed more cognitive delays. For children of single mothers living alone, increased time in child care yielded higher developmental scores.

Contrary to expectations, type of care was not predictive of child IQ. The best predictors of cognitive development observed in all children were high family income, high maternal WAIS vocabulary scores, authoritative parenting, and fewer maternal work hours. Kontos (1991) found similar results when studying an American sample of preschoolers.

Social Competence

As with the findings concerning cognitive development, the most interpretable findings on child care and social competence come from those studies that integrate and evaluate multiple influences on the child.

Perhaps the best example of research that incorporates family and center characteristics into predictive models of child outcome was conducted by

Lamb et al (1988). These investigators sampled equal numbers of boys and girls between the ages of 11 and 24 months of age from three types of care in Sweden: center-based care, family day care, and home care. They found social class and family background variables to be the best predictors of peer sociability and social competence, thus providing supportive evidence for the inclusion of family characteristics into models predicting child outcomes of children involved with some form of nonmaternal care. There were no differences among children who experienced different types of child care. A problem with this study was the uniformly high quality care. As noted above, greater differentiation of the quality of types of care might have produced effects of setting as well.

SOCIAL BEHAVIORS   Other studies report that children in child care exhibited more social behavior, were more popular with their peers, and more cooperative in their play (Ramey et al 1983; Howes & Olenick 1986; Schindler et al 1987; Balleyguier et al 1991). When contrasts were made between children who spent larger and smaller number of hours in care, more hours were associated with more social behavior (Field et al 1988). Within the early entry group, children in full-time care engaged in more social, cooperative play, sought the caregiver's attention more, and had generally more positive affect than early entry, part-time children (Field et al 1988).

Howes & Olenick (1986) found that children in child care centers were more likely than children at home to exhibit self-regulation, and that children in high quality child care centers were more compliant and less resistant than children in low quality centers. No effects were found for age or the interaction between age and type of child care.

CAREGIVER EFFECTS   The relationship between caregivers and children has also become an important research topic. Caregivers in high quality child care centers are more invested and involved in compliance than were caregivers in low quality child care centers (Howes & Olenick 1986; Kontos & Fiene 1987). Additionally, parents and caregivers rated children as more considerate, sociable, intelligent, and task oriented when caregivers engaged in more verbal interaction with the children. Phillips et al (1987a) found that overall quality affected social competence and adjustment.

These results are supported by other studies that found that children with involved and responsive caregivers displayed more exploratory behaviors (Anderson et al 1981), were more positive (Clarke-Stewart 1987), and had better peer relations (Howes et al 1992).

Howes & Hamilton (1992b) used the Waters and Deane Attachment Q-Set (1985) to study the relationship between children with their mothers and children with their caregivers. They assessed 441 children in either center-based care or family day care. The vast majority of these children (80%) had entered care before their first birthdays and attended child care full-time.

Children's relationships with the caregiver were important for predicting adjustment in the care setting. In contrast to children rated as avoidant or ambivalent, children rated as secure with the caregiver experienced more positive relationships with those caregivers, which were characterized by increased warmth and responsiveness, and more caregiver involvement.

To what can this pattern be attributed? Interactions observed in child care settings are likely to be the result of both the behavior the child brought to the relationship and the training of the caregiver. Recent work found that children direct proximity-seeking (Goossens & van Ijzendoorn 1990) as well as social-referencing behaviors (Camras & Sachs 1991) toward their caregivers. Others found that children with involved caregivers displayed more secure behaviors than did children with caregivers who were more remote and distant (Anderson et al 1981; Goossens & van Ijzendoorn 1991).

Emotional Outcomes

ATTACHMENT   Research indicates that compliance and peer socialization develop out of the mother-child attachment (Ainsworth et al 1978; Ainsworth 1982; Arend et al 1979; Bowlby 1969, 1973; Londerville & Main 1981; Sroufe & Fleeson 1986; Sroufe & Waters 1977). If the mother and child either have an avoidant or an insecure attachment, the literature suggests an increased chance for poor adjustment later. Such children are more likely to exhibit more negative affect, be less compliant, and exhibit less self-regulation than children judged to have secure relationships with their mothers (Egeland 1983; Main & Weston 1981; Maslin & Bates 1982).

Children in child care have higher security scores in attachments to their mothers than to caregivers (Clarke-Stewart & Fein 1983; Howes & Hamilton 1992a,b), but questions remain concerning the quality of mother-child relationships among children in nonmaternal care compared to those experienced by children of nonemployed mothers who care for their children at home (Lamb & Sternberg 1990)

The presence of a pattern of elevated incidence of aggression and insecure attachment in some research has concerned a number of investigators (Belsky 1988) who have targeted early entry of care and full-time care as potential causes of concern.

STRANGE SITUATION   Research on child care using the Strange Situation has become controversial, not only because of the results (Clarke-Stewart 1989; Phillips et al 1987b; Belsky 1989), but because of the mystique surrounding the measure itself. Although there has been no interruption in the number of studies using the Strange Situation paradigm to predict later development, other measures of emotional development are often included as well. Studies that find negative effects of child care on attachment in the Strange Situation (Farber & Egeland 1982; Schwartz 1983; Vaughn et al 1980; Barglow et al 1987; Belsky

& Rovine 1988) and those finding no child care effects on attachment (Blanchard & Main 1979; Brookhart & Hock 1976; Owen et al 1984) seem to present conflicting evidence. We will attempt to clarify the relationship between emotional development and child care.

EARLY ENTRY AND ATTACHMENT   In 1988, Belsky & Rovine presented data from a meta-analysis of five studies with a total sample of 491 children and focused on the effects of early entry into nonmaternal care. The authors concluded that the rates of insecurity for children in care more than 20 hours a week were significantly higher than for children in care less than 20 hours a week, and this pattern was more pronounced when care began during the first year of life.

Not all studies find this pattern (Field et al 1988), and the meaning of these findings has been debated much over the course of the last five years (Belsky 1992; Clarke-Stewart 1992). Perhaps the most influential study of attachment and child care experience (Farber & Egeland 1982; Vaughn et al 1980, 1985) was based on an improverished, high-risk sample of mothers (Phillips et al 1987b). More recent research on the long-term effects of infant child care clarifies the salience of these findings.

A review of the last five years by Hennessy & Melhuish (1991) considered the longitudinal effects of early child care entry. Only one study of early entry before the age of six months found no behavioral differences among children at ages five or six years who had displayed secure or insecure attachments earlier in life (Goldberg & Easterbrooks 1988). Two studies reported that early entry children displayed more behavior problems in preschool and later (Moore 1975; Vandell & Corasanti 1990). Six studies found early entry children to have higher levels of social competence and cognitive development (Andersson 1989; Cherry & Eaton 1977; Field 1991; Howes 1988; Howes 1990, 1991). In another study, the effects of early entry were separated from length of time in care (Park & Honig 1991). Analyses revealed increased aggression and noncompliance to be related to full-time care rather than to age at entry to care.

Three more recent studies are reviewed in some detail because they best integrate issues of context, quality, and family background. The first study (Howes 1990) measured social behavior between early and late entry groups in a group of kindergartners. Howes (1990) found an increase in social competence in the group of early entry children. These findings applied only to children from high quality care arrangements, however. Children who entered low quality care as infants appeared more maladjusted than those entering high quality care as infants. It should be noted that even in this group, only 4% of the children exhibited behaviors that could be identified within a recognized range of pathology. A limitation of this study was the inclusion of children who had entered care as late as 24 months into the early entry group.

Howes (1991) conducted another study of early entry and social competence at age 4 and found less competence in the early entry group, but only in children who had been judged to have insecure maternal attachments. This provides evidence that early entry per se may not be a risk factor, but the combination of early entry of children with insecure attachments may increase risk for later problem behavior.

Field (1991) also followed an early entry group and found that the length of time in quality care was positively related to number of friends in grade school, number of extracurricular activities, parent ratings of the child's emotional well-being, leadership, popularity, attractiveness, assertiveness, and less aggressiveness. A second group of early entry, full-time care children assessed at the sixth grade indicated the positive progression of these findings. Children who had experienced some child care early in life within centers of varying quality exhibited more assertive behavior than their late entry peers. This is consistent with observations of child behavior while in attendance at the center itself. However, this investigation also found lower levels of aggression to be inversely related to higher levels of assertiveness. This finding suggests two possibilities. First, behaviors identified as aggression in an infant group may be misidentified. Second, the positive experiences of quality center care may supercede any negative experiences, and positive behavior, rather than negative behavior, may remain over time.

These findings suggest that advantages of early entry into center care may linger well beyond early years of schooling. Unfortunately, no systematic evaluation of child care quality was possible for the sixth grade group, which made any interaction between levels of quality and behavioral displays of social competence impossible.

In spite of the breadth of each of these studies, they do not provide a definitive answer to the question of effects of early entry into child care on children's later development because the studies differ in their child care context, measures, definitions of early entry, as well as confounds between age at entry, stability of care, and parental characteristics. We do know that statistically reliable increases in levels of aggression among children with early and/or extensive child care experience do not translate into pathological aggressiveness. All studies find children within a normal range of variation, regardless of child care experience, and effect sizes should be considered in assessing the social importance of such results (Clarke-Stewart 1989; Phillips et al 1987b).

ELEVATED LEVELS OF AGGRESSION   A few investigations have found no differences between center care and home care (Braun & Caldwell 1973; Rubenstein & Howes 1979; Kagan 1982), while others reported higher levels of aggression and lower levels of compliance for children in child care (Cochran 1977; Haskins 1985; Schwarz et al 1973, 1974; Schwartz 1983).

It is interesting that some of these same studies have found increased levels of aggression accompanying other positive outcomes of child care attendance (Howes & Rubenstein 1985; Lally et al 1988; Schwarz et al 1974; Finkelstein 1982; Rubenstein et al 1981; Rubenstein & Howes 1983; Haskins 1985; Field et al 1988; see also Clarke-Stewart & Fein 1983).

Few studies have considered care setting, quality, and family characteristics in examining this pattern of increased aggression. However, the investigation by Field and her colleagues (1988) did allow for an examination of the relationship between a number of important variables such as timing of entry into care, extent of care, and care setting. Ratings of attachment as well as observational ratings of children who had entered care during their first six months were compared with a second group who had entered care after six months of age. These children were further identified within groups of full-time vs part-time care. It should be noted that these children were observed between the ages of 24 to 65 months and were further grouped by type of care arrangement.

Caregivers rated full-time children higher on aggression than did parents. However the total incidence of aggressive behavior remained quite low, and observational ratings of child behavior found no differences in rates of aggression between full-time and part-time children.

This discrepancy between caregiver ratings and observational ratings shows the importance of multiple respondent reports. Caregivers in charge of children for an entire day may have been more likely to rate children high on negative behaviors because of their own fatigue rather than because of any behaviors exhibited by the full-time child care child.

No one denies that an examination of children with extensive child care experience may reveal elevated levels of some negative behaviors. Regardless of methodology, increased aggression in children using center care has been found to be fairly robust and is no longer targeted for sole investigation. However, the behaviors of children in all groups where mean differences have been consistently found were within the normal range. The current emphasis is on the origins of aggression, and whether there are long-term negative consequences of child care for children.

AVOIDANT ATTACHMENT   Barglow et al (1987) examined the impact of non-maternal in-home care on infants, and found that this group was rated as more insecurely-avoidantly attached to mothers than a comparable group of infants cared for by their mothers at home. This study was important because it included a low-risk sample of middle-class mothers with substitute care in the child's home. The differences between maternal and nonmaternal care groups were quite small, but perhaps most importantly, there was no evaluation of the quality of care provided by the sitters while mothers were at work. In addition, while this study is frequently cited in the literature as evidence that nonmaternal care increases the risk of insecure attachment, the authors also note that over 50% of the infants in the substitute care group were rated as securely attached to their mothers. Here again, the behaviors observed for the majority of children are well within normal ranges. Barglow and his associates suggest that moderating variables may be influential in this pattern. They further note that the "routes to competence may well differ for infants of employed mothers" (p. 952).

In a study intended as a follow-up to the Barglow et al (1987) study, Belsky & Rovine (1988) included moderating variables, such as family stress and maternal personality. Infants in child care more than 20 hours per week were more likely to be rated as insecure only if they were boys, had nonresponsive mothers, and were rated as difficult by their mothers.

The strength of this study is that it was designed to test the salience of moderator variables and included measures of maternal role satisfaction, an area directly related to the prediction of child outcomes (Farel 1980; Hock 1978) and parental functioning (Stuckey et al 1982; Hock et al 1988).

Once more, however, the quality of care was not evaluated and the strength of the results reported was less than compelling. Only 6 of the 36 comparisons made were either "significant or near-significant" (Belsky & Rovine 1988). In their most recently published study of attachment and day care effects, Belsky & Braungart (1991) tested the hypothesis that the Strange Situation stresses child care infants less than home infants because they are routinely separated from mother. A sample of two groups of year old children, who had been rated as insecure-avoidant, were rated in the Strange Situation. Observers were blind to child care experience as well as to the goals of the investigation. Nine children experienced less than 20 hours per week of child care, while 11 children were in child care more than 20 hours per week. The 11 children with extensive child care experience displayed more negative reunion behaviors than did children in part-time child care arrangements.

The authors report that the group of children in child care more than 20 hours per week were rated more frequently as being distressed than those children in care less than 20 hours per week. Belsky & Braungart considered these data to support the Strange Situation as a valid measure of the emotional adjustment of children with extensive child care experience (Belsky 1992).

However, there are a number of limitations to this study. The study has a very small sample size, does not report the reliability of the original attachment classification, and the measure of negative affect was not standardized. Most importantly, the authors note that distress was a low frequency event in both groups of children.

Indeed, Phillips et al (1987b) conducted a meta-analysis of 16 investigations of child-mother attachment and essentially replicated findings of weak group differences between home care and extensive nonmaternal care. This analysis also revealed that group differences were more likely to be found when raters were not blind to group assignment. More recently, Lamb et al (1992) conducted another meta-analysis of 13 studies of attachment and child care. These investigators concurred with Belsky that elevated rates of avoidance and insecure attachment were consistently found in child care children.

However, they differ in the evaluation of the meaning of these findings, as do others who have observed greater proximity seeking in home-reared children (Pierrehumbert et al 1991). Lamb et al (1992) also note the absence of ratings of quality of care in any of these studies, the unrepresentative nature of the samples studied, as well as an almost singular reliance on the Strange Situation.

Other studies using measures of attachment to evaluate social and emotional development find no differences between maternal and non-maternal care even in early entry groups (Howes et al 1988; for reviews see Clarke-Stewart & Fein 1983; Belsky 1989).

PROBLEMS WITH ATTACHMENT RESEARCH   Exclusive reliance on the Strange Situation (Ainsworth et al 1978) as a measure of attachment has limited research on emotional development. The measure may not be ecologically valid for children in child care who experience routine separations from primary caregivers (Clarke-Stewart 1987, 1989; Lamb & Sternberg 1989). It is also difficult to evaluate the meaning of elevated levels of insecure attachment because it is not clear what is being measured in the Strange Situation (Clarke-Stewart 1989). Is attachment being measured or is temperament being evaluated (Braungart & Stifter 1991; Crockenberg 1981; Egeland & Farber 1984; Weber et al 1986)?

As noted above, attachment and temperament are conceptually orthogonal (Sroufe 1985); however, in practice there is ambiguity between the two domains for the regulation of affect observed in the Strange Situation (Ainsworth et al 1978). Vaughn and associates (Vaughn et al 1992) found that the effects of temperament and attachment may not be evaluated separately, although they maintained that the domains are conceptually distinct.

Other measures of attachment, such as ratings, Q-sorts, and observations, have not shown reliable differences between groups of children who differ in child care experience (McCartney & Marshall 1989).

Conclusions

The most recent investigations highlight that effects of child care experience depend on the quality of care, the family background of the child, and the child's characteristics (age, gender, temperament, and other vulnerabilities). Socially disadvantaged children and those from dysfunctional homes find child care a positive developmental influence. For other children, whose families are more advantaged and functional, the relationships between nonmaternal care and child outcomes are more complex. Compared to similar children at home with their mothers, children from well functioning, middle-class homes, whose mothers want to stay home, may be disadvantaged if they are placed in poor quality care, are male, and are temperamentally difficult. Most of these children will not be affected negatively or positively by reasonable quality child care. Any negative effects are more likely to be emotional than cognitive; any positive effects are likely to be greater social competence and better peer relations. But results from studies of child care in isolation from other aspects of the child, the family, and the larger context of their lives are not clear. There are many correlates of child care choices, and interactions abound (Scarr et al 1989).

The effects of nonmaternal care per se, if any, are small, so that from a practical standpoint it is impossible to predict the short-term effects of child care for any child. Long-term effects are even less likely to be predicted once appropriate controls for family background and later experiences have been applied.

SCIENTIFIC IMPLICATIONS

As the third wave of psychological research on child care continues there will be more carefully crafted studies that incorporate more of the child's characteristics and family ecology in order to study the effects of child care in context. In our current study of variation in child care quality (Scarr et al 1992), the results are clear: There is a small and consistent effect of child care quality on children's social and emotional development — not as large as that of the family, but reliably there. This is an expectable result for child care studies, in which variations in parent and child characteristics and in quality of care at home and elsewhere are sufficient to make a difference in development. We need to move on.

Wave of the future

Taking the first assumption about child care, that it is a support service for working parents, there are many questions that need to be asked about how the current system does and does not meet the needs of working parents. How should child care be integrated with other family service needs? What effects on family functioning can an expanded definition of child care services have (less depression, better marital relations, better parenting behaviors)? Very few psychologists have addressed such issues, in large part because those who study child care have adopted a child-centered assumption about the principal purpose of child care.

From a larger societal perspective, what effects can improving the quantity and quality of child care services have on women's employment, career advancement, income capacity, and job satisfaction (Eisenberg 1991)? Child care research should not be the domain of only those concerned with children's development but should expand to include psychologists concerned with political and societal issues. Research on child care in context requires more consideration on how child care services fit into a broader public support system for working parents. Most industrialized nations, and all European Community countries except the United Kingdom have (a) job-guaranteed, paid maternity leaves for approximately 12 weeks, (b) paid parental leaves for

4 months to 15 months of infant care, (c) family allowances to offset some of the costs of child rearing, (d) national health plans that cover the costs of health care, (e) unemployment and disability benefits that do not expire, (f) tax-supported child care (parents pay only 5–15 % of the cost of child care), and other social insurance provisions that insure a minimum, decent standard of care and living for everyone. The structure of the settings also differs. In many countries, parents expect community support in child rearing, and child care is part of that system.

To understand the stresses and strains of balancing work and family life in the US, psychologists need to look at how working parents juggle and make do, and what the psychic costs of our lack of family supports are. The lack of affordable child care has implications for how many families function or struggle to function. We need a second perspective on child care as a support system for parents. Policy-relevant research on such issues is badly needed.

PUBLIC POLICY

Good scientific research can inform public policy, but it can never determine public policy. Policy is made by a political process in which values usually play a larger role than information. Two value components underlie child care research: the scientific component (accuracy) and the value component (decisions; Hammond et al 1992). Psychological research on child care and its effects on children can inform public policy on families. And psychologists can advocate for better family supports.

First, we can stress that available and affordable, good quality child care is a necessity for the majority of families with infants and young children because in nearly two-thirds of those families parents (whether one or two) are in the labor force. Intact, middle-class families require child care just as much today as low income families (Caldwell 1987). Children under school age require adult care. School-age children under 12 or 13 years require after-school care.

Even if psychological research were to show (and it does not) that maternal care is always preferable to nonmaternal care, the fact that the majority of American mothers are employed makes this issue moot. Unfortunately, the US has not found the political will to make affordable child care available to all families who need it.

Second, low income working families and families on Aid to Families with Dependent Children need subsidized child care if they are to become self-sufficient. Many "welfare mothers" would work, if they could afford child care. For poor families, child care provides a setting for the delivery of other crucial services to children, such as health, nutrition, and social services.

Third, we should accept diverse sponsorship for child care services in our pluralistic society. Private and public sponsorship, for profit and nonprofit, independent and chain, ethnically centered and religiously sponsored will coexist. The corporate community should be involved in planning for, assisting employees with, and providing child care services for their workers.

Fourth, we need to provide training for a variety of roles in child care for professionals from different disciplines. Education, health, and social services are all essential to child care, as many European systems demonstrate. Career ladders in child care need to be developed, staff wages should be greatly improved, and training opportunities expanded. Only then can we improve the quality of care for children in the US.

Fifth, we need to be realistic. We are unlikely to persuade the voting public in the next decade that publicly supported child care for all children is essential to the national welfare. Parents in the US will continue to bear the financial burden of child care, unlike European families, whose governments long ago adopted child care. How much "quality" can US parents afford? Research shows that quality means more, better paid and better trained caregivers, and these caregivers cost more than parents can currently pay. We have the dilemma of where to allocate scarce resources.

Zigler, a devoted advocate of early education for disadvantaged children, drew the line at public support for middle-class children. The cost is too prohibitive for few if any educational gains (Zigler & Lang 1991). Early schooling may even be inappropriate and perhaps harmful for some four year olds. "Most parents need early child care not early childhood education. ... they do not need children who can read at age four, but they do need affordable, good quality child care" while they work.

Public support of child care is desperately needed for parents at low and middle income levels. Realistically, public support should first go to the needs of low income families. There is no question that support for child care for low income children is not readily available since federal and state support for child care has diminished since 1980. Child care help for mothers seeking to gain the training necessary to obtain jobs and income to move their families out of poverty is now even harder to find than it was a decade ago. As Zigler and others point out, US welfare policies punish families who make small steps toward independence; families are forced to remain poor to receive the most minimum of child care services. Additional public resources are necessary to meet the child care needs of single and low income parents.

Psychological research informs us that good quality child care is neither a clear benefit nor a detriment to the development of children from stable, low-risk families. Good child care has a positive influence on the development of children at risk. American families' needs for affordable child care are great. We require only the public will to put these facts into action. More research can help define the most effective ways to address these family problems.

Literature Cited

Ackerman-Ross, S., Khana, P. 1989. The relationship of high quality day care to middle-class 3-year-olds' language performance. *Early Child. Res. Q.* 4: 97–116

Ainslie, R. C., ed. 1984. *The Child and the Day Care Setting.* New York: Praeger

Ainsworth, M. D. S. 1982. Attachment: retrospect and prospect. In *The Place of Attachment in Human Behavior,* ed. C. M. Parkes, J. Stevenson-Hinde, pp. 3–30. New York: Basic Books

Ainsworth, M. D. S., Blehar, M. L., Waters, E., Wall, S. C. 1978. *Patterns of Attachment: A Psychological Study of the Strange Situation.* Hillsdale, NJ: Erlbaum

Alvarez, W. F. 1985. The meaning of maternal employment for mothers and their perception of their three-year old children. *Child Dev.* 56:350–60

Anderson, C. W., Nagel, R. J., Roberts, W. A., Smith, J. W. 1981. Attachment to substitute caregivers as a function of centre quality and caregiver involvement. *Child Dev.* 52:53–61

Andersson, B. E. 1988. *The effects of public day care—a longitudinal study.* Presented at a workshop on International Developments in Child Care, NAS Study Center, Woods Hole, Mass.

Andersson, B. E. 1989. Effects of public day care—a longitudinal study. *Child Dev.* 60:857–66

Anthony, E. J. 1987. Risk, vulnerability, and resilience: an overview. In *The Invulnerable Child,* ed. E. J. Anthony, B. J. Cohler. New York: Guilford Press

Arend, R., Gove, F. L., Sroufe, L. A. 1979. Continuity of individual adaptation from infancy to kindergarten: a predictive study of ego-resiliency and curiosity in preschoolers. *Child Dev.* 50:950–59

Aries, P. 1962. *Centuries of Childhood: A Social History of Family Life.* New York: Knopf. 447 pp.

Barglow, P., Vaughn, B. E., Molitor, N. 1987. Effects of maternal absence due to employment on the quality of infant-mother attachment in a low-risk sample. *Child Dev.* 58:945–54

Baydar, N., Brooks-Gunn, J. 1991. Effects of maternal employment and child-care arrangements on preschoolers' cognitive and behavioral outcomes: evidence from the children of the National Longitudinal Survey of Youth. Special section data analyses on developmental psychology. *Dev. Psychol.* 27:932–45

Balleyguier, G., Meudec, M., Chasseigne, G. 1991. Caretaking methods and temperament among young children. *Enfance* 45:153–69

Belsky, J. 1984. Two waves of day care research: developmental effects and conditions of quality. See Ainslie 1984, pp. 24–42

Belsky, J. 1986. Infant day care: a cause for concern? *Zero to Three* 6:1–9

Belsky, J. 1988. The "effects" of infant day care reconsidered. *Early Child. Res. Q.* 3:235–72

Belsky, J. 1989. Infant-parent attachment security and infant day care: in defense of the Strange Situation. See Lande et al 1989, pp. 23–48

Belsky, J. 1992. Consequences of child care for children's development: a deconstructionist view. See Booth 1992, pp. 83–94

Belsky, J., Braungart, J. 1991. Are insecure-avoidant infants with extensive day care experience less stressed by and more independent in the Strange Situation? *Child Dev.* 62:567–71

Belsky, J., Rovine, M. J. 1988. Nonmaternal care in the first year of life and the security of infant-parent attachment. *Child Dev.* 59:157–67

Belsky, J., Steinberg, L. D. 1978. The effects of day care: a critical review. *Child Dev.* 49:929–49

Belsky, J., Steinberg, L. D., Walker, A. 1982. The ecology of day care. In *Nontraditional Families,* ed. M. E. Lamb, pp. 71–116. Hillsdale, NJ: Erlbaum

Benn, R. 1986. Factors promoting secure attachment relationships between employed mothers and their sons. *Child Dev.* 57:1224–31

Berk, L. 1985. Relationships of educational attainment, child-oriented attitudes, job satisfaction, and career commitment to caregiver behavior toward children. *Child Care Q.* 14:103–29

Blanchard, M., Main, M. 1979. Avoidance of the attachment figure and social-emotional adjustment in day care infants. *Dev. Psychol.* 15:445–46

Bolger, K. 1991. *How family characteristics influence child care choices.* Presented at Soc. Res. Child Dev., Seattle, Wash.

Booth, A., ed. 1992. *Child Care in the 1990s: Trends and Consequences.* Hillsdale, NJ: Erlbaum. 245 pp.

Bowlby, J. 1969. *Attachment and Loss,* Vol. 1, *Attachment.* New York: Basic Books. 428 pp.

Bowlby, J. 1973. *Attachment and Loss,* Vol. 2, *Separation.* New York: Basic Books. 456 pp.

Braun, S. J., Caldwell, B. M. 1973. Emotional adjustment of children in day care who enrolled prior to or after age of three. *Early Child Dev. Care* 2:13–21

Braungart, J., Stifter, M. 1991. Regulation of negative reactivity during the strange situation: temperament and attachment in 12-

month-old infants. *Infant Behav. Dev.* 14:349–64

Bredekamp, S. 1989. *Measuring quality through a national accreditation system for early childhood programs.* Presented at Am. Educ. Res. Assoc., San Francisco, Calif.

Breitmayer, B. J., Ramey, C. T. 1986. Biological nonoptimality and quality of postnatal environment as codeterminants of intellectual development. *Child Dev.* 57:1151–65

Breslau, N., Salkever, D., Staruch, K. S. 1982. Women's labor force activity and responsibilities for disabled dependents: a study of families with disabled children. *J. Health Soc. Behav.* 23:169–83

Bronfenbrenner, U., Crouter, A. 1982. Work and family through time and space. In *Families That Work: Children in a Changing World,* ed. S. B. Kamerman, C. D. Hayes, pp. 39–83. Washington, DC: Natl. Acad.

Brookhart, J., Hock, E. 1976. The effects of experimental context and experiential background on infants' behavior toward their mothers and a stranger. *Child Dev.* 47:333–40

Caldwell, B. M., Freyer, M. 1982. Day care and early education. In *Handbook of Research in Early Childhood Education,* ed. B. Spadek. New York: Free Press

Caldwell, B. M. 1987. Professional child care. In *Group Care for Young Children: A Supplement to Parental Care,* ed. B. Caldwell, p. 214. Lexington, MA: Toronto

Caldwell, B. M., Wright, B., Honig, A., Tannenbaum, G. 1970. Infant day care and attachment. *Am. J. Orthopsychiatry* 40:397–412

Camras, L. A., Sachs, V. B. 1991. Social referencing and caregiver expressive behavior in a day care setting. *Infant Behav. Dev.* 14:27–36

Cherry, F. F., Eaton, E. L. 1977. Physical and cognitive development in children of low-income mothers working in the child's early years. *Child Dev.* 48:158–66

Chorvinsky, M. 1982. *Preliminary Enrollment 1980.* Washington, DC: Natl. Cent. Educ. Stats.

Clarke-Stewart, K. A. 1987. In search of consistencies in child care research. See Phillips 1987, pp. 43–56

Clarke-Stewart, K. A. 1989. Infant day care: malignant or maligned? *Am. Psychol.* 44:266–73

Clarke-Stewart, K. A. 1992. Consequences of child care for children's development. See Booth 1992, pp. 63–82

Clarke-Stewart, K. A., Fein, G. G. 1983. Early childhood programs. In *Handbook of Child Psychology,* Vol.2, ed. P. H. Mussen, M. Haith, J. Campos. New York: Wiley

Clarke-Stewart, K. A., Gruber, C. P. 1984. Day care forms and features. See Ainslie 1984, pp. 51–73

Cleary, P., Mechanic, D. 1983. Sex differences in psychological distress among married people. *J. Health Soc. Behav.* 24:111–21

Cochran, M. M. 1977. A comparison of group day and family-based childrearing patterns in Sweden. *Child Dev.* 48:702–7

Crittenden, P. M. 1989. Relationships at risk. In *Clinical Implications of Attachment,* ed. J. Belsky, pp.17–28. Hillsdale, NJ: Erlbaum

Crockenberg, S. 1981. Infant irritability, mother responsiveness, and social support influences on the security of infant-mother attachment. *Child Dev.* 52:857–65

Desai, S., Chase-Lansdale, P. L., Michael, R. T. 1989. Mother or market? Effects of maternal employment on the intellectual ability of four-year-old children. *Demography* 26:545–61

Egeland, B. 1983. Comments on Kopp, Krakow, and Vaughn's chapter. In *Minnesota Symposium in Child Psychology,* ed. M. Perlmutter, pp. 20–22. Hillsdale, NJ: Erlbaum

Egeland, B., Farber, E. A. 1984. Infant-mother attachment: factors related to its development and changes over time. *Child Dev.* 55:753–71

Eisenberg, M. M. 1991. *Work-family interference, coping strategies, and subjective well-being in working mothers.* Present at Soc. Res. Child Dev., Seattle, Wash.

Emery, R. E. 1988. *Marriage, Divorce, and Children's Adjustment.* Newbury Park, Calif.: Sage. 160 pp.

Etaugh, C. 1980. Effects of nonmaternal care on children: research evidence and popular wisdom. *Am. Psychol.* 35:309–19

Farber, E. A., Egeland, B. 1982. Developmental consequences of out-of-home care for infants in a low-income population. See Zigler & Gordon 1982, pp. 102–25

Farel, A. M. 1980. Effects of preferred maternal roles, maternal employment, and sociodemographic status on school adjustment and competence. *Child Dev.* 51:1179–96

Feiring, C., Fox, N., Jaskir, J., Lewis, M. 1987. The relation between social support, infant risk status, and mother- infant interaction. *Dev. Psychol.* 23:400–5

Fewell, R. 1987. Child care and the handicapped child. In *Group Care for Young Children: A Supplement to Parental Care,* ed. B.M. Caldwell. Lexington, MA: Lexington Books

Field, T. 1991. Quality infant day care and grade school behavior and performance. *Child Dev.* 62:863–70

Field, T., Masi, W., Goldstein, D., Perry, S., Parl, S. 1988. Infant day-care facilitates pre-school behavior. *Early Child. Res. Q.* 55:1308–16

Finkelstein, N. W. 1982. Aggression: is it stimulated by day care? *Young Child.* 37:3–12

Finkelstein, N. W., Wilson, K. 1977. *The influ-*

ence of day care on social behaviors towards peers and adults. Presented at Soc. Res. Child Dev., New Orleans

Gamble, T. J., Zigler, E. 1986. Effects of infant day care: another look at the evidence. *Am. J. Orthopsychiatry* 56:26–42

Goelman, H., Pence, A.R. 1987. Effects of child care, family and individual characteristics on children's language development: the Victoria Day Care Research Project. In *Quality in Child Care: What Does Research Tell Us?*, ed. D.A. Phillips. Washington, DC: Natl. Assoc. Educ. Young Children

Goldberg, W., Easterbrooks, M. A. 1988. Maternal employment when children are toddlers and kindergartners. See Gottfried & Gottfried 1988, pp. 32–49

Golden, M., Rosenbluth, L., Grossi, N. T., Policare, H. J., Freeman, H., Brownlee, E. M. 1978. *The New York City Infant Day Care Study*. New York: Med. Health Res. Assoc. New York City

Goossens, F. A., Ottenhoff, G., Koops, W. 1991. Day care and social outcomes in middle childhood: a retrospective study. *J. Reprod. Infant Psychol.* 9:137–50

Goossens, F. A., van Ijzendoorn, M. H. 1990. Quality of infants' attachments to professional caregivers: relation to infant-parent attachment and day-care characteristics. *Child Dev.* 61:550–67

Gottfried, A. E., Gottfried, A. W., eds. 1988. *Maternal Employment and Children's Development: Longitudinal Research*. New York: Plenum. 291 pp.

Hammond, K. R., Harvey, L. O., Hastie, R. 1992. Making better use of scientific knowledge: separating truth from justice. *Psychol. Sci.* 3:80–87

Haskins, R. 1985. Public aggression among children with varying day care experience. *Child Dev.* 57:692–703

Hennessy, E., Melhuish, E. C. 1991. Early day care and the development of school-age children: a review. *J. Reprod. Infant Psychol.* 9:117–36

Hock, E. 1978. Working and non-working mothers with infants: perceptions of their careers, their infants' needs, and satisfaction with mothering. *Dev. Psychol.* 14:37–43

Hock, E., DeMeis, D., McBride, S. 1988. Maternal separation anxiety: its role in the balance of employment and motherhood in mothers of infants. See Gottfried & Gottfried 1988, pp. 192–212

Hofferth, S. L. 1992. The demand for and supply of child care in the 1990s. See Booth 1992, pp. 56–62

Hoffman, L. W. 1980. The effects of maternal employment on the academic attitudes and performance of school-aged children. *School Psychol. Rev.* 9:319–35

Hoffman, L. W. 1984. Maternal employment and the child. In *Parent-Child Interaction and Parent-Child Relations in Development*, ed. M. Perlmutter. Hillsdale, NJ: Erlbaum

Holloway, S. D., Reichhart-Erickson, M. 1989. Child care quality, family structure, and maternal expectations: relationship to preschool children's peer relations. *J. Appl. Dev. Psychol.* 10:281–98

Howes, C. 1983. Caregiver behavior in center and family day care. *J. Appl. Dev. Psychol.* 4:99–107

Howes, C. 1988. Relations between early child care and schooling. *Dev. Psychol.* 24:53–57

Howes, C. 1990. Can the age of entry and the quality of infant child care predict adjustment in kindergarten? *Dev. Psychol.* 26:252–303

Howes, C. 1991. Caregiving environments and their consequences for children: the experience in the United States. See Melhuish & Moss 1991, pp. 185–98

Howes, C., Hamilton, C. E. 1992a. Children's relationships with caregivers: mothers and child care teachers. *Child Dev.* 63 859–66

Howes, C., Hamilton, C. E. 1992b. Children's relationships with child care teachers: stability and concordance with parental attachments. *Child Dev.* 63:867–78

Howes, C., Olenick, M. 1986. Family and child care influences on toddler's compliance. *Child Dev.* 57:202–16

Howes, C., Phillips, D. A., Whitebook, M. 1992. Thresholds of quality: implications for the social development of children in center-based child care. *Child Dev.* 63:449–60

Howes, C., Rodning, C., Galluzzo, D. C., Myers, L. 1988. Attachment and child care: relationships with mother and caregiver. *Early Child. Res. Q.* 3:403–16

Howes, C., Rubenstein, J. 1985. Determinants of toddler's experiences in day care: age of entry and quality of setting. *Child Care Q.* 14:140–51

Howes, C., Stewart, P. 1987. Child's play with adults, toys, and peers: an examination of family and child-care influences. *Dev. Psychol.* 23:423–30

Innes, R. B., Banspach, S. W., Woodman, J. D. 1982. A comparison of the ecologies of day care centers and group day care homes for 4-year-olds. *Early Child Dev. Care* 10:125–42

Kagan, J. 1982. *Psychological Research on the Human Infant: An Evaluative Summary*. New York: Grant Foundation. 201 pp.

Kagan, J., Kearsley, R., Zelazo, P. 1978. *Infancy: Its Place in Human Development*. Cambridge, Mass.: Harvard Univ. Press

Keister, M. 1970. *A Demonstration Project: Group Care of Infants and Toddlers*. Washington, DC: Dep. Health Educ. Welfare

Kermoian, R., Leiderman, P. H. 1986. Infant attachment to mother and child caretaker in an East African community. *Int. J. Behav. Dev.* 9:455–69

Kontos, S. 1991. Child care quality, family background, and children's development. *Early Child. Res. Q.* 6:249–62

Kontos, S., Fiene, R. 1987. Child care quality, compliance with regulations, and children's development: the Pennsylvania Study. See Phillips 1987, pp. 81–88

Lally, J. R., Mangione, P. L., Honig, A. S. 1988. The Syracuse University family development research program: long-term impact of an early intervention with low-income children and their families. In *Parent Education as Early Childhood Intervention: Emerging Directions in Theory, Research, and Practice*, ed. D. R. Powell. Hillsdale, NJ: Ablex

Lamb, M. E., Hwang, C., Bookstein, F. L., Broberg, A., Hult, G., Frodi, M. 1988. Determinants of social competence in Swedish preschoolers. *Dev. Psychol.* 24:58–70

Lamb, M. E., Sternberg, K. J. 1989. Day care. In *Handbuch der Kleinkind Forschung*, ed. H. Keller, pp. 587–608. Heidelberg: Springer-Verlag

Lamb, M. E., Sternberg, K. J. 1990. Do we really know how day care affects children? Erratum. *J. Appl. Dev. Psychol.* 11:499

Lamb, M. E., Sternberg, K. J., Ketterlinus, R. 1992. Child care in the United States. In *Child Care in Context*, ed. M. E. Lamb, K. Sternberg, C. P. Hwang, A. G. Broberg, pp. 207–22. Hillsdale, NJ: Erlbaum

Lamb, M. E., Thompson, R. A., Gardner, W., Charnov, E. L. 1985. *Infant-Mother Attachment: The Origins and Developmental Significance of Individual Differences in Strange Situation Behavior.* Hillsdale, NJ: Erlbaum

Lande, J., Scarr, S., Guzenhauser, N., eds. 1989. *Caring for Children: Challenge to America.* Hillsdale, NJ: Erlbaum. 327 pp.

Londerville, S., Main, M. 1981. Security, compliance, and maternal training methods in the second year of life. *Dev. Psychol.* 17:289–99

Main, M., Weston, D. R. 1981. The quality of the toddlers' relationship to mother and to father: related to conflict behavior and the readiness to establish new relationships. *Child Dev.* 52:932–40

Maslin, L., Bates, J. 1982. *Anxious attachment as a predictor of disharmony in the mother-toddler relationship.* Presented at the Int. Conf. Infant Stud., Austin, Tex.

McBride, S. L. 1990. Maternal moderators of child care: the role of maternal separation anxiety. *New Dir. Child Dev.* 49:53–70

McCartney, K. 1984. The effect of quality of day care environment upon children's language development. *Dev. Psychol.* 20:244–60

McCartney, K., Marshall, N. 1989. The development of child care research. *Div. Child Youth Family Serv. Newsl., Am. Psychol. Assoc.* 12:4, 14–15

McCartney, K., Scarr, S., Phillips, D. A., Grajek, S., Schwarz, J. C. 1982. Environmental differences among day care centres and their effects on children's development. See Zigler & Gordon 1982, pp. 128–51

McCartney, K., Scarr, S., Phillips, D. A., Grajek, S., 1985. Day care as intervention: comparisons of varying quality programs. *J. Appl. Dev. Psychol.* 6:247–60

Melhuish, E. C., Moss, P., Mooney, A., Martin, S. 1991. How similar are day-care groups before the start of the day care? *J. Appl. Dev. Psychol.* 12:331–46

Melhuish, E. C., Mooney, A., Martin, S., Lloyd, E. 1990. Type of day care at 18 months: I. Differences in interactional experience. *J. Child Psychol. Psychiatry* 31:849–60

Melhuish, E. C., Moss, P., eds. 1991. *Day Care for Young Children: International Perspectives.* London/New York: Tavistock/Routledge. 225 pp.

Moore, T. W. 1975. Exclusive early mothering and its alternatives; the outcome to adolescence. *Scand. J. Psychol.* 16:255–72

Mott, F. L. 1989. *Child care use during the first year of life: linkages with early child development.* Report to the US Dep. Labor, Bur. Labor Stat.

Mott, F. L. 1991. Developmental effects of infant care: the mediating role of gender and health. *J. Soc. Issues* 47:139–58

Murphy, L. B., Moriarty, A. E. 1976. *Vulnerability, Coping, and Growth.* New Haven: Yale Univ. Press

Owen, M. T., Easterbrooks, M. A., Chase-Lansdale, P. L., Goldberg, W. A. 1984. The relationship between maternal employment status and the stability of attachments to mother and father. *Child Dev.* 55:1894–1901

Park, K. J., Honig, A. S. 1991. *Infant child care patterns and later ratings of preschool behavior.* Presented at the Am. Psychol. Assoc., San Francisco, Calif.

Phillips, D. A., ed. 1987. *Quality in Child Care: What Does Research Tell Us? Research Monographs of the National Association for the Education of Young Children.* Washington, DC: Natl. Assoc. Educ. Young Child. 127 pp.

Phillips, D. A. 1991. Day care for young children in the United States. See Melhuish & Moss 1991, pp. 161–84

Phillips, D. A., McCartney, K., Scarr, S. 1987a. Child care quality and children's social development. *Dev. Psychol.* 23:537–43

Phillips, D. A., McCartney, K., Scarr, S., Howes, C. 1987b. Selective review of infant day care research: a cause for concern. *Zero to Three* 7:18–21

Pierrehumbert, B., Frascarolo, F., Bettschart, W., Plancherel, B., Melhuish, E. C. 1991. A longitudinal study of infant's social-emotional development and the implications of extra-parental care. *J. Reprod. Infant Psychol.* 9:91–103

Ramey, C. T., Bryant, D. M., Suarez, T. 1989. Preschool compensatory education and the modifiability of intelligence: a critical review. In *Current Topics in Human Intelligence,* ed. D. Detterman. Norwood, NJ: Ablex

Ramey, C. T., Dorval, B., Baker-Ward, L. 1983. Group day care and socially disadvantaged families: Effects on the child and the family. In *Advances in Early Education and Day Care,* ed. S. Kilmer. Greenwich, Conn.: JAI Press

Ramey, C.T., Farren, D. 1982. *Intervening with high-risk families via infant day care.* Presented at Soc. Res. Child Dev., Detroit, Mich.

Rosenthal, M. K. 1991. Daily experiences of toddlers in three child care settings in Israel. *Child Care and Youth Forum* 20:39–60

Roupp, R., Travers, J., Glantz, F., Coelen, C. 1979. *Children at the Center.* Cambridge, Mass.: ABT

Rubenstein, J. L., Howes, C. 1979. Caregiving and infant behavior in day care and in homes. *Dev. Psychol.* 15:1–24

Rubenstein, J. L., Howes, C. 1983. Socio-emotional development of toddlers in day care: the role of peers and of individual differences. In *Advances in Early Education and Day Care,* ed. S. Kilmer, 3:13–45. Greenwich, CT: JAI Press

Rubenstein, J. L., Howes, C., Boyles, P. 1981. A two year follow-up of infants in community based infant day care. *J. Child Psychol. Psychiatry* 22:209–18

Rubenstein, J. L., Pederson, F. A., Yarrow, L. J. 1977. What happens when mother is away: a comparison of mothers and substitute caregivers. *Dev. Psychol.* 13:525–30

Rutter, M. 1981. Socio-emotional consequences of day care for preschool children. *Am. Psychol.* 5:4–28

Scarr, S. 1984. *Mother Care/Other Care.* New York: Basic Books. 252 pp.

Scarr, S. 1985. Constructing psychology: Making facts and fables for our times. *Am. Psychol.* 40:499–512

Scarr, S. 1992. Developmental theories for the 1990s: development and individual differences. *Child Dev.* 63:1–19

Scarr, S., Lande, J., McCartney, K. 1989. Child care and the family: cooperation and interaction. See Lande et al 1989, pp. 1–22

Scarr, S., Phillips, D. A., McCartney, K. 1990. Facts, fantasies, and the future of child care in the United States. *Psychol. Sci.* 1:26–35

Scarr, S., Phillips, D. A., McCartney, K., Abbott-Shim, M. 1992. Quality of child care as an aspect of family and childcare policy in the United States. *Pediatrics* In press

Schindler, P. J., Moely, B. E., Frank, A. L. 1987. Time in day care psychology and so-

cial participation of young children. *Dev. Psychol.* 23:255–61

Schwartz, P. 1983. Length of day-care attendance and attachment behavior in eighteen-month-old infants. *Child Dev.* 54:1073–78

Schwarz, J. C., Krolick, G., Strickland, R. 1973. Effects of early day care experience on adjustment to a new environment. *Am. J. Orthopsychiatry* 43:340–66

Schwarz, J. C., Strickland, R. G., Krolick, G. 1974. Infant day care: behavioral effects at preschool age. *Dev. Psychol.* 10:502–6

Shiomi, T. 1990. The specialty of child care. *Hattatsu* 42:19–24

Sroufe, L. A. 1985. Attachment classification from the perspective of infant-caregiver relationships and temperament. *Child Dev.* 56:1–14

Sroufe, L. A., Fleeson, J. 1986. Attachment and the construction of relationships. In *The Nature and Development of Relationships,* ed. W. Hartup, Z. Rubin. Hillsdale, NJ: Erlbaum

Sroufe, L. A., Waters, E. 1977. Attachment as an organizational construct. *Child Dev.* 48:1184–99

Sternberg, K. J., Lamb, M. E., Hwang, C., Broberg, A. 1991. Does out-of-home care affect compliance in preschoolers? *Int. J. Behav. Dev.* 14:45–65

Stith, S., Davis, A. 1984. Employed mothers and family day care substitute caregivers. *Child Dev.* 55:1340–48

Strickland, B. 1992. Women and depression. *Curr. Dir. Psychol. Sci.* 1:132–35

Stuckey, M. F., McGhee, P. E., Bell, N. J. 1982. Parent-child interaction: the influence of maternal employment. *Dev. Psychol.* 18:635–44

Suwalsky, J., Zaslow, M., Klein, R., Rabinovich, B. 1986. *Continuity of substitute care in relation to infant-mother attachment.* Presented at Am. Psychol. Assoc., Washington, DC

Teti, D. M., Gelfand, D. M. 1991. Behavioral competence among mothers of infants in the first year: the mediational role of maternal self-efficacy. *Child Dev.* 62:918–29

Vandell, D. L., Corasanti, M. A. 1990. Variations in early child care: do they predict subsequent social, emotional andcognitive differences? *Early Child. Res. Q.* 5:55–72

Vandell, D. L., Ramanan, J. 1992. Effects of early and recent maternal employment on children from low-income families. *Child Dev.* 63:938–49

Vaughn, B. E., Deane, K. E., Waters, E. 1985. The impact of out-of-home care on child-mother attachment quality: another look at some enduring questions. *Monogr. Soc. Res. Child Dev.* 50:110–35

Vaughn, B. E., Gove, F. L., Egeland, B 1980. The relationship between out-of-home care and the quality of infant-mother attachment in an economically disadvantaged population. *Child Dev.* 51:1203–14

Vaughn, B. E., Stevenson-Hinde, J., Waters, E., Kotsaftis, A., Lefever, G. et al 1992. Attachment security and temperament in infancy and early childhood: some conceptual clarifications. *Dev. Psychol.* 28:463–73

Wasik, B. H., Ramey, C. T., Bryant, D. M.. Sparling, J. J. 1990. A longitudinal study of two early intervention strategies: Project CARE. *Child Dev.* 61:1682–96

Waters, E., Deane, K. E. 1985. Defining and assessing individual differences in attachment relationships: Q-methodology and the organization of behavior in infancy and early childhood. In *Growing Points of Attachment Theory and Research,* ed. I. Bretherton, E. Waters, pp. 41–65. Monogr. Soc. Res. Child Dev. 50 (1, Ser. No. 209)

Weber, R. A., Levitt, M. J., Clark, M. C. 1986. Individual variation in attachment security and Strange Situation temperament. *Child Dev.* 57:56–65

Weinraub, M, Jaeger, E., Hoffman, L.W. 1988. Predicting infant outcomes in families of employed and non-employed mothers. *Early Childhood Res. Q.* 3:361–78

Whitebook, M., Howes, C., Phillips, D. 1991. Who cares? Child care teachers and the quality of care in America. Final Rep. Natl. Staffing Study

Zaslow, M. J., Rabinovich, B. A., Suwalsky, J. T. 1986. From maternal employment to child outcomes. In *Employed Mothers and Their Children,* ed. J. V. Lerner, N. L. Galambos, pp. 237–82. New York: Garland

Zigler, E. 1989. Addressing the nation's child care crisis: the school of the twenty-first century. *Am. J. Orthopsychiatry* 59:484–91

Zigler, E. F., Gordon, E. W., eds. 1982. *Day Care: Scientific and Social Policy Issues.* Boston: Auburn House. 515 pp.

Zigler, E. F., Lang, M. E. 1991. *Child Care Choices: Balancing the Needs of Children, Families, and Society.* New York: The Free Press. 271 pp.

Ann,. Rev. Psychol. 1993. 44:645–74

PROGRAM EVALUATION

Lee Sechrest and Aurelio José Figueredo

Evaluation Group for Analysis of Data, Department of Psychology, University of Arizona, Tucson, Arizona 85721

KEYWORDS: quantitative methods, qualitative methods, social ecology, Newtonian paradigm, Darwinian paradigm

CONTENTS

INTRODUCTION 645
WORLD-VIEWS IN COLLISION... 646
CONCURRENT SOCIAL REVOLUTION 68
EVALUATION IS NOT A FIELD 650
THE QUALITATIVE MOVEMENT... 652
EVALUATIONS OF LARGE-SCALE SOCIAL PROGRAMS 656
PROGRAM EVALUATION: THE FUNDAMENTAL ISSUES.................................. 657
MULTIVARIATE METHODS IN PROGRAM EVALUATION.................................. 664
RECENT DEVELOPMENTS IN THE PROFESSION OF PROGRAM EVALUATION 671

INTRODUCTION

Notable attempts have been made of late (e.g. Shadish et al 1991) to take stock of the accumulated experience of the last three decades of program evaluation in order to draw both theoretical and practical lessons for the present edification and future development of that enterprise. This discussion is in no way intended to detract from the numerous valuable insights provided by such recent historical analyses, but in the ultimately constructive spirit of multiplism (Shadish 1989), we wish to emphasize a partially complementary and perhaps convergent perspective.

We are concerned with the changing social context, or social ecology, of program evaluation. Shadish et al (1991), for example, have described the historical evolution of evaluation theory in at least two complementary ways: (*a*) a confrontation between an initial naiveté on the part of evaluation researchers and the unanticipated complexities of social and political reality, and

645

0066-4308/93/0201-645$02.00

(b) a partially cumulative progression and refinement of ideas, both theoretical and practical, within the field over that time. We do not challenge the usefulness of either of these perspectives, but propose the addition of other historical forces to the list. These additional and complementary interpretations are: (a) a confrontation between an initial physicalistic, or Newtonian, paradigm dominant in the social sciences and the ecological, or Darwinian, realities of the sociopolitical environment, and (b) a complex of real social changes during the historical development of program evaluation from an industrial era, or Taylorite, mode of management, in both business and government, to a postindustrial era, or cybernetic, mode of social intervention in what has increasingly become an information-based society. These two forces have altered not only how contemporary program evaluators relate to the outside world, but also what they conceive to be their special role within it.

Behavioral ecology is the scientific study of the relationships of the behavior of organisms to the relevant characteristics of the environment (Alcock 1989). It rests on the assumption that the behavior of living things is adapted, whether genetically or experientially, or both, to critical and identifiable features of their material conditions of existence (James 1910; Mayr 1974). We believe that this approach can shed some light on some of the historical trends that have been identified (e.g. by Shadish et al 1991) in the evolution of program evaluation. For example, consider the following questions. What accounts for the initial naiveté of evaluation researchers with respect to the unanticipated complexities of social and political reality? Why were they unanticipated? What accounts for the evolution of ideas within the program evaluation community? Is it merely the presumably inexorable forward march of scientific progress, or did some ideas become more salient and others less so over time because of changing social and political conditions?

Ecologically conscious program evaluators (e.g. Tharp & Gallimore 1979) have discussed the role of what they called evaluation pressure upon the serial succession of elements within social programs undergoing formative evaluations. We propose a selective ecological pressure of ambient social and political factors upon the evolving practice of program evaluation, which also undergoes formative development as a discipline. This pressure is contrary to the natural trend in self-consciously emerging fields to define themselves in terms of their unique characteristics and, thus, to mark off their own particular disciplinary boundaries. We intend to call attention to how some of the trends within the field of program evaluation have either paralleled or reflected trends outside of it.

WORLD-VIEWS IN COLLISION

Shadish et al (1991) marshal a convincing argument that program evaluation is not merely applied social science. Conceding that particular point, the question remains, why not? Shadish et al (1991) appeal to the peculiar problems manifest in program evaluation. However, these various problems arise not merely in program evaluation but whenever one tries to apply social science. The problems, then, arise not from the perverse peculiarities of program evaluation but from the manifest failure of much of mainstream social science and the identifiable reasons for that failure.

This failure of mainstream social science derives from the chronically inadequate external validity of the results of the dominant experimental research paradigm. Historically, this failure has been largely attributable to the nearly universal institutionalization of Fisherian null-hypothesis testing, as has been well documented elsewhere (e.g. Cohen 1990; Meehl 1978, 1990). In academic psychology, for example, the research paradigm originally established more than a century ago by Fechner, Weber, and Wundt (see Stigler 1986), which has exerted great influence to this day, was physicalistic, mechanistic, elementistic, and universalistic. This paradigm was at least partially inspired by a self-conscious desire to appear more scientific by identification with the indubitably more prestigious field of physics. As has also been documented elsewhere (Brunswik 1952, 1955; Petrinovich 1979, 1989), this physicalistic paradigm resulted in the incorporation of a model for both theory and research in psychology that has historically proven itself catastrophically inappropriate to a biological science (Mayr 1982).

The hallmark of this approach in the pragmatics of research was the ideal of the completely randomized and controlled single-variable experiment, or where possible, its logical extension, the fully crossed orthogonal factorial design. The supporting technology was the maximization of experimental variance, the minimization of error variance, and the control of extraneous variance, concisely summarized by the expression *maxmincon* (Kerlinger 1973). The hallmark of this approach in the construction of theory was a brute force inductivistic, automatized, and mechanistic search for ways to manipulate behavior systematically without the necessity for understanding it (Cohen 1990). Although the gritty realities of program evaluation fortunately prevented anyone from actually implementing these sterile procedures, the ideals of this research tradition were nonetheless quite influential. Program evaluation developed in the shadow of this reflected glory, as poor relations of the experimentalists. Indeed, even the contemporary literature on quasi-experimentation still shows this apologetic streak (e.g. Cook & Campbell 1979). Arguably, for quasi-experimentation, the more powerful and sophisticated intellectual engines of causal inference are superior, by now, to those of the experimental tradition.

The inappropriate research methodology, however, through its obvious impracticability in the field, did the least damage of all because it was quickly superseded by the methodological ingenuity of the quasi-experimentalists. The conceptual grip retained was a world-view based on the ideology of Newtonian space. The metaphor of a "social physics," as some early enthusiasts dubbed it (see Stigler 1986), is explicitly patterned on that of celestial mechanics and the dynamics of nonliving material particles. The resultant image is of a mechanical universe governed by absolute and unalterable laws, made of indivisible and identical units, of a finite number of specifiable types, majestically floating along predetermined pathways in a limitless void. In Newtonian space, bodies in motion tend to remain in motion, and bodies at rest tend to remain at rest unless acted upon by an external force.

Was it mere naiveté that accounted for the initial failure of evaluation researchers to anticipate the complexities of social and political reality? These researchers were mentally prepared by the dominant Newtonian paradigm of social science for a bold exploration of the icy depths of interplanetary space. Instead, they found themselves completely unprepared for the tropical nightmare of a Darwinian jungle: A steaming green Hell, where everything is alive and keenly aware of you, most things are venomous or poisonous or otherwise dangerous, and nothing waits passively to be acted upon by an external force. This complex world is viciously competitive and strategically unpredictable because information is power, and power confers competitive advantage. The Darwinian jungle manipulates and deceives the unwary wanderer into serving myriads of contrary and conflicting ends. The sweltering space suits just had to come off.

For a simple illustration of the complicating ecology of social programs, let us make a schematic path model out of the typical story of any programmatic intervention. We often start by observing, in the world, that a certain outcome, *O1*, seems to be produced by a specific determinant, *D1*. This outcome produces a negative utility, *U1*, to a specified population, so we implement a given intervention, *I1*. Thus, *I1* is intended to influence *D1*, to reduce *O1*, to minimize *U1*. That is straight-line Newtonian thinking. The problem is that *O1* has other determinants, *D2* and *D3*, which *I1* does not affect. Or, worse, *I1* does affect *D2* and *D3*, but in counterproductive ways. Furthermore, *D1* has other, unanticipated outcomes, *O2* and *O3*, which *D2* and *D3* might also affect in unknown ways. It also turns out that *O1* has different utilities, *U2* and *U3*, to different populations of stakeholders, as, perhaps, do *O2* and *O3*. What is a Newtonian to do? We might strategically design interventions *I2* and *I3*, to adequately regulate the system, but this requires ecological, i.e. Darwinian, thinking. This abstract scenario may sound a bit farfetched, but concrete and recent examples of all of these (and worse) complex contextual effects in program evaluation were described in a recent American Evaluation Association Panel on this subject (Scott & Figueredo 1991).

CONCURRENT SOCIAL REVOLUTION

To add to the litany of woes resulting from ecological complexity, the social ecology in which program evaluation must operate has been undergoing a process of radical transformation during the development of the field. This transformation has changed not only the fundamental organization of the society around them, but the specific niche that program evaluators occupy within it. Thus, what program evaluators have been learning about social ecology has been changing all around them as they work. As a result, many views of the mechanisms of social action that were held decades ago now seem quaint and unrealistic. Perhaps they were, but perhaps not. It is quite possible that many such notions were originally valid in the context of an industrial society. When the practice of program evaluation was officially initiated in the 1960s, the shift toward a postindustrial information-based economy, and corresponding ways of thinking, had just begun. The succession of dominant ideas within the field may reflect not just a progressive maturation of thinking through experience, but an evolved adaptation to a changing social environment.

For example, it has been claimed (Lincoln & Guba 1985) that the so-called rational model of social decision-making is now dead and, with it, the role of the program evaluator as an intelligence agent (or, at least, information provider) for the defunct rational policymakers. But what precisely does that mean? Does it mean that decisions are now somehow to be made irrationally? If so, precisely what kind of information is now required for the making of irrational decisions?

Rejecting this *reductio ad absurdum,* we do not think that anyone really believes that modern humans have somehow lost their rational faculties in planning complex social strategy. What is really meant is that the so-called "rational decisions" are no longer considered the exclusive privilege of government bureaucrats who paternalistically decide what is best for everyone. It may be that everyone, government bureaucrats included, continues to pursue rational self-interests in social relations. What has changed is that the designs, implementations, outcomes, and assigned utilities of social programs are no longer seen as necessarily serving any single set of interests, public or private, rational or otherwise. By implication, program evaluators are not exclusively beholden to any monolithic set of interests, objectives, or policymakers. Their clientele is the entire social network involved in and influenced by the social program, not just some specially empowered managerial hierarchy or elite. To call the interests and perspectives of all interested others irrational, by implication, reflects a transparent political ruse for continued domination by intellectual intimidation.

Another relevant change wrought by the postindustrial revolution is the blurring of the formerly clear distinction between producer and consumer. Because the postindustrial product is largely composed of information, feedback from the consumer has now become an integral part of the production process. As the distributor of that critical information, the program evaluator is now moving into an unprecedentedly powerful position in the postindustrial production process. The program evaluator, where fully integrated and utilized, has now literally become part of the social program itself, and not just an afterthought. The formative evaluation is an explicit example of this, but even the summative evaluation has become an implicit equivalent for future and related social programs. As a result of this and other social pressures, the Newtonian stance of complete impartiality has been explicitly abandoned by many program evaluators who have become active participants, and thus stakeholders in the social programs they evaluate. It would also be naive to think that program evaluators have not yet discovered any special interests of their own.

This diversity of interests, however, would be politically impotent were it not for the concomitant decentralization of the decision-making power and responsibility that characterizes postindustrial processes of production. This decentralization has all but made heterogeneity of treatment implementation a permanent fact of life. Indeed, many program evaluators no longer decry it as a failure of centralized program management and a threat to inferential validity, but rather exploit it as a productive source of experimental variance, which represents a potentially informative set of adaptations to and interactions with the heterogeneity of local molar conditions. With the centralization of program planning authority, the subsidiary doctrine of strict management accountability has also been lost because it has become nearly impossible to determine precisely who is to be held accountable for what. These economic and political developments are radically altering the social and ecological niche in which program evaluators operate. We propose that some of the changing practices observed in the discipline may at least partially reflect these pressures from a changing ambient social ecology.

EVALUATION IS NOT A FIELD

Neither program evaluation nor, as more broadly construed, evaluation, constitute a field of inquiry. Evaluation is an enterprise aimed at deciding the worth of various activities, and that enterprise comes equipped with a variety of assumptions and methods. As noted by Shadish et al (1991), we can evaluate anything. But if evaluation as an intellectual or professional activity is defined too broadly, it loses most of its usefulness in focusing attention and effort. A central set of issues exists with respect to program evaluation, and it is those we address in this review.

No cumulative body of substantive knowledge is attached specifically to evaluation. Thus, it would make no sense to try to review the findings of evaluation across fields of inquiry. For example, no more than idle curiosity would be satisfied by a review of programs that have been found effective in the past five years. Progress in evaluation is not to be measured by positive or negative findings any more than progress in statistics ought to be measured by the number of statistically significant findings reported in journals during some period. Progress in evaluation is to be measured in terms of advances in conceptualization of the enterprise and in improvements in methods for realizing its aims.

It is questionable whether program evaluation is cumulative, or at least whether cumulation of knowledge is proceeding with any rapidity. An investigation of the references in Shadish et al (1991), started at a more or less random point, revealed that of the next 130 references only 5 were dated 1988 or later; 58 were dated 1979 or earlier. A similar check of 130 references (starting at a different alphabetical point) in Chen (1990) showed that only 11 references were from 1987 or later; 75 were from 1979 or earlier. Checks of two current textbooks (Posavec & Carey 1989; Rossi & Freeman 1989) showed similarly small proportions of citations of recent material. Just by contrast, a check of a textbook in health psychology (Serafino 1990), picked more or less randomly from the shelf, showed that 37 of 130 references were dated 1987 or later, and only 26 were dated more than 10 years prior to the publication date of the book. We suspect that the dearth of recent citations in program evaluation reflects (*a*) the relative irrelevance of specific program evaluation outcomes, (*b*) the slow pace of development of new research designs and methods, and (*c*) lack of recognition of the important contributions from new developments in statistics and data analysis.

Results of evaluation studies, i.e. actual attempts to determine worth, are reported in virtually the full spectrum of social science journals. In fact, only a small proportion of evaluation findings could be reported in *Evaluation Review* (*ER*) or *New Directions in Program Evaluation*. Of 44 articles that appeared in Volume 4 (1980) of *ER,* only 15 had the primary purpose of reporting evaluation outcomes as opposed to proposing methodological improvements (24 articles) or clarifying concepts (4 articles). Still under the same editorship as in 1980, *ER* currently seems even less likely to contain articles whose primary purpose is to report outcomes of evaluation efforts, both because fewer, albeit somewhat longer articles, are being accepted and because whole issues are being devoted to special topics. In 5 numbers of Volume 15 of *ER* (Number 6 was a special issue on correcting of biases in voting rights cases) only two articles appeared to have as their primary purpose the reporting of an outcome of an evaluation; 15 articles were primarily methodological in nature, and 1 additional article concerned conditions of utilization of evaluation findings. *New Directions in Program Evaluation* also does not often publish the results of evaluations.

We conclude that current publication policies in core evaluation journals show a preference for methodological and conceptual articles and relegate evaluation reports either to specialized subject matter journals or to the fugitive literature represented by technical reports and government documents. One consequence is that most persons working in evaluation may only infrequently see a full-fledged evaluation report. Even worse, they may rarely see an exemplary report, a model to follow in their own work or to use in teaching and training activities.

The foregoing indicates that a useful review of evaluation must be directed at determining advances, if any, in conceptual frameworks and methods for evaluation. Reviews of evaluation findings are the provinces of individual fields in which the evaluations have been undertaken.

THE QUALITATIVE MOVEMENT

Evaluation began as an unabashedly quantitative enterprise. Early leaders in the field—D. T. Campbell, L. J. Cronbach, P. Rossi, R. J. Light, C. Weiss, for example—had in mind that evaluation would take advantage of the methods of research and analysis prevalent in the most prestigious domains of social science. It should be remembered, though, that in 1974 Donald T. Campbell gave an address at the American Psychological Association meetings entitled "On Qualitative Knowing in Action Research." That event was four years prior to the publication of Patton's (1978) *Utilization-Focused Evaluation,* arguably the first widely disseminated plea for qualitative evaluation, although Guba (1978) had a monograph in that same year. Patton's *Qualitative Evaluation Methods,* apparently the first textbook of its kind, was not published until 1980 (Patton 1980).

In the years since 1980, however, interest in qualitative approaches to evaluation has grown rapidly, perhaps sufficiently to justify identifying it as a movement. One index of that interest is that current membership in the Qualitative Topical Interest Group of the American Evaluation Association is now several times as large as that of the Quantitative Topical Interest Group, with only a small number of persons holding membership in both Groups (Sechrest 1992).

The question naturally arises why interest in qualitative approaches has developed so rapidly and so extensively. We do not believe that the answer can be found in any remarkable successes of qualitative evaluation. We have looked in vain for a qualitative evaluation that is widely cited as exemplary. We could find no instances of large social programs that have been qualitatively evaluated with national prominence given to the findings. (One reason for the latter may be, of course, that so few instances of large social programs can be found these days.) Qualitative evaluation seems confined to local efforts and to be directed more at improving ongoing programs than in determining their larger impact (e.g. Fetterman 1988, 1991). In his study of educational programs for gifted children Fetterman (1988) promises to describe "what does work" (p. xiv) in classrooms, but no criteria for how programs are to be judged are presented. For example, one cannot determine that children in the classes for the gifted are actually better off in the longer run for having been in them, let alone that other children in more ordinary classes are not harmed in any way.

Perhaps the qualitative movement can be seen as an alternative response to the social changes we have described, especially the changing roles and social context of the program evaluator. This variant response is evidenced by, among other things, the dissatisfaction expressed with the perceived limitations of traditional quantitative methods and the stronger emphasis placed upon multiple stakeholder interests and values. Unfortunately, the flight into qualitative methods can also be seen to reflect a reaction of despair at maintaining an analytic research program in the face of increasing social complexities. As will be detailed below, we believe that this reaction is unwarranted in the light of all the recent progress in the power and sophistication of multivariate quantitative models. Perhaps unlike the qualitative researchers, contemporary quantitative modelers might be up to the challenge of representing postmodern complexity without sacrificing analytical and scientific modes of thought.

If qualitative methods are ever going to be fully exploited, their methodologies must be better explicated, rationalized, and standardized. A critical property and advantage of many quantitative methodologies is that they are formulaic in nature. One need only follow the rules reasonably well in order to produce findings that have a reasonable probability of meeting with acceptance and of being repeatable. (This does not imply that competence is not an issue in quantitative evaluation, e.g. see Barkdoll 1992.) The same cannot be said for phenomenology, hermeneutics, critical analysis, and other qualitative methods. Their results appear likely to depend heavily on the outlook and skills of individual users. Whether ethnography should be considered standardized, or likely to become so, is open to question. Fetterman (1989) has made a useful effort toward standardization of ethnographic methodology for use in evaluation. Thus far, though, we agree with Chen (1990) that qualitative, or as he terms them, naturalistic, methods have not yet produced dependable and valid data.

Examples of the kinds of exegeses of qualitative methods that we consider exemplary are descriptions of grounded theory (Strauss & Corbin 1990) and case studies (General Accounting Office 1987). Whatever one might think about the ultimate usefulness of grounded theory methodology, Strauss & Corbin (1990) at least provide a comprehensive prescription for doing it. Grounded theory methodology is the most clearly formulated of the qualitative methods, and two conscientious investigators doing such studies would at least be able to communicate effectively the specific procedures followed and the stage of their work at any given time. Case studies may serve a variety of purposes in evaluation projects, but the methodology for doing them has been generally neglected (although see Yin 1984). Kazdin (1981) has made the case for applying the same questions about the validity of inferences from case studies as are usually asked about quasi-experiments, and the General Accounting Office (GAO) transfer paper (GAO 1987) provides an excellent framework within which to carry out most case studies. Qualitative research, like any other research, is worth doing well if it is worth doing at all.

Early discussions of the distinctions between quantitative and qualitative research in evaluation centered on their complementarity (Campbell 1974; Cook & Reichardt 1978). That is, the two approaches were seen as contributing different sorts of information bearing on the same general problem. Later works (e.g. Patton 1980, 1990) seemed to imply that qualitative methods might complement quantitative methods by focusing more on questions of process, such as whether interventions are properly implemented or whether results are likely to be differentially accepted by various stakeholder groups.

More recently, though, some writers have insisted that quantitative methods are completely outmoded and should be replaced by, not be complementary to, qualitative methods. These claims have been made especially insistently by Guba & Lincoln (1989) in their exposition of what they term "fourth generation evaluation." As yet no example of fourth generation evaluation seems to exist (at least not one so labeled); therefore one cannot tell exactly how such an evaluation might be carried out, or to what kinds of conclusions it might lead. Guba & Lincoln seem to believe, however, that highly satisfactory evaluations can be done without any intervention, any particular research design, any data collection (as it is ordinarily understood), or any form of quantitative analysis, let alone inferential statistics. They do intend, however, that the values of the investigator should be an integral feature of the evaluation although nothing in their book indicates that they recognize the possibility that some investigators might have politically and economically conservative values.

We believe that some proponents of qualitative methods have incorrectly framed the issue as an absolute either/or dichotomy. Many of the limitations that they attribute to quantitative methods have been discoursed upon extensively in the past. The distinction made previously, however, was not between quantitative and qualitative, but between exploratory and confirmatory research. This distinction is perhaps more useful because it represents the divergent properties of two complementary and sequential stages of the scientific process, rather than two alternative procedures. For example, Popper (1959) distinguished between the "context of discovery" and the "context of justification." In the context of discovery, free reign is given to speculative mental construction, creative thought, and subjective interpretation. In the context of justification, unfettered speculation is superseded by severe testing of formerly favored hypotheses, observance of a strict code of scientific objectivity, and the merciless exposure of one's theories to the gravest possible risk of falsification. That Popper clearly embraced both of these twin goals is evidenced by the slogan: "Boldness in conjecture, austerity in refutation." In reaction to what they perceive as an excess of the latter, some qualitative researchers appear to have become fixated at the earlier stage. Perhaps a compromise is possible in light of the realization that although rigorous theory testing is admittedly sterile and nonproductive without adequate theory development, creative theory construction is ultimately pointless without scientific verification.

Evaluations of any kind are done for purposes of influencing decisions and, in the case of social program evaluations, for influencing social policy. In the long run, the evaluations of evaluations must be in relation to their actual effect on social policy. Thus in the past 15 years there has been so much anguish over the question whether evaluation results are actually used in any way. (A Topical Interest Group in the American Evaluation Association, "Utilizing Evaluations," has even been formed around that question.) Thus, the fate of qualitative evaluation, including fourth generation evaluation, will lie in its persuasiveness. Of interest is that Strauss & Corbin (1990) specifically consider the credibility of grounded theory, and their criteria come down to, in our opinion, the credibility of the individual investigator.

What are qualitative evaluations like? The published works investigated are, for the most part, directed toward questions concerning values held by different stakeholders toward assumptions (to some extent theory) underlying interventions and toward implementation of interventions (process). Relatively little of the published material argues directly for conclusions about outcomes—did the program work or not? Qualitative evaluations are often surprisingly quantitative; it is just that their quantitative statements are imprecise. For example, instead of reporting that "55 percent of those interviewed said ...," the qualitative evaluation will simply say that "many of those interviewed said ... ." One of us (LS) was commenting to friends on his amusement that a report on a meeting of qualitative researchers persistently reported the exact number of persons in attendance at sessions. One listener noted that the difference is that, while a quantitative reporter would say "Only ten persons were present ...," a truly qualitative reporter would say, "Attendance at the session was depressing."

A case that illustrates some of the differences between the two camps is the differing conclusions about Jesse Jackson's program PUSH/Excel. A team was commissioned to do an evaluation of Jackson's program, which was receiving substantial federal funding. The relatively orthodox quantitative evaluation team came to distinctly negative conclusions about PUSH/Excel, not only because they could not find any evidence of consistently positive outcomes but because they could not identify a program. PUSH/Excel was promoted as a program with a set of central, organizing principles—a philosophy perhaps—meant to drive activities at many local sites. The evaluation team could not, however, find any consistent activities across sites; every site was different. Thus, the evaluators concluded that PUSH/Excel did not constitute a program suitable for federal funding. The leading critic of that evaluation was House (1988), a strong proponent of qualitative approaches to evaluation. The main thrust of House's critique, though, was not to produce counter evidence for the effectiveness of PUSH/Excel but to argue that the evaluators were wrong in insisting on trying to identify program elements consistent across sites in the first place. PUSH/Excel, in House's view, had to be allowed to develop variously to fit local conditions and resources; presumably it also had to be trusted to produce locally useful outcomes. What House never addressed in his critique was how Congress and others responsible for national policy and national funds were to decide about funding for programs that could not be specified and evaluated across sites. One cannot help but feel that the issues here, as in many other disagreements between evaluators of different persuasions, are matters of values rather than facts.

EVALUATIONS OF LARGE–SCALE SOCIAL PROGRAMS

Although evaluations of large-scale social programs do not seem as frequent as in the early years of program evaluation, the genre still exists. An example is the 1988 evaluation of a federal program to improve prospects of homeless persons for obtaining nutritious meals (Burt & Cohen 1988). Put simply, the intervention enabled homeless persons to use food stamps to purchase prepared meals from authorized providers. The evaluation plan required obtaining interview data on nationally representative samples of both homeless persons using the service and providers of the service. The samples were drawn from a nationally representative sample of 20 cities with populations of 100,000 or more; ultimately 1704 homeless persons and 381 providers were interviewed. In addition a sample of 142 homeless persons who had not used the meal service in the week prior to the interview were interviewed. Obviously, the study was meant to be more in the nature of a monitoring effort than an attempt to arrive at any penetrating causal inferences.

The research plan sounds simple, but the data needed were diverse and difficult to collect. The plan required data to be obtained on adequacy of meals in relation to both variety and nutritional content, on the sources of food served by providers, on the family status of the homeless persons, on their customary eating habits, on their use of food stamps, and many other issues. Presumably the fact that many (36%) of those persons using the meal service went at least one day per week with no food at all and that about a third of all the persons had had no contact at all with the food stamp program would have been useful to program planners. It is difficult to see how equally useful and persuasive information might have been obtained by other means, e.g. qualitative evaluation.

Large-scale national evaluation is not dead in the United States. Fourteen different programs to assess the potential value of providing housing services to homeless alcoholics are being implemented in thirteen cities across the nation (National Institute on Alcoholism and Alcohol Abuse 1990). Each of the separate programs has its own evaluation plan, but a national evaluation is also being carried out in an attempt to derive from all the separate programs and evaluations more general conclusions and recommendations. An important feature of the national evaluation is that each of the individual programs has been helped to develop a logic model for its efforts, i.e. a theory of the intervention (Lipsey 1990a). The logic models describe all the features of the intervention, whether they are mediating or moderating variables (Baron & Kenny 1986) that connect the planned treatments to the proposed outcomes. These models are then linked to data collection and analysis plans. Programs are encouraged to use some common measures and schedules for data collection. The national evaluation plan required the specification of an entirely separate research protocol, in fact, a separate design that will constitute a meta-analysis of individual program results. This monumental effort, sponsored by the National Institute on Alcoholism and Alcohol Abuse, will be worth following closely as it may constitute a model for national evaluations that could be widely emulated.

PROGRAM EVALUATION: THE FUNDAMENTAL ISSUES

Shadish et al (1991) provide a potentially useful conceptual scheme for thinking about approaches (theory) to program evaluation, but their ideas also provide a more general framework for carrying out program evaluations and for research directed at improving that enterprise. Five fundamental issues are at the heart of practical program evaluation (Shadish et al 1991, p. 32):

> 1. Social programming: how social programs and policies develop, improve, and change, especially in regard to social problems;
> 2. Knowledge construction: how researchers learn about social action;
> 3. Valuing: how value can be attached to program descriptions;
> 4. Knowledge use: how social science information is used to modify programs and policies;
> 5. Evaluation practice: the tactics and strategies evaluators follow in their professional work, especially given their constraints.

These five points, in fact, encompass most of the activity in program evaluation today.

Social Programming and Theory-Driven Evaluation

The first issue is the focus on "theory driven evaluation" (Chen 1990; Chen & Rossi 1987, 1989). Many programs of social amelioration were launched with little thought to how they might actually have produced the expected effects. Moreover, when the programs were indifferently or even poorly implemented, as was almost always the case, no basis existed for determining the seriousness of departures from the original plans. In particular, Chen & Rossi advocate the explicit use of social science theory in order to devise, assess, and revise social programs. The longer range success of their prescription remains to be seen, but recent issues of *New Directions for Program Evaluation* have shown a distinct increase in emphasis on theory (e.g. Bickman 1990; Rog 1991), even when Chen & Rossi are not explicitly mentioned (e.g. Heilman 1991; Larson & Preskill 1991; Leviton et al 1990). Systematic application of social science theory could not help but be of some benefit both in the planning and evaluation of social programs, but for many social problems, e.g. drug addiction, crime, child abuse, domestic violence, the poverty of theory will be as evident as the theory of poverty.

Lipsey (1990a) argues strongly for more attention to theory of intervention as a complement to methodology. Under many circumstances, strong theory can compensate for relatively weak method. For example, strong theory can enable the development of more effective treatment, better measures, and more specific predictions about the exact circumstances under which effects are to be found. To argue, for example, that standardized outcome measures do not capture program effects (e.g. Hennessy & Grella 1992), is only helpful if alternative measures can be specified in advance. Theory helps to identify the focal and differential effects of treatments, saving both conceptual and statistical degrees of freedom.

Epistemology for Program Evaluation

The second critical issue raised by Shadish et al (1991), knowledge construction, is epistemological in nature: how do researchers obtain dependable knowledge about social programs. Perhaps it is an exaggeration to suggest that controversy rages, but the differences between those who urge rigorous and fundamentally quantitative approaches to evaluating social programs and those who urge more flexible and qualitative approaches are large and difficult to reconcile. As noted above, from the earliest years of program evaluation, it was assumed that both quantitative and qualitative information would be used in complementary ways to enhance understanding of programs and their effects. One has only to read the chapter titled "Approximations to knowledge" (Webb et al 1966), which was written early in the program evaluation movement, to have evidence of the commitment to multiple sources of knowledge. It is the recent insistence that qualitative evaluations can substitute for quantitative evaluations that is new (Guba & Lincoln 1989). This insistence is coupled with an increasing preoccupation with qualitative methods and their applications, and not accompanied by any concern at all for complementary quantitative data. None of three recent methodological books encouraging the use of qualitative methods for evaluation makes more than passing mention of any value of quantitative methods and data (Crabtree & Miller 1992; Fetterman 1989; Patton 1990).

Values and Evaluation

Valuing, the third issue listed by Shadish et al (1991), is related to another current and important controversy in program evaluation. Specifically, the issue is whether evaluation is, or ever could be, value free, and if it is not, whether evaluation should not operate openly in the service of particular values. Some writers (e.g. Guba & Lincoln 1989; House 1990; Sirotnik 1990) insist that evaluation can never be value free. Choice of perspectives, criteria, measures, methods, etc must necessarily reflect values. Therefore, these writers urge, evaluators should be partisan and carry out evaluations in the service of values. These writers also, however, seem to have a clear idea of which values should be served: Justice is the most frequently mentioned example.

Many conceptions of justice exist (Nozick 1974), but those writing about evaluation who insist on the explicit incorporation of values into the activity obviously have in mind a politically liberal version. Advocating the incorporation of values into program evaluation risks the very kind of partisanship that has aroused so much anger toward recent political regimes for their biased reviews of programs and policies.

It is not always easy to determine what the valuing controversy is all about. Early in the establishment of program evaluation as a formal enterprise, it was thought that evaluators would try to answer such questions as "Does this reading program improve reading skills?" or "Does this job training program help people get jobs?" Meta-questions such as "Why should these children be educated in a system that does not teach them to read by ordinary methods?" or "Where is the justice in a system that does not provide people with an adequate standard of living whatever their job status?" were scarcely imagined. The task of the evaluator was imagined rather like that of an appraiser who would give an objective estimate of the value of a piece of jewelry but who would not expect to be asked to give a special allowance for its sentimental value.

House (1990), to take but one example, seems to argue that the approach taken to the evaluation of two social programs, Follow Through and PUSH/Excel, were miscarriages of justice on largely sentimental grounds: The programs were for disadvantaged, largely minority populations and should have been valued for that reason. Nowhere in his critique of the evaluations does he provide any other basis for concluding that funding for the programs should have been continued, e.g. that they really were effective. Program evaluation may have to begin with values, but it will have to demonstrate objectivity if it is to retain any credibility at all.

Use of Program Evaluation Findings

The fourth issue raised by Shadish et al (1991) is knowledge use. The question whether program evaluation findings are used in any way once they are produced is one that has plagued the field since its beginning. For example, Weiss (1966) was writing about the problem well before the Evaluation Research Society was ever established. Early assumptions that evaluators would provide results of program evaluations to policymakers, who would then enact policies in accord with the results, now appear almost amusingly naive. On the other hand, that evaluation results would have had by this time such limited, irregular, and sometimes even perverse effects on social policy would likely have appalled the founders of program evaluation. Although such concepts as "enlightenment," proposed by Weiss (1977) and accepted by various other writers, have helped in understanding the complex relationships between evaluation results and public policy, it is still true that little can be stated with any confidence about the utilization of program evaluation findings, especially since much of the utilization that does occur may be conceptual rather than direct (Rossi & Freeman 1989).

Of special interest is the fact that most writing about utilization of program evaluation findings centers on public (usually national) policy. Very little is known about utilization of program evaluation results at state and local levels of government, and as far as we can tell, nothing at all may be known, at least systematically, about utilization of program evaluation results in the private sector. This is probably true in part because program evaluation in the private sector is proprietary and much of it is never published. Nonetheless, given that the private sector may be less political and somewhat less complex than the public policy sector, evaluation findings might have greater impact there. This is a prospect that merits examination and from which important lessons might be learned.

Evaluation Activities

The final issue mentioned by Shadish et al (1991) is evaluation practice: the specific activities carried out by program evaluators. Central to this issue, aside from the controversy over quantitative and qualitative approaches to evaluation, is formative versus summative evaluation. As originally conceived by Scriven (1967), formative and summative evaluation were two parts of the same process. Formative activities were those that guided program development to produce the best version possible of an intervention. Summative evaluation was then expected to follow in order to determine whether the best version possible had effects commensurate with original goals and with the costs and efforts required to produce the intervention. Summative evaluation was, though, hard to do. Determining whether programs worked required supporting a causal inference and, thus, a strong research design, careful attention to sample size and statistical power, and so on. Summative evaluation also required a commitment over a considerable period of time to the program and often to the evaluation itself. Finally, summative effects did not occur instantly. Unfortunately, evaluators and perhaps those commissioning their work have moved much in the direction of formative evaluation, which is, at least on a superficial level, easier. We admit that our assertion that evaluation has moved toward formative evaluation is a judgment, and in no way establishes that move with any certainty since published articles are a biased sample. We do not think it likely, though, that publication bias operates against summative evaluation. Three recent issues of *New Directions for Program Evaluation* aimed at evaluating training programs (Brinkerhoff 1989), AIDS prevention (Leviton et al 1990), and programs for the homeless (Rog 1991) do not contain a single article reporting outcomes of programs. This absence of material related to outcomes may be appropriate for the publication; nevertheless it is consistent with our point. Other evidence that leads us to believe that evaluators have shifted toward formative evaluations is the rapid growth of the Topical Interest Group on "Qualitative Methods" in the

AEA. Also an examination of the titles of papers from 12 randomly selected paper sessions of the 1991 meeting of the AEA, turned up only 12 of 51 titles that suggested that the papers might actually be reporting summative evaluation data.

We argued above that the ecology of evaluation has changed and, along with it, the roles and positions of evaluators and the nature of their activities. It is probably not in the nature of organizations and systems to seek summative evaluation of their own activities. The results of summative evaluation and even the rationale for doing it at all call into question the very reasons for existence of the organizations involved. Formative evaluation, by contrast, simply responds to the question, "How can we be better?" without strongly implying the question, "How do you know you are any good at all?" One has only to search for summative studies of university education, of which there are very few, to be reminded that even organizations with a tradition of intellectual inquiry have very little interest in evaluating themselves by their basic premises. Hence, if the relative prevalence of formative evaluation activities is increasing, relatively more evaluators may be employed within organizations that are commissioning the evaluations.

Still, we cannot escape the feeling that there has been, to some extent, a flight into qualitative, formative evaluation and away from the rigors of more quantitative, summative evaluation (Sechrest 1992). But we suspect also that focusing on formative evaluation helps to avoid the disappointments of summative evaluation. Rossi (1990) notes that, "Indeed, a good case can be made for the proposition that the expected value of the outcome of an impact assessment is zero or close to it" (p. 8). That expectation virtually guarantees that summative evaluation will be a discouraging activity. Even if formative evaluation is not easier to do, the findings are more comforting. Whatever else, one will at least be able to conclude that the program can be improved!

Program Development

In the 1970s, Tharp & Gallimore (1979) developed a model for program development, which they called the evaluation succession model. The model was seen as analogous to the biotic process (sere) by which a forest matures through a series of stages until finally reaching a climax stage of stability. Tharp & Gallimore postulated a similar progression for the development of effective social programs, and over a ten-year period they were able to construct a highly effective educational program for Hawaiian children. For example, their program increased reading scores of Hawaiian children from a very low level to a level about average for U.S. norms. Their program development process required use of the full array of research methods, data collection techniques, and so on. The process was iterative: At each step data from the previous step were fed back into the system to direct change and refinements. Although extensive use was made of the qualitative procedures, such as interviews and observations, and of formative evaluation approaches, summative (outcome) evaluations were required on a regular basis to determine the effectiveness of each successive version of the program. It is well known that the highly successful *Sesame Street* television program was developed by a similar iterative model of testing, feedback, and revision.

Unfortunately, the admirable model of Tharp & Gallimore appears to have gone unemulated. By and large, we are still at the level of either tinkering internally with programs by means of formative evaluation (without sufficient demonstration that the programs are effective) or conducting summative evaluations on one-shot programs (that are usually ineffective) and then proceeding to the next program. Why has the grand scheme of Tharp & Gallimore not caught on? First, their work is surprisingly little known in program evaluation, and awareness of the potentially far-reaching implications of their work is virtually zero. Two of the most recent textbooks in program evaluation (Posavac & Carey 1989; Rossi & Freeman 1989) do not even mention the Tharp & Gallimore project, although it remains one of the most successful intervention programs. The basic intervention program is proving highly effective in improving school performance of children in a Hispanic community in Los Angeles (R. Gallimore, personal communication, 1991). The second reason for the neglect of their model is more understandable: Their approach required ten years of continuing commitment and support from the funding agency and a matching commitment from the investigators. Few agencies, certainly not those of government, are in a position to make that kind of long term commitment and few investigators would be able and willing to stick with the same project for ten years, especially over the first several rather discouraging years. Still, if we are going to develop programs that are truly effective in our society, we must get beyond the notion of a quick fix, which is often implicit in our work. Tharp & Gallimore's funding agency, the Bishop Trust, in effect said, "We are going to solve this problem," not "Let's see if this idea works."

The essence of Tharp & Gallimore's evaluation succession is that one learns from one's mistakes. They started off their first year with what they thought was a reasonably good reading program. When that program proved a dismal failure, they did not set about finding another program to test. They asked themselves why what seemed like a good idea did not work at all, and they also asked other people, e.g. teachers, parents, even children. Then they built that feedback into the second year of their program, in the meantime also carrying out small-scale, controlled experiments of specific program elements. All over the country, shock incarceration is being tried as a way of getting youthful criminal offenders out of the criminal justice system and back into society. Predictably, it will prove disappointing in its outcomes, and equally predictably the response will be to close down the units and cast about for something else to do. Since shock incarceration is not a totally illogical intervention, and since it showed some promise in some places, a better response might be to try to figure out why it does not seem to work as well as expected and then, perhaps, try new versions of it, e.g. with better selection of candidates, better training of instructors, revised training schedule. Most of our social problems are of extreme difficulty. They will require commensurately strong efforts to deal with them, and program evaluation has, among its other important roles, the responsibility for giving policymakers the best information possible about the efforts that will be required.

Prospective Evaluation

Many children who are the offspring of disabled parents, e.g. drug addicts, mental patients, end up as public charges, although many others are taken in and cared for by relatives. A few years ago, it occurred to someone in New York that if more children were taken in by their relatives, the children would likely be better off and public expense for them would be reduced. Accordingly, a regulation was enacted that offered to pay relatives to take care of otherwise homeless children. The pay was fairly substantial but in line with responsibilities and savings to the public. In fairly short order the scheme collapsed because of extraordinarily high costs, which were way beyond what had been imagined. Suddenly people who had been taking care of children at their own expense wanted to be paid the same as anyone else. It is even likely that new cases were created when the natural mothers of children were forced out of their homes when it became apparent that their absence would result in a considerable increase in family income.

Could the result of the New York policy not have been foretold? In hindsight, exactly what happened seems an inescapable outcome. History is littered with stories of social interventions that did not have their intended effects or that had effects quite different from those intended, sometimes disastrous effects. The Program Evaluation and Methodology Division (PEMD) of the U.S. GAO is often asked by Congress to forecast the result of some program or policy change; they developed a process called "prospective evaluation" (GAO 1989c) to formalize the way they go about that task. The paper on prospective evaluation prepared by PEMD staff is a landmark in program evaluation. Much has yet to be learned about how to do prospective evaluations, but there is no reason to shirk the task. Prevention is better than cure, and if ways can be found to avert investments in ineffective or harmful programs, everyone will be better off.

New Evaluation Horizons

The title of this section is the same as the theme chosen for the 1991 meeting of the American Evaluation Association. That theme was meant to reflect the fact that the scope of evaluation has extended well beyond its original boundaries of public social programs. As noted, the concept of evaluation knows almost no bounds, and the methods employed are, for the most part, widely applicable and adaptable. Although not alone in doing so, the PEMD has been particularly notable for the increasing breadth of its evaluation efforts. The

USDA's commodity program, quality of the Federal workforce, the Paperwork Reduction Act, immigration policy, and accidental shootings have all been subjects of recent GAO/PEMD reports (GAO 1988a,b, 1989b, 1990c, 1991a). But PEMD has gone beyond even these areas to the evaluation of such physical systems as traffic congestion, hazardous waste management, highway safety, medical devices, and smart highways (GAO 1990b–e, 1990f, 1991b). A good bit of the work of GAO/PEMD is actually meta-evaluation, i.e. evaluation of the procedures by which other government agencies carry out their evaluations (GAO 1989c). Although GAO/PEMD is, perhaps, uniquely positioned to extend evaluation activities so greatly, other groups and persons could follow their lead, to the benefit of all concerned.

One of the consequences of extending evaluation to new areas is that one gets a sense of which issues and problems are general in nature and which may be limited to one or another area. Thus far, the issues and problems in evaluation appear much more general than specific. Proper specification of independent variables, construct validity of dependent variables, justifying causal inferences, and so on, are problems just as troubling in new areas as in the traditional ones of social services.

MULTIVARIATE METHODS IN PROGRAM EVALUATION

As noted elsewhere (Sechrest 1992), it is ironic that so much emphasis should now be placed on qualitative methods just when the development of quantitative methods is catching up to the demands of the complex tasks involved in program evaluation. Causal modeling with latent variables, growth curve analysis, regression-discontinuity analysis, and common factor measurement models are but a few examples of recent statistical developments or important improvements. These and other methods are now making it possible for data analysts to deal effectively with longitudinal data, unbalanced designs, multiple measures, and so on. Increased statistical sophistication, along with a much improved understanding of many of the basic design and logical issues put quantitative researchers in good position to respond to the challenges that qualitative methods are supposed to address.

It would be easy to exaggerate the influence of the philosophy of science on the everyday conduct of research, especially in program evaluation. By all the evidence, little of the research in program evaluation has been clearly guided by any particular philosophy of science. "Pointed in the right direction," might be about as far as one ought to go. Nevertheless, over the years the dominant philosophy of program evaluation has been Popper's, with its emphasis on falsification, i.e. the quest for residual truth. The time appears right for some reorientation.

Einhorn & Hogarth (1986) helped to clarify thinking about causality by showing the correspondence between everyday judgments of probable cause and both philosophical and empirical literature on the topic. A notable feature of their position is that causality becomes a positive rather than a residual inference. Cordray (1986) has elaborated on those ideas by suggesting that our usual criteria for positing causal relationships are impoverished. The situation is made worse by the inclination to treat quasi-experiments as only impoverished versions of true experiments rather than exploiting quasi-experiments fully for the information they do contain.

The change of emphasis advocated, then, is from a focus on ruling out rival causes or plausible rival hypotheses to a relatively stronger emphasis on ruling in causes, i.e. production of evidence and argument that makes our favored cause a plausible explanation for the data. In effect, this is what causal modeling attempts to do. The task of ruling in a cause may require casting our nets a bit wider for relevant evidence; it also puts more weight on theory. In the long run, though, we wish to generalize about causal relationships (Cook 1990), and these generalizations will best be supported by positive affirmation of the causal relationships. The good news is that increasingly powerful computers and statistical packages now offer researchers a wide range of statistical analyses capable of handling the large numbers of cases and variables required by an ecological systems approach. The bad news is that certain problems emerge from this cornucopia of statistical possibilities. Foremost among these is the possibility that researchers will end up using statistical analyses with little familiarity with their underlying assumptions and functional limitations. The use of unfamiliar statistical packages and procedures may, in turn, lead to inappropriate statistical analyses and unwarranted conclusions. The resulting problems can be very serious indeed, especially when conclusions are relevant to public policies. Another potential problem is that even technically competent researchers may become so immersed in and enamored of these new statistical techniques that their applications may cease to be the means to valid scientific ends and may instead become compulsive technological ends in themselves. One should avoid the technological imperative to apply them at every opportunity, regardless of the relative propriety of the occasion.

In order to support our strong claims with some concrete practical guidance, we review several of the more promising statistical options now available for the analysis of multiple predictors, multiple outcomes, multiple stakeholder utilities, and multiple independent replications.

Multiple Predictor Variables

Although widely accepted as a useful statistical tool, multiple regression/correlation analysis is fraught with dangers in estimating effect sizes when one uses a large number of predictor variables in the linear equation. For example, it is highly unlikely that a large number of naturally occurring predictors will be statistically independent. When two or more variables are relatively highly correlated, the statistical estimation method of squared error minimization used in multiple regression is incapable of sorting out their independent effects on the dependent variable. This condition is referred to as multicollinearity

(Pedhazur 1982) and results in highly unstable regression coefficients. Fortunately, useful diagnostic procedures for detecting multicollinearity exist (Pedhazur 1982; Cohen & Cohen 1983).

Because the least squares estimation procedure is unable to determine the independent effect of each variable, regression coefficients may be obtained that are actually: (*a*) higher than, (*b*) lower than, or (*c*) in a completely different direction from the bivariate correlation coefficient. Moreover, when correlations with another variable are nearly equal for two predictors, regression coefficients will be unstable across samples as first one predictor variable, then the other, happens to have the highest bivariate correlation (e.g. see Bingham et al 1991). Thus, correlated variables fed indiscriminately into a multiple regression equation may result in highly unstable and uninterpretable regression coefficients. Furthermore, serious possibilities of error lie in the interpretation of these unstable coefficients in regard to policy decisions (Figueredo et al 1991). Another substantial problem in using a large number of predictor variables in a multiple regression analysis is the possibility that coefficients may be reported as significant due to *alpha slippage*. Alpha slippage, sometimes known as capitalization on chance, can occur when testing large numbers of variables. The influence of multicollinearity and alpha slippage, although difficult to estimate, may cast considerable doubt on the validity and reliability of the final coefficients obtained by multiple regression.

Some researchers have fallen into the trap of using exploratory techniques of model specification, such as stepwise regression, to obtain a subset of predictors that can serve as proxies for the larger set through multicollinearity. The function of data reduction could be better served, however, not by using exploratory techniques of model specification, but by employing a common factor modeling technique. These multivariate methods capitalize on the problems of multiple regression by using the common variance, or multicollinearity, between predictor variables to construct hypothetical common factors, or latent variables, of which the measured variables are only manifest indicators. Hence, a large number of variables could be concisely represented by a few discriminable common factors; this would reduce the problem of alpha slippage and avoid the multicollinearity problems of multiple regression, while providing a parsimonious explanation of the phenomena. Another benefit of common factor modeling is that certain indicators that are clearly codetermined by more than one causal influence can be modeled as factorially complex, i.e. they indicate more than one hypothetical construct. By use of latent variable causal modeling, a factor analytic structural equation model can then be constructed in order to predict the outcomes of interest. At the very least, testing a common factor model can greatly facilitate understanding a complex data set. For instance, the inmate classification scale analyses reported by Bereccochea & Gibbs (1991) involved sets of 28 and 37 variables and a final set of 23 scorable items, developed by univariate tests and multiple logistic regressions. Because of weak theory and minimal data reduction, the final results are difficult to comprehend at any level of abstraction. Thus, an interpretable explanation need not be sacrificed for mere prediction as a goal of the analysis, and a conceptual virtue can be made out of a computational necessity.

Multiple Outcome Variables

In program evaluation, it is often the case that the multiple outcomes of a programmatic intervention need to be assessed. Moreover, these dependent variables are often selected to measure the impact of the intervention on several conceptually distinct outcomes rather than converge upon a single construct. Thus, multivariate data reduction methods, such as common factor modeling, may not be appropriate. Even where common factor modeling is appropriate, there remains the question how then to deal with the multiple dependent common factors that one has constructed. Because the programmatic intervention may exert a common causal influence on these multiple outcomes, whether manifest or latent, the dependent variables are likely to be at least spuriously correlated with each other. In addition, the multiple outcomes may also subsequently exert various causal influences on each other. Thus, separate causal analyses for each of these dependent variables may also not be appropriate.

Several statistical procedures are available for the analysis of multiple correlated dependent variables. One of these is structural equations modeling, or confirmatory path analysis, in which the hypothesized causal network between outcomes can be fully specified, estimated, and tested. This method, however, requires the guidance of a strong causal theory, which is often not available in program evaluation. Another multivariate method is simultaneous canonical analysis, which requires little theory. This method, however, produces empirically derived linear composites of dependent variables, or canonical variates, which are almost always difficult to interpret pragmatically in terms of concrete outcomes.

A third alternative is sequential canonical analysis, which combines some of the advantages of the previous two procedures. Rather than combining all dependent variables into uninterpretable linear composites, as in simultaneous regression of independent variables, it partitions their covariance sequentially, as in hierarchical regression, while maintaining their separate identity. This method isolates the direct effects of the independent variables or interventions sequentially on each of the dependent variables or outcomes, controlling for all indirect effects through the prior dependent variables. Because the only theoretical guidance required is a tentative specification of the causal order between the dependent variables, this sequential method is currently being developed into an exploratory form of path analysis (Gorsuch & Figueredo 1991).

One example of a potential application of sequential canonical analysis is the study of a juvenile justice program (Land et al 1990), which involved three outcome variables: delinquent offenses, status offenses, and judged overall success of the case. In the reported study, these three outcomes were separately analyzed as univariate indicators. A sequential canonical analysis would perhaps have determined first whether the intervention affected status offenses, then whether there was a significant residual effect on delinquent offenses after adjusting for status offense differences, and then whether judged success had a significant residual after removing any effect on delinquent offenses.

Multiple Utility Functions

In contrast to estimates of the relative effectiveness of programmatic interventions in producing specified objective outcomes, the estimates of the relative subjective utilities of those outcomes often used are only sometimes empirical in derivation, and then in varying degrees. One common index of utility is monetary cost (Kaplan 1985). Whereas few would recommend relying exclusively on money as the sole measure of utility, and thus (by default) the operational definition, most would recognize it as one important element in a multiple operationalization. Often, any nonmonetary outcome utilities are arbitrarily assigned, as when there is a clear and uncontroversial choice between outcomes with utilities of 1 and 0, such as life and death. Perhaps more often they are developed by consensus among a panel of expert judges. Technically, these judgments qualify as somewhat empirical estimates, but they may fail to hold up under critical scrutiny of methodological issues, such as parametric generalizability beyond the group of panel members sampled.

Quantifying utilities is the area of social decision-making that is least sophisticated in either methodological rigor or in just plain clear thinking about the nature of the problem. For example, assuming that adequate techniques are available for sampling utilities from a duly constituted representative sample, what precisely is the population of interest, or intended universe of generalization? One possible solution that has been suggested to this dilemma is to specify precisely what utilities are being estimated and what decision rules are being applied. A critical multiplist (Shadish 1989) alternative would be to simulate model predictions separately using the utilities obtained from different subject populations. Such substitution of values would constitute a kind of representative sensitivity analysis to the issue of what set of stakeholder interests are being considered. If they are to be applied as influential coefficients in our quantitative models, we need to know just what those numbers mean. If we do not know precisely what our assigned utilities represent, the whole result becomes uninterpretable.

Even with clear thinking on such thorny issues, there remain a number of quite formidable methodological obstacles to the very measurement of subjective utility. Unfortunately, psychological research has shown that many people are notoriously poor judges of numerical probability. Also, the alternatives posed in utility estimation are often also hypothetical: Subjects have had no direct experience with the outcomes in question. Another interesting feature of the current use of expected utility theory is that it appears to have been applied exclusively to the evaluation of discrete (e.g. binary) outcomes. There is, however, no immediately obvious mathematical reason to preclude its application to continuously graded outcomes. A certain degree of graded effect could be proportionately evaluated by a utility coefficient in much the same way that an all-or-nothing dichotomy is evaluated. Since the probabilities of discrete outcomes can be modeled as mere special cases of regression coefficients for which the criterion variables are dichotomous (Cohen & Cohen 1983), effect sizes from multiple regression analyses in general could perhaps be used to construct optimality models in which the graded levels of the dependent variables are weighted in such utility functions.

The graded equivalent of a discrete decision tree is a path model in which the multiplication of successive path regression coefficients in the computation of indirect effects is the exact functional equivalent of that of a series of Bayesian conditional probabilities. Utility coefficients could be represented as additional causal pathways to a single utility construct from all the dependent variables. This kind of continuous information might be even more difficult to obtain than the utilities of discrete outcomes. However, since a substantial proportion of the available parameter estimates of the effectiveness of means of intervention are reported in a continuous, rather than a discrete, metric, this adaptation would allow a more powerful and potentially widespread application of the benefits claimed for expected utility theory. The use of such decision-analytic path models is described more fully elsewhere (Sechrest & Figueredo 1992).

Despite the considerable attention paid to values in the literature on program evaluation, the concept of utility is almost completely missing. The notion of utility is, however, scarcely ever far from the surface of consciousness in evaluation studies. Utility refers to whatever comes after the immediate outcome of some intervention in terms of its impact on the lives of persons, organizations, communities. A drug to cure septicemia might well preserve many lives, but if many of those persons would be likely to die soon anyway of other problems, the drug might be regarded as successful but as having little utility. Suppose one developed a program that would keep some youth from dropping out of high school. But suppose one found that those students would not really be better off in any particular way for having finished high school. The latter involves the concept of utility. Few evaluation studies assess the utility of the programs that are the focus of interest.

Benefit-cost studies almost always seem to have disappointing results because the amount of money saved is scarcely ever more than marginally larger than the money spent. We would like to spend $1 on programs and get a return of $10. A more common result is $1.25. The reason for the low return is that monetized benefits tend to reflect utilities, the step(s) beyond immediate outcomes. That step represents an additional path in the path diagram and, hence, an extra multiplication. Even if the paths from intervention to outcome multiply out to .5, which would be a rather strong relationship, and if the relationship between outcome and utility is only .5, again a fairly strong relationship, then the overall path has a value of only .25. Put another way, variance in outcome accounted for of .25 is reduced to .06 variance in utility accounted for. Program evaluators may not like utility analyses when they get around to doing them.

Multiple Independent Replications

Meta-analysis of data sets is increasing in frequency and in influence on the field. The use of meta-analysis in program evaluation is likely to be somewhat restricted because of the relatively small number of programs that are ever tested in multiple sites and studies. Meta-analyses of medical and even psychological therapies often involve dozens of studies. Few social programs are likely to be tested so diversely. Too often the versions of interventions that are tested vary so greatly in almost all characteristics as to defy aggregation for purposes of meta-analysis. A partial exception is the ongoing multi-site study of programs for the homeless (National Institute for Alcohol Abuse and Alcoholism 1991). At least for those programs agreements were reached for some standardization of measures and for some common points of testing. A recent GAO report (GAO 1992) of unusual interest and potential importance offers new perspectives on synthesis of data across studies with different designs. In the long run, meta-analysis is likely to prove a good bit more useful for interpreting bodies of literature, e.g. for understanding our research and limitations on its generalizability, than for estimating overall effect sizes (Cordray 1990; Lipsey et al 1986).

One instructive meta-analysis (although it is nonquantitative) is the volume by Bloom et al (1988), for which they requested six papers summarizing evaluations of programs in six social problem areas. The editors then synthesized the lessons from across the six areas to produce the following five conclusions:

> 1. Effects of programs or policies are likely to be small but nonetheless may be quite important.
> 2. Treatments—even those that carry the same label—vary considerably. Looking inside the black box of treatment will help us to understand why programs succeed or not.
> 3. The effects of treatments are likly to vary substantially across the different target groups and locales.
> 4. Evaluations are often limited by small sample sizes, the implementation of weak and variable treatments, inadequate outcome variables, and poor research designs. These problems can be circumvented in many cases.
> 5. Results of individual, well executed evaluations contribute to our cumulative understanding of program theory, process, and outcomes.

Those five points sum up the current state of our knowledge of program evaluation.

Sechrest et al (1979) insisted quite some time ago that more attention should be paid to the concepts of strength and integrity of treatment and to their quantification. Although this idea is not yet ubiquitous, it may be catching on (e.g. see Chen 1990; Posavac & Carey 1989). Dennis and his colleagues (e.g. Dennis et al 1991) have been especially attentive to issues of strength and integrity of treatment in their evaluations of drug treatment programs. Quantification of strengths of social interventions would have the advantage of providing an important extra item of information in statistical analyses; intervention could be coded as a continuous rather than a binary variable. That would under many circumstances bring into play the concept of the dose-response relationship in outcome evaluations (Lipsey 1990). A second advantage of quantification of interventions would be much needed protection against Type 2 error in statistical conclusion validity. Low statistical power is as much a function of effect size as of sample size (Lipsey 1990), and if treatment strength were known to be low, failure to find an effect would not be as likely to be mistakenly attributed to ineffectiveness of the intervention.

RECENT DEVELOPMENTS IN THE PROFESSION OF PROGRAM EVALUATION

Just about the time of the last review in this series of program evaluation (Shadish & Cook 1986), the former Evaluation Research Society (ERS) and the Evaluation Network (ENet) merged to form the American Evaluation Association. That merger was not achieved without difficulty since it brought together a group (ERS) of predominantly academic and quantitative researchers with a group (ENet) often referred to as practitioners who are more interested in doing evaluation than in worrying about its theory and methods. A second signal event was the demise of the *Evaluation Studies Review Annual* (*ESRA*) with Volume 12 (Shadish & Reichardt 1987). Perhaps the ERS/ENet merger and the end of the *ESRA* are linked. *ESRA* was always a formidable volume that unquestionably appealed more to those evaluators with theoretical and methodological interests than to those with more pragmatic concerns. Indeed, it served as yearbook for the field (Shadish et al 1991), and the fact that it could not survive is not grounds for optimism about the future of the field. The AEA, itself, has languished to some extent, its membership hovering around the 2500 mark since its founding. Lack of growth in membership appears to reflect less the failure to recruit new members each year than the failure to retain the loyalties of enough of its members.

On the other hand, the AEA, in concert with the Canadian Evaluation Society, is planning the First International Congress on Evaluation, to take place in Vancouver, BC in 1995. Perhaps that international event may have a rejuvenating effect on the field.

Literature Cited

Alcock, J. 1989. *Animal Behavior: An Evolutionary Approach.* Sunderland, Mass: Sinauer.

Barkdoll, G. L. 1992. Strong medicine and unintended consequences. *Eval. Pract.* 13:53–57

Baron, R. M., Kenny, D. A. 1986. The moderator-mediator variable distinction in social psychological research: conceptual, strategic, and statistical considerations. *J. Pers. Soc. Psychol.* 51:1173–82

Bereccochea, J. E., Gibbs, J. B. 1991. Inmate classification: a program that works? *Eval. Rev.* 15:333–63

Bickman, L., ed. 1990. *Advances in Program Theory. New Directions for Program Evaluation,* No. 47. San Francisco: Jossey-Bass.

Bingham, R. D., Heywood, J. S., White, S. B. 1991. Evaluating schools and teachers based on student performance: testing an alternative methodology. *Eval. Rev.* 15:191–218

Bloom, H. S., Cordray, D. S., Light, R. J., eds. 1988. *Lessons from Selected Program and Policy Areas. New Directions for Program Evaluation,* No. 37. San Francisco: Jossey-Bass.

Brinkerhoff, R. O., ed. 1989. *Evaluating Training Programs in Business and Industry. New Directions for Program Evaluation,* No. 44. San Francisco: Jossey-Bass

Brunswik, E. 1952. The conceptual framework of psychology. In *International Encyclopedia of Unified Science,* ed. O. Neurath, R. Carnap, C. Morris, 1:655–760. Univ. Chicago Press

Brunswik, E. 1955. Representative design and probabilistic theory in a functional psychology. *Psychol. Rev.* 2:193–217

Burt, M. R., Cohen, B. E. 1988. *Feeding the homeless: does the prepared meals provision help? Rep. Congr. Prep. Meal Prov.,* Vol. 1. Washington, DC: The Urban Inst.

Campbell, D. T. 1974. On qualitative knowing in action research. In *Methodology and Epistemology for Social Science: Selected Papers of Donald T. Campbell,* ed. E. S. Overman, pp. 360–76. Chicago: Univ. Chicago Press

Chen, H. 1990. *Theory-Driven Evaluations.* Newbury Park, Calif: Sage. 336 pp,

Chen, H., Rossi, P. H. 1987. The theory-driven approach to validity. *Eval. Program Plan.* 10:95–103

Chen, H., Rossi, P. H. 1989. Issues in the theory-driven perspective. *Eval. Program Plan.* 12:299–306

Cohen, J. 1990. Things I have learned (so far). *Am. Psychol.* 45:1304–12

Cohen, J., Cohen, P. 1983. *Applied Multiple Regression/Correlation Analysis for the Behavioral Sciences.* Hillsdale, NJ: Erlbaum

Cook, T. D. 1990. The generalization of causal connections: multiple theories in search of clear practice. In *Research Methodology: Strengthening Causal Interpretations of Nonexperimental Data,* ed. L. Sechrest, E. Perris, J. Bunker, pp. 9–32. Rockville, MD: Agency Health Care Policy Res.

Cook, T. D., Campbell, D. T. 1979. *Quasi-Experimentation: Design and Analysis Issues for Field Settings.* Boston, Mass: Houghton Mifflin

Cordray, D. S. 1990. Strengthening causal interpretations of nonexperimental data: the role of meta-analysis. In *Research Methodology: Strengthening Causal Interpretations of Nonexperimental Data,* ed. L. Sechrest, E. Perrin, J. Bunker, pp. 151–72. Rockville, Md: Agency for Health Care Policy Res.

Crabtree, B. F., Miller, W. L., eds. 1992. *Doing Qualitative Research,* Vol. 3, *Research Methods for Primary Care.* Newbury Park, Calif: Sage

Dennis, M. L., Fairbank, J. A., Bonito, A. J., Rachal, J. V. 1991. *Treatment Process Study Design. Methadone Enhanced Treatment (MET) Trials Tech. Doc. 7.* Research Triangle Park, NC: Research Triangle Inst.

Einhorn, H. J., Hogarth, R. M. 1986. Judging probable cause. *Psychol. Bull.* 9:3–19

Fetterman, D. M. 1988. *Excellence and Equality: A Qualitatively Different Perspective on Gifted and Talented Education.* Albany: State Univ. New York Press

Fetterman, D. M. 1989. *Ethnography: Step by Step.* Newbury Park, Calif: Sage

Fetterman, D. M., ed. 1991. *Using Qualitative Methods in Institutional Research. New Directions for Institutional Research,* No. 72. San Francisco: Jossey Bass

Figueredo, A. J., Hetherington, J., Sechrest, L. 1991. Water under the bridge: A response to Bingham, Heywood, and White. *Eval. Rev.* 17:40–62

General Accounting Office 1987. *Case Study Evaluations. GAO/PEMD-87-9.* Washington, DC: US Gen. Account. Off.

General Accounting Office 1988a. *USDA's Commodity Program: The Accuracy of Budget Forecasts. GAO/PEMD-88-8.* Washington, DC: US Gen. Account. Off.

General Accounting Office 1988b. *Federal Workforce: A Framework for Studying Its Quality Over Time. GAO/PEMD-88-27.* Washington, DC: US Gen. Account. Off.

General Accounting Office 1989a. *Medical Devices: FDA's Implementation of the Medical Device Reporting Regulation. GAO/PEMD-89-10.* Washington, DC: US Gen. Account. Off.

General Accounting Office 1989b. *Paperwork Reduction: Mixed Effects on Agency Deci-*

sion Processes and Data Availability. GAO/PEMD-89-20. Washington, DC: US Gen. Account. Off.

General Accounting Office 1989c. *Prospective Evaluation Methods: The Prospective Evaluation Synthesis. GAO/PEMD-89-10.* Washington, DC: US Gen. Account. Off.

General Accounting Office 1990a. *Traffic Congestion: Federal Efforts to Improve Mobility. GAO/PEMD-90-2.* Washington, DC: US Gen. Account. Off.

General Accounting Office 1990b. *Hazardous Waste: EPA's Generation and Management Data Need Further Improvement. GAO/PEMD-90-3.* Washington, DC: US Gen. Account. Off.

General Accounting Office 1990c. *Immigration Reform: Major Changes Likely Under S358. GAO/PEMD-90-5.* Washington, DC: US Gen. Account. Off.

General Accounting Office 1990d. *Medical Device Recalls: Examination of Selected Cases. GAO/PEMD-90-6.* Washington, DC: US Gen. Account. Off.

General Accounting Office 1990e. *Highway Safety: Trends in Highway Fatalities 1975-87. GAO/PEMD-90-10.* Washington, DC: US Gen. Account. Off.

General Accounting Office 1991a. *Accidental Shootings: Many Deaths and Injuries Caused by Firearms Could Be Prevented. GAO/PEMD-91-9.* Washington, DC: US Gen. Account. Off.

General Accounting Office 1991b. *Smart Highways: An Assessment of Their Potential to Improve Travel. GAO/PEMD-91-18.* Washington, DC: US Gen. Account. Off.

General Accounting Office 1992. *Cross Design Synthesis: A New Strategy for Medical Effectiveness Research. GAO/PEMD-92-18.* Washington, DC: US Gen. Account Off.

Gorsuch, R. L., Figueredo, A. J. 1991. *Sequential canonical analysis as an exploratory form of path analysis.* Presented at Am. Eval. Assoc. Conf.: New Eval. Horizons. Chicago

Guba, E. G., Lincoln, Y. S. 1989. *Fourth Generation Evaluation.* Newbury Park, Calif: Sage

Heilman, J. G., ed. 1991. *Evaluation and Privatization: Cases in Waste Management. New Directions for Program Evaluation,* No. 51. San Francisco: Jossey-Bass

Hennessy, M., Grella, C. 1992. Evaluating "innovative" programs for homeless persons: case study of an unsuccessful proposal. *Eval. Pract.* 13:15–25

House, E. R. 1988. *Jesse Jackson and the Politics of Charisma: The Rise and Fall of the PUSH/Excel Program.* Boulder, Colo: Westview

House, E. R. 1990. Methodology and justice. See Sirotnik 1990, pp. 23–36

James, W. 1910. *Principles of Psychology.* Vol. I. New York: Holt

Kaplan, R. M. 1985. Quantification of health outcomes for policy studies in behavioral epidemiology. In *Behavioral Epidemiology and Disease Prevention,* ed. R. M. Kaplan, M. H. Criqui, pp. 31–54. New York: Plenum

Kazdin, A. E. 1981. Drawing valid inferences from case studies. *J. Consult. Clin. Psychol.* 49:183–92

Kerlinger, F. N. 1973. *Foundations of Behavioral Research.* New York: Holt, Rinehart & Winston

Land, K. C., McCall, P. L., Williams, J. R. 1990. Something that works in juvenile justice: an evaluation of the North Carolina Court Counselors' Intensive Protective Supervision Randomized Experimental Project, 1987–89. *Eval. Rev.* 14:574–606

Larson, C. L., Preskill, H., eds. 1991. *Organizations in Transition: Opportunities and Challenges for Evaluation. New Directions for Program Evaluation,* No. 49. San Francisco: Jossey-Bass

Leviton, L. C., Hegedus, A. M., Kubrin, A., eds. 1990. *Evaluating AIDS Prevention: Contributions of Multiple Disciplines. New Directions for Program Evaluation,* No. 46. San Francisco: Jossey-Bass

Lincoln, Y. S., Guba, E. G. 1985. *Naturalistic Inquiry.* Beverly Hills, CA: Sage

Lipsey, M. W. 1990a. Theory as method: small theories of treatments. In *Research Methodology: Strengthening Causal Interpretations of Nonexperimental Data,* pp. 33–52. Rockville, MD: Agency Health Care Policy Res.

Lipsey, M. W. 1990b. *Design Sensitivity: Statistical Power for Experimental Research.* Newbury Park, Calif: Sage

Lipsey, M. W., Crosse, S., Dunkle, J., Pollard, J., Stobart, G. 1986. Evaluation: the state of the art and the sorry state of the science. In *Evaluation Studies Review Annual,* ed. D. S. Cordray, M. W. Lipsey, 10:153–74. Beverly Hills: Sage

Mayr, E. 1974. Behavioral programs and evolutionary strategies. *Am. Sci.* 62:650–59

Mayr, E. 1982. *The Growth of Biological Thought: Diversity, Evolution, and Inheritance.* Cambridge, Mass: Harvard Univ. Press

Meehl, P. E. 1978. Theoretical risks and tabular asterisks: Sir Karl, Sir Ronald, and the slow progress of soft psychology. *J. Consult. Clin. Psychol.* 46:806–34

National Institute on Alcohol Abuse and Alcoholism. 1990. *Cooperative agreements for research demonstration projects on alcohol and other drug abuse treatment for homeless persons. RFA LA-90-01.* Washington, DC: Public Health Serv.

National Institute on Alcohol Abuse and Alcoholism. 1991. *National Evaluation Plan: Homelessness and Alcohol/Drug Abuse.* Rockville, MD: Natl. Inst. Alcohol Abuse and Alcoholism

Nozick, R. 1974. *Anarchy, State, and Utopia.* New York: Basic Books

Patton, M. Q. 1978. *Utilization-Focused Evaluation.* Beverly Hills, CA: Sage

Patton, M. Q. 1980. *Qualitative Evaluation Methods.* Beverly Hills, Calif: Sage

Patton, M. Q. 1990. *Qualitative Evaluation Methods and Research Methods.* Newbury Park, Calif: Sage

Pedhazur, E. J. 1982. *Multiple Regression in Behavioral Research: Explanation and Prediction.* New York: Holt, Rinehart & Winston

Petrinovich, L. 1979. Probabilistic functionalism: A conception of research method. *Am. Psychol.* 34:373–90

Petrinovich, L. 1989. Representative design and the quality of generalization. In *Everyday Cognition in Adulthood and Late Life,* ed. L. W. Poon, D. C. Rubin, B. A. Wilson, pp. 11–24. New York: Cambridge Univ. Press

Popper, K. 1959. *The Logic of Scientific Discovery.* New York: Basic Books. 479 pp.

Rog, D. J., ed. 1991. *Evaluating Programs for the Homeless. New Directions for Program Evaluation,* No. 52. San Francisco: Jossey-Bass

Rossi, P. H., Freeman, H. E. 1989. *Evaluation: A Systematic Approach.* Newbury Park, CA: Sage

Rossi, P. H. 1990. Foreword. See Chen 1990, pp. 7–10

Scott, A. G., Figueredo, A. J. 1991. Evaluating the ecological impact of social interventions. Discussed at Am. Eval. Assoc. Conf.: New Eval. Horizons. Chicago.

Scriven, M. 1967. The methodology of evaluation. In *Perspectives of Curriculum Evaluation,* ed. R. M. Tyler, R. M. Gagne, M. Scriven, pp. 39–83. Chicago: McNally

Sechrest, L. 1992. Roots: back to our first generations. *Eval. Pract.* 13:1–7

Sechrest, L., Figueredo, A. J. 1992. Approaches used in conducting outcomes and effectiveness research. In *A Research Agenda for Outcomes and Effectiveness Research,* ed. P. Budetti. Alexandria, Va: Health Adm. Press. In press

Sechrest, L., West, S. G., Phillips, M. A., Redner, R., Yeaton, W. 1979. Some neglected problems in evaluation research: strength and integrity of treatments. In *Evaluation Studies Review Annual,* ed. L. Sechrest, S. G. West, M. A. Phillips, R. Redner, W. Yeaton, 4:15–35. Beverly Hills, Calif: Sage

Serafino, E. P. 1990. *Health Psychology: Biopsychosocial Interaction .* New York: John Wiley

Shadish, W. R. Jr. 1989. Critical multiplism: a research strategy and its attendant tactics. In *Health Services Research: A Focus on AIDS,* ed. L. Sechrest, H. Freeman, A. Mulley, pp. 5–28. Rockville, MD: Agency Health Care Policy Res.

Shadish, W. R. Jr., Cook, T. D. 1986. Program evaluation: the worldly science. *Annu. Rev. Psychol.* 37:193–232

Shadish, W. R. Jr., Cook, T. D., Leviton, L. C. 1991. *Foundations of Program Evaluation: Theories of Practice.* Newbury Park, Calif: Sage

Shadish, W. R. Jr., Reichardt, C. S. 1987. *The Evaluation Studies Review Annual,* Vol. 12. Newbury Park, Calif: Sage

Sirotnik, K. A. 1990. Evaluation as critical inquiry: school improvement as a case in point. In *Evaluation and Social Justice: Issues in Public Education. New Directions for Program Evaluation,* No. 45, ed. K. A. Sirotnik, pp. 37–60. Newbury Park, Calif: Sage

Stigler, S. M. 1986. *The History of Statistics: The Measurement of Uncertainty Before 1900.* Cambridge, Mass: Harvard Univ. Press

Strauss, A., Corbin, J. 1990. *Basics of Qualitative Research: Grounded Theory Procedures and Techniques.* Newbury Park, Calif: Sage

Tharp, R. G., Gallimore, R. 1979. The ecology of program research and evaluation: A model of evaluation succession. See Sechrest et al 1979, pp. 39–60

Webb, E., Campbell, D. T., Schwartz, R. D., Sechrest, L. 1966. *Unobtrusive Measures: Nonreactive Measures in the Social Sciences.* Chicago: McNally

Weiss, C. H. 1966. Utilization of evaluation: toward comparative study. Paper presented at Am. Sociol. Assoc., Miami Beach

Weiss, C. H. 1977. Research for policy's sake: the enlightenment function of social research. *Policy Anal.* 3:531–45

Yin, R. K. 1984. *Case Study Research: Design and Methods.* Beverly Hills, Calif: Sage

Annu. Rev. Psychol. 1993. 44:675–708

ANIMAL BEHAVIOR: A Continuing Synthesis

William Timberlake

Department of Psychology and Center for the Integrative Study of Animal Behavior, Indiana University, Bloomington Indiana 47405

KEYWORDS: comparative methods, ethology, behavior systems, animal cognition, motivation

CONTENTS

INTRODUCTION 676
   The Historical Synthesis of Animal Behavior 676
   Current Status of the Synthesis 677
   A Reconsideration of the Synthesis 678
PERSISTENT RESEARCH DIFFERENCES 679
   Field vs. Laboratory Methods 679
   Genes vs. Environment 680
   Rules Guiding Research 680
METHODS OF COMPARING BEHAVIOR 682
   Protoevolutionary Comparisons 683
   Phylogenetic Comparisons 687
   Ecological Comparisons 689
   Microevolutionary Comparisons 691
   Integration 692
THE DYNAMICS AND STRUCTURE OF BEHAVIOR 694
   Motivation 694
   Learning 695
   Regulatory and Structural Behavior Systems 695
COGNITIVE ABILITIES 696
   Comparative Cognition 697
   Mental Life and Consciousness 698
   Animal Welfare and Rights 699
TOWARD CONTINUING SYNTHESIS 700

0066-4308/93/0201-675$02.00

INTRODUCTION

As a synthetic discipline, animal behavior lives by the wits, good will, and agreement of the scientists creating it. Current interest in animals is high, and powerful new techniques are available to establish the mechanisms, development, evolution, and function of behavior. Yet the coherence of the discipline is low, its conceptual center increasingly little more than a weighted average of new interests and old allegiances. Some of this lack of coherence can be traced to incomplete integration of parts of the original synthesis of the field. The present review considers four areas of conflict and truncated development for which further integration should contribute to a more stable base: (*a*) research differences, (*b*) methods of comparing behavior, (*c*) the dynamics and structure of behavior, and (*d*) cognitive abilities.

The Historical Synthesis of Animal Behavior

The discipline of animal behavior emerged in the late 1950s and early 1960s from the synthesis of comparative psychology and ethology. The initial interaction of these fields was dominated by sharp disagreement over the relative importance of instinct and learning in determining behavior (Lehrman 1953). Ethologists emphasized functional stereotyped motor movements and stimulus sensitivities that occurred without specific experience, presumably based on genetic programming. Psychologists emphasized the malleability of development, often focusing on nonfunctional outcomes as evidence of the importance of learning. A concise illustration of this conflict is Grohmann's (1939) demonstration that pigeons reared in confined boxes flew at the first opportunity, pitted against Dennis's (1941) discovery that vultures raised in similarly constricted circumstances failed to fly and fell to the ground when placed on a perch.

The unexpected outcome of this apparently intractable conflict was synthesis of the new and energetic discipline of animal behavior (Hinde 1966; Marler & Hamilton 1966). A major factor promoting this synthesis was the surprising number of interests shared by ethology and comparative psychology, including concern with development, motivation, evolution, adaptation, physiological mechanisms, small stimulus-response units, and stimulus control. Other shared concerns included a strong empirical orientation and a distaste for vitalism. A critical role in the synthesis also was played by personal ties between individual researchers, such as between the ethologist Lorenz and the psychologist Lehrman. The contributions of Frank Beach along these lines are described in a brief memorial (Dewsbury 1989b), while Tinbergen (posthumously) and Robert Hinde were recently honored with essay collections documenting their influence (Bateson 1991; Dawkins et al 1991).

Current Status of the Synthesis

The synthesis of comparative psychology and ethology has been quite successful. Authors of the last three chapters on this subject in the *Annual Review of Psychology* have documented the robustness of animal behavior research (Dewsbury 1989a; Mason & Lott 1976; Snowdon 1983). Opportunities for professional publication continue to increase with the expansion of old journals and the introduction of several new ones (*Journal of Biological Rhythms, Behavioral Ecology,* and *Journal of Cognitive Neuroscience* are recent examples). To stay current with just the titles of relevant books and chapters published each year requires a significant amount of time.

There are, however, some mixed indicators. The relative success of the field in securing government support for basic research is uncomfortably low. Though training funds in animal behavior recently received a slight increase, American government agencies typically fund only 10–15% of research proposals in this area (see Myers 1990, for an account of the process from the applicant's view). University positions related to animal behavior appear to have decreased. Research with dogs, cats, and rabbits has declined steadily (Viney et al 1990). Paranoid feelings remained high for years in reaction to E. O. Wilson's (1975) argument that comparative psychology had died and ethology and physiological psychology would follow by the year 2000, cannibalized by integrative neurophysiology, sociobiology, and behavioral ecology. Though concern has subsided, self-doubt continues. Bateson & Klopfer (1989) edited a volume entitled "Whither Ethology?" Demarest (1981) presided for several years over a self-examining newsletter on comparative psychology. Leger (1988: ix) noted, "I know of no discipline that has devoted so much time, effort, and printer's ink to a lengthy debate concerning its territorial limits … ."

At an accelerating pace important discoveries relevant to animal behavior come from outside the discipline. These discoveries provide fascinating opportunities for assimilation but also may bring into question the adequacy and stability of the synthesis. Recent advances in allometry (Gittleman 1989b) and the hormonal control of natural behavior (Wingfield & Moore 1988) have been dominated by physiologists. Molecular neuroscience has assumed a major portion of the search for basic mechanisms of learning, kin recognition, hormonal control of behavior, and rhythmicity (see Becker et al 1992; Martinez & Kesner 1991). Research in motivation has been co-opted by animal welfare concerns (Dawkins 1990; Hughes & Duncan 1988). The task of modeling animal behavior has leaned heavily on approaches developed in other fields. These approaches include: optimality, from economics and applied mathematics (Alexander 1982); connectionism, from cognitive psychology and computer science (Grossberg 1988); and stochastic dynamic modeling (Mangel & Clark 1988) and nonlinear dynamical systems (Beltrami 1987), from mathematics and physical systems.

Relevant new fields, such as artificial life, spring up without warning, complete with conferences, a newsletter (*Alife Digest*), and journals (*Adaptive Behavior* and *Artificial Life*). Slightly older fields, such as sociobiology and behavioral ecology, continue to pursue different visions of causation (though see the suggestion of Krebs & Davies 1991 and Bell 1991 that behavioral ecology return to mechanism). Other fields, such as neuroethology (Ingle & Crews 1985) and developmental psychobiology (Blass 1986) waver between animal behavior and closer ties to neuroscience. Changes in fundamental ideas, like the nature of evolution (Eldridge 1989), reinterpretations of the modern evolutionary synthesis (Provine 1988), and the active role of genes in daily behavior (Rusak et al 1990) provide continuing challenges to the task of constructing a coherent account. Because animal behavior remains a synthetic discipline, the critical issue for the field is maintaining an historically grounded coherence while assimilating the flood of new developments.

A Reconsideration of the Synthesis

In several respects the original synthesis was incomplete. For some the gap between comparative psychology and ethology has closed (Dewsbury 1990). But others still see marked differences in training, research focus, comparisons, procedures, and models—differences sufficiently large to promote separate professional allegiances. For example, the International Ethology Conference and the journal *Ethology* maintain a separate identity, as do the International Society of Comparative Psychology, the *Journal of Comparative Psychology*, and the *International Journal of Comparative Psychology*. Some even feel the name "animal behavior" is an issue because it might be seen as excluding humans. We are all animals here and we have a worthy heritage.

Much of the historical coherence of animal behavior has been provided by Tinbergen's (1951) four questions concerning evolution, function, mechanism, and development of behavior. These questions explicitly encourage a balance of approaches and causal levels, establish boundaries to the field, and help highlight research concerns overshadowed by rapid developments in other topic areas (e.g. Barlow 1989; Bateson & Klopfer 1989; Dawkins 1989). However, Tinbergen's questions by themselves do not provide a unifying picture of the fit between animal and environment. The clarity of the ethologist's original picture has been lost in the ensuing forty years. The purpose of the present review is to reconsider some unresolved conflicts and undeveloped strengths of the original synthesis in the hope that their further development and integration might help provide a more coherent center for the study of animal behavior. Even with this regrettable restriction it was possible to sample a only small portion of the thousands of excellent publications since the last review.

PERSISTENT RESEARCH DIFFERENCES

Field vs. Laboratory Methods

In the extreme view, comparative psychologists have been associated with a laboratory approach to research—the use of arbitrary stimuli, "artificial" laboratory-bred animals, automatic recording of arbitrary response elements, and extensive statistical analysis. Ethologists have been associated with a field approach to research—including extensive observation of animals in uncontrolled field conditions, a focus on highly complex behaviors, and impressionistic reporting. These stereotypes, always of doubtful accuracy, are inappropriate now that laboratory and field approaches have become increasingly difficult to distinguish (Blanchard et al 1989; Dewsbury 1990; Gibbons et al 1992). However, differences remain in how frequently individual investigators use the full range of research options.

Some researchers argue that field work must precede laboratory analysis (external validity first, see Kamil 1988). Others feel that phenomena must be established in the laboratory before dealing with the complexity of the field (internal validity first). The best long-term strategy is to include a range of approaches, thereby providing both sorts of validity and avoiding obstacles that arise simply from pursuing one approach exclusively. For example, a high degree of environmental control of stimuli allowed remarkable insight into the development of structure in birdsong, but the recent demonstration that live tutors produce different effects than tapes highlights the importance of also checking environmental influences on behavior in less constrained circumstances (see Marler 1991; Petrinovich 1990).

There is no single correct environment or species for research or observation, just the need to avoid downplaying either the contribution of the animal or the contribution of the environment. Different environments and species provide different opportunities to analyze the fit between animal and environment. Heidiger (1950) drew on this perception in arguing that the behavior of animals in zoos often was determined by so-called fight and flight distances. In a similar vein, Tinbergen & Perdeck (1950) and Hailman (1967) explored the possibilities of using artificial stimuli to analyze the mechanisms underlying begging in young birds. Even quite restricted environments can reveal characteristic animal/environment relations. For example, Olson (1991) used artificial learning problems to explore memory differences in corvids related to food caching, and Timberlake & Washburne (1989) used artificial moving stimuli to explore how the feeding ecology of rodent species affects conditioned reactions to movement predicting food.

Timberlake (1990) argued that behavior in even the most restricted laboratory environments is related to evolutionary determinants: first, because animals do not have a separate evolved repertoire for dealing with restricted environments; second, because even the most rigorous laboratory scientists carefully modify their procedures, apparatus, and measures to deal with the specific species under study (see Skinner's 1938, 1959 account of developing the leverpress for rats). To recapitulate, there need be no fundamental conflict between laboratory and field, provided we view them as different opportunities for reconstructing and predicting the fit between animal and environment.

Genes vs. Environment

The basic question of whether behavior is determined by genes or environment appeared to be resolved in the original synthesis. The concept of epigenesis captured the notion that development is not directed toward a preformed end, but occurs as an interaction between genes and environment (Oppenheim 1982). However, the nature of this interaction has proved difficult to analyze. Notions such as open instincts (Mayr 1974) and learning-instinct intercalation (Lorenz 1965) are not particularly epigenetic in the scope of interaction they allow for. Development does not occur as the programmed or even as the statistical interaction of genes and environment. Instead it seems to consist of individual, largely self-organizing processes involving genes, cells, physiological systems, and the "outer" environment (Thelen 1990; Wikler & Finlay 1989). Like evolution, development is not goal-directed but based on "spit and bailing wire"; that is, on making do with what is available. It is a vector that has direction in terms of its constituent processes (Oyama 1985).

Perhaps the most difficult point to grasp is that genes are not causal entities (Bateson 1988). Information about the "finished" animal does not reside exclusively in the genes any more than it resides in the environment. Identifying genes as causal agents remains a useful fiction because it makes possible simple manipulations and predictions of behavior in a particular environment. The fiction is made more attractive because proposed alternatives to simple causation often invoke maximal dialectical complexity (everything affects everything), a stance that gives only vague guidance to research (Kuo 1976). At present, the most rapid progress toward an understanding of development appears to come from using experimental manipulations to open windows during ontogeny that reveal how developmental processes work (Blass 1988; Moore 1990; Sinervo & Huey 1990; Thelen & Ulrich 1991).

Rules Guiding Research

Many successful scientists, just like successful authors and parents, often reconstruct their lives to yield a set of rules to follow (see Dewsbury 1985). Some recommend starting with first principles and deducing predictions that pit one hypothesis against another (strong inference). Others advise their students to observe extensively and without preconception, drop everything to follow a new lead, and then persist in the face of adversity. In practice most adept scientists appear to be more like game theorists, using conditional rather than absolute rules—deduction *and* induction, observation *and* manipulation, strong inference *and* demonstration, one species *and* many (Maynard-Smith

1982). Scientists also differ in individual abilities and predilections. Beer (1980) suggested that ethologists tend to be visually oriented, leading to their concern with behavioral form. Conversely, many psychologists began in physics and engineering, making them comfortable with the construction of apparatus and simple causal models.

Three additional suggestions may be useful in guiding integrative research: (a) assume "a modicum of ignorance" (a phrase of Nottebohm's), (b) try to view things from the animal's perspective, and (c) be aware of the functional systems that underlie behavior. On the issue of ignorance, it is often useful (after considerable training in an area) to return to being a little naive, to test the interpretation so obvious it's almost not worth checking, to question traditional procedures, to ask why the form of a response varies over time. Researchers inevitably accrue methods, measures, and models that constrain their questions and interpretations. A well-placed, simple question can reveal an important issue, e.g., Petrinovich (1990).

As to taking the animal's view, most scientists remain cautious because of the risk of falling into anthropomorphism—the projection of human thoughts and feelings into other animals. Though some have argued for its heuristic value and complexity (Fisher 1991), there is little evidence that research has been advanced in the long run by assuming that animals are fundamentally human in their thinking and behavior (Staddon 1989). The term theromorphism—meaning animal-centered as opposed to human-centered (von Uexkull 1934; see also Burghardt 1991; Simmons 1989)—better captures the present idea. Based on knowledge of an animal's sensory and motor equipment, its integrating and processing capabilities, and its motivational structure, dynamics, and decision rules, one attempts to enter into the animal's view of the circumstances. This is usually a difficult bootstrap endeavor involving asking repeated experimental and observational questions about an animal, and considering carefully the answers. It provides, though, an integration of intuition and experimental results that is essential both in setting up reasonable experimental manipulations and in interpreting and modeling more freely occurring behavior.

Finally, a recurrent theme in this discussion is that animals are sets of functional systems that operate within and influence the context of environment, physiology, behavior, social relations, and evolution. A simpler causal approach often dominates because researchers appreciate the power of analyzing and modeling the effects of one or two variables at a time. The problem with this simpler approach is the danger that our "picture" of the animal—our means of organizing knowledge—will become dependent primarily on our experimental procedures and simple causal models. Such a picture often is not transferable to new situations or even to different manipulations. For example, careful manipulation and measurement of copulation in single pairs of rats produced initial insight into the underlying physiological mechanisms (Rose 1990). However, broader comparisons of mammalian copulatory patterns

(Langtimm & Dewsbury 1991) introduced considerations of phylogeny and adaptation. Examining the social context of mating in rats clarified the roles of female and male choice as well as the selection pressures on the mechanisms (McClintock 1984). The hormonal analysis of reproduction provided further insight into evolutionary processes and mechanisms (Moore 1990).

Taking a systems approach has enabled researchers to organize information to develop a view of animal and environment that is conceptually and experimentally more tractable and heuristic.

METHODS OF COMPARING BEHAVIOR

Comparison has been touted as the heart of both comparative psychology and ethology (e.g. Dewsbury 1990; Lorenz 1950). Comparisons provide information about evolution and ecology, as well as suggesting and testing hypotheses about mechanism. Yet nowhere in animal behavior is the absence of a satisfying synthesis clearer than in the lack of agreement about the nature of appropriate comparisons. Thoughtful discussions have been offered by both psychologists and evolutionary biologists (Beer 1980; Bell 1989; Clutton-Brock & Harvey 1984; Dewsbury 1990; Gittleman 1989b; Hailman 1988; Harvey & Pagel 1991; Riley & Langley 1993). Given the diversity of answers, it is tempting to steal a page from philosophers of science and claim that the comparative method is whatever is used by scientists in making comparisons (see Adkins-Regan's 1990 review of comparative work on sex hormones and behavior).

In the absence of a single compelling rationale, it may be useful to categorize comparisons of behavior based on levels of concern with dimensions of genetic and ecological relatedness. Figure 1 shows four resultant categories: protoevolutionary comparisons (those not focused on either genetic or ecological relatedness), phylogenetic comparisons (focused on genetic but not ecological relatedness), ecological comparisons (focused on ecological but not genetic relatedness), and microevolutionary comparisons (concerned with both genetic and ecological relatedness).

Historically, comparative psychology focused on comparisons of mental life and physiology (protoevolutionary comparisons) combined with behavior genetics and development (microevolutionary comparisons). Ethologists focused on phylogenetic comparisons of behavior patterns in limited groups (homology), and ecological comparisons based on the form and function of behavior (convergence or divergence). Given these differences, it is not surprising that ethologists and psychologists often talked past each other (see Lorenz's, 1950, lament that comparative psychologists didn't do comparative research). As we shall see though, separations have blurred and empirical methods have emerged that cut across all categories (Harvey & Pagel 1991).

Protoevolutionary Comparisons

Faced with a large number of diverse species, most scientists are driven to impose some form of comparative order. A few scientists strive to add even more species for perspective and uniqueness (Adkins-Regan 1990). In neither case is the predominant focus on phylogeny or ecology, but on abstract relations such as trends, scales, and universal laws. I refer to such comparisons as protoevolutionary because their focus is not on the course of evolution but evolution is their broad concern.

CLASSIFICATION, TRENDS, GRADES, AND LEVELS   Comparisons across species in psychology readily can be traced to the interests of Darwin (1871) and Romanes (1884) in establishing a continuum of mental life from simpler animals to humans. Comparative psychologists developed more careful measures and reliable tests to document trends, grades, and levels in intelligence (e.g. Aronson 1984; Bitterman 1965; Krushinski 1965; Razran 1971) and in sensory-motor capabilities (Warden et al 1935). Recent examples of this analytic approach include development of a scale of categorization complexity (Herrnstein 1990) and the use of Piagetian stages of object permanence in human infants to grade species [e.g. primates (Parker 1990), dogs (Gagnon & Dore 1992), cats (Dumas & Dore 1991), and Psittacine birds (Pepperberg & Funk 1990)].

Biologists also have a history of classifying and grading species in a relatively nonevolutionary fashion, primarily with respect to morphology. For

Concern with Genetic Relatedness

	Low	High
High Concern with Ecological Relatedness	**Ecological** Convergence Divergence	**Microevolutionary** Genetics & Development Within-Species Strategies Micro-Model Systems
Low	**Protoevolutionary** Classifications, Trends, & Grades Scaling Functions & Allometry Universal Laws	**Phylogenetic** Homologies Series Animal Models

Figure 1   Types of comparison

example, animals have been classified grossly on the basis of radial vs. bilateral symmetry and polarized vs. unpolarized synapses, and more precisely on the basis of single cone vs. three cone retinas, and eusocial vs. asocial behaviors. Trends across groups have been noted, such as the decrease in genetic relatedness and increase in aggression in Wilson's pinnacles of sociality (1975), or changes from two-chambered to four-chambered hearts across classes of vertebrates (Hodos & Campbell 1990). Within smaller groups, behavior characteristics have been ordered in grades relating to differences in complexity of function or design features; for example, grades of cooperation in nest spinning ants (Holldobler & Wilson 1990), or sociality in primates (Martin 1974), or in bees (Michener 1974).

The major objection to such comparisons is the tendency to interpret trends, grades, and levels as progressive and as representing the actual course of evolution. Hodos & Campbell (1969, 1990) pointed out that many psychologists assumed they were documenting the progressive evolution of mental life from lower animals up to humans, an assumption often more clearly related to the scala naturae of Aristotle than to the course of evolution. Biologists, too, have inappropriately seen evolution and progress in some trends and grades (Gottlieb 1984; Nitecki 1988). For example, the three-chambered heart found in amphibians could be viewed as an intermediate evolutionary stage between the two-chambered heart found in fish and the four-chambered heart of mammals and birds. Instead, the three-chambered heart appears to be an adaptation of a four-chambered heart to the skin-aeration possibilities of an amphibian ecology (Hodos & Campbell 1990). The most conservative approach does not assume that classification schemes, trends, grades, and levels represent evolutionary history or progress. Instead, these comparisons must be reconciled individually with the course of evolution by working out the relations among mechanism, selection, and phylogeny.

SCALING FUNCTIONS AND ALLOMETRY   The process of scaling is based on fitting a function through a scatter plot relating variables such as body mass and basal metabolism rate (McNab 1989) or brain volume and body weight (Jerison & Jerison 1988). The result typically is a power function plotted as a straight line in log-log coordinates. The development of these relations is often referred to as allometry (Schmidt-Nielsen 1984; Thiessen 1990), because it typically involves the relation between body size and other variables, such as brain size, neural complexity, learning ability, metabolism, efficiency of locomotion, or reproductive success (e.g. Clutton-Brock & Harvey 1984; Gittleman 1989a). In most cases, each point is a species, but in recent comparative work many researchers (e.g. Gittleman 1989b) have made each point a genus in order to avoid influencing the function by correlated phylogenetic or ecological variables. Allometric functions are presumed to be determined by general physical relations and limitations, and thus should be present in all animals, though different taxa may have different exponents relating the variables.

Taken by themselves scaling functions deal with correlation rather than causation. They represent broad statements about the evolutionary landscape that make little contact with specific evolutionary history, development, or mechanisms. Recent research, though, has used deviations from allometric relations to indicate the effects of particular mechanisms and environments (e.g. McNab 1989). Also the use of convergent correlations and experimental manipulations can facilitate causal interpretations of allometric relations. For example, Sinervo & Huey (1990) tested the mechanisms underlying size-related locomotion differences in related lizard species. By directly manipulating adult body size through partial removal of yolk from the eggs of one species, they showed that burst speed but not stamina was affected by body size.

UNIVERSAL LAWS   A primary goal of science is to develop general principles or laws, preferably expressed as mathematical functions. In physics, the laws of mechanics hold true almost without regard to the entities involved. Laws of chemistry and biology more frequently require that the nature of the entity be taken into account. For example, to predict chemical reactions it is necessary to know the elements involved.

It is probably unfortunate that many behavior researchers have tried so hard to emulate physics (Bolles 1988) when chemistry would have made a better model. The fit of billiard ball and environment is not the same as the fit of an animal and its environment. Something like a dynamic "periodic table" relating animals, environments, and behavior is necessary before more accurate general laws are possible. Still, the development of general laws is a natural goal of science. Below are two examples of the search for laws of animal behavior.

Beginning in the 1930s many comparative psychologists focused attention on the development of universal laws of Pavlovian and operant conditioning. As more species were examined it became clear that similarities in learning were greater than differences (e.g. Macphail 1985; Skinner 1959). To be sure, similarities were highlighted by tuning apparatus and procedures to minimize differences attributable to the sensory, motor, and motivational aspects of a species (Timberlake 1990). Still, the similarities were remarkable, even across markedly divergent phyla (e.g. Maier & Schneirla 1935). More recently, Bitterman and his colleagues have shown that honey bees demonstrate a majority of the specific learning effects found in laboratory rats (e.g. Bitterman & Couvillon 1991). Neuroscientists have related universal learning laws to general cellular mechanisms (Hawkins & Kandel 1984). Some psychologists have attributed universal learning laws to the convergent evolution of associative processes (Dickinson 1980).

In biology, the past 20 years has seen a universal law approach emerge in behavioral ecology based on the principle of optimality. The basic assumption is that evolved behavior maximizes net benefit to the animal, both immediately (in terms of, for example, energy) and ultimately (in terms of individual reproduction and inclusive fitness). The principle of optimality is presumed to drive behavior regardless of ecology and without consideration of underlying mechanisms (Grafen 1991). Cleverly applied, it can predict a wide range of phenomena including foraging behavior (Stephens & Krebs 1986), group size (Pulliam & Caraco 1984) territoriality (Davies & Houston 1984), mating systems (Davies 1991), and parental care (Clutton-Brock & Godfray 1991). Kin selection (a form of optimality based on maximizing reproductive success at the level of the gene rather than the individual) has been used to explain altruistic behavior (Grafen 1991).

Most general principles of behavior, such as those concerned with learning and optimality, arise initially from a relatively narrow base of experimentation. Integration of concerns about mechanism, phylogeny and ecology comes later. To their credit, researchers in optimal foraging have shown increasing interest in the mechanisms (so-called "rules of thumb") that produce near-optimal behavior for a species in particular circumstances (Stephens & Krebs 1986).

For example, a bird may leave a patch based on the rule "search elsewhere after 20 seconds without food," or it may choose between alternative patches based only on the immediate probability of payoff (a hill-climbing rule). In some environments these rules produce optimal behavior, but in other environments they may fail miserably as optimal strategies.

Comparative learning researchers also have been concerned with the mechanisms that underlie learning. But, with a few exceptions they tend to regard deviations from expected results as constraints on general learning principles rather than as new information about specific adaptive mechanisms. In contrast, the research of Garcia and his coworkers (e.g. Garcia et al 1989) has consistently analyzed taste aversion learning as a specific functional adaptation.

MODEL SYSTEMS   A fourth class of protoevolutionary comparison is the model systems approach, an approach used frequently by physiologists to choose animals suitably qualified to test particular phenomena. The assumption underlying a model system is that a general substrate of action exists for many taxonomic groups and that its ruling principles can be investigated readily in particular preparations. Thus physiologists studied nerve conduction in squid because a giant axon was readily accessible in this species. More recently scientists have taken advantage of the relatively small number of pathways and neurons in simple marine molluscs to study the nature of learning (e.g. Alkon et al 1987). The many uses of chickens as a model system have been documented by Andrew (1991).

Ethology, sociobiology, and behavioral ecology have also begun to use data and general principles derived from work with other animals to analyze human behavior (e.g. Groebel & Hinde 1989; Hinde 1991 on Tinbergen). Wilson (1975) and those immediately following him bore the brunt of public dismay that the same analysis could be applied to human and nonhuman animals. But work has continued in this vein, appearing frequently in journals such as *Ethology and Sociobiology* (see Mulder 1991). For example, Daly & Wilson (1988a,b) melded an anthropological approach with that of genetic relatedness to predict patterns of parental solicitude and homicide in humans. Thornhill & Thornhill (1991) have examined the relation of characteristics of human rape to variables that have been shown to influence reproductive fitness in other animals. The evidence is compelling that some of the variance in human behavior is controlled by the same variables that determine the behavior of other species.

In sum, the precise procedures, generality, lawfulness, and heuristic value of protoevolutionary comparisons are the source of their attractiveness. Drawbacks often include lack of attention to phylogeny, specific selection pressures, mechanism, and development. Considerable care is required to avoid viewing all trends as progressive, attending to other species only as they relate to humans, or ignoring important species differences in the search for universal laws. Still, there seems little reason to shun protoevolutionary comparisons provided they are seen not as an endpoint, but as a starting place.

Phylogenetic Comparisons

Ethology began in this century with biologists comparing the form and development of motor acts in related species (Wheeler in ants; Heinroth in European songbirds and ducks; Whitman in pigeons and doves—see Thorpe 1979). Including the study of behavior was a natural extension of the taxonomic tradition in biology. Though enthusiasm for tracing phylogenetic relations waned for a bit, recent technical advances such as DNA finger-printing and multivariate statistics have provided some insight and a glut of information about phylogenetic relations among species (Brooks &McLennan 1991).

BEHAVIORAL HOMOLOGIES   Behavioral homologies refer to similarities in the topography (form) and sequencing of behavior based on phylogenetic linkage. The lack of a completely satisfying definition of behavioral homology has caused some investigators to dismiss the concept (Atz 1970). But the data acquired in the study of behavioral homologues appear potentially useful in filling in the phylogeny of behavioral and brain mechanisms, plus serving as another source of evidence about the overall course of evolution. For example, Lorenz (1950) used patterns of shared similarities and differences in courtship behavior to infer the course of evolution in a family of ducks (anatidae). The extent to which all species of ducks showed the same displays marked their closeness phylogenetically. Subgroups of ducks sharing unique displays were viewed as having split off from the root stock over evolutionary time. Later work combined evidence from behavior patterns with that based on morphological or physiological analysis to produce convergent evidence about phylogeny [e.g. Van Tets' (1965) work on Pelicaniformes; and Archibald's thesis work on unison calls in cranes, reported extensively in Grier & Burk (1992)].

A more recent form of specifying homologous relations is based on the uses of multivariate classification statistics. Typically, combinations of morphology and/or behavior are used to differentiate related groups of animals. For example, Eberhard (1982) combined data from web-building with information on predatory and courtship behavior to produce a taxonomy of related spiders. Losos' (1990) analysis of 13 species of lizards indicated that limb proportions and locomotor behavior evolved together, while Langtimm & Dewsbury (1991) showed that similarities in copulatory behavior among the Sigmodontiane rodents were traceable to a common ancestor.

BEHAVIORAL AND NEUROPHYSIOLOGICAL SERIES   A second method of phylogenetic comparison is to arrange living species in a sequence based on small and apparently systematic differences in behavior or neurophysiology. Such a sequence can present a compelling hypothesis of evolutionary development, though determining the validity of the sequence requires independent data relating the species. In behavior, a classic example is Kessel's (1955) arrangement of the courtship behavior of empid flies in a sequence beginning with courting males presenting the female with captured prey and culminating with a species in which the males present empty gossamer puffs. Similar series can be generated at the level of neurophysiology. A well-known example is the argument by MacLean (1990) for the triune evolution of control circuitry in the brain (first brain stem, then paleocortex, and finally neocortex). Masterton et al (1969) showed changes in brain development across branching phylogenetic groups of mammals, as did Kroodsma & Konishi (1991) in comparing songbirds with their suboscine relatives. Robinson (1991) warned that a large inductive database with many intermediate forms is necessary to infer a series that allows a distinction between evolutionary pressures and phylogeny. Brooks & McLennan (1991) argue strongly for a more computational approach in establishing such series.

ANIMAL MODELS   The (nonhuman) animal model approach is predicated on the notion that basic physiological substrates and behavioral qualities of a model species are homologous to those of humans. This approach has become a cornerstone of modern medical research (Alter et al 1991). Common laboratory animals are used as stand-ins for humans in determining, for example, the potency of a particular tranquilizer, or the physiological processes of aging (e.g. Gold & Stone 1988). Considerable objections have been raised (e.g. Regan 1983) to the extent and type of commercial product testing using animal models, resulting in changes in procedures and decreases in the amount of testing. The most sweeping objection, though, that work with nonhuman animals has no relevance to humans, is wrong, and even speciesist. Though no scientist would question the worth of continued research on determinants of the generalizability of results from animal models, specific results and principles stemming from animal models have long been useful in work with humans (for a nondisease example see Squire's 1992 review of converging human, primate, and rat data relating the hippocampus and memory).

A common interest in the use of animal models is in relating the behavior of other mammals to that of humans. For example, Young & Thiessen (1991) documented similarities between the cephalo-caudal organization of washing in humans and grooming in rodents. A less provocative finding is that all female mammals show a high degree of similarity in the hormonal regulation of their reproductive behavior (Rosenblatt 1989). The most explicit phylogenetic comparisons are between humans and the great apes, especially chimpanzees. For example, Tomonaga & Matsuzawa (1992) found that humans and chimpanzees showed the same dominance among perceptual categories in a matching to sample task. Outer contour elements were perceived the most readily and straight-line elements the least. The relation of language learning in apes and humans has been the source of fascinating data and continued debate (Gardner et al 1989; Savage-Rumbaugh 1988). In social behavior Manson & Wrangham (1991) have reported parallels in intergroup aggression in chimpanzees and humans. Some of the difficulties with behavioral homologies are considered at the end of the next section.

Ecological Comparisons

Ecological comparisons focus on the importance of selection pressures in producing divergence or convergence of behavior among species.

CONVERGENCE   The classic ecological comparison is based on behavioral and morphological similarities among species with dissimilar genetic make-up but similar environmental pressures. Usually an attempt is made to relate the similarities in a face-valid way to assumed selection pressures. Early work done by Hailman (1965) and others showed that unrelated cliff nesting shorebirds, such as gannets and gulls, exhibit quite similar behavior and morphology, presumably on the basis of the common selection pressures of the cliff environment. More recently, Logue (1988) provided evidence for a convergence of strategies among vertebrates to avoid poisonous foods, and Vander Wall (1990) discussed ecological similarities among diverse food hoarders. Sherry et al (1989) found that families of food-storing passerines show a larger hippocampus relative to the telencephalon and body weight than non-food-storing families.

LIFE HISTORY THEORY   In this view, selection for optimal strategies predicts general types of ecological convergence that approach the breadth of universal laws. Animals are grouped on the basis of their adaptations to common ecological pressures and a configuration of their behaviors is predicted. A now classic example is Ridley's (1983) demonstration that precopulatory guarding of the female by the male in invertebrates and anurans was predictable from whether females were receptive during predictable brief periods of time. More recent examples include the suggestion of Driver & Humphries (1988) that random movement by prey is the result of common predation pressure, and Davies (1991) review of the data used to support the view that mating systems follow from the defendability of resources (food for the female, and females for the male).

DIVERGENCE   Divergence comparisons involve looking for deviations from homologous behavior or morphology that can be related to changes in inferred selection pressures. For example, Glickman & Sroges (1966) investigated the exploratory behavior of zoo animals, looking for overall phylogenetic grades in reactivity. However, the data compelled a different interpretation relating exploratory behavior to the ecological variables of food variety, predator pressure, and the importance of social communication. More recently, Dewsbury (1988) used deviations and similarities in behavioral profiles to relate reproductive strategies to ecological circumstances, and Beecher (1990) predicted and showed that parent-offspring recognition was better in swallows that were colonial rather than solitary nesters. Also Brown (1989) developed evidence that the vocal repertoires and auditory sensitivities of old world monkeys are determined by their functions in conjunction with the acoustic characteristics of the habitats. Dukas & Real (1991) supported the prediction, based on the requirements of sociality, that a social bumblebee should show faster learning about reward than a solitary carpenter bee.

DEVIATIONS FROM ALLOMETRIC RELATIONS   This is a form of divergence comparison based on using allometric scaling functions as a central tendency against which to scale the deviations of individual species. For example, Jerison's (1973) encephalization quotient is based on the relation of the brain size to body weight ratio of a single species relative to the ratio typical of their taxonomic group. The resultant deviations can be related to ecological variables. McNab (1989) noted that the fundamental relation between basal rate of metabolism and body mass in carnivores is a power function with an exponent of .67 (Schmidt-Nielsen 1984), but it is influenced (in nonlinear ways) by the food type (vertebrates, invertebrates, leaves, fruit, and mixed diets), and the basic ecology (arboreal, burrowing, aquatic, arctic). Used in this way, allometric scaling becomes a type of ecological comparison (see also Harvey & Krebs 1990).

Finally, *adaptive correlation* is a form of divergence comparison based on demonstrating a suite of relations between morphology or behavior and presumed selection pressures. Cullen (1957) provided a classic example by documenting the differences in agonistic and reproductive behaviors between shore and cliff-nesting gulls and explaining them in terms of the different selection pressures produced by the cliff habitat. Another classic example is the correlation among feeding niche, morphological characteristics, and behavior in Darwin's finches (Grant 1986). A variant of this approach is the work of Gaulin et al (1990) and Gaulin & Wartell (1990) showing that across species and genders of rodents, average home range size is correlated with the spatial learning abilities shown by animals in laboratory tests.

There is a very long history of concern with the adequacy of the concepts of homology and convergence, a concern that has been compounded by applying these concepts to behavior (see Beer 1980). One fundamental difficulty is that each type of comparison considers only half of the evolutionary variables; one considers the evolutionary history, the other the selection pressure of the environment. Another difficulty is that most conclusions about phylogenetic and ecological relations are not checked by experimental manipulations. Studies such as Hailman's (1965) attempted to improve the accuracy of causal inferences by controlling rearing environments, but this approach appears to have gone out of favor. Recent statistical techniques provide alternative means of separating phylogenetic and ecological influences (e.g. Harvey & Pagel 1991).

Microevolutionary Comparisons

Microevolutionary comparisons are concerned with the contribution of both phylogeny and ecology to behavior. Historically, comparative psychologists focused on artificial selection (Plomin et al 1990) and ethologists focused on ritualization—the evolutionary process in which motor patterns become specialized for communication (Eibl-Eibesfeldt 1975). Both were concerned with general principles of development and the nature of critical periods (e.g. Immelman et al 1981).

GENETICS AND DEVELOPMENT   Much of the work on behavior genetics continues to focus on simple causal models, often statistical in nature. For example, Wheeler et al (1991) were able to change the rate of wing vibrations in *Drosophila* by the exchange of a single gene. An important window on the relation of genes and selection pressures has been provided by the use of DNA fingerprinting to link members of a population (Everitt et al 1991). DNA-based investigations of bees have shown that hormonal control of tasks differs within subpopulations in a hive (Robinson et al 1989). DNA-based investigations of birds have contradicted our assumption that many species are exclusively monogamous (Weatherhead & Montgomerie 1991).

Changes in behavior and development increasingly are treated as important contributors to evolution (Bateson 1988). Because development stands between genes and their expression, it can be selected for as a critical mediator of evolution. Arnold (1990) noted that development is a dimension of the phenotype and genotype instead of an alternative to direct inheritance. King & West (1990) proposed the concept of inherited niches to account for the effects of differences in ecological pressures on song development in cowbird subpopulations. A similar explanation may underlie the demonstration of Goldthwaite et al (1990) that ground squirrels do not show specialized defensive reactions to snakes in arctic populations that are now free from snakes.

Gottlieb (1992) argued that because of the large amount of "silent" DNA in all phyla, persistent changes in phenotype can occur in response to changes in the environment, with no change in genotype. For the more statistically oriented, allometric functions can be plotted with individuals (or individuals at different times) as the points, to look for similarities and differences in functional relations across development (Gittleman 1989a). Finally, as indicated previously, many processes of development have proved remarkably accessible to experimental investigation (Miller 1988).

BEHAVIORAL STRATEGIES WITHIN SPECIES   Tinbergen and his students provided evidence that populations show ranges of behavioral strategies associated with different reproductive success [e.g. Patterson (1965) on group vs. isolate nesters in gulls]. Work has expanded exponentially on within-species differences in life history strategies—such as body size at maturation, courtship method, mate choice, and parental care. Lessells (1991) reviewed a considerable body of literature relating life-history strategies to reproductive success and evolution. These strategies are often modified by different environmental conditions, and are even affected by the relative distributions of the strategies of other animals in the population. The notion of evolutionarily stable strategies (Maynard-Smith 1982) and the ideal free distribution approach (Milinski & Parker 1991) are designed to capture the conditional, frequency-based nature of appropriate behavior.

MICRO-MODEL SYSTEMS   The division between protoevolutionary and microevolutionary comparisons is not always clear, particularly in the areas of general principles and model systems. The assumption in both types of comparison is that careful analysis of the behavior of a small number of subjects will reveal information of general applicability. One distinction is that the microevolutionary approach focuses on comparisons within the same or closely related species. For example, Ketterson & Nolan (1992) and Marler & Moore (1991) used hormones to engineer new phenotypes in free-living male birds and lizards. These phenotypes were used to illustrate the effects of behavioral variation on fitness, and to infer general evolutionary trajectories within a population.

Integration

Explicit comparisons provide a powerful technique for disentangling the determinants of behavior, but it should be apparent that these four general categories of comparison are not fixed. They are intended to provide a framework acknowledging diversity while encouraging a more coherent approach. There may be considerable advantage in studying the same topic across all four categories. For instance, behaviors related to kin selection can be dealt with as a protoevolutionary trend, as a homologue, as examples of ecological convergence, and as the product of the genetic makeup of a particular population.

Similarly, the same empirical technique (e.g. allometric scaling, profiles, ideal free distribution) can be used in comparisons of any sort.

Should one of these types of comparison be preferred? In a recent paper Hailman (1988) argued that an adequate comparison requires including multiple species in all four categories of a table similar to the present one. Homology is inferred only if related animals in different niches show it and unrelated animals in the same niches do not. Convergence is indicated only if unrelated animals show similarities that their relatives in different circumstances do not. This is a worthy approach, but it focuses only on establishing homologues and convergence and the price is high in terms of subjects required.

Careful work in any single category provides useful data. Robinson (1991) cited several examples of how the painstaking accumulation of data from unrelated insects eventually led to insights concerning adaptation and phylogeny (Eberhard 1980; Robinson 1985). However, using several types of comparison probably will advance knowledge more rapidly than focusing on a single type. Phylogenetic or ecologically-based explanations often overlook simple proximal causes (Barlow 1989). On the other side, an exclusive focus on proximal determinants can produce general principles unconnected with function and evolution. For example, the general principles of learning established by laboratory psychologists are not very helpful in explaining or predicting naturally occurring phenomena such as song learning in birds (Timberlake & Lucas 1989). Finally, an exclusively ecological comparison may ignore the importance of general processes and exaptations (Riley & Langley 1993).

One effective approach to comparison would be to begin with protoevolutionary observation and analyses of the regularities and functional relations among the stimuli, responses, and states involved, move on to ecological and phylogenetic comparisons, and cross to microevolutionary analysis of mechanism and development. For an example of such a shift, consider that the study of learning began with the protoevolutionary approach of trends and grades, moved through general principles and model systems, into ecological comparisons (Balda & Kamil 1989) and the beginning of microevolutionary considerations (Arnold 1981; Bateson 1988).

It is assuredly not necessary that all research in animal behavior be explicitly comparative. For example, the sequence of research above is appropriate for any study of animal behavior whether comparative or not. In terms of Tinbergen's questions, this research example begins with an interest in mechanism, incorporates function and evolution, and returns to mechanism at a more profound level. However, this particular sequence of research types is not critical in advancing the field. What is important is the development of a picture of the animal and environment that helps integrate the results of different types of research.

THE DYNAMICS AND STRUCTURE OF BEHAVIOR

Motivation

At the time of the initial synthesis, the study of motivation was a critical substrate of both comparative psychology and ethology. Motivation fell out of favor with psychologists because neither deficit motivation nor incentive effects could be tied firmly to physiology, and the relations between deprivation manipulations and behavior differed with both the type of manipulation and the measure of behavior used. Perhaps most importantly, motivation was considered superfluous because, given a sentient organism with a few reflexes, researchers felt able to construct the form and dynamics of new behavior by employing operant and Pavlovian conditioning techniques. Motivation persisted only as a broad causal principle related to general arousal and attraction.

Ethologists from Tinbergen (1951) through Baerends & Drent (1970) began with a more complex view of motivation that combined regulation with hierarchical structures of states, releasers, and action patterns spread across levels of organization. However, despite its central position in ethological thinking, motivation declined in popularity for reasons similar to those in comparative psychology. Drive was not unitary (Hinde 1966), and the concept of action-specific energy failed to account for many examples of the initiation and cessation of behavior (e.g. Dethier 1976). Motivation became an unnecessary ghost in the machine.

To the surprise of many, motivation seems to be making a comeback. First Toates (1986) and then Colgan (1989) wrote small primers. The former surveyed motivational systems, the latter considered three basic research topics. The first topic was the motivational systems developed by ethologists, which they inferred from the timing, sequencing, and organization of behavior. The second topic was regulatory physiological systems for which control circuitry is inferred from lesions, stimulation, and measurement of hormonal levels and metabolic indicators (e.g. Stricker 1990; see also Mrosovsky 1990). The third topic was the adaptation and regulation of behavior from the viewpoint of optimality and game theory (e.g. Krebs & Davies 1991).

Three more research topics might have been added: one focusing on social contexts of motivation, particularly the developmental, ecological, and strategic aspects, including kin selection (Cheney & Seyfarth 1990; Slobodchikoff 1988); another focusing on the generation of response components and stimulus processing rules for particular states (Gallistel 1990); a final chapter could have dealt with recent work on computer simulations of animals. Imaginary animals can be taught to categorize inputs, learn sequential dependencies, and filter noise for signal (Grossberg 1988). Mechanical "insects" wander through their environments (Beer 1990), and complete worlds of computerized reproducing animals can be turned loose to evolve in sometimes wildly disparate ways (Langton et al 1991).

Learning

The study of learning very early became a protoevolutionary endeavor, one tied intimately to apparatus, procedures, and general principles. Within the last 20 years, a part of this massive literature (e.g. Spear et al 1990) has moved slowly in the direction of a functional ecological approach. Bolles & Beecher (1988), Gallistel (1990), Gould (1986), Kamil & Roitblat (1985), Kamil et al (1987), and Zentall & Galef (1988) deal with the role of learning in solving ecological problems in both restricted and relatively unrestricted circumstances. Other researchers have focused on laboratory versions of ecological learning problems, ranging from examples of perceptual learning (Suboski 1989), to the learning of the time and location of food availability by garden warblers (Biebach et al 1989), and how gouramis defend territories (Hollis 1990).

One of the most fascinating continuing research stories concerns memory for stored foods in the bird families of corvids and parids. An interesting recent outcome is that field differences in the memory of caching and noncaching corvids show up in tests of memory in an analogue of the radial arm maze (Balda & Kamil 1989), and also in even more constrained laboratory tests (Olson 1991; see Shettleworth 1990). Species that depend heavily on memory to retrieve caches in the field do better on even arbitrary laboratory tests of memory. Similar differences have been obtained for storing and nonstoring parids (Krebs et al 1990). Such evidence raises the possibility of using related species in studies of ecology and phylogeny (Kamil 1988). Similar opportunities appear to be developing in the study of bird song (Kroodsma & Konishi 1991; Nottebohm 1991).

Regulatory and Structural Behavior Systems

As the study of both motivation and learning moves toward ecological and microevolutionary comparisons, it will be necessary to provide an animal-based rather than a procedure- or apparatus-based framework. Such a framework may serve as a basis for integrating other research as well. Behavioral ecologists working on the determinants of foraging have begun to confront effectively the ways in which animals distribute their energy resources across feeding alternatives and the demands of different systems (McNamara & Houston 1990). Caraco & Lima (1987) and Lucas & Walter (1991) have examined the influence of metabolic balance on sensitivity to risk. Laboratory investigations have become concerned with the regulation of feeding by non-metabolic influences such as local cost and time windows (Collier & Johnson 1990; Cuthill et al 1990; Plowright & Shettleworth 1991). Other researchers have pressed for the consideration of the circadian and ultradian rhythmicity of behavior (Brady 1988; Silver 1990).

An approach compatible with much of this work is the concept of behavior systems deriving in part from traditional ethology (Davey 1989; Davis 1984;

Fanselow & Lester 1988; Heiligenberg 1991; Timberlake & Lucas 1989). This approach combines hierarchical motivational systems with a dimension of appetitive to consummatory motivational modes related to the physical and temporal proximity of incentives. Learning occurs in terms of integrating sensory-motor control circuitry, tying it to motivational states, and relating these elements to the environment. Such a systems approach encourages analysis of the levels of regulation (e.g. Cools 1985; Fentress 1991), consideration of interactions among different motivational states: for example, fear and thermoregulation in chicks (Rovee-Collier et al 1991), and comparison of regulation and learning in sexual systems (e.g. Domjan & Hollis 1988, Everitt 1990), and social systems relating to feeding in rats (Galef 1990, Timberlake 1983).

A behavior systems approach also makes ready contact with development (e.g. Hall 1990; Hogan 1988; Hogan et al 1991), and with the neurophysiological underpinnings of particular behaviors—for example, the reproductive behavior of reptiles and mammals (Bronson 1989; Crews 1988), and fear and aggression of rats in semi-natural environments (Blanchard & Blanchard 1990; see also Brain et al 1990). Fanselow (1989) and Fanselow & Lester (1988) have shown that avoidance and escape behavior is controlled by a sensory dimension of predatory imminence, associated with varying response probabilities, stimulus control, and brain structures. Lammers et al (1988a,b) have distinguished specific areas of the hypothalamus of rats related to social grooming, attack, teeth-chattering, flight, and escape jumps.

In short, amplifying the concept of behavior systems provides many opportunities for producing a more coherent and heuristic picture of the fit between animals and their environments. A system of behavior can provide a framework for integrating the answers to Tinbergen's questions and the results of different methods of comparing behavior. Finally, a systems approach can provide an organization for dealing with issues of animal cognition and animal welfare.

COGNITIVE ABILITIES

Even for normally reserved scientists, it is fascinating and delightful that chimpanzees sign (Gardner et al 1989), vervet monkeys warn of specific predators (Cheney & Seyfarth 1990), starlings mimic and rearrange human sounds and music (West & King 1990), rats and gray parrots count (Davis & Perusse 1988; Pepperberg 1990, and pigeons distinguish between slides of cats and chairs (Wasserman et al 1988).

Compared with the enthusiastic rebirth of interest in animal cognition, the behaviorist period of strict avoidance of the attribution of mental life appears at best a long fallow period (Wasserman 1993), and at worst an anomalous dark age that has finally been set right by the cognitive revolution. Nevertheless, behaviorism made a critical contribution to the study of animal cognition because it compelled scientists to try to ignore the projection of their own psychology onto animals long enough to begin to discern determinants of behavior in clearly defined external variables. The development of both comparative psychology and ethology required the rejection of poorly defined causal agents—mentalism and instincts in psychology, vitalism in biology—to allow science to emerge.

Comparative Cognition

Comparative cognition is the domain of scientists interested in how different species process and integrate stimuli (Boysen & Capaldi 1992; Honig & Fetterman 1992; Kesner & Olton 1990; Ristau 1991; Roitblat 1987). However, the field is split along much the same lines as traditional learning, into protoevolutionary approaches (anthropocentric) and ecological approaches (Shettleworth 1993). The anthropocentric stance is fueled partly by interest in the classic continuum of mental life (Wasserman 1993) and partly by the success of traditional research on universal laws of learning. Recent work on representation, counting, remembering, and categorization has been summarized in Gallistel (1989, 1990), Wasserman (1993), and Honig & Fetterman (1992). The processing of auditory stimuli by birds and mammals has also received attention (Dooling & Hulse 1989).

Much of the work relating nonhuman and human language and intelligence falls largely in the protoevolutionary camp (e.g. Gardner et al 1989 and Parker & Gibson 1990 on primates; Herman et al 1990 on dolphins). This work has profited from analytic efforts such as those pioneered by Premack (1983) to break down cognitive phenomena into components that can be tested separately, an approach followed by Washburn & Rumbaugh (1991) in studying counting in monkeys and by Gisiner & Schusterman (1992) in studying categorization in sea lions.

As for the ecological approach to cognition it is basically theromorphic, animal centered. The work of von Uexkull (1934) on the functional fit between the filtering of the sensory surround and behavior in the woodtick serves as a classic precursor. Gallistel (1990) recently reviewed studies of the ecological relevance of abilities such as memory, timing, and navigation. Yoerg (1993) also dealt generally with the relation of ecology and learning phenomena. The work on food storing in birds alluded to in the learning section provides examples of the ecological approach (see also Kallander & Smith 1990), as does the work of Cheney & Seyfarth (1990) on vervet monkeys, work on the critical evaluation of foraging "information centers" in social species (e.g. Richner & Marclay 1991; Zentall & Galef 1988), and Real's (1991) article on choice behavior and the evolution of cognitive "architecture" in bumblebees.

I believe cognitive research will be better served in the long run by moving in the same direction as other research in animal behavior, namely toward ecological, phylogenetic, and microevolutionary concerns. In maintaining an anthropocentric approach that is not clearly evolutionary, scientists tend to ignore the ecological and evolutionary basis of the phenomena they study, focusing instead on general principles and concerns of definition and experimental procedure. The result can be an unforseen limit on research procedures and interpretation. For example, the eight-arm radial maze has been used extensively to study memory, based on the presumption that rats were rewarded for efficient search by finding the maximum number of pellets in eight choices. However, Timberlake & White (1990) showed that rats efficiently search maze arms in the absence of any food at all, presumably based on evolved mechanisms facilitating foraging efficiency and increasing environmental familiarity in the absence of food.

Mental Life and Consciousness

For many scientists, the return to a concern with animal consciousness (e.g. Bateson & Klopfer 1991; Griffin 1981) is a return to a problematic approach to animals that it took centuries to escape (Burghardt 1985). Given there is little convincing data that the introspectively revealed contents of human consciousness play a primary causal role in most human behavior, how do we explain the fascination with animal consciousness? Beer (1992) has suggested that our interest in mental life is based on our "folk psychology," basically a "toolkit for coping with the cognitive and conative demands and tensions of human life." In other words, our interest in and ideas about consciousness reflect a human strategy for interacting with the world. Because of the questionable status of folk psychology and its intimate ties to human language, it is difficult to defend pouring large resources into a frontal attack on animal consciousness. The direct approach has failed badly in the past, and has yet to pay large dividends even in analyzing human behavior, despite high current interest and firsthand access to data.

There is more support for exploring mental states such as intentions (e.g. Dennett 1987). However, care must be taken. The use of such intentional terms as "Machiavellian" or "deceptive" to describe the behavior of nonhuman animals often has been more successful in stirring controversy than in specifying the determinants of behavior. Most scientists agree that mental terms must be treated experimentally as intervening variables for which we need to provide convergent behavioral, physiological, and comparative analysis.

Given the number of people concerned with mental states, some progress would be expected from an experimental approach analyzing components of processing and motivation. For example, Martin et al (1991) showed a separation in rats between determinants of discriminative and affective effects of opiates. The work of Povinelli et al (1991) suggests that rhesus monkeys are not able to infer the knowledge states of humans, though in similar circumstances chimpanzees apparently can (see also Whiten 1991).

In a way, the notion of deception is not necessarily more amorphous than the concept of, say, timing. Both involve stimulus processing and behavioral results. The difference is that the processes involved in timing are better analyzed and the concept has only a little explanatory value and interest by itself. In contrast, the concept of deception has compelling popular explanatory power for behavior, even though the concept is still clearly in transition. For example, Gyger & Marler (1988) inferred that deception in food calling is used by male domestic fowl to attract hens, but Moffatt & Hogan (1992) argued that hens so rapidly track the relation of calls to food that deception would not be effective. Research into both deception and timing would be served well by conceptualizing them within a functional system, and analyzing the component processes that comprise them (e.g. Adams & Caldwell 1990).

Animal Welfare and Rights

The historical inability of scientists to agree on how to study the mental life of nonhuman animals and its continuity with the mental life of humans, has come back to challenge the field of animal behavior. Freely ascribing mental states to other animals piques general interest, but it also allows activist philosophers to freely claim the existence of suffering in nonhuman animals without the convergent evidence and careful analysis that would be required for humans (e.g. Regan 1983; Singer 1990). Bekoff & Jamieson (1991) argue that because the criticisms of animal research raised by these philosophers are similar despite their differing "schools," the criticisms must point to a central truth. But an obvious alternative is that these activist philosophers began with their conclusions in place and reasoned backwards to produce a fit with their first principles.

A large number of scientists have become engaged in the laudable attempt to bring together concepts of animal welfare and research (e.g. Dawkins 1990; see Carlstead et al 1991 for application of a systems approach to the reduction of stereotyped behaviors). There are now many journals focused on animal welfare and conservation issues (e.g. *Anthropozoos, Applied Animal Behavior Science, Zoobiology*) while others (e.g. *American Journal of Primatology*) devote considerable space to and publish special issues on these topics.

Less fortunately, oversight committees and bureaucracies are increasing at every level, all with rules that can take on a life of their own independent of the good intentions with which they were created. For example, the expense of stainless steel caging and hospital-like stainless steel covering on all surfaces in animal housing rooms has unaccountably become a requirement of good care. The increased concern with animal welfare has in some ways improved the state of animals in science, but in too many cases it is still difficult to determine whether the importance and size of improvments outweighs the cost to research. The issues are many and complex (Novak & Petto 1991).

Equally problematic for research is the inability of scientists to communicate with the public as effectively as do animal rights groups. The knowledge of scientists ought to be more influential with the environmental and biodiversity movements and pet lovers than the anti-science stance of many animal rights groups. Yet too often important and well-intentioned remarks of visible scientists, such as Jane Goodall, fail to emphasize that our increased knowledge about animals and their cognitive processes comes from research not from intuition. Intuition alone usually produces contradictory and poorly founded beliefs.

In a recent radio interview, a leader of the largest animal rights organization in the United States stated with great feeling that her goal was to let every animal run free through meadows in the sunlight. Her sentiment was compelling but she utterly misunderstood a critical point. Given alternatives of cover or darkness most animals would prefer not to run through sunlit meadows, not even mammals, the small cladistic group she probably was thinking of [40% of mammals are rodents, and another 20% are bats (Vaughan 1978)]. We cannot allow such projections to represent nonhuman animals to the public or to governing officials. It is demeaning and even dangerous to us all.

TOWARD CONTINUING SYNTHESIS

A primary path of science is toward specialization, inevitably accompanied by fragmentation. Specialization is a sign of progress, but it is also both a problem and an opportunity for a synthetic field like animal behavior. The key to progress in such a field is continued synthesis. Wilson (1975) was basically right in his vision that sociobiology, behavioral ecology, and integrative neurobiology would combine with the classic study of behavior. What he failed to see was that behavior and its fit with the environment is the basis for this integration.

In any continuing synthesis Tinbergen's four questions are useful in encouraging balance in the ways phenomena are considered. The different methods of comparison reviewed above facilitate relating phenomena to trends, scales, general laws, and phylogenetic, ecological, and microevolutionary analyses. What ultimately defines a continuing synthesis, though, is not balance or methods, but the parsing and integration of the resultant knowledge by means of a flexible and heuristic picture of the fit between animal and environment. A picture I find attractive stems from modifying the basic behavior systems approach of the ethologists to emphasize greater roles for learning and development, stimulus processing and integration, response organization and coordination, and the co-regulation of hierarchical and interacting motivational states.

This view also treats behavior (including perception) as a bidirectional link between animal and environment in both local and ultimate senses. Locally, behavior creates environments as much as local environments create behavior. This point is particularly salient in highly social species. In an ultimate sense, behavior is the ambassador of environments to the genes as well as the representation of the genes in environments. Filling in this picture will require continuing research that combines elements of laboratory and field by providing sufficient stimulus support to engage processing mechanisms, response components, and motivational states relevant to the functional behavior system under study, but in a way that allows manipulation and measurement of the determinants of the fit between animal and environment.

Finally, continuing synthesis demands hard-nosed, innovative collaboration between disciplines, an ideal that faces important realities of finance and defended territories. J. P. Scott (1973:34) addressed both the promise and the problems of such research:

> Anyone who works on the new frontiers of science finds that the conventional disciplinary boundaries disappear, and become important only when we consider university organization and finance ... scientific progress is brought about through cooperation between involved individuals ... and segregation based on separation of disciplines may be just as harmful as that based on race.

ACKNOWLEDGMENTS

Preparation of this review was supported by NIMH Grant 37892 and NSF Grant IBN-9121647. I thank Ellen Ketterson, Meredith West, Gary Lucas, and Leslie Real for comments, and Holly Stocking for patience.

Literature Cited

Adams, E. S., Caldwell, R. L. 1990. Deceptive communication in asymmetric fights of the stomatopod crustacean Gonodactylus bredini. *Anim. Behav.* 39:706–16

Adkins-Regan, E. 1990. Is the Snark still a Boojum? The comparative approach to reproductive behavior. *Neurosci. Biobehav. Rev.* 14:243–52

Alexander, R. M. 1982. *Optima for Animals.* London: Edward Arnold

Alkon, D. L., Disterhoft, J., Coulter, D. 1987. Conditioning-specific modification of postsynaptic membrane currents in mollusc and mammal. In *The Neural and Molecular Bases of Learning,* ed. J. P. Changeux, M. Konishi, pp. 205–38. New York: Wiley

Alter, W. A. III, Hartgraves, S. H., Wayner, M. J. 1991. A review of animal to human extrapolation: issues and opportunities. *Physiol. & Behav.* 5:1–184

Andrew, R. J. 1991. *Neural and Behavioural Plasticity: The Use of the Domestic Chick as a Model.* Oxford: Oxford Univ. Press

Aronson, L. R. 1984. Levels of integration and organization: a reevaluation of the evolutionary scale. In *Behavioral Evolution and Integrative Levels,* ed. G. Greenberg, E. Tobach, pp. 57–81. Hillsdale NJ: Erlbaum

Arnold, S. J. 1981. The microevolution of feeding behavior. In *Foraging Behavior: Ecological, Ethological, and Psychological Approaches,* ed. A. C. Kamil, T. D. Sargent, pp. 409–53. New York: Garland

Arnold, S. T. 1990. Inheritance and the evolution of behavioral ontogenies. In *Developmental Behavior Genetics: Neural, Biomedical, and Evolutionary Approaches,* ed. M. E. Hahn, J. K. Hewitt, N. D. Henderson, R. Benno, pp. 167–89. New York: Oxford Univ. Press

Atz, J. 1970. The application of the idea of homology to behavior. In *Development and Evolution of Behavior,* ed. L. R. Aronson, E. Tobach, D. S. Lehrman, J. S. Rosenblatt, pp. 53–74. San Francisco: Freeman

Baerends, G. P., Drent, R. H. 1970. The herring gull's egg. *Behaviour* 17(Suppl.):1–416

Balda, R. P., Kamil, A. C. 1989. A comparative study of cache recovery in three corvid species. *Anim. Behav.* 38:486–95

Barlow, G. W. 1989. Has sociobiology killed ethology? See Bateson & Klopfer 1989, pp. 1–45

Bateson, P. P. G. 1988. The active role of behaviour in evolution. In *Evolutionary Processes and Metaphors,* ed. M. W. Ho, S. W. Fox, pp. 191–207. London: John Wiley & Sons

Bateson, P. P. G. 1991. *The Development and Integration of Behaviour: Essays in Honour of Robert Hinde.* Cambridge: Cambridge Univ. Press

Bateson, P. P. G., Klopfer, P. H. 1989. *Perspectives in Ethology.* Vol. 8. *Whither Ethology?* New York: Plenum

Bateson, P. P. G., Klopfer, P. H. 1991. *Per-*

spectives in Ethology Vol. 9. Human Understanding and Animal Awareness. New York: Plenum

Becker, J. B., Breedlove, S. M., Crews, D. 1992. Behavioral Endocrinology. Cambridge, MA: MIT Press

Beecher, M. D. 1990. The evolution of parent-offspring recognition in swallows. See Dewsbury 1990, pp. 360–80

Beer, C. G. 1980. Perspectives on animal behavior comparisons. In Comparative Methods in Psychology, ed. M. H. Bornstein, pp. 17–64. Hillsdale, NJ: Erlbaum

Beer, C. G. 1992. Conceptual issues in cognitive ethology. Adv. Stud. Behav. 21:69–110

Beer, R. D. 1990. Intelligence as Adaptive Behavior: An Experiment in Computational Neuroethology. New York: Academic

Bekoff, M., Jamieson, D. 1991. Reflective ethology, applied philosophy, and the moral status of animals. See Bateson & Klopfer 1991, pp. 1–47

Bell, J. 1989. A comparative method. Am. Nat. 133:553–71

Bell, W. J. 1991. Searching Behaviour: The Behavioural Ecology of Finding Resources. London: Chapman Hall

Beltrami, E. 1987. Mathematics for Dynamic Modeling. New York: Academic

Biebach, H., Gordijn, M., Krebs, J. R. 1989. Time-and-place learning by garden warblers, Sylvia borin. Anim. Behav. 37:353–60

Bitterman, M. E., 1965. Phyletic differences in learning. Am. Psychol. 20:396–410

Bitterman, M. E., Couvillon, P. A. 1991. Failures to find evidence of adaptive specialization in the learning of honey bees. In The Behavior and Physiology of Bees ed. L. J. Goodman, R. C. Fisher, pp. 288–305. Wallingford UK: CAB International

Blanchard, D. C., Blanchard, R. J. 1990. The colony model of aggression and defense. See Dewsbury 1990, pp. 410–30

Blanchard, R. J., Brain, P. F., Blanchard, D. C., Parmigiani, S., eds. 1989. Ethoexperimental Approaches to the Study of Behavior. Dordrecht: Kluwer Academic

Blass, E. M., ed. 1986. Handbook of Behavioral Neurobiology Vol. 8. Developmental Psychobiology and Developmental Neurobiology. New York: Plenum

Blass, E. M., ed. 1988. Developmental Psychobiology and Behavioral Ecology. Handbook of Behavioral Neurobiology, Vol. 9. New York: Plenum

Bolles, R. C. 1988. Nativism, naturalism, and niches. See Bolles & Beecher 1988, pp. 1–15

Bolles, R. C., Beecher, M. D., ed. 1988. Evolution and Learning. Hillsdale, NJ: Erlbaum

Boysen, S. T., Capaldi, E. J. 1992. The Development of Numerical Competence: Animal and Human Models. Hillsdale, NJ: Erlbaum

Brady, J. 1988. The circadian organization of behavior: time-keeping in the Tsetse fly, a model system. Adv. Stud. Behav. 18:153–91

Brain, P. F., Parmigiani, S., Blanchard, R. J., Mainardi, D., eds. 1990. Fear and Defence. London: Harwood Academic

Bronson, F. H. 1989. Mammalian Reproductive Biology. Chicago: Univ. Chicago Press

Brooks, D. R., McLennan, D. A. 1991. Phylogeny, Ecology, and Behavior. Chicago: Univ. Chicago Press

Brown, C. H. 1989. The acoustic ecology of East African primates and the perception of vocal signals by grey-cheeked mangabeys and blue monkeys. See Dooling & Hulse 1989, pp. 210–39

Burghardt, G. 1985. Animal awareness: current perceptions and historical perspective. Am. Psychol. 40:905–19

Burghardt, G. M. 1991. Cognitive ethology and critical anthropomorphism: a snake with two heads and hog-nose snakes that play dead. See Ristau 1991, pp. 53–90

Caraco, T., Lima, S. L. 1987. Survival, energy budgets, and foraging risk. In Quantitative Analyses of Behavior, ed. M. L. Commons, A. Kacelnik, S. J. Shettleworth, 6:1–20

Carlstead, K., Seidensticker, J., Baldwin, R. 1991. Environmental enrichment for zoo bears. Zoo-Biology 10:3–16

Cheney, D. L., Seyfarth, R. M. 1990. How Monkeys See the World: Inside the Mind of Another Species. Chicago: Univ. Chicago Press

Clutton-Brock, T. H., Harvey, P. H. 1984. Comparative approaches to investigating adaptations. See Krebs & Davies 1984, pp. 7–29

Clutton-Brock, T., Godfray, C. 1991. Parental investment. See Krebs & Davies 1991, pp. 234–62

Colgan, P. 1989. Animal Motivation. London: Chapman & Hall

Collier, G., Johnson, D. F. 1990. The time window of feeding. Physiol. Behav. 48:771–77

Cools, A. R. 1985. Brain and behavior: hierarchy of feedback systems and control of input. In Perspectives in Ethology, Vol. 6. Mechanisms, ed. P. P. G. Bateson, P. H. Klopfer, pp. 109–68. New York: Plenum

Crews, D., ed. 1988. Psychobiology of Reproductive Behavior. Englewood Cliffs, NJ: Prentice-Hall

Cullen, E. 1957. Adaptations in the kittiwake to cliff nesting. Ibis 9:275–302

Cuthill, I. C., Kacelnik, A., Krebs, J. R., Haccou, P., et al. 1990. Starlings exploiting patches: the effect of recent experience on foraging decisions. Anim. Behav. 40:625–40

Daly, M., Wilson, M. 1988a. Homocide. Hawthorne, NY: Aldine de Gruyter

Daly, M., Wilson, M. 1988b. Psychology of discriminative parental solicitude. See Leger 1988, pp. 51–144

Darwin, C. 1871. The Descent of Man and Selection in Relation to Sex. London: John

Murray

Davey, G. 1989. *Ecological Learning Theory.* New York: Routledge

Davies, N. B. 1991. Mating systems. See Krebs & Davies 1991, pp. 263–94

Davies, N. B., Houston, A. I. 1984. Territory economics. See Krebs & Davies 1984, pp. 148–69

Davis, H., Perusse, R. 1988. Numerical competence in animals: definitional issues, current evidence, and a new research agenda. *Behav. Brain Sci.* 11:561–615

Davis, W. J. 1984. Motivation and learning: Neurophysiological mechanisms in a "model" system. *Learn. Motiv., 15,* 377–93

Dawkins, M. S. 1989. The future of ethology, how many legs are we standing on? See Bateson & Klopfer 1989, pp. 47–54

Dawkins, M. S. 1990. From an animal's point of view: motivation, fitness and animal welfare. *Behav. Brain Sci.* 13:1–61

Dawkins, M. S., Halliday, T. R., Dawkins, R., eds. 1991. *The Tinbergen Legacy.* London: Chapman Hall

Demarest, J. 1981. *Comparative Psychology Newsletter.* W. Long Branch, NJ: Monmouth Coll.

Dennett, D. C. 1987. *The Intentional Stance.* Cambridge, MA: MIT Press

Dennis, W. 1941. Spalding's experiment on the flight of birds repeated with another species. *J. Comp. Psychol.* 31:337–48

Dethier, V. G. 1976. *The Hungry Fly: A Physiological Study of the Behavior Associated with Feeding.* Cambridge, MA: Harvard Univ. Press

Dewsbury, D. A. 1985. *Studying Animal Behavior.* Chicago: Univ. Chicago Press

Dewsbury, D. A. 1988. The comparative psychology of monogamy. See Leger 1988, pp. 1–50

Dewsbury, D. A. 1989a. Comparative psychology, ethology, and animal behavior. *Annu. Rev. Psychol.* 40:581–602

Dewsbury, D. A. 1989b. Frank Ambrose Beach 1911–1988. *Am. J. Psychol.* 102:414–20

Dewsbury, D. A. 1990. *Contemporary Issues in Comparative Psychology.* Sunderland, MA: Sinauer

Dickinson, A. 1980. *Contemporary Animal Learning Theory.* Cambridge: Cambridge Univ. Press

Domjan, M., Hollis, K. L. 1988. Reproductive behavior: a potential model system for adaptive specializations in learning. See Bolles & Beecher 1988, pp. 213–37

Dooling, R. J., Hulse, S. H. 1989. *The Comparative Psychology of Audition.* Hillsdale, NJ: Erlbaum

Driver, P. M., Humphries, D. A. 1988. *Protean Behavior: The Biology of Unpredictability.* Oxford: Clarendon Press

Dukas, R., Real, L. A. 1991. Learning foraging tasks by bees: A comparison between social and solitary species. *Anim. Behav.* 42: 269–76

Dumas, C., Dore, F. Y. 1991 Cognitive development in kittens (*Felis catus*): an observational study of object permanence and sensorimotor intelligence. *J. Comp. Psychol.* 105:357–65

Eberhard, W. G. 1980. Horned beetles. *Sci. Am.* 242:166–82

Eberhard, W. G. 1982. Behavioral characteristics for the higher classification of orb-weaving spiders. *Evolution* 36:1067–95

Eibl-Eibesfeldt, I. 1975. *Ethology: the Biology of Behavior.* New York: McGraw-Hill

Eldredge, N. 1989. *Macroevolutionary Dynamics: Species, Niches, and Adaptive Peaks.* New York: McGraw-Hill

Everitt, B. J. 1991. Sexual motivation: a neural and behavioural analysis of the mechanisms underlying appetitive and copulatory responses of male rats. *Neurosci. Biobehav. Rev.* 14:217–32

Everitt, J., Hurst, J. L., Ashworth D., Barnard, C. J. 1991. Aggressive behaviour among wild-caught house mice, *Mus domesticus* Rutty, correlates with a measure of genetic similarity using DNA fingerprinting. *Anim. Behav.* 42:313–16

Fanselow, M. S. 1989. The adaptive function of conditioned defensive behavior: an ecological approach to Pavlovian stimulus-substitution theory. See Blanchard et al 1989, pp. 151–66

Fanselow, M. S., Lester, L. S. 1988. A functional behavioristic approach to aversively motivated behavior: predatory imminence as a determinant of the topography of defensive behavior. See Bolles & Beecher 1988, pp. 185–212

Fentress, J. C. 1991. Analytical ethology and synthetic neuroscience. See Bateson 1991, pp. 77–120

Fisher, J. W. 1991. Disambiguating anthropomorphism: an interdisciplinary review. See Bateson & Klopfer 1991, pp. 49–85

Gagnon, S., Dore, F. Y. 1992. Search behavior in various breeds of adult dogs (*Canis familiaris*): object permanence and olfactory cues. *J. Comp. Psychol.* 106:58–68

Galef, B. G. 1990. An adaptationist perspective on social learning, social feeding, and social foraging in Norway rats. See Dewsbury 1990, pp. 55–79

Gallistel, C. R. 1989. Animal cognition. *Annu. Rev. Psychol.* 40:155–89

Gallistel, C. R. 1990. *The Organization of Learning.* Cambridge, MA: MIT Press

Garcia, J., Brett, L. P., Rusiniak, K. W. 1989. Limits of Darwinian conditioning. In *Contemporary Learning Theories: Instrumental Conditioning Theory and the Impact of Biological Constraints on Learning,* ed. S. B. Klein & R. R. Mowrer. *Hillsdale NJ: Erlbaum*

Gardner, R. A., Gardner, B. T., Van Cantfort, T. E. 1989. *Teaching Sign Language to Chimpanzees.* Albany, NY: SUNY Press

Gaulin, S. J., FitzGerald, R. W., Wartell, M. S. 1990. Sex differences in spatial ability and activity in two vole species (*Microtus ochrogaster* and *M. pennsylvanicus*). *J. Comp. Psychol.* 104:88–93

Gaulin, S. J., Wartell, M. S. 1990. Effects of experience and motivation on symmetrical-maze performance in the prairie vole (*Microtus ochrogaster*). *J. Comp. Psychol.* 104:183–89

Gibbons, E. G. Jr., Wyers, E. J., Waters, E., Manzel, E. W. Jr. 1992. *Naturalistic Environments in Captivity for Animal Behavior Research*. Albany, NY: SUNY Press

Gisiner, R., Schusterman, R. J. 1992. Sequence, syntax, and semantics: responses of a language-trained sea lion (*Zalophys californianus*) to novel sign combinations. *J. Comp. Psychol.* 106:78–91

Gittleman, J. L., ed. *1989a. Carnivore Behavior, Ecology, and Evolution*. Ithaca, NY: Cornell Univ. Press

Gittleman, J. L. 1989b. The comparative approach in ethology: aims and limitations. See Bateson & Klopfer 1989, pp. 55–83

Glickman, S. E., Sroges, R. W. 1966. Curiosity in zoo animals. *Behaviour* 26:151–88

Gold, P. E., Stone, W. S. 1988. Neuroendocrine effects on memory in aged rodents and humans. Special issue: experimental models of age-related memory dysfunction and neurodegeneration. *Neurobiol. Aging* 9:709–17

Goldthwaite, R. O., Coss, R. G., Owings, D. H. 1990. Evolutionary dissipation of an anti-snake system: differential behavior by California and Arctic ground squirrels in above- and below-ground contexts. *Behaviour* 112:246–69

Gottlieb, G. 1984. Evolutionary trends and evolutionary origins: relevance to theory in comparative psychology. *Psychol. Rev.* 91:448–56

Gottlieb, G. 1992. *Individual Development and Evolution: The Genesis of Novel Behavior*. New York: Oxford Univ. Press

Gould, J. L. 1986. The biology of learning. *Annu. Rev. Psychol.* 37:163–92

Grafen, A. 1991. Modelling in behavioural ecology. See Krebs & Davies 1991, pp. 5–31

Grant, P. 1986. *Ecology and Evolution of Darwin's Finches*. Princeton: Princeton Univ. Press

Grier, J. W., Burk, T. 1992. *Biology of Animal Behavior*. St. Louis: Mosby

Griffin, D. R. 1981. *The Question of Animal Awareness*. New York: Rockefeller Univ. Press. 2nd ed.

Groebel, J., Hinde, R. A., eds. 1989. *Aggression and War: Their Biological and Social Bases*. Cambridge: Cambridge Univ. Press

Grohmann, J. 1939. Modifikation oder Funktionsreifung? Ein Beitrag zur Klärung der Wechselseitigen Beziehungen zwischen Instinkthandlung und Erfahrung. *Z. Tierpsychol.* 2:132–44

Grossberg, S., ed. 1988. *Neural Networks and Natural Intelligence*. Cambridge, MA: MIT Press

Gyger, M., Marler, P. 1988. Food calling in the domestic fowl, *Gallus gallus:* the role of external referents and deception. *Anim. Behav.* 36:358–65

Hailman, J. P. 1965. Cliff-nesting adaptations of the Galapagos swallow-tailed gull. *Wilson Bull.* 77:346–62

Hailman, J. P. 1967. The ontogeny of an instinct. *Behaviour* (Suppl.) 15:1–159

Hailman, J. P. 1988. Operationalism, optimality and optimism: suitabilities versus adaptations of organisms. In *Evolutionary Processes and Metaphors,* ed. M. W. Ho, S. W. Fox, pp. 85–116. London: John Wiley & Sons

Hall, W. G. 1990. The ontogeny of ingestive behavior: changing control of components in the feeding sequence. See Stricker 1990, pp. 77–123

Harvey, P. H., Krebs, J. R. 1990. Comparing brains. *Science* 249:140–46

Harvey, P. H., Pagel, M. D. 1991. *The Comparative Method in Evolutionary Biology*. Oxford: Oxford Univ. Press

Hawkins, R. D., Kandel, E. R. 1984. Is there a cell-biological alphabet for simple forms of learning? *Psychol. Rev.* 91:376–91

Heidiger, H. 1950. *Wild Animals in Captivity*. London: Butterworths

Heiligenberg, W. 1991. The neural basis of behavior: a neuroethological view. *Annu. Rev. Neurosci.* 14:247–67

Herman, L. M., Morrel-Samuels, P., Pack, A. A. 1990. Bottlenosed dolphin and human recognition of veridical and degraded video displays of an artificial gestural language. *J. Exper. Psychol.: Gen.* 119:215–30

Herrnstein, R. J. 1990. Levels of stimulus control: a functional approach. *Cognition* 37:133–66

Hinde, R. A. 1966. *Animal Behaviour*. New York: McGraw-Hill

Hinde, R. A. 1991. From animals to humans. See Dawkins 1991 et al, pp. 31–39

Hodos, W., Campbell, C. B. G. 1969. The scala naturae: why there is no theory in comparative psychology. *Psychol. Rev.* 76:337–50

Hodos, W., Campbell, C. B. G. 1990. Evolutionary scales and comparative studies of animal cognition. See Kesner & Olton 1990, pp. 1–20

Hogan, J. A. 1988. Cause and function in the development of behavior systems. See Blass 1988, pp. 63–106

Hogan, J. A., Honrado, G. I., Vestergaard, K. 1991. Development of a behavior system: dustbathing in the Burmese red junglefowl (*Gallus gallus spadiceus*): II. Internal factors. *J. Comp. Psychol.* 105:269–73

Holldobler, B., Wilson, E. O. 1990. *The Ants*. Harvard: Harvard Univ. Press

Hollis, K. L. 1990. The role of Pavlovian conditioning in territorial aggression and reproduction. See Dewsbury 1990, pp. 197–220

Honig, W. K., Fetterman, J. G. 1992. *Cognitive*

Aspects of Stimulus Control. Hillsdale, NJ: Erlbaum

Hughes, B. O., Duncan, I. J. 1988. The notion of ethological "need," models of motivation and animal welfare. *Anim. Behav.* 36:1696–1707

Immelmann, K., Barlow, G. W., Petrinovich, L., Main, M. 1981. *Behavioral Development: The Bielefeld Interdisciplinary Project.* Cambridge: Cambridge Univ. Press

Ingle, D., Crews, D. 1985. Vertebrate neuroethology: definitions and paradigms. *Annu. Rev. Neurosci.* 8:457–94

Jerison, H. J. 1973. *Evolution of the Brain and Intelligence.* New York: Academic

Jerison, H. J., Jerison I., eds. 1988. *Intelligence and Evolutionary Biology.* New York: Springer-Verlag

Kallander, H., Smith, H. G. 1990. Food storing in birds: an evolutionary perspective. *Curr. Ornithol.* 7:147–208

Kamil, A. C., Roitblat, H. L. 1985. The ecology of foraging behavior: implications for animal learning and memory. *Annu. Rev. of Psychol.* 36:141–69

Kamil, A. C. 1988. A synthetic approach to the study of animal intelligence. See Lager 1988, pp. 257–308

Kamil, A. C., Krebs, J. R., Pulliam, H. R. 1987. *Foraging Behavior.* New York: Plenum

Kesner, R. P., Olton, D. S., eds. 1990. *Neurobiology of Comparative Cognition.* Hillsdale, NJ: Erlbaum

Kessel, E. L. 1955. Mating activities of balloon flies. *Syst. Zool.* 4:97–104

Ketterson, E. D., Nolan, V. Jr. 1992. Hormones and life histories: an integrative approach. *Am. Nat.* In press

King, A. P., West, M. J. 1990. Variation in species-typical behavior: a contemporary issue for comparative psychology. See Dewsbury 1990, pp. 321–39

Krebs, J. R., Davies, N. B. 1984. *Behavioural Ecology: an Evolutionary Approach* Sunderland, MA: Sinauer. 2nd ed.

Krebs, J. R., Davies, N. B. 1991. *Behavioural Ecology: An Evolutionary Approach.* Oxford: Blackwell. 3rd ed.

Krebs, J. R., Healy, S. D., Shettleworth, S. J. 1990. Spatial memory of Paridae: comparison of a storing and a nonstoring species, the coal tit, *Parus ater,* and the great tit, *P. Major. Anim. Behav.* 39:1127–37

Kroodsma, D. E., Konishi, M. 1991. A suboscine bird (eastern phoebe, *Sayornis phoebe*) develops normal song without auditory feedback. *Anim. Behav.* 42:477–87

Krushinski, L. V. 1965. Solution of elementary logical problems by animals on the basis of extrapolation. *Prog. Brain Res.* 17:280–308

Kuo, Z. Y. 1976. *The Dynamics of Behavior Development: An Epigenetic View* New York: Plenum. Enlarged ed.

Lammers, J. H. C. M., Kruk, M. R., Meelis, W., van der Poel, A. M. 1988a. Hypothalamic substrates for brain stimulation-in-duced attack, teeth-chattering and social grooming in the rat. *Brain Res.* 449:311–27

Lammers, J. H. C. M., Kruk, M. R., Meelis, W., van der Poel, A. M. 1988b. Hypothalamic substrates for brain stimulation-in-duced patterns of locomotion and escape jumps in the rat. *Brain Res.* 449:294–310

Langtimm, C. A., Dewsbury, D. A. 1991. Phylogeny and evolution of rodent copulatory behaviour. *Anim. Behav.* 41:217–25

Langton, C. L., Farmer, J. D., Rasmussen, S., Taylor, C., eds. 1991. *Artificial Life II.* New York: Addison-Wesley

Leger, D. W., ed. 1988. *Nebraska Symposium on Motivation, 1987: Comparative Perspectives in Modern Psychology.* Lincoln, NE: Univ. Nebraska Press

Lehrman, D. S. 1953. A critique of Konrad Lorenz's theory of instinctive behavior. *Q. Rev. Biol.* 28:337–63

Lessells, C. M. 1991. The evolution of life histories. See Krebs & Davies 1991, pp. 32–68

Logue, A. W. 1988. A comparison of taste aversion learning in humans and other vertebrates: evolutionary pressures in common. See Bolles & Beecher 1988, pp. 97–116

Lorenz, K. 1965. *The Evolution and Modification of Behavior.* Chicago: Univ. Chicago Press

Lorenz, K. Z. 1950. The comparative method in studying innate behaviour patterns. *Symp. Soc. Exp. Biol., IV.* 4:221–68

Losos, J. B. 1990. Concordant evolution of locomotor behaviour, display rate and morphology in *Anolis* lizards. *Anim. Behav.* 39:879–90

Lucas, J. R., Walter, L. R. 1991. When should chickadees hoard food? Theory and experimental results. *Anim. Behav.* 41:579–601

MacLean, P. D. 1990. *The Triune Brain in Evolution: Role in Paleocerebral Functions.* New York: Plenum

Macphail, E. M. 1985. Vertebrate intelligence: the null hypothesis. In *Animal Intelligence,* ed. L. Weiskrantz, pp. 37–51. Oxford: Clarendon Press

Maier, N. R. F., Schneirla, T. C. 1935. *Principles of Animal Psychology.* New York: McGraw-Hill

Mangel, M., Clark, C. W. 1988. *Dynamic Modeling in Behavioral Ecology.* Princeton, NJ: Princeton Univ. Press

Manson, J. H., Wrangham, R. W. 1991. Intergroup aggression in chimpanzees and humans. *Curr. Anthropol.* 32:369–90

Marler, C.A., Moore, M. C. 1991. Supplementary feeding compensates for testosterone-induced costs of aggression in male mountain spiny lizards, sceloporusjarrovi. *Anim. Behav.* 42:209–19

Marler, P. 1991. Song-learning behavior: the interface with neuroethology. *Trends Neurosci.* 14:100–206

Marler, P., Hamilton, W. J. 1966. *Mechanisms of Animal Behavior.* New York: Wiley

Martin, G. M., Bechara, A., Van der Kooy, D. 1991. The perception of emotion: parallel neural processing of the affective and discriminative properties of opiates. *Psychobiology* 19:147–52

Martin, R. D. 1974. The biological basis of human behavior. In *The Biology of Brains,* ed. W. B. Broughton, pp. 215–50. New York: Wiley

Martinez, J. L. Jr., Kesner, R. P. 1991. *Learning and Memory: A Biological View.* New York: Academic

Mason, W. A., Lott, D. F. 1976. Ethology and comparative psychology. *Annu. Rev. Psychol.* 27:129–54

Masterton, R. B., Heffner, H., Ravizza, R. 1969. Evolution of human hearing. *J. Acoust. Soc. Am.* 45:966–85

Maynard-Smith, J. 1982. *Evolution and the Theory of Games.* Cambridge: Cambridge Univ. Press

Mayr, E. 1974. Behavior programs and evolutionary strategies. *Am. Sci.* 62:650–59

McClintock, M. K. 1984. Group mating in the domestic rat as a context for sexual selection: consequences for the analysis of sexual behavior and neuroendocrine responses. In *Advances in the Study of Behavior,* ed. J. Rosenblatt, C. Beer, R. Hinde, pp. 1–15. New York: Academic

McNab, B. 1989. Basal rate of metabolism, body size, and food habits in the order Carnivora. See Gittleman 1989a, pp. 335–54

McNamara, J. M., Houston, A. I. 1990. The value of fat reserves and the tradeoff between starvation and predation. *Acta Biotheor.* 38:37–61

Michener, C. D. 1974. *The Social Behavior of the Bees.* Cambridge, MA: Harvard Univ. Press

Milinski, M., Parker, G. A. 1991. Competition for resources. See Krebs & Davies 1991, pp. 137–68

Miller, D. 1988. Development of instinctive behavior: an epigenetic and ecological approach. See Blass 1988, pp. 415–44

Moffatt, C. A., Hogan, J. A. 1992. Ontogeny of chick responses to maternal food calls in the Burmese Red Junglefowl (*Gallus gallus spadiceus*). *J. Comp. Psychol.* 106:92–96

Moore, C. L. 1990. Comparative development of vertebrate sexual behavior: levels, cascades, and webs. See Dewsbury 1990, pp. 278–99

Mrosovsky, N. 1990. *Rheostasis: The Physiology of Change.* Toronto: Univ. Toronto Press

Mulder, M. B. 1991. Human behavioural ecology. See Krebs & Davies 1991, pp. 69–98

Myers, G. 1990. *Writing Biology: Texts in the Social Construction of Scientific Knowledge.* Madison: Univ. Wisconsin Press

Nitecki, M. H., ed. 1988., *Evolutionary Progress.* Chicago, IL: Univ. Chicago Press

Nottebohm, F. 1991. Reassessing the mechanisms and origins of vocal learning in birds. *Trends Neurosci.* 14:206–11

Novak, M. A., Petto, A. J. 1991. *Through the Looking Glass: Issues of Psychological Well-being in Captive Nonhuman Primates.* Washington, DC: American Psychological Association

Olson, D. J. 1991. Species differences in spatial memory among Clark's nutcrackers, scrub jays, and pigeons. *J. Exp. Psychol.: Anim. Behav. Process.* 17:363–76

Oppenheim, R. W. 1982. Preformation and epigenesis in the origins of the nervous system and behavior: issues, concepts, and their history. In *Perspectives in Ethology,* ed. P. P. G. Bateson, P. H. Klopfer, 5:101–131. New York: Plenum

Oyama, S. 1985. *The Ontogeny of Information.* Cambridge: Cambridge Univ. Press

Parker, S. T. 1990. Origins of comparative developmental evolutionary studies of primate mental abilities. See Parker & Gibson 1990, pp. 3–64

Parker, S. T., Gibson, K. R., ed. 1990. "Language" and Intelligence in Monkeys and Apes. Cambridge: Cambridge Univ. Press

Patterson, I. J. 1965. Timing and spacing of broods in the black-headed gull, *Larus ridibundus. Ibis* 107:433–59

Pepperberg, I. M. 1990. Some cognitive capacities of an African Grey parrot (*Psittacus erithacus*). *Adv. Stud. Behav.* 19:357–409

Pepperberg, I. M., Funk, M. S. 1990. Object permanence in four species of psittacine birds: an African Grey parrot (*Psittacus erithacus*), an Illiger mini macaw (*Ara maracana*), a parakeet (*Melopsittacus undulatus), and a cockatiel (Nymphicus hollandicus*). *Anim. Learn. Behav.* 18:97–108

Petrinovich, L. 1990. Avian song development: methodological and conceptual issues. See Dewsbury 1990, pp. 340–59

Plomin, R., DeFries, J. C., McClearn, G. E. 1990. *Behavioral Genetics.* San Francisco: Freeman

Plowright, C. M., Shettleworth, S. J. 1991. Time horizon and choice by pigeons in a prey-selection task. *Anim. Learn. Behav.* 19:103–12

Povinelli, D. J., Parks, K. A., Novak, M. A. 1991. Do rhesus monkeys (*Macaca mulatta*) attribute knowledge and ignorance to others. *J. Comp. Psychol.* 105:318–25

Premack, D. 1983. The codes of men and beasts. *Behav. Brain Sci.* 6:125–67

Provine, W. B. 1988. Progress in evolution and meaning in life. See Nitecki 1988, pp. 49–74

Pulliam, H. R., Caraco, T. 1984. Living in groups: Is there an otpimal group size? See Krebs & Davies 1984, pp. 122-47

Razran, G. 1971. *Mind in Evolution.* New York: Houghton Mifflin

Real, L. A. 1991. Animal choice behavior and the evolution of cognitive architecture. *Science* 253:980–86

Regan, T. 1983. *The Case for Animal Rights.*

Berkeley, CA: Univ. California Press

Richner, H., Marclay, C. 1991. Evolution of avian roosting behaviour: a test of the information centre hypothesis and of a critical assumption. *Anim. Behav.* 41:433–38

Ridley, M. 1983. *The Explanation of Organic Diversity.* Oxford: Clarendon Press

Riley, D. A., Langley, C. M. 1993. The logic of species comparison. *Psychol. Sci.* In press

Ristau, C. A., ed. 1991. *Cognitive Ethology: The Minds of Other Animals: Essays in Honor of Donald R. Griffin.* Hillsdale, NJ: Erlbaum

Robinson, G. E., Page, R. E., Strambi, C., Strambi, A. 1989. Hormonal and genetic control of behavioral integration in honey bee colonies. *Science* 246:109–12

Robinson, M. H. 1985. Predator-prey interactions, informational complexity, and the origins of intelligence. *J. Washington Acad. Sci.* 75:91–104

Robinson, M. H. 1991. Niko Tinbergen, comparative studies and evolution. See Dawkins et al 1991, pp. 100–28

Roitblat, H. L. 1987. *Introduction to Comparative Cognition.* San Francisco: Freeman

Romanes, G. J. 1884. *Mental Evolution in Animals.* New York: Appleton

Rose, J. D. 1990. Forebrain influences on brainstem and spinal mechanisms of copulatory behavior: a current perspective on Frank Beach's contribution. *Neurosci. Biobehav. Rev.* 14:207–16

Rosenblatt, J. S. 1989. The physiological and evolutionary background of maternal responsiveness. *New Direct. Child Dev.* 1989:15–30

Rovee-Collier, C., Kupersmidt, J., O'Brien, L., Collier, G. 1991. Behavioral thermoregulation and immobilization: conflicting demands for survival. *J. Comp. Psychol.* 105:232–42

Rusak, B., Robertson, H. A., Wisden, W., Hunt, S. P. 1990. Light-pulses that shift rhythms induce gene-expression in the suprachiasmatic nucleus. *Science* 248:1237–40

Savage-Rumbaugh, S. 1988. A new look at ape language: comprehension of speech and syntax. See Lager 1988, pp. 201–55

Schmidt-Nielsen, K. 1984. *Scaling: Why Is Animal Size so Important?* Cambridge: Cambridge Univ. Press

Scott, J. P. 1973. The organization of comparative psychology. *Ann. NY Acad. Sci.* 223:7–40

Sherry, D. F., Vaccarino, A. L., Buckenham, K., Herz, R. S. 1989. The hippocampal complex of food-storing birds. *Brain Behav. Evol.* 34:308–17

Shettleworth, S. J. 1990. Spatial memory in food-storing birds. *Philos. Trans. R. Soc. London Ser. B* 329:143–51

Shettleworth, S. J. 1993. Where is the comparison in comparative cognition? *Psychol. Sci.* In press.

Silver, R. 1990. Biological timing mechanisms with special emphasis on the parental behavior of doves. See Dewsbury 1990, pp. 252–77

Simmons, J. A. 1989. A view of the world through the bat's ear: the formation of acoustic images in echolocation. *Cognition* 33:155–99

Sinervo, B., Huey, R. 1990. Allometric engineering: testing the causes of interpopulational difference in performance. *Science* 278:1106–9

Singer, P. 1990. The significance of animal suffering. *Behav. Brain. Sci.* 13:9–12

Skinner, B. F. 1938. *The Behavior of Organisms.* New York: Appleton-Century-Crofts

Skinner, B. F. 1959. A case history in the scientific method. In *Psychology: The Study of a Science,* ed. S. Koch, 2:359–79. New York: McGraw-Hill

Slobodchikoff, C. N., ed. 1988. *The Ecology of Social Behavior.* New York: Academic

Snowdon, C. T. 1983. Ethology, comparative psychology, and animal behavior. *Annu. Rev. Psychol.* 34:63–94

Spear, N. E., Miller, J. S., Jagielo, J. A. 1990. Animal memory and learning. *Annu. Rev. Psychol.* 41:169–211

Squire, L. R. 1992. Memory and the hippocampus: a synthesis from findings with rats, monkeys, and humans. *Psychol. Rev.* 99:195–231

Staddon, J. E. R. 1989. Animal psychology: the tyranny of anthropocentrism. See Bateson & Klopfer 1989, pp. 123–34

Stephens, D. W., Krebs, J. R. 1986. *Foraging Theory.* Princeton: Princeton Univ. Press

Stricker, E. M. 1990. *Handbook of Behavioral Neurobiology* Vol. 10. *Neurobiology of Food and Fluid Intake.* New York: Plenum

Suboski, M. D. 1989. Recognition learning in birds. In Bateson & Klopfer 1989, pp. 137–1

Thelen, E. 1990. Dynamical systems and the generation of individual differences. In *Individual Differences in Infancy: Reliability, Stability, and Prediction,* ed. J. Colombo, J. W. Fagen, pp. 77–117. Englewood Cliffs, NJ: Erlbaum

Thelen, E., Ulrich, B. D. 1991. Hidden skills. *Monogr. Soc. Res. Child Dev.* 561:1–106

Thiessen, D. 1990. Body size, allometry, and comparative psychology: locomotion and foraging. See Dewsbury 1990, pp. 80–100

Thornhill, N. W., Thornhill, R. 1991. An evolutionary analysis of psychological pain following human (*Homo sapiens*) rape: IV. The effect of the nature of the sexual assault. *J. Comp. Psychol.* 105:243–52

Thorpe, W. H. 1979. *The Origins and Rise of Ethology.* New York: Praeger

Timberlake, W. 1983. The functional organization of appetitive behavior: behavior systems and learning. In *Advances in Analysis of Behavior. Biological Factors in Learning,* ed. M. D. Zeiler, P. Harzem, 3:177–221. Chichester: Wiley

Timberlake, W. 1990. Natural learning in laboratory paradigms. See Dewsbury 1990, pp. 31–54

Timberlake, W., Washburne, D. L. 1989. Feeding ecology and laboratory predatory behavior toward live and artificial moving prey in seven rodent species. *Anim. Learn. Behav.* 17:2–11

Timberlake, W., Lucas, G. A. 1989. Behavior systems and learning: from misbehavior to general laws. In *Contemporary Learning Theories: Instrumental Conditioning Theory and the Impact of Biological Constraints on Learning,* ed. S. B. Klein, R. R. Mowrer, pp. 237–75. Hillsdale, NJ: Erlbaum

Timberlake, W., White, W. 1990. Winning isn't everything: rats need only food deprivation and not food reward to efficiently traverse a radial arm maze. *Learn. Motiv.* 21:153–63

Tinbergen, N. 1951. *The Study of Instinct.* Oxford: Clarendon Press

Tinbergen, N., Perdeck, A. C. 1950. On the stimulus situation releasing the begging response in the newly hatched herring gull chick (*Larus argentatus argentatus* Pont.) *Behaviour* 3:1–39

Toates, F. 1986. *Motivational Systems.* Cambridge: Cambridge Univ. Press

Tomonaga, M., Matsuzawa, T. 1992. Perception of complex geometric figures in chimpanzees (Pantroglodytes) and humans (Homosapeins): analyses of visual similarity on the basis of choice reaction time. *J. Comp. Psychol.* 106:43-52

Uexkull, J. von 1934. *Streifzüge durch die Umwelten von Tieren und Menschen.* Berlin: Springer. Transl. in Schiller, C. H. 1957. *Instinctive Behavior: The Development of a Modern Concept.* New York: International Universities Press

Van Tets, G. F. 1965. A comparative study of some social communication patterns in the Pelecaniformes. *Ornithol. Monogr.* 2:1–88

Vander Wall, S. T. 1990. *Food Hoarding in Animals.* Chicago: Univ. Chicago Press

Vaughan, T. A. 1978. *Mammalogy.* Philadelphia: Saunders

Viney, W., King, D., Berndt, J. 1990. Animal research in psychology: declining or thriving? *J. Comp. Psychol.* 104:322–25

Warden, C. J., Jenkins, T. N., Warner, L. H. 1935. *Comparative Psychology: A Comprehensive Treatise,* Vol. 1. New York: Ronald

Washburn, D. A., Rumbaugh, D. M. 1991. Ordinal judgments of numerical symbols by macaques (*Macaca mulatta*). *Psychol. Sci.* 2:190–93

Wasserman, E. A. 1993. Comparative cognition: beginning the second century of the study of animal intelligence. *Psychol. Bull.* In press

Wasserman, E. A., Kiedinger, R. E., Bhatt, R. S. 1988. Conceptual behavior in pigeons: categories, subcategories, and pseudo categories. *J. Exp. Psychol.: Anim. Behav. Process.* 14:235–46

Weatherhead, P. J., Montgomerie, R. D. 1991. Good news and bad news about DNA fingerprinting. *Trends Ecol. Evol.* 6:173–4

West, M. J., King, A. P. 1990. Mozart's starling. *Am. Sci.* 78:106–14

Wheeler, D. A., Kyriacou, C. P., Greenacre, M. L., Yu, Q., Rutila, J. E. 1991. Molecular transfer of a species-specific behavior from *Drosophila simulans* to *Drosophila melanogaster. Science* 251:1082–85

Whiten, A., ed. 1991. *Natural Theories of Mind: Evolution, Development and Simulation of Everyday Mindreading.* Oxford: Basil Blackwell

Wikler, K. C., Finlay, B. L. 1989. Developmental heterochrony and the evolution of species differences in retinal specializations. In *Development of the Vertebrate Retina,* ed. B. L. Finlay, D. R. Sengelaub, pp. 227–46. New York: Plenum

Wilson, E. O. 1975. *Sociobiology: The New Synthesis.* Cambridge, MA: Harvard Univ. Press

Wingfield, J. C., Moore, M. C. 1988. Hormonal, social, and environmental factors in the reproductive biology of free-living male birds. See Crews 1988, pp. 149–75

Yoerg, S. I. 1993. Ecological frames of mind: the role of cognition in behavioral ecology. *Q. Rev. Biol.* In press

Young, R. K., Thiessen, D. D. 1991. Washing, drying, and anointing in adult humans (*Homo sapiens*): commonalities with grooming sequences in rodents. *J. Comp. Psychol.* 105:340–44

Zentall, T. R., Galef, B. G. Jr. 1988. *Social Learning: Psychological and Biological Perspectives.* Hillsdale, NJ: Erlbaum

AUTHOR INDEX

A

Aarstad, H. J., 70
Abbott-Shim, M., 622, 636
Abelson, R. P., 36, 123, 170, 298, 587
Abma, J. C., 543
Abraham, L. M., 128
Abrahamson, D. J., 353
Abrams, D., 177
Abrams, D. B., 537
Abrams, R. A., 400
Abramson, L. Y., 44, 567, 571
Abu-Lughod, L., 499, 515
Achee, J. W., 169, 179
Achenbach, T. M., 572
Ackerman, K. D., 72
Ackerman, P. L., 32, 36, 251, 256
Ackerman, S. H., 70
Ackerman-Ross, S., 617, 627
Acorn, D. A., 161
Adams, E. S., 698
Adams, J. S., 200
Adams, M. J., 238, 241, 242, 245, 389
Adams, N. E., 37
Adams, R. D., 462, 466
Adapathya, R., 238, 245
Adelmann, P. K., 602
ADER, R., 53–85; 53, 55, 56, 60–70, 72, 75, 76
Adkins-Holmes, C., 249, 252
Adkins-Regan, E., 682
Adler, N. J., 221
Agler, H. L., 509
Ago, Y., 67
Agostinelli, G., 171
Agras, W. S., 352
Ahluwalia, P., 68
Ahmed, I. I., 69, 72
Ahmed-Ansari, A., 70
Ahrens, A. H., 44
Ai, W., 94
Aigner, T., 476
Ainsworth, M. D. S., 575, 619, 623, 625, 630, 635
Aird, P., 166
Ajjanagadde, V., 276, 307
Ajzen, I., 27, 123, 131, 133, 286
Akutsu, P. D., 364
Alba, J. W., 429
Albee, G. W., 550
Albert, M. L., 484
Albright, L., 157
Albus, J. S., 327

Alcock, J., 393, 646
Alexander, C. M., 364
Alexander, J., 284, 542
Alexander, J. F., 534
Alexander, P. C., 354
Alexander, R. A., 252
Alexander, R. M., 677
Alfert, E., 6
Alkon, D. L., 319, 686
Alksnis, O., 292
Allen, J. P., 544
Allen, N. J., 204
Allen, R., 283
Allen, V. L., 444, 591, 593, 597, 598, 604
Alley, W., 251
Allison, S. T., 169
Alloy, L. B., 567, 571
Allport, D. A., 397
Allport, G. W., 166, 435, 436
Alluisi, E. A., 256
Allwood, C. M., 105, 107
Altemeyer, B., 143, 145
Alter, W. A. III, 688
Altmaier, E. M., 351
Altman, D. G., 541, 542, 548
Alvarez, W. F., 621
Alvarez-Royo, P., 455
Alwin, D. F., 140
Amaiwa, S., 300
Amaral, D. G., 321, 462, 467, 469
Ambady, N., 158
Ames, C., 25, 567
Ames, R., 25, 567
Amkraut, A. A., 66
Amorim, M.-A., 283
Amrhein, P. C., 395
Anand, P., 138, 139
Anastasi, A., 89
Ancona, D. G., 204
Andersen, S. M., 165, 167, 175
Anderson, C. A., 129, 164, 170
Anderson, C. W., 620, 629, 630
Anderson, J. A., 415, 577
Anderson, J. R., 3, 28, 239, 267, 269, 275, 278, 281, 282, 287, 288, 290, 297, 300, 304, 384, 390, 393, 429, 474
Anderson, K., 280
Anderson, N. H., 119, 161, 413
Anderson, R. C., 591
Anderson, W., 550

Andersson, B. E., 623, 627, 628, 631
Andersson, T., 433
Andre, A. D., 249
Andrew, R. J., 686
Andrews, D. H., 256
Andriole, S. J., 241
Andrykowski, M., 63
Andrykowski, M. A., 63
Angel, R., 506, 507
Angell, J. R., 430
Angleitner, A., 162
Angyal, A., 435
Anisman, H., 57, 64, 67, 68, 70, 71, 74
Annett, J., 255
Annis, A. B., 590
Anthony, E. J., 623
Anthony, J. C., 530
Anthony, W. A., 527
Antonovsky, A., 3
Appadurai, A., 515
Applegate, C. D., 323
Appley, M. H., 31
Apter, M. J., 44
Arbit, J., 454
Arbona, C., 362
Arbuthnot, J., 534
Arce, A. A., 531
Archer, L., 320
Arcuri, L., 141, 164
Arend, R., 630
Aristotle, 17
Arkes, H. R., 137
Armfield, A., 70, 74, 75
Armfield, A. V., 69, 73
Armstrong, N. A., 119
Arneric, S., 321
Arnold, M. B., 6
Arnold, S. J., 693
Arnold, S. T., 691
Arnow, B., 352
Aronson, E., 118, 145, 587
Aronson, L. R., 683
Arthur, W. Jr., 252
Arvey, R. D., 128
Asarnow, J. R., 567, 568, 570, 571, 575, 577
Asch, S. E., 161, 597
Asendorpf, J. B., 445
Ashby, F. G., 392, 393
Asher, S. R., 568, 575, 576
Ashford, S. J., 204, 222
Ashforth, B. E., 213
Ashmore, R. D., 141, 166
Ashworth, D., 691
Assanah, P., 69
Asuncion, A. G., 137, 138,

169
Atkinson, D. R., 345, 362–
64, 366, 367
Atkinson, R. C., 384, 454,
456
Atz, J., 687
Austin, J., 604
Averill, J. R., 6–8, 10, 17,
498
Avis, N. E., 285
Avolio, B. J., 214
Axsom, D., 134
Aydin, C., 203, 223
Aydin, O., 567
Azmitia, M., 596

B

Baba, M., 58
Bachevalier, J., 465, 476
Bachorowski, J., 565, 566
Bachrach, L. L., 530
Backer, T. E., 368, 539
Backs, R. W., 246
Baddeley, A. D., 245, 251,
385, 454–56, 472
Baerends, G. P., 694
Bagley, W. C., 409
Bagozzi, R. P., 132, 133
Bailey, J., 123, 143
Bailey, T., 25
Baillargeon, R., 296, 465
Baird, J. C., 444
Baker, N. L., 350
Baker, S. L., 37
Baker, S. M., 140, 141, 166
Baker, T. J., 75
Baker-Ward, L., 622, 623,
628
Bakin, J. S., 319
Balasubramanian, S. K., 123
Balda, R. P., 693, 695
Baldo, J. V., 332, 478
Baldwin, M. W., 594
Baldwin, R. B., 326, 699
Bales, R. F., 163
Ball, K., 253, 254
Ballesteros, S., 480
Balleyguier, G., 629
Ballieux, R. E., 69
Balota, D. A., 400
Balthazard, C., 283
Banaji, M. R., 124, 179
Bandura, A., 3, 24, 25, 28,
30, 35–37, 39, 41, 43, 44,
347, 348, 353, 437, 441,
563, 577, 579
Banks, W. P., 408
Banspach, S. W., 626
Barber, A. V., 252
Barber, P. J., 105
Barcus, G. S., 235
Barcus, T. T., 235
Barefoot, J. C., 566
Bareket, T., 245
Bargh, J. A., 39, 122, 143,

156, 160, 175, 178, 179,
595
Barglow, P., 630, 633, 634
Bar-Hillel, M., 286
Barkdoll, G. L., 653
Barker, J. L., 60
Barley, S. R., 202, 220, 223
Barlow, G. W., 678, 691, 693
Barnard, C. I., 220
Barnard, C. J., 691
Barnett, B., 242
Barnett, W. P., 206
Barnston, J. L., 293
Baron, J. N., 220, 388
Baron, R. A., 222
Baron, R. M., 656
Baron, R. S., 589
Baron, S., 238
Barr, R. A., 253
Barr, W. B., 463
Barrett, G. V., 252
Barrios, H. A., 58
Barry, R. A., 68
Barsalou, L. W., 270, 500
Barta, S. G., 29
Bartholomew, H., 509
Bartlett, F. C., 429, 605
Barton, C., 534
Bartram, D. J., 480
Basar, E., 436
Bashore, T. R., 397
Bass, B. M., 210, 211, 213
Bassili, J. N., 123, 180
Bassok, M., 298, 299
Basu, K., 139
Batchelor, W. F., 368
Bates, J. E., 566, 579, 630
Bates, S., 567, 575, 577
Bates, S. E., 572
Bateson, P. P. G., 676–78,
680, 691, 693, 697
Batson, C. D., 143
Battle, J., 577
Batuman, O. A., 70, 72
Baudry, M., 319
Bauer, P. J., 465
Baum, A., 590
Bauman, K. E., 131
Baumeister, R. F., 43, 44, 140
Baumgartner, J., 132, 133
Baydar, N., 628
Bayer, B. M., 69
Bazerman, M. H., 211, 215
Beach, L. R., 248
Beachler, M., 533
Beard, R. L., 256
Bearden, W. O., 140
Beaudin, P. A., 537
Beauvois, J.-L., 164
Bechara, A., 698
Beck, A. T., 564, 577
Beck, L., 133
Becker, A. B., 246
Becker, J. B., 677
Becker, K. J., 69, 72, 74
Becker, R. E., 67

Becker, S. E., 44
Beckmann, J., 24, 43
Bedell, J. R., 537
Beden, S. N., 67
Bedford, S., 530
Beecher, M. D., 690, 694
Been-Zeev, A., 429
Beer, C. G., 680, 682, 690,
698
Beer, R. D., 694
Beere, C. A., 349, 350
Behar, L., 532, 533
Bekoff, M., 699
Bell, G., 682
Bell, N. E., 209
Bell, N. J., 634
Bell, R. Q., 434, 438
Bell, W. J., 677
Beller, D. S., 69, 70
Belsky, J., 614, 618, 620,
621, 623, 627, 630, 631,
634, 635
Beltrami, E., 677
Bem, D. J., 134, 444
Bem, S. L., 37
Bempechat, J., 587
Benassi, V. A., 571
Bender, B., 533
Benedetti, F., 330
Ben-Eliyahu, S., 65
Ben-Ezra, L. A., 368, 372,
373
Benfield, C. Y., 571
Benn, R., 623
Bennett, B. M., 408, 418
Bennett, C. C., 526
Bennett, E. M., 527
Bennett, M. B., 530
Bennett, M. I., 530
Bennett, S., 364
Bennett, T. L., 54, 65
Benson, D. F., 463
Benson, J. E., 180
Benson, R. W., 56, 67, 72
Bentin, S., 479
Bentley, A. F., 14
Benton, A. L., 462
Benware, C. A., 595
Benzing, W., 472
Beracochea, D., 464
Berczi, I., 75
Bereccochea, J. E., 666
Berg, D., 201
Berger, C. R., 37
Berger, T. W., 318, 319, 467,
477
Berglund, M. B., 444
Berglund, U., 444
Bergman, L. R., 443–46
Berk, L., 625
Berko, J., 388
Berkowitz, L., 14, 134
Berkowitz, N. N., 364
Berman, H. J., 533
Bermudez-Rattoni, F., 325
Bernal, M. E., 365

Bernard, H., 537
Berndt, J., 677
Berndt, R. S., 484
Bernier, J. E., 365, 366
Bernieri, F., 25
Berniger, D. B., 242
Berntson, G. G., 327
Berry, D. C., 279, 281, 283, 472, 473
Berry, D. S., 158, 166
Berry, S. D., 319
Bersoff, D. M., 500, 506, 509, 511, 515
Berthier, N. E., 327
Bertrand, J. T., 550
Besedovsky, H. O., 75, 76
Bettman, J. R., 212, 266
Bettschart, W., 635
Betz, A. L., 127, 161
BETZ, N. E., 343–81; 346–48, 350, 351
Bhatt, R. S., 696
Bickman, L., 657
Biebach, H., 694
Biederman, I., 276, 480
Biegel, D. W., 540
Bienenstock, J., 57, 60
Biernat, M., 141, 169
Biernat, M. R., 168
Bieschke, K. J., 348
Big Foot, D. S., 364
Biggart, N. W., 213
Billig, M., 602
Bilsky, W., 125
Bingham, R. D., 666
Biolsi, K. J., 239
Biran, M., 37
Bird, C., 159
Birk, T., 138
Birnbaum, M. H., 413
Birt, D., 319
Bissonnette, V., 157, 158, 600
Bitner, M. J., 125
Bitterman, M. E., 683, 685
Bizot, E., 280
Bjork, R. A., 278, 454, 478
Black, P. H., 69, 70
Black-Cleworth, P. A., 319
Blackford, S. P., 479, 480
Blackman, H. S., 244
Blackstone, T., 174, 591, 593
Blake, A. W., 181
Blakely, C. H., 534
Blalock, J. A., 358, 361
Blalock, J. E., 73, 75
Blanch, A., 528
Blanchard, D. C., 321, 322, 679, 696
Blanchard, F. A., 173
Blanchard, M., 630
Blanchard, R. J., 321, 322, 679, 696
Blanchard-Fields, F., 282, 284, 474
Blank, H., 286, 393, 413

Blankstein, K. R., 175
Blass, E. M., 678, 680
Blau, J., 530
Blau, P., 198
Blaxton, T. A., 482
Blaye, A., 294, 295
Blecha, F., 68, 73
Blehar, M. L., 619, 623, 625, 630, 635
Bleich, R. P., 480
Bless, H., 140, 141, 169, 179
Block, J., 435, 444, 445
Bloedel, J. R., 319, 332, 333
Bloom, B. S., 254
Bloom, H. S., 670
Bloom, J. R., 537
Bloxom, A. L., 359
Bloxom, B., 251
Boccia, M. L., 70
Boden, M. A., 290
Bodenhausen, G. V., 143, 175
Bodiford, C. A., 567
Boehm, L. E., 137
Boettger, R., 174
Boettger, R. D., 199, 217
Boff, K. R., 249
Boganski, R., 330
Bohner, G., 140, 141
Bohus, B., 67, 69
Boldizar, J. P., 570
Bolger, K., 621
Bolger, N., 9
Boller, F., 480
Bolles, R. C., 322, 685, 694
Bolstad, C. A., 243, 252
Bolten, S., 164
Bonanno, G. A., 24
Bond, C. F., 177
Bond, G. R., 529, 537
Bond, M. E., 350
Bond, M. H., 102, 108, 109, 162, 500, 508
Bond, R. N., 71, 75
Bonito, A. J., 670
Bonnano, G. A., 479
Bonneau, R. H., 64, 65
Booher, H. R., 233
Bookstein, F. L., 627, 628
Booraem, C., 548
Boose, J. H., 239
Booth, C., 534, 535
Booth, W., 547
Borgida, E., 166, 178
Borkenau, P., 163
Borkman, T. J., 537
Bornstein, R. F., 127
Borodovsky, L. G., 366
Boruch, R. F., 545
Borysenko, M., 72
Boselie, F., 408
Boss, A., 181
Bossert, S. T., 590, 604
Bothe, H. G., 436
Botkin, P. I., 593
Botwin, M. D., 162

Boucek, G. P., 241
Bouchard, T. J., 128
Boulette, M. D., 248
Bourne, E. J., 509, 515
Bovair, S., 239
Bovbjerg, D., 56, 63, 67, 72
Bovbjerg, D. H., 63
Bowen, K. M., 61
Bower, G. H., 285, 475, 477, 587
Bowers, C. A., 249
Bowers, K. S., 283, 429
Bowers, W., 68, 351
Bowlby, J., 575, 630
Bowles, S., 250
Boyacigiller, N., 221
Boyles, P., 633
Boysen, S. T., 696
Bracha, V., 319, 333
Bradburn, N., 124
Bradlyn, A. S., 567
Brady, J., 695
Brain, P. F., 67, 679, 696
Braine, M. D. S., 292, 293
Brand, M., 25
Brandon, S. E., 321
Brandtstädter, J., 25, 41, 429
Brannon, R., 361
Bransford, J. D., 589
Brasfield, T. L., 548
Braswell, L., 570
Braun, O. L., 177
Braun, S. J., 632
Braungart, J., 634, 635
Breakey, W. R., 530, 531
Bream, L. A., 568, 569
Breckler, S. J., 118–20
Bredekamp, S., 617
Breedin, S. D., 241
Breedlove, S. M., 677
Brehm, J. W., 37
Brehmer, B., 599
Breier, A., 71
Breitmayer, B. J., 622, 628
Breitmeyer, B. G., 400
Breneman, S., 66, 70
Brennan, S. E., 603
Brenner, G. J., 62, 65, 66, 68, 70
Brennis, D., 515
Brentano, E., 429
Breslau, N., 625
Bresnahan, J. C., 326
Bressi, S., 245
Brett, J. F., 206, 207
Brett, L. P., 686
Brewer, M. B., 129, 141, 142, 165, 166
Brewin, C. R., 40, 429
Brickman, P., 356
Briggs, J. L., 499, 515
Briggs, M. A., 161
Brill, N. Q., 64
Briner, R. B., 247
Brinkerhoff, R. O., 660
Brinkman, J. A., 252

Broad, W., 388
Broadbent, D. E., 65, 252, 279, 281, 283, 384, 472, 473
Broadbent, M. H. P., 65, 281
Broberg, A., 627, 628
Brod, C., 235, 247
Brodie, A. R., 70
Brodish, A., 75
Broduin, C. M., 535, 536
Brogmus, G. E., 253
Bronfenbrenner, U., 625
Bronson, F. H., 696
Brookhart, J., 630
Brooks, D. N., 472
Brooks, D. R., 687, 688
Brooks, L. R., 284, 345, 349, 388, 474
Brooks-Gunn, J., 543, 628
Brouillard, M. E., 37
Brouwer, W. H., 253
Brower, A. M., 43
Brown, A., 25, 530
Brown, A. L., 299, 589, 605
Brown, A. S., 479
Brown, C. H., 690
Brown, D., 69, 345
Brown, D. J., 328
Brown, J., 3, 137
Brown, J. S., 605
Brown, L. B., 88, 90
Brown, M. M., 568
Brown, M. W., 484, 560, 561, 568, 571
Brown, R., 56, 58, 180
Brown, S. D., 345, 348
Brown, S. L., 37
Brown, T. H., 324
Brown, Y., 598
Brownell, K. D., 25
Browning, C., 370
Brownlee, E. M., 627
Brownlow, S., 138, 166
Brubaker, R. G., 133
Bruch, M. A., 359
Bruner, J. S., 170, 498, 500, 502, 605
Brunswik, E., 647
Brushlinskii, A. V., 429
Bryant, D. M., 620, 622, 627
Bryant, H. U., 72
Bryden, M. P., 281
Bryson, J. B., 143
Bucher, B., 37
Buchsbaum, K., 566
Buchwald, J. S., 319, 477
Buck, M. L., 171
Buckenham, K., 689
Budesheim, T. L., 160
Buhrke, R., 368, 372, 373
Buhrke, R. A., 370
Buldain, R. W., 602
Bullemer, P., 280, 471, 472
Bullock, D., 39
Bullock, M., 296
Burgen, A., 438

Burgess, P., 245
Burghardt, G., 698
Burghardt, G. M., 681
Burgoon, J. K., 138
Burgos, A., 69
Burish, T. G., 63
Burk, T., 687
Burke, P. D., 530, 571
Burkhart, B. R., 353–55
Burleson, B., 570
Burnam, A., 531
Burnkrant, R. E., 135
Burns, B. J., 530, 532, 533
Burns, S., 537
Burnstein, E., 167, 601
Burris, C. T., 143
Burt, M. R., 656
Burt, R. S., 203
Burti, L., 539
Burton, A. M., 239
Busemeyer, J. R., 247
Bushyhead, J. B., 285
Buss, D. M., 162
Buss, R. R., 282, 284, 474
Butterfield, E. C., 384
Butters, N., 457, 463, 472, 480
Buttigieg, M. A., 250
Buttram, R. T., 181
Bycio, P., 205
Bye, L., 549
Bylsma, W. H., 595
Byrne, R. M. J., 275, 292, 304–6

C

Cacioppo, J. T., 124, 127, 134–36, 138, 172, 362, 597
Caggiula, A. R., 67, 69, 73
Cahill, L., 321
Cai, F., 105
Cairns, B. D., 577
Cairns, R. B., 430, 435–37, 576, 577
Calcagnetti, D. J., 321
Calderwood, R., 248
Caldwell, B. M., 616, 618, 627, 632, 637
Caldwell, D. F., 206, 207
Caldwell, R. L., 698
Calhoun, C., 10
Callahan, C. M., 548
Callan, J. W., 568, 570
Callaway, E., 60
Camaioni, L., 430
Camerino, M., 70
Cameron, J. E., 143
Campbell, C. B. G., 683, 684
Campbell, D. T., 600, 647, 653, 658
Campbell, J. A., 285
Campbell, J. D., 565
Campbell, V. E., 345
Campeau, S., 322, 324
Campione, J. C., 589

Campis, L. K., 139
Camras, L. A., 630
Canavar, A., 477
Cannon, W. B., 4
Cannon-Bowers, J. A., 235, 248, 255, 256
Cano, I., 169
Cantor, G., 281
Cantor, N., 24, 27, 28, 43, 50, 163
Cao, H. Q., 94
Cao, R. C., 90
Cao, Z. F., 98
Capaldi, E. J., 696
Capitanio, J. P., 70
Caporael, L. R., 129
Cappelli, P., 196, 220
Caraco, T., 685, 695
Caramazza, A., 484
Carballo-Dieguez, A., 372
Card, S. K., 238
Cardon, L., 129
Cardoze, S., 285
Carello, C., 419
Carey, M. P., 63
Carey, R. G., 651, 662, 670
Carey, S., 596
Carli, L. L., 138
Carlson, G. A., 571, 577
Carlson, R. A., 282, 435, 474
Carlson, S. L., 75
Carlstead, K., 699
Carlston, D. E., 159
Carney, C. G., 366
Carpenter, A. B., 67
Carpenter, C. B., 56
Carpenter, K. M., 40
Carpenter, P. A., 239, 252, 267
Carpenter, S., 161
Carr, D. J. J., 73, 75
Carr, T. H., 419
Carraher, D. W., 299
Carraher, T. N., 299
Carrell, S. E., 594
Carrera, P., 179
Carroll, B., 429
Carroll, L. A., 241, 243
Carroll-Wilson, M., 567
Carter, R. T., 363
Cartoof, V. G., 545
Cartwright, M., 333
Carugati, F., 597
Carver, C. S., 3, 24, 29, 33, 34, 36, 39, 40, 44, 589, 593
Casas, J. M., 363, 365, 366
Case, P., 548
Casey, E. J., 250
Caspi, A., 129, 434, 444
Casriel, C., 548, 549
Cassel, B. J., 541
Casselden, P. A., 165
Cassidy, J., 576
Catania, J. A., 549
Catanzaro, S. J., 40
Catrambone, R., 299

Cattarello, A. M., 132
Cattell, A. K. S., 445
Cattell, J. M., 411
Cattell, R. B., 445
Caul, W. F., 476
Cave, C. B., 454, 463, 468, 478–80
Cegavske, C. F., 318, 334
Celmer, V., 348
Cermak, L. S., 460, 478–80
Cervone, D., 25, 35–37, 40
Cesa, I. L., 299
Chace, P. M., 463
Chaiken, S., 118, 122, 125, 126, 128, 129, 133, 135, 136, 140, 172, 182, 597
Chalip, L., 498
Chalmers, M., 302
Chamberlin, J., 537, 538
Chamberlin, T. C., 388
Chambers, K. C., 318
Chambers, R. M., 252
Chan, C., 108
Chan, C. S., 372
Chandler, K., 478, 479
Chandler, M., 565
Channon, S., 477
Chao, C. C., 65
Chapanis, A., 232
Chapieski, M. L., 25, 35
Chaplin, W. F., 163
Chapman, G. B., 477
Chapman, P. F., 324, 327, 328, 331–33
Charnov, E. L., 625
Charters, W. W., 592
Chase, W. G., 268, 277, 415
Chase-Lansdale, P. L., 628, 630
Chasseigne, G., 629
Chater, N., 291, 292
Chatman, J. A., 207
Chattopadhyay, A., 139
Cheatham, H. E., 363
Check, J. V. P., 361
Chen, A. F., 98
Chen, C. C., 103, 214
Chen, D. Q., 90
Chen, H., 651, 653, 657, 670
Chen, H. Q., 90
Chen, H. Y., 106
Chen, K. J., 89
Chen, K. S., 471, 475, 476
Chen, K. W., 99
Chen, L., 90, 91, 94, 97, 101, 104, 109
Chen, L. (Long), 103, 104
Chen, M. J., 95
Chen, Q., 103
Chen, S. K., 105
Chen, S. Y., 91
Chen, X. Y., 101
Chen, Y. M., 95
Chen, Z. G., 91, 96, 102
Cheney, D., 236
Cheney, D. L., 694, 696, 697

Cheng, P. W., 292, 294, 296
Cheng, Y., 548
Cherry, F. F., 631
Cherubini, P., 295
Chester, J., 323
Cheung, F. M., 97
Chi, M. T. H., 298, 299
Chiapelli, F., 69
Chida, K., 323
Chilman, C. S., 543
Ching, C. C., 88, 90, 94
Chirigos, M., 69
Chiu, C.-Y. P., 278, 454, 478, 480
Cho, J., 282, 284
Cho, J. R., 474
Cho, Y. H., 464
Choi, K., 548
Choi, S. C., 509, 515
Chopko, B., 330
Chorine, V., 54
Chorvinsky, M., 623
Christal, R. E., 251
Christensen-Szalanski, J. J. J., 285
Christie, D., 330
Christner, R., 69
Christopher, F. S., 544
Chu, F. D., 527
Chu, L., 157
Church, A. T., 162
Church, B., 480
Ci, G. X., 104
Cialdini, R. B., 40, 138, 595, 597, 598
Ciampi, A., 61
Cicchetti, P., 321, 322
Cierpial, M. A., 69–73
Cioffi, D., 37
Cisterna, R., 69
Claire, T., 170
Clancy, R. L., 56
Clark, C. W., 677
Clark, G. A., 328
Clark, H. H., 603
Clark, L. F., 180
Clark, M. C., 253, 635
Clark, N. K., 602
Clark, R. D. III, 597
Clark, R. E., 328, 331, 333, 334
Clarke-Stewart, K. A., 617, 619, 620, 623, 626, 627, 629–33, 635
Clausen, J. A., 209
Clayton, S., 158
Cleary, P. D., 358, 621
Cleeremans, A., 280, 281, 284, 472
Clifford, J., 506
Clifton, C., 408
Clore, G. L., 10
Clugnet, M. C., 324
Clutton-Brock, T. H., 682, 684, 685
Coates, D., 356

Coates, T. J., 547, 549, 550
Cochran, M. M., 626, 632
Cochran, S. D., 367–69
Cochrane, J. I., 527
Cocke, R., 67, 69
Coe, C. L., 67, 70
Coelen, C., 617
Cohen, A., 280, 472
Cohen, B. B., 352
Cohen, B. E., 656
Cohen, B. F., 527
Cohen, J. J., 70, 547, 647, 665, 668
Cohen, M. M., 392, 396, 401
Cohen, M. R., 527
COHEN, N., 53–85; 55, 56, 60–63, 65–70, 72, 75, 76
Cohen, N. D., 527
Cohen, N. J., 457, 458, 463, 466–68, 472
Cohen, P. A., 604, 665, 668
Cohen, R. Y., 542
Cohen, S., 54, 64, 65, 67
Cohler, B., 500
Cohn, E., 356
Coie, J. D., 565, 566
Colburn, C. J., 295
Colbus, D., 571
Cole, M., 498, 499, 502, 591, 604, 605
Cole, N. S., 348
Cole, P., 500
Cole, S. W., 167
Coleman, N. C., 363
Coles, M. G. H., 397, 430
Colgan, P., 694
Collector, M. I., 69, 73
Collier, G., 695
Collins, A., 10, 605
Collins, C., 462, 466
Collins, R. L., 171
Collyer, C. E., 389
Colvin, C. R., 157, 158
Companion, M., 242
Companion, M. A., 243
Condiotte, M., 37
Conger, J., 367
Conlon, D. E., 201
Conlon, E. J., 223
Connine, C. M., 408
Conrad, F. G., 266
Contorer, A., 238
Converse, S., 235, 256
Converse, S. A., 235, 255
Conway, C. G., 24
Conway, M., 595
Cook, E. P., 356, 358
Cook, R. G., 455
Cook, R. L., 599
Cook, S. W., 145
Cook, T. D., 645–47, 650, 651, 653, 657, 665, 671
Cooke, N. J., 239, 241, 256
Cool-Hauser, V. A., 333, 334
Cools, A. R., 695
Cooper, C. L., 247

Cooper, D. M., 206, 207
Cooper, E. E., 480
Cooper, E. L., 69, 72
Cooper, J., 134, 592
Cooper, L. A., 479, 480
Coops, W., 431
Coovert, M. D., 159
Copeland, E. J., 366
Copeland, J., 548
Copper, C., 161
Corasanti, M. A., 631
Corbin, J., 653, 655
Corcoran, J. L., 346
Corcoran, K., 37
Cordray, D. S., 670
Corkin, S., 463, 466, 479, 481
Cornell, K. R., 127
Corsini, D. A., 565
Corso, G. M., 243
Cosmides, L., 294, 295, 393
Coss, R. G., 691
Costa, P. T., 163
Cota, A. A., 591
Cottle, T. J., 40, 41
Cottrell, N. B., 588
Coulter, D. A., 319, 686
Coury, B. G., 248, 252
Cousins, S., 508
Coussons, M. E., 60
Couvillon, P. A., 685
COWAN, N., 383–425; 400, 401, 405
Cowan, W. B., 25
Cox, D. J., 33
Cox, G. B., 527
Cox, S. L., 353
Cox, T. H., 206, 349
Crabtree, B. F., 658
Craig, J. W., 65
Craighead, L. W., 352
Crane, P. M., 242
Crane, S., 467
Crapanzano, V., 499
Crawford, C., 527
Crawford, I., 547, 548
Crawley, J. N., 60
Creer, T. L., 25
Crelia, R. A., 169, 174, 179
Crestani, F., 60
Crews, D., 677, 678, 696
Crick, F., 442
Crick, N. R., 562, 570
Cripps, A. W., 56
Crites, J. O., 346, 348
Crittenden, P. M., 575, 619
Crockenberg, S., 635
Crocker, J., 143, 177
Croiset, G., 69
Cropanzano, R., 128
Crosby, F., 158
Crosby, L. A., 125
Cross, S. E., 39
Cross, T., 532
Crosse, S., 670
Crouter, A., 625
Crow, T. J., 319

Crutchfield, J. P., 436
Crystal, G. S., 223
Csikszentmihalyi, M., 44
Cuellar, I., 363
Cullen, E., 690
Cummings, L. L., 197, 198, 209, 220, 224
Cummings, N., 71
Cummins, D. D., 292
Cummins, R. W., 60, 415
Cunitz, A. R., 454, 456
Cunnick, J. E., 58, 59, 67, 69–75
Curry, J. F., 533
Custeau, N., 71, 75
Cuthill, I. C., 695
Czaja, S. J., 253
Czapinski, J., 159
Czyzewska, M., 181, 472

D

Dagenbach, D., 391
D'Agostino, P. R., 174, 177, 180
Dahlstrom, W. G., 566
Dai, X. H., 105
Dallas, M., 470, 480
Dalton, M., 220
Daly, M., 686
Damasio, A. R., 484
Damon, W., 596
Damos, D. L., 244
Damrad-Frye, R., 134
Dandes, S. K., 576
Dandoy, A. C., 571
D'Andrade, R., 119, 294
D'Andrade, R. G., 498, 499, 502, 511
D'Andrea, M., 365
Daniels, J., 365
Dannefer, D., 446
Dansereau, D. F., 145
Dantzer, R., 60, 67, 69, 71, 75
Dark, K., 60
Dark, K. A., 60
Dark, W. J., 470
Darley, J. M., 172, 595, 603
Darlington, R. B., 433
Darwin, C., 683
Daum, I., 477
D'Aveni, R. A., 211, 215
d'Avernas, J. R., 133, 134
Davey, G., 695
David, R., 64
Davidson, W. S. II, 534
Davies, N. B., 677, 685, 689, 694
Davis, A., 617, 621
Davis, F. D., 131
Davis, G. F., 223
Davis, H., 696
Davis, J. H., 103, 599, 602
Davis, M., 321–25
Davis, R. T., 320, 352
Davis, S. A., 242

Davis, W. J., 695
Davis-Blake, A., 208, 210
Davison, L. A., 6
Dawis, R. V., 344, 346
Dawkins, M. S., 676–78, 699
Dawkins, R., 288, 676
Dawson, M. E., 477
Dawson, V. L., 178
Dean, L. M., 67
Deane, K. E., 619, 631
Deaux, K., 166
DeBono, K. G., 126, 140, 178
Dechambre, R.-P., 67
deCharms, R., 591
Deci, E. L., 24, 27, 41, 595
Decker, J., 36
DeCola, J. P., 324
DeCourville, N. H., 133, 134
Deese, J., 3, 18
Deffenbacher, K. A., 232
DeFries, J. C., 691
DeGraaf-Kaser, R., 529
de Groot, A. D., 431
Dekker, E., 62
Delacour, J., 455
de la Haye, A. M., 163
Dell, D. M., 359
Della Salla, S., 245
DeLongis, A., 9
del Rey, A., 75, 76
Deluty, R. H., 568, 570
Demaree, R. G., 221
Demarest, J., 677
Dember, W. N., 246
Dembo, T., 30
DeMeis, D., 615, 621, 634
DeMoya, D., 545
Denhaerinck, P., 168
Dennett, D. C., 698
Dennis, A., 443
Dennis, M. L., 670
Dennis, W., 676
De Paolis, P., 597
DePaulo, B. M., 565
Dépret, E. F., 173
Derrida, J., 500
Derry, P., 575
Dersarkissian, C., 332
Derthick, M., 416
Desai, S., 628
Desforges, D. M., 131, 145, 173
Desimone, R., 484
Des Jarlais, D. C., 548, 549
Desmond, J. E., 333
De Sousa, R., 10
Dessouky, M. I., 238, 245
Dethier, V. G., 694
Detterman, D., 251
DeUrioste, R., 565
Deutsch, M., 599
Deutsch, S. J., 249
Devgan, K. K., 319
Devillechabrolle, A., 67
Devine, P. G., 134, 144, 145, 166, 173, 176, 179, 182,

595
DeVos, J., 465
De Vries, N., 179
Dewey, G. I., 282, 474
Dewey, J., 14, 435
de Wied, D., 69
Dewsbury, D. A., 676, 681, 682, 687, 689
Deyo, R. A., 319, 477
DeYoe, E. A., 408
Diamond, A., 465
Diamond, D. M., 319
Diamond, R., 479
Diamond, R. J., 529
Diaz, Y. E., 549
Dick, A. O., 244
Dickinson, A., 685
Dickson, W. J., 220
Diehl, M., 169
Diemer, R. A., 370
Diener, C. I., 567
Diener, E., 40
Dienes, Z., 283, 284, 473
Dierolf, D. A., 249
Digman, J. M., 162
Dincin, J., 529, 537
Dinero, T. E., 353, 354
Ding, G., 69, 74
Dinstein, I., 250
Dion, K. L., 141, 591
DiScenna, P., 324, 463
Disterhoft, J. F., 318, 319, 332, 477, 686
Ditto, P. H., 180
Divak, J., 476
Djunghu, B., 550
Dobbin, F. R., 220
Dobkin, P. L., 63
DODGE, K. A., 559–84; 560–73, 576, 579
Doherty, K., 44
Doherty, M. E., 294
Doi, L. T., 500, 508
Doise, W., 596, 597, 604
Doktor, R., 221
Domjan, M., 695
Doms, M., 595
Donahue, S., 528
Donchin, E., 397
Donegan, N. H., 321, 330
Dong, Q., 98
Dooling, R. J., 697
Dore, F. Y., 683
Dorval, B., 622, 623, 628
Doty, R. M., 143
Douce, L. A., 346, 370
Dougherty, D., 532
Douglas, R. J., 465
Doumerc, S., 67
Dovenalina, I., 285
Doverspike, D., 254
Dovidio, J. F., 124, 127, 141, 142, 144, 145, 169, 173
Dovydaitis, A., 328
Dow, R. S., 327
Downing, J. W., 119, 127,

178
Downing, M., 548
Downing, P. E., 298
Downs, A. C., 361
Drachman, D. A., 454
Draucker, C. B., 353
Drent, R. H., 694
Dresel, K. M., 64
Driedger, S. M., 57
Drigotas, S. M., 43
Driscoll, D. M., 160, 161, 179
Driskell, J. E., 180, 249
Driver, P. M., 689
Drob, S., 537
Droge, C., 210
Drugan, R. C., 60, 71
Druhan, B., 267, 282, 284
Druian, P. R., 170
Dryfoos, J. G., 543, 547
Duan, C., 143, 160, 166
Dubois, N., 164
DuCette, J. P., 546
Duchnowski, A. J., 533
Duck, S. W., 602
Duffy, E., 10, 11
Duffy, S. A., 403
Dufour, C. L., 571
Duguid, P., 605
Dukas, R., 690
Dukerich, J. M., 218
Dulany, D. E., 27, 282, 474
Dull, V., 166
Dumas, C., 683
Dumont, L., 508, 515
Dunbar, K., 294
Duncan, I. J., 677
Duncan, J., 245, 403, 404
Duncan, J. C., 241
Duncker, K., 268
Dunér, A., 445
Dunkel-Schetter, C., 9, 431
Dunkle, J., 670
Dunn, D. S., 122
Dunn, L. T., 477
Dunning, D., 164, 171, 177
Dunn-Roberts, R. R., 235
Dupin, J. J., 598
Durant, C., 347
Durran, A., 365, 366
Dutka, M. E., 70
Dutton, J. E., 211, 218
Duval, S., 34, 44, 589
Duval, T. S., 44
Duval, V. H., 44
Dweck, C. S., 27, 567, 587
Dworkin, S. H., 370
Dyal, J. A., 108
Dyck, D. G., 57, 58, 64, 76
Dye, E., 354
Dyer, M. G., 271, 272
Dykstra, L. A., 60
Dynesius, R. A., 64

E

Eagly, A. H., 118, 123, 125, 126, 128, 133, 135, 136, 140, 141, 166, 169, 172, 595, 597
Eason, K. D., 234
East, P. L., 577
Easterbrooks, M. A., 630, 631
Eastman, C., 37
Eastman, R., 240
Eaton, E. L., 631
Eaves, L. J., 128
Ebeling, W., 436
Eberhard, J. W., 253
Eberhard, W. G., 687, 693
Eccles, J. C., 327
Eccles, J. S., 158
Echabe, A. E., 130, 169
Echemendia, R. J., 345, 365
Edeline, J. M., 319
Edelman, G., 436, 439
Edelson, S. M., 285
Eden, D., 204
Edgerton, R. B., 514
Edmunson, E. D., 537
Edwards, C. P., 500
Edwards, D., 602
Edwards, E. A., 67
Edwards, K., 121
Edwards, R. M., 323
Effrein, E. A., 592
Egan, T., 206, 207
Egeland, B., 630, 631, 635
Egeth, H., 391
Egger, G., 542
Egido, C., 603
Ehya, H., 70
Eibl-Eibesfeldt, I., 691
Eichenbaum, H., 458, 463, 467, 468
Eichenfield, G. A., 359, 362
Eikelboom, R., 57
Einhorn, H. J., 664
Eisen, M., 544
Eisenberg, H. M., 462
EISENBERG, N., 613–44
Eisenberg, M. M., 621, 636
Eisenberger, R., 32
Eisenhardt, K. M., 215, 223
Eisenstadt, C., 123, 143
Eisenstadt, T. H., 567
Eiser, J. R., 118, 131, 169
Eisler, R. M., 358, 360, 361
Eklund, G., 446
Ekman, P., 10
Ekstrand, M. L., 549
Elder, J. P., 537
Eldredge, N., 678
Eldridge, N. S., 369, 371
Elkind, D., 594
Elkind, J. I., 238
Ellen, P. S., 133
Elliot, A. J., 145, 173
Elliot, M. G., 470
Ellis, A., 35
Ellis, A. L., 595, 599, 601

Ellis, W. F., 534
Ellman, G., 60
Ellsworth, P. C., 14, 500, 515
Elman, J. L., 409, 410
Elmslie, S., 347, 348
Elsbach, K. D., 213
Embree, M. G., 537
Emery, E. J., 177
Emery, R. E., 619
Emmons, R. A., 28, 29, 40, 43, 429
Emptage, A., 568
Emshoff, J. G., 534
Endler, N. S., 429, 436
Endsley, M. R., 242, 243
Engleson, S. A., 361
Englis, B. G., 173
Enns, C. Z., 356, 357, 367
Enser, D., 319
Enzle, M. E., 134
Epstein, A. L., 515
Epstein, L. H., 67, 69, 73
Epstein, S., 3, 170, 430
Erber, R., 161, 180, 182, 602
Eriksen, C. W., 3
Ershler, W. B., 70
Erskine, N., 430
Esquenazi, V., 331
Esses, V. M., 144
Esterhay, R. J., 64
Esterling, B., 67, 73
Estes, W. K., 268, 272, 285, 416, 474, 475, 559, 560
Esveldt-Dawson, K., 571
Etaugh, C., 620
Etcoff, N. L., 591
Etringer, B. D., 351, 372
Evans, F. J., 460
Evans, J. St. B. T., 293, 294
Evans, M., 123
Everitt, B. J., 326, 477, 695
Everitt, J., 691
Ewart, C. K., 25, 30
Exon, J. H., 60
Eysenck, H. J., 128, 430

F

Fafel, J., 166
Fagan, A., 467
Fagan, J. F., 465
Fairbank, J. A., 670
Fairburn, C. G., 352
Faisal, M., 69, 72
Fajans, J., 515
Falbo, T., 100
Falender, V. J., 592
Falk, J., 76
Falkenhainer, B., 270
Fallon, P., 352
Fan, B. N., 104
Fan, J., 94
Fan, S., 69, 74
Fang, L. L., 107
Fang, X. C., 106
Fang, Z., 87

Fanselow, M. S., 321, 322, 324–26, 464, 695, 696
Fanshel, D., 500
Fantz, R. L., 465
Farah, M. J., 272, 484
Farb, C. F., 322, 324
Farber, E. A., 630, 631, 635
Farber, I. E., 3
Farel, A. M., 621, 634
Farhoody, N., 71, 75
Farioli, F., 295
Faris, M., 69
Farmer, J., 351
Farmer, J. D., 436, 439, 694
Farquhar, J. W., 542
Farr, R. K., 531, 604
Farren, D., 623, 627
Fassinger, R. E., 345, 346, 367, 368, 370–73
Faucheux, C., 597
Faulconer, J. E., 438
Fauman, M. A., 67
Fazio, R. H., 119, 122, 124, 126, 127, 129–33, 592
Feather, N. T., 125
Feffer, M., 593
Feigenbaum, E. A., 238
Fein, G. G., 620, 630, 633, 635
Fein, S., 168
Feinberg, L., 365, 366
Feingold, A., 141
Feiring, C., 622
Feldman, E., 565, 573
Felix, D., 75
Felix, M. R. J., 542
Felleman, D., 481
Felten, D. L., 72, 75
Felten, S. Y., 72, 75
Feltovich, P. J., 299
Feltz, D., 41
Feng, G. Q., 105
Feng, L., 94
Feng, N., 64, 65
Fennema, A. C., 481
Fentress, J. C., 695
Ferrara, R. A., 589
Ferrari, L., 129
Fertel, R., 65
Feshbach, S., 565
Festinger, L., 30, 220, 594
Fetterman, D. M., 652, 653, 658
Fetterman, J. G., 696, 697
Feucht, T. E., 548
Fewell, R., 625
Feyerabend, P. K., 389
Fiedler, K., 142, 164, 169, 500
Field, T., 624, 629, 631–33
Fiene, R., 617, 629
FIGUEREDO, A. J., 645–74; 648, 666, 667, 669
Filice, G. A., 65
Fincham, F. D., 567
Findling, R. L., 467

Fine, S., 567
Finke, R. A., 303
Finkelstein, N. W., 628, 632
Finlay, B. L., 680
Fischer, G. W., 167, 168, 574
Fischer, P. J., 530, 531
Fischhoff, B., 286
Fish, S. E., 500
Fishbein, M., 27, 123, 131, 133
Fisher, D. L., 403
Fisher, E. H., 356
Fisher, J. D., 132
Fisher, J. W., 681
Fisher, L. A., 131
Fisher, W. A., 132
Fisk, A. D., 253, 256
Fiske, A. P., 166, 498
Fiske, D. W., 162
FISKE, S. T., 155–94; 24, 44, 142, 143, 145, 155, 156, 159–62, 165–67, 169, 172, 173, 176–80, 182, 591, 595
FITZGERALD, L. F., 343–81; 346, 349, 350, 359, 367
FitzGerald, P., 281
FitzGerald, R. W., 690
Fitzgerald, T., 37
Fitzgerald, W., 542
Fitzpatrick, A. R., 595
Fitzpatrick, J. L., 346
Flach, J. M., 250
Flamenbaum, C., 129
Flanagan, O., 500
Flannagan, M. J., 281
Flannery, G. R., 56, 67, 72
Flavell, J. H., 593
Fleeson, J., 630
Fleeson, W., 27
Fleishman, E. A., 251, 252
Fleming, J. H., 603
Fleshner, M., 67, 73
Fletcher, G., 178
Fletcher, J. F., 123
Flett, G. L., 175
Flink, C., 157, 173
Flood, J. F., 57
Flowers, J. V., 548
Foa, E. B., 354
Fodor, J. A., 269, 271, 273, 291, 302, 387, 417, 418
Fogel, A., 432
Folkins, C. H., 7
Folkman, S., 4, 5, 8, 9
Follette, V. M., 354
Follette, W. C., 354
Fondacaro, R., 136
Fondacaro, R. A., 176
Fong, G. T., 548
Forbus, K. D., 270
Ford, D. H., 28, 30, 32, 38, 445
Ford, M. E., 27
Ford, T. E., 144, 168, 169, 172, 176, 178

Forehand, R., 577
Forrest, J. D., 543
Fortmann, S. P., 542
Foscarinis, M., 530
Fowler, C., 133
Fowler, H., 58, 59, 69–72
Fowler, H. S., 526
Fox, N., 622
Fox, P. T., 481
Foy, M. R., 327
Fozard, J. L., 252
Frable, D. E. S., 174, 591, 593
Fracker, M. L., 242
Frambach, M., 472
Frame, C. L., 564, 565, 577
Francescato, D., 527
Francis, J., 322
Frank, A. L., 629
Frank, R. H., 223
Frank, R. I., 351
Franke, S., 577
Franks, D. D., 223
Frape, G., 542
Frascarolo, F., 635
Fratianne, A., 296
Frazier, P., 353
Frazier, P. A., 352
Freed, D. M., 466
Freedman, D. G., 513
Freedman, S. M., 247
Freedman-Letofsky, K., 537
Freeman, H., 627
Freeman, H. E., 651, 659, 662
Freeman, R. B. Jr., 468, 470
Freeman, R. J., 567
Freeman, S. J., 537
French, N., 571
Frese, M., 25
Fretz, B. R., 345
Freud, S., 25, 464
Frey, K. S., 41
Freyer, M., 627
Fried, L. S., 281, 474
Friedlander, M. L., 352
Friedman, D., 392, 393, 396
Friedman, D. P., 465
Friedman, E. M., 70
Friedman, H. S., 40, 166
Friedman, R. M., 532, 533, 567
Friedman, S. B., 64
Friedman, S. R., 548, 549
Friedrich, J., 129
Frijda, N. H., 10, 14, 40, 515
Frodi, M., 627, 628
Frost, P., 197, 220, 221
Frost, P. J., 214
Fry, C. L. Jr., 593
Frysinger, R. C., 321, 323
Fuentes, I., 320
Fuhrman, R. W., 176, 595
Fujiwara, M., 67
Funder, D. C., 157, 158
Fung, H., 498, 500, 511

Funk, C. L., 144
Funk, M. S., 683
Furstenberg, F. F. Jr., 543
Fussell, S. R., 158, 603
Fuster, J. M., 484

G

Gable, R. K., 358, 360
Gabriel, S. W., 568, 577
Gabrieli, J. D. E., 479, 481
Gaelick-Buys, L., 37
Gaertner, S. L., 141, 142, 144, 145, 169, 173
Gagnon, S., 683
Gaillard, A. W. K., 430
Gaines, A. D., 515
Galanter, E., 30
Galaskiewicz, J., 203
Galatowitsch, S., 234, 236
Galavotti, C., 547, 549
Gale, K., 69
Gale, R. P., 65, 71, 74
Galef, B. G., 695
Galef, B. G. Jr., 694, 697
Galegher, J., 603
Galinsky, T. L., 246
Gallagher, M., 321, 323
Gallego, J., 282, 283
Gallimore, R., 646, 661
Gallistel, C. R., 694, 697
Gallo, K. L., 70
Galluzzo, D. C., 635
Galotti, K. M., 171
Galton, F., 430
Gamble, G., 439
Gamble, T. J., 618, 624
Gammage, P., 131
Gannon, L. J., 362
Ganong, W. F. III, 408
Gao, E. S., 97
Gao, J. F., 88, 91, 94
Garber, J., 560, 564, 566, 567, 569–71, 577, 578
Garcia, J., 686
Garcia, S., 157, 158, 600
Garcia, T., 25
Gardiner, J. M., 469, 470
Gardner, B. T., 689, 696, 697
Gardner, H., 417, 418, 480
Gardner, R. A., 689, 696, 697
Gardner, R. C., 141, 143, 169
Gardner, W., 625
Garfinkel, P. E., 351
Gargano, G. M., 590
Gariépy, J. L., 437
Garn, S. M., 543
Garner, D. M., 351, 352
Garnets, L., 367, 369, 371
Garnham, A., 293
Garrett, C. J., 533, 536
Garrison, W., 567
Garrod, A., 510
Garton, A. F., 596
Garvey, C., 500, 511
Gash, D. C., 220

Gastardo-Conaco, M. C., 594
Gatchel, R. J., 590
Gathercole, S. E., 456
Gattuso, S. M., 37
Gaudernack, G., 70
Gaulin, S. J., 690
Gauthier, J., 37
Gavanski, I., 171
Gay, J., 591
Gaylor, D. G., 124
Ge, L. Z., 105
Gebhard, P. H., 368
Geen, R. G., 589, 594
Geertz, C., 498, 499, 501, 508, 514
Geertz, H., 515
Gehrke, E. M., 182
Geiser, D. S., 54
Geiwitz, J., 239
Gelfand, D. M., 619
Gelman, R., 296, 596
Gelman, S. A., 280
Gelso, C. J., 345, 346, 368–70, 373
Gendlin, E. T., 500
Gentile, C. G., 321
Gentner, D., 270, 271, 298, 416
George, J. M., 216
Gerard, H. B., 127, 599
Gerber, E. R., 515
Gerbert, B., 547
Gergen, K. J., 500, 506
Gerhart, B., 222
Gersick, C. J. G., 209, 221
Geschwind, N., 463
Gesten, E. L., 542
Ghanta, V. K., 56, 60, 74
Ghirelli, G., 527
Ghoneum, M., 69, 72
Gibbons, E. G. Jr., 679
Gibbons, F. X., 589
Gibbons, P. A., 164, 166
Gibbs, B. W., 213
Gibbs, J. B., 666
Gibson, D. R., 548
Gibson, J. J., 419, 511
Gibson, J. M., 329
Gibson, K. R., 697
Gibson, R. S., 252
Gibson, W. A., 445
Gick, M. L., 284, 299
Gies, J., 234
Gifford, R. K., 142
Gigerenzer, G., 286, 295, 393, 413
Gilbert, B. J., 362
Gilbert, D. T., 137, 143, 176, 180, 181, 595
Gilbert, L., 371
Gilbert, L. A., 346, 350, 351, 355, 356
Gilfillan, D. P., 600
Gill, G., 69
Gill, H. K., 58
Gill, J. D., 125

Gillan, D. J., 241
Gilliam, P., 236, 256
Gilligan, C., 500, 501, 509
Gilliland, R. C., 139
Gilliom, J. D., 404
Gilly, M. C., 208, 294, 295
Gilman, S. R., 529
Gilovich, T., 157, 164, 589
Gim, R. H., 363
Ginsberg, B. I., 64
Giovanniello, O. A., 58
Girgus, J. S., 567
Girotto, G., 295
Girotto, V., 294, 295
Gisiner, R., 697
Gittleman, J. L., 677, 682, 684, 691
Giuliano, T. A., 180
Gjerde, P. F., 444
Glantz, F., 617
Glanzer, M., 454, 456
Glaser, R., 64, 65, 69, 240, 298, 299
Glasgow, L. A., 64
Glasgow, R. E., 37
Glass, A. L., 384
Glass, B., 166
Glass, G. V., 532, 535
Glasser, W., 25
Gleason, D. F., 537
Gleicher, F., 139–41, 174, 175
Gleick, J., 436
Gleitzman, M., 347
Glendon, A. I., 237
Glenn, W. G., 67
Glick, J. A., 591
Glickman, S. E., 689
Glickstein, M., 328, 330
Glidden, C. E., 356
Glisky, E. L., 459
Gluck, M. A., 285, 330, 475, 477
Gluckman, J. P., 246
Glushko, R. J., 388
Gochfeld, D., 274, 298
Godding, P. R., 37
Godfray, C., 685
Goelman, H., 620
Goering, P., 527
Goethals, G. R., 129
Goettl, B. P., 245
Goetz, T. W., 567
Gold, P. E., 323, 688
Goldberg, F., 463
Goldberg, L. R., 162–64
Goldberg, W., 631
Goldberg, W. A., 630
Golden, M., 627
Goldfine, P. E., 533
Goldman, J. A., 565
Goldman, S. K., 534
Goldman-Rakic, P. S., 456
Goldmeier, E., 459
Goldstein, D., 624, 629, 631, 633

Goldstein, I. L., 236, 254, 256, 257
Goldstein, L. H., 166
Goldstone, R. L., 271, 274
Goldthwaite, R. O., 691
Gollwitzer, P., 24
Gollwitzer, P. M., 37, 172, 176
Gonder-Frederick, L., 33
Gong, Y. X., 96
Gonso, J., 571
Gonzalez, E. G., 285
Good, B. J., 506, 515
Good, G. E., 356, 358, 359, 362
Goodall, T. A., 25
Goodchilds, J., 345, 367
Gooding, P., 480
Goodkin, H. P., 327, 334
Goodman, G., 532
Goodman, N., 500
Goodman, R. S., 212
Goodman-Brown, T., 575, 578
Goodnow, J. J., 500
Goody, E., 500
Goore, N., 589
Goossens, F. A., 619, 624, 627, 630
Gopher, D., 232, 238, 244, 245, 250–52
Gorczynski, R. M., 56, 58, 60, 61, 71–73
Gordijn, M., 694
Gordon, B. J., 533
Gordon, D. A., 534
Gordon, J. R., 25
Gordon, N. H., 571
Gordon, R. A., 131, 344
Gordon, R. E., 537
Gordon, R. M., 10
Gordon, T. P., 70
Gore, A., 530
Gormezano, I., 320, 327, 328, 333, 334
Gorsuch, R. L., 667
Gossard, D., 37
Gott, S. P., 238–40
Gottfredson, L. S., 344, 347
Gottlieb, G., 430, 684, 691
Gottman, J., 571
Gould, J. L., 694
Gould, S. J., 344
Gouze, K. R., 564
Gove, F. L., 630, 631
Govender, R., 122
Gowing, M. K., 235
Graf, P., 457, 470, 478–80, 483
Grafen, A., 685
Grafton, F., 251
Graham, F. K., 405
Grajek, S., 627
Granberg, D., 131
Grant, D., 64
Grant, P. R., 143, 690

Gray, E., 131
Gray, J. A., 430, 477
Gray, K. C., 237
Gray, T., 124
Greatorex, G. L., 253
Greaves, S., 439
Green, B. L., 138
Green, D. M., 384
Green, N., 56, 67, 72
Greenacre, M. L., 691
Greenberg, A. H., 57, 58, 64, 76
Greenberg, J., 44, 200
Greenberg, L., 240
Greenberg, M. T., 569
Greene, B. G., 250
Greenfield, P. M., 300, 604
Greeno, J. G., 390, 587
Greenwald, A. G., 34, 118–20, 124, 126, 130, 179
Gregory, L. W., 40
Gregory, R. L., 386
Grella, C., 658
Grice, H. P., 603, 604
Grier, J. W., 687
Griffin, D. R., 697
Griffin, D. W., 164, 286
Griffin, L., 236
Griffin, P., 605
Griffith, E. E. H., 528, 529
Grimm, L. G., 35
Grinker, R. R., 2, 6
Grochowicz, P., 61
Groebel, J., 686
Groen, G. J., 294, 390
Groen, J., 62
Groff, B. D., 589
Grohmann, J., 676
Gross, S., 595
Grossberg, S., 39, 677, 694
Grossi, N. T., 627
Grossman, J. D., 248
Grossman, L., 321
Grossman, S. P., 321
Grota, L. J., 56, 65, 67–70, 72, 76
Growdon, J. H., 463, 481
Grubb, P. D., 161
Grube, J. W., 132
Gruber, C. P., 626, 627
Grudin, J., 615
Gruen, E., 319
Gruen, R., 9
Gruenfeld, D. H., 137, 160
Gu, J. K., 93
Gu, X. Y., 97
Guarnaccia, P., 506, 507
Guarnaccia, P. J., 506
Guba, E. G., 649, 652, 654, 658
Guberman, S. R., 300
Gudeman, J. E., 530
Guerra, N. G., 562, 565, 566, 568, 570, 572
Guide, P. C., 252
Guigon, C., 15

Guilian, D., 75
Guion, R. M., 205
Gunasegaram, S., 170
Guo, J., 275, 277
Guo, Y. W., 105
Gurtman, M. B., 127, 179
Gust, D. A., 70
Gustafson, K. E., 534
Gustafson, S., 444
Guthrie, D., 571, 577
Guthrie, R. V., 362
Gutierrez, F., 370
Guydisch, J. R., 548
Guyre, P. M., 72
Guzman, L. P., 345, 365
Gyger, M., 698

H

Ha, Y., 293
Haaga, D. A., 37
Haapala, D., 534, 535
Haas, H., 75
Haccou, P., 695
Hackett, G., 345, 347, 348, 356, 357, 367
Hackett, R. D., 205
Hackley, S. A., 397, 398, 405
Hackman, J. R., 199, 209
Haddock, G., 123, 144
Hage, J., 219
Hagen, B. A., 250
Hagendoorn, L., 166
Hagerman, S., 30, 33, 43
Hailman, J. P., 679, 682, 689, 690, 692
Haist, F., 460, 462, 463, 470, 479
Hale, A. R., 237
Hale, C. R., 270
Haley, G. M. T., 567
Halford, G. S., 275, 277
Halford, W. K., 25
Halgren, E., 463
Hall, E. M., 239, 240
Hall, E. T., 590
Hall, G. B., 526
Hall, N. R. S., 68, 436
Hall, W. G., 695
Hallett, R., 131
Halliday, T. R., 676
Hallpike, C., 501
Hamburg, B. A., 543
Hamill, E., 67, 69, 73
Hamilton, C., 62
Hamilton, C. E., 619, 624, 629, 630
Hamilton, D. L., 118, 129, 141, 142, 158, 160, 161, 164, 166, 169
Hamilton, J. C., 44
Hamilton, W. J., 676
Hammann, S. B., 480
Hammen, C., 564, 575, 578
Hammond, K. J., 237
Hammond, K. R., 599, 637

Hampson, S. E., 162, 164, 165
Hancock, K. A., 367–69
Hancock, P. A., 242, 246, 247
Hankins, L., 323
Hannah, J. S., 347
Hansen, C. H., 161, 180
Hansen, J. C., 346
Hansen, R. D., 180
Hanson, G. R., 348
Hantzi, A., 166
Harackiewicz, J. M., 27
Harada, T., 58
Harbison-Briggs, K., 239
Harbluk, J. L., 460, 466
Hardesty, V. A., 533
Hardiman, M. J., 328, 330
Hardwood, R. L., 500, 511
Hardy, A. M., 550
Hardy, C., 69, 72
Harkins, S. G., 589, 590
Harlow, H. F., 320
Harman, P. J., 64
Harmon, L. W., 347, 348
Harnad, S., 414
Harper, R. M., 322
Harquail, C. V., 349
Harré, R., 10, 498
Harris, C., 3, 28
Harris, D. H., 248
Harris, L. C., 363, 529, 539
Harris, M. J., 158, 173, 178
Harris, P., 498
Harrison, J., 358
Harrison, P., 252
Hart, C. H., 570
Hart, H., 439
Hart, J., 484
Hart, S. G., 238
Harter, S., 41, 354, 575, 577
Hartgraves, S. H., 688
Hartig, M., 37
Hartley, L. H., 4
Hartman, M., 472
Hartry, A. L., 479
Hartup, W. W., 565
Hartwick, J., 602
Harvey, C. R., 107
Harvey, J. A., 329, 331–34
Harvey, J. H., 171
Harvey, L. O., 637
Harvey, P. H., 682, 684, 690, 691
Harwood, K., 242
Hasalm, A., 169
Haselton, J., 321
Hasher, L., 285, 429
Haskell, W. L., 542
Haskins, R., 622, 628, 632, 633
Haslam, N., 166
Hass, R. G., 123, 143
Hassard, J., 199
Hassig, S. E., 550
Hassner, V., 539

Hassoun, J. A., 243, 244
Hastie, R., 171, 600, 601, 637
Hatalla, J., 348
Hatano, G., 297, 298, 300
Hatfield, A., 63
Hatfield, A. B., 539, 541
Hatfield, G., 387, 388
Hatsopoulos, N., 285
Hauge, S. A., 319
Hauth, A. C., 549
Havercamp, B. E., 359
Hawkins, H. L., 400
Hawkins, R. D., 685
Hawley, K. J., 470
Hayden, B., 565
Hayes, J. A., 369, 370
Hayes, N. A., 279
Hayes, W. A., 256
Hayes-Roth, B., 37
Hayes-Roth, F., 37
Hayman, C. A. G., 459, 469, 479
He, B. Y., 91
He, C. D., 105
He, G. B., 104
He, S. J., 100
Healy, S. D., 695
Heath, A. E., 362
Heath, G. A., 533
Heath, S. B., 500
Heaton, A. W., 175
Heaton, R. K., 368
Heaven, P. C. L., 125
Hebb, D. O., 280
Heckhausen, H., 24, 27, 37, 43, 176
Heelas, P. L. F., 499
Heesacker, M., 362
Heesacker, R. S., 352
Heffner, H., 688
Hegedus, A. M., 657, 660
Heider, K. G., 515
Heidiger, H., 679
Heijnen, C. J., 69
Heiligenberg, W., 695
Heilman, J. G., 657
Heindel, W. C., 457, 472
Heinz, S. P., 404
Held, P. E., 67, 70, 73
Hell, W., 286, 393, 413
Heller, F. A., 103, 107
Heller, J. F., 163, 174
Heller, K., 551
Helms, B. J., 358, 360
Helms, J. E., 362, 363, 366
Helmstetter, F. J., 321
Helson, R., 435
Hembree, T. L., 328
Hempel, C., 293
Henderson, S., 347
Hendriks, L., 252
Henggeler, S. W., 535, 536
Henik, A., 250
Henle, M., 292
Hennessy, E., 631
Hennessy, M., 658

Henry, J. P., 67
Heppner, P. P., 349, 358
Herbener, E. S., 129
Herbert, H., 330
Herdt, G., 498, 502, 515
Herek, G. M., 367
Herman, L. M., 697
Hernandez, L. L., 322
Hernandez, M., 532, 534
Herrnstein, R. J., 683
Herschler, D. A., 243
Herz, R. S., 689
Hesketh, B., 347, 348
Hesson-McInnis, M., 349
Hetherington, C., 372
Hetherington, J., 666
Hettema, P. J., 430, 432, 436
Hewstone, M., 166, 169
Heywood, J. S., 666
Hibberd, A. D., 61
Higgins, D. L., 547
HIGGINS, E. T., 585–612;
  24, 34, 40, 136, 156, 160,
  176, 179, 587, 591–94,
  602, 603
Higgins, G. A., 321
Higgins, R., 43
Hilberger, M., 69
Hildebrand-Saints, L., 174
Hildemann, W. H., 68
Hilgard, E. R., 25
Hill, G. W., 600
Hill, L. E., 62
Hill, S. G., 244
Hill, T., 181, 280
Hillerbrand, E., 372
Hillery, J. M., 588
Hilsman, R., 560, 564, 567,
  571, 577, 578
Hilton, D., 168, 286
Hilton, D. J., 296, 596
Hilton, J. L., 129, 168, 172,
  182, 595
Himmelfarb, S., 123
Hinckley, E. C., 534
Hinde, R. A., 443, 676, 686,
  694
Hinkle, L. E. Jr., 2
Hinkston, J. A., 364
Hinrichsen, G. A., 537
Hinsz, V. B., 133, 602
Hinton, G. E., 272
Hintzman, D. L., 390, 454,
  474, 479, 574
Hippler, H., 124
Hiramoto, N. S., 56, 60
Hiramoto, R. N., 56, 60, 74
Hirsh, R., 457, 476
Hirst, W., 244, 469, 470
Hirt, E. R., 182
Hitch, G. J., 456
Hitchcock, J. M., 321, 322,
  325
Hixon, J. G., 143, 176, 181
Hochberg, J., 238
Hochschild, A. R., 223

Hock, E., 615, 621, 630, 634
Hockey, G. R. J., 44, 247,
  430
Hodell, M., 27
Hodges, K., 569
Hodos, W., 683, 684
Hoefler-Nissani, D. M., 598
Hoff, C. C., 549
Hofferth, S. L., 616, 617
Hoffman, C., 142, 166
Hoffman, D. D., 408, 418
Hoffman, H., 472
Hoffman, L. W., 621, 624,
  627
Hoffman, M. A., 368
Hoffman, R. R., 232
Hoffrage, U., 286
Hofmann, T., 14
Hofstadter, D. R., 266, 267,
  269
Hofstadter, P., 67, 73
Hogan, J. A., 695, 698
Hogarth, R. M., 664
Hogg, M. A., 177
Hoggson, N., 544
Hokoda, A., 567
Holding, D., 245, 256
Holland, D., 498, 502
Holland, J. H., 267, 273
Holland, J. L., 348
Holland, P. C., 477
Hollander, E. P., 214
Holldobler, B., 684
Holleran, S. A., 3, 28
Hollis, K. L., 694, 695
Hollis, M., 499
Holloway, S. D., 620
Holmberg, D., 161
Holmberg, S., 131
Holmes, J. G., 173
Holmes, W., 73
Holroyd, K. A., 25
Holt, P. A., 347
Holtgraves, T., 167, 174
Holton, B., 182
Holtz, R., 595
HOLYOAK, K. J., 265–315;
  267, 270, 272–74, 277,
  281, 284, 294, 296, 298,
  299, 384, 474
Hong, D. H., 96
Honig, A., 618, 627
Honig, A. S., 628, 631, 632
Honig, W. K., 696, 697
Honrado, G. I., 695
Hood, H. V., 548, 549
Hood, K. E., 430, 437
Hoogstra, L., 498, 500, 511
Hooker, K., 577
Hoosain, R., 108
Hoover, C. W., 33
Hopkins, N., 166, 169
Hopkins, W., 319
Horley, J., 429
Horner, C., 157
Hornik, K., 417

Hosmer, D. W., 443
House, E. R., 655, 658, 659
House, R. J., 214
Houston, A. I., 685, 695
Houston, B. C., 283
Houston, D. A., 130
Howard, A., 498, 502
Howard, D. J., 138
Howard, G. S., 24, 346
Howard, M., 543
Howard-Smith, S., 509
Howe, C. J., 597
Howe, C. W., 540, 541
Howe, J. W., 540, 541
Howell, J. M., 214
Howell, R. D., 124
HOWELL, W. C., 231–63;
  235, 256
Howes, C., 617–20, 622,
  624, 625, 627, 629–35
Hoyt, W. T., 346
Hsee, C. K., 36
Hu, B. Z., 108
Hu, L., 168, 180
Huang, H. L., 106
Huang, X. T., 101, 102
Huber, J., 198
Hudinburg, R. A., 235, 247
Huebner, A., 510
Huesmann, L. R., 560
Huey, B. M., 238, 246, 250
Huey, R., 680, 684
Hug, K., 295
Huggins, A. W. F., 242
Hughes, B. G., 25
Hughes, B. O., 677
Hughes, E. R., 243, 244
Hughs, J. M., 537
Hui, C. H., 108, 125
Hull, C. L., 54
Hull, J. G., 44
Hulse, S. H., 697
Hult, G., 627, 628
Humfleet, G., 548
Hummel, J. E., 276, 277
Humphrey, L. L., 351
Humphreys, G. W., 403
Humphries, C., 593
Humphries, D. A., 689
Humphries, G. W., 245
Humphries, L. G., 251
Hunt, P. J., 588
Hunt, S. P., 678
Huppert, F. A., 466, 467
Hurley, M. E., 368, 372, 373
Hurst, J. L., 691
Hurst, N., 142, 166
Hurwitz, J. B., 285
Husband, A. J., 56, 58, 60,
  61, 71
Hutcherson, H. W., 180
Hutchins, E., 502, 601, 602
Hutchinson, E. B., 351
Hutton, D. G., 140
Hwang, C., 627, 628
Hwang, K. K., 109

Hwang, M. T. Z., 108
Hyland, M. E., 30
Hymel, S., 576, 577
Hyson, R. L., 71

I

Ickes, W., 157, 158, 600
Idler, E. L., 506, 507
Idson, W. L., 401
Ikeda, H., 348
Ikemi, Y., 62
Ilgen, D. R., 196, 211
Immelmann, K., 691
Inagaki, K., 297, 298
Ingle, D., 678
Ingram, R. E., 560, 564
Innes, R. B., 626
Introini-Collison, I. B., 323, 325
Irle, M., 24
Ironson, G., 247
Irving, L. M., 3, 28
Irwin, D. E., 399, 419
Irwin, J., 67, 68, 70, 71, 74, 75
Isaacson, R. L., 321
Iscoe, I., 529, 539
Isen, A. M., 222
Isenberg, D. J., 601
Islam, M. R., 169
Ito, M., 327
Ito, Y., 67
Ivancevich, J. M., 247
Iverson, A. E., 548
Ivey, D., 348
Ivkovich, D., 328, 332
Ivry, R. B., 332, 478
Ivry, R. I., 280, 472
Iwata, J., 321–23
Izard, C. E., 10

J

Jackson, L. A., 180
Jackson, S. E., 206, 207
Jacobs, M., 532
Jacobs, R. C., 600
Jacobsen, P. B., 63
Jacobson, L., 592
Jacobson, N. S., 352
Jacobson, R. R., 466
Jacoby, L. L., 137, 457, 469, 470, 480, 482, 483
Jaeger, E.,, 627
Jaenicke, C., 564, 578
Jaffard, R., 464
Jagielo, J. A., 694
Jahoda, G., 498
James, J., 128
James, L. A., 222
James, L. R., 221, 222
James, W., 23, 155, 156, 162, 172, 182, 435, 454, 646
Jamieson, D. W., 126, 175,

178, 699
Janes, H. R., 547
Janis, I. L., 6, 601
Janiszewski, C., 139
Janoff-Bulman, R., 171
Janowsky, J. S., 460, 462, 466, 468, 470
Janz, L., 76
Jarrard, L. E., 326, 476
Jarrell, T. W., 321
Jarvis, P. E., 593
Jasechko, J., 137
Jaskir, J., 622
Jason, L. A., 542, 547, 548
Jasso, R., 363
Java, R. I., 470
Jemmott, J. B., 180, 548
Jemmott, J. B. III, 548
Jenkins, J., 515
Jenkins, L., 530
Jenkins, S. R., 348
Jenkins, T. N., 683
Jennings, P. D., 220
Jensen, M. P., 37
Jensen, P. S., 537
Jensen, R. A. Jr., 321, 324, 326
Jepson, C., 286
Jerison, H. J., 684, 690
Jerison, I., 684
Jernigan, T. L., 466
Jervey, J. P., 484
Jessop, J. J., 69
Jetter, W., 468, 470
Jex, S. M., 221, 222
Ji, G., 100
Ji, G. P., 94
Jiang, C. G., 69, 70
Jiang, J. Z., 104
Jiao, S., 100
Jiao, S. L., 94
Jin, Y., 96
Jing, Q., 100
Jing, Q. C., 91, 94, 95, 102, 105, 109
Jiwani, N., 25, 36, 37
John, O. P., 159, 162–64
Johnson, B. T., 123, 136
Johnson, C., 142, 169
Johnson, D. F., 695
Johnson, D. L., 540
Johnson, E. J., 266
Johnson, J. D., 180
Johnson, J. H., 567
Johnson, M. K., 469, 470, 500, 587
Johnson, S. D., 365
Johnson-Laird, P. N., 275, 292–94, 302, 304–6
Johnston, L., 166
Johnston, W. A., 404, 470
Johnston, W. B., 236
Johsua, S., 598
Jonas, K., 169
Jones, B. C., 68
Jones, D. K., 163

Jones, E. E., 155, 168, 591
Jones, J. M., 368
Jones, L. G., 4
Jones, P. M., 249
Jones, R. S., 415
Jones, W. A. Jr., 246
Jonides, J., 284
Jordan, D. D., 532, 534
Jordan, M. I., 269
Jöreskog, K. G., 443
Jorna, G. C., 250
Joseph, H., 549, 550
Joseph, J., 245
Joseph, L., 589
Josephs, L., 25
Joule, R., 134
Jourden, F. J., 37
Judd, C. M., 119, 127, 157, 168, 178
Judge, W. Q., 215
Juler, R., 323
Julin, J. A., 206, 207
Juni, S., 361
Jussim, L., 129, 156, 158
Jussim, L. J., 127
Just, M. A., 239, 252, 267
Justice, A., 64

K

Kaas, H., 439
Kacelnik, A., 695
Kagan, J., 10, 430, 618, 625, 627, 632
Kahn, K. B., 366
Kahn, S. E., 347
Kahn, W. A., 203
Kahneman, D., 170, 285, 286, 294, 296, 413
Kairiss, E. W., 324
Kaiser, M. K., 280, 281, 284
Kakar, S., 500
Kaldor, W., 347, 348
Kale, A. R., 127
Kalichman, S. C., 549
Kallander, H., 697
Kallman, H. J., 400, 401
Kalm, K. L., 124
Kalma, A., 167
Kalmar, D., 244
Kamakura, W. A., 123
Kameda, T., 599
Kamil, A. C., 679, 693–95
Kandel, E. R., 318, 454, 685
Kandil, O., 72
Kandler, K., 330
Kanfer, F. H., 25, 27, 30, 32, 33, 35–37, 42–44
Kanfer, R., 25, 32, 36
Kanter, R. M., 206
Kanzawa, S. A., 331
Kao, H. S. R., 108
Kapferer, B., 515
Kaplan, B., 435
Kaplan, C. A., 268, 418
Kaplan, D., 346

Kaplan, J. R., 67
Kaplan, M. F., 143, 175, 178, 599
Kaplan, R., 73
Kaplan, R. M., 668
Kapp, B. S., 320, 321, 323
Kaprow, M. L., 208
Kardes, F. R., 178
Karmiloff-Smith, A., 283, 289, 298
Karno, M., 515
KAROLY, P., 23–51; 25, 27–30, 33, 35–37, 41–43
Karuza, J., 356
Kashani, J. H., 571
Kashy, D. A., 157
Kaslow, M. J., 567
Kasper, P., 66
Kass, S. J., 243
Kassin, S. M., 281
Katigbak, M. S., 162
Katz, B. M., 131
Katz, I., 123, 143
Kaufman, J., 547, 548
Kaufman, L., 249
Kaufmann, A., 439
Kauth, M. R., 549
Kawamoto, A. H., 417
Kazdin, A. E., 33, 571, 653
Kazen-Saad, M., 24, 28, 32, 38, 39, 43
Ke, W. Q., 105
Keane, M., 298
Keane, M. M., 479, 481
Kearsley, R., 627
Keating, J. G., 327, 334
Keating, J. P., 127, 590
Keele, S. W., 280, 472, 474
Keeler, W., 515
Keenan, C. L., 324
Kegeles, S., 549
Kegeles, S. M., 547
Kehoe, E. J., 327
Keister, M., 627
Keith, C. R., 576
Kellam, K. L., 129, 170
Keller, S. E., 70–73, 75
Kellerman, H., 10
Kellerman, J., 134
Kelley, C. M., 480
Kelley, K. W., 67, 68, 71, 73, 75
Kelly, C., 137
Kelly, J. A., 548, 549
Kelly, J. G., 526
Kelly, P. L., 253
Kelly, T. M., 319, 332
Kemble, E. D., 321, 326
Kemeny, M. E., 54, 65
Kemper, T. D., 10
Kenardy, J., 352
Kendall, P. C., 570
Kendall-Tackett, K., 166
Kendrick, A., 144
Kendrick, D. F., 455
Kendzierski, D., 131

Kennedy, K., 533
Kennedy, M., 56, 58, 60, 61
Kennedy, P. T., 299
Kenny, D. A., 157, 656
Kenrick, D. T., 432
Kerlinger, F. N., 647
Kermoian, R., 619
Kerr, L., 57, 67
Kerr, N. L., 599
Kerr, P., 533
Kersteen-Tucker, Z., 479
Kesner, R. P., 323, 455, 677, 696
Kessel, E. L., 688
Ketterlinus, R., 634, 635
Ketterson, E. D., 692
Kettner, R. E., 328
Khan, A. U., 62
Khana, P., 617, 627
Khanna, A., 107
Kidder, L., 356
Kiecolt-Glaser, J. K., 69
Kiedinger, R. E., 696
Kieras, D. E., 239
Kierniesky, N., 129
Kiesler, C. A., 27, 531, 532
Kiesler, S., 595
Kiff, J., 65
Kihlstrom, J. F., 163, 278
Kijowski, B. A., 238, 245
Kilbride, P. L., 501
Kilgore, H. G., 549
Kim, H. H. W., 366
KIM, J. J., 317–42; 322, 324–26, 464
Kim, S. J., 363
Kim, U., 509, 515
Kim, Y. T., 56
Kimble, G. A., 39
Kimchi, R., 232, 244, 250, 384, 405
Kimmel, D., 369, 371
Kinchla, R. A., 405
Kinder, D. R., 179
King, A. C., 541, 542, 548
King, A. P., 691, 696
King, D., 677
King, G., 591, 598
King, L. A., 28, 29, 43
King, M. G., 56, 58, 60, 61, 71
King, W. R., 252
Kingsley, L. A., 548
Kinney, J. S., 250, 534, 535
Kinney, R. F., 176
Kinsbourne, M., 460
Kinsey, A. C., 368
Kintsch, W., 273
Kirby, D., 544
Kirkeby, J., 527
Kirkpatrick, J., 498, 501
Kirkpatrick, L. A., 170
Kirsch, I., 37, 40
Kirschenbaum, D. S., 42, 43
Kirsh, D., 508, 509
Kitayama, S., 179, 498, 500,

502, 506, 508, 515
Kite, M. E., 166
Kitto, C. M., 239
Klatzky, R. L., 165, 239
Klayman, J., 293
Klein, F., 367
Klein, G. A., 237, 238, 242, 248
Klein, H. J., 196, 211
Klein, J. G., 159, 182
Klein, R., 24, 34, 253, 617
Klein, S. B., 181
Klein, W. M., 177
Kleinbölting, H., 286
Kleinman, A. M., 506, 515
Kleinpenning, G., 166
Klemchuk, H. P., 351
Klerman, L. V., 545
Klineberg, S. L., 40, 41
Klinger, E., 28, 29, 32
Klinger, M. R., 429
Klonsky, B. G., 166
Klopfer, P. H., 677, 678, 697
Klopp, R. G., 70
Klosterhalfen, S., 60, 61
Klosterhalfen, W., 60, 61
Knerr, B. W., 256
Knight, D. B., 223
Knispel, J. D., 319
Knitzer, J., 532
Knopman, D. S., 472
KNOWLTON, B., 453–95
Knowlton, B. J., 284, 474, 475
Kobasa, S. C., 3
Koch, G. G., 131
Koedinger, K. R., 304
Koegel, P., 531
Koehler, D. J., 170
Koelega, H. S., 252
Koenig, O., 39
Koestner, R., 25
Koh, K., 281, 298
Kohl, D., 280
Kohlberg, L., 501
Kondo, D., 506
Kondratas, A., 530
Konishi, M., 688, 695
Kontos, S., 617, 628, 629
Koolhaas, J. M., 67, 69
Koops, W., 624, 627
Koota, D., 62, 66, 68, 70
Kopelman, M. D., 463, 467
Kopeloff, N., 54
Kopp, C. B., 25, 41
Koritsas, E., 244
Korman, M., 364
Korn, J. H., 476
Kornell, J., 239
Koskela, K., 542
Koss, M. P., 349, 352–54
Kosslyn, S. M., 39, 300, 481
Kotler-Cope, S., 282
Kotsaftis, A., 625, 635
Kott, T. L., 126
Kounios, J., 399

Kovach, J. K., 88
Kovner, R., 459
Kraft, D., 122
Kraft, J. K., 67
Krajicek, D., 408
Kramer, A., 244
Kramer, A. F., 403
Kramer, M., 530
Krank, M. D., 57
Krantz, D. H., 286
Krasnor, L. R., 560, 561
Krauss, D. H., 540, 541
Krauss, H. H., 603
Krauss, R. M., 158
Kraut, R. E., 603
Kravitz, D. A., 589
Krebs, J. R., 677, 685, 686, 690, 694, 695
Kristiansen, C. M., 125, 126, 173
Kritchevsky, M., 462, 468, 470
Kroemer, K. H. E., 253
Krolick, G., 627, 632
Kroodsma, D. E., 688, 695
Krosnick, J. A., 122, 123, 127, 140, 168, 178, 179, 286
Krueger, J., 167, 168
Kruglanski, A. W., 119, 157, 172, 175, 594, 595, 597
Kruk, M. R., 696
Krull, D. S., 137, 176, 180
Krumweid, R. D., 529
Krupa, D. J., 330
Kruschke, J. K., 475, 477
Kruser, D. S., 238
Krushinski, L. V., 683
Kuang, P. Z., 87, 91, 94, 105
Kubrin, A., 657, 660
Kucinski, B. J., 59, 69, 71–73
Kuhl, J., 24, 27, 28, 32, 38, 39, 41, 43
Kuiper, N., 575
Kuiper, N. A., 564
Kuklinski, J., 124
Kulik, C. C., 604
Kulik, J. A., 604
Kunda, Z., 129, 170, 177, 182, 286, 294, 595
Kunkel, M. A., 363
Kunst-Wilson, W. R., 479
Kuo, Z. Y., 680
Kupersmidt, J., 695
Kuperstein, M., 467
Kurtz, S. N., 498, 511
Kurzhanski, A. B., 436
Kusche, C. A., 569
Kushner, M., 280, 284
Kusnecov, A. W., 56, 60, 65, 71
Kutas, M., 482
Kuykendall, D., 127
Kwan, H. H., 318
Kwan, J. L., 598
Kyllonen, P. C., 251, 256

Kyriacou, C. P., 691

L

Laaksonen, O., 107
Lab, S. P., 533, 534
Labinsky, J., 76
Labov, W., 500
Lachman, J. L., 384
Lachman, L. B., 75
Lachman, R., 384
Ladd, G., 562, 570
Ladd, G. W., 568, 570, 577
Ladd, R. T., 221
Laessle, R. G., 351
La Greca, A. M., 576
Laird, J. D., 134
Laird, J. E., 267, 269, 297, 304, 414
Lajoie, S., 240
Lakoff, G., 269, 500
Lalljee, M., 170
Lally, J. R., 628, 632
Lalonde, R. N., 143, 169
Lamb, H. R., 531
Lamb, M. E., 625, 627, 628, 630, 634, 635
Lamb, R., 170
Lambert, A. J., 160, 162, 169
Lammers, J. H. C. M., 696
Lande, J., 616, 628, 636
Landeira-Fernandez, J., 324
Landers, D., 41
Lang, A. E., 475
Lang, E. J., 467
Lang, M. E., 616, 638
Langacker, R. W., 500
Lange, C., 178
Lange, T. E., 298
Langer, E. J., 33
Langley, C. M., 682, 693
Langston, C. A., 43, 270, 292, 295
Langtimm, C. A., 681, 687
Langton, C. L., 694
Lanzetta, J. T., 173
Lapan, R. T., 346
Larish, I., 238
Larkin, J., 304
Larkin, K. C., 348
Larson, C. L., 657
Larson, L., 71
Lashley, K. S., 335
Lassiter, G. D., 161
Laszlo, E., 436
Latane, B., 123, 589
Latham, G., 32, 199
Latham, G. P., 25, 31, 44
Latour, B., 604
Lau, R. R., 165, 177, 178, 180
Laudenslager, M. L., 67, 70, 71, 73, 75
Laughlin, P. R., 595, 599, 601
Launier, R., 5, 8, 14

Laux, L., 16
Laux, L. F., 253
Lave, J., 299, 500, 604, 605
LAVOND, D. G., 317–42; 320, 327, 328, 330–34
Law, J., 479
Lawrence, B. S., 206
Lawrence, D., 358, 360
Laws, J. V., 105
Lawton, M. P., 253
LAZARUS, R. S., 1–21; 3–10, 12, 14, 15, 40
Leaf, P. J., 528, 529
Leafgren, F., 362
Leaton, R. N., 320, 321, 326, 332
Lebra, T. S., 509
LeDoux, J. E., 321–24, 326, 477
Lee, B. A., 530
Lee, L. A., 349
Lee, P. H., 108
Lee, T. W., 32, 204, 222
Leeuwenberg, E., 408
Lefever, G., 625, 635
Lefkowitz, M. M., 571
Lefley, H. P., 540
Lefly, H., 365
Leger, D. W., 677
Legrenzi, P., 294, 295
Legrenzi, S. M., 294
Lehman, D. R., 168, 286
Lehrman, D. S., 676
Leiderman, P. H., 619
Leinbach, J., 388
Leiner, A. L., 327
Leiner, H. C., 327
Leippe, M. R., 118
Leitenberg, H., 567
LeMare, L. J., 569
Lemkau, J. P., 346
Le Moal, M., 60, 67, 71, 75
Lenerz, K., 577
Lennon, K., 25
Lent, R. W., 345, 348
Leo, G., 598
Leon, M., 413
Leong, F. T. L., 362, 366
Lepper, M. R., 27, 131
Lerner, J. V., 577
Lerner, M. J., 143
Lerner, R. M., 577
Lesgold, A., 240
Lesourd, B., 67
Lessells, C. M., 692
Lester, L. S., 695, 696
Letourneau, L., 479
Leung, K., 108, 508
Leung, S. A., 347, 348
Levant, R. F., 359
Levesque, H., 301, 303
Levin, H. S., 462
Levine, A., 551
LeVine, E. S., 365
Levine, I. S., 530, 531
LEVINE, J. M., 585–612;

587, 590, 594, 597, 600, 601
Levine, L. J., 515
LEVINE, M., 525–58; 526, 527, 532, 540, 551
Levine, N., 64
LeVine, R. A., 498, 501, 511, 514
Levine, S., 37, 64, 67
Levinson, S., 64
Leviton, L. C., 548, 645, 646, 650, 651, 657, 660, 671
Levitt, M. J., 635
Levitz, L. S., 537
Levy, A. S., 44
Levy, E. M., 69, 70
Levy, J., 277
Levy, L., 532
Levy, N. B., 359
Levy, R. I., 499, 506, 515
Lew, S., 363
Leweshow, S., 443
Lewicki, P., 181, 280, 472, 473
Lewin, K., 29, 30, 435, 444
Lewis, J., 62, 134
Lewis, J. L., 330
Lewis, J. W., 71, 74, 75
Lewis, L. L., 166
Lewis, M. A., 344, 515, 622
Lewis, M. W., 298
Lewis, S., 281
Lewontin, R. C., 286, 288
Leyens, J. Ph., 161–63, 165, 168, 182
Li, D., 96
Li, D. M., 94, 105
Li, F., 168, 286
Li, H. Y., 98
Li, L., 484
Li, S. Z., 105
Li, W., 102
Li, X. T., 94, 105
Li, X. Y., 103
Liang, K. C., 321, 323, 324, 326
Liberman, A., 122, 129, 135, 136, 172
Libet, B., 25
Lichtenberg, J. L., 370
Lichtenstein, E., 37
Liddle, C. L., 285
Lieberman, M. A., 537
Liebeskind, J. C., 65, 71, 74
Liebling, B. A., 589
Lienert, G. A., 445
Liew, F. Y., 58
Lifshutz, H., 537
Light, L. L., 253
Light, P. H., 294, 295
Light, R. J., 670
Lilly, T., 173
Lima, S. L., 695
Lin, C. D., 91, 98, 101
Lin, C. H., 364

Lin, C. T., 89
Lin, R. M., 108
Lin, S. H., 106, 164
Lin, W. Q., 103, 107
Lin, Z. X., 87, 91, 92
Lincoln, J. S., 320, 328
Lincoln, Y. S., 649, 654, 658
Lind, H. W., 533
Lindholm, C., 214
Lindsay, P. H., 416, 567
Lindsay, R. K., 415
Lindvall, T., 444
Link, B. G., 530
Lintern, G., 256
Linville, P. W., 167, 168, 574
Liotta, A. S., 71, 75
Lipkin, M., 320
Lippa, R., 139
Lipsey, M. W., 656, 657, 670
Lipshitz, R., 238, 248
Lishman, W. A., 466
Lisle, D. J., 122
Litt, M. D., 37
Little, B. R., 28, 29, 429
Littman, R., 71
Liu, F., 97, 98
Liu, J. H., 98, 101
Liu, J. X., 98
Liu, S. X., 87
Liu, X., 104
Lively, S. E., 250
Livnat, S., 69, 70, 72
Lloyd, E., 626
Lo, B., 547
Lo, W. D., 318
Lobel, S. A., 206
Lochman, J. E., 565
Lock, A. J., 499
Locke, E. A., 25, 31, 32, 44, 199
Loehlin, J. C., 430
Loerch, K. J., 349
Loftus, E. F., 429
Logan, C. G., 327, 328, 330, 332
Logan, G. D., 25, 403, 406
Logie, R., 245
Logue, A. W., 689
Loiacano, D. K., 372
Lollis, S., 569
Londerville, S., 630
Long, B. C., 349
Long, D., 94
Long, L. A., 532
Longergan, E. T., 253
Longo, L. C., 141, 166
Longshore, D., 548
Look, S. C., 134
Lopez, A., 292
Lopez, D. F., 594
Lopez, F. G., 348
Lord, C. G., 131, 145, 173, 174
Lord, R. G., 591
Lorenz, K., 680
Lorenz, K. Z., 682, 687

Lorion, R. P., 548, 550
Lorvick, J., 548
Losch, M. E., 134
Losos, J. B., 687
Lott, D. F., 677
LoTurco, J. J., 328, 330
Louis, M. R., 600
Lovallo, D., 286
Lovie, A. D., 387
Lown, B. A., 70
Lu, H. J., 96, 103
Lu, J., 96
Lu, S. Y., 97
Lu, S. Z., 91, 103
Lu, Z. Y., 106
Lubach, G. R., 70
Lubart, T., 292
Lucas, G. A., 693, 695
Lucas, J. R., 695
Lucy, J. A., 498
Luecken, L. J., 59, 61, 73
Luhtanen, R., 177
Lui, L., 166
Lui, L. N., 166
Luke, D. A., 538
Lukes, S., 499
Lumsden, D. P., 2
Luo, S. D., 87, 94
Lupfer, M. B., 180
Luthar, S., 500
Lutz, C., 498, 499, 501, 515
Lyall, W. A., 537
Lyman, R. D., 139
Lynch, J. G., 168
Lynch, L., 166
Lynch, O. M., 515
Lynn, A. R., 127
Lyons, J., 548
Lysaght, R. J., 244
Lysle, D. T., 58–61, 69–75
Lyte, M., 67, 69, 70, 72, 73
Lyter, D. W., 548

M

Ma, H. K., 108
Ma, N. Q., 99
Maass, A., 141, 142, 164, 169, 597, 598
Maccoby, N., 542
MacDonald, C., 468
MacDonald, C. A., 459
MacFarlane, S., 432
Macgregor-Morris, R., 159
MacIntyre, A., 499, 500
MacKay, D. M., 25, 386
Mackenzie, J. N., 61
Mackie, D. M., 118, 137, 138, 140, 141, 168, 169, 179, 593, 594, 597
MacLean, P. D., 688
MacMillan, I., 211, 215
Macphail, E. M., 685
MacQueen, G. M., 57, 60
Macrae, C. N., 181
Macrae, S., 56, 58, 60

MacWhinney, B., 388
Madden, T. J., 133
Maddi, S. R., 3
Maddux, J. E., 37
Madeira, E., 537
MAGNUSSON, D., 427–51;
    428–30, 433, 435, 436,
    440, 444–46
Maguire, B., 547
Mahapatra, M., 501, 506,
    509, 515
Mahapatra, M. M., 511, 515
Maher, J. T., 4
Maheswaran, D., 135, 139,
    182
Mahoney, M. J., 24, 37, 39,
    41, 388
Mahut, M., 461
Mai, H., 124
Maier, L. A., 63
Maier, N. R. F., 685
Maier, S. F., 67, 71, 73
Main, B. G., 223
Main, M., 630, 691
Mainardi, D., 696
Maioni, T. L., 565
Major, B., 143, 177, 595
Makani, B., 550
Makhijani, M. G., 141, 166
Makinodan, T., 57
Malamut, B. L., 457, 471,
    476
Malamuth, N. M., 361
Malloy, T. E., 157
Malone, P. S., 137, 180
Malovich, N. J., 349, 350
Manderlink, G., 27
Mandler, G., 10, 219, 457,
    469, 470, 478, 479, 483
Mandler, J. M., 269, 465
Mandler, R., 60
Mangel, M., 677
Mangge, H., 69, 70, 72
Mangione, P. L., 628, 632
Mani, K., 302
Manicas, P. T., 389
Manis, M., 168, 169, 285
Manktelow, K. I., 294, 295
Mann, B. J., 535, 536
Mann, J., 144, 169
Mann, J. A., 145, 173
Mann, L. M., 351
Mannes, S. M., 273
Manning, M. M., 37
Manske, S. R., 133, 134
Manson, J. H., 689
Manuck, S. B., 67
Manzel, E. W. Jr., 679
Mao, Y. Y., 100
March, J. G., 216, 225
Marchman, V., 388
Marclay, C., 697
Marcus, A. A., 212
Marcus, G. E., 506
Marcus, R. F., 564
Marcus-Newhall, A., 274

Margetts, I., 245
Marinkovic, K., 477
Markova, I., 567
Markovits, H., 293
Markowitsch, H., 462
Markowitsch, J. H., 468, 470
Marks, E., 63
Markus, H., 25, 27, 34, 39
Markus, H. R., 498, 500,
    502, 506, 508, 515
Marlatt, G. A., 25
Marler, C. A., 692
Marler, P., 676, 679, 698
Marr, D., 327
Marriage, K., 567
Marriott, M., 498, 509, 515
Marsh, J. T., 64
Marsh, K. L., 175
Marshall, B. S., 327
Marshall, J., 57, 60
Marshall, N., 614, 635
Marshall-Goodell, B. S., 127
Marsolek, C. J., 481
Martijn, C., 169
Martin, B., 589
Martin, C. E., 368
Martin, C. J., 251
Martin, C. L., 143
Martin, D. W., 249, 509
Martin, G. M., 698
Martin, L., 122, 181
Martin, L. L., 169, 174, 175,
    178, 179
Martin, N. G., 128
Martin, R. D., 684
Martin, S., 626
Martinez, J. L., 321, 324, 326
Martinez, J. L. Jr., 677
Marton, P., 537
Martone, M., 472
Maruyama, G., 166
Marzillier, J., 37
Masi, W., 624, 629, 631, 633
Maslin, L., 630
Maslonek, K. A., 59–61, 71–
    73
Maslow, A., 30
Mason, A. F., 235
Mason, J. A., 145, 173
Mason, J. W., 4
Mason, W. A., 677
MASSARO, D. W., 383–
    425; 384, 385, 387, 392–
    94, 396, 399–401, 405,
    407, 409, 411, 415
Massey, L. D., 255
Masson, M. E. J., 482
Mast, T., 253
Masterton, R. B., 688
Matheson, K., 125, 173
Mathews, A., 159
Mathews, P., 458, 467
Mathews, R., 267, 284
Mathews, R. C., 282, 284,
    474
Matlin, M. W., 589

Maton, K. I., 537
Matsui, T., 346, 348
Matsuzawa, T., 688
Matteson, M. T., 247
Matthews, G., 245
Matthews, R. W., 590
Mattis, S., 459
Mauk, M. D., 319, 328, 329,
    333
Mawer, R., 304
Maxeiner, M., 29
May, R., 30, 359
Mayer, J. D., 40
Mayes, A. R., 466–68, 480
Maynard-Smith, J., 680, 692
Mayr, E., 646, 680
Mays, V. M., 368, 550
Mayseless, O., 594, 598
Mazen, A., 346, 348
Mazursky, D., 139
Mazzocco, A., 295
McAlister, A. L., 544
McAllister, C. G., 71
McAndrews, M. P., 466
McBride, S., 615, 621, 634
McBride, S. L., 615
McCabe, J. B., 543
McCabe, P. M., 321
McCaig, L. F., 550
McCain, B. R., 206
McCann, C. D., 136, 176
McCann, I. L., 353
McCarl, R., 267, 269, 297,
    304
McCarn, S. R., 371, 373
McCarthy, E. D., 223
McCarthy, J., 271, 546
McCarthy, R. A., 484
McCartney, K., 614–18, 620,
    622, 623, 627–29, 631,
    632, 634–36
McCauley, C., 601
McCauley, E., 571
McClaskey, C. L., 560, 561,
    565, 568, 571
McClearn, G. E., 691
McClelland, J. L., 266, 272,
    281, 387, 388, 392, 396,
    409–12, 415, 417, 472,
    475, 484, 560, 562, 586
McClintock, M. K., 681
McCloskey, B. P., 239
McCloskey, M., 280, 416,
    417
McClure, H. M., 70
McCorduck, P., 238
McCormick, D. A., 320, 327–
    30, 332
McCrae, R. R., 163
McCune, W. J., 64
McCusker, C., 108, 125
McDaniels, S. M., 62
McDermott, D., 370
McDonald, D. R., 249
McDonald, J., 182
McDonald, J. E., 241

McDonald, S. M., 166
McDonell, D. M., 530
McDonough, J. H. Jr., 323
McFadden, L. S., 538
McFall, R. M., 33, 561
McFarland, C., 170, 595
McGarry, S. J., 299
McGaugh, J. L., 321, 323–26
McGee, R., 577
McGhee, P. E., 634
McGill, A. L., 139
McGonigle, B., 302
McGrath, E., 346
McGraw, K. L., 239
McGraw, K. M., 178
McGreen, P., 534
McGuire, T. W., 595
McGuire, W. J., 118, 120,
    136, 137, 587, 591
McIntosh, W. D., 175, 177
McIrvine, E. C., 385
McKechnie, P. I., 212
McKee, R., 465, 467, 479,
    480
McKeeman, D., 29
McKelvie, S. J., 280
McKenzie-Mohr, D., 179
McKinley, S. C., 475, 477
McKoon, G., 272, 298, 412
McKusick, L., 549
McLachlan, D., 480, 481
McLachlan, D. R., 460, 466
McLaughlin, B. P., 269
McLennan, D. A., 687, 688
McLeod, P. L., 206, 384, 419
McManus, J. A., 126
McMillan, D., 160
McMullen, P. A., 484
McNab, B., 684, 690
McNall, C. L., 323
McNally, J. W., 545
McNamara, J. M., 695
McNamara, K., 356
McNaughton, B. L., 463
McNeese, M. D., 238, 241
McNulty, S. E., 180
Mead, G. H., 593, 596
Mearns, J., 40
Mechanic, D., 6, 621
Medin, D. L., 266, 271, 274,
    285, 288, 474, 500, 574
Medina, N., 439
Medvene, L. J., 540, 541
Meehl, P. E., 647
Meeley, M. P., 321
Meelis, W., 696
Meichenbaum, D., 25, 37
Meier, P., 3
Meindl, J. R., 212, 214
Meissen, G. J., 537
Melhuish, E. C., 626, 631,
    635
Melia, K. R., 324
Meller, J., 439
Mellers, B. A., 413
Melton, G. B., 367, 368, 535,

536
Meltzoff, A. N., 465
Melz, E. R., 274
Men, Q. M., 91
Mendolia, M., 122, 181
Meng, Z. L., 94
Merleau-Ponty, M., 15
Merton, R. K., 592
Mesquita, B., 515
Messe, L. A., 602
Messick, D. M., 593
Messing, R. B., 321, 324, 326
Metal'nikov, S., 54
Metalsky, G. I., 571
Metcalfe, J., 283
Meth, R. L., 359
Metzler, J., 303
Meudec, M., 629
Meudell, P., 468
Meudell, P. R., 466
Meyer, A., 221
Meyer, D. E., 281, 397–99,
    406, 415, 419
Meyer, D. R., 320, 326
Meyer, G. W., 220
Meyer, J. P., 204
Meyer, J. W., 213
Meyer, M. F., 10
Meyer, M. M., 484
Meyer, P. M., 326
Meyers-Levy, J., 139, 140
Miao, X. C., 94, 107
Micco, D. J., 327
Michael, R. T., 628
Michaud, B., 67, 69, 71, 75
Michaut, R.-J., 67
Michener, C. D., 684
Middleton, D., 602
Miene, P., 126
Miezin, F. M., 481
Miki, H., 142, 165
Milberg, W., 479
Milburn, M. A., 118, 178
Milich, R., 565
Milinski, M., 692
Millar, K. U., 121
Millar, M. G., 121, 122, 181
Miller, A., 215
Miller, C. O., 237
Miller, D. T., 170, 171, 210,
    296, 691
Miller, E. K., 484
Miller, G. A., 30, 277
Miller, J. G., 164, 395–98,
    436, 500, 501, 506, 509,
    511, 515
Miller, J. S., 694
Miller, K., 108, 498
Miller, L. C., 38, 163, 170
Miller, L. D., 529
Miller, N. E., 29, 72, 73, 595
Miller, P., 498, 500, 511, 515
Miller, R. E., 476
Miller, T. E., 548
Miller, W. L., 658
Miller-Herringer, T., 40

Milligan, W. L., 320
Milner, B., 454, 455, 466,
    471
Milner, P. M., 463
Milner, T. A., 324
Milojkovic, J. D., 164
Milson, R., 288
Minde, K., 537
Mine, K., 67
Miner, J. B., 103
Minkiewicz-Janda, A., 68
Minsky, M., 270, 272, 291,
    510
Minsky, M. L., 586
Mintz, J., 498, 500, 511
Mintz, L. B., 350, 351, 358,
    359
Mischel, H. N., 27
Mischel, P. L., 198, 224
Mischel, W., 24, 27, 40, 158,
    163, 433
Miserendino, M. J. D., 321,
    324, 325
Mishkin, M., 455, 457, 461,
    465, 468, 471, 476, 484
Mitchell, C. M., 534
Mitchell, D. B., 479
Mitchell, J. R., 571
Mitchell, M., 267, 269
Mitchell, T. R., 196
Mitchell, V., 435
Mitroff, I. I., 388
Mitsuoka, A., 58
Miyashita, Y., 484
Mladinic, A., 169
Moely, B. E., 629
Moffatt, C. A., 698
Mogg, K., 159
Molino, A., 326
Molitor, N., 630, 633, 634
Moller, L., 568
Monaem, A., 542
Monat, A., 7
Money, J., 369
Monjan, A. A., 69, 73
Monro, A., 255
Monsell, S., 456
Montarolo, P. G., 330
Monteith, M. J., 145, 173
Montello, D. R., 432
Montepare, J. M., 166
Montgomerie, R. D., 691
Mooney, A., 626
Moore, B., 593
Moore, C., 480
Moore, C. L., 680, 681
Moore, D., 359, 362
Moore, D. S., 589
Moore, E. F., 390
Moore, J. J., 401
Moore, J. L., 587
Moore, J. W., 327, 328, 333,
    476
Moore, M. C., 677, 692
Moore, M. K., 354, 547
Moore, T. W., 624, 627, 631

Moran, J. S., 547
Moray, N., 235, 238, 245
Mordkoff, A. M., 6
Moreines, J., 480
Moreland, R. L., 590, 594, 600, 601
Moretti, M. M., 34, 567
Morgan, B. B. Jr., 249, 252
Morgan, K. S., 370
Morgan, M., 131, 132
Morgan, S. P., 543
Moriarty, A. E., 623
Morikawa, S., 58
Morin, S. F., 367, 368, 547
Morley, J. E., 54, 65
Morlock, L., 530
Mormede, P., 67, 69, 71, 75
Morrel-Samuels, P., 697
Morris, N. B., 239
Morrison, D. M., 544
Morrison, J. E., 255
Morrow, G. R., 63
Morrow-Tesch, J. L., 69, 70
Morten, G., 363, 364, 366
Morton, T., 532
Moruzzi, G., 327
Moscovici, S., 597, 598, 604
Moscovitch, M., 465, 479–81
Mosher, L. R., 539
Mosher, W. D., 545
Moskowitz, D. S., 158
Moskowitz, G. B., 180
Moss, M., 461
Moss, P., 626
Moss, S., 571
Mott, F. L., 543, 624, 625, 628
Mougey, E., 4
Moulias, R., 67
Mowbray, C. T., 530
MOWDAY, R. T., 195–229; 204, 222
Moyal, B. R., 567
Moyer, J. R., 319, 477
Moyer, R. J., 364
Moynihan, J. A., 62, 65–70, 72, 76
Mrosovsky, N., 694
Much, N. C., 498, 500, 511, 515
Mugnoini, E., 331
Mugny, G., 596, 597, 604
Mulaik, S. A., 221
Mulder, M. B., 686
Mulilis, J., 44, 139
Mullen, B., 142, 161, 168, 169, 180, 591
Mullennix, J. W., 250
Mullins, L. L., 569
Mumford, M. D., 251, 252, 444
Munck, A., 72
Munkel, T., 124
Muralidhar, K., 250, 252
Murdock, T. B., 354
Murino, M., 295

Murnighan, J. K., 201
Murphy, G., 88, 143
Murphy, J., 439
Murphy, K. R., 252
Murphy, L. B., 623
Murphy, M. D., 285
Murphy, R. R., 566
Murray, E., 468
Murray, F. B., 596
Murray, H. A., 29, 435
Murray, J., 165
Murrell, A. J., 145, 169, 173
MUSEN, G., 453–95; 463, 472, 479, 481
Mutter, S. A., 255
Myers, D. G., 166
Myers, F. R., 515
Myers, G., 677
Myers, H. F., 345, 365, 366
Myers, J. L., 399
Myers, L., 635
Mynatt, C. R., 294

N

Nadel, L., 457, 463, 465, 467
Naderer, G., 168, 286
Nagahara, A. H., 323
Nagar, D., 590
Nagel, J. A., 321, 326
Nagel, R. J., 620, 629, 630
Nagode, J., 467
Nagy, E., 75
Nakagawa, S., 62
Nakagawa, T., 67
Nakamura, Y., 479
Nantel, G., 293
Narrol, H., 567
Nasby, W., 565
Natelson, B. H., 70, 72
Navon, D., 34, 39
Naylor, J. C., 247
Nederhof, A. J., 131
Neimeyer, G. J., 362
Neimeyer, R. A., 354
Neisser, U., 384, 386, 464, 466, 509
Nelson, B. J., 331
Nelson, D. L., 208, 209, 222
Nelson, G., 274, 298, 526
Nelson, K., 466
Nelson, L. C., 133
Nelson, R. O., 33
Nelson, T. F., 168, 169
Nemeroff, C., 515
Nemeth, C., 598
Nemeth, C. J., 598
Nemeth, R., 57
Nesselroade, J. R., 430, 445
Netemeyer, R. G., 140
Neubauer, R. M., 181
Neuberg, S. L., 142, 160, 169, 172, 178, 182, 595
Neveu, P. J., 60, 71
Nevin, J. A., 407, 413
Nevis, E. C., 107

Newcomb, M., 353
Newcomb, T. M., 587, 592
Newell, A., 267, 269, 297, 304, 384, 389, 414, 560, 586
Newman, A., 37
Newman, D., 605
Newman, J. P., 563, 565, 566
Newman, L. S., 180
Newman, R. S., 25
Newman, S., 568, 605
Newsome, S. L., 389
Nguyen-Xuan, A., 294, 295
Ni, H., 322
Nicholls, J. G., 587
Nichols, C. W., 27
Nicholson, P., 235, 247
Nicolet, M., 596
Nicolis, G., 439
Niedenthal, P. M., 43
Niemeyer, G., 352
Nierenberg, A., 537
Nigo, Y., 67
Nisbett, R. E., 157, 164, 267, 270, 273, 286, 292, 294–96, 500, 507
Nissani, M., 598
Nissen, M. J., 280, 471, 472
Nissinen, A., 542
Nitecki, M. H., 684
Niu, J., 99
Niwembo, K. L., 550
Noel, R. W., 389
Nolan, V. Jr., 692
Nolen-Hoeksema, S., 567
Nomikos, M. S., 7
Nordholm, A. F., 332, 333
Norem, J. K., 43
Norman, D. A., 25, 37, 384, 399, 416, 429, 454, 456
Norman, N. M., 131
Norman, R. J., 319, 477
North, T. C., 139
Nosofsky, R. M., 393, 474, 475, 477
Nota, N. R., 58
Notgrass, C. M., 353
Nottebohm, F., 695
Novak, J. M., 455
Novak, M. A., 698, 699
Novelly, R. A., 463
Novick, L. R., 274, 296, 299
Nowak, A., 123
Nowak, A. J., 328
Nozick, R., 658
Nuckolls, C., 502
Nurius, P., 34
Nygren, T. E., 246

O

Oakes, P. J., 165, 169, 594
Oakhill, J., 293
Oakley, D. A., 319
Oaksford, M., 271, 275, 276, 291–93, 307

Oatman, L. C., 245
Oberlander, J., 275, 301
Obeyesekere, G., 499
O'Brien, D., 250
O'Brien, D. P., 292, 293
O'Brien, L., 695
Ochs, E., 511
Ochsner, K. N., 278, 454, 478, 480
Oden, G. C., 265, 411
Oden, S., 568
Odio, M., 75
Odum, H. T., 439
Offerman, L. R., 235
Ofir, C., 168
Ogan, T., 561
Ogawa, M., 67, 73
O'Grady, M. P., 68
O'Halloran, S. M., 348
Ohawa, T., 346, 348
Ohkuma, S., 68–70
Ohnishi, R., 348
Ohta, N., 479
Ojemann, J. G., 481
O'Keefe, D. J., 118
O'Keefe, J., 457, 467
Okimura, T., 67, 68, 73
Oldham, G. R., 199
Olds, D. L., 546
O'Leary, A., 37, 54
Olenick, M., 622, 624, 629
Olfson, M., 529
Olinger, J., 564
Oliver, L. M., 294
Olmstead, M. P., 351, 352
Olson, D. J., 679, 695
OLSON, J. M., 117–54; 118, 134, 141
Olson, J. R., 239
Olson, W. A., 250
Olton, D. S., 460, 696
Omar, A. S., 177
Omodei, M. M., 28
O'Neil, J. M., 357, 358, 360
O'Neill, J. B., 465
Onglatco, M. L. U., 346, 348
Oppenheim, R. W., 680
Opton, E. M. Jr., 6–8
Orasanu, J., 248, 252
Orasanu, J. M., 249
O'Reilly, C. A., 60, 196, 197, 205–7, 223
O'Reilly, K. R., 547, 549
Orive, R., 127
Orlansky, J., 251
Ormerod, A. J., 349
Ormerod, M., 350
Ormsby, G., 455
Orne, M. T., 359
Orr, E., 3
Orr, W. B., 319, 477
Ortega, S., 71
Orth, J. E., 35
Ortony, A., 10
Orzek, A., 372
Osachuk, T. A. G., 57, 58, 76

Osawa, K., 300
Osborne, R. E., 176, 595
Oscar-Berman, M., 478, 479
Osherson, D. N., 292
Osipow, S. H., 345, 346, 356, 358
Oskamp, S., 118, 128
Osler, S. F., 3
Osman, A. M., 397–99, 419
Ostendorf, F., 162
Ostergaard, A., 466
Ostergaard, A. L., 459, 479
Ostrom, T. M., 161
O'Sullivan, M. J., 527
Ottati, V. C., 124
Ottenberg, P., 62
Ottenhoff, G., 624, 627
Ottenweller, J. E., 70, 72
Otto, T., 463, 468
Over, D. E., 294, 295
Overman, W. H., 455, 465
Overton, W. F., 434
Owen, M. T., 630
Owen, N., 37
Owen, S. V., 358
Owens, J., 319
Owens, W. A., 444
Owings, D. H., 691
Owsley, C., 253, 254
Oyama, S., 680
Ozer, D. J., 129, 444
Ozer, E. M., 37, 353

P

Paap, K. R., 389
Pack, A. A., 697
Packard, M. G., 476
Packard, N. H., 436, 439
Packer, A. E., 236
Packer, M., 439
Pacteau, C., 282, 474
Padawer-Singer, A., 591
Padilla, A. M., 363, 365
Page, M. S., 181
Page, R. E., 691
Pagel, M. D., 682, 691
Pagniano, R., 65
Palca, J., 550
Palincsar, A. S., 605
Paller, K. A., 482
Palmer, C. T., 200
Palmer, D. J., 571
Palmer, S., 268, 270
Palmer, S. E., 384, 405
Palys, T. S., 28
Pan, S., 88, 90
Panak, W., 566, 567, 569, 570
Papagno, C., 456
Paquin, M. J. R., 535, 536
Parent, M. B., 326
Parham, T. A., 363
Parish, S., 510, 515
Park, B., 157, 168, 173
Park, K. J., 631

Park, L., 511, 515
Parker, D., 58
Parker, G. A., 692
Parker, N., 283
Parker, S. T., 683, 697
Parkes, K. R., 252
Parkin, A. J., 460, 466
Parkinson, J. K., 468
Parkman, J. M., 390
Parks, C. D., 599
Parks, J. M., 223
Parks, K. A., 698
Parl, S., 624, 629, 631, 633
Parmigiani, S., 679, 696
Parpal, M., 171
Pascoe, J. P., 323
Pashler, H., 404, 405
Pasick, R. S., 359
Pastoor, S., 250
Patel, V. L., 294
Pato, C. N., 71
Patrick, J., 255
Patterson, C. J., 40
Patterson, I. J., 691
Patterson, M. M., 318, 334
Patton, C. R., 249
Patton, M. Q., 652, 654, 658
Paule, M. G., 56, 67, 72
Paulhus, D. L., 143
Paulus, P. B., 399
Paunonen, S. V., 157
Pavelchak, M. A., 165, 172
Pavlidis, N., 69
Payne, J. W., 266
Payne, P., 472
Payne, R., 247
Peabody, D., 162
Peacock, J. L., 498, 502
Peak, L., 506
Pearl, D., 322
Pearl, J., 288
Pedersen, P. B., 362, 365, 366
Pederson, F. A., 626
Pedhazur, E. J., 665
Peeke, H. V. S., 60
Peeters, G., 159
Peio, K. J., 241
Pelham, B. W., 176
Pellegrini, D., 565
Pelser, H. E., 62
Pence, A. R., 620
Peng, D. L., 91, 94
Peng, K. P., 102
Peng, R. X., 95, 104
Pennebaker, J. W., 33, 171, 181, 182
Pennington, N., 171, 601
Pepitone, A., 286, 500, 506, 591
Peplan, L. A., 367–69
Peppe, R., 250
Pepperberg, I. M., 683, 696
Perdeck, A. C., 679
Perdue, C. W., 127, 179
Perdue, M., 57, 60
Perelson, A. S., 439

Perez, J. A., 597
Perie, M., 177
Perkins, D. N., 297
PERKINS, D. V., 525–58; 526, 540
Perlmuter, L. C., 39
Perlmutter, M., 446, 596
Perlow, M. J., 4
Perot, A. R., 349
Perret-Clermont, A.-N., 596, 597
Perrett, S. P., 329
Perruchet, P., 282, 283, 474
Perry, D. G., 570
Perry, G. P., 535, 536
Perry, L. C., 570
Perry, M., 506
Perry, S., 624, 629, 631, 633
Personnaz, B., 598
Perusse, R., 696
Pervin, L., 429, 438
Peschel, M., 436
Pesick, S. D., 543
Peterman, T. A., 547
Peters, G., 69, 72
Peters, R. D., 568
Petersen, S. E., 246, 481
Peterson, B. E., 143
Peterson, B. L., 566
Peterson, C., 107, 567
Peterson, D. R., 434
Peterson, G., 537
Peterson, M. F., 107
Peterson, P. D., 527
Peterson, P. K., 65
Petrakis, P. L., 537
Petrinovich, L., 647, 679, 681, 691
Pettigrew, T. F., 160, 168
Pettit, G. S., 560, 561, 566, 568, 571, 572, 579
Petto, A. J., 699
Petty, R. E., 122, 124, 127, 135, 136, 138–41, 172, 362, 589, 590, 595, 597
Petzold, A. S., 543
Pew, R. W., 238, 241, 242, 245, 278
Peyronnin, K., 206, 207
Pfau, M., 138
Pfeffer, J., 198, 205, 206, 208, 210, 212, 222
Pfefferbaum, B., 571
Phair, J., 548
Phelps, E. A., 469, 470, 596
Philippot, P., 179
Philliber, S., 544
Phillips, D. A., 615, 617, 618, 620, 622, 627–29, 631, 632, 634, 636
Phillips, J. S., 247
Phillips, M. A., 670
Phillips, R. G., 322, 326
Phillips, R. R., 476
Phillpotts, R., 65
Piaget, J., 596

Piazza, T., 144
Pichert, J. W., 591
Pickering, A., 466
Pickles, A., 441
Piercy, M., 466, 467
Pierrehumbert, B., 635
Pietras, C. M., 252
Pilkington, C. J., 177
Pillemer, D. B., 464, 466
Pincus, A. L., 162, 163
Pinker, S., 300, 303, 388
Pinney, N., 178
Pintrich, P. R., 25
Pirke, K. M., 351
Pisoni, D. B., 250
Pitman, D. L., 70, 72
Pitre, U., 177
Pittman, T. S., 163, 174, 177
Plake, B. S., 347
Plamondon, B. D., 244
Plancherel, B., 635
Platt, J. R., 388
Plaut, D. C., 416
Plaut, S. M., 64
Pleck, J. H., 358
Pliner, P., 175
Plomin, R., 430, 691
Plowright, C. M., 695
Plumert, J. M., 565
Plunkett, K., 388
Plutchik, R., 10
Pohajdak, B., 64
Pohlmann, L. D., 404
Poincaré, H., 440
Pokorny, R. A., 239, 240
Polanyi, M., 15
Policare, H. J., 627
Politzer, G., 292, 294, 295
Polivy, J., 351
Pollard, J., 670
Pollard, P., 293, 296
Pollatsek, A., 403
Polson, M. C., 255
Polson, P. G., 239
Pomales, J., 363
Pomare, M., 145, 173
Pomerantz, J. R., 300
Pomeroy, C., 65
Pomeroy, W. B., 368
Ponce, F. Q., 363
Ponterotto, J. G., 363, 364, 366
Ponton, J., 69
Pope, K. S., 355
Pope, R. L., 372
Popkin, S. J., 252
Popper, K., 388, 654
Poropatich, C., 70
Porta, S., 69, 70, 72
Porter, L. E., 143
Porter, M. E., 211
Porter, R., 199
Posavac, E. J., 651, 662, 670
Poser, U., 468, 470
Posner, M. I., 246, 384, 405, 419, 474

Posner, M. J., 41
Poston, D. L., 100
Potter, J., 604
Potts, G. R., 302
Potts, R., 498, 500, 511
Povinelli, D. J., 698
Powell, C. L., 236
Powell, D. A., 320, 322
Powell, M. C., 133
Power, T. G., 25, 35
Powers, W. T., 29, 37, 39
Prakash, C., 408, 418
Pratkanis, A. R., 118–20, 126, 130
Pratto, F., 122, 143, 159, 175
Premack, D., 697
Premkumar, G., 252
Prentice-Dunn, S., 139
Preskill, H., 657
Presson, J. C., 400
Pribram, K. H., 25, 30
Price, J. M., 143, 565, 566, 577
Prigogine, I., 439
Prince, A., 388
Proctor, R. W., 398
Proffitt, D. R., 280, 281
Prokasy, W. F., 318
Provine, W. B., 678
Pruitt, J., 351
Pryor, J. B., 126, 164
Pryor, R., 347
Psotka, J., 255
Puffer, S. M., 212
Pulkkinen, L., 444
Pulliam, H. R., 685, 694
Purcell, J. A., 252
Puska, P., 542
Putnam, H., 500, 514
Pylyshyn, Z. W., 269, 271, 291, 300, 302, 418
Pyszczynski, T., 44, 182

Q

Qi, X. L., 94
Qian, X. Y., 95
Qiu, Y. J., 106
Qiu, Z. L., 95
Quay, J., 69, 72
Quiggle, N. L., 566, 567, 569, 570
Quigley, A. M., 344
Quine, W. V. O., 273
Quinn, K. J., 332
Quinn, N., 498, 502
Quinn, S. C., 549, 550
Quinton, D., 443
Qunidos, G., 69

R

Raab, A., 69
Raaijmakers, J. G. W., 560
Rabacchi, S., 330
Rabany, J., 250

Rabin, B. S., 58, 59, 67, 69–75
Rabiner, D. L., 566
Rabinovich, B., 617
Rabinovich, B. A., 624
Rabinowitz, V. C., 356
Rachal, J. V., 670
Racine, J. P., 180
Raeburn, S. D., 352
Rafaeli, A., 201–3, 220
Rahe, R. H., 67
Raichle, M. E., 481
Raiff, N. R., 537
Rajecki, D. W., 118
Ralston, J. R., 250
Ramamurthy, K., 252
Ramanan, J., 621
Ramey, C. T., 620, 622, 623, 627, 628
Ramsey, S. L., 131, 145, 173
Ramsey, W., 415
Ramus, S. J., 284, 474
Ranck, J. B., 467
Ranney, M., 274
Rapapport, J., 538
Rapp, P. R., 321
Rappaport, J., 538
Rasinski, K. A., 119, 124
Raska, K., 37
Rasmussen, A. F. Jr., 64
Rasmussen, B., 571
Rasmussen, P., 570
Rasmussen, S., 694
Ratajczak, H., 176
Ratcliff, R., 272, 298, 399, 402, 412
Ratneshwar, S., 136
Ratterman, M. J., 298
Raudenbush, S. W., 159
Ravizza, R., 688
Rawlins, J. N. P., 477
Raymond, L. N., 68
Raymond, P., 161, 602
Razran, G., 683
Read, S. J., 38, 163, 170, 274, 299
Real, L. A., 393, 690, 697
Reardon, K. K., 118
Reber, A., 280, 284
Reber, A. S., 269, 278, 279, 281, 283, 284, 287, 288, 473, 474
Redd, W. H., 63
Redding, G., 108
Redner, R., 534, 670
Reed, S. E., 65
Reed, S. K., 474
Reeder, G. D., 126, 159, 164
Reese, H. W., 434
Reese, L., 37
Reeve, T. G., 398
Regal, D. M., 241
Regan, S., 283
Regan, T., 688, 699
Regehr, G., 283
Regian, J. W., 240, 255

Rehm, L. P., 571
Reich, P., 56, 64
Reichardt, C. S., 653, 671
Reichhart-Erickson, M., 620
Reid, J. C., 571
Reimann, P., 298
Reinisch, J. M., 369
Reis, D. J., 321, 322
Reischl, T. M., 538
Reisenzein, R., 14, 18
Reissman, F., 537
Reite, M., 70
Reite, M. L., 70
Rempel, J. K., 120
Rennke, H. G., 64
Renshaw, P. D., 568, 575, 576
Rentsch, J. R., 203, 223
Repp, B. H., 410
Reppucci, N. D., 543
Rescorla, R. A., 318, 330, 477
RESNICK, L. B., 585–612; 587, 599, 603
Rettura, G., 64
Reus, V. I., 60
Revenson, T. A., 537, 541
Revenstorf, D., 352
Reyes, E., 68
Reynolds, A. L., 370
Reynolds, A. R., 372
Rhoads, G. K., 124
Rhodes, G., 178
Rhodes, N., 136, 137
Rhymer, R. M., 445
Ricardo, M. J., 75
Rice, J., 65, 69
Rice, R. E., 203, 223
Richard, B. A., 569
Richardson, D., 539
Richardson, J. J., 255
Richardson-Klavehn, A., 278, 454, 478
Riches, I. P., 484
Richner, H., 697
Richter, K. J., 249
Richter, M., 57, 68
Rickard, K. M., 356
Rickard-Figueroa, K., 363
Rickel, A. U., 544, 546
Rickert, W., 352
Ridley, M., 689
Riecken, H. W., 220
Riggle, E. J., 124
Riley, D. A., 682, 693
Riley, T., 173
Rinaldo, C. R., 548
Ringo, J. L., 455
Rinner, I., 69, 70, 72
Rintoul, B., 571
Riordan, N., 547, 548
Rioux, M. H., 527
Ripley, J., 537
Rips, L. J., 266, 291, 292
Rising, C. E., 328
Risse, G., 469

Risss, D. S., 354
Rist, R., 292
Ristau, C. A., 696
Ritz, S. A., 415
Rizzo, N., 123, 143
Robbins, S. J., 477
Robbins, T. W., 326
Roberts, D. W., 56, 67, 72
Roberts, L. J., 538
Roberts, M., 410
Roberts, S., 392, 394
Roberts, W. A., 620, 629, 630
Robertson, G. C., 17
Robertson, H. A., 678
Robertson, J. R., 359, 367
Robertson, M. M., 234
Robinson, C. A., 73
Robinson, G. E., 691
Robinson, J. P., 118
Robinson, M. H., 688, 692, 693
Roccos, S., 125
Rock, I., 268
Rocklin, T., 107
Rodgers, A., 571
Rodgers, M. D., 245
Rodin, J., 71
Rodin, M. J., 143
Rodinone, S. N., 58
Rodning, C., 635
Rodriguez, M. L., 24
Roediger, H. L., 480, 481
Roediger, H. L. III, 278, 482, 483
Roemer, R. A., 318
Roethlisberger, F. J., 220
Rog, D. J., 530, 531, 657, 660
Rogers, J. L., 537, 545
Rogers, J. M., 527
Rogers, M. P., 56, 64
Rogers, R. W., 139
Rogers, W. A., 253, 256
Rogers, W. H., 241, 242
Roggeveen, J. P., 134
Rogoff, B., 500, 605
Roitblat, H. L., 694, 696
Rojahn, K., 160
Rokeach, M., 101, 125
Roland, A., 509
Rolls, E., 463
Romac, D. S., 348
Roman, R. J., 180
Roman, S. W., 548
Roman-Nay, H., 549, 550
Romanes, G. J., 683
Romano, A. G., 329
Romano, J. M., 37
Romanski, L. M., 322
Rommetveit, R., 600
Roosa, M. W., 544
Root, M., 352
Rosaldo, M. Z., 498, 509, 515
Rosanowski, J., 178
Rosch, E., 15
Rosch, E. H., 474
Rose, J. D., 681

Rose-Krasnor, L., 568, 569
Roseman, I. J., 14
Rosen, D. J., 327, 330
Rosen, J. B., 321, 323, 325
Rosenbaum, D. A., 269
Rosenbaum, M., 3, 37
Rosenberg, L. T., 67
Rosenberg, M. J., 587
Rosenberg, T. K., 571
Rosenberger, N. R., 498
Rosenblatt, J. S., 688
Rosenbloom, P. S., 267, 269, 297, 304, 414
Rosenbluth, L., 627
Rosenfield, M. E., 328
Rosenthal, J. A., 532, 535
Rosenthal, M. K., 617, 620
Rosenthal, R., 158, 592
Roskam, E. E., 435
Roskos-Ewoldsen, D. R., 169
Ross, B. H., 298, 299
Ross, L. L., 68, 157, 164, 500
Ross, M., 130, 161, 595
Ross, R. T., 477
Rossi, P. H., 530, 651, 657, 659, 661, 662
Rossiter, E. M., 352
Rosvold, H. E., 476
Roszman, T., 75
Roth, S., 354
Rothbart, M. K., 41, 168
Rothbaum, B. O., 354
Rothblum, E. D., 367, 368
Rothengatter, T., 253
Roudebush, R. E., 72
Rouillier, J. Z., 257
Roupp, R., 617
Rouse, W. B., 239, 254
Rousseau, D. L., 294
Routh, D. A., 166
Rovee-Collier, C., 695
Rovine, M. J., 618, 621, 623, 630, 631, 634
Rovira, D. P., 130, 169
Rowan, B., 213
Roy, A. W. N., 597
Rozin, P., 286, 479, 515
Rubens, A. B., 479
Rubenstein, J., 617, 632
Rubenstein, J. L., 626, 632, 633
Rubin, D. C., 283
Rubin, K. H., 560, 561, 565, 568, 569, 577
Rubini, M., 164
Rubinstein, P., 542
Rubinstein, T., 235
Ruble, D. N., 41, 160, 172
Ruderman, A. J., 591
Rudolph, J., 369, 370
Rudy, J. W., 460, 467, 477
Rueb, J. D., 243, 244
Ruehlman, L. S., 28, 29
Rugg, D. L., 549
Ruggiero, D. A., 322
Ruis de Gordioa, J. C., 69

Ruiz, B. P., 329
Rumbaugh, D. M., 697
Rumelhart, D. E., 266, 272, 387, 388, 411, 415, 475, 560, 562, 586
Ruprecht, L. J., 368, 372, 373
Rusak, B., 678
Rusbult, C. E., 43
Rusch, A. J., 138
Ruscher, J. B., 142, 143, 145, 165, 173, 182
Rush, M. C., 349
Rusiniak, K. W., 686
Russell, I. S., 319, 328
Russell, J. A., 500, 515
Russell, J. E. A., 349
Russell, M., 60
Russett, C. E., 344
Russo, E. M., 597
Rutherford, A., 239
Rutila, J. E., 691
Rutkowska, J. C., 289
Rutter, M., 441, 443, 620
Ruvolo, C. M., 129, 158
Ryan, A. M., 246
Ryan, C. S., 168
Ryan, R. M., 27, 41
Ryan, S. M., 71, 75

S

Sabnani, H. B., 366
Sachs, V. B., 630
Sackett, P. R., 251
Saenz, D. S., 174, 591
Sagar, H. H., 463
Sagiv, L., 125
Saint-Cyr, J. A., 475
Sajewski, D., 70, 72
Sakaguchi, A., 322
Sakai, K., 484
Sakheim, D. K., 353
Salancik, G. R., 212
Salas, E., 180, 235, 248, 249, 254–56
Salem, D. A., 526, 530, 538
Salfi, M., 60
Salina, D., 547, 548
Salinger, R., 62
Salkever, D., 625
Salmon, D. P., 457, 472
Salmon, M. H., 603
Salomon, G., 297
Salonen, J. T., 542
Salovey, P., 39, 40, 167, 168, 574
Salthouse, T. A., 253
Salvi, D., 141, 164
Salvin, S. B., 67, 69
Sameroff, A. J., 435
Sampson, E. E., 509
Samuel, A. G., 409
San, H. H., 106
Sananes, C. B., 321, 322, 324
Sanbonmatsu, D. M., 126, 132, 178

Sanchez, F. J., 143
Sancilio, M., 565
Sande, G. N., 129, 599
Sandelands, L. E., 211
Sanders, A. F., 394
Sanders, R. E., 285
Sanders, S. A., 369
Sanderson, P. M., 238, 250
Sandler, L. S., 64
Sands, S. F., 455
Sang, B., 94
Sanitioso, R., 182
Sansone, C., 27, 178
Santiago, H. C., 455
Santos, A. B., 530
Sapir, E., 498
Sarason, S. B., 526
Sarbin, T. R., 591, 593
Sarter, N. B., 238, 242, 243
Sarup, G., 124
Sato, K., 57
Satomi-Sasaki, Y., 67, 68
Satterlee, D. G., 68, 73
Saunders, R. C., 457, 458, 471, 476
Savage-Rumbaugh, S., 689
Savy, I., 283
Saxe, G. B., 299, 300
Saxe, L., 532
SCARR, S., 613–44; 430, 613, 615–20, 622, 627–29, 631, 632, 634, 636
Scavulli, J. F., 73
Scerbo, M. W., 246
Schachter, S., 220
Schachtman, T. R., 68, 70, 72
Schacter, D. L., 278, 286, 454, 457–60, 465, 466, 478–80, 483
Schadron, G., 165
Schaefer, C. E., 533
Schaeken, W., 304, 306
Schaffer, M. M., 474
Schaller, M., 142, 169
Schank, P., 274
Schank, R. C., 298
Schaubroeck, J., 250, 252
Schauenstein, K., 69, 70, 72
Schedlowski, M., 61
Scheel, M., 348
Schefft, B. K., 25
Schegloff, E. A., 603
Scheier, M. F., 3, 24, 29, 33, 34, 36, 39, 40, 44, 589
Schein, E. H., 204, 212, 600
Schell, A. M., 477
Scher, M., 356, 359, 362
Scher, S. J., 43, 134
Scherbaum, C., 174, 591, 593
Scherer, K. R., 10, 14, 15, 515
Schieber, F., 253
Schieffelin, B., 511
Schieffelin, E. L., 515
Schindler, P. J., 629
Schkade, J. K., 590

Schlegel, R. P., 133, 134
Schleifer, S. J., 70–73, 75
Schlenker, B. R., 44, 118
Schliemann, A. D., 299
Schmaltz, L. W., 319
Schmidt, D. E., 590
Schmidt, S. G., 65
Schmidt-Nielsen, K., 684, 690
Schmitt, B. H., 589
Schneider, B., 197, 206, 215
Schneider, D. J., 37, 181, 561, 573
Schneider, J. A., 352
Schneider, L. J., 345
Schneider, S. F., 550
Schneider, S. K., 40, 171
Schneider, W., 402, 406, 432, 560
Schneiderman, N., 320, 321
Schneirla, T. C., 685
Schnell, D. J., 547
Schoemaker, P. J. H., 393
Schofield, W., 359
Schon, D., 589
Schönpflug, W., 18
Schooler, J. W., 181
Schoonhoven, C. B., 215
Schriesheim, A., 236
Schubauer-Leoni, M.-L., 597
Schueren, J., 246
Schul, Y., 139, 167, 595
Schuller, G., 181
Schuller, R. A., 140, 141
Schulze, G. E., 56, 67, 72
Schunk, D. H., 32, 36
Schusterman, R. J., 697
Schvaneveldt, R. W., 241, 415
Schwaber, J. S., 321
Schwartz, C., 436
Schwartz, I. J., 532
Schwartz, M., 281, 567
Schwartz, P., 630, 632
Schwartz, R. D., 658
Schwartz, S. H., 125
Schwartz, S. P., 300
Schwartz, T., 498
Schwarz, J. C., 627, 632
Schwarz, N., 124, 140, 141, 168, 169, 179, 286, 6υ2
Schweickert, R., 391, 396, 400
Scott, A. G., 648
Scott, J., 348
Scott, J. P., 700
Scozzaro, P. P., 346
Scribner, S., 499
Scriven, M., 441, 660
Searle, J., 604
Sears, D. O., 144
Sears, L. L., 330, 331
Sears, P. S., 30
SECHREST, L., 645–74; 601, 652, 658, 661, 664, 666, 669, 670

Secord, P. F., 24, 389
Sedikides, C., 161, 164, 170, 176, 179, 595
Segal, N. L., 128
Seger, C. A., 279, 284
Seibel, C. A., 353
Seidensticker, J., 699
Seidman, E., 538
Seifert, C. M., 237, 298
Seifter, E., 64
Selcon, S. J., 244
Selden, N. R. W., 326
Self, C. A., 139
Selfridge, O. G., 415
Seligman, M., 567
Seligman, M. E. P., 567
Seljelid, R., 70
Selman, R., 565
Selman, R. L., 593
Selye, H., 4, 5
Selznick, P., 220
Semin, G., 141, 164
Semin, G. R., 164, 500
Semmer, N., 25
Sengelaub, D. R., 327, 330
Sentis, K., 601
Serafino, E. P., 651
Servan-Schreiber, E., 281, 282, 474
Sessa, V. I., 206, 207
Seta, J. J., 169, 174, 179, 590
Seton, J., 250
Settlage, P. H., 320
Seyfarth, R. M., 694, 696, 697
Seymour, S., 515
Shadbolt, N., 239
Shadish, W. R. Jr., 645, 646, 650, 651, 657, 668, 671
Shaffer, D. R., 138, 140
Shaffer, P., 119, 126, 135
Shafir, E., 292
Shafran, R., 355
Shallice, T., 25, 37, 245, 429, 456, 484
Shambes, G. M., 329
Shanks, D. R., 477
Shannon, C., 385
Shannon, J. W., 370
Shannon, L., 161
Shanon, B., 280
Shanteau, J., 252
Shao, R. Z., 91
Shapiro, D., 25
Shapiro, M., 467
Shapiro, P. N., 176, 177
Shapiro, S., 530
Sharp, B. M., 65
Sharp, D. W., 591
Sharpe, M. J., 358
Sharpe, N., 439
Shastri, L., 276, 307
Shaver, P. R., 118, 589
Shavit, Y., 71, 74, 75
Shavitt, S., 125, 126, 131
Shaw, K., 576

Shaw, M. L., 402, 403
Shaw, R. B., 436
Shell, P., 252
Shenck, R., 571
Sheng, D. L., 91
Sheng, J. P., 104
Sheng, J. X., 98
Shepard, R. N., 15, 303
Shepherd, J. W., 181
Shepherd, M., 277
Sheppard, B. H., 602
Sheppe, M. L., 256
Sherer, P. D., 196, 220
Sheridan, J. F., 64, 65
Sheridan, K., 548
Sherif, M., 600
Sherman, J. W., 164, 166, 598
Sherman, S. J., 129, 158, 169, 179, 587
Shern, D., 528
Sherry, D. F., 286, 458, 689
Shettleworth, S. J., 695, 696
Shi, K., 102
Shi, R. H., 101, 106
Shi, S. H., 101
Shields, S. A., 344
Shiffrin, R. M., 384, 402, 404, 406, 454, 456, 560
Shih, L.-C. N., 75
Shimamura, A. P., 459, 460, 462, 463, 466, 468, 470, 472, 478–81
Shinar, D., 253
Shindledecker, R. D., 70
Shinn, M., 530, 532, 537
Shiomi, T., 617
Shipley, M. T., 332
Shoda, Y., 24, 158
Shoqeirat, M. A., 467
Shortt, J. W., 181
Shosenberg, N., 537
Shostak, M., 499
Showers, C., 50
Shu, H., 95
Shulman, G. L., 405
Shults, C. W., 457
Shure, M. B., 568
Shute, V. J., 240, 251, 252, 255, 256
SHWEDER, R. A., 497–523; 498–502, 506, 509–12, 514, 515, 517, 604
Sieber, W. J., 71
Siegal, L. J., 569
Siegal, M., 591
Siegel, A. E., 593
Siegel, J., 595
Siegel, S., 57, 60, 593
Siegel, S. M., 352
Silva, P., 577
Silver, M., 24
Silver, R., 695
Silver, S., 568
Silverberg, R. A., 358, 359
Silverman, N., 532

Silverman, T., 346
Silverstein, B., 129
Silverstein, J. W., 415
Silverstein, L. D., 250
Silverstein, M., 500
Simmons, J. A., 681
Simon, B., 168
Simon, H., 34
Simon, H. A., 266–68, 277, 288, 299, 304, 384, 415, 418, 560, 586
Simons, H. W., 364
Simons, L., 67, 73
Simpkins, C., 532
Sinervo, B., 680, 684
Singer, E., 593
Singer, G., 56, 67, 72
Singer, J. L., 24, 39, 167
Singer, P., 699
Singh, J., 124
Singh, S., 543
Singley, M. K., 239
Sirotnik, K. A., 658
Siskind, G. W., 56
Sivyer, M., 56
Skelly, J. J., 594
Skidmore, J. R., 358, 360, 361
Skinner, B. F., 6, 679, 685
Skinner, W. F., 132
Skitka, L., 174
Sklar, L. S., 64
Skokan, L. A., 171
Skolnick, P., 60
Skowronski, J. J., 159, 161, 179
Slaby, R. G., 562, 565, 566, 568, 570, 572
Slaney, R. B., 363
Slater, P. C., 463
Slavin, R. E., 590, 605
Slaw, R. D., 161
Slobodchikoff, C. N., 694
Sloman, A., 40
Sloman, S. A., 479
Slovic, P., 285
Slugoski, B. R., 296
Small, R., 533
Smedslund, J., 515
Smelser, N. J., 4
Smith, A. C., 320
Smith, A. P., 65
Smith, C. A., 14, 15, 180
Smith, D. B. D., 252, 253
Smith, D. R., 587
Smith, E. E., 266, 270, 292, 295, 474
Smith, E. R., 142, 167, 169, 181
Smith, G. E., 300
Smith, G. H., 62
Smith, G. J., 180
Smith, G. R., 62
Smith, H., 439
Smith, H. G., 697
Smith, J. E. K., 398, 406

Smith, J. M., 70
Smith, J. W., 620, 629, 630
Smith, K., 201, 577
Smith, L., 434
Smith, L. A., 535, 536
Smith, M. B., 500
Smith, M. C., 320
Smith, M. E., 478, 479
Smith, P. B., 107
Smith, R. A., 165, 177, 178, 248
Smith, S. M., 138, 140
Smith Noricks, J., 509
Smolensky, P., 266, 272, 275, 416
Sniderman, P. M., 144
Snodgrass, S. E., 173
Snowdon, C. T., 677
Snyder, A. Z., 481
Snyder, C. R., 3, 28, 43
Snyder, C. R. R., 405
Snyder, D. E., 241
Snyder, H. L., 250
Snyder, M., 126, 172, 592
Socall, D., 167, 174
Soler, M., 532, 533
Solomon, G. F., 54, 65–67
Solomon, K., 359
Solomon, P. R., 319, 330, 476
Solomon, R. C., 10, 515
Solomon, R. L., 318
Soloway, E. M., 240
Solso, R. L., 384
Solvason, H. B., 56, 60, 74
Somberg, D., 562, 565
Song, J., 97
Song, W. Z., 96, 97
Sonnenfeld, G., 69, 73
Soong, S.-J., 60
Sorensen, J. L., 548
Sorkin, E., 75
Sorkin, R. D., 404
Sorrentino, R. M., 161, 587, 594, 598
Spangler, W. D., 214
Spangler, W. J., 327, 330
Sparling, J. J., 620
Spates, C. R., 35
Spear, N. E., 694
Spector, P. E., 221, 222
Speicher, C. E., 69
Speisman, J. C., 6
SPELLMAN, B. A., 265–315; 274
Speltz, M., 569
Sperry, L., 500, 515
Spiegel, D., 537
Spiegel, J. P., 2, 6
Spielman, L. A., 175
Spindler, G. D., 500
Spinnler, H., 245
Spiro, M. E., 506, 511, 516
Spivack, G., 568
Spokane, A., 358
Spokane, A. R., 345

SQUIRE, L. R., 453–96; 284, 454–57, 459, 460, 462, 463, 465–68, 470, 472, 474, 475, 478–81, 483
Srinivas, K., 480, 481
Sriram, N., 168
Sroges, R. W., 689
Sroufe, L. A., 436, 625, 630, 635
Srull, T. K., 39, 159, 160, 165, 167, 174, 592
Stablein, R., 197, 220, 221
Staddon, J. E. R., 681
Stadler, M. A., 280, 472
Stagner, R., 433
Stahler, G. J., 546
Stake, J. E., 349, 350
St. Lawrence, J. S., 548, 549
Stall, R., 549
Stall, R. D., 547
Standley, S., 332
Stangor, C., 118, 135, 143, 144, 160, 166, 168, 169, 172, 176, 178, 592
Stanley, M., 37
Stanley, W. B., 282, 284, 474
Stark, H., 457
Staruch, K. S., 625
Stasser, G., 599, 601
Stasson, M., 131, 133
Stasson, M. F., 599
Statham, A., 592
Staw, B. M., 197–99, 201, 209–12, 217
Stearns, C. Z., 498, 515
Stearns, P. N., 498, 515
Stebbins, S., 387
Steckler, N. A., 224
Steffen, V. J., 131
Stein, L. I., 528, 529
Stein, M., 62, 71–73, 75
Stein, N., 515
Steinberg, L. D., 620, 627
Steinberg, M. D., 565
Steiner, T. E., 390
Steinmetz, J. E., 327, 328, 330–33
Steinmetz, S. S., 332
Steller, B., 37, 176
Stelmach, G. E., 25
Stengers, I., 439
Stenning, K., 271, 275–77, 291, 293, 301, 307
Stephens, D. W., 685, 686
Stephens, L., 127
Stephens, P. M., 67
Stephens, R. C., 548
Stephenson, G. M., 602
Steplewski, Z., 70
Stern, W., 435
Sternberg, K. J., 630, 634, 635
Sternberg, R. J., 37
Sternberg, S., 26, 384, 386, 392, 401, 406, 415
Sterns, H. L., 254

Sternthal, B., 138, 140
Stevens, M., 359, 362
Stevens, W., 69
Stevenson, H. W., 299, 506
Stevenson, L. Y., 549
Stevenson, M. K., 44, 247
Stevenson, W. B., 208
Stevenson-Hinde, J., 625, 635
Stewart, B. L., 37
Stewart, J., 57
Stewart, J. E. M., 275, 277
Stewart, P., 617, 625
Stewart, T. L., 181
Stich, S. P., 415
Stifter, M., 635
Stigler, J. W., 108, 299, 498,
    500, 502, 506
Stigler, S. M., 647
Stillings, N. A., 479
Stillson, R. W., 358
Stinchcombe, M., 417
Stinson, L., 157, 158, 600
Stites, D. P., 54
Stith, S., 617, 621
Stobart, G., 670
Stokols, D., 590
Stoms, G. B., 545
Stone, K. M., 547
Stone, W., 576
Stone, W. S., 688
Story, A. L., 177
Stout, J., 65
Stout, J. C., 69
Stowe, M. L., 571
Strack, F., 124, 140, 141,
    168, 286, 602
Strader, M. K., 131
Strambi, A., 691
Strambi, C., 691
Strassberg, Z., 576
Strauman, T., 24, 34
Strauman, T. J., 576
Strauss, A., 653, 655
Strauss, C., 498, 499
Strauss, C. C., 577
Strayer, D. L., 403
Strebel, R., 64
Street, S., 533
Strelau, J., 429, 430
Stricker, E. M., 694
Stricker, G., 355
Strickland, B., 619
Strickland, R., 627, 632
Strickland, R. G., 632
Stroessner, S. J., 164, 166
Strom, T. B., 56
Stromquist, V. J., 576
Strong, S. R., 346, 364
Stroul, B. A., 528, 534
Struckman-Johnson, C. J.,
    139
Struckman-Johnson, D. L.,
    139
Stryker, S., 592
Stuckey, M. F., 634
Stucky, R. J., 43

Stumpf, C., 429
Stunkard, A., 542
Stunkard, A. J., 537
Stuss, D. T., 463
Styles, E. A., 252
Suarez, T., 622, 627
Subich, L. M., 346
Suboski, M. D., 694
Suchman, L. A., 603
Suchner, R. W., 124
Sue, D. W., 363–66
Sue, S., 364, 365, 373
Sugarman, B., 430
Sui, G. Y., 102
Suinn, R. M., 363
Sullins, E. S., 180
Sullivan, C., 244
Sullivan, L. A., 144, 169
Sullivan, M., 498, 499, 502
SULLIVAN, M. A., 497–523
Suls, J. M., 594
Summerfield, A. B., 515
Summerfield, Q., 410
Sun, C. F., 100
Sun, C. H., 98, 106
Sun, C. S., 98
Sun, F. L., 105
Sun, L. H., 94, 106
Sundar, S. K., 69, 72, 74
Sunderland, J., 177
Super, C. M., 513
Supple, W. F., 320, 326, 332
Surles, R., 528
Susman, L., 430
Sutherland, J. C., 64
Sutherland, R. W., 460, 467,
    477
Sutton, C., 208, 209, 222
SUTTON, R. I., 195–229;
    197, 201, 203, 209, 213,
    220
Sutton, S., 131
Suwalsky, J., 617
Suwalsky, J. T., 624
Suzuki, W. A., 463, 469
Swann, W. B. Jr., 156, 592
Swanson, A. J., 533
Swartz, M. J., 515
Sweeney, P. D., 571
Sweller, J., 298, 299, 304
Swets, J. A., 384
Swezey, R. W., 248
Swim, J., 166
Szamrej, J., 123
Szentagothai, J., 327
Szwarcbart, M. K., 476
Szymanski, K., 590

T

Tabossi, P., 304
Taghzouti, K., 69
Talbot, N., 478, 479
Talmy, L., 500
Tan, J. L., 97
Tan, L. H., 94

Tanenbaum, R. L., 567
Tang, C. H., 96, 97
Tang, C. M., 106
Tannenbaum, G., 618, 627
Tannenbaum, P. H., 587
Tannenbaum, S. I., 254–57
Tassinary, L. G., 124, 127
Tattersall, A. J., 247
Taube, C. A., 530
Taylor, A. E., 475
Taylor, A. N., 65
Taylor, A. R., 568, 576, 577
Taylor, B., 171
Taylor, C., 15, 498, 500, 694
Taylor, C. B., 37
Taylor, C. E., 68
Taylor, D. M., 143
Taylor, K. L., 594
Taylor, R. M., 244
Taylor, S. E., 24, 40, 44, 159,
    161, 167, 171, 172, 176,
    180, 591
Teasdale, J., 567
Teasley, S. D., 587
Teddlie, C., 590
Tedeschi, J. T., 131
Teel, J. E., 140
Teich, A. H., 321
Telch, C. F., 352
Telesca, C., 140
Tenenbaum, D. R., 166
Teng, G. R., 103
Tenney, Y. J., 238, 241, 242,
    245
Terman, G. W., 71, 74, 75
Terr, A. I., 54
Tesiny, E. P., 571
Tesser, A., 119, 122, 126,
    128, 135, 175, 177, 178,
    181
Test, M. A., 528, 529
Testa, M., 177, 595
Teti, D. M., 619
Tetlock, P. E., 144, 174, 595
Tetrick, L. E., 222
Teuber, H. L., 320
Teyler, T. J., 324, 463
Thach, W. T., 327, 334
Thagard, P. R., 267, 270,
    273, 274, 277, 298
Tharan, M., 479
Tharp, R. G., 25, 646, 661
Thebarge, R. W., 35
Theios, J., 319, 395
Thelen, E., 432, 680
Thelen, M. H., 351
Thiessen, D., 684
Thiessen, D. D., 688
Thoits, P., 506
Thomae, H., 432, 435
Thomas, D., 527
Thomas, E. A. C., 399
Thomas, J. P., 249
Thomas, S. B., 549, 550
Thompson, C. E., 362–64
Thompson, C. P., 161

Thompson, E., 15
Thompson, H. B., 430
Thompson, J. K., 327, 330, 332, 537
Thompson, K. S., 528, 529
Thompson, M. M., 123
Thompson, R. A., 625
THOMPSON, R. F., 317–42; 318–20, 327, 328, 330–34
Thoresen, C. E., 37
Thorn, W. A. F., 460
Thornhill, N. W., 686
Thornhill, R., 686
Thorpe, W. H., 687
Till, F. J., 349
TIMBERLAKE, W., 675–708; 679, 685, 693, 695, 697
Tinbergen, N., 678, 679, 694
Tindale, R. S., 601
Tinsley, D. J., 346
Tinsley, H. E. A., 346
Toates, F., 694
Tobin, J. J., 506
Tocco, G., 319, 332
Tokuda, S., 68
Tolman, E. C., 429
Tomaselli, M., 430
Tomaz, C., 326
Tomkins, S. S., 10
Tomlin, A., 565, 576
Tomonaga, M., 688
Torello, M. W., 327
TÖRESTAD, B., 427–51; 433, 440
TORO, P. A., 525–58; 526, 530, 531, 538
Torrey, E. F., 529, 531
Totman, R., 65
Toulmin, S., 431
Tourangeau, R., 119, 124
Tovar, A., 65
Towne, D. M., 255
Townsend, J. T., 390, 392, 393, 402
Tracey, T. J., 356
Trapnell, P. D., 163
Travers, J., 617
Travis, D. S., 250
Treisman, A., 405, 479
Trembley, R., 444
Trentham, D. E., 64
Trevarthen, C., 15
Trezza, G. R., 131
Triandis, H. C., 108, 119, 125, 500, 506, 509, 515
Tribus, M., 385
Trickett, E. J., 526, 530
Triplett, N., 588
Troiden, R. R., 371
Trolier, T. K., 161
Trotter, S., 527
Truax, C. B., 359
Trzebinski, J., 163
Tsang, P. S., 245
Tsui, A. S., 206, 207

Tsukahara, N., 333
Tubbs, M. E., 32
Tuckman, B., 215
Tudge, J., 597
Tuffin, K., 347
Tulving, E., 454, 457, 459, 460, 469, 478, 479
Tung, R. L., 221
Tuomilehto, J., 542
Turk, J. L., 58
Turnage, J. J., 235
Turnbull, W., 170
Turner, B. H., 325
Turner, C. W., 534
Turner, J. A., 37
Turner, J. C., 165, 169, 594
Turvey, M. T., 400, 419
Tuschl, R. J., 351
Tversky, A., 271, 285, 286, 294, 296, 413
Tweney, R. D., 273, 294
Tyler, L. E., 435
Tyler, R. B., 127
Tyler, T. R., 140
Tyndall, L., 370
Tyrell, D. A. J., 65
Tzelgov, J., 250

U

Ueki, S., 67
Uleman, J. S., 178, 180
Ulrich, B. D., 680
Ulrich, R., 397
Underwood, B. J., 560, 593
Underwood, M., 323
Ungerleider, L. G., 465
Ungson, G. R., 216
Unis, A., 571
Unnava, H. R., 135
Upchurch, D. M., 546

V

Vaccarino, A. L., 689
Vachon, M. L., 537
Valdiserri, R. O., 548
Valentine, T., 456
Vallacher, R. R., 29, 39
Vallar, G., 456
Vallis, T. M., 37
Vallone, R. P., 164
van Aken, M. A. G., 445
Van Avermaet, E., 595
Vanbeselaere, N., 169
Van Cantfort, T. E., 689, 696, 697
Van Cott, H. P., 246
Vandell, D. L., 621, 631
van der Heijden, A. H. C., 387
Van der Kloot, W. A., 163
Van der Kooy, D., 698
van der Poel, A. M., 696
Vander Schaff, E. F., 319
Vander Wall, S. T., 689

Van Dyke, D., 529
Van Essen, D. C., 408, 481
van Ijzendoorn, M. H., 619, 630
Van Knippenberg, D. V., 594
Van Leeuwen, M. D., 145, 173, 177
Van Maanen, J., 204, 600
Van Manen, S., 142, 165
Van Mechelen, I., 163
Van Schie, E., 169
Van Tets, G. F., 687
Van Tosh, L., 532
Van Wagoner, S. L., 370
VanWolffelaar, P. C., 253
Van Yperen, N. W., 179
Van Zandt, B. J. S., 479
Varela, F. J., 15
Varey, C. A., 170
Vasquez, B. J., 321, 324, 326
Vaughan, J. H., 73
Vaughan, T. A., 699
Vaughn, B. E., 625, 630, 631, 633–35
Vaughn, L. A., 173
Velazquez, V. L., 245
Veldhuis, H. D., 69
Velten, E., 40
Veno, A., 527
Vera, A. H., 299
Verbaten, M. N., 252
Vercruyssen, M., 253
Verfaellie, M., 479
Vergare, M. J., 531
Verschure, P. F. M. J., 415
Verwoerd, M., 412
Vessey, S. H., 67
Vestergaard, K., 695
Vetter, V. A., 355
Victor, M., 462, 466
Videen, T. O., 481
Videka, L. M., 537
Videka-Sherman, L., 537
Vidulich, M. A., 246
Vigil, P., 363
Villablanca, J. R., 319, 477
Vinacco, R. Jr., 126
Viney, W., 677
Vinokur, A., 601
Vitina, J. R., 285
Voelkl, K., 177
Vogel, W. H., 70
Vokey, F. R., 284
Vokey, J. R., 474
Vollrath, D. A., 602
Volpe, B. T., 469, 470
von Bertalanfy, L., 436
von Cranach, M., 604
von der Malsburg, C., 276
Voneida, T., 330
von Eye, A., 445
Von Glinow, M. A., 221
Von Hendy, H. M., 173, 595
von Hippel, W., 129, 168, 182
von Uexkull, J., 681, 697

Vygotsky, L., 596, 602

W

Waadt, S., 351
Waas, G. A., 565, 568
Wade, N., 388
Wagner, A. R., 321, 330, 477
Walbott, H. G., 515
Walden, T., 561
Waldman, I. D., 566
Waldmann, M. R., 296
Waldron, H., 534
Walicke, P. A., 457
Walker, A., 620
Wall, D. D., 526, 530, 531
Wall, S. C., 619, 623, 625, 630, 635
Wallace, J., 65
Wallace, W. T., 283
Waller, P. F., 252, 253
Walsh, J. P., 204, 216, 222
Walsh, L., 321
Walsh, W. B., 345
Walter, L. R., 695
Walters, J., 568
Walters, R. H., 577
Wan, K. C., 108, 508
Wan, M. G., 99
Wang, A. F., 105
Wang, A. S., 90, 95, 104
Wang, D., 103, 104
Wang, H. B., 94
Wang, J. M., 106, 476
Wang, J. S., 105, 106
Wang, S. X., 94, 105, 110
Wang, W. J., 100
Wang, X. P., 96
Wang, X. S., 102
Wang, Y. B., 103
Wang, Y. H., 96
WANG, Z.-M., 87–116; 89, 91, 94, 95, 102–5, 107, 109, 110
Wanous, J. P., 600
Wanshula, L. T., 143, 175, 178
Wapner, S., 435
Warboys, L., 532, 533
Warburton, J., 534
Ward, C. H., 358
Ward, G. F., 243, 244, 246
Ward, M., 304
Ward, R. S., 529
Warden, C. J., 683
Wareheim, L. E., 64
Warm, J. S., 246, 247
Warner, L. H., 683
Warner, M., 107
Warren, R. M., 409
Warrington, E. K., 454–57, 477, 484
Warshaw, P. R., 131
Wartell, M. S., 690
Washburn, D. A., 697
Washburne, D. L., 679

Wasik, B. H., 620
Wasmer, D., 529, 537
Wason, P. C., 294
Wasserman, A. A., 571
Wasserman, E. A., 696, 697
Wasserstein, J., 463
Waszak, C., 544
Waterink, W., 253
Waters, E., 619, 623, 625, 630, 631, 635, 679
Watkins, C. E. Jr., 345
Watson, D. L., 25, 157
Watson, J. B., 433
Watson, P. J., 327
Watters, J. K., 548
Watts, B., 602
Waugh, N. C., 454, 456
Wayner, E. A., 56, 67, 72
Wayner, M. J., 688
Wearing, A. J., 28
Weary, G., 174, 175
Weatherhead, P. J., 691
Weaver, J. L., 249, 252
Webb, E., 658
Webb, J., 529
Weber, A. L., 171
Weber, H., 16
Weber, M., 588
Weber, R. A., 253, 635
Webster, D. M., 175
Wegner, D. M., 29, 37, 39, 161, 181, 182, 602
Wei, S. L., 106
Wei, X., 106
Weick, K. E., 218, 219, 600
Weigold, M. F., 44, 118
Weil, M., 245
Weiler, E. M., 246
Weimer, W. B., 25
Weinberger, N. M., 319
Weiner, B., 14, 41, 102
Weiner, H., 64, 69, 438, 439
Weiner, S. G., 67
Weinert, F. E., 432
Weingarten, H., 323
Weinraub, M., 627
Weinstein, C. S., 604
Weiskrantz, L., 245, 456–58, 477
Weisner, T. S., 499
Weiss, B., 571, 572
Weiss, C., 319, 330, 332
Weiss, C. H., 659
Weiss, J. M., 69, 72–74
Weiss, P. A., 446
Weisse, C. S., 71
Weisz, C., 168
Weisz, D. G., 319
Weisz, D. J., 328
Weisz, J. R., 571
Weithorn, L. A., 532
Weitz, B. A., 212
Weitzman, B. C., 530
Weizmann, F., 128
Weksler, M. E., 56
Weldon, E., 590

Welker, W., 329
Wellenkamp, J., 515
Wellman, H. M., 280
Wells, G. L., 171
Wells, K., 533
Wells, P. H., 388
Welsh, A. A., 346
Welsh, J. P., 329, 331, 332
Wender, P. H., 359
Wenger, E., 298, 299, 605
Wenk, E. J., 64
Wenner, A. M., 388
Wenzlaff, R. M., 181
Werker, J. F., 513
Wermuth, L. A., 548
Wertheimer, M., 268
Wertsch, J., 498, 500
Wertsch, J. V., 602, 604
West, M. J., 691, 696
West, S. G., 597, 598, 670
Westcott, M. R., 24
Westley, F., 213
Westman, M., 3, 252
Weston, D. R., 630
Wetherell, M., 604
Wharton, C. M., 298
Wheeler, D. A., 691
Wheeler, V. A., 575, 576
Whelan, S. M., 280, 281
Wherry, R. J., 244
Whitaker, L. A., 242
White, G., 498, 501, 515
White, G. M., 498, 499, 501, 511
White, H., 417
White, N., 323
White, N. M., 476
White, S. B., 666
White, S. H., 464, 466
White, W., 697
Whitebook, M., 617, 620, 629
Whitehead, J. T., 533, 534
Whiteley, J. M., 344
Whiteley, S., 363
Whitely, B. E. Jr., 145
Whiten, A., 698
Whiting, B. B., 500
Whiting, J. W. M., 500
Whitmore, M., 252
Whorf, B. L., 512
Wible, C. G., 467
Wick, P., 576
Wickelgren, W., 399
Wickens, C. D., 40, 234, 237, 238, 242, 244–47, 249, 252
Wickens, T. D., 298
Wicklund, R. A., 34, 44, 177, 589
Wiebe, D., 283
Wiedenfeld, S. A., 37
Wiegand, S. J., 72
Wiener, N. I., 128
Wierzbicka, A., 500, 510, 515
Wiesenthal, D. L., 128
Wiethaff, M., 247

Wiggins, E. C., 120
Wiggins, J. S., 162, 163
Wikan, U., 515
Wikler, D. I., 529
Wikler, K. C., 680
Wilder, D. A., 138, 176, 177, 593, 598
Wiles, J., 275, 277
Wilfley, D., 352
Wilke, H., 594
Wilke, O., 292
Willemsen, T. M., 163
Williams, C. J., 133
Williams, C. L., 538
Williams, G., 576
Williams, K. D., 589
Williams, M. H., 355
Williams, N., 430
Williams, R. B., 566
Williams, R. N., 438
Williams, S., 577
Williams, V. W., 363
Williamson, G. M., 54, 64
Willingham, D. B., 280, 471
Wills, T. A., 431, 594
Wilson, B. R., 499
Wilson, E. O., 677, 683, 684, 686, 700
Wilson, F. A. W., 484
Wilson, G. F., 246
Wilson, G. T., 37
Wilson, J. R., 239, 430
Wilson, K., 628
Wilson, M. E., 70, 686
Wilson, T. D., 122, 181, 507
Wilson, W. H., 275, 277
Wilson, W. J., 526, 546
Wimsatt, W. C., 287
Windle, M., 577
Winer, J. L., 348
Winett, R. A., 541, 542, 548
Wingfield, J. C., 677
Winn, D. M., 550
Winocur, G., 464, 477, 480, 481
Winter, D. G., 143
Winter, L., 180
Wisden, W., 678
Wistar, R. T., 68
Witheridge, T. F., 528, 529, 537
Witherspoon, D., 457, 481
Witmer, B. G., 256
Wittgenstein, L., 500
Wohlford, P. F., 40, 345, 365
Wojciszke, B., 164
Wolbarst, L. R., 478, 479
Wolchik, S. A., 28, 29
Woloshyn, V., 480
Wong, D. B., 500
Wong, G. Y. Y., 108
Wood, F., 460
Wood, J. V., 594
Wood, P. D., 542
Wood, P. G., 69, 73
Wood, R., 25, 36, 37

Wood, R. E., 25
Wood, W., 136, 137
Woodman, J. D., 626
Woodruff-Pak, D. S., 328
Woods, D. D., 238, 242, 243
Woods, W. J., 370
Woody, C. D., 319, 333, 334
Wooley, T. W., 73
Worchel, S., 590
Word, C. O., 592
Worth, L. T., 129, 138, 140, 141, 160, 168, 169
Wortman, C. B., 431
Wortman, P. M., 601
Woycke, J., 214
Wrangham, R. W., 689
Wright, A. A., 455
Wright, B., 618, 627
Wright, J., 40
Wright, J. C., 158, 178
Wright, J. D., 530
Wright, J. W., 593
Wright, R. A., 37
Wright, S. C., 143
Wright, T. L., 37
Wrightsman, L. S., 118, 358, 360
Wu, J. M., 104
Wu, J. Z., 319, 333
Wu, L. J., 106
Wu, L. L., 91, 103
Wu, Z. P., 98
Wu, Z. Y., 96, 98
Wundt, W., 24, 430
Wurf, E., 25, 27
Wyatt, G. E., 353
Wyer, R. S., 39, 159, 160, 162, 165, 169, 592
Wyer, R. S. Jr., 124, 137
Wyers, E. J., 679

Yang, X. H., 106
Yang, Z. L., 106
Yantis, S., 398, 399, 406, 419
Yarowsky, P., 319
Yarrow, L. J., 626
Yarrow, M. R., 565
Yates, J. F., 247
Ye, R. M., 107
Yeaton, W., 670
Yeh, Y., 250
Yeo, C. H., 328–30, 332, 333
Yershak, R. N., 439
Yi, Y., 132, 133, 138
Yin, R. K., 653
Yirmiya, R., 65
Yoerg, S. I., 697
Yokaitis, M. H., 328
Yost, L. W., 567
Young, C., 403
Young, J., 538
Young, P., 385
Young, R. K., 688
Yu, B. L., 94, 95
Yu, K. C., 103
Yu, Q., 691
Yu, W. Z., 103, 104, 106
Yuen, J. C. K., 95
Yukl, G., 254, 257
Yzerbyt, V., 168
Yzerbyt, V. Y., 165, 182

X

Xiao, B. L., 96
Xie, X. F., 103
Xin, D. G., 106
Xu, B. H., 105
Xu, F., 96
Xu, G., 137
Xu, L. C., 96, 102–4, 107
Xu, S. L., 96, 98, 105, 106
Xu, W., 105
Xu, Z. J., 96
Xue, A. Y., 104

Y

Yalom, I., 537
Yamadori, A., 484
Yamatani, H., 540
Yamauchi, T., 67, 73
Yan, H. Q., 106
Yan, W. W., 106
Yang, C. F., 108
Yang, G. X., 104
Yang, K. S., 108, 162

Z

Zacharko, R. M., 68
Zacks, R. T., 285
Zaff, B. S., 238, 241
Zajac, E. J., 211, 215
Zajonc, R. B., 10, 127, 479, 588, 589, 595, 602
Zalcman, S., 57, 67, 68, 71, 74
Zaller, J., 177
Zamble, E., 124
Zane, C. J., 71, 74
Zane, N. W. S., 364, 365
ZANNA, M. P., 117–54; 118, 120, 123, 126, 133, 134, 136, 141, 143, 144, 175, 178, 179, 592, 599
Zárate, M. A., 167
Zaslow, M., 617
Zaslow, M. J., 624
Zebrowitz, L. A., 138, 156, 166
Zedeck, S., 235
Zeeman, E. C., 436
Zeitz, C. M., 178, 603
Zelazo, P., 627
Zellman, G. L., 544
Zenger, T. R., 206
Zentall, T. R., 694, 697
Zetterblom, G., 445
Zha, H., 69, 74
Zha, Z. X., 98
Zhang, A. A., 331, 333, 334
Zhang, C. X., 94

Zhang, D. R., 94
Zhang, H. C., 89, 91, 94–96
Zhang, H. Z., 105
Zhang, J. F., 101
Zhang, J. J., 94
Zhang, J. X., 322
Zhang, M., 94
Zhang, M. L., 101
Zhang, R. J., 108
Zhang, S. F., 99
Zhang, S. L., 101
Zhang, W. T., 95
Zhang, Z., 99
Zhang, Z. J., 98, 104
Zhang, Z. S., 91
Zhao, G. M., 94
Zhao, G. S., 105
Zhao, H. T., 102
Zhao, L. R., 91, 92, 108
Zhao, M. J., 99
Zhao, S. W., 98
Zhao, Y., 105

Zhao, Z. Y., 108
Zheng, Q. Q., 91
Zheng, R. C., 96
Zheng, Z. Y., 94
Zhong, J. A., 95, 103
Zhou, A. B., 94
Zhou, G., 106
Zhou, J. J., 96
Zhou, R., 98
Zhou, Y., 105
Zhu, M. S., 107
Zhu, P. L., 106
Zhu, Y. M., 94, 96, 97
Zhu, Z. X., 105
Zhu, Zi-Xian, 90, 91, 98, 99
Zhu, Zu-Xiang, 91, 104
Ziegler, J., 544
Ziegler, M., 128
Ziemba-Davis, M., 369
Ziff, P., 500
Zigler, E., 618, 624
Zigler, E. F., 616, 638

Zimbardo, P. G., 118
Zimmer, J., 325
Zimmerman, M. A., 538
Zimmerman, S. K., 599
Zirkel, S., 24, 28, 163
Zisblatt, M., 64
Zivin, G., 25
Zola-Morgan, S., 455, 457,
    461–63, 465, 467, 469,
    471, 475, 476
Zouzounis, J. A., 462
Zuckerman, M., 25
Zuffante, P., 479
Zukier, H., 286, 591
Zuo, C. C., 332
Zuo, M. L., 98, 99
Zupan, B. A., 564, 578
zur Oeveste, H., 445
Zuroff, D. C., 159
Zuwerink, J. R., 145, 173
Zwilling, B. S., 69

SUBJECT INDEX

A

Abecedarian Project, 622
Abortion
  adolescent, 545–46
Absenteeism
  temporal dimension and, 205
Accountability theory, 44
Acculturation
  measures of, 363
  rating scale for Asian self-identity, 363
  rating scale for Mexican Americans, 363
Accuracy
  consensus as proxy for, 157–58
  expectancy effects and, 158–59
  in memory, 159–61
  negativity effects and, 159
  in person perception, 156–61
  testing of, 157–58
Achievement motivation
  in China, 103
ACME model, 274
Acquaintance
  observer consensus and, 157–58
Acquaintance rape, 352–53
Acquired immune deficiency syndrome,
    367–68
  prevention of
    social/community intervention programs
      and, 547–50
Action theory
  individual in, 429
Activation
  psychological stress and, 4
ACT theory, 239
ACT UP, 213
Acupuncture
  psychological correlates of, 106
Adaptation
  biological factors for, 430
  ecological principle of, 526
Adaptive correlation
  animal behavior and, 690–91
Adaptive expertise, 298
Adaptivity
  standards of accuracy and, 156–57
Additive factor method
  information processing and, 386, 392,
    395–96
Ader, R., 53–77
Adolescent
  abortion and, 545–46
  alternatives to institutional care for, 532–36
  contraception education and, 544–45

mother
  programs for, 546
  parenthood
    prevention of, 543–47
AESOP theory
  adaptive behavior and, 321
Affect
  in attitude structure, 120–22
  persuasion and, 141
Affective perspective taking
  deficits in
    socially deviant/unpopular children and,
      564
Age/aging
  in engineering psychology, 252–54
  organizational behavior and, 206
  stereotyping and, 166
Aggression
  in children
    child care and, 632–33
  chronic reactive
    hostile attributional bias and, 566
  exposure to
    conduct disorder and, 579
    knowledge structures and, 575–77
Agreeableness
  as personality trait descriptor, 162
AIDS
  See Acquired immune deficiency syndrome
Air disaster
  organizational reactions to, 218–19
Alcohol dependence
  masculine gender-role stress and, 358
Alcoholics Anonymous, 537, 540
Allergic disease
  psychosocial factors in, 64
Alliance for the Mentally Ill, 537, 539–41
Allometry
  animal behavior comparisons and, 684–85
Alpha slippage, 666
Alzheimer's disease, 245
  forgetting rates in, 466–67
Ambivalence
  attitudinal, 123
Amino acid receptors
  fear conditioning and, 324
DL-Amino-5-phosphonovalerate
  fear-potentiated startle response and, 324
Amitriptyline
  conditioned immunosuppressive responses
    and, 73
Amnesia
  conditioning and, 477
  declarative memory and, 457

diencephalic, 466
episodic memory in, 459–60
forgetting rates in, 467
infantile, 464–66
priming and, 479
recall/recognition and, 469–70
retrograde, 462–64
short-term memory in, 454–55
skill learning and, 471–72
source, 460–61, 468
spatial memory in, 467–68
Amygdala
emotional learning and, 321
fear-conditioned responses and, 318, 322–26
Amygdalectomy
inhibitory/passive avoidance responses and, 321
Analogical reasoning
symbolic-connectionist models for, 273–74
Analogical transfer
relevance and, 298–99
Anger
appraisal pattern for, 14–15
Animal behavior, 675–700
cognition and, 696–99
dynamics and structure of, 693–96
ecological comparisons of, 689–91
field vs laboratory research methods in, 678–79
genes vs environment in, 680
historical synthesis of, 676
integration of comparisons of, 692–93
learning and, 694–95
methods of comparing, 682–93
microevolutionary comparisons of, 691–92
motivation and, 693–94
nonevolutionary comparisons of, 682–87
phylogenetic comparisons of, 687–89
rules guiding research in, 680–82
Animal models
behavior comparisons and, 688–89
Animal rights, 698–99
Animal welfare, 698–99
Anorexia nervosa, 350–52
two-component model of, 351
Anthropomorphism
animal behavior research and, 681
Anticipated interactions
cognition and, 595–96
Antigen
as unconditioned stimulus, 60–61
Antisocial personality disorder
masculine gender-role stress and, 358
Anxiety
gender-role conflict and, 358
impression formation and, 177
Anxiety test, 96
Appearance
stereotyping and, 166
Applied experimental psychology, 232
Appraisal
as cognitive mediator of stress reactions, 7
relational meaning and, 12
ARCS model, 274
Arthritis
psychosocial factors in, 64

Artificial-grammar learning, 279
classification performance in, 282–83
implicit, 473–74
remote transfer in, 284
Artificial intelligence, 234, 238
Artificial life, 677
Asian self-identity acculturation scale, 363
Assertive community treatment, 528–30
Associative learning
long-term potentiation and, 324
Asthma
psychosocial factors in, 64
Asynchronous discrete model
information processing and, 396–97
Attachment
avoidant
child care and, 633–35
child care and, 630
nonmaternal child care and, 618
Attachment Q-Set, 629
Attachment relationships
insecure
conduct disorder and, 579
Attachment theory
relationships and, 575
Attention
strategic control of, 244–45
Attentional effects
information processing and, 404–6
Attention work
self-regulation and, 39
Attitude(s), 574
accessibility of, 122
affective, cognitive, behavioral correlates in, 120–22
ambivalence of, 123
attributes of, 122–23
behaviors and, 131–35
conditioning of, 127–28
definitions of, 119–20
dissonance theory and, 134–35
as evaluations, 119
formation of, 127–29
functions of, 125–26
heritability of, 128–29
information processing and, 129–30
measurement of, 123–24
as representations in memory, 119–20
selective interpretation and, 129–30
selective memory and, 130
self-perception theory and, 134
sociocognitive model of, 120
structure of, 118–24
theory of reasoned action and, 131–32
values and, 125–26
See also Persuasion
Attitude-behavior relation
models of, 132–33
Attraction-selection-attrition model, 206–7
Authoritarianism
prejudice and, 143
Autoimmune disease
conditioning and, 61
psychosocial factors in, 64
Autokinetic effect, 600
Automaticity

cognitive efficiency and, 178–82
goal-dependent with intended effects, 181–82
goal-dependent with unintended effects, 180–81
postconscious, 179–80
preconscious, 179
Automobile accidents
masculine gender-role stress and, 358
Aversive conditioning, 317–35
specific/nonspecific
relation of, 320–21
Aversive racism, 144–45
Avoidant attachment
child care and, 633–35

B

Babyish appearance
stereotyping and, 166
Backward masking
information processing and, 386
Bacterial disease
psychosocial factors in, 64
"Battle fatigue", 2
Behavior(s)
attitudes and, 131–35
See also Organizational behavior
Behavioral ecology, 646, 677–78
Behavioral homologies, 687
Behaviorism, 2
information processing approach and, 387
Belief(s)
generation and evaluation of, 273
Belief bias
information processing and, 407–8
Berkeley Stress and Coping Project, 8
Betz, N. E., 343–75
Birth weight
low
teenage pregnancy and, 543
Bisexuality
research on, 372
Black racial identity, 362–63
Blame
anger and, 14
B lymphocytes
stressful stimulation and, 72
in vitro proliferation of
stimulation of, 59
Brain
declarative memory and, 461–64
Brain substrates
for nonspecific fear conditioning, 321–26
for specific conditioned responses, 327–34
Bulimia nervosa, 350–52
Bureacratic theory
organizational context and, 224
Bureaucratization, 208

C

California Personality Inventory, 96
Cancer
risk factors for, 541–42
Cancer chemotherapy
anticipatory nausea and, 63
Capitalization on chance, 666
CAPS, 267
Cardiovascular disease
risk factors for, 541–42
Career adjustment
gays/lesbians and, 372
women and, 349–50
Career choice
gays/lesbians and, 372
women and, 347–48
Career development
women and, 346–50
Career self-efficacy
cross-cultural generalizability of, 348
Caregiver effects
child care and, 629–30
Catastrophe theory, 436, 441
Catecholamines
immune/nonspecific defense responses and, 73
immunologic effects of, 74
Categorization, 165–70
core categories in, 166–67
individuation in, 167–68
meaning-making in, 168–70
rational analysis and, 288
social models of, 165–66
Category learning, 281
Cattell-16PF Test Battery, 96
Causal inference
rational analysis and, 288
Causality
in personality research, 434
Causal reasoning, 296
Cell-mediated immunity
conditioning and, 57–59
stress and, 66–69
Central nucleus
fear expression and, 321
Cerebellar cortex
classical conditioning and, 329
Cerebellar lesions
conditioned responses and, 328–29
lateral
eyelid conditioning and, 320
vernal
heart-rate conditioning and, 320
Cerebellum
eyelid conditioning and, 331
formation of memory and, 331
specific conditioned responses and, 318, 327–33
Cerebral cortex
complex learning and, 318
eye-blink conditioning and, 319
Challenge, 5
Chaos theory, 436
Charisma, 213–14
measure of, 214
Chemotherapy
anticipatory nausea and, 63
Child and Adolescent Service System
Program, 533
Child care
centers vs homes in, 626–27

cognitive effects of, 627–28
dimensions of quality of, 617
disabled children and, 625–26
early entry
  attachment and, 631–32
family pathology and, 619–20
gender and, 624–25
home care vs, 616
outcomes, 626–36
  emotional, 630–35
poor families and, 622–23
poor quality
  development and, 620
punitive families and, 621–22
as risk, 618–26
risky children and, 623–26
settings for, 616–17
social competence and, 628–30
temperament and, 625
Child care research, 613–38
  contexts of, 613–17
  public policy and, 637–38
  scientific implications of, 636–37
Child psychopathology
  social-information-processing theory and,
    563–71
Children
  alternatives to institutional care for, 532–36
Children's Attributional Style Questionnaire,
  567
Children's Cognitive Ability Scale, 96
China
  ancient
    psychological thinking/practice in, 88–89
    professional associations and journals in,
      91–92
    psychological testing/measurement in, 96–97
  psychology in, 87–110
    cross-cultural, 106–7
    developmental, 97–100
    development of, 89–91
    educational/school, 100–2
    engineering, 104–5
    experimental/physiological, 94–96
    managerial, 102–4
    medical/clinical, 105–6
    social/sports, 106
  research institutions and training programs
    in, 92–94
Chinese Adolescent Non-Intellectual
  Personality Inventory, 96
Chinese Association of Mental Health, 92
Chinese Binet-Simon Test, 96
Chinese characters
  shapes of
    comprehension and, 94–95
    short-term memorability of, 95
Chinese Educational Association, 92
Chinese Ergonomics Society, 92
Chinese National Association of Science and
  Technology, 92
Chinese National Foundation of
  Social Sciences, 93
Chinese National Science Foundation, 93
Chinese people
  psychology of, 108–9

Chinese Psychological Society, 91–92
Chinese Social Psychological Association, 92
Chinese Society of Behavioral Sciences, 92
Chlorpromazine
  conditioned immunosuppressive responses
    and, 73
Chronic reactive aggression
  hostile attributional bias and, 566
Chunking, 414
Circadian cycles
  stereotyping and, 175
Civil service examination
  in ancient China, 89
Classical conditioning
  alternative loci for, 333–34
  cerebellar cortex and, 329
  engram for, 318
  immune response and, 54–55
Clinical Memory Test, 96
Clinical psychology
  in China, 105–6
Cluster analysis, 445
Cognition
  animal behavior and, 696–99
  anticipated interactions and, 595–96
  attitude structure and, 121–22
  child care and, 627–28
  as collaboration, 599–603
  communication and, 602–3
  comparative, 696–97
  conflict and, 596–97
  crowding and, 590
  evolutionary history of, 286–89
  goal, 28–29
  group composition and, 590–91
  group decision making and, 599
  group memory and, 602
  majority/minority influence and, 597–98
  mental representations of others and, 593–96
  modeling of
    frames and, 270
  motivation and, 587
  parallel search process in, 391
  reference groups/individuals and, 593–94
  role-taking and, 593
  shared
    development in groups, 600–2
  social, 155–83
    automaticity in, 178–82
    goals and control in, 171–82
    trait descriptors in, 162–65
  social comparison and, 594–95
  social facilitation and, 588–89
  social foundations of, 585–605
  social identity and, 592–93
  social interaction and, 596–99
  social loafing and, 589–90
  social position and, 592
  social role and, 591
  sociocultural perspective on, 604
  symbolic approach to, 267
Cognitive continuum theory, 248
Cognitive efficiency
  automaticity and, 178–82
Cognitive mediation
  psychological stress and, 5–7

Cognitive psychology, 585–605
Cognitive task analysis
 in engineering psychology, 238–41
Cohen, N., 53–77
Coherence
 sense of
  psychological stress and, 3
Combat
 emotional breakdown due to, 2
Commitment
 goal cognition and, 28
Commitment propensity, 204
Common factor modeling, 667
Communication
 cognition and, 602–3
Community intervention, 525–51
 assertive, 528–30
 homelessness and, 530–32
 lifestyle change and, 541–50
 prevention of AIDS and, 547–50
Community mental health
 developments in, 527
 lifestyle-related problems in, 527
 resource-related problems in, 526–27
Community Mental Health Centers Act, 526
Comparative cognition, 696–97
Comparative psychology
 comparison in, 682
 ethology and, 676–77
 motivation in, 693–94
Compensatory conditioning
 host-defense reactions and, 57
Compliance
 cognition and, 597–98
Computer networking, 235
Computer simulation
 attitude measurement and, 123
Conditioned responses
 specific
  brain substrates for, 327–34
Conditioning, 476–78
 of attitudes, 127–28
 aversive, 317–35
  relation of specific/nonspecific, 320–21
 cell-mediated immunity and, 57–59
 classical
  alternative loci for, 333–34
  cerebellar cortex and, 329
  engram for, 318
  immune response and, 54–55
 compensatory
  host-defense reactions and, 57
 eye-blink
  hippocampus and, 319
 eyelid
  cerebellum and, 331
  lateral cerebellar lesions and, 320
 fear
  brain substrates for, 321–26
 heart-rate
  cerebellar vernal lesions and, 320
 human subjects and, 61–63
 humoral immunity and, 55–57
 memory traces for, 318
 nonimmunologically specific reactions and,
  59–60

therapeutic potential of, 61
Conduct disorder
 developmental psychopathology of, 578–80
Configural frequency analysis, 445
Confirmatory path analysis
 multiple correlated dependent variables and,
  667
Conflict
 cognition and, 596–97
Conformity
 cognition and, 597
Connectionism
 information processing and, 415–17
Connectionist paradigm
 thinking and, 266–77
Conscientiousness
 as personality trait descriptor, 162
Consciousness
 animal behavior and, 697–98
Consensus
 as proxy for accuracy, 157–58
Consensus accuracy model, 158
Constraint
 organizational behavior and, 200–1
Constraint satisfaction
 in reasoning, 275
Constructive thinking
 psychological stress and, 3
Contextual proximity
 organizations and, 202
Continuum model, 165
Contraception education
 adolescents and, 544–45
Control
 in social cognition, 171–82
Convergence
 animal behavior and, 689
Conversion
 cognition and, 597–98
Cooperative interdependence
 impression formation and, 173
Coping
 emotion and, 16–17
 emotion-focused, 8
 physiological analogue of, 4
 problem-focused, 8
 psychological stress and, 8–9
Coronary heart disease
 masculine gender-role stress and, 358
Corticosteroids
 psychological stress and, 4–5
Corticostriatal system
 skill/habit learning and, 475
Counseling
 cross-cultural
  counselor-client match in, 363–64
Counseling psychology, 343–75
 career development and, 346–50
 diverse populations and, 362–67
 eating disorders and, 350–52
 gay, lesbian, bisexual individuals and,
  367–73
 gender issues in, 346–62
 male socialization in, 357–58
 male violence and, 361–62
 men and, 357–62

men in therapy and, 358–60
multicultural training and, 364–66
sexual violence and, 352–55
women and, 346–57
Counterfactual simulation
social understanding and, 170–71
Covariation
implicit learning of, 281
Cowan, N., 383–420
Coxsackie B virus
susceptibility to
stress and, 64
Creative drawing
role of internal representations in, 289
Creativity test, 96
Cross-cultural counseling
counselor-client match in, 363–64
Cross-cultural psychology
in China, 106–7
Crowding
cognition and, 590
Cue-probability learning, 281
Cultural diversity
counseling psychology and, 362–67
Cultural learning
as inherited complexity, 512–13
Cultural psychology, 497–517
disciplinary context, 499–503
"experience-near" concepts in, 507–12
historical context, 503–4
inherited complexity in, 512–13
institutional context, 504–5
universalism in, 514–17
Cyclophosphamide
immunologic reactivity and, 58
Cytokines
hypothalamo-pituitary-adrenal axis and, 75

D

Data
information compared, 386
Decision bias
information processing and, 407–8
Decision making
distress and, 211
in engineering psychology, 247–49
group
cognition and, 599
information processing and, 413
social
rational model of, 649
Declarative memory, 457–59
brain system supporting, 461–62
time-limited function of, 462–64
development of, 464–66
skills and habits distinguished from, 475–76
Deductive reasoning
mental-models approach to, 306
relevance and, 293
Defensive evaluative avoidance
self-regulation and, 43–44
Deinstitutionalization, 527
homelessness and, 530
Demography
relational

organizational behavior and, 205–7
Denial, 6–7
Depression
attentional processes in, 174–75
in children
distorted mental representations in, 567
response accessing and, 569
response evaluation and, 570–71
developmental psychopathology of, 578–80
gender-role conflict and, 358
information processing in, 564
knowledge structures and, 577–78
learned helplessness model of, 567
Developmental psychobiology, 678
Developmental psychology
in China, 97–100
Diencephalic amnesia, 466
Diencephalon
declarative memory and, 457, 462
Differential psychology, 344
Disability
child care and, 625–26
Disagreement
cognition and, 598
Discrepancy reduction
self-regulation and, 36–37
Discrimination reversal
hippocampus and, 319
Dissonance theory
attitudes and, 134–35
Distal causation
information processing approach and, 393–94
Distancing, 6–7
Distress, 5
decision making and, 211
Divergence
animal behavior and, 689–90
Dodge, K. A., 559–80
Dominance ranking, 167
Drug dependence
masculine gender-role stress and, 358
DSM-III-R, 350, 354, 356
Dual-process model, 165
Dual-task performance
multiple-resource model and, 245
resource theory and, 245
strategic facets of, 245
Dynamic binding
reflexive reasoning and, 275–77
Dynamic processes, 437–39
levels of, 438–39
prediction in, 440–41

E

Earth First!, 213
Eating disorders, 350–52
Eating disorders inventory, 351
ECHO model, 274
Ecological comparison
animal behavior and, 689–91
Ecological model, 526
Ecological realism
information processing and, 419
Economic theory

organizational behavior and, 223–24
Education
    organizational behavior and, 206
Educational psychology
    in China, 100–2
Ego-defense theory, 6
Eisenberg, M., 613–38
Elaboration likelihood model, 135–36, 362
Emotion(s)
    appraisal components of, 14–16
    cognitive-motivational-relational theory of,
        12–17
    coping and, 16–17
    core relational themes of, 13–14
    cultural psychology of, 516
    psychological stress as subset of, 10–12
Emotional arousal
    impression formation and, 177
Emotional breakdown
    psychodynamics of, 2
Emotional contrast strategies
    distance dimension and, 203
Emotional learning
    amygdala and, 321
Enactment
    child psychopathology and, 571
    social information processing and, 562
Encoding
    child psychopathology and, 563–64
    social information processing and, 561
Engineering psychology, 231–57
    aging in, 252–54
    in China, 104–5
    cognitive task analysis in, 238–41
    customized training in, 254–57
    decision making in, 247–49
    knowledge elicitation in, 238–41
    mental workload in, 244–47
    research topics in, 252
    situation awareness in, 241–44
    social change and, 235–37
    system design and, 233
    task demands in, 237–50
    technological innovation and, 234–3
    theoretical developments in, 251–52
Engram(s)
    for classical conditioning, 318
    localization of, 319
Environment
    animal behavior and, 700
Epigenesis, 680
Episodic memory, 459–61
Epstein-Barr virus infection
    psychosocial factors in, 64
Ethnicity
    counseling psychology and, 362–67
    occupation type categorized by, 503–4
    residential patterns based on, 503
Ethology
    comparative psychology and, 676–77
    comparison in, 682
    motivation in, 693–94
Eustress, 5
Evaluation(s)
    attitudes as, 119
    in attitude structure, 120–21

Evaluation succession model
    for program development, 661–63
Event-related potentials
    word recall/recognition and, 482
Evolutionary change
    cognition and, 286–89
Evolutionary theory
    information processing and, 393–94
Examplar(s), 574
Expectancy congruence
    information processing and, 159–61
Expectancy effects
    target behavior and, 158–59
Experimental psychology, 232
    in China, 94–95
Explanatory coherence
    symbolic-connectionist model of, 274
Explicit knowledge, 289–90
Explicit thinking, 289–90
Extraversion
    consensus and, 157
    as personality trait descriptor, 162
Eye-blink conditioning
    hippocampus and, 319
Eyelid conditioning
    lateral cerebellar lesions and, 320
    plasticity associated with
        cerebellum and, 331
Eysenck Personality Questionnaire, 96, 105

F

Facial expressiveness
    persuasiveness and, 138
Falsification strategy
    information processing and, 388–89
Family pathology
    risky child care and, 619–20
Fear appeals
    persuasiveness and, 139–40
Fear conditioning
    nonspecific
        brain substrates for, 321–26
Feminist therapy, 356–57
Figueredo, A. J., 645–71
Fiske, S. T., 155–83
Fitzgerald, L. F., 343–75
Five-factor model, 162
Flow continuity principle
    information processing and, 385
Flow dynamics principle
    information processing and, 385
Focal set, 296
Follow Through, 659
Foraging behavior
    optimality and, 685
Forgetting
    rates of, 466–67
Fragmentation
    in personality research, 431–32
Frames
    cognition and, 270
Freezing response
    amygdala stimulation and, 323
Frontal-lobe lesions
    amnesia due to, 466

delayed response deficits due to, 320
Fully intentional thinking, 182
Fuzzy logical model of perception,
  392, 396, 409, 411–12

G

Gay client
  therapist attitudes and, 369–71
Gay identity
  development of, 371
Gay lifestyle
  research on, 371–73
Gay parenting
  research on, 372–73
Gender
  career decision-making process and, 347
  child care and, 624–25
  in counseling psychology, 346–62
  counselor behavior and, 355–56
  organizational behavior and, 206
  same-sex relationships and, 371–72
  stereotyping and, 166
Gender harassment, 349
Gender-role conflict
  masculine, 357–58
Gender-role conflict scale, 358, 360–61
General adaptation syndrome
  psychological stressors and, 4
Generation of organized inferences
  deficits in
    socially deviant/unpopular children and,
    565
Gestalt psychology
  thinking in, 268–69
Goal(s)
  in social cognition, 171–82
Goal cognition, 28–29
Goal definition process, 27
Goal-referent thinking, 38
Goal-setting theory, 31–32
Group(s)
  composition of
    cognition and, 590–91
  norm formation in, 600
  powerful
    influence on organizations, 215
  shared cognitions in
    development of, 600–2
Group decision making
  cognition and, 599
  in engineering psychology, 247–49
Group memory, 602
"Groupthink", 601
Groupware, 235
GROW, 537, 538–39

H

Habits, 471–75
  distinguished from declarative memory,
  475–76
Habitual routines
  task-performing groups and, 209
Halstead-Reitan Neuro-Psychological Test
  Battery, 96

Hardiness
  psychological stress and, 3
  stress and performance and, 252
Harm, 5
Healthy behavior
  promotion of, 541–43
Heart disease
  reducing risk for, 542
Heart-rate conditioning
  cerebellar vernal lesions and, 320
Hebb digits task, 281–82
Heritability
  of attitudes, 128–29
Herpes simplex virus
  murine response to
    physical restraint and, 65
  susceptibility to
    stress and, 64
Herpes virus infection
  manifestation of
    psychosocial factors in, 65
Heterophilia, 369
Heterosexual bias, 368
Heuristic-systematic model, 135–36
Higgins, E. T., 585–605
Hippocampus
  complex learning and, 318
  declarative memory and, 457–58, 461–62
  discrimination reversal and, 319
  eye-blink conditioning and, 319
  fear memory and, 325–26
  short-term memory and, 455
  spatial memory and, 467
Histamine
  conditioned release of, 60
HIV infection, 368, 547
  media campaigns and, 548
  multiple approaches to, 549
Holyoak, K. J., 265–307
Homebuilders program, 534–35
Homeless
  organizational reactions to, 218
Homelessness
  community intervention/policy and, 530–32
Homeostasis
  psychological stress and, 4
Homophilia, 369
Homophobia, 368
Homosexuality
  destigmatization of, 367–68
  therapist attitudes and, 369–71
Hong Kong
  psychology in, 108–9
Hong Kong Psychological Society, 108
Hope
  psychological stress and, 3
Hospitalization
  assertive community treatment and, 528–29
  homeless and, 531
Host-defense reactions
  compensatory conditioning of, 57
  conditioned modulation of, 54–55
Hostile attributional bias, 565–66
  chronic reactive aggression and, 566
Howell, W. C., 231–57
Human-computer interface, 234

display-design in, 249–50
Human resource management
in ancient China, 89
Humoral immunity
conditioning and, 55–57
stress and, 66–69
Huntington's disease
skill learning in, 472
Hyperspecificity
nondeclarative memory and, 459
Hypervigilance
aggressive children and, 564
Hypothalamo-pituitary-adrenal axis
cytokines and, 75
Hypothesis testing, 293–94

I

Identifiability
information processing approach and,
390–93
Image theory, 248
Immune response
classical conditioning and, 54–55
Immunity
behaviorally induced changes in
mediation of, 71–76
cell-mediated
conditioning and, 57–59
stress and, 66–69
conditioned changes in
biologic impact of, 61
conditioned modulation of, 54–63
humoral
conditioning and, 55–57
stress and, 66–69
stress and, 63–71
Implicit knowledge
access and use of, 282–86
acquisition of, 278–82
Implicit learning, 278–82
Implicit thinking, 278–90
Impression formation
control in, 172–75
typing in, 165
Incest
disordered eating behavior and, 352
long-term effects of, 353
Indeterminancy
memory and inference and, 302
Individual(s)
as biological beings, 429–30
as intentional, active beings, 428–29
powerful
influences on organizations, 210–15
as social beings, 430–31
Individual counseling
adolescent behavior change and, 536
Individuation
stereotyping and, 167–68
Induction
central task of, 273
Infant care, 623–24
Infantile amnesia, 464–66
Inference
indeterminancy and, 302

systematicity and, 270–71
Inferential boundaries
self-regulation and, 40–41
Inferior olive
lesions of
conditioned responses and, 330
Information
data compared, 386
definition of, 385–86
Informational description
information processing and, 384
Information exchange
joint decision making and, 601
Information processing
attentional/strategic effects and, 404–6
attitudes and, 129–30
connectionism and, 415–17
decision making and, 413
definition of, 386–87
discrete vs continuous, 395–401
ecological realism and, 419
knowledge structures guiding, 573–78
memory and, 412
models of, 383–420
characteristics of, 384–87
justifications of, 387–89
metatheoretical issues and, 389–94
modularity and, 417–18
parallel modes of, 429
physical symbol systems and, 414–15
psychophysics and, 406–8
reading and, 411–12
recognition effects and, 160
serial vs parallel, 401–4
speech perception and, 409–11
stages of
evidence for, 394–95
visual perception and, 408
Information-processing theory
social, 560–73
child psychopathology and, 563–71
single behavioral events and, 562–63
Informativeness principle
social communication and, 137
Innovation
cognition and, 597
Insecurity
impression formation and, 177
Institutional care
alternatives to, 532–36
Integrated computer-aided manufacturing, 241
Integration
psychological functioning and, 438
Intellectualization, 6
Intelligent tutoring systems, 255
Intention
animal behavior and, 698
conditionability of, 27
Intention-behavior relation, 131–32
Intention-cue detection deficit, 566
Interactive activation model, 411
Interdependence
psychological functioning and, 437
International Union of Psychological Science,
92, 108
Interpersonal conflict

cognitive change and, 596–97
Interpersonal disagreement
  cognition and, 598
Interpersonal interaction
  relational demography and, 206
Interpersonal traits
  in social psychology, 163
Interpositus nucleus
  lesions of
    new learning and, 328
  stimulation of
    responses evoked by, 327–28
Interpretation
  selective
    attitudes and, 129–30
Intersubjectivity
  coordinated cognitive activity and, 600
Involvement
  outcome-relevant, 136
  persuasion and, 136
  value-relevant, 136

J

Juvenile delinquency
  community-based care and, 533–34
Juvenile justice program
  sequential canonical analysis of, 667

K

Karoly, P., 23–45
Ke's Personality Scale, 108
Kim, J. J., 317–35
Kin preference
  altruistic behavior and, 685
Knowledge
  explicit, 289–90
  implicit
    access and use of, 282–86
    acquisition of, 278–82
  procedural, 573–74
  structural, 573–74
  systematicity of, 269–70
Knowledge construction
  program evaluation and, 658
Knowledge elicitation
  in engineering psychology, 238–41
Knowledge structures
  aggressive behavior and, 575–77
  depression and, 577–78
  information processing and, 573–78
Knowlton, B., 453–85
Korsakoff's syndrome
  amnesia due to, 466

L

Language
  transmission/persistence of stereotypes and, 142
Latent profile analysis, 445
Lateralized readiness potential, 397–98
Lateral pons
  lesions of
    conditioned responses and, 330

Lavond, D. G., 317–35
Law of cognitive structure activation, 179
Lazarus, R. S., 1–18
Leader(s)
  charismatic, 213–14
  organizational legitimacy and, 213
Leadership psychology
  in China, 103–4
Learned resourcefulness
  psychological stress and, 3
Learning
  animal behavior and, 694–95
  associative
    long-term potentiation and, 324
  category, 281
  cue-probability, 281
  cultural
    as inherited complexity, 512–13
  emotional
    amygdala and, 321
  implicit, 278–82
  paired-associate, 484–85
  prototype
    declarative memory and, 475
  sequence, 280–82
  specific/nonspecific
    cerebellar lesions and, 320
Learning-instinct intercalation, 680
Lesbian client
  therapist attitudes and, 369–71
Lesbian identity
  development of, 371
Lesbian lifestyle
  research on, 371–73
Levine, J. M., 585–605
Levine, M., 525–51
Levorphanol
  attenuation of fear learning due to, 323
Lidocaine
  conditioned responses and, 331–32
  inhibitory avoidance responses and, 324
Life events
  psychological stress and, 11
Life history theory
  animal behavior and, 689
Lifestyle change
  promotion of, 541–50
Limited-capacity model
  information processing and, 403
Linear regression models
  personality research and, 432
Linguistic interaction
  cognition and, 602–3
LISREL, 443
Long-term memory, 457–61
Long-term potentiation
  N-methyl-D-aspartate receptors and, 324
Low birth weight
  teenage pregnancy and, 543
Luria-Nebraska Test Battery, 96
Lymphoid organs
  innervation of, 75

M

Macrophages

suppression of
  stress and, 69
Madison model, 528
Magnusson, D., 427–48
Majority influence
  cognition and, 597–98
Male sexual aggression, 362
Male socialization, 357–58
  psychotherapy and, 358–60
Male violence
  counseling psychology and, 361–62
Mammillary nuclei
  memory functions and, 462
Managerial psychology
  in China, 102–4
MANPRINT, 233
Masculine gender-role conflict, 357–58
Masculine gender-role stress scale, 360–61
Massaro, D. W., 383–420
Maternal separation anxiety
  child care and, 621
Mathematical problem solving
  analogical transfer in, 274
Mating systems
  optimality and, 685
Maxmincon, 647
Meaning-making
  stereotyping and, 168–70
Medial geniculate nucleus
  lesions of
    conditioning to sensory stimuli and, 322
Medial temporal lobe
  declarative memory and, 457, 461–62
Medical psychology
  in China, 105–6
Medical rehabilitation
  in ancient China, 88–89
Mediodorsal nucleus
  declarative memory and, 462
Memory
  accuracy issues in, 159–61
  attitudes as representations in, 119–20
  conditioning and, 476–78
  declarative, 457–59
    brain system supporting, 461–64
    development of, 464–66
    skills and habits distinguished from,
      475–76
  episodic, 459–61
  formation of
    cerebellum and, 331
  group, 602
  indeterminancy and, 302
  long-term, 457–61
  nondeclarative, 471–82
  organization of, 453–85
  priming and, 478–82
  rational analysis and, 288
  recall, 469–71
  recognition, 469–71
  reconstructive, 605
  selective
    attitudes and, 130
  semantic, 459–61
  short-term, 454–57
  spatial, 467–69

transactive, 602
Memory traces
  for conditioning, 318
  essential, 319
  localization of, 319
Men
  counseling psychology and, 357–62
Mental health
  community
    developments in, 527
    lifestyle-related problems in, 527
    resource-related problems in, 526–27
Mental life
  animal behavior and, 697–98
Mentally ill
  assertive community treatment for, 528–30
  self-help groups for, 538–41
Mental rehabilitation
  in ancient China, 88–89
Mental representation
  child psychopathology and, 564–58
  of others
    cognition and, 593–96
    social information processing and, 561
Mental retardation
  in China, 100
Mental workload
  in engineering psychology, 244–47
Message reception
  persuasion and, 136–37
Meta-analysis
  attitude measurement and, 123
  program evaluation and, 669–70
Metacognition, 589
Metaskills
  self-regulation and, 38–40
Metatheory
  information processing and, 389–94
N-Methyl-D-aspartate receptors
  fear conditioning and, 324
Mexican Americans
  acculturation rating scale for, 363
Microevolutionary comparison
  animal behavior and, 691–92
Middle cerebellar peduncle
  lesions of
    conditioned responses and, 329–30
Minnesota Multiphasic Personality Inventory,
  96–97
Minority influence
  cognition and, 597–98
Mitogens
  nonimmunologically specific actions of,
    59–60
Mobilization-minimization hypothesis
  negativity effects and, 159
Model systems
  animal behavior comparisons and, 686–87
MODE model
  of attitude-behavior relation, 132–33
Modularity
  information processing and, 417–18
Moloney sarcoma virus
  susceptibility to
    stress and, 64
Mood

persuasion and, 140–41
Morphine
natural killer cells and, 74
Motion
dynamic processes and, 438
Motivation
animal behavior and, 693–94
cognition and, 587
reasoning and, 294
Motor nuclei
engram for classical conditioning and, 333–34
Mowday, R. T., 195–225
Multicollinearity, 665–66
Multicultural counseling, 362–67
research and, 366–67
training and, 364–66
Multi-determination
psychological functioning and, 437
Multiple regression models
personality research and, 432
Multisystemic therapy
adolescent behavior change and, 535–36
Multivariate analysis
program evaluation and, 664–70
Multivariate P-technique factor analysis, 445
Musen, G., 453–85

N

Nadolol
B-cell mitogenesis and, 73
Naloxone
acquisition of conditioned fear and, 323
memory-enhancing effect of, 323
nonspecific defense responses and, 74
Naltrexone
nonspecific defense responses and, 74
Narratives
importance in social understanding, 170–71
National Alliance for Research on
Schizophrenia and Depression, 539
National Alliance for the Mentally Ill, 539–41
Naturalistic decision making
in engineering psychology, 247–49
Natural killer cells
conditioned enhancement of, 60
electric shock stimulation and, 71, 74–75
morphine and, 74
nonimmunologically specific actions of, 59–60
norepinephrine and, 74
Natural object categorization model
negativity effects and, 159
Negative feedback control
self-regulation and, 30–31
Negativity effects
accuracy and, 159
Neuroethology, 678
Neurons
sensory
receptive-field properties of, 319
Neuroticism
as personality trait descriptor, 162
Next-in-line effect, 177
Nictitating membrane reflex, 334

Nondeclarative memory, 471–82
Nonlinearity
psychological functioning and, 438
Norepinephrine
natural killer cells and, 74
Nuclear power
unsuccessful management commitment to, 219–20
Null-hypothesis testing, 647

O

Object appraisal
attitudes and, 125–26
Observer theory
perception and, 408
Occupational stress
in China, 105
Olson, J. M., 117–46
Openness
as personality trait descriptor, 162
Operational boundaries
self-regulation and, 41
Opioid(s)
nonspecific defense responses and, 74
Opioid antagonists
memory-enhancing effect of, 323
Opportunity
organizational behavior and, 199–200
Opportunity-vs-socialization hypothesis
career choice and, 348
Optimality
animal behavior and, 685–86
Optimism
psychological stress and, 3
Organization(s)
aggregate member attributes and, 215–17
contextual influences in, 198–208
contextual proximity and, 202
development in China, 104
group influence in, 215
leader influence in, 212
powerful individuals and, 210–15
Organizational behavior, 195–225
constraint and, 200–1
distance dimension and, 202–4
economic theory and, 223–24
individual-organization fit and, 207–8
macro, 196
micro, 196
opportunity and, 199–200
relational demography and, 205–7
research on
methodological implications in, 220–22
substantive implications in, 222–25
temporal dimension in, 204–5
Organizational culture profile, 207
Outcome dependency
impression formation and, 173

P

Paired-associate learning, 484–85
Parahippocampal cortex
spatial memory functions and, 469
Parallel constraint satisfaction, 273

Parental care
  optimality and, 685
Parental consent
  abortion and, 545
Parenthood
  adolescent
    prevention of, 543–47
Parenting
  attitudes toward work and, 621
PARI, 240
Parkinson's disease
  recall/recognition in, 475
Pathfinder, 240–41
Pattern analysis
  in personality research, 444–45
Pattern description, 444–45
Pattern dynamics, 445
Peer socialization
  mother-child attachment and, 630
Perceived Self-Competence Scale, 575
Perception
  fuzzy logical model of, 392, 396, 409,
    411–12
  high-level thinking and, 269
  person
    accuracy in, 156–61
    goals and control in, 171–82
  social, 155–83
    interpersonal dimension of, 157
Perceptual priming
  neural basis of, 481
Performance operating characteristic, 245
Periodicity
  biological processes and, 438
Perirhinal cortex
  visual memory functions and, 469
Perkins, D. V., 525–51
Personal engagement/disengagement
  psychological distance and, 203–4
Personality, 427–48
  development of
    genetic factors in, 430
  models of
    developmental, 428
    holistic, dynamic, 435–39
Personality impression ratings
  testing of accuracy and, 157–58
Personality research
  biological factors in, 430
  causality in, 434
  characteristics of, 431–35
  empirical, 435
  fragmentation in, 431–32
  methods and statistics in, 434–35
  pattern analysis in, 444–45
  person-oriented analyses in, 444
  prediction in, 433–34
  scientific
    goal of, 442
  trait descriptors in, 162–65
  variable-oriented approach in, 443–44
  variables in, 432–33
Personality trait(s)
  psychological stress and, 3
Personality trait descriptors, 162–65
  five-factor model of, 162

Person perception
  accuracy in, 156–61
  goals and control in, 171–82
Persuasion, 135–41
  message characteristics and, 138–40
  message reception and, 136–37
  models of, 135–36
  mood and, 140–41
  recipient characteristics and, 140–41
  source characteristics and, 138
Phylogenetic comparison
  animal behavior and, 687–89
Physical abuse
  in childhood
    conduct disorder and, 579
Physical attractiveness
  stereotyping and, 166
Physical embodiment principle
  information processing and, 385
Physical Strain Questionnaire, 358
Physical symbol systems
  information processing and, 414–15
Physiological psychology
  in China, 94–95
Physiological stress
  psychological stress and, 4–5
Pinyin, 95
Polyinosinic-polycytidylic acid
  pharmacological tolerance to
    role of conditioning in, 57
Positivism, 2
Postconscious automaticity, 179–80
Post-traumatic stress disorder
  psychological sequelae of rape as, 354
Pragmatic reasoning
  relevance and, 293–97
Pragmatism
  standards of accuracy and, 156–57
Preconscious automaticity, 179
Prediction
  in dynamic processes, 440–41
  as goal/tool, 441
  in personality research, 433–34
Pregnancy
  teenage
    reducing risk of, 543–44
Prejudice, 143–45
  determinants of, 143–44
  reduction of, 145
Prematurity
  teenage pregnancy and, 543
Priming
  memory and, 478–82
  memory research and, 412
  neural basis of, 481
Problem solving
  mathematical
    analogical transfer in, 274
    rational analysis and, 288
    symbolic paradigm and, 267–68
Procedural knowledge, 573–74
Program development
  evaluation succession model for, 661–63
Program evaluation, 645–71
  activities of, 660–61
  epistemology for, 658

issues in, 657–64
of large-scale social programs, 656–57
multiple independent replications in, 669–70
multiple outcome variables in, 666–67
multiple predictor variables in, 665–66
multiple utility functions in, 667–69
multivariate methods in, 664–70
qualitative movement in, 652–56
recent developments in, 671
theory-driven, 657–58
use of findings, 659–60
valuing and, 658–59
Project Care, 622
"Proletarianization", 208
Prolonged exposure
post-traumatic stress disorder and, 354
Propranolol
inflammatory response and, 73
inhibitory avoidance response and, 323
Protection motivation theory
dual-process models of persuasion and, 139–40
Prototype(s), 574
Prototype learning
declarative memory and, 475
Proximal causation
information processing and, 393–94
Psychological Association of China, 91
Psychological distance
personal engagement/disengagement and, 203–4
Psychological functioning
individual
characteristics of, 428–31
as dynamic process, 437–39
holistic view of, 436
lawfulness of, 439–42
Psychological research
information processing and, 388–89
Psychological stress
cognitive mediational approach to, 5–7
coping process and, 8–9
physiological stress and, 4–5
research approaches to, 2–5
as subset of emotions, 10–12
Psychological stress theory
cognitive mediational principle in, 13
Psychological testing
in China, 89, 96–97
Psychology
in China, 87–110
development of, 89–91
in Taiwan/Hong Kong, 108–9
Psychoneuroimmunology, 53–77
Psychopathology
child
social-information-processing theory and, 563–71
development of
mental process mechanisms in, 574
Psychophysics
information processing and, 406–8
Psychotherapy
in China, 105–6
with diverse populations, 362–64
male socialization and, 358–60

sex bias in, 355
Public policy
child care research and, 637–38
PUSH/Excel, 655, 659

Q

QiQong, 105–6
Q-sort technique, 445

R

Race
counseling psychology and, 362–67
residential patterns based on, 503
stereotyping and, 166
Racial identity
development of, 362–63
Racism
aversive, 144–45
symbolic, 144
Rape
acquaintance, 352–53
long-term effects of, 352–53
risk variables in, 354
RAPIDS, 255
Rational analysis, 287–89
Raven's Standard Progressive Matrices, 96
Reading
context effects in, 411–12
Reasoning
analogical
symbolic-connectionist models for, 273–74
causal, 296
constraint satisfaction in, 275
deductive
mental-models approach to, 306
relevance and, 293
motivation and, 294
pragmatic
relevance and, 293–97
reflective, 276
reflexive
dynamic binding and, 275–77
soft constraint satisfaction in, 273–75
syllogistic, 275
vivid representations for, 300–7
See also Thinking
Recall, 469–71
Reciprocity
psychological functioning and, 437–38
Recognition, 469–71
Recognition effects
information processing and, 160
Recognition-primed decision model, 248
Reconstructive memory, 605
attitudes and, 130
Recursive decomposition
information processing and, 384–85
Red nucleus
engram for classical conditioning and, 333
stimulation of
responses evoked by, 328
Reductive analysis, 13–14
Reference groups
cognition and, 593–94

Reference individuals
  cognition and, 594
Reflective reasoning, 276
Reflexive reasoning
  dynamic binding and, 275–77
Regression models
  personality research and, 432
Rehospitalization
  assertive community treatment and, 528–29
Relational correspondences
  systematicity of, 271
Relational demography
  organizational behavior and, 205–7
Relational meaning, 13–14
  appraisal and, 12
Relationships
  attachment theory and, 575
Relevance
  pragmatic reasoning and, 293–97
Religiosity
  prejudice and, 143
Residential care
  effectiveness of, 532–33
Resnick, L. B., 585–605
Resource theory
  dual-task performance and, 245
Respiratory infection
  psychosocial factors in, 64
Response accessing
  child psychopathology and, 568–69
  social information processing and, 561–62
Response effects
  attitude measurement and, 124
Response evaluation
  child psychopathology and, 569–71
  social information processing and, 562
Reticular formation
  engram for classical conditioning and, 333–34
Retrograde amnesia, 462–64
Rhythm
  biological processes and, 438
Robotics, 234
Rokeach Value Survey, 101, 125
Role-taking
  cognition and, 593
Rumination, 181

S

SAGAT, 243
Salience effects
  postconscious automaticity and, 180
SART, 244
Scaling functions
  animal behavior comparisons and, 684–85
Scarr, S., 613–38
Schemata, 574
Schooling and Training Approaches Measurement Program, 256
School psychology
  in China, 100–2
Scientific careers
  women's underrepresentation in, 348
Scripts, 575
Sechrest, L., 645–71

Seduction, 349
Selection task
  reasoning in, 294–95
Selective interpretation
  attitudes and, 129–30
Selective memory
  attitudes and, 130
Self
  cultural psychology of, 508–12
Self-blame
  rape outcome and, 353–54
Self-concept
  negative
    information processing and, 577
Self-efficacy
  definition of, 28
  psychological stress and, 3
  self-regulation and, 37–38
Self-esteem
  appraisal of injury to
    anger and, 14
  gender-role conflict and, 358
  impression formation and, 177
  persuasibility and, 137
Self-help
  homelessness and, 532
Self-help intervention, 537–41
Self-identity acculturation scale
  Asian, 363
Self-monitoring
  object appraisal function of attitudes and, 126
Self-organization
  biological systems and, 439
Self-perception theory
  attitudes and, 134
Self-protection
  impression formation and, 177
Self-regulation
  boundedness in, 40–41
  discrepancy reduction in, 36–37
  failure in, 42–44
  goal cognition in, 28–29
  goal selection in, 27
  goal setting in, 31–32
  mechanisms of, 23–45
  metaskills in, 38–40
  models of, 25–30
  proximal volitional regulators in, 30–38
  self-efficacy in, 37–38
  self-evaluation in, 35–36
  self-monitoring in, 32–33
  use of standards in, 33–35
Self-reporting
  attitude measurement and, 123
Self-schema
  negative
    information processing and, 577–78
Semantic memory, 459–61
Separation anxiety
  maternal
    child care and, 621
Sequence learning, 280–82
Sequential canonical analysis
  multiple correlated dependent variables and, 667

Sex bias
  in psychotherapy, 355
Sexual abuse
  in childhood
    eating disorders and, 352
    long-term effects of, 353
Sexual activity
  teenage
    lowering rate of, 543–44
Sexual aggression
  male, 362
Sexual behavior
  cross-orientation, 369
Sexual bribery, 349
Sexual coercion, 349
Sexual Experiences Questionnaire, 349
Sexual harassment, 349–50
Sexual imposition, 349
Sexual orientation
  defining, 368–69
Sexual violence, 352–55
"Shell shock", 2
Short-term memory, 454–57
Shweder, R. A., 497–517
Signal-detection theory
  information processing and, 407, 409,
    411–13
Significant others
  categorization and, 167
SIMNET, 243
Simultaneous canonical analysis
  multiple correlated dependent variables and,
    667
Situation awareness
  in engineering psychology, 241–44
Situation awareness global assessment, 243
Skills, 471–75
  distinguished from declarative memory,
    475–76
SOAR architecture, 267, 414
Social adjustment
  of children
    child care and, 620
Social attention
  allocation of, 182
Social behavior
  child care and, 629
  information processing theory and, 560–73
  mental processes in, 560
Social category models, 165–66
Social change
  engineering psychology and, 235–37
Social cognition, 155–83
  automaticity in, 178–82
  goals and control in, 171–82
  trait descriptors in, 162–65
Social-cognitive theory, 31–32
  self-efficacy in, 37
Social communication
  informativeness principle and, 137
Social comparison
  cognition and, 594–95
Social competence
  child care and, 628–30
  of children
    child care and, 620

Social decision making
  rational model of, 649
Social facilitation
  cognition and, 588–89
Social identity
  cognition and, 592–93
Social information
  models of memory for, 159
Social interaction
  cognition and, 596–99
Social intervention, 525–51
  lifestyle change and, 541–50
  prevention of AIDS and, 547–50
Social intimacy
  gender-role conflict and, 358
Socialization
  male, 357–58
    psychotherapy and, 358–60
  multicultural, 363
Social judgment
  examplar model of, 167
Social loafing
  cognition and, 589–90
Social perception, 155–83
  interpersonal dimension of, 157
Social perspective taking
  deficits in
    socially deviant/unpopular children and,
      564
Social position
  cognition and, 592
Social programs
  large-scale
    evaluation of, 656–57
Social psychology
  in China, 106
Social reasoning
  deficits in
    socially deviant/unpopular children and,
      565
Social relations model, 157
Social role
  cognition and, 591
Social understanding
  importance of stories in, 170–71
Sociocognitive model, 120
Sodium-channel blockers
  inhibitory avoidance responses and, 325
SOP theory
  discrete response learning in, 321
Source amnesia, 460–61, 468
Spatial memory, 467–69
Speech perception
  information processing and, 409–11
  selective adaptation in, 410
  TRACE model of, 392
Spellman, B. A., 265–307
Sports psychology
  in China, 106
Squire, L. R., 453–85
STAMP, 256
Startle response
  amygdala stimulation and, 323
Statistics
  in personality research, 434–35
Stereotype(s), 141–43, 165–70, 575

categories of, 166–67
development of, 141–42
individuation and, 167–68
meaning-making and, 168–70
perceivers and, 142–43
social category models of, 165–66
Stereotyping
circadian cycles and, 175
Stewart B. McKinley Homeless Assistance
Act, 530
Stigma
impression formation and, 174
Stochastic interactive activation, 412
Stories
importance in social understanding, 170–71
Story model, 171
Strain
temporal dimension of, 204–5
Strange Situation
child care research and, 630–31
Strategic effects
information processing and, 404–6
Streptococcal infection
psychosocial factors in, 64
Stress
in China, 105
disease and, 64–66
immunity and, 63–71
nonimmunologically specific reactions and,
69–71
temporal dimension of, 204–5
See also Psychological stress
Stress inoculation training
post-traumatic stress disorder and, 354
Stressors
See Psychological stressors
Structural equations modeling
multiple correlated dependent variables and,
667
Structural knowledge, 573–74
Subjective rating index, 244
Subordinate role
impression formation and, 173–74
Subtraction method
information processing and, 386, 395
Sufficiency principle, 135–36
Suinn-Lew Asian self-identity acculturation
scale, 363
Sullivan, M. A., 497–517
Supportive counseling
post-traumatic stress disorder and, 354
Supratrigeminal nucleus
engram for classical conditioning and, 333
Sutton, R. I., 195–225
SWORD, 244, 246
Syllogistic reasoning, 275
Symbolic architectures, 414
Symbolic beliefs
intergroup attitudes and, 144
Symbolic paradigm
thinking and, 266–77
Symbolic racism, 144
Symbolism
in systematic reasoning, 270
Symbolization
transformation through, 512

Systematicity
of knowledge, 269–70
of relational correspondences, 271
rules of inference and, 270–71
Systematic reasoning
symbols in, 270
System design
cognitive task analysis in, 238–41
decision making in, 247–49
engineering psychology and, 233
knowledge elicitation in, 238–41
mental workload in, 244–47
situation awareness in, 241–44
technological innovation and, 234–35
Systems theory, 436

T

Tactical decision making under stress, 248
TADMUS, 248–49
Taiwan
psychology in, 108–9
Taiwan Psychological Association, 108
Taiwan Psychological Testing Association,
108
Task demands
in engineering psychology, 237–50
Task revision
goal setting and, 199–200
Technical careers
women's underrepresentation in, 348
Technology
engineering psychology and, 234–35
interpersonal relationships and, 202
Technostress, 247
Teenage pregnancy
reducing risk of, 543–44
Temperament
biological characteristics of, 430
child care and, 625
Temporality
psychological functioning and, 438
Temporal-lobe lesions
concept formation deficits due to, 320
Temporal synchrony
visual perception and, 275–76
Tenure
organizational behavior and, 206
Territoriality
optimality and, 685
Tetrodotoxin
inhibitory avoidance responses and, 325
Text comprehension
ambiguity resolution in
symbolic-connectionist model for, 273
Thalamus
declarative memory and, 461–62
Thematic Apperception Test, 96
Theorem proving
thinking vs, 290–93
Theory of planned behavior, 133
Theory of reasoned action
attitudes and, 131–32
Therapist bias
women and, 355–57
Theromorphism, 681

Thinking, 265–307
connectionist paradigm and, 266–77
content in, 290–307
evolutionary history of, 286–89
explicit, 289–90
Gestalt perspective on, 268–69
implicit, 278–90
symbolic paradigm and, 266–77
systematicity and, 269–72
theorem proving vs, 290–93
vivid representations for, 300–7
See also Reasoning
Thompson, R. F., 317–35
Threat, 5
Timberlake, W., 675–700
Time pressure
stereotyping and, 175
T lymphocytes
stressful stimulation and, 72
in vitro proliferation of
stimulation of, 59
Törestad, B., 427–48
Toro, P. A., 525–51
Torrance Tests of Creative Thinking, 96
TRACE model, 392, 409
Training in community living, 528
Transactive memory, 602
Transference, 167
Trigeminal nucleus
engram for classical conditioning and, 333
Tumors
development of
psychosocial factors in, 64–65
Type A Behavior Pattern Questionnaire, 105

U

Unidirectional causality
in personality research, 434
Universalism
in cultural psychology, 514–17
Universal laws
animal behavior comparisons and, 685–86
Utility
definition of, 157

V

Value(s)
attitudes and, 125–26
Value expression
attitudes and, 125–26
Valuing
program evaluation and, 658–59
Variables
in personality research, 432–33

Videoconferencing, 235
Vigilance
subjective workload and, 246
Violence
male
counseling psychology and, 361–62
sexual, 352–55
Virtual reality, 235
Visual perception
information processing and, 408
object representations in
temporal synchrony and, 275–76
Vivid representations
for reasoning, 300–7
Vocal pleasantness
persuasiveness and, 138
Vocational choice
accident theory of, 348
Vocational interests
self-efficacy expectations and, 348
Voluntary action management
See Self-regulation

W

Wait-list control
post-traumatic stress disorder and, 354
Wang, Z-M., 87–110
"War neurosis", 2
Wechsler Adult and Children Intelligence
Scales, 96
Women
career adjustment among, 349–50
career choice among, 347–48
career development and, 346–50
counseling psychology and, 346–57
eating disorders among, 350–52
sexual harassment and, 349–50
sexual violence and, 352–55
therapist bias and, 355–57
Word priming
right posterior cortex and, 481
Word superiority effect, 411
Work
bureaucratization of, 208
Workload
in China, 105
Work motivation
in China, 103
Work preferences
parenting and, 621

Z

Zanna, M. P., 117–46

CUMULATIVE INDEXES

CONTRIBUTING AUTHORS, VOLUMES 35–44

A

Achenbach, T. M., 35:227–56
Adelmann, P. K., 40:249–80
Ader, R., 44:53–85
Alkon, D. L., 36:419–93
Amir, Y., 37:17–41
Anastasi, A., 37:1–15
Applebaum, M. I., 40:23–43
Arabie, P., 43:169–202
Aslin, R. N., 39:435–74

B

Badura, L. L., 41:81–108
Baer, J. S., 39:223–52
Banks, W. P., 42:305–31
Bargh, J. A., 38:369–425
Barlow, D. H., 43:235–67
Bassok, M., 40:631–66
Baum, A., 36:349–83
Bednar, R. L., 39:401–34
Beer, M., 38:339–67
Ben–Ari, R., 37:17–41
Berry, J. W., 40:493–531
Bettman, J. R., 37:257–89;
  43:87–131
Betz, N. E., 44:343–81
Binder, A., 39:253–82
Bjork, R. A., 39:475–544
Blanchard, D. C., 39:43–68
Blanchard, R. J., 39:43–68
Borgen, F. H., 35:579–604
Boynton, R. M., 39:69–100
Brédart, S., 43:505–29
Brehm, J. W., 40:109–31
Brewer, M. B., 36:219–43
Brown, T. A., 43:235–67
Browne, M. A., 35:605–25
Brugge, J. F., 36:245–74
Burlingame, G. M., 39:401–34
Buss, D. M., 42:459–91

C

Cairns, R. B., 35:553–77
Cantor, N., 36:275–305
Carnevale, P. J., 43:531–82
Carson, R. C., 40:227–48
Cascio, W. F., 35:461–518
Chaiken, S., 38:575–630
Chakravarti, D., 41:243–88
Chase, M. H., 41:557–84
Clark, M. S., 39:609–72
Cohen, J. B., 41:243–88
Cohen, N., 44:53–85
Cohn, T. E., 37:495–521
Collins, W. A., 41:387–416

Cook, T. D., 37:193–232
Cooper, J., 35:395–426
Cowan, N., 44:383–425
Coyne, J. C., 42:401–25
Cross, D. R., 37:611–51
Croyle, R. T., 35:395–426
Cutting, J. E., 38:61–90

D

Dark, V. J., 37:43–75
Darley, J. M., 41:525–56
Datan, N., 38:153–80
Day, R. H., 39:375–400
Deaux, K., 36:49–81
de Boer, E., 38:181–202
Denmark, F., 38:279–98
Depue, R. A., 40:457–92
Dewsbury, D. A., 40:581–602
Diaz-Guerrero, R., 35:83–112
Digman, J. M., 41:417–40
Dodge, K. A., 44:559–84
Donovan, D. M., 39:223–52
Downey, G., 42:401–25
Dreschler, W. A., 38:181–202
Duncan, C. C., 37:291–319

E

Edelbrock, C. S., 35:227–56
Eisenberg, M., 44:613–44
Estes, W. K., 42:1–28

F

Farley, J., 36:419–93
Fassinger, R. E., 41:355–86
Feder, H. H., 35:165–200
Figueredo, A. J., 44:645–74
Fischer, K. W., 36:613–48
Fiske, S. T., 44:155–94
Fitzgerald, L. F., 44:343–81
Foss, D. J., 39:301–348
Fowles, D. C., 43:303–36
Fraisse, P., 35:1–36

G

Gallistel, C. R., 40:155–89
Geen, R. G., 42:377–99
Gelman, S. A., 43:337–75
Gelso, C. J., 41:355–86
Gescheider, G. A., 39:169–200
Gesten, E. L., 38:427–60
Gibson, E. J., 39:1–42
Gibson, W. M., 39:349–74
Glaser, R., 40:631–66
Goldfried, M. R., 41:659–88

Goldman, B. D., 41:81–108
Goldstein, M. J., 39:283–300
Gopher, D., 40:431–55
Gorsuch, R. L., 39:201–22
Gould, J. L., 37:163–92
Green, B. F., 35:37–53
Green, D. M., 42:135–59
Greenberg, L., 41:659–88
Grunberg, N. E., 36:349–83
Guion, R. M., 39:349–74
Gunnar, M., 41:387–416

H

Hakel, M. D., 37:135–61
Hall, J. A., 35:37–53
Hall, W. G., 38:91–128
Harris, L. C., 35:333–60
Harvey, J. H., 35:427–59
Hasher, L., 38:631–68
Hay, D. F., 37:135–61
Heller, J. F., 38:461–89
Heller, K., 41:141–68
Hellige, J. B., 41:55–80
Helzer, J. E., 37:409–32
Hendersen, R. W., 36:495–529
Hertz, R. M., 43:235–67
Higgins, E. T., 38:369–425
Higgins, E. T., 44:585–612
Hilgard, E. R., 42:79–107
Hintzman, D. L., 41:109–39
Hodapp, R. M., 42:29–50
Holahan, C. J., 37:381–407
Holyoak, K. J., 44:265–315
Honzik, M. P., 35:309–31
Horn, J. M., 39:101–34
Horton, D. L., 35:361–94
House, R., 38:669–718
Howell, W. C., 44:231–63
Hubert, L. J., 43:169–202
Hughes, F., 38:153–80
Hunt, E., 40:603–29
Hunter, J. E., 43:627–70
Hurvich, L., 40:1–22
Hyman, R., 40:133–54

I

Iacono, W. G., 40:457–92
Ilgen, D. R., 40:327–51
Iscoe, I., 35:333–60

J

Jagielo, J. A., 41:169–211
Jameson, D., 40:1–22
Janssen, P. J., 43:505–29
Jason, L. A., 38:427–60

Jenkins, J. M., 43:55–85
Johnson, E. J., 43:87–131
Johnson, M. K., 38:631–68
Johnston, W. A., 37:43–75
Jones, L. V., 40:23–43
Judd, C. M., 40:281–326

K

Kaas, J. H., 38:129–51
Kagitcibasi, C., 40:493–531
Kamil, A. C., 36:141–69
Karoly, P., 44:23–51
Kazdin, A. E., 41:21–54
Keesey, R. E., 37:109–33
Kelley, H. H., 43:1–23
Kessler, R. C., 36:531–72
Kihlstrom, J. F., 36:385–418
Kim, J. J., 44:317–42
Kimchi, R., 40:431–55
Kinchla, R. A., 43:711–42
Kivlahan, D. R., 39:223–52
Klaber, M., 36:115–40
Klein, H. J., 40:327–51
Knowlton, B., 44:453–95
Kolligian, J., Jr., 38:533–74
Kozma, R. B., 37:611–51
Krajicek, D., 42:305–31
Kramer, A., 36:307–48
Kramer, R. M., 36:219–43
Krantz, D. S., 36:349–83
Krumhansl, C. L., 42:277–303

L

Lam, Y. R., 36:19–48
Lanyon, R. I., 35:667–701
Lasley, D. J., 37:495–521
Latham, G. P., 39:545–82
Lavond, D. G., 44:317–42
Lazarus, R. S., 44:1–21
Leary, D. E., 42:79–107
Leon, M., 43:377–98
Leventhal, H., 37:565–610
Levine, J. M., 41:585–634;
  44:585–612
Levine, M., 44:525–58
Light, L. L., 42:333–76
Loehlin, J. C., 39:101–34
London, P., 37:321–49

M

Mackie, D. M., 40:45–81
Magnusson, D., 44:427–51
Mahoney, M. J., 35:605–25
Markus, H., 38:299–337
Marlatt, G. A., 39:223–52
Marmar, C., 41:659–88
Marshall, J. F., 35:277–308
Massaro, D. W., 44:383–425
Masters, K. S., 39:401–34
Matthies, H., 40:381–404
McGinty, D., 39:135–68
McGuire, C. B., 42:239–76
McGuire, G. R., 42:79–107

McKeachie, W. J., 37:611–51
McReynolds, P., 40:83–108
Medin, D. L., 35:113–38
Messick, D. M., 40:45–81
Middlebrooks, J. C., 42:135–59
Miller, D. T., 37:291–319
Miller, J. S., 41:169–211
Mills, C. B., 35:361–94
Milner, P. M., 43:443–71
Mineka, S., 36:495–529
Mirsky, A. F., 37:291–319
Misumi, J., 41:213–41
Mitchell, G., 42:239–76
Morales, F. R., 41:557–84
Moreland, R. L., 41:585–634
Mowday, R. T., 44:195–229
Musen, G., 44:453–95

N

Nelson, R. J., 41:81–108
Newell, K. M., 42:213–37
Nosofsky, R. M., 43:25–53

O

Oatley, K., 43:55–85
Oden, G. C., 38:203–27
O'Leary, K. D., 42:191–212
Olson, J. M., 44:117–54
Ones, D. S., 43:627–70
Oppenheim, R. W., 38:91–128
O'Reilly, C. A., 42:427–58
Osipow, S. H., 38:257–78

P

Panksepp, J., 37:77–107
Park, B., 40:281–326
Parloff, M. B., 37:321–49
Payne, J. W., 43:87–131
Perkins, D. V., 44:525–58
Pervin, L. A., 36:83–114
Petersen, A. C., 39:583–608
Peterson, M., 41:213–41
Phillips, D. P., 36:245–74
Pincus, A. L., 43:473–504
Pintrich, P. R., 37:611–51
Pittman, T. S., 38:461–89
Pitz, G. F., 35:139–63
Plomin, R., 42:161–90
Porras, J. I., 42:51–78
Powley, T. L., 37:109–33
Price, R. H., 36:531–72
Pruitt, D. G., 43:531–82

Q

Quay, H. C., 38:491–532

R

Raaijmakers, J. G. W., 43:205–34
Reis, H. T., 39:609–72
Rende, R., 42:161–90
Resnick, L. B., 44:585–612

Rheingold, H. L., 36:1–17
Richardson-Klavehn, A., 39:475–544
Richelle, M., 43:505–29
Rips, L. J., 41:321–53
Robertson, I., 41:289–319
Robins, L. N., 37:409–32
Rodeheaver, D., 38:153–80
Rodin, J., 40:533–79
Roitblat, H. L., 36:141–69;
  43:671–710
Rompre, P., 40:191–225
Routh, D. K., 38:491–532
Russo, N. F., 38:279–98

S

Sachs, N. J., 35:139–63
Saegert, S., 41:441–77
Salovey, P., 40:533–79
Sarason, S. B., 36:115–40
Scarr, S., 44:613–44
Schlenker, B. R., 43:133–68
Schmidt, F. L., 43:627–70
Schmitt, N., 41:289–319
Schneider, B., 36:573–611
Schneider, D. J., 42:527–61
Sears, D. O., 38:229–55
Sechrest, L., 44:645–74
Segall, M. H., 37:523–64
Self, E. A., 40:109–31
Shadish, W. R., Jr., 37:193–232
Shaffer, D., 41:479–523
Shapiro, S. K., 38:491–532
Shapley, R., 41:635–58
Sherman, S. J., 40:281–326
Shiffrin, R. M., 43:205–34
Showers, C., 36:275–305
Shultz, T. R., 41:525–56
Shweder, R. A., 44:497–523
Siegler, R. S., 40:353–97
Silvern, L., 36:613–48
Silvers, R. C., 42:51–78
Simon, H. A., 41:1–19
Simon, N. G., 35:257–76
Singer, J. L., 38:533–74
Singh, J. V., 38:669–718
Smith, D. A., 42:191–212
Smith, E. E., 35:113–38
Smith, L. B., 39:435–74
Snow, R. E., 43:583–626
Spear, N. E., 41:169–211
Spellman, B. A., 44:265–315
Squire, L. R., 44:453–95
Stangor, C., 38:575–630
Staw, B. M., 35:627–66
Stern, P. C., 43:269–302
Sullivan, M. A., 44:497–523
Sutton, R. I., 44:195–229
Swanson, J., 43:583–626
Szymusiak, R., 39:135–68

T

Taft, R., 39:375–400
Tannenbaum, S., 43:399–441

Teas, D. C., 40:405–29
Tesser, A., 41:479–523
Tetlock, P. E., 42:239–76
Thompson, R. F., 44:317–42
Timberlake, W., 44:675–708
Tomarken, A. J., 37:565–610
Törestad, B., 44:427–51
Toro, P. A., 44:525–58
Traub, R. E., 36:19–48
Trull, T. J., 42:109–33
Turnbull, W., 37:233–56

V

Valsiner, J., 35:553–77
von Fersen, L., 43:671–710

W

Wallach, H., 38:1–27
Walton, E., 38:339–67
Wang, Z.-M., 44:87–116
Weary, G., 35:427–59
Weigold, M. F., 43:133–68
Weinstein, C. S., 42:493–525
Wellman, H. M., 43:337–75
Westheimer, G., 35:201–26
Wexley, K. N., 35:519–51
Whalen, R. E., 35:257–76
White, N. M., 43:443–71
Wickens, C. D., 36:307–48
Widiger, T. A., 42:109–33
Wiggins, J. S., 43:473–504
Wilcox, R. R., 38:29–60
Willerman, L., 39:101–34
Wimer, C. C., 36:171–218
Wimer, R. E., 36:171–218
Winkel, G., 41:441–77

Wise, R. A., 40:191–225
Wolfe, B., 37:321–49
Woody, C. D., 37:433–93
Wortman, C. B., 36:531–72
Wurf, E., 38:299–337

Y

Young, F. W., 35:55–81
Yukl, G., 43:399–441

Z

Zajonc, R. B., 40:249–80
Zanna, M. P., 44:117–54
Zedeck, S., 35:461–518
Zigler, E., 42:29–50
Zinbarg, R. E., 43:235–67

CHAPTER TITLES, VOLUMES 35–44

PREFATORY CHAPTER

Perception and Estimation of Time	P. Fraisse	35:1–36
Development as the Acquisition of Familiarity	H. L. Rheingold	36:1–17
Evolving Concepts of Test Validation	A. Anastasi	37:1–15
Perceiving A Stable Environment When One Moves	H. Wallach	38:1–27
Exploratory Behavior in the Development of Perceiving, Acting, and the Acquiring of Knowledge	E. J. Gibson	39:1–42
Essay Concerning Color Constancy	D. Jameson, L. Hurvich	40:1–22
Invariants of Human Behavior	H. A. Simon	41:1–19
Cognitive Architectures from the Standpoint of an Experimental Psychologist	W. K. Estes	42:1–28
Common-Sense Psychology and Scientific Psychology	H. H. Kelley	43:1–23
From Psychological Stress to the Emotions: A History of Changing Outlooks	R. S. Lazarus	44:1–21

ATTENTION

Selective Attention	W. A. Johnston, V. J. Dark	37:43–75
Attention	R. A. Kinchla	43:711–42

BIOLOGICAL PSYCHOLOGY

Hormones and Sexual Behavior	H. H. Feder	35:165–200
Brain Function: Neural Adaptations and Recovery from Injury	J. F. Marshall	35:277–308
Animal Behavior Genetics: A Search for the Biological Foundations of Behavior	R. E. Wimer, C. C. Wimer	36:171–218
Cellular Mechanisms of Learning, Memory, and Information Storage	J. Farley, D. L. Alkon	36:419–93
The Neurochemistry of Behavior	J. Panksepp	37:77–107
Developmental Psychobiology: Prenatal, Perinatal, and Early Postnatal Aspects of Behavioral Development	W. G. Hall, R. W. Oppenheim	38:91–128
The Organization of Neocortex in Mammals: Implications for Theories of Brain Function	J. H. Kaas	38:129–51
Ethnoexperimental Approaches to the Biology of Emotion	D. C. Blanchard, R. J. Blanchard	39:43–68
Human Behavior Genetics	J. C. Loehlin, L. Willerman, J. M. Horn	39:101–34
Neuronal Unit Activity Patterns in Behaving Animals: Brainstem and Limbic System	D. McGinty, R. Szymusiak	39:135–168
Brain Dopamine and Reward	R. A. Wise, P. Rompre	40:191–225
Hemispheric Asymmetry	J. B. Hellige	41:55–80
The Atonia and Myoclonia of Active (REM) Sleep	M. H. Chase, F. R. Morales	41:557–84
Visual Sensitivity and Parallel Retinocortical Channels	R. Shapley	41:635–58

Human Behavioral Genetics   R. Plomin, R. Rende   42:161–90
The Neurobiology of Filial Learning   M. Leon   43:377–98
Psychoneuroimmunology: Conditioning and
  Stress   R. Ader, N. Cohen   44:53–85
Mammalian Brain Substrates of Aversive Clas-
  sical Conditioning   D. G. Lavond, J. J. Kim,
    R. F. Thompson   44:317–42

CHEMICAL SENSES
See SENSORY PROCESSES

CLINICAL AND COMMUNITY PSYCHOLOGY
Social and Community Interventions   I. Iscoe, L. C. Harris   35:333–60
Individual Psychotherapy and Behavior Change   M. B. Parloff, P. London,
    B. Wolfe   37:321–49
Diagnosis and Clinical Assessment: The Cur-
  rent State of Psychiatric Diagnosis   L. N. Robins, J. E. Helzer   37:409–32
Social and Community Interventions   E. L. Gesten, L. A. Jason   38:427–60
Systems of Family Treatment: Substance or Se-
  mantics?   R. L. Bednar, G. M.
    Burlingame, K. S. Mas-
    ters   39:401–34
Diagnosis and Clinical Assessment Current
  Status and Major Issues   P. McReynolds   40:83–108
Social and Community Intervention   K. Heller   41:141–68
Individual Psychotherapy: Process and Outcome   M. R. Goldfried, L.
    Greenberg, C. Marmar   41:659–88
Diagnosis and Clinical Assessment   T. A. Widiger, T. J. Trull   42:109–33
Marital Interactions   K. D. O'Leary, D. A.
    Smith   42:191–212
Cognitive-Behavioral Approaches to the Nature
  and Treatment of Anxiety Disorders   R. E. Zinbarg, D. H. Bar-
    low, T. A. Brown, R.
    M. Hertz   43:235–67
Schizophrenia: Diathesis-Stress Revisited   D. C. Fowles   43:303–36
Social and Community Interventions   M. Levine, P. A. Toro,
    D. V. Perkins   44:525–58
See also PSYCHOPATHOLOGY

COGNITIVE PROCESSES
Concepts and Concept Formation   D. L. Medin, E. E. Smith   35:113–38
Judgment and Decision: Theory and Application   G. F. Pitz, N. J. Sachs   35:139–63
Concept, Knowledge, and Thought   G. C. Oden   38:203–27
Experimental Psycholinguistics   D. J. Foss   39:301–48
Animal Cognition: The Representation of
  Space, Time, and Number   C. R. Gallistel   40:155–89
Cognitive Science: Definition, Status, and Ques-
  tions   E. Hunt   40:603–29
Reasoning   L. J. Rips   41:321–53
Behavioral Decision Research: A Constructive
  Processing Perspective   J. W. Payne, J. R.
    Bettman, E. J. Johnson   43:87–131
Thinking   K. J. Holyoak, B. A.
    Spellman   44:265–315
Information Processing Models: Microscopes of
  the Mind   D. W. Massaro, N.
    Cowan   44:383–425

COMPARATIVE PSYCHOLOGY, ETHOLOGY, AND ANIMAL BEHAVIOR
The Biology of Learning   J. L. Gould   37:163–92
Comparative Psychology, Ethology, and Ani-
  mal Behavior   D. A. Dewsbury   40:581–602
Comparative Cognition: Representations and
  Processes in Learning and Memory   H. L. Roitblat, L. von

| | Fersen | 43:671–710 |
| Animal Behavior: A Continuing Synthesis | W. Timberlake | 44:675–708 |

COUNSELING

| Individuality and Diversity: Theory and Research in Counseling Psychology | N. E. Betz, L. F. Fitzgerald | 44:343–81 |

See EDUCATION AND COUNSELING; CLINICAL AND COMMUNITY PSYCHOLOGY

DEVELOPMENTAL PSYCHOLOGY

Life-Span Development	M. P. Honzik	35:309–31
Child Psychology	R. B. Cairns, J. Valsiner	35:553–77
Stages and Individual Differences in Cognitive Development	K. W. Fischer, L. Silvern	36:613–48
Infancy	D. F. Hay	37:135–61
Adult Development and Aging	N. Datan, D. Rodeheaver, F. Hughes	38:153–80
Perceptual Development	R. N. Aslin, L. B. Smith	39:435–74
Adolescent Development	A. C. Petersen	39:583–608
Mechanisms of Cognitive Development	R. S. Siegler	40:353–97
Social and Personality Development	W. A. Collins, M. Gunnar	41:387–416
Memory and Aging: Four Hypotheses in Search of Data	L. L. Light	42:333–76
Cognitive Development: Foundational Theories of Core Domains	H. M. Wellman, S. A. Gelman	43:337–75
Social Foundations of Cognition	J. M. Levine, L. B. Resnick, E. T. Higgins	44:585–612
Child Care Research: Issues, Perspectives, and Results	S. Scarr, M. Eisenberg	44:613–44

EDUCATION AND COUNSELING

Counseling Psychology	F. H. Borgen	35:579–604
The School as a Social Situation	S. B. Sarason, M. Klaber	36:115–40
Instructional Psychology	P. R. Pintrich, D. R. Cross, R. B. Kozma, W. J. McKeachie	37:611–51
Counseling Psychology: Theory, Research, and Practice in Career Counseling	S. H. Osipow	38:257–78
Learning Theory and the Study of Instruction	R. Glaser, M. Bassok	40:631–66
Counseling Psychology: Theory and Research on Interventions	C. J. Gelso, R. E. Fassinger	41:355–86
The Classroom as a Social Context for Learning	C. S. Weinstein	42:493–525
Instructional Psychology: Aptitude, Adaptation, and Assessment	R. E. Snow, J. Swanson	43:583–626

EMOTION

| Emotion: Today's Problems | H. Levanthal, A. J. Tomarken | 37:565–610 |
| Facial Efference and the Experience of Emotion | P. K. Adelmann, R. B. Zajonc | 40:249–80 |

ENVIRONMENTAL PSYCHOLOGY

| Environmental Psychology | C. J. Holahan | 37:381–407 |
| Environmental Psychology | S. Saegert, G. Winkel | 41:441–77 |

GENETICS OF BEHAVIOR
See BIOLOGICAL PSYCHOLOGY

GERONTOLOGY (MATURITY AND AGING)

See DEVELOPMENTAL PSYCHOLOGY

HEARING
See SENSORY PROCESSES

HYPNOSIS
Hypnosis   J. F. Kihlstrom   36:385–418

INDUSTRIAL PSYCHOLOGY
See PERSONNEL-ORGANIZATIONAL PSY-
  CHOLOGY

LEARNING AND MEMORY
Human Learning and Memory   D. L. Horton, C. B. Mills   35:361–94
The Ecology of Foraging Behavior: Implica-
  tions for Animal Learning and Memory   A. C. Kamil, H. L. Roit-
      blat   36:141–69
Understanding the Cellular Basis of Memory
  and Learning   C. D. Woody   37:433–93
Human Learning and Memory   M. K. Johnson, L. Hasher   38:631–68
Measures of Memory   A. Richardson-Klavehn,
      R. A. Bjork   39:475–544
Neurobiological Aspects of Learning and Mem-
  ory   H. Matthies   40:381–404
Human Learning and Memory: Connections
  and Dissociations   D. L. Hintzman   41:109–39
Animal Memory and Learning   N. E. Spear, J. S. Miller,
      J. A. Jagielo   41:169–211
Models for Recall and Recognition   J. G. W. Raaijmakers, R.
      M. Shiffrin   43:205–34
Mammalian Brain Substrates of Aversive Clas-
  sical Conditioning   D. G. Lavond, J. J. Kim,
      R. F. Thompson   44:317–42
The Structure and Organization of Memory   L. R. Squire, B. Knowl-
      ton, G. Musen   44:453–95

MOTIVATION
Biological Motivation   R. E. Whalen, N. G. Si-
      mon   35:257–76
Controllability and Predictability in Acquired
  Motivation   S. Mineka, R. W. Hen-
      dersen   36:495–529
The Regulation of Body Weight   R. E. Keesey, T. L.
      Powley   37:109–33
Social Motivation   T. S. Pittman, J. F. Heller   38:461–89
The Intensity of Motivation   J. W. Brehm, E. A. Self   40:109–31
Facial Efference and the Experience of Emotion   P. K. Adelmann, R. B.
      Zajonc   40:249–80
Mechanisms of Seasonal Cycles of Behavior   R. J. Nelson, L. L.
      Badura, B. D. Goldman   41:81–108
Social Motivation   R. G. Geen   42:377–99
Human Emotions: Function and Dysfunction   K. Oatley, J. M Jenkins   43:55–85
The Psychobiology of Reinforcers   N. M. White, P. M. Mil-
      ner   43:443–71

PERCEPTION
Perception and Information   J. E. Cutting   38:61–90
Perception   W. P. Banks, D. Krajicek   42:305–31

PERSONALITY
Personality Assessment   R. I. Lanyon   35:667–701
Personality: Current Controversies, Issues, and
  Directions   L. A. Pervin   36:83–114

Personality: Developments in the Study of
    Private Experience   J. L. Singer, J. Kolligian,
                                            Jr.   38:533–74

Personality: Developments in the Study of Private Experience	J. L. Singer, J. Kolligian, Jr.	38:533–74
Personality	R. C. Carson	40:227–48
Social and Personality Development	W. A. Collins, M. Gunnar	41:387–416
Personality Structure: Emergence of the Five-Factor Model	J. M. Digman	41:417–40
Evolutionary Personality Psychology	D. M. Buss	42:459–91
Personality: Structure and Assessment	J. S. Wiggins, A. L. Pincus	43:473–504
A Holistic View of Personality: A Model Revisited	D. Magnusson, B. Törestad	44:427–51

PERSONNEL-ORGANIZATIONAL PSYCHOLOGY

Psychological Issues in Personnel Decisions	S. Zedeck, W. F. Cascio	35:461–518
Personnel Training	K. N. Wexley	35:519–51
Organizational Behavior: A Review and Reformulation of the Field's Outcome Variables	B. M. Staw	35:627–66
Engineering Psychology	C. D. Wickens, A. Kramer	36:307–48
Organizational Behavior	B. Schneider	36:573–611
Consumer Psychology	J. R. Bettman	37:257–89
Personnel Selection and Placement	M. D. Hakel	37:351–80
Organizational Behavior: Some New Directions for I/O Psychology	R. House, J. V. Singh	38:669–718
Organization Change and Development	M. Beer, E. Walton	38:339–67
Personnel Selection and Placement	R. M. Guion, W. M. Gibson	39:349–74
Human Resource Training and Development	G. P. Latham	39:545–82
Organizational Behavior	D. R. Ilgen, H. J. Klein	40:327–51
Engineering Psychology	D. Gopher, R. Kimchi	40:431–55
Consumer Psychology	J. B. Cohen, D. Chakravarti	41:243–88
Personnel Selection	N. Schmitt, I. Robertson	41:289–319
Organization Development and Transformation	J. I. Porras, R. C. Silvers	42:51–78
Organizational Behavior: Where We've Been, Where We're Going	C. A. O'Reilly	42:427–58
Training and Development in Work Organizations	S. Tannenbaum, G. Yukl	43:399–441
Personnel Selection	F. L. Schmidt, D. S. Ones, J. E. Hunter	43:627–70
Organizational Behavior: Linking Individuals and Groups to Organizational Contexts	R. T. Mowday, R. I. Sutton	44:195–229
Engineering Psychology in a Changing World	W. C. Howell	44:231–63

PSYCHOLINGUISTICS

See COGNITIVE PROCESSES

PSYCHOLOGY AND CULTURE

Culture and Behavior: Psychology in Global Perspective	M. H. Segall	37:523–64
Political Psychology	D. O. Sears	38:229–55
Cross-Cultural Psychology: Current Research and Trends	C. Kagitcibasi, J. W. Berry	40:493–531
Cultural Psychology: Who Needs It?	R. A. Shweder, M. A. Sullivan	44:497–523

PSYCHOLOGY IN OTHER COUNTRIES

| Contemporary Psychology in Mexico | R. Diaz-Guerrero | 35:83–112 |
| Psychology in a Developing Society: The Case of Israel | R. Ben-Ari, Y. Amir | 37:17–41 |

Psychology in Australia   R. Taft, R. H. Day   39:375–400
Psychology in Japan   J. Misumi, M. Peterson   41:213–41
Psychology in Belgium   M. Richelle, P. J.
   Janssen, S. Brédart   43:505–29
Psychology in China: A Review Dedicated to
   Li Chen   Z.-M. Wang   44:87–116

PSYCHOPATHOLOGY

Psychopathology of Childhood   T. M. Achenbach, C. S.
   Edelbrock   35:227–76
Social Factors in Psychopathology: Stress, So-
   cial Support, and Coping Processes   R. C. Kessler, R. H.
   Price, C. B. Wortman   36:531–72
Etiology and Expression of Schizophrenia:
   Neurobiological and Psychosocial Factors   A. F. Mirsky, C. C. Dun-
   can   37:291–319
Psychopathology of Childhood: From Descrip-
   tion to Validation   H. C. Quay, D. K. Routh,
   S. K. Shapiro   38:491–532
The Family and Psychopathology   M. J. Goldstein   39:283–300
Neurobehavioral Aspects of Affective Disorders   R. A. Depue, W. G. Ia-
   cono   40:457–92
Psychotherapy for Children and Adolescents   A. E. Kazdin   41:21–54
Social Factors and Psychopathology: Stress, So-
   cial Support, and Coping Processes   J. C. Coyne, G. Downey   42:401–25
Social-Cognitive Mechanisms in the Develop-
   ment of Conduct Disorder and Depression   K. A. Dodge   44:559–84
See also CLINICAL AND COMMUNITY
   PSYCHOLOGY

PSYCHOPHARMACOLOGY

See BIOLOGICAL PSYCHOLOGY

RESEARCH METHODOLOGY

Quantitative Methods for Literature Reviews   B. F. Green, J. A. Hall   35:37–53
Scaling   F. W. Young   35:55–81
Latent Structure and Item Sampling Models for
   Testing   R. E. Traub, Y. R. Lam   36:19–48
Program Evaluation: The Worldly Science   T. D. Cook, W. R.
   Shadish, Jr.   37:193–232
New Designs in Analysis of Variance   R. R. Wilcox   38:29–60
Psychophysical Scaling   G. A. Gescheider   39:169–200
Psychometric Methods   L. V. Jones, M. I. Appel-
   baum   40:23–43
Similarity Scaling and Cognitive Process Mod-
   els   R. M. Nosofsky   43:25–53
Combinatorial Data Analysis   P. Arabie, L. J. Hubert   43:169–202
Program Evaluation   L. Sechrest, A. J.
   Figueredo   44:645–74

SENSORY PROCESSES

Spatial Vision   G. Westheimer   35:201–26
Progress in Neurophysiology of Sound Localiza-
   tion   D. P. Phillips, J. F.
   Brugge   36:245–74
Visual Sensitivity   T. E. Cohn, D. J. Lasley   37:495–521
Auditory Psychophysics: Spectrotemporal Rep-
   resentation of Signals   E. de Boer, W. A. Dre-
   schler   38:181–202
Color Vision   R. M. Boynton   39:69-100
Auditory Physiology: Present Trends   D. C. Teas   40:405–29
Sound Localization by Human Listeners   J. C. Middlebrooks, D.
   M. Green   42:135–59

SEX ROLES

Sex and Gender   K. Deaux   36:49-81

SLEEP

See BIOLOGICAL PSYCHOLOGY

SOCIAL PSYCHOLOGY

Attitudes and Attitude Change	J. Cooper, R. T. Croyle	35:395–426
Current Issues in Attribution Theory and Research	J. H. Harvey, G. Weary	35:427–59
The Psychology of Intergroup Attitudes and Behavior	M. B. Brewer, R. M. Kramer	36:219–43
Social Cognition: A Look at Motivated Strategies	C. Showers, N. Cantor	36:275–305
Expectancies and Interpersonal Processes	D. T. Miller, W. Turnbull	37:233–56
The Dynamic Self-Concept: A Social Psychological Perspective	H. Markus, E. Wurf	38:299–337
Social Cognition and Social Perception	E. T. Higgins, J. A. Bargh	38:369–425
Attitudes and Attitude Change	S. Chaiken, C. Stangor	38:575–630
Interpersonal Processes in Close Relationships	M. S. Clark, H. T. Reis	39:609–72
Intergroup Relations	D. M. Messick, D. M. Mackie	40:45–81
Social Cognition	S. J. Sherman, C. M. Judd, B. Park	40:281–326
Social and Personality Development	W. A. Collins, M. Gunnar	41:387–416
Attitudes and Attitude Change	A. Tesser, D. Shaffer	41:479–523
Progress in Small Group Research	J. M. Levine, R. L. Moreland	41:585–634
Social Cognition	D. J. Schneider	42:527–61
Interpersonal Processes Involving Impression Regulation and Management	B. R. Schlenker, M. F. Weigold	43:133–68
Negotiation and Mediation	P. J. Carnevale, D. G. Pruitt	43:531–82
Attitudes and Attitude Change	J. M. Olson, M. P. Zanna	44:117–54
Social Cognition and Social Perception	S. T. Fiske	44:155–94

SPECIAL TOPICS

Sport Psychology	M. A. Browne, M. J. Mahoney	35:605–25
Health Psychology	D. S. Krantz, N. E. Gruneberg, A. Baum	36:349–83
Contributions of Women to Psychology	N. F. Russo, F. Denmark	38:279–98
The Dynamic Self-Concept: A Social Psychological Perspective	H. Markus, E. Wurf	38:299–337
Psychology of Religion	R. L. Gorsuch	39:201–22
Addictive Behaviors: Etiology and Treatment	G. A. Marlatt, J. S. Baer, D. M. Donovan, D. R. Kivlahan	39:223–52
Juvenile Delinquency	A. Binder	39:253–82
The Psychology of Deception	R. Hyman	40:133–54
Health Psychology	J. Rodin, P. Salovey	40:533–79
Moral Judgments: Their Content and Acquisition	T. R. Shultz, J. M. Darley	41:525–56
Behavioral Functioning in Individuals with Mental Retardation	E. Zigler, R. M. Hodapp	42:29–50
History of Psychology: A Survey and Critical Assessment	E. R. Hilgard, D. E. Leary, G. R. McGuire	42:79–107
Motor Skill Acquisition	K. M. Newell	42:213–37
Psychological Perspectives on Nuclear Deterrence	P. E. Tetlock, C. B. McGuire, G. Mitchell	42:239–76

Music Psychology: Tonal Structures in Perception and Memory	C. L. Krumhansl	42:277–303
Psychological Dimensions of Global Environmental Change	P. C. Stern	43:269–302
Mechanisms of Self-Regulation: A Systems View	P. Karoly	44:23–51

VISION

See SENSORY PROCESSES

ANNUAL REVIEWS INC.

a nonprofit scientific publisher
4139 El Camino Way
P. O. Box 10139
Palo Alto, CA 94303-0897 • USA

Annual Reviews Inc. publications may be ordered directly from our office; through booksellers and subscription agents, worldwide; and through participating professional societies. **Prices are subject to change without notice.** California Corp. #161041 • ARI Federal I.D. #94-1156476

- **Individual Buyers:** Prepayment required on new accounts by check or money order (in U.S. dollars, check drawn on U.S. bank) or charge to MasterCard, VISA, or American Express.

- **Institutional Buyers:** Please include purchase order.

- **Students/Recent Graduates:** $10.00 discount from retail price, per volume. Discount does not apply to Special Publications, standing orders, or institutional buyers. **Requirements:** [1] be a degree candidate at, or a graduate within the past three years from, an accredited institution; [2] present proof of status (photocopy of your student I.D. or proof of date of graduation); [3] Order direct from Annual Reviews; [4] prepay.

- **Professional Society Members:** Societies that have a contractual arrangement with Annual Reviews offer our books to members at reduced rates. Check your society for information.

- **California orders** must add applicable sales tax.

- **Canadian orders** must add 7% General Sales Tax. GST Registration #R 121 449-029. Now you can also telephone orders Toll Free from anywhere in Canada (see below).

- **Telephone orders,** paid by credit card, welcomed. **Call Toll Free 1-800-523-8635** from anywhere in USA or Canada. From elsewhere call 415-493-4400, Ext. 1 (not toll free). Monday – Friday, 8:00 am – 4:00 pm, Pacific Time. Students or recent graduates ordering by telephone must supply (by FAX or mail) proof of status if current proof is not on file at Annual Reviews. Written confirmation required on purchase orders from universities before shipment.

- **FAX: 415-855-9815** – 24 hours a day.

- **Postage paid** by Annual Reviews (4th class bookrate). UPS ground service (within continental U.S.) available at $2.00 extra per book. UPS air service or Airmail also available at cost. UPS requires a street address. P.O. Box, APO, FPO, not acceptable.

- **Regular Orders:** Please list below the volumes you wish to order by volume number.

- **Standing Orders:** New volume in series is sent automatically each year upon publication. Please indicate volume number to begin the standing order. Each year you can save 10% by prepayment of standing-order invoices sent 90 days prior to the publication date. Cancellation may be made at any time.

- **Prepublication Orders:** Volumes not yet published will be shipped in month and year indicated

- **We do not ship on approval.**

ANNUAL REVIEWS SERIES *Volumes not listed are no longer in print*	Prices, postpaid, per volume. USA / other countries (incl. Canada)	Regular Order Please send Volume(s):	Standing Order Begin with Volume:
Annual Review of **ANTHROPOLOGY**			
Vols. 1-20 (1972-1991)............................ $41.00/$46.00			
Vol. 21 (1992)...................................... $44.00/$49.00			
Vol. 22 (avail. Oct. 1993)................... $44.00/$49.00	Vol(s). _____	Vol._____	
Annual Review of **ASTRONOMY AND ASTROPHYSICS**			
Vols. 1, 5-14 (1963, 1967-1976)			
16-29 (1978-1991)............................ $53.00/$58.00			
Vol. 30 (1992)...................................... $57.00/$62.00			
Vol. 31 (avail. Sept. 1993)................... $57.00/$62.00	Vol(s). _____	Vol.____	
Annual Review of **BIOCHEMISTRY**			
Vols. 30-34, 36-60 (1961-1965, 1967-1991) .... $41.00/$47.00			
Vol. 61 (1992) .... $46.00/$52.00			
Vol. 62 (avail. July 1993) .... $46.00/$52.00	Vol(s). _____	Vol.____	

ANNUAL REVIEWS SERIES	Prices, postpaid, per volume. USA / other countries (incl. Canada)	Regular Order Please send Volume(s):	Standing Order Begin with Volume:
Volumes not listed are no longer in print			

Annual Review of **BIOPHYSICS AND BIOMOLECULAR STRUCTURE**
Vols. 1-20	(1972-1991)............................. $55.00/$60.00		
Vol. 21	(1992)...................................... $59.00/$64.00		
Vol. 22	(avail. June 1993)................. $59.00/$64.00	Vol(s). _____	Vol._____

Annual Review of **CELL BIOLOGY**
Vols. 1-7	(1985-1991)............................. $41.00/$46.00		
Vol. 8	(1992)...................................... $46.00/$51.00		
Vol. 9	(avail. Nov. 1993).................. $46.00/$51.00	Vol(s). _____	Vol._____

Annual Review of **COMPUTER SCIENCE**
| Vols. 1-2 | (1986-1987)............................. $41.00/$46.00 | | |
| Vols. 3-4 | (1998-1989/1990)................... $47.00/$52.00 | Vol(s). _____ | Vol._____ |

Series suspended until further notice. Purchase the complete set for the special promotional price of $100.00 USA / $115.00 other countries, when all four volumes are ordered at the same time. Orders at the special price must be prepaid.

Annual Review of **EARTH AND PLANETARY SCIENCES**
Vols. 1-19	(1973-1991)............................. $55.00/$60.00		
Vol. 20	(1992)...................................... $59.00/$64.00		
Vol. 21	(avail. May 1993)................... $59.00/$64.00	Vol(s). _____	Vol._____

Annual Review of **ECOLOGY AND SYSTEMATICS**
Vols. 2-12, 14-22	(1971-1981, 1983-1991)......... $40.00/$45.00		
Vol. 23	(1992)...................................... $44.00/$49.00		
Vol. 24	(avail. Nov. 1993).................. $44.00/$49.00	Vol(s). _____	Vol._____

Annual Review of **ENERGY AND THE ENVIRONMENT**
Vols. 1-16	(1976-1991)............................. $64.00/$69.00		
Vol. 17	(1992)...................................... $68.00/$73.00		
Vol. 18	(avail. Oct. 1993)................... $68.00/$73.00	Vol(s). _____	Vol._____

Annual Review of **ENTOMOLOGY**
Vols. 10-16, 18	(1965-1971, 1973)		
20-36	(1975-1991)............................. $40.00/$45.00		
Vol. 37	(1992) .... $44.00/$49.00		
Vol. 38	(avail. Jan. 1993) .... $44.00/$49.00	Vol(s). _____	Vol._____

Annual Review of **FLUID MECHANICS**
Vols. 2-4, 7, 9-11	(1970-1972, 1975, 1977-1979)		
14-23	(1982-1991) .... $40.00/$45.00		
Vol. 24	(1992) .... $44.00/$49.00		
Vol. 25	(avail. Jan. 1993) .... $44.00/$49.00	Vol(s). _____	Vol._____

Annual Review of **GENETICS**
Vols. 1-12, 14-25	(1967-1978, 1980-1991) .... $40.00/$45.00		
Vol. 26	(1992)...................................... $44.00/$49.00		
Vol. 27	(avail. Dec. 1993).................. $44.00/$49.00	Vol(s). _____	Vol._____

Annual Review of **IMMUNOLOGY**
Vols. 1-9	(1983-1991) .... $41.00/$46.00		
Vol. 10	(1992) .... $45.00/$50.00		
Vol. 11	(avail. April 1993) .... $45.00/$50.00	Vol(s). _____	Vol._____

Annual Review of **MATERIALS SCIENCE**
Vols. 1, 3-19	(1971, 1973-1989).................. $68.00/$73.00		
Vols. 20-22	(1990-1992) .... $72.00/$77.00		
Vol. 23	(avail. Aug. 1993) .... $72.00/$77.00	Vol(s). _____	Vol._____